Nineteenth-Century Literature Criticism

Guide to Gale Literary Criticism Series

When you need to review criticism of literary works, these are the Gale series to use:

If the author's death date is:

You should turn to:

After Dec. 31, 1959
(or author is still living)

CONTEMPORARY LITERARY CRITICISM

for example: Jorge Luis Borges, Anthony Burgess,
William Faulkner, Mary Gordon,
Ernest Hemingway, Iris Murdoch

1900 through 1959

TWENTIETH-CENTURY LITERARY CRITICISM

for example: Willa Cather, F. Scott Fitzgerald,
Henry James, Mark Twain, Virginia Woolf

1800 through 1899

NINETEENTH-CENTURY LITERATURE CRITICISM

for example: Fedor Dostoevski, George Sand,
Gerard Manley Hopkins, Emily Dickinson

1400 through 1799

LITERATURE CRITICISM FROM 1400 TO 1800
(excluding Shakespeare)

for example: Anne Bradstreet, Pierre Corneille,
Daniel Defoe, Alexander Pope,
Jonathan Swift, Phillis Wheatley

SHAKESPEAREAN CRITICISM

Shakespeare's plays and poetry

Gale also publishes related criticism series:

CONTEMPORARY ISSUES CRITICISM

Presents criticism on contemporary authors writing
on current issues. Topics covered include the social
sciences, philosophy, economics, natural science, law,
and related areas.

CHILDREN'S LITERATURE REVIEW

Covers authors of all eras. Presents criticism on
authors and author/illustrators who write for the
preschool to junior-high audience.

Volume 6

Nineteenth-Century Literature Criticism

Excerpts from Criticism of the
Works of Novelists, Poets, Playwrights,
Short Story Writers, and Other Creative Writers
Who Died between 1800 and 1900,
from the First Published Critical
Appraisals to Current Evaluations

Laurie Lanzen Harris
Sheila Fitzgerald
Editors

Emily B. Tennyson
Associate Editor

Gale Research Inc. · DETROIT · LONDON

STAFF

Laurie Lanzen Harris, Sheila Fitzgerald, *Editors*

Emily B. Tennyson, *Associate Editor*

Cherie D. Abbey, Jelena Obradovic Kronick, Patricia Askie Mackmiller,
Janet S. Mullane, Gail Ann Schulte, *Assistant Editors*

Sharon K. Hall, Anna C. Wallbillich, *Contributing Editors*

Robert J. Elster, *Production Supervisor*

Lizbeth A. Purdy, *Production Coordinator*

Denise Michlewicz, *Assistant Production Coordinator*

Eric F. Berger, Paula J. DiSante, Amy Marcaccio, *Editorial Assistants*

Karen Rae Forsyth, *Research Coordinator*

Jeannine Schiffman Davidson, *Assistant Research Coordinator*

Victoria B. Cariappa, Robert J. Hill, James A. MacEachern,
Leslie Kyle Schell, Valerie J. Webster, *Research Assistants*

Linda Marcella Pugliese, *Manuscript Coordinator*

Donna D. Craft, *Assistant Manuscript Coordinator*

Colleen M. Crane, Maureen A. Puhl, Rosetta Irene Simms Carr, *Manuscript Assistants*

L. Elizabeth Hardin, *Permissions Supervisor*
Filomena Sgambati, *Permissions Associate*
Janice M. Mach, *Permissions Coordinator*
Patricia A. Seefelt, *Assistant Permissions Coordinator, Illustrations*
Susan D. Nobles, *Senior Permissions Assistant*
Margaret A. Chamberlain, Mary M. Matuz, Joan B. Weber, *Permissions Assistants*
Josephine M. Keene, Virgie T. Leavens, Diana M. Platzke, *Permissions Clerks*
Margaret Mary Missar, Audrey B. Wharton, *Photo Research*

Frederick G. Ruffner, *Publisher*
James M. Ethridge, *Executive Vice President/Editorial*
Dedria Bryfonski, *Editorial Director*
Christine Nasso, *Director, Literature Division*

The paper used in this publication meets the minimum requirements
of American National Standard for Information Sciences—Permanence
Paper for Printed Library Materials, ANSI Z39.48-1984. ∞™

Printed in the United States of America.

Published simultaneously in the United Kingdom
by Gale Research International Limited
(An affiliated company of Gale Research Inc.)

Library of Congress Catalog Card Number 81-6943
ISBN 0-8103-5806-9
ISSN 0732-1864

CONTENTS

Preface 7

Authors to Appear in Future Volumes 9

Appendix 531

PREFACE

The nineteenth century was a time of tremendous growth in human endeavor: in science, in social history, and particularly in literature. The era saw the development of the novel, witnessed radical changes from classicism to romanticism to realism, and contained intellectual and artistic ideas that continue to inspire authors of our own century. The importance of the writers of the nineteenth century is twofold, for they provide insight into their own time as well as into the universal nature of human experience.

The literary criticism of an era can also give us insight into the moral and intellectual atmosphere of the past, for the criteria by which a work of art is judged reflect current philosophical and social attitudes. Literary criticism takes many forms: the traditional essay, the book or play review, even the parodic poem. Criticism can also be of several kinds: normative, descriptive, interpretive, textual, appreciative, generic. Collectively, the range of critical response helps us to understand a work of art, an author, an era.

The Scope of the Work

The success of Gale's two current literary series, *Contemporary Literary Criticism (CLC)* and *Twentieth-Century Literary Criticism (TCLC),* which excerpt criticism of creative writing from the twentieth century, suggested an equivalent need among students and teachers of literature of the nineteenth century. Moreover, since the critical analysis of this literature spans almost two hundred years, a vast amount of critical material confronts the student.

Nineteenth-Century Literature Criticism (NCLC) presents significant passages from published criticism on authors who died between 1800 and 1900. The author list for each volume of *NCLC* is carefully compiled to represent a variety of genres and nationalities and to cover authors who are currently regarded as the most important writers of an era as well as those whose contribution to literature and literary history is significant. The truly great writers are rare, and in the intervals between them lesser but genuine artists, as well as writers who enjoyed immense popularity in their own time and in their own countries, are important to the study of nineteenth-century literature. The length of each author's entry is intended to represent the author's critical reception in English. Articles and books that have not been translated into English are excluded. Each author entry represents a historical overview of the critical response to the author's work: early criticism is presented to indicate initial responses, later selections represent any rise or decline in the author's literary reputation. We have also attempted to identify and include excerpts from the seminal essays on each author, and to include recent critical comment providing modern perspectives on the writer. Thus, *NCLC* is designed to serve as an introduction for the student of nineteenth-century literature to the authors of that period and to the most significant commentators on these authors.

NCLC entries are intended to be definitive overviews. Approximately 20 authors are included in each 600-page volume, compared with about 65 authors in a *CLC* volume of similar size. Because of the great quantity of critical material available on many authors, and because of the resurgence of criticism generated by events such as an author's centennial or anniversary celebration, the republication of an author's works, or publication of a newly translated work or volume of letters, an author may appear more than once.

The Organization of the Book

An author section consists of the following elements: author heading, biocritical introduction, principal works, excerpts of criticism (each followed by a bibliographical citation), and an annotated bibliography of additional reading.

- The *author heading* consists of the author's full name, followed by birth and death dates. The unbracketed portion of the name denotes the form under which the author most commonly wrote. If an author wrote consistently under a pseudonym, the pseudonym will be listed in the author heading and the real name given in parentheses on the first line of the biocritical introduction. Also located at the beginning of the biocritical introduction are any name variations under which an author wrote, including transliterated forms for authors whose languages use nonroman alphabets. Uncertainty as to a birth or death date is indicated by a question mark.

- A *portrait* of the author is included when available.

- The *biocritical introduction* contains biographical and other background information that elucidates the author's creative output. When applicable, biocritical introductions are followed by references to additional entries on the author in biographical and critical reference series published by Gale Research Company. These include *Dictionary of Literary Biography, Children's Literature Review,* and *Something about the Author.*

- The list of *principal works* is chronological by date of first book publication and identifies genres. In those instances where the first publication was in other than the English language, the title and date of the first English-language edition is given in brackets. Unless otherwise indicated, dramas are dated by the first performance, rather than first publication.

- *Criticism* is arranged chronologically in each author section to provide a perspective on any changes in critical evaluation over the years. In the text of each author entry, titles by the author are printed in boldface type. This allows the reader to ascertain without difficulty the works discussed. For purposes of easier identification, the critic's name and the publication date of the essay are given at the beginning of each piece of criticism. Unsigned criticism is preceded by the title of the journal in which it appeared. For an anonymous essay later attributed to a critic, the critic's name appears in brackets in the heading and in the bibliographical citation.

- Important critical essays are prefaced with *explanatory notes* as an additional aid to students using *NCLC.* The explanatory notes provide several types of useful information, including: the reputation of the critic, the importance of a work of criticism, the specific approach of the critic (biographical, psychoanalytic, structuralist, etc.), and the growth of critical controversy or changes in critical trends regarding an author's work. In many cases, these notes will include cross-references to related criticism in the author's entry or in the annotated bibliography.

- A complete *bibliographical citation* designed to facilitate the location of the original essay or book follows each piece of criticism. An asterisk (*) at the end of the citation indicates that the essay is on more than one author.

- The *annotated bibliography* appearing at the end of each author section suggests further reading on the author. In some cases it includes essays for which the editors could not obtain reprint rights. An asterisk (*) at the end of a citation indicates that the essay is on more than one author.

Beginning with Volume 6, *NCLC* will include a cumulative index to authors listing all the authors who have appeared in *Contemporary Literary Criticism, Twentieth-Century Literary Criticism, Nineteenth-Century Literature Criticism,* and *Literary Criticism from 1400 to 1800,* along with cross-references to the Gale series *Children's Literature Review, Authors in the News, Contemporary Authors, Dictionary of Literary Biography, Something about the Author,* and *Yesterday's Authors of Books for Children.* Users will welcome this cumulated author index as a useful tool for locating an author within the various series. The index, which lists birth and death dates when available, will be particularly valuable for those authors who are identified with a certain period but whose death date causes them to be placed in another, or for those authors whose careers span two periods. For example, Fedor Dostoevski is found in *NCLC,* yet Leo Tolstoy, another major nineteenth-century Russian novelist, is found in *TCLC.* In addition, each volume of *NCLC* includes a cumulative index to critics. Under each critic's name are listed the authors on whom the critic has written and the volume and page where the criticism appears. *NCLC* also includes a cumulative nationality index to authors. Authors are listed alphabetically by nationality, followed by the volume number in which they appear.

An appendix is included which lists the sources from which material in the volume is reprinted. It does not, however, list every book or periodical consulted for the volume.

Acknowledgments

No work of this scope can be accomplished without the cooperation of many people. The editors especially wish to thank the copyright holders of the excerpts included in this volume, the permissions managers of the book and magazine publishing companies for assisting us in securing reprint rights, and the staffs of the Detroit Public Library, University of Michigan Library, and Wayne State University Library for making their resources available to us. We are also grateful to Jeri Yaryan for her assistance with copyright research and Norma J. Merry for her editorial assistance.

Suggestions Are Welcome

The editors welcome the comments and suggestions of readers to expand the coverage and enhance the usefulness of the series.

Authors to Appear in Future Volumes

About, Edmond Francois 1828-1885
Aguilo I. Fuster, Maria 1825-1897
Ainsworth, William Harrison 1805-1882
Aksakov, Konstantin 1817-1860
Aleardi, Aleadro 1812-1878
Alecsandri, Vasile 1821-1890
Alencar, Jose 1829-1877
Alfieri, Vittorio 1749-1803
Alger, Horatio 1834-1899
Allingham, William 1824-1889
Almquist, Carl Jonas Love 1793-1866
Alorne, Leonor de Almeida 1750-1839
Alsop, Richard 1761-1815
Altimirano, Ignacio Manuel 1834-1893
Alvarenga, Manuel Inacio da Silva
  1749-1814
Alvares de Azevedo, Manuel Antonio
  1831-1852
Andersen, Hans Christian 1805-1875
Anzengruber, Ludwig 1839-1889
Arany, Janos 1817-1882
Arene, Paul 1843-1893
Aribau, Bonaventura Carlos 1798-1862
Arjona de Cubas, Manuel Maria de
  1771-1820
Arnault, Antoine Vincent 1766-1834
Arneth, Alfred von 1819-1897
Arnim, Bettina von 1785-1859
Arnold, Thomas 1795-1842
Arriaza y Superviela, Juan Bautista
  1770-1837
Asbjornsen, Peter Christian 1812-1885
Ascasubi, Hilario 1807-1875
Atterbom, Per Daniel Amadeus
  1790-1855
Aubanel, Theodore 1829-1886
Auerbach, Berthold 1812-1882
Augier, Guillaume V.E. 1820-1889
Azeglio, Massimo D' 1798-1866
Azevedo, Guilherme de 1839-1882
Bagehot, Walter 1826-1877
Bakin (pseud. of Takizawa Okikani)
  1767-1848
Bakunin, Mikhail Aleksandrovich
  1814-1876
Banville, Theodore de 1823-1891
Baratynski, Jewgenij Abramovich
  1800-1844
Barnes, William 1801-1886
Batyushkov, Konstantin 1778-1855
Beattie, James 1735-1803
Beckford, William 1760-1844
Becquer, Gustavo Adolfo 1836-1870
Bentham, Jeremy 1748-1832
Beranger, Jean-Pierre de 1780-1857
Berchet, Giovanni 1783-1851
Berzsenyi, Daniel 1776-1836
Black, William 1841-1898
Blair, Hugh 1718-1800
Blake, William 1757-1827

Blicher, Steen Steensen 1782-1848
Bocage, Manuel Maria Barbosa du
  1765-1805
Boratynsky, Yevgeny 1800-1844
Borel, Petrus 1809-1859
Boreman, Yokutiel 1825-1890
Borne, Ludwig 1786-1837
Borrow, George 1803-1881
Botev, Hristo 1778-1842
Brackenridge, Hugh Henry 1748-1816
Bremer, Fredrika 1801-1865
Brinckman, John 1814-1870
Bronte, Emily 1812-1848
Brown, Charles Brockden 1777-1810
Browning, Robert 1812-1889
Buchner, Georg 1813-1837
Burney, Fanney 1752-1840
Campbell, James Edwin 1867-1895
Campbell, Thomas 1777-1844
Carlyle, Thomas 1795-1881
Castelo Branco, Camilo 1825-1890
Castro Alves, Antonio de 1847-1871
Channing, William Ellery 1780-1842
Chatterje, Bankin Chanda 1838-1894
Chivers, Thomas Holly 1807?-1858
Clare, John 1793-1864
Claudius, Matthais 1740-1815
Clough, Arthur Hugh 1819-1861
Cobbett, William 1762-1835
Colenso, John William 1814-1883
Coleridge, Hartley 1796-1849
Coleridge, Samuel T. 1772-1834
Collett, Camilla 1813-1895
Comte, Auguste 1798-1857
Conrad, Robert T. 1810-1858
Conscience, Hendrik 1812-1883
Cooke, Philip Pendleton 1816-1850
Corbiere, Edouard 1845-1875
Cowper, William 1731-1800
Crabbe, George 1754-1832
Crawford, Isabella Valancy 1850-1886
Cruz E Sousa, Joao da 1861-1898
Desbordes-Valmore, Marceline
  1786-1859
Deschamps, Emile 1791-1871
Deus, Joao de 1830-1896
Dickinson, Emily 1830-1886
Dinis, Julio 1839-1871
Dinsmoor, Robert 1757-1836
Dumas, Alexandre (pere) 1802-1870
Dumas, Alexandre (fils) 1824-1895
Du Maurier, George 1834-1896
Dwight, Timothy 1752-1817
Echeverria, Esteban 1805-1851
Eden, Emily 1797-1869
Eichendorff, Joseph von 1788-1857
Eminescy, Mihai 1850-1889
Engels, Friedrich 1820-1895
Espronceda, Jose 1808-1842
Ettinger, Solomon 1799-1855

Euchel, Issac 1756-1804
Ferguson, Samuel 1810-1886
Fernandez de Lizardi, Jose Joaquin
  1776-1827
Fernandez de Moratin, Leandro
  1760-1828
Fet, Afanasy 1820-1892
Feuillet, Octave 1821-1890
Fitzgerald, Edward 1809-1883
Fontane, Theodor 1819-1898
Forster, John 1812-1876
Foscolo, Ugo 1778-1827
Frederic, Harold 1856-1898
Freiligrath, Hermann Ferdinand
  1810-1876
Freytag, Gustav 1816-1895
Gaboriau, Emile 1835-1873
Ganivet, Angel 1865-1898
Garrett, Almeida 1799-1854
Garshin, Vsevolod Mikhaylovich
  1855-1888
Gezelle, Guido 1830-1899
Ghalib, Asadullah Khan 1797-1869
Godwin, William 1756-1836
Goldschmidt, Meir Aron 1819-1887
Goncalves Dias, Antonio 1823-1864
Griboyedov, Aleksander Sergeyevich
  1795-1829
Grigor'yev, Appolon Aleksandrovich
  1822-1864
Groth, Klaus 1819-1899
Grun, Anastasius (pseud. of Anton
  Alexander Graf von Auersperg)
  1806-1876
Guerrazzi, Francesco Domenico
  1804-1873
Gutierrez Najera, Manuel 1859-1895
Gutzkow, Karl Ferdinand 1811-1878
Ha-Kohen, Shalom 1772-1845
Halleck, Fitz-Greene 1790-1867
Harris, George Washington 1814-1869
Hayne, Paul Hamilton 1830-1886
Hazlitt, William 1778-1830
Hebbel, Christian Friedrich 1813-1863
Hebel, Johann Peter 1760-1826
Hegel, Georg Wilhelm Friedrich
  1770-1831
Heiberg, Johann Ludvig 1813-1863
Herculano, Alexandre 1810-1866
Herder, Johann Gottfried 1744-1803
Hernandez, Jose 1834-1886
Hertz, Henrik 1798-1870
Herwegh, Georg 1817-1875
Herzen, Alexander Ivanovich 1812-1870
Hoffman, Charles Fenno 1806-1884
Holderlin, Friedrich 1770-1843
Holmes, Oliver Wendell 1809-1894
Hood, Thomas 1799-1845
Hooper, Johnson Jones 1815-1863
Hopkins, Gerard Manley 1844-1889

Horton, George Moses 1798-1880
Howitt, William 1792-1879
Hughes, Thomas 1822-1896
Imlay, Gilbert 1754?-1828?
Irwin, Thomas Caulfield 1823-1892
Issacs, Jorge 1837-1895
Jacobsen, Jens Peter 1847-1885
Jean Paul (pseud. of Johann
    Paul Friedrich Richter) 1763-1825
Jippensha, Ikku 1765-1831
Kant, Immanuel 1724-1804
Karr, Jean Baptiste Alphonse 1808-1890
Keats, John 1795-1821
Keble, John 1792-1866
Khomyakov, Alexey S. 1804-1860
Kierkegaard, Soren 1813-1855
Kinglake, Alexander W. 1809-1891
Kingsley, Charles 1819-1875
Kivi, Alexis 1834-1872
Klopstock, Friedrich Gottlieb 1724-1803
Koltsov, Alexey Vasilyevich 1809-1842
Kotzebue, August von 1761-1819
Krasicki, Ignacy 1735-1801
Kraszewski, Josef Ignacy 1812-1887
Kreutzwald, Friedrich Reinhold
    1803-1882
Krochmal, Nahman 1785-1840
Krudener, Valeria Barbara Julia de
    Wietinghoff 1766-1824
Lamartine, Alphonse 1790-1869
Lamb, Charles 1775-1834
Lampman, Archibald 1861-1899
Landon, Letitia Elizabeth 1802-1838
Landor, Walter Savage 1775-1864
Larra y Sanchez de Castro, Mariano
    1809-1837
Lautreamont (pseud. of Isodore Ducasse)
    1846-1870
Lebensohn, Micah Joseph 1828-1852
Leconte de Lisle, Charles-Marie-Rene
    1818-1894
Le Fanu, Joseph Sheridan 1814-1873
Lenau, Nikolaus 1802-1850
Leontyev, Konstantin 1831-1891
Leopardi, Giacoma 1798-1837
Leskov, Nikolai 1831-1895
Lever, Charles James 1806-1872
Levisohn, Solomon 1789-1822
Lewes, George Henry 1817-1878
Lewis, Matthew Gregory 1775-1810
Leyden, John 1775-1811
Lobensohn, Micah Gregory 1775-1810
Longstreet, Augustus Baldwin 1790-1870
Lopez de Ayola y Herrera, Adelardo
    1819-1871
Lover, Samuel 1797-1868
Luzzato, Samuel David 1800-1865
Macedo, Joaquim Manuel de 1820-1882
Macha, Karel Hynek 1810-1836
Mackenzie, Henry 1745-1831
Malmon, Solomon 1754-1800
Mangan, James Clarence 1803-1849
Manzoni, Alessandro 1785-1873
Mapu, Abraham 1808-1868
Marii, Jose 1853-1895

Markovic, Svetozar 1846-1875
Martinez de la Rosa, Francisco
    1787-1862
Mathews, Cornelius 1817-1889
McCulloch, Thomas 1776-1843
Merriman, Brian 1747-1805
Meyer, Conrad Ferdinand 1825-1898
Montagu, Elizabeth 1720-1800
Montgomery, James 1771-1854
Moodie, Susanna 1803-1885
Morike, Eduard 1804-1875
Morton, Sarah Wentworth 1759-1846
Muller, Friedrich 1749-1825
Murger, Henri 1822-1861
Nekrasov, Nikolai 1821-1877
Neruda, Jan 1834-1891
Nestroy, Johann 1801-1862
Newman, John Henry 1801-1890
Niccolini, Giambattista 1782-1861
Nievo, Ippolito 1831-1861
Nodier, Charles 1780-1844
Novalis (pseud. of Friedrich von
    Hardenberg) 1772-1801
Obradovic, Dositej 1742-1811
Oehlenschlager, Adam 1779-1850
Oliphant, Margaret 1828-1897
O'Neddy, Philothee (pseud. of
    Theophile Dondey) 1811-1875
O'Shaughnessy, Arthur William
    Edgar 1844-1881
Ostrovsky, Alexander 1823-1886
Paine, Thomas 1737-1809
Parkman, Francis 1823-1893
Pater, Walter 1839-1894
Patmore, Coventry Kersey Dighton
    1823-1896
Peacock, Thomas Love 1785-1866
Perk, Jacques 1859-1881
Pisemsky, Alexey F. 1820-1881
Pompeia, Raul D'Avila 1863-1895
Popovic, Jovan Sterija 1806-1856
Praed, Winthrop Mackworth 1802-1839
Prati, Giovanni 1814-1884
Preseren, France 1800-1849
Pringle, Thomas 1789-1834
Procter, Adelaide Ann 1825-1864
Procter, Bryan Waller 1787-1874
Pye, Henry James 1745-1813
Quental, Antero Tarquinio de 1842-1891
Quinet, Edgar 1803-1875
Quintana, Manuel Jose 1772-1857
Radishchev, Aleksander 1749-1802
Raftery, Anthony 1784-1835
Raimund, Ferdinand 1790-1836
Reid, Mayne 1818-1883
Renan, Ernest 1823-1892
Reuter, Fritz 1810-1874
Rogers, Samuel 1763-1855
Ruckert, Friedrich 1788-1866
Runeberg, Johan 1804-1877
Rydberg, Viktor 1828-1895
Saavedra y Ramirez de Boquedano,
    Angel de 1791-1865
Sacher-Mosoch, Leopold von 1836-1895
Saltykov-Shchedrin, Mikhail 1826-1892

Satanov, Isaac 1732-1805
Schiller, Friedrich 1759-1805
Schlegel, August 1767-1845
Schlegel, Karl 1772-1829
Scott, Sir Walter 1771-1832
Scribe, Augustin Eugene 1791-1861
Sedgwick, Catherine Maria 1789-1867
Senoa, August 1838-1881
Shelley, Mary W. 1797-1851
Shelley, Percy Bysshe 1792-1822
Shulman, Kalman 1819-1899
Sigourney, Lydia Howard Huntley
    1791-1856
Silva, Jose Asuncion 1865-1896
Slaveykov, Petko 1828-1895
Slowacki, Juliusz 1809-1848
Smith, Richard Penn 1799-1854
Smolenskin, Peretz 1842-1885
Southey, Robert 1774-1843
Stagnelius, Erik Johan 1793-1823
Staring, Antonie Christiaan
    Wynand 1767-1840
Stendhal (pseud. of Henri Beyle)
    1783-1842
Stifter, Adalbert 1805-1868
Stone, John Augustus 1801-1834
Taine, Hippolyte 1828-1893
Taunay, Alfredo d'Ecragnole 1843-1899
Taylor, Bayard 1825-1878
Tennyson, Alfred, Lord 1809-1892
Terry, Lucy (Lucy Terry Prince)
    1730-1821
Thompson, Daniel Pierce 1795-1868
Thompson, Samuel 1766-1816
Thomson, James 1834-1882
Thoreau, Henry David 1817-1862
Tiedge, Christoph August 1752-1841
Timrod, Henry 1828-1867
Tommaseo, Nicolo 1802-1874
Tompa, Mihaly 1817-1888
Topelius, Zachris 1818-1898
Turgenev, Ivan 1818-1883
Tyutchev, Fedor I. 1803-1873
Uhland, Ludvig 1787-1862
Valaoritis, Aristotelis 1824-1879
Valles, Jules 1832-1885
Verde, Cesario 1855-1886
Very, Jones 1813-1880
Vigny, Alfred Victor de 1797-1863
Villaverde, Cirilio 1812-1894
Vinje, Aasmund Olavsson 1818-1870
Vorosmarty, Mihaly 1800-1855
Wagner, Richard 1813-1883
Warren, Mercy Otis 1728-1814
Weisse, Christian Felix 1726-1804
Welhaven, Johan S. 1807-1873
Werner, Zacharius 1768-1823
Wescott, Edward Noyes 1846-1898
Wessely, Nattali Herz 1725-1805
Whitman, Sarah Helen 1803-1878
Whittier, John Greenleaf 1807-1892
Wieland, Christoph Martin 1733-1813
Woolson, Constance Fenimore
    1840-1894
Wordsworth, William 1770-1850
Zhukovsky, Vasily 1783-1852

Louisa May Alcott

1832-1888

(Also wrote under the pseudonyms of Flora Fairfield, A. M. Barnard, Cousin Tribulation, A.M., Abba May Alcott, and A.M. daughter of Amos Bronson Alcott) American novelist, short story and fairy tale writer, poet, essayist, editor, and dramatist.

Alcott is best known for her sentimental yet realistic depictions of nineteenth-century domestic life. Her *Little Women* series attracted young and old readers alike and remains popular today. Alcott's continuing appeal is generally attributed to her characterization and her simple, charming style, reflected in her adage: "Never use a long word when a short one will do as well." Though she became somewhat of a literary celebrity, Alcott remained reclusive throughout her life. She wrote solely to finance her family's comfort, and avoided fame and recognition.

Alcott, the second of four daughters, was born in Germantown, Pennsylvania and raised in Concord, Massachusetts, and Boston. Her father, Amos Bronson Alcott, was a noted New England Transcendentalist philosopher and educator who worked without pay through Alcott's childhood. Her mother, Abigail May Alcott, was descended from the witch-burning Judge Samuel Sewall and the noted abolitionist Colonel Joseph May. Alcott's childhood was apparently happy, though severely impoverished. She never forgot the sparse vegetarian diet imposed on the family by her father, nor his frequent absences as he spread his experimental philosophies through New England. Later, Alcott often remarked that her entire career was inspired by her desire to compensate for her family's early discomfort.

Alcott was educated by her father, whose experimental approach to education combined spiritual, physical, and intellectual training with the writings of his friends and fellow Transcendentalists, Henry David Thoreau, Ralph Waldo Emerson, and Theodore Parker. When her father's schools failed, however, Alcott, her sisters, and her mother sought work to offset the family's financial hardship. Alcott taught school, took in sewing, and worked briefly as a domestic servant. At age sixteen, she began writing, convinced that she could eventually earn enough money to alleviate the family's poverty. In 1851, her first poem was published in *Peterson's Magazine* under the pseudonym of Flora Fairfield, bringing Alcott little money but a great deal of confidence. It was during the ensuing years that Alcott published, as A. M. Barnard, a number of sensational serial stories, which were both popular and lucrative.

In 1862, Alcott went to Washington, D.C. to serve as a nurse to soldiers wounded in the American Civil War. It was a short-lived experience, however, for she contracted typhoid pneumonia within a month, from which she nearly died. Her health, undermined by the long illness, never fully recovered. Alcott later recounted her experiences as a nurse in her popular *Hospital Sketches*, which was originally published in the periodical *Commonwealth*. Her first novel, *Moods*, pronounced immoral by critics, sold well nonetheless, and its success encouraged Alcott to continue writing. In 1865, Alcott traveled

through Europe as a companion to a wealthy invalid and wrote for periodicals. While abroad, she was offered the editorship of *Merry's Museum*, an American journal featuring juvenile literature. She accepted the position and became the journal's chief contributor.

The turning point of Alcott's career came with the publication of *Little Women; or, Meg, Jo, Beth, and Amy*. An autobiographical account of nineteenth-century family life, the novel traces the development of Alcott, depicted as Jo March, and her three sisters. The work was an immediate success and established Alcott as an author. She published four sequels to *Little Women* entitled *Good Wives* (volume two of *Little Women*), *Little Men: Life at Plumfield with Jo's Boys, Aunt Jo's Scrap Bag*, and *Jo's Boys and How They Turned Out*. Alcott was regarded as a celebrity and was easily able to support her family with her earnings.

Alcott's literary career can be divided into three periods. The first phase, spanning the 1840s to the late 1860s, is characterized by the lurid, sensational short stories which were published anonymously and pseudonymously in various New England periodicals. Critics generally agree that the characters in these early efforts are well drawn and colorful and that the plots are intricate and tightly woven. Most of these tales feature a mysterious, vengeful woman bent on manipulation and destruction. Alcott also included ghosts, opium eaters, and mercenaries in these serials. These melodramatic stories were extremely popular and provided Alcott with a steady income as she worked on lengthier pieces.

The publication of *Moods* inaugurated Alcott's most profitable and popular period. The *Little Women* books, which were the most successful series of their time, illustrate the struggles between adolescence and maturity. *Little Women* depicts the March family with a strong sense of realism, and represents New England manners and customs with documentary accuracy. Critics have noted that its organization, in which each chapter comprises a well-rounded episode with a moral commentary, succeeds as a study of adolescent psychology. In particular, commentators praise Alcott's insightful characterization, which they regard as the essential reason for the book's enduring popularity.

From 1875 onward, as her health deteriorated, Alcott primarily produced popular juvenile literature. Most of her later works, particularly *Work: A Story of Experience* and *Rose in Bloom*, depict heroines who have acquired inner strength through personal hardship and achieved personal satisfaction through careers and without marriage. In general, these works provoked mixed reviews. Most critics applaud the feminist tone reflected in these later pieces, but consider their characters and plots to be weak.

Henry James called Alcott the "novelist of children . . . the Thackeray, the Trollope, of the nursery and the schoolroom . . . ," and other contemporaries remarked that her spirited, wholesome stories were destined to become American classics. The twentieth century, however, witnessed a change in the critical assessment of Alcott's works. Although still popular with an adolescent audience, Alcott's *Little Women* has been criticized for its blatant moralizing. In 1920, Katharine Fullerton Gerould carried the criticism further, calling the March girls "underbred" and "unworldly." Gerould found the novel dated and sentimental, and attacked the work for its "inexcusable amount of love-making." She insisted that Alcott wrote as one who had never loved. Both *Little Women* and *Little Men* have been faulted by some early-twentieth-century scholars for their organization. They maintain that the books read as volumes of single sketches rather than integrated novels and therefore are lacking in unity. More recent critics, however, value this method of construction and maintain that it provides an excellent representation of life from the adolescent point of view. The last decade has seen a renewed interest in Alcott's melodramatic early work. The noted Alcott critic Madeleine Stern has reprinted two collections of these colorful stories and introduced them to a new audience.

Alcott remains an enduring figure in American literature. Although some regard her portrayals of nineteenth-century domestic life as dated, she will be remembered for her sympathetic and realistic depictions of the maturing adolescent. Her most popular work, *Little Women*, displays her perfection of the moral tale and was instrumental in changing the focus of juvenile literature so that it included sensitive portrayals of young adults.

(See also *Children's Literature Review*, Vol. 1; *Dictionary of Literary Biography*, Vol. 1: *The American Renaissance in New England;* and *Yesterday's Authors of Books for Children*, Vol. 1.)

PRINCIPAL WORKS

Flower Fables   (fairy tales)   1855
''Pauline's Passion and Punishment'' [as A. M. Barnard]   (short story)   1862; published in newspaper *Frank Leslie's Illustrated Newspaper*
Hospital Sketches   (letters and sketches)   1863
Moods   (novel)   1864; also published as *Moods* [revised edition], 1882
Little Women; or, Meg, Jo, Beth, and Amy. 2 vols.   (novel) 1868-69; also published as *Little Women and Good Wives,* 1871
An Old-fashioned Girl   (novel)   1870
Little Men: Life at Plumfield with Jo's Boys   (novel)   1871
Aunt Jo's Scrap Bag. 6 vols.   (short stories)   1872-82
Work: A Story of Experience   (novel)   1873
Eight Cousins; or, The Aunt-Hill   (novel)   1875
Rose in Bloom   (novel)   1876
A Modern Mephistopheles   (novel)   1877
Under the Lilacs   (novel)   1878
Jack and Jill: A Village Story   (novel)   1880
Jo's Boys and How They Turned Out   (novel)   1886
Louisa May Alcott: Her Life, Letters, and Journals   (letters and journals)   1889
Comic Tragedies   (drama)   1893
Behind a Mask: The Unknown Thrillers of Louisa May Alcott   (short stories)   1975
Plots and Counterplots: More Unknown Thrillers of Louisa May Alcott   (short stories)   1976

HARPER'S WEEKLY   (essay date 1865)

["**Moods**"] is a short story of great power and absorbing interest by a new writer, whose "**Hospital Sketches**" were remarkable for a humor and insight which ought to have made them much more widely known. In the present tale the conflict of passion in noble characters is drawn with great delicacy and skill, and with a freedom and firmness which promise remarkable works hereafter. "**Moods**" is neither sentimental nor morbid nor extravagant. It has freshness and self-reliance. Greater experience and resolute study will correct the imperfect literary art; nor is it a disheartening failure not to have succeeded in a satisfactory discrimination between the two heroes of the tale. Such likeness in unlikeness demands a Shakespearian subtlety of skill fully to delineate. It is something to have suggested it. After Hawthorne we recall no American love-story of equal power.

> A review of "Moods," in Harper's Weekly, Vol. IX, No. 421, January 21, 1865, p. 35.

[HENRY JAMES]   (essay date 1865)

[*James was an American-born English novelist, short story writer, critic, essayist, and playwright of the late nineteenth and early twentieth centuries who is considered one of the greatest novelist in the English language. Although best known for his novels, James is also admired as a lucid and insightful critic. James's review of Alcott's Moods is mixed. He states that "with the exception of two or three celebrated names, we know not, indeed, to whom, in this country, unless to Miss Alcott, we are to look for a novel above the average." This positive assessment is tem-*]

pered, however, by the critic's reservations about Alcott's ability to create believable characters. James's largely favorable attention, however, proved crucial to her increasing popularity.]

[In "**Moods**"] Miss Alcott has given us her version of the old story of the husband, the wife, and the lover. This story has been told so often that an author's only pretext for telling it again is his consciousness of an ability to make it either more entertaining or more instructive; to invest it with incidents more dramatic, or with a more pointed moral. Its interest has already been carried to the furthest limits, both of tragedy and comedy, by a number of practised French writers: under this head, therefore, competition would be superfluous. Has Miss Alcott proposed to herself to give her story a philosophical bearing? We can hardly suppose it.

We have seen it asserted that her book claims to deal with the "doctrine of affinities." What the doctrine of affinities is, we do not exactly know; but we are inclined to think that our author has been somewhat maligned. Her book is, to our perception, innocent of any doctrine whatever.

The heroine of "**Moods**" is a fitful, wayward, and withal most amiable young person, named Sylvia. We regret to say that Miss Alcott takes her up in her childhood. We are utterly weary of stories about precocious little girls. In the first place, they are in themselves disagreeable and unprofitable objects of study; and in the second, they are always the precursors of a not less unprofitable middle-aged lover. We admit that, even to the middle-aged, Sylvia must have been a most engaging little person. One of her means of fascination is to disguise herself as a boy and work in the garden with a hoe and wheelbarrow; under which circumstances she is clandestinely watched by one of the heroes, who then and there falls in love with her. Then she goes off on a camping-out expedition of a week's duration, in company with three gentlemen, with no superfluous luggage, as far as we can ascertain, but a cockle-shell stuck "pilgrim-wise" in her hat. It is hard to say whether the impropriety of this proceeding is the greater or the less from the fact of her extreme youth. This fact is at any rate kindly overlooked by two of her companions, who become desperately enamored of her before the week is out. These two gentlemen are Miss Alcott's heroes. One of them, Mr. Geoffrey Moor, is unobjectionable enough; . . . but the other, Mr. Adam Warwick, is one of our oldest and most inveterate foes. He is the inevitable *cavaliere servente* [faithful servant] of the precocious little girl; the laconical, satirical, dogmatical lover, of about thirty-five, with the "brown mane," the quiet smile, the "masterful soul," and the "commanding eye." Do not all novel-readers remember a figure, a hundred figures, analogous to this? Can they not, one of his properties being given,—the "quiet smile" for instance,—reconstruct the whole monstrous shape? When the "quiet smile" is suggested, we know what is coming: we foresee the cynical bachelor or widower, the amateur of human nature, "Full of strange oaths, and bearded like the pard," who has travelled all over the world, lives on a mysterious patrimony, and spends his time in breaking the hearts and the wills of demure little school-girls, who answer him with "Yes, sir," and "No, sir."

Mr. Warwick is plainly a great favorite with the author. She has for him that affection which writers entertain, not for those figures whom they have well known, but for such as they have much pondered. Miss Alcott has probably mused upon Warwick so long and so lovingly that she has lost all sense of his proportions. There is a most discouraging good-will in the manner in which lady novelists elaborate their impossible he-roes. There are, thank Heaven, no such men at large in society. We speak thus devoutly, not because Warwick is a vicious person,—on the contrary, he exhibits the sternest integrity; but because, apparently as a natural result of being thoroughly conscientious, he is essentially disagreeable. (pp. 276-77)

The two most striking facts with regard to "**Moods**" are the author's ignorance of human nature, and her self-confidence in spite of this ignorance. Miss Alcott doubtless knows men and women well enough to deal successfully with their every-day virtues and temptations, but not well enough to handle great dramatic passions. The consequence is, that her play is not a real play, nor her actors real actors.

But beside these facts are others, less salient perhaps, upon which it is pleasanter to touch. Chief among these is the author's decided cleverness; that quality to which we owe it that, in spite of the absurdities of the action, the last half of her book is replete with beauty and vigor. What shall we call this quality? Imagination does not seem to us too grand a word. For, in the absence of knowledge, our authoress has derived her figures, as the German derived his camel, from the depths of her moral consciousness. If they are on this account the less real, they are also on this account the more unmistakably instinct with a certain beauty and grace. If Miss Alcott's experience of human nature has been small, as we should suppose, her admiration for it is nevertheless great. . . . For inanimate nature, too, she has a genuine love, together with a very pretty way of describing it. With these qualities there is no reason why Miss Alcott should not write a very good novel, provided she will be satisfied to describe only that which she has seen. When such a novel comes, as we doubt not it eventually will, we shall be among the first to welcome it. With the exception of two or three celebrated names, we know not, indeed, to whom, in this country, unless to Miss Alcott, we are to look for a novel above the average. (pp. 280-81)

[Henry James], in a review of "Moods," in The North American Review, *Vol. CI, No. CCVIII, July, 1865, pp. 276-81.*

THE NATION   (essay date 1868)

Miss Alcott's new juvenile [novel, *Little Women,*] is an agreeable little story, which is not only very well adapted to the readers for whom it is especially intended, but may also be read with pleasure by older people. The girls depicted all belong to healthy types, and are drawn with a certain cleverness, although there is in the book a lack of what painters call atmosphere—things and people being painted too much in "local colors," and remaining, under all circumstances, somewhat too persistently themselves.

A review of "Little Women; or, Meg, Jo, Beth, and Amy," *in* The Nation, *Vol. VII, No. 173, October 22, 1868, p. 335.*

LOUISA M. ALCOTT   (essay date 1869)

[*Hospital Sketches,* which are] taken from letters hastily written in the few leisure moments of a very busy life, make no pretension to literary merit, but are simply a brief record of one person's hospital experience. As such, they are republished, with their many faults but partially amended, lest in retouching they should lose whatever force or freshness the inspiration of the time may have given them.

To those who have objected to a "tone of levity" in some portions of the sketches, I desire to say that the wish to make the best of every thing, and send home cheerful reports even from that saddest of scenes, an army hospital, probably produced the impression of levity upon those who have never known the sharp contrasts of the tragic and comic in such a life. (p. i)

> Louisa M. Alcott, "Preface to 'Hospital Sketches'" *(1869), in her* Hospital Sketches and Camp and Fireside Stories, *Roberts Brothers, 1872, pp. i-ii.*

BRONSON ALCOTT   (journal dates 1861-69)

[*The father of Louisa May Alcott, Alcott was a noted nineteenth-century transcendental philosopher. In his journal entries, which have been collected in* The Journals of Bronson Alcott, *Alcott follows the progression of his daughter's career. He praises her insight and concludes that, in her writings, especially in her novel* Moods, *she has "succeeded better in her treatment of the social problem than did Goethe or George Sand. . . ."*]

[Louisa's book *Moods*] is entertaining and witty, her characters are drawn in lively colors, and there are several fine scenes. The chapters on "Nemesis" and "Herbs" are especially excellent. The book has merits, and should be popular. Her discriminations are metaphysical; there is a variety of character and a wealth of fancy expended in it; nor is it the less attractive to us for the personal and family history, but slightly shaded, scattered along its pages. She writes with unusual ease, and in a style of idiomatic purity. Her culture has come from the writing of letters and the keeping of a diary, chiefly. (pp. 336-37)

• • • • •

I read Louisa's [*Moods*] with admiring interest, and think I am not overestimating its merits when I say that she has succeeded better in her treatment of the social problem than did Goethe or George Sand, justifying its laws to the moral sense without their lapse into murder or adultery. Her style, too, is vigorous and clear, suited to the dignity of her theme, her characters being forcibly drawn and making a deep impression on the imagination and heart of her readers. She has written a better book than she knows, opening for herself, I trust, a career of wide usefulness, if not of permanent fame as a novelist and a woman. (pp. 367-68)

• • • • •

[Louisa] writes but little, but has various literary works in thought—among others a novel embodying our family adventures which she entitles *The Cost of an Idea.* If written out with the dramatic genius with which she is gifted, the story will be a taking piece of family biography, as attractive as any fiction and having the merit of being purely American. She is among the first to draw her characters from New England life and scenes, and is more successful in my judgement, in holding fast to nature, intermingling less of foreign sentiment than any of our novelists. Her culture has been left to nature and the bias of temperament and she comes to her pen taught simply by an experience that few of her age have had the good fortune to enjoy—freedom from the trammels of school and sects, helps that her predecessors in fiction—Hawthorne, Judd, and Mrs. Stowe—had not. (p. 396)

> Bronson Alcott, *in extracts from three of his journal entries from February 25, 1861 to April 30, 1869, in his* The Journals of Bronson Alcott, *edited by Odell*

Shepard (copyright 1938 by Odell Shepard; copyright renewed © 1965 by Odell Shepard; reprinted by permission of Little, Brown and Company), Little, Brown, 1938, pp. 336-37, 367-68, 396.

HARPER'S NEW MONTHLY MAGAZINE   (essay date 1869)

Little Women, Part II., by Louisa M. Alcott, is a rather mature book for the little women, but a capital one for their elders. It is natural, and free from that false sentiment which pervades too much of juvenile literature. Autobiographies, if genuine, are generally interesting, and it is shrewdly suspected that Joe's experience as an author photographs some of Miss Alcott's own literary mistakes and misadventures. But do not her children grow rather rapidly? They are little children in Part First, at the breaking out of the civil war. They are married, settled, and with two or three children of their own before they get through Part Second. (pp. 455-56)

> *A review of* "Little Women," *in* Harper's New Monthly Magazine, *Vol. XXXIX, No. CCXXXI, August, 1869, pp. 455-56.*

LOUISA M. ALCOTT   (essay date 1870)

[*In the following preface to* An Old-fashioned Girl, *Alcott explains that the novel, although published in one volume, was actually written in two separate parts. The second part was written in response to reader requests, according to Alcott, which "rendered it necessary to carry* [her] *heroine* [Polly] *boldly forward some six or seven years into the future."*]

As a preface is the only place where an author can with propriety explain a purpose or apologize for shortcomings, I venture to avail myself of the privilege, to make a statement for the benefit of my readers.

As the first part of **"An Old-Fashioned Girl"** was written in 1869, the demand for a sequel, in beseeching little letters that made refusal impossible, rendered it necessary to carry my heroine boldly forward some six or seven years into the future. The domestic nature of the story makes this audacious proceeding possible; while the lively fancies of my young readers will supply all deficiencies, and overlook all discrepancies. . . .

The **"Old-Fashioned Girl"** is not intended as a perfect model, but as a possible improvement upon the Girl of the Period, who seems sorrowfully ignorant or ashamed of the good old fashions which make woman truly beautiful and honored, and through her, render home what it should be,—a happy place, where parents, and children, brothers and sisters, learn to love and know and help one another.

If the history of Polly's girlish experiences suggests a hint or insinuates a lesson, I shall feel that, in spite of many obstacles, I have not entirely neglected my duty toward the little men and women, for whom it is an honor and a pleasure to write, since in them I have always found my kindest patrons, gentlest critics, warmest friends.

> Louisa M. Alcott, *in a preface to her* An Old-Fashioned Girl, *Roberts Brothers, 1870, p. v.*

THE ATLANTIC MONTHLY   (essay date 1870)

If we said that Miss Alcott, as a writer for young people just getting to be young ladies and gentlemen, deserved the great good luck that has attended her books, we should be using an unprofessional frankness and putting in print something we might be sorry for after the story of the **"Old-fashioned Girl"** had grown colder in our minds. And yet it *is* a pretty story, a very pretty story; and almost inexplicably pleasing, since it is made up of such plain material, and helped off with no sort of adventure or sensation. It is nothing, in fact, but the story of a little girl from the country, who comes to visit a gay city family, where there is a fashionable little lady of her own age, with a snubbed younger sister, a gruff, good-hearted, mischievous brother,—as well as a staid, sensible papa, a silly, sickly mamma, and an old-time grandmother. In this family Polly makes herself ever so lovely and useful, so that all adore her, though her clothes are not of the latest fashion, nor her ideas, nor her principles. . . . That is about all; and as none of these people or their doings are strange or remarkable, we rather wonder where the power of the story lies. There's some humor in it, and as little pathos as possible, and a great deal of good sense, but also some poor writing, and some bad grammar. One enjoys the simple tone, the unsentimentalized facts of common experience, and the truthfulness of many of the pictures of manners and persons. Besides, people always like to read of kindly self-sacrifice, and sweetness, and purity, and naturalness; and this is what Polly is, and what her character teaches in a friendly and unobtrusive way to everybody about her. The story thus mirrors the reader's good-will in her well-doing, and that is perhaps what, more than any other thing, makes it so charming and comfortable; but if it is not, pleasing the little book remains nevertheless; and nobody can be the worse for it. (pp. 752-53)

A review of "An Old-fashioned Girl," in The Atlantic Monthly, *Vol. XXV, No. CLII, June, 1870, pp. 752-53.*

THE ATHENAEUM   (essay date 1870)

Let whoever wishes to read a bright, spirited, wholesome story get the **'Old-Fashioned Girl'** at once! It is not our fault if the male readers who follow our advice should close the book with a pang of regret that Polly, the heroine—Polly the darling—is an entirely unattainable treasure. Neither will it be our fault if a standard is set up of a nice girl,—so high that most of the young ladies of their acquaintance shall seem to fall short of it; for Polly is a heroine in a book, and perhaps, after all, they would not have recognized how very good and pleasant she was, unless Miss Alcott had been there to tell them and to open their eyes. **'The Old-Fashioned Girl'** is an American story, and there are little traits of life and manners which give a pleasant flavour of novelty to the tale: we have had several hearty laughs over the book, for it is full of fun. The picture of society amongst the young people in America is, we would hope, an exaggeration; and we heartily trust that the like fashions may never prevail in the school-rooms and nurseries of England; but if they should show themselves, we hope some "old-fashioned girl" like Polly Milton will come and drive them away.

A review of "An Old-Fashioned Girl," in The Athenaeum, *No. 2225, June 18, 1870, p. 803.*

HARPER'S NEW MONTHLY MAGAZINE   (essay date 1871)

[It can hardly be asserted that **"Little Men"**] is a natural story, or doubted that it is an entertaining one. The description of an actual boarding-school, with its humdrum life, would be as tedious as any thing that can well be conceived of, and that Miss Alcott is able to invest a story of boarding-school life with any interest must be taken as one of the evidences of her genius. There is hardly enough in the story itself to sustain the reader's interest in it; and despite the author's bright style and vivid descriptions, and, best of all, her hearty sympathy with youth, the book drags a little if one attempts to read it directly through. It is more entertaining read as a series of sketches than as a single connected story. We beg leave to doubt whether, on the whole, it would be for the best interest of any well-ordered school for the boys to have unlimited liberty to slide down the balusters at the risk of broken heads, and every Saturday night, after their bath, to chase each other over the house in a sham battle with the pillows. . . . Had we been present, we should have been tempted to admonish Mother Bhaer that it was not a safe operation to let her baby suck the spoon in which she had just administered a dose of medicine to a ragged urchin just picked from the street, the nature of whose disease she did not know. But, after all, the lesson which these improbable incidents are meant to teach, and do teach, is a good one—this, namely, that personal sympathy with children, in all their life, even their pranks and good-natured mischief, is the first condition of acquiring influence over them, and hence is the first condition of any true and good government in school or family. The children will be sure to read **"Little Men"** with interest, and the parents can read it with profit.

A review of "Little Men," in Harper's New Monthly Magazine, *Vol. XLIII, No. CCLV, August, 1871, p. 458.*

OVERLAND MONTHLY   (essay date 1871)

Miss Alcott says, the unprejudiced criticism of children is not to be despised, and she has need to be gratified with the lavish praise offered her by her many youthful admirers. Though their flattering comments be not always couched in the most elegant phraseology, and a superabundance of adjectives—among which "awful nice" gains force by constant repetition—seems necessary to relieve their delighted hearts, yet are they none the less sincere and acceptable. Perhaps no book of the season has been so eagerly sought after as [*Little Men*], or has given such genuine satisfaction, which is saying a great deal, for *Little Women* raised expectations that we feared would not be realized. We are agreeably disappointed. We welcome *Little Men* heartily, and find them thoroughly enjoyable. Though "little men," they are full-grown, rollicking, hearty boys. Boys in the rough, but as such easily understood and appreciated by their many prototypes; boys to be admired for their frank good-heartedness, and boys to be envied for the "splendid times" they have. . . . Chief among the many pleasant things in this pleasant book, is the thorough insight displayed in the portrayal of children's characters, and the tender sympathy shown toward them. As we read of "Demi," "Nat," "Jack," "Ned," and the rest of "Jo's" boys, we take them to our hearts, and feel they are real, living children. And one who has ever been with, or known any thing of little folks, can not fail to be charmed with the naturalness of the scenes described. (p. 293)

A review of "Little Men," in Overland Monthly, *Vol. VII, No. 3, September, 1871, pp. 293-94.*

THE ATHENAEUM   (essay date 1872)

[*Aunt Joe's Scrap Bag*] is a collection of fugitive tales and sketches, which we should have been very sorry to lose. Miss

Alcott's boys and girls are always delightful in her hands; she throws a loving glamour over them, and she loves them herself so heartily that it is not possible for the reader to do otherwise. The story called **'Tessa's Surprises'** is the one we like best, though we laughed heartily over **'The Children's Joke'**; but it is altogether so revolutionary, or, as Kitty expresses it, "everything is so turned round," that although we cordially subscribe to the moral, that children ought not to be worried by constant fault-finding and petty injunctions, it still remains a fact, that children are *not* the best judges of what is good for them, and that, on the whole, parents love them better than any one is ever likely to do in this world. It gives a rather startling glimpse into the precocious freedom of American children that the idea of the "joke" could ever have occurred of changing places with their papa and mamma for a whole day, and exercising upon *them* all the rules and regulations which have been such heavy burdens! But, in spite of this protest, we have found the book very pleasant to read.

> *A review of "Aunt Joe's Scrap Bag," in* The Athenaeum, *No. 2341, September 7, 1872, p. 303.*

THE ATHENAEUM   (essay date 1873)

'Work: a Story of Experience,' is full of good and excellent passages; but we miss the cheery energy there was in the **'Old-Fashioned Girl,' 'Little Women,' 'Good Wives,'** and other works, too numerous to specify, for which we have to thank Miss Alcott. She uses her present heroine, Christie Devon, worse than ever the traditional step-mother in fairy-tales used the neglected child:—much worse; for she does not even leave her to be "happy ever after," when her tasks are finished and the rightful Prince has come! Poor Christie Devon, after turning her hand to everything that a woman's hand can find to do, and doing it heartily, though she is bruised, and battered, and all but beaten in her battle with the world, has just attained a comfortable haven, and married a good man whom she loves, when the authoress swoops down upon her once more, with "the uses of adversity," and heaps upon her more sorrow, bent on distilling the very coldest, purest, and dreadfully precious elixir from it all. The reader feels that a little bit of happiness would have been much better for everybody, and much more like the real "Providence that shapes our ends." The story of **'Work'** is too restless; and the result is so fatiguing, that we should not be surprised if the reader, after finishing it, gives up, and refuses to do anything whatever for the rest of the day.

> *"Two American Tales," in* The Athenaeum, *No. 2887, July 26, 1873, p. 111.**

HARPER'S NEW MONTHLY MAGAZINE   (essay date 1873)

Miss Alcott's name will give to this pleasant story [**Work**] a circulation and a celebrity which otherwise it would not attain. The book would not have made her reputation, but her reputation will make the book. The first thing that strikes the reader after he gets fairly under way is that the novel is not a novel at all, but a serious didactic essay on the subject of woman's work. Not, indeed, that Miss Alcott has loaded it with instruction, or put on any unwomanly vestments and taken to preaching in the guise of a story-teller; but the bee on the cover, the motto on the title-page, the title itself, and the current and course of the story, all point in the same direction. Miss Alcott wished to exhibit the various phases of woman's work, and the story was the instrument she chose for that purpose. (p. 618)

The first half of the story is without even the semblance of a plot. Miss Alcott appears to have sat down to write the first chapter without knowing what the next chapter would be, and to have drifted along in the current of her own thoughts till she found a novel growing under her hands. Then, under a sense that a novel needs design, she conceived a simple one, and finished off her series of sketches in a very simply constructed story. But despite this defect, and it is a serious one, she has written what is both an interesting and an entertaining narrative. Some of her pictures are exceedingly pretty; some of her characters are exceedingly well drawn. The best bit of painting in the book is Mrs. Wilkins and her home; and the contrast between the tireless energy of the wife and the nerveless quiet of the husband gives vividness to both. In Mrs. Wilkins's home the unmanageable children play a principal part; and with them Miss Alcott is unmistakably in her element. Mr. Power may be a portrait, as some of the critics have thought it, of Theodore Parker; if so, it is a portrait drawn by a feminine admirer, and clothed with traits that woman's admiring imagination easily attributes to her heroes. A pleasant humor sparkles in the book, and a cheerful good nature imparts to it a singularly pleasant flavor. It is this sunny cheerfulness infused through all its pages by the glow of a woman's bright, trusting, and loving heart, and which imbitters even the death of David "Sunrise," which gives to the book its peculiar charm, and will make it acceptable to hundreds of readers, who will rise from its perusal stronger for the battle of life because of its inspiration, and who will hardly recognize, though they may vaguely feel, the defects which impair it as a work of art. In brief, passing by the externals of this story, which are not above criticism, and getting at its heart, we may say of it what Mrs. Wilkins said of Mr. Powers's preaching: "Ain't it fillin'? Don't it give you a kind of spiritual h'ist, and make things wuth more, somehow?" (pp. 618-19)

> *A review of "Work," in* Harper's New Monthly Magazine, *Vol. XLVII, No. CCLXXX, September, 1873, pp. 618-19.*

[HENRY JAMES]   (essay date 1875)

[*Although James's review of* Moods (1865) *was somewhat favorable, this review of* Eight Cousins; or, The Aunt-Hill *is more negative. He calls Alcott "the Thackeray, the Trollope, of the nursery and the schoolroom," but adds that the novel "strikes us as a very ill-chosen sort of entertainment to set before children." He concludes that in* Eight Cousins "there is no glow and no fairies; it is all prose, and to our sense rather vulgar prose."*]

Miss Alcott is the novelist of children—the Thackeray, the Trollope, of the nursery and the school-room. She deals with the social questions of the child-world, and, like Thackeray and Trollope, she is a satirist. She is extremely clever, and, we believe, vastly popular with infant readers. In [**"Eight Cousins; or, The Aunt-Hill"**] she gives us an account of a little girl named Rose, who has seven boisterous boy-cousins, several grotesque aunts, and a big burly uncle, an honest seaman, addicted to riding a tilt at the shams of life. He finds his little niece encompassed with a great many of these, and Miss Alcott's tale is chiefly devoted to relating how he plucked them successively away. We find it hard to describe our impression of it without appearing to do injustice to the author's motives. It is evidently written in very good faith, but it strikes us as a very ill-chosen sort of entertainment to set before children. It is unfortunate not only in its details, but in its general tone, in the constant ring of the style. The smart satirical tone is the last one in the world to be used in describing to children their elders and betters and the social mysteries that surround them. Miss Alcott seems to have a private understanding with the youngsters she depicts, at the expense of their pastors and masters; and her idea of friendliness to the infant generation seems to be, at the same time, to initiate them into the humorous view of them taken by their elders when the children are out of the room. In this last point Miss Alcott does not perhaps go so far as some of her fellow-chroniclers of the nursery (in whom the tendency may be called nothing less than depraved), but she goes too far, in our opinion, for childish simplicity or parental equanimity. All this is both poor entertainment and poor instruction. . . . What have become of [Jacob Abbot's] "Rollo" books of our infancy and [his] delightful "Franconia" tales? If they are out of print, we strongly urge that they be republished, as an antidote to this unhappy amalgam of the novel and the story-book. These charming tales had, relatively speaking, an almost Homeric simplicity and "objectivity." The aunts in "Rollo" were all wise and comfortable, and the nephews and nieces were never put under the necessity of teaching them their place. The child-world was not a world of questions, but of things, and though the things were common and accessible to all children, they seemed to have the glow of fairy-land upon them. But in **"Eight Cousins"** there is no glow and no fairies; it is all prose, and to our sense rather vulgar prose. (pp. 250-51)

> *[Henry James], in a review of "Eight Cousins; or, The Aunt-Hill," in* The Nation, *Vol. XXI, No. 537, October 14, 1875, pp. 250-51.*

THE ATLANTIC MONTHLY   (essay date 1881)

Miss Alcott's **Jack and Jill** has the merits of her writing more conspicuously than the faults. There is the generous confidence in children which she always shows, the rosy light in which she looks upon the hobbledehoy period, and the persistent lesson of kindness, charity, and amiable sacrifice. The scenes are lively, the incidents varied, and a cheerfulness predominates which is justified by the unfailing success of every character in the book. Yet there is nothing like real character drawing, and the air of life in the book is secured not by an endowment of the persons represented, but by the animation and cheeriness of the author. Nor can we altogether find satisfaction in the suppressed love-making of these young people. The author protests that she is only drawing the picture of a natural society of boys and girls who are soon to be young men and young women, but there is a self-consciousness about the book on this side which impairs its simplicity. We are, no doubt, unreasonable readers; we object to the blood-and-thunder literature, and when in place of it we have the milk-and-sugar we object again. What do we want? (pp. 123-24)

> *A review of "Jack and Jill," in* The Atlantic Monthly, *Vol. XLVII, No. CCLXXIX, January, 1881, pp. 123-24.*

G. K. CHESTERTON   (essay date 1907)

> [*Remembered primarily for his detective stories, Chesterton was also an eminent biographer, essayist, novelist, poet, journalist, dramatist, and critic. His essays are characterized by their humor, frequent use of paradox, and rambling style. His* The Victorian Age in Literature *is considered a standard source. Chesterton here ranks Alcott with Jane Austen and states that "Little Women was written by a woman for women. . . ." He praises the work*

> *for its "unmistakable material truth," as well as for its moral philosophy, and remarks that "even from a masculine standpoint, the* [Little Women] *books are very good. . . ."*]

Little Women was written by a woman for women—for little women. Consequently it anticipated realism by twenty or thirty years; just as Jane Austen anticipated it by at least a hundred years. For women are the only realists; their whole object in life is to pit their realism against the extravagant, excessive, and occasionally drunken idealism of men. . . . There is, indeed, a vast division in the matter of literature (an unimportant matter), but there is the same silent and unexplained assumption of the feminine point of view. There is no pretence, as most unfortunately occurred in the case of another woman of genius, George Eliot, that the writer is anything else but a woman, writing to amuse other women, with her awful womanly irony. Jane Austen did not call herself George Austen; nor Louisa Alcott call herself George Alcott. These women refrained from that abject submission to the male sex which we have since been distressed to see; the weak demand for masculine names and for a part in merely masculine frivolities; parliaments, for instance. These were strong women; they classed parliament with the public-house. But for another and better reason, I do not hesitate to name Miss Alcott by the side of Jane Austen; because her talent, though doubtless inferior, was of exactly the same kind. There is an unmistakable material truth about the thing; if that material truth were not the chief female characteristic, we should most of us find our houses burnt down when we went back to them. To take but one instance out of many, and an instance that a man can understand, because a man was involved, the account of the quite sudden and quite blundering proposal, acceptance, and engagement between Jo and the German professor under the umbrella, with parcels falling off them, so to speak, every minute, is one of the really human things in human literature; when you read it you feel sure that human beings have experienced it often; you almost feel that you have experienced it yourself. There is something true to all our own private diaries in the fact that our happiest moments have happened in the rain, or under some absurd impediment of absurd luggage. The same is true of a hundred other elements in the story. The whole affair of the children acting the different parts in *Pickwick,* forming a childish club under strict restrictions, in order to do so; all that is really life, even where it is not literature. And as a final touch of human truth, nothing could be better than the way in which Miss Alcott suggests the borders and the sensitive privacy of such an experiment. All the little girls have become interested, as they would in real life, in the lonely little boy next door; but when one of them introduces him into their private club in imitation of *Pickwick,* there is a general stir of resistance; these family fictions do not endure being considered from the outside.

All that is profoundly true; and something more than that is profoundly true. For just as the boy was an intruder in that club of girls, so any masculine reader is really an intruder among this pile of books. There runs through the whole series a certain moral philosophy, which a man can never really get the hang of. For instance, the girls are always doing something, pleasant or unpleasant. In fact, when they have not to do something unpleasant, they deliberately do something else. A great part, perhaps the more godlike part, of a boy's life, is passed in doing nothing at all. Real selfishness, which is the simplest thing in the world to a boy or man, is practically left out of the calculation. The girls may conceivably oppress and torture each other; but they will not indulge or even enjoy themselves—not, at least, as men understand indulgence or enjoyment. . . . But two things are quite certain; first, that even from a masculine standpoint, the books are very good; and second, that from a feminine standpoint they are so good that their admirers have really lost sight even of their goodness. (pp. 164-66)

> G. K. Chesterton, "Louisa Alcott" (1907), in his A Handful of Authors: Essays on Books and Writers, edited by Dorothy Collins (reprinted by permission of Miss D. E. Collins), Sheed and Ward, Inc., 1953, pp. 163-67.

KATHARINE FULLERTON GEROULD (essay date 1920)

[Twentieth-century critics have found less to praise in Little Women than previous commentators. Gerould is one of the best known of Alcott's detractors and notes that she is "content to be typical. All her people have the same background. . . ." In this excerpt, Gerould agrees that Alcott's perception of New England is accurate and well-represented, but dislikes the "inexcusable amount of love-making" in the novels, as well as the "blatant" moral tone she perceives throughout Alcott's works.]

The astounding result of re-reading Miss Alcott at a mature age is a conviction that she probably gives a better impression of mid-century New England than any of the more laborious reconstructions, either in fiction or in essay. The youth of her characters does not hinder her in this; for childhood, supremely, takes life ready-made. Mr. [William Dean] Howells's range is wider, and he is at once more serious and more detached. Technically, he and Miss Alcott can be compared as little as [Gustave Flaubert's] Madame Bovary and the Bibliothèque Rose. Yet, although their testimonies often agree, his world does not "compose" as hers does. . . . Miss Alcott is content to be typical. All her people have the same background, live in the same atmosphere, profess the same ideals. Moreover, they were ideals and an atmosphere that imposed themselves widely during their period. Mr. Howells gives us modern instances in plenty, but nowhere does he give us clearly the quintessential New England village. It is precisely the familiar experiences of life in that quintessential village that Miss Alcott gives us, with careless accuracy, without arrière-pensée [a hidden motive]. (pp. 184-85)

[What] strikes one on first re-reading her, is the extraordinary success with which she has given us our typical New England. Some of her books, obviously, are less successful in this way than others—**Under the Lilacs,** for example, or **Jack and Jill,** where . . . there is an inexcusable amount of love-making. There is an equally inexcusable amount of love-making, it is interesting to remember, in much of the earlier Howells. But for contemporary record of manners and morals, you will go far before you match her masterpiece, **Little Women.** What Meg, Jo, Beth, Amy, and Laurie do not teach us about life in New England at a certain time, we shall never learn from any collected edition of the letters of Emerson, Thoreau, or Hawthorne.

The next—and equally astounding—result of re-reading Miss Alcott was [that her characters] . . . were, in some ways, underbred. Bronson Alcott (or shall we say Mr. March?) quotes Plato in his family circle; but his family uses inveterately bad grammar. "Don't talk about 'labelling' Pa, as if he was a pickle-bottle!"—thus Jo chides her little sister for a malapropism. Bad grammar we might expect from Jo, as a wilful freak; but should we expect the exquisite Amy (any little girl will tell you how exquisite Amy is supposed to be) to write to

her father from Europe, about buying gloves in Paris, "Don't that sound sort of elegant and rich?"

The bad grammar, in all the books, is constant. And yet, I know of no other young people's stories, anywhere, wherein the background is so unbrokenly and sincerely "literary." Cheap literature is unsparingly satirized; Plato and Goethe are quoted quite as everyday matters; and "a metaphysical streak had unconsciously got into" Jo's first novel. In **The Rose in Bloom,** Miss Alcott misquotes Swinburne, to be sure, but she does it in the interest of morality. . . . (pp. 185-87)

Breeding is, of course, not merely a matter of speech. . . . Miss Alcott's people are, as the author herself says of them, unworldly. They are even magnificently so; and they score the worldly at every turn. (p. 188)

Granted their unworldliness, their high scale of moral values, where, then, is the trace of vulgarity that is needed to make breeding bad? They pride themselves on their separation from all vulgarity. "My mother is a lady," Polly reflects, "even if"—even if she is not rich, like the Shaws. The March girls are always consoling themselves for their vicissitudes by the fact that their parents are gentlefolk. Well, they are underbred in precisely the way in which, one fancies, the contemporaries of Emerson in Concord may well have been underbred. It is the "plain-living" side of the "high thinking." They despised externals, and, in the end, externals had their revenge. Breeding, as such, is simply not a product of the independent village. . . . The villagers have not—and who supposes that Bronson Alcott and Thoreau had it?—the gift of civilized contacts. A contact, be it remembered, is not quite the same thing as a relation. Manners are a natural growth of courts. Recall any mediaeval dwelling of royalty; then imagine life lived in those cramped chambers, in the perpetual presence of superiors and inferiors alike—and lived informally!

In Miss Alcott's world, all that is changed. According to the older tradition, a totally unchaperoned youth would mean lack of breeding. Here, on the contrary, all the heroines are unchaperoned, while the match-making mamma is anathema. . . . The reward of the unchaperoned daughter is to make a good match. In that rigid school, conventions are judged—and nobly enough, Heaven knows!—from the point of view of morals alone (of absolute, not of historic or evolutionary morals) and many conventions are thereby damned. . . . "Underbred" is very likely too strong a word; yet one does see how the social state described in **Little Women** might easily shock any one brought up in a less provincial tradition. There is too much love-making, for example. Though sweethearting between five-year-olds is frowned on, sweethearting between fifteen-year-olds is quite the thing. In real life, it would not always be safe to marry, very young, your first playmate. Any one who has lived in the more modern New England village knows perfectly well that people still marry, very young, their first playmates, and that disaster often results. Nor can Una always depend on the protection of a lion that is necessarily invisible. Granted that Jo's precocious sense was right, and that it would have been a mistake for her to marry Laurie; which of us believes that, in real life, she would not have made the mistake? (pp. 188-90)

The whole tissue of the March girls' lives is a very commonplace fabric. You know that their furniture was bad—and that they did not know it; that their aesthetic sense was untrained and crude—and that they did not care; that the simplicity of their meals, their household service, their dress, their every day manners (in spite of the myth about Amy) was simplicity of the common, not of the intelligent, kind. You really would not want to spend a week in the house of any one of them. Nor had their simplicity in any wise the quality of austerity. Remember the pies that the older March girls carried for muffs (the management whereof was one of the ever unsolved riddles of my childhood).

No: in so far as breeding is a matter of externals, one must admit that there is some sense in calling Miss Alcott's people underbred. Perhaps we do not choose to call breeding a matter of externals. In that, we should perfectly agree with Miss Alcott's people themselves; and to that we shall presently come. For what is incontrovertible is that Miss Alcott's work is a genuine document. (p. 191)

There are not, I believe, any other books in the world so blatantly full of morality—of moral issues, and moral tests, and morals passionately abided by—and at the same time so empty of religion. The Bible is never quoted; almost no one goes to church; and they pray only when very young and in extreme cases. The only religious allusion, so far as I know, in **Little Women**, is the patronizing mention of the Madonna provided for Amy by Aunt March's Catholic maid. And even then, you can see how broad-minded Mrs. March considers herself, to permit Amy the quasi-oratory; and Amy does not attempt to disguise the fact that she admires the picture chiefly for its artistic quality. (pp. 192-93)

The New English literary tradition seems to be fairly clear: either passion must be public, or, if it is private, it must be thwarted. There is a good deal of public passion—for philanthropy, for education, and what-not—in the books, after all. There is no private passion at all: though the books brim with sentiment, Miss Alcott writes as one who had never loved. It would be difficult to find, anywhere, stories so full of love-making and so empty of emotion. (p. 195)

> *Katharine Fullerton Gerould, ''Miss Alcott's New England,'' in her* Modes and Morals *(copyright, 1920, by Charles Scribner's Sons; copyright renewed 1948 by Gordon Hall Gerould; reprinted with permission of Charles Scribner's Sons), Charles Scribner's Sons, 1920, pp. 182-98.*

ELIZABETH VINCENT   (essay date 1924)

Why do people republish [Alcott's books]? . . . [In **Little Women**, the] characters are perfectly categorical—each patterned on a simple formula like this: Mr. March, father, philosopher and friend; Mrs. March, Mother and All That Stands For; Meg, fastidious womanliness; Amy, a perfect little lady; Beth, angel in the house. Even Jo is not the person to cut much ice with the current 'teens. . . .

The so-called plot holds few apparent thrills. . . . Miss Alcott herself admitted it was not ''sensational,'' and at that she exaggerated. Except for the uncomplicated chronicle of their loves and marriages the Marches have really nothing to offer in the way of plot at all. The structure of the book is largely segmental, each chapter a neatly rounded episode, loaded with its lesson, and capped with repentance and tears and a few words of comfort from Mrs. March.

And yet—and yet: one does have to admit that these impossible Marches are real people. The children who get so absorbed in them are not wrong in finding them alive and true. The only wonder is that any child raised this side of 1900 has been able

to put up with the things they do and the things they say, these all too real people. Of course the Marches *were* real people. Except for the trussing up of episodes and the simplification of character which passes for Miss Alcott's art, she has merely reported her own family.

I can see . . . why little girls still read [Miss Alcott's] books. They are bad for them of course. Could any but pernicious influence hold such a fascination for so long? The fact is that little girls have a natural depraved taste for moralizing. They like to see virtue rewarded and evil punished. They like good resolutions. They like tears and quarrels and loving reconciliations. They believe in the ultimate triumph of good, in moral justice, and honeymoons in Valarosa. And Miss Alcott panders to these passions!

Let modern mothers bob their hair and talk the neopsychic talk. Let children spell by drawing rabbits; let them study the city water works. Yet it will not avail. For unless we take to censorship to protect them against the subversions of the past, little girls will read **Little Women** still.

> *Elizabeth Vincent, ''Subversive Miss Alcott,'' in* The New Republic, *Vol. XL, No. 516, October 22, 1924, p. 204.*

MADELEINE B. STERN   (essay date 1949)

[*Stern elucidates the numerous reasons for* Little Women's *enduring popularity. Calling the novel ''far more than a picture of childhood,'' Stern praises Alcott's depictions of adolescent psychology and claims that* Little Women's *episodic organization ''results in a mighty architecture'' of structure.*]

[Louisa May Alcott's] muse was, first and foremost, domestic. She unlatched the door to one house, and her readers speedily discovered that it was their own house that they entered. She unroofed every dwelling in the land by unroofing the home of the four March girls. **Little Women** is great because it is a book on the American home, and hence universal in its appeal. As long as human beings delight in ''the blessings that alone can make life happy,'' as long as they believe, with Jo March, that ''families are the most beautiful things in all the world,'' the book will be treasured. It is a domestic drama, indeed, and Louisa Alcott knew, as her representative did, that when she wrote of her own home ''something got into that story that went straight to the hearts of those who read it.'' Like Jo, the author had ''found her style at last.'' The jolly larks, the plays and tableaux, the sleigh rides and skating frolics are enjoyed not by an isolated heroine, but by a family. The poverty, the domestic trials, . . . are the troubles and the joys of family life. The omissions indicate as notably as the actual content the writer's contributions to the domestic novel. (pp. 476-77)

To the domestic novel the author made still another contribution in **Little Women**. While her glorification of family life is universal in its appeal, her details offer a local flavor that gives the work a documentary value. . . . By its documentary value alone, **Little Women**, as an index of New England manners in the mid-century, would be accorded a place in literary history. It is the great merit of the book that it is at once a documentary account of a given locality and a universal delineation of any American home. By those two contributions, the one local, the other universal, the author raised the domestic novel from the state of trite insipidity in which it had remained so long, and carved for herself a niche in American letters.

Louisa Alcott added no less to juvenile literature than to the domestic novel. *Little Women* is far more than a "picture of a happy childhood." . . . The author's knowledge of adolescent psychology reveals itself in twofold form throughout the work, for it consisted first of an appeal to adolescents, the skill of making them laugh or cry, and secondly of an ability to describe adolescents, to catch and transfix the varied emotions and thoughts of the young. (pp. 477-78)

Louisa Alcott remembered her adolescence and recorded it before the memory faded. . . . *Little Women* runs the gamut of the adolescent heart and mind, and supplies a case book of adolescent psychology far surpassing any text on the subject.

By combining her local and universal contributions to the domestic novel with her knowledge of adolescent psychology, Louisa Alcott cleared the ground of juvenile literature and wrote a best-seller for the generations. The means whereby she arrived at such an end are less apparent than the end itself. She forgot none of the varied techniques she had tried when she sat down to produce a girls' book. . . . She remembered her apprenticeship in the short story, and the method she evolved in *Little Women* is therefore episodic. Each chapter in turn is granted almost invariably to one of the sisters, so that Meg's married life alternates with Amy's experiences abroad or Jo's tussles with herself at home. This segmental structure results in a mighty architecture when it houses human beings, for the author knew that "our lives are patchwork." . . . [The] episodic technique requires a short attention span for young readers and at the same time gives the effect of verisimilitude in the lives of human beings which do indeed resemble patchwork. (pp. 478-80)

[Realism] provided the finest grist for [Louisa Alcott's] mill. (p. 480)

The use of "good strong words, that mean something," the grammar that is as natural as it is unpolished aided her in producing that "mannerless manner" by which verisimilitude is achieved. She was well aware of the value of never using a long word when a short one would do as well. Her defenses of impure English were not written until later, but they were practised in *Little Women*. It is better to "let children write their own natural letters . . . than to make them copy the Grandisonian style." (p. 481)

The author was less successful in her attempts at repeating her characterizations of adolescence [in her later works following *Little Women*]. By reason of her hearty good will and honest realism, Polly, of *An Old-Fashioned Girl*, narrowly escapes being a "little prig in a goody story-book." She is at once a symbol of the old-fashioned virtues and a genuine little girl who heartily enjoys a coast down the mall, dolls' dresses, and Grandma Shaw's stories. The March girls were individuals who never deteriorated into symbols. Once the writer converted Polly into "Sweet P.," "Polly Peacemaker," she ran the risk of weakening the verisimilitude of her character. . . . The boys of *Little Men* . . . lack the three-dimensional qualities of the March girls. . . . To each the author endowed one glaring fault awaiting correction by the Plumfield methods; hence the reader is likely to think of Ned as the braggart, Stuffy as the glutton, Tommy as the mischievous youth, and Dan as the wild boy rather than as fully rounded individuals. Nan . . . was modeled from the mold of Jo March, but she lacks Jo's completeness and becomes a mere symbol of the tomboy. The symbols continue to pursue the readers of *Eight Cousins,* where the characterizations were touched off boldly with broad strokes, each

of the *dramatis personae* possessing one distinguishing trait adumbrated in the beginning and continually stressed. . . . Louisa Alcott was never to repeat the more minute characterizations of *Little Women*. Bab of *Under the Lilacs* . . . is simply another Nan, the tomboy who inherits Jo March's gallantry and allows Ben to win the archery contest. Jack of *Jack and Jill* is a symbol of pluck rather than a plucky adolescent; Merry Grant is a representative of household art rather than an artistic girl. Jo's Boys continue to be the stereotypes of *Little Men*. . . . The author had no time to add full-length portraits to her gallery of adolescents or to complete with minute touches the sketches too broadly painted in her *Little Women* Series. (pp. 482-84)

So aware was the author of the means of titillating the minds of her readers that when she could no longer invent fresh incidents she repeated the old to delight them. Where Amy March had nearly met her death after a fall through the ice, Rob of *Jo's Boys* . . . narrowly escapes hydrophobia because of Ted's wilfulness. Where Laurie had asked to pull forever in the same boat with his beloved, Tom expresses the wish to go on cycling with his angel. . . . As the years drew on, the author found it impossible to resist the temptation of repeating her themes with or without variation. She knew her public and she catered to their demands. . . . Children, she believed, were "good critics . . . , and to suit them was an accomplishment that any one might be proud of." Suit them she did, and she will continue to suit them as long as their tastes remain unchanged. (p. 484)

From all the authors whose influence she acknowledged, Louisa Alcott took only what she could apply to her own purposes—from Bunyan, the picturesque progress of an Everyman from the Slough of Despond to the Celestial City; from Dickens, a few obvious and sentimental characterizations; from Carlyle, a simple and a single doctrine; from Thoreau, a flowery fairyland and its gardener; from Emerson, a lofty ethic; from Parker, exaltation of strength of character. She selected precisely such material as would be intelligible to youthful readers. When she borrowed from Hawthorne, however, the author found that she was borrowing from writings composed in an intellectual twilight, haunted by shadows and the ghosts of shadows. By no amount of literary skill could such material be worked into wholesome tales for *Harper's Young People* or *St. Nicholas.* Hence it is that Hawthorne's influence is most apparent in a book written neither for nor about children, but in a book issued anonymously in the No Name Series of Roberts Brothers, that freed the author from fulfilling her obligations to her young public and from adding fresh laurels to her reputation as a juvenile writer.

[This book,] *A Modern Mephistopheles,* is less interesting, however, as a demonstration of Hawthorne's influence upon Louisa Alcott than as an instance of what the successful author wrote when she pleased herself instead of her admirers. It is, indeed, the only book written after 1868 that gives any indication of what Louisa Alcott might have become had she not devoted herself to juvenile literature. The result is disappointing. Instead of using her journalistic skill to report the domestic life of her day, or incorporating in the novel her observations of adolescents, she reverted to the sensationalism of her early career, combining with it a verbose intellectuality based upon her readings in Hawthorne and Goethe. *A Modern Mephistopheles* is a bookish and spurious attempt at "literature," a study, almost in abstract, of good contending with evil, of crime and the punishment consequent upon it.

The characters of the novel are pegs upon which the author hung her theme, artificial puppets lacking all reality. Felix

Canaris, the Adonis who sells his liberty and his love for fame, the young Bacchus who revels in "olives and old wine," surely never lived in Concord; Jasper Helwyze, the Sybarite with a Mephistophelian love of power, who believes "in nothing invisible and divine," whose god is intellect and who studies the subtle evil of men's minds, bears little resemblance to any human being. Olivia, the mellow beauty, and Gladys, the artless, "white-souled" girl, are contrasting symbols rather than contrasting women.

When Louisa Alcott wrote anonymously she borrowed as much from the effusions of "A. M. Barnard" (the pseudonym she had frequently used in her own thrillers), as from Hawthorne or Goethe, for *A Modern Mephistopheles* follows not only in its characterizations but in its episodes the pattern of the penny dreadfuls. Mesmerism is substituted for more obvious violence, and hashish, enclosed in a "*bonbonnière* [candy box] of tortoise-shell and silver" takes the place of opium. The style itself is reminiscent of the mannerisms of "A. M. Barnard," for it is peppered with exotic descriptions of "lustrous silks sultanas were to wear," of "odorous woods and spices, . . . with fragrance never blown from Western hills," of "skins mooned and barred with black upon the tawny velvet, that had lain in jungles, or glided with deathful stealthiness along the track of human feet." . . . The ghost of "A. M. Barnard" had not been laid.

Yet it must be admitted that the threads of these sensational phrases and themes have been woven upon a more mature framework than any used by "A. M. Barnard." The plot itself, consisting of "the contest between good and evil," the struggle between the world, the flesh and the devil, on the one hand, and virtue on the other is, as it was designed to be, a modern debate between the body and soul. (pp. 494-96)

Louisa Alcott will be remembered first for her accurate depiction of the domestic life of the nation in *Little Women* especially, but also in *An Old-Fashioned Girl, Eight Cousins,* and *Jack and Jill.* She will be remembered secondly for her studies of adolescent psychology exhibited in the three-dimensional characters of the March girls, and thirdly for her astounding ability to appeal to youthful readers revealed in the *Little Women* Series. Her contribution to the domestic novel have a value at once universal and local, to be treasured by adult readers as well as by an adolescent public, for the household which she chose to delineate is indeed a "microcosm of the world outside." It is and ever will be valid that "the incidents of any life truly set forth in their human interest will take hold of humanity as with a spell." Louisa Alcott's translation of the incidents of family life to the domain of literature will take hold of humanity as long as family life abides. Her twofold contribution to the more limited field of juvenile literature, her characterization of adolescence and her ability to appeal to adolescents, will likewise be cherished as long as youth endures. (p. 497)

> *Madeleine B. Stern, "Louisa M. Alcott: An Appraisal," in* The New England Quarterly, *Vol. XXII, No. 4, December, 1949, pp. 475-98.*

BRIGID BROPHY (essay date 1964)

[*Brophy calls the characters of* Little Women *masochists and is especially critical of Alcott's excessive sentimentality in the depiction of Beth and Laurie.*]

You can measure Alcott's technical skill by asking any professional novelist how he would care to have to differentiate the characters of four adolescent girls—particularly if he were confined to a domestic setting, more-or-less naturalism and the things which were mentionable when Alcott wrote. Greater scope in at least the first and last of those departments has not prevented more than one recent novel from making a hash of almost the identical technical problem. Alcott, of course, triumphed at it (that is why we have heard of her), incidentally turning out for one of her four, Meg, a brilliant portrait of the sort of girl whose character consists of having no character. Girls of this sort are the commonest to meet in life and the rarest in literature, because they are so hard to depict (the problem is a variant of the old one about depicting a bore without being boring): usually it takes the genius of a Tolstoy (who specialised in them) to bring them off.

Whereas Meg was a commonplace of Alcott's own—or any—time, in Amy Alcott actually shewed sociological prescience. Or, rather, I think, it shewed despite her. Try as she will to prettify and moralise, she cannot help making Amy the prototype of a model which did not become numerous in the United States until the twentieth century—the peroxided, girl-doll golddigger. *Of course* it's Amy who gets Laurie in the end (he's rich, isn't he?): she's had 'Good pull-in for Laurie' emblazoned on her chest from the moment her chest began to bud. (p. 117)

[With Beth,] Alcott went altogether too far. Beth's patience, humility and gentle sunniness are a quite monstrous imposition on the rest of the family—especially when you consider at what close, even cramped, quarters they live (two bedrooms to four girls): no one in the household could escape the blight of feeling unworthy which was imposed by Beth. I concur in the judgment of the person with whom I watched the film (and who wept even more than I did) in naming her the Black Beth. (I also concur in his naming Marmee Smarmee.) I think Louisa Alcott may herself have had an inkling that in designing a fate for Beth she was inspired by revenge. She seems, perhaps through suspicion of her own motives, to have faltered, with the result that she committed the sort of blunder only a very naïve technician would fall into and only a very self-assured one could, as she does, step out of in her stride. She brings Beth to the point of dying in *Little Women,* and then lets her recover; whereupon, instead of washing her hands—as not ruthless enough to do it—of the whole enterprise, she whips the situation up again in *Good Wives* and this time does ('As Beth had hoped, "the tide went out easily"') kill her off.

As for Laurie: well, of course, Laurie is awful, tossing those awful curls (though in *Good Wives* he has them cropped and is told off for it): yet though I will go to my death (may the tide go out easily) denying that Laurie has a millionth part of the attractions he thinks he has and the girls think he has, I cannot deny that he is lifelike. If you want to see the romanticized implausibility which even an intelligent woman of the world (and great novelist into the bargain) could make of a curly-haired young man, look at George Eliot's Will Ladislaw. Laurie by contrast is—if awfully—probable.

In the most important event affecting Laurie, the fact that Jo refuses him, Alcott goes beyond verisimilitude and almost into artistic honesty. No doubt she found the courage for this, which meant cutting across the cliché-lines of the popular novel and defying her readers' matchmaking hopes, in the personality of Jo. Jo is one of the most blatantly autobiographical yet most fairly treated heroines in print. All that stands between her and Emma Woodhouse is her creator's lack of intellect. Alcott is not up to devising situations which analyse and develop, as distinct from merely illustrating, her characters. (pp. 118-19)

As sentimentalists go, Louisa M. Alcott is of the gentler and less immoral sort. Beth's is the only really lushed-over death (the canary who dies in Chapter Eleven of *Little Women* is virtually a throw-away): on the whole, Alcott prefers to wreak her revenges on her characters by making them unhappy in their moments of happiness. (They make it easy for her to do so, through their own proneness to sentimentality.) Even here, one can morally if not aesthetically justify her. It's all, so to speak, between consenting adolescents. All four girls are quite masochists enough to enjoy what she does to them.

I rest on Louisa M. Alcott my plea—hedged about with provisos, reduced, indeed, to a mere strangled sob—that we should recognise that, though sentimentality mars art, craftsmanship in sentimentality is to be as legitimately enjoyed as in any of those genres (thrillers, pornography, ghost stories, yarns, science fiction—whichever way your taste lies) which, because they suppress some relevant strand in artistic logic, are a little less than literature. The spasm across the eyelids is not inherently more despicable than the frisson of the supernatural or the muted erotic thrill imparted by a brilliant sado-erotic literary craftsman like Raymond Chandler. It is, however, more dangerous. (p. 119)

Brigid Brophy, "Sentimentality and Louisa M. Alcott," in The Sunday Times, *London (© Times Newspapers Limited 1964), December 20, 1964 (and reprinted in her* Don't Never Forget: Collected Views and Reviews, *Holt, Rinehart and Winston, 1967, pp. 113-20).*

ELIZABETH JANEWAY   (essay date 1968)

[Janeway comments on the remarkable equality between Jo and Laurie in Little Women. *Jo, Janeway maintains, "is a unique creation: the one young woman in 19th-century fiction who maintains her individual independence . . . and gets away with it."]*

["**Little Women**"] is dated and sentimental and full of preaching and moralizing, and some snobbery about the lower classes that is positively breathtaking in its horror: that moment, for instance, when old Mr. Laurence is improbably discovered in a fishmarket, and bestows his charity on a starving Irish woman by hooking a large fish on the end of his cane, and depositing it, to her gasping gratitude, in her arms. It is as often smug as it is snug, and its high-mindedness tends to be that peculiar sort that pays. . . .

Its faults we can see in a moment. . . . "**Little Women**" does harp on our nerves, does play on our feelings, does stack the cards to bring about undeserved happy outcomes here and undeserved come-uppance there. But that is not the whole story, and couldn't be, or there wouldn't be all those girls with their noses in the book right now, and all those women who remember the supreme shock of the moment when Jo sold her hair; when Beth was discovered on the medicine chest in the closet with scarlet fever coming on; when Meg let the Moffats dress her up; when Amy was packed off, protesting and bargaining, to Aunt March's stiff house.

No, "**Little Women**" does manipulate life, but it is also *about* life, and life that is recognizable in human terms today. Miss Alcott preached, and the conclusions she came to are frequently too good to be true; but the facts of emotion that she started with were real. She might end by softening the ways to deal

with them, but she began by looking them in the eye. Her girls were jealous, mean, silly and lazy; and for 100 years jealous, mean, silly and lazy girls have been ardently grateful for the chance to read about themselves. If Miss Alcott's prescriptions for curing their sins are too simple, it doesn't alter the fact that her diagnoses are clear, unequivocal and humanly right. When her girls are good, they are apt to be painful; but when they are bad, they are bad just the way we all are, and over the same things. . . .

This general background of human interest makes "**Little Women**" still plausible, but it is hardly enough to keep it a perennial classic. The real attraction is not the book as a whole, but its heroine, Jo, and Jo is a unique creation: the one young woman in 19th-century fiction who maintains her individual independence, who gives up no part of her autonomy as payment for being born a woman—and who gets away with it. Jo is the tomboy dream come true, the dream of growing up into full humanity with all its potentialities instead of into limited femininity: of looking after oneself and paying one's way and doing effective work in the real world instead of learning how to please a man who will look after you, as Meg and Amy both do with pious pleasure. (So, by the way, does Natasha [in Leo Tolstoy's "War and Peace"]). It's no secret that Jo's story is the heart of "**Little Women**." . . . (p. 42)

[The relationship between Laurie and Jo] has always been that of two equals, which in 19th-century America (and in some places today) implies two equals of the same sex. Twice at least Laurie suggests that they run off together, not for lovemaking, but for adventure; very much in the manner and mood in which [Mark Twain's] Tom Sawyer and Huck Finn plan to run away from comfort and civilization. Again when Jo speaks to her mother about the possibility of marriage to Laurie, Mrs. March is against it "because you two are too much alike." So they are, and so—with no explanations ever given—Jo refuses Laurie, and the reader knows she is right, for Jo and Laurie are dear friends, competitors and not in the least a couple. It is worth nothing that the two other adored 19th-century heroines who say "No" to the hero's proposal give way in the end, when circumstances and the hero have changed: Elizabeth Bennet and [Charlotte Brontë's] Jane Eyre. But Jo says "No" and does not shift.

The subtlety of Miss Alcott's character drawing (or self knowledge, if you will) comes through here, for Jo is a tomboy, but never a masculinized or Lesbian figure. She is, somehow, an idealized "New Woman," capable of male virtues but not, as the Victorians would have said, "unsexed." Or perhaps she is really archaic woman, re-created out of some New-World-frontier necessity when patriarchy breaks down. For Jo marries (as we all know! Who can forget that last great self-indulgent burst of tears when Professor Bhaer stops, under the umbrella, and asks "Heart's dearest, why do you cry?"). Yes, Jo marries and becomes, please note, not a sweet little wife but a matriarch: mistress of the professor's school, mother of healthy sons (while Amy and Laurie have only one sickly daughter), and cheerful active manager of events and people. For this Victorian moral tract, sentimental and preachy, was written by a secret rebel against the order of the world and woman's place in it, and all the girls who ever read it know it. (pp. 44, 46)

Elizabeth Janeway, "Meg, Jo, Beth, Amy and Louisa," in The New York Times Book Review *(copyright © 1968 by The New York Times Company; reprinted by permission), September 29, 1968, pp. 42, 44, 46.*

CORNELIA MEIGS (essay date 1968)

[In *Little Women*, Miss Alcott] contributed not only sympathy and understanding to her characters but also a complete and generous honesty which gave the book its strong sense of reality. She pretended nothing and concealed nothing; all of her persons were fully and frankly themselves. People who read the book could see reflected their own failings, their own small and secret temptations, and be reassured by the account of other people trying to get the better of their shortcomings. Particularly in relation to herself, Miss Alcott showed Jo in all her hasty-tempered errors, all her doubts and hesitations and her many failures in trying to avoid them. With her instinctive keenness of observation she was able to describe how people could and did change, could develop and make the most of themselves as they went forward. . . .

In certain ways the book inevitably shows that it was written in another age, one in which people felt free to express their feelings and their spiritual and inner thoughts more fully than they would today. In spite of that, the book showed a long step forward for its time. In books for young people it was then the custom to weigh down the narrative with moral platitudes, strewn with an all too heavy hand. Louisa was fully aware of the dangers of too much preaching. (p. x)

Mrs. March's occasional little lectures have their own solid worth; they are, actually, only made up of matters that all parents would like to put before their children. Jo's mother, when the two consult together over Jo's impulsive difficulties in the conduct of her life, does not hesitate to meet her troubled daughter on her own ground and exposes all of her own failures in learning to control a hot and explosive temper.

The natural progress of events which is involved in the growing up of four lively girls and the boy who lives next door would make plot enough, but the course of the story follows a more distinctive pattern which should not be overlooked. There is an illuminating scene in the earlier part of the book which ought not to be too hastily passed over. On a certain summer afternoon Laurie sees the girls going up the hill behind the house, wearing big hats, with bags hanging on their shoulders and with staffs in their hands. When he joins them he finds that they are playing a game which they have been fond of since they were small children, that of being people in *Pilgrim's Progress,* the book to which every one of the Alcotts was so devoted. Sitting on the grass the girls and Laurie fall to talking of the future and each one voices his or her ambition, telling of the thing that is at the back of every growing young person's mind, "What would I like to be?" (pp. x-xi)

While the reader is not aware of it, one of the things that holds the story together is the fact that all these cherished schemes do, in actual fact, come to their desired ends but only after each person has accepted the modification and compromise that circumstances and his or her own character have made inevitable. The happy and irresponsible materialism and youthful vanity that clothe these ambitious plans are shed away and replaced by something far more valuable. It is the highest proof of Louisa Alcott's mastery of storytelling that none of us realize this until we look back long after we have read the book. (pp. xi-xii)

[Perhaps] the thing for which we can be most thankful was that travel brought [Miss Alcott the image of the character] Laurie.

She met him in Vevey where she and her friend had stayed a month. He was Ladislas Wisinewski, the Polish boy who had

taken part in the resistance to Russian rule, who had been in prison, who was ill and an exile, who was such a fine musician and such an immediate and devoted friend. . . . It was, of course, pure imagination which brought him, in her unfolding story, to live next door to the March family and to become part of all they did and thought. He is, except for Jo, Louisa's most perfectly drawn character, with his charm, his musical temperament, his dash of foreign inheritance and his slight leaning toward irresponsibility of which all four sisters try so conscientiously to cure him. With it all he has his grandfather's strong integrity, besides his own affectionate and generous heart, which has its particular link with each member of the March family. He and Jo are the principal figures of the book, both of them unsparingly shown as having their own faults, but both irresistibly likable beyond all the rest. (p. xiii)

Cornelia Meigs, "Introduction" (copyright © 1968 by Little, Brown and Company (Inc.); reprinted by permission of Little, Brown and Company), in Little Women; or, Meg, Jo, Beth and Amy *by Louisa May Alcott, Little, Brown, 1968, pp. vii-xiv.*

THOMAS H. PAULY (essay date 1975)

Set against the background of the Civil War and its disruption of life in America, [*Little Women*] implies that the solidarity of the home is an equally critical test of the nation's health, the final result depending on the fortitude of the women who struggle to sustain it. (p. 585)

This is not to say that *Little Women* is merely a hornbook in female propriety. Perhaps the greatest achievement of the work derives from its successes in presenting these "burdens" as neither an ordeal nor a tedious lesson in manners, but rather a colorful array of concerns and diversions, sorrows and joys, with which Alcott's audience could identify. . . . [The] March girls participate in activities and events which could easily have been part of their readers' own lives. Their love of parties, their delight in games, their fear of alienation, their desire for recognition make the girls' experiences both exciting and familiar. However much Meg's vanity, Jo's temper, Beth's aestheticism or Amy's disobedience may appear ridiculously venial transgressions in comparison to the Bunyan vices with which they are associated, they are faults which their audience recognized and shared. The pronounced disparity between the sensational, romantic literature with which the girls are constantly involved . . . and the very plausible, even plain lives they lead suggests that Alcott may have been signalling her departure from the prevailing literary standard of her audience and calling attention to the drama and impact that could attend the commonplace. (pp. 585-86)

However much Jo wishes to align herself with the example of her mother, whose disciplined temper, loving devotion to her children, and selfless commitment to her domestic responsibilities define her as an ideal Victorian woman, the daughter's attempts at being a "little woman" only show her to be a distinct nonconformist. Her willingness to wear a dress with scorch marks stems not only from a real lack of concern for her appearance and a realization that she would merely ruin a nice dress, but also from an underlying reluctance to assume a role she cannot play; whether or not her dress is marred, the strict social demands of a formal dance leave her much more comfortable behind a curtain with the ineffectual Laurie. In other words, the marred dress simply becomes an overt symbol of Jo's sense of disharmony with her outer role. She is at ease only in the "unfashionable" flop hat she wears to the picnic because it proclaims her uniqueness and visually anticipates the indecorous outbursts of ''Christopher Columbus!'' she cannot repress.

This impropriety in dress, manners and conversation gives her the reputation of being ''boyish.'' Yet, for all her domination of Laurie and her croquet victory over Fred, Jo is no more masculine than she is childish. Her repeated wishes that she always remain the same age . . . , that she have an iron upon her head to keep her from growing up . . . , like her reference to herself as ''the man of the family,'' tell the reader not what she is, but rather her sense of deviance from what is conventionally expected of her. At the same time, both references reveal her essentially female nature, by virtue of her accord with the prevailing association of the woman with the home. Her wish to prolong her childhood stems from a desire to retain the intimacy she enjoys with her mother and sisters. Similarly, as ''man of the family,'' she eagerly assumes the burden of responsibility for preserving this closely knit circle. However, these efforts to assume the responsibilities of the parent while preserving the security of the child leave Jo in the awkward position of opposing marriage, not only for herself but for her sisters. She makes a concerted effort to prevent the match between Mr. Brooke and Meg, not because of Mr. Brooke's lack of means, as she first insists . . . , nor out of jealousy, but in order to preserve the integral intimacy of the family. . . . (pp. 586-87)

By way of extension, she insistently refuses to allow her involvement with Laurie to advance beyond that of a brother-sister relationship. Jo's determination to break up the Meg/Mr. Brooke match leads her to the expectation that Meg will marry Laurie ''by and by.'' . . . Alcott herself resisted the pairing of Jo and Laurie to the extent that she would only agree to writing a sequel on the condition that they not be married; ''I won't marry Jo to Laurie, to please anyone,'' she insisted. However intrusive may be the Freudian overtones of this stance, Jo's reluctance to accept the responsibilities of marriage and motherhood is nonetheless a logical extension of her persistent rejection of the prevailing standards of womanhood. In the totally female world of the March household, Jo's strong personality has been allowed to flourish so that, despite her resolution to control her strong will, she still cannot abide the stifling constraints of the male-dominated society outside. Appropriately, Jo's story of ''The Rival Painters,'' which wins her literary acclaim, financial reward and some consequent independence, is a tale of unrequited love ending with the death of both hero and heroine. Such a conclusion, as the narrator points out . . . , eliminates any possibility of a sequel which would presumably cover the lives of the pair together. In trying to interest us in a rather similar depiction of Jo's development, Louisa May Alcott makes a concerted effort to win sympathy for a spirited heroine confronting the same plight she herself faced. Jo, indeed, has her faults, it is made clear, yet they are integral to her uniqueness as a passionate supporter of the Victorian home who rejects the debilitating role it imposed on the women who maintained it. (p. 587)

> *Thomas H. Pauly, '''Ragged Dick' and 'Little Women': Idealized Homes and Unwanted Marriages,'' in* Journal of Popular Culture *(copyright © 1975 by Thomas H. Pauly), Vol. IX, No. 3, Winter, 1975, pp. 583-92.**

PATRICIA MEYER SPACKS (essay date 1975)

[*Sparks interprets* Little Women *as a portrait of feminine nature— passive, altruistic, disciplined, and repressed.*]

Little Women is usually remembered, sometimes even referred to in print, as a study of four girls with an absent father. In fact, the father is on hand for half the narrative. He provides spiritual advice to his daughters (his tone and language eerily identical with his wife's), confiscates the wine at Meg's wedding, teaches his grandson the alphabet: guide, rebuker, pedagogue—man. Yet he seems invisible: in a deep sense this is a women's world. On the other hand, there is no doubt about which sex really *does things*. The novel—one hesitates to call it that, since the narrative complexity is on the level of a child's story: all, of course, it purports to be—exhaustively examines the feminine role of ''taking care,'' yet makes clear from the outset that the masculine kind of taking care—providing financial and serious moral support—is the kind that counts. The girls dispute about who is to have the privilege of buying their mother some new slippers. Jo wins, saying, ''I'm the man of the family now papa is away, and I shall provide the slippers, for he told me to take special care of mother while he was gone.'' Unfortunately for her psychic well-being, she can only temporarily occupy the comforting role of ''man of the family''; her father returns to supplant her.

The book is not one an adult is likely to reread with pleasure, yet children—even college students—still respond strongly to Jo as a fictional character. And the pure didacticism that governs the narrative gives it special clarity as a revelation of nineteenth-century feminine assumptions about feminine nature and possibility. Louisa May Alcott's ideas about what women should and can be, and what men naturally are, shape the simple narrative structure, which moves from one ''lesson'' to another. These pieces of didacticism reveal how completely women can incorporate unflattering assumptions about their own nature, using such assumptions as moral goads. (pp. 96-7)

The nature of women, this book suggests, is to be frivolous, foolish, vain, and lazy. They must be laboriously taught to be otherwise. Only in relative isolation can they learn to be good, since female society is thoroughly corrupt. Confining themselves within the family, learning at the knee of a virtuous mother, controlled from afar by a vague but stern father, they may hope to acquire goodness, which will be rewarded, at best, by marriage or at least by the opportunity to exercise positive influence on a man. Boys, on the other hand, are naturally enterprising, gay, and bold. Masculine society may lead a young man to play pranks; such boyish high spirits will be admired and envied by young women, who beg to be told of them. At worst, such society leads the man to drinking— but a word from a good woman will make him swear off. A man may fall into depression; a woman can bring him out of it. Such power is her highest achievement. In most cases her other nondomestic accomplishments represent only ways of passing time until she is married. It is true that Jo writes successfully—but Jo is a special, and complicated, case. (p. 97)

[The March girls] must learn to repress emotion, specifically anger. The expression of anger, it seems, is always unforgivable. When Meg's husband brings home an unseasonable guest, she reveals her anger and frustration in an explosion. He conceals his, so he wins: she apologizes. When Meg is extravagant with her husband's money, he says almost nothing, but quietly sacrifices his winter overcoat. He wins. Mrs. March has learned almost total repression of hostile emotions: this is a source of her power. She urges the lesson on Jo particularly, whose curse is a temper. Girls are not expected, not *allowed*, to have tempers. When a boy, their neighbor Laurie, has a fit of temper, Jo goes over to soothe him and his grandfather and bring them together by feminine wiles. No one objects to the boy's directly expressed resentment and hostility. When Jo has a fit of temper, her sister almost dies as a result. Her mother reveals that she has once had the same fault, but "I've learned to check the hasty words that rise to my lips and when I feel that they mean to break out against my will, I just go away a minute, and give myself a little shake, for being so weak and wicked." It is "weak and wicked" for a woman ever to express hostility . . . ever to express even vitality, except in limited prescribed forms. Jo's mother has learned from her husband to be good. "He never loses patience—never doubts or complains—but always hopes, and works, and waits so cheerfully that one is ashamed to do otherwise before him." For men virtue seems natural; for women, in most cases, it must be bitterly acquired.

If girls are to be passive in their relations with men, repressed in their emotional lives, they yet are allowed that familiar sphere of service to others. The glorification of altruism as feminine activity in ***Little Women*** reaches extraordinary heights. The good woman *serves,* she subordinates herself always to the will of others—to husband, to employer, but also to the poor family down the street—she demonstrates her worthiness by sacrificing her self, in the most literal sense: one comes to feel that no *self* remains for the book's ideal woman. (pp. 98-9)

Jo is remarkable. She is of course a version of the author herself: if we didn't know that, we'd be forced to surmise it. Her fictional vitality comes from the fact that she alone is in essential conflict with herself. The other girls, with superficial conflicts, deeply accept the values inculcated by their mother. Jo, more ardent than the rest in her resolutions to do good, her professions of virtue, her efforts to control her temper, cook dinners, be agreeable to her disagreeable aunt, fails no more often than anyone else. Still, she is different. The difference is exemplified by her reservations about being a girl. . . . She learns to behave more like a girl; her father congratulates her at length, when he returns, on having become more womanly. But her preference for boys' work and manners stems from a deep awareness of how the limitations on feminine possibility make it difficult for her to express what's in her. Indeed, she is, as a girl, constantly being told that she is not supposed to express what's in her—yet her vocation is to be a writer. (pp. 99-100)

Writing provides the promise of escape. She justifies the activity on altruistic grounds—if she earns money by her writing, she can help her parents and the other girls—but the need for it is far deeper than the need to earn money. It appears to be a quite genuine vocation, although Jo has no guidance about how to develop it and promptly falls into the corruption of writing sensational stories, a trap from which she is rescued, of course, by a wiser man. The writing of trash appeals to her because she is paid for it—and to be paid is to be valued. She is interested in the occupation in itself, unlike Amy, for example, whose narcissistic desire to paint disappears promptly when she is married. But she is also interested in being valued. To be valued for expressivity contradicts what she has been taught at home: the conflict becomes ever more intense. (p. 100)

Louisa May Alcott does not enter deeply into the problems of marriage, although she examines Meg's match on a ladies' magazine level (what do you do when your currant jelly refuses to jell? what do you do when your husband starts spending the evening elsewhere?). She . . . sees marriage as reward for virtue and as enlarged sphere for feminine activity; but she also sees it as discipline. Mrs. March's husband helps her control her temper; Meg's husband by example teaches her the beauties of self-sacrifice and self-control; Amy's husband insists that she help him spend his money doing good; Jo's husband, after all, is a middle-aged professor who has begun his relationship with the girl by showing her that she is wrong to write newspaper fiction. Discipline, ***Little Women*** suggests, is what women little and big require. They must be controlled or their passion for pickled limes and finery and freedom will precipitate chaos. Jo is a dangerous figure. She reveals her creator's awareness that women have needs deeper than Mrs. March allows herself to know. (p. 101)

Patricia Meyer Spacks, "Taking Care" (originally published in a different form as "Taking Care: Some Women Novelists," in Novel: A Forum on Fiction, *Vol. 6, No. 1, Fall, 1972), in her* The Female Imagination *(copyright © 1972, 1975 by Patricia Meyer Spacks; reprinted by permission of Alfred A. Knopf, Inc.), Knopf, 1975, pp. 78-112.*

ADDITIONAL BIBLIOGRAPHY

Adams, Mildred. "When the Little Angels Revolted." *The New York Times Magazine* LXXXVII, No. 29261 (6 March 1936): 10-11, 24.

A brief survey of the role of children in literature. Adams maintains that Alcott's juvenile characters possess both the moral and domestic traits evident in most nineteenth-century writing, and that they also foreshadow their counterparts in modern fiction. In particular, Adams notes Jo's desire for a career in *Little Women,* and Rose's ambition to become a "healthy, active and popular girl" in *Rose in Bloom.*

Anthony, Katharine. *Louisa May Alcott.* New York, London: Alfred A. Knopf, 1938, 315 p.

A biography that questions the morality and upbringing of the Alcott family. Anthony's biography has been the subject of controversy, most notably from Odell Shepard, who believes that Anthony's conjectures about the family are not based on adequate evidence.

Beach, Seth Curtis. "Louisa May Alcott, 1832-1888." In his *Daughters of the Puritans: A Group of Brief Biographies,* pp. 251-86. Boston: American Unitarian Association, 1905.

A brief biographical study of Alcott. Beach outlines Alcott's literary accomplishments and her political contributions to the women's suffrage movement.

Cheney, Ednah D., ed. *Louisa May Alcott: Her Life, Letters, and Journals.* Boston: Little, Brown, and Co., 1907, 404 p.

A biography sanctioned by Alcott's sister, Anna Alcott Pratt, which relies heavily on Alcott's journal entries and correspondence. Also included in the biography are excerpts of Alcott's poetry, previously unpublished.

Goldman, Suzy. "Louisa May Alcott: The Separation Between Art and Family." *The Lion and the Unicorn* I, No. ii (1977): 91-7.

Discusses the evolution of Alcott's female characters from domestic "ladies" to feminist heroines. Goldman cites examples from early and late works.

Hamblen, Abigail Ann. "Louisa May Alcott and the 'Revolution' in Education." *The Journal of General Education* XXII (April 1970-January 1971): 81-92.

Appraises the educational theories Alcott advocated in her works.

Hamblen, Abigail Ann. "Louisa May Alcott and the Racial Question." *The University Review-Kansas City* XXXVII, No. 4 (Summer 1971): 307-13.

A brief consideration of the works that reflect Alcott's abolitionist position. Hamblen notes that while Alcott is sympathetic to blacks and the abolitionist cause, she herself berates other immigrant minority races, particularly the Irish.

The Horn Book, Special Number XLIV, No. 5 (October 1968): 158 p.
A special issue that commemorates the centennial of *Little Women*'s publication. This issue contains essays from several Alcott critics, including Cornelia Meigs and Lavinia Russ.

Payne, Alma J. "Louisa May Alcott (1832-1888)." *American Literary Realism* 6, No. 1 (Winter 1973): 27-43.
An extensive bibliography of critical writings on Alcott through 1968, the centennial year of *Little Women*'s publication.

Porter, Maria S. "Recollections of Louisa May Alcott." *The New England Magazine* n.s. IV, No. I (March 1892): 2-19.
A biographical study that examines the family influence in Alcott's writings. Porter, a personal friend, recalls her relationship with Alcott and describes the author's reactions to fame.

Russ, Lavinia. "Not To Be Read on Sunday." *The Horn Book* XLIV, No. 5 (October 1968): 520-35.
Contradicts Brigid Brophy's assertion that Alcott's literature is "masochistic," (see excerpt above, 1964) and claims that "girls are right to love *Little Women* . . . because it is a story about good people." Russ calls Alcott's characters "rebels" because they work to change their worlds.

Shepard, Odell. "The Mother of *Little Women*." *The North American Review* 245, No. 2 (Summer 1938): 391-98.
An unfriendly review of Katharine Anthony's biography, *Louisa May Alcott*. Shepard remarks that "Miss Anthony has failed to master even the surface of her topic." In particular, Shepard disputes Anthony's suggestion that Alcott's mother was romantically involved with her father's partner, Charles Lane.

Stern, Madeleine B. "Louisa Alcott, Trouper: Experiences in Theatricals, 1848-1880." *The New England Quarterly* XVI (June 1943): 175-97.
An account of Alcott's experiences in the theater and her attempts at writing dramas.

Stern, Madeleine [B]. Introduction to *Behind a Mask: The Unknown Thrillers of Louisa May Alcott,* edited by Madeleine [B.] Stern, pp. vii-xxxiii. New York: William Morrow & Co., 1975.
An excellent introduction to the pseudonymous works of Alcott. Stern traces each story's origin, the periodical in which each piece was originally published, and the critical reception each received.

Stern, Madeleine [B]. Introduction to *Plots and Counterplots: More Unknown Thrillers of Louisa May Alcott,* edited by Madeleine [B.] Stern, pp. 7-29. New York: William Morrow & Co., 1976.
The introduction to the second volume of Alcott's pseudonymous thrillers.

Yellin, Jean Fagan. "From Success to Experience: Louisa May Alcott's *Work*." *Massachusetts Review* XXI, No. 3 (Fall 1980): 527-39.
Explores the background of Alcott's *Work: A Story of Experience*. Yellin suggests that this work differs from other nineteenth-century fiction by "proposing that women extend their actions into the public sphere." Alcott fails in this novel, according to Yellin, because she does not deal consistently with her topic.

Matthew Arnold

1822-1888

Arnold is considered one of the most influential authors of the later Victorian period in England. His elegiac verse often expresses a sense of modern malaise, and critics rank such poems as "Dover Beach" and "The Forsaken Merman" with the finest of the era. While Arnold is well known today as a poet, in his own time he asserted his greatest influence through his prose writings. As a social critic, he denounced materialism and called for a renewal of art and culture. His forceful literary criticism, which is based on his humanistic belief in the value of balance and clarity in literature, significantly shaped modern theory; T. S. Eliot stated, for example, that "the valuation of the Romantic poets, in academic circles, is still very largely that which Arnold made." In his effort to establish high artistic standards, Arnold sought to deter the loss of faith that he perceived among his contemporaries and expressed so eloquently in his verse.

Arnold was the eldest son of Dr. Thomas Arnold, an influential educator who became headmaster of Rugby School in 1828. Arnold attended Rugby and Balliol College, Oxford, where he was known as somewhat of a dandy. At Oxford he met Arthur Hugh Clough, who became his close friend and correspondent and whose death Arnold mourned in his well-known pastoral elegy, "Thyrsis." Even Arnold's early poetry, such as the privately issued *Alaric at Rome*, had the brooding tone which was to become characteristic of his mature work. After the publication of *The Strayed Reveller and Other Poems*, Arnold was appointed inspector of schools, a position that he held, with the exception of his ten years as Professor of Poetry at Oxford, for the rest of his life. In the eight years following the publication of *The Strayed Reveller*, Arnold published the bulk of his poetry, including *Poems* in 1853. That volume contains his famous preface outlining the reasons for deleting from the collection the title poem from his earlier book, *Empedocles on Etna and Other Poems*. Arnold declared that "Empedocles on Etna" did not fulfill the requirements of a good poem and therefore did not qualify as meaningful art. In his emphasis on the purpose of poetry in the preface, Arnold indicated the direction that his writing and thought were to take.

Arnold's election to the position of Professor of Poetry at Oxford in 1857 marked the beginning of his transition from poet to literary, educational, and theological critic. *On Translating Homer*, based on lectures he delivered at Oxford, and *The Popular Education of France; With Notices of That of Holland and Switzerland*, a study made for the education commission, evidence his turn toward prose. His first volume of *Essays in Criticism* advances Arnold's belief in the scope and importance of literary criticism: he describes it as "a disinterested endeavor to learn and propagate the best that is known and thought in the world, and thus to establish a current of fresh and true ideas." After the publication of *Culture and Anarchy: An Essay in Political and Social Criticism* in 1869, Arnold's interests tended increasingly towards social criticism and centered on the issue of the deterioration of faith in the modern world. In *Literature and Dogma: An Essay towards a Better Apprehension of the Bible*, Arnold proposed a new approach

to scripture. He contended that the Bible had been misread as prose and therefore taken literally, while it should have been read as poetry and taken figuratively. *God and the Bible: A Defense of Literature and Dogma* and *Last Essays on Church and Religion* are also concerned with the importance of religion and faith in an age of skepticism. Arnold toured America in 1883, and later published the lectures he had delivered there as *Discourses in America*. Arnold's most noted essays, *Essays in Criticism, second series*, were published posthumously in 1888. The essays are generally considered Arnold's tour de force; in them he gives final expression to his conviction that the humanities are an essential and nurturing force for society. With this conviction, he implicitly elevates the status of criticism from an intellectual pastime to a creative occupation with vital repercussions.

Many critics have viewed the pervasively melancholy tone of Arnold's verse as a reflection of the dilemma of the Victorian, who, in the words of Arnold's "The Scholar-Gypsy", published in *Poems*, is caught between "two worlds, one dead / The other powerless to be born." Though not overtly didactic, Arnold in his poetry as in his prose often concerns himself with the diagnosis of the maladies of his time. Many critics have particularly applauded Arnold's awareness of and sensitivity to the spirit of the day. Stylistically, Arnold's poetry is subtle and unadorned, particularly in comparison with that of the Romantics and his Victorian contemporaries. He strove to achieve a classical sense of balance and unity in his works, yet some critics feel that he sacrificed meaning and depth to achieve this goal, and he has been accused of lacking the breadth of true poetic imagination. Arnold was not a popular poet in his day, and his elegiac tone may have been responsible; nevertheless, several of his poems, notably "The Scholar-Gypsy," "Empedocles on Etna," "Thyrsis," and "Dover Beach," are still studied and respected today, and are considered among the best of the Victorian period.

While Arnold's poetry has been labeled passionless, his critical writings have been termed overly poetic and emotional. What some critics regard as an overriding concern with structure is considered by some responsible for the obvious flaws in his critical arguments. Many critics have faulted what they consider Arnold's inattention to scholarship, and cite his devaluation of Geoffrey Chaucer, Percy Bysshe Shelley and Alfred, Lord Tennyson as evidence of his narrow critical vision. As one critic stated, Arnold's criticism has endured "more because of its general principles than its estimates of individual authors." Arnold's greatest attribute as a prose writer is generally considered his crisp and simple prose which is marked by what have become enduring catch-phrases, such as "high seriousness" and "Grand Style." Arnold used these phrases to sum up his theories in a way which has been called overly simplistic. It has been suggested, however, that because he made his ideas readily understandable, Arnold was instrumental in making literary criticism accessible to the average reader.

Arnold is remembered today for several poems that critics consider to be extraordinary. In his revolutionary role as a critic, he is valued for clearing the way for twentieth-century literature and critical theory.

PRINCIPAL WORKS

Alaric at Rome (poetry) 1840
*The Strayed Reveller and Other Poems (poetry) 1849
Empedocles on Etna and Other Poems (poetry) 1852
Poems (poetry) 1853
Poems, second series (poetry) 1855
Merope [first publication] (drama) 1858
On Translating Homer (lectures) 1861
*The Popular Education of France; With Notices of That of
     Holland and Switzerland* (essay) 1861
Essays in Criticism (criticism) 1865
**New Poems (poetry) 1867
On the Study of Celtic Literature (criticism) 1867
*Culture and Anarchy: An Essay in Political and Social
     Criticism* (essay) 1869
*Friendship's Garland: Being the Conversations, Letters, and
     Opinions of the Late Arminus, Baron von Thunder-Ten-
     Tronckh* (humorous letters) 1871
*Literature and Dogma: An Essay towards a Better
     Apprehension of the Bible* (essay) 1873
God and the Bible: A Defense of Literature and Dogma
     (essay) 1875
Last Essays on Church and Religion (essays) 1877
Mixed Essays (essays) 1879
Irish Essays and Others (essays) 1882
Discourses in America (lectures) 1885
Essays in Criticism, second series (criticism) 1888
Letters of Matthew Arnold, 1848-1888 (letters) 1895

*This work includes the poem "The Forsaken Merman."

**This work includes the poems "Dover Beach" and "Thyrsis."

[WILLIAM EDMONSTONE AYTOUN] (essay date 1849)

The *Strayed Reveller* is rather a curious compound of imitation. [The poet] claims to be a classical scholar of no mean acquirements, and a good deal of his inspiration is traceable to the Greek dramatists. . . . The language, though hard, is rather stately; and many of the individual images are by no means destitute of grace. The epithets which he employs bear the stamp of the Greek coinage; but, upon the whole, we must pronounce these specimens failures. The images are not bound together or grouped artistically, and the rhythm which the author has selected is, to an English ear, utterly destitute of melody. (p. 342)

If any one, in possession of a good ear, and with a certain facility for composing verse, though destitute of the inventive faculty, will persevere in imitating the style of different poets, he is almost certain at last to discover some writer whose peculiar manner he can assume with far greater facility than that of others. The *Strayed Reveller* fails altogether with Mrs. Browning, because it is beyond his power, whilst following her, to make any kind of agreement between sound and sense. He is indeed very far from being a metaphysician, for his perception is abundantly hazy; and if he be wise, he will abstain from any future attempts at profundity. But he has a fair share of the painter's gift, and were he to cultivate that on his own account, we believe that he might produce something far superior to any of his present efforts. As it is, we can merely accord him the praise of sketching an occasional landscape, very like one which we might expect from Alfred Tennyson. He has not only caught the trick of Tennyson's handling, but he can use his colours with considerable dexterity. (p. 344)

[In] spite of his many faults, the *Strayed Reveller* is a clever fellow; and thought it cannot be averred that, up to the present time, he has made the most of fair talents and a first-rate education, we are not without hope that, some day or other, we may be able to congratulate him on having fairly got rid of his affected misanthropy, his false philosophy, and his besetting sin of imitation, and that he may yet achieve something which may come home to the heart, and secure the admiration of the public. (p. 346)

> [*William Edmonstone Aytoun*], "'The Strayed Reveller'," in *Blackwood's Edinburgh Magazine*, Vol. LXVI, No. CCCCVII, September, 1849, pp. 340-46.

MATTHEW ARNOLD (essay date 1853)

[*In this famous preface to his* Poems, *Arnold defends his decision to exclude his poem "Empedocles on Etna" from the collection, and, in so doing, outlines his philosophy of poetry.*]

I have, in the present collection, ommitted the Poem from which the volume published in 1852 took its title [*Empedocles on Etna*]. I have done so, not because the subject of it was a Sicilian Greek born between two and three thousand years ago, although many persons would think this a sufficient reason. Neither have I done so because I had, in my own opinion, failed in the delineation which I intended to effect. (p. 3)

A poetical work . . . is not yet justified when it has been shown to be an accurate, and therefore interesting representation; it has to be shown also that it is a representation from which men can derive enjoyment. In presence of the most tragic circumstances, represented in a work of Art, the feeling of enjoyment, as is well known, may still subsist: the representation of the most utter calamity, of the liveliest anguish, is not sufficient to destroy it: the more tragic the situation, the deeper becomes the enjoyment; and the situation is more tragic in proportion as it becomes more terrible.

What then are the situations, from the representation of which, though accurate, no poetical enjoyment can be derived? They are those in which the suffering finds no vent in action; in which a continuous state of mental distress is prolonged, unrelieved by incident, hope, or resistance; in which there is everything to be endured, nothing to be done. In such situations there is inevitably something morbid, in the description of them something monotonous. When they occur in actual life, they are painful, not tragic; the representation of them in poetry is painful also.

To this class of situations, poetically faulty as it appears to me, that of Empedocles, as I have endeavoured to represent him, belongs; and I have therefore excluded the Poem from the present collection. (pp. 4-5)

"The Poet," it is said, and by an apparently intelligent critic, "the Poet who would really fix the public attention must leave the exhausted past, and draw his subjects from matters of present import, and *therefore* both of interest and novelty."

Now this view I believe to be completely false. It is worth examining, inasmuch as it is a fair sample of a class of critical dicta everywhere current at the present day, having a philosophical form and air, but no real basis in fact; and which are calculated to vitiate the judgment of readers of poetry, while they exert, so far as they are adopted, a misleading influence on the practice of those who write it.

What are the eternal objects of Poetry, among all nations, and at all times? They are actions; human actions; possessing an inherent interest in themselves, and which are to be communicated in an interesting manner by the art of the Poet. Vainly will the latter imagine that he has everything in his own power; that he can make an intrinsically inferior action equally delightful with a more excellent one by his treatment of it: he may indeed compel us to admire his skill, but his work will possess, within itself, an incurable defect.

The Poet, then, has in the first place to select an excellent action; and what actions are the most excellent? Those, certainly, which most powerfully appeal to the great primary human affections: to those elementary feelings which subsist permanently in the race, and which are independent of time. These feelings are permanent and the same; that which interests them is permanent and the same also. The modernness or antiquity of an action, therefore, has nothing to do with its fitness for poetical representation; this depends upon its inherent qualities. To the elementary part of our nature, to our passions, that which is great and passionate is eternally interesting; and interesting solely in proportion to its greatness and to its passion. A great human action of a thousand years ago is more interesting to it than a smaller human action of to-day, even though upon the representation of this last the most consummate skill may have been expended, and though it has the advantage of appealing by its modern language, familiar manners, and contemporary allusions, to all our transient feelings and interests.

These, however, have no right to demand of a poetical work that it shall satisfy them; their claims are to be directed elsewhere. Poetical works belong to the domain of our permanent passions: let them interest these, and the voice of all subordinate claims upon them is at once silenced.

Achilles, Prometheus, Clytemnestra, Dido—what modern poem presents personages as interesting, even to us moderns, as these personages of an "exhausted past?" We have the domestic epic dealing with the details of modern life which pass daily under our eyes; we have poems representing modern personages in contact with the problems of modern life, moral, intellectual, and social; these works have been produced by poets the most distinguished of their nation and time; yet I fearlessly assert that *Hermann and Dorothea, Childe Harold, Jocelyn, The Excursion,* leave the reader cold in comparison with the effect produced upon him by the latter books of the *Iliad,* by the *Oresteia,* or by the episode of Dido. And why is this? Simply because in the three latter cases the action is greater, the personages nobler, the situations more intense: and this is the true basis of the interest in a poetical work, and this alone. (pp. 5-7)

But for all kinds of poetry alike there was one point on which [the Greeks] were rigidly exacting; the adaptability of the subject to the kind of poetry selected, and the careful construction of the poem.

How different a way of thinking from this is ours! We can hardly at the present day understand what Menander mean, when he told a man who enquired as to the progress of his comedy that he had finished it, not having yet written a single line, because he had constructed the action of it in his mind. A modern critic would have assured him that the merit of his piece depended on the brilliant things which arose under his pen as he went along. We have poems which seem to exist merely for the sake of single lines and passages; not for the sake of producing any total-impression. We have critics who seem to direct their attention merely to detached expressions, to the language about the action, not to the action itself. I verily think that the majority of them do not in their hearts believe that there is such a thing as a total-impression to be derived from a poem at all, or to be demanded from a poet; they think the term a commonplace of metaphysical criticism. They will permit the Poet to select any action he pleases, and to suffer that action to go as it will, provided he gratifies them with occasional bursts of fine writing, and with a shower of isolated thoughts and images. That is, they permit him to leave their poetical sense ungratified, provided that he gratifies their rhetorical sense and their curiosity. Of his neglecting to gratify these, there is little danger; he needs rather to be warned against the danger of attempting to gratify these alone; he needs rather to be perpetually reminded to prefer his action to everything else; so to treat this, as to permit its inherent excellences to develop themselves, without interruption from the intrusion of his personal peculiarities: most fortunate, when he most entirely succeeds in effacing himself, and in enabling a noble action to subsist as it did in nature.

But the modern critic not only permits a false practice; he absolutely prescribes false aims.—"A true allegory of the state of one's own mind in a representative history," the Poet is told, "is perhaps the highest thing that one can attempt in the way of poetry."—And accordingly he attempts it. An allegory of the state of one's own mind, the highest problem of an art which imitates actions! No assuredly, it is not, it never can be so: no great poetical work has ever been produced with such an aim. (pp. 9-10)

The present age makes great claims upon us: we owe it service, it will not be satisfied without our admiration. I know not how it is, but their commerce with the ancients appears to me to produce, in those who constantly practise it, a steadying and composing effect upon their judgment, not of literary works only, but of men and events in general. They are like persons who have had a very weighty and impressive experience: they are more truly than others under the empire of facts, and more independent of the language current among those with whom they live. They wish neither to applaud nor to revile their age: they wish to know what it is, what it can give them, and whether this is what they want. What they want, they know very well; they want to educe and cultivate what is best and noblest in themselves: they know, too, that this is no easy task . . . and they ask themselves sincerely whether their age and its literature can assist them in the attempt. If they are endeavouring to practise any art, they remember the plain and simple proceedings of the old artists, who attained their grand results by penetrating themselves with some noble and significant action, not by inflating themselves with a belief in the pre-eminent importance and greatness of their own times. They do not talk of their mission, nor of interpreting their age, nor of the coming Poet; all this, they know, is the mere delirium of vanity; their business is not to praise their age, but to afford to the men who live in it the highest pleasure which they are capable of feeling. (pp. 14-15)

A host of voices will indignantly rejoin that the present age is inferior to the past neither in moral grandeur nor in spiritual health. He who possesses the discipline I speak of will content himself with remembering the judgments passed upon the present age, in this respect, by the men of strongest head and widest culture whom it has produced; by Goethe and by Niebuhr. It will be sufficient for him that he knows the opinions held by these two great men respecting the persent age and its literature; and that he feels assured in his own mind that their aims and demands upon life were such as he would wish, at any rate, his own to be; and their judgment as to what is impeding and disabling such as he may safely follow. He will not, however, maintain a hostile attitude towards the false pretensions of his age; he will content himself with not being overwhelmed by them. (pp. 15-16)

I am far indeed from making any claim, for myself, that I possess this discipline; or for the following Poems, that they breathe its spirit. But I say, that in the sincere endeavour to learn and practise, amid the bewildering confusion of our times, what is sound and true in poetical art, I seemed to myself to find the only sure guidance, the only solid footing, among the ancients. They, at any rate, knew what they wanted in Art, and we do not. It is this uncertainty which is disheartening, and not hostile criticism. How often have I felt this when reading words of disparagement or of cavil: that it is the uncertainty as to what is really to be aimed at which makes our difficulty, not the dissatisfaction of the critic, who himself suffers from the same uncertainty. (p. 16)

Two kinds of *dilettanti*, says Goethe, there are in poetry: he who neglects the indispensable mechanical part, and thinks he has done eough if he shows spirituality and feeling; and he who seeks to arrive at poetry merely by mechanism, in which he can acquire an artisan's readiness, and is without soul and matter. And he adds, that the first does most harm to Art, and the last to himself. If we must be *dilettanti*: if it is impossible

for us, under the circumstances amidst which we live, to think clearly, to feel nobly, and to delineate firmly: if we cannot attain to the mastery of the greater artists—let us, at least, have so much respect for our Art as to prefer it to ourselves: let us not bewilder our successors: let us transmit to them the practice of Poetry, with its boundaries and wholesome regulative laws, under which excellent works may again, perhaps, at some future time, be produced, not yet fallen into oblivion through our neglect, not yet condemned and cancelled by the influence of their eternal enemy, Caprice. (pp. 16-17)

> *Matthew Arnold, "Matthew Arnold's 'Poems',"* (originally a preface to his Poems, revised edition, Longman & Co., 1853), in his The Poems of Matthew Arnold: 1840 to 1866, E. P. Dutton & Co., 1908, pp. 3-18.

THE LEADER (essay date 1853)

Empedocles on Etna and other Poems, is really a delightful volume, and issues from a highly-cultured, highly tempered mind. (p. 41)

The principal poem we regard as altogether a mistake. Empedocles, disheartened with the world, ascends Etna, and after a due amount of monologue precipitates himself into the crater. But what then? Wherefore the poem? It is not a poetic exposition of the philosopher's life, nor of his doctrines. It is but a slender thread upon which "A." may string stray thoughts and images. Moreover, the classicality of the poem is intensely modern. (pp. 41-2)

[The volume] cannot be read without admiration; but as poetry, it wants *individuality*, and that choice felicity of phrase which follows individuality. Let a man speak or sing of what he has actually seen and felt, as he saw and felt it, and the right phrase is sure to come; but, in repeating what others have seen and felt, he repeats their language. (pp. 42-3)

> *A review of "Empedocles on Etna and Other Poems,"* in The Leader, Vol. IV, No. 146, January 8, 1853, pp. 41-3.*

[ARTHUR HUGH CLOUGH] (essay date 1853)

> [*Clough, an English poet, was a close friend and schoolmate of Arnold and the subject of Arnold's poem "Thrysis." The two men often disagreed about matters relating to poetry, and Clough's review of* Empedocles on Etna and Other Poems *is indeed somewhat unenthusiastic. Arnold did not fail to note this; in a letter to Clough he stated: "There is no one to whose aperçus I attach the value I do to yours—but I think you are sometimes—with regard to me especially—a little cross and wilful."*]

Empedocles on Etna and other Poems, with its earlier companion volume, *The Strayed Reveller and other Poems,* are, it would seem, the productions . . . of a scholar and a gentleman; a man who has received a refined education, seen refined "society," and been more, we dare say, in the world, which is called the world, than in all likelihood has a Glasgow mechanic. More refined, therefore, and more highly educated sensibilities,—too delicate, are they, for common service?—a calmer judgment also, a more poised and steady intellect, the *siccum lumen* of the soul; a finer and rarer aim perhaps, and certainly a keener sense of difficulty, in life;—these are the characteristics of him whom we are to call "A." (p. 12)

Does the reader require morals and meanings to [the stories in these volumes]? What shall they be, then?—the deceitfulness of knowledge, and the illusiveness of the affections, the hardness and roughness and contrariousness of the world, the difficulty of living at all, the impossibility of doing any thing,—*voilà tout?* A charitable and patient reader, we believe, (such as is the present reviewer,) will find in the minor poems that accompany these pieces, intimations—what more can reader or reviewer ask?—of some better and further thing than these; some approximations to a kind of confidence, some incipiences of a degree of hope, some roots, retaining some vitality, of conviction and moral purpose. . . . In the future, it seems, there is something for us; and for the present also, which is more germane to our matter, we have discovered some precepts about "hope, light, and *persistence*," which we intend to make the most of. Meantime, it is one promising point in our author of the initial, that his second is certainly on the whole an improvement upon his first volume. There is less obvious study of effect; upon the whole, a plainer and simpler and less factitious manner and method of treatment. This, he may be sure, is the only safe course. Not by turning and twisting his eyes, in the hope of seeing things as Homer, Sophocles, Virgil, or Milton saw them; but by seeing them, by accepting them as he sees them, and faithfully depicting accordingly, will he attain the object he desires. (p. 18)

Let us remark also in the minor Poems, which accompany **"Empedocles,"** a disposition, perhaps, to assign too high a place to what is called Nature. It may indeed be true, as the astronomers say, though after all it is no very great piece of knowledge, that the heavenly bodies describe ellipses; and go on, from and to all the ages, performing that self-repeating, unattaining curve. But does it, therefore, of necessity follow that human souls do something analogous in the spiritual spaces? Number is a wonderful thing, and the laws of nature sublime; nevertheless, have we not a sort of intuition of the existence, even in our own poor human selves, of something akin to a Power superior to, and transcending, all manifestations of Nature, all intelligible forms of Number and Law. (pp. 22-3)

It is wonderful what stores of really valuable thought may lie neglected in a book, simply because they are not put in that form which serves our present occasions. But if we have been inclined to yield to a preference for the picture of simple, strong, and certain, rather than of subtle, shifting, and dubious feelings, and in point of tone and matter to go along with the young mechanic, in point of diction and manner, we must certainly assign the palm to "A," in spite of a straining after the rounded Greek form, such as, to some extent, vitiates even the style of Milton. (p. 24)

> [*Arthur Hugh Clough*], *in a review of "Empedocles on Etna, and Other Poems" and "The Strayed Reveller and Other Poems," in* The North American Review, *Vol. LXXVII, No. CLX, July, 1853, pp. 1-30.**

G. H. LEWES (essay date 1853)

> [*Lewes was one of the most versatile men of letters of the Victorian era. A prominent English journalist, he also made original contributions in the fields of physiology, psychology, and philosophical history. His life of Goethe is regarded as a biographical masterpiece. In his review of* Poems, *Lewes finds the classical elements of the verse attractive, but overall regards Arnold as a scholar rather than poet.*]

Mr. Arnold, as a scholar, and one of poetical tendencies rather than of poetical genius, a man of culture, reflection, and sensibility, but not forming one of that small band of Singers who "sing as the birds sing," naturally looks towards Greece for inspiration. His poems will delight scholars, who will with curious pleasure follow him in his undisguised imitations of works which long have been their ideals; they will note his curiosities of verse, and his Graecism of imagery. Nor will the larger public read without delight. Poems such as these are not common. Some of the qualities most easily appreciable these poems possess, and they will secure an audience. But the fit audience is that of the cultured few. The longest poem in the volume, **Sohrab and Rustum,** will be the greatest favourite, for it tells an intelligible and interesting story, and the story moves through pictures and pathos such as we rarely meet in "volumes of poetry." It has its Graecisms, but they are little more than ornaments of questionable tastes; the real attractiveness lies in the qualities just named. . . .

The poem, indeed, is not an ordinary production; but we should have an easy task to show that its excellencies are not derived from the Greek, although most of its defects are. More than this, its defects are often the mere defects of rude art, which are copied from Homer; such, for example, as the practice of conducting the narrative through lengthy similes, elaborately circumstantial, positively retarding and encumbering what they are meant to accelerate and lighten. If Homer lived in our days he would not write like Homer's imitators. In fact the mistake of all imitation is that it naturally fastens on the fleeting modes, and not on the eternal spirit. (p. 1170)

Criticism might have something to say in other directions if this poem were to be closely scrutinised. We point in passing to such prosaisms as "fate" treading something or other down with an "iron heel". . . . But we need not dwell on them. Our purpose is gained if we have directed the reader's attention to an unusual but delightful volume of poems and if we have, at the same time, indicated the real position which the poet is to hold, with respect to both Ancients and Moderns. (p. 1171)

> *G. H. Lewes, "Arnold's 'Poems'," in* The Leader, *Vol. IV, No. 193, December 3, 1853, pp. 1169-71.*

[W. R. ROSCOE] (essay date 1854)

Once taken in hand, [Mr. Arnold's **The Strayed Reveller and Other Poems**] must bring genuine pleasure to every one whose judgment it is worth a man's while to interest. Mr. Arnold measures himself too justly to claim a place among the kings of song, but below the topmost heights of Parnassus lie many pleasant ranges and happy pastures, among whose denizens he may enjoy a not ignoble rank. He starts from a vantage ground rare in these days. He possesses the uncommon and valuable conviction that poetic art has its nature and its rules which admit of being studied with advantage. Nor does he want the more intrinsic attributes of a poet. A keen and refined sense of beauty, sometimes finding its expression in phrases of exquisite felicity, a mind and artistic faculty, trained, and disciplined to reticence, and an imagination of considerable scope and power, are no mean qualifications. (pp. 99-100)

Mr. Arnold's are eminently the poems of a gentleman, and what is, perhaps, part of this characteristic, they are thoroughly genuine and sincere, the author is always himself and not a pretence at any one else; there is no affectation, no strained effort, no borrowed plumage; he presents himself without disguise, and without false shame; is dignified, simple, and self-restrained. If not always profound, at least he does not affect profundity; his strokes bring his thought or sentiment out clear and decisive; he is never guilty of false show and glitter, and those who have read some of our modern poets, will recognise the inestimable comfort of not having to press through an umbrageous forest of verbiage and heterogeneous metaphors in order to get at a thin thought concealed in its centre. There is artistic finish too in his verse (though, as we wish hereafter to remark, not in his conceptions); not the finish of high polish, but the refined ease and grace of a taste pure by nature and yet conscientiously cultivated. (p. 100)

A considerable portion of these poems are self-descriptive, or more properly, self-betraying. These owe their interest chiefly to any fresh indication they may afford us of the tone of feeling and mode of thought prevalent among some of our recent Oxford scholars. Mr. Arnold will perhaps be startled to hear that he belongs to an unchristian school, but we hasten to assure him that by saying this we do not mean to charge him with a limited faith in the eternity of punishment, or with nourishing views of his own on baptismal regeneration, or even declining to rest implicit confidence on the verbal inspiration of the Bible. . . .

Probably, however, an error in dogmatic convictions can alone entitle us to call a man unchristian in his views; and that it would be more correct to say that Mr. Arnold is of a *non-*Christian school. "Oh, how shocking!" exclaimed a lady, on hearing a certain sonnet of Wordsworth's read aloud; "he'd rather be a Pagan!" And so Mr. Arnold (or his Muse, for it is with the poet not the man we deal) prefers to be a Pagan. (p. 101)

Perhaps it is hardly fair to quarrel so much with Mr. Arnold's personal philosophy, when his poetry is so much better. He brings this sort of observation on himself however, by inflicting so much of the subject-matter of it upon his readers. His pages are crowded with personal poems when he has it in his power to write others infinitely superior to them. He must pardon us for saying that his own sensations and emotions are scarcely varied and profound enough, his philosophy and meditations on life scarcely valuable enough, to make a poetry employed in developing them capable of deeply moving and widely profiting the public mind. . . . We seek him, not to be reminded of our short-comings and imbecilities, but to be lifted into a clearer air which may revive our spirit and purge our eyesight for a new and more vigorous contest in the dusty plain. And Mr. Arnold can do this for us if he will. His fine, often exquisite sense of beauty, his power of felicitous narration, his command over varied sentiment and feeling (he has not attempted the delineation of violent passion), open a field to him where he might occupy not only a high place, but one peculiarly his own. Wordsworth and Tennyson have both left a tinge of their peculiar characteristics in the fountain of Mr. Arnold's poetry, and there is something very charming in having poems analogous to the short narrative or descriptive pieces in which Tennyson so often revels, less gorgeous and rich in their beauty, but at the same time less turbid and sensuous, and purified by something of the quieter insight and higher refinement of Wordsworth. (pp. 106-07)

"Tristram and Iseult" is by far the most pleasing of these *quasi* narrative poems, and is, on the whole, the best thing in these volumes; and the mould in which the story is cast, though at the first glance a little perplexing, is ingenious, and has a charm of its own. (p. 107)

"Sohrab and Rustum" is a fine poem, but less to our taste. Mr. Arnold's forte is description, but here there is a little too much of it. The poem is too long for the action: but throughout the diction is stately and sustained, and the ornament and imagery rich, and in keeping with it. Yet it interests us more by the mode of its narration and its decorations, than by the inner kernel of sentiment and action. It is more like a fine carving than a good picture. One merit it has which is very rarely to be found in its author. It is conceived as a whole and executed as a whole, a poem—not a piece of joinery. We wish Mr. Arnold could be prevailed on to bestow more pains on some of the main requisites of his art. If he would read his own preface with attention, he might profit by some excellent observations contained in it. No man ever insisted more strongly on the excellence of wholeness and of a due subordination of details to the main composition, on the importance of the choice of a subject and the careful construction of the poem; few men have ever more systematically disregarded their own preaching. It is the one great and prominent defect of these poems that they give the reader no satisfaction as poems, but only scattered rays of enjoyment. Mr. Arnold's conceptions want force and unity: what is worse, they sometimes want substance. His minor poems especially, even when delighting us most, are apt to leave us with a sense of shortcoming, arising from the want of unity in their thought, or some hidden weakness in their conclusion. (pp. 108-09)

[Mr. Arnold] has both delicacy and purity of finish, and this is one thing which makes his book such agreeable reading. In this respect his classical education and tastes have stood him in good stead; and it is disappointing to find them exercising so disproportionately small an influence over the form of his conceptions and the choice of his subjects.

So fully is Mr. Arnold himself aware of the importance of this latter point, that he has excluded one of his larger poems from the last edition on the grounds that the situation embodied in it is one from which no poetical enjoyment can be derived. Apropos of this, and of some difference with his critics, as to the field afforded by ancient subjects for the exercise of modern art, he has written a preface [to his *Poems,* see excerpt above] in which he develops a theory of poetry, defends the ancients as models for the artist, and rebukes the false pretensions of the age and of his own critics—but distantly and politely. He is a little sore; but he keeps a steady countenance. (p. 110)

[W. R. Roscoe], "The Poems of Matthew Arnold, and of Alexander Smith," in The Prospective Review, Vol. X, No. XXXVII, February, 1854, pp. 99-118.*

THE ECLECTIC REVIEW   (essay date 1855)

The mind of Mr. Arnold seems to be more essentially critical than creative. Now, the province of the poet is the creative—not the critical. It is his province to produce the rare result, and not to hold a light to reveal the working of his machinery, or state publicly wherefore he produced it. The poet includes the critic, as the greater includes the less, but his criticism works silently, and his poetry will be the best exponent of his critical creed, if he have any. Our author's poetry does not furnish satisfactory illustrations of the truth of his prose propositions. He is strongest and most poetical when he overleaps his theories. (p. 279)

[One] cannot read these two volumes [*Poems* and *Poems, Second Series*] through without coming to the conclusion that [Mr.

Arnold] is a poet, and that Parnassus has room for such a denizen. We cannot define genius, notwithstanding all our attempts; but it always defines itself, and makes its presence felt. So of poetry; we always know it when we meet with it, although we may fail to define the wherefore. . . . Many men have their hints without their motions of fury and pride of soul, because they want fire enough to agitate their spirits; and these we call cold writers. Others, who have a great deal of fire, but have not excellent organs, feel the fore-mentioned motions, without the extraordinary hints. We take Mathew Arnold to represent the former. Our author is too cold and colourless. He does not thrust his hand into ours pulsing divine inspirations, and warm with human feeling. He is not sensuous enough to be widely popular. He appeals to the intellect, to the neglect of passion and feeling, from which poetry still draws much of its richest life. . . . There seems to be some strange remoteness in Mr. Arnold's mind, resulting, we think, form his greater book-education than life-experience. A more perfect acquaintance with human life and its many-sided mystery—a larger fulfilment of his own being—will doubtless bring him nearer to us.

Yet, although his subjects may be remote, he never writes without a strong, clear purpose. He does not sit down to 'make' poetry, by stringing together pretty images, and saying fine things. What he sees, that he sees clearly, and without a mist of metaphor. (pp. 281-82)

> *"Arnold's 'Poems',"* in The Eclectic Review, *n.s. Vol. IX, March, 1855, pp. 276-84.*

[W. R. ROSCOE] (essay date 1858)

Mr. Arnold is no doubt following his own true bent when he devotes himself to what is called the classical school of literature. Certainly no living poet is so well qualified to familiarise the English mind (if that be possible) with the forms and substance of the Greek drama. The limits, as well as the quality, of his genius give him more than common facilities for such a task. His love of beauty is profound, and he loves best, perhaps by nature, and certainly from study, its more abstract manifestations, especially those of form. He uses the emotions as a field for the intellect, not the mind to subserve the heart, and his imagination is bound up with the former rather than the latter; it is a lamp that shines, not a fire that glows. He lays a cold hand on sensuous imagery; and there is a keen clear atmosphere about his pictures from nature, as if his muse had steeped his eyes in Attic air and sunshine. Thus gifted, he devotes himself to reproducing Greek poetry in an English dress, and presents us with an Athenian tragedy in our own language. (p. 259)

[*Merope*] is professedly an attempt on the part of the author to give English readers a knowledge of what Greek tragedy was—to teach them the secret of its beauty and power. And it is not impossible that something may be thus taught. True, there is no royal road which can give us any adequate knowledge and real appreciation of ancient art; true that this process is rather beginning at the wrong end, and that instead of *Merope* teaching us what Greek tragedy is, we ought to know what Greek tragedy was to understand what *Merope* is; true that those will read it with the greatest pleasure and the highest appreciation who have got a standard with which to compare it. . . . (p. 263)

We have said that the limitations of Mr. Arnold's genius drew him towards Greek art; and it is so in this particular. We have given him full credit for his love of finish and proportion; but

his poems have every where shown that he is deficient in the higher power of conception, which requires unity. He balances strophe against antistrophe; but he gives us a play with two distracting interests. He is pure in language and clear in verse; but instead of a tragedy, he writes a melodrama with a separate tragical end to it. (p. 270)

[The play's] main interest—the anxiety of Merope for her son, her agony of grief for his supposed loss, and her narrow escape of killing him, followed by the joyful recognition between them—lies wide of tragedy. We do not say there are no models for such a drama in Greek literature—the *Electra* of Sophocles is very much in point; but we say there were far higher models, such as either play of *Oedipus* or the *Antigone,* and that there is an essential difference between melodrama and tragedy, and that the latter is of a nobler class in art. (p. 271)

Merope . . . is not a subject that affords scope for the highest kind of dramatic art. Our interest in her story is one not tragical in its nature, but of *transient* grief and terror. Moreover, it ceases when, long before the conclusion of the play, the mother clasps her uninjured and recognised child in her arms. Henceforth for them the tale is told, and the play played out. All the passion and life of the poem are here concentrated: the author has carefully and skilfully used all the materials of the play to develop this crisis with simplicity and dramatic effect, and has employed the utmost vigour and pathos of which he is master to heighten the effect and to stir the emotions. (p. 272)

Matthew Arnold's is a symmetrical rather than a harmonious genius. He creates parts, and adjusts them together. He wants depth and largeness of artistic power; but he has an exquisite taste, the faculty that detects at least minor disproportions and discrepancies. He has a nice sense of fitness and proportion, and, in all that goes to furnish beauty and finish of execution, it would not be easy to rival him among living poets. His poetry wants power: this play does not move you deeply, nor leave as a whole any profound impression; but step by step it is to be read with a high degree of pleasure, and of a high kind. For the author is rich in poetic instincts, and not devoid of the true poet's insight, and his work is informed throughout with an unfailing life of imagination and fancy. Moreover, his faculties are never strained—he strikes no note above his natural compass. . . . He has a reticence which enables you to enjoy him with a sense that there is more power in reserve, and sometimes a glowing coal breaks out through the lambent play of imaginative diction which generally characterises him—and it is imaginative, not fanciful. Almost always he writes from the deeper hold of the imagination, not from the lighter grasp of fancy. (p. 277)

> [W. R. Roscoe], *"'Merope: A Tragedy',"* in The National Review, *London, Vol. VI, No. XII, April, 1858, pp. 259-79.*

[H. H. LANCASTER] (essay date 1865)

Mr. Arnold's [*Essays in Criticism*] can hardly be classed as good popular writing, and will hardly recommend themselves to ordinary and hasty readers. Their publication in this form can be justified on a higher ground—on the ground of their intrinsic merit. On the other hand, doubts may be entertained as to their probable popularity. They are all in the strictest sense critical, and criticism is never popular. Most of the sources of attraction which have made the success of so many similar publications are wanting here: we have not the attractiveness of biography, the power of history, or the yet livelier interest which attaches to social and political questions. Nor is the style of the criticism calculated to conciliate. No prejudices are flattered; no faults are left unexposed: and the standards appealed to are not such as will readily be recognized, or even comprehended, by the every-day reader. . . . It is no part of our present purpose to enter into any criticism of Mr. Arnold's poetical labors. It must be conceded that the highest imaginative power is not his; but he possesses many eminent poetical gifts notwithstanding. His varied and musical versification; his diction, of great beauty, yet never overloaded with gaudy richness—indeed he sometimes carries his horror of mere verbal ornament to excess; his cultivated thought; a good taste which is never forgotten; a repose which dwells upon his page,—all these things combine to give his poetry a peculiar charm. It is refreshing to turn from the feverish obscurities which, under the name of poems, so trouble our literature, to the vigor of *Mycerinus,* the Homeric echoes of *Sohrab and Rustum,* the pathos and romantic beauty of *Tristan and Iseult* [*sic*]. Beyond question, Mr. Arnold can claim to be numbered among the licensed critics. . . . (pp. 67-8)

But it is Mr. Arnold's prose writings which will gain for him the greatest and most enduring reputation. For some years he has been in the habit of contributing to various reviews and magazines, papers which had power to command attention even amid the turmoil of periodical literature. Marked beyond common by originality of view and fearlessness of expression, they often excited dissent, sometimes provoked hostility; but they never failed to arouse interest and to stimulate thought. (p. 68)

[Criticism] has its origin in a love of truth, and its real aim is to discover and foster excellence, though, as a means to this end, it may be sometimes necessary to expose pretence and incompetence. To be impatient of the restraints of criticism, to disparage it, to rail at it, to affect an unreal independence of its judgments, are certain signs of weakness in an author.

To prove all this, and illustrate it, and exemplify it, has been the aim of much of Mr. Arnold's writing. . . . In the present volume he has collected together essays, ranging over a great variety of subjects, but all of them in the strictest sense, critical. In the first of these, called *The Functions of Criticism at the Present Time,* he not only explains those functions, but also vindicates their dignity and utility. (p. 70)

We must not, however, suppose that Mr. Arnold would limit the sphere of criticism to literature alone. On the contrary, he maintains that criticism, being truly an endeavor to see things as they really are, can not be limited in its scope, but must extend its efforts in all things relating to man and human life,— society, politics, religion. He admits, indeed, that where these burning matters are concerned, it is most likely to go astray; nevertheless, it must set out on the dangerous wayfaring, and take its chance. Safety, according to Mr. Arnold, lies in this only, that criticism must "maintain its independence of the practical spirit and its aims." It must abandon altogether the sphere of practical life, and rest content with discovering and impressing on the world adequate ideas, trusting that those ideas will bring forth their fruit in a fitting, though it may be a distant season. Such a work may be slow and obscure, but it is not the less the only proper work of criticism. Now this is a striking thought, but we doubt whether it be a sound one. It seems to rest on a confusion between the direct and the indirect influence of the critical spirit on the affairs of life. The indirect influence is exerted, of course, through literature. It is in this sense that Mr. Arnold upholds the justice of Goethe's claim to have been "the liberator" of the Germans, because

he taught the German poets that men must live from within outwards, placing the standard inside the man instead of outside him,—a doctrine, as Mr. Arnold says, "absolutely fatal to all routine thinking." (p. 71)

On the other hand, when comment or criticism, or whatever we choose to call it, applies itself directly to matters of action, it seems impossible but that it must take a practical turn. Let us test the thing by Mr. Arnold's own instances. When extreme or ill-timed demands for political change are met by dwelling on our present "unrivalled happiness," he objects to the answer, not on behalf of the reformers, but in the interests of a correct theory of criticism. But what style of answer does he suggest as in accordance with his own theory? Why, the somewhat rude one of taking an aggravated case of child-murder from the newspapers, and tabling it against the "unrivalled happiness" notion. Now, we say nothing as to the value of this answer, nor pause to inquire how far the fact of child-murders taking place in England from time to time is inconsistent with the position that the people of England as a body enjoy more happiness than the people of any other nation; but we ask, is not this of Mr. Arnold's a most *practical* answer? (pp. 71-2)

Again, the illustration given by Mr. Arnold of how criticism should approach religious themes, succeeds in keeping quite clear of any practical tendency, but this at the expense both of distinctness and utility. He objects to Bishop Colenso's criticism on the ground that it strengthens the common confusion between science and religion. . . . If the truths of science and the truths of religion are to be kept always distinct—the one delivered only by men of science, the other delivered only by men of religion, what are we to make of their seeming opposition? That there is a *seeming* opposition no one will deny, and must we, then, accept the opposition as inexplicable? Can we make no endeavor to get beyond this seeming? Can criticism do nothing to reconcile? Is the task of showing that there is no real opposition between science and religion too "practical?" It rather seems to us that this might be attempted without placing any harsh restraints on the free play of thought, and that, if accomplished, it would be the greatest and happiest step ever made in spiritual progression; in a word, criticism might herein exercise not only its appropriate, but its noblest functions. (p. 72)

Now, if all this merely means, that criticism, being an honest endeavor to get at truth, must keep itself free from party catchwords, from party considerations, ay, even from party ideas, there can hardly be room for dispute. Surely so simple a truth need not have been so elaborated. But if it mean more than this, if it mean that criticism can be applied with profit, or, indeed, can be applied at all to questions of active life, yet in no way concern itself with results, keeping above all practical considerations, then we think Mr. Arnold altogether mistaken, and we are sure that his criticism will be for ever barren. . . . [When] he turns to religion, his criticism only ceases to be practical by becoming totally useless, and not a little obscure.

To say the truth, it is not when dealing with these weighty matters that Mr. Arnold is at his best. He does not understand them; he does not, we suspect, greatly care to understand them; his interest in them strikes us as being forced. When he passes from confuting Mr. Adderley and Mr. Roebuck to analyzing the beauties of Maurice de Guérin, he carries his readers into a new atmosphere of warmth and light. His principles of criticism will be found safe guides in the region of the fine arts, though he does not seem to possess the special knowledge required in an art-critic; but literature is the theme he knows best, likes best—where he is, in all respects, most at home. His natural qualifications for the work of literary criticism have been enhanced by assiduous cultivation. No man can be a good critic who does not possess a familiarity with at least one great literature besides his own. (pp. 72-3)

Mr. Arnold's mind is open to foreign thought from many sources. His scholarship shows itself in the only way in which scholarship can show itself becomingly, *i.e.*, in its results, its influence on the judgment and the style. It has given him what Pope considers the rarest quality of the critic, good taste:

> In poets, as true genius is but rare,
> True taste as seldom is the critic's share.

But he has much that is higher than mere scholarship, though unfortunately separable, and too often separated from it; he has caught "the secret of antiquity"—has penetrated to the spirit of the ancient writers. The influence of Germany seems to have been but slight upon him; on the other hand, he has a perfect familiarity with French literature—the literature of criticism *par excellence;* some will say that he surrenders himself too unreservedly to its dominion. His Gallicism is perhaps extreme, and this, combined with his devotion to classical models, may give a certain narrowness to his judgments; but in these days of utter lawlessness, when there is truly no king in Israel, and every man writes as seems good in his own eyes, we welcome any ruler even though his laws be rigid and his rule severe. Coming to his work of criticism with such powers and such resources, he magnifies his office, very naturally, and not, we think, unduly. (p. 73)

It would be too strong to call the critique on Heine disappointing, yet we may say that its very excellence makes us wish there were more of it. Some of his best poetry is translated by Mr. Arnold into prose—into pure and beautiful prose certainly; but still we thus lose the grace, the nameless charm, the divine light; and a writer who is himself a poet might, we think, have attempted a metrical rendering. Moreover, this paper, though, like all the rest, rich in subtle observation and suggestive thoughts, as an estimate of Heine is insufficient. We are told distinctly enough what he was, but we get no idea of what he did. (p. 75)

Mr. Arnold, indeed, is very strong on the necessity for urbanity in criticism; and in his essay on the Influence of Academies, condemns more than one English critic for undue vehemence. But those who love justice rather than mercy, will gladly learn that, with Mr. Arnold . . . , urbanity does not by any means involve gentleness. It is not too much to say that the tone of his lectures on Homer was in some instances quite insulting. . . . (pp. 75-6)

Nor do we quite recognize as a leading characteristic in Mr. Arnold that he is "*modestly* bold," though herein also he improves with age and experience. Formerly his arrogance astonished even the *Saturday Review;* now, however, while far from observing the precept to "speak, though sure, with seeming diffidence," he offends less than he did. We wish we could add that a similar improvement is observable in another of Mr. Arnold's faults—the fault of affectation. (pp. 76-7)

One form of affectation, frequent with Mr. Arnold is specially objectionable, we mean the inappropriate use of scriptural phraseology. Thus he took as the motto for his "Last words," *multi, qui persequuntur me, et tribulant me; a testimoniis non declinavi;* to those who laugh at the grand style, he "repeats, with compassionate sorrow, the Gospel words, 'Ye shall die

in your sins;'" and he illustrates the uncertainty of literary success by quoting, "many are called, but few are chosen." We assure Mr. Arnold that this sort of thing can not fail to offend. . . . (p. 77)

We confess that even Mr. Arnold's egotism and arrogance has for our minds we know not what curious charm; but we can not feel assured that other readers will feel the same; and we therefore regret these and such-like blemishes, exactly in proportion as we estimate highly the services which a writer like Mr. Arnold is capable of rendering to English literature. . . . Many will be impatient of his cultivated criticism. Many will be abashed by his usual good sense and moderation. He, more than most men, should be careful to afford no vantage-ground of attack to his enemies, to show no weakness which his friends will find it hard to defend. He owes this not only to his own reputation, he owes it also to the hopes of doing good to literature, which he is justly entitled to entertain. Why should he give occasion for triumph to the sons of the Philistines?

What, then, are these hopes? or, in other words, what benefits can be expected to come from sound criticism? Mr. Arnold, as we have seen, claims for it high and useful functions, as the servant and pioneer of the creative faculty, discovering, or at least rousing into activity the ideas with which that faculty must work. (pp. 77-8)

[It] is the function of criticism to impress moderation—*sanity* both in thought and expression. It is as an aid to criticism in discharging this function that Mr. Arnold thinks an academy would be of value—at once supplying a standard of judgment and forming a court of appeal. We think he overrates the utility of such an institution. It might, and probably would do something for the form, but we can not share Mr. Arnold's expectations of what it would do for the matter of our literature. We can see how it might cure "notes of provincialism" in expression; but how could it affect notes of provincialism arising from poverty of thought? . . . At all events, English criticism must be content to labor without such aid. And the work to be done, at least in our day, is mainly a work of correction. Hence the common remark, that it is the duty of the critic to welcome merit rather than discover faults, is not true. (p. 78)

[Mr. Arnold] is sometimes spoken of as an upholder of the classical as opposed to the Romantic style, and in a sense he is so. Thus he can not yield to the dogma frequently announced now-a-days, that "the poet who would really fix the public attention must leave the exhausted past, and draw his subjects from matters of present import, and *therefore* both of interest and novelty." He believes, on the contrary, that the best materials for poetry are to be found not in situations and incidents in themselves mean and disagreeable, however they may be elevated by the power of the imagination, but rather in events and ideas in themselves grand and beautiful, possessing an immediate dignity and interest, irrespective of the force of association; and, so far, he holds with the classicists. He believes, further, that distance from ourselves, either in time or idea, tends to bestow this immediate dignity and interest, while nearness to ourselves tends to take it away. Poetry, according to his idea, should approach, as with the most classic of the great poets it did approach, to sculpture, at once in natural beauty of subject, and in perfection of form. Yet he is far from confining poetry to classical themes in the strict sense of the word. He does not so limit his own choice. Most of his largest poems come from very different sources—from Northern mythology, from Eastern legend, from the cycle of Arthurian romance. His view, in short, is, that all noble subjects are fitting for poetry, only that the more distant the subject the more likely it is to possess this element of nobility, not having been exposed to the vulgarizing influences of familiarity. (p. 80)

But while it would be incorrect to call Mr. Arnold a disciple of the classic style, as the expression is employed by Schlegel, no man can have a truer appreciation of classical literature, or value a familiarity with it more highly. Men, he says, who often enjoy commerce with the ancients, seem to him ''like persons who have had a very weighty and impressive experience, they are more truly than others, under the empire of facts, and more independent of the language current among those with whom they live.'' Now, no one can reproach Mr. Arnold with admiring the ancient beyond due measure, because of ignorance of modern literature. He but adds another to the many instances which show that it is the most accomplished and most cultivated men who most value the cultivation of antiquity. (p. 81)

Readers who have accompanied us thus far do not need to be told that, in our judgment, Mr. Arnold's little volume is a work at once of sterling merit and of great value. That he may be, as indeed we believe him to be, wrong in many of his practical results—such as his admiration for academies, and his choice of English hexameters as a vehicle for rendering Homer—is a thing of no real moment. The virtue of his teaching consists in the excellence of the standard he sets up, and in the soundness of the principles he applies. The more widely he is read, the greater the influence he obtains, the brighter the prospects of our literature. (p. 82)

> [*H. H. Lancaster*], '' *Essays in Criticism*,'' in The Eclectic Magazine, *n.s. Vol. II, No. II, July, 1865, pp. 67-82.*

[HENRY JAMES]   (essay date 1865)

[*James was an American-born English novelist, short story writer, critic, essayist, and playwright of the late nineteenth and early twentieth centuries who is considered one of the greatest novelists in the English language. Although best known for his novels, James is also admired as a lucid and insightful critic. James was essentially a great admirer of Arnold. While he here criticizes Arnold's prose style and faults his logic in places, he praises Arnold's willingness to take the ''high ground'' in criticism and his seriousness in approaching his subject. James's increased regard for Arnold can be seen in his later review in the* English Illustrated Magazine *(see Additional Bibliography).*]

Mr. Arnold's *Essays in Criticism* come to American readers with a reputation already made,—the reputation of a charming style, a great deal of excellent feeling, and an almost equal amount of questionable reasoning. . . .

Mr. Arnold's style has been praised at once too much and too little. Its resources are decidedly limited; but if the word had not become so cheap, we should nevertheless call it fascinating. This quality implies no especial force; it rests in this case on the fact that, whether or not you agree with the matter beneath it, the manner inspires you with a personal affection for the author. (p. 206)

His Preface is a striking example of the intelligent amiability which animates his style. His two leading Essays were, on their first appearance, made the subject of much violent contention, their moral being deemed little else than a wholesale schooling of the English press by the French programme. Nothing could have better proved the justice of Mr. Arnold's re-

marks upon the ''provincial'' character of the English critical method, than the reception which they provoked. (p. 207)

For Mr. Arnold's critical feeling and observation, used independently of his judgment, we profess a keen relish. He has these qualities, at any rate, of a good critic, whether or not he have the others,—the science and the logic. It is hard to say whether the literary critic is more called upon to understand or to feel. It is certain that he will accomplish little unless he can feel acutely; although it is perhaps equally certain that he will become weak the moment that he begins to ''work,'' as we may say, his natural sensibilities. The best critic is probably he who leaves his feelings out of account, and relies upon reason for success. If he actually possesses delicacy of feeling, his work will be delicate without detriment to its solidity. The complaint of Mr. Arnold's critics is that his arguments are too sentimental. . . . [Sentiment] has given him, in our opinion, his greatest charm and his greatest worth. Hundreds of other critics have stronger heads; few, in England at least, have more delicate perceptions. (p. 208)

We may here remark, that Mr. Arnold's statement of his principles is open to some misinterpretation,—an accident against which he has, perhaps, not sufficiently guarded it. For many persons the word *practical* is almost identical with the word *useful,* against which, on the other hand, they erect the word *ornamental.* Persons who are fond of regarding these two terms as irreconcilable, will have little patience with Mr. Arnold's scheme of criticism. They will look upon it as an organized preference of unprofitable speculation to common sense. But the great beauty of the critical movement advocated by Mr. Arnold is that in either direction its range of faction is unlimited. It deals with plain facts as well as with the most exalted fancies; but it deals with them only for the sake of the truth which is in them, and not for *your* sake, reader, and that of your party. It takes *high ground,* which is the ground of theory. It does not busy itself with consequences, which are all in all to you. (p. 211)

Some of the parts in these *Essays* are weak, others are strong; but the impression which they all combine to leave is one of such beauty as to make us forget, not only their particular faults, but their particular merits. If we were asked what is the particular merit of a given essay, we should reply that it is a merit much less common at the present day than is generally supposed,—the merit which pre-eminently characterizes Mr. Arnold's poems, the merit, namely, of having a *subject.* Each essay is *about* something. . . . If we were questioned as to the merit of Mr. Arnold's book as a whole, we should say that it lay in the fact that the author takes high ground. The manner of his *Essays* is a model of what criticisms should be. . . . [Mr. Arnold] says a few things in such a way as that almost in spite of ourselves we remember them, instead of a number of things which we cannot for the life of us remember. There are many things which we wish he had said better. . . . [But] Mr. Arnold's excellent spirit reconciles us with his short-comings. . . . [His] supreme virtue is that he speaks of all things seriously, or, in other words, that he is not offensively clever. The writers who are willing to resign themselves to this obscure distinction are in our opinion the only writers who understand their time. That Mr. Arnold thoroughly understands his time we do not mean to say, for this is the privilege of a very select few; but he is, at any rate, profoundly conscious of his time. This fact was clearly apparent in his poems, and it is even more apparent in these *Essays.* It gives them a peculiar character of melancholy,—that melancholy which arises from the spectacle of the old-fashioned instinct of enthusiasm in conflict (or at all events in contact) with the modern desire to be fair,— the melancholy of an age which not only has lost its *naïveté*, but which knows it has lost it. (pp. 212-13)

[Henry James], ''Arnold's 'Essays in Criticism','' in The North American Review, *Vol. CI, No. CCVIII, July, 1865, pp. 206-13.*

ALGERNON CHARLES SWINBURNE   (essay date 1867)

[Swinburne was an English poet, dramatist, and critic. He was renowned during his lifetime for his lyric poetry, and he is remembered today for his rejection of Victorian mores. In the following review of New Poems, *Swinburne lavishes Arnold with praise, likening him to John Milton, William Shakespeare, and Percy Bysshe Shelley.]*

The supreme charm of Mr. Arnold's work is a sense of right resulting in a spontaneous temperance which bears no mark of curb or snaffle, but obeys the hand with imperceptible submission and gracious reserve. Other and older poets are to the full as vivid, as incisive and impressive; others have a more pungent colour, a more trenchant outline; others as deep knowledge and as fervid enjoyment of natural things. But no one has in like measure that tender and final quality of touch which tempers the excessive light and suffuses the refluent shade; which as it were washes with soft air the sides of the earth, steeps with dew of quiet and dyes with colours of repose the ambient ardour of noon, the fiery affluence of evening. . . . For the instinctive selection of simple and effectual detail he is unmatched among English poets of the time, unless by Mr. [William] Morris, whose landscape has much of the same quality, as clear, as noble, and as memorable—memorable for this especially, that you are not vexed or fretted by mere brilliance of point and sharpness of stroke, and such intemperate excellence as gives astonishment the precedence of admiration: such beauties as strike you and startle and go out. . . . The description does not adorn or decorate the thought; it is part of it; they have so grown into each other that they seem not welded together, but indivisible and twin-born. (pp. 420-21)

At times [Mr. Arnold] writes simply as [Wordsworth] might have written, without sensible imitation, but with absolute identity of style and sentiment; at times his larger tone of thought, his clearer accent of speech, attest the difference of the men. So perfect and sweet in speech, so sound and lucid in thought as the pupil is at his best, the master perhaps never was; and at his best the pupil is no more seen, and in his stead is a new master. He has nothing of Wordsworth's spirit of compromise with the nature of things, nothing of his moral fallacies and religious reservations; he can see the face of facts and read them with the large and frank insight of ancient poets; none of these ever had a more profound and serene sense of fate. But he has not grasped, and no man, I suppose, will ever grasp, the special and imperial sceptre of his elder. (pp. 426-27)

Less adorable and sublime, not less admirable and durable, Mr. Arnold's [sonnets] hold their own in the same world of poetry with [Wordsworth's]. All in this new volume [*New Poems*] are full of beauty, sound and sweet fruits of thought and speech that have ripened and brought forth together; . . . all, I repeat, have a singular charm and clearness. I have used this word already more than once or twice; it comes nearest of all I can find to the thing I desire to express; that natural light of mind, that power of reception and reflection of things or thoughts, which I most admire in so much of Mr. Arnold's

work. I mean by it much more than mere facility or transparency, more than brilliance, more than ease or excellence of style. It is a quality begotten by instinct upon culture; one which all artists of equal rank possess in equal measure.

There are in the English language three elegiac poems so great that they eclipse and efface all the elegiac poetry we know; all of Italian, all of Greek. It is only because the latest born is yet new to us that it can seem strange or rash to say so. The "**Thyrsis**" of Mr. Arnold makes a third, with [the] "Lycidas" [of Milton] and [the] "Adonais" [of Shelley]. . . . "**Thyrsis,**" like "Lycidas," has a quiet and tender undertone which gives it something of [the] sacred. (p. 429)

Such English-coloured verse [as found in "**Thyrsis**"] no poet has written since Shakespeare, who chooses his field-flowers and hedgerow blossoms with the same sure and loving hand, binds them in as simple and sweet an order. All others, from Milton downward to Shelley and onward from him, have gathered them singly or have mixed them with foreign buds and alien bloom. No poem in any language can be more perfect as a model of style, unsurpassable certainly, it may be unattainable. . . . [Mr. Arnold] is the most efficient, the surest-footed poet of our time, the most to be relied on; what he does he is the safest to do well; more than any other he unites personality and perfection; others are personal and imperfect, perfect and impersonal; with them you must sometimes choose between inharmonious freedom and harmonious bondage. Above all, he knows what as a poet he should do, and simply does that; the manner of his good work is never more or less than right. His verse comes clean and full out of the mould, cast at a single jet; placed beside much other verse of the time, it shows like a sculptor's work by an enameller's. (p. 430)

"**Thyrsis**" has all the accomplished and adult beauty of a male poem. In the volume which it crowns there is certainly no new jewel of equal water. . . . "**Dover Beach**" marks another high point in the volume; it has a grand choral cadence as of steady surges, regular in resonance, not fitful or gusty, but antiphonal and reverberate. But nothing of new verse here clings closer to the mind than the overture of that majestic fragment from the chorus of a "**Dejaneira.**" (pp. 431-32)

Where the thought goes wrong, the verse follows after it. In Mr. Arnold's second book there was more of weak or barren matter, and therefore more of feeble or faulty metre. Rhyme is the native condition of lyric verse in English; a rhymeless lyric is a maimed thing, and halts and stammers in the delivery of its message. There are some few in the language as good as rare; but the habit or rule is bad. The fragments of his "**Antigone**" and "**Dejaneira**" no reader can wish other than they are; and the chorus for example in "**Merope**" which tells of Arcas and Callisto is a model of noble form and colour; but it does not fasten at once upon the memory like a song of Callicles, or like the "**Merman,**" or like any such other. (p. 433)

Algernon Charles Swinburne, ''Mr. Arnold's New Poems,'' in The Fortnightly Review, *Vol. X, October 1, 1867, pp. 414-45.*

BLACKWOOD'S MAGAZINE   (essay date 1871)

And what shall we say of '**Friendship's Garland**'? Is it amusement—is it instruction—which Mr. Matthew Arnold is minded to convey to us in this quaint publication, by which, we have no doubt, many honest brains will be bewildered? Perhaps his name is sufficient to warrant the supposition that the latter is what is chiefly intended; and we cannot but in all humility venture a doubt whether Mr. Matthew Arnold—whose literary powers we admire, if not as much as he does himself (for that is a very high standard), at least as much as a defective education permits—has been adapted by nature to afford any vivid amusement to his fellow-creatures. When he does so to any high degree, we fear it will not be wittingly or willingly, but in his own despite. . . . Fun is not the forte of the editor of this interesting collection of papers; the play is elephantine, the jokes creak on their hinges like doors hard to open, and the central figure, which is Mr. Matthew Arnold himself, is distressingly prominent and deeply self-conscious. He was always so, to be sure, in or out of masquerade, and so are all the personages in this little drama. We have great doubt, indeed, whether the effect of the volume upon the obtuse British intelligence to which it is meant to be so very cutting, will be at all commensurate with the trouble taken; for, oddly enough, Mr. Arnold does not seem to take into consideration the important, and we should say essential, matter of reaching the special audience to which he preaches. His discussion of the shortcomings of the British Philistine, which are uttered in a voice much too finely pitched ever to reach that culprit's veritable ear, remind us somewhat of the awakening sermons aimed at brutal vice which evangelical clergymen often thunder at a meek score of innocent women, guilty of no enormity greater than a bit of scandal. (p. 458)

"Arnold's 'Friendship's Garland'," in Blackwood's Edinburgh Magazine, *Vol. CIX, No. DCLXVI, April, 1871, pp. 458-60.*

RICHARD HOLT HUTTON (essay date 1871)

[*Hutton was a preeminent English critic, theologian, and editor, and for many years Arnold's greatest advocate among English critics. In the following he offers a comparison of Arnold with Johann Wolfgang von Goethe and William Wordsworth, whom he cites as being representative of Arnold's two leading characteristics. According to Hutton, Arnold adopted Goethe's "calm critical eye for human life and its confusions" in his objective delineation of the spiritual malaise of his age, while he drew from Wordsworth his exaltation of nature and the "lyrical cry" that animates his verse. The dichotomy between Arnold's critical and poetic impulses was further explored in the twentieth century by William A. Madden in his study of Arnold and the aesthetic temperament (see Additional Bibliography).*]

Mr. Arnold, in borrowing from Goethe the artist and critic, and from Wordsworth the poet, something of what I have called their style of clear heroic egotism, has not borrowed from either of them the characteristic motive and individuality which in them justifies that style. Had he done so he could not be the original poet he is. He is neither the poet of mere self-culture, nor the solitary interpreter of Nature, but something between the two; a careful student and graphic, as well as delicate, expositor of the spiritual pangs and restlessness of this age on the one hand, and of the refreshments and anodynes to be derived from Nature on the other. And he is more or less conscious, moreover, in spite of some youthful theories of the true function of poetry which he has had to disregard, that it is in the elaborate delineation of his own poetic individuality that these distresses and these consolations receive their reconciliation and their best chance of being practically combined. He feels that his poetic personality has a certain grandeur and meaning in it; that while he has something of Goethe's calm critical eye for human life and its confusions, he has also something of the meditative thirst and meditative pleasures of

Wordsworth; and that the combination of these two poetic qualifications gives him a distinctive power of his own. (pp. 314-15)

In all his poetical successes, it is easy to distinguish two distinct strands: first, the clear recognition (with Goethe) of our spiritual unrest, and the manful effort to control it; next, the clear recognition (with Wordsworth) of the balm to be found in sincere communion with Nature. To the treatment of both these elements indeed he has given a certain freshness and individuality of his own.

I will first indicate generally his treatment of the former point. His characteristic effort on this side has been to introduce into a delineation, at once consistent and various in its aspects, of the intellectual difficulties, hesitations, and distresses of cultivated minds in the nineteenth century, a vein of imperious serenity—what he himself calls "sanity" of treatment—which may stimulate the mind to bear the pain of constantly disappointed hope. Yet, oddly enough, his early theory of poetry would have restrained him from giving us such a picture of moral and intellectual sufferings at all; and he did for a time suppress a poem, **"Empedocles on Etna,"** which had already gained a certain reputation, and which, beneath a thin disguise of antiquity, discussed half the religious difficulties of modern days, simply because he declared it poetically faulty to choose a situation in which "everything is to be endured, nothing to be done" [see excerpt above by Matthew Arnold, 1853]. (p. 317)

What alone renders all the delineation of spiritual bewilderment which pervades this poem endurable, is that there is a steady current of resistance, a uniform "sanity" of self-control in the treatment of the painful symptoms so subtly described. Empedocles, in the course of his meditations on suicide on the slopes of Etna, no doubt dwells much on the feeble and false religious philosophy of the time, the credulous self-flatteries of human sophistry, and the sharp antagonism between clear self-knowledge and the superstitions of the age; but he also makes a vigorous appeal to the manliness, fortitude, and sobriety of spirit with which all the disappointments and failures of humanity ought to be met, asserts that it is the part of a man of true wisdom to curb immoderate desires, to bow to the might of forces he cannot control, and, while nursing no "extravagant hope," to yield to no despair. . . . It seems to me striking enough that the very charm of Mr. Arnold's method in dealing with this hectic fever of the modern intellect,—for Empedocles, if a true ancient, is certainly a still truer modern in his argument,—is due to his own inconsistency; is due, that is, to the fact that when his subject required him to paint and justify the last stages of moral despondency, and when his intellectual view was sceptical enough to be in sympathy with his subject, he could not help expending his chief strength in cutting away the moral ground from under his hero's feet, by insisting that the well-spring of despair was, after all, not in the hostility of Nature or of human circumstances, but in the license of immoderate desires and of insatiable self-will. And it is so throughout his poems. (pp. 318-19)

He has not the impulse or *abandon* of nature for a pure lyric melancholy, such as Shelley could pour forth in words that almost make the heart weep, as, for instance, in the "Lines Written in Dejection in Naples." Again, Mr. Arnold has nothing of the proud faith that conquers melancholy, and that gives to the poems of Wordsworth their tone of rapture. Yet he hits a wonderful middle note between the two. The "lyrical cry," as he himself has finely designated the voice in which the true poetic exaltation of feeling expresses itself, is to be found in a multitude of places in his poems; but in him it neither utters the dejection of the wounded spirit, nor the joy of the victorious spirit, but rather the calm of a steadfast equanimity in conflict with an unconquerable, and yet also unconquering destiny—a firm mind, without either deep shadows of despair or high lights of faith, only the lucid dusk of an intellectual twilight. (p. 320)

[The] general nature of the human strand in Mr. Arnold's poetry [is] the restless spiritual melancholy which he pictures, resists, and condemns. But there is another permanent strand in it, that due partly to his love for Wordsworth, and partly to his love for Nature, of whom Wordsworth was the greatest of modern priests. Mr. Arnold finds in the beauty and sublimity of natural scenes the best assuagement of intellectual unrest and moral perplexities. Nature is his balm for every woe. He does not find in her, as Wordsworth did, the key to any of life's mysteries, or the source of hope, but only the best kind of distraction, which, while it does not relax but rather elevates the tone of the spirit, and even furnishes it with a certain number of symbols for its thought and emotion, also lightens the burden of the mystery by its cooling and refreshing influence. . . . Throw off the yoke of the world sufficiently to steep yourself in Wordsworth, and no doubt the refreshment is more complete and the flow of new strength more full than you can expect from the verse of Mr. Arnold; for Mr. Arnold's poetry of Nature is not like Wordsworth's, a newly-created meditative universe, distilled by the poet's mind out of Nature; it is a delicate transcript of Nature, painted in the clear, dewy water-colours of tranquil memory. . . . In Mr. Arnold's studies of Nature you see the quiet external scene with exquisite lucidity; but you see also, instead of a mirror of laborious and almost painful elaboration, as you do in Gray, a tranquillised spirit, which reflects like a clear lake the features of the scene. . . . [It] is characteristic of Mr. Arnold, that in closing his longer poems, even when they are poems of narrative, he is very fond of ending with a passage of purely naturalistic description which shadows forth something more than it actually paints, and yet leaves the field of suggestion absolutely to the reader's own fancy. (pp. 321-27)

Mr. Arnold always seems to feel that the proper anodyne for the pain of lacerated hearts is the contemplation of the healing and the peace which are to be found inherent in the vital energies of Nature; but his view never seems to be to use these natural analogies as a vague augury of happier fortunes for his characters than it suits his purpose as a poet to paint, but rather simply to recall that there is a great restorative power in the life of Nature to which we ought to turn for relief, whenever the spectacle of disease and disorder and distress becomes overpowering. (pp. 328-29)

A more perfect intellectual anodyne for the pain of a sick mind, doubting if its own true life could be harmonised with the life of the great universe, it would be difficult to conceive; it solves no problem, it lifts no veil, but it sings of perfect beauty, human effort, and celestial rest, as if they could really be harmonised in the same bright vision, and so hushes for a moment the tumultuous pulses of the heart. And this is Mr. Arnold's habitual use of Nature. He loves to steep his poems in the colours of the great mountain landscapes, or the cool mountain pastures, or the star-lit summer sea; but it is as a refuge from restlessness and doubt, a draught in which he can find not joy but relief, not peace but a sad serenity. (pp. 330-31)

His power of poetic expression is founded on a delicate simplicity of taste—such a simplicity as we might fairly expect

from the student of Goethe and Wordsworth; from one, moreover, who shows the finest insight into Greek poetry, and who has a highly cultivated appreciation both for the specific aroma of words and for the poetical atmosphere of thought. Simplicity is the characteristic fruit of all these studies and tastes, and perhaps Mr. Arnold's bitterest reproach against this modern world of "change, alarm, surprise," is the medley of unblest emotions, and turbid, obscure feelings which it thrusts upon us. Hence his own poetic style is remarkable for its scholarlike delicacy and genuine simplicity of touch . . . ; and if his ear for rhythm is not equal to his insight into the expressive power of words, it is only in the poems of *recitative* that this fault is observable. He has not caught from his fine studies of Homer the exquisite music of the Homeric wave of rhythm; but he has caught his clearness of atmosphere, what he himself has so finely termed "the pure lines of an Ionian horizon, the liquid clearness of an Ionian sky."

So much as I have yet said of Mr. Arnold's power of expression has relation only to form—to all which is implied in delicacy of discernment of the force of language, and preference for simplicity of subject in what he treats. But the special direction in which Mr. Arnold's power of poetic expression is chiefly shown is . . . that of sedate and half-intellectual emotions, especially those which turn towards Nature with tender and melancholy yearning. (pp. 332-33)

Mr. Arnold hardly exercises the full magic of his characteristic power of poetical expression until he is in the mood in which some sad, though calm, emotion is the predominant thread of his thought, and natural beauty only the auxiliary to it; till he is in the mood in which, if his heart flies to his eyes, it is only to find some illustration for the enigmas pent up within it, some new image for the incommunicability of human joy and grief, for the pain that results from the division of the soul against itself, for the restlessness which yearns inconsistently for sympathy and for solitude, and rebounds like a shuttlecock from the one desire to the other. (p. 335)

                    Richard Holt Hutton, "The Poetry of Matthew Arnold" (1871), in his Literary Essays, *revised edition, Macmillan and Co., Limited, 1896 (and reprinted by Gregg International Publishers Limited, 1969), pp. 310-60.*

LIPPINCOTT'S MAGAZINE OF POPULAR LITERATURE & SCIENCE   (essay date 1873)

[*Literature and Dogma: An Essay toward a Better Apprehension of the Bible*] is a tract issued in the author's apprehension that our popular view of Christianity is false, our conception of the Hebrew and Greek Bible altogether hidebound and deadening, our notion of the Deity a picture that is doomed to destruction in the face of science. As it is a sincere scheme of individual opinion (though not of original opinion, being largely made up of graftings from a certain recognizable class of modern scholars), it could only be finally disposed of by following it up root and branch in nearly all its details, at the cost of writing a much larger book. No opponent will be likely to give it so much importance. (p. 126)

We should perhaps begin with Mr. Arnold's matter, but it is hard to represent him at all without doing some preliminary justice to his manner—his attitude toward the Christian public, his dogma of urbanity, and the value of his way of putting things as a likelihood of making converts. This is the more appropriate as he thinks the Founder of Christianity, and its chief promulgators, such as Peter and Paul, gained most of their successes through manner. "Mildness and sweet reasonableness" he believes to be the characteristic of Christ's teaching—a presentment of truths long afloat in the Jewish mind so winningly and persuasively that they became new and profound convictions in all minds; and he believes that when these characteristics were withdrawn or veiled the teaching was so far ineffectual; that when Christ, addressing the Pharisees, abandoned "the mild, uncontentious, winning, inward mode of working," there was no chance at all of His gaining the persons at whom His sayings were launched; and that Saint Paul certainly had no chance of convincing those whom he calls "dogs." Now, it is inevitable for us to ask ourselves what chance Mr. Arnold, undertaking the most delicate and critical crusade that can possibly be imagined against the dearest opinions of almost everybody, will have with *his* method. . . . Not much more "sweetly reasonable" will be seem to the ordinary Cantab, when he says that the Cambridge addiction to muscularity would have sent the college, but for the Hebrew religion, "in procession, vice-chancellor, bedels, masters, scholars, and all, in spite of the professor of modern philosophy, to the temple of Aphrodite;" nor any more "sweetly reasonable" will he seem to the ordinary innocent, conventional Churchman in asserting that the God of righteousness is displeased and disserved by men uttering such doggerel hymns as "Out of my stony griefs Bethel I'll raise," and "My Jesus to know, and feel His blood flow;" or in asserting that the modern preacher, who calls people infidels for false views of the Bible, should have the epithet returned upon him for his own false views; and that it would be just for us to say, "The bishop of So-and-so, the dean of So-and-so, and other infidel laborers of the present day;" or "That rampant infidel, the arch-deacon of So-and-so, in his recent letter on the Athanasian creed;" or "*The Rock, the Church Times,* and the rest of the infidel press;" or "The torrent of infidelity which pours every Sunday from our pulpits! Just it would be," pursues the author, "and by no means inurbane; but hardly, perhaps, Christian." The question is not so much whether such allocutions are Christian—which they possibly may be in Mr. Arnold's clearer aether—as whether they are adapted to his purpose of winning. He manages here and there, indeed, in trying on his new conceptions of old truths, to be exquisitely offensive. . . . But he becomes most elaborately and carefully outrageous when, combating [the] idea of Personality in the Holy Trinity, he calls it "the fairytale of the three Lord Shaftesburys," in allusion to a parable which he is at the pains of constructing about a first Lord Shaftesbury, who is a judge with a crowd of vile offenders, and a second Lord Shaftesbury, who takes their punishment, and a third Lord Shaftesbury, "who keeps very much in the background and works in a very occult manner." This seems like the talk not of a man who wishes to convince, but who wishes to wound: it appears to be completely parallel with the method of those dissenters, whom Mr. Arnold is never tired of inveighing against, who use invective because Christ used it, and who hurl epithets at a state church or titles. (pp. 126-27)

> *A review of "Literature and Dogma: An Essay Toward a Better Apprehension of the Bible," in* Lippincott's Magazine of Popular Literature & Science, *Vol. XII, July, 1873, pp. 126-28.*

THE NEW ENGLANDER   (essay date 1876)

["**God and the Bible**"] is a review of the objections which have been urged against the author's "**Literature and Dogma.**"

The author's design in this work, as in that, is "to show the truth and necessity of Christianity, and its power for the heart, mind, and imagination of man, even though the praeternatural, which is now its popular sanction, should be given up." "At the present moment two things about the Christian religion must surely be clear to anybody with eyes in his head. One is that men cannot do without it; the other that they cannot do with it as it is." . . .

The work is a further unfolding and defense of the author's well-known views, with the usual charm of his felicitous style. His attempt to reconstruct a Christian faith is vitiated by the fundamental error of recognizing religious belief as grounded only in the feelings, and receiving its form from the imagination; religion is an alliance between imagination and conduct. Religious belief can be firmly established only as we find a synthesis of it with reason. (p. 403)

> *A review of "God and the Bible," in* The New Englander, *Vol. XXXV, No. CXXXV, April, 1876, pp. 403-04.*

THE CRITIC, NEW YORK   (essay date 1882)

There is something highly Hibernian in the composition of this volume of '**Irish Essays.**' Here are three or four articles on Ireland and two or three on British Liberalism; and both sets are sermons from the same old text—the need of good education for the 'middle classes,' and the necessity for the reform of a state of affairs in Great Britain which materializes the 'upper classes,' vulgarizes the 'middle,' and brutalizes the 'lower.' Though the text was old, the sermons were none the less salutary. Mr. Arnold's preaching has worked a reform in the tone and manner of English literary criticism, though much yet remains to be done. His preaching on politics will also have its effect in due time. Politics, indeed, is only the apparent subject of these essays; in reality they quickly go behind politics into the educational question. . . . While one is inclined to go far with Mr. Arnold in declaring the very decided inferiority of the French language to the English, and of French rhythms as a medium for poetry of the highest order, still it is evident that he proves his case a little too easily. He should have re-read his own preface of 1853, reprinted here, before setting up some of Shakspeare's finest lines against some of Hugo's emptiest.

> *"Matthew Arnold's Latest Essays," in* The Critic, New York, *Vol. 11, No. 35, May 6, 1882, p. 126.*

[JOSEPH JACOBS]   (essay date 1885)

[*A native of Australia who resided in England, Jacobs regularly wrote literary criticism in addition to pursuing Jewish studies. In the following review of* Discourses in America, *Jacobs praises Arnold's logic and his method of presentation, which he describes as "that of a lay sermon."*]

[*Discourses in America*] consists of only three discourses—the Rede Lecture adapted to American audiences and the specially American lectures on Numbers and Emerson. . . . Small as it is, the volume differs favourably from some of the recent republications of Mr. Arnold's utterances in that it contains only specimens of his best work, and we may perhaps add that in it he dismounts from his over-ridden hobby—state schools for the middle classes. Each of the three essays attracted attention when first delivered—readers will remember the ludicrous blunders made by the American reporters with the goddess

Lubricity in **'Numbers'**—and they were as eagerly read when republished in magazines. Now collected in a volume they will be as popular as any in the series in which they are published. . . .

The analysis of the French character and its threefold strain— Gallic, Latin, and Germanic—recalls some of the best parts of the **'Celtic Literature.'** The admirable quotations from Newman, Carlyle, Goethe, and Emerson, in the opening passage of the essay on the last, together with the remarks on each author—often but a word, but what an instructive word!— exhibit Mr. Arnold at one of his best moments; as, indeed, the whole discourse on Emerson shows him to us in one of his happiest hours of inspiration, and might be selected as giving an admirable specimen of his peculiar qualities as a critic of letters and of life; or, as Mr. Arnold would say, it gives us his method and his secret.

There is an apt phrase—we believe, of Prof. Huxley's—which exactly expresses the *differentia* of Mr. Arnold's studies: they are lay sermons. The object of the sermon may be assumed to be the moral regeneration of the hearers. This is clearly and avowedly the object of most of Mr. Arnold's utterances. Notice how he invariably picks out the favourite sin of his audience. At the Royal Institution, in the midst of the London season, he lectures on equality. At Cambridge he avers that with the majority of mankind a little of mathematics goes a long way, and that science cannot satisfy the soul of man. He crosses to America, and there he chooses as his special topic Numbers, preaching to the text, "The majority are bad." (p. 817)

His method, then, is that of the lay sermon. Would that clerical sermons were ever as good! His secret is his subacid reasonableness and his serious levity or frivolous seriousness. What strikes one in his criticisms of life even more than their penetration is their sanity and completeness. Many a controversial victory he has won in discussions about letters or life, or sometimes even in politics, by attending to the one question, What are the actual and complete facts of the case? He takes human nature all round, and sees how far a proposed remedy answers to all its needs. Herein he is really penetrated by the scientific spirit in its best aspect, and he has been no insufficient teacher of the higher anthropology. That in part is the secret of his influence. Men see that what he says tallies in the main with what they know, and at the same time they are half attracted, half repelled by the tone in which he says it. If we may so put it, he pretends not to be serious, and by the very pretence convinces one of his seriousness. It is, in fact, this seriousness, the conviction his words convey that his deepest concern is with the things of moral import, that gives such authority to his word among Englishmen. The things of conduct are, after all, what both he and they have most at heart, and they listen to him as he discourses on things of sweetness and light— now, alas! becoming rarer and rarer with him—because they know that in his hands they have intimate bearing on conduct. . . .

[One] cannot help thinking what a force Mr. Arnold would be if he dropped his cloak of levity. He has given a clever sermon on Gray, text "He never spoke out." One feels that Mr. Arnold has never spoken out the faith that is in him. He began life as an Hellene of the Hellenes, and was as one of those who are at ease in Zion. He has gradually become more Hebraic than the Hebrews, but yet retains the easy manner of the sons of light. What a motive force he might be if he adapted his style to his matter! Mr. Arnold has some admirable words on Carlyle here in the pages before us. Carlyle is weighed in the balance

and found wanting; but if we may deplore the want of sweetness in Carlyle might we not regret its overabundance in Mr. Arnold's nature? (pp. 817-18)

[Joseph Jacobs], in a review of "Discourses in America," in The Athenaeum, *Vol. I, No. 3009, June 27, 1885, pp. 817-18.*

THE NATION   (essay date 1885)

The three lay sermons which Mr. Arnold delivered in America [and which have recently been published as **Discourses in America,**] were at the time the text of criticisms innumerable, though rather of the author than of his matter. . . . Lay-sermons we call them because they deal so exclusively with universal truths. The first, that on Numbers, enunciates a truth confessedly from "the sages and saints," Greek and Jew, and declares it applicable to every nation and every age indifferently; to wit, that wisdom and virtue belong to an aristocracy which is the leaven of the state, and if they fail, then, to speak after the vulgar, your bread is dough. In the second lecture, an academical polemic with Huxley, this same addiction to generalities— in the main, the assertion that education should by preference include knowledge operating intimately and directly on conduct—was so complete that audiences as a rule were as little interested in it as in a discussion of lunar optics. In the case of the last lecture, too—that on Emerson, which has been a puzzle to many and an offence to more—an explanation of its effect may be found in that same remoteness which in the others had caused their neglect. Emerson was treated as if he were already a classic, known only through his books, and the criticism applied to him rested on what may be called the universals of literature; but at Concord and Boston Bay Emerson is not a book, but a man—not a classic, an utterer of universal and time-dissociated truth, but the utterer of truth that had a special propriety to the hour's need, a particular applicability and force at a stage of New England thought. . . . To his audience [Mr. Arnold's] words had often the magical power of releasing vague aspiration into the form of intellectual light; by others, who only apprehend his meaning as thought without at the same time experiencing it as a mode of seemingly miraculous power, the very same words may be very differently rated. The critic reads *Open Sesame* quite plainly, and says they are pretty syllables enough; but when they were spoken, what a treasure they revealed! That treasure Mr. Arnold could not see, just as Prince Posterity and his Regent, Time, will have no eyes for it. Mr. Arnold wrote of his subject like one born in the next century, and he suffers only the common fate of men who insist on being in advance of their age. He used in his analysis only the materials open in the case of all classics who are a voice and no more, and thus was obliged to restrict himself to the universals of literature, as has been said; whether his conclusions are sound, it would be premature to inquire. . . . (pp. 98-9)

A review of "Discourses in America," in The Nation, *Vol. XLI, No. 1048, July 30, 1885, pp. 98-9.*

MRS. OLIPHANT   (essay date 1892)

[*A prolific English novelist, biographer, and critic, Oliphant discusses Arnold's poetry with the general rather than serious reading public in mind. She faults Arnold for being overly academic and for writing with a diffuseness that, according to her, will always keep his verse "outside the popular heart." She praises, however, the "music and freshness and reality" of "Thyrsis" and "The Scholar Gipsy."*]

The younger section of the poets who have illustrated [the Victorian age] could not be headed by any name so appropriate as that of Matthew Arnold—younger not so much in time, for he was not more than a dozen years in age after Lord Tennyson—but because not only of much later publication, but of a mind and temper which never got far beyond the Academic circle, or remembered that the atmosphere of the classics is not that most familiar and dear to all men. It is perhaps this atmosphere more than anything else which has prevented him and others of his brethren from ever penetrating into the heart of the country, and which forms a kind of argument against that careful training which it is now the fashion to claim for every literary workman. . . . (p. 430)

[We find among Mr. Arnold's poems] two poems on which most of those who esteem him most highly are willing to rest his fame,—"**Thyrsis**" and the "**Scholar Gipsy**," both of them comparatively short, and so much more individual than most of his poetical works as to touch a chord of sympathy wanting in many of the others. The extreme diffuseness of much of this poetry is indeed one of the faults which will always keep it outside the popular heart. There is something in the flow of even rhyme, page after page, long, fluent, smooth, looking as if it might go on forever, which appalls the reader. (p. 432)

To return, however, to the special poems which we have selected as the most living and individual of Matthew Arnold's poetry, both the "**Scholar Gipsy**" and "**Thyrsis**" are full of the atmosphere of Oxford and of youth. They are indeed rather two different parts of the same poem than independent inspirations, though the latter embodies rather the regretful looking back of the elder man upon those early scenes, than the actual musings of the young one. Their music and freshness and reality interest all readers; yet we can more readily imagine these poems to be conned over and repeated to each other, with that enthusiasm which adopts and dwells upon every word by those who "wear the gown" than by any other class. . . . The two poems naturally hang together, two parts of one elegy, mildly mournful, nothing like despair in either, the friend shading into the more distant vision, the shadow becoming more distinct in the friend, and both full of charm—the atmosphere of the evening, the breath of Nature, the City close at hand with all its teeming young life—and wandering figures here and there, roaming as Thyrsis roamed in his time, keeping up the long continuance, which is never more dreamy nor more persistent than in such a place, where the generations follow each other so quickly, with so little interval between. These are poems of Oxford, of a phase of life which has become very prominent in recent times—but also of a purely vague emotion, a visionary sentiment which touches no depths. (pp. 434-36)

Mrs. Oliphant, in her The Victorian Age of English Literature, Vol. II, *Lovell, Coryell & Company, 1892, 647 p.*

LESLIE STEPHEN (essay date 1893)

[*Stephen is considered to be one of the most important literary critics of the Victorian age. In his moral criticism, Stephen argues that all literature is nothing more that an imaginative rendering, in concrete terms, of a writer's philosophy or beliefs. It is the role of criticism, he contends, to translate into intellectual terms what the writer has told the reader through character, symbol, and plot. Stephen's analyses often include biographical judgments*

of the writer as well as the work. As Stephen once observed: "The whole art of criticism consists in learning to know the human being who is partially revealed to us in his spoken or his written words." Stephen often attacked Arnold's work from an agnostic point of view, yet he accorded him great respect in the following essay, which is a carefully considered, appreciative assessment of Arnold's achievement.]

[We] feel, when dealing with such a man as Arnold, at a loss. He has intuitions where we have only calculations; he can strike out vivid pictures where we try laboriously to construct diagrams; he shows at once a type where our rough statistical and analytical tables fail to reveal more than a few tangible facts; he perceives the spirit and finer essence of an idea where it seems to slip through our coarser fingers, leaving only a residuum of sophistical paradox. (pp. 459-60)

I may certainly say at once that Arnold, whatever else he was, was a genuine poet. . . . Matthew Arnold's poetry has, in an eminent degree, the quality—if not of inevitableness—of adhesiveness. . . . In certain of his more laboured poems, I am conscious rather that I ought to admire than that I do admire. To my brutal mind, the recollection of the classical models is a source of annoyance, as suggesting that the scholar is in danger of suppressing the man. But there are other poems which I love, if not because, at any rate in spite of, the classical propensities which they reveal. "**Sohrab and Rustum**" is to me among the most delightful of modern poems, though in it Arnold indulges, perhaps more than enough, in the long-tailed Homeric metaphor, which drags in upon principle all the points on which the thing compared does not resemble the object. I can always read "**Tristram and Iseult**," and the "**Church of Brou**" and "**Empedocles on Etna**"; and know that they leave behind them a sense of sweetness and delicacy and exquisite feeling, if they do not present those vivid phrases into which the very greatest men—the Dantes or Shakespeares—can infuse the very life-blood. . . . At his best Arnold reaches a felicity of style in which Tennyson alone, of all our modern poets, if Tennyson himself, was his superior. The comparison, much as I dislike comparisons, may suggest at least the question why Arnold's popularity is still, as I think it is, below his deserts. One answer is obvious. I cannot doubt that Arnold fully appreciated the greatest of contemporary artists. (pp. 460-61)

What is latent in the poet is made explicit in the critic. Arnold, himself, even when he turned to criticism, was primarily a poet. His judgments show greater skill in seizing characteristic aspects than in giving a logical analysis or a convincing proof. He goes by intuition not by roundabout logical approaches. No recent English critic, I think, has approached him in the art of giving delicate portraits of literary leaders; he has spoken, for example, precisely the right word about Byron and Wordsworth. Many of us who cannot rival him may gain, from Arnold's writings a higher conception of what is our true function. He did, I think, more than any man to impress upon his countrymen that the critic should not be a mere combatant in a series of faction fights, puffing friends and saying to an enemy, "This will never do." The weak side, however, of the poetical criticism is its tendency to be "subjective," that is, to reflect too strongly the personal prejudices of the author. It must virtually consist in giving the impression made upon the critic; and, however, delicate his perception and wide his sympathy, he will be scarcely human if his judgments are not affected by his personal equation. No one could be more alive to the danger than Arnold, and his most characteristic teaching turns upon the mode of avoiding it. There are times, no doubt, when he relies too confidently upon the fineness of his perception, and then obviously has a slight spasm of diffidence. I have noticed how, in his *Essays on Celtic Literature,* he uses the true poetical or intuitive method: he recognizes the precise point at which Shakespeare or Keats passes from the Greek to the Celtic note; he trusts to the fineness of his ear, like a musician who can detect the slightest discord. And we feel perhaps that a man who can decide, for example, an ethnological question by such means, who can by simple inspiration determine which are the Celtic and which are the Teutonic and which are the Norman elements in English character, is going a little beyond his tether. . . . Arnold is, perhaps, too much inclined to trust to his intuitions, as if they were equivalent to scientific and measurable statements. The same tendency shows itself in his curious delight in discoursing catch-words, and repeating them sometimes to weariness. He uses such phrases as "sweetness and light" with a certain air of laying down a genuine scientific distinction, as clear-cut and unequivocal as a chemist's analysis. He feels that he has thoroughly analyzed English characteristics when he has classified his countrymen as "Philistines, Barbarians, and the Populace." To fix a certain aspect of things by an appropriate phrase is the process which corresponded with him to a scientific analysis. But may not this method merely lead to the substitution of one set of prejudices for another; the prejudices, say, of the fastidious don for the prejudices of the coarser tradesman? (pp. 464-66)

[There] is room for poets as well as for arithmeticians; and Arnold, as at once poet and critic, has the special gift—if I may trust my own experience—of making one feel silly and tasteless when one has uttered a narrow-minded, crude, or ungenerous sentiment; and I dip into his writings to receive a shock, unpleasant at times, but excellent in its effects as an intellectual tonic. (p. 477)

> Leslie Stephen, "Matthew Arnold," in The National Review, *London, Vol. XXII, No. 130, December, 1893, pp. 458-77.*

THE SPECTATOR   (essay date 1895)

Matthew Arnold was not at his full height in letter-writing, as he was in writing his poems. His letters [in *Letters of Matthew Arnold: 1848-1888*] are pleasant, affectionate, wholly unaffected, but they are a faint reflection of the poet, and not even a bright or vivid reflection of his conversation. They are himself a little subdued, not as the letters of a born letter-writer should be, himself a little exalted. (p. 719)

Matthew Arnold's letters of travel, again, hardly suggest the vividness with which his imagination brooded over the loveliness of the scenes he visited. They are pleasant letters of travel, but they do not in any sense supplement or lend new colour to the poems. Take the letters from Switzerland. They are lively, unaffected letters, but they do not glow at all as the poems glow. We never see him pouring out his heart in his letters as we do in his poems. . . . The truth is that it took something more than letter-writing fully to kindle Matthew Arnold. The sympathy elicited by living personal intercourse did it, and the mingled toil and passion of imaginative composition did it, but correspondence did not usually do it. His letters are genial, tender, sometimes playful, but they are not often passionate in the sense in which his poems are passionate,—that is, written in the mood in which the inner depths of his nature showed themselves. In a very interesting letter to his sister, Mrs. Forster, written from Martigny in 1858, he expresses his sympathy with Goethe's feeling that he could not

write his best while distracted by practical duties and cares. Goethe, he says, thought that he could have written several good tragedies, but that in order to write them he must have been "sebr zerrissen,"—in other words, moved to the very bottom of his heart,—and that he dared not be so moved while there was so much that he needed a calm judgment and a busy mind in order to do well. And Arnold felt the same. His mind was too full of his practical duties to spare for poetry the full room needed to kindle intense imaginative life. His letters are pleasant, interesting, simple, unaffected, often even lively. But they have not the buoyancy and *élan* either of his poetry or even of his conversation. He was not excited by letter-writing. He only half-realised that living contact of mind with mind which sometimes kindles correspondence even more than it kindles talk. He was not a reserved man in talk. He seems almost a reserved man in his letters. They are written in a tone much more subdued than that of his talk or of his compositions whether in verse or often even in prose. (pp. 719-20)

> *"Matthew Arnold's Letters," in* The Spectator, *Vol. 75, No. 3517, November 23, 1895, pp. 719-20.*

GEORGE SAINTSBURY   (essay date 1895)

[*Saintsbury was an English literary historian and critic of the late nineteenth and early twentieth centuries. A prolific writer, Saintsbury composed a number of histories of English and European literature as well as several critical works on individual authors, styles, and periods; his* Matthew Arnold, *published in 1899, was the first full-length study of the author (see Additional Bibliography). In the following, Saintsbury surveys Arnold's poetry, which he considers outstanding if somewhat uneven, and he maintains that the verse in* Poems *is Arnold's best. Saintsbury briefly discusses Arnold's criticism, which he praises, although he finds Arnold occasionally narrow in his sympathies and unsure of his own theories. In a 1904 essay, Saintsbury made a lengthier and far more positive assessment of Arnold's critical writings (see excerpt below).*]

[Perhaps] Mr. Arnold's critical abilities, if not overrated, were wrongly estimated. It was difficult to praise too highly the expression of his criticism when it was at its best; but it was easy to set the substance too high. Even his subtlety and his acuteness, two faculties in regard to which I suppose his admirers would put him highest, were rather more apparent than real, and were constantly blunted and fettered by the extraordinary narrowness and crotchettiness of his range of sympathies. He was always stumbling over his own formulas; and he not unfrequently violated his own canons. (pp. 144-45)

The real value of Mr. Arnold as a critic—apart from his indirect merit of providing much delightful English prose shot with wit and humour, and enclosing endless sweetmeats if not solids of sense—consisted chiefly in the comparative novelty of the style of literary appreciation which he adopted, and in the stimulus which he accordingly gave to literary study. . . . Though well read, [Mr. Arnold] was not extremely learned; and though acute, he was the very reverse of judicial. He had fortunately been brought up on classical literature, to which he pinned his faith; and it is impossible that any one with this advantage should be a literary heretic of the worst description. But he constantly committed the fault of Shylock in regard to his classics. What was not in the classical bond, what "was not so expressed," could not be good, could not at least be of the best. Now I will yield to no man in my respect for the classics; and I do not think that, at least as far as the Greeks are concerned, any one will ever do better the things that they did.

But it is absurd to suppose or maintain that the canon of literary perfections was closed when the Muses left Philemon's house.

Mr. Arnold, then, as a critic seemed to me at first, and has always seemed to me, flawed with these very faults of freak and crotchet against which he was never tired of protesting, and, though a very useful alternative-stimulant, and check, not a good model, and a still worse oracle. I should say of him, and I think I have always recked my own rede from 1865 to the present day in this respect, "Admire, enjoy, and be thankful for Mr. Arnold as a critic; but be careful about imitating him, and never obey him without examination." Of Mr. Arnold as a poet there is much more to be said.

The book in which I first made acquaintance with any considerable quantity of Mr. Arnold's poetry was the so-called second edition of the "Poems," containing the first issue of the celebrated Preface [see excerpt above, 1853]: perhaps the best piece of criticism (though I do not agree with its main position) that the author ever did. . . . I venture to think—divorcing criticism as much as possible from any pathetic or egotistic fallacy—that the collection was and is an extremely favourable one for the purpose of doing full but friendly justice to Mr. Arnold's poetical talent. . . . [The] best things of all are [contained in this volume]—the best sonnets, **"Requiescat," "The Church of Brou," "Tristram and Iseult," "Sohrab and Rustum," "The Forsaken Merman," "The Strayed Reveller,"** and **"Switzerland,"**—this last without its most unfortunate *coda,* **"The Terrace at Berne."** When I find myself ranking Mr. Arnold higher as a poet than some do whose opinions I respect, I always endeavour to make sure that the cause is nothing illegitimate connected with this first acquaintance. And I do not think it is. For, though he himself would not have admitted it, a poet is to be judged by his best things, by his flashes, by his highest flights; and there are more of these to be found in this volume than in all the rest of Mr. Arnold's verse. (pp. 145-50)

I still like to try first to raise and then to correct the impressions of a new-comer, taking the standard edition as it too comes. He must, I should think, be staggered and disappointed by the respectable but imitative Wordsworthianism of the first two sonnets, **"Quiet Work"** and **"To a Friend."** But the Shakespeare piece is truly magnificent, and as Dryden's famous sentence has said the best and most final thing about Shakespeare in prose, so has Mr. Arnold said the best and most final thing in verse. Then we relapse heavily, to be uplifted again after pages by the strains, a little Wordsworthian still but freed from Wordsworthian woodenness, of **"Mycerinus"** with its splendid close. But the problem and puzzle—a problem and a puzzle which in thirty years I do not pretend to have solved—of the Arnoldian inconsistency and inequality meet us full in **"The Church of Brou."** Part I. is prosaic doggerel which any smart boy of sixteen could have written at any time during this century. Part II. is a little better. And then Part III. is poetry,—poetry not indeed free from Wordsworthian and Miltonic echoes, but poetry indisputable, marmoreal, written for all time. **"A Modern Sappho"** drops to Moore, and not very good Moore; and then with **"Requiescat"** we are in upper air again. It is not faultless; it has lapses, flatnesses, *clichés,* but it is one of the great lyrical dirges of English. (pp. 150-51)

In considering the longer narrative poems we must remember Mr. Arnold's pet theory that "all depends on the subject," that the epic and the drama stand high above all other forms of poetry, and so forth. I own that they do not interest me greatly, despite the magnificent close of **"Sohrab and Rus-**

tum," or that sudden lyric burst which lightens the darkness of **"Tristram and Iseult"**. . . . The truth is that Mr. Arnold had neither the narrative nor (to take in **"Merope"**) the dramatic gift. For to possess either you must possess the other power of "keeping your own head out of the memorial," and that he could never do. Nevertheless it is something wonderful that he should be as bad as he sometimes is. And the inequality is the same in his ballads. **"St. Brandan,"** with a magnificent and not wholly unsuccessful strain in it, is yet not quite a success. . . . But **"The Forsaken Merman"** is very nearly supreme. He is not popular now, I believe, and certainly he might not have been written if there had been no Tennyson; but he is good,—good all through, good in sentiment, good in music, good (which is the rarest thing in poetry) in composition, not easily surpassable in finale. The man who wrote **"The Forsaken Merman"** was a poet *sans phrase.* (pp. 152-53)

"The Scholar Gipsy" I would fain think nearly faultless, and fain hope that it is not old Oxford prejudice that makes me think it so. . . . **"Dover Beach,"** though I do not in the least agree with it, and though the metaphor of the retreating tide is a singularly damaging one for the poet's meaning . . . has a majestic music. (p. 154)

Mr. Arnold's poetical position is remarkable in our literature, and not wholly benign in its influence. He provides for those who know and love letters an interesting and admirable example of a literary poet. He provides for those who can appreciate poetry some exquisite notes nowhere else heard, and not to be resigned even if the penalty for hearing them were twenty times as great. But he provides also a most dangerous model. For he may seem to suggest, and has, I think, already suggested to some, that the acquisition by dint of labour of a certain "marmoresque" dignity of thought and phrase will atone for the absence of that genius which cometh not with labour, neither goeth with the lack of it. (p. 156)

George Saintsbury, "Matthew Arnold" and "Matthew Arnold (Concluded)," in his Corrected Impressions: Essays on Victorian Writers, *Dodd, Mead and Company, 1895, pp. 138-47, 148-56.*

W. C. BROWNELL   (essay date 1901)

What especially singularizes Arnold, personally, among the writers of his time and for his public is that, in a more marked and definite way than is to be said of any of them, he developed his nature as well as directed his work in accordance with the definite ideal of reason. He had probably little disposition originally to swerve from the pursuit of this ideal, but he made of it an aim so constant and so conscious as to illustrate it with great distinctness in his life as well as in his writings. The pursuit of perfection that he preached he practised with equal inveteracy. But in this pursuit he sought first of all completeness of harmonious development, and to the Greek he added the Christian inspiration. His own translation of the quality celebrated by St. Paul, "sweet reasonableness," was the chief trait of his character—the "note," to use the expression he borrowed from Newman and popularized, of his personality. His reasonableness was tinctured with feeling, his stoicism was human, his temper affectionate, his aim benevolent, and his manner gentle. But he rarely lost the poise that he advocated so sedulously, and his gentleness for being ingrained failed no whit in vivacity or in force. (pp. 152-53)

The **"Letters"** were disappointing to readers who perhaps unwarrantably looked in them for the literature which he limited to his writings, though the fact that he did so attests the precision, almost inconsistent with spontaneity, with which he ordered his activities. The **"Letters"** have been subjected to an unknown quantity of editing, but it is evident that they were adjusted to the measure of his correspondents' capacities and not expressive of his own. This, nevertheless, is a circumstance that has its advantage and shows a very charming side of him. The **"Letters"** leave the impression of a singularly elevated soul, living habitually on a high plane. Spite of their lack of accent and incident they repay more than one reading, for this reason; and they bring out into a stronger light the qualities deducible from his works. They testify happily to shortcomings rather than defects.

He lacked the edge at least of the aesthetic faculty. . . . In the matter of art he speculated only; and in a general way, after the fashion of the "Laocoön." Nor is his sense of humor conspicuously spontaneous. It has the aptness of wit even where it is not, as is generally the case with him, distinctly wit rather than humor at all. His wit, however, is distinguished. It seasoned even—or I may say, especially—his controversy to an extent that makes literature of it. (pp. 154-55)

His wit, however, thoroughly personal in its pungency as it is, is an instrument rather than a medium with him. . . . Outside of it he certainly lacked that indefinable but very definite element of character that we know as temperament. Lacking energy, he lacked also the genius of which he himself affirmed energy to be the main constituent. He freely acknowledged this, and made the best of it. He made, in fact, a great deal of it. Without in the least overrating himself he took himself with absolute seriousness, and his work from first to last is informed with the high sincerity of a consistent purpose—the purpose of being nobly useful to his time and country by preaching to them precisely the gospel he conceived they most vitally needed. (p. 156)

To the advocacy of these ends he brought an essentially critical spirit. He was in endowment and in equipment the first of English critics. Among English critics, indeed, he stands quite alone. No other has his candor, his measure of disinterestedness, his faculty of extracting their application from the precedents indicated by culture. But he is also eminently an English critic. Disinterestedness pure and simple, disinterestedness to the point of detachment he neither illustrated nor believed in—much as he advocated the free play of consciousness in dealing with subjects of vital concern. (pp. 156-57)

It is natural, therefore, that his criticism, even his purely literary criticism, should be altogether synthetic. It is even didactic. He had, it is true, a remarkable gift for analysis—witness his Emerson, his clairvoyant separation of the strains of Celtic, Greek, Teutonic, inspiration in English poetry, his study of Homeric translation, his essays on Keats and Gray. But in spite of his own advocacy of criticism as the art of "seeing the object as in itself it really is," and his assertion that "the main thing is to get one's self out of the way and let humanity judge," he was himself never content with this. He is always concerned with the significance of the object once clearly perceived and determined. (pp. 157-58)

Moreover, no pure analyst (such as Sainte-Beuve), occupied with the endeavor to see the object as in itself it really is, would evince so much interest in its connotation. Arnold is interested in removing—often in satirizing—the current misconceptions of it. He does not write of Milton and Goethe, but of **"A French Critic on Milton," "A French Critic on Goethe,"** to show how differently these popular idols are estimated by a disinterested critic from the way in which they are estimated popularly. (pp. 158-59)

He had, however, unmistakably his own way of being an Englishman, and if his concern was moral and his aim didactic, as they certainly were, the disinterestedness he inculcates appears in his method. One may say, in fact, that his motive is didactic and his method disinterested. His criticism thus becomes truly constructive. In form he does not dogmatize, he deduces; he does not argue, he elucidates; he uses his subject to illustrate his idea. His idea, indeed, is his formal subject, however near his heart its application may be. He deals with ideas directly, and his genius for generalization appears even where he is most pointedly and pithily specific. The essay on **"Equality"** is an excellent instance. He is concerned about the specific advantage of restricting the English freedom of bequest and the consequent distribution of wealth. But he advocates the reform by presenting the *idea* of equality in the most attractive, disinterested, and detached way, as if it were merely a literary thesis. (p. 160)

It is obvious, therefore, that his criticism differs in kind from that of other writers. It differs especially from that most in vogue at the present time. It is eminently the antithesis of impressionist criticism. It has behind it what may fairly pass for a body of doctrine, though a body of doctrine as far as possible removed from system and pedantry. It is wholly unfettered by academic conventions, such as, citing Addison, he calls "the sort of thing that held our fathers spellbound in admiration." But it is still more removed from the irresponsible exercise of the nervous system however attuned to taste and sensitized by culture. Certain definite *ideas,* held with elastic firmness but not developed into any set of procrustean principles, formed his credo, and his criticism consisted in the application of these as a test and measure of quality and worth. (p. 161)

His criticism is distinguished also from much that is currently popular in being wholly non-scientific. To begin with, it is interested very largely in the one element that eludes the scientific spirit—the element of personality. It does not ignore the substantial contributions that the scientific spirit has made to the theory and the practice of criticism. It merely concerns itself, and in a personal way mainly, with material that is too highly organized to be satisfactorily considered when considered materially, according to Taine's famous method. It is not occupied with origins—a subject that has an almost universal interest at the present day—nor much with relations, the study of which for being more literary is hardly less scientific. To Arnold apparently the study of heredity and environment involved in literary criticism based on "the man, the moment and the *milieu*" theory, has very much the interest that the process of running up all our manifold appetites and emotions into the two primitive instincts of self-preservation and reproduction would have, and no more. It is sound enough, no doubt, but in large measure superfluous—at any rate elementary. (pp. 163-64)

[His subject] is often ideas illustrated or exemplified in some personality. It is what Joubert, Keats, the Guérins, Heine, Byron were themselves and what, in relation to ideas, they stand for, in each instance. It is not at all how they came to be what they were, their evolution, the influences of their environment of time and place, or their influence in turn upon their age and succeeding ones. In brief, though their general interest is always drawn out, in contradistinction to the specific interest of pure portraiture, they are not generalized. (p. 166)

Arnold performed a signal service in characterizing literature as "a criticism of life" and thereby revealing even to the unreflecting the essentially critical nature and function of the truly creative "thought of thinking souls"—to recall Carlyle's definition of literature itself. His emphasis was of course on the word "life," but the incidental implication as to *how* literature is concerned with its proper "content" has a value of its own. (pp. 167-68)

Public questions interested Arnold acutely and his discussion of them was always suggestive if not conclusive. He dealt most successfully perhaps with those that were mainly social in their nature. The essay on **"Equality,"** for example, is one of his best. That on **"Democracy"** is hardly its equal. Both are, however, eminently stimulating because they deal with general principles and are, as the former asserts, "for the thoughts of those who think," at the same time that the commendation of equality as an ideal is convincingly buttressed by the salutary way in which laws of bequest are shown to operate in correction of the natural tendency to inequality; and that such penetrating remarks as "We have never yet been a self-governing *democracy,* nor anything like it," illustrate and enforce his discussion of the more political theme. (pp. 169-70)

Culture, of course, is his central theme. His name is popularly and rightly more closely associated with it than with anything else. It is his notable reliance and recommendation in every department of thought and action with which he occupies himself—religious, poetic, critical, political, social—his gospel, in a word. Culture he defines as "a pursuit of our total perfection by means of getting to know, on all matters which most concern us, the best which has been known and thought in the world; and through this knowledge, turning a stream of fresh and free thought upon our stock notions and habits which we now follow stanchly but mechanically, vainly imagining that there is a virtue in following them stanchly which makes up for the mischief of following them mechanically." (pp. 171-72)

He was not particularly happy in dealing with America. He could not let us alone. He seemed to be haunted by the desire to subject us, also, to his discrimination. But he could not, I fancy, quite characterize us to his satisfaction. (p. 173)

The **"Discourses in America"** undoubtedly read better to-day than they sounded then. That on Emerson is surely one of the most appreciative as well as most discriminating things ever written about its subject, and is on a very high plane. The **"Literature and Science"** is delightful, a real *vade mecum* for the humanist. The discourse on **"Numbers,"** however, which is the one most specially American in its subject and address, is, like the rest of his writings on America, decidedly less authoritative than his writings on almost any other theme. . . . But even in his writings on America, where their application is occasionally less apt than elsewhere, Arnold's general principles are, as elsewhere, cogent, stimulant, and suggestive. (pp. 174-76)

> W. C. Brownell, "Matthew Arnold," in his Victorian
> Prose Masters: Thackeray—Carlyle—George Eliot—
> Matthew Arnold—Ruskin—George Meredith, *Charles
> Scribner's Sons, 1901, pp. 149-202.*

GEORGE SAINTSBURY (essay date 1904)

[*In a review centering on Arnold's critical writings, Saintsbury accords Arnold far greater praise than he had in his briefer,* *earlier assessment (1895), and he ranks him with the greatest nineteenth century critics.*]

[As] I look back over European criticism for the years (approaching a century) which have passed since his birth, I cannot find one critic, born since that time, who can be ranked above or even with [Matthew Arnold] in general critical quality and accomplishment. (p. 516)

[Here] is a critic who knows what he means, and who means something not, directly, or as a whole, meant, or at least said, by any earlier critic. That "all depends on the subject" had been said often enough before: but it had not been said by any one who had the whole of literature before him, and the tendency—for half a century distinctly, for a full century more or less—had been to unsay or gainsay it. Further, the critic has combined with the older Neo-classic adoration of the "fable" something perhaps traceable . . . to the Wordsworthian horror of poetic diction, a sort of cult of baldness instead of beauty, and a distrust, if not horror, of "expression." In fact, though I do not believe that he in the least knew it, he is taking up a position of direct and, as it were, designed antagonism to Dryden's, in that remarkable preface to *An Evening's Love.* . . . It is hardly possible to state the "dependence"— in the old duelling sense—of the great quarrel of Poetics, and almost of Criticism, more clearly than is done in [the *Preface* of 1853 and the preface to *An Evening's Love*] by these two great poet-critics of the seventeenth and the nineteenth centuries in England. (p. 520)

[The] matter of more than a decade's production, by which [Mr. Arnold] chose to stand, is included in the three well-known volumes, *On Translating Homer* and *The Study of Celtic Literature* for the Oxford Lectures, and the famous *Essays in Criticism.* . . .

In these three books the expression of critical attitude, displayed, as we have said, unmistakably in the *Preface* of 1853 [see excerpt above], is not only developed and varied into something as nearly approaching to a *Summa Criticismi* as was in Mr Arnold's not excessively systematic way, but furnished and illustrated by an extraordinarily interesting and sufficiently diversified body of critical applications in particular. (p. 521)

[We] shall see that, right or wrong, partial or impartial, capricious or systematic as he may be, Mr Arnold applies himself to the actual appreciation of actual literature, and to the giving of reasons for his appreciation, in a way new, delightful, invaluable.

The really important part or feature of the [*On Translating Homer*] for us is its famous handling of "the Grand Style." He had used this phrase, italicising it, in the *Preface* itself, had declared that the ancients were its "unapproached masters," but he had not said much about it or attempted to define it. Here he makes it almost his chief battle-charger—presenting Homer, Dante, and Milton as the greatest masters of it, if not the only sure ones, denying any *regular* possession of it to Shakespeare, and going far to deny most other poets, from Tennyson down to Young, the possession of it at all. It was impossible that this enigmatic critical phrase, applied so provocatively, should not itself draw the fire of critics. (pp. 522-23)

[Mr. Arnold's Grand Style] is, in fact, a fresh formulation of the Classical restraint, definiteness, proportion, form, against the Romantic vague, the Romantic fantasy. . . . It is a doctrine like another: and, in its special form and plan, an easily comprehensible reaction from a reaction—in fact, the inevitable ebb after the equally inevitable flow. But when we begin to examine it (especially in comparison with its Longinian original) as a matter of theory, and with its own illustrations as a matter of practice, doubts and difficulties come thick upon us. . . . (p. 524)

[It] is difficult, on examining Mr. Arnold's instances and his comments, in the most impartial and judicial manner possible, to resist the conclusion that his definition only really fits Dante, and that it was originally derived from the study of him. To that fixed star of first magnitude in poetry it *does* apply as true, as nothing but true, and perhaps even as the whole truth. Nobility, quintessential poetry, simplicity in at least some senses, severity and seriousness in almost all,—who will deny these things to the *Commedia?* But it is very difficult to think that it applies, in anything like the same coequal and coextensive fashion, to either Homer or Milton. There are points in which Homer touches Dante; there are points in which Dante touches Milton; but they are not the same points. It may, further, be very much doubted whether Mr Arnold has not greatly exaggerated both Homer's universal "simplicity" and his universal "seriousness." The ancients were certainly against him on the latter point. While one may feel not so much doubt as certainty that the application of "severity" to Milton—unless it means simply the absence of geniality and humour—is still more rash.

But when we look back to Longinus we shall find at least a hint of a much more serious defect than this. Why this unnecessary asceticism and grudging in the connotation of grandeur? why this tell-tale and self-accusing limitation further to a bare three poets, two of them, indeed, of the very greatest? . . . How much wiser is it, instead of fixing such arbitrary limits, to recognise that the Grand Style has infinite manifestations; that it may be found in poets who have it seldom as well as in those who have it often. . . . (pp. 524-25)

The other "chair"-book, *The Study of Celtic Literature*, is tempting in promise, but disappointing in performance. Much of it is not literary, and when it becomes so, there are difficulties. In the *Preface* itself, and in the *Homer*, Mr Arnold had sometimes been unjust or unsatisfactory on what he did not know or did not like—Mediaeval literature, the Ballad, &c.,— but his remarks and his theories had been, in the main, solidly based upon what he did not know thoroughly and did appreciate—the Classics, Dante, Milton, Wordsworth. . . . Whether Mr Arnold knew directly, and at first-hand, *any* Welsh, Breton, Cornish, Irish, or Scotch Gaelic, I do not know. He certainly disclaims anything like extensive or accurate knowledge, and it is noticeable that (I think invariably) he quotes from translations, and only a few well-known translations. . . . Yet he proceeds to pick out (as if directly acquainted with the literatures themselves, at dates which make the matter certain) divers characteristics of "melancholy," "natural magic," &c., in Celtic literature, and then, unhesitatingly and without proof of any kind, to assign the presence of these qualities, in writers like Shakespeare and Keats, where we have not the faintest evidence of Celtic *blood,* to Celtic influence. (pp. 526-27)

In that central citadel or canon of the subject, *Essays in Criticism,* this contraband element, this theory divorced from history, makes its appearance but too often: it can and need only be said, for instance, that Mr Arnold's estimate of the condition of French, and still more of German, literature in his own day, as compared with English, will not stand for five minutes the examination of any impartial judge, dates and books in hand. . . . The two first Essays, **"The Function of Criticism at the Present**

Time" and the **"Influence of Academies,"** take up, both in the vivacious and in the sober manner, the main line and strategy of the old *Preface* itself. We may, not merely with generosity, but with justice, "write off" the, as has been said, historically false parallels with France and Germany which the writer brings in to support his case. That case itself is perfectly solid and admissible. Those who are qualified to judge—not perhaps a large number—will admit, whether they are for it or against it, that no nonsuit is possible, and perhaps that no final decision for it or against is possible either, except to the satisfaction of mere individual taste and opinion. (pp. 527-28)

[For] acute, sensitive, inspired, and inspiring *remarks* on the man, or the work, or this and that part of work and man— attractively expressed, ingeniously co-ordinated, and redeemed from mere desultoriness by the constant presence of the general critical creed—no critic is [Mr Arnold's] superior. . . .

He may be said—imperfectly Romantic, or even anti-Romantic, as he was—to have been the very first critic to urge the importance, the necessity, of that comparative criticism of different literatures, the half-blind working of which had helped to create, if it had not actually created, the Romantic movement. (p. 535)

His services, therefore, to English Criticism, whether as a "preceptist" or as an actual craftsman, cannot possibly be overestimated. In the first respect he was, if not the absolute reformer,—these things, and all things, reform themselves under the guidance of the Gods and the Destinies, not of men,— the leader in reform, of the slovenly and disorganised condition into which Romantic criticism had fallen. In the second, the things which he had not, as well as those which he had, combined to give him a place among the very first. He had not the sublime and ever new-inspired inconsistency of Dryden. . . . He had not the robustness of Johnson; the supreme critical "reason" (as against understanding) of Coleridge; scarcely the exquisite, if fitful, appreciation of Lamb, or the full-blooded and passionate appreciation of Hazlitt. But he had an exacter knowledge than Dryden's; the fineness of his judgment shows finer beside Johnson's bluntness; he could not wool-gather like Coleridge; his range was far wider than Lamb's; his scholarship and his delicacy alike gave him an advantage over Hazlitt. Systematic without being hidebound; well-read (if not exactly learned) without pedantry; delicate and subtle, without weakness or dilettanteism; catholic without eclecticism; enthusiastic without indiscriminateness,—Mr Arnold is one of the best and most precious of teachers on his own side. And when, at those moments which are, but should not be, rare, the Goddess of Criticism descends, like Cambina and her lion-team, into the lists, and with her Nepenthe makes men forget sides and sects in a common love of literature, then he is one of the best and most precious of critics. (pp. 536-37)

George Saintsbury, "English Criticism from 1860-1900," in his A History of Criticism and Literary Taste in Europe from the Earliest Texts to the Present Day: Modern Criticism, Vol. III, *William Blackwood & Sons Ltd., 1904, pp. 515-61.**

WILLIAM MORTON PAYNE (essay date 1907)

Arnold confronts the dark problem of the grave, not, as Tennyson did, with the agony of a self-tortured spirit, passionately clinging to the one solution upon which the heart is set, and finding no possibility of solace in any other, but rather with a spirit which is ready to acquiesce in the order of the universe, whatever that order may be, and to live a life no less strenuous for the abandonment of the certainty of its conscious prolongation after death. "Hath man no second life?—Pitch this one high!"—Such is Arnold's essential message, and it has an inspiration, an ethical energy, that we do not get from Tennyson's utterances upon the same theme. . . . It is the fashion to call Arnold a poet of despair, and it is easy to make selections from his verse which will lend colour to that view. Certainly, "his sad lucidity of soul" has little in common with the burly temper of such an optimist as Browning, or with the buoyancy of spirit that we often find in Tennyson and always in Shelley. It would be difficult to express the mood of pure pessimism more absolutely than it is expressed in the closing lines of **"Dover Beach."** . . . And the many passages in which the poet seems to bewail the fate that made him the child of an age of lapsing faith, and to look longingly back upon those earlier ages when men might believe things now impossible to the cultured mind, fill us, no doubt, with the sense of spiritual tragedy. Yet the note of calmness, of spiritual serenity, which, as I have already urged, is more than the merely stoical acceptance of the common lot of human suffering, seems to me, on the whole, the prevailing note of Arnold's poetry. (pp. 259-60)

In dealing with the great intellectual and spiritual movements of civilisation, Arnold showed a fine historical sense, which enabled him to enter with deep sympathy into modes of thought which had become for himself outworn. This is particularly true of his study of historical Christianity, and he was unfailing in his sympathy with a faith to which he could not give intellectual assent. (p. 264)

Arnold is not likely to have his turn as a poet in the sense in which Browning and Tennyson have had theirs, but he is likely to hold his audience, and even to increase it, during the coming years. He has hardly more of the elements of popularity than Landor had, but he has equal reason to be proud of the quality of his limited following.

Among the preoccupations which Arnold carried over into his prose from his verse, none are more important than those which relate to ethical and religious questions. That conduct is three-fourths of life, is a maxim he never ceased to reiterate, and to enforce with a seriousness none the less real because sometimes disguised by the playful vivacity of his manner. The influence exercised upon religious thought by those famous books, **"Literature and Dogma"** and **"God and the Bible,"** has been both far-reaching and profound. It is an influence which professional theologians, with a sense of alarm heightened by the suspicion that there was even more in the argument than they could understand, have done their best to minimise. Those books, so unlike the dull tomes which their subjects naturally suggest, may be lacking in exact scholarship, and the latest developments of the higher criticsm may have rendered some of their positions untenable, but their fundamental logic remains unanswerable, and the spirit of sweet reasonableness which informs them will long remain potent to shape the religious consciousness of open-minded readers. (pp. 269-70)

There is one aspect of Arnold's work which has not usually received the attention it deserves, and which I would be unwilling to neglect even in so summary an account of his leading ideas as that now attempted. The fact is apt to be forgotten that during a long period of the best years of his life his literary pursuits constituted an avocation, and that his real work was the very practical one of inspecting schools and marking examination papers. In his capacity as an officer of public education he prepared many reports of his work, and also wrote those volumes upon the schools of France and Germany which no one engaged in the work of education can afford to neglect. These educational writings have something less than the full charm of his manner at its best, but they are no less stimulating in their influence than his more popular books, and no less weighty in their judgments. It is so rare a thing for an intelligence of the first order to be applied to the technical questions of teaching that Arnold's writings in this department have a value that is well-nigh unique. That value is as great now as it ever was, for Arnold's discussion of educational questions, however closely concerned with the matter immediately in hand, never loses sight of the permanent principles that underlie all sound educational work. These writings have particular value in our own time, for they serve as a corrective to what must be regarded as the two most unfortunate tendencies in the current educational movement—the tendency to place faith in machinery, and the tendency to demand for subjects of secondary importance a recognition equal to that given to the humanities. It is hardly necessary to say that the weight of Arnold's influence was always thrown against machinery and in favour of the humanities. (pp. 277-78)

Concerning the general sanity and acuteness of his literary judgments it is not easy to speak in terms of praise sufficiently high. It is the simple truth to say that he was the greatest English critic of his time. And yet, for all his balance and insight, he occasionally gave utterance to opinions to perverse and exasperating that they produce a feeling of blank amazement. When he tells us, for example, that Shelley's prose is better than his poetry, we can only say with Swinburne that it would not take many such dicta to ruin the reputation of any critic, however eminent. But if I have taken occasion to dissent, with all the emphasis at my command, from certain of Arnold's vagaries, I feel bound to add a tribute of the deepest gratitude to the critic who has, on the whole, done more than any of his contemporaries to aid men in clear thinking and right feeling about literature. His instinct in such matters was nearly always sure, and his guidance is nearly always safe. (pp. 280-81)

William Morton Payne, "Matthew Arnold," in his The Greater English Poets of the Nineteenth Century, *Henry Holt and Company, 1907 (and reprinted by Books for Libraries Press, 1967; distributed by Arno Press, Inc.), pp. 251-83.*

WALTER RALEIGH   (essay date 1912)

[*A popular lecturer and respected literary critic, Raleigh was appointed Oxford's first professor of English literature in 1904. His critical approach to literature, however, was not that of a scholar, but rather that of a sensitive, urbane commentator whose literary exegesis served to assist the nonacademician's understanding of English literature. In the following discussion of Arnold's* Essays in Criticism, *Raleigh proposes that Arnold's criticism of England and of English literature is harmed by his lack of affection for England.*]

The *Essays in Criticism* cannot be fully appreciated and understood if they are taken as a mere collection of discourses composed on various occasions and inspired by various subjects. They are something more, or at least they are something other, than that. Taken together they are a manifesto, an attempt to define, and to illustrate in practice, the vital functions of criticism. (p. 300)

A sure instinct governed [Arnold's] poetic adventures, and made him refuse subjects and occasions which did not rouse and inspire him. Most of his poetry was born, not made. Yet there is little evidence that he remembered this when he became a preacher. He is too fond of speaking as if there were a saving grace in method. Ben Jonson's Roman plays conform much more perfectly to his standards than do any of the Roman plays of Shakespeare. But what profit is that, to them or to us, when nobody can read them? The curse that rests on the academics of modern literature has sent **Merope** to join *Sejanus* in the limbo where everything is measured and correct.

It will be observed that among the names which are the subjects of these essays there is no English name. The ideals that are set before us are European or cosmopolitan, not national. That is at once their strength and their weakness. The classic doctrine belongs to the Latin civilization; the doctrine of ideas, of the pure intelligence, freed from all local and temporal prejudices, belongs to those intellectual wayfarers who are citizens of the world, and refuse to contract themselves in narrower bonds. If London or Berlin were destroyed, they could live no less happily in Paris. Wherever they find intelligence and art, there they are among their own people. They are in no way attached to the soil. It is significant that what is perhaps the finest of these essays, the essay on Heinrich Heine, is an essay on a Jew. From Heine's mocking attacks on German middle-class complacency Matthew Arnold learned how to make war on his own countrymen; the very term *Philistine*, a weapon with which he did so much execution, was borrowed from Heine's armoury. The attitude that was natural to Heine, standing aloof, as he did by necessity, from national custom and national sentiment, whether in France or Germany, seems less graceful in Matthew Arnold. There is no evidence that he ever understood the English character. . . . The love which makes the world go round is not the love of the pure idea; and the defect of Matthew Arnold, as a critic of England, is that he had too little affection for England. It is not easy to divine how the English people, if, by the operation of some mad miracle, they had moulded themselves on his teaching, could have remained English. All that is peculiar to them seems to offend him. (pp. 304-05)

These considerations are not irrelevant, for Matthew Arnold became more and more, in his later work, a critic of English literature, which is an intensely national literature, and can be only imperfectly criticized from the cosmopolitan point of view. That, and no other, was his point of view, from first to last. His criticism is a good antidote to parochialism. His condemnations, based as they are on a knowledge of the great work that has been done in other countries and in bygone ages, are sound and often illuminative. But every literature is attached, by a myriad of invisible threads, to the life of its native speech, which is the creature, not of pure reason, but of national custom and habit. . . . In a certain sense, Matthew Arnold's attitude to English literature was that of a foreigner. He had nourished his youth on other pastures, and had no taste for many flavours that are racy of the English soil. When he wishes to show how poetry should be written, it is commonly a line of Homer, or Dante, or Goethe, that he quotes. (pp. 305-06)

The method of his criticism is essentially and wholly dogmatic. He believed in dogma and authority as engines of practical good, and in an academy as a means of literary salvation. He wanted only the best and highest things from poetry; he was very quick to discern them, and was so confident in his judgment that he cared not at all to reason about them, or to analyse the causes of their greatness. . . . In his critical essays [Arnold] presents us with many sound rules, and many memorable sen-

tences, but no live man. How Shelley appeared to Shelley, what Keats thought of Keats—this most fascinating inquiry, not in itself very difficult to pursue, seems to interest him not at all. But when they write anything, or do anything, he is willing enough to judge it. (pp. 306-07)

> *Walter Raleigh, in an introduction to* Essays in Criticism *by Matthew Arnold, Gowans and Gray, 1912 (and reprinted as "Matthew Arnold," in* Some Authors: A Collection of Literary Essays, 1896-1916 *by Walter Raleigh, Oxford at the Clarendon Press, Oxford, 1923, pp. 300-10).*

G. K. CHESTERTON (essay date 1913)

[*Regarded as one of England's premier men of letters during the first half of the twentieth century, Chesterton is best known today as a witty essayist and creator of the Father Brown mysteries and the fantasy* The Man Who Was Thursday. *His essays are characterized by their humor, frequent use of paradox, and chatty, rambling structure.*]

Against Mill's "liberty" and Carlyle's "strength" and Ruskin's "nature," [Matthew Arnold] set up a new presence and entity which he called "culture," the disinterested play of the mind through the sifting of the best books and authorities. Though a little dandified in phrase, he was undoubtedly serious and public-spirited in intention. He sometimes talked of culture almost as if it were a man, or at least a church (for a church has a sort of personality): some may suspect that culture was a man, whose name was Matthew Arnold. But Arnold was not only right but highly valuable. If we have said that Carlyle was a man that saw things, we may add that Arnold was chiefly valuable as a man who knew things. Well as he was endowed intellectually, his power came more from information than intellect. He simply happened to know certain things, that Carlyle didn't know, that Kingsley didn't know, that Huxley and Herbert Spencer didn't know: that England didn't know. He knew that England was a part of Europe: and not so important a part as it had been the morning after Waterloo. He knew that England was then (as it is now) an oligarchical State, and that many great nations are not. He knew that a real democracy need not live and does not live in that perpetual panic about using the powers of the State, which possessed men like Spencer and Cobden. He knew a rational minimum of culture and common courtesy could exist and did exist throughout large democracies. He knew the Catholic Church had been in history "the Church of the multitude": he knew it was not a sect. He knew that great landlords are no more a part of the economic law than nigger-drivers: he knew that small owners could and did prosper. He was not so much the philosopher as the man of the world: he reminded us that Europe was a society while Ruskin was treating it as a picture gallery. He was a sort of Heaven-sent courier. His frontal attack on the vulgar and sullen optimism of Victorian utility may be summed up in the admirable sentence, in which he asked the English what was the use of a train taking them quickly from Islington to Camberwell, if it only took them "from a dismal and illiberal life in Islington to a dismal and illiberal life in Camberwell?" (pp. 73-6)

As a critic he was chiefly concerned to preserve criticism itself; to set a measure to praise and blame and support the classics against the fashions. It is here that it is specially true of him, if of no writer else, that the style was the man. The most vital thing he invented was a new style: founded on the patient unravelling of the tangled Victorian ideas, as if they were matted hair under a comb. He did not mind how elaborately long he made a sentence, so long as he made it clear. He would constantly repeat whole phrases word for word in the same sentence, rather than risk ambiguity by abbreviation. His genius showed itself in turning this method of a laborious lucidity into a peculiarly exasperating form of satire and controversy. . . . If his opponent had said something foolish, like "the destiny of England is in the great heart of England," Arnold would repeat the phrase again and again until it looked more foolish than it really was. Thus he recurs again and again to "the British College of Health in the New Road" till the reader wants to rush out and burn the place down. Arnold's great error was that he sometimes thus wearied us of his own phrases, as well as of his enemies'. (pp. 77-9)

> G. K. Chesterton, "The Victorian Compromise and Its Enemies," in his The Victorian Age in Literature (copyright © 1913 by Henry Holt and Company; reprinted by permission of Miss D. E. Collins), Holt, Rinehart and Winston, 1913, pp. 12-89.*

LAFCADIO HEARN   (essay date 1915)

[*Considered one of modern America's leading prose impressionists, Hearn wrote sketches, short stories, and novellas that demonstrate a vision of evil and the supernatural reminiscent of the work of Edgar Allan Poe and Charles Baudelaire. Hearn is also recognized as a perceptive literary critic whose theories reflect his devotion to the beautiful and the bizarre. In both his criticism and his fiction Hearn emphasized the emotional effects of art rather than its social and ethical functions.*]

[Arnold] loved beauty and truth for their own sake, and found himself everywhere confronted by a narrow and vulgar conservatism that imposed restrictions upon thought, and refused all privileges to opinions at variance with its own small and somewhat brutal dogmatism. Arnold fought against the spirit bravely, and succeeded in breaking a great deal of it down before his death. But he was able to do this very largely for the reason that he was not a great thinker. Had he been a great thinker, the world would not have listened to him so well, and his struggle would have been much more bitter. As it was, the melancholy of his life has given to most of his poetry a peculiar dark tinge, which borders upon pessimism without actually expressing it. His longer poems are his least great; his briefer lyrical pieces best represent his genius. For genius of a certain kind he really had; but the work of no other Victorian poet is so uneven. (p. 342)

Undoubtedly "Merope" is a fine imitation of Greek tragedy, but when this cold poem is compared with the fiery splendour and sonorous music of Swinburne's "Atalanta in Calydon," it suffers enormously. Had it been written in another age it would have had a better chance.

Again, Arnold was unfortunate even in his choice of subjects, when there was no comparison to be made. "Empedocles on Ætna" is certainly a very remarkable poem, but how unfortunate is the choice of subject. . . . Arnold makes Empedocles commit suicide because of doubts and despondencies; he makes Empedocles a very interesting character, capable of making very wonderful verses upon the difficulty of understanding the universe and of bearing the pains of life. The long soliloquy of Empedocles is really the soliloquy of no Greek, but of Matthew Arnold himself. But Arnold had no sense of humour. The ridiculous side of the story never perhaps occurred to him, until George Meredith produced a savage little satire upon

Empedocles with his heels in the air. . . . There is yet another reason why the best of Arnold's poems of the longer class are not likely ever to become really popular. His beautiful dirge on the death of his friend Clough, entitled "Thyrsis," by many thought almost equal to Milton's "Lycidas," appeals chiefly to the feelings of a class, not human feelings at large. It reflects personal remembrances, and it describes, very beautifully, the country in the neighbourhood of Oxford University; but it does not touch those deep common feelings which make poetry immortal. The same thing must be said of his "Scholar Gipsy"— it is an Oxford poem, rather than an English poem. And finally, it may be said that Arnold never found out where his own poetical strength really lay, and wasted himself upon subjects that might have been left alone. One of these subjects was Norse Mythology. "The Death of Balder" is fine verse, but it will never move us like the strong grand prose of the Scandinavian Edda. "Sohrab and Rustum" is a very fine poem, but who would not prefer the original of the same story in the great Firdusi's "Shah Nameh," now translated into so many European tongues? It is in his briefer pieces alone that Arnold will live. (pp. 342-44)

[The] verses from the beautiful piece entitled "Human Life" really represent the habitual feeling of the poet—doubt and sorrow. Perhaps this is why his poetry, or at least some of it, will long continue to appeal to the old rather than to the young— to the men who are disillusioned, who have known the same doubts, the same sorrows and the same unfulfilled aspirations. But I think the student ought to be warned against over-estimation of Arnold either as a poet or as a philosopher. The fact that he was able to do so much good, to break down the barriers of prejudice, to give new life to English criticism, is proof itself that he was not much in advance of his age as a thinker. (p. 345)

> Lafcadio Hearn, "Pessimists and Their Kindred," in his Interpretations of Literature, Vol. 1, edited by John Erskine (reprinted by permission of Dodd, Mead & Company, Inc.; copyright 1915 by Mitchell McDonald; copyright renewed 1942 by Kazuo Koizumi), Dodd, Mead, 1915 (and reprinted by Kennikat Press, 1965), pp. 321-47.*

WILLIAM PATON KER   (lecture date 1922)

The tragedy of *Merope,* with its preface, seems to me to be one of those strange 'visitings' that have to be noted along with the inspiration of the Muses: besides the Muses there are Powers of the air, *aeria animalia,* 'eyrisshe bestes', as Chaucer calls them; demons, in short, that occasionally fill the minds even of good artists with vanity. *Merope* is a return to the worst idolatry of the Renaissance, the belief in the formal pattern, especially of classical drama. It is touching to see the poet struggling with the enemy. The light that leads astray is light from Heaven; the poet sets out from true sincere worship of Greek tragedy, and his enterprise is no mean one: to express the beauty of Greek form in English verse. But then he falls into the cold empty space, where nothing lives but vacuity, the pithless phantoms of mere Form. (p. 150)

The fault of the drama of *Merope* is that the fable is not *lecta potenter.* It is merely found suitable; the author does not take it to heart, and it does not carry the author with it. (p. 152)

The poet who believes so strongly, so rightly and truly, in the force of Greek tradition, the irresistible value of Greek legend, takes for his epic a Persian story, *Sohrab and Rustum;* a piece of old Northern mythology, the death of Balder. He loses much in the choice: he loses what was not lost by the authors of *Hyperion* and *Prometheus Unbound.* The scene and the story of *Sohrab and Rustum* need explaining: the story of Balder may indeed by nearer to us, nearer by ancestry, in one sense, than anything of Thebes or Troy; but the mythology of Asgard is not really part of our inheritance, though we have rights in it. Again I say it is strange that the poet who lectured at one time on Homer, at another on the *Mabinogion,* should not have said anything, apart from citation of authorities, about his Persian and Norwegian epic poetry. Are they, as some think, artificial poetry, Homeric or Virgilian parodies? I left this difficulty in order to speak of *Merope,* which is imitation in a different way, copying the mere abstract form; whereas *Sohrab and Rustum* and *Balder Dead* repeat forms of imagination which have an eternally fresh life in them. *Merope,* copying Greek tragedy, uses *stichomythia,* the dialogue in single lines which is a mark of all modern classical tragedies, a fashion that has no value in it except as recalling one of the least attractive formalisms of Greek drama. (pp. 153-54)

> *William Paton Ker, "Matthew Arnold" (originally a lecture delivered on June 10, 1922), in his* The Art of Poetry: Seven Lectures, 1920-1922 *(reprinted by permission of Oxford University Press), Oxford at the Clarendon Press, Oxford, 1923, pp. 139-60.*

WILLIAM S. KNICKERBOCKER (essay date 1925)

[Arnold's poetry] is frequently cited as representative of the prevailing *mal de siècle,* of Victorian disillusion and despair. Arnold himself has been called "the Hamlet of the nineteenth century." . . .

To question a characterization which has become so fixed and generally accepted is perilous; yet if it be true, then Arnold's practice violated some of his own principles of poetry. One need not accept this theory as adequate, but if his art is to be understood, it is necessary to discover whether his practice did indeed violate his theory. If his idea of the function of the Poet and of the nature of poetry be considered against the background of his own achievement, one may catch some glimpse of his ambitious effort to make the art something more than an outlet for creative fancy, or even, indeed, than as a vehicle for the expression of Byronic feelings engendered in a spirit of militant unrest. (p. 439)

Arnold's view was rooted in his experience. For a poet, he had an unusual historical sense and an aptitude for discerning the trend of ideas and social movements. Unlike most of his fellow craftsmen, he had had considerable contact with politics and social ideas before he published a line of verse. (p. 442)

Seldom since the Greeks, he believed, had poetry kept touch with the movement of European ideas and aspirations. One of the tragedies of English poetry in the generation preceding his was that, though an effort had been made to bring the art into closer touch with modern life, it had not succeeded in making the liaison. (p. 443)

Victorian poetry, continuing the ideals and tendencies of the romantic era, showed . . . [few] signs of contact with its milieu. Arnold found himself in a generation which idealized the romantics, but what was true of Wordsworth's contemporaries was equally true of his own. Tennyson's poems on poetry and the poet merely versified what Wordsworth, Coleridge, and Shelley had stated in prose. The poet was one whose word "shook the world"; he was a seer who alone, unaided, remote,

had intimate touch with unseen wisdom, giving voice to its otherwise unutterable mysteries. (p. 444)

While the main drift of English poetry was veering away from contact with social forces or with ideas, Arnold stood out with a protest, insisting that poetry was basically "a criticism of life in terms of poetic truth and beauty." He was deeply conscious of dissent from prevailing practice. "It might fairly be urged," he said, "that I have less poetical sentiment than Tennyson, and less intellectual power than Browning; yet because I have, perhaps, more of a fusion of the two, and have more regularly applied that fusion to the main line of modern development, I am likely to have my turn as they have had theirs." The emphasis is laid upon the relationship of poetry to social forces; his use of the word "development", indeed suggests his belief in the Victorian doctrine of progress. Poetry must have intimate contact with society, and not only reflect its movement but direct it. In order to do this, the Poet must be a critic. . . .

> It is important to hold to this . . . that the greatness of a poet lies in his powerful and beautiful application of ideas to life, to the question: How to Live. . . . A poetry of revolt against moral ideas is a poetry of revolt against *Life:* a poetry of indifference towards moral ideas is a poetry of indifference towards *Life.*

Behind his own art we can discern such an effort and such a recognition of the moral quality of life. His poems emanated from the mind of a disciplined man who had renounced much, a note too prominent to permit one to suppose that his frequent use of the first personal pronoun refers always to himself as an individual. It has a generic ring; he is identifying himself with his age. (pp. 444-45)

A new age was in the throes of birth; he, too, with agony and pain, felt its fever, and knew its struggle for deliverance. Through the pressure of the "daemonic spirit" he gave it lyric utterance. Two of his poems preëminently illustrate the point: *The New Age* and *The New Laocoon.* But he was not a victim of his age. That fact most of his critics have missed. *The Strayed Reveller,* the song of Callicles which ends *Empedocles on Etna, Stanzas from the Grande Chartreuse,* and the two *Obermann* poems, read in their entirety, are radiant in their notes of hope and peace.

How, then, may one explain the presence of the note of the prevailing *mal de siècle* in *The Scholar Gypsy, Thyrsis,* and in numerous lines and stanzas in other poems? With tremendous social changes going on everywhere about him, with such continuous stirrings of the human spirit on all sides, his broad human interest in and passion for them inevitably swept into his art. With keen insight he perceived that he lived in an age of transition; that in such an age the one hope of man was to interpret humanity afresh as a being of great moral and spiritual powers. *The Youth of Nature* and *The Youth of Man* clearly sounded that note. With the detachment of one who held constant commerce with the greatest thinkers and poets he touched the pulses of modern life like Goethe, and, like his Master, said: "Thou ailest here, and here!" It makes all the difference, then, if we are rightly to catch the meaning of Arnold's poetry, whether we read it as the cry of anguish of one who was crushed by his age, or as the lyrical catharsis of one of its physicians after the order of Goethe. (pp. 448-49)

Discriminative readers know well that Arnold's poetry has on it some shreds of the days of its gestation, but they also know that it has an abiding element which makes it estimable quite apart from the spiritual or intellectual conditions out of which it arose. If it is not more extensively read or appreciated at its true value, the reason may possibly be found in the fact that it has suffered somewhat at the hands of critics, earnest enough in their effort to interpret it historically, but who have nevertheless, by a subconscious process of which they were hardly aware, read themselves into his work. They have perverted the main drift of his intention by directing attention to his diagnosis of the spiritual malady of his age instead of to his remedy. Or, if they have not done that, they have weighed and tested him by a criterion romantic in origins and somewhat conventionally persisting in the face of the need for poetry to make clearer the deeper meanings of life. Against that criterion Arnold threw the whole strength of his powers, and his critical influence is now beginning to tell. (pp. 449-50)

If there is disillusion in Arnold, there is no despair. For all of his effort to restore poetry to vivid contact with modern life, he became at length aware that the time had not yet come; but that it would come some day he was firmly convinced. In that sense, and perhaps in that sense alone, he was—

> A wanderer between two worlds,
> One dead, the other powerless to be born.

(p. 450)

William S. Knickerbocker, "Matthew Arnold's Theory of Poetry," in The Sewanee Review *(reprinted by permission of the editor; published in 1925 by The University of the South), Vol. XXXIII, No. 4, Autumn, 1925, pp. 439-50.*

G. R. ELLIOTT   (essay date 1929)

Matthew Arnold is in general so confidently clear as to the nature of his own poetry that the reader is apt to credit him when he insists upon the contemporary sources of its melancholy. But those sources will appear much dimmer as time goes on. The "two worlds" that the poet wandered between, so sadly, will doubtless be rather nebular on the rear horizon, and the carefully wrought stanzas concerning them may seem the "strechèd-metre of an antique song." The future cursory reader, when he reaches the poem *On Growing Old,* may toss the volume aside with the remark that "this old fellow carefully architectured his gloom but added, here, a gable far too quaintly obtrusive." The discerning reader, however, will be in a better position than now to find, flowing beneath Arnold's verse, a profounder melancholy than the clear Arnoldian eye itself could fathom. (p. 58)

[In] nineteenth-century poetry there appears, more and more, an overstrained joy dogged by an overstrained sorrow: Shelley ecstatic, leading on Shelley miserable; Browning twisting hope, and then Hardy spinning gloom.

Arnold's position in this moody company will seem, to the future eye, quite natural but also very distinctive. For his melancholy will appear more essential than that of the others,—not so fully resolvable into temperamental and temporary conditions. Unlike the other poets, notably unlike Browning, Arnold had a firm and open-eyed serenity, which he cultivated more and more. In his prose, it wins a larger and steadier swing than in his verse, adding to itself a kind of cheerfulness; but at the same time it develops a guarded elaboration that prevents the finest quality of prosaic art. In his poetry his serene mood, though not so commanding, is intimate and native. And the main charm of his verse lies precisely in the quiet, upward push of this serenity upon his melancholy; like a spring of water in autumn rising again beneath a settled pool, moving, lifting, and clarifying it.

Such is the fine flow of poetry that went on in this man's spirit. But rarely has it a complete and natural circulation in his style; continually we are aware of pipes and pressure. For, in addition to the comparative tenuity of his poetic gift, Arnold was so intent upon clarifying Hippocrene, in reaction from current confusion, that clearness became in him a process too distinct and conscious for full poetic reality,—except in the didactic and satiric mode. In this kind of verse he could be superbly satisfying, and the meditative stanzas in *Empedocles on Etna* make the reader wish he had done more of it. But under the influence of that Romantic reaction from eighteenth-century forms which is still too current today, he underestimated the poetry of ethical wit. He wanted to be very lyrical. His fondness for lyric magniloquence was larger than his aptitude for it. In his odes and elegies, the true chanting is less present than excellently imitated. Often we can feel his music in the very process of freezing into architecture, under the pressure of his insistent effort at motivational clarity. (pp. 58-9)

The profoundest thing in [Arnold's] poetry is precisely his sense of the homelessness of the human spirit in its yearning that Perfection should come upon earth. The deepest source of his melancholy did not lie between his official "two worlds," did not lie between two conflicting times, but rather between a time and an eternity. More than any other Englishman of his century, Arnold succeeded, like Goethe, in mentally envisaging the full nature of Poetry, as a living norma, ever going on before mankind. He remarkably shaped his daily life in its light, while his century was doing alternate homage to "madman and slave"—as every century, in some degree, has done and will do. In the chasm between the life of the centuries and the life of Poetry lie the deepest waters of Arnoldian melancholy; and up through them and mingling with them, deriving indeed from the same ultimate source, rises his loveliest serenity. Arnold's verse is at its best when this autumnal spring flows out spontaneously, and notably where it mixes with his love of seas and streams. (p. 62)

[Its] fullest and loveliest tone comes in *The Scholar Gipsy.* Significantly enough, Arnold is here under guidance of Keats, instead of his more frequent masters, Wordsworth and Byron. The shade of the fullest poetic temperament of the century broods here upon him who saw so fully what Poetry means for human life. Hence, though scenic and temporal motifs are elaborate, they have not in this poem their usual danger for Arnold. He does not get caught in his own mental geography. . . . If, in the last third of the poem, the theme tends to wind too long among contemporary conditions, it saves itself superbly in the two closing stanzas; flowing back through the old clear Mediterranean, "betwixt the Syrtes and soft Sicily," and recapturing its reflection of eternity. Arnold's verse at its best has the melancholy "which there is in life itself": the melancholy of life yearning toward the full life of Poetry, and still "waiting for the spark from heaven to fall." (pp. 62-3)

G. R. Elliott, "The Arnoldian Lyric Melancholy" in PMLA, 38 *(copyright © 1923 by the Modern Language Association of America; reprinted by permission of the Modern Language Association of America), Vol. XXXVIII, No. 4, December, 1923 (and reprinted in a different form in his* The Cycle of Modern Poetry: A Series of Essays toward Clearing Our Present Poetic Dilemma, Princeton University Press, 1929, pp. 58-63).*

T. S. ELIOT   (essay date 1930)

[*Perhaps the most influential poet and critic of the first half of the twentieth century, Eliot is closely identified with many of the qualities denoted by the term Modernism: experimentation, formal complexity, artistic and intellectual eclecticism, and a classicist view of the artist working at an emotional distance from his or her creation. He introduced a number of terms and concepts that strongly affected critical thought in his lifetime, among them the idea that poets must be conscious of the living tradition of literature in order for their work to have artistic and spiritual validity. Another of Eliot's concepts, the "objective correlative," is often cited as a major contribution to literary analysis. In the following excerpt, drawn from a comparison of Arnold and Walter Pater, Eliot centers on Arnold's notion of Culture, particularly as delineated in his books* Culture and Anarchy *and* Essays in Criticism. *For a more general assessment by Eliot of Arnold's poetry and criticism, see excerpt below (1933).*]

Arnold had little gift for consistency or for definition. Nor had he the power of connected reasoning at any length: his flights are either short flights or circular flights. Nothing in his prose work, therefore, will stand very close analysis, and we may well feel that the positive content of many words is very small. Culture and Conduct are the first things, we are told; but what Culture and Conduct are, I feel that I know less well on every reading. Yet Arnold does still hold us, at least with *Culture and Anarchy* and *Friendship's Garland.* To my generation, I am sure, he was a more sympathetic prose writer than Carlyle or Ruskin; yet he holds his position and achieves his effects exactly on the same plane, by the power of his rhetoric and by representing a point of view which is particular though it cannot be wholly defined. (pp. 346-47)

We go to him for refreshment and for the companionship of a kindred point of view to our own, but not as disciples. And therefore it is the two books I have mentioned that are most readable. Even the *Essays in Criticism* cannot be read very often; *Literature and Dogma, God and the Bible,* and *Last Essays on Church and Religion,* have served their turn and can hardly be read through. In these books he attempts something which must be austerely impersonal; in them reasoning power matters, and it fails him; furthermore, we have now our modern solvers of the same problem Arnold there set himself, and they, or some of them, are more accomplished and ingenious in this sort of rationalizing than Arnold was. Accordingly, and this is my first point, his Culture survives better than his Conduct, because it can better survive vagueness of definition. But both Culture and Conduct were important for his own time.

Culture has three aspects, according as we look at it in *Culture and Anarchy,* in *Essays in Criticism,* or in the abstract. It is in the first of these two books that Culture shows to best advantage. And the reason is clear: Culture there stands out against a background to which it is contrasted, a background of definite items of ignorance, vulgarity and prejudice. As an invective against the crudities of the industrialism of his time, the book is perfect of its kind. Compared with Carlyle, it looks like clear thinking, and is certainly clearer expression; and compared with Arnold, Ruskin often appears long-winded and peevish. Arnold taught English expository and critical prose a restraint and urbanity it needed. And hardly, in this book, do we question the meaning of Culture; for the good reason that we do not need to. (p. 347)

Already, in the *Essays,* Culture begins to seem a little more priggish—I do not say "begins" in a chronological sense—and a little more anaemic. Where Sir Charles Adderley and Mr. Roebuck appear, there is more life than in the more literary

criticism. Arnold is in the end, I believe, at his best in satire and in apologetics for literature, in his defence and enunciation of a needed attitude.

To us, as I have said, Arnold is rather a friend than a leader. He was a champion of "ideas" most of whose ideas we no longer take seriously. His Culture is powerless to aid or to harm. But he is at least a forerunner of what is now called Humanism. . . . How far Arnold is responsible for the birth of Humanism would be difficult to say; we can at least say that it issues very naturally from his doctrine, that Charles Eliot Norton is largely responsible for its American form, and that therefore Arnold is another likely ancestor. But the resemblances are too patent to be ignored. The difference is that Arnold could father something apparently quite different—the view of life of Walter Pater. The resemblance is that literature, or Culture, tended with Arnold to usurp the place of Religion. From one point of view, Arnold's theory of Art and his theory of Religion are quite harmonious, and Humanism is merely the more coherent structure. Arnold's prose writings fall into two parts; those on Culture and those on Religion; and the books about Christianity seem only to say again and again—merely that the Christian faith is of course impossible to the man of culture. They are tediously negative. But they are negative in a peculiar fashion: their aim is to affirm that the emotions of Christianity can and must be preserved without the belief. From this proposition two different types of man can extract two different types of conclusion: (1) that Religion is Morals, (2) that Religion is Art. The effect of Arnold's religious campaign is to divorce Religion from thought.

In Arnold himself there was a powerful element of Puritan morality, as in most of his contemporaries, however diverse. And the strength of his moral feeling—we might add its blindness also—prevented him from seeing how very odd might look the fragments of the fabric which he knocked about so recklessly. (pp. 348-49)

For Arnold's Culture, at first sight so enlightened, moderate and reasonable, walks so decorously in the company of the will of God, that we may overlook the fact that it tends to develop its own stringent rules and restrictions.

> Certainly, culture will never make us think it an essential of religion whether we have in our Church discipline "a popular authority of elders," as Hooker calls it, or whether we have Episcopal jurisdiction.

Certainly, "culture" in itself can never make us think so, any more than it can make us think that the quantum theory is an essential of physical science: but such people as are interested in this question at all, however cultured they be, hold one or the other opinion pretty strongly; and Arnold is really affirming that to Culture all theological and ecclesiastical differences are indifferent. But this is a rather positive dogma for Culture to hold. When we take *Culture and Anarchy* in one hand, and *Literature and Dogma* in the other, our minds are gradually darkened by the suspicion that Arnold's objection to Dissenters is partly that they do hold strongly to that which they believe, and partly that they are not Masters of Arts of Oxford. Arnold, as Master of Arts, should have had some scruple about the use of words. . . . The total effect of Arnold's philosophy is to set up Culture in the place of Religion, and to leave Religion to be laid waste by the anarchy of feeling. And Culture is a term which each man not only may interpret as he pleases, but must indeed interpret as he can. (pp. 350-51)

T. S. Eliot, "Arnold and Pater" (1930), in his Selected Essays: 1917-1932 (copyright, 1932, 1936,
1950 by Harcourt Brace Jovanovich, Inc.; renewed
1960, 1964 by T. S. Eliot, 1978 by Esme Valerie
Eliot; reprinted by permission of the publisher and
Faber and Faber Ltd.), Harcourt, Brace Jovanovich,
1932, pp. 346-57.*

T. S. ELIOT   (lecture date 1933)

[*Eliot here offers an assessment of Arnold's poetry and criticism
and of the character of Arnold's intellect. For additional commentary by Eliot on Arnold, see excerpt above, 1930.*]

Arnold represents a period of stasis; of relative and precarious
stability, it is true, a brief halt in the endless march of humanity
in some, or in any direction. Arnold is neither a reactionary
nor a revolutionary; he marks a period of time, as do Dryden
and Johnson before him.

Even if the delight we get from Arnold's writings, prose and
verse, be moderate, yet he is in some respects the most satisfactory man of letters of his age. (pp. 103-04)

Arnold's poetry has little technical interest. It is academic
poetry in the best sense; the best fruit which can issue from
the promise shown by the prize-poem. When he is not simply
being himself, he is most at ease in a master's gown: *Empedocles on Etna* is one of the finest academic poems ever written.
He tried other robes which became him less well; I cannot but
think of *Tristram and Iseult* and *The Forsaken Merman* as
charades. *Sohrab and Rustum* is a fine piece, but less fine than
Gebir; and in the classical line Landor, with a finer ear, can
beat Arnold every time. But Arnold is a poet to whom one
readily returns. It is a pleasure, certainly, after associating with
the riff-raff of the early part of the century, to be in the company
of a man *qui sait se conduire;* but Arnold is something more
than an agreeable Professor of Poetry. With all his fastidiousness and superciliousness and officiality, Arnold is more intimate with us than Browning, more intimate than Tennyson
ever is except at moments, as in the passionate flights in *In
Memoriam.* He is the poet and critic of a period of false stability. All his writing in the kind of *Literature and Dogma*
seems to me a valiant attempt to dodge the issue, to mediate
between Newman and Huxley; but his poetry, the best of it,
is too honest to employ any but his genuine feelings of unrest,
loneliness and dissatisfaction. (pp. 105-06)

[When] we know his poetry, we are not surprised that in his
criticism he tells us little or nothing about his experience of
writing it, and that he is so little concerned with poetry from
the maker's point of view. One feels that the writing of poetry
brought him little of that excitement, that joyful loss of self in
the workmanship of art, that intense and transitory relief which
comes at the moment of completion and is the chief reward of
creative work. As we can forget, in reading his criticism, that
he is a poet himself, so it is all the more necessary to remind
ourselves that his creative and his critical writings are essentially the work of the same man. The same weakness, the same
necessity for something to depend upon, which make him an
academic poet make him an academic critic. (pp. 107-08)

The valuation of the Romantic poets, in academic circles, is
still very largely that which Arnold made. It was right, it was
just, it was necessary for its time; and of course it had its
defects. It is tinged by his own uncertainty, his own apprehensions, his own view of what it was best that his own time
should believe; and it is very much influenced by his religious

attitude. His taste is not comprehensive. He seems to have
chosen, when he could—for much of his work is occasional—
those subjects in connexion with which he could best express
his views about morals and society: Wordsworth—perhaps not
quite as Wordsworth would have recognised himself—Heine,
Amiel, Guérin. He was capable of learning from France and
from Germany. But the *use* to which he put poetry was limited;
he wrote about poets when they provided a pretext for his
sermon to the British public; and he was apt to think of the
greatness of poetry rather than of its genuineness.

There is no poetry which Arnold experienced more deeply than
that of Wordsworth. . . . We may expect to find in the essay
on Wordsworth, if anywhere, a statement of what poetry meant
to Arnold. It is in his essay on Wordsworth that occurs his
famous definition: 'Poetry is at bottom a criticism of life.' At
bottom: that is a great way down; the bottom is the bottom.
At the bottom of the abyss is what few ever see, and what
those cannot bear to look at for long; and it is not a 'criticism
of life'. If we mean life as whole—not that Arnold ever saw
life as a whole—from top to bottom, can anything that we can
say of it ultimately, of that awful mystery, be called criticism?
We bring back very little from our rare descents, and that is
not criticism. Arnold might just as well have said that Christian
worship is at bottom a criticism of the Trinity. We see better
what Arnold's words amount to when we recognise that his
own poetry is decidedly critical poetry. A poem like *Heine's
Grave* is criticism, and very fine criticism too; and a kind of
criticism which is justified because it could not be made in
prose. (pp. 110-11)

The poem about Heine is good poetry for the same reason that
it is good criticism: because Heine is one of the *personae*, the
masks, behind which Arnold is able to go through his performance. The reason why some criticism is good (I do not care
to generalise here about all criticism) is that the critic assumes,
in a way, the personality of the author whom he criticises, and
through this personality is able to speak with his own voice.
Arnold's Wordsworth is as much like Arnold as he is like
Wordsworth. Sometimes a critic may choose an author to cri-
ticise, a role to assume, as far as possible the antithesis to
himself, a personality which has actualised all that has been
suppressed in himself; we can sometimes arrive at a very satisfactory intimacy with our anti-masks. (p. 112)

We must remember that for Arnold, as for everyone else,
'poetry' meant a particular selection and order of poets. It
meant, as for everyone else, the poetry that he liked, that he
re-read; when we come to the point of making a statement
about poetry, it is the poetry that sticks in our minds that
weights that statement. And at the same time we notice that
Arnold has come to an opinion about poetry different from that
of any of his predecessors. For Wordsworth and for Shelley
poetry was a vehicle for one kind of philosophy or another,
but the philosophy was something believed in. For Arnold the
best poetry supersedes both religion and philosophy. (p. 113)

[Arnold's] charm and his interest are largely due to the painful
position that he occupied between faith and disbelief. Like
many people the vanishing of whose religious faith has left
behind only habits, he placed an exaggerated emphasis upon
morals. Such people often confuse morals with their own good
habits, the result of a sensible upbringing, prudence, and the
absence of any very powerful temptation; but I do not speak
of Arnold or of any particular person, for only God knows.
Morals for the saint are only a preliminary matter; for the poet

a secondary matter. How Arnold finds morals in poetry is not clear. He tells us that:

'A poetry of revolt against moral ideas is a poetry of revolt against *life;* a poetry of indifference towards moral ideas is a poetry of indifference towards *life*,' but the statement left in suspension, and without Arnold's illustrating it by examples of poetic revolt and poetic indifference, seems to have little value. A little later he tells us why Wordsworth is great:

> Wordsworth's poetry is great because of the
> extraordinary power with which Wordsworth
> feels the joy offered to us in nature, the joy
> offered to us in the simple primary affections
> and duties; and because of the extraordinary
> power with which, in case after case, he shows
> us this joy, and renders it so as to make us
> share it.'
>
> (pp. 114-15)

Arnold's account seems to me to err in putting the emphasis upon the poet's feelings, instead of upon the poetry. We can say that in poetry there is communication from writer to reader, but should not proceed from this to think of the poetry as being primarily the vehicle of communication. Communication may take place, but will explain nothing. Or Arnold's statement may be criticised in another way, by asking whether Wordsworth would be a less great poet, if he felt with extraordinary power the horror offered to us in nature, and the boredom and sense of restriction in the simple primary affections and duties? Arnold seems to think that because, as he says, Wordsworth 'deals with more of *life*' than Burns, Keats and Heine, he is dealing with more of moral ideas. A poetry which is concerned with moral ideas, it would appear, is concerned with life; and a poetry concerned with life is concerned with moral ideas. (pp. 115-16)

To ask of poetry that it give religious and philosophic satisfaction, [as Arnold did], while deprecating philosophy and dogmatic religion, is of course to embrace the shadow of a shade. But Arnold had real taste. His preoccupations, as I have said, make him too exclusively concerned with *great* poetry, and with the greatness of it. His view of Milton is for this reason unsatisfying. But you cannot read his essay on *The Study of Poetry* without being convinced by the felicity of his quotations: to be able to quote as Arnold could is the best evidence of taste. The essay is a classic in English criticism: so much is said in so little space, with such economy and with such authority. Yet he was so conscious of what, for him, poetry was *for,* that he could not altogether see it for what it is. And I am not sure that he was highly sensitive to the musical qualities of verse. His own occasional bad lapses arouse the suspicion; and so far as I can recollect he never emphasises this virtue of poetic style, this fundamental, in his criticism. What I call the 'auditory imagination' is the feeling for syllable and rhythm, penetrating far below the conscious levels of thought and feeling, invigorating every word; sinking to the most primitive and forgotten, returning to the origin and bringing something back, seeking the beginning and the end. It works through meanings, certainly, or not without meanings in the ordinary sense, and fuses the old and obliterated and the trite, the current, and the new and surprising, the most ancient and the most civilised mentality. Arnold's notion of 'life', in his account of poetry, does not perhaps go deep enough.

I feel, rather than observe, an inner uncertainty and lack of confidence and conviction in Matthew Arnold: the conserva-

tism which springs from lack of faith, and the zeal for reform which springs from dislike of change. Perhaps, looking inward and finding how little he had to support him, looking outward on the state of society and its tendencies, he was somewhat disturbed. He had no real serenity, only an impeccable demeanour. Perhaps he cared too much for civilisation, forgetting that Heaven and Earth shall pass away, and Mr. Arnold with them, and there is only one stay. He is a representative figure. A man's theory of the place of poetry is not independent of his view of life in general. (pp. 118-19)

> *T. S. Eliot, "Matthew Arnold" (originally a lecture delivered at Harvard University on March 3, 1933), in his* The Use of Poetry and the Use of Criticism: Studies in the Relation of Criticism to Poetry in England *(copyright © 1933 by the President and Fellows of Harvard College; copyright 1961 by T. S. Eliot; reprinted by permission of the publisher; in Canada by Faber and Faber Ltd),* Harvard University Press, 1933, Faber and Faber, 1933 (and reprinted by Barnes & Noble, Inc., 1959, pp. 103-19).

JOSEPH WARREN BEACH (essay date 1936)

It is well known that Matthew Arnold was strongly under the influence of both Wordsworth and Goethe. He was not averse to philosophical speculation in poetry. And one might expect him to have turned out nature-poetry of high significance. But as a matter of fact his references to nature in the abstract show a certain confusion of attitude. Sometimes they are conventional and admiring; more often perhaps they are critical and disparaging. And throughout they are lacking in the warmth and richness that marked the romantic treatment of nature. This is presumably due to his want of enthusiasm for either science or religion, the two main inspirers of nature-worship. One feels at once, in reading Arnold, that one has reached a period distinctly more "modern" than that of Wordsworth; that the poet no longer makes those religious assumptions in regard to the universe which were latent in Wordsworth's philosophy of nature. He is the least transcendental of English poets; and no German inspirations had come in, as with Emerson and Whitman, to give a new lease of life to nature.

Equally marked is a certain aloofness, in his poems, from the scientific movement of his day. There is very slight reference to evolution. (p. 397)

While Arnold indicates several different lessons to be learned from nature, it is almost invariably the sharp distinction between nature and man which forms the point of his departure. In his early sonnet, **"In Harmony with Nature,"** he points out the absurdity of this phrase, taken from some foolish preacher. . . . The doctrine of this poem, that of the "new humanists," is identical with Goethe's in "Das Göttliche," a poem with which I think it probable that Arnold was familiar. The English and German poems illustrate equally well the ambiguity inherent in the use of the word nature unless it is carefully defined. The two poets are here using this word to designate the "world of things" as opposed to the moral world of man; whereas it is often used to designate the natural order which includes man and his moral world together with the world of things. But Arnold's poem reminds us how hard it is to maintain the distinction. The world of things, which is cruel, evidently includes the lower animals to which man is so close akin; and the cruelty, fickleness, and vengefulness of "nature" are obviously characteristics of man in so far as he shares in the world of things. The division comes within man himself between that which is from his lower "nature," and those godlike traits which we choose to call "human." (pp. 398-99)

At other times Arnold maintains the distinction between nature and man in order to exalt the moral qualities felt in nature above the restlessness of man. Most doubtful humanism! Here indeed Arnold is himself frankly indulging in the pathetic fallacy, attributing to inanimate nature moods and qualities which are lent her by ourselves. They are variously described in different poems. In **"Resignation"** . . . he is recommending to his Fausta the stoical character that seems to be impressed on the country scene, or the peace which he feels at the heart of the cosmos. . . . (p. 400)

In other poems, Arnold, more conventionally, celebrates the steadfastness or the greatness of nature. In **"The Youth of Nature,"** the poet is rowing on a lake near where Wordsworth lies dead, and musingly debates the question whether the beauty and inspiration of nature are in nature herself or in the poet who so well sings her praises. Whereupon she herself replies, assuring him that loveliness, magic and grace are actually here, are set in the world. (p. 401)

[In **"Morality"**] he pictures a light-hearted and debonair Nature puzzling over the moral strenuousness of man, and wondering where he got it from—surely not from her? And then she recollects that she too has once felt "that severe, that earnest air." . . . This is indeed neat, and it does suggest, for once, that man's moral being is not completely without relation to the natural order in which it flowers. But it involves, at the same time, the notion of a divine origin of nature—the notion of God, so thin and uncongenial to Arnold. His conception of divinity has none of the richness of Coleridge's, drawn from metaphysics and mystic theology; nor of Wordsworth's, drawn from natural theology and his passion for the earth; nor of Goethe's, drawn from his passion for beauty and his devotion to science. And if there is a hint of Shelley's platonism in Arnold's imagery, it is but a cold and fleeting glimmer. What we most feel in the whole poem is Arnold's wistful loneliness in this no-man's-land where he wanders, between an old faith weakly grasped and a new faith not yet surmised.

If Arnold has little of the positive faith of the nature-poets, he has at least something of the negative and critical, the disciplinary side of that faith. He has not the glow and hopefulness of Wordsworth, nor the revolutionary enthusiasm of Shelley. Science does not exalt him as it did Goethe; nor does the concept of evolution lift his heart as it did Goethe and Swinburne and Meredith. What he does share with the nature-poets—and in him it stands out in high relief, owing to the comparative want of the other elements of their faith—is their implicit or explicit disapproval of the supernatural. . . . (pp. 402-03)

[The] disciplinary aspect of nature-philosophy is set forth in **"Empedocles upon Etna"** . . . , in the long sermon of the philosopher to his disciple Pausanias. Empedocles deprecates man's disposition to struggle and rave against the order of things, his dream that the world exists for his benefit, and that he has a right to happiness. Instead of studying the actualities of things in order to determine the limits within which he is free to move, man invents gods to gratify the dreams of his heart. . . . The consequence is that, looking to supernatural powers for aid, we neglect the means we have at our disposal in our own breasts. (p. 403)

In this discourse of Empedocles, Arnold rises to a conception of the universal order to which we belong, though we are reluctant to acknowledge it, unwilling to conform to its decrees,

and fain instead to invent evil gods, whom we blame for our distresses, and kind gods who may be relied on to bring to fulfilment our feeble undertakings. (p. 404)

Man has an ambition to understand the universe and the secrets of his own mind. But soon growing discouraged with the enormity of the task, he gives it up and weakly concludes that the search for knowledge is a sin, since "man's measures cannot mete the immeasurable All." He abandons to imaginary gods the business of comprehending the universe. And since the world has failed to gratify his craving for joy, he assumes that the gods will provide a realm beyond death to make up for this want.

The leading ideas of this discourse of Empedocles will be found later, in much more splendid poetic garb, in Swinburne and Meredith, combined with more heartening articles of the nature-faith. Again, Arnold's suspicion of nature as pagan and immoral will be found vigorously expressed in Tennyson and Hardy. His preference of man's ideal morality to nature's cruelty is echoed by Tennyson, who conceives of man's ideals in more explicitly religious terms. It is Arnold's anticipation of the sterner and more critical side of the later poets that constitutes his only significant contribution to the philosophy of nature in English poetry. (p. 405)

> *Joseph Warren Beach, "Arnold," in his* The Concept of Nature in Nineteenth-Century English Poetry *(reprinted with permission of the Literary Estate of Joseph Warren Beach), The Macmillan Publishing Company, 1936 (and reprinted by Pageant Book Company, 1956), pp. 397-405.*

F. R. LEAVIS (essay date 1938)

[*Leavis is an influential English critic. His critical methodology combines close textual criticism with predominantly moral, or social-moral, principles of evaluation. Leavis views the writer as that social individual who represents the "most conscious point of the race" in his or her lifetime. In the following examination of Arnold's criticism, Leavis responds to T. S. Eliot's comments (see excerpts above, 1930, 1933) and explores the nature of Arnold's critical intellect.*]

In *The Sacred Wood*, speaking of Arnold with great respect, Mr. Eliot calls him 'rather a propagandist for criticism than a critic', and I must confess that for years the formula seemed to me unquestionably just. Is Arnold's critical achievement after all a very impressive one? His weaknesses and his irritating tricks one remembers very well. Is it, in fact, possible to protest with any conviction when we are told (in the later essay, *Arnold and Pater*)?—

> Arnold had little gift for consistency or for definition. Nor had he the power of connected reasoning at any length: his flights are either short flights or circular flights. Nothing in his prose works, therefore, will stand very close analysis, and we may very well feel that the positive content of many words is very small.

And yet, if the truth is so, how is it that we open our Arnold so often, relatively? For it is just the oddity of Arnold's case that, while we are apt to feel undeniable force in such judgments as the above, we nevertheless think of him as one of the most lively and profitable of the accepted critics. Let us at any rate seize on the agreement that as a propagandist for criticism he is distinguished. On the view that has been quoted the first two essays in *Essays in Criticism: First Series* would be the texts to stress as exhibiting Arnold at his strongest, and they have, indeed, seemed to me such. And re-reading confirms the claim of *The Function of Criticism at the Present Time* and *The Literary Influence of Academies* to be remembered as classical presentments of their themes. (pp. 319-20)

Arnold's distinction as a propagandist for criticism cannot be questioned. At the same time, perhaps, it must be admitted that these essays do not involve any very taut or subtle development of an argument or any rigour of definition. They are pamphleteering—higher pamphleteering that has lost little of its force and relevance with the passage of time.

Yet it must surely be apparent that the propaganda could hardly have had its virtue if the pamphleteer had not had notable qualifications in criticism. The literary critic, in fact, makes a direct appearance, a very impressive one, in the judgment on the Romantics, which, in its time, remarks Mr. Eliot (who elsewhere justly pronounces it incontrovertible) 'must have appeared startlingly independent.' It seems plain that the peculiar distinction, the strength . . . is inseparable from the critical qualifications manifested in that judgment: the sensitiveness and sure tact are essentially those of a fine literary critic.

But does any actual performance of Arnold's in set literary criticism bear out the suggestion at all convincingly? Again it is characteristic of his case that one should be able to entertain the doubt. How many of his admirers retain very strongly favourable impressions of the other series of *Essays in Criticism?*—for it is to this, and to the opening essay in particular, *The Study of Poetry*, that the challenge sends one back. For myself, I must confess to having been surprised, on a recent re-reading of that essay, at the injustice of my recollection of it. The references to Dryden and Pope tend (in my experience) to bulk unfairly, and, for that reason and others, there is a temptation to talk too easily of the essay as being chiefly memorable for having standardized Victorian taste and established authoritatively what, in the academic world, has hardly ceased to be the accepted perspective of poetic history. And it is, actually, as a review of the past from the given period angle that the essay claims its classical status. But it is classical—for it truly is—because it performs its undertaking so consummately. Its representative quality is of the highest kind, that which can be achieved only by the vigorously independent intelligence. If it is fair to say that Arnold, in his dismissal of Dryden and Pope by the criterion of 'soul' and his curious exaltation of Gray, is the voice of the Romantic tradition in his time, we must note too that he is the same Arnold who passed the 'startlingly independent' judgment on the Romantics. And with whatever reservations, protests and irritations we read *The Study of Poetry*, it is impossible in reading it (I find) not to recognize that we have to do with an extraordinarily distinguished mind in complete possession of its purpose and pursuing it with easy mastery—that, in fact, we are reading a great critic. Moreover, I find that in this inconsequence I am paralleled by Mr. Eliot. (pp. 321-22)

How is this curious inconsistency of impression—this discrepancy of report which, I am convinced, many readers of Arnold could parallel from their own experience of him—to be explained? Partly it is, I think, that, taking critical stock at a remove from the actual reading, one tends to apply inappropriate criteria of logical rigour and 'definition.' And it is partly (a not altogether separable consideration) that the essay 'dates' in various ways; allowances have certainly to be made with reference to the age to which it was addressed, certain things

'date' in the most damaging sense, and it is easy to let these things infect one's general impression of the 'period' quality of the essay.

The element that 'dates' in the worst sense is that represented by the famous opening in which Arnold suggests that religion is going to be replaced by poetry. Few now would care to endorse the unqualified intention of that passage, and Arnold as a theological or philosophical thinker had better be abandoned explicitly at once. Yet the value of the essay does not depend on our accepting without reservation the particular terms in which Arnold stresses the importance of poetry in those introductory sentences, and he is not disposed of as a literary critic by pointing out that he was no theologian or philosopher; nor is it proved that he was incapable of consistency and vigour of thought. Many who deplore Arnold's way with religion will agree that, as the other traditions relax and social forms disintegrate, it becomes correspondingly more important to preserve the literary tradition. When things are as already they were in Arnold's time, they make necessary, whatever else may be necessary too, the kind of work that Arnold undertook for 'Culture'—work that couldn't have been done by a theologian as such. No doubt Arnold might have been able to do it even better if he had had the qualifications that actually he hadn't; he would at any rate have known his limits better, and wouldn't have produced those writings of his which have proved most ephemeral and which constitute the grounds on which Mr. Eliot charges him with responsibility for Pater. But his actual qualifications were sufficiently remarkable and had their appropriate use. His best work is that of a literary critic, even when it is not literary criticsm: it comes from an intelligence that, even if not trained to some kinds of rigour, had its own discipline; an intelligence that is informed by a mature and delicate sense of the humane values and can manifest itself directly as a fine sensibility. (pp. 322-23)

The seriousness with which he conceived the function and the importance he ascribed to poetry are more legitimately expressed in the phrase, the best-known tag from the essay, 'criticism of life.' That it is not altogether satisfactory the animadversion it has been the object of must perhaps be taken to prove: at best we must admit that the intention it expresses hasn't, to a great many readers, made itself satisfactorily clear. Nevertheless Arnold leaves us with little excuse for supposing—as some of his most eminent critics have appeared to suppose—that he is demanding doctrine or moral commentary on life or explicit criticism. Nor should it be necessary to point out that all censure passed on him for having, in calling poetry 'criticism of life,' produced a bad definition is beside the mark. For it should be obvious to anyone who reads the phrase in its context that Arnold intends, not to define poetry, but, while insisting (a main concern of the essay) that there are different degrees of importance in poetry, to remind us of the nature of the criteria by which comparative judgments are made. (pp. 323-24)

[We] can certainly not say that 'Art for Art's sake' is the offspring of Arnold's 'criticism of life.' In fact, Arnold's phrase is sufficiently explained—and, I think, vindicated—as expressing an intention directly counter to the tendency that finds its consummation in 'Art for Art's sake.' Aestheticism was not a sudden development: the nature of the trend from Keats through Tennyson and Dante Gabriel Rossetti was, even in Arnold's mid-career, not unapparent to the critic who passed the judgment on the great Romantics. The insistence that poetry must be judged as 'criticism of life' is the same critic's reaction to the later Romantic tradition; it puts the stress where it seemed to him that it most needed to be put.

In so far as Arnold ever attempts to explain the phrase it is in such terms as those in which, in the essay on Wordsworth, he explains why it is that Wordsworth must be held to be a greater poet than the 'perfect' Gautier. But with no more explanation than is given in *The Study of Poetry* the intention seems to me plain enough for Arnold's purposes. To define the criteria he was concerned with, those by which we make the more serious kind of comparative judgment, was not necessary, and I cannot see that anything would have been gained by his attempting to define them. His business was to evoke them effectively (can we really hope for anything better?) and that, I think, he must be allowed to have done. (pp. 324-25)

There is still to be met the pretty general suspicion to which Mr. Eliot gives voice when he says [in *The Use of Poetry*] that Arnold 'was apt to think of the greatness of poetry rather than of its genuineness.' It is a suspicion that is the harder to lay because, with a slight shift of accent, it turns into an unexceptionable observation:

> The best of Arnold's criticism is an illustration of his ethical views, and contributes to his discrimination of the values and relations of the components of the good life.

This very fairly accords due praise while suggesting limitations. We have, nevertheless, to insist that, but for Arnold's gifts as a literary critic, that criticism would not have had its excellence. (pp. 325-26)

[Some] pages of *The Study of Poetry* are explicitly devoted to considering 'genuineness'—the problem of how the critic makes those prior kinds of judgment, those initial recognitions of life and quality, which must precede, inform and control all profitable discussion of poetry and any evaluation of it as 'criticism of life.' Towards the close of the essay we read:

> To make a happy fireside clime
> 　　To weans and wife,
> That's the true pathos and sublime
> 　　Of human life.

> There is criticism of life for you, the admirers of Burns will say to us; there is the application of ideas of life! There is undoubtedly.

And Arnold goes on to insist (in terms that would invite the charge of circularity if we were being offered a definition, as we are not) that the evaluation of poetry as 'criticism of life' is inseparable from its evaluation as poetry; that the moral judgment that concerns us as critics must be at the same time a delicately relevant response of sensibility; that, in short, we cannot separate the consideration of 'greatness' from the consideration of 'genuineness.' The test for 'genuineness' Arnold indicates in this way:

> Those laws [of poetic truth and poetic beauty] fix as an essential condition, in the poet's treatment of such matters as are here in question, high seriousness;—the high seriousness which comes from absolute sincerity. The accent of high seriousness, born of absolute sincerity, is what gives to such verse as

> "In la sua volontade è nostra pace . . . "

> to such criticism of life as Dante's, its power.

Is this accent felt in the passages which I have been quoting from Burns? Surely not; surely, if our sense is quick, we must perceive that we have not in those passages a voice from the very inmost soul of the genuine Burns; he is not speaking to us from these depths, he is more or less preaching.

This passage is old-fashioned in its idiom, and perhaps 'high seriousness' should be dismissed as a mere nuisance. But 'absolute sincerity,' a quality belonging to the 'inmost soul' and manifested in an 'accent,' an 'accent that we feel if our sense is quick'—this phrasing, in the context, seems to me suggestive in a wholly creditable and profitable way. And actually it has a force behind it that doesn't appear in the quotation: it is strengthened decisively by what has come earlier in the essay.

The place in question is that in which Arnold brings out his critical tip, the 'touchstone.' Whatever that tip may be worth, its intention should be plain. It is a tip for mobilizing our sensibility; for focussing our relevant experience in a sensitive point; for reminding us vividly of what the best is like. (pp. 326-28)

And the succeeding couple of pages might seem to be mainly a matter of irritating repetition that implicitly admits an inability to get any further. Nevertheless, there is development, and the varied reiteration of associated terms, which is certainly what we have, has a critical purpose. . . .

His procedure is a way of intimating that he doesn't suppose himself to have said anything very precise. But he seems to me, all the same, to have done the appropriate directing of attention upon poetry. . . . (p. 329)

Inquiry, then, into the main criticisms that have been brought against *The Study of Poetry* yields reports decidedly in Arnold's favour. If he speaks in that essay with economy and authority, it is because his critical position is firmly based, because he knows what he is setting out to do, and because he is master of the appropriate method. The lack of the 'gift for consistency or for definition' turns out to be compensated, at his best, by certain positive virtues: tact and delicacy, a habit of keeping in sensitive touch with the concrete, and an accompanying gift for implicit definition—virtues that prove adequate to the sure and easy management of a sustained argument and are, as we see them in Arnold, essentially those of a literary critic.

However, it must be confessed that none of the other essays in that volume can be called a classic in English criticism. The *Milton* is a mere ceremonial address. (But it may be noted at this point that the reader who supposes Arnold to have been an orthodox idolator of Milton will be surprised if he turns up in *Mixed Essays* the essay called *A French Critic on Milton*). The *Gray* dates most of all the essays in the series—dates in the most damaging sense; though it may be said to have gained in that way a classical status as a document in the history of taste. Neither the *Keats* nor the *Shelley* makes any show of being a model critique of poetry; but nevertheless the rarely gifted literary critic is apparent in them. (p. 330)

[What] has to be stressed is his relative valuation of the great Romantics: Wordsworth he put first, then Byron (and for the right reasons), then Keats, and last Shelley. It is, in its independence and its soundness, a more remarkable critical achievement than we easily recognize to-day. (The passage on the Romantics in the *Heine* essay should not be overlooked).

If any other particular work of his is to be mentioned, it must be the long essay *On Translating Homer*. It was . . . an extraordinary original undertaking at the time, and it was carried out with such spirit and intelligence that it is still profitable reading.

The actual achievement in producible criticism may not seem a very impressive one. But we had better inquire where a more impressive is to be found. As soon as we start to apply any serious standard of what good criticism should be, we are led towards the conclusion that there is very little. If Arnold is not one of the great critics, who are they? . . . [We] read Arnold's critical writing because for anyone who is interested in literature it is compellingly alive. I can think of no other English critic who asks to be considered here, so I will say finally that, whatever his limitations, Arnold seems to me decidedly more of a critic than the Sainte-Beuve to whom he so deferred. (pp. 331-32)

> *F. R. Leavis, "Arnold As Critic," in* Scrutiny *(reprinted by permission of Cambridge University Press), Vol. VII, No. 3, December, 1938, pp. 319-32.*

ALLEN TATE   (essay date 1941)

Matthew Arnold's war on the Philistines was fought, as everybody knows; but nobody thinks that it was won. Arnold conducted it in what he considered to be the scientific spirit. The Philistines had a passion for "acting and instituting," but they did not know "what we ought to act and to institute." This sort of knowledge must be founded upon "the scientific passion for knowing." But it must not stop there. Culture, which is the study of perfection and the constant effort to achieve it, is superior to the scientific spirit because it includes and passes beyond it. Arnold was, in sort, looking for a principle of unity, but it must be a unity of experience. There was before him the accumulating body of the inert, descriptive facts of science, and something had to be done about it.

Yet if it is true, as T. S. Eliot said many years ago, that were Arnold to come back he would have his work to do over again, he could at any rate have to do it very differently. His program, culture added to science and perhaps correcting it, has been our program for nearly a century, and it has not worked. For the facts of science are not inert facts waiting for the poet, as emblematic guardian of culture, to bring to life in the nicely co-operative enterprise of scientist and poet which the nineteenth century puts its faith in. In this view the poet is merely the scientist who achieves completeness. "It is a result of no little culture," Arnold says, "to attain to a clear perception that science and religion are two wholly different things." Religion had yielded to the "fact" of science, but poetry on a positive scientific base could take over the work of religion, and its future was "immense." The "fact" had undermined religion, but it could support poetry.

Although Arnold betrayed not a little uneasiness about this easy solution, it was his way of putting literature upon an equal footing with science. If Arnold failed, can we hope to succeed? . . . While Arnold's poet was extending the hand of fellowship to the scientist, the scientist did not return the greeting; for never for an instant did he see himself as the inert and useful partner in an enterprise of which he would not be permitted to define the entire scope. He was not, alas, confined to the inertia of fact; his procedure was dynamic all along; and it was animated by the confident spirit of positivism which has since captured the modern world.

Had he been what Arnold thought he was, how conveniently the partnership would have worked! For what was Arnold's scientist doing? He was giving us exact observation and description of the external world. The poet could give us that, and he could add to it exact observation and description of man's inner life, a realm that the positivist would never be so bold as to invade. But the poet's advantage was actually twofold. Not only did he have this inner field of experience denied to the scientist, he had a resource which was his peculiar and hereditary right—figurative language and the power of rhetoric.

If the inert fact alone could not move us, poetic diction could make it moving by heightening it; for poetry is "thought and art in one." This is an injustice to Arnold; he was a great critic of ideas, of currents of ideas, of the situation of the writer in his time; and from this point of view his theory of poetry is of secondary importance. But since I am now interested in the failure, ours as well as his, to understand the relation of poetry and science, it has been necessary to put his poetic theory in terms that will bring out its defects. On one side it is an eighteenth-century view of poetic language as the rhetorical vehicle of ideas; and it is connected with Arnold's famous definition of religion as "morality touched with emotion." Poetry is descriptive science or experience at that level, touched with emotion.

If Arnold had taste, he had very simple analytical powers, and we are never quite convinced by his fine quotations from the poets. Why is this so? Because he admires good things for bad reasons; or because at any rate his reasons invariably beg the question. . . . He cites his "touchstones" for the purpose of moving us, and the nice discrimination of feeling which awareness of the touchstones induces will permit us to judge other passages of verse in terms of feeling. The "high seriousness" is partly the elevated tone, a tone which is a quality of the poet's feeling about his subject: it is the poet's business to communicate it to the reader.

This attitude, this tone, centers in emotion. But its relation to what it is about, whether it is external to the subject or inherent in it, Arnold refuses to make clear. The high seriousness may be said to reflect the subject, which must have Aristotelian magnitude and completeness. Arnold had a shrewd sense of the disproportions of tone and subject which he developed into a principle in the Preface to the 1853 edition of his poems [see excerpt above]. He was suppressing the very fine **"Empedocles on Aetna"** because, he said, it has no action; it is all passive suffering; and passive suffering is not a proper subject for poetry. Action, then, is the subject of the greatest poetry. This conviction is so strong—who will question its rightness, *as far as it goes?*—that he actually puts into quotation marks words which are not quoted from anybody at all but which represent for him the consensus of the ancients on the importance of action: "'All depends upon the subject; choose a fitting action, penetrate yourself with the feeling of its situations; this done, everything else will follow.'" But will everything else follow? Does a great style follow? To a gift for action Shakespeare "added a special one of his own; a gift, namely, of happy, abundant, and ingenious expression. . . ." I think we should attend closely here to the words "added" and "ingenious," for they reveal Arnold's view of the function of language. And suppose you have lyric poetry which may be, like Arnold's own fine lyrics, more meditative than dramatic, and more concerned with the futility of action than with action itself? It has never, I believe, been pointed out that the Preface of 1853 cuts all the props from under lyric poetry. The lyric at its best is "dramatic," but there is no evidence that Arnold thought it so; for the lyric, though it may be a moment of action, lacks magnitude and completeness; it may be the beginning, or the middle or the end, but never all three. What, then, is the subject of the lyric? Is it all feeling, nothing but feeling? It is feeling about "ideas," not actions; and the feeling communicates "power and joy."

This gross summary of Arnold's poetics omits all the sensitive discriminations that he felt in reading the poets; it omits all but the framework of his thought. Yet the framework alone must concern us on this occasion. Arnold is still the great critical influence in the universities, and it is perhaps not an exaggeration of his influence to say that debased Arnold is the main stream of popular appreciation of poetry. It would be fairer to say that Arnold the critic was superior to his critical theory; yet at the distance of three generations we may look back upon his lack of a critical dialectic—he even had a certain contempt for it in other critics—as a calamity for that culture which it was his great desire to strengthen and pass on.

His critical theory was elementary, and if you compare him with Coleridge a generation earlier, he represents a loss. His position is nearer to the neo-classicism of Lessing, whom he praises in **Culture and Anarchy** for humanizing knowledge, a leveling-off of distinctions of which Lessing as a matter of fact was not guilty. He shares with Lessing the belief—but not its dialectical basis—that the language of poetry is of secondary importance to the subject, that it is less difficult than the medium of painting, and that, given the action, all else follows. (pp. 16-20)

Arnold's view contains a fundamental truth. But it is not the whole truth; asserted in his terms, it may not be a truth at all. The important question goes further. It is: What is the relation of language to the "subject," to the dramatic and narrative subject as action, or to the lyrical subject as "idea"? The question may be pushed even further: Is it possible finally to distinguish the language from the subject? Are not subject and language one?

For Arnold the subject is what we commonly call the prose subject; that is to say, as much of the poetic subject as we can put into ordinary prose. The poet takes it up at the level at which the scientist—or Arnold's simulacrum of him—takes it: the level of observation and description. The poet now puts it into langauge that will bring the inert facts to life and move us. The language is strictly what Mr. Richards calls the "vehicle"—it does not embody the subject; it conveys it and remains external to it.

For what are action and subject? The positivists have their own notion of these terms; and their language of physical determinism suits that notion better than the poet's. The poet's language is useless. (p. 20)

Allen Tate, "Literature As Knowledge," in his Reason in Madness: Critical Essays *(© 1941 by Allen Tate; reprinted by permission of the Literary Estate of Allen Tate), G. P. Putnam's Sons, 1941 (and reprinted in his* Limits of Poetry: Selected Essays, 1928-1948, *Swallow Press, 1949, pp. 16-48).*

GEOFFREY TILLOTSON   (lecture date 1942)

[Matthew] Arnold was solemn as a steel bar by nature, and by nature also he was flippant, gay, loud. He had it in him to be a delicious satirist. He had all the necessary sensitiveness (de-

spite everything else, he was one of the first of the aesthetes), and he had the wish to inflict pain. And this potential satirist was actualised in flashes and stretches of his prose. We are all familiar with the satire in his social criticism, but satire exists in the more purely literary criticism too. (p. 54)

Arnold's wicked gifts, suppressed in verse, jetted in prose. The gift of the satirist, however, is no solid help to the critic because the satirist sees things too quickly, too summarily, with little of the loafing sympathy that ends in understanding.

And there were other subtle deflections from disinterestedness. Arnold . . . was an egotist. There is always a strong presence in his essays. His way of writing compels attention, but that attention is directed, not on his object, but on himself and his object together. In the essay on Amiel he stands like an unyielding rock washed around by the waves of Amiel. His essays are monologues. We cannot imagine him employing, as Dryden did, the dialogue form. Arnold's egotism accounts for the high-pitched conversational tone, the ripple of inspired extemporisation, the French grace, the lizard slickness. It accounts for the posturings. We sometimes find him hovering in pretended apprehension when his theme nears a knot that he is perfectly well prepared for. (pp. 55-6)

There is . . . another deflection. For Arnold, unlike some at least of his contemporaries, had almost no sense of the historical. He thought he had. But what he possessed was a much flimsier thing—a sense of 'the spirit of the age'. Arnold preferred reading books that philosophised about the past rather than books that doggedly recorded or re-created it. If one has an active mind, a creative mind, nothing is easier than to let it draw coloured fume out of a few 'significant' facts and to treasure that distorting mirage as history. And accordingly there are times when one feels that Arnold knew as much about the English past as a foreigner does. . . . Arnold lacked an adequate sense of the places originally occupied by old things and by things in foreign lands, and when he criticised them, he was a critic not so much of them themselves as of his personal reactions to them. . . . He would group together lines from Homer, Chaucer, Milton, because they had in common a capacity to make a similar impression on Matthew Arnold in the nineteenth century. It follows that Arnold was a good critic, a good literary critic, only within limits—i.e., when the quality of the things criticised had not suffered the almost inevitable fate of deteriorating along with the quite inevitable fate of ageing, or when, criticising contemporary things, he was an authentic historical critic without knowing it.

Arnold's sense of the nineteenth century was historically sound because he had lived in it and was still engaged in doing so. Outside his memory and his sense of the present, history scarcely existed. But within those shining limits, it existed comprehensively, substantially and vividly. (pp. 57-8)

Geoffrey Tillotson, "Matthew Arnold: The Critic and the Advocate" (reprinted by permission of the Literary Estate of Geoffrey Tillotson; originally a lecture delivered on March 30, 1942), in Essays by Divers Hands, *n.s. Vol. XX, 1943 (and reprinted in his* Criticism and the Nineteenth Century, *The Athlone Press, 1951, pp. 42-60).*

GEOFFREY TILLOTSON   (essay date 1951)

It is perhaps because so much of Arnold's day went in school inspecting, and so much of his leisure in keeping abreast of his own age, that he achieved only a vague notion of the past.

Vagueness is a disabling disease of the historian because the one thing certain about the past (we infer this from our own experience of the present) is that it was lived through particular by particular. It is the business of the historian to discover these particulars for himself and for us. He will not always, of course, present them as particulars; he will sometimes generalise. But generalisations are concrete things when derived from an adequate number of particulars. They are the pattern made by the particulars; they are the expression (to adapt a phrase of Wordsworth's) on the countenance of knowledge. Arnold's generalisations are not pattern, expression: they are the speculations of a mind interested in ideas independently of the material that alone should generate and govern them. (pp. 65-6)

Arnold . . . was not a victim: it was not a lack of leisure which imposed vagueness on him, but a preference for seeing vague things. The verse shows it equally with the prose, though vagueness, of course, is not necessarily so fatal to verse as to prose. . . . A gift for clarity of manner is often expended on presenting vague thoughts and a vague conception of the concrete. As a secular historian he remained vague to the end. With the result that much of his history exists in a sort of poetical sanctuary. Its impressionistic vagueness makes it inaccessible to argument. (p. 68)

> *Geoffrey Tillotson, "Matthew Arnold and Eighteenth-Century Poetry," in* Essays on the Eighteenth Century: Presented to David Nichol Smith in Honour of his Seventieth Birthday *(reprinted by permission of Oxford University Press), Oxford at the Clarendon Press, Oxford, 1945 (and reprinted in a revised form in his* Criticism and the Nineteenth Century, *The Athlone Press, 1951, pp. 61-91).*

JOHN HOLLOWAY (essay date 1953)

Arnold's polemics were less irresponsible than those of Carlyle, because his effort to persuade was much more sustained and planned; and his task was a more elusive one than Newman's, because he had no rigid doctrines to argue for, only attitudes. His work inculcates not a set of ultimate beliefs—a 'Life-Philosophy'—but simply certain habits and a certain temper of mind. (p. 203)

Others could start with the same premises and probably reach any detailed conclusions they liked. What significance they had for Arnold is determined in the whole texture of his writing. If he offers anything of wisdom or sanity or mental poise, it is to be found in the whole experience of reading him, in a sense of what intellectual urbanity is that transpires rather from his handling of problems than from his answers to them. He mediates not a view of the world, but a habit of mind. (p. 207)

To a degree quite unusual among polemical writers, Arnold's persuasive energy goes to build up, little by little, an intimate and a favourable impression of his own personality as an author, and an unfavourable impression, equally clear if less intimate and more generalized, of the personalities of his opponents. Over and over again one finds the discussion taking shape between these two poles; and this is natural, because Arnold's chief purpose is to recommend one temper of mind, and condemn another, and such things are more readily sensed through contact than understood through description. No author, of course, can give a favourable impression of his own temper of mind, except obliquely and discreetly. When Arnold writes of himself at length, it is usually in a depreciatory vein;

but he causes us to glimpse his personality through various devices, and of these, as with Newman, perhaps the most conspicuous is tone. Indeed he adopts a tone not unlike Newman's, save that it is usually less grave and calm, more whimsical and apologetic. Newman, after all, thought he had a powerful silent ally as Arnold did not. (pp. 207-08)

Arnold is also like Newman, and unlike Carlyle (and George Eliot in her discursive works), in developing our sense of his temper of mind, and of the kind of thinking he is doing, through the distinctive forms of his argument. Newman and Arnold both employ the *argumentum ad hominem*. In Newman this form is common, it is constantly employed on points of detail, and the effect of its frequency is to amplify our sense of the great integrated system of reality, as the author conceives it. Arnold uses the argument much less often, and then in respect only of some fundamental issue. . . . In *Literature and Dogma* he writes approvingly of how Newman relies on this form of argument. But in his own case its oblique contribution is less to give the impression of system and precision than of circumspection in argument and modesty on the part of the author.

Again, like Newman, Arnold enlists the negative evidence. Scientists are likely to have an incomplete understanding of human nature not through their limitations, but actually through their special talents and interests. (pp. 209-10)

Perhaps the two forms of argument most distinctive of Arnold are *distinguo* arguments which keep the reader sensitized to his unrelaxing circumspection, and concessive arguments which emphasize his modesty. "'Let us distinguish'', replied the envious foreigners' (who here are speaking for Arnold himself) 'let us distinguish. We named three powers . . . which go to spread . . . rational humane life. . . . Your middle class, we agreed, has the first. . . . But this only brings us a certain way. . . .' (pp. 211-12)

The reader must have noticed that through the forms of his arguments Arnold does something to develop our notion of his opponents, as well as of himself. The abiding consciousness of those with whom he disagrees—it is something quite distinctive in Arnold's work—finds remarkable expression in *Friendship's Garland*. This is very largely a work discrediting the opinions of others; and in the main it proceeds by methods of irony. . . . One cannot help noticing that Arnold offers almost no objections of substance to the practical measures he most clearly condemns. But three times—coloured and half-concealed, certainly, by his satirical flashes—an argument does appear. . . . [These] arguments take the form of the *reductio ad absurdum;* and above all, what they contribute to is our sense of the personality and the intellectual temper of those with whom Arnold disagrees. Caricature of the arguments is done in a style that indicates the true nature of the authors: it is Arnold's opponents, ultimately, who are being reduced to the absurd.

Arnold's preoccupation . . . is with what states of mind and what attitudes are desirable in human society, and more particularly with what is the desirable temper of mind in which to conduct an enquiry. Apart from a rationalist historical determinism, which plays a minor rôle in his thought, he had no metaphysics which might form apparent premises for the moral principles he wished to assert. But because a certain temper of mind—the characteristic urbanity and amenity of Arnold—is so pervasively recommended to the reader by the whole texture of his writing, he had a quite distinctive means for both making and justifying value-judgements in other fields. He could praise and justify praise, or condemn and justify condemnation, by suggesting that the topic or the belief under discussion would appeal, or fail to appeal, to the frame of mind which appears throughout his work as the fundamental good.

This distinctive method is to preface or envelop the main assertion in clauses which invite the reader to view it with favour or disfavour, and suggest grounds for the attitude he is to adopt. These *value frames,* as they might be called, serve several different purposes in Arnold's work, and are sometimes very elaborate. Although by their nature they do not obtrude on the casual reader's notice, yet their influence on the texture of argument is great. It should perhaps be said that when they are quoted, one feels at first that the mere trimmings of a sentence have been given and its substantial part omitted: but this impression rapidly fades. Consider an example first: 'The aspirations of culture, which is the study of perfection, are not satisfied unless [what men say when they may say what they like, is worth saying]'. Here the two elements, first praise, second the grounds for praise, are fairly clear: first, a condition such as the assertion describes would satisfy one whose concern was for *perfection,* and this is as much as to call it *good;* second, it would satisfy the *cultured, aspiring* and *studious,* and these qualities—which **Culture and Anarchy** from beginning to end has endeared to us—are here the grounds of goodness. (pp. 213-16)

It is easy to see how much these value frames do, not only to recommend assertions and offer grounds for them, but also to elucidate and recommend the temper of mind to which they seem true, and above all to show that their strength lies in their appeal to such a temper. . . . On the other hand, there are negative instances that show equally clearly how some false proposition is born of the mental temper which Arnold condemns. . . . In either case it is clear that in cultivating this sense of a right 'habit of mind' throughout his argument, Arnold equipped himself with a precise and powerful instrument for giving effect to judgements of value. (p. 217)

It transpired above that the value frame might not only put one of Arnold's keywords, like 'culture', to use, but that it could also control its meaning; and this is to say that the value frame may be inverted in function (or have, as is more likely, two simultaneous functions), and serve as a kind of defining formula. Since definitions proved to be so important a persuasive device in Carlyle, George Eliot and Newman, it is high time to trace the contribution they make in Arnold. But we find that it is surprisingly small. (pp. 219-20)

[Definitions] are to be found, doubtless, from time to time—it would be inconceivably odd if Arnold were never to define a term anywhere. But by comparison they are certainly few in number, and what is more important, they lack the characteristic quality of such arguments, because they are trite. The typical re-definition seems to transform the import of a word, giving it a more pointed, provocative, pregnant, influential meaning by seeming to draw on some insight of unusual keenness. By contrast, Arnold's definitions are often textbook definitions; they are dull; they are diaphanous. It is not merely that they cannot facilitate interesting inferences; they preclude them, and this is their job. (pp. 220-21)

The desire to have distinctive names for whatever he is discussing is a feature of much of Arnold's work. . . . How Arnold introduces the terms 'sweetness and light', or 'Barbarians, Philistines, Populace', is perhaps too well known to need further remark. The effect of some of these is clear enough—they

are what may simply be called *hangdog* names. But Arnold gives a reason for using the last three which indicates how they can contribute to the general texture of his prose. 'The same desire for clearness', he writes, '. . . prompts me also to improve my nomenclature . . . a little, with a view to making it thereby more manageable'. This is important. To be clear and manageable are not new concepts in Arnold's work. They were the distinctive qualities of his tone, because he made this represent his temper of mind. By providing convenient names for his main topics, he not only influences our attitude through the nuance of those names, but articulates his argument with nodal points that soon become familiar, and easy to trace again. The kind of argument that is his at his most typical, an argument that moves gently forward with a smooth, unruffled urbanity, owes not a little to the familiarity of these coinages, as they so constantly reappear. They do not affect the logic of his discussion, but they transform its quality. (pp. 225-26)

It is widely agreed that by irony an author can seem to the casual or uninformed reader to say one thing, but really say something quite different, clear only to the reader who is initiated or more attentive. (p. 234)

Arnold makes his irony show both what he is like, and what his opponents are like. Images can do this as well as descriptions. In **A Courteous Explanation** he finds occasion to write: '(Horace) and his friends have lost their tails, and want to get them back'. The tail here is a symbol of political liberty. But it is not long before Arnold is utilizing its ironic possibilities:

> I think our 'true political Liberty' a beautiful
> bushy object . . . it struck me there was a danger of our trading too extensively upon our
> tails, and, in fact, running to tail altogether. . . . Our highest class, besides having
> of course true political liberty,—that regulation
> tail that every Briton of us is blessed with,—
> is altogether so beautiful and splendid (and above
> all, as Mr. Carlyle says, polite) that for my part
> I hardly presume to enquire what it has or has
> not in the way of heads.

Clearly, this beautiful bushy tail is—may one say it?—a two-edged weapon. (p. 236)

Arnold uses irony to widen his range of assertion, while still remaining within the range of tone that his outlook demands. It is one further method whereby he conveys a certain temper of mind by example rather than description, and it emphasizes once more that this temper is essentially what his work strives to express. This explains, too, why he is so prominent himself in his writings, why his personality is progressively revealed in a favourable light that the hostile reader, revolting from Arnold's whole attempt to persuade, labels complacency. Nothing will rigorously prove this label mistaken; but we tend less, perhaps, to call Arnold's method complacent, once we have equipped ourselves with a proper knowledge of its detail, and its function. (p. 243)

> *John Holloway, "Matthew Arnold," in his* The Victorian Sage: Studies in Argument *(copyright 1953 Macmillan & Co., Ltd.; reprinted by permission of the author), Macmillan, 1953 (and reprinted by Archon Books, 1962), pp. 202-43.*

JOHN SHEPARD EELLS, JR. (essay date 1955)

How did Arnold's "personal affinities, likings, and circumstances" sway his judgment? That is a question of great importance, and the [following seeks] to discover the real, the underlying reason for Arnold's choice of the passages themselves; and, having done so, to assess their value as touchstones. (pp. 15-16)

The touchstone passages are eleven in number; three each from Homer, Dante, and Milton; two from Shakespeare. They are "lines and expressions of the great masters," "short passages, even single lines," "the poet's comment," "the address of Zeus," "the words of Achilles," "Ugolino's tremendous words," "the lovely words of Beatrice," "the simple, but perfect, single line," "Henry the Fourth's expostulation," "Hamlet's dying request," "that Miltonic passage," "the exquisite close."

We now come to the generalization which purports to unite these fragments. Though differing widely from one another they have, we are told, a common poetic cement.

1. They have in common the possession of the very highest poetical quality; a quality revealed in matter, substance, manner, and style.
2. In substance and matter they are characterized by an eminent degree of truth and seriousness.
3. The special character of the style and manner is given by diction and movement.
4. Two and three are inseparable.

Such is Arnold's generalization on the touchstone passages taken together. (p. 17)

[The touchstone passages] may be regarded as essences, not, . . . of the poetry from which they are taken, but of certain states of mind. Given, for instance, the mood which contemplates the abiding pathos of young death. Has it in all literature found utterance more concise, more beautifully economical, more quintessential than in Helen's comment on her brothers? Given, again, the state of mind joyously aware of that peace which flows from an identification with God's will through love. Its perfect expression Arnold has garnered in that line which tells the truth of all religion: "e la sua volontate è nostra pace." So one might run through all the passages; and, with the possible exception of King Henry's words, the same might be said of each. If further evidence of this miracle of compression be needed, one has only to consider, for a moment, passages expressive of the same moods to which the touchstone lines allusively direct the mind. It instantly becomes apparent that such passages, though in themselves beautiful and memorable, are, in comparison with the touchstone lines, discursive and rambling. They lack density, they lack fusion. For whatever else may be said of the touchstones, this much is sure; they are, in almost every instance, supreme examples of condensation and economy. They are, as expressions of certain moods, the best words in the best order.

But the power of these lines becomes all the more apparent as soon as, forsaking the method of isolation, one reads and ponders them in their contexts. (p. 205)

[The] touchstones must, to a great extent, absorb their richness from their contests. But this is not to say . . . that they are of the essence of the poetry—that they cannot be detached without violation of artistic unity. I do not intend to imply that Arnold was aware of these sources of contextual richness, which sluice into the touchstones the gold of poetry. I intend merely to suggest what a critic greater and more objective than Arnold, one more attentive to contextual relations, and not subject to

Arnold's idiosyncrasies, might have said about the [touchstone] passages. . . . (p. 207)

What is the relation between Arnold's characteristic states of mind and those reflected by the touchstone passages? Were the passages selected by an unconscious exercise of what personal estimate against which Arnold himself has warned us? (p. 209)

Of the eleven moods with which we have to deal, ten are entirely characteristic of Arnold. The lines describing the fallen Satan are the only ones which cannot be identified with his settled habits of mind. And these habits seem to fall into a broad pattern. Thus, eight of the passages reflect varying degrees of melancholy: Helen's comment on her brothers; the lines on the grief of the horses; the words of Achilles, Ugolino, King Henry and Hamlet; the description of the ruined Satan; the pain of Ceres' search. Of the remaining three, two constitute, for Arnold, the cornerstones of Christianity; one expresses tonic fortitude under suffering. (p. 213)

In the light of all that has thus far been said, the second question may now be asked: Were the touchstone passages selected by an unconscious exercise of that personal estimate against which Arnold himself has warned us? And again the answer can only be *yes*. For although most of the passages, especially when read in their contexts, are examples of poetry intrinsically great, nevertheless, in choosing at least ten out of the eleven he responded to inner, deep-seated compulsions, emotionally and personally affinitive. (p. 214)

That he selected these passages partly to suit personal predilection does not, however, necessarily imply that the touchstones are not representative of poetry at its best. In the first place, some personal evaluation is nearly always present in the judgment of poetry. Second, I have already maintained that these lines are quintessential poetic expressions of certain states of mind, and that their imaginative excellence is all the more apparent when they are taken contextually. If, then, the states of mind presented in them are both universal and significant, there is firm ground for arguing that these touchstones—*so far as they go*—are indeed representative of poetry at its best, and as such are valid as touchstones, whatever one may think of the validity of the touchstone method itself. (p. 215)

[Although] Arnold, in selecting the touchstones, was dominated by states of mind habitual to him, these states of mind (once they have been ascertained) are, with a possible exception or two, universal and of significant value in the history of the race.

It develops, therefore, that now the universal significance of nearly all the states of mind may be conjoined with a quintessential poetic expressiveness to justify nearly all the passages—*so far as they go*—as such touchstones as Arnold intended.

But if the states of mind of these passages are severally constricted to suit Arnold's habitual moods and mental attitudes . . . do they then still preserve a universal significance? (pp. 217-18)

[We] must recur to the contention that Arnold had a defective intake. Neither by means of scholarly acumen nor of many-sided Coleridgean sensitiveness was he able successfully to channel into his own mind the complete thought of a great poet. It was not his habit to take a passage of poetry, to unload from it all the richness and significance with which it was freighted, to analyze, rearrange, and store the material in his mind; to be, in short, a methodical critic who subjects his first responses to the control of the context. He tended, on the other hand, to treat such a passage with surprising nonchalance, as though it were a ship without a cargo; or one whose load could be shifted to make room for the emotional and affinitive freightage which he wished to bestow upon it. (p. 218)

As we review, then, [the] discrepancies between the touchstone moods as Arnold saw them, and the states of mind revealed by their larger contexts; as we see in constant operation his habit of diluting the richess of poetry to suit his own taste; as we note his lack of scholarly insight, his tendency to load a passage with the freightage of his own mind, we realize that the emotional and affinitive urge which led him to select lines in which he found supreme utterances of states of mind characteristic of himself was supplemented and strengthened by an intellectual disregard for the actual intent and full meaning of the poet. His defective intake, in other words, not only made his use of the personal estimate all the more inevitable, but, what is more important, dimmed, deflected, and gave a peculiar Arnoldean twist to the significance and universality of the states of mind really presented in the touchstones. This is a disappointing, disenchanting conclusion: all the more so because Arnold himself constantly stressed what he called a ''real'' estimate as against a personal one. If what he meant by a ''real'' estimate involved contextual control of responses, he fell short of attaining it. (p. 221)

[The touchstone] passages, if they are . . . read in careful relation to contexts, appear to be quintessential, highly imaginative, poetic expressions of . . . universally significant states. Therefore—so far as the passages go—they may be said to be valid touchstones.

But in his own reading of them, Arnold did not sufficiently control his responses by contextual interpretation. He endowed them with those personal and habitual states of mind which governed their choice. He gave, in fact, a peculiar Arnoldean twist to their universal significance. A realization of this fact comes only after detailed and comprehensive study, for Arnold himself insufficiently explained *what* he read into his touchstones. Moreover, because he is not at pains to explain just what he read into the passages, an ordinary reader is puzzled by these brief lines and fragments lifted so casually from their contexts.

If he supposes that Arnold *did* read them in the light of their contexts, he will find upon careful examination, as we have done, that Arnold missed much. Then the reader's puzzlement issues in confusion. But Arnold himself confused his own readings of the touchstone passages with contextual readings, and so was unaware that, forsaking the ''real'' estimate he demanded, he had himself exercised the personal estimate against which he protests. Therefore, despite the fact that in the lines high and universal values are to be found, especially if they are read contextually, confusion and contradiction reign both in Arnold's procedure and in the reader's understanding.

Perhaps the matter may be stated thus: Arnold did not sufficiently control his responses and subsequent values by studious knowledge of contexts. . . . (pp. 247-48)

[Futhermore], the general control under which Arnold *did* bring his personal preferences—(and this we have ascertained by a study of his notebooks, prose, and poetry)—was an attitude of profound earnestness toward the grimness and darkness of the human adventure. The result is a narrow choice of touchstones, so that they are not widely enough representative. . . .

Arnold's touchstones and his application of them make for confusion in actual procedure and chaos in method; and even

if this were not the case they lack inclusiveness; they do not cover great poetry in general.

Arnold's principal fault as a critic of poetry is not that he is swayed by the personal estimate, for all critics, in varying degrees, are intuitive and are so swayed. His principal fault is that the controls which govern his intuitions are insufficiently definitive, insufficiently rational, socially incommunicable. They are, moreover, static and retrospective, while intuition should be dynamic and prospective. They are tied up with his own past, and with the literature of the past. They are petrifactive rather than vivifying. And although our intuitions are properly based on personal experience and on a sound knowledge of such works of the past as are commonly held to be classics, we must not, by subjecting them to static controls, sacrifice a sense of novelty and freshness, an eager anticipation of growth, a vision of other stately mansions. (p. 248)

John Shepard Eells, Jr., in his The Touchstones of Matthew Arnold *(copyright 1955 by Twayne Publishers; reprinted with the permission of Twayne Publishers, a division of G. K. Hall & Co., Boston), Bookman Associates, 1955 (and reprinted by College and University Press, 1963), 280 p.*

MURRAY KRIEGER   (essay date 1956)

Matthew Arnold's **''Dover Beach''** bears and rewards contemplation from the vantage point of the modern—and yet ancient—concept of time which has stirred our consciousness through writers like Mann, Proust, Virginia Woolf, T. S. Eliot— a concept of time as existential rather than as chronologically historical, as the flow of Bergson's dynamics, as the eternal present. This awareness which we associate with our sophisticated contemporary can be seen somehow to emerge from Arnold's highly Victorian **''Dover Beach.''** . . . [The] very weaknesses that characterize Arnold's poetic imagination generally—his chronic melancholy as a would-be faithful man in a faithless world and his easy didacticism as a ''poetic'' observer extorting symbolic instruction out of his natural surroundings—serve here to create this tragic and extremely modern vision. It is a vision which Arnold achieves neither as a nineteenth century optimist nor as a vague and confused rebel of his period who turns to an equally nineteenth century pessimism and simple melancholy; it is a vision which he achieves by transcending his period completely and foreseeing the intellectual crisis which is so peculiarly of our own century.

A cursory reading of the poem discloses that all the stanzas but the second are built on a similar two-part structure and that each recalls the ones which have gone before. The first section in each of these stanzas deals with that which is promising, hopeful; the second undercuts the cheer allowed by the first section and replaces the illusory optimism with a reality which is indeed barren, hopeless. In these subdivisions of stanzas there is also a sharp contrast in tone between the pleasant connotations of the first section of these stanzas and the less happy ones of the second. In each of them, too, there is a contrast between the appeal to the sense of sight in the first section and the appeal to the sense of hearing in the second.

And yet, these three stanzas are not, of course, mere repetitions of each other. Each marks a subsequent development of the image—the conflict between the sea and the land. The sea with each succeeding stanza takes on a further meaning. . . . [This], like most of Arnold's poems, deals with a natural scene and the moral application of the meaning perceived within it: the vehicle of the metaphor and then the tenor carefully stated for us. In this poem, however, the development from the natural scene to the human levels into which it opens is much more successfully handled than elsewhere in his work. Each level grows into the succeeding one without losing the basic natural ingredients which initiated the image. (pp. 73-4)

As nature has . . . naturally merged with man [in the first part of the poem], so, through the use of the middle part of the poem, has history merged with the present, has the recurrence, of which the sea, the tides, the meeting of land and sea have always stood as symbols, merged with the ever-historical present. This is why the second stanza of the poem is excluded from the parallel development of the others. It is the stanza which makes the poem possible, which brings us to "the ebb and flow of *human* misery," and brings us to the past even as we remain in the present. The image and its archetypal quality are indispensable to the poem. For the tidal ebb and flow, retreat and advance, and the endless nature of these, are precisely what is needed to give Arnold the sense of the eternal recurrence which characterizes the full meaning of the poem. (p. 74)

The "eternal note of sadness," . . . caused by the endless battle without victory and without truce between sea and land; [the] note representing the give-and-take of the tide which symbolically echoes the basic rhythmic pattern of human physio-psychology—this eternal note of sadness, heard also by Sophocles, connects the past at once with the presentness of the past, and connects also this rhythmic pattern with the humanity who has taught it to serve them and yet ironically, as the Greeks among others have shown us, have instead served it. (p. 76)

The handling of the metrics and rhyme scheme reflect the other elements we have observed in the poem. The inexorable quality of the unending struggle as it is felt in such passages as:

> . . . the grating roar
> Of pebbles which the waves draw back, and fling,
> At their return, up the high strand,
> Begin, and cease, and then again begin . . .

is obvious enough. But perhaps more significant is the development of the patterns of line-length and rhyme which begin as relatively undefined and conclude as firm and under full control. Through the first three stanzas the intermixture of pentameter lines with shorter ones is unpredictable, and, similarly, there is no determinate rhyme scheme. While the poem clearly is written in rhyme, the echoes of the final syllables of the lines surprise us since there is no pattern which enables us to foresee when the sounds will recur. And yet they continually do recur in this seemingly undetermined way. (p. 78)

[Until] the last stanza is reached, the patternless rhymes suggest a continual recurrence, but one on which human meaning and form have not yet been bestowed. The echoes multiply, but they have not yet been cast into a significant mold. In the final stanza a clear rhyme scheme at last emerges (*abbacddcc*), and further, for the first time the line-lengths even out. . . . The problem of the poem, while certainly not resolved (poems rarely resolve problems, or ought to), has at last emerged as fully comprehensible, in terms of the poem at least. The meaning of the recurrence has become tragically and profoundly clear.

It may—and perhaps with some justice—be claimed that, if my prosodic analysis is valid, this manipulation of line-length

and rhyme is, after all, a not very cunning trick, indeed is a highly mechanical contrivance. . . . [The] versification, like the structure, the diction, and the archetypal imagery, marks out the repetitive inclusiveness of the human condition and its purposeless gyrations. The poem's form thus comes to be a commentary on the problem being poetically explored, a mirror which allows the poem to come to terms with itself.

But if the form helps indicate the price of eternal recurrence for a world robbed of its faith—the fate of being pitilessly bound by the inescapable circle—in the regularity it finally achieves it indicates too the sole possibility for victory over the circle and freedom from it—the more than natural, the felt human awareness of its existence and its meaning. The tragic is at least an attainment, an attainment through the painful process of utter realization, realization of self, of nature, and of history. And the contemporaneity of the western tradition in the poem is Arnold's way of proving that he has realized *it* and himself as its child. (pp. 78-9)

Murray Krieger, "'Dover Beach' and the Tragic Sense of Eternal Recurrence," in The University of Kansas City Review *(copyright University of Kansas City, 1956), Vol. XXIII, Autumn, 1956, pp. 73-9.*

A. E. DYSON (essay date 1957)

The Scholar Gipsy confronts the joyful illusions of an earlier age with the melancholy realism of the nineteenth century, and . . . in this confrontation, with its complex emotional tensions, the really moving quality of the poem is to be found. Arnold was as aware of the difficulties of 'belief' as any Victorian, and as determined as George Eliot to live and think 'without opium'. (p. 258)

In *The Scholar Gipsy* Arnold's attitude to the gipsy is closely analogous to that of an adult towards a child. He appreciates and even envies its innocence, but realizes that no return to such a state is possible for himself. The child loses its 'innocence' not by some act of sin, nor by a defect of intellect, but merely by gaining experience and developing into an adult. The realities of adult life turn out to be less agreeable, in many respects, than childish fantasies, but there can be no question of thinking them less true.

The gipsy, like a child, is the embodiment of a good lost, not of a good temporarily or culpably mislaid. When Arnold contrasts the gipsy's serenity with the disquiets and perplexities of his own age, he is not satirizing the nineteenth century, or renouncing it, or criticizing it, or suggesting a remedy. He is, rather, exploring its spiritual and emotional losses, and the stoic readjustment which these will entail for it. (pp. 259-60)

The scholar gipsy embodies . . . the optimistic but chimerical hopes of an earlier age. He waits for 'the spark from Heaven to fall' . . . , but he waits in vain: the spark does not fall, as the nineteenth century has discovered for itself. . . . This realization is in the rhythms and tone of the poem, which is reflective and melancholy in the elegiac mode, not filled with dynamic hope. The gipsy is committed to a discredited art, and so exiled from Oxford. In [stanza] 8, as he looks down on the lighted city at night, he looks not as a presiding deity but as a long superseded ghost from the past. His very nature forbids him to enter, since one touch of Victorian realism would reveal him for the wraith he is. . . . The situation is not unlike that of the young Jude gazing eagerly towards the lights of that same city—not to Oxford itself, however, but to the ideal city which his childish dreams have superimposed. The scholar gipsy turns away from the real Oxford, and seeks his 'straw' in 'Some sequester'd grange'. His place is with the primitive, the uncultured, the unintellectual. Only so can he survive at all, so late in history.

In *Literature and Dogma* and *God and the Bible* Arnold insists that he is writing not for those who are still happy with their Christian illusions (the Victorian version of 'simple faith'), but only for those highly serious few who still value the illusions whilst being unable honestly to accept them. The scholar gipsy would not have been one of the readers Arnold had in mind: he would have been one of the happier (though perhaps less honest) band who enjoyed the faith of earlier ages simply because they had not been intellectually awakened to reality in Oxford. The gipsy is essentially outside Oxford; and his exclusion, though it tells against the happiness of Oxford, tells even more against the acceptability of the gipsy. (p. 261)

The Victorian predicament, in so far as Arnold represents it, was a tragic one—to desire with the heart what was rejected by the head, to need for the spirit what was excluded by the mind. . . . [This] is the tradition in which *The Scholar Gipsy* stands. (p. 262)

When Tennyson's head had assimilated honest doubts to the edge of scepticism, his 'heart stood up and answered "I have felt"'. When Strauss had undermined the historicity of the Bible, he tried to reinstate it as a myth. Matthew Arnold, also, tried to find an emotional cure for the loss of faith. In his case, it took the form of an attempt to substitute culture and poetry for religion, and to find a few axioms that could be made real on the moral pulses. But when it came to the trail, his head gained the day, honesty won the victory over expediency. *The Scholar Gipsy* is a poem of unbelief. Arnold did not discover anything adequate to replace the hopes of the earlier world. (p. 265)

       A. E. Dyson, ''The Last Enchantments,'' in The Review of English Studies *(reprinted by permission of Oxford University Press), n.s. Vol. VIII, No. 31, 1957, pp. 257-65.**

W. STACY JOHNSON (essay date 1961)

Whether it takes the form of soliloquy, of monologue, or of dialogue, virtually all of Arnold's best poetry involves, . . . what he calls in his Preface of 1853 the ''dialogue of the mind with itself'' [see excerpt above]. This process, Arnold asserts, had commenced by the time of the historical Empedocles, and apparently it continues in the minds of modern men; for, unlike a Platonic dialogue, the conversation of inner voices does not often conclude with the wisdom of one master voice. Arnold's dialogue between disillusioned Tristram and faithful Iseult and his contrast between the songs of Empedocles and those of Callicles make these several voices seem to represent the several sides of a dialogue, as it were, within the poet's own mind, just as the opposites of land and sea do in **''The Forsaken Merman''** and **''Dover Beach.''** But, perhaps because literal dialogue can so easily be reduced to unsettled debate on points of philosophy and religion, as it is in Clough's ''Dipsychus,'' or to simple preaching, as it begins to be in the first act of **''Empedocles,''** the dialogue of the poet's mind with itself is often represented less strikingly in the speeches of his characters than in contrasts implied by the more indirect and symbolic means.

In Arnold's narrative poetry, too, the inner tensions are realized by contrasts in imagery and setting, along with the speeches that reveal the differences between Sohrab and Rustum or between Balder and his fellows. Although the weaker narratives, like **''Saint Brandan,''** amount at last to fairly single-minded moralities, the most successful of Arnold's poetic tales involve these contrasts and are essentially double visions. The voice of the narrator does not intrude upon the stories as it does sometimes in **''Tristram''**—where the pronouns *I, we,* and *you* introduce the author's and the reader's points of view and where, in the third part, a moralizing *I* comments directly on the poem—but it describes actions and settings so as to reveal differences not only between several people's lives but also between several ways of viewing their lives.

The views implied, the messages carried, in **''The Neckan''** and **''Saint Brandan''** are comparatively simple: each of these short narratives versifies a folk tale which shows that there may be divine grace given to one who is apparently lost. The first piece is another version of the tale that Arnold tells in **''The Forsaken Merman,''** but now the story is rendered almost as a ballad, and in the third person; and, although the words of the sea-creature are again plaintive, his attitude, that of his wife, and the implicit attitude of the narrator are much less painfully ambivalent than those in the better poem. . . . A quatrain added to [**''The Neckan''**] in 1869 . . . takes emphasis away from the miracle to make this point explicit:

> He said: 'The earth hath kindness,
>   The sea, the starry poles;
> Earth, sea, and sky, and God above—
>   But, ah, not human souls!'

The mood of these lines is almost directly opposed to that of **''Dover Beach,''** where the earth is seen to lack the sympathy that human love may provide. But this poem is not, like **''Dover Beach,''** qualified by any imagery in contrast to its message: it never makes us feel strongly why the earth and his mate are so attractive to the neckan, and so it realizes only one side of the contrast between the natural and the human orders. The difference, however, between **''The Neckan''** and some other less impressive poems is that the Christian God now seems to be on the side of this lonely creature who is more human than the human beings in his sadness, not that of the smug priest, the horrified knights and ladies and the weeping wife. And that difference, after all, helps to give interest to this rather tight and limited version of the pathetic story.

''Saint Brandan,'' too, Arnold's verse rendering of the Celtic legend about Judas on the iceberg, carries some interest as evidence of the poet's desire to make the most of the most humane elements in religion. It is a crisply told tale of the Saint's vision on the ''sea without a human shore,'' a vision of the archtraitor momentarily relieved from his torment each Christmas eve because of one good deed done in his lifetime. But these stanzas, which include dialogue within the narrative (and Judas' narrative within his speech), are less dramatic than parabolic, are simple and fanciful rather than complex and serious. (pp. 118-20)

It is not so easy to sum up the sense of his longer narrative **''The Church of Brou,''** a poem that lacks the richness of Arnold's greatest verse tales but one that has, nevertheless, some fine passages, especially in the last part. . . . Like **''The Neckan,''** **''The Church of Brou''** must suffer by comparison with the larger work it resembles; but the contrast is not now so distinct or even so extreme. (p. 121)

"Balder Dead," a poem obviously comparable with "Sohrab and Rustum"—Arnold compared the two and preferred "Balder," although his readers have rarely done so—brings more complication into its storytelling than "Sohrab" and departs somewhat more from its source in its ordering of events and use of narrative detail. If it is not quite so fine a poem as the more celebrated work, "Balder" nevertheless makes a better narrative, with its beginning *in medias res,* its omens and foreshadowings, journeys and quests. It adapts a Homeric manner and an ultimately Virgilian tone to another kind of classical material, the Norse, dealing with an heroic society and with the death of a hero: "Balder" begins as "Sohrab and Rustum" ends, with the death of and the mourning for a mighty father's mighty son. But "Balder" makes more use of dialogue between characters, so that it is rather more vigorous and less stately in its diction and movement. (p. 122)

In fact, "Balder" is a poem of polarities, of ironies and even of paradoxes. It is filled with a visionary knowledge of the future—the knowledge that Frea possesses and Odin, and finally Balder too—which makes its action seem inevitably futile, and yet the gods are apparently fated to will and act against the decrees of fatality. Its central figure is the ideal hero of a Valhalla to whose heroic code he is opposed. And its imagery again and again contrasts the value of heavenly warfare with the value of heavenly rest.

To the tensions implicit within this dark story the narration gives emphasis, especially in its use of imagery. First, there is a contrast between epic characters, setting, and movement, all of which are magnified and formal, and the details that give a specific, even personal, quality to the poem. This contrast is enforced almost always by the Homeric similes, which Arnold introduces with reference neither to Homer nor to the Edda. Hoder's touch on Hermod's arm is like the touch of honeysuckle brushing across a tired traveler's face (surely English honeysuckle and an English traveler), and the road to Hell is blocked by a maiden just as a mountain pass is blocked by cattle. (pp. 122-23)

But it is not only through the epic similes, with their yoking of heroic events and pastoral or domestic terms, that the Eddic story takes on its new dimensions. Images and themes that are symbolic and recurrent in Arnold's poetry, those of light and shadow, of battle in life and repose in death, are embodied in the settings and metaphors of this poem, and they again express duality, tension, or dialogue between contrasting attitudes. The most striking contrast, perhaps, is that between the dark and the sunlit places. There is daylight in Heaven, and none in the place of obscure spirits; Odin would, on entering Hell, "set the fields of gloom ablaze with light," did not Frea insist that he could not rightly violate Hela's darkness. Both Thok's iron wood and Hela's world are dark, cold regions, and their shadows are associated with the dreary and morbid. And yet the brilliance of Odin's Asgard is a harsh brilliance, one that is not at last so clearly preferable to the peaceful gloom of Hela. (pp. 123-24)

The final paradox of the poem has to do with the nature of death. Within the hall where heroes live after their valiant deaths, a god has died, only to find rest in his underworld and to anticipate a new life. The name of the poem and its first lines introduce us to the subject of life in death—we never see Balder *alive,* literally, but he is quite as alive in another sense as any of the gods—and the titles of its parts remind us of it. Like "Tristram" and "The Church of Brou," the narrative has a threefold division, with sections called "Sending,"

"Journey to the Dead," and "Funeral." The task that Hermod is sent upon is the recovery of Balder from the realm of ghosts, the mythical quest of Orpheus, but his journey is to be vain, for the guile of Lok the enemy, who caused Balder's downfall by giving blind Hoder the mistletoe to throw at him, prevents the gods from meeting Hela's demand that all things grieve for Balder before he be returned to life. And so the god's funeral, with his ship a pyre sent blazing out to sea, is for Asgard final, if not for Balder. The most nearly invincible of the gods, after Odin himself, seems at last to be subject to death's power, and not only in the body but in his mind and will. Arnold's version of the story, filled with forebodings and ominous signs of a Götterdämmerung, suggests some promise too, through Balder's vision of a new Heaven and a new earth, but it concludes literally in darkness and withdrawal, not only with life in death but with a sense of death in life—or, rather, with a melancholy sense of how imperfect, in the world as it is, both energy without peace and peace without energy must be.

Balder's vision of peace and wholeness, then, the Arnoldian vision, is only that, a vision of the longed-for future. Even the god's acceptance of his death cannot make us forget the contrast, the opposition, at the heart of the poem between darkness and light, between the pathetic picture of life as essentially passive, resigned at best to the inevitable, and the picture of an heroic existence as a series of quests or battles which the gods delight to watch if not to enter. (pp. 125-26)

The paradox of "Balder Dead," that the pagan Hell offers peace with gloom and the heroic Heaven weariness with glory, is very closely related to an ironic quality of "Sohrab and Rustum," in which two images of human existence are even more clearly opposed one to the other. Partly because "Sohrab and Rustum" has a somewhat less complex plot and partly, perhaps, because it ends with the narrator's description of a scene rather than a character's speech, the effect of the work is more formal and "poetic"; but in its exploiting of the subject, involving a conflict of father and son, and in its extensive use of imagery both Homeric and symbolic, "Sohrab" finally achieves, if less rapidity, then an even more moving effect of pathos than "Balder Dead."

Implicit in Arnold's Persian material is the psychological significance of a son's search for his father and the battle between the two, followed by reconciliation. No doubt the poet's own feelings as the son of a famous father are reflected in his choice of this story about Sohrab's defeat by Rustum (Sohrab is in effect defeated by his filial piety, for it is his father's name that vanquishes him). . . . Just as it is possible for the action in the poem to occur because father and son do not recognize each other, so it is possible for Arnold to narrate the action, and the death of the young warrior, because he has not fully recognized Sohrab and Rustum, because the conflict does not have to be presented as a distinct and personal irreconciliation of old earnestness and young enthusiasm.

Even so, the death of Sohrab is painful, and the fair amount of skill Arnold displays in using narrative devices of irony (Rustum's "Be as a son to me," for instance) and fore-shadowing (as in the initial scene between Sohrab and the paternal Peran-Wisa, who predicts "danger or death") might not be enough to make the finest poetry of this pattern that is so painfully resolved—at least, not according to the critical doctrine that led Arnold to withdraw his "Empedocles." The most striking parts of the poem, striking because of their conjunction with the narrative, are those metaphorical and symbolic passages that once more transform violence into beauty and death into peace; one is likely to remember these pictures rather than the intermittent dialogue or the details of the main action. (pp. 127-28)

"Sohrab and Rustum" makes somewhat more extensive use of the Homeric simile than **"Balder,"** again with the effect of adding immediacy and pathos to the military events of the poem; at the same time, the similes provide relief from and dramatic contrast to the tension which gradually builds up all the way through the first half of the poem. And so the imagery, rather like that of the *Iliad,* often evokes scenes basically unlike those of camp and battle, recalling either peaceful settings from nature or domestic life. (pp. 128-29)

Perhaps the two most striking epic similes are those which compare the dying Sohrab with a flower, first with a hyacinth and then with a violet—similes that may remind us of the deaths both of Gorgythion in the *Iliad,* whose head droops in death like a poppy, and of Euryalus in the *Aeneid.* The device works well for Arnold as it has for Homer and Virgil, and the images are strangely beautiful. They are, of course, in extreme contrast with the literal scene, for they draw our attention from the plain which has become a scene of death to the cultivated garden, where flowers are destroyed merely by carelessness. Both similes occur after the tension of the conflict has been suddenly relaxed, while Sohrab is slowly dying, and they do not follow the tendency that has made the earlier images reflect the minds of actors within the poem, leaping to pictures of cranes and eagles, Caucasus mountains and Persian deserts; the feeling of the similes becomes less subjective now as it becomes less violent. (p. 130)

The sense of death as consummation is yet more beautifully embodied in the water imagery of the poem. The whole scene, the challenge, the fierce battle, and the death of Sohrab, has taken place by the river Oxus, which is alluded to again and again, even in the midst of the fighting. (p. 131)

Just as the metaphors are fine only in the context of the narrative, however, [the poem's final] passage of description gains its power from the terrible and finally pathetic events that precede it. We know that the old warrior has defeated himself in defeating his enemy, and we have seen a poignant outcome of the conflict between generations. With the change of mood from urgent vigor to quiet grief, from heroic to elegiac, the poem concludes in what might be called a brief comment of the narrator's—but a comment made by indirection—which reveals another way of viewing this action. Now a new contrast is implied, between the story of two human lives reaching their climax in the battle of ignorant forces on a darkling plain and the imaging forth of human life as essentially a natural flowing of waters toward their consummation in the ultimate and inevitable sea. (pp. 132-33)

In **"Sohrab and Rustum,"** as in **"Balder Dead,"** the contrasts are implicit in action, speech, and setting: the dialogue of the mind with itself is represented but does not become a debate. The narrator of **"Balder"** makes no specific comment on the Eddic values that his transcription of the story must reveal when the inhabitants of Hell are described as women, cowards, and old men who had the misfortune to die in bed rather than in battle; but the final mood of Balder is comment enough. . . . Arnold is like some other Victorian poets in drawing largely from mythical and legendary materials for his narrative poems, and his plotting of these materials is less masterly than Tennyson's or even Morris's; in his ability to translate legendary

scenes into not only contemporary terms but timeless human situations, however, he far surpasses Morris and easily rivals Tennyson. **"Balder Dead"** is infused with a moving quality that the more truly Eddic **"Sigurd the Volsung"** rarely achieves, and **"Tristram and Iseult"** is a more beautiful poem than any of the *Idylls.* One might go so far, indeed, as to compare the death of Balder favorably with the more thrilling but very slightly stagy death of Arthur.

Although narrative invention is not his *forte* and his production of strictly narrative verse is slight, Arnold can, in the last of **"Tristram"** and especially in **"Balder Dead"** and **"Sohrab and Rustum,"** add even to good stories a heightening and enriching quality that is peculiarly his own: a quality of pathos deep and genuine and touched at best with a sense of the dignity of human suffering. His double vision, of men and gods as heroic forces, and of Nature or Fate as the single dominant principle in the life of the world, reflects two sides, two voices, of his imagination: voices that can fairly be represented if not perfectly reconciled in the action and imagery of these poems, in the one voice of the narrator. (pp. 133-34)

W. Stacy Johnson, in his The Voices of Matthew Arnold: An Essay in Criticism *(© 1961 by Yale University Press, Inc.), Yale University Press, 1961, 146 p.*

RENÉ WELLEK   (essay date 1965)

[*Wellek's* A History of Modern Criticism *is a major, comprehensive study of the literary critics of the last three centuries. Wellek's critical method, as demonstrated in* A History *and outlined in his* Theory of Literature, *is one of describing, analyzing, and evaluating a work solely in terms of the problems it poses for itself and how the writer solves them. For Wellek, biographical, historical, and psychological information is incidental. Although many of Wellek's critical methods are reflected in the work of the New Critics, he was not a member of that group and rejected their more formalistic tendencies.*]

The position of Matthew Arnold . . . as the most important English critic of the second half of the 19th century seems secure. His eminence is due not only to his literary criticism but also to his standing as a poet and general critic of English society and civilization. (p. 155)

Arnold is, first of all, a very important apologist for criticism. Criticism, of course, means for him not simply literary criticism but rather the critical spirit in general, the application of intelligence to any and all subjects. Arnold is an eloquent advocate of "disinterestedness," curiosity, flexibility, urbanity, a free circulation of ideas. . . . Arnold's ideal of "disinterestedness" must not be understood as Olympian aloofness or escape to the ivory tower. It is easy to show that Arnold himself was deeply absorbed in the problems of his age and was not above engaging in polemics and even losing his temper. But "disinterestedness" surely means for him something quite specific: a denial of immediate political and sectarian ends, a wide horizon, an absence of prejudice, serenity beyond the passions of the moment. . . . [Arnold] had the gentleman-scholar's dread of pedantic learning and disparages his own erudition with some mock humility. But while one should admit that he was no Sainte-Beuve, Dilthey, or Croce (he was, after all, a poet and a busy inspector of schools), he read Greek and Latin, German and French (and some Italian), and knew enough for a critic who does not even pretend to be a professional literary historian or classical philologist. Arnold's advocacy of the critical spirit, of an atmosphere conducive to the free exchange of ideas, his praise of objectivity, disinterestedness, and curiosity (properly understood) are valuable and sound even today. (pp. 156-57)

Contrary to the usual opinion, Matthew Arnold is . . . primarily a historical critic who works with a historical scheme in his mind. Society is often conceived as an independent, fixed, given force that even genius cannot change. (p. 161)

Yet Arnold does not think merely in terms of genius versus age, individual versus society, poet versus current or staple of ideas. He just as often thinks in collectivist terms of race and the march of history. He is preoccupied almost as much as Taine with racial theories. All his writings play variations on the contrasts appearing among the Latin, Celtic, and Germanic races, or in that between the Hebraic and the Greek spirit. But the distinction between national spirit (*Volksgeist*) and race is not clear to him. He sketches the history of France in terms of the conflict between Gaul, Latin, and Teuton. His lectures *On the Study of Celtic Literature* turn upon the concept of race. . . . He confidently assigns to the Celts (with whom he sometimes includes the French) specific literary characters: a turn for style, a turn for melancholy, and a turn for natural magic, while he denies them other literary abilities, such as a sense of over-all form. He never raises the obvious question whether these qualities could not be found elsewhere in the world where there were no Celts—in the Orient, for instance—and he never seems to doubt the cogency of his argument that the occurrence of these qualities in English literature is a proof of Celtic nature in the English. (pp. 161-62)

The contradictions in Arnold's concept of poetry and its limitations—the alternatives of mere didacticism or soulful religious seriousness—are connected with Arnold's lack of clarity on such central problems of poetics as the relation between content and form, between totality and local detail. Arnold (like his time in general) has a feeble grasp of the difference between art and reality. Imagination, illusion, the special world of art, mean little to him. In some sense he acknowledges the unity of form and content, but mostly he conceives of the subject of poetry as something given and fixed, something capable of being judged as poetic or unpoetic outside a work of art. Form just as often is conceived of as a hard vessel into which the poet pours his content. Even reality is often seen as something given and fixed, either good or bad for the artist, and art often means only artifice, technique, virtuosity. The poet, Arnold assumes, should deal with a beautiful world, but, unfortunately, he is not always able to do so. (p. 167)

Arnold is well aware of the central importance of totality and unity in art. The idea of "totality" appears early in his critical vocabulary: the 1853 **"Preface"** [see excerpt above] makes much of the "grandiose effect of the whole," the "total-impression" (Arnold spells the term with a hyphen) and of *architectonice,* something suggested to him by Goethe's reflections on dilettantism. The ancients are contrasted with the moderns on this point. "They regarded the whole, we regard the parts." These terms recur in later essays and are varied by the addition of such phrases as the "spirit which goes through her [George Sand's] work as a whole," or "a supreme total effect," or "the *symmetria prisca* of the Greeks," or "composition," or "grouping" used in a painter's sense. These terms are used to express standards of judgment. (pp. 170-71)

Arnold's more celebrated proposal to use "touchstones," "infallible touchstones," "short passages, even single lines" as a norm for judging poetry is an obvious contradiction of the

insight into unity, an atomistic principle that may be used to justify the most willful and erratic prejudices. Arnold himself, however, warns against a mechanical application of the touchstones. "These few lines, if we have tact and can use them, are enough even of themselves to keep clear and sound our judgments about poetry, to save us from fallacious estimates of it, to conduct us to a real estimate." But he admits that it is not easy to apply such lines to other poetry. "Of course we are not to require this other poetry to resemble them; it may be very dissimilar." The touchstones enumerated in **"The Study of Poetry"** are eleven passages, three each from Homer, Dante, and Milton, two from Shakespeare, all in a tone of sadness, melancholy, or resignation. . . . They are, no doubt, all fine passages but, as specimens of great poetry, extremely limited in range. They are not always representative of their authors and often hardly comprehensible outside of their context. (p. 171)

Arnold's stereotyped phrases and formulas are unfortunately the best remembered side of his criticism. He knew it himself and treated his pet phrases with proper irony. . . . The range and variety of Arnold's criticism belie such a superficial indictment. It seems necessary to survey his essays in an attempt to rank them and to point out some of their virtues and shortcomings. (p. 173)

The two first essays in [*Essays in Criticism*], **"The Function of Criticism at the Present Time"** and **"The Literary Influence of Academies,"** are Arnold's most formal and most eloquent pleas for criticism and the critical spirit. The whole volume clearly shows the influence of Sainte-Beuve; not only are the essays on the two Guérins and on Joubert suggested by Sainte-Beuve's essays on these writers: they are also (as is the essay on Marcus Aurelius) portraits in Sainte-Beuve's sense: deft blends of biography, liberal quotation, and psychological observation. Arnold has been blamed for wasting his energy on three minor French writers, but he wanted to paint unknown figures as part of his program of arousing "curiosity," and he was drawn to them by sympathetic interest in the religious and contemplative temper of his sitters. (pp. 173-74)

The essay on Heine, which has been much admired, seems to me the least satisfactory of the literary essays in the volume. Arnold, from a perspective which is French in its sources, considers Heine the follower and heir of Goethe, on whom "incomparably the largest portion of Goethe's mantle fell." The emphasis on Heine as the "brilliant soldier in the Liberation War of humanity" is quite speciously linked up with Goethe's very differently meant saying about himself that he had been the Liberator of the Germans. The admiration for Heine's "culture" . . . seems excessive if one knows Heine's gross simplifications of German philosophy, while the condescending attitude to his morals strikes one as unpleasantly smug. (p. 174)

Arnold's newly found certainty and authority are most boldly and memorably expressed in the series of essays devoted to the English romantic poets. . . . (p. 177)

Arnold's preference for Wordsworth is admirably defended. The anthology shows in detail that he loved the pastoral, serene Wordsworth above the speculative and mystical. The protest against the attempt to extract a philosophy of nature and ethics from Wordsworth is perfectly defensible if one remembers Arnold's desire to dismiss Wordsworth's *formal* philosophy. But one should not forget that Arnold actually values Wordsworth for the cognitive element in him, for "seeing into the life of things." Arnold, however, does not quite recognize the intellectual subtlety and profundity of Wordsworth's poetry and overstates his "provincialism" and lack of book learning. (pp. 177-78)

The preference for Byron as the second greatest poet is harder to defend. . . . Byron seems to Arnold "an ordinary nine-teenth-century English gentleman, with little culture and with no ideas." But in spite of all these reservations Arnold exalts Byron as "the greatest natural force, the greatest elementary power" in English poetry since Shakespeare. His admiration has mainly political motives: Byron is an enemy of cant and Philistinism, a great fighter in the war for the liberation of mankind. Byron, Arnold feels strongly, is fundamentally sin-cere in spite of all his theatrical preludings. . . . Arnold's an-thology shows clearly what he liked in Byron: descriptive and narrative passages, rhetorical reflections. But any defense of Byron as a poet must be based largely on *Don Juan* and *The Vision of Judgment*. Arnold gives only small fragments of the satires and thus cannot present a persuasive argument for By-ron's importance as a poet. (p. 178)

Keats stands highest among these poets in Arnold's eyes. . . . He acknowledges that Keats' passion for the Beautiful was "an intellectual and spiritual passion." He emphasizes, however, Keats' "natural magic," in which "he ranks with Shake-speare." He underscores, excessively to my mind, the idea that Keats was not ripe for "moral interpretation." He admires rightly the great odes for their "rounded perfection," but does not think *Hyperion* a success. Keats, though greatly admired, is seen too much as a mere promise.

Shelley is criticized as a man and hardly as a writer. But there are scattered passages that concern his work. To say that the pieces by Shelley in Palgrave's *Golden Treasury* are "a gallery of his failures" shows a complete lack of appreciation even for the best in Shelley, and to prefer the translations, the "de-lightful Essays and Letters," to the poetry seems puzzling. (p. 179)

[However] much we may disagree with Arnold's ranking of the poets and ages, he accomplished the main task of a practical critic: the sifting of the tradition, the arrangement or rearrange-ment of the past, the discrimination among currents, major and minor. The table of the English poets was fixed by Arnold for a long time to come. But Arnold's defense of the critical spirit, his theory of criticism with its emphasis on the real estimate, and even his discussion of the concept of poetry (limited as it is by his didacticism) were a great contribution to English criticism. Arnold, almost single-handedly, pulled English crit-icism out of the doldrums into which it had fallen after the great Romantic Age. (p. 180)

> *René Wellek, "Arnold, Bagehot, and Stephen," in his* A History of Modern Criticism, 1750-1950: The Later Nineteenth Century *(copyright © 1965 by Yale University), Yale University Press, 1965, pp. 155-90.**

WARREN D. ANDERSON (essay date 1965)

In 1849 *The Strayed Reveller, and Other Poems,* by "A.," revealed a poet who acknowledged his classical training but was not sure what role it ought to play. Arnold's uncertainty at once sets him apart from eighteenth century writers. Unlike Pope and Johnson he did not turn unhesitatingly to a Horace or a Juvenal; his lyricism owes nothing to the "pindaric" cultivated by earlier poets. To take for granted the time-honored preconceptions of classical values was no longer a possibility.

The writer's task was now to define these values anew for his own purposes and establish what seemed to have a continuing significance. (p. 15)

[Arnold's earliest poems] show a notable variety of approaches to the classical. They do not, however, give evidence of any common element. Matthew Arnold's long apprenticeship in Greek and Latin, a training then unsurpassed outside Germany, evidently had included no detached consideration of the nature of classicism or the classical. . . . Once he had taken up the writing of poetry, however, some attitude became increasingly necessary. Sooner or later he had to decide for himself.

Two ways of avoiding the decision were possible. He might have declared his poetic independence from antiquity; at the other extreme, he might have joined the ranks of its conven-tional imitators. But like every Victorian poet of substance he scorned a mere imitative classicism; and as for breaking with the past, he possessed neither the temperament nor the vision-ary powers of a Blake. In poem after poem Arnold sought a means of reunion with antiquity. It seemed that the goal might be realized in **"The Strayed Reveller"**; and here he turned away, apparently lacking the resolve for a final decision. . . .

Arnold's [early] poems lacked a common factor in approaching the classical. It follows that he had not committed himself to any ordered principle which could be termed classicism. He continued nevertheless to search for a viable relationship with antiquity, and the record of the crucial phases of his search may be found in his double portrait of Empedocles and Cal-licles. (p. 35)

In its most immediate origins the larger structure [of **"Em-pedocles on Etna"**] owes a good deal to Romanticism. Parallels with Byron's "Manfred" are too numerous and important to be accidental, and it has been plausibly argued that Arnold simplified and rearranged some of Byron's materials to get a pattern for his poem. The demonstration can be taken one step further: "Manfred" is a descendant of *Prometheus Bound*. Instances of structural and textual correspondence make clear the relationship, which Byron himself declared to be real though unintended. Thus **"Empedocles on Etna"** is Aeschylean at two levels—directly, through Arnold's knowledge of the Greek play, and also indirectly, through the use he apparently made of Byron. Yet its structure is not a cobbling together of Byronic and Aeschylean scraps. Arnold planned his poem with the greatest care, as if determined to produce the major work that critics now recognize it to be. (p. 36)

[In **"Empedocles on Etna"**, two] opposed outlooks have been set forth by means of a dramatic device, not at all classical but thoroughly Victorian, which rules out any possibility of set debate or philosophical dialogue. Arnold deliberately chose this method of presentation, and it may be suggested that he did so to demonstrate the impossibility of communication be-tween the inner worlds represented by Callicles and Empe-docles. The introspective man of thought brooding upon his wrongs and the barrenness of the time, ill at ease in solitude as in society, has no common language with the poet, whose thought radiates outward. Arnold himself embodied this di-lemma. He lacked the power of systematic exposition and be-littled its value; his critical method remained essentially intu-itive. Possibly this lack ultimately explains the poem's distinctive structure.

It was a discerning critic, therefore, who pointed out that **"Em-pedocles on Etna"** is what you make of it when you have read the whole poem. The assessment to which the reader has looked forward, the final reckoning, is not forthcoming; incommensurables have no calculus. But while Arnold may not arrive at any rationale, he clearly makes a choice between the two ways of responding to life. It speaks ill for mid-nineteenth-century criticism that he felt compelled to dissociate his own views from those of his protagonist. Empedocles' beliefs, he pointed out, ought not to have led to suicide. The point is badly stated and disregards the Stoic justification of suicide, but there is truth in it. Callicles embraces life, Empedocles death. The latter view may prevail in the end: of his youth Empedocles says . . . , "The smallest thing could give us pleasure then." What took away his Calliclean delight in life was too great contact with men in a world grown hostile; this is the contagion of which Arnold's works so often show an awareness. A Calliclean spirit may not be able to retain its serenity in the midst of the jarring shocks of existence. Nevertheless, it is the way of Callicles that Arnold chooses as an ideal. (pp. 45-6)

"**Empedocles on Etna**" contains a further choice. The classical-Romantic antithesis does not come in question here; the poet has already revealed his feelings, particularly in "**The New Sirens.**" The question is rather how he will employ classical form and content—whether they are to penetrate him and become embodied in poetry such as the great passages of "**The Strayed Reveller**" or to serve instead as graceful external ornament.

If the interpretation we have proposed is a valid one, an answer to this question can already be discerned. The emotional agitation of Greek lyricism must give way to an impersonal Apolline serenity even as Callicles' themes, at first inspired by Pindar, conclude within the range that Homer assigned to the bard. . . . Arnold's classicism now begins to take refuge in externals—first, Homeric and then tragic form, but always form of some kind. It is within the frame of classical convention that his restless melancholy and sense of isolation must find expression henceforth when he deals with the past; often they cannot do so without incongruity. Nevertheless they demand expression, as the Empedoclean elements of his nature that cannot be merely wished out of existence. The tension created by their presence removes some of the chill from this hieratic classicism, but it remains cold. Arnold in fact cannot realize within himself the Calliclean ideal of the remarkable poem we have been considering. He is determined to circumscribe it with Aristotelian formalism, with the doctrine of Longinus that great writing bespeaks a great soul. . . . (pp. 46-7)

This poem has rightly been called the most ambitious of Matthew Arnold's works, because the most filled with tensions; but it also signalizes his turning away from personal involvement towards a Parnassian objectivity. . . . "**Empedocles on Etna**" marks the close of a period in Matthew Arnold's development and indicates what his classicism is to be. (p. 47)

[These] early poems show Arnold tending towards involvement with deep classical feeling of the kind often called Dionysiac. In "**The Strayed Reveller**" that tendency became pronounced. It reached a crisis with the writing of "**Empedocles on Etna**," where he chose the serenity of Apollo in preference to the raptures of Dionysus. The reveller had already forsaken the established, public Dionysiac rites but not the god himself: in the later poem Arnold seems to decide against the god as well. If the essence of the classical is passion made significant through order, then he chose the ordered over the passionate.

This explanation endeavors to account for the change which clearly occurred in Arnold's work. It is less evident, and somewhat less generally accepted, that any profound change occurred in his nature. We have chosen to study the more limited problem of whether his classicism shifted essentially at any time. If the arguments presented here are sound, it did shift. What remains to be considered is how this fact affects an estimate of his role as lifelong mediator between the classical and modern worlds.

Here one faces the task of distinguishing between subjective and objective validity. A writer achieves the first of these when he is true to himself; Arnold was never anything else. . . . As for objectivity, it is at best a relative term. We do expect it, nevertheless, in an interpreter of cultures past or present; at least we look for a broad awareness of the main factors and proportions. This expectation Arnold was unable to satisfy. Whenever he deals with classical material at length, the stresses and omissions give evidence of his inability. Bad faith is not in question: the instances of one-sided or even misleading argument in his presentation are hardly the manipulations of a conscious imposture. They should be viewed as the loci of a highly individual personality; they place in a commonsense perspective the protestations about "seeing the thing as in itself it really is."

Misgivings about subjective bias or scholarly inadequacy cannot alter the fact that Arnold's classicism rendered a notable service to Victorian thought. He came to an age which had no clear attitude towards the cultural achievement of Greece and Rome; and he came bringing forthright doctrines, memorable phrases, catchwords that lodged stubbornly in the memory, all of them phrased with a virtuosity capable of charming and irritating the reader almost in the same moment. . . . Arnold revealed Homer's true place, no longer in the customary narrow classical setting but in the whole sweep of Western literature. His Oxford lectures opened a new age of English criticism, and the new comparative approach which they embodied was to be the foundation of his literary method. Precisely because he lacked that type of objectivity known as the historical sense, he was able to travel in an instant between Victorian London and the Athens of Pericles without any real consciousness of being on a journey at all. No doubt this makes for shocking scholarship and deserves to be condemned on many grounds, but it does have the quality of its defects: it is undeniably lively. No such Athens as he described ever existed; yet this may after all be less important than the fact that, for a considerable part of literate England, Matthew Arnold's brilliance compelled it to exist. (pp. 201-02)

Warren D. Anderson, in his Matthew Arnold and the Classical Tradition *(copyright © by University of Michigan 1965), The University of Michigan Press, 1965, 293 p.*

A. DWIGHT CULLER (essay date 1966)

[The] first thing we would have to say [about Arnold's elegies] is that they are the poetic counterpart of his imaginative world. We have perhaps obscured this fact by saying that the elegy is divided into two parts by means of the elegiac reversal. So it is in its actual structure, but the complete world which the elegy presupposes is divided into three parts by means of two elegiac reversals. The first of these is simply the death of the subject, and therefore the first part of the world occurs before the poem opens. To use . . . the example of *Lycidas*, the first part consists of the happy days when

> we were nursed upon the self-same hill,
> Fed the same flock by fountain, shade, and rill.

This part is terminated by the first elegiac reversal, "But O the heavy change now thou art gone." The second part, then, consists of the body of lamentation and is terminated by the more usual reversal,

> Weep no more, woeful shepherds, weep no more,
> For Lycidas your sorrow is not dead.

The third part is the final phase of recovery and reconciliation. It is obvious that Arnold's poetic myth corresponds exactly with this structure: his forest glade is the happy times together, his burning plain the body of lamentation, and his wide-glimmering sea the period of reconciliation. Moreover, his image of the gorge or strait which connects one part of his world with another corresponds to the structural device of the elegiac reversal, and the River of Life corresponds to the current of thought or feeling which sweeps him through his song. This last device is of great value to Arnold, for it not only gives a strong compulsive movement to his thought, but it also enables him to attribute his views to some power larger than himself. Just as in his essays he will attribute to History or the Zeitgeist the unfavorable judgments which he passes upon his countrymen, so in the elegies he will attribute them to muses, breezes, or fate. In *A Summer Night* it is the midnight breeze which "checks his strain" and reminds him that no one is more worthy of a romantic resting-place than an English gentleman of noble feeling. In *Heine's Grave* it is the Bitter Spirits of Heine's own poetry which mock his efforts to claim the bard as his own and remind him that Heine wanted love and so also wanted charm. And in *Haworth Churchyard* it is again the Muse which interrupts him and angrily denies to the Brontës the reawakening which the poet has promised. In this way Arnold is able to give weight and objectivity to value judgments which are his own.

This correspondence of the elegy to the myth explains the different forms which the elegy takes in Arnold's work. If the subject is an inhabitant of the forest glade, as in the case of Wordsworth, then we get the first elegiac reversal but not the second, for in 1850 Arnold did not believe that the forest glade could ever be recreated again. But if the subject is an inhabitant of the burning plain, then we do not get a first reversal, since his death is not a "heavy change," and the second reversal is a reversal in reverse. This is the form of the elegies on Obermann, Charlotte Brontë, and Heine. Then, when Arnold is a little further along in his own myth, he discovers that persons whom he had thought to be on the burning plain actually were not, and this revisal of opinion constitutes a conventional elegiac reversal in which the subject dies in Arnold's estimation as one thing and is reborn as another. *Thyrsis* is an ambiguous example, *A Southern Night* a much clearer one. (pp. 264-66)

[Taking] this larger view of the elegies, we can now see that a great deal of Arnold's poetic production is elegiac in character. *Balder Dead* . . . is essentially an elegy drawn out, by the insertion of inert matter, into epic proportions. *Sohrab and Rustum*, initially entitled *The Death of Sohrab*, is an elegy for lost youth. *The Church of Brou* is an elegy for the Duke of Savoy in which the poet reproduces in words the elegy which the Duchess has carved in stone. The *Sick King in Bokhara* is a double elegy, both for the King, who becomes well, and for the Moollah, who is redeemed through punishment and understanding. *Tristram and Iseult* is another double elegy, Tristram dying as himself to be reborn in the form of his own children, Iseult dying as Ireland to be reborn as Brittany. All the love poems taken together constitute one large elegy in which woman dies as Marguerite and is reborn as Mrs. Arnold.

Likewise, the poet dies as passionate lover and is reborn as son or brother. *Empedocles on Etna* is a truncated elegy in which Empedocles dies with only the promise of rebirth when he shall poise his life at last. But more largely, the drama *Empedocles on Etna* "dies" as morbid art through the "elegiac reversal" of the Preface of 1853 [see excerpt above] in order to be reborn as wholesome art in *Sohrab and Rustum*. Indeed, in this sense both of Arnold's first two volumes die in order to be reborn as their successor. (pp. 266-67)

[Imaginative] reason is that synthesis of intellect and feeling which is characteristic of the modern spirit. It does not deny the evidence of the senses and understanding, but neither does it deny that of the heart and imagination. It is at once profoundly satisfying and profoundly true. As such, it combines the best elements of science and religion and yet transcends these by remaining poetry. In the late essays **"Literature and Science"** and **"The Study of Poetry"** Arnold explores the interrelationships of science, poetry, and religion in such a way as to make religion analogous to the forest glade, science to the burning plain, and poetry to the wide-glimmering sea. . . . [In *Essays in Criticism* Arnold states]: "For poetry the idea is everything; the rest is a world of illusion, of divine illusion. Poetry attaches its emotion to the idea; the idea *is* the fact."

Modern readers, interpreting this passage in terms of their own theories of poetry as an autonomous art, tend to overlook the fact that Arnold distinguishes between "the idea," which *is* the fact, and "the rest," which is a world of illusion. And they also overlook that Arnold is here speaking not of all poetry but only of that which is "worthy of its high destinies," the poetry of the imaginative reason. For some poetry does attach its emotion to the illusion, the divine illusion, and the illusion can fail it. In Arnold's view this is what had happened to the poetry of the English Romantic movement. It was too exclusively a product of the imagination. It was too personal and private, too transitory and unenduring. It "did not know enough" in the sense simply of knowing the great, substantial ideas which had operated in human history. It was very beautiful, but it was essentially a dream. Keats says of Adam that he awoke and found his dream true, but the Romantic poets awoke and found their dreams were false. One after another they awoke upon the "cold hillside" of a purely phenomenal world. Arnold himself began life upon that cold hillside and was forced to write the greater part of his poetry from that situation. For a long time he wrote it in terms of the senses and understanding. But the late paganism of Epictetus and Lucretius and even Marcus Aurelius was not enough. Religion was morality "touched with emotion," and poetry, if it was not pure imagination, was not pure reason either—it was the imaginative reason. And so, in *Obermann Once More*, Arnold dreamed a dream whose substance was neither the dry rationalism of Empedocles nor the sensuous myth of Callicles but was his own personal myth embodied in human history. And he awoke and found it true. The morning which broke in his dreams actually was breaking when he emerged from his dream. Whereas in *The Scholar-Gipsy* he awoke and found himself back in the phenomenal world, here he awoke and found himself forward in his dream. He had actually dreamed himself off the burning plain into the next phase of human history.

Arnold did this in the same way that Adam did it, by realizing his dream in himself. His elegies repudiate a lower nature and create a higher nature, and insofar as his whole poetry had an elegiac character, this was its larger function. It did not hang nostalgically over the past, lamenting a lost paradise, but tried with honesty and integrity to create a "paradise within thee, happier far." (pp. 282-84)

It has always been something of a problem why Arnold turned from poetry to prose, and the answer may be given in various ways. But one way of stating it is simply to say that the task of the poetry was done. It told the story of a river which descended from the hills, all but lost itself in the sands of the desert, and finally emptied into the sea. Once it reached the sea its story was done. (p. 285)

> *A. Dwight Culler, in his* Imaginative Reason: The Poetry of Matthew Arnold *(copyright © 1966 by Yale University), Yale University Press, 1966, 303 p.*

JAMES DICKEY (essay date 1966)

"**Dover Beach**" has been called the first modern poem. If this is true, it is modern not so much in diction and technique—for its phrasing and its Miltonic inversions are obvious carryovers from a much older poetry—but in psychological orientation. Behind the troubled man standing at the lover's conventional moon-filled window looking on the sea, we sense—more powerfully because our hindsight confirms what Arnold only began to intuit—the shift in the human viewpoint from the Christian tradition to the impersonal world of Darwin and the nineteenth-century scientists. The way the world is seen, and thus the way men live, is conditioned by what men know about it, and they know more now than they ever have before. Things themselves—the sea, stars, darkness, wind—have not changed; it is the perplexed anxiety and helplessness of the newly dispossessed human being that now come forth from his mind and transmute the sea, the night air, the French coast, and charge them with the sinister implications of the entirely alien. What begins as a rather conventional—but very good—description of scenery turns slowly into quite another thing: a recognition of where the beholder stands in relation to these things; where he *really* stands. It is this new and comfortless knowledge as it overwhelms for all time the old and does away with the place where he thought he stood, where his tradition told him he stood, that creates the powerful and melancholy force of the poem.

In statement, "**Dover Beach**" goes very easily and gravely, near prose and yet not too near. It has something of the effect of overheard musing, though it is addressed, or half-addressed, to someone present. Its greatest technical virtue, to my mind, is its employment of sound-imagery, particularly in the deep, sustained vowels of lines like "Its melancholy, long, withdrawing roar." The lines also seem to me to *break* beautifully: " . . . on the French coast, the light / Gleams, and is gone." I have tried many times to rearrange Arnold's lines, and have never succeeded in doing anything but diminish their subtlety, force, and conviction.

The one difficulty of the poem, it seems to me, is in the famous third strophe wherein the actual sea is compared to the Sea of Faith. If Arnold means that the Sea of Faith was formerly at high tide, and he hears now only the sound of the tide going out, one cannot help thinking also of the cyclic nature of tides, and the consequent coming of another high tide only a few hours after the present ebb. In other words, the figure of speech appears valid only on one level of the comparison; the symbolic half fails to sustain itself. Despite the magnificence of the writing in this section, I cannot help believing that it is the weakest part of the poem when it should be the strongest; the explicitness of the comparison seems too ready-made. Yet I

have the poem as it is so deeply in memory that I cannot imagine it changed, and would not have it changed even if I knew it would be a better poem thereby.

In the sound of waves rolling pebbles, an eternal senseless motion, unignorable and meaningless, Arnold hears—as we ever afterwards must hear—human sadness, the tears of things. It links us to Sophocles and to all men at all times who have discovered in such a sound an expression of their own unrest, and have therefore made of it "the eternal note of sadness." Yet our sadness has a depth that no other era has faced: a certainty of despair based upon our own examination of empirical evidence and the conclusions drawn by our rational faculty. These have revealed not God but the horror and emptiness of things, including those that we cannot help thinking beautiful: that *are* beautiful. By its direct, slow-speaking means, the poem builds toward its last nine lines, when the general resolves into the particular, divulging where *we* stand, what these things mean to *us*. The implication is that if love, morality, constancy, and the other traditional Western virtues are not maintained without supernatural sanction, there is nothing. The world that lies before us in such beauty that it seems to have come instantaneously from God's hand does not include, guarantee, or symbolize the qualities that men have assumed were also part of it. It is beautiful and impersonal, but we must experience it—and now suffer it—as persons. Human affection is revealed as a completely different thing than what we believed it to be; as different, in fact, as the world we were mistaken about. It is a different thing but also a new thing, with new possibilities of terror, choice, and meaning. The moment between the lovers thus takes on the qualities of a new expulsion from Eden: they tremble with fear but also with terrible freedom; they look eastward. The intense vulnerability of the emotional life takes place in an imperiled darkness among the sounds of the sea and against the imminence of violence, wars, armies blundering blindly into each other for no reason. Yet there is a new, fragile center to things: a man and a woman. In a word, it is love in what we have come to call the existential predicament. Nearly a hundred years ago, Arnold fixed unerringly and profoundly on the quality that more than any other was to characterize the emotion of love in our own century: desperation. (pp. 235-38)

> *James Dickey, "Arnold: 'Dover Beach'," in* Master Poems of the English Language: Over One Hundred Poems Together with Introductions by Leading Poets and Critics of the English-Speaking World, *edited by Oscar Williams (copyright © 1966 by, Trident Press; reprinted by permission of Simon & Schuster, Inc., a Division of Gulf & Western Corporation), Trident Press, 1966 (and reprinted in his* Babel to Byzantium: Poets & Poetry Now, *Grosset & Dunlap, 1971, pp. 235-38).*

BEVERLY TAYLOR (essay date 1982)

Although "**Tristram and Iseult**" reveals theme through image and situation more successfully than do the lyrics [in *Empedocles on Etna; and Other Poems*, the volume in which it first appeared], Arnold's overt exposition of destructive passion may be termed "thinking aloud." Yet in this intricately crafted artifact, Arnold's narrative devices—codas, flashbacks, alternating speakers and modes, for example—demonstrate his consciousness of "making" as well as "thinking." Principally through these techniques or texturing devices, Arnold obliquely treats a larger concern, of which Tristram's passion is but one aspect: the relative values of actuality and fantasy. Indeed, much of Arnold's "thinking" in the poem involves the importance of man's "making," in dreams and fantasies, and more overtly in statues, tapestries, and stories. Given so many imaginative re-creations of experience, one may conclude that the poem concerns art and the imagination no less than it concerns love. (pp. 633-34)

In the years preceding the appearance of "Tristram and Iseult" Arnold sometimes emphasized aesthetic elements more than message, and sometimes focused on meaning more than on artifice. "Tristram and Iseult" furnishes both an explicit ethical message about consuming passions and an implicit aesthetic indication of the importance of "making," of exercising imagination to re-create experience in art. The created form—whether tapestry, poem, or dream—can be accepted and interpreted precisely because it is art rather than life. Extrapolated from experience, art gives enjoyment and truth, both of which are too often destroyed in the "gradual furnace of the world."

Arnold suggests this idea in such earlier works as "The Strayed Reveller" and "Resignation," which emphasize the poet's need to know life directly but to remain aloof from its pains. Art is thus meaningful in being at once a part of life and something distinct from it. Similarly, in the title poem of the 1852 volume, *Empedocles on Etna,* Arnold explores the relation between art and life and the value of aesthetic re-creation of experience. (pp. 634-35)

Although the importance of making is a theme revealed only obliquely in "Tristram and Iseult," it is a major concern. Whereas Arnold advances much of his thinking about the destructiveness of passion explicitly—through the editorial comment of the narrator or through the incontrovertible evidence of Tristram's unhappiness and untimely death—he reveals his thinking about the significance of aesthetic creativity only implicitly. Most of the significant implications are to be found in his embellishments on the medieval legend, his modern touches. The old subject matter presumably appealed to Arnold in part because it countered his sense of the aesthetic impoverishment of his own time. (p. 635)

But neither the setting nor the situation of the Tristram romance itself provides the poetic charm of the work. Rather, Arnold's innovations as a "maker" create the work's appeal. These innovations include alternating a narrator's voice with characters' monologues and dialogues and manipulating chronology through flashbacks and through setting an ostensible "present" against the "long-ago" of the Tristram tale. (p. 636)

Though the importance of creativity becomes most prominent in the final coda, Arnold suggests the significance of art for life throughout the poem. From the opening lines, he complicates our sense of what is actual and what is produced by the imagination. The narrative creates uncertainty about the objective validity of Tristram's words—is he waking or dreaming? And the dreams of his children in the first coda emphasize both the parallels and the contrasts between actuality and illusion. . . .

Arnold throughout the poem piles fantasy upon fantasy. In part one, the dreams of both Tristram and his children are recounted—or created—by the narrator, whose imaginative speculations also lead him in part two to depict Tristram and Iseult's deaths as a sculpture or tableau. This artifact is observed—again in the narrator's mind—by a character, the tapestry Huntsman, who is himself actually an artifact produced by an unknown weaver. (p. 638)

The narrator's treatment of the stories of Tristram and Merlin obliquely emphasizes man's need to escape from actuality by dreams, memory, and fable. The destructiveness of unrestrained passion is but one aspect of the experience from which the narrator insulates himself with art. (pp. 638-39)

The narrator judges that each character's success in coping with life matches the vitality of his imagination. Tristram's passion for Iseult of Ireland, although destructive, demonstrates his continuing capacity to feel and is expressed through fantasy. We see the results of Tristram's love—his illness and death—as actual events, but we see that love itself through his dreams and feverish recollections. In one sense Tristram's love provides an escape from the immediate environment, but because his dreams inevitably touch remembered actual events, they fail to remove him from anxiety and torment. . . .

In one respect, Tristram's death releases Iseult of Brittany from the turbulence of frustrated love, but she is incapable of enduring the "gradual furnace" of normal society. Instead, she finds refuge in fantasy . . . and creates days that are artifacts of sorts, each an "effigy" of its predecessor. By withdrawing from the passions and activities of the normal adult world and by simulating innocent childhood, Iseult of Brittany creates an artificial identity. . . . (p. 639)

Her principal companions, her children, embody a kind of reality that approximates fantasy, for the child's vision is private, inexperienced, and unrealistic. Despite their liveliness, the children know only the circumscribed realm that Iseult permits. Their experience is filtered through fantastic tales that entrance both their mother and themselves. . . . Unlike the adults, whose dreams involve recollection necessarily assailed by painful experience, the children dream of ideal beauty which lives only in an enchanted world. In a chamber flooded with moonlight that creates the illusion of daylight, they dream of such evanescent joys as pursuing fragile butterflies. (p. 640)

Throughout the poem, Arnold's narrator contrasts fantasy with actuality by setting contained, insulated scenes against an expanding landscape. Refugees from pain have dreams, tell their stories, and create their fictions in carefully bounded areas beyond which the narrative portrays a widening physical world. . . . The great world lies always just beyond the limit of attention for Arnold's characters who replace consuming actualities with consoling fancies. While resembling external experience, fictive creation provides refuge within the lovely or familiar. (pp. 640-41)

Even death can be metamorphosed by the creative will. Though for Tristram and Iseult of Ireland death may be mere extinction, to the imagination their death becomes a kind of fantasy or artifact, a peaceful scene endowed with magical dreaminess by the narrator's fable of the Huntsman in the arras. The tapesty, created by an unknown artist of long ago, contains for the narrator a second imaginative creation—the story of the Huntsman's response to the lovers. Although static, the Huntsman represents the active life formerly pursued by Tristram. He seems to move through the vast forest, surprised to discover himself in an enclosed room. To him the still scene seems like a tapestry. . . .

All the levels of fiction in the poem are focused in the final coda. The embodiment of fantasy, the bard and enchanter Merlin nonetheless falls prey to the same sort of passion that consumes Tristram and his Iseult. Although Merlin's fate is not death or the living death of Iseult of Brittany, his transformation provides a final commentary on the story of Arnold's principal characters and the narrator as well, all of whom represent escape through fantasy. As in the other instances of fantasies that provide relief from the real, unpleasant world, Merlin actively creates his escape. (p. 642)

In **"Tristram and Iseult"** Arnold explores two poles of response to life—attitudes expressed in the brief poem **"Youth and Calm,"** which was probably initially intended as part of the Tristram poem. Tristram acts on the desires of youth but in death achieves the calm that, despite youth's vast hunger for more, is finally the best that man can expect. . . . The Breton narrator of **"Tristram and Iseult"** offers an alternative to this unenthusiastic conclusion, which presents the ultimate calm of death as a meager prize. (p. 644)

In **"Tristram and Iseult"** Merlin represents an imagination that escapes ordinary passions by means of the peace, beauty, and permanence of art. But, as the subject of legend told over centuries—by Breton dames, the widowed Iseult, the poem's narrator, and by Arnold—Merlin also serves the instructive purposes of didactic art. The characters in **"Tristram and Iseult"** illustrate varying degrees of success in using their imaginations to cope with the barrenness and "unpoetrylessness" of life. Those who remain most fully immersed in mundane experience are least able to derive lasting benefit from their imaginations. Iseult of Brittany employs her creativity, it seems, only to escape from pain. The narrator, safely distanced from the unhappy experiences, shares them only vicariously. Yet his frustrated editorializing and spluttering against life in general suggest his failure to achieve control over his art or the life on which he comments. It is, finally, Arnold and his reading audience who can use art not just as an escape or an anodyne, but as a fundamental remedy for the maladies of existence. (p. 645)

> Beverly Taylor, "Imagination and Art in Arnold's 'Tristram and Iseult': The Importance of 'Making'," in Studies in English Literature, 1500-1900 (© 1982 William Marsh Rice University), Vol. 22, No. 4, Autumn, 1982, pp. 633-45.

ADDITIONAL BIBLIOGRAPHY

Alexander, Edward. *Matthew Arnold, John Ruskin, and the Modern Temper.* Columbus: Ohio State University Press, 1973, 210 p.*
  A comparative biography. Alexander states that in spite of their ideological, epistemological, and psychological differences, Arnold and John Ruskin invite comparison because their views are "eminently the views of artists who are seeking the means of sharing with others the beauty and truth which they themselves have glimpsed."

Allott, Kenneth, ed. *Matthew Arnold.* Athens, Ohio: Ohio University Press, 1976, 353 p.
  A collection of essays by ten scholars exploring such issues as Arnold's attitude toward religion, his social and political thought, and his relationship to Johann Wolfgang von Goethe and Arthur Hugh Clough.

Baum, Paull F. *Ten Studies in the Poetry of Matthew Arnold.* Durham, N.C.: Duke University Press, 1958, 139 p.
  Close explications of eight of Arnold's poems, including "Dover Beach" and "Tristram and Iseult," in addition to an analysis comparing "The Scholar Gypsy" with "Thyrsis," and a study of the Marguerite poems.

Bradley, A. C. "Shelley and Arnold's Critique of His Poetry." In his *Miscellany,* pp. 139-62. London: Macmillan, 1931.*

Evaluates Arnold's criticism of Shelley as a poet and attempts to reveal the strength of Arnold's arguments.

Brown, E. K. *Matthew Arnold: A Study in Conflict.* 1944. Reprint. Chicago: University of Chicago Press, 1966, 224 p.
  A biography. The critic set out to write, as he states in his preface, neither a biography of the man nor his mind, but a work that would "illuminate Arnold's writings by tracing the history of a lifelong conflict with his personality."

Buckley, Vincent. "Matthew Arnold: Poetry as Religion." In his *Poetry and Morality: Studies on the Criticism of Matthew Arnold, T. S. Eliot, and F. R. Leavis,* pp. 25-53. London: Chatto & Windus, 1961.
  Considers Arnold the most interesting of all English literary critics, and states that Arnold considered writing poetry a religious act.

Chambers, E. K. *Matthew Arnold: A Study.* 1947. Reprint. New York: Russell & Russell, 1964, 144 p.
  A biographical study examining Arnold's various roles, including poet, professor, and philosopher.

Coulling, Sidney. *Matthew Arnold and His Critics.* Athens: Ohio University Press, 1974, 351 p.
  A study of Arnold's responses to his contemporary critics. Coulling states in his preface that he is concerned with "those exchanges between [Arnold] and his reviewers that comprised a kind of dialogue which shaped a significant portion of his prose work."

Dawson, Carl, ed. *Matthew Arnold: The Poetry.* The Critical Heritage Series, edited by B. C. Southam. London: Routledge & Kegan Paul, 1973, 466 p.
  A comprehensive compilation of critical commentary written on Arnold's poetry between 1849 and 1900. The excerpts are drawn from such sources as periodical essays, books, and letters and are prefaced by useful notes on the critics and criticism. In addition, the editor's introduction provides a concise overview of critical reaction to the poetry. Dawson also coedited a companion to this volume which covers Arnold's prose writings (see annotation below).

Dawson, Carl, and Pfordresher, John, eds. *Matthew Arnold: Prose Writings.* The Critical Heritage Series, edited by B. C. Southam. London: Routledge & Kegan Paul, 1979, 458 p.
  A companion to *Matthew Arnold: The Poetry* (see annotation above). This collection follows the same format as the earlier book, providing a thorough selection of critical commentary written on Arnold's prose works between 1861 and 1899. Like its counterpart, the volume contains an introductory overview of the criticism in addition to informative annotations to individual essays.

DeLaura, David J. *Matthew Arnold: A Collection of Critical Essays.* Englewood Cliffs, N.J.: Prentice-Hall, 1973, 186 p.
  An anthology of twelve previously published essays by noted modern Arnold critics, including T. S. Eliot, U. C. Knoepflmacher, Kenneth Allott, John P. Farrell, and A.O.J. Cockshut. Several of the articles center on Arnold's poetry; other subjects include Arnold's theory and practice as a prose writer and Arnold as a conservative revolutionary.

Eliot, George [pseudonym of Mary Ann Evans]. *Westminster Review* n.s. LXIV, No. VII (July 1855): 297-99.*
  A brief commentary on *Poems, second series.* Eliot finds Arnold's earlier poems superior to those in his second collection, and, while she praises the powerful effect of Arnold's verse, she considers his rhythm defective.

Fulweiler, Howard W. *Letters from the Darkling Plain: Language and the Grounds of Knowledge in the Poetry of Arnold and Hopkins.* Columbia, Mo.: University of Missouri Press, 1972, 173 p.*
  A linguistic and epistemological study of Arnold and Gerard Manley Hopkins. Fulweiler attempts to show how these poets "faced the dilemma of language in a changed world and devoted the greater share of their creative energies to establishing under new

conditions the grounds of knowledge in relation to the function of poetic art.''

Gosse, Edmund. ''Matthew Arnold.'' In his *More Books on the Table,* pp. 381-87. New York: Charles Scribner's Sons, 1923.
A charming reminiscence of Arnold.

Gottfried, Leon. *Matthew Arnold and the Romantics.* Lincoln: University of Nebraska Press, 1963, 277 p.*
Explores and evaluates the full range of Arnold's reaction to the major Romantic poets.

Hecht, Anthony. ''The Dover Bitch: A Criticism of Life.'' In *Matthew Arnold: A Collection of Critical Essays,* edited by David J. DeLaura, p. 54. Englewood Cliffs, N.J.: Prentice-Hall, 1973.
Hecht's well-known satire of Arnold's ''Dover Beach.'' The poem reviews Arnold's nineteenth-century melancholy through twentieth-century eyes.

James, Henry. *English Illustrated Magazine* I (January 1884): 241-46.
A laudatory overview stating that readers owe Arnold a ''debt of gratitude for his admirable example, for having placed the standard of successful expression, of literary feeling and good manners, so high.''

Jamison, William A. *Arnold and the Romantics.* Anglistica, edited by Torsten Dahl, Kemp Malone, and Geoffrey Tillotson, vol. X. Copenhagen: Rosenkilde and Bagger, 1958, 167 p.
Evaluates Arnold's acumen as a literary critic ''by examining his judgment of the five major Romantic poets . . . , especially in relation to the critical thought of his age.'' The five, each of whom is treated in a separate chapter, are William Wordsworth, George Gordon, Lord Byron, John Keats, Percy Bysshe Shelley, and Samuel Taylor Coleridge.

Jump, J. D. *Matthew Arnold.* London: Longmans, Green and Co., 1955, 185 p.
An interpretation and reassessment of Arnold regarded from three aspects: ''The Man,'' ''The Poet,'' ''The Critic.''

Madden, William A. Poetry as Religion. *Matthew Arnold: A Study of the Aesthetic Temperament in Victorian England.* Bloomington: Indiana University Press, 1967, 242 p.
A study of Arnold's place in the debate which accompanied the emergence of the aesthetic consciousness in England. Madden attempts to demonstrate through Arnold's writings the conflict between his innate aesthetic temperament and the ethical and critical sense of duty which inhibited that aesthetic drive.

McCarthy, Patrick J. *Matthew Arnold and the Three Classes.* New York: Columbia University Press, 1964, 257 p.

A detailed account of Arnold's theory of classes as depicted in *Culture and Anarchy.* The critic traces Arnold's development of his theory throughout life.

Meredith, G. E. ''The Source of Mr. Arnold's Power.'' *Church Review* LII, No. CLXXXVI (July 1888): 65-70.
A fond reminiscence of Arnold.

Middlebrook, Jonathan, ed. *Matthew Arnold: ''Dover Beach''.* The Merrill Literary Casebook Series, edited by Edward P. J. Corbett. Columbus, Ohio: Charles E. Merrill Publishing Co., 1970, 159 p.
A ''casebook'' designed to aid students in evaluating and writing research papers on ''Dover Beach.'' The volume includes the text of the poem itself in addition to several well-known critical essays on ''Dover Beach,'' suggestions for papers, a list of additional readings, and general instructions for writing a research paper.

Miller, J. Hillis. ''Matthew Arnold.'' In his *The Disappearance of God,* pp. 212-69. Cambridge, Mass.: The Belknap Press, 1963.
An approach to Arnold's poetry and poetic theory as a reflection of the nineteenth-century's troubled struggle with godlessness.

Raleigh, John Henry. *Matthew Arnold and American Culture.* Berkeley: University of California Press, 1957.
Explores Arnold's critical influence in the United States. Raleigh attributes Arnold's great impact on American culture to the lack of American literary tradition.

Robbins, William. *The Ethical Idealism of Matthew Arnold: A Study of the Nature and Sources of His Moral and Religious Ideas.* University of Toronto Department of English Studies and Texts, no. 7. Toronto: University of Toronto Press, 1959, 259 p.
A study of Arnold's ethical idealism based on an examination of his ''ideas, their source in his reading and environment, their relation to currents of thought and belief in his own day, and their relevance to some of the currents still moving within the main stream.''

Roper, Alan. *Arnold's Poetic Landscapes.* Baltimore: The Johns Hopkins University Press, 1969, 268 p.
An evaluation of Arnold as a landscape poet.

Saintsbury, George. *Matthew Arnold.* Modern English Writers Series. Edinburgh: William Blackwood and Sons, 1899, 230 p.
A biographical-critical study. Saintsbury's was the first book-length work devoted to Arnold.

Trilling, Lionel. *Matthew Arnold.* New York: Norton, 1939, 465 p.
A sympathetic and insightful analysis of Arnold's concepts. This is considered the definitive critical biography of Arnold.

Trilling, Lionel. Introduction to *The Portable Matthew Arnold,* edited by Lionel Trilling, pp. 1-30. New York: The Viking Press, 1949.
Provides a brief overview of Arnold's works. Trilling calls Arnold ''the great continuator and transmitter of the tradition of humanism.''

Charles Baudelaire

1821-1867

French poet, critic, translator, essayist, novelist, and playwright.

Baudelaire is considered one of the world's greatest lyric poets, and his masterpiece, *Les fleurs du mal (The Flowers of Evil)*, is ranked among the most influential volumes of French poetry. Though a critical and popular failure at the time of its publication, *The Flowers of Evil* is now hailed for its innovative, influential verse. Baudelaire's modernity is evident in the diversity and controversial nature of his subject matter, the amoral tone of his writings, and his evocation of degradation and despair. In *The Flowers of Evil*, Baudelaire chose to analyze, often in shocking terms, his urban surroundings, erotic love, and the conflicts within his own soul. The spiritual discontent he depicts has inspired a variety of critical interpretations. Some detect a Catholic philosophy in his work, while others find satanic overtones. Some note a vague mystical quality. Underlying these concepts is Baudelaire's belief that the individual, if left to his own devices, is inherently evil and will be damned. Only that which is artificial can be construed as absolutely good. Poetry, according to Baudelaire, should in turn serve only to inspire and express beauty. Like the Decadents and Symbolists he influenced, Baudelaire aspired to a beauty separate from the natural or moral world. This aesthetic doctrine forms the basis of both his poetry and his critical writings. Baudelaire valued his criticism as much as his poetry, and recent commentators suggest that one must study Baudelaire's criticism alongside his poetry to fully grasp his artistic and philosophic principles.

Born in Paris, Baudelaire had a happy childhood until age six, when his father died. In the year following his father's death, Baudelaire grew very close to his mother; later he remembered their relationship as "ideal, romantic . . . as if I were courting her." When Mme. Baudelaire married Jacques Aupick, a military officer, Baudelaire became deeply resentful. Though he had initially excelled in school, as he grew older he increasingly neglected his studies in favor of a dissipated, rebellious lifestyle. In 1841, the Aupicks sent him on a two-year trip to India. Although the trip failed to reform him as they had hoped, it was productive from a literary standpoint, for it was during this time that he experimented with verse, and wrote the first poems that would be included in *The Flowers of Evil*.

When Baudelaire returned to Paris, he received a sizeable inheritance and, for a short time, lived a frivolous dandy's life. Dandyism, as Baudelaire conceived it, involved the glorification of the ego as the ultimate spiritual and creative power. In his essay "Le Dandy" he described his conception of the dandy as a heroic individualist in revolt against a decadent society. At this time, Baudelaire fell in love with Jeanne Duval, a Parisian woman of mixed race. Though she cared little for poetry and perhaps less for him, she inspired the poems which formed the cycle of the "Black Venus," his first series of love poems. The sensuality indicated in this early verse eventually erupted in a volatile passion which dominated his writing as well as his life. The darker side of his love for Jeanne is expressed in "Le vampyre" ("The Vampire") which describes a figure representing Jeanne, who stands ready to thrust a

dagger into his heart. His relationship with Jeanne deteriorated, and he denounced romance, writing that "woman is abominable . . . sinning comes to her as naturally as eating and drinking." Now introspective and solemn, Baudelaire continued to write and also began to experiment with hallucinogens. Later, he documented his drug usage in *Les paradis artificiels: Opium et haschisch (Artificial Paradises: On Hashish and Wine as a Means of Expanding Individuality)*, a volume which contains his translation of Thomas De Quincey's *Confessions of an English Opium Eater*, and his own "Poème du Haschisch."

After his mother obtained a court order blocking his inheritance, Baudelaire supported himself by writing. During this time, he established friendships with such painters as Eugene Delacroix and Gustave Courbet, who inspired his interest in art. Baudelaire's first critique of art, the "Salon of 1846," is considered one of the nineteenth century's most perceptive analyses of Romantic painting. His critical output increased dramatically during this period, and he developed the style and aesthetic concepts that would aid his poetic technique. He read a great deal in English and, in 1846, discovered the works of Edgar Allan Poe; later, Baudelaire said that in Poe he had found his "twin soul." Poe, like Baudelaire, stressed technical perfection and the creation of an absolute beauty; in him, Baudelaire found confirmation of his own philosophies. Determined that Poe should achieve recognition in Europe, Baudelaire devoted a number of years to translating his works. These translations, which include the *Histoires extraordinaires*, *Nouvelles histoires extraordinaires*, and *Aventures d'Arthur Pym*, are considered among the finest translations in French literature. In 1855, after achieving acclaim for his early Poe translations, Baudelaire published a number of poems in the journal *Revue des deux mondes*. Although his poems were condemned by some critics for their scandalous subject matter, he was encouraged by such noted literary figures as Victor Hugo.

In 1857, Baudelaire published *The Flowers of Evil*, a collection which he had written over several years. *The Flowers of Evil* combines the passion of Romanticism with a Parnassian perfection of form, yet its subject is wholly original. Baudelaire found man and his world to be evil; only art, he claimed, could bring redemption. Like Théophile Gautier, to whom he dedicated the volume, Baudelaire sought to depict "l'horreur et l'extase de la vie," the horror and ecstasy of life. Like his mentor, Poe, Baudelaire found beauty in the horrific. He took as his main subject the perplexities of a soul both sinful and repentant.

Baudelaire organized *The Flowers of Evil* according to its themes, which include "spleen," "idéal," "luxe," and "ennui." The most prevalent of these, "spleen" and "idéal," juxtapose the idea of a perfect existence with the knowledge of the dream's futility. "Spleen," to Baudelaire, signifies nostalgia and desperation, a masochistic, sterile mood that reinforces his belief in damnation. "Ennui," too, figures prominently in these poems. "Ennui" depicts the horrors of daily tedium and embodies, for Baudelaire, the inherent evil in nature. "Luxe," or luxury, and "extase," or ecstasy, are alternately embraced and disdained as fleshly pleasures that are natural, appealing, and ultimately, repellent. These contradictions reveal Baudelaire's spiritual crisis. Though Baudelaire had no orthodox religious affiliation, he profoundly felt the presence of both Satan and God. Satanic imagery, synonymous with vice and man's unclean nature, pervades *The Flowers of Evil*. The images reappear throughout the volume, evoking man's conflict between temporal enjoyment and spiritual redemption. While Baudelaire maintained that he did not aspire to Heaven, the final poem, "Le voyage" ("The Voyage") poignantly details his desire to escape life's misery. *The Flowers of Evil* also contains some of the first French poetry to depict the displaced and unwanted citizens of Paris. While Baudelaire's Parnassian predecessors found beauty in *objets d'art*, Baudelaire found poetry in the outcasts of the city. In their misfortune, he found a metaphor for his concept of original sin, and the paradox of good and evil existing side by side. The beauty and cruelty of Parisian existence, he felt, represented humanity's own complicated and irrational nature.

The love poems of *The Flowers of Evil* are Baudelaire's most controversial. Besides the cycle of the "Black Venus," he included poetry written for his two other mistresses, Apollonie Sabatier and Marie Daubrun. Apollonie, the "White Venus," inspired a cycle of reverent, celestial verse reminiscent of his early adoration for his mother. Baudelaire, in fact, referred to Apollonie as his "Madonna and Angel." In a different tone, Baudelaire's cycle of the "Green Venus" depicts his unrestrained passion for Marie. While evoking a sensuality similar to the "Black Venus" cycle, the poems composed for Marie are more explicitly erotic and display elements of sadism. Collectively, the love poems provide an important and, to some, frightening commentary on Baudelaire's conflicting feelings

about women. He alternately worshipped and loathed them; critics speculate that from the time of his mother's remarriage, he never had an enduring or successful relationship with any woman.

Upon the publication of *The Flowers of Evil*, Baudelaire was critically attacked. Reviewers called him a "sick poet," and even friends such as the critic Charles Sainte-Beuve refused to praise the book. Subsequently, Baudelaire and his publisher were prosecuted and convicted of immorality. Six offending poems were removed from the book and published later the same year in Belgium as *Les épaves*. For both the 1861 and posthumous 1868 editions, some poems were added and others reworked, but the ban on his suppressed poems was not lifted in France until 1949. After the publication of *Artificial Paradises* and the second edition of *The Flowers of Evil*, Baudelaire's publisher went bankrupt. Though Baudelaire published more Poe translations, the revenue proved insufficient and, in an attempt to regain both his reputation and his financial solvency, he traveled to Belgium on a lecture tour. The trip failed and, in 1866, he returned to Paris. Shortly after his return, he suffered a stroke. His mother, with whom he had recently reconciled, nursed him until his death.

A number of Baudelaire's works were published posthumously, including *Petits poemès en prose: Le spleen de Paris (Poems in Prose from Charles Baudelaire)*. These poems represent a new literary genre, the prose poem. Written in prose form, these writings contain all the lyrical imagery and language of his earlier poetry. Like *The Flowers of Evil*, they convey, in melancholy tones, Baudelaire's desire to escape earth's misery. The influence of Baudelaire's prose poems is strongly evident in the poetry of Stéphane Mallarmé, Paul Claudel, and Arthur Rimbaud. In particular, Rimbaud's *Le bateau ivre* and *Une saison en enfer* show the influence of Baudelaire's stylistic innovations.

Twentieth-century critics maintain that Baudelaire's criticism is as valuable as his poetry. According to Baudelaire, criticism allows one to contemplate art, while poetry crystallizes artistic concepts, and he believed that every great artist would one day become a critic. Commentators generally agree that Baudelaire's critical essays revolutionized nineteenth-century aesthetic theory. Though few critics, including Algernon Swinburne and Théophile Gautier, initially championed Baudelaire, he received more attention after Joris Karl Huysmans praised him in his novel *À rebours (Against Nature)*. Soon, other Symbolist poets such as Jules Laforgue acknowledged their debt to Baudelaire, and his influence extended to the works of T. S. Eliot and W. B. Yeats. Arthur Symons called his work "satanic," an outlook disputed by later critics. Wallace Fowlie and T. S. Eliot both noted the religious aspects of Baudelaire's writings, and Enid Starkie, in her biography of Baudelaire, maintained that *The Flowers of Evil* is essentially religious poetry. Jean-Paul Sartre denied any moral concepts in Baudelaire's poetry and interpreted him as a nihilist. Other critics have focused on Baudelaire's juxtaposition of Romanticism and classicism. S. A. Rhodes, in 1929, pointed out classical elements such as Baudelaire's balanced versification, adherence to traditional poetic form, and an objective appreciation of beauty coupled with Romantic tendencies which included his reliance on intuition and exaltation of the emotions and senses. Interpretations continue to vary. However, critics generally agree that *The Flowers of Evil* is among the greatest achievements in literature, combining numerous literary elements and influences, yet creating a unified and compelling whole.

PRINCIPAL WORKS

La fanfarlo (novel) 1847
Histoires extraordinaires [translator; from the short stories
   of Edgar Allan Poe] (short stories) 1856
Les épaves (poetry) 1857
Les fleurs du mal (poetry) 1857, 1861, 1868
   [*The Flowers of Evil*, 1909]
Nouvelles histoires extraordinaires [translator; from the short
   stories of Edgar Allan Poe] (short stories) 1857
Aventures d'Arthur Pym [translator; from the novel *The
   Narrative of Arthur Gordon Pym* by Edgar Allan Poe]
   (short stories) 1858
Les paradis artificiels: Opium et haschisch [translator; from
   the autobiography *Confessions of an English Opium
   Eater* by Thomas De Quincey] (autobiography and
   poetry) 1860
   [*Artificial Paradises: On Hashish and Wine as a Means of
   Expanding Individuality*, 1971]
Curiosités esthetiques (criticism) 1868
Oeuvres complètes. 7 vols. (poetry, letters, essays, and
   criticism) 1868-70
L'art romantique (criticism) 1869
Petits poèmes en prose: Le spleen de Paris (poetry) 1869
   [*Poems in Prose from Charles Baudelaire*, 1905]
Journaux intimes (diaries) 1887
   [*Intimate Journals*, 1930]
Lettres: 1841-1866 (letters) 1905
The Letters of Charles Baudelaire (letters) 1927
The Mirror of Art: Critical Studies (criticism) 1955
*Art in Paris, 1845-1862: Salons and Other Exhibitions
   Reviewed by Charles Baudelaire* (criticism) 1965

*This work includes the diaries ''Fusées'' and ''Mon coeur mis à nu.''

[ALGERNON CHARLES SWINBURNE] (essay date 1862)

[*Swinburne was an English poet, dramatist, and critic, who is
remembered for his lyric poetry and his rejection of Victorian
mores. With this essay, Swinburne brought Baudelaire to the
attention of English-speaking readers. He praises Baudelaire's
delicate verse and his technical skill. Unlike many critics, who
considered* The Flowers of Evil *immoral and repellent, Swinburne
found the poems to be truthful, graceful, and founded upon a
''distinct and vivid background of morality.''*]

[M. Baudelaire] has more delicate power of verse than almost
any man living, after Victor Hugo, Browning, and (in his
lyrics) Tennyson. The sound of his metres suggests colour and
perfume. His perfect workmanship makes every subject admirable and respectable. Throughout the chief part of [the *Fleurs
du Mal*], he has chosen to dwell mainly upon sad and strange
things—the weariness of pain and the bitterness of pleasure—
the perverse happiness and wayward sorrows of exceptional
people. It has the languid lurid beauty of close and threatening
weather—a heavy heated temperature, with dangerous hot-
house scents in it; thick shadow of cloud about it, and fire of
molten light. It is quite clear of all whining and windy lamentation; there is nothing of the blubbering and shrieking style
long since exploded. The writer delights in problems, and has
a natural leaning to obscure and sorrowful things. Failure and
sorrow, next to physical beauty and perfection of sound or

scent, seem to have an infinite attraction for him. In some
points he resembles Keats, or still more his chosen favourite
among modern poets, Edgar Poe; at times, too, his manner of
thought has a relish of Marlowe, and even the sincerer side of
Byron. From Théophile Gautier, to whom the book is dedicated, he has caught the habit of a faultless and studious simplicity; but, indeed, it seems merely natural to him always to
use the right word and the right rhyme. How supremely musical
and flexible a perfect artist in writing can make the French
language, any chance page of the book is enough to prove;
every description, the slightest and shortest even, has a special
mark on it of the writer's keen and peculiar power. The style
is sensuous and weighty; the sights seen are steeped most often
in sad light and sullen colour. As instances of M. Baudelaire's
strength and beauty of manner, one might take especially the
poems headed *Le Masque, Pärfum Exotique, La Chevelure, Les
Sept Vieillards, Les Petites Vieillas, Ilrumes et Pluies*. . . .

[The sonnet titled *Causerie* is a complete] specimen of the
author's power. The way in which the sound and sense are
suddenly broken off and shifted, four lines from the end, is
wonderful for effect and success. M. Baudelaire's mastery of
the sonnet form is worth remarking as a test of his natural bias
towards such forms of verse as are most nearly capable of
perfection. . . . Not the luxuries of pleasure in their simple
first form, but the sharp and cruel enjoyments of pain, the acrid
relish of suffering felt or inflicted, the sides on which nature
looks unnatural, go to make up the stuff and substance of this
poetry. Very good material they make, too; but evidently such
things are unfit for rapid or careless treatment. The main charm
of the book is, upon the whole, that nothing is wrongly given,
nothing capable of being re-written or improved on its own
ground. Concede the starting point, and you cannot have a
better runner.

Thus, even of the loathsomest bodily putrescence and decay
he can make some noble use. . . .

Another of this poet's noblest sonnets is that *A une Passante*,
comparable with a similar one of Keats, ''Time's sea hath been
five years at its slow ebb,'' but superior for directness of point
and forcible reality. Here for once the beauty of a poem is
rather passionate than sensuous. . . .

There is noticeable also in M. Baudelaire's work a quality of
drawing which recalls the exquisite power in the same way of
great French artists now living. His studies are admirable for
truth and grace; his figure-painting has the ease and strength,
the trained skill, and beautiful gentle justice of manner, which
come out in such pictures as the *Source* of Ingres. . . .

It may be worth while to say something of the moral and
meaning of many among these poems. Certain critics, who will
insist on going into this matter, each man as deep as his small
leaden plummet will reach, have discovered what they call a
paganism on the spiritual side of the author's tone of thought.
Stripped of its coating of jargon, this may mean that the poet
spoken of endeavours to look at most things with the eye of
an old-world poet; that he aims at regaining the clear and simple
view of writers content to believe in the beauty of material
subjects. To us, if this were the meaning of these people, we
must say it seems a foolish one; for there is not one of these
poems that could have been written in a time when it was not
the fashion to dig for moral motives and conscious reasons.
Poe, for example, has written poems without any moral meaning at all; there is not one poem of the *Fleurs du Mal* which
has not a distinct and vivid background of morality to it. Only

this moral side of the book is not thrust forward in the foolish and repulsive manner of a half-taught artist; the background, as we called it, is not out of drawing. . . .

[Those] who will look for them may find moralities in plenty behind every poem of M. Baudelaire's; such poems especially as *Une Martyre.* Like a mediaeval preacher, when he has drawn the heathen love, he puts sin on its right hand and death on its left. (p. 999)

[We] may note a few others in which [a] singular strength of finished writing is most evident. Such are, for instance, *Le Cygne, Le Poison, Tristesses de la Lune, Remord Posthume, Le Flacon, Ciel Brouillé, Une Mendiante Rousse* (a simpler study than usual, of great beauty in all ways, noticeable for its revival of the old fashion of unmixed masculine rhymes), *Le Balcon, Allegorie, L'Amour et le Crâne,* and the two splendid sonnets marked xxvii. and xlii. We cite these headings in no sort of order, merely as they catch one's eye in revising the list of contents and recall the poems classed there. Each of them we regard as worth a separate study, but the *Litanies de Satan,* as in a way the key-note to this whole complicated tune of poems, we had set aside for the last. . . .

Here it seems as if all failure and sorrow on earth, and all the cast-out things of the world—ruined bodies and souls diseased—made their appeal, in default of help, to Him in whom all sorrow and all failure were incarnate. As a poem, it is one of the noblest lyrics ever written; the sound of it between wailing and triumph, as it were the blast blown by the trumpets of a brave army in irretrievable defeat. . . .

[*Litanies de Satan* is not] more finished than the rest; every verse has the vibration in it of naturally sound and pure metal. It is a study of metrical cadence throughout, of wonderful force and variety. . . . We know that in time it must make its way. . . . (p. 1000)

> [*Algernon Charles Swinburne*], "Charles Baudelaire: 'Les fleurs du mal'," in The Spectator (© 1862 by The Spectator), No. 1784, September 6, 1862, pp. 998-1000.

EVERY SATURDAY   (essay date 1867)

There is no tenderness, not a smile, not a tear in all [Baudelaire's] works. There is nothing in them but jeerings and sarcasms, anguish, desire, screams of revolt and blasphemies. He never summons emotion, nor still gentler pity. He invokes death and night, graveworms and horrid skeletons. Seated on a tomb amid darkness, when the moon is muffled by thick clouds, he shakes a blood-stained spangled shred and the burying-ground's mournful haunters, its night hawks and its owls, and bats and moths flit round and round the sinister charmer. He believed himself pursued by destiny, and gazed in the chalice to see if it still held more dregs that he might exhaust them. By dint of feeling the prosaic and persisting in rowing against the stream, he fell into antithesis and exaggeration. He somewhat resembles Byron; he looked upon himself as accursed, his imagination was diseased and it killed him. Baudelaire was a moral curiosity, a singular manifestation; I was about to say an exceptional "case," a precious "subject." But that peculiar disposition, that mood of feeling and comprehension, that irresistible thirst, those screams, those aspirations towards the Unknown, that vertigo, that *nostalgia* of the abyss and the maelstrom found their formula, and we are obliged to raise our head and listen to the sonorous rhythm. I am not afraid to

say that in matter of form of prose or verse, the author of *Fleurs du Mal* is one of the masters of the present time. He had the lofty tradition of the close of the seventeenth century. His phrases have something noble and severe in their movement, which reminds one of the great masters, while his own individuality is very marked in them. Pompous, without being theatrical, clear, absolutely accurate, he exhibits his ideas with such method and classification they assume a shape and full relief even when they are ultra-speculative, and transport us into ideal regions and into "artificial paradises," whose scenes the most daring imaginations have never dreamed of evoking.—Things bizarre, things extraordinary, and a diseased curiosity about new and unknown things led him to exercise his admirable talents of author on ideas with which the mob had little sympathy, and the mob did not know him. He made this ignorance of the mob his boast. His ambition was to inhabit alone a lofty peak, and M. Sainte Beuve was able with truth to say of him, he built himself, at the very extremity of the romantic peninsula, a lodge of his own, in which exquisite sonnets were recited. . . . Under the empire of what hallucination, what sickly dreams, what feverish excessive excitement, could a poet be led to write the *Fleurs du Mal,* to make of these morbid thoughts a nosegay of a magnificent tone and perfect form? (p. 528)

As a poet, Baudelaire is remarkable for the form, number, and rhythm of his verse. He was not a spontaneous writer. He created with painful travail, and his verse is redolent of labor and difficulty. Nevertheless, he is the author of exquisite and complete poems. His imagery is grand, although his inspiration is weak. The sonnet is his favorite form; if the effort to write it is great, it does not last long. He had the talent for giving relief, but 't is plastic relief, 't is the jutting of marble or bronze, not of life. It is a curious detail of the subject treated by him. In the admirable sonnet *La Géante,* the imagination struck by its beautiful verse evokes the "charms moulded for Titans' mouths" by the mighty bards of a Michael Angelo or of a Puget, 't is a marble statue, 't is not a woman, 't is not a human being. It is in the *Fleurs du Mal* . . . that the artist reveals himself in the most curious light. It is well known that this book was prosecuted and condemned. These legal proceedings were mistaken. Free course should be allowed these bitter thoughts, doubts, despair, and lamentations. . . . [Baudelaire] required (if the expression may be used) the acute in a chronic state. It was his doating love for that which in art is called "character," which, developed to strangeness, superinduces this ideal and produces the painful exception we are now studying like some unusual case in medicine, as 't were a moral *elephantiasis.* But we are, nevertheless, artists, and Baudelaire was an artist to very delirium, and as he discovered his harmonious formula, and cast his nightmares in a bronze mould, we are interested, and we remember his name. (pp. 529-30)

Les Paradis Artificiels Opium et Haschish is a very curious book. If the reader bears in mind this idea, which was a favorite of the author: "It is not necessary for the writer's contentment that any book should be understood except by him for whom it was written," he will understand this strange book, in which Baudelaire, under pretence of studying the sensations produced by excitants, has advanced dangerous ideas. He said, in one of his works, he had so little taste for the world of the living, like those sensitive and idle women who send through the post-office their confessions to imaginary friends, he was half tempted to write only for the dead. Evidently the angel Azrael had touched with his wing him who in this way pursued the discovery of our secret destiny. He spoke likewise in his preface of his "frightful slumbers." We have the key of his life and the secret of his death in reading these pernicious studies, written by a learned hand in admirable language. . . . [Baudelaire] did not write a work of pure physiology, but a moral work, and with great energy and certainty he deduced the conclusion that "seekers of paradise attain hell," and deepen their hell, with a success which, had they foreseen, would have appalled them. Here as elsewhere he was pursued by an insatiable thirst of new sensations. He sought to develop sensibility to delirium, and note with *sang froid* [cold blood] the progress of sensations. He wished to see heaven with its glorious splendors, its magnificent effulgence, its cascades of liquid gold, and its dazzling apotheoses. . . . If you accept the subject, you must admit the book to be an original work. He has noted in it, with extraordinary precision and great affluence of resources, the incredible deformations of objects, the aberrations of the eyes, the ecstasies and the ravishment. . . .

Baudelaire's translations [of Edgar Poe] are as perfect as a translation can be. He made them with extraordinary care and resolved the difficult problem of giving the equivalent of the word and the meaning of the idiomatic phrases while at the same time he wrote a work of thorough elegance and accomplished style. . . . Edgar Poe is an eccentric writer, who borrowed nothing from any one and belonged to no school. This was enough of itself to attract Baudelaire's attention. Poe enlarged the domain of drama by making dramatic emotion spring from an unexpected source, a source which has hitherto never raised emotion, joy, or terror. Before Poe, precision and exactness had invariably engendered coldness, lassitude, and fatigue; he made imperative, inflexible deduction and fatal logic engender for the first time nervous terror. Baudelaire, the *blasé* artist and inquisitive author, was doubtless grateful to Poe for having astonished him,—him, whom nothing could astonish. Moreover, the poetical character of that vexed spirit attracted him. Poe had a power of nerve, a factitious joy, a real sorrow flowing from imaginary woes, something acrid and morbid which corresponded with the frame of his own mind, an inextinguishable ardor and an insatiable appetite of inquisitiveness which he understood because he had felt them. (p. 530)

As a critic of art, Baudelaire deserves to be taken into serious consideration, although he carried into his judgments some of the bizarre tendencies of his mind. [The pamphlet entitled *Salon de 1846*] . . . violently attacked those then regarded as demigods; but it attacked them in the name of very lofty aesthetics, with arguments drawn from the highest intelligence of the plastic arts. Time has ratified the judgments of the author, and those made great artists by fashion are already forgotten, while day by day the fame of those then so sharply discussed, increases. Baudelaire became a critic, not only from taste of art; he had an aesthetic of his own, based on a profound knowledge of the different manifestations of art from East Indian idols, Egyptian pylons, and the gods of Olympus, to the Italian revival and the French dainty, affected painters. It need not be said his sympathies and his predilections did not lay down their arms, and he felt attracted towards them who attracted his sympathies and his predilections, but he knew how to rise above his own individuality and to place himself at the proper point of view to judge genius which differed essentially from his own nature. He said of Delacroix's women: "He does not in general paint pretty women, at least not what fashionable people so call." Near all of his women are ailing, and are effulgent with a certain inner beauty. "It is not only grief which Delacroix best knows how to express, but, above all, prodigious

mystery of his painting, moral grief." This is what, besides Delacroix's color, attracts and seduces him; that great and profound melancholy is all his own. He says masterly of Ingres: "M. Ingres draws admirably well and draws rapidly. He natively is ideal in his sketches. His drawing, often slight, does not contain many lines, but *each of them expresses an important contour.*" Note this sentence, it expresses in a few words the essential, indispensable idea of high art. "Each of them expresses and important contour," in other words, those, from Phidias to M. Ingres, who have executed work of high art, have made form monumental. He defined the Romantic in these words: "The Romantic does not exactly lie in the choice of subject, or in the exact truth, but in the manner of feeling. Whoever uses the expression Romantic, means Modern Art, namely, spirituality, color, aspirations towards the infinite, expressed by every means at the Art's command." He sought the soul under the contours, and was lenient to form in favor of everything which beamed and which came from the heart. He sometimes became enamored in painting and sculpture of those sickly sentiments and those morbid ideas which he had expressed in literature. . . . Baudelaire had a horror of pretty things. Graceful things, so near affectation, exasperated him; as he was of exquisite sensibility in these matters, and his pen gritted, he unbosomed his anger in frightful epithets. Often, in turning over collections of drawings with him, we saw him gaze on works which seemed to us scarcely worthy of attention. . . . Even when he descended from the summits of Art, he retained his principles. (p. 531)

Baudelaire should be studied as a moral curiosity. We should note his exquisite form while regretting that it does not contain healthier and more human ideas. "The question here is art, nothing but art." Was Baudelaire the architect of his misfortune? I doubt it. To ascertain the secret sorrows, the terrible deceptions, the infinite griefs of any man, we must fathom his heart of hearts. Baudelaire was a sick poet. (p. 532)

"Charles Baudelaire," in Every Saturday, Vol. IV, No. 95, October 26, 1867, pp. 528-32.

WILLIAM STIGAND (essay date 1871)

The *Fleurs du Mal* comprise a series of poems, whose subjects almost exclusively are drawn from the corruptions and vices of our advanced state of civilisation. . . . Baudelaire is not the only poet of his time in whom doubt and despair and a choice of unfit themes is remarkable; but gleams of new spritual light, rays of glorious hope, are to be found in sufficient abundance scattered about in the works of others to atone for their scepticism. The accusation to which Baudelaire has laid himself subject is, that he has with premeditation taken more loathsome forms of corruption and vice as matter meet for song than ever were so employed before, and that he has raised in their behalf diabolic chants of adoration, sometimes mingled with hate, in which he appears to resign himself wholly and in ghastly delight to the domination of evil. (pp. 438-39)

[Baudelaire's] readers must be a compound of all the vices, unredeemed by a single virtue, except want of courage, to prevent them from committing murder, arson, &c.; and he himself was as bad as they were. It is not suggested that man possesses a beam of light to enlighten him, or a virtue of any kind to appeal to. Why, then, appeal to him at all? A saint is said to have once addressed a sermon to fishes; but in these days one can expect to attain little by addressing an audience of panthers, and vipers, and vermin. The poems of the *Fleurs de Mal,* as a whole, carry out the gloomy character of the preface; there are, however, a few pieces which form exceptions; the best of these is one called **'Elévation.'** . . .

The poem ironically called **'Bénédiction'** is another piece which shines like a glowworm amid the desolate darkness of the rest of the volume; but even here there are passages gloomy and overstrained enough. (p. 440)

Love has been the theme of poets since the beginning of time, to which each true poet has added a fresh charm and a fresh pathos. It is curious to see how Baudelaire treats this passion. A number of women flit across the lurid stage of his morbid imagination; the majority of them are the priestesses of venal passion. The power and the fatal beauty of such women, the delusive and impotent ravings of unrestrained desire, the self-imposed tortures of profaned and vainly-lavished adoration—such are the topics which form matter for some of Baudelaire's most powerful love-poems. (p. 442)

[The] general impression derived from the perusal of Baudelaire's volume is one of extreme pain. All the nightmares, morbid fancies, blind, wild, and insatiable desires, deluded and mocked by appearance of fruition—all the disillusions, all the agonies of doubts and despairs, ending in adoration of the powers of evil—which tortured the morbid brain of an arrogant and eccentric genius, found place in the pages of the *Fleurs du Mal;* so that the reading leaves a sense of nightmare on the soul. Is it any relief to such impressions to know that Baudelaire has done this in verse which, from the point of view of manufacture, is of extreme merit? The greater the loathsomeness and wickedness of the result produced, the greater is the crime of the artist. (pp. 443-44)

Baudelaire sought after originality, and he may fairly be allowed this originality—that he is, perhaps, the only man since the beginning of time who has attempted to combine obscenity, bad odours, and a putrefying carcass into a love-ditty [*Une charogne—Carrion*]. Hamlet moralising on a skull in a churchyard, we all know; but in the highest ecstasy of madness one cannot imagine his composing a sonnet of this fashion to present to Ophelia—though possibly this very scene in *Hamlet* may have suggested Baudelaire's poem. (p. 446)

The poetry of Baudelaire places us face to face with the gravest questions of art. Is a moral end to be left out of sight altogether in writing and criticising a poet's work? Baudelaire and his admirers declare that morals have nothing to do with poetry. Baudelaire says that poetry must have no other end but itself. Others say the end of art is to please, without any moral ambition at all. Baudelaire, however, admits with others that poetry is aspiration towards a higher form of beauty.

Baudelaire, we imagine, would not consent to agree with those who say the end of art is to please. However, we have nothing to do with the fine distinctions which those who agree in denying the possibility of any alliance between morality and art may choose to draw: any quantity of specious logic may be produced on this vexed question. To us it seems as absurd to deny the use of moral power to the poet and the artist, as it would be to deny it to the orator, or to any form of human expression. (p. 449)

[Those] who declare that moral considerations should have nothing to do with our æsthetic judgments, and form no part of a true poem, leave out of sight altogether the fact that moral beauty is one of the highest forms of beauty, and that its contemplation is capable of affording the highest pleasure; and

a poet who omits to use moral power as an ally in his service omits to appeal to emotions which are capable, if excited, of giving the purest satisfaction, and lacks also one of the most inspiring, invigorating, and enduring elements of his art. (p. 450)

[It] cannot be denied that fleeting gleams of better convictions than those to which [Baudelaire] has given his main energies are to be found in his verse and prose. We cannot accept the fatalistic conclusion that Baudelaire was necessarily what he was, and could be no other; it is a question how far external influences, and a more wholesome social and intellectual atmosphere, might have aided in saving from wreck a man who certainly had an intellect worth the saving.

> William Stigand, "Baudelaire," in Belgravia, *Vol. XV, October, 1871, pp. 438-52.*

THÉOPHILE GAUTIER   (essay date 1872)

[*Gautier, to whom Baudelaire dedicated* The Flowers of Evil, *holds an important place in French letters as a transitional figure between Romanticism and Realism. Like Baudelaire, he adhered to the doctrine which he expressed as "art pour l'art," or art for art's sake. Gautier maintains that in* The Flowers of Evil *Baudelaire wished to excite "in the reader's mind the sensation of the Beautiful." Further, he states that, though the volume's intention and execution are Romantic, Baudelaire is not to be confined to any literary school or movement. He praises the work's musical metre and prosody, and terms* The Flowers of Evil *"new and unexpected."*]

[Baudelaire] loved what is inaccurately called the decadent style, which is simply art that has reached the extreme point of maturity which marks the setting of ancient civilisations. It is an ingenious, complex, learned style, full of shades and refinements of meaning, ever extending the bounds of language, borrowing from every technical vocabulary, taking colours from every palette and notes from every keyboard; a style that endeavours to express the most inexpressible thoughts, the vaguest and most fleeting contours of form, that listens, with a view to rendering them, to the subtle confidences of neurosity, to the confessions of aging lust turning into depravity, and to the odd hallucinations of fixed ideas passing into mania. This decadent style is the final expression of the Word which is called upon to express everything, and which is worked for all it is worth. (pp. 39-40)

When Baudelaire is not engaged in expressing a yet untold side of the soul or of things, he makes use of so pure, clear, correct, and accurate a tongue that the most critical can find nothing in it to blame. This is particularly noticeable in his prose, in which he treats of matters more generally current and less abstruse than in his verse, which is almost always extremely condensed. (pp. 42-3)

[Baudelaire] did not believe that man was born good, and he admitted original sin as an element that is ever to be found in the depths of the purest souls, sin, that is an evil counsellor urging man to do what is harmful to him, precisely because it is deadly to him and for the sole pleasure of running counter to law, without any other inducement than disobedience, apart from any sensuality, any profit, any charm. . . . He might have engraved as a motto on his seal the two words, **"Spleen and Idealism,"** which form the title of the first part of [**"The Flowers of Evil"**]. If it be urged that his bouquet is composed of strange, metallic-leaved flowers, with intoxicating perfumes, their calyxes filled with bitter tears or aqua-tofana instead of dew, his answer is that scarce any others grow in the black loam, saturated with rottenness like the soil of a grave-yard, which is formed by the decrepit civilisations, in which the corpses of former ages are dissolving amid mephitic miasmata. (pp. 43-5)

[Baudelaire] believed art should be absolutely autonomous, and refused to admit that poetry had any end other than itself, or any mission to fulfil other than that of exciting in the reader's mind the sensation of the Beautiful, in the strictest meaning of the word. . . . He banished from poetry, to the utmost of his power, eloquence, passion, and the too accurate reproduction of truth. (pp. 46-7)

These principles may surprise one, when reading certain poems of his in which he seems to have deliberately set out to be horrible; but if they be carefully examined, it will be seen that the horrible is always transformed by the character and the effect of it, by a Rembrandt-like flash, by a grand stroke, like that of Velasquez, that reveals the high breeding under the foul difformity. (p. 47)

Although few poets have been endowed with more spontaneous originality and inspiration, Baudelaire, no doubt through disgust at the sham lyricism that pretends to believe that a tongue of fire settles upon the head of the writer who is striving hard to rime a stanza, maintained that a true writer called up, directed and modified at will the mysterious power of literary production. . . . (p. 51)

Baudelaire's nature was more subtle, complex, logical, paradoxical, and philosophical than that of poets in general. The æsthetics of his art preoccupied him greatly; he had a wealth of systems which he endeavoured to apply, and he planned out whatever he did. In his belief, literature should be *predetermined*, and the share of the *accidental* restricted as much as possible. (pp. 55-6)

"The Flowers of Evil" was a happy title, and happy titles are far more difficult to hit upon than is believed. It summed up in brief, poetic fashion the general idea of the book and indicated its tendency. Although quite plainly Romanticist in its intention and its execution, Baudelaire cannot be connected by any very visible bond with any one of the great masters of the school. His verse, with its refined and erudite structure, its occasionally too great conciseness, clothing objects as with a suit of armour rather than with a garment, appears at the first reading to be difficult and obscure. (p. 57)

The volume opens with a poem addressed **"To the Reader,"** whom the poem, contrary to custom, does not attempt to win over, but to whom he speaks the harshest of truths, accusing him, in spite of his hypocrisy, of having all the vices he blames in other men, and of bearing in his heart the great modern monster, Weariness, which with bourgeois cowardice, idiotically dreams of Roman ferocity and debauchery, like the bureaucratic Nero, the shop-keeping Heliogabalus it is. (pp. 58-9)

In **"Elevation"** we see the poet soaring in the very vault of heaven, beyond the starry spheres, in the luminous ether, on the very confines of our universe which has vanished like a cloudlet in the depths of the infinite, drinking in deeply the healthy rarefied air free from the foul odours of earth and perfumed by the breath of angels. For it must not be forgotten that Baudelaire, though he has often been accused of materialism—a reproach fools never fail to address to men of talent—is on the contrary endowed to an eminent degree with the gift of *spirituality,* as Swedenborg would say. He also possesses

the gift of *correspondence,* if I may still use these mystical terms; that is, he is able to discover through a secret intuition relations invisible to other people, and thus to connect by unexpected analogies, which a *seer* alone can note, objects apparently utterly removed from and most opposed to each other. Every true poet is endowed with this quality to a greater or less degree, for it is the very essence of his art.

No doubt, in this book devoted to the representation of modern depravity and perversity, Baudelaire has placed repugnant pictures, in which vice laid bare wallows in all the hideousness of its shame; but the poet, filled with utter disgust, with indignant contempt, and with a return to the ideal that is often lacking in satirists, stigmatises and brands with a red-hot iron the unhealthy flesh, plastered over with unguents and powder. Nowhere does the thirst for pure, untainted air, for immaculate whiteness, for spotless azure, for inaccessible light manifest itself more ardently than in those poems which have been charged with immorality; as if the flagellation of vice and vice itself were one and the same thing, or a man were a poisoner because he had described the toxic pharmaceutics of the Borgias. (pp. 60-1)

[Baudelaire] more than once dedicated to cats beautiful poems—there are three in **"The Flowers of Evil"**—in which he sings of their moral and physical qualities, and he very often brings them in as characteristic accessories in his compositions. Cats are as numerous in Baudelaire's verse as dogs are in Paolo Veronese's paintings, and are equivalent to a signature. (p. 65)

Diverse female figures show in Baudelaire's poems, some veiled, others semi-nude, but to none can a name be given. They are types rather than persons; they represent the *eternal woman,* and the love the poet expresses for them is *abstract love,* and not *concrete love,* for we have seen that his theory did not admit individual passion, which he looked upon as too crude, familiar, and violent. (pp. 65-7)

At the end of **"The Flowers of Evil"** come a number of poems on "Wine" and the different forms of intoxication it produces, according to the kind of brain on which it acts. It is unnecessary to say that these are not bacchanalian songs in which the fruit of the vine is honoured, or anything resembling them. They are terrible and hideous descriptions of drunkenness, but unprovided with a Hogarthian moral. The painting needs no inscription, and one shudders at **"The Workingman's Drink."** **"The Litanies of Satan,"** the god of evil and the prince of this world, are a cold piece of irony of the kind the poet indulges in, and which it would be a mistake to consider impious. Impiety did not form part of Baudelaire's nature, for he believed in a higher law established by God from all time, the least violation of which is punished in the severest way, not in this world only, but also in the next. (pp. 69-70)

I must draw attention to some of the most remarkable poems in **"The Flowers of Evil,"** especially the one called **"Don Juan in Hades."** It is a tragically grand picture, painted with a sober masterliness of colouring upon the sombre flaming background of the infernal regions. (pp. 70-1)

The serene melancholy, the luminous peace, and the slumbrousness of the poem entitled **"The Former Life,"** form a pleasant contrast to the sombre descriptions of monstrous modern Paris, and testify to the fact that by the side of the blacks, bitumens, browns, umbers, and siennas on the artist's palette, there is a whole range of cool, light, transparent, delicately rosy, ideally blue hues like those in the distances in Paradise

Breughel's pictures, which are fitted to reproduce Elysian landscapes and the mirages of dreams.

The feeling for the *artificial* should be mentioned as characteristic of the poet. By this must be understood a creation due wholly to art and whence nature is excluded. . . . [A striking instance of this curious tendency is] the poem called **"A Parisian Dream."** (pp. 71-2)

Is it not strangely fanciful, this composition made up of rigid elements among which nothing lives, breathes, or moves, in which no blade of grass, no leaf, no flower, breaks the implacable symmetry of fictitious forms invented by art? Does not one seem to be in an untouched Palmyra or Palenque which has remained intact and erect in some dead planet from which the atmosphere has vanished?

Unquestionably such fancies are fantastic, anti-natural, bordering on hallucination, and they betray a secret desire for impossible novelty, but for my part I prefer them to the sickly simplicity of so-called poems that embroider with old faded wools upon the canvas of worn-out commonplaces, trite, trivial, and idiotically sentimental patterns. . . . Barbarism is superior to platitude, to my thinking, and Baudelaire has this advantage, so far as I am concerned: he may be bad, but he is never vulgar; his faults are as original as his qualities, and even when he is unpleasant, it is because he has willed to be so, in accordance with long matured æsthetics and reasoning. (pp. 73-4)

Baudelaire rightly considered that metre, disdained by all who lack feeling for form,—and there are plenty such nowadays,—is most important. (p. 75)

[While] he accepted the chief improvements or reforms introduced by Romanticism, such as richness of rimes, the displacement at will of the cæsura, the running into or encroaching upon the next line, the use of exact or technical terms, the fulness and firmness of rhythm, the casting of the great Alexandrine in one unbroken length, and the whole of that careful mechanism of prosody and cadence in stanzas and strophes, Baudelaire nevertheless exhibits in his verse his own peculiar architectonics, his own individual formulæ, his own easily recognised structure, his own professional secrets, his own knack. . . . (p. 77)

Baudelaire often seeks to produce his musical effects by the use of one or more peculiarly melodious lines that form a refrain, and that reappear in turns, as in the Italian stanza called sextain. . . . He uses this form, which has something of the faint swing of a magical incantation dimly heard in a dream, in subjects of sorrowful remembrances and unfortunate love. The stanzas, with their monotonous soughing, bear the thought away and bring it back, rocking it the while as a flower fallen from the bank is rocked in the regular volutes of the billows. (p. 81)

From the structure of the verse let us pass to the woof and warp of the style. Baudelaire weaves in it threads of silk and gold with strong, rough threads of hemp, as in those stuffs of the East, at once superb and coarse, in which the most delicate ornaments are embroidered in a delightfully fanciful way upon a ground of harsh camel's-hair or coarse cloth, rough to the touch as sail-cloth. The most coquettish refinements, the most subtle, even, are thrown side by side with grim brutalities, and the reader passes suddenly from the boudoir with its heady scents and its voluptuously languorous conversations, to the vile

pot-house where drunkards, mingling blood with their wine, are knifing each other for the sake of a street Helen.

"The Flowers of Evil" are the finest gem in Baudelaire's poetic crown. It is in them that he sounded a note wholly his own, and proved that even after the incalculable number of volumes of verse, which seemed to have exhausted every possible subject, it was still possible to bring to the light something new and unexpected, without necessarily indulging in absurdities or causing the whole procession of universal history to file past as in a German fresco. (pp. 84-5)

Medically speaking, **"The Artificial Paradises"** constitute a very well written monograph of hascheesh, and science might find in it reliable information; for Baudelaire piqued himself on being scrupulously accurate, and not for the world would he have allowed the smallest poetic imagery to slip into a subject that was naturally adapted to it. He specifies quite correctly the peculiar character of hascheesh hallucinations, which does not create anything, but merely develops the particular temperament of the individual while exaggerating it to its highest power. What is seen is one's own self, enlarged, rendered more acutely sensitive, excited beyond all reason, outside the confines of time and space, of which the very notion vanishes, in surroundings that are real to begin with, but which are speedily deformed, intensified, exaggerated, and in which every detail, extreme in its intensity, assumes supernatural importance, that, however, is readily apprehended by the hascheesh eater, who perceives mysterious relations between images often incongruous. (pp. 103-04)

Baudelaire brought out a precious, dainty, and odd side of his talent. He has managed to get closer to the inexpressible, and to render the fleeting shades that hover between sound and colour, and thoughts that resemble motives of arabesques or musical themes.

This form is applied successfully not to physical nature only, but to the most secret motions of the soul, to fanciful melancholy, to the splenetic hallucinations of nervous temperaments. The author of **"The Flowers of Evil"** has drawn marvellous effects from it, and it is surprising at times to find that speech manages to show objects apparently impossible to describe, and hitherto never *reduced* by verbs, now through the transparent gauzy veils of dreams, now with the sudden sharpness of a sunbeam that brings out vividly, in the bluish openings in the distance, a ruined tower, a mountain crest, or a clump of trees. It will be part of Baudelaire's glory, if not his greatest claim to it, to have brought within the possibilities of style numbers of objects, sensations, and effects, unnamed by Adam, the great nomenclator. No writer can wish for higher praise, and he who wrote the **"Short Prose Poems"** [**"Petits poèmes en prose"**] undoubtedly deserves it. (pp. 122-23)

Théophile Gautier, "Charles Baudelaire" (1872), in his The Complete Works of Théophile Gautier, *Vol. XII, edited and translated by F. C. DeSumichrast, Bigelow, Smith & Co., 1903, pp. 17-126.*

[HENRY JAMES] (essay date 1876)

[*James was an American-born English novelist, short story writer, critic, essayist, and playwright of the late nineteenth and early twentieth centuries. Although he is best known as one of the greatest novelists in the English language, he is also admired as a lucid and insightful critic. James calls* The Flowers of Evil *a "sincere book," but finds little else to praise. He considers Bau-*

delaire's interest in Edgar Allan Poe to be the "mark of a de-
cidedly primitive stage of reflection." Instead, James points to
Nathaniel Hawthorne as the model that Baudelaire should have
emulated. While James admits that Baudelaire had extraordinary
facility with language and admires several of his poems, he ul-
timately considers Baudelaire to be the "victim of a grotesque
vision."]

'Les Fleurs du Mal' is evidently a sincere book—so far as
anything for a man of Baudelaire's temper and culture could
be sincere. Sincerity seems to us to belong to a range of qualities with which Baudelaire and his friends were but scantily
conversant. His great quality was an inordinate cultivation of
the sense of the picturesque, and his care was for how things
looked, and whether some kind of imaginative amusement was
not to be got out of them, much more than for what they meant
and whither they led, and what was their use in human life at
large. . . . Baudelaire had a certain groping sense of the moral
complexities of life, and if the best that he succeeds in doing
is to drag them down into the very turbid element in which he
himself plashes and flounders, and there present them to us
much besmirched and bespattered, this was not a want of good-
will in him, but rather a dulness and permanent immaturity of
vision. For American readers, furthermore, Baudelaire is compromised by his having made himself the apostle of our own
Edgar Poe. . . . With all due respect to the very original genius
of the author of the 'Tales of Mystery,' it seems to us that to
take him with more than a certain degree of seriousness is to
lack seriousness one's self. An enthusiasm for Poe is the mark
of a decidedly primitive stage of reflection. Baudelaire thought
him a profound philosopher, the neglect of whose golden utterances stamped his native land with infamy. Nevertheless,
Poe was vastly the greater charlatan of the two, as well as the
greater genius.

'Les Fleurs du Mal' was a very happy title for Baudelaire's
verses, but it is not altogether a just one. Scattered flowers
incontestably do bloom in the quaking swamps of evil, and the
poet who does not mind encountering bad odors in his pursuit
of sweet ones is quite at liberty to go in search of them. But
Baudelaire has, as a general thing, not plucked the flowers—
he has plucked the evil-smelling weeds (we take it that he did
not use the word flowers in a purely ironical sense), and he
has often taken up mere cupfuls of mud and bog-water. He
had said to himself that it was a great shame that the realm of
evil and unclean things should be fenced off from the domain
of poetry; that it was full of subjects, of chances and effects;
that it had its light and shade, its logic and its mystery; and
that there was the making of some capital verses in it. So he
leaped the barrier, and was soon immersed in it up to his neck.
Baudelaire's imagination was of a melancholy and sinister kind,
and, to a considerable extent, this plunging into darkness and
dirt was doubtless very spontaneous and disinterested. But he
strikes us on the whole as passionless, and this, in view of the
unquestionable pluck and acuteness of his fancy, is a great
pity. He knew evil not by experience, not as something within
himself, but by contemplation and curiosity, as something outside of himself, by which his own intellectual agility was not
in the least discomposed, rather, indeed (as we say his fancy
was of a dusky cast), agreeably flattered and stimulated. In the
former case, Baudelaire, with his other gifts, might have been
a great poet. But, as it is, evil for him begins outside and not
inside, and consists primarily of a great deal of lurid landscape
and unclean furniture. . . .

A good way to embrace Baudelaire at a glance is to say that
he was, in his treatment of evil, exactly what Hawthorne was

not—Hawthorne, who felt the thing at its source, deep in the
human consciousness. Baudelaire's infinitely slighter volume
of genius apart, he was a sort of Hawthorne reversed. . . . [In
Baudelaire's] pages we never know with what we are dealing.
We encounter an inextricable confusion of sad emotions and
vile things, and we are at a loss to know whether the subject
pretends to appeal to our conscience or—we were going to
say—to our olfactories. "*Le Mal?*" we exclaim; "you do yourself too much honor. This is not Evil; it is not the wrong; it
is simply the nasty!" Our impatience is of the same order as
that which we should feel if a poet, pretending to pluck "the
flowers of good," should come and present us, as specimens,
a rhapsody on plum-cake and on cologne-water. Independently
of the question of his subjects, the charm of Baudelaire's verse
is often of a very high order. He belongs to the class of geniuses
in whom we ourselves find but a limited pleasure—the laborious, deliberate, economical writers, those who fumble a long
time in their pockets before they bring out their hand with a
coin in the palm. But the coin, when Baudelaire at last produced
it, was often of a high value. He had an extraordinary verbal
instinct and an exquisite felicity of epithet. . . . Baudelaire is
extremely remarkable in his talent for suggesting associations.
His epithets seem to have come out of old cupboards and
pockets; they have a kind of magical mustiness. Moreover, his
natural sense of the superficial picturesqueness of the miserable
and the unclean was extremely acute; there may be a difference
of opinion as to the advantage of possessing such a sense; but
whatever it is worth, Baudelaire had it in a high degree. (p. 280)

Baudelaire repudiated with indignation the charge that he was
what is called a realist, and he was doubtless right in doing
so. He had too much fancy to adhere strictly to the real; he
always embroiders and elaborates and endeavors to impart that
touch of strangeness and mystery which is the very *raison
d'etre* of poetry. Baudelaire was a poet, and for a poet to be
a realist is of course nonsense. The idea which Baudelaire
imported into his theme was, as a general thing, an intensification of its repulsiveness, but it was at any rate ingenious. . . .
Occasionally he treats agreeable subjects, and his least sympathetic critics must make a point of admitting that his most
successful poem is also his most wholesome and most touching:
we allude to **"Les Petites Vieilles"**—a really masterly production. But if it represents the author's maximum, it is a note
which he very rarely struck. (pp. 280-81)

[On the whole, Baudelaire] was the victim of a grotesque illusion. He tried to make fine verses on ignoble subjects, and
in our opinion he signally failed. He gives, as a poet, a perpetual impression of discomfort and pain. He went in search
of corruption, and the ill-conditioned jade proved a thankless
muse. . . . What the poet wished, doubtless, was to seem to
be always in the poetic attitude; what the reader sees is a
gentleman in a painful-looking posture, staring very hard at a
mass of things from which we more intelligently avert our
heads. (p. 281)

> [Henry James], "Charles Baudelaire," *in* The Na-
> tion, *Vol. XXII, No. 565, April 27, 1876, pp. 279-
> 81.*

GEORGE SAINTSBURY (essay date 1878)

[*Saintsbury was an English literary historian and critic of the late
nineteenth and early twentieth centuries. A prolific writer, Saintsbury composed a number of histories of English and European
literature as well as several critical works on individual authors,
styles, and periods. In the following, he praises Baudelaire's*

*critical aptitude and judges him to be more adept as a critic of
literature and music than of painting. Saintsbury maintains that
one must understand Baudelaire's criticism in order to grasp his
poetic concepts. Saintsbury also provides commentary on Baudelaire's prose poems, which he describes as a "tour de force of
the most wonderful kind."*]

The characteristics of Baudelaire's picture-criticism are not
difficult to discover and describe. It is singularly fluent and
pleasant to read, possessing like all his works excellent literary
qualities. . . . Baudelaire not unfrequently reminds us of Diderot, and this is of itself high praise. But it is undeniable that
his peculiar style of criticism shows its faults . . . , more particularly when it is applied to painting. Baudelaire's criticism
is not only intensely, but also narrowly and fragmentarily,
subjective. With its subjectivity there is no fault to find. There
can be nothing better for us, there can be nothing more true
to the truth, than that a critic should simply tell us, in the best
manner he can, the effect produced on his own mind by a given
work of art. But he should at the same time take care to let
his mind contemplate the object fully, so that the copy may
fairly represent with due difference the phenomenon presented
to it. Now Baudelaire is not quite free from the charge of
occasionally, indeed not seldom, letting himself go off at a
tangent, after very slight contact with a very small portion of
the work he has before him. He observes too little and imagines
too much, so that his criticism, though it is perhaps in itself
more interesting than it would be easy to make it compatibly
with faithful representation, is very often far from representing
the complete effect of the subject on his own or any mind. In
other words, to read a criticism of Baudelaire's without the
title affixed, is by no means a sure method of recognising the
picture afterwards. (p. 504)

Baudelaire is far more successful as a critic when he is dealing
with literature and music; arts which aiming at less minuteness
of delineation leave more to the recipient, and are therefore
capable of vaguer and more manifold interpretation. It is natural
that Baudelaire, who is nothing if not literary, should incline
to this style of criticism, and a curious evidence of his unconscious thoroughness therein is his preference, a preference far
more singular a dozen years ago than it is now, for etching.
For it is just in this point that etching differs from kindred arts
of design, that it is far more literary and less pictorial; it aims,
just as poetry does, rather at calling up in the mind of the
beholder an effect similar to something in the mind of the artist,
than at the elaborate representation of the artist's own idea. In
the recognition of an aim of this sort, Baudelaire is unrivalled
among critics; but he does not always escape the imminent
danger of this sort of criticism, the danger of seeing in the
picture or the poem all sorts of things which are not there, and
are not even directly suggested by anything there, but come
by a complicated process of association. . . . It is sufficient
praise to say of Baudelaire that his fault, if it be a fault, is
only the result of excessive critical sensibility, and so is not
far from being a virtue.

He has, moreover, the one merit which is, perhaps more than
any other, the mark of the true critic. He judges much more
by the form than by the matter of the work submitted to his
notice. (pp. 504-05)

It is necessary . . . for the reader who is to understand and
appreciate fully and fairly the *Fleurs du Mal* and the *Petits
Poëmes en Prose,* to bear in mind the idiosyncrasies of the
author as to taste and temperament, and to comprehend fully
the aim and object of the work. This latter is, in few words,
to give poetical expression and currency to the vague joys and
sorrows, the faint and fleeting impressions and beliefs, that
occupy with more or less obstinacy and continuity the modern
cultivated mind. Possessing himself a typical mind of this sort,
open to all influences, able to detect all motives, and to analyse
whatever strange fancy or feeling may present itself, Baudelaire
possesses at the same time a singular faculty of projecting
himself out of the circle of his individual tastes and sentiments,
and of depicting these at once with the impassive accuracy of
an impartial observer, and with the sympathetic accuracy of a
fellow-sufferer. He is further qualified for the task by the possession of a quite extraordinary spirit of precision and concentration. . . . Dealing as he does with a class of subjects in
which vague treatment is particularly tempting, and precise
treatment peculiarly difficult, he is as accurate in the choice
and conduct of his expressions as in the choice and conduct
of his verse. . . . The pieces included [in the section of *Fleurs
du Mal* entitled *Spleen et Idéal*] go far to present a complete
picture of the mind and its wanderings in what may be called
the second romantic stage. The first, of which Byron is the
natural representative and spokesman, contented itself, as was
indeed natural in a child of the eighteenth century, with simple
discontent at the limited capacity of its own stomach. A universe not materially differing from the present save in two
points, greater attainability of sweet victuals and a total absence
of headache and indigestion, would have exactly met the views
of this school. But as La Mettrie produced Diderot, so does
Byron produce Baudelaire. . . . The Romantic of the second
stage suffers from a disorder radically different from the mea-
sles incidental to his predecessor. He has not as a rule any very
glaring outward symptoms. He does not think it necessary to
go to bed at six o'clock A.M., to drink half-a-dozen of claret,
or to wear collars of peculiar cut. . . . He has a kind of general
aspiration towards the infinite, the vague, the impossible, but
he does not go about the streets shouting out these words and
his desire for the things they signify. His heart is not worn on
his sleeve. Sometimes he takes an interest in things political
and religious, and believes in the millennium; but in this case
his disease is not incurable, and he is hardly of the purest
breed. In art, and above all in literature, he finds a certain
solace—a solace which to some natures is all but sufficient.
To science he is indifferent, if not absolutely hostile. Of such
a mind as this the poems entitled *Spleen et Idéal*, miscellaneous
as they may appear at first sight, will be found to present a
tolerably correct diorama. (pp. 507-09)

It is not difficult to appreciate the general features of Baudelaire's poetry. The first thing, perhaps, which strikes a careful
observer is that it is singularly *unfrench*. The characteristics
which one is accustomed to look for in French poetry, even in
that which has been most exposed to the denationalizing influences of the Romantic movement, are almost entirely absent.
The medium of expression is for the first time entirely under
the control of the artist. Even Victor Hugo and Théophile
Gautier, able as they undoubtedly are to say anything, show
more traces of the restraining influence of the language than
does Baudelaire. . . . [His] great peculiarity and excellence is
that he manages to produce almost endless variety of metrical
and rhythmical effect without having recourse to any mechanical aids of complicated metre and rhythm, by far the larger
number of his poems being written in ordinary Alexandrines
or eight-syllabled verses, arranged in simple four-line stanzas.
It is not at all improbable that the superior poetical merit of
his Alexandrines is owing to his never having written for the
stage; but whatever be the cause of the merit it certainly exists,
and his verses stand almost alone in their singular variety of

cadence and consequent flexibility of expression. In many of his poems, notably in **"Une Martyre,"** he has managed to stamp such a character of sombre horror on the verse, that if syllables of similar sound but unknown sense were substituted, the general effect would still be retained. It is undoubtedly in the production of this kind of effect, varied and enhanced by touches of quiet beauty, that he chiefly excels. . . . (pp. 512-14)

[*Petits Poëmes en Prose*] is simply the *ne plus ultra* of word-painting, a *tour de force* of the most wonderful kind, executed in most attractive manner, and with matchless felicity and taste, but still a *tour de force*. What is the province of one art is *ipso facto* not the province of another art, and this Baudelaire's finer literary sense enabled him to perceive. There is accordingly in the *Petits Poëmes en Prose* much less of the merely pictorial, and much more appeal to the intellect and the imagination. He has also rejected the division into staves or fragments. Every one of the *Petits Poëmes* is a strictly proper and legitimate piece of prose, in which no ornament or device of an unusual or unprosaic kind is employed. But it is prose employed to serve a new purpose, the presentation of a definite and complete image, thought, or story in a definite, complete, and above all, brief form. The precise presentation within contracted limits, and the employment of an extraordinarily refined and polished style, are the sole differentiating factors, but the variety and originality which their introduction produces are unmistakable. Such pieces as *Un Hemisphère dans une Chevelure*, and *Les Bienfaits de la Lune* show what prose can do, if not to the utmost extent possible, certainly to the utmost extent known to the present writer. Others, as *La Belle Dorothée* and *L'Invitation au Voyage,* have an additional interest, because we can compare them with the poet's own treatment of the same subjects in verse. But all, with hardly any exception, display the same extraordinary supremacy of composition and the same mastery over language. . . . [There] can be no doubt that the *Petits Poëmes en Prose* are of almost equal merit with [Baudelaire's poetical works] and deserve almost equal attention. (p. 515)

Baudelaire's position in regard to [morals] is so strange that it is impossible to pass it over. The author of a condemned book . . . , he has naturally seemed to virtuous men of letters a perfectly safe figure, when they happen to be in need of a vituperative parallel. But if these virtuous persons, in quest (of course only in the pursuit of knowledge) of inspiring indecency, should happen to invest in a copy of the *Fleurs du Mal,* even with the condemned pieces attached, we are afraid they will meet with a disappointment similar to that which Mr. Charles Reade has described so graphically in [his novel] *It is never too late to mend.* Indeed, on reading the book it is impossible not to understand and sympathize with the poet's astonishment at the prosecution and its result. The pervading tone, from a moral point of view, is simply a profound and incurable discontent with things in general, a discontent which may possibly be unchristian, but which is not yet an indictable offence in any country that I know of. . . . We all know of course that you may write about murder as often as you like, and no one will accuse you of having committed that crime. You may depict an interesting brigand without being considered a thief. Nor in either case will you be thought an inciter to either offence. But so soon as you approach the other deadly sin of luxury in any one of its forms, instantly it appears self-evident that you not only do these things but also take pleasure in those who do them. (p. 516)

[Baudelaire's] work measured by volume is not great. But in that work there is no line of careless or thoughtless execution, no paragraph where taste or principle has been sacrificed for praise or pay, for fear or favour, no page where the humanist and literary ideal is not steadily kept in view and exemplified. Valuable and delightful as he is for private study with no further end, he should be yet more valuable and productive of multiplied delight as a model and a stimulant. (p. 518)

George Saintsbury, "Charles Baudelaire," in The Fortnightly Review *(reprinted by permission of Contemporary Review Company Limited), n.s. Vol. CVI, 1878, pp. 500-18.*

J. K. HUYSMANS   (essay date 1884)

[*Huysmans was a French novelist, critic, essayist, and short story writer. Although he began his writing career as a strict naturalist and ended it as one of the most important Catholic novelists of the nineteenth century, his most influential work is his novel* A rebours (Against Nature), *which became a manifesto of the decadent movement in European literature. The novel, which is excerpted below, describes the exotic tastes of its protagonist Des Esseintes in literature, art, romance, and decor. The high regard of the fictional character for Baudelaire indicates the great extent to which Baudelaire influenced Huysmans. Through* Against Nature, *Huysmans encouraged and renewed French interest in Baudelaire.*]

[Des Esseintes' admiration for Baudelaire] knew no bounds. In his opinion, writers had hitherto confined themselves to exploring the surface of the soul, or such underground passages as were easily accessible and well lit, measuring here and there the deposits of the seven deadly sins, studying the lie of the lodes and their development, recording for instance, as Balzac did, the stratification of a soul possessed by some monomaniacal passion—ambition or avarice, paternal love or senile lust. (p. 146)

Baudelaire had gone further; he had descended to the bottom of the inexhaustible mine, had picked his way along abandoned or unexplored galleries, and had finally reached those districts of the soul where the monstrous vegetations of the sick mind flourish.

There, near the breeding-ground of intellectual aberrations and diseases of the mind—the mystical tetanus, the burning fever of lust, the typhoids and yellow fevers of crime—he had found, hatching in the dismal forcing-house of *ennui*, the frightening climacteric of thoughts and emotions.

He had laid bare the morbid psychology of the mind that has reached the October of its sensations, and had listed the symptoms of souls visited by sorrow, singled out by spleen; he had shown how blight affects the emotions at a time when the enthusiasms and beliefs of youth have drained away, and nothing remains but the barren memory of hardships, tyrannies, and slights, suffered at the behest of a despotic and freakish fate.

He had followed every phase of this lamentable autumn, watching the human creature, skilled in self-torment and adept in self-deception, forcing its thoughts to cheat one another in order to suffer more acutely, and ruining in advance, thanks to its powers of analysis and observation, any chance of happiness it might have.

Then, out of this irritable sensitivity of soul, out of this bitterness of mind that savagely repulses the embarrassing attentions of friendship, the benevolent insults of charity, he witnessed the gradual and horrifying development of those middle-aged passions, those mature love-affairs where one partner goes on blowing hot when the other has already started blowing cold, where lassitude forces the amorous pair to indulge in filial caresses whose apparent juvenility seems something new, and in motherly embraces whose tenderness is not only restful but also gives rise, so to speak, to interesting feelings of remorse about a vague sort of incest.

In a succession of magnificent pages he had exposed these hybrid passions, exacerbated by the impossibility of obtaining complete satisfaction, as well as the dangerous subterfuges of narcotic and toxic drugs, taken in the hope of deadening pain and conquering boredom. In a period when literature attributed man's unhappiness almost exclusively to the misfortunes of unrequited love or the jealousies engendered by adulterous love, he had ignored these childish ailments and sounded instead those deeper, deadlier, longer-lasting wounds that are inflicted by satiety, disillusion, and contempt upon souls tortured by the present, disgusted by the past, terrified and dismayed by the future.

The more Des Esseintes re-read his Baudelaire, the more he appreciated the indescribable charm of this writer who, at a time when verse no longer served any purpose except to depict the external appearance of creatures and things, had succeeded in expressing the inexpressible—thanks to a solid, sinewy style which, more than any other, possessed that remarkable quality, the power to define in curiously healthy terms the most fugitive and ephemeral of the unhealthy conditions of weary spirits and melancholy souls. (p. 146-48)

> *J. K. Huysmans, in a chapter from his novel* Against Nature, *translated by Robert Baldick (copyright © 1959 by the Estate of Robert Baldick; reprinted by permission of Penguin Books Ltd; originally published as* À rebours, *G. Charpentier, 1884), Penguin Books Inc., 1959, pp. 144-65.*

JULES LAFORGUE   (essay date 1887?)

[*A noted French Symbolist poet, short story writer, and critic, Laforgue was among the first commentators to observe Baudelaire's candor and objectivity. In particular, Laforgue notes Baudelaire's distance from the public and his refusal to create poetry for the masses. The date of the essay is unknown; the critic died in 1887.*]

[Baudelaire] was *the first* to relate his experiences in the subdued tones of the confessional and did not assume an inspired air.

He was the first to speak of Paris like any ordinary lost soul of the capital . . . , the street lamps tormented by the wind, "the prostitution which lights up in the streets", the restaurants and their ventilators, the hospitals, gambling, the wood that is sawn into logs which echo on the paving-stones of courtyards, the chimney corner, cats, beds, women's stockings, modern makes of perfume, but all of it in a noble, distant, superior manner. . . .

He is the first who is not triumphant, but accuses himself, reveals his wounds, his laziness, his bored uselessness in the midst of this hardworking, devoted century.

The first who brought into literature the feeling of apathy in pleasure . . . and its bizarre décor . . . *spleen* and sickness (not poetical Consumption but neurasthenia) without once using the word.

He was the first to discover after the daring of the Romantics the crude comparison which casually introduces a note of flatness into the middle of a harmonious period. . . .

He was the first to break with the public.—The poets addressed themselves to the public—human repertoire—but he was the first to say to himself:

> Poetry will be something for the initiated.
> I am damned on account of the public.—
>   Good.—The public is not admitted.

(pp. 36-7)

> *Jules Laforgue, in an extract translated by Martin Turnell, from* Baudelaire: A Study of His Poetry *by Martin Turnell (reprinted by permission of the Literary Estate of Martin Turnell), Hamilton, 1953 (and reprinted by New Directions, 1954), pp. 36-7.*

H. McCULLOCH, JR.   (essay date 1890)

Baudelaire's poetry is always deeply serious and earnest. This of itself is sufficient to place him apart from most French poets, whose language seems to limit them to light, graceful verses on wine and love, and equally graceful, and almost equally light, laments for the inevitable death, and when it is seen how very different he was from his contemporaries, and how little he owed to his predecessors, the importance of his position will be understood.

There was never any one like him, except, in some degree, his master, Poe. He discovered his province in poetry himself; a land never before explored. It is the land of the unusual, of the bizarre. . . . To him virtue is a name only; to Shelley and Victor Hugo it is the great power of the world. In the whole *Fleurs du Mal* there is scarcely a mention of what the world considers virtue.

Artistic virtues there are in plenty, for Baudelaire was an artist before all else. He was no believer in the inspiration of the moment, of the eye in fine phrensy rolling. To him a poem was a work of art like a picture or a statue, and words were the colors on whose arrangement depended the value of the whole. To arrange them rightly the artist must be collected, and least of all should he yield to impulse. (p. 203)

Unlike most makers of maxims, Baudelaire lived up to his. His formula of art was derived from his practice. More than one of his poems remind the reader of that picture of Corot where the landscape's gray tones are lit up and intensified by the bright details of the peasants' costume in the foreground. Not less simple than this are many of the details wherewith he perfects his poems, nor less effective in rendering them artistically perfect. (pp. 203-04)

Chiefly he laid great stress on the climax. He considered that a sonnet, like a drama, should constantly increase in intensity and interest, until a skilfully wrought and impressive line should mark the culmination; that the author should never write the first line until he had composed the last. Here again, he is obedient to his own rule. Some of his poems begin in a manner commonplace enough; a sunrise, or reflections at the grave of a dead mistress. Gradually the interest increases; we leave the commonplace behind. Then comes the final phrase; the purpose for which the poem was written. There is *never* an anti-climax.

When poetry is written in this way, it is easy to see that the finding of a subject is by no means the hardest part. When a subject has been found, even when it has been developed, only the first step has been taken. The author has the skeleton; he has next to clothe it in flesh. He has to translate his thought into words, choosing carefully the best possible ones. The choice of words is difficult enough, even in a commonplace poem, or one in which the idea is everything. In poems like Baudelaire's, where the best words express the thought imperfectly, where the whole structure is strange and unearthlike, and where the effect depends almost entirely on the sound of a word or the turning of a phrase, it is of consummate difficulty. Yet Baudelaire's art is rarely deficient. There is scarcely a false note in the whole of the *Fleurs du Mal*. (p. 204)

One of the first things that strikes a reader of Baudelaire is his fondness for an almost grotesque use of definite images. One would think that a painter of the vague would delineate shadowy forms; that he would express vagueness by vague metaphors. But Baudelaire does not employ this means. Take, for instance, *L'Aube Spirituelle*—the breaking of day upon a room full of revellers still sleeping from the effects of their night's debauch. Amongst these, when the pale dawn has broken in, an angel awakes out of the stupified *débauchées*. The sun has quenched the light of the candles; so the flesh is overcome by the spirit. There is so little difference between the spiritual man and the brutal man. . . . [Even] in the room reeking with the fumes of debauch, the heavens open. All this is mystical enough; yet with all the spiritual and mystical thought, there is no vagueness of outline. (pp. 205-06)

[In] one of his most powerful poems, *Don Juan aux Enfers,* he takes us down to Hell. Like Dante's, Baudelaire's Demons are clothed in flesh. Here there are no long, mysterious reaches, no inaccessible cliffs and unfathomable gulfs like those Doré imagined. . . . There are no devils with pitchforks or red-hot tongs; none of the horrors that fail to terrify the men of our time, but which could frighten our fathers. Here are only earthly things, made terrible by their new surroundings. (p. 206)

Any one will admit, I think, that this is impressive poetry. And it is more impressive, it seems to me, from the very absence of the symbols of damnation—the fire and flames, the brimstone and the bottomless pit. Even more impressive from the absence of the great gates whose harsh clangor filled Hell with dread. The conventional Hell has become a jest; but this place of baffled passions which Baudelaire gives us is too terrible to play with. For here men are not purged of their passions but scourged by them. (p. 207)

[In *Femmes Damnées*], Baudelaire takes us to the throne of Satan. But it is a Satan of his own, differing from the conventional Devil of the schools, and from Goethe's Mephistopheles, the mocker. He is pity, while God is stern justice. No one is too abandoned, too altogether lost for his sympathy. He relieves and succors those whom God has cast off. To this being, great with the attributes of love and pity, Baudelaire wrote *Les Litanies de Satan*. As he had transferred to him many of the qualities ascribed by the schools to the Creator, so he borrowed the form consecrated by the mediaeval church to the Mother of God. He preserves the form and the spirit of devotion and humility. (p. 208)

The ruling power of [Baudelaire's] life was a great ennui. . . . It was this ennui which incited his most terrible poems, and which forced him to describe obscure forms of vice for which he had no liking. Satiated in his youth with conventionality,

in his manhood he took a perverse pleasure in dwelling on the other side—took pleasure in it, if one can enjoy gazing on an object which inspires intense horror. It was rather a fascination that vice had for him; he was forced to dwell upon it when he loathed it the most. He writes of the loathsomeness of vice, not of the raptures; he has an infinite pity for its votaries. He is rather the surgeon who dissects than the subject. He writes of debauch, but not of its madness. It is rather the spiritual sun breaking in upon a party of revellers, or naked souls gaming away their eternity.

Baudelaire had his milder side, too, which is faithfully reflected in the *Fleurs du Mal*. He was a lover as well as a hater, and rebelled as fiercely against the conventions of love, as against the other conventions of life. He was an admirer of the delicate, fragile, somewhat artificial beauty of the *mondaine* [everyday] rather than of the healthy rustic beauty which most poets have dwelt on much. His love poems are as bizarre and original as the rest of his work. There is nothing in them of the conventional reproaches for past or present cruelty; indeed the love is usually taken for granted. (pp. 208-09)

Most of his love poetry is pervaded by the peculiar conceptions that are characteristic of his other poems; conceptions that in any other would be affectations, but which are part of the man. His love, like all of his emotions, lives in a land of its own, undiscovered of men. (p. 209)

As the years go on he will probably be read less and less. Yet he is an interesting man, and exerted not a little influence on the poets of his time. . . . He was not like other men, yet he sympathized with them. He was a worshipper of the grotesque, a slave of the perverse. (p. 210)

> *H. McCulloch, Jr., "The Poetry of Baudelaire," in*
> The Harvard Monthly, *Vol. IX, No. 5, February,*
> *1890, pp. 203-10.*

JEAN CARRÈRE (essay date 1904?)

I have always loved Baudelaire. Even now, when I propose to dissect his work and analyse the unwholesome perfumes which rise from his "sickly flowers," I find, for the hundredth or the thousandth time, an unutterable pleasure in plunging into the warm, enfolding atmosphere of his genius. There have been, and will again be, perhaps, certainly more bracing and more uplifting poets; but there was never one who was more captivating, more sincere, and more profound. If you read him once, you can never forget him. His verses grip a man's memory as if with iron claws which cauterise and tear, and leave red scars for ever. In the energy, the conciseness, and the sober splendour of his style he is the most classical of all the poets of the nineteenth century. In boldness of metaphor, the startling character of his figures, the boldness of his ellipses, and the sprightliness of his lyrics, he is the greatest innovator amongst the romanticists. From the literary point of view he is complete. . . . (p. 139)

He remains, with Flaubert, a severe lesson in literary conscientiousness, and his example teaches us that the first duty of a true poet is to devote his whole life and work to the glorification of the language he has inherited; and that to sustain and augment the prestige of that language is the best means of showing oneself piously loyal to the race from which one has sprung.

Yet the magician in the art of style and the science of the heart, this great writer, is, in spite of all, a "bad master" [*mauvais maitre*]. Possibly no other has had a more disturbing, more saddening, more discouraging influence on the generations that followed him. (p. 141)

Baudelaire was not immoral, as his short-sighted critics said; but he was demoralising, which is quite a different thing. He was a dissipator of energy. In his own person first, then in others, he broke the mainspring of action and strength.

His evil was, *the fear of action*. This he hides from himself under the pleasant title, *the love of dreaming*. But they are merely two different expressions for the same weakness, and that is *cowardice in face of life*. (p. 142)

The coward's dream—that is what Baudelaire enjoyed, what he expressed in all its forms. His despair, his misanthropy, his revolts, his troubles, his terrors, his love of non-existence, are only so many developments of this initial weakness—the fear of life. With all his gifts as a humanist and all his marvellous gifts as a poet he had also, to the degree of genius, the state of soul of the vagabond who wanders off to sleep in the fields, shunning the lodging and the workshop, and at night soaks in the public-house. He refused manly action. All the rest is the penalty for this.

We may take the whole of his work, the *Flowers of Evil* as well as the *Poems in Prose,* and we shall see that, line by line, word by word, we may reduce everything to these sentiments:

1. Fear and disgust of life, boredom, dislike and contempt of men.

2. Refuge in the dream, in travel, and in the night.

3. Refuge in pleasure, debauch, and artificial paradises.

4. Regret for the loss of healthy life, action, and time.

5. Remorse and anguish.

6. Refuge in death, desire for non-existence, appeal to an unknown life.

And all these succeed each other as logically as the successive leaps of a waterfall in a gorge. (p. 144)

The love of travelling which Baudelaire, like all slaves of the dream, had in a passionate degree, is merely one way of fleeing from life. Travel is a dream materialising in constantly renewed forms.

In the *Poems in Prose* there is a page that expresses with penetrating emotion the sentiment felt by all who have known the joy of being cradled in the voluptuousness of the waves during a long voyage, so that one's heart tastes the delight of an infinite dream:

> Like some priest from whom his divinity has been stolen, I could not, without heart-rending bitterness, tear myself away from this monstrously seductive sea. . . .
>
> In saying farewell to this incomparable beauty I was stricken to death; and that is why, when my companions cried "At last!" I could only exclaim "Already!"

The whole fear of life weeps in that simple "Already"; the whole love of dreams breathes in it. (p. 146)

[What] need is there for us to wander through the whole of Baudelaire's works? One single poem is enough. It contains all the others. It is synthetic; as formidable as some mirror in

which the rays of a black sun are focussed. It is called *The Voyage,* and is a masterpiece of beauty. Read that attentively, for it closes and sums up the *Flowers of Evil.* Passing from verse to verse, you go through all the mazes of impotence and dizziness of brain, until you reach the sonorous and magnificent appeal at the end:

> O death, old Captain, it is time, put forth!
> We have grown weary of the gloomy north.
>
> (p. 151)

Can you tell me any way in which we can defend ourselves against the magic of Baudelaire's poems? Endowed, as he was, to produce the finest verse, such a poet could, if he had so willed, have borne us into the world of heroes. What can he not do, then, when he drags us with him to the facile instincts of the Dream and Inaction? He finds too many echoes in the obscure depths of our being for us to fail to respond to him; his voice, moreover, is irresistible. Immense, therefore, is the evil for which he is responsible! Baudelaire was, like Musset, a propagator of moral cowardice. It is to those two that whole generations owe it that they were not able to live, or that they lingered too long in the non-existence of revery. (pp. 152-53)

In spite of their difference in temperament and genius, Musset and Baudelaire did the same unhealthy work, for both, unfortunately, were tainted with the same inability to act. Both sought refuge in dreaming and all the horrors which follow upon it. . . . [From] both one learned easily that there was a high distinction in shunning life. (p. 153)

That is why, while we may love these harmonious and seductive poets, we cannot too carefully guard ourselves against the disturbing influence of their genius. . . . *Flowers of Evil,* terrible mandragoras, magical and funereal flowers that spring up in the malediction of the dark, who will come with breath strong enough to blow away for ever the perfume of your poisoned corollas? Who will bring out toward new mornings the lovely and sane flowers of light, the victorious lilies and triumphant roses, whose happy colours will, on the festivals of the soul, be the bright flags of works of strength and joy that are yet to come? (pp. 154-55)

> *Jean Carrère, "Charles Baudelaire" (1904?) in his* Degeneration in the Great French Masters: Rousseau—Chateaubriand—Balzac—Stendhal—Sand—Musset—Baudelaire—Flaubert—Verlaine—Zola, *translated by Joseph McCabe (originally published as* Les mauvais maîtres: Rousseau—Chateaubriand—Balzac—Stendhal—Sand—Musset—Baudelaire—Flaubert—Verlaine—Zola, Plon, 1922), T. Fisher Unwin, Limited, 1922, pp. 139-54.*

ALBERT LEON GUÉRARD   (essay date 1913)

[*A French-born American critic, Guérard calls Baudelaire "the best-known exponent of depraved Catholicism" and maintains that Baudelaire "found satisfaction in the more sombre aspects of its mysticism and theology." He questions Baudelaire's sincerity, and disputes the common assumption that* The Flowers of Evil *is a confession of Baudelaire's own life. Guérard states that, on the contrary, Baudelaire's verse was "the mirror of his own dreams."*]

It is difficult to determine the limits of Baudelaire's sincerity. *The Flowers of Evil* is not a straight confession—that much is certain. There is a Baudelaire legend—that of an eccentric, half-crazy personage, subtly corrupt, addicted to poisonous drugs and monstrous vices. The poet resented this opprobrious legend; but, impelled by his inner demon of perverse mystification, he could not help encouraging its growth. It had some slight foundation in fact: not enough to give *The Flowers of Evil* the value of a clinical document. It is not a scientific study either. This was Baudelaire's specious plea when the book was prosecuted. But the very title is antiscientific: it implies a double judgment, one of moral reproof, the other of esthetic admiration. His daily life was not pictured in his verse; his whole soul was not in his work, but his imagination at least was there. His poetry was the mirror of his dreams.

Now, to Baudelaire, the dream-life meant more than to many of his healthier, happier contemporaries. Cramped in his material circumstances, isolated in his pride, "yawning his life" . . . , he sought a refuge in "the ideal," as he chose to call it, and when he came into contact with reality, he used it only as a stuff to make dreams of. Thus it became impossible to disentangle his fancies from his true self. They were unreal, and yet the only reality he cared for. His poems were a pageant which he gave to charm the ennui and solitude of his soul, and the pageant became his very soul. (pp. 37-8)

That dream-life of his was coloured by his own sad experience and by his intense desire for originality. Heredity, failure, disease, had made him morbid; the influence of low Romanticism fixed vague tendencies into a permanent, semi-conscious attitude; pride sought for this attitude a philosophical sanction. The beauty of sanity and harmony came to strike him as offensively vulgar. Goodness and truth were good and true enough for the "modern rabble" he so thoroughly despised. All religions of healthy-mindedness, optimism, progress, nature, were hateful to [Baudelaire]. Catholicism was at hand to provide him with a doctrine. As a man, as an artist, as a thinker, he found satisfaction in the more sombre aspects of its mysticism and theology. The doctrine of total depravity, the corruptedness of the flesh, the constant presence of the enemy, the haunting fear of death and of eternal punishment—he needed such notions as these for imparting to his fancies the *haut-goût* [stronger taste] he was craving for. At the same time, their spirituality gave them distinction, kept them far above the brutal pessimism of materialists like Taine. Theological and ecclesiastical terms and images are constantly found in his poetry: angels and demons, sin, hell, damnation, sacraments, priests, monks, bells, cathedrals, incense, ex-voto. This is not a mere literary trick, but the expression of his habitual train of thought. (pp. 38-9)

But the Catholic poet remained, first of all, a seeker after sensations and a sentimentalist. He was not satisfied with the mere description of sin and its horrors; he must needs taste and analyse the enjoyableness, the fascination of that very horror, the *flower of evil*. . . .

The three pieces [from *The Flowers of Evil*] entitled *Révolte* are not in harmony with the true Baudelairian spirit. They proceed from the assumption that Satan and Cain were "wronged," that there is, as Vigny said, a great historical case to be judged anew before the court of our conscience. Such a view is an unnatural, inverted form of moralism, a paradoxical but genuine craving for justice and truth; it may be depraved, it is not perverse. Baudelaire affirmed that these three pieces were mere pastiches; and it seems safe to accept his word for it. (p. 39)

Baudelaire's imagination was one-sided and wholly diseased. He never woke to normal life again, as Goethe did after *Werther*.

Yet there are in his poetry notes which seem to herald the dawn: all too few, but all the more precious. Such are:—

> Through the operation of some avenging mystery
> In the slumbering brute an angel awakens

and the closing lines of *Le Voyage à Cythère:*—

> Ah, Lord! give me the force and the courage
> To contemplate my heart and my body without disgust.

In these outbursts of remorse, Baudelaire rivals Verlaine at his best. . . .

[*The Flowers of Evil*] is a remarkable feat of poetic skill; it has psychological merit and even some moral interest; but it does not ring true as religious literature. Its intermittent sincerity is smothered by downright affectation, sensationalism, and sentimentalism; in its mixture of mysticism and sensuality, the latter is evidently the predominant element. A faith used for adding spice to lustful pleasure must be of a very equivocal character. Catholicism was for Baudelaire a good working hypothesis; had Pantheism inspired him with more enjoyable dreams, he would have adopted it with the same degree of semi-sincerity. (p. 40)

Baudelaire is the best known exponent of depraved Catholicism. He was neither a great thinker nor a supreme artist. . . . But Baudelaire never left his own narrow field, and he showed in it a rare power of poetic concentration. (p. 41)

> Albert Leon Guérard, "Catholicism," in his French Prophets of Yesterday: A Study of Religious Thought Under the Second Empire (*reprinted by permission of the Literary Estate of Albert Leon Guérard*), D. Appleton and Company, 1913, pp. 25-69.*

MARCEL PROUST (essay date 1919?)

[*A French novelist and critic, Proust is best known for his multi-volume novel,* À la recherche du temps perdu (Remembrance of Things Past), *which is considered one of literature's greatest achievements. Proust's most important early work is to be found in the critical writings of* Contre Sainte-Beuve (By Way of Sainte-Beuve), *where he puts forth his personal view of literature in opposition to the doctrines of the noted critic Charles Sainte-Beuve. While Sainte-Beuve failed to make a distinction between the author's life and his work, Proust contended that a work of literature offers a perspective unique to itself. The following essay, which is drawn from* By Way of Sainte-Beuve, *discusses Sainte-Beuve's failure to review much of Baudelaire's work in his weekly columns, an act which hindered Baudelaire's career. Proust's enthusiastic championing of Baudelaire is thought by many to be an effort to compensate for Sainte-Beuve's neglect.*]

[Baudelaire] is merciless in his poetry, merciless with the utmost sensibility, his ruthlessness the more startling since one feels that he had had felt to his nerves' ends the sufferings he makes a mock of and describes with such composure. To be sure, in such a poem as the magnificent *Les Petites Vieilles* no item of the old women's sufferings escapes him. It is not only their vast unhappiness:

> Those eyes are well-heads which thousands of tears
>   have brimmed. . . .
> Each of them could have made a river with her tears;

he lives in their bodies, winces with their nerves, quakes with their trembling limbs. . . . Yet for all the beauty of statement and characterisation in [his] picture, he does not recoil before any cruel detail. . . . (p. 129)

[To] love Baudelaire, to love him, I mean, to the point of infatuation, in [his] most piteous and human poems, is not necessarily a token of great sensibility. The picture he draws of those sights which I am convinced really pained him is so powerful, and yet so divorced from any expression of feeling, that purely ironic and sensation-hunting minds, truly hard hearts, can take pleasure in it. The line about the old women:

> Rubble of humankind, ripe for eternity,

is a noble line, and dear to the high-minded and the generous-hearted. But how often have I not heard it quoted, and with full appreciation, by a woman who was extremely intelligent, but of all the women I've met the stoniest-hearted, the most devoid of kindness or conscience, and who, adding it to her repertory of jests and gibes, amused herself by letting fly with it, after the exit of this or that old woman whom she loathed, as a prophecy of impending death. To feel every variety of pain, but to have such mastery over oneself that one can watch it undistressed, to be able to bear the pain that an impulse of malice has artificially provoked (when one quotes it, one overlooks the cruelty of that lovely line:

> The fiddle trembling, like a heart that one gives
>   pain to. . . .

Oh, that quivering of a heart one has given pain to!—a minute ago, it was only the nerves of old women, quivering at the rolling din of omnibuses); perhaps this subordination of sensibility to truth and statement is ultimately a sign of genius, of the force of art overcoming a personal compassion. But there are stranger things than this in Baudelaire. When he is giving the noblest possible expression to certain feelings, he seems to be describing them from outside and without being involved in them. (pp. 130-31)

He understands the nature of [the virtues he describes], yes, indeed, but he seems to banish their spirit from his poetry. There is the whole fervour of piety in these lines from the *Petites Vieilles:*

> All these thrill me. But yet among these heirs of dust
> Some there are who, sucking a nectar out of woe,
> Have said to Piety, laying hold on her wings:
> "O soaring Griffin, bear my soul up to the skies!"

It is as though he were employing this extraordinary and unprecedented power of language (a hundred times more powerful than Hugo's, for all that people may say), in order to state for all time a feeling that he tries not to feel at the time he speaks of it, and which he paints rather than expresses. He finds these unmatched phrases for all the pains, for all the balms—phrases torn up by the roots from his own heaven and hell and unfindable in any other man's, phrases from a planet which he alone has lived in and which is like nothing we know of. Over every type of humankind he puts one of these great phrases, all warm and supple, full of scent and sap, one of these bags that could hold a bottle of wine, or a ham; but though he says it with lips that can speak like thunder, one would say he is trying to speak from the lips outward, though at the same time one feels he has experienced it all, understood it all, and has the most quivering sensibility and the profoundest comprehension. (pp. 132-33)

[Among Baudelaire's poetic idioms], invented by him and enveloping the bare facts he catalogues with their warm, multi-coloured great phrases, a certain number are really idioms bearing on the classic idea of *patria.*

> One by her country long-schooled in adversity. . . .

> Some glad of heart to flee an infamous country. . . .

> The poor man's purse, and the dear land of his
>   fathers. . . .

like the splendid idioms on the idea of the Family: *Others, the horror of their childhood*—which quickly take their place in the category of biblical idiom, and all those figures of speech which make up the force and vehemence of a poem like **Bénédiction,** where everything is on a larger scale because of that solemn diction:

> In the meat and in the drink they set before him
> They have intermingled ashes and gobs of spit. . . .

[This] poem contains some of those beautiful images from the Catholic liturgy which are wings to . . . [Baudelaire]:

> Of Thrones and Virtues and of Principalities. . . .

> I know that sorrow is the classic dignity
> Of man which neither earth nor Hades can corrode,
> And that if I would wear the crown laid up for me
> I must weave in all time and every universe.

(Not an ironical image of suffering, this, like those I quoted about charity, and Christian piety, but still very impassive, and owing its beauty mainly to idiom and allusions to mediaeval religious art, more pictorial than emotional.) . . . I think I could begin to conjure up for you, phrase by phrase, this world of Baudelaire's mind, this country of his genius, of which each poem is only a part and which as soon as we read it rejoins other parts we know already. . . . But for this, I would have to give you all the harbours, not only *a harbour thronged with sails and masts,* and those

> Where ships swimming in gold and watered silk, hold out
> Their vast arms to embrace the splendour of a clear
> Sky and the quiver of interminable heat,

but those which are only doorways

> That the sea-faring suns have fired with countless hues,

and *the doorway opening upon unknown skies,* and the African palm-trees, pale as ghosts. . . . (pp. 133-36)

[How] can one count up all these phrases, when there is nothing he spoke of (and he spoke with the whole span of the soul) that he did not present by a symbol, and that symbol always so concrete, so striking, so living, and in the strongest, most usual, most dignified language? . . . [All] his women, and his springtimes with their scents, and his mornings with the dust blown from the garbage-tins, and his towns tunnelled like ant-hills, and his "voices" that promise worlds, those that speak out of book-shelves, those that call the ships after them, those that say the earth is a sweet-flavoured cake, those that say:

> here are for the plucking
> Hesperidean fruits that your heart hungers for.

And all the true, modern, poetic colours, it was he, remember, who discovered them—unobtrusive, delicious, his pinks above all, with blue, or gold, or green:

> You are an autumn sky, clear and pink and lovely. . . .

> And balconied twilights, with the pink mists rising,

and all the evenings that have a rosy sky. (pp. 137-38)

[Within] this world there is another, even more secluded, the world of scents; but that, we should never come to the end of; and if we should take no matter which poem of his (I don't mean his great major poems that you love as much as I do, *Le Balcon, Le Voyage,* but the lesser ones), you would be astounded to see at every third or fourth line a famous line, not wholly Baudelairean, so that (compared with lines that are perhaps more typically and supremely his) you would not know where it came from:

Rich caskets without gems, lockets that hold no tress,

a parent line, it would seem, being so universal and so new, of thousands of other kindred lines, though no one else has done them so well; and lines in every manner, lines like:

And the wide skies that bring eternity to mind,

which you might think was Hugo's, like:

And your compelling eyes, such as a portrait has,

which you might think was Gautier's, like:

O thou I should have loved, O thou aware of it. . . .

It is very interesting in the Baudelaire poems with those great lines, that his inspiration, swept on through the turning-point after the previous hemistich, is preparing itself in mid-career to replenish them for the whole length of their enormous course, and that this gives one the utmost impression of the wealth and eloquence and boundlessness of a genius:

Whose aspect would have loosed a flow, a flood of alms,

(into)

But for the spitefulness which glittered in their eyes.

that little river
Scant, sorry looking-glass, wherein aforetime blazed

(into)

The pomp and stature of your grieving widowhood,

and scores of other examples. (pp. 138-40)

> *Marcel Proust, "Sainte-Beuve and Baudelaire" (1919?), in his* Marcel Proust on Art and Literature 1896-1919, *translated by Sylvia Townsend Warner (© 1958 by Meridian Books, Inc.; reprinted by permission of Georges Borchardt, Inc., as agents for the author; in Canada by the translator's Literary Estate and Chatto & Windus; originally published as* Contre Sainte-Beuve, *Librairie Gallimard, 1954), Meridian Books, 1958, pp. 120-43 [published in England as his* By Way of Sainte-Beuve (Contre Sainte-Beuve), *translated by Sylvia Townsend Warner, Chatto & Windus, 1958].**

ARTHUR SYMONS (essay date 1920)

[*An English critic, poet, dramatist, short story writer, and editor, Symons initially gained notoriety as an English decadent in the 1890s, and eventually established himself as one of the most important critics of the modern era. His sensitive translations of Paul Verlaine and Stéphane Mallarmé offered English poets an introduction to the poetry of the French Symbolists. Though he was a gifted translator and linguist, it was as a critic that Symons made his most important contribution to literature. Symons's* Charles Baudelaire: A Study, *from which the following is drawn, is the first full-length study in English devoted to Baudelaire. Symons terms* The Flowers of Evil *the "most curious, subtle, fascinating, and extraordinary creation of an entire world ever fashioned in modern ages." While Symons sees in Baudelaire's despair a satanic vision, he ultimately finds Baudelaire to be more mystical, visionary, and confessional than satanic. Symons considers Bau-*

delaire the first writer to bring "into modern literature the chagrin that bites at our existence like serpents."]

Baudelaire's genius is satanical; he has in a sense the vision of Satan. He sees in the past the lusts of the Borgias, the sins and vices of the Renaissance; the rare virtues that flourish like flowers and weeds, in brothels and in garrets. He sees the vanity of the world with finer modern tastes than Solomon; for his imagination is abnormal, and divinely normal. In this age of infamous shames he has no shame. His flesh endures, his intellect is flawless. He chooses his own pleasures delicately, sensitively, as he gathers his exotic *Fleurs du Mal,* in itself a world, neither a *Divina Commedia* nor *Une Comédie Humaine,* but a world of his own fashioning.

His vividly imaginative passion, with his instincts of inspiration, are aided by a determined will, a self-reserve, an intensity of conception, an implacable insolence, an accurate sense of the exact value of every word. In the Biblical sense he might have said of his own verse: "It is bone of my bone, and flesh of my flesh." The work, as the man, is subtle, strange, complex, morbid, enigmatical, refined, paradoxical, spiritual, animal. (p. 29)

Fascinated by sin, he is never the dupe of his emotions; he sees sin as the Original Sin; he studies sin as he studies evil, with a stern logic; he finds in horror a kind of attractiveness, as Poe had found it; rarely in hideous things, save when his sense of what I call a moralist makes him moralize, as in his terrible poem, *Une Charogne.* He has pity for misery, hate for progress. He is analytic, he is a learned casuist. . . .

His soul swims on music played on no human instrument, but on strings that the Devil pulls, to which certain living puppets dance in grotesque fashion, to unheard-of rhythms, to the sound of violins strummed on by evil spirits in Witches' Sabbats. Some swing in the air, as hanged dead people on gallows, and, as their bones rattle in the wind, one sees Judas Iscariot, risen out of Hell for an instant's gratification, as he grimaces on these grimacing visages.

Les Fleurs du Mal is the most curious, subtle, fascinating, and extraordinary creation of an entire world ever fashioned in modern ages. Baudelaire paints vice and degradation of the utmost depth, with cynicism and with pity, as in [*Une Charogne*], where the cult of the corpse is the sensuality of ascetism, or the ascetism of sensuality: the mania of fakirs; material by passion, Christian by perversity. (p. 31)

Les Fleurs du Mal are grown in Parisian soil, exotics that have the strange, secretive, haunting touch and taint of the earth's or of the body's corruption. In his sense of beauty there is a certain revolt, a spiritual malady, which may bring with it the heated air of an alcove or the intoxicating atmosphere of the East. Never since Villon has the flesh of woman been more adored and abhorred. (pp. 32-3)

Certain of these Flowers of Evil are poisonous; some are grown in the hotbeds of Hell; some have the perfume of a serpentine girl's skin; some the odour of woman's flesh. Certain spirits are intoxicated by these accursed flowers, to save themselves from the too much horror of their vices, from the worse torture of their violated virtues. And a cruel imagination has fashioned these naked images of the Seven Deadly Sins, eternally regretful of their first fall; that smile not even in Hell, in whose flames they writhe. One conceives them there and between the sun and the earth; in the air, carried by the winds; aware of their infernal inheritance. They surge like demons out of the Middle Ages; they are incapable of imagining God's justice.

Baudelaire dramatizes these living images of his spirit and of his imagination, these fabulous creatures of his inspiration, these macabre ghosts, in a fashion utterly different from that of other tragedians—Shakespeare, and Aristophanes in his satirical Tragedies, his lyrical Comedies; yet in the same sense of being the writer where beauty marries unvirginally the sons of ancient Chaos.

In these pages swarm (in his words) all the corruptions and all the scepticisms; ignoble criminals without convictions, detestable hags that gamble, the cats that are like men's mistresses; Harpagon; the exquisite, barbarous, divine, implacable, mysterious Madonna of the Spanish style; the old men; the drunkards, the assassins, the lovers (their deaths and lives); the owls; the vampires whose kisses raise from the grave the corpse of its own self; the Irremediable that assails its origin: Conscience in Evil! There is an almost Christ-like poem on his Passion, *Le Reniement de Saint-Pierre,* an almost Satanic denunciation of God in *Abel and Cain,* and with them the Evil Monk, an enigmatical symbol of Baudelaire's soul, of his work, of all that his eyes love and hate. Certain of these creatures play in travesties, dance in ballets. For all the Arts are transformed, transfigured, transplanted out of their natural forms to pass in magnificent state across the stage: the stage with the abyss of Hell in front of it. (pp. 34-5)

It is Baudelaire who, in Hell as in earth, finds a certain Satan in such modern hearts as his; that even modern art has an essentially demoniacal tendency; that the infernal pact of man increases daily, as if the Devil whispered in his ear certain sardonic secrets. (pp. 35-6)

Yet, tainted as the style is from time to time, never was the man himself tainted: he who in modern verse gave first of all an unknown taste to sensations; he who painted vice in all its shame; whose most savorous verses are perfumed as with subtle aromas; whose women are bestial, rouged, sterile, bodies without souls; whose *Litanies de Satan* have that cold irony which he alone possessed in its extremity, in these so-called impious lines which reveal, under whatever disguise, his belief in a mathematical superiority established by God from all eternity, and whose least infraction is punished by certain chastisements, in this world as in the next. (pp. 36-7)

Has Baudelaire *l'amour du mal pour le mal* [an evil love of evil]? In a certain sense, yes; in a certain sense, no. He believes in evil as in Satan and God—the primitive forces that govern worlds: the eternal enemies. He sees the germs of evil everywhere, few of the seeds of virtue. He sees pass before him the world's drama: he is one of the actors, he plays his parts cynically, ironically. He speaks in rhythmic cadences.

But, above all, he watches the dancers; these also are elemental; and the tragic fact is that the dancers dance for their living. For their living, for their pleasure, for the pleasure of pleasing others. So passes the fantastic part of their existence, from the savage who dances silent dances—for, indeed, all dancers are silent—but without music, to the dancer who dances for us on the stage, who turns always to the sound of music. There is an equal magic in the dance and in song; both have their varied rhythms; both, to use an image, the rhythmic beating of our hearts. (pp. 37-8)

The greatest French poet after Villon, the most disreputable and the most creative poet in French literature, the greatest

artist in French verse, and, after Verlaine, the most passionate, perverse, lyrical, visionary, and intoxicating of modern poets, comes Baudelaire, infinitely more perverse, morbid, exotic than these other poets. In his verse there is a deliberate science of sensual perversity, which has something almost monachal in its accentuation of vice with horror, in its passionate devotion to passions. Baudelaire brings every complication of taste, the exasperation of perfumes, the irritant of cruelty, the very odours and colours of corruption to the creation and adornment of a sort of religion, in which an eternal mass is served before a veiled altar. There is no confession, no absolution, not a prayer is permitted which is not set down in the ritual. (p. 38)

There is something Oriental in Baudelaire's genius; a nostalgia that never left him after he had seen the East: there where one finds hot midnights, feverish days, strange sensations; for only the East, when one has lived in it, can excite one's vision to a point of ardent ecstasy. He is the first modern poet who gave to a calculated scheme of versification a kind of secret and sacred joy. He is before all things the artist, always sure of his form. And his rarefied imagination aided him enormously not only in the perfecting of his verse and prose, but in making him create the criticism of modern art.

Next after Villon, Baudelaire is the poet of Paris. Like a damned soul (to use one of his imaginary images) he wanders at nights. . . . [A] kind of intense curiosity, of excitement, in his frequentation of [Parisian] streets, comes over him, like one who has taken opium. . . . (pp. 39-40)

He is the first who ever related things in the modulated tone of the confessional and never assumed an inspired air. The first also who brings into modern literature the chagrin that bites at our existence like serpents. He admits to his diabolical taste, not quite exceptional in him; one finds it in Petronius, Rabelais, Balzac. In spite of his magnificent *Litanies de Satan,* he is no more of the satanical school than Byron. Yet both have the same sardonic irony, the delight of mystification, of deliberately irritating solemn people's convictions. Both, who died tragically young, had their hours of sadness, when one doubts and denies everything; passionately regretting youth, turning away, in sinister moods, in solitude, from that too intense self-knowledge that, like a mirror, shows the wrinkles on our cheeks. (p. 40)

Arthur Symons, in his Charles Baudelaire: A Study *(reprinted by permission of George Allen & Unwin (Publishers) Ltd), Elkin Mathews, 1920, 116 p.*

BENEDETTO CROCE   (essay date 1923)

[*Croce was an Italian philosopher, historian, editor, and literary critic whose writings span the first half of the twentieth century. According to Croce, the only proper form of literary history is the* caratteristica, *or critical characterization, of the poetic personality and work of a single artist; its goal is to demonstrate the unity of the author's intention, its expression in the creative work, and the reader's response. Croce maintains that, unlike many nineteenth-century artists and philosophers, Baudelaire believed in the concept of original sin and thought that both nature and romantic love were evil. Croce discusses Baudelaire's view of ultimate beauty and his disdain for philosophic poetry. While Croce praises Baudelaire's creations, he adds that Baudelaire's poetry "seems to lack [a] purity of form towards which he nevertheless was striving with all his force."*]

Charles Baudelaire was among those who was keenly conscious of what there is of fatuous in the doctrine of natural goodness and human perfectibility, otherwise called progress, as imagined in the eighteenth century and invested with romantic colours by the liberal thought of the nineteenth. He laughed at the freethinkers and humanitarians who proposed to abolish the death penalty and hell out of friendship for humanity; or war by means of a popular subscription at a halfpenny a head; at the fanatics who imagined that "the devil would one day be gobbled up" by manufactories and machines; and finally at everything that he described as modern *sottise* [foolishness]. Against this he upheld the doctrine of "original sin," stressing the evident truth of the daily observation that "man is always in the savage state." (p. 281)

But Baudelaire covered with sarcasm and contempt yet another ethical conception of more recent origin, foreign to the libertine eighteenth century (clear-sighted as to this question), and proper to the nineteenth century and romanticism: the religion of love, of love as the expression of what there is of most lofty and noble and gentle in man, love-passion as a heroic form, and erotic adoration, which consecrates its object. Fixing his eye upon the depths of eroticism, he discovered that "the one supreme delight of love lies in the certainty of doing wrong, and man and woman know from birth that in evil all pleasure is found." He used jestingly to remark that love is a crime, "the most tiresome part of which is the necessity of always having an accomplice." All attempts at moralizing it are vain, by introducing "honesty" into the things of love, which would be like wishing "to unite shade and heat in mystic union, night and day." And woman, who is all love, has the right and in a certain way the duty of seeking to "seem magical and supernatural," encircling herself with fascination and mystery. She performs this work of seduction to evil even as mother, as nurse, as sister, surrounding man in swaddling-clothes, not only by her cares for him, but with "her caresses and sensual pleasure." (pp. 282-83)

Baudelaire turned against the cult of nature, both of "nature" as it was understood in the eighteenth century and of nature as the romantics understood it. The whole of nature seemed to him to share in "original sin," and he often fancied that "maleficent and horrible animals are nothing but the vivification, corporification and disclosing in material existence of the evil thoughts of man." Woman is certainly a "natural" being and thus "abominable." (p. 284)

[Baudelaire's criticism] is altogether negative, on the one hand taking from him the possibility of relying upon ordinary, vulgar or middle-class beliefs, as they are called, that faith of the laity in human brotherhood and progress with the duties which it implies, and on the other tearing every veil from the illusions which irradiate sensual and erotic desire, but substituting nothing for the faith destroyed and opposing nothing to the inrush of turbulent sensuality. Indeed, this remained nevertheless his only rule of life, with the sole difference that it was no longer for him as for others evil unconscious of itself. (p. 285)

[The] world of Baudelaire was dominated by two sisters, two amiable girls, Dissoluteness and Death (*"La Débauche et la Mort sont deux aimables filles . . ."* [Dissoluteness and Death are two amiable girls]). He believed one day that he had found a definition of the Beautiful as something that should be at once "ardent and sad," and "a little vague," and such as "opens the way to the imagination." He symbolized beauty as a female figure, mingling "voluptuousness and sadness, melancholy, weariness, satiety, with ardour, avidity for life, and the bitterness which results from deprivation, desperation

and complaint. Joy could not be associated with it save in an accidental way, as "a vulgar ornament." (p. 286)

For Baudelaire, as for other artists, it is very difficult to draw the line between real life and the life of the imagination, and for him, as for them, the latter was certain to gain the upper hand. (p. 287)

Baudelaire opposed philosophic poetry, which was then the fashion in France, and from which he must have the more keenly desired to discriminate his lyrical production, for the reason that it occupied a neighbouring field. From his lips . . . fell [the] words: "great poetry is essentially *bête* [crazy]: believe that there lies its strength and its glory." Philosophical poetry, on the contrary, returned to *imagerie* [imagery], usual in the infancy of a people, at a period when it could not compete in power of bringing conviction with an article of the *Encyclopaedia*. For this reason it was useless. Not only was it useless, but harmful, since it artificially introduces philosophy into art, whereas art has its own implicit and spontaneous philosophy. . . . (p. 288)

Baudelaire felt how inartistic was passion when it tyrannizes over art, for "the principle of poetry is strictly and simply this, human aspiration to a superior beauty, and it manifests itself by means of an enthusiasm, a transport of soul, altogether independent of passion, which is an intoxication of the heart, and of truth, which is the food of reason." (p. 289)

[Baudelaire's] mind was so clear and exact that he was never led by his constant polemic against formless art into the assertion and exaltation of the abstract form; indeed, he utters a warning against "the monstrous disorders due to an immoderate taste for form, and against "the frantic passion for art," which is "a cancer that devours all the rest" and leads to nothing, "as does every excessive specialization of faculty." Acute observations throng his pages, such as those upon the true draughtsmen "who always draw according to the image written on their brains and never according to nature." He also speaks of the necessity to enlarge the history of art so as to include all the infinite forms of universal beauty excluded by [the German art historian Johann Joachim] Winckelmann; and of restricting ourselves to *l'impeccable naïveté* [flawless simplicity] in lack of a satisfactory system; or of the history of fashion and dress; or of that good sort of artistic barbarism, which we find even in perfect art, and which is due to the need of "seeing things in the large and of considering them above all in their total effect." (p. 290)

[It] would be to misunderstand [Baudelaire] if, letting ourselves be deceived by certain appearances in his work, we were to attribute to him something of that frivolous spirit which plays with its own object and which is one of the forms of caprice and arbitrary choice, which he abhorred in art. His inspiration drawn from lubricious, sad and bestial sources, remains lofty and serious; bound to a sensual world which he cannot overcome, he succeeds in rendering it colossal, tragical, sublime, and here too he appears as a "rebel angel": a heroic poet compressed and yet unable to abandon his heroics, which he creates upside down, by means of the lustful and the horrible. What there is in his creations that flashes out in irony, or rather in satire, is nothing but the consciousness of evil, inseparable from his mode of embracing the evil. Satan sometimes laughs, because, if he did not, he would be a maniac or a madman, and no one has yet insulted him with such a name. But Satan is also sometimes seized with nausea and disgust of himself, because he is not altogether able to suffocate the memory of the nobility that once was his. (p. 291)

[Not] infrequently Baudelaire's poetry seems to lack [a] purity of form towards which he nevertheless was striving with all his force. The reason of this failure is that he has within him other loves extraneous to the love of perfect form, which he does not always succeed in conquering. These were, on the one hand, intellectuality or reflection, which insinuate themselves here and there in his composition, owing to which he insisted so strongly upon having given a general design, a beginning, middle and end to his book; and on the other, the sensualism of images and lines, which greatly attracts him, inducing him to coin lines more vigorous and resonant than clear in their imagery, or to unite discordant images, or hyperboles which stand out from the original motive and seem to be sought for themselves. For this reason, the composition is somewhat confused in some of his lyrics, in others too symmetrical, at others glosses are attached or intercalated, at others again it allows us to discover lacunas and leaps beneath the severity of the form. . . . It is possible that the two last strophes of the **Vin des chiffonniers** containing considerations and conclusions may fail to please others as they fail to please me, for they are useless and empty beside the liveliness of the representations that precede them, and say all that is needed. But what a representation is that of the old rag-picker, rolling drunken along the streets as he dreams and expresses in gesture the heroic and generous dream of humanity; how completely it seems to express at the same time that the sublime is in man, but that he does not discover it save at the bottom of his folly! Yes, enthusiasm and sarcasm, perfectly fused: irrationality: poetry. (pp. 293-94)

> *Benedetto Croce, "Baudelaire," in his* European Literature in the Nineteenth Century, *translated by Douglas Ainslie (reprinted by permission of the Literary Estate of Benedetto Croce; originally published as his* Poesia e non poesia: Note sulla letteratura europea del secolo decimonono, *G. Laterza & Figli, 1923), Alfred A. Knopf, 1924, pp. 281-96.*

S. A. RHODES   (essay date 1929)

[*Rhodes provides an in-depth study of Baudelaire's cult of beauty. In his analysis, Rhodes describes elements of Romanticism and classicism in Baudelaire's poetry, which fuse together in what Rhodes considers to be a unique modernism. Rhodes maintains that although Baudelaire strives for flawlessness and reason in his art like the classicists, he glorifies emotion and sensation like the Romantics, and thus is "the first poet to be modern in the sense that he dared to be a full man." Rhodes also discusses Baudelaire's criticism, which he finds to be "lucid, pervadingly intelligent, and epoch-making."*]

Baudelaire's persistent search for a new realization of beauty, for a new way of apprehending the ecstatic moments in modern life, set him apart and ahead of the Romanticists of the earlier generation whose ideals he reinterpreted and modified to meet the exigencies of a changing world. He cultivated his senses and his mind to feel and understand the soul of nature, to sense the drama and the mystery of life, to perceive the relations between himself and his universe. He oriented Romantic aesthetics in this manner towards a more realistic conception of life, and one more susceptible of coming to complete fruition in art. (p. 115)

Let the poet, insisted Baudelaire, be the smelter of every transitory, fugitive instant in life, of the trivial as well as the memorable. Let him study absorbingly the parade of spectacles, crowds, lights, shadows, harmonies and discordances at once

so soothing and so disturbing to the modern soul. . . . [The] poet who can crowd and rush the thrill of life into his solitude can also remain master of his individuality in a crowd. He may thus be at once himself and incarnate the soul of every man in his. By this universal transmutation, he can distill the celestial drop of divinity inherent in every human life. . . . This was, in a real sense to Baudelaire, the essence of the heroism and the epic grandeur of modern life. He saw beauty surrounding us on all sides, flourishing in our midst, becoming at every moment, and in a variety of ways, the source of our aesthetic and moral happiness. All life, he declared, is rich in poetic and wonderful motives. From the upper strata of social, fashionable life, to the dark avenues of the underworld, life is filled with heroism. . . . To him, the spectacle daily unfolded to his gaze and meditation is a cause for wonder, and in Baudelaire this wonder was the beginning, the inspiration often, of his creative work. Modern life, he held, is no less fruitful in sublime motives than the ancient, albeit our sublimity seemed to him, by the nature of things, more tragic, deeper, and more spiritual. In every phase of daily life he saw an evidence of this, in our inner struggles, passions, vices and torments of which even the simple and dark-colored clothes we wear are a constant symbol. It is beauty such as this that modern art must seek, express and render eternal. This, in Baudelaire's estimation, was the true function of Romanticism, as Balzac well understood it, he says, because he turned into poetry the meanest aspects of life. (pp. 145-47)

The essence of Baudelaire's Romanticism, then, lies in its subjective realism, a realism *sui generis,* drawn from the inner fibers of his own consciousness in contact with reality. It synthesizes the whole of life in the inner laboratory of the poet's sentient being. It is an unconscious effort, at first, slowly rising to consciousness, to grasp the significance of the invisible mystery of things. That is why his sensual state approached often a condition of ecstasy, something almost akin to hallucination. . . . He was not content with giving the surface delineations of things only and sought to discover their spiritual concomitants. His aesthetic reactions are therefore from unconsciousness to consciousness, from sensual groping to artistic lucidity. He gets at the true reality of life by taking the shortest route to its center through his intuitions and sensations, and he rises from it to the heaven of his idealism by an even shorter flight through his aesthetic and spiritual aspirations. In so doing he discloses views of both the visible and invisible worlds of reality that shift swiftly from the depths of sensual experience to the heights of transcendental visions. His Romantic spirit thus achieves its culmination by going through reality and not by skirting it. He may often exaggerate or magnify the depths or heights of his aesthetic experiences. But because they are implicit in the very existence of reality, he cannot avoid or falsify them. (pp. 147-48)

[Baudelaire] favored a freer avenue for the expression of the grotesque in art not merely as an antithesis to what is sublime, but as another phase of nature, as a means of bringing the most of life into art. He desired to attach its expression to the main current of aesthetic values, since the hideous, horrible, distorted and frenzied passions of life, the fear of death, of the unknown and of the incomprehensible are the only avenues through which to express a certain mysterious and symbolic beauty that lurks in the unfrequented depths of nature and life.

But in spite of his extreme modernism, or rather because of it, Baudelaire's art entailed a reversion to the classic dependence upon reason and analysis in artistic creation, for in proportion as life seems to be ruled by forces which are beyond the control of the intelligence is the latter required more in controlling and coordinating its elements in art. The classic ideal subordinated the imagination to the intellect. . . . [Unlike the classicists, however], Baudelaire made the share of the imagination and intuition as great as that of the intelligence in art. His Romanticism or modernism is thus characterized by the fusion of two spiritual heritages, the Romantic and the classic. His cult of an impeccable form in art, his psychological analysis of the emotions, his pervading intelligence, are manifestations of a classic nature. His cultivation and exaltation of the sensations for aesthetic experience, his reliance on the intuition, his desire to seek in himself an expression of the world beyond external appearances, are manifestations of a Romantic order. These two tendencies, instead of being mutually exclusive, were complementary in him. They combined to constitute a new aesthetic principle the purpose of which was to cause to see and to interpret modern life fully, realistically, and, at the same time, spiritually. It enabled Baudelaire to reach toward a complete grasp of the strain and stress of all the dynamic forces of life about him and within him, and to incorporate them in a new aesthetic synthesis which is his art. . . . Baudelaire, like the Romanticists, freed himself from the undue restraint imposed upon the expression of human passions in poetry by classic prosody. But unlike them, and more like the classicists, he did not allow his reason to be drowned by their rising tide. Instead, he deepened the channels along which they run, and thus he increased and controlled at once their scope in art. His raising of all the sensations to the level of artistic interpretation committed him to an aesthetic doctrine of mutation in which his instincts formed the motive power and his imaginative intelligence the guiding beacon. The classical notion that life is always the same, in time and space, contributed to exteriorizing it, to its becoming symmetrical and exclusive. By going to the other extreme, the Romanticists made it lose consistency and reality in art. The former did away with all mystery. The latter shrouded everything in it. What was needed was the sensitive emotionalism of the latter combined with the lucid reasoning of the former to render the darkness visible, and the mystery of life lucent. Baudelaire possessed both qualifications. (pp. 153-55)

Even from a poet like Vigny, so much nearer to him poetically than any other Romantic poet, Baudelaire is distinguished by his deeper sense of human sorrow and beauty. For even when, in his highest lyric flight, Vigny succeeds in reaching the portals of the eternal problems of life, his poetic vision ends in an impasse. His outburst of poetry ends in a eulogy of silence or disdain. Baudelaire's ends in a eulogy of sorrow and beauty, in life and art. . . . [Such] poems of Baudelaire as *Élévation, Bénédiction, Recueillement* are seen to be really what Vigny called them, "des Fleurs du bien [the flowers of goodness]." . . . (pp. 161-62)

[Baudelaire is] the first poet to be truly modern in the sense that he dared to be a full man. He dared to submit his spirit to the full sway of his instincts, while still holding the whip of reason over them in his art. He dared to be in his heart and in his poetry a perfect characterization of the complex modern man; a palpitating image and echo of a palpitating reality. (p. 162)

[Baudelaire] becomes a guide to the perplexed through the dark avenues of the human heart. And because of this, because his spirit was able to pierce through the outer shell of his complex experiences to express itself in beauty, he succeeded not only

in making of both his spirit and reality the two terms of a poetic impression, but also in making of them the very essence of his poetry, in converting them into pure poetry. With him, and after him, lyric poetry ceases to be a reaction to life, to become its inner impulse as well as its goal; its ultimate aspiration as well as its highest justification. (p. 165)

Baudelaire's lyricism represents a return or an evolution to the expression not only of inwardness, but also of mental energy in poetry. His lyric flight is not a blind urge tearing heedlessly through the passions of man, but an intelligent survey aiming to apportion their hold over and place in his rational and spiritual life. His poetic intelligence is not abstract and didactic, however, but imaginative and intuitive. That is why he can become conscious of the interrelation between all the elements that make up reality—of their "correspondances." And that is why, in spite of the depth of his analytical vision, he does not destroy reality, but acquires instead a directness of vision akin to that of children. His intuitive intelligence gives him a clear vision in the dark, and at last reason and sensation tend toward the same goal, the apprehension of the spirit, of the mystery of life. He recreated the ideal of a pure lyric poetry by the union of its two chief elements, intelligence and sensibility, in a crucible of pure spirituality. (pp. 184-85)

[Whereas] Romantic poetry is primarily picturesque and sentimental, Baudelaire's is psychological and intuitive. A sensation and an idea sing jointly in it. The latter is carried on the wings of the former. It is never expressed, and yet it is felt. We come to know life through it because we sense it, not because we are delivered a harangue about it. The procession of images and symbols in this poetry leaves upon a sensitive organism an impression that resembles something like a contagious spread of the inspiration that created it. . . . Baudelaire exhibits no . . . metaphysical, abstract concern with the questioning mystery of the sky [as Victor Hugo does in his poetry]. He does not consider it the proper subject for pure poetry. His inquiry into the mystery of the human heart is more vital to his poetical nature than any versified conjectures over the silent heavens. He does not ask from an indifferent universe the secret of man's destiny. He knows that secret is in his heart, and therein he seeks it. . . . Baudelaire wrestles with the aching and unyielding passions which he finds entrenched in life until he unmasks them, so that, at last, the human heart stands exulting in the intoxication of its own nakedness, unashamed any longer to look at its tragic depths and its sublime heights. And that is the essence of Baudelaire's contribution to an ideal of pure poetry. . . . With Baudelaire it becomes a lyric vehicle to express not ideas and conjectures and prophetic orations, but feelings, sensations, sorrows and sobs; the doubts and pains of the heart and mind, and also the ecstatic aspirations, the unsullied idealism, and the thrilling music of the soul. And it came nearer and nearer to being, like music, the voice of life expressing itself directly through the senses and the spirit. Thus truly does he bring us nearer to the unknowable, the unconscious, the transcendental, and set us face to face at last with the bare enigma of life. (pp. 186-88)

[Baudelaire believed that while] it is nearly impossible for a critic to become a poet, it is quite fatal that a poet should contain a critic. By the force of circumstances, he is the best qualified to become a judge of artistic excellence. The moment when the intuitive impulses of the creator are illumined by the analytic faculties of the critic is the moment when the artist tries to bring his vision and his contribution to beauty in line with the eternal stream of art. Criticism becomes then a phase of the creative activity. . . . (p. 263)

To analyze the idea that underlies a work of art, its development, its affiliations, its inspiration, its composition, is to write a spiritual biography more dramatic than one filled with events and adventures. This is the sort of study [Baudelaire] made of [Gustave Flaubert's] *Mme. Bovary,* dissecting the novel into its constituent elements, disclosing its hidden channels, its conception, development, construction, and spiritual significance. The result was that he wrote the best review of the book ever penned. (p. 268)

The groundwork for such criticism lies in the faculty of the critic to enjoy and delight in a work of art, as well as to analyze and explain it. Baudelaire, however, avoided throughout that excess of the qualities that are evident in the Romantic "critique admirative" [admiring criticism], and in the dispassionate, abstract, and frigid criticism of the "esprit de géométrie" [spirit of geometry]. From the former he differed by his power of selective and intelligent appreciation; and from the latter by his undoubted possession of an "esprit de finesse" [spirit of finesse]. "I believe sincerely," he says, "that the best criticism is the kind that is ingratiating and poetic; and not that cold, algebraic variety, which, under pretext of explaining everything, expresses neither like nor dislike, and divests itself of all vestige of personality. For example, a beautiful painting being an image of nature seen through an artist, the best criticism of it will be a reflection of it upon an intelligent and sensitive spirit. Thus the best review of a painting might be a sonnet or an elegy." . . . [Analyzing] the paintings of Delacroix, and the rare effects the painter achieved by the harmony, the melody, and the tonality of his colors, he turns . . . to some verses from his poem **"Les Phares."** This he does even when, as in two instances, he has to quote poems by other poets to emphasize the impression he wishes to convey, quoting Th. Gautier once in connection with Delacroix, and Victor Hugo in connection with some water colors by Meryon. This is not within the reach of every critic, of course, but neither is creative criticism within the reach of every book-reviewer. . . . [As] an aesthetic critic, [Baudelaire] could not keep his personality out of the subject of his criticism. It is noteworthy that all the characters he has studied passionately, Poe, Delacroix, Wagner, Guys, Gautier, bear some traits that affiliate them to him; or it might be said that he found in them all something germane to his spirit, whose expression was for him another means of self-expression. (pp. 268-70)

Baudelaire's aim was always to discover the beautiful qualities in a work of art, those by which it deserved to live. He preferred to ignore minor shortcomings and flaws when they did not obscure the splendor of the main theme. But when they crowded in the foreground, he chose to ignore both author and work completely. . . . Baudelaire especially avoided confusing criticism of a work of art with criticism of the life of its author. He would not condemn a book because its writer led a sad and unhappy existence, as his own detractors . . . were prompt to do in his case. . . . His own attitude is distinguished by a luminous judiciousness that keeps him from falling into such pitfalls. He is constantly aware of the fact that above all personality is art; that ultimately it is by his qualities that an artist must be judged; that it is by his positive achievements that he appeals to posterity, and not by his negative traits. (pp. 273-75)

[His] criticism is very often, not unlike that of Sainte-Beuve, enlivened and seasoned with biographical traits and anecdotes. Trivial and fugitive incidents in the life of an author are revealed, not necessarily, however, to explain, justify, or con-

demn his work, but rather to bring out more fully the many-sidedness of his genius. And it is always the truly human, touching angles of his character that arrest his attention. (p. 275)

[Baudelaire believed that whatever] be the nature and the origin of an artistic creation, the criterion by which it is to be judged must be its own intrinsic merits. "It is a specimen of the universally beautiful; but, in order to be understood," says Baudelaire, "it is necessary that the critic, the spectator, undergo himself a change which is in the nature of a mystery, and that, through the secret working of his will upon his imagination, he should become acclimated to the atmosphere which gave birth to this unusual creation. Few men have—in its fullest extent—this divine grace of cosmopolitanism; but all can acquire it in various degrees." No better word is needed to define the supreme quality that Baudelaire gives to and looks for in the highest form of criticism: cosmopolitanism—as he says, a grace divine. All those who are gifted with it have no other incentive than the love of the beautiful and of justice. (p. 280)

Baudelaire was never concerned with the particular methods to be employed in the study of a work with a view to its criticism, because that is primarily a question of mere technique. There might be differences of opinion as to the amount of research and the lengths to which a critic must go to place a work in its background for purposes of historical accuracy and understanding. But that he would consider of secondary importance in any form of aesthetic criticism. No critic had more respect for exact data than he. . . . So while Baudelaire would, without doubt, approve of the fundamental *raison d'être* [reason of state] of the historical method of criticism, he would, after all, consider its immediate results to be subsidiary to real criticism. For in all creative criticism the presence of two factors is of primary importance: 1st, the work of art to be studied; 2d, the possession by the student of a critical faculty. All else is either a help or an encumbrance, depending upon the nature of the first two prerequisites. That is why Baudelaire declared that the great critic can and must make up for any defects in his training and his technical knowledge, as well as remedy tendencies in him to pedantic dogmatism. . . . Baudelaire never approached a work of art in any other spirit than that of delight, to seek and feel that aspect of beauty it brought forth into life. He attacked the pseudo-classicists who thrive not by intuition, but through imitation. (pp. 280-83)

One of the beautiful traits of Baudelaire's criticism lies in its freedom from the polemical. This contributes to make it lucid, pervadingly intelligent, and epoch-making. For a critic to grasp the significance of the work of the artists of his time, and to reveal it absolutely in the form which posterity will accept as final, surely this is creative criticism, and Baudelaire did this in all his studies. (pp. 287-88)

Baudelaire could enter with absolute sympathy into the spirit of a work of art, but his sympathy never obscured his critical judiciousness. . . . He is never intolerant except against mediocrity and hypocrisy, but even then he takes no pleasure in condemning, yielding to it rather from a sense of duty. He was a tower of strength in defense of artists who deserved it, displaying a rare vision and a ready willingness to identify himself with what seemed lost causes. (pp. 288-89)

Both his unbounded enthusiasm for all great art, and the austerity of his aesthetic taste, tended to broaden and heighten Baudelaire's critical standards. His whole criticism is a continuous attempt at understanding. The words that flow from his pen are not cold and pedantic. They are the words of an artist who takes a book, a painting for his inspiration. He recreates for the reader the vision of beauty the artist sought to convey. He possessed a quality without which criticism is bare and ineffectual: intellectual sympathy—culture supplemented by warmth of understanding and moral honesty. He brought into play a lucid intelligence always at the service of a broad artistic concept; supple and yet firm enough to embrace all that is beautiful and exclude what is not. Criticism was for him a spiritual venture; pioneering in an intellectual forest whose thick undergrowth renders it inaccessible to the layman. It was to enter into the innermost recesses of a spirit; to lay bare its resources, its secrets. . . . Reading Baudelaire's critical studies, one passes constantly from passages illumined with analytical insight to outbreaks of pure lyricism, in which the poet in the critic grasps as if by inspiration the full import of the artist's aim and achievement, and he conveys it to the reader with the emotional flush of a newly discovered aspect of beauty and truth. (pp. 289-91)

> *S. A. Rhodes, in his* The Cult of Beauty in Charles Baudelaire, Vols. I & II *(copyright, 1929, by G. L. van Roosbroeck; reprinted by permission of the publisher), Columbia University Press, 1929, 283 p.*

T. S. ELIOT   (essay date 1930)

[*An American-born British writer, Eliot is one of the most influential poets and critics of the first half of the twentieth century. In the following, he discusses Baudelaire's personality as it is manifested in his* Intimate Journals. *In contrast with Arthur Symons (1920), Eliot views Baudelaire as "essentially Christian." However, Eliot asserts, Baudelaire displays a "theological innocence"; his primary concern is the problem of good and evil in the Christian tradition, but he is confused by both concepts. Eliot judges Baudelaire to be the "greatest exemplar in modern poetry" for his "renovation" of verse and language as well as for his "renovation of an attitude towards life. . . ."*]

Baudelaire has, I believe, been called a fragmentary Dante, for what that description is worth. It is true that many people who enjoy Dante enjoy Baudelaire; but the differences are as important as the similarities. Baudelaire's inferno is very different in quality and significance from that of Dante. Truer, I think, would be the description of Baudelaire as a later and more limited Goethe. As we begin to see him now, he represents his own age in somewhat the same way as that in which Goethe represents an earlier age. . . . [In] Baudelaire, as well as in Goethe, is some of the out-moded nonsense of his time. The parallel between the German poet who has always been the symbol of perfect "health" in every sense, as well as of universal curiosity, and the French poet who has been the symbol of morbidity in mind and concentrated interests in work, may seem paradoxical. But after this lapse of time the difference between "health" and "morbidity" in the two men becomes more negligible; there is something artificial and even priggish about Goethe's healthiness, as there is about Baudelaire's unhealthiness; we have passed beyond both fashions, of health or malady, and they are both merely men with restless, critical, curious minds and the "sense of the age"; both men who understood and foresaw a great deal. (pp. 372-73)

It was once the mode to take Baudelaire's Satanism seriously, as it is now the tendency to present Baudelaire as a serious and Catholic Christian. Especially as a prelude to the *Journaux Intimes* this diversity of opinion needs some discussion. I think that the latter view—that Baudelaire is essentially Christian—is nearer the truth than the former, but it needs considerable

reservation. When Baudelaire's Satanism is dissociated from its less creditable paraphernalia, it amounts to a dim intuition of a part, but a very important part, of Christianity. Satanism itself, so far as not merely an affectation, was an attempt to get into Christianity by the back door. Genuine blasphemy, genuine in spirit and not purely verbal, is the product of partial belief, and it is as impossible to the complete atheist as to the perfect Christian. It is a way of affirming belief. This state of partial belief is manifest throughout the *Journaux Intimes.* What is significant about Baudelaire is his theological innocence. He is discovering Christianity for himself; he is not assuming it as a fashion or weighing social or political reasons, or any other accidents. He is beginning, in a way, at the beginning; and being a discoverer, is not altogether certain what he is exploring and to what it leads; he might almost be said to be making again, as one man, the effort of scores of generations. His Christianity is rudimentary or embryonic. . . . His business was not to practise Christianity, but—what was much more important for his time—to assert its *necessity.* (pp. 373-74)

[Baudelaire] was one of those who have great strength, but strength merely to *suffer.* He could not escape suffering and could not transcend it, so he *attracted* pain to himself. But what he could do, with that immense passive strength and sensibilities which no pain could impair, was to study his suffering. And in this limitation he is wholly unlike Dante, not even like any character in Dante's Hell. But, on the other hand, such suffering as Baudelaire's implies the possibility of a positive state of beatitude. (pp. 374-75)

From the poems alone, I venture to think, we are not likely to grasp what seems to me the true sense and significance of Baudelaire's mind. Their excellence of form, their perfection of phrasing, and their superficial coherence, may give them the appearance of presenting a definite and final state of mind. In reality, they seem to me to have the external but not the internal form of classic art. . . . Now the true claim of Baudelaire as an artist is not that he found a superficial form, but that he was searching for a form of life. In minor form he never indeed equalled Théophile Gautier, to whom he significantly dedicated his poems: in the best of the slight verse of Gautier there is a satisfaction, a balance of inwards and form, which we do not find in Baudelaire. He had a greater technical ability than Gautier, and yet the content of feeling is constantly bursting the receptacle. His apparatus, by which I do not mean his command of words and rhythms, but his stock of imagery (and every poet's stock of imagery is circumscribed somewhere), is not wholly perdurable or adequate. His prostitutes, mulattoes, Jewesses, serpents, cats, corpses, form a machinery which has not worn very well; his Poet, or his Don Juan, has a romantic ancestry which is too clearly traceable. Compare with the costumery of Baudelaire the stock of imagery of [Dante's] Vita Nuova . . . , and you find Baudelaire's does not everywhere wear as well as that of several centuries earlier. . . . (pp. 375-76)

To say this is only to say that Baudelaire belongs to a definite place in time. Inevitably the offspring of romanticism, and by his nature the first counter-romantic in poetry, he could, like any one else, only work with the materials which were there. It must not be forgotten that a poet in a romantic age cannot be a "classical" poet except in tendency. If he is sincere, he must express with individual differences the general state of mind—not as a *duty,* but simply because he cannot help participating in it. For such poets, we may expect often to get much help from reading their prose works and even notes and diaries; help in deciphering the discrepancies between head and heart, means and end, material and ideals.

What preserves Baudelaire's poetry from the fate of most French poetry of the nineteenth century up to his time, and has made him . . . the one modern French poet to be widely read abroad, is not quite easy to conclude. It is partly that technical mastery which can hardly be overpraised, and which has made his verse an inexhaustible study for later poets, not only in his own language. (p. 376)

[His] invention of language, at a moment when French poetry in particular was famishing for such invention, is enough to make of Baudelaire a great poet, a great landmark in poetry. Baudelaire is indeed the greatest exemplar in *modern* poetry in any language, for his verse and language is the nearest thing to a complete renovation that we have experienced. But his renovation of an attitude towards life is not less radical and no less important. In his verse, he is now less a model to be imitated or a source to be drained than a reminder of the duty, the consecrated task, of sincerity. From a fundamental sincerity he could not deviate. The superficies of sincerity . . . is not always there. . . . [Many] of his poems are insufficiently removed from their romantic origins, from Byronic paternity and Satanic fraternity. The "satanism" of the Black Mass was very much in the air; in exhibiting it Baudelaire is the voice of his time, but I would observe that in Baudelaire, as in no one else, it is redeemed by *meaning something else*. He uses the same paraphernalia, but cannot limit its symbolism even to all that of which he is conscious. . . . Baudelaire is concerned, not with demons, black masses, and romantic blasphemy, but with the real problem of good and evil. It is hardly more than an accident of time that he uses the current imagery and vocabulary of blasphemy. In the middle nineteenth century, . . . an age of bustle, programmes, platforms, scientific progress, humanitarianism and revolutions which improved nothing, an age of progressive degradation, Baudelaire perceived that what really matters is Sin and Redemption. It is a proof of his honesty that he went as far as he could honestly go and no further. To a mind observant of the post-Voltaire France . . . , a mind which saw the world of *Napoléon le petit* more lucidly than did that of Victor Hugo, a mind which at the same time had no affinity for the *Sainte Sulpicerie* of the day, the recognition of the reality of Sin is a New Life; and the possibility of damnation is so immense a relief in a world of electoral reform, plebiscites, sex reform and dress reform, that damnation itself is an immediate form of salvation—of salvation from the ennui of modern life, because it at last gives some significance to living. It is this, I believe, that Baudelaire is trying to express; and it is this which separates him from the modernist Protestantism of Byron and Shelley. It is apparently Sin in the Swinburnian sense, but really Sin in the permanent Christian sense, that occupies the mind of Baudelaire.

Yet, . . . the sense of Evil implies the sense of good. Here too, as Baudelaire apparently confuses, and perhaps did confuse, Evil with its theatrical representations, Baudelaire is not always certain in his notion of the Good. The romantic idea of Love is never quite exorcised, but never quite surrendered to. In *Le Balcon,* . . . there is all the romantic idea, but something more: the reaching out towards something which cannot be had *in*, but which may be had partly *through*, personal relations. (pp. 377-79)

[In] the adjustment of the natural to the spiritual, of the bestial to the human and the human to the supernatural, Baudelaire is a bungler compared with Dante; the best that can be said, and

that is a very great deal, is that what he knew he found out for himself. In his book, the *Journaux Intimes,* and especially in *Mon coeur mis à nu,* he has a great deal to say of the love of man and woman. . . . Baudelaire has perceived that what distinguishes the relations of man and woman from the copulation of beasts is the knowledge of Good and Evil (of *moral* Good and Evil which are not natural Good and Bad or puritan Right and Wrong). Having an imperfect, vague romantic conception of Good, he was at least able to understand that the sexual act as evil is more dignified, less boring, than as the natural, "life-giving," cheery automatism of the modern world. (pp. 379-80)

[Baudelaire's] human love is definite and positive, his divine love vague and uncertain: hence his insistence upon the evil of love, hence his constant vituperations of the female. In this there is no need to pry for psychopathological causes, which would be irrelevant at best; for his attitude towards women is consistent with the point of view which he had reached. Had he been a woman he would, no doubt, have held the same views about men. He has arrived at the perception that a woman must be to some extent a symbol; he did not arrive at the point of harmonising his experience with his ideal needs. The complement, and the correction to the *Journaux Intimes,* so far as they deal with the relations of man and woman, is the *Vita Nuova,* and the *Divine Comedy* [by Dante Alighieri]. But—I cannot assert it too strongly—Baudelaire's view of life, such as it is, is objectively apprehensible, that is to say, his idiosyncrasies can partly explain his view of life, but they cannot explain it away. And this view of life is one which has grandeur and which exhibits heroism; it was an evangel to his time and to ours. (p. 381)

T. S. Eliot, "Baudelaire" (1930), in his Selected Essays *(copyright 1950 by Harcourt Brace Jovanovich, Inc.; renewed 1978 by Esme Valerie Eliot; reprinted by permission of the publisher and Faber and Faber Ltd.), Harcourt Brace Jovanovich, 1950, pp. 371-81.*

PAUL VALÉRY (essay date 1930)

[*A prominent French poet, Valéry is one of the leading practitioners in modern literature of nineteenth-century Symbolist aestheticism. Valéry's work reflects his desire for total control over his creation. His absorption with the creative process forms the method of his criticism as well. Here, Valéry maintains that* The Flowers of Evil *is the most important work in the history of French literature. Like earlier critics such as S. A. Rhodes (1929), Valéry recognizes the juxtaposition of Romantic and classical elements in Baudelaire's verse. Valéry also notes Baudelaire's debt to Edgar Allan Poe and discusses their common desire to create "absolute poetry." Finally, Valéry assesses the influence of* The Flowers of Evil *on such later French poets as Paul Verlaine, Stéphane Mallarmé, and Arthur Rimbaud.*]

Baudelaire is at the height of his glory.

The little volume, *Les Fleurs du Mal,* which contains less than three hundred pages, outweighs, in the esteem of the literary, the most illustrious and bulkiest works. . . . [It] is, I believe, without precedent in the history of French Letters. (p. 71)

[With] Baudelaire, French poetry at length passes beyond our frontiers. It is read throughout the world; it takes its place as the characteristic poetry of modernity; it encourages imitation, it enriches countless minds. Men like Swinburne, Gabriele d'Annunzio and Stefan George bear magnificent witness to the Baudelairian influence in foreign countries.

Thus I can say that, though there may be French poets greater and more powerfully endowed than Baudelaire, there is none more *important*.

Whence comes this extraordinary importance? How has a man so peculiar, so far removed from the average as Baudelaire, been able to engender so widespread a movement?

This great posthumous favour, this spiritual richness, this supreme glory, must depend not only upon his own value as a poet but also upon exceptional circumstances. Critical intelligence associated with poetic proficiency is such a circumstance. Baudelaire owes to this rare alliance a capital discovery. He was born sensual and exacting; he had a sensibility whose exigencies led him to make the most delicate formal experiments; but these gifts would doubtless have made him merely a rival to Gautier or an excellent Parnassian artist, had his mental curiosity not led him to the discovery of a new intellectual world in the works of Edgar Allan Poe. . . . [In Poe's works, so] many original views and extraordinary promises enthralled him; his talent was transformed by them, his destiny magnificently changed. (pp. 72-3)

[The second remarkable circumstance of the moulding of Baudelaire was that he] arrived at man's estate when romanticism was at its height; a dazzling generation was in possession of the empire of Letters. Lamartine, Hugo, Musset, Vigny were the masters of the day. (p. 74)

His literary existence provoked and nourished by them, thrilled by their fame, determined by their works, is, however, necessarily dependent upon negation, upon the overthrow and replacement of those men who seemed to him to fill all fame's niches and to deny him: one, the world of forms; another, that of sentiments; a third, the picturesque; a fourth, profundity.

The point was to distinguish himself at any cost from a group of great poets whom some stroke of chance had exceptionally assembled in full vigour in the same period.

Baudelaire's problem then might, and probably should, be thus stated: ''To be a great poet but to be neither Lamartine nor Hugo nor Musset.'' (pp. 74-5)

In short, he is led, constrained, by the state of his soul and its environment, more and more clearly to oppose the system, or the absence of system, called romanticism. (p. 75)

Baudelaire had the greatest interest—a vital interest—in picking out, in calling attention to, in exaggerating all the weaknesses and lapses of romanticism observed at close quarters in the work and personalities of its greatest men. (p. 78)

[Baudelaire] had to choose the shortest road, to limit himself in his gropings, to be sparing of repetitions and divergencies. He had therefore to seek by means of analysis what he was, what he could do and what he wished to do; and to unite, in himself, with the spontaneous virtues of a poet, the sagacity, the skepticism, the attention and reasoning faculty of a critic.

This is why Baudelaire, although originally a romantic, and even a romantic by taste, sometimes appears as a *classic*. There are infinite ways of defining the classic, or of thinking to define him. For today we shall adopt this one: *a classic is a writer who carries a critic within him and who associates him intimately with his work.* (pp. 81-3)

[There] appeared about this time [Edgar Allan Poe], a man who was to consider the things of the mind with a clearness, a sagacity, a lucidity which had never been encountered to such

a degree in a head endowed with poetic invention. And among these things was literary production. Until Poe, never had the problem of literature been examined in its premises, reduced to a psychological problem and approached by means of an analysis where the logic and the mechanics of effects were deliberately employed. For the first time, the relations between the work and the reader were elucidated and given as the positive foundations of art. (pp. 85-6)

Baudelaire and Edgar Allan Poe exchanged values. Each gave to the other what he had, received from the other what he had not. The latter communicated to the former a whole system of new and profound thought. He enlightened him, he enriched him, he determined his opinions on a quantity of subjects: philosophy of composition, theory of the artificial, comprehension and condemnation of the modern, importance of the exceptional and of a certain strangeness, an aristocratic attitude, mysticism, a taste for elegance and precision, even politics. . . . Baudelaire was impregnated, inspired, deepened by them.

But, in exchange for what he had taken, Baudelaire gave Poe's thought an infinite extension. He proffered it to the future. (p. 88)

I only wonder what Baudelaire's poetry, and more generally French poetry, may owe to the discovery of the works of Poe. Some poems in *Fleurs du Mal* derive their sentiment and their material from Poe's poems. . . . [Poe's] conception, which he set forth in various articles, was the principal factor in the modification of Baudelaire's ideas and art. (p. 89)

[Poe] analyses the psychological requirements of a poem. Among these, he puts in the first rank, the ones which depend upon the *dimensions* of poetical works. He gives exceptional importance to the consideration of their length. He moreover examines the very conception of these works. He easily establishes that there exists a great number of poems concerned with notions for which prose would have been an adequate vehicle. (pp. 91-2)

Poe understood that modern poetry should conform to the tendency of an age which drew a sharper and sharper distinction between forms and provinces of activity. He understood that it could claim to realize its own object and produce itself, to some degree, in a *pure state*.

Thus, by analysing the requirements of poetic delight and defining *absolute poetry* by *exhaustion*, Poe showed a way and taught a very strict and fascinating doctrine in which he united a sort of mathematics with a sort of mysticism. . . .

If we now regard *Les Fleurs du Mal* as a whole and take the trouble to compare this volume with other poetic works of the same period, we shall not be surprised to find that Baudelaire's work is remarkably consistent with Poe's precepts and consequently remarkably different from the productions of romanticism. *Les Fleurs du Mal* contains neither historical nor legendary poems; nothing based upon a narrative. There are no flights into philosophy. Politics here make no appearance. Descriptions are rare and always *pertinent*. But all is charm, music, powerful, abstract sensuality. . . . *Luxe, forme et volupté* [Luxury, form, and voluptuousness].

In Baudelaire's best poems there is a combination of flesh and spirit, a mixture of solemnity, warmth and bitterness, of eternity and intimacy, a most rare alliance of will with harmony, which distinguishes them clearly from romantic verse as it distinguishes them clearly from Parnassian verse. . . . [The] resonance, after more than sixty years, of Baudelaire's unique and far from copious work, still fills the whole poetic sphere; . . . it is still influential, impossible to neglect, reinforced by a remarkable number of works which derive from it and which are not imitations but the consequences of it. Consequently, to be just, it would be necessary to join to the slender collection of *Les Fleurs du Mal* several first-rate works and a number of the most profound and finest experiments that poetry has ever undertaken. The influence of *Poèmes Antiques* and *Poèmes Barbares* has been less diverse and less surprising.

It must be recognized, however, that this same influence, had it been exerted on Baudelaire, would perhaps have dissuaded him from writing or from retaining some very slack verses which are to be found in his book. Out of the fourteen lines of the sonnet *Recueillement,* one of his most charming pieces, there are five or six which, to my never-failing surprise, are undeniably weak. But the first and last verses of this poem are so magical that we do not feel the ineptitude of the central part and are quite ready to hold it for null and void. Only a very great poet can effect a miracle of this kind. (pp. 92-4)

Baudelaire's poetry owes its duration and the ascendency it still has to the plenitude and the unusual clearness of its timbre. At times, this voice yields to eloquence, as happened a little too frequently in the case of the poets of the period; but it almost always retains and develops an admirably pure melodic line and a perfectly sustained sonority which distinguish it from all prose. (p. 96)

To render less imprecise and less incomplete this attempt to explain Baudelaire's importance today, I must now recall what he was as an art critic. . . . [On] the whole, his judgments, invariably motivated and accompanied by the finest and most substantial considerations on painting, remain models of their kind, which is so terribly facile, hence so terribly difficult.

But Baudelaire's greatest glory . . . is without question to have inspired several great poets. Neither Verlaine, nor Mallarmé, nor Rimbaud would have been what they were had they not read *Les Fleurs du Mal* at the decisive age. (p. 97)

Paul Valéry, "The Position of Baudelaire," in his Variety, second series, *translated by William Aspenwall Bradley (copyright 1938 by Harcourt Brace Jovanovich, Inc.; renewed 1966 by Jenny E. Bradley; reprinted by permission of the publisher; originally published as "Position de Baudelaire," in his* Variété II, Gallimard, 1930), Harcourt Brace Jovanovich, 1938, pp. 71-100.

JOHN MIDDLETON MURRY (essay date 1931)

[*A noted twentieth-century critic and journalist, Murry here assesses the label of "decadent" which many have attached to Baudelaire. In relation to art or literature, according to Murry's interpretation, the word decadent can refer either to that which is created "during an age of decadence, or it can be used to describe the literature of a period of transition between two literary ideals." Murry believes that while Baudelaire belonged to a historically decadent period, he was not himself a decadent poet. The critic maintains, rather, that Baudelaire recognized the decadence of his age and protested against it in his poetry.*]

Many poets were branded as decadents in the nineteenth century. All of them suffered by the name; some deserved to suffer, and some did not. Charles Baudelaire, who was the first and greatest of the line, suffered most and deserved it least. He suffers still, because every critic who is convinced of his high

excellence as a poet and is anxious to elucidate it is driven to dwell on the element of decadence in the man and his work. The word is as necessary to the understanding of Baudelaire as a particular instrument to a surgeon for a particular operation.

Decadence is essentially a word of the historian who applies it to those periods in the history of a society when its old institutions are breaking down and being obscurely replaced by new; to ages when the transition is being made from one social ideal, one social fabric, to another. The word can be applied to literature, or art in general, in one of two ways. It can be used historically to distinguish the literature that is created during an age of decadence, or it can be used metaphorically to describe the literature of a period of transition between two literary ideals. (pp. 115-16)

Baudelaire is the poet of an historical decadence; he is not in any useful sense of the word a decadent poet. On the contrary, he was one of the greatest and most assured poets that France has produced. As a poet, he was strong, masculine, deliberate, classical; not a puny successor of great men, but the heroic founder of a line; and the peculiar quality of his work derives from the interaction of these two very different factors, the decadence of the age in which he lived and his own poetic strength and determination. Not that his choice of subject may not sometimes be called perverse; but the perversity of his work is the least important, the least relevant, and, to the unbiased reader, the least noticeable of its qualities. It is easy for any poetaster to be perverse; it is extremely difficult for a poet to be perverse in Baudelaire's way. For Baudelaire was not a furtive dabbler in unclean things; he was the deliberate and determined poet of an attitude to life to which we cannot refuse the epithet heroic. The driving impulse of his work was not a predilection, but a conviction.

Baudelaire was convinced that the age in which he lived was a decadence. . . . Against [the tyranny of the age he] conceived it his duty to protest, not merely by the poetic utterance of cries of revolt but by the actual conduct of his life. The French romantic movement as a whole was animated to some extent by a spirit of protest against the sordidness of the age; but Baudelaire belonged to a curious section of the movement which had very little in common with romanticism as we generally conceive it now. His affinities were with the disciplined and contemptuous romanticism of Stendhal and Mérimée. This romanticism was rather a kind of sublimated realism, based upon an almost morbid *horreur d'être dupe* [fear of being tricked]—romantic in its aspiration away from the *bourgeois* society which it loathed, realistic in its determination to accept the facts as they were. It was romantic also in its conception and elaboration of the attitude which it considered inevitable for the chosen spirits who would not bow the knee to Baal.

It is important to grasp these two intimately woven strands of realism and romanticism in Baudelaire and his two predecessors. This strange but natural combination plays a great part not in the literature of France only, but in that of Europe as a whole during the last century. A single thread runs through the work of Stendhal, Mérimée, Baudelaire, Nietzsche, and Dostoevsky; in spite of their outward dissimilarity, and the great differences between their powers, these men are united by a common philosophical element which takes bodily shape in their conceptions of the hero. They are all intellectual romantics, in rebellion against life, and they imagine for themselves a hero in whom their defiance should be manifested. The three Frenchmen had in common, and put into actual practice, the ideal of 'le Dandy'. . . . On the one side the conception of the

Dandy touches the romantic literary ideal of the poet in his *tour d'ivoire* [ivory tower], on the other it reaches out in anticipation towards the superman of Nietzsche and the still subtler and more impressive antinomian hero of Dostoevsky's novels. In both these forms it influenced Baudelaire's life as a man and activity as a poet.

From this angle it is perhaps easier to understand and analyse the almost massive impression of unity we receive from so small a work as Baudelaire's. . . . What is really original in [his work] could easily be contained in three pocket volumes. Yet the abiding impression made by them is one of solidity. This is in the main because the inspiration is single and the foundations firm and invariable. As an artist Baudelaire works from a single centre; his attitude to life and his attitude to art lend each other aid and confirmation. Even his vices as a poet have the merit of being deliberate, and of contributing to the total effect at which he aimed. They are the vices proper, one might almost say essential, to his achievement. When Baudelaire is rhetorical, his rhetoric is never entirely empty; it has a dramatic propriety and significance in the mouth of the *âme damnée* [damned soul], the rebellious angel hurling defiance at the powers of heaven. When he indulges his desire to astonish, he is asserting his immunity from conventional fears. (pp. 116-19)

It is Baudelaire's chief distinction that, in spite of these one or two failures, he made a successful and undeviating effort to translate his ethical attitude towards life into a purely poetical gesture. He might so easily have been a poet of the confessional, pouring out his wounded soul in lyrical *cris de coeur* [cries of the heart]; but his 'Dandyism' helped him to a more truly poetic conception of his task. (pp. 119-20)

Baudelaire's power of concentration saved him from rhetorical disaster. In the matter of prosody he willingly accepted the severest limitations. He made no technical innovations himself, and he rejected some of those which Victor Hugo had made before him. He saw that for him it was much more important to blow a few blasts that were piercing than many that were merely loud; and he early set himself to the task of finding an equivalent in pure poetry to his detestation of the world and his defiance of the powers that ordained it. He sought the equivalent by making his poetry as metallic in sound and suggestion as he could; he would change the psychological oppression of life into a plastic oppression. To make concrete the immaterial is, of course, a familiar process of the poet's activity, and the effort lies at the source of all metaphor. But Baudelaire went far beyond this phase; he made it his deliberate aim to expel all elasticity from his verse, all bright and ethereal perspectives from his vision. (pp. 121-22)

His methods of achieving his end were manifold. The most obvious and the most successful is his endeavour to reduce all living things to a condition of immobile solidity. . . . [In his writing] Baudelaire makes solid everything he can. His very ideal of Beauty is an absolute immobility. . . . In Baudelaire's vision of the cosmos . . . steel is opposed to steel. The oppressor and the oppressed are equally ruthless, equally immobile, equally conscious, and equally beautiful. . . . Baudelaire conceived himself as working like a smith at an anvil on the very words of his poems, hammering and shaping them till they rang with a steely resonance. (pp. 122-24)

[Baudelaire's] main road of escape from his iron-walled world . . . was as ample as the prison-house was huge. His symbol of deliverance was the sea. The sea appears as often in his poetry as the metals themselves. It was for him a terrestrial infinite that led 'anywhere out of the world'; and even in that famous and beautiful poem *Le Voyage,* the last of *Les Fleurs du Mal,* when the voyagers have returned with their mournful message that in every corner of the world 'the eternal bulletin' is the same, the poet calls to Death as the great ship's captain. (p. 126)

[Few can] fail to respond to the suggestion of his recurrent imagery of the sea. We may call it a simple or a naïve emotion that finds in a 'splendid ship with white sails crowding' the perfect symbol of the freedom and happiness that are hidden beyond our mortal horizon; it is a profound emotion, and, what is more, an emotion peculiarly of our time. An age of industrialism drives men to treasure the symbol of the sea and its ships. (p. 127)

The sea is life, and the ship that rides over it is that triumphant, impossible beauty which haunts the mind with the promise that by its power the terrors of life may be overcome. It is only a dream, as Baudelaire well knew, but he dreamed it continually.

For Baudelaire was truly an *âme damnée,* because he was in love with the ideal. The fox of disillusion and disgust really tore at his vitals. Like Ivan Karamazov [from Dostoevski's novel *The Brothers Karamazov*], he persisted in his determination to give God back the ticket; because his sensitiveness was such that the degradation and misery of life left him no peace. . . . [He] sought to transform the reactions of his sensibility into the elements of a cosmos of his own making, a little universe that should produce in us the emotions that had tormented him in the world of everyday. Sometimes the original emotions show through the mask he wore; not through any artistic failure on his part, for no man was ever more resolute in his determination to sacrifice himself to his achievement, but because in the later work in prose he was intentionally loosening the rigour of his artistic creed. He was looking for a more precise equivalence to his feeling. In the texture of the *Poèmes en Prose* we can distinguish the separate threads of emotion which are lost in the still brocade of *Les Fleurs du Mal.* The prose is more lightly and in a sense more delicately woven; the unity of effect which the little pieces give derives more from complicated harmony than from the resonant unison which marks the poetry. In his prose Baudelaire is content to be ironical, compassionate, lyrical, and symbolic by turns; each piece has the contour of a single mood, together they have the complex solidity of an attitude. (pp. 128-29)

Baudelaire was a great poet of a decadence. In other words, he was a great modern poet; for the decadence which shaped him by compelling him to revolt against it was the 'civilization of industrial progress' which has endured from his day to our own. Baudelaire confronted the reality like the hero he strove to be; he had the courage both of his attitude and his art, and the result of his unremitting exercise of will in transforming his keen emotions is a poetic achievement that makes a single and profound impression upon our minds. . . . He was indeed the poet of rebellion; but the resolution of his defiance was subtly modulated by doubts and dreams which he would entertain and cherish for a while and then dismiss with an ironical contempt for his own unworthy weakness. Underneath his steely surface lay an infinity of sensitive responses. We could have deduced it; deep resentments are born only of deep wounds, and the solidity of permanent poetry is the work only of the most delicate fingers. But the finest artist seldom permits the precise quality of his personal response to appear. He makes his sacrifice to his own universality. (p. 135)

John Middleton Murry, "Baudelaire," in his Countries of the Mind: Essays in Literary Criticism, first series (reprinted by permission of Oxford University Press), revised edition, Oxford University Press, London, 1931 (and reprinted by Books for Libraries Press, 1968; distributed by Arno Press, Inc.), pp. 115-36.

WALLACE FOWLIE   (essay date 1943)

[*Fowlie is among the most respected and versatile scholars of French literature. His works include translations of major dramatists and poets of France, including Baudelaire, in addition to critical studies of the major figures and movements of modern French letters. Like T. S. Eliot (1930), Fowlie maintains that* The Flowers of Evil *clearly reflects Baudelaire's Christian faith. He states that Baudelaire proves the Roman Catholic dictum that it is "impossible to dispossess oneself of the spirit of Christianity." The critic adds that Baudelaire certainly loved God, even though he "seemed to require extreme debauchery in order to feel afterwards the need of purification."*]

[Baudelaire's] greatness is the sinister cold beauty he created. *Les Fleurs du Mal* is a book made with the fury of a child and the patience of an artist. One may pity all the romantic poets of the nineteenth century, nightingales whose song is measureless. But one can be afraid of Charles Baudelaire. He was very far from his contemporaries: Gautier, Hugo, Leconte de Lisle. He was very near Villon. . . . Baudelaire welcomed, in the midst of nineteenth century ruins, the true state of man.

The spirit of man is submitted to incessant metamorphoses and it is true that Baudelaire's book teaches that happiness is essentially what does not last. But the Christian spirit receives a special mark which is as clearly visible in *Les Fleurs du Mal* as in St. Augustine's *Confessions.* Christian thought possesses itself and never leaves itself. Baudelaire's solitude is filled and penetrated. It is the solitude of an exile who keeps the memory of a distant voyage he has never taken. (p. 95)

Les Fleurs du Mal is . . . a book of human courage and, moreover, a book of chastity. Readers today are becoming more aware of these two values of Baudelaire. His courage is his moment in history. . . . His chastity is his knowledge that one must desire the good even with an impoverished will. His passion attained the same purity of the great idealistic poets: Dante, Cavalcanti, Petrarch, but with more clairvoyance. The specifically French sign of passion is the clairvoyance of the heart which accompanies it.

Baudelaire's lyric humanism unquestionably played an important part in the creation of the epic humanism of Proust and Joyce. The richness and coherence of the Middle Ages will perhaps return. But the new order, as we are able to distinguish it today through the smoke and noise of war, has not yet gone beyond the search for order.

We like to consider Baudelaire's malady an incapacity to approach the good, the result of that myth of the modern age that man no longer needs God. But Baudelaire did not hesitate to proclaim that sin is a deicide. The ransom of the genius is heavy, heavier for Baudelaire and the modern artist than for Dante and Pascal. His terrible lucidity about the ransom explains why Baudelaire became one of the greatest critics of all time. His criticism is his real renovation because it is his psychological and theological knowledge, his understanding of man's reality. (pp. 96-7)

In the history of nineteenth century French poetry Baudelaire occupies a double place as announcer; on the one hand, as announcer of a spiritual restlessness . . . , and on the other hand as announcer of a new poetic preoccupation. It is difficult to dissociate the art of Baudelaire's poetry from the poet's experience. One engenders the other. The experience itself is not narrated however, but a "state" resulting from emotion or shock is transcribed. The transcription is the essence of what is most vacillating and most ineffable: a spiritual communication. The means used to produce this transcription are the most universal sensorial experiences of man apt to evoke or connote the particular personal experience of the poet. In this way the unique becomes the multiple, the unfathomable becomes the revealed. (p. 100)

The spectacle of the exterior world exists for Baudelaire only in so far as it reflects the spectacle of an inner peace or an inner disquietude. Both of these spectacles, the one materialistic and the other immaterial, are dark and discreet, guardians of strange secrets. Man, or more exactly the poet, builds his existence on the double rhythm of exploring the spectacle of life and the spectacle of himself. Both are fortresses impossible of capture in any ordinary manner. Both require a mystical approach. (p. 101)

Baudelaire as the artist eternally seeking unity, analogy, precision, is the poet of the short poem and, indeed, the artist of the single line. The image condensed, at times brutally explosive, harmonizes with the intense poetic state so difficult of attainment and so prone to vanish. (pp. 101-02)

If the imagery isn't striking in some of the poems, the musical element and the purely sensual vitality dominate. *Le Balcon,* for example, without condensing any images, except in one of its thirty lines, fuses various sentiments and evocations into a unified state. The setting sun and the warmth of the fire indicate that perishing light has called into the poet's mind the concept of imperishable love. . . . The dream of Baudelaire, evoked in a rare music of nostalgia, reaches its climax in the mystery of rejuvenation and rebirth. The rhythm of man's happiness is not even or sustained. A crescendo in order to become greater must sink first. *Le Balcon,* which is doubtless a memory of Jeanne Duval, develops the same plan as most of his spiritual pieces. Any approximation to a sense of order implies a previous state of disorder, a spiritualization of love follows the physical experience, an aspiration toward the Good results from a knowledge of Evil.

If the world is, in the words of Baudelaire, a vast system of contradictions, the preoccupation of the artist is to discover order where chaos exists. What is order in the world must of necessity be spiritual. The words themselves "esprit" and "spirituel" [spirit and spiritual] are the words most often used by Baudelaire. His art not only announces a conquest of the spiritual; it is the conquest itself. *Les Fleurs du Mal,* as truly as the *Divine Comedy,* and with greater personal anguish than the poem of Dante, is an art which both in its essence and in its adornments is the annunciation of God. One may object that Baudelaire defines Beauty as something ardent and sad, and that Beauty in God should be purity and joy. But a state outside of grace cannot be joyful, and does not exclude belief. Baudelaire, as an artist, is condemned to paint on darkness. But because this art is for him a magic in which he will use formulas of incantation, the darkness is black and yet luminous, "noire et pourtant lumineuse." In his prose writings he claims two literary qualities: supernaturalism and irony. Their commingling is the witchcraft which is the necessary procedure for

Baudelaire's communication. Satan has his own beauty in *Les Fleurs du Mal.*

Baudelaire has no illusions about the Demon at his side. He compares the influence of evil to the air around him. . . . Baudelaire seeks to reach a state of poetry. He does this, and very often he does more. The profound experience of his art succeeds in making the state of poetry a poetic state of grace. (pp. 102-04)

[Baudelaire] was a visionary who never knew ecstasy. The barrier (to use a favorite word of the mystics) which prevented Baudelaire from seeing more clearly was unquestionably eroticism. (p. 104)

But Baudelaire is an excellent proof for a belief the Church has always held; namely, that once a Christian, it is impossible to dispossess oneself of the spirit of Christianity. The sacraments leave an indelible mark. Baudelaire notes that as a child he held conversations with God; later, in the very midst of incredulity, he experienced a need for prayer. (pp. 104-05)

With a power comparable to Dante's, although not so sustained, Baudelaire paints the picture of sin in some of its blackest aspects. Curiously enough in this poetry, sin is rarely pictured without death. It is death in the true Villon style, the physical horror of decomposition. (p. 105)

Acedia is the sin which Baudelaire characterizes in his *Journaux Intimes* as the malady of monks. Acedia is also Baudelaire's sin which, coupled with eroticism, made his case one of the most hopeless. A lustful desire, if it exists by itself, may be conquered by exercise of the will. Acedia is precisely the sin of spiritual indolence. . . . [For] Baudelaire it was the "spleen," the spiritual impotency, which was at the base of his cerebral suffering.

In a sonnet to which he gave as a title the Biblical phrase, *De Profundis Clamavi,* Baudelaire synthesizes the major themes in *Les Fleurs du Mal:* his own tragic experience of twenty years, the spectacle of the universe which remains in his memory as a dull grey horizon . . . and, more precisely, the night of his disorder. . . . The whole sonnet is worthy of a mystic who has known the world and who has renounced it, a Jacopone da Todi or a Saint Augustine. It is the confession of a man who has experienced in the flesh the death of himself. The remarkable part of the piece is that it doesn't treat a pure pessimism, a pessimism like de Vigny's for example, which would reject all existence. Baudelaire's pessimism is mitigated by his understanding of it and by his prayer for aid. Even in the poems which are blasphemous, the poems of Baudelaire's so-called "satanism," his belief in Satan presupposes a belief in God [see excerpt above by T. S. Eliot, 1930]. (pp. 105-06)

Baudelaire seemed to require extreme debauchery in order to feel afterwards the need of purification. He would experience voluptuousness only when he would be conscious of sinning. He has recorded that after sin he experienced a great thirst for purity and beauty. This he calls an avenging mystery. In the brute an angel awakens. (p. 106)

The moment [Baudelaire] felt remorse and hope coincided with disgust for sin. This is a mystical experience which has been recorded in the narratives of countless conversions. When Baudelaire comments on the art of Daumier, he expresses a truth about his own work. The artist has used satire and mockery in depicting the spirit of evil in the world, but in the very energy and sincerity of his conception of evil, he has revealed the beauty of his heart. His laughter is impure: it has an element

of horror. His ribaldry is impure: it has an element of disgust. (p. 107)

In the cases of both Baudelaire and Racine, we can see a man convinced of a reality greater than himself and, at the same time, of a man who, after touching eternity and recognizing it to be such, lost his grasp on it. Their unhappiness lay in the intermittence of the pure vision which they knew existed beyond the cloud of worldliness. (p. 108)

The irony of Baudelaire, which is absent only from his most elevated pieces, is never the sign of spiritual raillery; it is rather the indication of his heart which has not been tricked. Baudelaire unquestionably loved God. But he knew another love which prevented the first from acting. It was his love for the lie. The poet in love with a woman never effaced the man intelligent enough to see through the mask of woman's deceit. (p. 110)

It was not only the dichotomy of Baudelaire's loves that engendered his irony and frustration; it was also his search for God within himself. All the Catholic practices imposed upon the faithful are built upon the belief that God is outside of man and that He has to be met in a meeting place. . . . Reason in man must desire God, but the will must act in order to find Him. Reason and Nature are imperfect in themselves. They demand the aid of grace which alone is able to give them supernatural life. (p. 111)

Wallace Fowlie, "Charles Baudelaire: The Experience of Religious Heroism," in his Clowns and Angels: Studies in Modern French Literature, *Sheed and Ward, Inc., 1943, pp. 93-111.*

JOSEPH D. BENNETT (essay date 1944)

[*In his full-length study of Baudelaire, Bennett analyzes Baudelaire's dandyism, which he characterizes as a combination of pride and wisdom. Like T. S. Eliot (1930) and Wallace Fowlie (1943), Bennett considers Baudelaire a religious man; he maintains that "Baudelaire used the Christian concept of human nature and destiny as a touchstone to expose the falsity of the ideas of the nineteenth century." Bennett also discusses several of Baudelaire's individual poems in relation to dandyism and religion.*]

[Baudelaire's dandyism] was a consciousness of his own uniqueness as a genius, a child of the gods. It was not dandyism, but monarchism; and he was the sole and absolute monarch: "The dandy should aspire to be sublime, without interruption. He ought to live and to sleep before a mirror." This mirror is his court, his palace, his Versailles. . . . (pp. 5-6)

The dandy is a Romantic projection of an ideal self which is pride incarnate. The dandy strives to be completely *a se;* uncaused, uncreated, independent of every social tie to family, friends, or nation. His only function is to exist; he is superb and his leisure is creative. (p. 7)

[We may] inquire whether or not the dandy represents the Devil, since he is an incarnation of unlimited egotism and cruel pride. His elegance and his politeness are refined expressions of this hateful vanity. From the picture of the early dandyism of Baudelaire, we can appreciate the amount of travail and suffering which was required to purge him of it. The rest of his life is a story of slow agonizing *purgation,* by which the dandy, the pride-devil, was torn out of him, leaving alone within him the man of charity. Baudelaire, as dandy, was

Pascal's man of intellect (*esprit*). But the man of the greatest intellect is infinitely far below the man of charity. . . .

The early dandyism is not completely diabolical; it is mixed with unusual wisdom. (p. 8)

We know that when Baudelaire says "to be a useful man has always appeared to me as something quite hideous," he means that the man "useful" for the production of material goods and services in a bourgeois or a socialist economy is useful merely as a machine is useful. Such a man has no spiritual life and no excesses. But Baudelaire at [his dandy] stage will not pity this automaton; he must triumph over him and give vent to his *superbia* by implying "Thank God that I am not as other men" in his remark. His dandy's pride is involved with his wisdom. His dandyism is even the starting point for his brilliant analysis and denunciation of the doctrines of natural goodness, the danger of which he sensed. As he became more convinced of the natural evil in man and in his impulses, his dandyism came to be a barrier of artificial restraints—of courtesy, of religious restraints in the ethical sphere—which he set up against his natural impulse toward evil. But the danger of pride is still resident in dandyism when he infuses it with the ideal of sainthood, the life of religious restraint. He is constantly tempted to be proud of his momentary and infrequent successes in restraint, or of his mere advocacy, without enactment, of restraint. Then he uses his ideal of sainthood as an instrument of scorn, as in his attack on George Sand. Every word he says about her is true. But he cannot avoid making his unusual wisdom and insight a sort of triumph-festival, or field day for his own pride.

We can see this demon of pride ineradicably haunting his Journals and his criticism. The fact that he can scarcely suppress it gives us an idea of the intensity of his suffering. His pride was a much greater obstacle to him than his lust, or his use of alcohol and drugs. The dandy would of course consider himself able to suppress his lust and his use of stimulants. It would be part of his pride, his independence. A demon would certainly not be subject to these fleshy weaknesses; his diabolical pride would prevent them.

Baudelaire's suffering comes from tearing out his demon by the roots. If Baudelaire had been only a demon, he would not have suffered, nor would his flesh have been so weak as to cry out with pain when Black Jeanne was separated from him. The Journals give us the record of this suffering. We know that he suffered equally from himself and from "the tyranny of the human face." But when he had to confront both at once, he was sorely tried. When this exquisite man went abroad in the city, it seemed that he gave himself out, prostituted himself, exhausted his energy in facing every visage he saw. (pp. 9-10)

[In one of Baudelaire's last writings, he] remembers and extols the Lord's law and judgeship even though he is condemned by this law. He is grateful for the terror which God has put into him, for it has brought him to fear his Lord. He knows he has been a monster of pride and lust; he feels the closeness of lunacy, "the wind from the wing of imbecility" at his ear. He blames himself for having made himself a monster. He does not blame God, but is utterly humble, opened out flat for his Creator to inspect, like a cloth on the ground. The process of Purgation is complete and he is ready to die. (p. 11)

At the end of his purgatory, we found Baudelaire a religious man, ready for his Creator. But what sort of a religion? His religious feeling was all important to his life at the end. He

was in the process of being saved; he had undergone severe religious experience in which he had been clawed open by Irresistible Grace. He certainly believes in the God of the Jews and the Christians. A sinner, he appeals to this God as both just Judge and dispenser of forgiveness. It is the same God that Descartes discovered at the end of his syllogism of universal doubt: the God about whom he had been taught, as a child, in the French Catholic schools. But did he believe in the divinity of Christ? Christ had been for some time "of Gods, the most incontestable." Yet, even by the time of his death, Baudelaire had not assumed belief in the Trinity. It is probable that at the time of his death, he was headed in that direction.

Baudelaire is close to the orthodox view of human nature. He stresses the natural depravity and original sinfulness of human nature. His religious consciousness develops from his knowledge of the evil within him and of the Devil attacking him through his corruption. He is thus orthodox on the most important point, the one which the nineteenth century refused to believe. But he is heretical in his constant emphasis on the absolute empire of evil and Satan over human nature. (p. 12)

He grew up in a literary atmosphere which considered Satan the hero of *Paradise Lost*. Satan was the rebellious Hernani defying his unjust ruler. He was a Byronic hero, wronged and defiant, the companion of Alpine scenery and thunderstorms.

The Satanism of his adolescence did serve to represent the attractiveness of vice throughout his life. It remained as a melodramatic background for his few unsuccessful poems—poems cluttered with the machinery of horror, rats, corpses, and demons. But Satan, though attractive, is never a sympathetic figure in the mature poems. . . . We must remember, too, that Baudelaire is not a theologian. As a poet, he has a right to exploit Satan as a symbol. (p. 13)

The poet is concerned with arousing, juxtaposing, and fusing the paradoxes which inform our cogent experience. In doing so he orders it, or reconciles it. But he avoids systematization insofar as it is formal and deductive. He may feel (and generally does) that he has exceeded this level of discourse in that he has achieved suggestion and polysignification, that he has actualized rather than baldly stated the content of the situation which he exploits. He lays no claim to nor has he any desire to incur the laborious but necessary systematization of the responsible theologian.

The stylistic precursor of Baudelaire's Journals is Pascal, which whets their surgical and dissective tactic; but more important, their ideological atmosphere is to a considerable extent Pascalian, and, insofar as it is, it supplies Baudelaire with standards for criticism which enabled him to exhaust the evils of his time as he concentrated his gaze upon the certain alternatives which the psychology, eschatology, and ethic of the tradition of Paul, Augustine, and Pascal afforded him. (pp. 13-14)

Baudelaire used the Christian concept of human nature and destiny as a touchstone to expose the falsity of the ideas of the nineteenth century. (p. 14)

Baudelaire attacked especially those ideas which cover up the contradictions and paradox in our experience by omitting those parts of it which give us difficulty. The doctrine of progress violates his experience of the depravity and destructiveness rooted in human nature which certainly cannot be removed by human craft or ingenuity. (pp. 14-15)

For Baudelaire, the devotion of the century to utility and commerce is evidence of its retrogression. It is a blatant and self-congratulatory display of egotism of the crudest sort. All functions except those of poet, priest, and warrior are given up to cupidity and utility. (p. 15)

In detecting his existence and in appraising his great power, Baudelaire has a defense against Satan; he has exposed him. Baudelaire is not duped by evil; he has branded evil as evil and in the act of naming, or identification, he has thrown up a protective buttress. We cannot say then that for Baudelaire Satan, having deposed God, is omnipotent. That would be true only for a man who does not believe in the existence of the Devil and who is thereby in bondage to him.

Baudelaire violently rejected the idea of man possessing natural goodness. Whatever charity man possesses comes as a result of spiritual effort and supernatural grace. (pp. 15-16)

Baudelaire's attack on the doctrines of natural goodness comes directly from his cardinal conviction and experience of the original, natural, universal sinfulness of man. It is this belief which informs all of his writings. Man is piteous, lamentable, surely damned; and all the more so because he feels he needs no help, that he can save himself by his own secular effort.

For Baudelaire then, the central problem is a religious problem. And the religious problem to him and to most men is most seriously apparent in the constant encroachment of evil upon them. Baudelaire has the clairvoyance which can see evil as evil in spite of *volupté* [sensual pleasure], and that "It is the devil who holds the strings which move us." His religious theme is the play of concupiscence and voluptuousness upon us; the terror and delight which our slow decline into hell brings us. Baudelaire's hell, like Dante's, is not for the other people; it is for us. (pp. 16-17)

Behind the poems is persistent and meticulous scholarship which searches the problem of evil. Evil is not abstractly conceived in a proposition for metaphysical speculation. It is presented as it feeds on the marrow of men, as it incubates, and circulates within them. It tinges every thought and act, and instigates most of them, for morality, to the religious man, is mainly criticism, restraint upon previously incubated selfishness. Evil is irrational, inexplicable, impossible, and yet ingrained in every particular. In Baudelaire's poems, no corners are lopped off the problem to make it easy to get evil rationally explained.

In the ordered and climactic experience which these poems arouse, the central paradox is still a paradox, unresolved. Stimulating and evocative, it works out in many concentric combinations which spread away from the poem and into our sensibilities as readers and bystanders, until we too are involved in the drama and participate in the evil thereof, like toy boats set rocking by the concentric, expanding ripples started in the water by the plunge of a rock. We *correspond* to the poem and to the paradox of evil much as the poet corresponds to the poem or snail-shell he leaves behind, and as the elements fusing within the crucible of the poem itself correspond to each other. The elements are selectively induced as representatives of experience. (pp. 17-18)

Baudelaire's poems are concrete, which is another way of saying that they are paradoxical. Every concrete object is a mystery because, like a paradox, it cannot be solved or decided. It is in this respect that poetry renders our experience. It presents the paradoxes but does not explain them. It refines, channels, and sharpens for presentation the subtleties of the interplay and interdevelopment of these conjunctions of opposites. And it is the conjunction of opposites which lies at the basis of poetry, by its very form and technique, its rhythm, and especially by its central power and tool: the trope, or figure of speech. All figures of speech and metaphor depend on comparison. They harness two objects or facts in our physical or emotional cosmos which on the surface seem to have no relation. (pp. 18-19)

What did Baudelaire accomplish within and beyond the barriers of his time? He accepted the doctrine of Gautier and Poe against moralization and didacticism. Poetry has only itself as an object. It should not be used for metaphysical speculation, for the development of ethical notions, or for any political or economic end. Thus Baudelaire opposes the philosophic poetry of Leconte de Lisle while admiring his small number of purely descriptive poems, such as the ones about animals. Nor does he follow Gautier's aesthetic. He takes objectivity as a discipline only and surcharges it with personal feeling—with anguish, with knowledge of sin, or with enjoyment of the harmony of *volupté*.

The discipline prevents the personal feeling in the poems from overflowing their objective frame into the subjective flood of Lamartine, Musset, and Hugo. Baudelaire does not wish to divert us with melancholy and joy, but to awaken us, to make us see clearly the mystery which surrounds our life. He brings us directly before the genuine problems by making them evident with unusual clarity. And clarity is out of place in the poems of his immediate predecessors. Vagueness of imagery and language chosen for sound give them a fuzzy effect. The images in such a poem may be interchanged; for the vague longing which they arouse and picturize is identical from image to image. The emotion aroused in such a poem is constant likewise. In this way the average poem, written in Baudelaire's period and before it, is a whole which is merely the sum of all its parts. (p. 26)

The fascination of the poems of Baudelaire is that they are surds; they cannot be dissolved; they are suggestive in that they actualize the genuine problems, but do not solve them. These problems and paradoxes are the ones outlined earlier in connection with the nature of evil and sin.

There is also paradox in the relation of the poet to the external world—paradox for which they keys are symbol, metaphor, trope—paradox in developing that external world to *correspond* with what we call an internal experience. The poet is then not only the maker, but the synthesizer; he who makes the forms to correspond; he who orders, reconciles, coheres our experience, preserving intact its paradoxical (that is, real, unresolved, integral, irreducible, inexplicable) nature. (p. 27)

The harmonies, reverberations, and correspondences between sounds, colors, and perfumes exist in Baudelaire's mind as it is projected into external nature. These harmonies are, therefore, all dependent upon the basic correspondence between the internal and external worlds of the poet and are valid insofar as the poet integrates the external world with himself, coloring it with his individuality.

In relation to the problems of composition and form, Baudelaire was a dandy. Rejecting the concept of genius-inspiration, he substituted artifice for natural overflow. His revisions are infinite, his labor is painstaking. His artifice is built up with a search for the exact word and the exact sound. Even when he uses "abyss" and "gulf," his language is clear and precise. He has a horror of vagueness and facility. . . . (p. 28)

Baudelaire's success, like that of all great art, comes as a product of the tension between the spontaneity that gives birth to the organism and the discipline that shapes and prunes it. The discipline is the part which the artist adds to the unformed stuff; it is in this sense that the artist is said to create.

There are obstacles to Baudelaire's attainment of perfection aside from the universal poetic obstacle of the rock which must be hewn, and may possibly never be hewn correctly. One of these is his abuse of oratory and rhetoric. Another is his apparatus of horror imagery by which we often imagine he is merely trying to scare us. (p. 29)

The opening poem ["**Au Lecteur**"] of *Les Fleurs du Mal* broaches the central religious paradox: the question of the joint existence of good and evil; the problem of sin. (p. 32)

"**Au Lecteur**" begins the treatment of the attractiveness of evil. Our spirits are *occupied* by evil; they are its demesne. It alone directs our bodies . . . , working them for its purposes, as a selfish foreman would work and abuse a gang of day laborers. Our sorrow for wrongdoing is ironically exposed. . . . The most real and apparent force in our cosmos is Satan Trismegistus—thrice-powerful. . . . He rules us and we delight in his rule; we proceed to his hell *sans horreur* [without horror]. But our subjection to him is underlaid by irony. We mock ourselves for being his puppets. And when we find the exact, the superb metaphor which expresses our pleasure at his rule, we find that it is a witty one: . . .

> Like an impoverished debauchee who kisses and eats
> The martyred breast of an antique whore
> We steal in passing a clandestine pleasure
> Which we press very strongly like an old orange.

Its irony gives it its strength, makes it the exact metaphor, because it introduces the paradox. Evil is not an unmixed delight. It violates our dignity; it makes us beasts. The superb mutually contributory metaphors of the harlot's breast and the orange make us see this; but in the subtlest way possible. We seem to discover this fact for ourselves, unaided by the poem. Seeking pleasure, we squeeze a shrunken breast as we would squeeze an old orange, clamping our strong teeth to it, draining it dry. We devour it without ceremony and without restraint, seeking immediate efficient satisfaction of our desire. But we are then paradoxically gaining pleasure from a disgusting, ugly object. We are beasts because we require no beauty for the satisfaction of our desire. We find pleasure in ugliness. Thus the suggestive and precise metaphor has given a vivid knowledge of the nature of evil which a thousand lines of didactic, moralistic poetry could never bring home. We have knowledge because we have contributed our effort to that of the poem. It has enabled us to find out the nature of evil for ourselves. This is characteristic of all of Baudelaire's successful imagery. . . . (pp. 32-4)

In hitting upon the exact phrase, Baudelaire has harmonized or *corresponded* the external and internal worlds, the natural and spiritual realms. All are bound up together.

It is in this sense that the poet sees in nature *forêts de symboles* [forests of symbols] and calls nature *un dictionnaire* [a dictionary]. There exists in nature a correspondence to every psychological state. It is the poet's job to find that correspondence—not merely to state his psychological state, . . . but to find it in nature and actualize it in metaphor and symbol. Thus the poet tends to create his own exterior world and to project

himself into it. He orders it and arranges it to express his sensibility. . . .

"**Au Lecteur**" is unusually rich in successful metaphor. Baudelaire strikes the perfect phrase with amazing accuracy. (p. 35)

[In this poem], evil rides high in every human breast, held back and increased in attractiveness by timidity and fear. The soul of the bourgeois Pharisee (whether a devotee of religious or commercial Pharisaism) is as rotten with vice and egotism as the murderer's:

> Si le viol, le poison, le poignard, l'incendie,
> N'ont pas encor brodé de leurs plaisants dessins
> Le canevas banal de nos piteux destins,
> C'est que notre âme, hélas! n'est pas assez hardie.
>
> If rape, poison, the dagger, and arson
> Have not yet embroidered with their pleasant designs
> The banal canvas of our pitiful destinies,
> It is because, alas, our spirit is not bold enough.

Le canevas banal! It strikes you immediately. We conceive our destinies pictorially. But they are *banal, piteux*. They are Watteau and Fragonard canvases—conventional reproductions of the "Eldorado banal." We long to give them the grandeur of sin—to achieve the damnation denied to shopkeepers and bank presidents. If we could attain genuine vice, we could find adventure and relish in life. Genuine vice is not excess, as most people understand it to be. It is the struggle that goes on in evil against good and that goes on within good to attain evil, just as virtue is the struggle in good against evil. We are all secret criminals. (pp. 37-8)

Baudelaire, in his famous apostrophe to the reader: *Hypocrite lecteur,—mon semblable—mon frère!* (Hypocritical reader—my likeness—my brother!) is indicating that the attraction of evil is not peculiar to him, but is *au lecteur*—for the reader. He is also indicating his powers of absorption of the external world and self-projection. . . . (p. 38)

The poet knows that the self-satisfied *lecteur* is *hypocrite*, because he has examined the race of *lecteurs*. . . . He has observed that his own experience is true archetype of that of his fellows; he projects himself into his fellows and so orders their experience in his poem that it is index of the evil within them when they read it. Their experience is no longer a confused mass of temptations, consolations, and self-satisfaction as it was before they came to the poem. (p. 39)

"**Au Lecteur**" concludes with the celebrated statement that ennui is the most evil vice and crime in which we can indulge. . . . Ennui, it would seem certainly cannot be a crime, worse than murder or adultery. It appears on the surface merely to be innocent lassitude. . . . [For Baudelaire], "all our unhappiness comes from having wished a change in place." Ennui, the desire for a change in place, is thus one of the principal circles in Baudelaire's Inferno. (pp. 39-40)

[Ennui] is also for Baudelaire a state of abstraction, of removal from the paradox which gives tension and significance to our life. Ennui removes us from the world of good and evil to an *abstract* world of moral and spiritual unconsciousness, where we are not troubled by the asymmetry of the principal paradoxical problems of life. Ennui convinces us that the Devil does not exist; that he is a childish or a medieval superstition, fantastic and impossible. So rid of the Devil, the person possessed by ennui does evil, not knowing that it is evil. He is then firmly in the Devil's grasp, having fallen victim to his strongest ruse. . . . Satan *lives* in the victim of ennui; he *attacks* the conscious sinner. The consciousness of sin can release from ennui. The consciousness that the evil in our lives is overcoming the good makes life dramatic and gives significance to every moment of it, just as the reverse process in the saintly Christian makes every moment significant in view of ultimate redemption.

Baudelaire's Satan is not a Byronic hero, although that idea is present in his youthful poems, where God is presented as "the tyrant gorged by the sobs of tortured martyrs," where Cain "mounts to the sky and throws God upon the earth," and where Satan is Bacchus, god of pleasure. The idea of Satan represents the fact that as free agents we have the power to transgress divine law. The concept of Satan is the necessary concomitant of the concept of free will. Paradoxically, we cannot be free without also being subject to evil. The religious life is the purification and perfection of freedom, so that it may, with Divine grace, be proof against evil. The religious life is laid in the cosmos of Pascal; it is tension, strife, paradox. Though he is relieved from the subtler pangs of ennui, the sinner is tormented by the realization of his abandonment to evil all along the route of degradation. (pp. 40-2)

"Au Lecteur" introduced us to Baudelaire's Inferno, which is for us; not for the other fellow or the conventional villain, such as the capitalist or the labor leader. It entails a belief in both the divine and sinful potentialities of the fallen human spirit. It is a belief in the validity and all-importance of spiritual phenomena which are ignored in the modern world of abstractions, ennui, control-techniques, and therapy. . . . (p. 42)

"Femmes Damnées" is the best example of Baudelaire's presentation of a situation which is developed as an illumination of the moral problem, but deftly, imperceptibly, without didacticism. . . .

The Lesbian women, Delphine and Hippolyte, are symbols expressing in their deed and their spiritual distress Baudelaire's conception of the sterility of lust. Their particular lust, as most sterile of all, is but the type of all lust. Lust rages and wrenches the spirit which can never be consumed by its fires and thus can never find surcease. (p. 52)

Baudelaire possibly chose Lesbian rather than heterosexual lust for "Femmes Damnées" because he wished to illustrate that deformity and perversity—unnatural qualities—are part of vice and crime; that the sinful is what revolts against the harmony and order which is the basis for the moral life—moral life which is at the same time the truly aesthetic life. Morality and aesthetics are nearly the same. . . . (p. 56)

[The longer poems, of which "Femmes Damnées"] is the best example, are well sustained performances, but seem overgrown. One well-executed stanza succeeds another, but their development seems inconclusive. The poems have been allowed to ramble and ruminate. The result is dissipation of cumulative impact. Each stanza is in itself marshaled for attack. But the links between stanzas present not transitions to fresh developments and perspectives, but extensions and supplements. When a genuine modulation or movement is made, the effect is lost. The poem seems merely to ruminate within a succession of new channels which are in turn exhausted of complementary material. The individual stanzas are tightly composed and well stocked with brilliant metaphor. But they do not combine to form an organism. (pp. 159-60)

For this reason, the shorter poems . . . are Baudelaire's aesthetic and formal achievement. Certain larger poems, "Au

Lecteur" and "La Béatrice," which are not so well made as the best shorter poems, possess considerable structural strength and good sustention of intensity of language and rhetorical impetus. There is subtlety in their use of nexus. Among the larger poems, "Femmes Damnées" is a well-sustained performance. But most of the longer important poems have in addition to the structural faults of "Femmes Damnées" a number of mediocre stanzas. Poems such as "A Celle Qui Est Trop Gaie," "L'Imprévu," "Les Petites Vieilles," "Une Voyage à Cythère," "Le Beau Navire," "L'Irrémédiable," "Le Voyage," and others, I have considered only in part. Each contains brilliant verses which make the poems memorable. And each contains dependable standard verses which fill in adequately, but are not distinguished. (p. 160)

Notwithstanding his failure to sustain a high level of intensity in most of his poems, it is apparent that Baudelaire was striving for the perfectly reduced poem, one of uniform high excellence, of which one verse could not be compared to the disadvantage of another. This was *ipso facto* [by that very fact] the poem of perfect structure, because it was so skillfully joined that it could not be dismantled for the purpose of critical comparison of some of its components at the expense of others. The poorly constructed poems may be dismantled easily. . . .

The shorter poems cannot be sectioned. They are rigorously ordered. There are no seams, no crevices, no soft spots. Mr. R. P. Blackmur has remarked that Baudelaire, a disordered, excruciated man, expressed his disorder in a carefully ordered and disciplined poetic form. (p. 161)

We must accord Baudelaire his seat within the poetic hierarchy. His skill in form and language broke him off from his predecessors, and made him the stem and starting point for subsequent French poetry and for English poetry from Pound and Yeats onward. Modern poetry learned from him the use of precise and compelling metaphor, the use of language both exactly clear and connotative, and the discriminating utilization of paradox, all of which had fallen into disuse since the seventeenth century. Baudelaire announces the decline of the era of vagueness, sentiment, and loose outpourings of personality. He upholds precision and clarity. He discloses precisely and clearly the nature of a given act or state of mind.

His language, in addition to this, produces subsurface relations of meaning which enhance the initial precision by delimiting more closely the quality of the act or state of mind described. To obtain this quality, precision is required first of all in the denotative, or apparent, surface meaning. This initial precision is refined by the addition of subsurface meanings which pare down the possibilities of meaning to the one or two which will satisfy all the conditions exacted by the metaphors. When this precision is applied, the hypocrisy which surrounds the principal dramatic situations found in the world falls away, and poetry of great power and passion may result. This precision is an intensity of focus which allows for maximum penetration by language of those surfaces of hypocrisy and euphemism which conceal the world of the conscience and which obstruct our attempt to use the natural world as a source for metaphors and symbols of spiritual states.

Baudelaire's excruciation likewise entitles him to a seat in the hierarchy, seeing that his disorder was expressed in an orderly form. His disorder presents a nakedness and lack of pretense which enables his skilled language to work up metal which is drawn directly from the furnace of lust, egotism, and the nonsensual desires. He was spiritually alive even in his degradation. He was never utterly lost because he knew that what he was involved in was evil. (pp. 162-63)

Joseph D. Bennett, in his Baudelaire: A Criticism *(copyright 1944; copyright © 1972 renewed by David P. Bennett, Jr. and George Bennett; excerpts reprinted by permission of Princeton University Press), second edition, Princeton University Press, 1944, 165 p.*

JEAN-PAUL SARTRE   (essay date 1947)

[*Sartre is regarded as one of the most influential contributors to world literature in the twentieth century. As with all his work, the basis of Sartre's criticism is existentialism: a philosophy that places a greater emphasis on existence than on essence. For the existentialist, human reason cannot adequately explain the problems of existence, and it is through action rather than intellection that the individual finds meaning in life. In his study* Baudelaire, *from which the following excerpt is drawn, Sartre examines the author in relation to the social conditions under which he wrote and the changes he underwent as a result of historical events. Critics have referred to this volume as an example of a new genre: existentialist biography. Sartre discusses Baudelaire's philosophy of sin and suffering; Sartre maintains that Baudelaire enjoyed sinning, and that his suffering served to express his own lack of satisfaction and dismay at being part of the world. Baudelaire only accepted ultimate Good, Sartre states, in order to violate it.*]

Through pride and rancour [Baudelaire] tried all his life to *turn himself into a thing* in the eyes of other people and in his own. He wanted to take up his stand at a distance from the great social fête like a statue, like something definitive and opaque which could not be assimilated. In a word, we can say that he wanted to *be*—and by that we mean the obstinate, carefully defined mode of being which belongs to an object. But Baudelaire would never for a moment have tolerated in this being, which he wanted to force on the attention of others and enjoy himself, the passiveness and unconsciousness of a utensil. He certainly wanted to be an object, but not a thing which had come into being by mere chance. This thing was to be his very own; it would achieve salvation if it could be established that it had created itself and that it alone maintained its own being. . . . He clung to a ready-made universe where Good and Evil were settled in advance and in which he occupied his appointed place. He chose to have a conscience which was always tormented, was always a bad conscience. His insistence on man's perpetual dualism, on the double postulation, on body and soul, on the horror and ecstasy of life, reflected his divided spirit. Because he wanted at the same time to be and to exist, because he continually fled from existence to being and from being to existence, he was nothing but a gaping wound. All his actions and each of his thoughts had two meanings—were dominated by two contradictory intentions which issued commands to one another and destroyed one another. He preserved Good in order to be able to do Evil, and if he did Evil it was in order to pay tribute to Good. If he departed from the Norm, it was in order to bring home to himself the power of Law, so that a look could judge him and classify him in spite of himself in the universal hierarchy; but if he recognized this Order and this supreme power explicitly, it was in order to escape from them and to become conscious of his solitude in sin. In these monsters which he worshipped he found first and foremost the indefeasible laws of the World in the sense that 'the exception proves the rule'; but he found them parodied and derided. Nothing about him was simple; he ended by losing himself in

them and by writing in a state of despair: 'I have such a strange soul that I don't even recognize myself in it.' . . . Baudelaire's feelings had a sort of interior emptiness. He tried by a perpetual frenzy, by an extraordinary nervousness to make up for their insufficiency. In vain. They sounded hollow. He reminds us of the neurasthenic who was convinced that he had an ulcerated stomach and who rolled shrieking and trembling on the floor, drenched in perspiration; but there was no pain. If we could put out of our minds the exaggerated vocabulary which Baudelaire used to describe himself, forget words like 'frightful', 'nightmare' and 'horror' which occur on every page of the *Fleurs du mal,* and penetrate right into his heart we should perhaps find beneath the anguish, the remorse and the vibrating nerves something gentler and much more intolerable than the most painful of ills—Indifference. (pp. 79-82)

[The] sufferings of which Baudelaire complained were in the nature of an alleviation of his wrongdoing. They established a sort of reciprocity between the sinner and the judge. The sinner had offended the judge, but the judge was the cause of the sinner's unjust sufferings which represented, symbolically, the impossible transcendence of Good in the attempt to achieve freedom. They were credits drawn by Baudelaire on the theocratic universe in which he had chosen to live. (p. 93)

The function of Baudelaire's particular form of suffering was to express non-satisfaction. 'The sensitive modern man' did not suffer for this or that reason in particular, but in a general way because nothing on this earth could satisfy his desires. People have claimed that this was an appeal to heaven; but, as we have already seen, Baudelaire never had the faith except during a period when he was enfeebled by sickness. His non-satisfaction resulted rather from the consciousness that he suddenly acquired of man's transcendence. Whatever the circumstances, whatever the pleasure offered, man was perpetually beyond them; he transcended them in order to attain other goals and finally in order to possess himself. . . . Baudelaire, who was incapable of action and who found himself bounced into short-term enterprises which he used to abandon only to fall into a stupor, discovered in himself, if one can say so, an unfulfilled transcendence. . . . Baudelaire's non-satisfaction drove him to transcend for the sake of transcending. It was a form of suffering because nothing could overcome or assuage it. (pp. 96-7)

Baudelaire's suffering was the empty exercise of his transcendence in face of the given. His suffering enabled him to adopt the pose of not being of this world. It was another form of his revenge on Good. To the extent, indeed, to which he deliberately submitted to the divine Rule, which was paternal and social, Good enveloped and crushed him. He lay, so to speak, at the bottom of Good as though it were a well. But his transcendence avenged him: even though crushed and battered by the waves of Good, man is always something else. There was only one thing. If Baudelaire had gone on living his transcendence to the end, it would have led him to challenge Good itself, to move forward to other goals which really would have been his goals. He refused; he stifled the positive impulse; he only wanted to experience it in its negative form of non-satisfaction which was like a continual mental reservation. Through suffering the loop was looped, the system made a closed one. Baudelaire submitted to Good in order to violate it; and if he violated it, it was in order to feel its grip more powerfully; it was in order to be condemned in its name, labelled, transformed into a guilty *thing*. But through suffering he once more escaped condemnation; he discovered once more that he was spirit and freedom. The game was free from risk; he did not challenge Good; he did not transcend it; he simply found it unsatisfying. (pp. 97-8)

[It] was not by chance that Baudelaire saw in Satan the perfect type of suffering beauty. Satan, who was vanquished, fallen, guilty, denounced by the whole of Nature, banned from the universe, crushed beneath the memory of an unforgivable sin, devoured by insatiable ambition, transfixed by the eye of God, which froze him in his diabolical essence, and compelled to accept to the bottom of his heart the supremacy of Good—Satan, nevertheless, prevailed against God, his master and conqueror, by his suffering, by that flame of non-satisfaction which, at the very moment when divine omnipotence crushed him, at the very moment when he acquiesced in being crushed, shone like an unquenchable reproach. In this game of 'whoever loses wins', it was the vanquished who, *precisely because he was vanquished,* carried off the victory. Proud and vanquished, penetrated by the feeling of his uniqueness in the face of the world, Baudelaire identified himself in the secrecy of his heart with Satan. Human pride has never, perhaps, been pushed farther than this cry, which is always stifled, always repressed, but which echoes all through Baudelaire's work: '*I am* Satan!' But at bottom what was Satan except the symbol of disobedient sulky children who asked that their father's look should freeze them in their singular essence and who did wrong in the framework of Good in order to assert their singularity and to have it consecrated?

The reader will no doubt be a little disappointed with this 'portrait'. . . . For many people, indeed, Baudelaire is, rightly, purely and simply the author of the **Fleurs du mal;** and they regard any form of research as useless which does not increase our appreciation and understanding of Baudelaire's poetry. (pp. 99-100)

He possessed, as it were, a profound intuition of the obstinate, amorphous contingency which is life—it was the precise opposite of work—and he was horrified by it because it seemed to him to reflect the gratuitousness of his own consciousness which he wanted to conceal from himself at any price. As a townsman, he loved the geometrical object which was subjected to human rationalization. . . . He wanted work to leave its impress even on the fluidity of water; and since it was impossible to give it a solidity which was incompatible with its natural properties, he would have liked, on account of his horror of its subsidence and its wandering ductility, to imprison it between walls, to give it a geometrical shape. . . . Baudelaire was a townsman and for him *real* water, *real* light and *real* heat meant those which one found in towns and which were already works of art unified by a governing idea. For work had conferred on them a function and a place in the human hierarchy. . . . Baudelaire dreamed of an existence in a moral hierarchy where he would have had a function and a value in exactly the same way that a de luxe suitcase or the tractable water in jugs exists in the hierarchy of utensils.

But first and foremost what Baudelaire called Nature was life. When he spoke of Nature he always mentioned plants and animals. Vigny's *impassible Nature* was the sum total of physico-chemical laws. Baudelaire's was more pervasive. It was a vast, warm, abundant force which penetrated everywhere. He had a horror of this damp warmth, this abundance. This natural prolificness, which knocked off a million copies of the same model, was bound to clash with his love of rarity. He too could say: 'I love the thing that will never be seen a second time.' And he intended it as a eulogy of absolute sterility. What he

could not abide about paternity was the continuity of life between the progenitor and his descendants, which meant that the first begetter was compromised by those who came after him and went on leading an obscure and humiliating life in them. This biological eternity seemed intolerable to him: the rare being took the secret of his creation with him to the grave. Baudelaire wanted to be completely sterile because it was the only means of putting a price on himself. (pp. 104-07)

The form of *creation* which he lauded to the skies was the opposite of parturition. It did not involve one in compromise. No doubt it was still a form of prostitution, but in this case the cause—the infinite and inexhaustible spirit—remained unchanged after producing its effect. As for the created object, it did not live; it was imperishable and inanimate like a stone or an eternal truth. Yet one must not create with too great an abundance under pain of a *rapprochement* with Nature. Baudelaire often showed his repugnance for Hugo's gross temperament. If he wrote little, it was not on account of impotence. His poems would have seemed less rare to him if they had not been the product of exceptional acts of the mind. Their small number like their perfection was intended to underline their 'supernatural' character; Baudelaire pursued *infecundity* all his life. And in the world which surrounded him, the things which found grace in his eyes were the hard, sterile forms of minerals. In the *Poèmes en prose,* he wrote:

> This town stands at the edge of the water. It is said that it is built of marble and that the inhabitants have such a hatred of plant life that they uproot all the trees. It is a landscape which suits (my) taste: a landscape composed of light and minerals with water to reflect them.
>
> (pp. 107-08)

[For] him metal and, in a general way, minerals reflected the image of the mind. One of the results of the limits of our imaginative powers is that all those who, in their endeavours to understand the opposition between the spirit and life and the body, have been driven to form a non-biological image of it, have necessarily had to appeal to the kingdom of inanimate things —light, cold, transparency, sterility. . . . [Steel]—the most brilliant, the most highly polished of metals and the one which offers least grip—always appeared to [Baudelaire] to be the exact objectification of his Thought in general. If he felt a tenderness towards the sea, it was because it was a mobile mineral. It was because it was brilliant, inaccessible and cold with a pure and, as it were, an immaterial movement. Because it possessed those forms which succeeded one another, that changed without anything which changed, and sometimes that transparency, that it offered the most adequate image of the spirit. It *was* spirit. Thus Baudelaire's horror of life led him to choose materialization in its purest form as a symbol of the immaterial.

Above everything else, he had a horror of feeling this vast, soft fecundity in himself. (pp. 108-09)

Nature was the first movement, spontaneity, immediacy, pure uncalculating goodness. It was first and foremost the whole of creation, the hymn which rises up to its Creator. If Baudelaire had been *natural,* he would no doubt have been lost in the crowd but he would also have had a clear conscience, would have carried out effortlessly the divine commandments, would have been completely at home and at his ease in the world. This was the very thing that he did not want. He hated Nature and sought to destroy it *because it came from God* just as Satan sought to undermine creation. Through suffering, non-satis-faction and vice he tried to create for himself a place apart in the universe. His ambition was the solitude which belongs to the accursed and the monster, to 'counter-nature' precisely because Nature is everything and everywhere. His dream of artifice was indistinguishable from his desire of sacrilege. He lied, and he lied to himself, when he identified virtue with an artificial construction. For him Nature was transcendent Good to the extent to which it had become something *given*, a reality which surrounded him and insinuated itself into him without his consent. It revealed the ambiguity of Good which is pure value in so far as it imposes itself and pure *donnée* in so far as it *is* without my having chosen it. Baudelaire's horror of Nature was coupled with a profound attraction towards Nature. The poet's ambivalent attitude is found in those who either will not consent to transcend all the Norms by their choice of themselves or to submit themselves completely to an external system of Morality. Baudelaire himself submitted to Good in so far as it appeared as a Duty which had to be accomplished, but he rejected and scorned it in so far as it was a quality which was given in the universe. And yet it was the same Good which was both of these things because Baudelaire had chosen irre-vocably not to choose it.

These observations enable us to appreciate Baudelaire's cult of frigidity. In the first place coldness stood for *himself*—sterile, gratuitous and pure. In contrast to the warm, soft, mucous life, every object which was cold reflected his own image. He had a complex about coldness; he identified it with polished metal and also with precious stones. *Coldness* meant the vast flat spaces without vegetation; and these flat deserts were like the surface of a metal cube or the facet of a jewel. Coldness and paleness merged into one another. White was the colour of coldness not merely because snow is white, but chiefly because absence of colour was a pretty clear sign of infecundity and virginity. That is why the moon became the emblem of frigidity; the precious stone isolated in the sky turns its chalky steppes towards us and during the coldness of night sheds on the earth a white light which kills the thing it illu-minates. The light of the sun appears nourishing; it is golden and thick like bread, and it warms. The light of the moon can be identified with pure water. Through its intermediary, trans-parency—an image of lucidity—it becomes associated with frigidity. Let us add that the moon with its borrowed brightness and its continual opposition to the sun which lights it, is a tolerable symbol of the satanic Baudelaire illuminated by Good and doing Evil. That is why there remained in this very purity something unhealthy. Baudelaire's coldness was a region where neither spermatozoa, bacteria nor any other germ could exist; it was at once a white light and a transparent liquid, close enough to the limbo of consciousness where the animalcules and solid particles dilute one another. It was the clarity of the moon and of liquid air, the great mineral power which freezes us in winter on the mountain tops. It was avarice and impas-sibility. (pp. 116-18)

> *Jean-Paul Sartre, in his* Baudelaire, *translated by Martin Turnell (copyright 1950 by Martin Turnell; reprinted by permission of New Directions Publish-ing Corporation; originally published as* Baudelaire, *Gallimard, 1947), New Directions, 1950, 192 p.*

HENRI PEYRE (essay date 1951)

[*Peyre, a noted critic of the Symbolist movement, is the author of a full-length study of Baudelaire which is not available in*

English in its entirety. The following is excerpted from a chapter translated from that work. Here Peyre shares the focus of S. A. Rhodes (1929) and Paul Valéry (1930) regarding the Romantic and classical elements of Baudelaire's work. Peyre states that Baudelaire "represents the most modern interweaving of those eternally hostile and fraternally bound features which we like to call romantic and classical—and of many others besides."]

In Baudelaire, there cannot be said to have been a marked evolution, in the conventional sense of the word, or an as-cending and then declining curve. Even as a critic, he rose no higher in 1859 than he had done in 1846. He never endeavored to reconcile his contradictions or to mutilate, through weariness and resignation or the need for easy intellectual comfort, the rebellious sides of his being. . . . What we may call his ro-manticism and his classicism were not the manifestations of a calculated alternation or of an orderly succession. . . . The romantic and the classicist in him interpenetrated each other, corrected and reinforced each other. T. S. Eliot may have simplified things when he defined him peremptorily as "in-evitably the offspring of romanticism and by his nature the first counter-romantic in poetry" [see excerpt above, 1930].

The doctrines and the superficial agitation of the Romantic *cénacles* [literary societies] impressed Baudelaire but little. He saw beyond that and further; with lucid insight he declared, at the outset of his career, that romanticism was an infernal or a celestial grace to which he and others owed eternal stigmata. (p. 21)

Baudelaire is a romantic first because of his life, or rather because of the way in which he lived his poetry and allowed himself to be devoured by his own creation. . . . More surely than any of his predecessors in France, Baudelaire reached that "authenticity" of which the moderns make so much; all else was sacrificed to that pursuit. The phrase which he borrowed from his elder brother from overseas, E. A. Poe's "my heart laid bare," well conveys the tense obsession which haunted him to mirror the secrets of his deeper self as faithfully as possible.

The fragments which Baudelaire left and which are grouped under that title, **"Mon coeur mis à nu,"** do not come anywhere near to rivalling, as Baudelaire had for a time rashly hoped, Rousseau's *Confessions*. They are devoid of the aesthetic dis-tance with which even a self-portraying author should view himself, too vibrant with the poet's hatreds, fits of anger and of self-blame. Yet his own drama, half divined through some incensed cursing of God, of women, or of men, or through a few snatches of abject confession closer to Dostoevsky than to Montaigne or Gide, grips us all the more powerfully. There lingers no rhetoric in those bare avowals. . . . Of all the French poets of the last century, Verlaine excepted, Baudelaire is the last of those who confided to the reader or—as he put it in a famous letter to the man whom he judged least able to under-stand him, Ancelle—poured "into an atrocious book [*The Flowers of Evil*] all his heart, all his tenderness, all his religion, all his hatred." (p. 22)

Baudelaire is profoundly romantic also through the role which he grants, in the work of art, to sensibility and to sensual-ity. . . .

Baudelaire loudly scorned Musset's elegiac and complacent histrionics and sided with Flaubert and the stern Parnassian, Leconte de Lisle, who insisted on the concealment of the self in art. If, however, he wished to purify and sublimate, or perhaps to transpose and disguise his sensibility in his poetry, he never attempted to stifle it altogether. His own sensitiveness, as he well knew, was acute. . . . Many of his stanzas are pleas to be understood and loved: . . .

> And yet, love me, tender sister! Be a mother
> Even to an ungrateful, even to a wicked one.

However, behind that tidal wave of sensibility submerging the whole being, under that vaporous and languid language which many romantics had cast as a deceptive veil over their sensibility, Baudelaire perceived the full originality of the discovery made by the late eighteenth century: that sensuality also must have its place in the work of art. With Laclos, Rétif, Sade, Casanova himself (who is often a man of great delicacy and a piercing psychologist), with Diderot and Rousseau, sensation became one of the primary foundations of modern letters. Baudelaire realized that angelism, an almost Platonic attempt to transcend the body, could not satisfy a reader of poetry who had also reveled in the vivacious prose of the previous century. His own sensations were keen. . . . He provoked them, he prolonged them, he blended them in a whirlpool where they underwent what he calls ''a mystical metamorphosis.'' (p. 23)

Lastly, Baudelaire is romantic in two more senses of the adjective: in his passionate advocacy of modernity and through the role which he grants to strangeness as a component of beauty. To him, the word romantic denoted modern art, as it had for Stendhal, whose definition seems to have attracted him. . . . [With] Delacroix, Balzac, and Hugo, romanticism had flown in the face of the timid aesthetes or conservative doctrinaires for whom beauty had to be stylized, idealized, stripped of all that might make it the thing of one country and of one age. Baudelaire's **''Tableaux parisiens''** may occasionally recall Boileau or Gay and eighteenth century urban realism. But because the poet had understood how poetical we can be in our cravats and our patent leather boots he was able to rediscover the poetry of the past preserved in the streets of the metropolis.

Baudelaire succeeded better than anyone else before him in extracting from the modern what is all the more seductive in it for being short-lived, all the more dearly to be cherished because, as Vigny put it, it will not be seen twice. . . . ''The Beautiful always is bizarre,'' he pronounced. To him, astonishment and surprise made up the most valuable element of beauty. Several of Baudelaire's aesthetic dicta, perhaps acquired from Poe, recall the romantics of Great Britain: Coleridge at times; Blake even more, for whom everything exists in human imagination; or Keats, who wanted poetry to surprise by a fine excess and proclaimed beauty to be truth when it was perceived by human imagination. Baudelaire's discovery of ''the loneliness of terror,'' and of the enjoyment of ugliness by temperaments powerful enough to drink that strong potion, can be logically traced back to the romantics.

No less romantic, in its deeper manifestations, was Baudelaire's fondness for ''la révolte'' [the revolt]: a rebelliousness which expanded and exalted the nature of man and was to acquaint him with all vices, all excesses, to make him hover on the verge of many an abyss and to cherish death itself in order to live more courageously, since, as Camus later exclaimed, ''True artists are always on the side of life, not of death.'' ''The intoxication of art,'' Baudelaire clear-sightedly declared, ''is better fitted than any other to throw a veil over the terrors of the abyss.'' The lucid aesthetician who complemented and supported the poet in Baudelaire always protested against any general and insipid conception of beauty which

reduced it to an unbodied common denominator. From romanticism, he had learned the value of the concrete and the primacy of passion. . . . The subtitle of **''Revolt''** given to a whole section of his poems was no mere caprice or desire to antagonize the bourgeois who misjudged him. There may have been in it, as Sartre stubbornly contends, some adolescent need for compensation and some pose, a desire to flout the conventions which he was in fact observing. But it was also a metaphysical revolt, as that of Sade had been, as that of Rimbaud, of Henri Michaux, of Camus was later to be: a refusal of the terms meted out to existence, an aspiration to the lost innocence of childhood or to some forsaken Eden. . . . [Baudelaire] must be counted among those many French rebels who, in the century of Dostoevsky's Kirilov [from the novel *The Possessed*] and of Nietzsche, dreamt of transcending man by becoming Satanic or angelic supermen.

The paradox is that many successors of Baudelaire have lauded the classic in him and turned to him to defend themselves, through his example, against romantic spells and wiles. T. S. Eliot went so far as to hint that he was close, not to Dante, but rather to ''a later and more limited Goethe'' [see excerpt above, 1930]. There was indeed in Baudelaire a being who needed to fight precisely that in him which nurtured his genius and to maintain the validity of two contradictory and simultaneous positions.

First, he was perspicacious enough as a man of letters to realize how ruinous might have been for him the role of an imitator. There are artists who, fully confident of their creative force, may accumulate materials which they fetch and hew in quarries as yet unexplored. Baudelaire admired, with some envy, those brutal, violent, imaginative creators. He praised Delacroix, Balzac, Hugo himself, and Wagner more glowingly than he did Ingres, Stendhal, Vigny, or Mozart. . . . He belonged to another family of minds: those who polish materials already hewn and carved, and, by dint of reflection and impregnation of the material by the intellect and by memory, succeed in transmuting what has appeared familiar into something rare and strange. His originality is deliberate, acquired, refined. Valéry rightly presented Baudelaire as one who chose to differ from his romantic predecessors, who had shared among themselves the realm of poetry and only left for him to extract the beauty lurking in evil. In 1845, Baudelaire clearly understood that one no longer could be a romantic as others had been in 1830. It was necessary to become a classic of romanticism. (pp. 24-6)

Baudelaire's poetry as well as his poetics are characterized by the virtues of lucidity and patient calculation. Therein, he parts company with those romantic temperaments which would rather trust the enthusiasm of inspiration.

He too celebrated enthusiasm, but, he made clear, as ''quite independent from the passion which is the intoxication of the heart and from the truth which is the nourishment of reason.'' His most sardonic barbs were aimed at those sophisms and confusions which had been ushered into France by ''the disorderly era of romanticism'' and the ridiculous motto of ''the poetry of the heart.'' (p. 26)

Baudelaire is classical through his fondness for analysis, in which he tapped springs of poetry still richer than the fountains of imagination. French romanticism had been tempted to lose itself in exoticism, picturesqueness, nature, in a word, in all the world without. (p. 27)

If *The Flowers of Evil* bear being read over and over again after a century, it is because they fulfill our need for analysis and for classical values, in the very midst of lyricism.

Baudelaire is also classical through the eminent role which he granted to the virtues of order; and architecture is the quality which he most wished critics to discover in his individual poems and in his volume. Therein also Baudelaire indicated his affinity with those men of the seventeenth century who lauded the beauty of order as primary among the forms of beauty: Bouhours, Malebranche. His poetry never rolls turbidly like a torrent. . . . Even in its evocation of madly rebellious or of morbidly destructive moods, it maintains the orderliness of a Racinian tirade, the lucid moderation of a landscape by Claude Lorrain, the serene nobleness of a La Tour interior illumined by a mystical candle. "I wish to illuminate things with my spirit," declared Baudelaire.

The paradox of Baudelaire's life, often distorted by his biographers, lies in the total transference of his will power from his life, abjectly deprived of planned organization, to his art. (pp. 27-8)

Through his fondness for constraints and gleefully confronted difficulties, Baudelaire is classical, in the sense that Goethe before him and Valéry after him were. He praised rhetoric and prosody as "rules demanded by the very organization of the spiritual being." Those rules, he added in his [essay on the art work of France's] 1859 salon, have always helped originality to emerge. He stubbornly clung to rhythm as conditioning poetical thought. In one of his most curious letters, he begged his correspondent to acknowledge that a patch of blue sky framed by a dormer-window and thus limited produced a more powerful impression of the infinite than the whole sky expanding above our heads. His definition of beauty is famous: "It is the infinite within the finite." Through consenting on the surface to those limits and restraints which, in Goethe's oft-quoted phrase, reveal the true master, Baudelaire dug more deeply his voluntarily restricted, but in truth inexhaustible domain. He plunged low into the mud and evil, then ascended all the higher for that previous descent into infernal depths, and, reaching artistic balance, recovered the very essence of classicism. (p. 28)

Baudelaire is a complete poet and a supremely moving one also because he aspired to classicism but never stayed secure in it and never imprisoned himself in it as in a set attitude. The very same man who praised the deliberate calculation of the poet as craftsman confessed, at other times, that the role of the will in art is not so vast as is believed. He who had railed at the romantic display of sentiment elsewhere gave the warning: "Do not scorn anyone's sensibility; the sensibility of each person is his genius." He pretended at times to survey his work with the haughty glance of his Don Juan in hell, "staring at the wake and not deigning to see anything," but the creator in him was one with his creation and desperately involved in it. Never is his work serene or still; it unceasingly tends upward or it is drawn downward by carnal and satanic impulses. It aims at a formal classicism, the better to set off an inner disorder which ravaged the poet. Never did Baudelaire find God with any finality, or the serene satisfaction of concentration in his work of which he naïvely dreamt, or perfected beauty, or any degree of triumph over his nerves and his emotions, or any control over his fear of the abyss. He never ceased to search. He remained a dual creature. If to be modern means, as Valéry once put it, to unite in oneself the most contradictory features and to live with that monstrous juxtaposition of op-

posites, Baudelaire represents the most modern interweaving of those eternally hostile and fraternally bound features which we like to call romantic and classical—and of many others besides. (p. 29)

> *Henri Peyre, in a chapter in his* Connaissance de Baudelaire *(copyright 1951 by José Corti; reprinted by permission), Corti, 1951 (and reprinted as "Baudelaire, Romantic and Classical," in* Baudelaire: A Collection of Critical Essays, *edited by Henri Peyre, Prentice-Hall, Inc., pp. 19-29).*

P. MANSELL JONES (essay date 1952)

[*Jones focuses on the various sections of* The Flowers of Evil *and provides a balanced technical and thematic overview of each subsection. Jones singles out the final sub-section titled* La Mort (Death) *as "one of the most attractive of the groups." He perceives "The Voyage," the final poem, as a poem of departure that summarizes Baudelaire's melancholy in a "fusion of strange serenity with mastery of the long, nervous, solemn yet exultant rhythm."*]

As we pass from *Au Lecteur* to *Bénédiction* [in *Les Fleurs du Mal*] we perceive the antithesis from which the tragic interest of the entire series draws its strongest effects—the judgment of man in error under the curse: the magnification of art as a supernatural and vicarious grace. That the artist has a chance of redemption through pleading the cause of mankind in the anguish of its predicament is the positive implication of his task. And this faith is the intermittent rainbow against that 'thick shadow of cloud and fire of molten light' in which Swinburne found the poems to be steeped [see excerpt above, 1862].

[The subsection] *Spleen et Idéal* elaborates and diversifies this fundamental contrast to the extent of two-thirds of the whole collection. In *Bénédiction* the position of the poet in society is contrasted with his divine function. The poet belongs to the spiritual order to which, when his arduous work is done, he returns. (p. 31)

The romantic cliché of the poet's fate, misunderstood and victimized in an indifferent society, is developed with unexampled ferocity; though, characteristically, it is the intimate hostilities that are emphasized. The mother's lamentations at having given birth to a poet are almost as harsh as the threats of his harpy-fingered wife. The rhythmic vituperation rises to a stridency that verges on the melodramatic but to evaporate in the notably fine stanzas of the close. Redemption through suffering, the price of ransom, is, however precarious its credal foundations, a note struck never more impressively than when, as here, hope can dictate chords of such clear perfection as to dissolve the orchestrated din of mockeries and aspersions. The poem is not a masterpiece; it strains one's suspension of disbelief more, I think, in its virulent denunciations than in its soaring finale. . . .

Most of the pieces in this subsection [*Spleen et Idéal*] symbolize the spiritual task of the artist. In *Les Phares* the theme is illustrated from the work of great painters who, like beacons aflame on citadels, pass on the cry of humanity.

The light five-stanzaed *Élévation* which followed *Bénédiction* in the first edition sings of the joyous ascension of the spirit uninhibited by notions of retribution or reward, with a purity of timbre we should not miss in Baudelaire's orchestration. Its implication of intuition into the language of flowers and mute things leads by clear design to the sonnet, *Correspond-*

ances. . . . Itself a fascinating meditation in fourteen lines rather than a perfect sonnet, this compact repository of mystical reveries, analogies and synaesthesia concentrates a considerable number of ingredients in Baudelaire's thought. Here (to use a favourite image of his) many influences are condensed as in a phial of perfumes, whence they spread out again with effects covering the whole field of modern poetry. (p. 32)

Originality is more flagrantly achieved in another sonnet, *La Géante*. Here the author's plethoric sensuality is powerfully symbolized in the huge female figure which, lying across the countryside seems, under the spell of the long rhythms which trace her outlines, to become the ample nonchalant naked Earth herself and to prefigure the lure to which the poet will succumb in body and spirit: the obverse of his mystical aspirations and their contamination.

Unlike Leconte de Lisle Baudelaire has no statuesque fixation. Soon he is crying out against the abuse of 'that frightful word, "plastic"', which makes his flesh creep; nor do themes of abstract beauty satisfy him for long. Two pieces seem arranged to cut through this pictorialism with a singular blend of novelty and premonition. (pp. 34-5)

[The] pieces inspired by Jeanne Duval are not mere exhibitions of corruption; still less are they crude records of debauchery. They are involved in a metaphysique of the conscience—eddies in the vortex of an *âme en peine* [soul in pain] round which the series whirls, from which it rebounds and into which it plunges again. (p. 36)

Distraught power, a desperate sincerity and an impulse of provocation went into the making of many of these pieces, the more interesting of which escape crudity through the intimations they give of a mind at work in reactions of abhorrence and misery—but a mind in fundamental error. The inescapable fury of animal desire is not merely an outrage committed on the flesh; the intimacy is damned in its inception and the pleasure of union is derived from the conviction of its iniquity. . . . At times it would seem as if the sexual relationship was conceived as *the* original sin, redeemed, if at all, by the law of procreation. . . . (pp. 36-7)

Never since Villon had a major French poet declared so emphatically that the wages of sin is the putrescence of wasted flesh and carious bone. And the question, as I have suggested, is not whether the lesson is driven home with sufficiently revolting detail—few things in literature can equal that notorious *tour de force*, **La Charogne**,—but whether the antithesis is not at times so abruptly juxtaposed that the mind of the common reader registers *truquage*—shock for shock's sake—even when he may notice the moral so many offended critics seem to have missed? (p. 37)

Considered together the pieces inspired by the Black Venus make a remarkable group. Baudelaire's introspection is a lucid, not a saving grace. But the vitality of his treatment has extracted an astonishing variety of moods out of the liaison and has transmuted them, through the expert manipulation of complex resources, into a set of love poems as distinctive as if they had been written before Romanticism had begun to abuse the theme of the *femme fatale*. . . .

Of all his associations [Baudelaire's romantic liaison with Marie Daubrun] seems to have been the most beneficent to the poet. To **L'Invitation** some critics seem to prefer the equally perfect, though even less personal, **Chant d'Automne**. . . . But while the pieces known to have been inspired by Marie are free from

dross, they are not all euphoric. **L'Irréparable** is one of the most disquieting of the collection. . . . [This] mysterious and powerful poem is built up of two elements: the conviction of the irremissible felt by a soul smitten with remorse and a set of images and formulae precisely related to a play of which Marie was the principal interpreter. The perfect fusion of these images used as symbols with the favourite reversible form produces a strange fascination. (p. 42)

[Finally,] the Ideal withdraws, while Spleen progressively invades all avenues and contaminates all feelings. It is remarkable how much interest romanticism has extracted from the analysis of ennui; and even more remarkable that Baudelaire could have extended the field of morbid interest so as to make it almost his own. What appears from [the final pieces in the book] is the variety of treatment applied to *taedium vitae* [boredom of life] experienced in its many forms: moral paralysis, reaction from excesses, claustrophobia of the void which is a cell, a vault, the dropped lid of asphyxiation, the weight of dead bodies on wounded limbs. . . .

As with all French poetry of the mid-nineteenth century—apart from the persistent virtuosity with which Hugo in exile challenged Ronsard—line and stanza are insufficiently varied to satisfy our restless taste for protean forms. (p. 43)

[The] two pieces in octosyllabic quatrains, **L'Héautontimorouménos** and **L'Irrémédiable** revert to the more sinister vein. . . . [These] pieces reflect the most intense preoccupation with their author's sombre predicament. (p. 44)

The series of about [twenty poems] that compose the **Tableaux Parisiens** are very unequal in value. The uninitiated should not be put off by the first two or identify the climax with the last of all—pedestrian pieces of moralizing, in the manner of Sainte-Beuve, amongst the earliest of those collected and obviously immature. They do however contribute to the greater objectivity of this phase; and many in the subsequent sections could find their place under the same rubric. The three central poems show an acute sense of types of personal tragedy involved in the social order. Baudelaire was not even a 'Socialiste mitigé' (a phrase scribbled against a stanza which he suppressed). What criticism of society he indulges in shows a sense of wrongs more deeply interfused than social injustices. It is not the social or even the moral order that is wrong but the vindictiveness of the mysterious order of the universe—and this order is not branded as Satanic. The pariahs of society and the pariah poet himself are the victims, not of God's vengeance, but of his inscrutable law. From the pathos of his own plight Baudelaire reacts in a superb effort of compassion: he is the founder of the modern order of pariah poets, the order that feeds on destitution to-day.

Le Cygne is a poem of exile. Formally it is perhaps the most original piece in the collection, combining a number of classical, romantic and modern themes in a quasi-symphonic arrangement. Though some commentators ignore the musical character of the composition, this aspect seems inescapable, based as it is on an expert use of recurrent motifs, not regularly disposed, their discords of tempo, tone and imagery resolving into the harmonies and psychological unity of a new kind of incantatory poem, a prototype for much Symbolist experimentation. (pp. 45-6)

The poem is arranged in two movements. The second picks up the theme of Paris through whose contemporary transformation the earlier scene re-emerges. The incidents are distanced and recur, as it were, in the depths of reverie or meditation. . . . (pp. 46-7)

The three poems, *Le Cygne, Les Sept Vieillards, Les Petites Vieilles,* are each dedicated to Victor Hugo and owe a degree of their impulsion to his example. (p. 47)

Less than thirty poems are distributed under the rubrics, *Le Vin, Fleurs du Mal, Révolte, La Mort.* But they contain some significant additions to the presentation of the poet's philosophy interspersed with a few of the most perfect examples of his art. . . . [This] section reveals, along with the temerity, the *limits* of Baudelaire's genius: it delimits his actual achievement as that of a major, not a great, poet. For all his fascination with human error, the range of evils analysed in his work is narrow: they are predominantly, though not exclusively, sexual. And they are regarded as *secret* sins, sins against the self or against God, not as sins against society. Even when they are felt to be sins against the *other,* they are still not envisaged as sins against society. Adultery, the social form of sexual transgression . . . , is of no interest to Baudelaire. In this alone his inferiority to Racine is such as to differentiate him as a great introspective from a great dramatist and, for all the maturity he demands of his readers, to prompt the question whether he himself had time to survive his 'stormy' adolescence?

But whatever else they reveal or lack, few of these pieces fail to bear witness to that vigilance of the judgment already differentiated. Indeed the most celebrated poem in this group, *Un Voyage à Cythère,* is at once the most brilliant and the most realistic sermon in verse he ever extemporized on the text, 'The wages of sin is death'—if one can use the word 'extemporized' of a theme he returned to so often. (pp. 50-1)

Révolte comprises three short pieces which might, for the little they add to the total effect, have been distributed among the rest. Presumably intended to mark an essential attitude, they lack the strength to demonstrate it distinctively as compared with its expression elsewhere in the collection. The first, in which God is conceived as a tyrant, indifferent to the torments of the martyred, is addressed to the supreme Martyr who is reminded of the successful days of his mission and of the desertion he suffered at the end. Did Christ feel remorse? (p. 51)

[*Les Litanies de Satan*] are a version, showing some slight novelty of form, of the romantic apotheosis of the Devil as patron saint of exiles and outcasts. Though the language is not free from clichés, nothing Baudelaire wrote could lack originality of phrase. . . .

The final section on Death is, if not one of the richest, at least one of the most attractive of the groups. It is composed of five sonnets, simple in structure but of subtle charm, followed by the longest and, many think, the greatest of all Baudelaire's poems. The first sonnet, *La Mort des Amants,* is one of his most perfect trifles—if a thing so perfect can be called a trifle. Worked, as it were, in soft colours on shot silk yet free from languorousness, touched but not steeped in the sheen of luxury, it illustrates the significance of that self-sufficing objective so fondly characterized as writing a poem for the poem's sake. (p. 52)

The lightness which characterizes these sonnets is not absent from the finale. *Le Voyage* is a poem, not of death, but of departure. Not an escapist poem either, but a piece of inspired meditation on the fatuity of escapism. Anything but a poem written for its own sake, it is full of restrained irony at the illusions of restless *déplacement* [displacement]. Baudelaire

professed a hatred of direct moralizing; but meditation on the fruits of desire and activity is one of the strengths of his collection. *Le Voyage* is a poem which conforms to the definition, a 'criticism of life'.

A noble exhilaration carries the quatrains on with a fine swing of controlled rapture toward the unknown. . . . The famous envoy constitutes a supreme achievement in its fusion of strange serenity of feeling with mastery of the long, nervous, solemn yet exultant rhythm. . . . (p. 53)

P. Mansell Jones, in his Baudelaire *(copyright 1952 by Yale University Press; copyright renewed © 1980 by Richard Mansell Jones; reprinted by permission of The Bodley Head Ltd for Bowes & Bowes), Bowes & Bowes, 1952, 63 p.*

MARTIN TURNELL   (essay date 1953)

[*Turnell has written widely on French literature and has made significant translations of the works of several important French authors. In* Baudelaire: A Study of His Poetry, *the critic provides an examination of the primary themes of* The Flowers of Evil. *Turnell sees* The Flowers of Evil *as an epic of the loss of spiritual unity and considers the central theme to be ''the tragic disproportion between aspiration and reality.'' Though Turnell notes the recurrence of religious terminology and imagery in* The Flowers of Evil, *he does not consider Baudelaire's Christian faith genuine. Rather, Turnell sees it as a symbol of the ''Ideal'' to which Baudelaire aspired; according to Turnell, the poet uses these religious terms in a personal fashion. For additional commentary on Baudelaire's conception of Christianity and its evidence in his work, see T. S. Eliot (1930), Wallace Fowlie (1943), Joseph D. Bennett (1944), and Enid Starkie (see Additional Bibliography).*]

In nearly all Baudelaire's greatest work the theme is contained in embryo in the opening image and the poem seems to unfold like a tapestry in a series of images which follow one another logically. The underlying theme of *Le Voyage* is the tragic disproportion between aspiration and reality. The poet begins by evoking the 'cosy' world of childhood—the world of lamplight, maps, and prints—in which there is no gap between the two, and in which the human being feels for the first and last time secure and satisfied. . . .

The movement of expansion and contraction is the basic movement of the poem. It is used to express the changing feelings of the travellers, and through them the poet's own attitude to civilization. The travellers are constantly buoyed up by fresh hopes which are invariably the source of fresh disillusionment. (p. 82)

Le Voyage is rightly regarded as one of Baudelaire's supreme achievements. It is remarkable for its extraordinary range and variety of tone, for its sardonic, astringent humour, and for its extreme poise and sophistication. The main theme is also the main theme of the *Fleurs du mal*. Baudelaire's poetry is filled with voyages and plans for voyages. There are voyages round the world, voyages to fabulous islands, voyages round Paris, and even the 'voyage' of a bored monk pacing ceaselessly round and round his narrow cell. Although a passionate interest in travel is characteristic of modern poetry, it is not altogether new. It had already made its appearance in medieval poetry, but there is a world of difference between the journeys described in [Dante Alighieri's] *The Divine Comedy* or [Geoffrey Chaucer's] *The Canterbury Tales* and those described in *Le Voyage* or [Arthur Rimbaud's] *Le Bateau ivre.* The medieval traveller was a pilgrim moving steadily towards a known goal and overcoming all obstacles in a spirit of Christian fortitude. In spite of the use of the word in **Bénédiction,** Baudelaire was no 'pilgrim'. He was in a special sense a tourist whose goal remained tantalizingly unknown. . . . (p. 88)

[In Baudelaire's work,] the setting as well as the purpose of the journey has changed. Dante's careful logical universe, with its heaven above and its hell below, and Chaucer's wide tranquil English countryside have been replaced by the shapeless indifference of the great modern city. . . . Baudelaire's Paris is not a local affair, a mere emanation of his personal sensibility. . . . Its significance is universal. It is the modern world and it is a sign of Baudelaire's greatness that he manages to present it as a physical—a terrifyingly oppressive physical—reality.

His choice of theme gives his poetry its distinctive style. When we look into it, we find that it possesses a highly personal movement. This movement is reflected not merely in the general structure of the **Fleurs du mal,** but in the six 'chapters' into which the book is divided, in the different 'cycles' of certain of these chapters, and in some of the most characteristic of the individual poems like **La Chevelure, Le Beau navire, Un Voyage à Cythère,** and **Le Voyage.** It contributes largely to the internal coherence of his poetry, making us feel that the whole work is present in the separate poems. It is not a *forward*, but a *circular* movement. A monologue of Racine's moves steadily forward from one fixed point to another and carries the entire play a stage further. Baudelaire uses a different method. He takes a scene or a situation and examines it from every angle until the last drop of feeling has been extracted from it, but in the end he always returns to his starting-point. (pp. 89-90)

The sea is a symbol of liberation in his poetry, but it is also a symbol of ceaseless, exhausting movement which brings no rest and no relief. Desires revolve in circles, rising and falling, shifting and changing, until at last feelings destroy themselves by their own internal friction. (p. 90)

The *Fleurs du mal* is . . . a record not merely of a circular tour of the modern world, but of the progressive loss of spiritual unity. The world described by the poet is continually growing smaller and the sense of stifling oppression greater. He had seen at the outset that his problem was the resolution of the conflict between man and his environment, between the inner and the outer life, and the recovery of unity. He had tried to achieve it through art and love, but all his attempts had failed. He found himself driven further and further into himself, into the desolating inner solitude. His revolt was short-lived and destructive, and we leave him waiting in a mood of resignation for death which is the prelude to dissolution, but which alone offers a way out of a world where he is at once a 'prisoner' and an 'exile'.

The drama is twofold. It lies in the impact of a hostile environment on his consciousness which continually cheats his dream of reaching a unity outside him, and in the sudden eruption of destructive impulses from the depths of the unconscious which destroys internal unity. For this reason the 'tour' is an exploration of the inner and the outer worlds. . . . [In the fourth **Spleen** Baudelaire brings] home to us the sense of constriction and oppression which weighs on the poet imprisoned—the familiar image is there—in a 'circle'. (pp. 224-25)

[There] are two processes at work in Baudelaire's poetry. The domination of metal and stone, the sense of the human becoming part of the soulless machine, gives his world its night-mare quality. This quality is heightened by the reverse process, by the disconcerting way in which cracks and fissures suddenly appear and the surface disintegrates to reveal the 'gulf' which threatens to swallow him up. (p. 226)

The desire to resolve tension, to break out of prison, which is apparent in the general construction of the **Fleurs du mal,** is also reflected in the imagery of the individual poems. . . . [*Ennui*] and *spleen* correspond to the positives, *extase* and *volupté;* but . . . images expressing constriction and frustration like 'prison', 'tomb', and 'abyss' are matched by their opposites which at least provide a temporary release, or more precisely, a tantalizing hope of release. 'Ships' and the 'sea' are the commonest, but in addition there are the images of 'oases', 'gourds', and 'drinking'. . . . (pp. 226-27)

It is characteristic of Baudelaire that many of his key-words are used in both a positive and a negative sense. One of the most striking examples of the reversal of meaning is a line from **Le Voyage** where the 'oasis' becomes

> Une oasis d'horreur dans un désert d'ennui.

> [An oasis of horror in a desert of boredom.]

while in **L'Ennemi** water, instead of irrigating and fertilizing the poet's garden, is the agent of destruction. . . . (p. 227)

[Baudelaire's] habit of perpetually pitting words and images against one another is a further reflection of the insoluble conflict at the heart of the **Fleurs du mal.** For every emotion and every sensation is balanced by its opposite or by the hope or fear of its opposite, and is undermined by it the moment it comes into being. The poignancy of much of his finest work lies in his immense appreciation of life coupled with the simultaneous feeling that what he wants is just out of reach or just behind him. In

> Le Printemps adorable a perdu son odeur!

we are conscious of a muffled note of doom which is faintly heard in the repeated d's, and it is fatal. The passionate desire for new life behind the 'Printemps adorable' [Adorable springtime] can never be realized, and the poet is left contemplating the dry scentless spring which has lost its magic and its tremulous beauty.

Baudelaire is with Racine the greatest master of the single line in French poetry, but if we examine his most famous and beautiful lines we find that they express an almost unbearable sense of loss, absence, distance. When he writes

> L'air est plein du frisson des choses qui s'enfuient,

the very essence of life seems to slip away in the sighing f's and s's. (pp. 227-28)

Discussion of the structure of the **Fleurs du mal** leads naturally to an examination of individual poems and images, but in order to discover the ultimate meaning it is necessary to make the return journey and analyse the main themes. Three of the most important are religion, art, and love. (p. 228)

The **Fleurs du mal** is filled with images and words drawn from the Christian religion. The devil stalks through its pages. We are continually reading of angels, evil, sin, repentance, vices, and ecstasy. Yet we have to admit with the Abbé Jean Massin that Baudelaire's Christianity is 'a very odd form of Christianity'. Although he often uses theological terms in an orthodox sense, he gives them just as often a personal nuance. The devil is sometimes the Christian devil and sometimes the devil of the Romantics. His angels are sometimes guardian angels, avenging angels, or angels of evil; but the word is also used to describe a mistress or the divine element in man. There is one significant omission. The term 'grace' is frequently used to denote the elegance and beauty of woman, but it is never used in the poetry as distinct from the prose in its theological sense. On the other hand, 'ecstasy' is used as a rough equivalent; but . . . it means the temporary rapture of *La Chevelure,* never the ecstasy of the religious mystics. (pp. 228-29)

[Baudelaire was] obliged to create a new 'framework' in which religion, so far from imposing its pattern, appears in a fragmentary mutilated form. It follows that though religion is present in his poetry it only exists *à l'état de mythe* [in the state of the myth]. It is a convenient poetic fiction—a 'hypothesis'—which provides an explanation of the dark forces that pervade his work. It is not a faith in which as a *poet* or a *man* he believes, but it is a symbol of the order or 'Ideal' towards which he was striving, and as such it is of great importance. (p. 230)

[His] negative aim in the *Fleurs du mal* was to resolve tension and his positive aim the recovery of unity—the unity as opposed to the multiplicity of experience, the 'centralisation' as opposed to the 'vaporisation' of the '*Moi*' [me]. This could only be accomplished in an order which was in the widest sense religious. For in the religious order man has his appointed place; there can be no conflict between him and his milieu and no internal division of the self. The attempt to achieve this unity through poetic experience accounts at one level for his preoccupation with what must be called the transcendental element in experience and at the technical level for his preoccupation with form as a means of organizing experience. In some of the poems of positive vision, the momentary sense of unity comes either through the identification of the poet with a work of art or through union with another person. In *L'Invitation au voyage* it seems to be largely Dutch art:

> Là, tout n'est qu ordre et beauté,
> Luxe, calme et volupté.

> [All is order there, and beauty,
> luxury, calm and sensual pleasure] . . .

['Ordre'] is a symbol of unity in the sense of everything having its appointed place. 'Beauté' is an equivocal word. It often has transcendental associations both in Baudelaire's poetry and in his prose, and it can be applied to the supernatural and the natural orders. 'Calme' is absence of tension, while 'luxe' and 'volupté' emphasize the material element in his personal vision of beatitude. It can be put in another way by saying that his 'Ideal' is based on a compromise between two orders, that instead of hierarchy there is an attempt to fuse elements which are heterogeneous and to invest them with a quasi-religious aura. (p. 231)

'Mystique' is a word that occurs frequently in the *Fleurs du mal* and its meaning varies. In its present context it gives a vague religious overtone to 'métamorphose' [metamorphosis] and is, at the same time, a disguised superlative. 'Métamorphose' is the operative word and it stands not for unity but for the constant twisting and turning of the poet in search of his goal, of the alchemist trying to find the right formula.

This brings me to the parallel between religion and love. Baudelaire aimed at a religious-aesthetic unity on one plane, but on the human plane he also aimed at emotional unity through personal relationships which was to be the symbol of or the path to a higher unity. (p. 232)

'Prostitution' is another of the words on which Baudelaire set his personal stamp, but its meaning varied. . . . [The] prostitute was a symbol of rebellion, but in its present context prostitution stands for degradation. The conjunctions, 'art-prostitution', 'amour-prostitution', are striking examples of the way in which opposites either balance or undermine one another. Love is debased and degraded from within and becomes a form of prostitution. The poet's predicament is plain. As a man, he feels the need to 'go out of himself' in order to achieve union with another; but this simply causes an internal division without real union with the other. The genius strives to create an internal unity at the price of remaining within himself, but in doing so he is exposed to the internal stresses and divisions which make unity impossible. The first term of the equation may vary, but the final term is always 'prostitution' which is the negation of any form of unity.

The contrast goes still deeper. The prostitute, who degrades love, is the symbol of those forces which were undermining man in modern civilization. For in the last resort it is not only the man of genius, but every man who wishes to remain 'one' and to preserve the inner citadel against the forces of destruction which were perpetually undermining the unity of the individual. Religion, art, and love represent the three highest ideals of man, but instead of becoming the means of unity and wholeness by imposing their form on man, it is man who drags them down to his level, robbing them of their efficacity and making them an excuse for the dispersal instead of the organization of his potentialities. (pp. 232-33)

'Original sin', said Baudelaire in the diaries, 'is unity become duality.' The ultimate explanation of his predicament is metaphysical. The whole of his poetry . . . is dominated by the search for unity. Now since 'duality', which is the root of the dilemma, was caused by original sin and since there was no place in his world for grace and redemption, it follows that the attempt was condemned to failure and frustration from the start. The drama of the *Fleurs du mal* lies therefore in an intense desire for unity coupled with the knowledge that it is impossible. (p. 233)

[Baudelaire's] successors tried to solve the problem by turning poetry into an autonomous activity and by denying the relevance of religious and metaphysical problems. Baudelaire himself occupies an intermediate position. He recognized that the origin of the dilemma was metaphysical or religious, but he tried to solve it by aesthetic means. He translated his opposites into subjective terms—'the horror of life and the ecstasy of life'—and attempted to reconcile them in the act of poetic creation. The result is paradoxical. The greatest poetry written in the nineteenth century is not merely the record of an *échec* [failure]; it is the record of the final collapse and ruin of the individual trying in vain to 'remain one'. (pp. 233-34)

Baudelaire's poetry is the picture of a general breakdown of traditional relationships: the relations between Man and God—a world without redemption; between Man and Man—the community dissolves into the anonymous crowd of 'exiles'; between Man and Woman—a fragmentary mutilated religion is matched by a fragmentary mutilated love; and between the different faculties of the Individual—the destruction of the self. (p. 234)

Martin Turnell, in his Baudelaire: A Study of His Poetry *(reprinted by permission of the Literary Estate of Martin Turnell), Hamilton, 1953 (and reprinted by New Directions, 1954), 328 p.*

ROLAND BARTHES   (essay date 1954)

[*Barthes was among the most influential and revolutionary writers in modern critical thought. His importance derives less from persuasive illumination of his themes or from his introduction of certain nonliterary perspectives into his writing (he has at various times employed viewpoints adopted from Marxism, psychoanalysis, and structuralism), than it does from a dominant method of critical analysis. This method is based on the insight that language—or any other medium of communication: painting, fashion, advertising—is a "system of signs." Here, Barthes discusses the dramatic fragments composed by Baudelaire. Their date of publication is unknown, and they are virtually ignored by other critics. Barthes analyzes the theatrical elements of Baudelaire's work, which he defines as a "density of signs and sensations . . . it is that ecumenical perception of sensuous artifice."*]

What is interesting about Baudelaire's plays [*Ideolus, La Fin de Don Juan, Le Marquis du Ier Houzards,* and *L'Ivrogne*] is not their dramatic content but their embryonic state. . . . It would be futile—and probably cruel to Baudelaire's memory—to imagine the plays these germs might have produced; it is not so to seek out the reasons which kept Baudelaire in this state of imperfect creation, so far from the esthetic of *Les Fleurs du mal.* (p. 25)

One notion is essential to the understanding of Baudelairean theater: theatricality. What is theatricality? It is theater-minus-text, it is a density of signs and sensations built up on stage starting from the written argument; it is that ecumenical perception of sensuous artifice—gesture, tone, distance, substance, light—which submerges the text beneath the profusion of its external language. . . . One thing strikes us [in *La Fin de Don Juan, Le Marquis du Ier Houzards,* and *L'Ivrogne*] (I set no store by *Ideolus*): these are purely narrative scenarios whose theatricality, even potentially, is very weak.

We must not let Baudelaire deceive us by such naïve indications as "very active, bustling production, great military pomp, settings of a poetic effect, fantastic statue, costumes of various nations," etc. This concern for externals, manifested intermittently, like a sudden remorse, affords no profound theatricality. Quite the contrary, it is the very generality of the Baudelairean impression which is alien to the theater: here, as elsewhere, Baudelaire is too intelligent; he substitutes concept for object, replaces the tavern of *L'Ivrogne* by the idea, the "atmosphere" of the tavern, offers the pure concept of military pomp instead of the materiality of flags or uniforms. Paradoxically, nothing attests better to impotence in the theater than this *total* character, somehow romantic, at least exotic, of vision. Each time Baudelaire refers to "production values," he sees them, naïvely, with a spectator's eye—in other words, fulfilled, static, ready-made, precooked and offering a seamless deception which has had time to do away with all traces of its own artifice. The "color of crime" necessary, for example, in the last act of *L'Ivrogne* is a critic's truth, not a dramatist's. In its initial movement, the production can be based only on the plurality and the literalness of objects. Baudelaire, on the other hand, conceives things in the theater only as accompanied by their dreamed-of doubles, endowed with a spirituality vaporous enough to unify them, to alienate them all the more. (pp. 26-7)

It is therefore not when Baudelaire speaks of production, of staging, that he is closest to a concrete theater. His authentic

theatricality is the sentiment, indeed one might say the torment, of the actor's disturbing corporeality. In one scenario he proposes that Don Juan's son be played by a girl, in another that the hero be surrounded by lovely women each assigned a domestic function, and in a third that the drunkard's wife offer in her very body that appearance of modesty and fragility which call down rape and murder upon her. This is because for Baudelaire the actor's condition is a prostitution ("In a spectacle, in a dance, each takes his pleasure from all the participants"); his charm is therefore not experienced as an episodic and decorative character (contrary to the "bustling" staging, the movements of gypsies or the atmosphere of taverns), it is necessary to the theater as the manifestation of a primary category of the Baudelairean universe: artificiality.

The actor's body is artificial, but its duplicity is much more profound than that of the painted sets or the fake furniture of the stage; the grease paint, the imitation of gestures or intonations, the accessibility of an exposed body—all this is artificial but not factitious, and thereby a part of that delicate transcendence, of an exquisite, essential savor, by which Baudelaire has defined the power of the artificial paradise: the actor bears in himself the very overprecision of an excessive world, like that of hashish, where nothing is invented, but where everything exists in a multiplied intensity. (p. 27)

Baudelaire put his theater everywhere except, precisely, in his projects for plays. It is, moreover, a general fact of creation, this kind of marginal development of the elements of a genre—drama, novel, or poetry—within works which nominally are not made to receive them. For instance, France has put her historical drama everywhere in her literature except on stage. Baudelaire's theatricality is animated by the same power of evasion: wherever we do not expect it, it explodes; first and foremost in *Les Paradis artificiels:* here Baudelaire describes a sensory transmutation which is of the same nature as theatrical perception, since in both cases reality is assigned an emphatic accent, which is the stress of an ideality of things. Then in his poetry, at least wherever objects are united by the poet in a kind of radiant perception of matter, amassed, condensed as though on a stage, glowing with colors, lights, and cosmetics, touched here and there by the grace of the artificial; in every description of scenes, finally, for here the preference for a space deeper and stabilized by the painter's theocratic gesture is satisfied in the same manner as in the theater (conversely, "scenes" abound in the scenario of *Le Marquis du Ier Houzards,* which seems to come all of a piece out of Gros or Delacroix, just as *La Fin de Don Juan* or *L'Ivrogne* seem to come from a poetic rather than a strictly theatrical intention).

Thus Baudelaire's theatricality evades his theater in order to spread through the rest of his work. By a converse process, though one just as revealing, elements deriving from extra-dramatic orders abound in these scenarios, as if this theater were striving to destroy itself by a double movement of evasion and intoxication. As soon as it is conceived, the Baudelairean scenario is immediately steeped in novelistic categories. . . . (p. 28)

Time and place, each time they are indicated, testify to the . . . horror of the theater, at least of the theater as we can imagine it in Baudelaire's day: act and scene are units which immediately hamper Baudelaire, which he repeatedly overflows and whose regulation he always postpones: sometimes he feels that the act is too short, sometimes too long: in Act III of *Le Marquis du Ier Houzards* he inserts a flashback which even today only the cinema could manage; in *La Fin de Don Juan,* the scene gradually shifts from city to country, as in some abstract theater . . . ; in a general manner, even in its germ, this theater explodes, turns like an unstable chemical mixture, divides into "scenes" (in the pictorial sense of the term) or narratives. This is because, contrary to any true man of the theater, Baudelaire imagines a story entirely narrated, instead of starting from the stage; genetically, the theater is the subsequent creation of a fiction around an initial datum, which is always of a gestural order (liturgy in Aeschylus, actors' intrigues in Molière); Baudelaire evidently conceives the theater as a purely formal avatar, imposed after the fact upon a creative principle of a symbolic order (*Le Marquis du Ier Houzards*) or an existential one (*L'Ivrogne*). (p. 29)

Not that Baudelaire's scenarios are absolutely alien to an esthetic of performance; but precisely insofar as they belong to a generally novelistic order, it is not theater but cinema which might best articulate them, for it is from the novel that cinema derives and not from the theater. The shifting locales, the flashbacks, the exoticism of the scenes, the temporal disproportion of the episodes, in short that torment of laying out the narration, to which Baudelaire's pretheater testifies, might nourish a pure cinema. From this point of view, *Le Marquis du Ier Houzards* is a complete scenario: even the actors in this drama suggest the classical typology of cinema roles. This is because the actor, deriving from a novelistic character and not from a corporeal dream (as is still the case for Don Juan's son, played by a woman, or the drunkard's wife, object of sadism), has no need of the stage's dimension in order to exist: he belongs to a sentimental or social typology, not a morphological one: he is a pure narrative sign, as in the novel and as in the cinema.

What remains, then, which is strictly theatrical in Baudelaire's projects? Nothing, except precisely a pure recourse to the theater. It is as if the mere intention of someday writing plays had sufficed for Baudelaire and had exempted him from sustaining these projects with a strictly theatrical substance, suggested throughout his work but rejected in just those places where it might have been fulfilled. For to this theater which Baudelaire momentarily sought out, he eagerly lent the features most likely to eliminate it at once: a certain triviality, a certain puerility (surprising in relation to Baudelairean dandyism), deriving visibly from the supposed pleasures of the crowd, the "Odeonic" imagination of spectacular scenes (a battle, the emperor reviewing troops, a country dance hall, a gypsy camp, a complicated murder), a whole esthetic of crude impressiveness, cut off from its dramatic motives or, one might say, a formalism of the theatrical act conceived in its effects most flattering to *petit bourgeois* sensibility. (pp. 29-30)

This theater is trivial, but it is a triviality painful precisely insofar as it is pure conduct, mutilated as though deliberately of any poetic or dramatic depth, cut off from any development which might have justified it, crudely indicating that zone in which Baudelaire created himself from project to project, from failure to failure, until he built up that pure murder of literature, which we know since Mallarmé to be the torment and the justification of the modern writer.

It is therefore because the theater, abandoned by a theatricality which seeks refuge everywhere else, then fulfills to perfection a vulgar social nature, that Baudelaire chooses it briefly as the nominal site of an impulse and as the sign of what we would today call a commitment. By this pure gesture (pure because it transmits only his intention, and because this theater exists only as a project), Baudelaire rejoins, but this time on the level

of creation, that sociability he pretended to postulate and to flee. . . . (pp. 30-1)

[Baudelaire's theatrical projects belong] to that vast background of negativity against which rises finally the success of *Les Fleurs du mal* like an act which no longer owes anything to talent, that is, to literature. . . . Baudelaire's fulfilled work [was a] responsible choice which made, in the end, his life into a great destiny. We would be ungrateful for *Les Fleurs du mal* if we failed to incorporate into its creator's history this agonizing Passion of vulgarity. (p. 31)

Roland Barthes, "Baudelaire's Theater" (1954), in his Critical Essays, *translated by Richard Howard (copyright © 1972 by Northwestern University Press, Evanston, Ill.; originally published as* Essais critiques, *Éditions de Seuil, 1964), Northwestern University Press, 1972, pp. 25-31.*

ERICH AUERBACH   (essay date 1959)

[*A noted German critic, Auerbach is best known for* Mimesis, *a study of European literature. Auerbach believes that to fully grasp Baudelaire's significance, one must be aware of the influence on Baudelaire of sexuality in the European literary tradition. In Baudelaire's verse, the relationship between lovers is "an obsession mingled with hatred and contempt," which Auerbach believes has its roots in the medieval Christian tradition. Auerbach also compares* The Flowers of Evil *and Christian philosophy. To Auerbach,* The Flowers of Evil *exalts nothingness rather than beatitude, hopelessness rather than redemption, and escape rather than salvation.*]

[Baudelaire] is authentic, and his conceptions are large; his poetry is in the grand style. But even among those whose intentions were similar, he is an extreme case; he is distinguished even from Rimbaud by his inner stagnation, his lack of development. He was the first to treat matters as sublime which seemed by nature unsuited to such treatment. The "spleen" of [his poem **"Spleen"**] is hopeless despair; it cannot be reduced to concrete causes or remedied in any way. A vulgarian would ridicule it; a moralist or a physician would suggest ways of curing it. But with Baudelaire their efforts would have been vain. He wrote in the grand style about paralyzing anxiety, panic at the hopeless entanglement of our lives, total collapse— a highly honorable undertaking, but also a negation of life. German slang has an apt term for this spleen: *das graue Elend*, the gray misery. . . . Baudelaire himself found a very similar term for his spleen, "ma triste misère" [my bitter misery]. It occurs in his poem **"Le Mauvais Moine";** after a half ironic picture of the medieval monks, who painted pictures of death and the truths of religion to console them for the ascetic austerity of their lives, he concludes as follows: . . .

> My soul is a tomb which, miserable monk,
> I have paced for all eternity. There I live
> In a hateful cloister to which nothing lends beauty.
>
> O idle monk! When shall I learn
> To turn the living vision of my bitter misery
> Into the work of my hands, the beloved of my eyes?
>
> (pp. 154-55)

It is characteristic of the gray misery that it incapacitates one for all activity. . . . [But Baudelaire] managed to form his *triste misère* into poetry, to leap directly from his misery into the sublime, to fashion it into the work of his hands, the beloved of his eyes. His passion for expressing himself drove him into an unremitting struggle with his gray misery, a battle in which he was sometimes victorious; not often, and never completely enough to cast it off; for strange to say, the gray misery was not merely the enemy, but also the beginning and object of his activity. What could be more paradoxical? The misery that paralyzed and degraded him was the source of a poetry that seems endowed with the highest dignity; it was the source both of the sublime tone produced by the fact of working under such desperate conditions and of the breaches of style that sprang directly from the subject matter.

The poet's misery had still other aspects, the most painful being his sexuality. . . . (pp. 155-56)

If we are fully to understand the profound significance of Baudelaire we must recall the place of [sexuality] in the European literary tradition. Traditionally, physical love was treated in the light style. In the older poetry the perverse or abject is scarcely mentioned in any category of style. In Baudelaire it is dominant. . . . The intimate tenderness that had gained a place beside the sublime in the love poetry of the early romantics also appears here and there in Baudelaire . . . , but it is not the same idyllic intimacy as in the romantics, which would have been quite incompatible with Baudelaire's temperament; in him it has a new and strange aftertaste.

Almost everywhere in Baudelaire the relation between lovers—or more accurately between those bound by sexual attraction—is represented as an obsession mingled with hatred and contempt, an addiction which loses none of its degrading, tormenting force for being experienced in full (yet defenseless) awareness. Love is a torment, at best a numbing of the senses; true, it is also the source of inspiration, the actual source of the mystical intuition of the supernatural; nevertheless it is torture and degradation. Sometimes the loved one is sick and no longer young, more often she is a kind of bestial idol, soulless, barren, and morally indifferent. Baudelaire's masterly rendition of synesthetic impressions, in which the sense of smell is dominant . . . helps to create a unique impression, at once sensuous, cold, bestial, painful, demonic, and sublime. (pp. 158-59)

[The] degradation of the flesh, and particularly the equations of woman-sin and desire-death-putrefaction belong to a Christian tradition that was particularly strong toward the end of the Middle Ages. It was inevitable that certain critics should have related Baudelaire to this tradition, especially since he was sharply opposed to the tendencies of the Enlightenment and since prayers or something very close to it already make their appearance in Les Fleurs du mal. It is certainly true that like the romantics before him, he was influenced by Christian-medieval images and ideas. It is also true that Baudelaire had the mind of a mystic; in the world of the senses he looked for the supernatural, and found a second sensory world that was supernatural, demonic, and hostile to nature. Finally it may be said—and indeed it has been said—that the view of sensory reality that we find in Les Fleurs du mal would have been inconceivable in the pagan world. But that is as far as one may go. We owe it to the Christian tradition to point out that although the central trend of Les Fleurs du mal would have been unthinkable without the Christian tradition, it is fundamentally different from the Christian tradition, and incompatible with it. Here we shall sum up the essential points of difference:

1. What the poet of Les Fleurs du mal is looking for is not grace and eternal beatitude but either nothingness, or a kind of sensory fulfillment, the vision of a sterile, but sensuous artificiality. . . . (pp. 162-63)

2. In any Christian interpretation of life, redemption by the Incarnation and Passion of Christ is the cardinal point of universal history and the source of all hope. There is no place for Christ in Les Fleurs du mal. He appears but once, in "Le Reniement de Saint-Pierre," and here he is at odds with God. (p. 163)

3. The corruption of the flesh means something very different in Les Fleurs du mal and in the Christianity of the late Middle Ages. In Les Fleurs du mal the desire that is damned is most often a desire for the physically corrupt or misshapen; the enjoyment of young, healthy flesh is never held up as a sin. In the warnings and castigations of the Christian moralists, on the other hand, the object of carnal temptation may have been represented as the creature of an hour, but for the present she was endowed with youth and full-blown earthly health. There was nothing decrepit about Eve with the apple; her apparent soundness is what made the temptation so insidious, and in Christian morality it is condemned. The poet of Les Fleurs du mal knows youth, vitality, health, only as objects of yearning and admiration—or else of malignant envy. Sometimes he wants to destroy them, but in the main he tends to spiritualize, admire, and worship them.

4. In Les Fleurs du mal, Baudelaire is not striving for humility, but for pride. To be sure, he degrades himself and all earthly life, but in the midst of his degradation he does his best to sustain his pride. (pp. 163-64)

[Les Fleurs du mal] is a work of despair and of the bitter pleasures of despair. Its world is a prison; sometimes the pain is deadened or appeased, and sometimes, too, there is the ecstatic pleasure of artistic self-exaltation; but escape from the prison there is none. Nor can there be. . . . In order to determine the historical position of Les Fleurs du mal, it is important to observe that in the middle of the nineteenth century a man was able to fashion this character and this biography and that this kind of man was able to achieve full expression at just this time, so that he disclosed something that was latent in his age, which many men gradually came to perceive through him. The periods of human history prepare their prospective representatives; they seek them out, shape them, bring them to light, and through them make themselves known. (p. 164)

In an entirely new and consummate style, [Baudelaire], whose character and life were so strange, expressed the naked, concrete existence of an epoch. For his style was not based on his personal situation and his personal needs; it became apparent that his extreme personality embodied a far more universal situation and a far more universal need. Now that the crisis of our civilizations (which at Baudelaire's time was still latent, presaged by only a few)—now that the crisis is approaching a decision, we may perhaps expect a decline in Baudelaire's influence; in a totally changed world that is perhaps moving toward a new order, the coming generations may lose contact with his problems and his attitude. But the historic importance of Les Fleurs du mal can never be shaken. The human structure that appears in these poems is just as significant for the transformation, or perhaps one should say the destruction, of the European tradition as the human structure of Ivan Karamazov [of Fedor Dostoevski's novel The Brothers Karamazov]. (p. 168)

[Les Fleurs du mal] is a book of gruesome hopelessness, of futile and absurd attempts to escape by inebriation and narcosis. Accordingly, a word should be said in defense of certain critics who have resolutely rejected the book. Not all of them, but a few, had a better understanding of it than many contemporary and subsequent admirers. A statement of horror is better understood by those who feel the horror in their bones, even if they react against it, than by those who express nothing but their rapture over the artistic achievement. . . . It seems to us that aesthetic criticism alone is unequal to the task, though Baudelaire would scarcely have shared our opinion: he was contaminated by the idolatry of art that is still with us. What a strange phenomenon: a prophet of doom who expects nothing of his readers but admiration for his artistic achievement. "Ponete mente almen com' io son bella" ("consider at least how beautiful I am")—with these words Dante concludes his *canzone* to the movers of the third heaven. But can such words be applied to poems whose meaning is so actual and urgent, whose beauty is as bitter as that of *Les Fleurs du mal*? (pp. 168-69)

> Erich Auerbach, "The Aesthetic Dignity of the 'Fleurs du mal'," in his Scenes from the Drama of European Literature: Six Essays *(copyright 1959 by Meridian Books, Inc.; reprinted by permission of the Literary Estate of Erich Auerbach), Meridian Books, 1959 (and reprinted in* Baudelaire: A Collection of Critical Essays, *edited by Henri Peyre, Prentice-Hall, Inc., 1962, pp. 149-69).*

D. J. MOSSOP (essay date 1961)

The second edition of *Les Fleurs du Mal* may be considered as a tragedy in six parts corresponding to the six books into which it is divided. The tragedy is primarily the personal one of the anonymous poet-hero but he is clearly intended to represent also the 'jeunesse moderne' [modern youth]. . . . The sweeping nature of the indictment contained in the introductory poem, *Au Lecteur,* indicates moreover that the poet-hero is ultimately representative of Everyman, and that impression is confirmed by the tragedy itself. For in the action from which it springs, religious, moral and aesthetic issues which are particularly, but not exclusively, the concern of a nineteenth-century French poet and Catholic, have been superimposed on a problem which is the universal one of appetence—the quest for happiness envisaged in its basic, instinctive form. (p. 16)

[The] conflict which opposes the poet-hero to himself and to his environment is a struggle to escape from Spleen towards the Ideal. This struggle determines the primary motif revealed by the architecture of the work: it may be thought of figuratively as a movement upward or outward followed by a return to rest. From Spleen comes an aspiration towards the ideal state of pleasurable excitement, some degree of satisfaction is achieved, the energy needed to maintain this state is temporarily exhausted, and the aspiration collapses with a consequent return to Spleen. Each of the six books of *Les Fleurs du Mal* represents at least one such cycle. The movement is as simple as that of breathing, the simplest and most regular of all rhythmic patterns and an archetype of every kind of physical or moral movement (the *voyage* in the flesh or in the imagination and the *transport* of the emotions) which returns to its point of departure. Few works of literature can show such a rigid adherence to so simple a basic plan: few can show such remarkable structural coherence and unity.

The value of coherence in art is, however, relative to the degree of complexity that enters into it. And the basic pattern in *Les Fleurs du Mal* is not repeated without constant variations. These affect, not the type of movement involved, but its direction— that is to say, the precise form of the Ideal at which it is aimed, and, less obviously, the precise form of the Spleen in which

it begins and ends. Although the Ideal remains constant in the sense that it is always an emotional excitement which is felt as pleasurable, it may be derived from very different kinds of experience and assume correspondingly different forms: religious, artistic, sexual and so on. Not only has Baudelaire introduced such variations, but he has presented them in an order which is itself necessary, logical and coherent. It imposes on successive examples of the primary movement, a secondary movement which determines the progress of the action of the tragedy. . . . The successive forms of the poet-hero's ideal are here arranged in the order in which they appear in *Les Fleurs du Mal:* those of God, art and woman (with the transitional ideal of beauty) are treated in *Spleen et Idéal,* the life of Paris (or of the world in general) in *Tableaux parisiens,* drugs in *Le Vin,* sexual vice in *Fleurs du Mal* (anticipated, of course, by the cycles dealing with woman in *Spleen et Idéal*), Satan in *Révolte,* death in *La Mort.* In respect of his struggle to escape from Spleen, the poet-hero's situation is the same at the end as it was at the beginning; the primary pattern of the architecture remains unchanged. But in respect of the form taken by his ideal, his situation changes constantly, and even if one limits one's view of the matter to the primary level of purely appetitive, non-rational experience, one can see something of the logic of the order in which the successive ideals are explored. The logic lies in the degree of unpleasantness or pain which enters into the later forms of the Ideal as compared with the earlier ones. The poet-hero becomes a man whose instinctive tastes in pleasurable excitement (the Ideal) become more and more degraded in so far as they make excitement and pleasure itself conditional upon an ever-increasing admixture of pain. (pp. 17-19)

[The poet-hero's sado-masochistic complex] is of the greatest importance in the architecture since it constitutes [his] tragic 'flaw'. It is the perversion of his aspiration towards the Ideal, which is, or should be, his noblest attribute. To avoid a gross misunderstanding, it must indeed be insisted from the start that although the poet-hero may share with the brute this attraction towards what pains and repels, it is not in him a sign of brutality. It is, on the contrary, a sign of the very intensity of his revulsion from brutality, ugliness, immorality and sin in all its forms. Therein lies the full irony of his tragedy. (pp. 19-20)

Considered in terms of aesthetic values, the poet-hero's struggle to escape from Spleen towards the Ideal is synonymous with his struggle to convert his experience of life into great poetry. The Ideal, in its aesthetic form, therefore remains constant throughout, in the sense that it is aimed at in every poem and enjoyed as the 'principe de la poésie' [principal of the poetry], the specific kind of pleasurable emotional excitement which characterizes successful poetic activity for poet and reader alike. What varies is not the pure aesthetic ideal but the kinds of ideal that serve the poet as *subject-matter* for his art at different stages of his poetic career. These are so varied and so arranged as to allow him to treat the whole range of human passions from the most beautiful to the most ugly. All are transformed with equal success into the specifically artistic beauty of the pure aesthetic ideal and the poet-hero achieves an artistic triumph. He nevertheless lives the tragedy which is unfolded in the subject-matter of his poems and his very aspiration towards the aesthetic form of the Ideal helps to bring about his moral and spiritual ruin and indeed the ruin of his basic mental health. For although the aesthetic ideal is itself a perfectly pure and healthy one, closely connected, moreover, with the highest form of the religious ideal, pursuit of it encourages him to give expression to morally dangerous tendencies in the appetent or instinctive level of his personality which underlies (and, to a large extent, assimilates) the rational levels formed by aesthetic and religious culture. He thereby fosters the development of tastes which cause him to be gradually seduced from his original allegiance to the ideal of God and led down through what he hopes is a neutral position (the ideal represented by the contemplation of the life of Paris in *Tableaux parisiens*) to the extreme of moral and spiritual evil (allegiance to the ideal of Satan) before seeking a final, morally neutral ideal in and beyond death. (pp. 22-3)

The poet-hero of *Les Fleurs du Mal* is . . . a being whose destiny it is to be pulled in two seemingly opposed directions by forces which must, in the final analysis, be deemed super-human. . . . In the case of his poet-hero, God and Satan tug, it seems, with exactly equal strength—except when his own efforts to cleave to one, confer upon the other an increase in strength just sufficient to restore the balance. It is from the poet-hero's initial aspiration towards God that there develops the movement which carries him through intermediate positions and ideals to the ideal of Satan. But for reasons which are grounded in psychology no less than in theology, . . . the further the poet-hero moves away from God in the direction of Satan, the stronger becomes the pull of the force that binds him to God. And when at last the aspiration towards Satan himself weakens, the poet-hero's soul relapses into a state of frustrated inertia in which the two *postulations* cancel each other out completely. This spiritual inertia is the specifically religious and moral form assumed by Spleen—for it must be remembered that Spleen, as the negation of the Ideal, has as many different forms as the Ideal itself. It also has different intensities: the mildest form of religious Spleen, suggested rather than expressed in the final stanza of *Les Phares,* is merely the consciousness of the separation of man from God. In its worst form, in *La Destruction* and Part VI of *Le Voyage* for example, it is a bitter consciousness of the satanic *postulation;* it is a horrified and despairing consciousness of being spiritually torn apart by forces that hold man forever suspended between God and Satan, Heaven and Hell, unable to identify himself with either of the two absolutes whose conflict makes him suffer. (pp. 24-5)

[This] grim view of human destiny is incorporated, through the hero, into the dramatic structure of the volume and does indeed dominate it. The human drama is presented as an episode in a dimly-seen cosmic drama which enriches and completes the work by making it communicate with the mystery of the infinite. Although the poet-hero retains ultimate responsibility for his fate, the hand of God or of Satan must be seen even in the simplest manifestations of appetence within him. It is both a sign of Satan's power and a condition of it, that the values of appetence conflict with religious and moral values. The poet-hero's religious and moral convictions force him to regard God as the Ideal and Satan as the opposite of the Ideal. Thanks to the sado-masochistic complex, however, he discovers in the appetent level of his personality a taste for a pleasure mingled with pain which he interprets as a *postulation* towards Satan, and this obliges him to contradict the religious and moral judgement to the extent of regarding both God and Satan as ideals, having a common opposite or negation in the state of Spleen. What is more, he finds that the conflict between the values of appetence and those of religious morality is contained in another conflict between the latter and aesthetic values. It is in this clash of values that God and Satan join battle for the soul of the poet-hero, and from it Baudelaire develops the tragic action. (pp. 26-7)

Poems I to XXI form an exposition which introduces the reader to a poet who is not precisely at the outset of his career, but who is at a sufficiently early stage of it to be able to contemplate making a fresh and more systematic start. To this end, he is engaged in taking stock of the vocation of poet and artist (Poems I-VI), of his personal poetic talent (Poems VII-XI) and of certain enigmatic characteristics of his moral nature (Poems XII-XVI). His ideal is presented as a very pure and lofty one in which God and art are closely associated, thanks to his conception of the sacrificial, semi-divine role which the artist must play. (p. 27)

The opening movement of aspiration culminates in Poem XVII (*La Beauté*) in which the poet personifies as a celestial goddess the austerely Platonic ideal of absolute beauty which must be the goal of the efforts of all artists. But, as the first of the group of five poems devoted to the ideal of beauty, this same sonnet marks the beginning of a critical phase in the poet-hero's development. . . . For it is here that the poet-hero becomes fully aware of the conflict of values which divides his own nature, and ultimately the cosmos itself, into two warring camps.

To attain to the absolute beauty of art envisaged in *La Beauté,* the poet-hero must write great poems. To write great poems he requires inspiration in the shape of subject-matter. For not any subject-matter will do: if he is to give of his best, it must be subject-matter of the kind which holds the greatest interest and appeal for him personally, subject-matter which will itself be 'beautiful' in the loose, relative sense that it affords him pleasurable excitement. In the next three poems of the exposition (*L'Idéal, La Géante, Le Masque*), he therefore proceeds to take stock, more consciously and deliberately than before, of his tastes in this relative kind of beauty. And by a natural association of ideas, he is led to envisage it in the particular form of the physical and moral attractions of types of womanhood. The results are disconcerting and not what one might expect from the poet of *Bénédiction* and *La Beauté* who quite genuinely aspires to very high and pure religious and artistic ideals. They confirm earlier hints as to the sombre depths of this nature, by revealing, alongside the more elevated aspirations and indeed not wholly distinguishable from them, incipient sado-masochistic tendencies which cause the poet to be attracted to what, in some measure, is painful, to find a strangely stirring beauty, distinct from the absolute beauty of art, in what is in some measure ugly or evil.

This is the problem which the poet-hero envisages with remarkable lucidity in the final poem of the group and the exposition, the *Hymne à la Beauté.* He shows complete awareness of the spiritual and moral ambiguity with which his ideal of Beauty has come to be invested, for on the one hand there is the semi-divine beauty of art itself, and on the other, the satanic beauty of the tragic, ugly and evil experiences which can serve the artist as material for his art—and serve the man as a source of pleasurable excitement and an escape from Spleen in everyday life. Quite clearly, the spiritual and moral values which he tacitly recognizes in aspiring to the ideal of God, demand the sacrifice of the ideal of satanic beauty both in his art and his personal life. But his aesthetic ambitions join with appetence to persuade him that the sacrifice is too great. As the concluding stanzas of the poem show clearly, he determines to accept all forms of beauty, including the satanic, into his Ideal, his art and his life. By this acceptance to which the *Hymne* bears witness, he assumes complete moral responsibility for his subsequent tragedy. He takes the right course as a poet, but the wrong course as a man—a piece of irony which Baudelaire, with his tragic view of life, was not in the least concerned to explain away. And like the conventional tragic hero, he is at once innocent and guilty. (pp. 27-9)

At the end of *Spleen et Idéal* the poet-hero has progressed so far from the ideal of God that its attraction can be felt only as pain: it may be the pain that is an essential ingredient in the satanic pleasure of conscious wrongdoing, or the undiluted pain of the periods of remorseful Spleen which follow such orgies of excitement. But although he realizes that he cannot go back, the poet-hero is loath to go forward and continue with his own perdition. He therefore tries to stay where he is, and, like an invalid at a window, to seek forgetfulness of self, or at least some peace of mind, in contemplating the life of the city around him and using it as material for his poetry. This is the innocent, morally neutral ideal of pleasure towards which he cautiously aspires at the opening of the second book, *Tableaux parisiens.* It proves to be as ambiguous as the ideals of beauty and woman, for despite his attempt to forget God and Satan, he and the city are both in their grip, and within the city he can and does find a reflection of his own vice and his own Spleen. This ideal also becomes corrupted in so far as he uses it to indulge his vice by finding pleasurable excitement in the pain, the ugliness and the evil that he uncovers. But the excitement itself seems perilously close to Spleen and the end of the book may be taken to indicate abandonment of this ideal and a reversion to the state of Spleen itself.

Having failed to achieve peace of mind and forgetfulness of self by natural methods, the poet-hero seeks the artificial consolation of drink, as suggested by the third book, *Le Vin.* As it stands, however, the book is clearly the weakest of all. . . . When one remembers the effort expended by Baudelaire on his *Paradis artificiels,* one cannot but agree with Marcel Ruff that the significance of *Le Vin* within the architecture of the volume must be understood in relation to the work in prose. To understand it thus is to see in this ideal also an ambiguity which the poems of *Le Vin* do not bring out with sufficient clarity and force. (pp. 31-3)

The poet's ideal has become more corrupt in the sense that a higher degree of repulsion and pain has entered into the excitement that is his pleasure. But this means that the ideal, which is the only escape from Spleen, has been brought a step nearer the level of pure repulsion and pure pain which is the state of Spleen itself. The only step which can increase the diminishing efficacity of the Ideal has, in the end, the opposite effect. The same paradox can be expressed in terms of religious morality by saying that the pleasure which the poet finds in vice depends in very large measure upon his inward adherence to the principles of virtue. So the greater his vice, the closer his state of mind to actual remorse and revulsion from vice. All the more quickly and surely therefore does this ideal lead him back to Spleen in the poems of moral and physical destruction which end this book.

The same laws govern the passage to the ideal of Satan in the fifth book, *Révolte,* and the eventual abandonment of this ideal also. The fascination of the supreme sin depends more than ever on consciousness of sinfulness; the fascination of adherence to Satan depends upon tacit adherence to the law of God; such adherence can never be absolute and the excitement that it brings must sooner or later be replaced by remorseful Spleen.

So at last the poet turns his back on Satan, God and life and seeks his last ideal in death. For a time the mere contemplation

of death is emotionally exciting and sufficient in itself as an escape from Spleen. In *Le Voyage,* however, the poet turns to the only possible solution of his problem which remains—that offered by the concrete reality of death and whatever may lie beyond. (pp. 34-5)

D. J. Mossop, in his Baudelaire's Tragic Hero: A Study of the Architecture of "Les fleurs du mal" *(© Oxford University Press 1961; reprinted by permission of Oxford University Press), Oxford University Press, London, 1961, 254 p.*

GEORGES POULET   (essay date 1961)

[*Poulet is a modern Belgian critic who often focuses on the elements of time and space in his explications of works of literature. His early criticism demonstrates his belief that authors create in an isolated world and thus cannot be understood solely through an examination of the historical era in which they wrote. In contrast to his early critical approach, Poulet in his later work has suggested that an author is indeed influenced by the philosophical and artistic climate of his or her era. Here, Poulet examines sensory awareness, time, and movement in Baudelaire's work. Poulet states that the movement in Baudelaire's verse symbolizes Baudelaire's vast universe and extensive vision. Ultimately, Poulet finds the symbol of "the center and the circle both moving" to be the most accurate representation of Baudelaire's creation.*]

"Nature . . . quivers with a supernatural and galvanic quivering." It is by this quivering that everything in Baudelaire begins. . . . An exceptional energy makes everything tremulous. They sparkle, resound, trepidate. To be is no longer enough with them, they come alive. To this intensity bursting everywhere outside, there corresponds a similar intensity within. . . . Things vibrate, thought vibrates. A vibration which is in every contour, noise, or color without, in every idea within. Or rather, there is neither within nor without, simply the sudden and multiple apparition, somewhere, in the perceptive field, of the same vibrating intensity. All things are touched and exalted by a translating, nay, a transfiguring power, metamorphosing them; so to speak, on the spot!

This is the first unforgettable experience of Baudelaire's imagination. It is equivalent to a birth. The birth of the world, the birth of the being who apprehends the world. Everything happens as though, in a moment of such intensity that no previous or later moment could be likened to it, the world of exterior objects attests its exclusive presence, if by nothing more than the violence by which it manifests its sensible qualities. And at first this profusion seems absolutely satisfying. It inspires an immediate happiness, a feeling of physical ecstasy. Nothing is lacking in a world which is content with living and affirming its existence by the intensity of its lines, its colors, and its sounds. But the existence of this world is without duration, and even without space. The moment in which it springs forth is not linked with other moments. (pp. 266-67)

To roll, to swim, to fly, to sail, are the almost equivalent terms by which Baudelaire expresses the movement of the senses protracting itself in free space. Free but not empty, for if the flight of images is similar to a flying bird, to a swimmer who breasts the waves, it resembles also, the element, ethereal or liquid which, in unrolling itself, upholds this swim or this flight. It is a flood, but a flood which spreads out, which not only overruns places, but occupies them, an energy which in dilating itself actually creates the milieu, aqueous or aerial, in which its vibratory thrust is pursued. And this mobile milieu, pouring itself out on all sides, sweeps along the thought it envelops in such a manner that, simultaneously, two phenomena are accomplished, that by which the wave of sensation invades space, and that by which, situated at the crest of the wave, thought progressively occupies the same expanses. Thus objective space and subjective space, that which is *covered over* by the vibration of things, and that which is *discovered* by the vibration of thought, are but one. It little matters yet that these two movements are condemned to get separated, because of the limitation of one and the infinity of the other. (p. 268)

[If] Baudelaire is more the bard of perfumes, than of any other sense-data there is no reason to believe that it is because of an abnormally developed olfactory faculty. It is not with Baudelaire, but with others, Colette, for example, that one finds the manifestation of a hypersensitive sense, rare with men and frequent with animals, which is called flair. More than sound and even more than color, odor seems to Baudelaire the primary sense power, that which is most capable of occupying space and of being able to reveal its amplitude. . . . [As] perfume diffuses itself, space becomes atmosphere, as a liquid or a gas reveals itself when one mixes with it a coloring. All the energies of feelings, but odor, to the highest degree, impregnate, and in impregnating, make space apparent.

It also makes time apparent. To swim, to fly, to roll, to sail, all these terms of Baudelaire, far from implying a sort of instantaneous irradiation, express a continuous movement, which, at the same time, consumes and realizes duration. As in Aristotle's universe, we are here in the presence of an operation which, to be fulfilled, needs a certain becoming. But becoming for Baudelaire is not the passing from potentiality to act. No substantial form guides here the movement toward its end. Or rather, there is no end. The only action that is required of things is that they should vibrate, and that their vibration should prolong itself. To become means simply to continue to act, and as, in spatial reality, to continue to act signifies to progress, to occupy more and more of space, so in the temporal reality it signifies to vibrate unceasingly, to occupy more and more of duration.

Hence, from the point of view of time, the expansion of all feelings with Baudelaire first appears as a movement toward the future. But this future differs only from the present, by the fact that it extends indefinitely into the distance. . . . (pp. 269-70)

There is nothing less celestial than Baudelaire's paradise. There is nothing less different from the ''paradisical'' states experienced on earth in the actuality of perception. The dream is simply a continued sensation. The future, even the eternal future, even the terminal paradise, is, on a far vaster scale, the sheer repetition of what vibrates in the senses, of what is already present in the mind. In the same way that the spatial expanse is, little by little, filled by the effusion of a perfume, so the temporal space is, little by little, filled with the diffusion of a dream. . . .

But sound, color, scent, do not only grow in the direction of the future. The moment they begin to vibrate, that is to say to project their resonances toward the future, they instigate in the depths of the soul the echo of an analogous movement accomplished in the past. When the colors flame, when sounds resound, and perfumes become fragrant, corresponding forces make echo to them in the depth of memory. It is as though sensations had the faculty of extending their vibrations in the direction, not only of the future, but of the past. . . . (p. 270)

Baudelaire does not in the least wish to establish, outside of time, an identity of essences between the separated moments, but, on the contrary, to suggest that in the interval between the moments, time has never ceased to reign, an always-identical time. (p. 271)

In time as in space the phenomenon of vibration . . . appears as a double extension: extension of the vibrating object, and of the place where it is vibrating. On the one hand, Baudelaire, in imagination, follows the dilation of all that he perceives, so that any object becomes susceptible, to his eyes, of an immense development, to the point that he imagines his mistress in the form of a giant who ''grows freely in her terrifying games.'' But on the other hand, and this is the more frequent, to the dilation of beings there is added the dilation of the expanse in which these beings inflate themselves, and this second dilation can coincide with the first, but can also differ from it in two ways. Sometimes the movement by which the resonances invade the expanses of space and of duration is less rapid than the elongation of the expanse itself. The wave of images is as though outstripped by the expansion of the field in which they unfold. They propagate themselves within a field whose limits are fleeing away. And sometimes, too, the movement of expansion appears as if realized in the interior of a space and a time already extended, so that beyond this space and time which have already been invaded there are still a space and a duration infinitely to be invaded, and in spite of their effort to fill up these expanses, the images constantly find before them an unoccupied zone. It little matters that this impression in Baudelaire is due—as with De Quincey—to a narcotic. It is not the cause that is important here, but the effect. (pp. 271-72)

To have the sensation of space is not only to feel space, it is, thanks to the sensation of space, to feel oneself as vast as space. And what is true for space, is even more valid for duration. If for Baudelaire, the profundity of space is an ''allegory of the profundity of time,'' it is because time here is, so to speak, spread out so that its parts are placed side by side in the manner of parts of space; but it is also because Baudelaire's time, in ridding itself of almost all its specifically temporal characteristics—succession, change, discontinuity, irreversibility—and in substituting specifically spatial qualities, nevertheless never loses, in Baudelaire's eyes, its most authentically temporal characteristic, which is to be lived by a human being, to have as substance, a human experience. So that time being spatialized, it is all of lived experience which also shows itself as spatialized, and consequently, as identical to space. In rendering space sensible, Baudelaire's thought makes time visible, that is to say, renders the extent of existence visible. (p. 273)

In being able to experience the sensation of space, Baudelaire is able to experience as the same sensation, the sensation of duration; a duration which . . . is to say a *lived duration,* with only this difference, but it is an essential one, that for Baudelaire the experienced duration is, not the opposite, but the same thing as space. In Baudelaire's experience, experienced duration and experienced space are exactly analogous one to the other. When Baudelaire speaks of the profundity of space and of the profundity of time, nothing is farther from his thinking than scientific or cosmic time and space. Profound space, profound time, are the same things as the profound milieu, or the ''profound years.'' They are the time and space of Baudelaire's individual existence. . . . (pp. 273-74)

In certain almost supernatural states of soul, the profundity of life is entirely revealed. (p. 274)

In the same profundity, time, space, and the feeling of existence coalesce. At the utmost of their limits, if they have limits, time and space appear as identical to life. . . . In his happiest, most forceful moments, Baudelaire's vision hovers far above existence.

This continuity of existence has the smooth amplitude of a plain or a sea. It has the marvelous simplicity of free space. But this simplicity engenders a complication. For I am at the same time he who contemplates, and the object of this contemplation. . . . When Baudelaire writes a phrase like this one: ''He looks with a certain melancholy delight across the profound years and audaciously plunges into infinite perspectives,'' in this apparently simple phrase, three different states of the same being are, in the most complex fashion, evoked and linked: Baudelaire as a melancholy spectator, placed in a certain moment, as though on a shore; Baudelaire as a distant object identified with the profound years, and a third Baudelaire who, by an audacious movement, links the Baudelaire of the shore and the Baudelaire of the distance and the horizon. This movement is very exactly a movement of *perspective,* an act by which, to reach profundity, one opens an avenue in the visual field across which the gaze travels. The magical perspective which Baudelaire disposes in his landscapes, exactly corresponds to the perspectives which he arranges in the ''pictures'' of his own existence. (pp. 274-75)

The amplification of life therefore becomes a complication, a multiplication. Life is not only an infinite expanse, but also an infinity of possible rapports between the various points included in this expanse. Even more, these infinite rapports are not fixed rapports, but changing rapports. (p. 275)

As time lived, finally identified itself for Baudelaire with space lived, so, for him, space lived became identified, in the end, with a multiplication of the self, with, so to speak, a *number lived.* . . . In the same way that the total spread of existence is enlarged by the vibrating expansion of the sensations unfolding in it, so every moment and every place of existence are multiplied by the number of vibrations whose seat they are. It is not only the whole which is extended, it is also every individual particle at the interior of the whole. . . . [Sensation] can simultaneously multiply its ricochet in all the spatial and temporal dimensions of living. The moment it vibrates, it vibrates here and there, near and far, in the future as in the past. It is a particular happening, and yet a universal one, since it manifests itself simultaneously in the most diverse points of existence. Such is for Baudelaire the phenomenon of *echo,* or reverberation. It is only possible because, on the one hand, thanks to the continual spreading of the vibration, the poet takes cognizance of the totality of the vibrating extent; but also because, on the other hand, against this background, he perceives particular notes, which are emitted or sent back by different points. (pp. 275-76)

Baudelaire's greatest verses are those which express reverberation. Reverberation of sounds, colors, light, reverberation of various happenings in life, which, at a distance one from another, send to one another a strange, and yet familiar call, since it is always the characteristic call of the same being. So much so, that of all the diversities of tone, shades, forms, and feelings, which cross and meet one another, only the better accentuate by their diversity the ''shadowy and profound unity'' of the mental space. Distance separates them, but unites them too, since it is a traversed distance. And this distance crossed and recrossed and rendered visible, by the thousand movements which are accomplished in it, is not an anonymous space, it

is the very space of the being, the whole of its spatial and temporal dimensions. (p. 276)

[He] who represents his own life to himself as the ascension and expansion of an ensemble of images, finally sees these dissipate themselves into vapor at the zenith of their motion. (p. 277)

[In] Baudelaire there is a general phenomenon of the dissolution of living forces. They vanish at the horizon in a mist of light. The sound, even the scent of things, and the echoes and reflections which generally last more than they, soon are no more than shadows. Through propagating themselves in space, they lose in it, degree by degree, the power of their vibration and their reverberation. In the expanse which they filled, which they animated, there is nothing left but a whirlwind of volatile essences. Dissolving themselves into vapor, they dissipate themselves into space. Everything empties itself out into windings, becoming fainter and more attenuated. . . .

Vaporization is . . . the decomposition and the disappearance of the mental world, at the extreme limit of its excentric development. In the final analysis, everything is dissolved in space. Everything, too, is dissolved in forgetfulness. (p. 278)

The vaporized lands are the expanses of time and space. They constitute a horizon, that is to say, a distant limit, beyond which the gaze may not diffuse itself and from which he who gazes is separated. Very far away a sort of circular barrier forms itself which the eye barely reaches, and which it cannot pierce. And yet it is beyond this barrier, in the distance, in the past, that happiness and life have withdrawn:

> I think of the Negress, thin and consumptive,
> Trampling in the mud, searching, with a haggard eye,
> *Behind the immense wall of the fog,*
> The *missing* coco palms of superb Africa.

Baudelaire's poetry is no longer a poetry of presence: the presence of things, the presence of oneself in the vibration of things, the presence of space. Behind the immense wall of the fog a universal retreat has occurred. The immensity is now only the immensity of an absence. (pp. 278-79)

Baudelaire's impotence is the impotence of the being who cannot extend himself, because he has extended himself too far, because all his imagination and even will power have evaporated all around, in the distance, in peripheric space. (p. 279)

Tobacco, wine, opium, dreams, all vivid sensation, all effort of the expansive imagination ends, in the long run, in the exhaustion of the will. . . .

[To] dream amply, profoundly, is precisely to disperse, in the long run, one's energy in amplitude and in profundity. From concentration to dispersion, and so on, by an infinitely renewed processus, the soul exhausts itself, like a fish which the fisherman maneuvers at the end of his line. This fisherman is Satan. His prey is the soul; and to ''lead'' it, all he needs to do is to ''tire'' it. . . .

Dissolution, vaporization, are . . . also terms for chemistry and alchemy. In any case, the soul is the captive of a fatal movement. In place of the free world in which the imagination joyously moves, a prison space stands out. It is the same space, but inverted, a travesty, hideously transformed. (p. 280)

The expansion of our dreams ends not only in the volatilization of our will, but also, at the same time, to our incapacity to direct our dreams, and consequently to the horrible meta-morphosis of these, beyond our reach, in a mental universe over which we have no influence except by the ugliness of phantoms which, despite ourselves, we project into it. (p. 281)

Turning around themselves and turning around ourselves, curiosity, passions, evil ideas, form a circular movement which not only encloses us in its vertigo, but which also constitutes a sort of mobile screen beyond which our gaze and our will cannot go. The sky lowers. The horizon shrinks. To the universal movement of expansion which opened and uncovered the surrounding expanses, an inverse movement of constriction and obstruction succeeds. No one has more often or more tirelessly described the closing of the horizons than Baudelaire: "Impermeable horizon," "black lid of the great stew-pot," "splenetic cupola of the sky," "blood-red horizon walled in on all sides," these are some of the terms by which he has described the circumscription of space of which, like Poe, he has experienced a horror, but whose tragic conditions he has been incapable of utilizing. For, differently from Poe, Baudelaire cannot resign himself to forgetting the blue horizon and free space. Or, if he accepts or even calls for forgetfulness, it is not the better to accommodate himself to the "narrow" life, which is the only one possible in the monstrously reduced circle in which he is forced to live. (pp. 281-82)

Like a blind man whose gaze searches the sky, or a bat knocking itself on the vault of a dungeon, an obstinate hope prevents Baudelaire from renouncing the very act which is, for him, creator of beauty and joy, the act of expansion. (p. 282)

If expansion is no longer possible, if, all around the being, the blood-red horizon is walled in on all sides, if the circle is well closed, and the shadows black, if "in the mirey and leaden Styx no eye of Heaven ever penetrates," and if the eye of the damned never pierces, around and above the Styx, the leaden cover of Heaven, there is still a possible solution, that which consists no longer in extending oneself but in digging down, not in diffusing oneself but in thrusting down. For Baudelaire as for Nerval, the last possible movement is the descent, a movement, too, that is circular, made up of increasingly narrow circles, approaching more and more closely to the center. . . . (pp. 282-83)

If Baudelaire chooses hell's direction, it is, without any doubt, and as he has often explained, in part because of the fascination exerted on him by evil. But the beauty of evil, quite simply, is the beauty of movement, the final possible movement. At the extremity of this narrowing movement there is, as Baudelaire knows, the terminal fixity, the absolute paralysis of the being. . . . (p. 283)

For Baudelaire can renounce neither movement nor space. He cannot renounce the possession, by movement, of space. If it is indeed impossible to live in infinite space because, through an infinite series of motions, one disseminates there one's life, and if it is no less impossible to live in constricted space, because at the extremity of this constriction there is no longer any movement, nor, consequently, life, is there no way of conceiving a space in which one could move without losing oneself, and concentrate oneself without becoming immobilized in it? (pp. 283-84)

Thus Baudelaire conceives a double movement, all of whose characteristics would always be associated with opposite traits: a movement at once both sinuous and rectilinear, diverse and simple, intentional and imaginative, in a space at once infinite and finite, vast and narrow, distant and near. This double space,

possessed by a double movement, is not inconceivable if one considers the elements which compose it.

First, the point. The point is center. It is without dimensions, without imagination. It is pure will. It is fixed. The point is the final place, absolute concentration, the extremity of the movement of profundity, the eternal stop in a place without space.

But it is also the initial place, the line's starting point.

The straight line is infinitely superior to the point. It is the point which moves out of its inertia and directs itself. It is still concentration, since it has but one dimension, but a moving concentration which projects itself in space. Nevertheless it is "dry and naked." It is like a stick. (pp. 284-85)

The curved line is therefore preferable to the straight. It is, as Leonardo and Hogarth said, the line of beauty. Of all the curves, the most perfect is that of the circle. . . . For the circle is without movement. It is an achieved curve, a movement at its termination, the final point co-incident with the initial point. No more than the center, can the circumference satisfy Baudelaire, for in one case as in the other, there is not possession but only determination in space, not a movement but a fixation. Of all the thinkers and poets who have meditated on the figure of the center and the circle, Baudelaire is the only one who has refused to give into the magic of a representation which is nevertheless the most adequate symbol of the ideal (divine or infernal). And if he rejects it, it is precisely because it is the symbol of the attained ideal, the ideal in oneself and not in its moving rapport with the spirit which approaches it. Baudelaire therefore detested the circle, he doesn't even want to think of it as the circle. . . .

The outlining line is . . . the deadest, the least natural of all. Like the straight line, it is the symbol of a will without imagination. Worse still, it is like the central point, a will without movement, stopped.

Hence the sinuous line, dear to the artists of the eighteenth century, is the only remaining one. It is more alive, more imaginative. Humanly speaking, it is the most beautiful of all. None better than Baudelaire has detailed the graces of the sinuous line. (p. 285)

A straight line around which is wound a sinuous line, such is . . . the form, even the formula, of the poetic activity, of the possession of space, of happiness, of the poem.

For Goethe, this took the form of the first plant, original, typical, that is to say, of nature; for Baudelaire, this was to be the form of art, that is to say, counter-nature.

This is already, in a slight way the form of the chandelier, suspending its crystalline complications at the end of a stem. . . .

Above all, it is the symbol of woman. . . .

Symbol of woman, but even more generally, of the human being, since the complete human being is at once man and woman, serpent and stick, will and laxity. For Baudelaire, the superior genius is the man-woman. . . .

A symbol, therefore, of the complete man, but the complete man is not the stationary man, on the contrary, it is man on the march, the wayfarer. . . . (p. 287)

The wayfaring man is a moving center which traverses and links the circumference, incessantly re-begun, caused by the eddies of the crowd. The association of the straight with the sinuous line is therefore, in general, the association of all moving objects in space, since—around the straight line depicted by a specific object—space, by an immense and eurhythmic process, varies and joins all its positions:

> . . . The infinite and mysterious charm which lies in the contemplation of a ship, especially a ship in motion, is held . . . in the successive multiplication and in the generation of all the imaginary curves and forms operated in space by the real elements of the object.

Space possessed by the conjunction of the straight line and the sinuous line is therefore a rhythmic space, a musical space. . . .

Imagination clothes the nakedness of the will, and in dressing it, it endows it with a splendor which is made up of the possession and the joy of space. . . .

The poetical act is therefore a spiral that is wound and unwound around a directed thought. It is a thyrsus. . . . (p. 288)

In the symbol of the thyrsus, which Baudelaire has borrowed from De Quincey, the author of the *Fleurs du mal* finds the most adequate expression of his enterprise. Not the symbol of the perfect circle, closed upon itself, because this form represents a divine beauty, inhuman, an achievement impossible for the double and imperfect beings which we are; not the symbol of the central point, the sign of a concentration no less inhuman and rightly satanic; but the symbol of the center and the circle both moving, a true representation of imperfect and human beauty which, by an effort of will and through forms always unfinished, lifts itself like an immense twisted column toward perfection, and, in so lifting itself, envelops and carries space in its ascending movement. (p. 289)

> *Georges Poulet, ''Baudelaire,'' in his* The Metamorphoses of the Circle, *translated by Carley Dawson and Elliott Coleman with Georges Poulet (copyright © 1966 by The Johns Hopkins Press; originally published as* Les metamorphoses du cercle, *Librairie Plon, 1961), The Johns Hopkins University Press, 1966, pp. 266-89.*

SUZANNE NALBANTIAN (essay date 1977)

The extent to which the word 'soul' appears in Baudelaire's poetry and the variety of connotations it assumes are striking. He uses the word frequently but advisedly in very specific contexts which enable us to discern certain tendencies and implications in his allusions to the soul. Baudelaire shares with the Romantic poets . . . a spiritual nostalgia for the ideal. (p. 49)

As we examine the notion of soul in Baudelaire, we find that in many respects he adheres to the standard Romantic connotation of soul and to the concept of elevation. A poem by that name, **'Elevation',** clearly demonstrates this survival of association of soul with elevation.

As we examine the imagery in which the soul is contained, however, we notice new uses of the word. The soul's aspiration for the ideal is never more than a mortal's longing with no promise of eternity. Baudelaire's concept of reversibility in all values such as the beautiful and the ugly, the good and the evil, applies equally to the soul, giving it double direction, projecting and recoiling, ethereal and heavy, but always subject to the precarious human condition. (pp. 49-50)

[In] the uses of soul imagery, Baudelaire takes one step backward before surging forward to grant the soul new vistas and new contexts. In an *oeuvre* in which dichotomy is the rule rather than the exception, and in which the extremes in sensibility are the ingredient of the poetic imagination, it is not surprising that the notion of the soul ranges widely. In **'L'Invitation au Voyage'** the use of the word 'soul' exemplifies one end of the spectrum. In alluding to a terrestrial paradise, Baudelaire writes:

> Tout y parlerait
> A l'âme en secret
> Sa douce langue natale. . . .

There, all would speak to the soul secretly, its soft, native language.

The dichotomy of the soul and the body is suggested here by the reference to the special language of the soul. The soul escapes to an earthly paradise designated by 'there' or 'là'. Although the paradise seems to be an ideal place, distinctly separate from the world of everyday experience, the description of its landscape is nevertheless concrete and earthly.

Although we have observed Baudelaire's images of elevation of soul and sublimation of its earthly habitat, these are not persistent characteristics but exceptions. One might say that the instances just cited are archaic in relation to newer uses of the word which we shall observe, and which diverge drastically from the previous ones.

The soul undergoes a dialectical process in the poetry of Baudelaire as it vacillates between two distinct representations. On the one hand, it is a quintessence which man tries to preserve although he knows it to be ephemeral. The soul in this guise goes through a process of distillation and is purified. On the other hand, the soul is frequently embodied in an earthly substance as the wounded self. (p. 50)

The expansion of the soul is conveyed primarily through the strong sensations which lift the soul and purify it to its essence. Sensations serve to put the soul in a state of suspension. In **'La Chevelure',** the soul expands through the intermingling of powerful senses which act upon it and transport it into infinity:

> Un port retentissant où mon âme peut boire
> A grands flots le parfum, le son et la couleur. . . .

> A resounding port, where my soul can take
> deep draughts of scent, of sound, of colour.

In this poem the soul is immersed in memory through the means of the senses which are incited by the synaesthesia of perfume, sound and colour. It is endowed with the capacity to transform the initial input of sense experience into a more permanent substance which is memory. The depth of the soul is suggested through the image of the sea which pervades the entire poem and which becomes mingled with the soul. In the poem **'Parfum Exotique',** a similar *sorcellerie* or magic operates on the soul and makes it receptive to exotic sensations. . . . Sense and soul are united in the common feeling of expansion. The mingling of scent and song intensifies the total experience.

In the poem **'Hymne'** the soul's longing for eternity is particularly noticeable as the beloved imbues it with a sense of the eternal. . . . (p. 51)

The poem is reminiscent of Hugo's 'Extase'. However, when the two poems are juxtaposed we see that although they both demonstrate an aspiration to the eternal the difference in the language of the two poems is symptomatic of a change in attitude. . . . The soul functions through the piercing eye which is imbued with nature's manifestations of the eternal and through the attentive ear which is receptive to the harmonies of the eternal. In Baudelaire the soul's longing for eternity is couched in concrete, physical terms whereas in Hugo there is saturation with the divine presence in abstract and lofty dimensions. (p. 52)

When we examine the soul's expansion in a poem such as Baudelaire's 'L'Ame du Vin', we find that there is added significance in the distinctly physical language used to express the soul's communion with the divine. Above all, there is the outright association of soul with the expansion that wine provokes. The distillation process which acts on the soul is here conveyed literally as the soul migrates from its life in wine to that of ambrosia in what resembles an alchemic transformation. The purification of the soul is manifest as the soul enters into the sweet liqueur of the gods. (p. 53)

We find that in 'L'Ame du Vin', a dislocation of the soul has occurred. The prison in which the wine is contained is the glass, and when it is liberated it migrates to man, not to the divine in the hereafter:

> Un soir, l'âme du vin chantait dans les bouteilles:
> 'Homme, vers toi je pousse, ô cher déshérité,
> Sous ma prison de verre et mes cires vermeilles,
> Un chant plein de lumière et de fraternité!'

> One evening, the soul of the wine was singing
> in the bottles: 'Sir, towards you I send forth,
> o dear disinherited one, from under my prison
> of glass and my ruddy seals of wax, a song full
> of light and of fraternity!'

The divine act is granted to man in his capacity for artistic creation, and man becomes what Baudelaire had termed in his aesthetics, 'l'Homme Dieu' [The Man-God]. What is interesting, then, is that the soul functions in the realm of the human and is the basis for the poetic act which makes of the human a divinity. Second, we observe that the soul is personified: it engages in discourse, demonstrates an effervescent personality, speaks, in particular, of a love affair. From this poem we begin to notice a significant pattern by which the soul's assumption of personality correlates with the human dimension which it acquires in the course of the century as it gradually approaches the notion of the ego and is set in the worldly context.

But where the basis of the impact of the soul on the poet in 'L'Ame du Vin' is expansion, more instances in other poems show the opposite image of the soul. More often Baudelaire expresses the calcification of the soul. This is particularly true when Baudelaire wants to suggest that the soul is deeply hurt. In the poem 'La Cloche Fêlée' the concrete image of a wounded dying man enters into the metaphoric delineation of the soul and reflects the nature of the soul depicted. . . . The soul is humanized and made vulnerable. Concrete physical images translate the inner spiritual wound of the soul. The 'lac de sang' [lake of blood] vividly emphasizes the wounded condition. (pp. 54-5)

[A] mood identified with the soul's suffering in Baudelaire's poetry is the spleen. It expresses a violent horror of life and overwhelming depression. In the poem 'Le Crépuscule du Soir', the soul is exposed to a hellish night which discloses the ills of human existence. In the poem the mood of horror is suggested through objects relating to sordid urban life and through references to the miseries of the sick. (p. 55)

In a number of Baudelaire's poems the soul is tossed here and there, thrown into abysses, plunged into seas. . . .

What distinguishes the plunging of the soul in Baudelaire's poetry is the fact that there is concrete territory surrounding this particular activity of the soul. Furthermore, there are elements of horror concerned with life 'here' rather than awe concerned with life 'there'. (p. 57)

'Le Flacon' and 'Le Poison' are two of Baudelaire's poems in which the soul's wound is conveyed in terms of vertigo. In 'Le Flacon' the soul is seized and controlled by memory, which throws it into a state of intense suffering. Baudelaire suggests that the memory is a painful one, of a lost love:

> Voilà le souvenir enivrant qui voltige
> Dans l'air troublé; les yeux se ferment; le Vertige
> Saisit l'âme vaincue et la pousse à deux mains
> Vers un gouffre obscurci de miasmes humains. . . .

> There's the intoxicating remembrance which
> hovers in the troubled air; the eyes close; vertigo seizes the conquered soul and thrusts it
> with both hands into an abyss darkened by human miasmas.

It is clear that the sensation of vertigo is an inner one. The eyes are closed, and the horror goes on in the soul beneath. Such words as 'seize', 'vanquished', and 'push' emphasize the violence of the sensation. They are precise physical words which succeed in rendering concrete a metaphysical anguish. Here is a strikingly graphic portrait of a soul that is terrorized. The two hands that act upon it give it a three-dimensional character as a concrete object. The 'gouffre' image further points to the abyss of nothingness into which this very real entity is thrust. As memories are suddenly awakened in it, the soul is exposed to a condition of dire brutality. (pp. 57-8)

In 'Le Poison' the soul receives a . . . brutal treatment . . . from the standpoint of forgetfulness. Baudelaire sadistically envisages his beloved in terms of poison. The poison is personified by a beautiful woman who seduces the poet. In the second stanza of the poem, Baudelaire refers to the power that opium has to fill the poet with a passion which inundates the soul:

> L'opium agrandit ce qui n'a pas de bornes . . .
>   Et de plaisirs noirs et mornes
> Remplit l'âme au delà de sa capacité. . . .

> Opium enlarges the limitless . . . and with dark
> and gloomy pleasures fills the soul beyond its
> capacity.

But the passion which the beloved evokes in the poet is a far greater force. The poet's soul is hurt by the very pleasure which it enjoys. The poem traces the destruction of a soul tortured by the excess of its fiery desire. (pp. 58-9)

In both 'Le Flacon' and 'Le Poison' the soul is overwhelmed and devastated. In 'Le Poison' voluptuous pleasure seizes and rules the soul while in 'Le Flacon' a spiritual force controls the soul. In both cases, however, the setting of water, the abyss, and the thrust by an exterior force are concrete manifestations of the process of annihilation which the soul undergoes. (p. 59)

In 'Les Sept Vieillards', Baudelaire identifies the soul with a 'vieille gabarre' or old barge which rides aimlessly on the monstrous seas:

> Vainement ma raison voulait prendre la barre;
> La tempête en jouant déroutait ses efforts,
> Et mon âme dansait, dansait, vieille gabarre
> Sans mâts, sur une mer monstrueuse et sans bords! . . .

In vain my reason would take the helm; the
tempest, sporting, countered its essays, and my
soul danced and danced, an old mastless barge
on a monstrous sea without shores!

In this poem, the soul is thrown into a state of confusion after
the poet has contemplated a nightmarish image of seven odious
old men filing before him. . . . [The] soul is conveyed as a
heavy, degenerate entity which lacks direction, being 'without
masts', and is on the verge of annihilation. (p. 60)

Baudelaire addresses his soul as a dear friend. When in '**Le
Crépuscule du Soir**' he warns his soul to close its ears to the
dangerous movement in the atmosphere which will only hurt
it, the poet addresses the soul with compassion. In '**Les Sept
Vieillards**', the split between the self and the soul is explicit
in the fact that the poet carries on a conversation with his
soul. . . . In most instances Baudelaire addresses the soul directly; he either pities it, warns it of impending dangers or
shares with it the ills of human existence. The integrity of the
soul is further stressed by the designation of particular senses
to the soul such as sight, hearing and smelling. The dichotomy
between the poet and his inner self leads us to believe that the
soul is the alter ego.

The other self or alter ego which the soul frequently constitutes
is conveyed also by the existence of the soul as the subconscious. In many instances the soul is evoked in the midst of
dark tombs, alleys and general areas of blackness, all indications of the landscape which traditionally suggests the subconscious. The most outright identification of the soul with the
subconscious is expressed in the poem entitled '**Le Mauvais
Moine**'. . . . The soul is associated with the darkness and infinitude triggered by the sea image. The soul, in its identification with a subterranean habitat, resembles the hidden deep
regions of the subconscious. (pp. 63-4)

From the examination of Baudelaire's poetry, we can conclude
that the mortality of the soul is more often expressed through
the laden sense of its oppression than through its frustrated
longing for other shores. The intoxicating images of wine and
sensuality suggest only momentary transcendence and the traditional boat image of flight is doomed by obstruction. In fact,
the soul in Baudelaire's imagery becomes heavy with spleen,
gloom and horror as it is increasingly contaminated with the
poet's mortality. (p. 65)

> *Suzanne Nalbantian, "Baudelaire and His Contem-
> poraries: The Mortal Soul," in her* The Symbol of
> the Soul from Hölderlin to Yeats: A Study in Me-
> tonymy *(copyright © 1977 Suzanne Nalbantian; re-
> printed by permission of the publisher), Columbia
> University Press, 1977, pp. 49-65.*

ADDITIONAL BIBLIOGRAPHY

Auden, W. H. Introduction to *Intimate Journals,* by Charles Baudelaire, translated by Christopher Isherwood, pp. 13-28. Hollywood:
Marcel Rodd, 1947.
> Discusses Baudelaire's conception of the individual in society.
> Auden focuses on Baudelaire's dandyism, which he considers a
> strong aspect of his creative persona.

Barlow, Norman H. *Sainte-Beuve to Baudelaire: A Poetic Legacy.*
Durham, N.C.: Duke University Press, 1964, 226 p.*
> A scholarly study of Charles Sainte-Beuve's influence on Bau-
> delaire's poetry. Barlow states that the poetry Sainte-Beuve wrote
at the beginning of his career was the primary source of *The
Flowers of Evil.* He cites a number of stylistic parallels and pro-
> vides letters written by Baudelaire that indicate his debt to Sainte-
> Beuve.

Benjamin, Walter. *Charles Baudelaire: A Lyric Poet in the Era of
High Capitalism.* Translated by Harry Zohn. London: NLB, 1973,
179 p.
> A detailed explication of *The Flowers of Evil.* Benjamin examines
> the book's structure and content, but focuses primarily on Bau-
> delaire's poetic vocabulary. His study of Baudelaire is incorpo-
> rated in a broader cultural analysis of nineteenth-century France
> during Baudelaire's era.

Berman, Marshall. "Baudelaire: Modernism in the Streets." *Partisan
Review* XLVI, No. 2 (1979): 205-33.
> Maintains that Baudelaire, more than any nineteenth-century art-
> ist, experienced "modernity as a basis for self-definition." Ber-
> man defines modernity as a form of self-awareness which did not
> exist before Baudelaire's era.

Cargo, Robert T. *Baudelaire Criticism, 1950-1967: A Bibliography
with Critical Commentary.* University, Ala.: University of Alabama
Press, 1968, 171 p.
> An annotated bibliography listing Baudelaire studies that were
> published between 1950 and 1967.

Cargo, Robert T., ed. *A Concordance to Baudelaire's "Les fleurs du
mal."* Chapel Hill: The University of North Carolina Press, 1965,
417 p.
> An alphabetical index of principal words in *The Flowers of Evil.*

De Casseres, Benjamin. "Baudelaire: Ironic Dante." In his *Forty
Immortals,* pp. 206-11. New York: Joseph Lawren, 1926.*
> A rumination on Baudelaire's artistic nature. De Casseres briefly
> contrasts Baudelaire with Dante Alighieri, and notes that, while
> the hell of Dante is fictional and theological, Baudelaire's is real
> and psychological.

Emmanuel, Pierre. *Baudelaire: The Paradox of Redemptive Satanism.*
Translated by Robert T. Cargo. University, Ala.: The University of
Alabama Press, 1970, 189 p.
> Views Baudelaire as a Christian and analyzes his artistic creations
> as the manifestation of his spiritual aspiration.

Friedrich, Hugo. "Baudelaire." In his *The Structure of Modern Poetry
from the Mid-Nineteenth to the Mid-Twentieth Century,* pp. 19-38.
Evanston, Ill.: Northwestern University Press, 1974.
> Considers *The Flowers of Evil* an example of "pure poetry."
> Friedrich defines pure poetry as that which emphasizes sound and
> structure rather than meaning.

Gilman, Margaret. *Baudelaire the Critic.* New York: Columbia University Press, 1943, 264 p.
> The foremost study of Baudelaire's critical writings. Gilman
> stresses the importance of his criticism to the creation of *The Flowers of
> Evil* and analyzes the roots of Baudelaire's critical theory. Ac-
> cording to Gilman, Baudelaire believed that the best critic is one
> who is also an artist.

Hemmings, F.W.J. *Baudelaire the Damned: A Biography.* New York:
Charles Scribner's Sons, 1982, 251 p.
> An insightful, coherent biography. Hemmings focuses on the issue
> of satanism as manifested in Baudelaire's writings and personal
> philosophy.

Huxley, Aldous. "Baudelaire." In his *Do What You Will,* pp. 171-
202. London: Chatto & Windus, 1929.
> Examines the satanic imagery of *The Flowers of Evil.* Huxley
> maintains that "Baudelaire was not merely a satanist; he was a
> bored satanist . . . the poet of ennui."

Isherwood, Christopher. Preface to *Intimate Journals,* by Charles Baudelaire, translated by Christopher Isherwood, pp. 5-12. Hollywood:
Marcel Rodd, 1947.
> An insightful biographical note.

Kuhn, Reinhard. "The Draining of the Clepsydra." In his *The Demon of Noontide: Ennui in Western Literature*, pp. 279-329. Princeton: Princeton University Press, 1976.*
     Probes the element of ennui in Baudelaire's verse.

Leakey, F. W. *Baudelaire and Nature*. Manchester, England: Manchester University Press, 1969, 382 p.
     Traces the evolution of Baudelaire's treatment of nature in both his poetry and his criticism.

Lloyd, Rosemary. *Baudelaire's Literary Criticism*. Cambridge, England: Cambridge University Press, 1981, 338 p.
     A detailed study of Baudelaire's art criticism. Lloyd states that Baudelaire's critical writings served as the inspiration for his creative writings.

Morgan, Edwin. *Flower of Evil: A Life of Charles Baudelaire*. New York: Sheed & Ward, 1943, 179 p.
     Focuses on the profoundly negative aspects of Baudelaire's life. Morgan concentrates on Baudelaire's relationship with Jeanne Duval and his mother, and provides only minimal commentary on his literary career.

Peyre, Henri, ed. *Baudelaire: A Collection of Critical Essays*. Englewood Cliffs, N.J.: Prentice-Hall, 1962, 184 p.
     A collection of essays by the foremost commentators on Baudelaire.

Quennell, Peter. "Charles Baudelaire (1821-1867)." In his *Baudelaire and the Symbolists,* 2nd rev. ed., pp. 1-55. London: Weidenfeld and Nicolson, 1954.*
     A study of Baudelaire and his literary successors. Quennell considers Baudelaire "one of the noblest spirits of the nineteenth century, both as an insightful critic and visionary poet." In addition, he maintains that Baudelaire provided the poetic direction for subsequent writers.

Read, Herbert. "Baudelaire As Art Critic." In his *The Tenth Muse: Essays in Criticism*, pp. 113-17. London: Routledge & Kegan Paul, 1957.
     An analysis of Baudelaire's art criticism and his view of painting. Read states that "painting for Baudelaire was an evocation of spontaneity."

Rexroth, Kenneth. "The Ennobling Revulsion." In his *Bird in the Bush: Obvious Essays*, pp. 59-64. New York: New Directions, 1959.
     An analysis of Baudelaire's artistic persona as expressed in his correspondence. Rexroth interprets Baudelaire as both disgusting and pathetic, characteristics which he believes are integral to Baudelaire's genius.

Sainte-Beuve, Charles. "Baudelaire." In his *Sainte-Beuve: Selected Essays,* translated and edited by Francis Steegmuller and Norbert Guterman, pp. 275-79. London: Methuen and Co., 1963.
     An essay written in 1863 that provides the only critical commentary on Baudelaire by Sainte-Beuve available in English. While Baudelaire revered Sainte-Beuve, most critics believe that Sainte-Beuve resented the younger poet's talent. Here, Sainte-Beuve begrudgingly acknowledges Baudelaire's creative ability. Many critics believe that, had Sainte-Beuve provided a fair assessment of *The Flowers of Evil,* the book's critical reception would have differed tremendously.

Shanks, Lewis Piaget. *Baudelaire: Flesh and Spirit*. 1930. Reprint. New York: Haskell House Publishers, 1974, 265 p.
     A general biographical study.

Starkie, Enid. *Baudelaire*. London: Faber and Faber, 1957, 622 p.
     The definitive biography in English. Starkie considers Baudelaire deeply Catholic, and maintains that the strongest emotion in his work was his disgust for human weakness and sin. According to Starkie, Baudelaire's writing indicates his desire to rid himself of vice and reflect "the beauty of God's creation," an interpretation that had been presaged by the commentary of Wallace Fowlie and T. S. Eliot.

Welch, Cyril, and Welch, Liliane. *Emergence: Baudelaire, Mallarmé, Rimbaud*. State College, Pa.: Bald Eagle Press, 1973, 134 p.*
     A discussion of Baudelaire, Stéphane Mallarmé, and Arthur Rimbaud as the three French poets who first broke with classical poetic style. The critics argue that Baudelaire's primary accomplishment was the development of poetry as an extension of human existence rather than a purely imaginary creation.

Aubrey Beardsley

1872-1898

English poet and novelist.

Beardsley is considered one of the most representative figures of the fin de siècle Decadent period in English letters and art. Best-known for his flamboyant, stylized drawings, Beardsley employed subtly rhythmic lines and an exaggerated eroticism to create images which dominated and scandalized the Victorian art world. The juxtaposition of ornamentation and sensuality is also apparent in the richly descriptive prose and candid sexual themes of *Under the Hill*, the unfinished novel that is Beardsley's lengthiest literary work. Beardsley hoped to become an accomplished author, but published, in addition to *Under the Hill*, only two poems, "The Ballad of a Barber " and "The Three Musicians." Though minor, these writings are regarded by many as quintessential examples of Decadent literature. Critics note with particular interest the formal and thematic relationship of Beardsley's visual and literary art.

Born in Brighton, Beardsley was exposed to the arts at an early age and both he and his sister Mabel were musical prodigies. When, at six, he went to boarding school, he had already displayed a talent for art and by age eleven had sold several drawings. In 1888, Beardsley left school to become an architect's apprentice; this, in addition to a brief period at a London art school, constitutes the whole of his formal artistic training. While in London, Beardsley met the noted painter Edward Burne-Jones, who helped him to secure a commission to illustrate Thomas Malory's *Le morte Darthur*. These illustrations feature sensuous, flowing lines and an underlying sexual element that shocked the public. While Victorian critics questioned the morality of Beardsley's drawings, none could deny their visual appeal and mastery of form, and his fame grew among the artists and writers of London. Oscar Wilde hired Beardsley to illustrate the English publication of his play, *Salomé*, but unlike most critics, who praised the pictures, Wilde disliked the drawings. He called Beardsley a "monstrous orchid," and declared that the drawings were not appropriate for his work. Some sources believe that Wilde was, in fact, jealous of Beardsley's talent and feared that the illustrations would draw attention away from his play. The popularity of Beardsley's artwork steadily increased, but critics and readers continued to question its morality. Critics labeled the drawings "gross," "excellent in technique, detestable in spirit," and "full of monsters and vile sensuousness." Beardsley agreed that his work was unnatural and, in fact, stated that his ultimate aim was the grotesque.

In 1894, Beardsley was appointed editor of *The Yellow Book*, a journal that published a variety of Symbolist and Decadent literature. The Decadent trend flourished until later that year when Wilde was arrested and convicted of committing homosexual acts, an occurrence which precipitated a paranoid reaction against the Decadents. Beardsley, being closely associated in the public mind with Wilde, was fired from his post at *The Yellow Book*. His problems were further aggravated by the decline of his health brought on by tuberculosis.

Shortly after Beardsley lost his position with *The Yellow Book*, Leonard Smithers, a lawyer and publisher of controversial

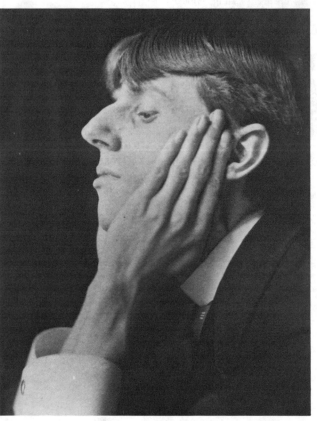

literature, asked him to join the staff of his new periodical, *The Savoy*, which was to be edited by the noted critic Arthur Symons. In the premier issue of 1896 Beardsley published, in addition to sketches and decorations, an expurgated version of *Under the Hill*. Based on the German legend of Venus and Tannhäuser, the tale had been made famous by Richard Wagner in his opera *Tannhäuser*, and Beardsley had long been interested in its literary possibilities. Beardsley's version is an elaborate recreation of an eighteenth-century French novel; some critics suggest that it is a parody of the genre. Due to its explicit sexual content, the uncensored version did not appear until 1907, when it was published in book form as *The Story of Venus and Tannhäuser*. Though Beardsley was unable to finish the work due to his illness, the Canadian poet John Glassco completed it in 1959. The completed version received little critical attention, however, and most commentators feel that Glassco's style is too dissimilar to Beardsley's to merit praise. The original portion, however, is generally recognized as a masterpiece of Decadent literature, and both *Under the Hill* and *The Story of Venus and Tannhäuser* are notable for the insight they provide into Beardsley's aesthetic. Many critics also praise the novel as an impressive record of Beardsley's rich knowledge of literature and music. After *Under the Hill*, Beardsley published his two poems in *The Savoy*, but in 1897 he abandoned all work due to his failing health. As his illness progressed, he converted to Roman Catholicism and denounced some of his more erotic and sensational drawings, requesting in particular that the ribald illustrations to Aristophanes's *Lysistrata* be burned. Hoping to find a more hospitable climate, Beardsley traveled in 1898 to France, where he died on March 16.

Beardsley's artwork has inspired almost unanimous praise and his method of design and literary illustration stand among the prominent aesthetic influences on twentieth-century art. While Beardsley had no followers, his first champions included Arthur Symons and Max Beerbohm. The latter made the famous statement "I belong to the Beardsley period," a comment indicative of Beardsley's preeminence during the 1890s. For Beerbohm, the Beardsley period symbolized a reaction against staid Victorian mores. Symons, defining Beardsley as "the satirist of an age without conviction," interpreted Beardsley's work as an attempt to separate pretense from reality. Other early critics, such as Henry Strong, maintained that Beardsley's writing displays workmanship and dedication rather than talent. Strong asserted that Beardsley's writing is decorative and admirable, but that his artistic aptitude did not translate well into literature.

Later, Holbrook Jackson called Beardsley a literary man who drew as he thought. Brigid Brophy challenged Jackson's argument, maintaining that Beardsley's artwork is not literary but stems rather from its own medium. In 1967, Annette Lavers provided the first extensive analysis of Beardsley's writings. She noted the similarity between his artwork and literature and pointed in particular to the profusion of detail in both text and illustration. Lavers's study is indicative of the reevaluation of Beardsley's work begun in the 1960s. During that decade, *Under the Hill* was analyzed, and critics studied his literary allusions, recurring symbols, and treatment of the Venus and Tannhäuser myth. Few commentators, however, find deep meaning in the novel or the poems; like his illustrations, they are considered highly visual expressions of an aesthetic which stresses the artificial nature of the created object. While critics generally believe that Beardsley failed to finish his novel because of poor health, a few suggest that he denounced the Decadent movement completely upon his conversion to Catholicism. These sources maintain that Beardsley ultimately rejected Decadence as a spiritual and artistic death.

PRINCIPAL WORKS

Under the Hill [censored edition]   (unfinished novel)
    1896; published in journal *The Savoy;* also published as
    The Story of Venus and Tannhäuser [uncensored
    edition], 1907
*Under the Hill, and Other Essays in Prose and Verse
    (unfinished novel, poetry, essays, and letters)   1904

**This work includes the poems "The Three Musicians" and "The
Ballad of a Barber."*

HERBERT SMALL   (essay date 1895)

Mr. Aubrey Beardsley is the hero of such a vogue in London as no mere pen draughtsman ever excited before. Everybody is wondering—in laughter, disgust, or admiration—at the extraordinary black-and-white drawings by which he has made himself famous in only two short years. (p. 26)

A good many people look upon Mr. Beardsley as a joke in the worst possible taste. . . . But the horrible faces of his little monsters, which he has drawn from models no one ever had the audacity to select before, are much more than half serious. Many of his women, with their exquisite hands and their thick lips, seem bred by piquancy out of a vile sensuousness; but they are usually human—humanity stripped bare of everything but good manners—and they are always art. . . . Mr. Beardsley is oppressed by a peculiarly hideous phase of the cynicism of youth, which he prefers to express as it suits him, instead of imitating, like other young men, the work of the schools. One may think as one chooses of Mr. Beardsley's artistic morality. His decorative scheme is never at fault, thanks to his magnificent treatment of his blacks and whites . . . and thanks to his unequalled, rocking line.

More than this, it would be unfair not to admit that Mr. Beardsley has done work to which no objections whatever can be made. No more beautiful piece of book illustration has been done for a long time than his frontispiece to Oscar Wilde's "Salome." Except for a trace of mawkishness in the boy and girl who are looking across the terrace to the rising moon, it is as cool and calm as a stanza out of Keats's odes. (pp. 27-8)

Herbert Small, "Aubrey Beardsley," in The Book
Buyer (copyright, 1895, by Charles Scribner's Sons;
reprinted with permission of Charles Scribner's Sons),
Vol. XII, No. 1, February, 1895, pp. 26-9.

THE BOOK BUYER   (poem date 1895)

[*The anonymous author of the following poem protests the "disgusting" elements of Beardsley's art and draws a number of literary comparisons to Beardsley's artwork.*]

Somebody writes to an English paper a formula for making the species of art which Mr. Aubrey Beardsley delights in.

> Take of Swinburne's ballads three—
>   Choose the most erotic—
> Let them simmer in a pan,
>   Steeped in some narcotic.

To this mixture he adds some other disagreeable things, including "Several Green Carnations," and

>   . . . when a scum
>   Thick and green is on it,
> Throw a scene from Maeterlinck,
>   And one hot Richepin sonnet;
> Grate some cankered Dead-Sea fruit,
>   And withered flowers of passion,
> Drench with sauce à-Schopenhauer
>   Mixed in latest fashion;
> Add a paradox or two
>   (See they're Oscar Wilde-ish);
> Sprinkle in some draughtsmanship,
>   Absolutely childish;
> And, when all these things you've mixed
>   In a hotch-potch baleful,
> Chinese white and ivory black
>   Dash in by the pailful.
> Take the mixture off the fire
>   When it is well heated,
> Put it in the sink to stand
>   Till it grows quite fetid.

Pour it in a tainted mould,
    Like to nothing human,
Shut your eyes and hold your nose,
    And serve the Beardsley woman!

> "'Another View'," in The Book Buyer, *Vol. XII,*
> *No. 1, February, 1895, p. 29.*

MARGARET ARMOUR (essay date 1896)

[Armour praises the "excellent technique" of the Decadents although she states that they inspire "more repugnance than praise."]

Mr. Beardsley might adapt the *mot* [saying] of Louis XIV., and say, almost without arrogance, "L'Art décadent, c'est moi" [I am Decadent art]. In his work we have the most complete expression of what is typical of the movement— disdain of classical traditions in art, and of clean traditions in ethics; the *fin de siècle* outlook on the husk of life, and brilliant dexterity in portraying it; also, perhaps, a finer feeling for the tools of art than for its materials.

Mr. Beardsley's career has been meteoric in brilliance, yet at present he has all the appearance of a fixed star. He is one of those in whom genius is no smouldering ember, but a many-tongued flame. (p. 9)

There is hardly an adjective in the dictionary too ugly to sling at the hectic vice, the slimy nastiness of [the faces in Beardsley's art]. And they can be pure and glad—some of them are— but Beardsley is a Decadent, and must do as the Decadents do: he must gloat upon ugliness and add to it; and when it is not there, he must create it. Compare his impression of a familiar object—[the painting of] Mrs. Patrick Campbell, for instance—with our own; the Beardsley trail is on her face, and it is curious to think what the Duchess of Devonshire would have been in his hands instead of Gainsborough's. But this fact, while it exasperates, has its own comfort for those who would see the world fair; for if we find an artist besmirching his model when we can test results by our own experience, the chances are he is always at it, and the ugliness he dresses out for us is in his own eye.

To be a devout Decadent, too, you must not only be wicked; you must be worse—as *Punch* would say—you must be vulgar. Mr. Beardsley has a trick of superimposing one style on another—Japanese on mediaeval, mediaeval on Celtic. That does not matter so long as he has the genius to unify; but what does matter is that the groundwork of them all should be Cockney, and the coster be so prominent in the *motifs*. (p. 10)

The art like Beardsley's, so excellent in technique and so detestable in spirit, wakes more repugnance than praise—proves us a nation stronger in ethics than in art. We are true to the Teutonic strain in us, and are not Goths for nothing. But there is Latin blood in us as well—enough, let us hope, to temper harshness, and allow us to give the Decadents the honour which is their due. In the externals of art they are doing good work, and even their flippancy may have its uses, if it jeer us out of conceit with the *bourgeois* sentimentality of the average painter. (p. 12)

> *Margaret Armour, "Aubrey Beardsley and the Decadents," in* The Magazine of Art, *Vol. 20, November, 1896, pp. 9-12.*

MAX BEERBOHM (essay date 1897)

[A friend of Beardsley who made the famous statement: "I belong to the Beardsley period," Beerbohm was an English satirist, critic, caricaturist, and short story writer. He is chiefly associated with the fin-de siècle *period, particularly for his witty sophistication and mannered elegance. As a champion of Beardsley's work, Beerbohm sometimes made exaggerated claims for his friend, maintaining for example that Beardsley "never had one title of instruction" and "scarcely drew a line before he was fourteen years of age." Yet many critics concur with his assessment of Beardsley as an exuberant and sensational artist.]*

[I], having a real admiration for Mr. Beadsley's genius, am rather loth to write of it. There is no knowing what may not happen before I have finished. But, possibly, the fact that I am a personal friend of Mr. Beardsley may suffice to guide my pen in reverence and in truth. For do not imagine that friendship can generally discount the value of praise given! If it be (it should be) the critic's aim to appreciate all that is good in the work that he has selected, and if that work be (it is) the expression of the artist's own temperament, then has that critic, who is also the personal friend, a high advantage over the other critics, though they be, for the rest, his equals. (pp. 257-58)

Mr. Beardsley's genius is so swift that his critics' process must be strangely congested. At a time when most artists are still throwing about for ideals, and cursing their ineffectual fingers, he is—Aubrey Beardsley. What strikes one first in his . . . drawings is his unique exuberance. . . . Mr. Beardsley's work is not the careful, slender outcome of a merely exquisite mind. It is a thing of utterly colossal bulk. Three short years! When we know that this artist hardly drew a line before he was fourteen years of age, that he has never had one tittle of instruction, and that he has been always the prey of physical delicacy, which prostrates him only too often and makes activity of any kind impossible, what can we do but throw up our hands and wonder at the miracles which Nature is still working in this flat world? Mr. Beardsley forces us to rëadjust all our ordinary scale of judgment. He is most comparable, perhaps, with the painter-children of the Renaissance. (p. 259)

Can one wonder at the sensation made by [the first drawings of the *Yellow Book*], with their simple ordering of black blots and cobweb lines, so flawless in their accomplishment, so very decorative, so very strange? (p. 260)

[Perhaps] the favourite charge against Mr. Beardsley's work was the charge of indecency. Some professed to see actual indecency in the drawings, others declared it was rather the spirit of them that was indecent. I have no wish to enter into a discussion on this point. I would merely have suggested to the indignant that they should not look at the drawings, nor talk about them. If they supposed that they could cure Mr. Beardsley by newspaper diatribes, they were much mistaken. An artist may alter his method, but the impulse is always within himself. Critical anger tends, if anything, to make him more strenuous in his own method. If he be not quite indifferent, he probably retaliates by a wilful exaggeration of what offends. I think there is some evidence, in the *Savoy* especially, that Mr. Beardsley tried, now and again, in a spirit of sheer mischief, to scandalise the public. (pp. 261-62)

[But there is in] the later drawings, evidence of another kind. Mr. Beardsley's bent is no longer the bent to pure fantasy and curious conventions. The "Catalogue Cover" shows an agreeable faun, in a glade by a river, reading to a lady. There, as elsewhere, we have a straight tendency to realism. The trees, the reflections on the surface of the water, are all imitated from nature. (p. 262)

Now, these new [more realistic] elements will secure for the artist less tardy homage from the public. To me, they are interesting as steps in the process of a unique mind. But, of course, the important thing in these drawings is their decorative value. Some of them, I think, suffer from an excessive elaboration. As, in his Japanese days, Mr. Beardsley, unable to restrain his abundance, did sometimes overfill his pictures from the cornucopia of his fancy; so, now that he loves the things of the eighteenth century, do a few of his pictures suffer from a plethora of exquisite inventions. (pp. 262-63)

> *Max Beerbohm, "Mr. Beardsley's Fifty Drawings" (reprinted by permission of Mrs. Eva Reichmann; originally published in* Tomorrow, *London, January, 1897), in* Beardsley: A Biography *by Stanley Weintraub, George Braziller, 1967 pp. 257-63.*

ARTHUR SYMONS (essay date 1898)

[*An English critic, poet, dramatist, short story writer, and editor, Symons initially gained notoriety as an English decadent of the 1890s and eventually established himself as one of the most important critics of the modern era. His sensitive translations of Paul Verlaine and Stéphane Mallarmé provided English poets with an introduction to the poetry of the French Symbolists. Though he was a gifted translator and linguist, it was as a critic that Symons made his most important contribution to literature. His* The Symbolist Movement in Literature *provided his English contemporaries with an appropriate vocabulary with which to define their new aesthetic—one that communicated their concern with dreamlike states, imagination, and a reality that exists beyond the boundaries of the senses. As Beardsley's editor on the journal* The Savoy, *Symons was well-acquainted with the various elements of his art. In the following essay, he analyzes Beardsley's desire to disturb the public, a tendency which, according to Symons, occasionally inhibited his artwork. Symons equates Beardsley with Charles Baudelaire; like Baudelaire, Symons asserts, "Beardsley is the satirist of an age without convictions, and he can but paint hell as Baudelaire did."*]

No artist of our time, none certainly whose work has been in black and white, has reached a more universal, or a more contested fame; none has formed for himself, out of such alien elements, a more personal originality of manner; none has had so wide an influence on contemporary art. [Aubrey Beardsley] had the fatal speed of those who are to die young; that disquieting completeness and extent of knowledge, that absorption of a lifetime in an hour, which we find in those who hasten to have done their work before noon, knowing that they will not see the evening. (p. 752)

Like most artists who have thought much of popularity, he had an immense contempt for the public; and the desire to kick that public into admiration, and then to kick it for admiring the wrong thing or not knowing why it was admiring, led him into many of his most outrageous practical jokes of the pen. He was partly right and partly wrong, for he was indiscriminate; and to be indiscriminate is always to be partly right and partly wrong. The wish to "épater le bourgeois" [shock the bourgeois] is a natural one, and, though a little beside the question, does not necessarily lead one astray. The general public, of course, does not in the least know why it admires the right thing to-day though it admired the wrong thing yesterday. But there is such a thing as denying your Master while you are rebuking a servant-girl. Beardsley was without the very sense of respect; it was one of his limitations.

And this limitation was an unfortunate one, for it limited his ambition. With the power of creating beauty, which should be pure beauty, he turned aside, only too often, to that lower kind of beauty which is the mere beauty of technique, in a composition otherwise meaningless, trivial, or grotesque. (pp. 753-54)

Pierrot [the character of French pantomime drawn by Beardsley and described as "Pierrot gamin" by Paul Verlaine] is one of the types of our century, of the moment in which we live, or of the moment, perhaps, out of which we are just passing. Pierrot is passionate; but he does not believe in great passions. He feels himself to be sickening with a fever, or else perilously convalescent; for love is a disease, which he is too weak to resist or endure. He has worn his heart on his sleeve so long, that it has hardened in the cold air. He knows that his face is powdered, and if he sobs, it is without tears; and it is hard to distinguish, under the chalk, if the grimace which twists his mouth awry is more laughter or mockery. He knows that he is condemned to be always in public, that emotion would be supremely out of keeping with his costume, that he must remember to be fantastic if he would not be merely ridiculous. And so he becomes exquisitely false, dreading above all things that "one touch of nature" which would ruffle his disguise, and leave him defenceless. (pp. 755-56)

And Beardsley, with almost more than the Parisian's deference to Paris, and to the moment, was, more than any Parisian, this "Pierrot gamin." He was more than that, but he was that: to be that was part of what he learnt from France. It helped him to the pose which helped him to reveal himself. . . . He had that originality which surrenders to every influence, yet surrenders to absorb, not to be absorbed; that originality which, constantly shifting, is true always to its centre. . . . [He] was always drawing to himself, out of the order of art or the confusion of natural things, the thing he wanted, the thing he could make his own. And he found, in the French art of the moment, a joyous sadness, the serving of God or Mephistopheles, which his own temperament and circumstances were waiting to suggest to him.

"In more ways than one do men sacrifice to the rebellious angels," says St. Augustine; and Beardsley's sacrifice, together with that of all great decadent art, the art of Rops or the art of Baudelaire, is really a sacrifice to the eternal beauty, and only seemingly to the powers of evil. And here let me say that I have no concern with what neither he nor I could have had absolute knowledge of, his own intention in his work. A man's intention, it must be remembered, from the very fact that it is conscious, is much less intimately himself than the sentiment which his work conveys to me. So large is the subconscious element in all artistic creation, that I should have doubted whether Beardsley himself knew what he intended to do, in this or that really significant drawing. Admitting that he could tell exactly what he had intended, I should be quite prepared to show that he had really done the very contrary. Thus when I say he was a profoundly spiritual artist, though seeming to care chiefly for the manual part of his work; that he expresses evil with an intensity which lifted it into a region almost of asceticism, though attempting, not seldom, little more than a joke or a caprice in line; and that he was above all, though almost against his own will, a satirist, a satirist who has seen the ideal; I am putting forward no paradox, nothing really contradictory, but a simple analysis of the work as it exists.

At times he attains pure beauty, has the unimpaired vision; in the best of the "Salome" designs, here and there afterwards.

From the first it is a diabolic beauty, but it is not yet divided against itself. The consciousness of sin is always there, but it is sin first transfigured by beauty, and then disclosed by beauty; sin, conscious of itself, of its inability to escape itself, and showing in its ugliness the law it has broken. His world is a world of phantoms, in whom the desire of the perfecting of mortal sensations, a desire of infinity, has overpassed mortal limits, and poised them, so faint, so quivering, so passionate for flight, in a hopeless and strenuous immobility. They have the sensitiveness of the spirit, and that bodily sensitiveness which wastes their veins and imprisons them in the attitude of their luxurious meditation. They are too thoughtful to be ever really simple, or really absorbed by either flesh or spirit. They have nothing of what is "healthy" or merely "animal" in their downward course towards repentance; no overwhelming passion hurries them beyond themselves; they do not capitulate to an open assault of the enemy of souls. It is the soul in them that sins, sorrowfully, without reluctance, inevitably. (pp. 756-57)

Here, then, we have a sort of abstract spiritual corruption, revealed in beautiful form; sin transfigured by beauty. And here, even if we go no further, is an art intensely spiritual, an art in which evil purifies itself by its own intensity, and by the beauty which transfigures it. (p. 757)

In those drawings of Beardsley which are grotesque rather than beautiful, in which lines begin to grow deformed, the pattern, in which now all the beauty takes refuge, is itself a moral judgment. Look at that drawing called "The Scarlet Pastorale." In front a bloated harlequin struts close to the footlights, outside the play, on which he turns his back; beyond, sacramental candles have been lighted, and are guttering down in solitude, under an unseen wind. And between, on the sheer darkness of the stage, a bald and plumed Pierrot, holding in his vast, collapsing paunch with a mere rope of roses, shows the cloven foot, while Pierrette points at him in screaming horror, and the fat dancer turns on her toes indifferently. Need we go further to show how much more than Gautier's meaning lies in the old paradox of "Mademoiselle de Maupin," that "perfection of line is virtue"? That line which rounds the deformity of the cloven-footed sin, the line itself, is at once the revelation and the condemnation of vice, for it is part of that artistic logic which is morality.

Beardsley is the satirist of an age without convictions, and he can but paint hell as Baudelaire did, without pointing for contrast to any contemporary paradise. He employs the same rhetoric as Baudelaire, a method of emphasis which it is uncritical to think insincere. In that terrible annunciation of evil which he called "The Mysterious Rose-Garden," the lantern-bearing angel with winged sandals whispers, from among the falling roses, tidings of more than "pleasant sins." The leering dwarfs, the "monkeys," by which the mystics symbolised the earthlier vices; those immense bodies swollen with the lees of pleasure, and those cloaked and masked desires shuddering in gardens and smiling ambiguously at interminable toilets; are part of a symbolism which loses nothing by lack of emphasis. And the peculiar efficacy of this satire is that it is so much the satire of desire returning upon itself, the mockery of desire enjoyed, the mockery of desire denied. It is because he loves beauty that beauty's degradation obsesses him; it is because he is supremely conscious of virtue that vice has power to lay hold upon him. And, unlike those other, acceptable satirists of our day, with whom satire exhausts itself in the rebuke of a drunkard leaning against a lamppost, or a lady paying the wrong

compliment in a drawing-room, he is the satirist of essential things; it is always the soul, and not the body's discontent only, which cries out of these insatiable eyes, that have looked on all their lusts, and out of these bitter mouths, that have eaten the dust of all their sweetnesses, and out of these hands, that have laboured delicately for nothing, and out of these feet, that have run after vanities. They are so sorrowful because they have seen beauty, and because they have departed from the line of beauty.

And after all, the secret of Beardsley is there: in the line itself rather than in anything, intellectually realised, which the line is intended to express. With Beardsley everything was a question of form: his interest in his work began when the paper was before him and the pen in his hand. And so, in one sense, he may be said never to have known what he wanted to do, while, in another, he knew very precisely indeed. He was ready to do, within certain limits, almost anything you suggested to him; as, when left to himself, he was content to follow the caprice of the moment. (pp. 758-59)

[It] must never be forgotten, Beardsley was a decorative artist, and not anything else. From almost the very first he accepted convention, he set himself to see things as pattern. Taking freely all that the Japanese could give him, that release from the bondage of what we call real things, which comes to one man from an intense spirituality, to another from a consciousness of material form so intense that it becomes abstract, he made the world over again in his head, as if it existed only when it was thus re-made, and not even then, until it had been set down in black line on a white surface, in white line on a black surface. Working, as the decorative artist must work, in symbols almost as arbitrary, almost as fixed, as the squares of a chess-board, he swept together into his pattern all the incongruous things in the world, weaving them into congruity by his pattern. (p. 760)

In the "Salome" drawings, in most of the "Yellow Book" drawings, we see Beardsley under this mainly Japanese influence; with, now and later, in his less serious work, the but half admitted influence of what was most actual, perhaps most temporary, in the French art of the day. . . . [But] in the interval between the last drawings for the "Yellow Book" and the first drawings for the "Savoy," a new influence has come into the work, the influence of the French eighteenth century. This influence, artificial as it is, draws him nearer, though somewhat unquietly nearer, to nature. . . . The four initial letters to "Volpone," the last of which was finished not more than three weeks before his death, have a new quality both of hand and of mind. . . . [They] bring, at the last, and with complete success, nature itself into the pattern. And here, under some solemn influence, the broken line of beauty has reunited; "the care is over," and the trouble has gone out of this no less fantastic world, in which Pan still smiles from his terminal column among the trees, but without the old malice. Human and animal form reassert themselves, with a new dignity, under this new respect for their capabilities. Beardsley has accepted the convention of nature itself, turning it to his own uses, extracting from it his own symbols, but no longer rejecting it for a convention entirely of his own making. And thus in his last work, done under the very shadow of death, we find new possibilities for an art, conceived as pure line, conducted through mere pattern, which, after many hesitations, has resolved finally upon the great compromise, that compromise which the greatest artists have made, between the mind's outline and the outline of visible things. (pp. 760-61)

Arthur Symons, "Aubrey Beardsley," in The Fort-nightly Review (reprinted by permission of Contem-porary Review Company Limited), n.s. Vol. LXIII, No. CCCLXXVII, May 1, 1898, pp. 752-61.

HENRY MELANCTHON STRONG   (essay date 1900)

[*Strong provides commentary on Beardsley's novel,* Under the Hill. *Though he praises the novel's painstaking workmanship, Strong maintains that Beardsley's writing lacks the "tragic intensity" of his drawings.*]

The satirical import of many of [Beardsley's] drawings may perhaps be traced to [a] feeling of bitterness with which he regarded the pleasures and vanities of a world in which he moved only as a shadow. His satire is uncompromising, and when he "scourges the town," he does it with a thoroughness worthy only of a Juvenal or a Swift. But his portraiture is usually exaggerated to such an extent that the people at whom it is levelled often fail to apply the ridicule to themselves. And it is the glory of his satire that it is in no way ephemeral. He has ridiculed the foibles, the gross conceits of the age as no one living has done; but he has achieved something beyond this. He has succeeded in rending asunder the veil which obscures the souls of men, and has revealed them in their utter nakedness. . . . The secret of such a revelation is far to seek, but this much is certain: that Beardsley has seized upon essentials and has reproduced them as they have never been reproduced before. When an authoritative account of his work comes to be written, the explanation of his unprecedented success will possibly be found to consist largely in this: in his penetrating insight and in his marvellous power of seeing and reproducing the essential. (p. 89)

Beardsley's literary attempts, few as they are, emit an interesting side-light upon his temperament. Here we see none of that tragic intensity, that feverish expression of nameless sin, which characterise so many of his drawings. The more we come to consider the spirit of his writings the more the thought suggests itself that Beardsley could hardly have realised the full force and horror which he imparted to his grotesques, and that these terrible apotheoses of evil were rather the outcome of levity than of a mind deeply attracted by the artistic manifestation of vice. His three poems published in the *Savoy* [one of which was his translation of Catullus CI] were the product of the genius which has been called "the infinite capacity of taking pains," rather than of the divine fury. Such, too, is *Under the Hill,* a tale curiously compounded of the mediaeval spirit and of eighteenth-century conceits. It is the old story of Venus and Tannhauser over again, presented under a new and witty light. The characters are trifling; the incidents are equally so. The story has no ending, hardly, indeed, a beginning; we can see no purpose in view; in short, we are finally led to consider it in the light of a choice piece of Dresden china which has no other *raison d' être* than to stand on the dainty dressing-table of some latter-day Madame de Pompadour. It is hardly possible to say that the writing betrays any so gross a thing as style. Each sentence is a little hymn of itself, elfishly dainty, of exquisite workmanship. Whimsicality of thought and treatment, curious little flashes of imagination, now humorous, now half divine—these are what strike us at every turn. (p. 93)

Henry Melancthon Strong, "Aubrey Beardsley," in The Westminster Review, Vol. CLIV, No. 1, July, 1900, pp. 86-94.

HALDANE MACFALL   (essay date 1904)

No man drew from line the music that is in it as Aubrey Beardsley drew it by the strange and haunting magic of his genius. Whether his pen drew the dotted line that so wondrously suggests muslin and the like woman's light fripperies; whether it drew the swinging line that sings like a violin's music; whether he drew the beautiful outline of a woman's shoulder so that it seems to contain the very dainty flesh itself; whether he tricked in the charming landscape or the dandy's dressing-room or the anterooms of the beaux and belles of Pope's day, it was all done with a resonant sense that is like very music. It may be that he too often plays with the indecencies; but he sets down even the naughtinesses with consummate art. Look at the Ali Baba—surely in that figure he has stated the full-bellied voluptuary so that it seems to breathe the whole bestiality of the East. It is a perfectly legitimate statement—as legitimate as Hogarth or Rabelais. It is when he sniggers and winks and nods that he is really unforgivable; and he is sometimes wholly unforgivable.

But how intensely beautiful he could be! Take that exquisite *cul-de-lampe* [end piece] from "The Pierrot of the Minute"; the beauty of the thing is a marvel. Or take the "Frontispiece" to "Das Rheingold," surely as perfect a piece of decorative line as we shall ever see!

With Aubrey Beardsley died one of the greatest masters of line that the world has known. There is something appallingly pathetic in the death of this young fellow at the very moment when his powers were developing to the full, his imagination perfecting, his fancy becoming orderly and dainty. The quality of his artistic achievement places him not only in the front rank of the masters of his century, but of all time. (p. 463)

Haldane Macfall, "Aubrey Beardsley," in The Academy and Literature, *Vol. LXVII, No. 1697, November 12, 1904, pp. 462-64.*

HOLBROOK JACKSON   (essay date 1913)

[*A contemporary of Beardsley, Jackson asserts that the "only real and lasting influence in the art of Aubrey Beardsley was literature." Under the Hill, to Jackson, is the ultimate indication of Beardsley's love and knowledge of literature. Jackson disputes Arthur Symons's contention that Beardsley was a satirist (see excerpt above, 1898), maintaining that Beardsley did not intend to satirize so much as to merely decorate. Jackson assesses Beardsley's importance in the history of art as "an idea, not an accomplishment so much as a mood."*]

The appearance of Aubrey Beardsley in 1893 was the most extraordinary event in English art since the appearance of William Blake a little more than a hundred years earlier. With that, however, or almost so, the resemblance ends. Blake was born "out of his due time," not alone because he baffled the understanding of his age, but because his age scarcely knew of his existence. Beardsley, on the other hand, was born into an age of easy publicity; and that circumstance, combined with the fact that he was so peculiarly of his period, instantly made him a centre of discussion, a subject for regard and reprehension. (p. 91)

[Arthur Symons described Beardsley as a "Pierrot gamin" (see excerpt above, 1898).] But Beardsley was something more than that, something more purposeful, although his early death left his purpose unrealised. His youth made him the infant prodigy of the decadence; and the Pierrot in him was an attitude, and even then it was a bigger attitude than that of its namesake. Innocence always frustrated the desires of Pierrot and left him desolate, but Aubrey Beardsley introduced into art the desolation of experience, the *ennui* of sin. It required the intensity of youth to express such an attitude, although the attitude savours not of the conventional idea of youth, but of the conventional idea of experienced age. Perhaps it is only the young who are ever really morbid, for youth more than age regrets that "spring should vanish with the rose." But youth that has heard the beatings of the wings of death, as Beardsley must have done, grows so hungry for the joys and beauties of spring that it becomes aged by the very intensity of desire. (p. 95)

Aubrey Beardsley was all mannerism; his genius all whim. That is the explanation of its suddenness; its surprise. But it does not explain the extraordinary vision of humanity associated with his work.

An interviewer once asked him whether he used models. "All humanity inspires me. Every passer-by is my unconscious sitter," Beardsley replied, "and," he added, "strange as it may seem, I really draw folk as I see them. Surely it is not my fault that they fall into certain lines and angles." Contradictions of actuality as each of these statements may be, they yet throw light on Beardsley's attitude. Those who know his work, eclectic as it is, know that "all humanity" did not inspire it; that "every passer-by" was not an "unconscious sitter"; that his confession of drawing folk as he saw them was merely the art cant of the hour, which he tacitly admits by the suggestion that such a confession is strange, in the light of his own drawings and what he and the interviewer knew to be actually true. It was not, of course, his fault that these folk under his pencil fell into "certain lines and angles," it was the natural outcome of his genius. But that genius was never pictorial in the realistic sense. Beardsley was not an Impressionist, like Manet or Renoir, drawing the thing as he *saw* it; he was not a visionary, like William Blake, drawing the thing as he *dreamt* it; he was an intellectual, like George Frederick Watts, drawing the thing as he *thought* it. Aubrey Beardsley is the most literary of all modern artists; his drawings are rarely the outcome of pure observation—they are largely the outcome of thought; they are thoughts become pictures. And even then they are rarely if ever the blossoming of thought derived from experience; they are the hot-house growths of thought derived from books, pictures and music. (pp. 99-100)

The only real and lasting influence in the art of Aubrey Beardsley was literature. All who have written about him concur as to his amazing booklore. He himself admitted to having been influenced by the writers of the eighteenth century. "Works like Congreve's plays appeal far more vividly to my imagination than do those belonging to the age of Pericles," he said, in the interview already quoted. He was well versed in the literature of the decadence, and was fond of adventuring in strange and forbidden bookish realms of any and every age. The romance, **Under the Hill,** especially in its unexpurgated form, suggests deep knowledge of that literature generally classed under . . . *erotica* by the booksellers, and there are passages which read like romanticised excerpts from the *Psychopathia Sexualis* of Krafft-Ebing. **The Last Letters of Aubrey Beardsley** reveal on almost every page an extraordinary interest in books, equalled only by the keenness of his insight into literature. They reveal also how he was gradually being drawn from the literature of time to that of eternity. "Heine," he writes, "certainly cuts a poor figure beside Pascal. If Heine is the great warning, Pascal is the great example to all artists and thinkers.

He understood that to become a Christian the man of letters must sacrifice his gifts, just as Magdalen must sacrifice her beauty." (pp. 101-02)

In his literary predilections, more even than in his art, you can see the mind of Aubrey Beardsley. All the restlessness, all the changefulness of modernity were there. His art was constantly changing, as Oscar Wilde's was, not necessarily progressing, for, properly understood, Beardsley said his say in [his drawing] "The Fat Woman," just as the essence of Wilde is in *The Harlot's House.* All afterwards was repetition, restatement, intensification and elaboration. As with all the work of the decadence, Aubrey Beardsley's represented a consistent search after new and more satisfying experiences: the soul-ship seeking harbourage. But unlike so many decadents he possessed humour. You hear the laugh, often enough satyric, behind his most sinister design; and there is something in Max Beerbohm's belief that many of his earlier drawings, which seemed morbid and horrible, were the outcome of a very natural boyish desire to shock conventional folk [see excerpt above, 1897]. But that does not explain away his undeniable interest in all phases of sexual experience. . . . Beardsley loved the abnormal and he invented a sort of phallic symbolism to express his interest in passionate perversities. His prose work, **Under the Hill,** is an uncompleted study in the art of aberration. He is seldom frankly ribald, after the manner of youth, although, strangely enough, the most masterly of all his drawings, the illustrations to the *Lysistrata,* if it were not for their impish cynicism, are sufficiently Rabelaisian to satiate the crudest appetite for indecencies. It has been urged that Beardsley was engaged with such matters as a satirist, that his designs had the ultimate moral objective of all satire [see excerpt above by Arthur Symons, 1898]. Such apologies would make of him an English Félicien Rops. But there is little genuine evidence to support the contention, and what there is fades away in the light of an unpublished letter, written after his conversation during his very last days, imploring his friends in a few tragic, repentant words to destroy all indecent drawings. (pp. 102-03)

Aubrey Beardsley, although he died a saint, represents a diabolonian incident in British art. He was essentially a decorator; but with the perversity of one phase of his generation he made decoration a thing in itself. None of the books he illustrated are illustrated or decorated in the best sense. His designs overpower the text—not because they are greater but because they are inappropriate, sometimes even impertinent. The diabolical thumb-nail notes in the "Bon Mot" series have nothing whatever to do with the texts. Where the designs for the *Morte d'Arthur* approximate to the work of William Morris and Burne-Jones they serve their purpose, but where they reveal the true Beardsley they miss the point; the *Salomé* drawings seem to sneer at Oscar Wilde rather than interpret the play. *The Rape of the Lock* is eclipsed, not explained, by Beardsley. But, outrageous as his decorative comments on the *Lysistrata* may be, they are at least logical commentations on the text of the play; as are also the illustrations to his own **Under the Hill.** "No book ever gets well illustrated once it becomes a classic," wrote Beardsley, but that does not explain his own failure as an illustrator. He failed as an illustrator because his art was decoration in the abstract: it lacked the rhythm of relationship—just as he himself lacked obvious relationship with the decades that preceded and followed him. He is entombed in his period as his own design is absorbed in its own firm lines.

But Beardsley as a fact is the significant thing, not Beardsley as an artist. It does not matter how or where he stands in art, for he represents not art so much as an idea, not an accomplishment so much as a mood. The restless, inquisitive, impudent mood of the Nineties called him forth, and he obeyed and served and repented. (pp. 103-04)

> *Holbrook Jackson, "Aubrey Beardsley," in his* The Eighteen Nineties: A Review of Art and Ideas at the Close of the Nineteenth Century *(reprinted by permission of The Society of Authors as the literary representative of the Estate of Holbrook Jackson),* Grant Richards, 1913 *(and reprinted by Humanities Press, 1976, pp. 91-104).*

JOYCE KILMER   (essay date 1916)

[*A noted American poet of the early twentieth century, Kilmer calls Beardsley perverse and sick and labels him "the one genuine decadent." However, Kilmer adds that Beardsley's Catholic conversion enabled him to turn away from his evil work and "to see in the lamp which is beauty the light which is God."*]

For Aubrey Beardsley I have the greatest sympathy and admiration. That being the case, let me say that for the honor of his memory I wish that every drawing that he made, every one of those deftly-made arrangements in black and white, might be destroyed. It seems to me that he was of all the men of the eighteen-nineties the one genuine decadent. It is not only in such openly vicious things as the illustrations to Wilde's "Salome" that we find deliberate immorality in intention and expression, there is in all his work, however simple and even noble may be the theme, as for instance his illustrations to Malory's "Morte D'Arthur," a definite and unmistakable perversity, a sure sign of physical, mental and moral sickness.

Aubrey Beardsley's mental and moral sickness at first showed itself only in a contempt for the conventions of art and in especial for the conventions of proportion and prospective. It has sometimes been said that it is as absurd to rebel against the moral law as against the law of gravitation. The first revolt of a consumptive young architectural draughtsman with an extraordinary talent for line was against natural law—against the law of proportion. The first drawings which brought him any notoriety were extraordinary for two things—their admirable draughtsmanship and their deliberate eccentricities of proportion. He drew nothing but monsters—men eight feet tall with microscopic heads, women with arms as long as their entire bodies. The revolt against the moral law came later—the selection of hideously obscene subjects, the painful obsession with sex. Then came the sick boy's discoveries that after all beauty was no more in the weird ugliness he had celebrated than it was in the smug conventions of sentimental Victorian painting. A few weeks before his death Aubrey Beardsley found the immortal abiding place of beauty. Received into the Church, Aubrey Beardsley repented bitterly his misuse of his talents, and plead with his friends to destroy all his immoral drawings, of which he was now thoroughly ashamed. "Burn all my bawdy pictures," he wrote—a dying prayer which his pagan friends utterly disregarded. He had striven to find beauty in sin, and he knew that this seeking was in vain. For now he had found beauty, now he had learned to see in the lamp which is beauty the light which is God. (pp. 240-41)

> *Joyce Kilmer, "Lionel Johnson, Ernest Dowson, Aubrey Beardsley," in his* The Circus and Other Essays *(copyright, 1916, by Laurence J. Gomme; copyright renewed © 1944 by Kenton Kilmer and Christopher Kilmer; reprinted by permission of Doubleday & Company, Inc.),* Gomme, 1916 *(and reprinted as his*

> The Circus and Other Essays and Fugitive Pieces, *edited by Robert Cortes Holliday, Doran, 1921, pp. 237-52).**

W. B. YEATS   (essay date 1917?)

[*The leading figure of the Irish Renaissance and a major twentieth-century poet, Yeats wrote extensively on Beardsley's artwork. Here, Yeats provides a personal reminiscence of Beardsley and echoes Arthur Symons's assertion that Beardsley was essentially a satirist (see excerpt above, 1898.)*]

In Beardsley I found that noble courage that seems to me at times, whether in man or woman, the greatest of human faculties. I saw it in all he said and did, in the clear logic of speech and in [the] clean swift line of his art. His disease presented continuously before his mind, as one of its symptoms, lascivious images, and he drew them in their horror, their fascination, and became the first satirist of the soul English art has produced. I once said to him, 'Beardsley, I was defending you last night in the only way possible by saying that all you draw is inspired by fury against iniquity.' 'If it were so inspired,' he said, 'it would be no way different.' So great was his pride in his own sincerity. And yet certainly at the time I write [of] there was no fury, nothing but an icy passion for all reality. He had had a beautiful mistress, and I remember his coming to our flat of a morning with some painted woman with whom he had, I suppose, spent the night. And yet sexual desire under the pressure of disease became insatiable, and I was told at the time of his death that he had hastened it by masturbation. It was natural, perhaps, that so much of his nature should be uncontrollable, for I had in his presence a greater sense of power than has come to me from any young man of his age. I cannot imagine to myself the profession where he would not have made himself a foremost man. (p. 92)

> *W. B. Yeats, "Autobiography" (1917?), in his* Memoirs, *edited by Denis Donoghue (reprinted with permission of Macmillan, Limited, London and Anne Yeats; © 1972 by M. B. Yeats and Anne Yeats),* Macmillan, 1972, pp. 19-136.**

[ROGER ELIOT] FRY   (essay date 1920)

One might . . . argue that to some extent Beardsley's moral perversity actually prevented him, in spite of his extraordinary specific talent for design, from ever becoming a great designer. It is just that *mesquinerie* [meanness] of line, that littleness and intricacy of the mere decorator, that love of elegance rather than beauty, which on purely artistic grounds one finds to be his great failing, that he cherished as a means of expressing his diabolism. But if Beardsley was corrupt, he was certainly sincere in his corruption. There is no suggestion in his work, as in that of some modern artists . . . that corruption is an affectation taken up in order to astonish the *bourgeoisie*. Beardsley is never funny or amusing or witty; his attempts in this direction are contemptible; still less is he voluptuous or seductive; he is very serious, very much in earnest. There is even a touch of hieratic austerity and pomp in his style, as becomes the arch-priest of a Satanic cultus. He has, indeed, all the stigmata of the religious artist—the love of pure decoration, the patient elaboration and enrichment of surface, the predilection for flat tones and precision of contour, the want of the sense of mass and relief, the extravagant richness of invention. It is as the Fra Angelico of Satanism that his work will always have an interest for those who are curious about this recurrent phase of complex civilisations. But if we are right in our analysis of his work, the finest qualities of design can never be appropriated to the expression of such morbid and perverted ideals; nobility and geniality of design are attained only by those who, whatever their actual temperament, cherish these qualities in their imagination. (p. 155)

> [Roger Eliot] Fry, "Aubrey Beardsley's Drawings" (originally published in a different form in The Athenaeum, 1904), in his Vision and Design, Wm. Clowes & Son, 1920, pp. 153-55.

E. T. RAYMOND   (essay date 1921)

[The Decadents] stood for something which can perhaps be best described as a revolt without a standard, a rebellion without object or hope. They were in arms against everything that had happened, but had no idea whatever of what they wanted to happen. Indeed, they appeared to be pretty certain that nothing genuine could happen. They seemed to be really impressed by the accident that they were near the end of a century. (p. 193)

Aubrey Beardsley was very typical of the Nineties in his unenjoying luxuriousness, his invalid indecorum, his trammelled originality, and his pert pessimism. He was in pictorial art much what Wilde was in literature, except that he possessed a certain conscience of the hand, so to speak, a pride and care for technical quality, which few considerable draughtsmen lack, while Wilde, though an artist also, lacked such fastidiousness, and was just as pleased with a cheap victory as with a dear one. Both he and Wilde were in revolt against convention, but each would have died rather than do anything naturally. Both were at war with the great Victorian commandment of decorum, but both respected slavishly the little law of a little clique. Both suggested the futility of all things, the one in the most precious prose, the other in the most austerely thought-out design. Both offended against all laws, human and divine, in order to be brilliant and exceptional, and both were under the thraldom of taboos with the force of the Decalogue and crotchets elevated to the dignity of a religion. Each was guilty of most extraordinarily bad taste, not a simple but a complex bad taste, reminiscent of the decaying Roman world; there was something barbaric in their over-sophistication, and something common in their over-refinement. (p. 194)

Pessimism is always barren; a pessimism which needs continual conscious cultivation is merely ridiculous. Aubrey Beardsley was saved from being merely ridiculous by [a] conscience of the hand. . . . (p. 195)

Beardsley had one great talent apart from the mere mastery of line. Over-civilised himself, he was unequalled in suggesting the tragedy of over-civilisation, though quite possibly he did not feel it. He could portray with remorseless truth, though in a convention as strict as that of an old Chinese artist, certain types of modern men and women. He is the limner of the pinched soul, the pampered body, the craving without appetite, the animalism without animal health. . . . To Beardsley the greater light and the less only existed as astronomical facts of minor interest; his real element was the arc-light of the street or the shaded glow of the interior. There is a sense of joyless depravity about his men and women, as if vice were a routine, and even a solemn social ritual; and his illustrations of the "Morte d'Arthur" are made ridiculous by the perpetual recurrence of the haggard eyes and small, evil features of people Beardsley had studied in a Piccadilly restaurant or the Casino at Dieppe. Anachronism, so often the joy and life of literature,

is no necessary fault in the decorative artist, and nobody need quarrel with Beardsley for taking liberties with the gowning of Isolde. But it was an anachronism without excuse to swap souls as well as dresses. (pp. 196-97)

> E. T. Raymond, "Aubrey Beardsley," in his Portraits of the Nineties (reprinted with permission of Charles Scribner's Sons), Charles Scribner's Sons, 1921, pp. 192-99.

OSBERT BURDETT   (essay date 1925)

[Burdett repeats Arthur Symons's statement that Beardsley was "the satirist of an age without convictions" (see excerpt above, 1898). Yet Burdett believes that, rather than merely satirizing corruption, Beardsley depicted "the state of a soul to which an age without convictions is reduced." Burdett also discusses Beardsley's love of the grotesque, which he considers a rebellion against Victorian principles.]

[The 1890s were] rich in personalities, in men who were interesting apart even from the work that has distinguished them, but if one were lacking without whose art the decade would feel its greatest loss, that personality is unquestionably Aubrey Beardsley's. He alone has earned without reserve the epithet of a great artist, and his personality is remarkable because in his short and crowded years almost every ounce of energy that disease left him was transmuted into his drawings. (p. 98)

He was something of a dandy, like Wilde; he was something of a wit also; he wrote prose and verse as characteristic as any of the prevailing point of view, and he could be considered under any of these aspects of his talent. His art is the principal product of the time, perhaps the only characteristic product of which we never weary, the suggestions and beauty being as inexhaustible as the resource that created them. (p. 99)

The vivid, eager life in Beardsley's designs gives an intense, almost a dramatic, quality to every curve and line within them. All excrescences, all confusion, have been pruned away. The design springs to life with the swiftness of a perfected miracle, nor is this effect an effect merely. Each design will bear strict and curious examination. Every foliation can be traced to its authentic source; nothing is weak or wayward, or intruded merely to fill a corner or disguise an unrelated fragment of the pattern. The blank spaces are as much alive as the revealing lines that are traced upon them. Often with a sparing amount of pattern each page is scrupulously filled, for the spacing becomes an integral part of the design, and is always more than a background to it.

From this it follows that the critical intellect of the artist has been no less severely awake than his imagination. The two go hand in hand, to produce work that, in the strict sense of the word, is beyond criticism because every criticism has been already allowed for. The result is a strange effect of austerity, an intense, almost cold, perfection, which we know not whether to call passionless or impassioned, to such a pitch has it been brought. The treatment of the folds of the draperies is classic in its economy of means, and yet the lines are troubled by the souls of the figures, which move in a bitter ecstasy of contemplation or thought, for their bodies have become transparent with the feverish life within and can hardly sustain the burden of an existence so intense. There had been a fragile innocence in Burne-Jones's figures; a spiritual refinement had paled their faces and hollowed their cheeks, but in Beardsley's the very children were living in an age of experience, and his figures suffer from their souls as from a malady of the nerves. (pp. 103-04)

The intellect of an artist cannot be so critical of the form that his imagination creates, or subdue it so thoroughly, without the suggestion of satire; for the intellect is an analysing faculty, sad under the doom that it must take its material to pieces and, as it were, reverse the process of creation that the imagination has achieved, since it works in detachment rather than in sympathy with its material. Therefore, when we find the flowerlike or merely fanciful forms of [his] designs refashioned by Beardsley to express no more than the essence of themselves, we should expect the quality of his genius to be even more apparent in his figures, where a detachment that seems malicious betrays itself. The introduction of beings as of flowers would suggest ideas to him, and to him every idea was a piece of intellectual criticism. His imagination would make mischief for his intellect, and his intellect would dispassionately criticize his imagination, and from this curious detachment we should expect the satirical suggestion that we find. It was not so much that he started deliberately to satirize his subjects, but that his glance was penetrating, so that his intelligence coldly and quickly responded to every image recorded by his eye. He penetrated immediately to the soul, and compared it with the substance, as we ourselves contrast ourselves with our own shadows when we happen to stand before a strong light. Beardsley's eye was like such a light, and when his eye fell upon an object it placed that object in intense relief, an opaque form on a brilliant background.

If we glance merely at the vignettes that decorate the vacant corners of the *Morte d'Arthur,* vignettes in many of which the forms of flowers are the principal motives, we observe the same treatment as that which was to inspire his terrible figures later on. The flower-forms seem, intellectually, to be the satire of their originals because the pattern that they have suggested is a form beyond their own consciousness, and has been rigidly controlled by a critical intellect which has cared for them merely as motives, to be bent and shapen to the decorative scheme he had in mind, a scheme which represents more nearly than life itself their inner nature, their hidden soul. At the same time, the result is exquisitely beautiful: more beautiful than the original suggestion, for nothing competes or falls short because the conditions of the pattern have been fulfilled with an unnatural, that is to say a flawless, integrity. A new kingdom seems to have been conquered because some heaven of imagination has been reached.

So vivid are the whites and the blacks that all colours seem to have been absorbed by them. By denying himself every resource of the painter's palette, the artist produces an effect more vivid than that of colour. This, indeed, carried him to a point which seems not surpassed in the range of black-and-white drawing: the power of drawing white on white and black on black. . . . Black and white, keeping the while in the utmost strictness their several qualities, become capable of suggesting varied grades of tone. The effect is uncanny, because black and white are made to do more than had seemed possible, so strict was the intellect which controlled and the imagination which suggested their combinations. (His coloured drawings and single picture are less good, but then he died too young to be judged by them.)

It is well to insist on this quality at the very foundation of Beardsley's work, because we are accustomed to observe it chiefly in the decorations of his later manner. There has rarely been a greater play of fancy than in the details with which his designs abound. (pp. 104-07)

This decorative sense was his master-gift, and to it form, flower, figure or convention even, was subdued successfully. The untrammelled imagination, which saw everything that could be represented by space and line merely as a motive for decorative effect, was most startling when the human face and figure were introduced. These last, being treated with equal artistic detachment, were bound to seem satirical because all treatment of them that is not mainly representative must appear in some degree a caricature to the human observer. At this point in his development it was as if the forms of nature in plant and spray had been given their revenge. Human imagination had evoked them for a delight of its own, for an alien purpose, and now it was to mete the same treatment to its kindred. (pp. 107-08)

In that beautiful drawing, *The Mysterious Rose-Garden,* we can see a symbol of the artistic instinct of the century set in the cultivated garden of the time, which first subdued and then was to be questioned by itself. The rose-garden was the Victorian parterre in which the spirit of imagination was domesticated, and employed to beautify and delight its contented guardians. A virgin art she was, protected from all disturbing influences, and allowed to wander, like another Eve, in this sanctified precinct that had been retrieved from nature. . . . We are shown no more in this design than the roses, the figured voice, and the listening virgin, but we know that she is destined to yield, and that in the moment of yielding she has become a different creature, mysteriously deeper than the child of yesterday. The forces that have wrought this miracle are forces of freedom and growth. It is conventional art listening to the whisper of creative imagination in the familiar and formal garden of Victorian times; it is the return of Pan, the repudiation of authority. (pp. 109-10)

Mr. Thomas Hardy has remarked that there is no better sign of the vitality of art than the delight of its master-spirits in grotesque. One reason why Beardsley was great was that he shared and indulged this impulse to the full. The true artistic criticism of Victorian art is that it lacked this playfulness, that it created a convention in which there was no room for the grotesque; the final gaiety (even in Dickens) was beyond its power. It barely tolerated Punch, until it had made him a pillar of respectable society. It is the only recent age that attempted to ignore Pan and Punch and Pierrot. The Beardsley period was the moment of their long-delayed revenge. This explains why Beardsley's imagination seemed so alien to his contemporaries. A grotesque is the invention of a form that does not exist in nature, and is usually a fusion of animal and human shapes. Beardsley devised innumerable examples, which were as true to his artistic ideal as those on the walls of Gothic buildings to the mediaeval. (p. 113)

The beauty of [his] designs is evident, but the appearance of satire, which the technique natural to his genius encouraged, became dominant when the subjects became symbols of human appetite or passion, or human beings drawn to typify the corruption of human souls. To what was due this apparent preoccupation with diabolical manifestations, with an extremity of beauty that infused malignant forms? It was partly an accident, partly a criticism. . . . Through the oppression of popular standards, of the crowd upon each man, the imagination of the time became preoccupied with the sport of sin. . . . (pp. 113-14)

[Beardsley] was reacting from an exhausted convention, and being constitutionally indifferent to motives from his artist's delight in all that his imagination divined, was impelled on every side to concentrate on the hidden and the evil. Our convention that evil consists in *admitting* unpalatable truth, shocked his conscience, for an imaginative conscience is one that suffers acutely from the dread of being deceived. To forbid the mention of evil things encourages their further invasion, and decorum, which is often the polite name for censorship, may become a form of suppressing the truth, and be loved by men for the same reason that they prefer darkness to light, because their deeds are evil. The source of man's energies is his instincts, and the Victorian convention imposed, in the name of decency, a conspiracy of silence concerning them. Its effect produced a result directly contrary to that which had been first intended: the elimination of words led to an ignoring of facts; it enthroned a lie in the soul because the soul had lost the vision of evil. . . . Evil had become our good, and good our evil, and the only remedy was ruthlessly to strip the masks from the realities.

When pretence and reality have become divorced to this extent, men cease to be aware of the extent of either, and there arrives an age without convictions. Mr. Symons' summary verdict: "Beardsley was the satirist of an age without convictions," is the final verdict on this aspect of Beardsley's art, and the subject of his satire is not usually this or that corruption, but the state of soul to which an age without convictions is reduced. Sometimes, indeed, he shows us side by side the pretension and the reality, but this is the exception. . . . In *Lady Gold's Escort,* [a] group of young men is paying court to an old woman, whose possession of a purse is the real object of their hospitable courtesies. When the pretence and the reality were thus placed side by side, an obvious piece of satire resulted, the effect of which is immensely heightened by the beauty of the black and white design. But neither comes home to the conscience of the observer, because, being localized, he does not recognize his own portrait there. The satire is not less real and becomes far more wounding when the instincts and the soul are the only subject of the drawing. (pp. 115-17)

The line of beauty in Beardsley's drawings is the current of vigour in a decay; and it may be regarded either as the principle of vitality in the completion of a necessary process, or as the final survival of a higher life departure from which has occasioned the ruin. Only a spiritual force can create convincing images of spiritual corruption, and the eye of the soul must be stricken indeed with blindness if it cannot see, beyond the evil depicted, the line of beauty by which it is circumscribed in Beardsley's work. . . .

[The] word satirist applied to Beardsley does not mean that he was on the side of the conventions, but on the side of the reality that they ignored. It came to him directly as a vision of evil, and he transcribed his vision, not with a self-conscious satirical purpose, but simply as a decorative artist. It is this artistic single-mindedness, indeed, which makes the designs terrible. . . . (p. 119)

Beardsley's most characteristic style was not the invention of evil in a virtuous age, but the depiction of an underlying corruption. After these drawings had appeared, people professed to see Beardsley faces in the streets, as they had previously seen Rossetti ones. A characteristic whim of the period was that life copies art, and excellent play was made with it. But the deeper truth is otherwise. Fogs did not arrive in London upon the tips of Whistler's brushes, but he was the first artist to see them imaginatively, and when he had opened our eyes to their quality, we began to refer the images on our own retina to the canvases that we remembered. The same is true of the

faces created by Rossetti, Burne-Jones and Aubrey Beardsley. We were on the look out for such faces among the people whom we met, and felt flattered when we discovered them. . . . The evil that informs the Beardsley drawings was an evil that informed the typical soul, and so the typical face, of his contemporaries. We can admit this without boasting much difference, because in the meantime we have learnt more than they of the causes and nature of this corruption. That is why I [would not call] Beardsley a satirist without explaining that a great satirist is one with an eye for corruption that seems inevitable, and even respectable, to smaller men. . . . We may apply to the artist the remark of Gautier in his preface to *Mademoiselle de Maupin:* "Books follow morals, and morals do not follow books. The Regency made Crébillon, and not Crébillon the Regency. . . . The centuries succeed each other and each bears its own fruit. Books are the fruits of morals."

The art of Beardsley is another example of this truth, which also enables us to do justice to the good side of the early Victorian reaction from the Regency, and to the truth to that effort of the best Victorian art. But a convention endures longer than the original impulse which produces it, and the Victorian convention came to mask a corruption which it was a return to sanity to reveal. This is the revelation of the Beardsley drawings. . . . (pp. 126-28)

> *Osbert Burdett, in his* The Beardsley Period: An Essay in Perspective, *Boni and Liveright, 1925, 302 p.*

JOHN K. M. ROTHENSTEIN (essay date 1928)

The promoters of the fabulous legend of the 'nineties have insisted that Aubrey Beardsley was its epitome. . . . Looking back upon that age across a space of more than thirty years we are able to perceive that certain strong affinities existed between certain artists. There was a similarity in their unconscious reactions towards the two most significant factors affecting modern art, namely, industrialism and classicism. (p. 163)

If Beardsley could not epitomise the spirit of an exclusive and exotic clique which never had any existence save in the minds of its inventors, his art was profoundly characteristic of the actual group which we are able to see so clearly in retrospect. His instinctive attitude towards industrialism is clearly shown by his constant attempt to create a world of his own, a fantastic and exotic refuge from the present. From this refuge all things significant of the modern world were excluded.

Hardly less clear is his attitude to classicism. I say "hardly" because his eclecticism led him to borrow from classic art as he borrowed from every other, so slightly obscuring the purely romantic nature of his own creations. His disregard for the classical canon, his insistence upon character, his predilection for the exaggerated and the grotesque, all testify to the absence of the classic spirit from his nature.

More pronounced than his antipathy for industrialism and classicism was his hatred of the conventions which had been built up by the middle classes during the reign of Victoria. (pp. 163-64)

[The] victorian conspiracy of silence had been attacked neither so remorselessly nor so boldly nor so effectively as by the dying consumptive boy, Aubrey Beardsley. (p. 165)

His work passed through four clearly marked phases. The second of these alone is dominated by the satirical motive. (p. 166)

[These phases] were expressions of his own inner development. He borrowed what he needed at each stage, instead of being dragged hither and thither by one enthusiasm after another, as [some] critics pretend. The orderly nature of his progress is sufficient in itself to confute any such idea.

His development was of a peculiar kind. It must be remembered that from a very early age he knew that he had not long to live. The significance of this knowledge to anyone who was so greatly in love with life, so avid of experience as he, was that everything must be compressed into the few years which remained. Although there was about his progress an element of self-consciousness, it was never so strong as to make him attempt to force its pace. What he did was so to stimulate his mind, by constant contact with his fellow men (he became a considerable social figure), by reading (he always read prodigiously), by hearing music (he was a regular frequenter of concerts), by experiencing much (he experienced in certain directions more than his biographers are inclined to concede), that it should miss no opportunity of completing its evolution. (pp. 167-68)

[During his first phase, no] very definite motive beyond the purely decorative appeared in his work. . . . The *Morte d'Arthur* is a fine testimony to his courage and his perseverance, but it also shows that he did not express himself naturally on such a scale. Even Beardsley's most fervent admirers admit that the effect of such sustained effort was to make the work uneven in quality. But uneven and derivative as it is, the *Morte d'Arthur* places the fact of Beardsley's technical skill beyond doubt. (pp. 168-69)

His was the skill of the mediaeval craftsman. Had he lived in the middle ages instead of our own the demands which would have been made upon his ability might have created an artist of the highest rank. As it was, one immense task was given him, and afterwards so much of his great talent was allowed to go to waste in the expression of trivial morbidities. (p. 169)

[During his second phase, Beardsley] combined the character of inexorable exposer of the evil which convention hid, with that of its high priest. His work began to take on something of the austere hieratical quality characteristic of religious art. The illustrations to Wilde's play, *Salome,* and those published in *The Yellow Book* were the most important products of the second phase.

Towards the end of 1895 a new element entered Beardsley's art. Like the Japanese and the Greek, the conventions of the French eighteenth century were now taken and subordinated to purely beardsleian ends. The significance of this change does not lie in the introduction of elements of French eighteenth century decoration into his design, but in the decline of his satiric mood.

The way of the satirist is to place profession and reality side by side, so that the discrepancy between them may shock the onlooker. Therefore any man who is a satirist must feel such discrepancy keenly. I believe that Beardsley, often as he revelled obviously in the evil which he satirised, was oppressed by it. Hypocrisy was alien to a mind so imperturbably clear. (pp. 171-72)

The eighteenth century, with its clear limited objective, its rational outlook and its acknowledgement of human frailty, was able to achieve a greater harmony between profession and practice than those which immediately preceded or followed it. And so, when Beardsley, largely owing to his friendship

with Conder, discovered the age of Watteau, Fragonard, Crébillon, and Chesterfield, a certain unhappy tenseness which had before been present in his work now left it. In this third phase it was as though he were rejoicing in a subject in which he could believe. Since he believed in it, satire was no longer necessary: his entire energies were concentrated upon beautiful rendering. The illustrations of *The Rape of the Lock* are as characteristic of this as are those of *Salome* of the preceding stage. If the later drawings have a richness and finish which the earlier ones have not, they are without something of their bizarre and fascinating atmosphere.

Of the final phase, upon which Beardsley entered so shortly before his death, it is difficult to speak with precision. For the time between the last momentous change and the end was so brief, so fraught with suffering, that the artist could do little. One fact at least stands out clearly; that Beardsley, who had borrowed from every art to aid his own expression, began to turn towards Nature herself. Of becoming a naturalistic artist he showed no sign. His own vision remained as clear and individual as it had always been, but he clothed it in the garments of Nature rather than of art. (pp. 171-72)

Beardsley's final mood could only be expressed aesthetically in naturalistic, and emotionally in religious, terms. The difference between such terms and any he had used before was very great. (p. 174)

That he already loved the externals of the Catholic Church, and one of his closest friends was a member of her priesthood, predisposed him in her favour.

Far more important was the fact that the Church stood in a particular relationship to certain forces which underlay Beardsley's ideas and conduct. . . . [However] diversely it manifested itself, the profoundest spirit, which unknown to themselves, animated the men of the 'nineties, was the protest against industrialism. Now it is clear that the Catholic Church, whose concern, before everything else, is the salvation of the individual, must be hostile to certain important conditions of an industrialised society. . . . Since the action of such a society tends to deprive the individual of both the will and the ability to be answerable to himself, and to make of him a mere standardised mechanism, it follows inevitably that it challenges the responsibility of each man to himself, which the Church holds to be the necessary condition of salvation.

There is no evidence, indeed there is little likelihood, that Beardsley's mind worked consciously along these lines. But the drabness and disorder against which he and the other artists of the 'nineties uttered their vehement if largely unconscious protest, was the direct result of the working of the standardising tendencies inherent in modern society. The majority of them sought refuge from it in the practice of their art rather than the practice of religion. Of those who can be termed ''of the 'nineties'' the proportion who either maintained their Catholicism intact or afterwards entered the Roman Communion is surprisingly large. (pp. 175-76)

Despite the surprising nature of his artistic talent Beardsley often asserted—without affectation, his friends thought—that he would rather have been a writer. Certainly his writings have qualities akin to those in his drawings, which give them a unique if modest place in English literature. As a reader his capacity was extraordinary. The way in which, in the course of a few years, he managed, in addition to his vast output of drawings, full social life, and interest in music, to absorb the greater part of English and French literature, from the most learned works to the most trivial, to say nothing of great quantities of the classics, is little short of miraculous. (p. 177)

John K. M. Rothenstein, "Beardsley," in his The Artists of the 1890's *(reprinted by permission of Routledge & Kegan Paul PLC), Routledge, 1928, pp. 163-78.*

ROBIN IRONSIDE (essay date 1946)

Beardsley's [*Under the Hill,* an] unfinished romantic *nouvelle*, as he might have called it, has many painful phrases; the affectations in his published letters, the use of 'touchant' for 'touching', of the adverb 'vastly' or of the epithet 'simply too, too' embarrass us today; and even in his drawings our appreciation is apt to be interrupted by a vulgarity of affectation which has no sanction beyond its special appeal to the so-called 'decadent' artistic circles of the early 'nineties. His illustrations to the *Rape of the Lock* are almost too, too *dix-huitième* [eighteenth-century] for unquestioning enjoyment, those for *Salome* too japanesque; and it was not, probably, the impulse of a colourist that led him to propose that he should tint the drawings for *Lysistrata* in pale mauve. The defect in his art that arose from the subjection of his taste to literary and artistic fashion cannot be dismissed as superficial. There is every likelihood, even a certainty, that he would have outgrown it, had he lived; but it was present in nearly everything he did up to a few months before his death. . . . (pp. 190-91)

As the victim mainly of circumstance, the Aesthetic Movement was short-lived and valetudinarian. Such as it was, Beardsley epitomized it, and his art, despite the contemporary affectations he was unable to overcome, embodies a force and a specific expression which compels us to reckon with, to pierce the preciosities which are its outward and sometimes ludicrous vesture. Beardsley's authentic poetic energy was not manifest in his art only. We do not have to reconcile the strength of his best drawings with the conceits of *Under the Hill*. . . . (p. 192)

Beardsley has regularly been praised as a superb craftsman. In fact, his method was that which most amateurs instinctively employ. . . . [There] was nothing of the craftsman's systematic, acquired acumen in his method. . . . 'Finish', however, is certainly one of the obtrusive qualities of Beardsley's art, not the finish of legibility or adequate representation (his more complex drawings have no immediate clarity of subject and he was apparently indifferent to the accident of representing a figure with two left hands), but the finish that results from the melodious fulfilment, of some linear rhythm or from the tonal or atonal harmonies that may be produced by the painstaking disposition and variation of darks and lights. All his work shows this self-conscious deliberation in the choice of a line that must flow even if it should fail to describe or suggest, or of a shape that must be graceful whatever may be the normal features of the natural object of which it is the image. (pp. 197-98)

Beardsley's inspiration was erotic before it was decorative, and it is as an altar, irreproachably graven, to the erotic ambitions of the period—as he intensely experienced them—that his art preserves its idiosyncratic spirit. Whatever the degree of formalization, the abstract elements in his work may be seen to be the shrine of a breathing Eros. (p. 199)

The unexpurgated story [of *Under the Hill, The Story of Tannhäuser and Venus*], though it was to end with Tannhäuser's disillusioned withdrawal from the delights of the Venusberg,

must dispose of any obstinate notion that Beardsley accepted certain forms of licence and rejected others. Its value is as a key to the suggestive or mysteriously disturbing features in the drawings; it more than confirms, in unambiguous but absurd language, our extreme suspicions of the excesses of which the Abbé in the illustration to *Under the Hill* might be capable; it degrades Helen in more ways than even the advised sweetness of her appearance in the second illustration seems to invite; and it proves that the delicate attendants of Salome are able and ready to accomplish feats of which, in the drawings, only their eyes and what Beardsley would have called their massive 'chevelure' are the pledge. The story in itself has no merits beyond those that an exacting connoisseur would require of that dubious channel of near-literature to which its theme is confined and whence . . . it presumes in vain to emerge in spite of the care that Beardsley spent upon its composition— the same care, incited by the same inspiration, that he bestowed with such beautiful, reticent results upon his drawing. (p. 201)

Robin Ironside, "Aubrey Beardsley," in Horizon, *Vol. XIV, No. 81, September, 1946, pp. 190-202.*

ANNETTE LAVERS (essay date 1967)

[*Lavers's essay is an extensive study of Beardsley's writings, particularly* Venus and Tannhäuser. *The critic discusses the correspondence between Beardsley's fiction and artwork, terming* Venus and Tannhäuser *the "perfect literary equivalent" of Beardsley's drawings. In addition, Lavers examines the influence of eighteenth-century French literature on Beardsley and explores his prosodic technique.*]

Beardsley laid considerable stress on the flavour of isolated words and phrases, on the rhythm of sentences. He also felt it essential to describe with absolute fidelity certain quite definite conceptions and effects of sensibility. He was not prepared to rely on felicities which arise from technique alone. It was precisely this somewhat Flaubertian behaviour which led Symons to deduce that Beardsley lacked the literary temperament and made desperate attempts to force nature. Yet sufficient evidence exists of Beardsley's literary facility; in his letters, his small humorous poems, in that pleasure in the pure act of writing itself. . . . But, whether Beardsley realized it or not, literature for him was more than a gratuitous game. . . .

[Pure] artist as he virtually was, Beardsley was not well equipped to defend his writings on a purely intellectual level. He preferred to allow meanings shape and body in his work and in his life. (p. 244)

[How] are we to interpret [*Under the Hill,* a] *Fête Galante* [elegant party] in which a puerile Venus and Tannhäuser settle on a Babylonian terrace to a supper as epic as that of Trimalchio, followed by a bacchanalia and a ballet worthy of the French *Régence* to the strains of a music which strongly reminds one of [Claude Debussy's] *Prélude à l'Après-Midi d'un Faune*—this work in which all influences are amalgamated; in which all the contrasts, beloved by this period, between decadence and barbarism are resolved, thanks to the brisk pace of a tale as gay and as irreverent as if it had been written by a Voltaire or a Crébillon fils?

Let us first note that misunderstandings about its meaning are only too easily explained by the fragmentary state of the 'novel'. (p. 245)

Why did Beardsley discontinue his novel? After a year, the *Savoy* itself stopped appearing for lack of financial support.

Then there were the difficulties naturally surrounding publication of a work which had been in part published already, and of which the greater part was certainly unpublishable. There was failing health. But a deeper reason than any of those may be found in Beardsley's psychological evolution, which . . . made him bring his story to a conclusion in his own life: indeed most of his work can be viewed as an attempt to reach a satisfactory synthesis of his various tendencies.

It is interesting to notice that expurgation brings new devices: a way, for instance, of presenting events elliptically and with *non sequiturs,* which has analogues in the design and stylization of the drawings. Some of the censored material is introduced as seemingly erudite footnotes, a device Beardsley had probably come upon in that seventeenth-and eighteenth-century fiction he so relished. Interesting in themselves, such devices nonetheless merely increase the impression of mere artificiality left by **Under the Hill** and altogether break the brisk pace of the original version.

Someone who had been struck by the extraordinary images which people Beardsley's drawings once asked him whether he had fantastic visions. He allowed himself, Beardsley answered, only to have them on paper. But several things seem directly to contradict this. Each scene in **Venus and Tannhäuser** is first described with the fantastic precision which is Beardsley's hallmark; the tableaux then become animated and the story resumes its momentarily interrupted course. Settings and characters first come to the author as if they were petrified by a magic wand, and it is this first state which is illustrated. But all the details appearing in the drawings play a part in the story, which is a perfect literary equivalent. There exists, therefore, a vision which could be expressed as a story, as a drawing, or as both of these. The story is conceived as a string of scenes (chapters, in **Venus and Tannhäuser**), but conversely the drawings have a literary background. (pp. 246-47)

What was to be the meaning of the completed **Venus and Tannhäuser**? A long sub-title imitated from those of the seventeenth and eighteenth centuries gives the synopsis of the story:

> The story of *Venus and Tannhäuser,* in which is set forth an exact Account of the Manner of State held by madam Venus, Goddess and Meretrix, under the famous Horselberg, and containing the Adventures of Tannhäuser in that place, his journeying to Rome, and return to the loving mountain.

Was it to have been a parody where nothing would have differed from the original except in a very *fin de siècle* irony? That would have been in keeping with the historicism typical of the nineteenth century. . . . (pp. 253-54)

[There is] in **Venus and Tannhäuser** a triple desecration: religious, medieval, and Wagnerian, a desecration of all that [Beardsley] once revered, although whether this is genuine or whether it expresses a liberation is difficult to say. Beardsley's title has no mention of Elizabeth, no mention either of the final absolution. Does this indicate a return to the medieval ending, or an ironical twist in the tail, the return to the Venusberg being welcomed by Tannhäuser? (p. 254)

[It is essential] to realize that the typical rhythm in Beardsley is to become totally engrossed in a particular [aesthetic] atmosphere, expressed in a definite technique, and then to abandon it completely. It would be rash indeed to attempt to confine

Beardsley, as some have done, within a single phase and its supposed implications. Yet one must insist that **Venus and Tannhäuser** was written at the height of Beardsley's fad for the eighteenth century, and the French eighteenth century in particular, with all its refinements and vanities, its art of enjoyment, its gay corruptions, its passion for opera and ballet. The keynote of text and illustration is profusion. The most typical feature, frequent enumerations in the text (of decorations, shoes, masks, names, and habits, etc.), reflects an attempt to grasp reality by the means of saturation and excess. The illustrations of the *Rape of the Lock* had contrived to give an impression of spaciousness, derived mainly from variation in thickness of line, equivalent to musical *pianissimo* and *fortissimo.* In **Under the Hill**, Beardsley goes knowingly too far: the monstrous proliferation of rococo detail devours space, stifles the characters, rapturously exists for its own sake. There remain none now of the empty spaces which so mysteriously acquired colour and texture by juxtaposition; characters and planes are now only distinguished by a close weave of hatching and stipple. In the opposition, so charmed for Beardsley, between the beautiful and the grotesque, it is the latter which triumphs here, characterized as always by inexhaustible licence, where only surprise and ingenuity are the law, and where more than in any other realm of art the sole rule is to please, and success establishes *a posteriori* the canon. It is Carnival, where everything is allowed.

The *Ancien Régime* [pre-Revolutionary France] and its myth seem specially designed to slake this transient thirst for pure decoration, even at the expense of meaning. It is the age of senseless survivals, of pompous spellings, of sumptuous names, and complicated etiquette. . . . In the nostalgic dedication to an imaginary cardinal which opens the book, Beardsley, typically in half-earnest, assumes the subservient part of the artist of those days, very different from the priestly prestige which had been acquired since the days of Romanticism. This dedication, moreover, reminds us that there had been an aesthetic conversion to catholicism before a religious one. It is easy to see what in that religion attracted Decadents, and Beardsley in his present state of mind more than anyone else. It is the religion of rites and traditions, of fossils and relics, of symbols as powerful as realities. (pp. 256-57)

[Beardsley's work] contains a real 'comédie humaine' [human comedy] (a repertoire of which can be seen, for instance, in the drawing entitled 'The Toilet of Helen'), and it is precisely Beardsley's fidelity to certain types, in spite of their unsuitability for some commissioned work, which could expose him to the charge of perversity. The most striking are two, whose physical interpretation can vary slightly but whose significance remains the same.

After the first phase in which his masters were Burne-Jones, Mantegna, and Botticelli, Beardsley did not try any longer to represent Beauty. Even to that point, it had not been pure beauty, but a beauty permeated with history, literature, and feeling. The ideal he painted, so difficult to express without mawkishness, is, grace, 'loveliness', 'irritating' because it 'can never be entirely comprehended or ever enjoyed to the utmost'. It can be seen in Venus, in the singer in **The Three Musicians,** in the princess of the **Ballad of the Barber** 'as lyrical and sweet as one of Schubert's melodies'. In front of this image of purity we find the entirely corrupt characters, often at the same time inhibited and full of sadistic obsessions. To render their psychological complexity, Beardsley's art, which consists essentially of lyrical lines, endeavours to reach the particular: stippling, a veritable uniform, attempts to indicate on their faces blemishes and wrinkles. They are the Barber, Priapusa, or that curious personage in the drawing significantly chosen by the artist for his own book plate . . . , laden with books, who does not dare to look directly at a buxom naked lady. This latter type must not be confused with what could be called Beardsley's *roués,* his Laclos, his Messalina, his Valmont, his Herodias, august monsters who carry their heads high and whom the author has endowed with a robust dignity.

One image seems to have held a perpetual attraction for Beardsley. It is that of the 'toilette' scenes, which he has interpreted in all his successive manners. These are nearly always characterized by the contrast between the pure and the corrupt, which gives them their well-known aspect of a Black Mass. Here, for instance, is Venus sitting at a dressing-table on which are piled candles, flowers, perfumes, and fashionable books. . . . By an assimilation which recalls eighteenth-century erotic vocabulary, the dressing-table becomes an altar on which is accomplished a strange ceremony. Beauty, the equivocal substitute of the ultimate good, passively appears as a victim on whom the desires of all converge and who offers a strong contrast with the motley crowd which surrounds her. She abandons herself to the care of the officiant, one of the corrupt, but whose experience gives an impression of security because it suggests a bottomless and properly maternal indulgence. Both live together in a symbiotic relationship which seems obscurely to express the fundamental ambiguity of life; which is at the same time experience (and therefore corruption or qualified morals at least) and ideal, faceless depth and brilliant surface.

After the angelism of the first drawings, and perhaps in reaction to the hard labour of the *Morte D'Arthur,* sadistic fantasies seem briefly to have fascinated Beardsley.

Reading Wilde's *Salome* (from which he soon felt remote enough to begin scattering his illustrations of that work with caricatures of its author), Beardsley was first moved by the climax of the drama, entirely of Wilde's invention, where Salome proudly claims all responsibility for her behaviour. . . . (pp. 257-59)

[Sadistic] is the poem of the **Barber,** which Beardsley illustrated with a 'toilette' scene and which shows very well that for him sadism was not sought out for its own sake as the extreme form of sensation, but on the contrary adopted when for some reason normal reactions were impossible. Sadism is significantly absent from *Venus and Tannhäuser,* where the whole point is to suppress all such taboos. (p. 259)

Other works represent the triumph of mental equilibrium. It is that of happiness normally obtained in the poem of **The Three Musicians;** but it is significantly obtained as a defiance of the moralists personified by the prudish English tourist, who 'sent up a prayer for France'. For this takes place in France, the only country according to Beardsley which knew how to achieve happiness. Many French words in **Venus and Tannhäuser** show to what an extent his sensibility had been fashioned by his readings in French literature which ranged widely. . . . Beardsley's Tannhäuser is not a dandy but a fop, whose nostalgia of the earth gives way to a hundred trivial preoccupations. His Venus is a universal prostitute without being divested of the radiant sovereignty which characterizes her in the drawing *Venus between Terminal Gods.* She is the type of 'toilette' heroine, who knows all about corruption but lends to it her smiling complicity. Conversely, the main feature of corruption here is its reassuring aspect, due to its limitless experience. For the real divinity of the Venusberg is not Venus; it is Priapus, or,

rather, a significantly feminine Priapusa. A tutelary personage, at the same time mother and procuress, she intrudes in all the lovers' activities, rejoicing in these incarnations without which she cannot really exist. And vice, thus tamed, becomes as venerable as Erda or the Mothers in the second *Faust.* (pp. 259-60)

[The] 'voyeur' tourist is also present implicitly: this is what the reader is forced to become, since he is constantly needled by the challenges of the author to follow him if he dares. For [*Venus and Tannhäuser*] is not a novel, it is a tale where the teller ceaselessly watches the reaction of the hearer. Recognition of this fact allows us to avoid certain pitfalls of interpretation. . . . Detachment, humour, and a Voltairean irony (he greatly enjoyed Voltaire's *La Pucelle*) play a great part in his book, as well as changes in tone like those found in Laforgue, and without their manic vulgarity. And there can be felt through such changes the mixture of admiration and compassion at the sight of the infinite variety of human desires which is also found in a Brantôme, a Restif, or a Sade. But a phrase of modern psychology, although inelegant, can probably best account for the work; it describes the child as a 'polymorphous pervert', and indeed the impression one derives from **Venus and Tannhäuser** is that love is a marvellous game, full of infinite possibilities, and suited to adults as well as to children. (p. 261)

[**Venus and Tannhäuser** is] a tale told by a voice, suave, singing, and with analogies even to the line in Beardsley's drawings. To declare, as does Symons, that 'every sentence' is 'meditated over, written for its own sake, and left to find its way in its own paragraph' atomized, amounts merely to parading one's own lack of ear. Like the drawings, the novel is full of hidden ironies and curious *double-entendres,* and like them derives most of its charms from a double contrast: that between the stylization and a selective and sensitive realism which reaches the essence of the thing depicted, and that between the abundance of the details and the precision of the pattern, as in those cadenzas by which the virtuoso demonstrates not only his ingenuity but also his control. (pp. 261-62)

The technique of **Venus and Tannhäuser** has a triple function. It helps to charm, to divert the reader; but, on the other hand, it helps also, like Nessus' shirt, to torment him at leisure. More profoundly, it allows the author to unify what must seem the ill-assorted elements of the work; to marry, in Baudelarian terms, the 'spleen' to the 'ideal'. And this ideal is a world of fantasy and evasion, with the specific 'decadent' nostalgia for the morning and virginal things. It is yet another version of pastoral: dream of innocence, of the Golden Age; lost paradise, vast enough, though, to contain all aberrations; but, strangely, giving an impression of artless simplicity, which is expressed, so Beardsley says, by 'a perfect fifth'. That it should exert such a powerful influence is surely an indication that the attempted synthesis was unsuccessful. . . . It is only by keeping reality at arms length that Beardsley can surrender to lyricism. . . . [Adolphe] is the only character in the novel whose behaviour expresses feelings and not the physiological whim of the minute; but his animal form forbids him any direct contact with his divine mistress, by whom he daily fears to be abandoned. It is in Adolphe, rather than in the paltry Tannhäuser, that we find the symbol of the artist. The significance of this episode is confirmed by the allusion to St Rose of Lima's legend in **Under the Hill,** she, who had taken a vow of chastity and to whom on her wedding day the Virgin (significantly coming out of a painting, art in this manner rescuing the dreamer when reality becomes too pressing) came to assume her into heaven. According to his own testimony, Beardsley found some particular charm in the drawing (quite one of his best) which he made to illustrate this episode. He seems to have been fascinated by the pattern of seclusion from the world for the sake of a divine partner (the pattern already of the Tannhäuser legend). . . . (pp. 262-63)

This flight before life is actually conspicuous in the tale in a sense more profound than that expressed by the ostensible flight 'under the hill' (granting all the Freudian implications of that) and reveals itself by a continual game of hide-and-seek, a movement to and fro between life on the one hand, and on the other art, artifice, books, civilizations. Just this laid Beardsley open to the charge of decadence. . . . In the Venusberg . . . , smart people have their adornments painted on their skins and play with fans made of live moths. One finds there a sort of Balzacian 'concurrence à l'état-civil' to the second power, in the matter of names, showing that the experience of life is constantly born from the experience of books: the plants there are 'unknown to Mentzelius', Venus is 'not at all like the lady in Lemprière'. One is at first surprised to hear that Beardsley did not like [Huysmans's novel] A Rebours. This is doubtless because of the coldness emanating from Huysmans' learned lists, for his book has something deliberate about it, while Beardsley's is the catalogue of all he so passionately relished.

There is in the tale yet another episode whose meaning is not at first very discernible but which becomes clear in view of our previous arguments. It has the beauty and the typical features of Rimbaud's *Illuminations,* and its mysterious character shows the profoundly phantasmagoric origin of much of *Venus and Tannhäuser.* It is reprinted in *Under the Hill* with the title *The Woods of Auffray* . . . and tells about 'a still argent lake— a reticent, romantic water that must have held the subtlest fish that ever were' and of 'its unruffled calm, its deathly reserve', and ends with this astonishing sentence: 'Perhaps the lake was only painted, after all. He had seen things like it at the theatre.' What was elsewhere the pleasant charm of reverie becomes here the narcotic attraction of nirvâna. The fascinating and ever changing waters of the pond which so attract and frighten Tannhäuser at the same time, while undoubtedly having a sexual significance, symbolize an exile still more radical than Tannhäuser's flight to the Venusberg, and betray a taste for nothingness. (pp. 263-64)

[The] decadent aspect of Beardsley's work had not been chosen from any superficial perversity: it corresponded to very deep exigencies. Applied to the Tannhäuser theme, it strikes a singularly deep note and makes us see, in this apparently disjointed work, the proof of a prolonged reflection on man, the plaything of pleasure, 'divertissement' and death. (p. 264)

Annette Lavers, "'Aubrey Beardsley, Man of Letters'," in Romantic Mythologies, *edited by Ian Fletcher (© Routledge & Kegan Paul Ltd 1967; by permission of Barnes & Noble Books, a Division of Littlefield, Adams & Co., Inc.), Barnes & Noble, 1967, pp. 243-70.*

PETER MICHELSON   (essay date 1968)

[Aubrey Beardsley's] artistic elegance—both graphically and literarily—satisfies our desperation for the beautiful, while his blatant pornography adds another raspberry to the popular assault on moral transcendentalism. The dilemma is that poeti-

cally we want the beautiful without its constant companion, the ideal good. But the tradition of our aesthetics makes them inseparable. The "decadent" art with which Beardsley was much involved made the first direct hit against the monolith of aesthetic idealism. Beardsley, in keeping with the central principle of decadence, demonstrated that artistic beauty was not obliged to traditional morality in any way for its being. His two most extreme statements of this are of course the *Lysistrata* illustrations and his unfinished pornographic novel, *The Story of Venus and Tannhauser.* Beardsley was one of the first to present pornographic satire in a lyrical guise and make both satire and lyricism convincing. His story of Venus and Tannhauser is at once a rebuttal of the transcendental melodrama of Wagner's libretto, on the one hand, and a parody of pornographic "romance," on the other. Simultaneously it is also a lyrical tour de force celebrating its own purely artistic beauty. Whereas Wagner's libretto is patterned on the morality play—Tannhauser's despair, *for example,* is at last resolved in Christian faith and spiritual beauty—Beardsley's treatment denies the artistic potency of moral conflict by simply dismissing it, and thereby he exorcises morality and celebrates style. . . . The decadent Tannhauser, unlike Wagner's moralistic counterpart, relishes losing himself in the Hill of Venus, and is neatly poised in the face of his ambiguous perdition: "Goodbye, Madonna," he says casually, and then sighs to heaven for "the assurance of a looking glass before I make my debut!" . . . Beardsley proves the decadent thesis by creating a pornographic narrative at once denying the necessary connection between either pornography and vulgarity, or immorality and ugliness. Characteristically he casts hard-core pornographic images into elegance and wit. . . . The appeal of Beardsley's brilliant rhetoric to the literati in an age of fading aristocracy was ironically similar to his appeal for ourselves. To his time Beardsley represented the triumph of an aristocratic, classically oriented aesthetic taste over a modern puritanic, know-nothing moralism. To a contemporary (democratic, middle-class) mind he recalls a traditional aesthetic— line, symmetry, and representation highly stylized—without its vestigial moralism. Thus Beardsley is the kind of avantgarde gift the man who has everything can understand and feel comfortable with. His popularity is a pop culture analogue of the now famous "forward-looking return to the past." In short, *The Story of Venus and Tannhauser* is a tour de force carrying formal poetic tradition to extremity and at the same time ridiculing the moral idealism so long concomitant with that poetic tradition.

Of the four major treatments of the Venus and Tannhauser legend that I know in the nineteenth century, only Beardsley's has artistic potential for us today because his was the only treatment that was in touch with poetic evolution in a really vital way. Not simply because his is pornographic (although a good pornographer is no mean thing), but because he used pornography to make a statement about the nature of art. (pp. 61-4)

Beardsley's pornographic novel is important because it shows how completely the decadents were persuaded that, as Oscar Wilde put it in "The Decay of Lying," "Things are because we see them, and what we see, and how we see it, depends on the Arts that have influenced us." The decadents could produce Beardsley's effete *tour de force* because it affirmed for them what Zola denied, that art brings reality to man rather than bringing man to reality. But in fact they could not really accept it—it is not altogether accidental I think that Beardsley never finished [his novel]—because it was the nihilistically logical conclusion of their poetics. For in saying that nothing mattered but artistic beauty they had sooner or later to confront the implication that beauty did not matter either. . . . Beardsley's pornography carried the grand decadence as far as it could go in creating a cosmos where morality was non-existent, sentiment was merely an ironic rhetorical device, and classical artifice was the nature of being. It is more than a little historically prophetic when Yeats laments that that place where "Fish, flesh, or fowl, commend all summer long whatever is begotten, born, and dies" is no country for old men or monuments of unaging intellect. In recent years art and literature have been much more concerned with those dying generations, their long, hot summer, than with the artifice of eternity. (pp. 65-7)

Peter Michelson, "Beardsley, Burroughs, Decadence, and the Poetics of Obscenity" (© 1968 by TriQuarterly, Northwestern University; reprinted by permission of the publisher and the author), in TriQuarterly, No. 12, Spring, 1968 (and reprinted as "Decadence and the Poetics of Obscenity," in his The Aesthetics of Pornography, Herder and Herder, 1971, pp. 61-87).

BRIGID BROPHY (essay date 1968)

[*In Brophy's book-length study,* Black and White: A Portrait of Aubrey Beardsley, *from which the following excerpt is drawn, the critic examines the various characteristics that distinguish Beardsley's art. Primarily, Brophy considers Beardsley a lyrical artist; she states that this lyricism, juxtaposed with the knowledge that his life would be brief, lent an element of tension to Beardsley's drawings and writings. Like Holbrook Jackson (1913), Brophy finds that Beardsley's style is Mannerist, characterized by sensual imagery and elongated, graceful figures. However, Brophy disputes Jackson's labeling of Beardsley as a "literary" artist and maintains, rather, that there are no literary characteristics to be found in his work. To Brophy, "the tension that dominates all his compositions is entirely in the design and in the medium." Though Brophy concedes that style and image are literary elements, she adds that both are common to every form of the arts. She rejects other exterior influences on Beardsley, and states that his art was ultimately controlled by his own imagination.*]

Live (love) now: die sooner or later.

That, classically, is the purport of lyrical art. Aubrey Beardsley was above all a lyrical artist—but one who was pounded and buckled into an ironist by the pressure of knowing, which he did virtually from the outset, that for him death would be not later but sooner. (p. 11)

Beardsley is lyrical by virtue of his gift of line, which resembles the gift of melodic invention. Sheerly, Beardsley's lines, like great tunes, go up and down in beautiful places. It is true that they often, by the same stroke, represent objects: but never for purposes of reportage or narrative. Not a dot is put in for description's sake. Beardsley inserts nothing on the grounds that it was or would be there. He attends only to what, by compulsion of the design, should be there.

Illustrator though he was by choice, and sometimes of his own literary fictions, and though he was also (which not all writers are) a devouring reader, Beardsley the draughtsman isn't in the least 'literary'. The tension that dominates all his compositions is entirely in the design and the medium. None of it is borrowed from the incidents, and still less the characters, of any story he may adopt. This makes it less strange than it superficially looks, in a personality so passionately literate,

that Beardsley *didn't*, after the Hamlet picture of his teens, much draw on or from Shakespeare. (pp. 11-12)

What Beardsley plunders from literature are matters common to all the arts: pure style, pure image. Pope figures to him as the epitome of the rococo, Ben Jonson of the baroque. (In this sense, Shakespeare *has* no style.) Out of the given style Beardsley sets his virtuoso line to pluck a pure, self-sufficient image. His sequences of drawings establish series of related images or conduct a single image through metamorphic variations. A Beardsley sequence is like a sonnet sequence. Yet it is never the literary content of an image that concerns him. His portraits, including those of himself, are less portraits than icons. He is drawing not persons but personages; he is dramatizing not the relationships between personalities but the pure, geometric essence of relationship. He is out to capture sheer tension: tension contained within, and summed up by, his always ambivalent images.

Sometimes the image is presented, in its complete irony and ambiguity, through a single piercing contrast—a solo black outline that severs a white area into two spaces. The second . . . of the two drawings Beardsley made, for his Juvenal illustrations, of Bathyllus . . . lies as firm, fine and inscrutable in its white oblong as a Greek vase-painting on its ground. Indeed, Beardsley has borrowed from the vase-painters' technique—and from their subjects' physique: in both cases, to satiric purpose. The implicit homosexuality of Greek boxers and athletes Beardsley has expanded into the explicit gesture of an invitation to buggery; and the over-muscled heroic Greek body he has bloated out into Roman blowsiness. The flabby femaleness of Bathyllus's flesh Beardsley decorates by comically flinging over his shoulder something remarkably like a Wagnerian maiden's plait—which is yet also a displaced horse's tail: the very blatancy with which Bathyllus prances with monumentally spread buttocks turns on the ironic joke that his pose is one which, in equestrian monuments, is conventionally noble. The metamorphic suggestion that Bathyllus is animal from the waist down renders him on the instant a monster. That he is a monster simultaneously attractive and repulsive (people who are blatantly sexually available are available to *us* but not *exclusively* to us, so that they provoke jealousy simultaneously with desire) is incarnated, by the most economic of means, in the brilliant *contrapposto* [representation of the human body in a curving axis, producing an appearance of asymmetry and imbalance], between his lewd, inviting left hand and his crude, sign-posting right (which indicates so plainly what the horse's tail has been displaced in favour of); and this contraposition is in turn made meaningful by the simple, masterly intellectual *rightness* of the figure's placing in its space, whose organic importance to the composition Beardsley has emphasized by framing it in a double line.

The economy of the Bathyllus drawing is the opposite of impoverished: the rich imaginative material is all condensed into the single outline. By the converse process, Beardsley could tease material out from the image and spin it into a decorative setting which, because its metaphors repeat those of the image itself, intensifies the image it enshrines. Beardsley's conversion to Catholicism, which his recent commentators rightly do not take very seriously as a religious act, was a logical continuation of his work. The contemplation—the cult—of an image is the essence of Beardsley's art. (pp. 12, 14, 16)

[He] was destined pre-eminently to the Catholic cult of the Madonna. In Beardsley's life, his mother is as regularly there, and his father as regularly absent or unnoticeable, as the Madonna and Saint Joseph in Christian iconography. His elder sister, Mabel . . . , figured to Beardsley as the mother writ one size smaller. . . . As a child, he probably felt an unusual material dependence on his mother, since, unusually for the period, she, as well as the father, worked. And as a dying man Beardsley returned to the child's state of bodily dependence on his mother. In Beardsley's novel [*Under the Hill*], after Venus and Tannhäuser have made love, Venus is literally carried—'in a nice, motherly way'—to bed in the arms of her 'manicure', Mrs Marsuple, who ends the chapter with a speech that must have often been made to the young Mabel and Aubrey Beardsley (who were perhaps in some sense lovers, too): 'Come along, children . . . it's time you were both in bed.' . . . In 'The Ascension of Saint Rose of Lima' . . . , the child, though grown-up, is still enfolded within the outline of the protector's mantle, and is, as in the Barber drawing, female. So, it should be supererogatory to say, is the Madonna. It is by a singular infelicity, of the kind ironic artists seem fated to in their interpreters, that a recent study of Beardsley's eroticism mistakes the erotic point of the drawing by supposing the saint to be ascending 'in the embrace of the heavenly bridegroom'. Not she. As a matter of fact, the Madonna is saving her from an earthly bridegroom. The very pretty . . . [and camp] passage in Beardsley's novel *Under The Hill* which this drawing illustrates recounts how, on the morning of her wedding day, Saint Rose 'perfumed herself and painted her lips, and put on her wedding frock, and decked her hair with roses' and then, from a hill outside Lima, spent 'some moments calling tenderly upon Our Lady's name'. (pp. 20, 22, 24)

Even when she is not present and personified, the mother dictates Beardsley's very point of view. Beardsley was a latter-day Mannerist. The common complaint of his contemporaries against his figures, especially his women, was the complaint made at all periods against all mannered figures, that they are too tall and have necks like giraffes. His lovely, gentle and unsentimental drawing . . . of Mrs Patrick Campbell was said to make her 'nine feet high'. Mannerism: mama-ism. The elegance of these elongated persons, who are so au fait in the world, is a memory of adults, and quintessentially the mother, seen in child's-eye-view; the slight melancholy they so exquisitely wear is draped on them by the child's sense of their high inaccessibility.

Mannerism is in itself a style that murmurs of perversity, its elongations a visual drawl that mimics sexual languor. It shews a child's-eye-view, but the child is precocious. . . . It is the characteristic of precocious children that, in childhood, they are astonishing because they resemble adults. In adulthood, they are often—like Mozart and Beardsley—astonishing because they resemble children. The genius of Beardsley's eroticism is precisely the quality Freud ascribed to the sexuality of children: polymorphous perversity.

It is only the most obvious manifestation of this quality that Beardsley's subject-matter, by his own choice, encompasses virtually the whole sexual spectrum, from delicate bestiality (Venus, in his novel, masturbates her pet unicorn, Adolphe, every morning before breakfast) to flagellation. . . . (pp. 26, 28, 32)

[In imagination he] was incestuous: he was, in imagination, everything; and for him the imagination was everything. Although it was Tannhäuser he plundered from Wagner for his novel, it was very likely the brother-sister incest theme in *The Ring* that caused Beardsley to make a personal cult of (instead of just admiring, as he did Beethoven) Wagner. He recognized,

moreover, the eroticism, the fetishism, in the general cult of Wagner by Wagnerites. His most successful transposition of Wagner's eroticism does not depict the Wagnerian personages at all, but simply the sensuality with which the audience listens to *Tristan und Isolde* [in his drawing 'The Wagnerites']. (p. 32)

Beardsley's perversity goes well beyond his signing his work with an emblem said to be (in, presumably, the anthropological sense) a fetish symbolizing sexual intercourse; and his polymorphism goes worlds beyond his alertness to the fetishist value (in the psychosexual sense) of hair . . . , of tiny pointed shoes . . . , and of hats. . . . Rather, his imagination seems to be in at the actual infantile origin of fetishism. His vision is permanently that of a child lying in bed watching his mother dress for a dinner-party. His fantasy hangs this here, tries the effect of that there: everything is a jewel, and everything is a sexual organ. (pp. 32, 36)

Beardsley's imagination is for ever lying in bed dressing and re-dressing his mother—and doing it inappropriately. The child's protest against his inexperience, against the ban on touching, is to glory in his ignorance. He does not know which sexual organs are appropriate to which sex; he makes deliberate howlers in order to howl against his exclusion from adult knowledge. And even that bitter intellectual howl is a mask for a yet earlier cry of pure terror, the boy child's terror at the discovery that his mother does not possess the organ he so values as a pendant and ornament on his own body. (p. 36)

It is his own polymorphism that animates the metamorphism of Beardsley's images. His decorative forms are ambiguous in matter, caught in the act of changing from one substance into another; his human figures are ambiguous in sex. (p. 38)

Alternatively, Beardsley translates the male/female mixture into a human/animal mixture. He does this to grotesque effect (the grotesquerie being borrowed from the dressed-up animals of circuses and organ-grinders) in his frontispiece to Juvenal, where a sedan-chair is carried by monkeys in livery. . . . Elsewhere Beardsley adopts a ready-made motif, like his favourite one of the satyr, and presses an ironic poetry from the fact that the male/female mixture created by infantile muddle and infantile fantasy has already been transformed by mythology into the nostalgic figure of a human/animal mixture belonging to a golden, partly heroic, partly alarming and wholly irrecoverable past.

Beardsley translates mythology back into the language of the unconscious, wherein the golden age equals childhood, by the very piquancy with which he disposes his satyr . . . in the rôle of precocious child. . . .

And, even so, a further metamorphosis is possible, for Beardsley, in the already human/animal mixture. The animal portion may be further transformed—into a thing. (p. 42)

The elasticity which Beardsley needed in order to exploit his temperamental eclecticism he acquired, I suspect, thanks to what looks like a childish method of work. The fastidiousness of his final drawings evidently represents a naive perfectionism. . . .

Beardsley's novel underwent so many important changes, its title being at various times *Venus and Tannhäuser* and *Under The Hill* and its hero varying from Tannhäuser to the Abbé Aubrey to the Abbé Fanfreluche, that it looks as though Beardsley applied the same method to literature—and was, perhaps, to judge from his inability to finish his book, surprised that it was there less practical. (p. 50)

PAT BARNETT (essay date 1971)

The most prominent and important of Beardsley's symbols is
the candle. This object has a useful double meaning, suggesting
simultaneously the dim religious world of church and worship,
and also the dim Decadent world of secret affairs and artificial
lights. Both aspects evoke the mysterious, the romantic and
the sensual—and obviously therefore appealed strongly to
Beardsley's nature. Candles became important to him, not only
as a delightfully ambiguous symbol in his work, but as part of
the Decadent pose of his whole life. (p. 33)

In his literary masterpiece [*The Story of Venus and Tannhäuser*], as well as in his drawings, candles are vitally important to Beardsley, and symbolize perfectly the delicious Decadence of his prose. It is 'taper-time' at the beginning of **"Venus
and Tannhäuser,"** an artificial word describing the coming of
darkness to Nature in the terms of man's invention of light.
For the great supper-scene of Chapter III, the terrace is 'lit
entirely by candles', described with a visual detail and exquisite
care through which the drawn line is echoed by the precision
of the written word:

> There were four thousand of them, not num-
> bering those upon the tables. The candlesticks
> were of a countless variety, and smiled with
> moulded cochonneries. Some were twenty feet
> high, and bore single candles that flared like
> flagrant torches over the feast, and guttered till
> the wax stood round the top in tall lances. Some,
> hung with dainty petticoats of shining lustres,
> had a whole bevy of tapers upon them, devised
> in circles, in pyramids, in squares, in cunei-
> forms, in single lines regimentally and in cres-
> cents.

Beardsley obviously gets some satirical fun out of the dangers
of symbolism here, and points out at the same time the phallic
suggestiveness of his favorite candle-symbol: one of the 'games'
at the supper is for everyone to find 'a delightful meaning in
the fall of festoon, turn of twig, and twist of branch. . . .
Sporion, too, had delicate perceptions, and was vastly entertained by the disposition of the candelabra.' Everything here
seems artificially and seductively lit by the 'warm haze of
candle light', and saturated by a 'faint amatory perfume', both
adding to the sensual and depraved atmosphere of the story.

It is fascinating to note that Beardsley's famous Japanese signature can itself be taken as a symbolic representation of candles, of the triple candelabrum of which he was so fond. (pp.
38-9)

It is easy to carry a study of symbolism too far in the work of
any poet or artist; with Beardsley, particularly, it is hard to
know when to stop. So many objects—the foetus, insects, great
flat flowers, feet, women's breasts and men's sexual parts, to
name a few—were unusually important to him, and thus naturally appear frequently in his work. I believe, though, that
the candle symbol is one of extra-ordinary importance for its
suggestiveness, its usefulness in elegance and design, and its
dual symbolism, and one which throws greater light upon some
of the subtleties of his work. It is also a highly appropriate

figure to symbolize some of the warring contrasts and paradoxes in the strange life of Aubrey Beardsley himself. (p. 42)

*Pat Barnett, "Some Aspects of Symbolism in the
Work of Aubrey Beardsley" (copyright 1971 by Pat
Barnett; used by permission of the publishers), in*
The Antigonish Review, *Vol. 1, No. 4, Winter,
1971, pp. 33-45.*

GEOFFREY HARPHAM (essay date 1975)

[*Harpham maintains that* The Story of Venus and Tannhäuser
*was intended as the tale of an "aesthete who pursues life as an
art." In the same way that Beardsley abandoned his Decadent
philosophies to join the Catholic church, Harpham believes Tannhäuser prepared to "repent of his aestheticism." Had Beardsley
completed the story, Harpham suggests he would have depicted
a conversion in Tannhäuser similar to Beardsley's own.*]

The legend of Venus and Tannhäuser was one of the guiding
myths of the aesthetic movement. After serving Wagner, Swinburne and Morris, the tradition expires with Beardsley's parody, *The Story of Venus and Tannhäuser*. The struggle, which
had dominated so much late Victorian literature, between Venus and Christ for the hero's soul comes to no conclusion, and
the hoped-for reconciliation is never realized. In fact, the central critical question concerning Beardsley's story would seem
to be its incompleteness. (p. 24)

The primary reason for the incompleteness of the story seems
to me to be not that Beardsley abandoned it arbitrarily, but
that it was moving simultaneously in two directions, seeking
an impossible resolution; as Beardsley progressed with his story—
which occupied him more than half his creative life—he progressed in his journey into the bosom of the Church. It is
impossible to tell what Arthur Symons meant when he said
that the story "could never have been finished for it had never
been really begun," but one possible sense is that Beardsley
had not solved the problems posed by the legend before he
started. For in this spiritual self-portrait (in another version of
the story, Tannhäuser was called the "Abbé Aubrey"), Beardsley is both sinner and penitent.

On one level, Tannhäuser's "sin" is merely conventional indulgence in sensualism. Beardsley's Jansenist inclinations led
him, near the end of his life, to condemn this weakness in
particular; he ordered, for example, the destruction of the *Lysistrata* drawings he considered obscene. And the structure of
the Tannhäuser legend lent itself perfectly to an indictment of
gross fleshliness.

But if this was Tannhäuser's only offense against virtue, the
story would scarcely deserve our attention. Two factors complicate the issue of Tannhäuser's corruption. First, the kind of
sexuality portrayed on the Venusberg has a quality of childish
innocence, of, as Dr. Lavers points out, "polymorphous perversion" [see excerpt above, 1967], with a characteristically
decadent yearning for the dawn and virginal things. The world
of the Venusberg is not the world of de Sade; its inhabitants
seem scarcely even conscious that the pleasures of the flesh
are sinful. And Beardsley is at pains to stress this quality of
reversion in Tannhäuser's retreat from the world. . . . The
second complicating factor is that a much more dominating
and consuming sin is aestheticism—precisely the offense of
which Beardsley came to feel most guilty. After beginning
instruction in the Roman Catholic faith, Beardsley had written
his spiritual mentor, André Raffalovich, that the true Christian
man of letters "must sacrifice his gifts, just as Magdalen must
sacrifice her beauty." And in this aesthete's parody, artistic

gifts and the artistic perspective serve as the sin of which
Tannhäuser must repent. This aestheticism is expressed, for
example, in the sense of ritual which absolutely dominates the
early part of the story. In this extravaganza, this pagan carnival,
Beardsley is always in total control. On the Venusberg, as well
as in Beardsley's unerring sense of stylistic nuance, of calculated disorder, the laws of harmony and ritual prevail. Tannhäuser himself is nothing if not an aesthete. Even his dress and
the timing of his entry into the Venusberg are dominated by a
strong sense of symbolism. . . . And he adjusts to a world in
which sex might be the primary form of expression or communication, but in which aesthetics is the ruling passion.
Beardsley's description of Tannhäuser's first meal on the
Venusberg could apply equally to the Venusberg's approach
to sex: "Mere hunger quickly gave way to those finer instincts
of the pure gourmet." The main characters seem more inclined
to the appreciation of beauty through sex than vice versa. . . .
Beardsley as narrator complements this aestheticism. One of
the dominant metaphors for intercourse and the whole sexual
process is music. Tannhäuser tunes Venus' body "as a violinist
tunes his instrument before he plays upon it," and when Adolphe
the unicorn squeals in pleasure as Venus plays upon his "tight-
strung instrument," it is an "astonishing vocal accompaniment." Furthermore, the style is characterized by such mod-
ifiers as "subtle," "fascinating," "extraordinary," "astonishing," and "perfect"—is itself ritualistic, reinforcing the
absolute isolation of the Venusberg from the mundane world.
(pp. 24-6)

It seems that Beardsley intended us to interpret his story not
only as the story of a guilty sensualist, but also as a tale of an
aesthete who pursues life as an art. To this end he created a
world entirely of artifice, so that Tannhäuser could repent of
his aestheticism as well as of his licentiousness, completing,
in effect, an allegory of the '90s. The very incompleteness of
the story contributes to this sense of it as an allegory for the
doomed solipsistic aestheticism of the generation, itself cut
short by the Wilde trial and the early, tragic deaths of many
of its most talented artists—including Beardsley himself. . . .

[While] the plot was leading Tannhäuser-Beardsley in the direction of papism and penitence, the poetry of the style was
manifesting a kind of aesthetic hedonism much closer in spirit
to the pagan Venusberg. Who speaks of Tannhäuser's damnation? The plot, but not the poetry. Beardsley was in trouble
from the outset. While it is not entirely unknown for authors
to create narrators who change and grow along with their protagonists, in this case the style was too much a part of the story
itself—and was too *extreme* a style—to be significantly altered
without destroying the story. On the other hand, to continue
the story in this mode would have been to make a mockery of
Tannhäuser's spiritual growth. Most important, Beardsley obviously took far too much passionate delight in his style to
trade it in for a sackcloth-and-ashes prose. (p. 27)

Perhaps the limitations of [Beardsley's] "decadent consciousness" can provide an explanation for the subtle changes which
begin to appear in the sixth chapter. Here, the story, disre-
garding the impasse of sinner *vs.* penitent, begins to move in
a third direction, circumventing that decision altogether. Near
the end of this chapter Venus and Tannhäuser, greatly taken
with each other after meeting at the banquet, have their first
"amorous encounter"; afterwards, they are tired. Beardsley
explains this atypical fatigue by pointing out that, while "It
is, I know, the custom of all romancers to paint heroes who
can give a lady proof of their dalliance at least twenty times

a night," yet "Tannhäuser had no such gargantuan facility. . . ." Priapusa then enters the bedroom.

> "How tired the dear baby looks," said Pria-
> pusa. "Shall I put him in his little cot?"
>
> "Well, if he's as sleepy as I am," yawned
> Venus, "you can't do better."
>
> Priapusa lifted her mistress off the pillows, and
> carried her in her arms in a nice, motherly way.
>
> "Come along, children," said the fat old thing,
> "come along; it's time you were both in bed."

In comparison to what had preceded it, this is a remarkable
passage. Not only is it the first hint of sexual limitation of
satiety, it is the first actual dialogue, the first verbal exchange
between characters. Prior to this, the only dialogue was in the
form of ejaculations, such as "Ah, I'm famished," or "All
the rorty little things."

In Chapter 9 especially, life reasserts itself against the icy
artificiality of the earlier chapters. Venus expresses real jealousy when Tannhäuser looks at other women or men from the
carriage window. "Is it all mine?" she asks, slipping the "fingers of comfort under the lace flounces of his trousers." The
narrative voice adapts itself slightly to accomodate the changed
situation, and we find such commonplaces as, "The Chevalier
was very happy," and, "Venus looked so beautiful," which
indicate a retreat into less "subtle" or "astonishing" attitudes
and situations. . . . [Tannhäuser sees] "a reticent, romantic
water." At this sight, he "fell into a strange mood. . . . It
seemed to him that the thing would speak, reveal some curious
secret, say some beautiful word. . . ." While the word seems
clearly to be Death, these waters have sexual significance as
well, indicating an attachment to Life, and the kind of reality
which would, if fully understood, shatter the world of the
Venusberg. . . . (pp. 28-9)

Chapter 9 begins, in contrast to the previously episodic progress
of the narrative, to establish a sense of mortality and progressive time. With this development comes a change of scene. In
Chapter 10, Venus and Tannhäuser arrive at the casino, and
later, they visit De La Pine's studio. Still on the Venusberg,
but out of the palace itself, these places seem midway between
the upper and the underworld. Here, mundane events such as
a civilized "little dinner" for four people can occur.

The plot was heading towards a limited realism—and, it seems,
away from Beardsley's original intention regarding Tannhäuser's repentence. He had planned to show the Chevalier leading
a life of sin and dissipation before going to Rome to seek
forgiveness. When Tannhäuser looks out the carriage window
at the lake, he is turning toward Rome. And life, which had
seemed, according to Pater's recipe, an endless parade of sparkling moments, undergoes a sea-change. Beneath the pale translucent surface of the water lies hidden a revelation of the end
of time.

The moral view of life, for which Beardsley was preparing
Tannhäuser, depends upon an integrated time sense, with penitence for past sins and fear of future retribution. After the
lake, Tannhäuser is almost ready. But by the time Tannhäuser
can understand the concept of penitence, he is no longer a
sinner. Having committed themselves to each other, Tannhäuser and Venus are respectably monogamous. Taking trips together, paying calls together, dining with close friends—they
share the same little pleasures and tensions of any newly mar-

ried couple; and the glittering, hollow shell Beardsley had constructed shows signs of cracking up. In the final chapter, they are non-participants in the rape of the alto, nor are they sought out by the others, as they were in Chapter 6. At this point, Tannhäuser is something of a fool—far from being either a first-rate sinner or a first-rate penitent—but a sincere fellow with potential for development.

The Story of Venus and Tannhäuser stands as a testament to Beardsley's integrity both as artist and Roman Catholic. Refusing to compromise art or dogma—and fully understanding the implications of both—he "sacrificed his gifts," leaving his literary *opus magnus* unfinished. But perhaps in its incompleteness lies its greatest value. Too skimpy to be truly impressive or ennobling from a purely literary standpoint, it yet commands respect as a document of transition, a kind of war diary of an intense inner struggle. (pp. 29-30)

> Geoffrey Harpham, *"The Incompleteness of Beardsley's 'Venus and Tannhäuser',"* in English Literature in Transition *(copyright © 1975 Helga S. Gerber), Vol. 18, No. 1, 1975, pp. 24-32.*

LINDA C. DOWLING   (essay date 1978)

[*Dowling analyzes the elements of parody and self-satire in* The Story of Venus and Tannhäuser.]

Beardsley, like Beerbohm and Wilde, found in satire and self-parody a way of evading the ideological claims of conventional late-Victorian aesthetic culture. Moreover they perceived that self-parody offered an amusing if unstable mode of self-transcendence, as when Wilde, for instance, conflates and lampoons the plots of his early social comedies in order to overthrow in *The Importance of Being Earnest* his own earlier notions of language and self. On the other hand, avant-garde artists and writers knew that satire and self-parody need not accomplish anything at all: self-delighting amusements, they need have no object beyond mere play. It is precisely this sort of divided perception of satire and self-parody, or wavering allegiance to them, that we discover in Beardsley's *Venus and Tannhäuser.*

Beardsley launches his satire by reducing the heroic legend that Wagner had made splendid to the level of pornographic travesty. Yet at the same time, Beardsley qualifies his own satire by mocking the conventions of pornographic romance: his Tannhäuser effetely lacks the prodigious appetites, the "Gargantuan facility" of the usual erotic hero, and indeed is rather relieved when later on in an evening of debauch Venus is taken off his hands by more indefatigable revelers. This satiric diminution of the spiritual and physical dimensions required by the two literary genres Beardsley burlesques is paralleled by a mock-heroic treatment of narrative structure and by language that deflates by trivializing. And this in its turn has its analogue in Beardsley's caricatures of contemporary types, thumbnail portraits that belittle his real-life acquaintance even as they insist upon the importance of such figures to his fiction. Beardsley's characteristically uncommitted play with the artistic possibilities offered by satire and self-parody is, indeed, nowhere more fully expressed than in these caricatures. Like such figures as G. S. Street's Tubby or Beerbohm's Enoch Soames, they exist in a teasingly indeterminate range between public and private identification, most convincing when most ambiguous.

Yet on another level the coy irresolution of Beardsley's prose caricatures itself, satirizes the personal dilemmas of the fin de siècle avant-garde, just as his continually qualified and re-qualified notions of art and life in *Venus and Tannhäuser* suggest the self-conscious hesitations and refinements of its aesthetic—the very aesthetic, of couse, that had offered itself as a boldly innovative alternative to established Victorian culture. Full of conflicting ambitions and evasions, fin de siècle Decadence seemed to Beardsley to expose itself perversely—because invitingly—to the forces that would compromise and truly corrupt it. This is why, for example, Beardsley creates a type of Oscar Wilde in Spiridion, "that soft incomparable alto," and makes him sing for the entertainment of the company the Virgin's part in Rossini's *Stabat Mater:*

> A miraculous virgin, too, he made of her. To begin with he dressed the role most effectively. His plump legs up to the feminine hips of him, were in very white stockings clocked with a false pink. He wore brown kid boots, buttoned to midcalf, and his whorish thighs had thin scarlet garters round them. His jacket was cut like a jockey's, only the sleeves ended in manifold frills, and round the neck, and just upon the shoulders, there was a black cape. His hair, dyed green, was curled into ringlets, such as the smooth Madonnas of Morales are made lovely with, and fell over his high eggshaped forehead, and about his ears and cheeks and back.

(pp. 28-30)

[The singer's situation offers] amusing possibilities for satire: the effeminate Spiridion's impersonation of an innocent Virgin grieving over the loss of her Son wickedly parallels [Oscar Wilde's loss after his trial and conviction for committing homosexual acts]—even more so since Wilde's artful charade of sexual innocence at his trial contrasted, as Beardsley well knew, so completely with the unrestrained license of his actual conduct. The episode concludes, as episodes generally do in *Venus and Tannhäuser,* with the chaster seductions of art giving way to the heartier ravishments of the flesh: Spiridion is assaulted by the appreciative men of the audience who enthusiastically penetrate his disguise. (p. 30)

In Beardsley's imperturbably indulgent underworld, the prohibitions of ordinary life melt away, suppressed desires surface, and private fantasies become public occasions, for in the Venusberg what everyone does not do to everybody else he or she naturally talks of doing. And once the duplicity and dividedness of ordinary inhibited life have collapsed, everything appears in its true and singular aspect: what was disguised as the pure motives of art, for example, will be disclosed as simply the impulse of sex. It is an easy matter, of course, for Beardsley to turn the radical reductiveness of pornography to satirical purposes, to expose the sexual underworld which he knew to lie beneath the art and experience of his contemporaries to the innocent morning light of the Venusberg. The sublimations and evasions of sex by which art in the 1890s officially existed seemed to Beardsley like so many "unwilling disguises" which were put on by artists and connoisseurs for the sake of propriety but which sadly hampered their real purpose. To help them consummate this purpose Beardsley's satire strips away their involved veils, and artistic pursuits are revealed as what they are, sexual performances.

"So white and light and matinal," Beardsley's Venusberg is thus the underworld of art as well as love. Here, in the capital of joyfully lubricious excess, the cautious and self-conscious daring of literary Decadence is laughed away: for Beardsley sees that though Decadence pretends to live beyond good and evil, it is almost obsessively dependent upon the clear demarcation of moral categories. To be "Decadent" in word or deed meant to defy, to transgress, to trespass on forbidden and thus dangerous terrain. In the absence of any posted warning, however, no one, least of all the Decadent who defined himself through opposition, could know where he was. (pp. 35-6)

[Beardsley's] rattling chatter, the gushing confidences alternating with coy reticence, and his peculiarly campy patois . . . deflate the pretensions of Decadence. The narrator who apologizes profusely for being unable "to tell you what occurred round table 15, just at this moment" does not hesitate to confide in fullest detail Venus' morning performance with Adolphe, her pet unicorn. This sort of blithe authorial inconsistency is paralleled on the structural level by narrative discontinuity. The loose episodic pattern of romance is further exaggerated in *Venus and Tannhäuser* by the pornographic motive which loves to linger, never to conclude. Beardsley's digressions, however, tend to spend as much time on matters of food and dress as they do on sex. And this characteristic pattern is parallelled on the level of diction by a rococo rhetoric which delights in assembling the most heterogenous materials—shells, droppings, petals, eyebrows—and painting the assemblage over in pastels and gilt. The narrator tells us, for instance, that Tannhäuser's "torso"—a word with high cultural associations borrowed from art criticism and suggesting marmoreal nudes—is "scrumptious"—a word expressive of childish appetites or homosexual gush. (p. 36)

Beardsley's indiscriminate embrace in *Venus and Tannhäuser* of verse and prose usages, of vulgarity and preciosity, of housemaid and goddess, emphasizes the pleasurableness of language as language, just as it celebrates the promiscuity of selves such highly rhetorical language can create.

In the same way, the tone of exquisite fastidiousness Beardsley adopts throughout *Venus and Tannhäuser,* whether he is describing the "dear little coat of pigeon rose silk that hung loosely about his hips, and showed off the jut of his behind to perfection" or the crotted paper treasured up by Venus' faithful Felix, serves to efface distinctions even as it seems scrupulously to honor them. In doing so, Beardsley turns quite upside down the pretensions of Decadence to efface distinctions while actually observing them. (p. 37)

Like the others of his day who were engaged in reassessing through satire and self-parody contemporary aesthetic assumptions, Beardsley was not particularly interested in reform except as a rhetorical motive. For him as for them, the point of parody as self-criticism was the pose it allowed one to strike and the momentary perspective it granted; what mattered was self-delighting impersonation, not dutiful improvement. The avant-garde critique of aesthetic attitudes—of which *Venus and Tannhäuser* is a part—thus in the end embodied one of the chief tenets of the avant-garde aesthetic theory it satirized: the disinterestedness of criticism. (p. 38)

Linda C. Dowling, "'Venus and Tannhäuser': Beardsley's Satire of Decadence," in The Journal of Narrative Technique *(copyright © 1978 by* The Journal of Narrative Technique*), Vol. 8, No. 1, Winter, 1978, pp. 26-41.*

JOSEPH H. GARDNER (essay date 1979)

[*The Story of Venus and Tannhauser*] seems as elusive as it is impressive. One can, like one recent biographer [Stanley Wein-

traub (see Additional Bibliography)], identify it as a pornotopia, or, like another [Brigid Brophy (see excerpt above, 1968)], stress its necessity to Beardsley's fragile hold on life. Both are correct, but neither fully answers the question: what are we to make of this novel as a novel? My own sense is that while it may indeed frustrate traditional modes of literary analysis, it can be approached by way of definition. It *is* a pornotopia, but a mock-heroic pornotopia that attempts to cope with the problematic nature of human sexuality in a post-Romantic world.

Unlike her classical prototype, Beardsley's Venus did not spring from the foam of the sea. Rather she grows directly out of the nineteenth century's fascination with the Tannhauser legend, and her genealogy can be traced through such disparate works as Heine's *The Gods in Exile,* Wagner's opera [*Tannhauser*], Baudelaire's essay on that opera, Pater's *The Renaissance,* [and] Swinburne's "Laus Veneris." . . . I would emphasize Beardsley's achievement in fusing the two major, and seemingly antithetical, modes of treating the legend adopted by his nineteenth-century predecessors. On the one hand there is the delicately ironic and essentially comic approach growing out of Heine's essay with its accounts of the "painful embarrassments" suffered by "the gods of the older world at the time of the definite triumph of Christianity," embarrassments which "greatly resembled certain tragical situations of their earlier life." . . . On the other hand, there is the tradition represented by Wagner, Baudelaire, and Swinburne, which approaches the legend with what even a Matthew Arnold would accept as the highest of high seriousness. For them, the story, far from being funny, embodies an inherently tragic aspect of the human predicament. Beardsley's treatment is deliciously comic, but the comedy paradoxically serves only to underscore, by mitigating against, Beardsley's sense of the significance of his theme.

The paradox can be dramatically seen in the contrast between two of his graphic representations of Tannhauser himself. In "The Chevalier Tannhauser," published to illustrate the expurgated serialization of the novel in *The Savoy* . . . , the treatment is clearly comic. Tannhauser appears as the epitome of the fantastical, set against a dense background of vegetation, which writhes and contorts itself into a seemingly endless series of female *pudenda* while the impish faces of children's book insects mock the central figure. In "The Return of Tannhauser to the Venusberg" (second version), which was intended to be an illustration to the novel but was not published until after Beardsley's death, the mood is radically different. Here the inherent tragedy of the story takes force. . . . What is perhaps most striking in the two drawings is the way in which the latter serves not simply to complement but also to explicate the former. If "The Chevalier Tannhauser" is conceived in the spirit of comedy, one is nonetheless forced to recognize the epic proportions of the central figure and the heroic cast of his face. If he is the absurd epitome of dandydom, it is clearly that philosophical tradition of dandyism of which Baudelaire, D'Aurevilly, and Wilde are the great theoreticians. (pp. 3-4, 6)

The heroic defiance in the dandyism of the "Chevalier Tannhauser" design points to that deep element of faith on Beardsley's part which allows him to cast his story in the comic mode without ever losing sight of its tragic implications, his "decadent," if you will, faith in the transforming and redemptive power of the imagination and art, the ability of imaginative art to transmute the disturbing, the tragic, the terrible or loathsome into images of beauty and repose. (p. 7)

The same paradox lies behind Beardsley's decision to cast his retelling of the Tannhauser story into the form of a "pornotopia,'' a term coined by Steven Marcus to describe a kind of writing in which the entire universe is conceived in sexual terms. . . . To the abbreviated version . . . [of his novel, Beardsley] gave the title *Under the Hill,* an explicit indication that, in his own vision, the Venusberg of myth and the *mons veneris* of anatomy are one. One also recalls the description mentioned earlier of Tannhauser entering the Venusberg with all ''the admirable aplomb and unwrinkled suavity of Don John.'' It is a twofold metamorphosis: Tannhauser becomes Don Juan, and Don Juan becomes John Thomas.

By casting the novel as a pornotopia, Beardsley reveals that the originating impulses behind the story are those which give rise to sexual fantasy and are, in turn, associated with the psychological and physiological processes of masturbation. But for Beardsley, fantasy, even masturbatory fantasy, leads to the enchanted world of the imagination. The masturbatory impulse dissolves into an imaginary voyage to an artificial paradise as the fantasy is jewelled and enamelled, removed from the exigencies of time and space, transformed into art and made an object of decadently inverted beauty, beyond good and evil, freed from the guilt-ridden, the destructive, and the disturbing. The autoerotic impulse is both fulfilled and short-circuited; what began as one thing ends as another. For if *The Story of Venus and Tannhauser* is a pornotopia, it is not pornography . . . . [Pornography] [It] never entirely divorces itself from its function as masturbatory stimulus. Unlike art, it is a means to an end, not an end in itself, and as good a working definition of pornography as any is that it is literature designed to be read with one hand. But in *The Story of Venus and Tannhauser* the end toward which the fantasy moves is always the unfolding of its own inherent beauty. (pp. 7-8)

One of the most remarkable features of Beardsley's story is the way in which Venus and Tannhauser move through the world of the polymorphous perverse without ever losing their almost Blakean innocence. Images of evil and excess modulate into the benign and even the protective. There is, for example, Madame Priapusa, ''the fat manicure and fardeuse,'' who serves as Venus's mistress of revels. The initial description of her . . . is decidedly sinister. . . . But after presiding over an evening's activities that included acts of masturbation, fornication, transvestism, fellatio, cunnilingus, sodomy, and urolangia, Priapusa bundles off her charges with the soothing accents of maternal tenderness: '''Come along, children,' said the fat old thing, 'come along; it's time you were in bed.''' (pp. 9-10)

For Beardsley's post-Romantic generation, the ability of art to transform the disturbing and destructive into harmless beauty was crucial. The Venus of Romantic cosmology had, by and large, approximated the *alma Venus* [nourishing Venus] of Lucretius: *hominum divomque voluptas* [pleasing to both men and gods]. Human sexuality presented few theoretical problems since it could be seen as part and parcel of benevolent cosmic process. Thus Blake, for example, could celebrate ''Happy Copulation, bliss upon bliss!'' and Whitman could sing ''The Body Electric'' because, in his words, ''the kelson of creation is love.'' . . . But in the essentially Darwinian world of post-Romanticism, the kelson of creation is not love but random, and hence meaningless, suffering, pain, and death. Accordingly, the *alma Venus* of the Romantics had, in Swinburne's phrase, ''grown diabolical among ages that would not accept her as divine.'' Swinburne is, I think, referring to more than just the psychological process by which the sexual impulse, when suppressed and denied, goes underground and turns in upon itself, only to erupt later in perverse and destructive forms.

He is also referring to the mythic dimensions in sexuality which cause it to become problematical when it no longer serves as the expression of a benevolent cosmic order. (p. 10)

In the penultimate chapter of Beardsley's novel Tannhauser sets out to tour Venus's kingdom [and he eventually reaches a lake]. . . . The episode, as it continues embodies both the terror faced by the post-Romantic and Beardsley's means of coping with it. Like many images of depths of water in Romantic and post-Romantic literature, the lake is a symbol of the subconscious mind, a paradoxical world which can be either a realm of profound beauty where one drinks the milk of paradise or a kingdom of equally profound horror where the soul is destroyed. . . . For Tannhauser the lake may be the source of the *logos* [divine wisdom], for in its depths may lie some ''beautiful word,'' and on its other side there may be ''other gardens, other gods''—but he also recognizes that he dare not wrinkle its gleaming surface. He would like to bathe in it, but he is sure that if he did he would be drowned. Under his gaze, it swells to an enormous size, and he is terrified by the ''big eyes and monstrous wet feet'' of the huge, foetus-like frogs that inhabit it. His self-preserving response is twofold. First he attempts to see the lake as a work of art, art which, we are reminded, ''does not hurt us'': ''Perhaps the lake was only painted, after all. He had seen things like it at the theatre.'' But he also marshalls his imagination to shrink the lake into ''a miniature of itself.'' . . . (pp. 12-13)

Like Tannhauser, Beardsley does not trust simply in the transforming and prophylactic powers of art; he too must also shrink the frogs into playroom figures of delight and fun. If the form is pornotopia, the mode with which Beardsley works within the form is mock-heroic. . . . On the one hand it reduces the disturbing and potentially dangerous, or at least disruptive, to the level of the harmless and absurd. Tannhauser, who in the old myth was man enslaved and damned by sexual passion, becomes in Beardsley's new setting a fantastical dandy whose martial valor is devoted solely to ''quelling the little mutinies of cravat and ruffle.'' . . . The keynote is sounded at the very beginning in Beardsley's mock-dedication of the work to the ''most eminent and reverend'' Cardinal Pizzoli, ''Bishop of S. Maria in Trastavere and Nuncio to the Holy See in Nicaragua and Patagonia,'' and it is maintained to the final episode with which the manuscript breaks off, a performance of Rossini's *Stabat Mater* which results in the rape of the castrato who has performed the role of the Virgin dressed in ''white stockings clocked with false pink,'' his hair ''dyed green'' and curled into ringlets. Only once is it broken, in the momentary vision of the monstrous wet feet of the frogs. For if the mock-heroic is reductive, it is also capable of conveying themes of high seriousness. It paradoxically elevates that which it reduces. If Beardsley reduces potentially tragic sexual passion to the level of the charmingly ridiculous, he does so without lessening his, or our, sense of its imperatives, of its centrality in human experience, and of man's need to find a means of looking upon his body and his heart without disgust. Beardsley's fragment (and I am convinced that in good Alexandrian fashion he planned it as a fragment) is not only, esthetically, one of the finest works of literary art to come out of the English ''decadence,'' it is also a significant and fascinating document in the history of man's attempt to come to terms with a force he can neither deny nor fully accept. (pp. 13-14)

Joseph H. Gardner, ''Beardsley and the Post-Romantic Venus,'' in The Denver Quarterly *(copyright ©1979 by The University of Denver), Vol. 13, No. 4, Winter, 1979, pp. 3-14.*

ADDITIONAL BIBLIOGRAPHY

Benkovitz, Miriam J. *Aubrey Beardsley: An Account of His Life*. New York: G. P. Putnam's Sons, 1981, 226 p.
   A recent biography that focuses on Beardsley's personal development and his relationship with his sister, Mabel.

Clark, Kenneth. *The Best of Aubrey Beardsley*. New York: Doubleday and Co., 1978, 173 p.
   Analyzes the nature of Beardsley's genius and lists his artistic influences, which the critic claims range from Sandro Botticelli to Edward Burne-Jones.

Easton, Malcolm. *Aubrey and the Dying Lady: A Beardsley Riddle*. London: Secker & Warburg, 1972, 272 p.
   A discussion of Beardsley's relationships with his sister Mabel and with Julian Sampson, a wealthy young man. Easton analyzes Beardsley's sexual interests and questions the sincerity of his conversion to Catholicism.

Gallatin, Albert E. "Note on the Literary Element in Beardsley's Art." *The Critic* XLI, No. 6 (December 1902): 561-69.
   A consideration of literary allusions in Beardsley's drawings, with particular attention to his *Salomé* illustrations.

Good, W. G. "Aubrey Beardsley: A Reappraisal." In *The Saturday Book*, edited by John Hadfield, pp. 61-81. Boston, Toronto: Little, Brown and Co., 1965.
   An assessment of Beardsley's drawings for *Salomé*. The critic maintains that Beardsley has been too closely associated with the Art Nouveau movement and not appreciated sufficiently on his own.

Macfall, Haldane. *Aubrey Beardsley: The Man and His Work*. London: John Lane The Bodley Head, 1928, 109 p.
   A biographical study of Beardsley by one of his contemporaries. Macfall includes a general discussion of Beardsley's artistic development.

Marillier, H. C. "Aubrey Vincent Beardsley." In *The Early Work of Aubrey Beardsley*, by Aubrey Beardsley, pp. 1-18. 1899. Reprint. New York: Da Capo Press, 1967.
   An analysis of "the Beardsley craze" and an appreciation of Beardsley's artistic innovations.

Praz, Mario. "Byzantium: *Under the Hill*, by A. Beardsley." In his *The Romantic Agony*, translated by Angus Davidson, pp. 342-43. 1933. Reprint. New York: Meridian Books, 1956.
   Calls *Under the Hill* the "essence of the English Decadent School."

Reade, Brian. "Aubrey Beardsley." In his *Aubrey Beardsley*, pp. 12-23. New York: The Viking Press, 1967.
   A biographical introduction to a collection of Beardsley's drawings. Reade suggests that Beardsley's artwork expresses the "Ideal." In addition, he discusses sexual symbolism in the drawings.

Ross, Robert. *Aubrey Beardsley*. New York: Jack Brussel, 1967, 112 p.
   A study of Beardsley's use of the grotesque. Ross considers the grotesque elements in his work to be the result of his skill and "scholarly originality."

Trail, George Y. "Beardsley's *Venus and Tannhäuser:* Two Versions." *English Literature in Transition* 18, No. 1 (1975): 16-23.
   A comparison of the expurgated and unexpurgated versions of *Under the Hill*. Trail explores the reasons why the novel was censored, who its censors were, and how their changes altered the work's style.

Weintraub, Stanley. *Beardsley: A Biography*. New York: George Braziller, 1967, 285 p.
   The definitive biography. Weintraub states that he wants to "enrich our view of the marvelous boy as human being and artist." Weintraub discusses all aspects of Beardsley's personal and artistic development and favorably compares *Under the Hill* to the works of John Keats.

Weintraub, Stanley. *Aubrey Beardsley: Imp of the Perverse*. University Park, London: The Pennsylvania State University Press, 1976, 292 p.
   Updates Stanley Weintraub's earlier biography (see annotation above). Weintraub has added new material and amended some data.

William Cullen Bryant

1794-1878

American poet, editor, critic, travel sketch writer, translator, short story and sketch writer, satirist, and historian.

Considered the most accomplished poet of his time in the United States, Bryant was also the first American poet to receive substantial international acclaim. His poetic treatment of the themes of nature and mutability identifies him as one of the earliest figures in the Romantic movement in American literature. Bryant's editorial career, among the longest in the history of American journalism, also contributes to his historical importance. Though Bryant's significance in American literary history is acknowledged today, his reputation has declined considerably in the twentieth century.

Bryant was born in Cummington, Massachusetts and grew up under the conflicting influences of his father, a liberal Unitarian physician, and his maternal grandfather, a conservative Calvinist farmer. As a boy, Bryant read the Bible, eighteenth-century English literature, and the English Romantic writers, particularly William Wordsworth. In addition, he studied and was influenced by the writings of William Shakespeare, John Milton, Sir Walter Scott, and the Scottish associationist philosophers Thomas Reid and Dugald Stewart. Bryant attended Williams College, but soon returned to Cummington because of financial hardship. He began studying the law and practiced as an attorney from 1815 to 1825.

Feeling encouraged by some of his earlier literary successes, Bryant traveled to New York in 1825 to try to build a literary career. In New York, Bryant co-founded the *New York Review and Atheneum Magazine* and became associated with the famous Knickerbocker group that included such authors as Washington Irving, Fitz-Greene Halleck, James Fenimore Cooper, and Gulian Verplanck, in addition to the artists Asher Durant and Thomas Cole. From 1829 to 1878, Bryant served as editor-in-chief of the *New York Evening Post*. Under his leadership, the *Post* became a leading liberal newspaper. Bryant's support for such causes as free speech, workers' rights, abolitionism, and the Union cause made him a prominent and controversial public figure. After breaking with the Democratic party over support for the Free Soilers in 1848, Bryant became one of the founders of the American Republican party. He remained politically active throughout his life and struggled to encourage liberal political causes.

Bryant's first published poem, *The Embargo; or, Sketches of the Times*, a verse satire of Thomas Jefferson's laws limiting free trade, appeared when the poet was fifteen years old. "Thanatopsis," Bryant's most famous poem, was composed in 1811 and published anonymously in the *North American Review* in 1817. "Thanatopsis" did not assume its final form until its appearance in Bryant's volume *Poems* (1821), however. The poem's evolution toward a Unitarian view of death—in which man becomes one with all the processes of nature—testifies to Bryant's improvement and maturation as a poet during these years. Bryant produced several more poetry collections: *Poems* (1832), *The Fountain and Other Poems, Hymns*, and *Thirty Poems*. However, his editorial responsibilities propelled Bryant in the direction of prose writing, and he pub-

lished two suspense stories, "Medfield" and "The Skeleton's Cave" in an anthology entitled *Tales of the Glauber-Spa*. His other prose works are collections of travel sketches, including *Letters of a Traveller; or, Notes of Things Seen in Europe and America, Letters of a Traveller, second series, Letters from the East*, and a popular historical survey entitled *A Popular History of the United States from the First Discovery of the Western Hemisphere . . . to the End of the First Century of the Union of the States*. Bryant also wrote several critical biographies, including *Discourse on the Life and Genius of Cooper, A Discourse on the Life, Character, and Genius of Washington Irving, Some Notices of the Life and Writings of Fitz-Greene Halleck*, and *A Discourse on the Life, Character, and Writings of Gulian Crommelin Verplanck*. His final literary projects were translations of *The Iliad* and *The Odyssey* of Homer.

Critics have singled out simplicity, didactic purpose, idealism, and a conscious concern for craftsmanship as the most prominent features of Bryant's poetic style. His poems express ideas derived from the Enlightenment, from English Romanticism, and from his study of German, Spanish, and Portuguese poetry. The recurring themes of these poems include mutability, loneliness, and the passing of innocence, and both Bryant's prose writings and his poetry attest to his interest in politics, folk themes, the American landscape and history. Bryant's chief stylistic hallmark, however, is his treatment of nature, especially his belief that it consoles as well as provides lessons about history and divine purpose. His poetry embodies an acceptance of the cycles of change in nature and in life and a belief that change is providential because it leads to an individual's spiritual progress and moral improvement.

Bryant's critical reputation has varied over the course of the nineteenth and twentieth centuries. After the *North American Review* published "Thanatopsis," the magazine discontinued its verse department, fearing that the standard Bryant's poems had set was so high that no other contributors could equal it. In fact, Bryant's place as the most eminent American poet was generally unquestioned until the middle of the nineteenth century. Though most critics agree that Bryant's earliest poems are his best work, there has been some variation in critical opinion about his work in general. Edgar Allan Poe, Edmund Clarence Stedman, and Gay Wilson Allen have praised Bryant's skillful and often innovative handling of prosody. Other critics single out Bryant's sincerity and simplicity of tone as his best trait, while Walt Whitman valued Bryant's high moral tone above all of his other qualities. James Russell Lowell and Henry B. Sedgwick, Jr. perceived a lack of passion in Bryant's poems. He has also frequently been criticized for the lack of flexibility and depth in his poetic subjects and themes, as well as for his over-reliance on didactic endings. The question of whether Bryant's sensibility is more Puritan or Romantic is often debated. Norman Foerster and Fred Lewis Pattee assert that Bryant's Puritan traits dominate his style, whereas Tremaine McDowell and Albert F. McLean, Jr. emphasize Bryant's Romantic characteristics. Stedman praised Bryant's journalistic prose, as did Vernon Louis Parrington, who proposed that Bryant's editorial contributions are equal in importance to his poetry.

Several critics, Charles Leonard Moore and Stedman among them, consider Bryant second only to Poe in literary importance during the pre-Civil War period in America. He is recognized as one of the first poets in the United States to challenge the dominance of traditional eighteenth-century poetic styles. His development of lofty philosophic themes, his editorial contributions, and his verse experiments with iambic rhythm make Bryant an important, if eclipsed, figure in American literature.

(See also *Dictionary of Literary Biography*, Vol. 3: *Antebellum Writers in New York and the South*.)

PRINCIPAL WORKS

The Embargo; or, Sketches of the Times (poetry) 1809
*Poems (poetry) 1821
"Medfield" (short story) 1832; published in *Tales of the Glauber-Spa*
Poems (poetry) 1832
"The Skeleton's Cave" (short story) 1832; published in *Tales of the Glauber-Spa*
The Fountain and Other Poems (poetry) 1846
The White-Footed Deer and Other Poems (poetry) 1846
Letters of a Traveller; or, Notes of Things Seen in Europe and America (travel sketches) 1850
Discourse on the Life and Genius of Cooper (criticism) 1852
Letters of a Traveller, second series (travel sketches) 1859
A Discourse on the Life, Character, and Genius of Washington Irving (criticism) 1860

Hymns (poetry) 1864
Thirty Poems (poetry) 1864
Letters from the East (travel sketches) 1869
Some Notices of the Life and Writings of Fitz-Greene Halleck (criticism) 1869
A Discourse on the Life, Character, and Writings of Gulian Crommelin Verplanck (criticism) 1870
The Iliad of Homer [translator] (poetry) 1870
The Odyssey of Homer [translator] (poetry) 1871
The Poetical Works of William Cullen Bryant (poetry) 1876
A Popular History of the United States from the First Discovery of the Western Hemisphere . . . to the End of the First Century of the Union of the States. 4 vols. (history) 1876-81
The Letters of William Cullen Bryant. 3 vols. (letters) 1975

*This work includes the poems "Thanatopsis" and "To a Waterfowl."

THE MONTHLY ANTHOLOGY, AND BOSTON REVIEW (essay date 1808)

If [*The Embargo; or, Sketches of the Times*] be really written by a youth of thirteen, it must be acknowledged an extraordinary performance. We have never met with a boy at that age, who had attained to such command of language and to so much poetick phraseology. Though the poem is unequal, and there are some flat and prosaick passages, yet is there no small portion of fire and some excellent lines. . . .

We regret that the young poet has dared to aim the satirick shaft against the breast of our most excellent President [Thomas Jefferson]. (p. 339)

If the young bard has met with no assistance in the composition of this poem, he certainly bids fair, should he continue to cultivate his talent, to gain a respectable station on the Parnassian mount, and to reflect credit on the literature of his country. (p. 340)

> *A review of "The Embargo; or, Sketches of the Times," in* The Monthly Anthology, and Boston Review, *Vol. V, No. VI, June, 1808, pp. 339-40.*

[WILLARD PHILLIPS] (essay date 1821)

There is running through the whole of [*Poems*], a strain of pure and high sentiment, that expands and lifts up the soul and brings it nearer to the source of moral beauty. This is not indefinitely and obscurely shadowed out, but it animates bright images and clear thoughts. There is every where a simple and delicate portraiture of the subtle and ever vanishing beauties of nature, which she seems willing to conceal as her choicest things, and which none but minds the most susceptible can seize, and no other than a writer of great genius, can body forth in words. There is in this poetry something more than mere painting. It does not merely offer in rich colours what the eye may see or the heart feel, or what may fill the imagination with a religious grandeur. It does not merely rise to sublime heights of thought, with the forms and allusions that obey none but master spirits. Besides these, there are wrought into the composition a luminous philosophy and deep reflection, that make the subjects as sensible to the understanding, as they are splendid to the imagination. There are no slender lines and unmeaning epithets, or words loosely used to fill out the measure. The whole is of rich materials, skilfully compacted. A throng of ideas crowds every part, and the reader's mind is continually and intensely occupied with 'the thick coming fancies.'

The first poem ["**The Ages**"] is in the majestic and flexible stanza of Spenser; the last ["**Thanatopsis**"] is in the common heroic blank verse; and in both there is a powerful sway of versification, and a sure and ready style of execution. The others are shorter than these. They have great freedom and propriety of language, and are abundantly rich in sentiment, and marked by the utmost fineness and delicacy of perception. (pp. 380-81)

The pictures [in "**The Ages**"] of man, in a savage and semi-barbarous state, are given with great strength of colouring. The views are broad and full of light, and the tone of the versification deep, solemn, and powerful. The reader is borne away with an irresistible influence, while his mind is entirely filled and satisfied. (p. 381)

The striking features of the national character and state of society in Greece and Rome are . . . sketched [in the same poem] with distinct and bold strokes. A notice of the reformation follows, when 'the web, that for a thousand years had grown o'er prostrate Europe, crumbled, as fire dissolves the flaxen thread.' These are proper topics, for the ideas and principles derived from these sources are the elements of which modern society, or rather modern mind and character, are compounded. Though they are necessarily touched upon but generally, yet there is no vagueness or obscurity; the images are illustrative, and grand, and commensurate with the subject; and it is hardly too much to say, that they are as close, as intelligible, and as full fraught with meaning, as are those of Spenser himself. The imagery and poetry of this part are not more beautiful and great, than the thoughts are just and philosophical. (p. 382)

Those who had singled out "**Thanatopsis**," and put it in their number of admirable things, will be concerned to learn that the author has made considerable additions and some alterations. But he has not, we think, marred his work, and in its new form it will deserve to be a favorite no less than before. (p. 383)

Of the shorter pieces, that "**To a Waterfowl**" is thought by some the best. It has, perhaps, conceptions of greater novelty and strength, but we can imagine nothing finer than the "**Inscription for the Entrance into a Wood**," "**Green River**," and "**The Yellow Violet**." (p. 384)

> [Willard Phillips], "Bryant's Poems," in The North
> American Review, Vol. XIII, No. XXXIII, October,
> 1821, pp. 380-84.

THE UNITED STATES LITERARY GAZETTE (essay date 1824)

> [*Though this review of Bryant's* Poems *(1821) generally praises his abilities and talent, the reviewer carefully emphasizes the fact that the volume is "a promise rather than a performance," and that the poems indicate "rather the possession of extraordinary powers, than their exertion." Later critics conclude that Bryant failed to fulfill his early promise.*]

We have no hesitation in saying, that no American, whose productions are within our knowledge, has written so good poetry as Mr. Bryant; and we confess, that in our opinion, no volume can be indicated more honorable to the literature of our country than this thin duodecimo [*Poems,* published in 1821]. . . .

Mr. Bryant does not seem to be wanting in ambition, or in the disposition to attempt arduous things; but he sustains himself at his loftiest height with so strong a wing, we cannot but think he might have gone higher. We hope he is not lazy; we hope he is willing to do what no American has done; what no one but himself has given presumptive proof, that he can do. We trust he will attempt, with earnestness and determination, to make one poem, long enough to task all his powers, and good enough to reward his severest toil. Parts of this volume are truly admirable, and have already won for their author an exalted and extended reputation; but he must know, that it is regarded as a promise rather than a performance; as indicating rather the possession of extraordinary powers, than their exertion. . . . If he adds not to the talents he has already exhibited, a capacity for more sustained and persevering effort, than so small a work,—elaborate as it is,—could require, he may make more odes and songs, beautiful as such things well can be, but will never build up a lasting monument of mighty power, strenuously, resolutely, and successfully put forth. . . .

The poetry in this volume, is strongly marked with every characteristic which could be impressed upon it, by the most watchful, laborious, and repeated revision. . . .

Most of the pieces are . . . upon subjects sufficiently trite; yet there is very little of commonplace in any of them. This is a striking characteristic of Mr. Bryant's poetry, and seems to arise, not from a determination to be eccentric, when he can be nothing better, but because his mind has its own character, and will impress it upon all its works. He is a good thinker, and never uses fine words to adorn or conceal thoughts, which have no intrinsic value or beauty. . . .

We were not pleased with all [the poems] . . . , for the construction of some lines in "**The Ages**," and in "**Thanatopsis**" reminded us rather too strongly of the Lake School; but the ode "**To a Waterfowl**," is a beautiful and harmonious blending of various beauties into one. (p. 8)

> *A review of "Poems," in* The United States Literary
> Gazette, *Vol. I, No. 1, April 1, 1824, pp. 8-9.*

THE SOUTHERN REVIEW (essay date 1832)

The diction of [*Poems*] is unobjectionable—and that is saying a great deal. It is simple and natural—there is no straining after effect, no meretricious glare, no affected point and brilliancy. It is clear and precise. . . . This is to us the charm of Mr. Bryant's verses. They flow spontaneously from a heart softened by the most touching sensibilities, and they clothe themselves in the very language which nature has adapted, and as it were consecrated to the expression of those sensibilities. (pp. 444-45)

There are some translations from [Spanish] that strike us (by analogy, for we do not remember to have read the originals) as admirably well executed. They are full of the life and soul of those spirited and lofty, though simple effusions of a heroic age. Some of Mr. Bryant's own verses, in the same style and measure, are particularly well done. Another set of pieces are in an elegiacal strain—though not properly elegies or monodies. They are the expression of feelings rather deeper than a mere poetical melancholy, and yet not deep enough to be very pathetic or tragical. There are two or three very lively little poems that form a separate and third class. (p. 445)

The poems that aim at solemnity and grandeur, and those of a sadder and darker mood, do not strike us as equal to the [Spanish translations]. Still some of them possess no ordinary merit. . . . (p. 456)

Mr. Bryant's [sonnets], besides their wanting the legitimate form, are not master-pieces in other respects. Still they are very good. (p. 460)

There are three or four pieces of a livelier mood than the rest, that pleasingly diversify the character of this little volume. They are not remarkable for a very high degree of *vis comica* [comic power], but their gay and ironical good humour makes them agreeable. (p. 461)

Of the more serious pieces, we ought to mention that the **"Hymn of the Waldenses"** is very good, but **"The Hurricane"** strikes us as a failure. We do not think poems of that sort the *fort* of Mr. Bryant.

Upon the whole, we have great pleasure in strongly recommending this excellent little volume to the attention and patronage of the public. (pp. 461-62)

> *"Bryant's 'Poems',"* in The Southern Review, *Vol. VIII, No. XVI, February, 1832, pp. 443-62.*

[W. J. SNELLING]   (essay date 1832)

Bryant is not a first-rate poet; but he has great power, and is original in his way. In saying this, we do not mean to be understood, that he has struck out an entirely new path. Others before him have sung the beauties of creation, and the greatness of God; but no one ever observed external things more closely, or transferred his impressions to paper in more vivid colors. A violet becomes, in his hands, a gem fit to be placed in an imperial diadem; a mountain leads his eyes to the canopy above it. The woods, the hills, the flowers,—whatever, in short, is his subject, is brought before our eyes with a fidelity of delineation, and a brightness of coloring, which the actual pencil cannot rival. The picture is always finished to the minutest particular. (pp. 502-03)

Mr. Bryant has a [noble] language. He has communed with Nature in all her 'visible forms,' and understands her, whether she whispers in the breeze, or speaks in the storm. There is a very beautiful description of a forest in winter after a rain [in **'The Rivulet'**]. . . . **'Summer Wind,' 'Autumn Woods,'** and the lines written **'After a Tempest,'** are among the best of many excellent pieces of this kind. (pp. 503-04)

To equal, if not excel Thomson, in his own department of literature, would be distinction enough for any one man; but his excellence in descriptive poetry is not Mr. Bryant's chief merit. The bent of his mind is essentially contemplative. He loves to muse in solitude, in the depths of the forest, and on the high places of the hills. Whatever is great, whatever is fair, is felt by him as soon as seen. . . . He owes little to books, and hence his ideas are not marked by the technicality of any of the schools of poetry. His course, like the course of nature, whose poet he emphatically is, is even and steady. There is nothing dazzling, no concentrated fire, no 'word that burns,' in his writings. His verse never makes the cheek glow, and the veins tingle. He is never carried out of sight of common sense by his imagination. His strength is never impetuous, his boldness never extravagant. He is pensive, but not sad, or even

melancholy. He is too much of a philosopher to entertain visions of gloom. . . . The **'Hymn to Death'** is one of the noblest sermons that were ever written. There is as much poetry in **'The Old Man's Funeral,'** as in any poem of equal length, which we remember to have read, and a great deal more practical wisdom.

There have been greater poets than Mr. Bryant. He cannot crowd so many brilliant thoughts into the same compass, as Shakespeare could. He cannot harrow up the soul or appeal to the darker feelings like Byron. He cannot change from grave to gay. He has no versatility of talent; but he knows the exact extent of his powers, and never attempts any thing for which he is not qualified. He never strains after effect, like some we could mention, or fails as they do. The fact is highly honorable to him. 'Know thyself,' is a lesson too hard for most minds. Mr. Bryant has learned it. (pp. 504-05)

'Thanatopsis' is the most generally known and esteemed of Bryant's *Poems,* and perhaps deserves its reputation. It is sublime throughout. We do indeed recognise old acquaintances in some lines, the ideas of which are derived from the book of Job. Bryant has improved upon them, and thereby made them his own. He cannot be charged with plagiarism, for it is impossible to think that he intended to make any part of a work so well known as Job, pass for his. . . .

There is much cheerful philosophy in a little poem, called **'The Lapse of Time.'** The lines **'To the Evening Wind,'** are of a different character. With one or two trifling exceptions, the versification is perfect. It is in Bryant's best manner. . . . (p. 507)

If there be any thing within the whole compass of literature more delicate, more pure, more exquisitely sweet than [**'To the Evening Wind'**], it has not yet fallen under our observation. And this is not a solitary emanation of the spirit that produced it. [*Poems*] abounds with verses of the same character.

The relations of men and things to their Maker, never fail to call forth Bryant's utmost strength. Those of his pieces which are of this cast, are his very best. We would particularly notice . . . **'The Forest Hymn.'** (p. 508)

Some of [the translations in this volume] are very fine, particularly the **'Life of the Blessed,'** and **'Mary Magdalene.'** We should, however, prefer, that Mr. Bryant should employ his leisure in adding to the stock of English poetry. (p. 511)

There are some other articles which we never saw before, and which we are sorry to see now. We could not have affirmed, that Mr. Bryant would not succeed in humor, but we should not have expected him to attempt it. No one would recognise the hand of the author of **'Thanatopsis'** in things so much beneath mediocrity, or even believe them to be his, were it not for his somewhat amusing repeated escapes from such poor conceits, into a train of thoughts more worthy of him. On the whole, we may pronounce the book before us, the best volume of American poetry that has yet appeared. (p. 512)

[Bryant] has set up a high standard, and reached it. He has kept his pieces nine years. We do not believe that he will ever be the favorite of the multitude. . . . Bryant does not address the feelings or sympathies of common readers. He communes not with others, but himself. His poetry is entirely spiritual. Hence it will not be esteemed by the unthinking; but it will charm those for whom it was written,—men of sound judgment and cultivated taste. (pp. 513-14)

[W. J. Snelling], "Bryant's 'Poems'," *in* The North American Review, *Vol. XXXIV, No. LXXV, April, 1832, pp. 502-14.*

[T. H. LISTER] (essay date 1832)

[*In this English review of Bryant's* Poems *(1832), Lister compares Bryant with numerous English poets. He praises Bryant's "unconscious originality," "unaffected propriety," and "philosophic spirit." Even though Lister feels that Bryant's translations are not "distinguished," and that his poems sometimes lack "metrical polish," he assigns him "an honourable station in the second class" of poets.*]

We do not find [in *Poems by William Cullen Bryant, an American*] the rich mosaic work of Gray—the faultless delicacy of Goldsmith—the polished brilliancy of Moore—and that unexceptionable elegance of thought and expression which appear in the "Pleasures of Memory," and in many of the writings of Campbell. The rare finish which the works of these writers exhibit, is not very apparent in Mr. Bryant's. We do not feel, as in the foregoing instances, that the most careful elaboration could hardly have made them better; and yet there are, perhaps, few poems in which it would be more difficult to discover distinct blemishes than in those of the American poet. Mr. Bryant is not a writer of marked originality, but neither is he a copyist. It is true we are often reminded by him of other writers—of Thomson, of Young, of Akenside, of Cowper, not unfrequently of Wordsworth, and sometimes of Campbell and of Rogers. We are reminded of them by discovering passages which we feel they might have written, and which partake of the spirit which breathes in their works; but we perceive no traces of direct imitation, no resemblance which does not seem to arise rather from the congeniality of our author's mind than from his study of their productions. He cannot be truly called the follower of any one of them. Like each of them, he has, though unmarked by strong peculiarities, a manner of his own, and is, like them, original. This may not be very evident on the first hasty glance at his writings; for his is an unpretending, unconspicuous originality, not that which results from eager straining after novelty of effect, but such as will be naturally unfolded in the works of him who, drawing little from books, records the impressions of his own mind, the fruits of his own observation. It does not occur to us, in reading his poems, that he has ever tried to be thought original—that he has at all considered whether such or such a sentiment has been previously uttered by others—that he has ever studiously striven to be unlike his predecessors. Accordingly, he digresses slightly from off the broad straight highway of truth—deals little in novel illustrations and ingenious conceits, and has no epigrammatic points or bright quick turns of wit. The merit of his sentiments lies rather in their justness than in their novelty—the merit of the language in which he clothes them, in its unaffected propriety rather than in its point. There are hardly any short passages of his which, taken out of their *setting,* would sparkle alone, and have much isolated merit, independent of the poem of which they are a part. They must be viewed with reference to the whole. Alone they seem scarcely more than well-worded truisms, excellent in their way, but rather common-place—and yet they are, perhaps, the constituents of a poem to which the term "common place" would be utterly inapplicable.

Mr. Bryant is not a literary meteor; he is not calculated to dazzle and astonish. The light he shines with is mild and pure, beneficent in its influence, and lending a tranquil beauty to that on which it falls. But it will be little attractive, except to sobered minds, which do not seek their intellectual pleasures in the racy draught of strong excitement. He does not possess the requisite qualifications for the attainment of extensive popularity. No writer will be extensively popular who does not employ notes more stirring than those of Mr. Bryant—who does not transport us somewhat more out of the realms of contemplation into those of action—who does not excite our sympathies by moving exhibitions of human passion—or who, in default of these means, does not possess the resources of versatility, of wit, or of those attractive artifices of polished style, to the fascination of which many are sensible who disregard the more intrinsic germ of poetical excellence. But if the popularity of Mr. Bryant will not be extensive, it will, in its contracted sphere, be of a kind which is eminently creditable. He will have pampered no evil passion—he will have distorted no moral truth—he will have penned (as we conceive) "no line which dying he would wish to blot."—He will have addressed himself with unambitious simplicity, and modest knowledge of his own powers, to the pure of heart, and will have earned, not perhaps a loud applause, but a just and heartfelt approbation. He will not be the founder of a style—his manner is not sufficiently marked—nor has he those glaring peculiarities which will ensure his being either vehemently censured or vehemently applauded by any literary sect.

The turn of his mind is contemplative and pensive, disposed to serious themes, such as are associated with solemnity and awe. He is a Jaques without his moroseness. The mutability, the uncertainty of all around us, and even Death itself, are to him welcome themes. Yet he is not a gloomy poet. There is nothing misanthropic, nothing discontented, nothing desponding in his tone. On the contrary, there is in it a calm and philosophic spirit, which disposes rather to tranquil cheerfulness; and he treats subjects which in other hands might be food for melancholy, in the happy consciousness of being able to extract from them that germ of comfort which, if rightly considered, they are calculated to afford. We recommend to notice the short poem entitled **"The Lapse of Time,"** not so much for its poetical merits, as for an example of that true philosophy which discovers the materials of happiness in circumstances on which many a dismal poetaster has strung only notes of the deepest anguish. More strongly still, for the same reason, do we commend a poem with a startling title, his **"Hymn to Death;"** a poem of no mean power, yet a power not shown in terrific exaggeration or heated enthusiasm, but in its philosophical calmness, its justness of thought, and, strange as it may seem, its cheerfulness. . . . **"Thanatopsis"** [is] similar in tone and subject, and little inferior in poetical merit. (pp. 122-24)

In poetry descriptive of the aspects of nature Mr. Bryant principally excels. He has evidently observed accurately, and with the eye of a genuine lover of natural scenery, and he describes eloquently and unaffectedly what he has seen—selecting happily, using no tumid exaggeration and vain pomp of words, not perplexing us with vague redundancies, but laying before us with graceful simplicity the best features of the individual scene which has been presented to his eye. Nor is he limited in his sphere. Nature, under aspects the most different, seems alike congenial to his pen. Winter and summer—storm and sunshine—the hurricane and the zephyr—the rivulet and the mighty Hudson—a humble flower and the solemn magnificence of boundless forests—are alike depicted, and with equal beauty. He has much of the descriptive power of Thomson, divested of the mannerism which pervaded that period of our poetry—much of the picturesqueness of touch which shines in the verse of Sir Walter Scott, but ennobled by associations which that great writer did not equally summon to his aid—much of the fidelity of Wordsworth, but without his minuteness and occasional overstrained and puerile simplicity, yet closely following him in that better characteristic, his power of elevating the humblest objects by connection with some moral truth. In this Mr. Bryant eminently shines. His descriptions of nature are never mere barren descriptions, undignified by association, unproductive of pure and generous feelings, unaccompanied by some great lesson. . . . He is singularly happy in touching the relations of inanimate objects to man and his lot, and of all to their Creator. To him the aspect of nature seems ever associated with grateful and religious feelings, and he renders it a means of praise and worship. He treats it, however, not like the sceptic, who deifies nature, that he may exclude revelation and make religion as vague as possible. The view which Mr. Bryant takes of it suggests to us no such idea. (pp. 129-30)

The longest and one of the best poems in the collection is his first, "The Ages," written in the metre of Childe Harold [by Lord Byron], reminding us not a little of that great poem, and compensating for inferior power and brilliancy by superior justness of sentiment. It is a rapid and eloquent sketch of the rise and fall of nations, and the vicissitudes of man's condition, written in a strain of hope—the grateful "optimism" of a well-attempered mind—and ending with a truly patriotic anticipation of the progressive welfare of his native country. (p. 133)

There are some pretty translations, chiefly from the Spanish; but we cannot counsel Mr. Bryant to pursue this branch of composition. Not only is it secondary to that in which he is capable of excelling, but he is not possessed of those qualities which would enable him to be distinguished as a translator. He wants versatility and pliancy of style. He can not invest himself easily in a foreign garb, and dismiss all marks of individual manner. The translations are very pleasing, but they differ scarcely at all from his original poems, except in having less force. They do not enable us to forget the identity. They are still evidently from the hands of Mr. Bryant. Mr. Bryant cannot, perhaps, be said to have a bad ear for metrical rhythm, but neither has he shown a very good one. Some of his experiments in metre certainly cannot be called successful. Such are his "Mary Magdalen"—"Autumn Woods"—Lines "To a Cloud"—"Hymns of the City." The short poem called "The Gladness of Nature" halts awkwardly. . . . The "Indian Story," which has in it much good poetical imagery, shambles . . . in weak emulation of [Matthew Gregory Lewis's] "Alonzo the Brave." (pp. 136-37)

Mr. Bryant does not, we think, always well understand how to adapt his metre to his subject, or he would not have written on "The Hurricane" in such dancing sing-song. . . .

His want of metrical polish is rendered very evident by comparison whenever he has adopted the measure of Moore. His blank verse is good, and more satisfactory to the ear than his other poetry. This may be thought minute criticism, but, if Mr. Bryant's faults had not been few, we should not have stopped to notice such as these. We cannot advise him to prosecute the sportive style. He does not trifle lightly and gracefully. He has rarely attempted it, and with little success. His "Meditations on Rhode Island Coal," his lines "To a Mosquito," and "Spring in Town" are not worthy of his talents. Mr. Bryant is in the main a very unaffected writer, but there is a little occasional tendency to *prettiness*—to the namby-pamby Rosa-Matildaism

of modern album poetry, against which we would warn him. We have no flagrant instances to adduce; but whoever will look at his "Song of the Stars" will see plainly what we mean. These flaunting tags of garish embroidery consort ill with the correct and simple garb in which his thoughts are usually clothed. (p. 137)

We do not consider [Mr. Bryant] a first-rate poet, but we would assign him an honourable station in the second class, and regard him as eminently entitled to that respect which both in this and in his native land his poetical labours will, we trust, never fail to receive. (pp. 137-38)

> [*T. H. Lister*], "American Poetry," in *The Foreign Quarterly Review, Vol. X, No. XIX, August, 1832, pp. 121-38.*

[EDGAR ALLAN POE] (essay date 1837)

[*Considered one of America's most outstanding men of letters, Poe was a distinguished poet, novelist, essayist, journalist, short story writer, editor, and critic. Poe stressed an analytical rather than emotive approach to literature and emphasized the specifics of style and construction in a work, instead of concentrating solely on the importance of the ideological statement. Although Poe and his literary criticism were subject to controversy in his own lifetime, he is now valued for his literary theories. Poe notes several metrical faults in Bryant's poems, and censures Bryant's "didactics." At the same time, he points out Bryant's "air of calm and elevated contemplation," and concludes that "in all the minor merits Mr. Bryant is preeminent." Poe concludes that while Bryant had not yet achieved the stature of such poets as John Keats and William Wordsworth, he showed promise of attaining it.*]

Mr. Bryant's poetical reputation, both at home and abroad, is greater, we presume, than that of any other American. . . .

The four initial lines [of **The Ages**] arrest the attention at once by a quiet dignity of manner, an air of placid contemplation, and a versification combining the extremes of melody and force—

> When to the common rest that crowns our days,
> Called in the noon of life, the good man goes,
> Or full of years, and ripe in wisdom, lays
> His silver temples in their last repose—

The five concluding lines of the stanza, however, are not equally effective—

> When, o'er the buds of youth, the death-wind blows,
> And blights the fairest; when our bitterest tears
> Stream, as the eyes of those that love us close,
> We think on what they were, with many fears
> Lest goodness die with them, and leave the coming years.

The defects, here, are all of a metrical and of course minor nature, but are still defects. The line

> When o'er the buds of youth, the death-wind blows

is impeded in its flow by the final *th* in *youth,* and especially in *death* where *w* follows. The word *tears* cannot readily be pronounced after the final *st* in *bitterest*; and its own final consonants, *rs,* in like manner render an effort necessary in the utterance of *stream* which commences the next line. In the verse

> We think on what they were, with many fears

the word *many* is, from its nature, too rapidly pronounced for the fulfilment of the *time* necessary to give weight to the foot of two syllables. (p. 41)

The other metrical faults in *The Ages* are few. Mr. Bryant is not always successful in his Alexandrines. Too great care cannot be taken, we think, in so regulating this species of verse as to admit of the necessary pause at the end of the third foot—or at least as not to render a pause necessary elsewhere. We object, therefore, to such lines as

> A palm like his, and catch from him the hallowed
>   flame.
> The truth of heaven, and kneel to Gods that heard them
>   not. . . .

Stanza VI is, throughout, an exquisite specimen of versification, besides embracing many beauties both of thought and expression.

> Look on this beautiful world and read the truth
> In her fair page; see every season brings
> New change, to her, of everlasting youth;
> Still the green soil with joyous living things
> Swarms; the wide air is full of joyous wings;
> And myriads, still, are happy in the sleep
> Of ocean's azure gulfs, and where he flings
> The restless surge. Eternal love doth keep
> In his complacent arms the earth, the air, the deep.

The cadences, here, at the words *page, swarms,* and *surge* respectively, cannot be surpassed. We shall find, upon examination, comparatively few consonants in the stanza, and by their arrangement no impediment is offered to the flow of the verse. Liquids and the most melodious vowels abound. *World, eternal, season, wide, change, full, air, everlasting, wings, flings, complacent, surge, gulfs, myriads, azure, ocean, soil,* and *joyous,* are among the softest and most sonorous sounds in the language, and the partial line after the pause at *surge,* together with the stately march of the Alexandrine which succeeds, is one of the finest imaginable of finales—

> Eternal love doth keep
> In his complacent arms, the earth, the air, the deep.

The higher beauties of the poem are not, we think, of the highest. It has unity, completeness,—a beginning, middle and end. The tone, too, of calm, hopeful, and elevated reflection, is well sustained throughout. There is an occasional quaint grace of expression, as in

> Nurse of full streams, and lifter up of proud
> Sky-mingling mountains that o'erlook the cloud—

or of antithetical and rhythmical force combined, as in

> The shock that hurled
> To dust in many fragments dashed and strown
> The throne whose roots were in another world
> And whose far-stretching shadow awed our own.

But we look in vain for something more worthy commendation. At the same time the piece is especially free from errors. Once only we meet with an unjust metonymy, where a sheet of water is said to

> *Cradle,* in his soft *embrace,* a gay
> Young group of grassy islands.

We find little originality of thought, and less imagination. But in a poem essentially didactic, of course we cannot hope for the loftiest breathings of the Muse. . . .

In the second quatrain [of *To the Past*], the lines

> And glorious ages gone
> Lie deep within the shadow of thy womb

are, to us, disagreeable. Such images are common, but at best, repulsive. In the present case there is not even the merit of illustration. The womb, in any just imagery, should be spoken of with a view to things future; here it is employed, in the sense of the tomb, and with a view to things past. In Stanza XI the idea is even worse. The allegorical meaning throughout the poem, although generally well sustained, is not always so. In the quatrain

> Thine for a space are they—
> Yet shalt thou yield thy treasures up at last;
> Thy gates shall yet give way
> Thy bolts shall fall, inexorable Past!

it seems that *The Past,* as an allegorical personification, is confounded with *Death.* . . .

[*The Old Man's Funeral*] is nearly perfect in its way—the thoughts striking and natural—the versification singularly sweet. The third stanza embodies a fine idea, beautifully expressed. (p. 43)

[*The Prairies*] possesses features which do not appear in any of the pieces above mentioned. Its descriptive beauty is of a high order. The peculiar points of interest in the Prairie are vividly shown forth, and as a local painting, the work is, altogether, excellent. (p. 44)

The Living Lost has four stanzas of somewhat peculiar construction, but admirably adapted to the tone of contemplative melancholy which pervades the poem. We can call to mind few things more singularly impressive than the eight concluding verses. They combine ease with severity, and have antithetical force without effort or flippancy. The final thought has also a high ideal beauty. . . .

The Damsel of Peru is in the fourteen syllable metre, and has a most spirited, imaginative and musical commencement—

> *Where olive leaves were twinkling in every wind that blew,*
> There sat beneath the pleasant shade a damsel of Peru.

This is also a ballad, and a very fine one—full of action, chivalry, energy and rhythm. Some passages have even a loftier merit—that of a glowing ideality. (p. 45)

Rispah is a scriptural theme from 2 Samuel, and we like it less than any poem yet mentioned. The subject, we think, derives no additional interest from its poetical dress. (pp. 45-6)

Of the seven original sonnets in [*Poems*], it is somewhat difficult to speak. The sonnet demands, in a great degree, point, strength, unity, compression, and a species of completeness. Generally, Mr. Bryant has evinced more of the first and the last, than of the three mediate qualities. (p. 47)

The Waterfowl is very beautiful, but still not entitled to the admiration which it has occasionally elicited. There is a fidelity and force in the picture of the fowl as brought before the eye of the mind, and a fine sense of *effect* in throwing its figure on the back ground of the "crimson sky," amid "falling dew," "while glow the heavens with the last steps of day." But the merits which possibly have had most weight in the public estimation of the poem, are the melody and strength of its versification, (which is indeed excellent) and more particularly its *completeness*. Its rounded and didactic termination has done wonders. (pp. 47-8)

Like *The Waterfowl*, [*Thanatopsis*] owes much to the point, force, and general beauty of its didactic conclusion. In the commencement, the lines

> To him who, *in the love of nature,* holds
> Communion with her visible forms, &c.

belong to a class of vague phrases, which, since the days of Byron, have obtained too universal a currency. The verse

> Go forth under the open sky and list—

is sadly out of place amid the forcible and even Miltonic rhythm of such lines as

> Take the wings
> Of morning, and the Barcan desert pierce,
> Or lose thyself in the continuous woods
> Where rolls the Oregan.

But these are trivial faults indeed, and the poem embodies a great degree of the most elevated beauty. (p. 48)

In all the rhapsodies of Mr. Bryant, which have reference to the beauty or the majesty of nature, is a most audible and thrilling tone of love and exultation. As far as he appreciates her loveliness or her augustness, no appreciation can be more ardent, more full of heart, more replete with the glowing soul of adoration. Nor, either in the moral or physical universe coming within the periphery of his vision, does he at any time fail to perceive and designate, at once, the legitimate items of the beautiful. Therefore, could we consider (as some have considered) the mere enjoyment of the beautiful when perceived, or even this enjoyment when combined with the readiest and truest perception and discrimination in regard to beauty presented, as a sufficient test of the poetical sentiment, we could have no hesitation in according to Mr. Bryant the very highest poetical rank. But something more, we have elsewhere presumed to say, is demanded. Just above, we spoke of "objects in the moral or physical universe coming within the periphery of his vision." We now mean to say, that the relative extent of these peripheries of poetical vision must ever be a primary consideration in our classification of poets. Judging Mr. B. in this manner, and by a *general* estimate of the volume before us, we should, of course, pause long before assigning him a place with the spiritual Shelleys, or Coleridges, or Wordsworths, or with Keats, or even Tennyson, or Wilson, or with some other burning lights of our own day, to be valued in a day to come. Yet if his poems, as a whole, will not warrant us in assigning him this grade, one such poem as the last upon which we have commented, is enough to assure us that he may attain it.

The writings of our author, as we find them *here,* are characterized by an air of calm and elevated contemplation more than by any other individual feature. In their mere didactics, however, they err essentially and primitively, inasmuch as such things are the province rather of Minerva than of the Camenae. Of imagination, we discover much—but more of its rich and certain evidences, than of its ripened fruit. In all the minor merits Mr. Bryant is pre-eminent. His *ars celare artem* [art is to conceal art] is most efficient. Of his "completeness," unity, and finish of style, we have already spoken. As a versifier, we know of no writer, living or dead, who can be said greatly to surpass him. . . . In regard to his proper rank among American poets there should be no question whatever. Few—at least

few who are fairly before the public, have more than very shallow claims to a rivalry with the author of *Thanatopsis*. (p. 49)

> [*Edgar Allan Poe*], ''Bryant,'' *in* The Southern Literary Messenger, *Vol. III, No. 1, January, 1837, pp. 41-9.*

[JAMES RUSSELL LOWELL]   (poem date 1849)

[*Lowell was a celebrated nineteenth-century American poet, critic, essayist, and editor. In the following excerpt from* A Fable for Critics, *his book-length poem featuring witty critical portraits of his contemporaries, Lowell chides Bryant for his ''ice-olation'' and lack of ''kindling enthusiasm.'' Lowell does, however, grant Bryant praise as a nature poet, and admires his ''grace, strength, and dignity.'' The name ''Griswold,'' which appears early in the excerpt, is a reference to their contemporary, the American reviewer, Rufus Wilmot Griswold.*]

> There is Bryant, as quiet, as cool, and as dignified,
> As a smooth, silent iceberg, that never is ignified,
> Save when by reflection 'tis kindled o' nights
> With a semblance of flame by the chill Northern Lights.
> He may rank (Griswold says so) first bard of your
>   nation,
> (There's no doubt that he stands in supreme ice-
>   olation,)
> Your topmost Parnassus he may set his heel on,
> But no warm applauses come, peal following peal
>   on,—
> He's too smooth and too polished to hang any zeal on:
> Unqualified merits, I'll grant, if you choose, he has
>   'em,
> But he lacks the one merit of kindling enthusiasm;
> If he stir you at all, it is just, on my soul,
> Like being stirred up with the very North Pole.
>
> He is very nice reading in summer, but *inter
> Nos,* we don't want *extra* freezing in winter;
> Take him up in the depth of July, my advice is,
> When you feel an Egyptian devotion to ices.
> But, deduct all you can, there's enough that's right
>   good in him,
> He has a true soul for field, river, and wood in him;
> And his heart, in the midst of brick walls, or where'er
>   it is,
> Glows, softens, and thrills with the tenderest
>   charities,—
> To you mortals that delve in this trade-ridden planet?
> No, to old Berkshire's hills, with their limestone and
>   granite.
> If you'r one who *in loco* (add *foco* here) *desipis,*
> You will get of his outermost heart (as I guess) a piece;
> But you'd get deeper down if you came as a precipice,
> And would break the last seal of its inwardest fountain,
> If you only could palm yourself off for a mountain.
> Mr. Quivis, or somebody quite as discerning,
> Some scholar who's hourly expecting his learning,
> Calls B. the American Wordsworth; but Wordsworth
> Is worth near as much as your whole tuneful herd's
>   worth
> No, don't be absurd, he's an excellent Bryant;
> But, my friends, you'll endanger the life of your client,
> By attempting to stretch him up into a giant:

If you choose to compare him, I think there are two
  per-
sons fit for a parallel—Thomson and Cowper;
I don't mean exactly,—there's something of each,
There's T.'s love of nature, C.'s penchant to preach;
Just mix up their minds so that C.'s spice of craziness
Shall balance and neutralize T.'s turn for laziness,
And it gives you a brain cool, quite frictionless, quiet,
Whose internal police nips the buds of all riot,—
A brain like a permanent strait-jacket put on
The heart which strives vainly to burst off a button,—
A brain which, without being slow or mechanic,
Does more than a larger less drilled, more volcanic;
He's a Cowper condensed, with no craziness bitten,
And the advantage that Wordsworth before him has
  written.

  But, my dear little bardlings, don't prick up your
    ears,
Nor suppose I would rank you and Bryant as peers;
If I call him an iceberg, I don't mean to say
There is nothing in that which is grand, in its way;
He is almost the one of your poets that knows
How much grace, strength, and dignity lie in Repose;
If he sometimes fall short, he is too wise to mar
His thought's modest fulness by going too far;
'Twould be well if your authors should all make a trial
Of what virtue there is in severe self-denial,
And measure their writings by Hesiod's staff,
Which teaches that all has less value than half.

                                              (pp. 39-42)

[James Russell Lowell], in his A Fable for Critics:
A Glance at a Few of Our Literary Progenies, *second
edition, G. P. Putnam, 1849, 80 p.**

THOMAS POWELL (essay date 1850)

What Mr. Bryant gains as a philosopher, he loses as a poet.
Not that a poet should *not* be a philosopher, for indeed he
cannot be one without, but because he makes the secondary
the ascendant. Poetry includes philosophy, but it should be
hidden by the poetical glow, as the color of blooming health
hides the white skin of the fair maiden's cheek. This substitution of the lower for the higher faculty is very apparent in
the fine poem called the **"Ages."** This is the longest and most
ambitious of Mr. Bryant's attempts. The subject is admirably
fitted for the display of power. What can be more susceptible
of poetical thought and expression than a rapid review of the
history of the world? The theme is a half-inspiration of itself.
Mr. Bryant, however, looks with the eye of a philosopher on
the varying phases of humanity, and although we read with an
attentive pleasure, we do not feel that delight which we know
the subject is so admirably calculated to afford. We miss those
vigorous golden passages, which compel us to pause, and read
again out of the mere enthusiasm of admiration. (pp. 190-91)

In the [poem's] apostrophe to Rome we feel the philosophical
coolness of Mr. Bryant in its full force of negativing his poetry.
There is too much of the abstract. More can be gathered often
from a small event than from a dry balance-sheet of the result.
(p. 193)

[We] think Mr. Bryant has injured a fine subject by throwing
over it too frigid a mantle of philosophy. (p. 194)

It may be affirmed that his intention was to take a calm general
view of the ages of the world; if so, he has perfectly succeeded
as a philosopher, but failed somewhat as a poet. We may also
observe that we do not think he shines in the Spenserian stanza.
(pp. 195-96)

The tendency to moralize is an evil when indulged in indiscriminately; and a greater one when it is superinduced. Mr.
Bryant's productions are, however, so pervaded by this pre-
disposition that it is the leading faculty of his mind. It is,
indeed, his very nature. This will always give a value to his
reflections over the mere artificial moralist. We feel that it is
genuine thought—no make-believe—it is deep from the poet's
soul. He looks on nature with a sad calmness, like Wordsworth's muse in many of his finest moods. He, however, falls
short of the art shown by the author of "Netley Abbey," of
hiding his intention. . . . Mr. Bryant labors to obtrude his
design; this, with all deference to so true a poet, we think an
error, either of judgment or execution. (p. 196)

[In] his **"Thanatopsis,"** there is too much ostentation of purpose expressed in the opening. (p. 197)

It seems as though Mr. Bryant could not begin a subject in
blank verse, without a superfluity of explanation, which materially destroys the pleasure of the perusal. It is very much
like impairing the unexpectedness of a play by unnecessarily
announcing the denouement before it begins. All writing, more
especially poetry, is dramatic, and very much of all its interest
depends upon curiosity. In addition to this besetting tendency,
alike characteristic of Wordsworth and Bryant, is a prolixity
in the opening sentences in many of his poems. Few poets can
write simpler, closer English than Mr. Bryant, but mark how
feeble is the commencement of a very fine poem:

    The time has been that these wild solitudes,
    Yet beautiful as wild, were trod by me
    Oftener than now; and when the ills of life
    Had chafed my spirit—when the unsteady pulse
    Beat with strange flutterings—I would wander forth
    And seek the woods.

There is a homely phrase of "putting one's best leg foremost;"
but our poet seems to take a delight in putting his dullest thought
and feeblest verse at the porch of his otherwise fine structures
of verse. (pp. 197-98)

In the **"Forest Hymn,"** we see a better system at work [than
in **"Thanatopsis"**]. Instead of a needless introduction, the poet
at once opens boldly and truly into the subject. (p. 208)

In the later poems we do not see much advance on his earlier
effusions. The same calm spirit looking on men, not as one of
them fighting in the throng of battle, giving and receiving
blows, but on an eminence, where, above the smoke of the
conflict and the tumult of the conflict, he can see as a spectator:
removed from the turmoil, he can draw his conclusions.

In his verses **"To the Apennines,"** he combines the ideal of
paradise with the locale of Peru.

    Your peaks are beautiful, ye Apennines!
      In the soft light of these serenest skies;
    From the broad highland region, black with pines,
      Fair as the hills of Paradise they rise,
    Bathed in the tint Peruvian slaves behold
    In rosy flushes on the virgin gold.

This is . . . proof how much some poets *feel* with the *brain*.
Reflection here has yoked the dissimilar. We must confess that

we had hoped for a more personal, humanizing conclusion, than the frigid summing up of—

> In you the heart that sighs for freedom seeks
>   Her image; there the winds no barrier know,
> Clouds come and rest and leave your fairy peaks;
>   While even the immaterial Mind, below,
> And Thought, her winged offspring, chained by power,
> Pine silently for the redeeming hour.

Mr. Bryant very seldom originates his subject; he generally selects some well-known fact, and after amplifying it, he then closes his poem by drawing a moral. That there is a moral in everything we need no instructor to assure us; but as this propensity to point it out seems part of our poet's nature, we must not blame him for it. We may, however, be permitted to express our opinion, that it very greatly interferes with his immortality as a master of song. (pp. 210-11)

It is impossible to rise from the study of Mr. Bryant's poems without feeling more in harmony with nature and man than the spirit generally feels. We know that we have been calmly, kindly reasoned with by a good, calm, sad, Christian man, who, having no turbulence in himself, endeavors to throw the quiet mantle of his own reflective spirit over his companions. (p. 220)

> *Thomas Powell, "William Cullen Bryant," in his* The Living Authors of America, first series, *Stringer and Townsend, 1850, pp. 189-221.*

EDMUND CLARENCE STEDMAN   (essay date 1864)

[*A major nineteenth-century American critic and anthologist, Stedman gained wide critical influence as the author of* Victorian Poets *(1875) and* Poets of America *(1885). In conjunction with his popular* American Anthology *(1900), the latter work helped to establish greater interest in and appreciation for American literature. A foe of the "heresy of the didactic," Stedman wrote criticism which is often informed by his belief that "a prosaic moral is injurious to virtue by making it repulsive." Stedman praises Bryant's dispassionateness and "self-restraint," as well as his technical mastery in the poems. In a later assessment (see excerpt below, 1885), Stedman's comments, while largely favorable, proved to be more acerbic.*]

[Bryant's] *Thirty Poems,* by their very tranquillity, will at first repel those who have been stall-fed on the seething excitement of the latest modes, and flattered to the top of their bent with the jingling variety of its cadences.

But give them another study, and their simplicity will have a most seductive charm. . . . Mr. Bryant rarely goes beyond his sight and knowledge, and we say that the secret of his simplicity is his self-restraint. This is at once the safeguard of his poetry, of his prose, and of his almost blameless life. (pp. 113-14)

["**The Planting of the Apple-Tree**"] affords an illustration of the limit to which Mr. Bryant, as a melodist, is subjected. With a purpose evidently to give spirited abruptness to the refrain, the last verse of each stanza is a foot shorter than its correspondent. This has a certain effect, but jars harshly on the even cadence of the author's style; and a more *facile* artist would have found a better way to achieve the desired result. When Mr. Bryant ventures beyond the established metres, it is with uncouthness and an air of doubt. He is in unknown waters, and would gladly touch firm land; but then, as we have said, he seldom ventures. The poem in question is followed by the perfectly beautiful "**Snow Shower**"; a little further on

we have "**Robert of Lincoln,**" full of bird music and delicate humor; and, toward the middle of the volume, the finely imaginative "**Song of the Sower**" teems with the richness of a fruitful theme. These four poems, though cast in moulds of the author's own devising, are, with the slight exception hitherto noted, in forms as well suited to the author's genius, because as evenly and nobly balanced, as those of his well-remembered "**June**" and "**The Conqueror's Grave.**" (pp. 114-15)

If there are any pieces which could have been omitted from this collection, they are, "**An Invitation to the Country,**" the "**Song for New Year's Eve,**" "**The Wind and Stream,**" "**These Prairies Glow with Flowers,**" and "**The Mother's Hymn.**" It seems to us that many feebler singers might have printed these. Nor do the two poems evoked by the present war at all compare with that ringing clarion blast, "**The Song of Marion's Men,**" which has stirred the pulses of every school-boy in the land, and to which no bugle but that of Motherwell could ever make response.

There are two simple and affluent forms of English verse in whose mastery Mr. Bryant is without an American rival. The first is the iambic quatrain, of which a familiar stanza, "**Truth crushed to Earth,**" in "**The Battle-Field,**" may be cited as a specimen. Perhaps the most finished poem of this volume is the "**Day-Dream.**" (pp. 115-16)

The second of the forms above-named is that blank verse of which Mr. Bryant's handling is always recognized. . . . His imprint stamps every line which he has thus written. The "**Thanatopsis**" and "**Forest Hymn**" are embalmed in literature. Nor has his hand lost its cunning. In [*Thirty Poems*], "**A Rain Dream,**" "**The Night Journey of a River,**" and "**The Constellations,**" are poems which none but Bryant could have written, and in his loftiest method. They are compact of high imaginings. (p. 117)

The verse of ["**Sella**" and "**The Little People of the Snow**"] is light and graceful, melodiously adapted to their themes, and greatly modified from Mr. Bryant's reflective style. They are imaginative throughout, but especially attractive for the rare fancy which sparkles in every line. The author's heart seems budding with a greenness which it somewhat lacked in the springtime of his life, and thus, by natural piety, could we also wish our days "bound each to each." (p. 119)

With Spanish poetry Mr. Bryant is entirely successful. His verse renders the grave Roman feeling of the Castilian muse to our outer and inner senses. Every reader will be repaid by a study of that Latinesque production, "**The Ruins of Italica**"; and "**The Lost Bird**" (by Carolina Colorado de Perry) is suggestive and melodious as the Spanish lyric itself.

Throughout the volume are evidences of a serene and joyous prime, which age cannot wither, nor the rust of years corrode. "**The Life That Is,**" "**A Sick Bed,**" "**The New and the Old,**" "**The Cloud on the Way,**" are all recognitions of the season to which the singer and his life-companions have arrived; but they breathe compliance with the sweet law of Nature's successions, and are radiant with faith that looks beyond the vail. His philosophy, like his poetic art, resembles a tranquil river still widening toward the close. (pp. 122-23)

> *Edmund Clarence Stedman, "Mr. Bryant's 'Thirty Poems'" (originally published as an unsigned essay entitled "Mr. Bryant's 'Thirty Poems'," in* The Round Table, *Vol. 1, No. 5, January 16, 1864), in his* Genius

and Other Essays, *Moffat, Yard and Company, 1911, pp. 111-24.*

RALPH WALDO EMERSON   (journal date 1864)

[An American essayist and poet, Emerson was the founder of the Transcendental movement and the shaper of a philosophy which embraced optimism, individuality, and mysticism. He stressed the presence of ongoing creation and revelation by a god apparent in all things, who exists in everyone, as well as the essential unity of all thoughts, persons, and things in the divine whole. Critics consider Emerson one of the most influential figures of the nineteenth century. Here, Emerson admires the way in which all of nature seems to "recall the name of Bryant." He addresses Bryant's sincerity, but also the "cold and majestic" quality noted in Bryant's style by such previous critics as James Russell Lowell (1849).]

Bryant has learned where to hang his titles, namely, by tying his mind to autumn woods, winter mornings, rain, brooks, mountains, evening winds, and wood-birds. Who speaks of these is forced to remember Bryant. [He is] American. Never despaired of the Republic. Dared name a jay and a gentian, crows also. His poetry is sincere. I think of the young poets that they have seen pictures of mountains, and sea-shores, but in his that he has seen mountains and has the staff in his hand. (pp. 76-7)

• • • • •

[Bryant's] sincere, balanced mind has the enthusiasm which perception of Nature inspires, but it did not tear him; only enabled him; gave him twice his power; he did not parade it, but hid it in his verse. His connection with party *usque ad aras* [even to the altars]. "True bard, but simple," I fear he has not escaped the infirmity of fame, like the presidential malady, a virus once in, not to be got out of the system: he has this, so cold and majestic as he sits there,—has this to a heat which has brought to him the devotion of all the young men and women who love poetry, and of all the old men and women who once were young. 'T is a perfect tyranny. Talk of the shopmen who advertise their drugs or cosmetics on the walls and on the palisades and huge rocks along the railways;—why, this man, more cunning by far, has contrived to levy on all American Nature and subsidized every solitary forest and Monument Mountain in Berkshire or the Katskills, every waterfowl, every partridge, every gentian and goldenrod, the prairies, the gardens of the desert, the song of the stars, the Evening Wind,— has bribed every one of these to speak for him, so that there is scarcely a feature of day and night in the country which does not—whether we will or not—recall the name of Bryant. This high-handed usurpation I charge him with, and on the top of this, with persuading us and all mankind to hug our fetters and rejoice in our subjugation. (pp. 80-2)

> *Ralph Waldo Emerson, in journal entries on October 20 and November 26, 1864, in his* Journals of Ralph Waldo Emerson: 1864-1876, *edited by Edward Waldo Emerson and Waldo Emerson Forbes (Copyright, 1914, by Edward Waldo Emerson. Copyright renewed 1941 by Houghton Mifflin Company. Reprinted by permission of Houghton Mifflin Company), Houghton Mifflin, 1914, pp. 76-7, 80-2.*

CHARLTON T. LEWIS   (essay date 1871)

Mr. Bryant's translation of [*The Iliad of Homer*] has peculiar claims upon critical attention, both because it is the work of

a poet eminent for his original writings, and because it has already won much favor with the people. (p. 328)

In the accuracy with which the sense of the Greek is expressed [in the translations of Bryant and Lord Derby, his most illustrious predecessor,] there is little to choose between them upon scholarly grounds. An idle student, seeking aid in construing the original, would find more of it in the Earl of Derby's translation than in Mr. Bryant's. It is more literal, preserving more closely the construction and order of the text. There are also many passages in which it shows a nicer appreciation of the shades of meaning in the Greek words and phrases. But it contains a large number of errors from which Mr. Bryant's care has saved him, and cannot be said as a whole to be more faithful to the sense of the old bards than his. When the translations are compared, however, in respect of their artistic accuracy, of the imaginative sympathy with which the thought of the bard has been appreciated and appropriated, the superiority of the American poet over the British statesman is immeasurable. (p. 359)

Mr. Bryant has long been known, by his original poems, as resembling the old epic poets, in his language, more than any other living writer of English. It may be said that contemporary poets have excelled his verse, one in splendor, another in suggestiveness, another in fulness of knowledge and in reach of thought, and more than one in nearness to the great mental conflicts of the age; but he has certainly not been surpassed, perhaps not approached by any writer since Wordsworth, in that majestic repose and that self-reliant simplicity which characterized the morning stars of song. He has adhered to the permanent element in our language; and the common perversions in the meaning of good old words, which make it so nearly impossible even for most men of culture to write a sentence that Chaucer could have understood, seem to be unknown to him. No qualification for a translator of Homer could be more essential than this; and the reader who has duly considered its importance will find that it has given Mr. Bryant's translation a vast superiority over all others. . . . [The ballad verse] of Mr. Bryant is at once majestic and direct, at once noble, rapid, and vigorous; it is, in a large degree, the simplicity of Homer. (pp. 360-61)

[Mr. Bryant] is a master of our heroic blank verse, as even the earliest of his poems proved. . . . [His translation] is varied, easy, and pleasing, and is not excelled by any other in its power of rising to an exalted solemnity, and of sinking to a natural familiarity; of sympathizing in its movement with all forms of passion, and of reflecting, without abruptness, all changes of tone. . . . Mr. Bryant has succeeded in giving to his verse something of the charm which the scholar finds in the grand roll of the inimitable Greek hexameter. . . . (p. 362)

Mr. Bryant's excellence, in all these respects, is not uniform. Passages may be found in which he has misunderstood the meaning of the Greek; but they are very few. . . . Passages may be found in which he has lost much by a somewhat loose paraphrase, when a translation in his best style is to be desired. A few lines may be detected by a nice ear, which interrupt the nearly unbroken flow and melody of his verse. But if the imperfections be not merely counted, but weighed, they will be found inconsiderable in comparison with those of any other English version. They may be remedied upon revision, without affecting the general tone and style; and were they all corrected, so that no positive error or marked defect could be found, few readers would notice any change. There is no other English *Iliad* which could be made by corrections to represent Homer, on the whole, as well as Mr. Bryant's represents him now; and until that distant day, when a poet no less eminent than he shall, with fuller knowledge, and before a world of richer intelligence, be content to give his maturest years of labor to the singing of these old songs again, Mr. Bryant's translation will assuredly be recognized wherever our mother tongue is read as its best echo of the old Greek epic. (pp. 367-69)

[One] may learn of Homer, and more impressively through Mr. Bryant than any other interpreter, the first lesson of noble art, that simplicity is the richest fertility, and a single eye the best guide to suggestive work. (p. 370)

> *Charlton T. Lewis, "Mr. Bryant's Translation of the 'Iliad'," in* The North American Review, *Vol. CXII, No. CCXXXI, April, 1871, pp. 328-70.*

WALT WHITMAN (essay date 1882-83)

[*American poet, essayist, novelist, short story writer, journalist, and editor, Whitman is regarded as one of America's finest poets, and a great literary innovator. His poetry collection,* Leaves of Grass, *in which he celebrates the "divine average," democracy, and sexuality, is regarded as a major influence on modern free verse. In this brief testimonial, Whitman singles out Bryant's excellence as a nature poet, and praises his ability to convey morals "grim and eternal" through his poetry.*]

In a late magazine one of my reviewers, who ought to know better, speaks of my "attitude of contempt and scorn and intolerance" toward the leading poets—of my "deriding" them, and preaching their "uselessness." If anybody cares to know what I think—and have long thought and avow'd—about them, I am entirely willing to propound. I can't imagine any better luck befalling these States for a poetical beginning and initiation than has come from Emerson, Longfellow, Bryant, and Whittier. Emerson, to me, stands unmistakably at the head, but for the others I am at a loss where to give any precedence. Each illustrious, each rounded, each distinctive. . . . Bryant pulsing the first interior verse-throbs of a mighty world—bard of the river and the wood, ever conveying a taste of open air, with scents as from hayfields, grapes, and birch-border—always lurkingly fond of threnodies—beginning and ending his long career with chants of death, with here and there through all, poems, or passages of poems, touching the highest universal truths, enthusiasms, duties—morals as grim and eternal, if not as stormy and fateful, as anything in Eschylus. (pp. 31-3)

> *Walt Whitman, "My Tribute to Four Poets," in his* Specimen Days & Collect, *Rees Welsh & Co., 1882-83 (and reprinted in his* Rivulets of Prose: Critical Essays, *edited by Carolyn Welts and Alfred F. Goldsmith, Greenberg Publishers, 1928, pp. 31-3).**

EDWIN P. WHIPPLE (essay date 1885)

The genuineness of Bryant is, perhaps, too austerely conscientious, and, if any fault can be found with him in this respect, it is his repression of poetic instincts, which might, if cultivated, have given more variety to his muse. Surely, the little poem of **"The Mosquito"** indicates a vein of sentiment, delicate, playful, and genial, that might have been developed into many a piece of exquisite poetical wit and gracefully fanciful humor, which would have relieved the sad, sweet, earnest tone of his ordinary meditations.

Another characteristic of Bryant's poetical diction is its fulness of matter. Every line is loaded with meaning. This weight and wealth and compactness of thought sometimes fail to impress the reader in his blank verse, on account of its swift and slipping freedom of movement; but in his ringing rhyme they are forced upon the attention. (pp. 306-07)

This solidity of thought is perhaps exhibited too much in one direction, but still the one-sidedness proceeds from a limitation of poetical sympathy, not from a limitation of intellectual power. (pp. 307-08)

Bryant has a true sentiment for external nature, . . . but he has not, in addition to [this], the sentiments which lead the intellect to explore the depths of human character, and find a joy in the concrete facts of human life. (p. 309)

There is no genial delineation of men and women, as individuals, in his writings. When he glows at the mention of a name, we find it is not a person he is celebrating, but some qualities of that person, abstracted from his personality, and idealized. His general tone toward society is harsh. . . . In his poems he continually speaks of escaping from the crowd, of despising the frivolity of society, of hating the every-day work by which man, in this life, keeps up that interesting and slightly important connection between body and soul called "getting a living." In this we are, of course, speaking of Bryant as a poet, and of the feelings which animate him as he contrasts the nature he poetically conceives with the social life he prosaically apprehends. The result is that, though perhaps the first of poets in America, he is not especially an American poet, for what nationalizes genius is not so much the scenery it describes as the human life it idealizes. . . . He appears rather to have for [the real concrete life of the nation] a subtle and supercilious antipathy, when, as a poet, he gives himself up to the influences of nature. (pp. 310-11)

> *Edwin P. Whipple, "Bryant," in his* Literature and Life, *seventh edition, Houghton Mifflin and Company, 1885, pp. 303-21.*

EDMUND CLARENCE STEDMAN (essay date 1885)

Bryant is, in one respect, peculiarly unmodern. . . . Our poet's learning [of nature] was not scientific; he lacked the minor vision which, an added gift, enables Tennyson and others to give such charm and variety to their work. . . . Bryant regarded nature in its phenomenal aspect, careless of scientific realities. What he gained in this wise was the absence of disillusionizing fact, and a fuller understanding of the language of nature's "visible forms"; what he lost was the wide and various range opened by the endless avenues of new-found truth.

Right here it is well for us to observe his limitations as a poet,—limitations so undeniable as to be a stumbling-block in the way of those who lightly consider his genius, and sometimes to throw him out of the sympathetic range of elegant and impartial minds. His longevity was not allied with intellectual quickness and fertility, but seemed almost the biologic result of inborn slowness and deliberation. He was not flexible, not facile of ear and voice. He consorted with nature in its still or majestic moods, and derived wisdom and refreshment from its tenderness and calm. . . . The most fervent social passions of his song are those of friendship, of filial and fraternal love; his intellectual passion is always under restraint, even when moved by patriotism, liberty, religious faith. There is still less of action and dramatic quality in his verse. Humor, the overflow of strength, is almost absent from it,—when present, sufficiently awkward; yet it should be noted that in conversation, or in the after-dinner talks and speeches so frequent in his later years, his humor was continuous and charming. . . . There are few notable expressions and separable lines in his poetry. In his stanzaic verse, following the established eighteenth-century patterns, he scarcely can be said to have a style of his own. . . . Where Bryant was most impressive—that is to say, in his blank-verse poems—he had a positive and unmistakable style, quite distinct even from that of his master, Wordsworth. Finally, his diction, when not confined to that Saxon English at every man's use, is bald and didactic,—always sententious, but less frequently rich and full. He had a limited vocabulary at command; I should think that no modern poet, approaching him in fame, has made use of fewer words. His range is like that of Goldsmith, restricted to the simpler phrases of our tongue. Other poets, of an equally pure diction, show here and there, by rare and fine words, the extent of their unused resources, and that they voluntarily confine themselves to "the strength of the positive degree." (pp. 69-71)

[Bryant] never, by any chance, affected passion or set himself to artificial song. He had the triple gift of Athene, "self-reverence, self-knowledge, self-control." He was incapable of pretending to rapture that he did not feel, and this places him far above a host of those who, without knowing it, hunt for emotions and make poetry little better than a trade. As for his diction, he began when there was no Feast of Pentecost with its gift of tongues. . . . No doubt Bryant's models confirmed his natural restrictions of speech. But even this narrow verbal range has made his poetry strong and pure; and now, when expression has been carried to its extreme, it is an occasional relief to recur to the clearness, to the exact appreciation of words, discoverable in every portion of his verse and prose. It is like a return from a florid renaissance to the antique; and indeed there was something Doric in Bryant's nature. His diction, like his thought, often refreshes us as the shadow of a great rock in a weary land. He refused to depart from what seemed to him the natural order of English verse,—that order which comes to the lips of childhood, and is not foreign to any life or age. The thought was like the measure, that which was old with the fathers and is young in our own time, the pure philosophy of nature's lessons. Give his poems a study, and their simplicity is their charm. (pp. 76-7)

Verse, to Bryant, was the outflow of his deepest emotions; a severe taste and discreet temperament made him avoid the study of decoration. Thus he was always direct and intelligible, and appealed to the common people as strongly as to the select few. . . . Among others Daniel Webster might be mentioned as one whose mood and rhetoric are in keeping with the poetry of Bryant. Like Webster, our poet always selected the leading, impressive thought, and brushed the rest aside. This he put in with a firm and glowing touch. Many have thought the works of both the statesman and the poet conventional, but the adjective might be brought to apply to all simple and essential truth and diction. Adopting Arnold's distinction, we see that Bryant's simplicity was not *simplesse*, but *simplicité*. (pp. 77-8)

One [of Bryant's favorite chosen measures] was the iambic quatrain, in octosyllabic verse, of which the familiar stanza, "Truth crushed to earth will rise again," may be recalled as a specimen. Many of his best modern pieces are composed in this measure, so evenly and firmly that the slightest change would mar their sound and flow. **"A Day Dream,"** written in

the poet's old age, is perfect of its kind, and may rank almost with Collins's nonpareil, "To fair Fidele's Grassy Tomb." (pp. 78-9)

His variations upon the iambic quatrain, as in the celebrated poems, **"To a Waterfowl"** and **"The Past,"** are equally successful. The second of the forms [Bryant favored] . . . is that blank-verse in which his supremacy always was recognized. Among the distinct phases of our grandest English measure that have been observed in literature, Bryant's may be classed with the Reflective, of which Wordsworth, succeeding the didacticians, held unquestioned control; but from the outset it was marked by a quality plainly his own. The essence of its cadence, pauses, rhythm, should be termed American, and it is the best ever written in the New World. . . . In this measure Bryant was at his height, and he owes to it the most enduring portion of his fame. However narrow his range, we must own that he was first in the first. He reached the upper air at once in **"Thanatopsis,"** and again and again, though none too frequently, he renewed his flights, and, like his own waterfowl, pursued his "solitary way."

The finest and most sustained of his poems of nature are those written in blank-verse. At intervals so rare throughout his life as to resemble the seven-year harvests, or the occasional wave that overtops the rest, he composed a series of those pieces which now form a unique panorama of nature's aspects, moving to the music of lofty thoughts and melodious words. Such are **"A Winter Piece,"** the **"Inscription for the Entrance to a Wood,"** **"A Forest Hymn,"** **"Summer Wind,"** **"The Prairies,"** **"The Fountain,"** **"A Hymn of the Sea,"** **"A Rain-Dream"**; also a few written late in life, showing that the eye of the author of **"Thanatopsis"** had not been dimmed, nor was his natural force abated: these are **"The Constellations,"** **"The River, by Night,"** and **"Among the Trees."** In all the treatment is large and ennobling, and distinctly marks each as Bryant's. The method, that of invocation, somewhat resembles the manner of Coleridge's Hymn in the Vale of Chamouni. When in a less enraptured strain, they exhibit repose, feeling, wise and reverent thought.

In the same eloquent verse, and with like caesural pauses and inflections, we find his more purely meditative poems, upon an equal or still higher plane of feeling,—**"Thanatopsis,"** the **"Hymn to Death,"** **"Earth,"** **"An Evening Revery,"** **"The Antiquity of Freedom,"** and one of his latest and longest, **"The Flood of Years."** Yet, in both his reflective verse and that devoted to nature, he often employed lyrical measures with equal excellence; as in the breezy, exquisite poem on **"Life,"** **"The Battle Field,"** **"The Future Life,"** and **"The Conqueror's Grave,"**—the latter one of his most elevating pieces. Especially in his lyrics he seemed like a wind-harp yielding tender music in response to every suggestion of the great Mother whom he loved. Such poems as **"June,"** **"The Death of the Flowers,"** and **"The Evening Wind"** show this, and also indicate the limits within which his song was spontaneous. (pp. 79-81)

At last, then, we are brought to a recognition of the power in Bryant's verse which has given him a station above that which he could hope to win by its amount or range. It is the *elemental quality* of his song. Like the bards of old, his spirit delights in fire, air, earth, and water,—the apparent structures of the starry heavens, the mountain recesses, and the vasty deep. These he apostrophizes, but over them and within them he discerns and bows the knee to the omniscience of a protecting Father, a creative God. Poets, eminent in this wise, have been gifted always with *imagination*. The verse of Bryant often is full of high imaginings. . . . [Our] rising men must acknowledge Bryant as a laurelled master of the early American School. He seldom touched the keys, yet they gave out an organ tone.

Indeed, when he essayed piano-music, and was in a light or fanciful mood, he was unable to vie with sprightlier and defter hands. His lyrics, in swift and simple measures, had a ringing quality, noticeable in the **"Song of Marion's Men,"** the best of them, and in **"The Hunter of the Prairies."** A pleasant surprise awaits us in certain later pieces, such as **"The Planting of the Apple-Tree,"** the delicate **"Snow-Shower,"** and **"Robert of Lincoln,"**—so full of bird-music and fancy. Usually it was with an air of uncouthness and doubt that he ventured beyond established precedents, as if he were in strange waters and would gladly touch firm land; but then, he seldom ventured. As he grew older, beyond the asperities of life, he became less brooding, sad, and grave. His Fancy, what there was of it, came in his later years, and suggested two of his longest pieces, **"Sella"** and **"The Little People of the Snow,"** tales of folk-lore, in which his lighter and more graceful handling of blank-verse may be studied without fatigue. (pp. 81-3)

There was something in [Bryant] which his admirers called Homeric; and there were these traits, at least, common to the genius of the epics and that of their translator,—a primitive way of regarding things, a stately utterance, a vision clear and suited to the theme. The best characteristics of Bryant's *The Iliad* and *The Odyssey* are: (1), general, though not invariable, fidelity to the text, as compared with former versions by poets of equal rank; (2), simplicity of phrase and style; (3), approximate transfusion of the heroic spirit; (4), a purity of language that pleases a sensible reader. . . . His choice of words is meagre, and so—in a modern sense—was that of Homer; there is no lack of minstrels, nowadays, who ransack their vocabularies to fill our jaded ears with "words, words, words." As a presentment of standard English the value of these translations is beyond serious cavil. When they are compared with the most faithful and poetic blank-verse rendering which preceded them, the work of Cowper, they show an advance in both accuracy and poetic quality. Lord Derby's contemporaneous version is dull and inferior. Bryant naturally handled to best advantage his descriptive passages,—the verses in the Fifth Odyssey, which narrate the visit of Hermes to Calypso, furnishing a case in point. His rendering of these is more literal than the favorite transcript by Leigh Hunt, and excels all others in ease and choice of language. . . . His paraphrases of the Greek idioms are noticeable for English idiomatic purity, so much so that the idea of a translation frequently absents itself from the reader's mind. While in one respect this is the perfection of such work, in another it is the loss of that charm pertaining to the sense of all rare things which are foreign to our own mode and period. His restraint, also, is carried to the verge of sterility by the repetition of certain adjectives as the equivalents of Greek words varying among themselves. The words "glorious" and "sagacious," for example, not uncommon in this translation, do not always represent the same, or even synonymous, expressions in the original text. But some of his epithets and renderings . . . give a more elevated and poetical tone to the work. (pp. 83-6)

[Bryant's] swelling poem, **"The Death of Slavery,"** was not needed to assure us that the cause of freedom touched his heart. For, secondly, his true counterpart to Whittier's work was to be found in the vigorous antislavery assaults he made for years

in the journal [*New York Evening Post*] of which he died the editor. (p. 92)

His prose labors were an outlet, constantly afforded in his journalism, through which much of that energy escaped which otherwise would have varied the motives and increased the body of his song. On the whole, though he was without a philologist's equipment, there were few better writers of simple, nervous English. He made it for half a century the instrument of his every-day thought and purpose; as a leader-writer, a traveller and correspondent, an essayist and orator, a political disputant. His polemic vigor and acerbity were worked off in his middle-life editorials, and in defence of what he thought to be right. There he was, indeed, unyielding, and other pens recall the traditions of his political controversies. He never confused the distinct provinces of prose and verse. Refer to anything written by him, of the former kind, and you find plainness, well-constructed syntax, free from any cheap gloss of rhetoric or the "jingle of an effeminate rhythm." (p. 93)

> *Edmund Clarence Stedman, "William Cullen Bryant," in his* Poets of America, *Houghton Mifflin Company, 1885, pp. 62-94.*

WILLIAM ROSCOE THAYER (essay date 1894)

Bryant's typical and best work is comprised in a dozen poems, the longest not exceeding 140 lines. Read **"Thanatopsis,"** **"The Yellow Violet,"** **"Inscription for the Entrance to a Wood,"** **"To a Waterfowl,"** **"Green River,"** **"A Winter Piece,"** **"The Rivulet,"** **"A Forest Hymn,"** **"The Past,"** **"To a Fringed Gentian,"** **"The Death of the Flowers,"** and **"The Battlefield,"** and you have Bryant's message; the rest of his work either echoes the notes already sounded in these, or represents uncharacteristic, and therefore transitory, moods. (p. 324)

Bryant is one of the few poets of genuine power whose poetic career shows no advance. The first arrow he drew from his quiver was the best, and with it he made his longest shot; many others he sent in the same direction, but they all fell behind the first. This accounts for the singleness and depth of the impression he has left; he stands for two or three elementals, and thereby keeps his force unscattered. He was not, indeed, wholly insensible to the romanticist stirrings of his time, as such effusions as **"The Damsel of Peru," "The Arctic Lover,"** and **"The Hunter's Serenade,"** bear witness. He wrote several pieces about Indians,—not the real red men, but those imaginary noble savages, possessors of all the primitive virtues, with whom our grandfathers peopled the American forests. He wrote strenuously in behalf of Greek emancipation and against slavery; but even here, though the subject lay very near his heart, he could not match the righteous vehemence of Whittier, or Lowell's alternate volleys of sarcasm and rebuke. Like Antaeus, Bryant ceased to be powerful when he did not tread his native earth. (p. 327)

> *William Roscoe Thayer, "Bryant," in* The American Review of Reviews, *Vol. X, No. 4, October, 1894 (and reprinted in his* Throne-Makers, *Houghton Mifflin Company, 1899, pp. 309-29).*

JOHN VANCE CHENEY (essay date 1895)

With Bryant, as with Whittier, poetry is not the vocation; if Whittier gave his best years to the liberation of the slave, Bryant gave his—a half-hundred of them—to the general guidance and advancement of his countrymen. Always a moralist, he is at times a poet. Meditation on the great theme of life and death in the calm presence of Nature,—this was Bryant's rest from the toil of a long and busy life. (p. 132)

It is a current notion that Bryant, rearing his altar in the woods and fields, is the high priest of Nature. Nature is the altar; but the goddess is morals. Bryant is skilful in depicting the place of his solemn ceremony, he is second to none of our poets as a "Nature painter." A painter, however, is not a priest. Painter of Nature, priest of morals, Bryant uses his skill as an artist to frame the features, to enforce the message, of the lofty goddess,—Duty. (pp. 133-34)

While Bryant is, perhaps, our most correct "Nature painter," the treatment of Nature is external compared with the treatment of his own remote, lofty soul. He stands at the altar, stately and calm, compelling the elements to bend to his one high mood,—the mood of him that would rise to the Author of all things, and stand, unspotted, before him.

Wordsworth received from Nature, Bryant gave to her; Bryant masters, Wordsworth is mastered. Here is the key to Bryant's limitation; and here may we begin to account for his slight production in point of quantity. The rare purity and nobility of spirit being once cast in language noble and pure as the spirit itself, the task was ended. Material so precious is soon exhausted. (pp. 134-35)

Bryant's reliance was not on the poet's rock of strength, inspiration, but on a substitute for it,—as good a one as may be,—meditation. Nor is this all; the meditation, though in a high, broad field, is in that one field and that only. Even the Nature wherein he sets up his altar is of the one realm, the upper realm of quiet and peace, the region of "supreme repose":—

> Be it ours to meditate,
> In these calm shades, thy milder majesty,
> And to the beautiful order of thy works
> Learn to conform the order of our lives.

So strong is the tendency toward tranquillity that the burden of the song is less the life than the fate of the race. Bryant is the laureate of gentle, restful death. Plainly as this is shown in the "Hymn to Death," it is as plain in "Thanatopsis," "A Forest Hymn," "The Prairies;" in nearly all the poems, long and short; it is the theme of the perfect lyric, embodying the loveliest and most familiar lines [that Bryant wrote]. (pp. 135-36)

> John Vance Cheney, "William Cullen Bryant," in his That Dome in Air: Thoughts on Poetry and the Poets, A. C. McClurg and Company, 1895, pp. 127-43.

HENRY D. SEDGWICK, JR.   (essay date 1897)

[Sedgwick echoes Edmund Clarence Stedman's comment (see excerpt above, 1885) that Bryant lacked "modernity" in viewing nature without an eye for science. Bryant's early verses, Sedgwick states, "show a lack of art," as well as too little passion and flexibility; he terms Bryant's prose "baldly simple." Sedgwick sums up by saying that "Bryant's chief attractiveness is in his modesty."]

This intimate interdependence of poet and people is very obvious in our best known group of poets. Bryant, Longfellow, Whittier, Lowell, and in their several ways Poe and Whitman, utter the common human feelings that enter the hearts of common men. This is particularly true of Bryant. He says what a large body of people feel, understand, and hold in sympathy. This trait in his poetry is the result of his character, which is essentially American. If we take as the two ideal types of our American character George Washington and Abraham Lincoln, we are struck by a change from the repose and self-control of Washington to the emotion and self-control of Lincoln. This difference between the two serves fairly to illustrate the tendency of our American type. Bryant is an excellent specimen of the earlier. He was calm, intelligent, self-respecting, abounding in common sense, contemplative, gentle, peaceful, almost austere. He was like the country in which he was born. Hampshire County, Massachusetts, his birthplace, is in sight of the Berkshire Hills. If Bryant's verses were to be turned into meadow, hill, dale, and river, we should have almost the counterpart of western Massachusetts. It is somewhat significant that his two best poems, "Thanatopsis" and the lines "To a Waterfowl," were written there, in his early youth, before he had had experience of the greater emotions and incidents of life. It is on them that his fame chiefly rests, and it is they that best indicate the characteristics of his talents. Early in his long life they gave him public distinction, and at its close they still were his best titles to honor. (pp. 539-40)

"Thanatopsis" is a very extraordinary feat for a boy of eighteen years. Its language shows honest familiarity with the English Bible. Its thoughts are elevated, its manner is quiet and restrained. Dignity and ease, sensibility and self-command, stand out conspicuous. But can we read a chapter from the book of Job, and then turn to it and not be aware of a falling off? Can we set "Thanatopsis" beside Gray's "Elegy in a Country Churchyard," and not miss Gray's wider thoughtfulness, deeper tenderness, and surpassing art? Can we match it with [William Wordsworth's] "Lines composed near Tintern Abbey?" No, most assuredly. "Thanatopsis" does not rank with these great poems, but it is a noble poem, and disappointing only in this, that it gives promise of a greater excellence, which Bryant never attained. (p. 540)

Bryant's verses, except at their best, show a lack of art. They are a little undisciplined; they betray truancy to the classics. . . . Bryant holds so high his independence that he will not submit enough to discipline, and therefore he says, "The sun was near his set;" he speaks of "sylvan lakelet," and then before that has dribbled out of our memory "wavelets" come splashing along. There may be high authority for these expressions, but they were not meet for Bryant's purposes. This incivility to English that appears in Bryant, seldom, yet too often, is due partly to his willful independence, partly to his lack of training, and also in a measure to his lack of sensitiveness. A man keenly alive to delicate impressions, to "shadows and sunny glimmerings," will do one of two things: either he will try and try again until he shall succeed in making his readers partakers of his sensations, or he will forbear; he will not put up with inadequate expression. (p. 541)

Bryant only makes us see what he sees,—beautiful inanimate nature, fruitful in suggestion, quick to catch the color of our imaginings, ready to reflect our moods, but at most only tinged with us and painted with our thoughts. Certainly we need to be reminded that beauty lies about us. . . . Yet this is work of a less degree of excellence than that of drawing aside the veil from the temple of God.

Bryant shows us many, but not all the aspects of nature. His love of nature is simpler than nature. He enjoys her calm, he finds repose in her inaction; he does not enter into all her joyousness, her delicate growths, her childlike activities. . . . Bryant falls into seriousness as soon as he is in a wood. So, too, nature's sorrowful fadings and fallings pass him by unheeded except as he draws a sorrowful inference for man.

We cannot but feel the great difference between Bryant's poems on nature and those of Wordsworth. In most of Wordsworth's familiar poems we find this sensitive recognition of nature "through the veil that seems to hide" her,—nature, as we would fain believe her, our young virgin mother, a Primavera singing out of the very dust from which our bodies are wrought. In Bryant we find nature is but an echo of himself. High, serene, calm, and sometimes beautiful, she rises like an eidolon of Bryant. Through Wordsworth we learn love and reverence for nature; he teaches us that she will suffer us like little children to come unto her, and we find rest, refreshment, and delight. (pp. 541-42)

In Bryant nature is a patch on a New England hillside. There is much beauty, much tenderness, much room for virtuous reverie and noble thought, but nature for him does not vary with its changing seasons. It is October, sunshine or shade, all the year; there is but one music in the pines, but one rustle in the fallen leaves; the grasses speak in monotone. Sometimes, it is true, Bryant is half conscious of a girlish spirit in nature, as if she were dodging round his subject, too quick to catch. He attempts to lay hold of her, and writes **"Sella"** and **"Little Children of the Snow."** But nature, the wood nymph, is denied to him. . . . (p. 542)

Although Bryant does not reveal to us the holy spirit of nature as Wordsworth does, or nature the forest nymph as Theocritus does, or even portray all her outward aspects, he does show the most important significance of nature for us. . . . The difficulties of belief cannot be overcome without the help of beauty, which bare laws of cause and effect, probable rules for escaping evils, cannot of their own nature put on. We need poets to make that moral law beautiful in our eyes, to "endue it with heavenly gifts," to cover it with "thoughts beyond the reaches of our souls" or with an authority that we will not question. . . . Bryant, in narrow limits, perhaps, and with uneven powers, has done this for us. Men with need of metaphysical and subtle reasonings, and men too much in the glare of common sense, may not feel the value of his work, but . . . [ordinary people] will feel that Bryant has added a touch of poetry to that moral law, has helped to show more clearly a loveliness which our hearts accept as inherent in it. . . . **"The Forest Hymn," "The Planting of the Apple Tree," "The Death of the Flowers," "O Fairest of the Rural Maids," "Green River,"** and a number of other poems, incompletely perhaps, and with various degrees of excellence, bear witness to this great service which he has thus rendered to us. (pp. 542-43)

Bryant is didactic; he dwells upon the pleasure and innocence in nature, in contemplation, in the colors of flowers and the noise of falling waters. . . . It is well to encourage and develop such a habit and such a disposition. But contemplation is too narrow a school in which to study ethics. In this generation, when the metaphysical aspects of religion have a less firm foundation in the minds of men, morality is sought, not in communion with Deity, but in coming closer to humanity, and in a world of such beliefs the poet must reckon with them.

We do not find among Bryant's poems any which stir our sympathies with passion or with joy. After reading every poem he has written, the reader is not richer in any fresh knowledge of mankind. He has learned no more of yearning, of despair,

of all the doubts and perplexities that hedge us in. (pp. 544-45)

The limitations encompassing Bryant's powers appear as soon as he departs from the narrow path of reverie in the meadows. Take **"The Ages"** as an example. . . . When the poet reaches the year of his poem, 1821, he alludes to the United States and to Europe in these lines:—

> Here the free spirit of mankind at length
> Throws its last fetters off; and who shall place
> A limit to the giant's unchained strength,
> Or curb his swiftness in the forward race?
>
> .   .   .   .   .   .
>
> Europe is given a prey to sterner fates,
> And writhes in shackles.

This is commonplace. It is poor in form, and narrow-minded in substance. (pp. 545-46)

The mechanical work of Bryant's poetry is generally well done: the rhymes rhyme, the rhythm moves along, the blank verse does not halt. His language is good, yet it is not flexible enough for lyrical poetry. Perhaps it is not fanciful to trace the influence of Pope, which fell upon him in boyhood, in much of his work all through life. A correct, monotonous metre shows in many passages, where his inspiration is scant of breath. Bryant, however, rarely tries to do what he cannot do fairly well. His fine self-sobriety taught him what to eschew. Sometimes his form is his misfortune, in that it recalls Campbell or Moore; for a marked metre, of course, calls to memory the best poems in that metre, and the comparison suggested is not always fair. His blank verse is very good; not majestic, but simple and severe. It fails to impress us as the handiwork of a man who is confident in perfect mastery. There is none of the flush of victory that shows in Milton's verse. . . . Bryant's blank verse is at its best in **"Thanatopsis."** In his translation of Homer it struggles to produce the effect of the Greek hexameters, and it rejects this alien duty. In **"Sella"** it sometimes reads too much like prose, wherein the words are shifted out of deference to the beat of the verse. Simplicity is the most serviceable slave, but the worst master, and Bryant occasionally felt the weight of its yoke. His sonnets are very poor sonnets, feeble imitations of Wordsworth. Bryant is said to have had correct knowledge of metre, but he had not sufficient flexibility and delicacy, not enough effeminacy of taste, we might say, to use that knowledge well and successfully.

Bryant's prose consists of his editorials in the *New York Evening Post*, of various letters gathered into two volumes, entitled *Letters of a Traveller*, and of sundry discourses and orations. His style is simple, direct, and clear. It is almost too baldly simple. It has the shrewd simplicity of the prose of a Yankee storekeeper. It discloses a mind with almost childlike curiosity, which picks up the things immediately in front of it, and then, those dropped, reaches towards one new object after another. Some men are born to write of travels; they establish a human relation with bridges, towers, cornpatches, chance passengers in the omnibus, and they can give on paper an interesting account of these intimacies. . . . Bryant tells us facts, conscientiously and intelligently. He has one great merit: he tells what he sees, he describes it as it appears to his mind. There is no mixture of the opinions of art critics and amateurs; there is the blunt delineation of the prospect as it was reflected on the retinas of Bryant's eyes. . . . Bryant's chief attractiveness is in his modesty. It always is by him. He omits all gossip of famous men from his letters, he leaves out all special courtesies shown to him. This modesty is not tinged with affectation, but it is a union of native self-respect and early training. (pp. 546-47)

Henry D. Sedgwick, Jr., ''Bryant's Permanent Contribution to Literature'' (copyright © 1897 by Henry D. Sedgwick, Jr.; reprinted with permission), in The Atlantic Monthly, Vol. LXXIX, No. CCCCLXXIV, April, 1897, pp. 539-49.

CHARLES LEONARD MOORE (essay date 1905)

Without meaning anything but praise, it may be said of Bryant's poems in general that Wordsworth forgot to write them. A few of them rise to the height of Wordsworth's best, and they never sink to the level of his worst. But of course in mass, in range, in fire, the English poet is immeasurably beyond his American double or pupil. There is a difference, too, in their view of Nature and outlook on man's destiny. Wordsworth is the poet of immortality—of resurrection; the Nature he loved was ablaze with Spirit. Bryant's Nature is the Nature of the chemists and geologists and geographers. He lacked metaphysics. (p. 223)

Bryant has in poetry the felicity which the Psalmist prayed for,—neither poverty nor riches. Yet his severe taste saved him from that inevitable instinct for the second-best which has ruined so much American verse. He always recalls the masters; and when it is not Wordsworth's star which is in the ascendant, it is that of Milton, or Gray, or Collins. He was perhaps the most careful student of verse we have had. But his music is too often a recollected air. His pictures,—achieving, as they frequently do, the virgin phrase, cool, dewy, and unravished of man,—lack yet the ecstacy of more daring souls. The sacred spark in him was a lambent phosphorescence, incapable of communicating heat or fire. (p. 224)

The largest division of Bryant's work is the group of blank-verse pieces, including 'Thanatopsis,' 'The Forest Hymn,' 'The Prairies,' 'Earth,' 'Hymn to Death,' 'The Flood of Years,' and a few others. As far as theme and matter are concerned, they are practically all one,—the same thoughts in varied settings. The earliest written of them sums up their whole message, and the world has accepted it as the greatest. In manner, however, they are equally good; and it is a manner which makes a small thing seem almost colossal. The blank-verse is studied from Wordsworth, who got his by inheritance through Cowper from Milton. Neither in Wordsworth nor in Bryant, however, is there anything which much resembles Milton's sidereal style. And the two later poets differ from each other. In Wordsworth's best blank-verse there is a sense of growth, a pulsating vitality, a pushing upward as of forest trees, each trying to be tallest. In Bryant's lines there is the faltering, soundless fall of Autumn leaves detaching themselves without wind. His verse, however, is a most fit instrument for the meditative mood. Inferior in passages to Wordsworth's similar work, it is superior in single lines, and has far fewer lapses into prose.

Bryant's poems which bear upon wild-life in America, aboriginal or that of the early settlers, such as 'The Disinterred Warrior,' 'The Hunter of the Prairies,' 'Catterskill Falls,' have all a stamp of deep and grave sincerity. They are miniatures, and require a magnifying-glass to bring out their merits. But even after Cooper's great canvasses, painted with a broad brush, these little vignettes repay study.

There are a good many of Bryant's minor pieces which have a sort of faded elegance, as if they were originally written for the old Books of Beauty—the Annuals of our early literature. They are not in the least vital,—they are purely manufactured; but their artifice is well done. A list of these would to too long to give, but in it would be 'The Song of the Greek Amazon,' 'Song of Pitcairn's Island,' 'The Damsel of Peru.' A poem like 'The Lapse of Time' is of a higher mood; yet it too is irritating: it is so near the commonplace, yet manages to evade actual prosaism. It reminds one of some of the slighter, prelusive strains of Collins, which have nothing in them but an ineffable grace—the classic air.

But I must come to the handful of lyrics which are Bryant's real title-deeds to fame signed and sealed by the Muse. Two little odes I would first mention, not for any special mark of thought or phrase which they possess, but because of their originality in metre. They are 'The Greek Partisan' and an 'Ode for a Celebration.' Most poets, when they try to bring a variety of rhythm into a short compass, merely change the length of their lines; but Bryant here changes the key of the music, as Gray did. These brief poems have in consequence a dancing movement which is most effective.

'The Siesta' is probably the nearest approach to a real song that Bryant ever wrote. Some other of his things which are labelled songs are as wooden as clothes-pegs, as cold as icicles. The 'Song of Marion's Men' is a martial lyric, and a fine one, though it comes far short of equalling the war-poems of Burns and Campbell, or even two more recent American patriotic strains, 'The Blue and the Gray,' and 'The Bivouac of the Dead.' Bryant's 'Greek Boy' is also a Tyrtarean poem, and has real rather than painted fire. It is of course reminiscent of Byron's 'Isles of Greece.'

In 'June' for almost the first time we find Bryant standing unpropped by any other poet. All the art he had learned from Gray and Collins and Wordsworth was in his mind when he wrote it, but for the nonce he forgot them and spoke straight from his soul. The diction of the piece is full of floating gold which concentrates into one or two ingot-like phrases. 'Oh, Fairest of the Rural Maids' is almost equally good, but here Bryant leans again on Wordsworth's shoulder, as he does in 'The Fringed Gentian.' 'Autumn Woods' is entirely original and absolutely flawless. Singularly enough, Bryant, usually so grave, not to say drab, in his coloring, here gives the gayest picture of American Autumn which exists in our literature. Mark the art or the unconscious truth with which he assembles all the bright aspects of the season,—the woods which have put their glory on, the colored landscape, the gay company of trees, the painted leaves, the sun's quiet smile, the absence of gloom where many branches meet, the stream that shines with the image of its golden screen, the roseate canopy where a maiden's blush would be unmarked! The word 'colored' is repeated three times, probably with intention. Altogether it is the most perfect piece of objective work which Bryant ever achieved, and needs only a touch of magical imagination to place it fairly by the side of Keats's best. Hardly less admirable is 'The Death of the Flowers,' a little elegy whose sweet and gentle perfection make of it a sister-song to Collins's 'Fidele,' and even render it worthy to stand, at some remove, in the presence of the Death Song in [William Shakespeare's] 'Cymbeline.' The simple fitness of the epithets throughout the piece is Greek; and the exquisitely modulated metre is perhaps the most lyrical movement in all Bryant's verse.

There remain Bryant's three crowning poems—'To the Past,' 'Lines to a Waterfowl,' and 'The Battlefield.' The first has an air of antique greatness. Its bareness is impressive as of a Spanish Hidalgo presiding at his empty board with an inestimable jewel or two, heirlooms spared by Fate, glittering on his fingers. The piece contains what is probably Bryant's finest line,—

> And features, the great soul's apparent seat,

although

> Old ocean's gray and melancholy waste,

from '**Thanatopsis**,' and

> The desert and illimitable air,

of the '**Lines to a Waterfowl**,' are near rivals. The last-named poem is the quintessence of Bryant's genius. Neither in motive nor manner does it recall any other poet, and there is none throughout time who would not be proud to own it. Yet I think '**The Battlefield**' is his final and supreme triumph. Beauty and splendor of picture are here, and a grandeur of utterance which might have been thundered from Sinai.

What is Bryant's rank among our American singers? Poe is greatest in prose, his verse being merely the gold fringe on his prose suit of sables; yet even in poetry he keeps his precedence. . . . In weight and felicity of single phrase, however, he is certainly not equal to either Bryant or Emerson; and by virtue of this felicity, allied to a considerable gift of design, Bryant, I should say, must rank second. (pp. 224-25)

> *Charles Leonard Moore, "Our Pioneer American Poet," in* The Dial, *Vol. XXXVIII, No. 451, April 1, 1905, pp. 223-26.**

WILLIAM ASPENWALL BRADLEY   (essay date 1905)

Bryant's poetry is national poetry because it deals with what is national and local in a way that is natural and universal. It is primarily nature poetry and therefore limited in scope, for physical environment is but one element among the many that act upon the life of a race. Even as nature poetry it has its limitation, in that its treatment of nature is almost exclusively descriptive and reflective, and does not therefore take account of all the ways in which this physical environment is felt and reacted upon. But although the representation of the national spirit is limited in Bryant's poetry, it is no less genuine and profound. It bears witness to the awaking of an eager and intense delight in the very face of the country, that for a new generation of Americans, born after the storm and stress of the Revolutionary period, was no longer regarded merely as the land they happened to inhabit, but as the nation's precious inheritance from nature. (p. 118)

[Bryant's] moral seriousness might amount to nothing more than mere didacticism if it were not so sweetly and naturally expressive of a genuinely poetic spirit. As it is, Bryant's moralizing bears little relation to the didacticism of certain phases of eighteenth-century English poetry or of Wordsworth. It does not rise from any conscious consideration of the proper method of art to elevate and exalt the soul. It is not an artistic prepossession. It is a spiritual trait inherited from ancestors wholly preoccupied with the problem of good and evil in the practical sphere, and it breathes as gently and easily through his verse as the evening wind or the sound of the rustling of the leaves of his great forests. Like his close and accurate observation of nature, it is raised to poetry by the profound imaginativeness of its expression. (pp. 123-24)

[Bryant's diction] is simple at times almost to the point of baldness; but most often its simplicity is felt rather as a support to the elevation and austerity of the mood in which he wrote. Even his occasional baldness has in it something that consorts well with the note of elemental grandeur which enters into his descriptions, and which was called for by the rugged character of his favourite landscape. While his vocabulary is limited, its limitation arises less from poverty than from a rigid selective sense which sought precision and accuracy rather than mere opulence of verbal expression. From this careful attention to the choice of words, as well as in his reliance on simple metrical forms, it is easy to see the influence of those standards of eighteenth-century taste on which his own style was founded. Yet this influence is felt rather in the purity of his diction than in any marked traces of conventionality. There is a certain stiffness at times and an employment of words and phrases that have passed out of modern poetical usage. But for the most part his vehicle is the natural idiom of the English tongue that was restored to poetry by Cowper and Wordsworth. As a result there is in his best poetry a preponderance of the Anglo-Saxon over the Latin elements of our language; and this is one of the sources of his vitality, one of the things that give his descriptions a vividness and his moral reflections a pithiness of expression, as in the line that has passed into common currency,

> Truth crushed to earth will rise again,

that are among their most striking characteristics. For, while Bryant's expression is luminously transparent, it is not colourless. The very precision with which he chooses his words, especially descriptive words of form, colour, and motion, and limits them to those that best render the desired effect, while it often detracts from the musical flow of his numbers, heightens the painter-like quality which makes a constant appeal through the eye. Indeed, the definiteness and vividness of Bryant's descriptions often result in a very close approximation to the peculiar effect of pictorial art. It is as if he were handling lines and colours, and not the mere symbols of these things, with the added advantage of being able to suggest that perpetual motion of wind-blown grass and moving shadows that must forever remain suspended in any vision of nature as rendered by the painter. Finally, Bryant has a high imaginative instinct in the selection and use of words as in themselves objects having intrinsic value apart from all ideas and associations. Alliteration may be either a great vice or a great virtue. With Bryant, since he employs it not as an ill-considered rhetorical ornamentation, but as a reënforcement of the general effect, it is most often the latter. It completes the circuit, as it were, and helps to vitalize the expression into something complete and organic. (pp. 128-29)

[Bryant] does not make his appeal to any very wide range of human sympathies, or solicit lively personal interest in himself through the extreme moods of romantic self-expression. His poetry is in the best sense of the word impersonal; it is an embodiment of that element of beauty which hovers between earth and the sky and fills the sensitive soul with a kind of spiritual ardour akin to worship. (p. 130)

> *William Aspenwall Bradley, in his* William Cullen Bryant *(copyright, 1905, by The Macmillan Company), Macmillan, 1905, 229 p.*

WILLIAM ELLERY LEONARD   (essay date 1917)

[*Leonard addresses earlier critics' attacks on Bryant by stating that "it is ungracious, as well as superficial, to quarrel with*

[*Bryant's limitations*].'' *The repetition and clarity of the "same few ideas, emotions, modes, methods," make Bryant's work harmonious, Leonard points out. Like Charles Leonard Moore (1905), Leonard ranks Bryant behind Ralph Waldo Emerson and Walt Whitman and finds him "not pre-eminently endowed with intellectual intensity and imaginative concentration."*]

Bryant's poems stress perpetually a certain few ideas, grow perpetually out of a certain few emotional responses, and report in a few noble imaginative modes a certain few aspects of man and nature, with ever recurring habits of observation, architectonics, and style. This absence of complexity is, again, emphasized by the elemental clarity and simplicity of those same few ideas, emotions, modes, methods. Within his range he is complete, harmonious, and, in a deeper sense than above, impressively one. It is for this, perhaps, that of all American poets he makes the strongest impression of an organic style, as contrasted with an individual . . . literary style, consciously elaborated, as in Poe and Whitman. It is partly for this, perhaps, that the most Puritan of our poets is also the most Greek. Bryant's limitations, then, are intimately engaged in the peculiar distinction of his work; and it is ungracious, as well as superficial, to quarrel with them.

Bryant's ideas, stated in bald prose, are elementary,—common property of simple minds. His metaphysics was predominantly that of the Old Testament: God is the Creator and His works and His purposes are good. Bryant communicated, however, little sense of the loving fatherhood and divine guidance in human affairs: perhaps once only, in *To a Waterfowl,* which originated in an intensely religious moment of young manhood. His ethics stress the austerer loyalties of justice and truth rather than those of faith, hope, and charity. His politics in his poems, however analytic and specific he might be as publicist, reiterate only the ideals of political freedom and progress, with ever confident reference to the high destinies of America, that "Mother of a Mighty Race." His assurance of individual immortality for all men, which scarcely touches the problem of sin, rests not on revelation, not on a philosophy of the transcendental significance of intellect, struggle, and pain but mainly on primitive man's desire to meet the loved and lost, the father, the sister, the wife. There is nothing subtle, complex, or tricky here; there are no philosophers, apparently, on his reading desk. . . . There is in these ideas, as ideas, nothing that a noble pagan, say of republican Rome, might not have held to, even before the advent of Stoic and Academician. But there is a further paganism in the emphasis on the phenomena of life as life, on death as death. Man's life, as individual and type, is what it is—birth and toil in time; and death is what it is, save when he mentions a private grief—for men and empires it is a passing away in a universe of time and change. The original version of *Thanatopsis* is more characteristic than its inconsistent introductory and concluding lines, now the oftenest quoted of all his writings. If Bryant was the Puritan in his austerity and morale, he was quite as much the Pagan in the universality of his ideas, and in his temperamental adjustment to brute fact.

On nature and man's relation to nature, one who reads without prepossession will find the American Wordsworth equally elemental. He raises his hymn in the groves, which were God's first temples,—venerable columns, these ranks of trees, reared by Him of old. And "the great miracle still goes on"; and even the "delicate forest flower" seems

> An emanation of the indwelling Life,
> A visible token of the upholding Love,
> That are the soul of this great universe.

But more frequently nature is herself enough, in the simple thought that personifies and capitalizes: it is She herself that speaks to man, in his different hours, a various language. But it is only casually, as in *Among the Trees,* that he wonders if the vegetable world may not have some

> dim and faint
> . . . sense of pleasure and of pain,
> As in our dreams;

only casually, for conscious mysticism was foreign to Bryant's intellect, and the conception had yet to be scientifically investigated in the laboratories of the Hindoo botanist Bose. Here nature, as herself the Life, is simply an hypostasis of the racial imagination in which Bryant so largely shared, just like his intimate personifications of her phenomena, her flowers, her winds, and waters; it is not a philosophic idea, but a primitive instinct. "Nature's teachings" for men are simply the ideas that suggest themselves to Bryant himself (not inevitably to everyone) when he observes what goes on, or what is before him:

> The faintest streak that on a petal lies,
> May speak instruction to initiate eyes.

But this apparently Wordsworthian couplet can be related in no system of thought or Wordsworthian instruction. These ideas are sometimes merely analogies, where in effect the flower (be it the gentian), or the bird (be it the waterfowl), is the firm term in a simile on man's moral life; in this phase Bryant's thought of nature differs from that of Homer, the Psalmist Jesus, or any sage or seer, Pagan or Christian, only in the appositeness, more or less, of the illustrative symbol. It implies no more a philosophy of nature than similes drawn from the action of a locomotive or a motor-boat would imply a philosophy of machinery. As a fact, Bryant's one abiding idea about nature is that she is a profound influence on the human spirit, chastening, soothing, encouraging, ennobling—how, he does not say; but the fact he knows from experience, and mankind knows it with him, and has known it from long before the morning when the sorrowful, chafed soul of Achilles walked apart by the shore of the many-sounding sea. (pp. 265-68)

[Bryant's] primary feelings were equally deep: awe in the presence of the cosmic process and the movements of mankind, reverence for holiness, pity for suffering, brooding resentment against injustice, rejoicing in moral victory, patriotism, susceptibility to beauty of outline and colour and sound, with peculiar susceptibility to both charm and sublimity in natural phenomena. These emotions, in Bryant, ring out through his poetry, clear, without blur or fringe, like the Italian vowels. He had no emotional crotchets, no erratic sensibilities. . . . (p. 269)

Bryant's imagination has its characteristic modes of relating its objects. Three or four huge and impressive metaphors underlie a great part of his poetry: the past as a place, an underworld, dim and tremendous, most poignantly illustrated in the poem *The Past* with its personal allusions, and most sublimely in *The Death of Slavery,* a great political hymn, with Lowell's *Commemoration Ode,* and Whitman's *When Lilacs Last in the Dooryard Bloomed,* the highest poetry of solemn grandeur produced by the Civil War; death as a mysterious passageway, whether through gate or cloud, with the hosts ever entering and disappearing in the Beyond; mankind conceived as one vast company, a troop, a clan; and, as suggested above, nature as a multitudinous Life.

Bryant wonderfully visualized and unified the vast scope of the racial movement and the range of natural phenomena. His "broad surveys," as they have been called, are more than surveys: they are large acts of the combining imagination, presenting the significance, not merely the catalogue. These acts take us home to the most inveterate habit of his poet-mind. As method or device they seem to suggest a simple prescription for writing poetry; superficially, after one has met them again and yet again in Bryant, one might call them easy to do, because easy to understand. The task is, however, not to make a list, but to make the right list; a list not by capricious association of ideas, but by the laws of inner harmony of meaning. Again, in Bryant the list is itself often a fine, far look beyond the immediate fact—the immediate fact with which all but the poet would rest content. . . . Often the "survey"—the word is convenient—starts from some on-moving phenomenon in nature—again an immediate fact—and proceeds by compassing that phenomenon's whence or whither, what it has experienced or what it will do: let one re-read his tale of *The River,* by what haunts it flows (like, but how unlike, Tennyson's brook); *The Unknown Way,* the spots it passes (becoming a path symbolic of the mystery of life); *The Sea,* what it does under God (like and unlike Byron's apostrophe); *The Winds,* what they do on sea and land; *A Rain-Dream,* imaging the waters of the globe. Sometimes the phenomenon is static and calls his imagination to penetrate its secret history, or what changes it has seen about it, as when he looks at the fountain or is among the trees. Sometimes the vision rides upon or stands beside no force in Nature, but is his own direct report, as in *Fifty Years,* on the changes in individual lives, in history, in inventions, especially in these States, since his class graduated at Williams. "Broad surveys" of human affairs and of the face of earth, so dull, routine, bombastic as far as attempted in Thomson's *Liberty,* in Blair's *Grave,* in White's *Time,* become in Bryant's less pretentious poems the essential triumph of a unique imagination. The mode remained a favourite to the end: large as in *The Flood of Years,* intimate and tender in *A Lifetime.* No American poet, except Whitman, had an imagination at all like Bryant's, or, indeed, except Whitman and Emerson, as great as Bryant's. (pp. 270-71)

[In his Homeric translations, Bryant wanted] to see if he might not, by closeness to the original and simplicity of straightforward modern English, supersede the looseness and artificial Miltonic pomp of Cowper. His translation, by detailed comparison line for line with the Greek and with the English poet, will be found to be exactly what Bryant intended it. By block comparison of book for book, or version for version, it will be found to be the better translation, from the point of view of limpid and consequent story-telling—perhaps the best in English verse. (p. 273)

[Bryant's] qualities of thought, feeling, imagination, were communicated, were indeed only communicable, because [they were] so wrought into his diction, his rhymes, cadences, and stanzas. Indeed, there is no separating a poet's feeling, say, for a beautiful flower from his manner of expressing it—for all we know about his feeling for the flower is what he succeeds in communicating by speech. It is tautology to say that a poet treats a sublime idea sublimely—for it is the sublimity in the treatment that makes us realize the sublimity of the idea. We can at most conceive a poet's "style" as a whole; as, along with his individual world of meditation and vision another phase of his creative power—as his creation of music. Possibly it is the deepest and most wonderful of the poet's creations, transcending its manifestation in connection with any single

poem. . . . Certainly this is the more true the more organic the style is; and, as said before, Bryant's style was highly organic. (p. 274)

Bryant's diction was severe, simple, chaste, narrower in range than that of his political prose; . . . his rhymes were dignified, sonorous, exact and emphatic rather than subtle or allusive, and narrow in range—not from artistic poverty but because the rhymed vocabulary of the simple and serious moods is in English itself narrow, and much novelty and variety of rhyme is in our speech possible only when, like Browning, one portrays the grotesque and the eccentric, or like Shelley the fantastic, or like Butler the comic, or like Chaucer the familiar. Such a mind would deduce Bryant's most fundamental rhythm, the iambic; his most fundamental metre, the pentameter; together with his preference for stanzaic, or periodic, treatment, whether in blank verse or in rhyme, rather than for couplets; yet, together with the most characteristic cadences,—like the curve of a distant mountain range, few and clear but not monotonous like the waves of a broad river, slow and long but not hesitant or ponderous, never delighting by subtle surprises, nor jarring by abrupt stops and shifts. Indeed . . . the very pitch of his voice in verse—strongest in the lower octaves—as well as the intrinsic alliteration,—an alliteration as natural as breathing, in its context unobtrusive as such to the conscious ear because so involved in a diction which is itself the outgrowth of very mood and meaning? In quite different ways, Bryant is, with Poe, America's finest artist in verse. Perhaps this is, with Bryant's genuineness of manhood, a reason why Bryant was the one native contemporary that Poe thoroughly respected.

What to puzzled readers seems "characteristically Bryant's blank verse" is really the total impression of both materials and manner, manner itself including diction as well as metrics. But the metrics alone do have their peculiarities, which can, however, hardly be examined here: line endings like "and the green moss," caesuras at the end of the first and of the fourth foot, the tendency to repeat the same caesura and cadence through a succession of lines, a stanza group of five or more lines with full stop followed by a single line or so, inverted accent at the beginning of a line, and a differentiated, strong cadence at the conclusion of the whole poem which gives the effect of a completion, not of a mere stopping,—these are all contributing factors.

Yet Bryant is not one of the world's master-poets. It is not so much that he contributed little or nothing to philosophic thought or spiritual revolution, not altogether that his range was narrow, not that he never created a poem of vast and multitudinous proportions, drama, epic, or tale, not that he knew nature better than human life and human life better than human nature, not that he now and then lapsed from imaginative vision into a bit of sentiment or irrelevant fancy,—not either that there is not a single dark saying, or obscure word, construction, allusion, in all his verse, for the judicious to elucidate at a club or in a monograph. He is not one of the world's master-poets, because he was not pre-eminently endowed with intellectual intensity and imaginative concentration. The character of his whole mind was discursive, enumerative, tending, when measured by the masters, to the diffuse. Thus, among other results, his report of things has given man's current speech but few quotations, of either epigrammatic criticism or haunting beauty. (pp. 274-76)

And if he was and is a true poet, he belongs to our best traditions also as critic. He was never, to be sure, the professional guide of literary taste, like Arnold and Lowell. Apart from sensible but obvious memorial addresses on Irving, Halleck, and Cooper, his best known essay is introductory to his *Library of Poetry and Song;* it enunciates fewer keen judgments on individuals, fewer profound principles, than does Emerson's introduction to his *Parnassus,* but it does enunciate the primacy of "a luminous style" and of themes central to common man, in noble paragraphs that should not be forgotten, certainly not by any one who believes that criticism gains in authority when it is the concentrated deduction of experience. (p. 276)

> William Ellery Leonard, "Bryant and the Minor Poets," in The Cambridge History of American Literature: Colonial and Revolutionary Literature, Early National Literature, Part I, Vol. I, edited by William Peterfield Trent & others (reprinted with permission of Macmillan Publishing Company; copyright 1917 by Macmillan Publishing Co., Inc.; renewed 1945 by Macmillan Publishing Co., Inc.), Macmillan, 1917 (and reprinted by Macmillan, 1933, pp. 260-83).*

NORMAN FOERSTER (essay date 1918)

William Cullen Bryant found in [American scenery] the material for poetry. He has the same large, free handling of nature, united with a regard for detail absent in the romancer [James Fenimore Cooper]; he has the same feeling for the magnificence of the scene, united with a more penetrating sympathy and more speculative power. No longer an impressive setting merely, nature is now conceived as a profoundly moving symbol of God, speaking, to the devout beholder, a various language. (p. 7)

Of the qualities of his poems of nature, most readers of Bryant, apparently following Stedman [see excerpt above, 1885], have emphasized the "elementary" aspect of his themes and of his mood—his interest in earth, air, and water, as distinguished from an interest in insect, bird, and tree; and although something is said of his accuracy in detail, one receives the impression that he tended to avoid detail on account of his preference for the universal. From **"Thanatopsis,"** his most popular poem, one might very well reach this conclusion, since in the entire poem he mentions only the oak—no other tree, and no bird or flower. But as a matter of fact, Bryant, if not often minutely descriptive, is quite as concrete as most American poets, and mentions more species of flowers and trees than any other American poet—more than Lowell or Whittier or even Whitman. Insects alone seemed of slight interest to him, or else he regarded them as alien to the dignity of poesy. Only the bee occurs with any frequency, and even in this case one suspects that the alliterative association with "brooks" and "birds" and "blossoms" had something to do with the matter. Of mammals he introduced into his verse, like Whitman, an assortment that would suffice for a zoölogical garden. The deer, the squirrel, the wolf, or the panther graces almost every page; the deer, indeed, if one may judge by the number of poems in which it appears, was to him a symbol of the great forests that had kindled his youthful imagination. Birds, whose music rather than beauty of color attracted him, he used in his verse more often than any other American poet save Whitman—in all, some thirty species—and he devoted entire poems to the song sparrow, the English sparrow, the bobolink, and a nameless waterfowl: the last of these being the inspiration of his best poem. Of trees and flowers his knowledge, and the use of his knowledge, was still more extensive. . . . The trees of his poetry number nearly thirty, and many of them, in particular the oak, the beech, the pine, the maple are used repeatedly,

the oak for instance, occurring in some twenty poems. Lastly, the flowers of his poems, though but a small bouquet compared with those he could name, are about forty-five in number, and the use of them indicates a faithfulness of observation that well-nigh exceeds Thoreau's. Three—the yellow violet, the fringed gentian, and the painted cup—are the themes of separate poems. Of the forty-five species it is rather odd that none, save the violet, appears more than once or twice; when he wanted a flower, he generally picked a new one—the water-lily, the dandelion, the meadowsweet, and a dozen others blossom only once in the poetical work of over seventy years.

Clearly, though remaining a poet of the elements, of "The earth, the air, the deep," Bryant did not disdain to mention in his poetry the concrete details of nature, to mention them, moreover, both incessantly and accurately. And, we may add, sympathetically. Like other modern poets, he recognized in nature, not only a thing of beauty, but also a precious healing power, which seemed to him to stream into his spirit through the senses. Bryant's genius, after all, was by no means altogether didactic and mortuary; sensuous pleasure, despite the alleged "coldness" of his temperament, is prominent in his relation to external nature. The fact that so little has been said of his sensuousness is to be explained, not by its absence from his life, but by the moral inflexibility that held it in check. The kind of sensuousness that we shall observe in Whitman, and even in Thoreau, we can find no trace of in Bryant. But that his senses did not respond with normal eagerness to the blandishments of nature is refuted by **"Green River,"** the **"Inscription,"** and a dozen other poems. No one, I believe, has pointed out his particular pleasure in the wind, especially the mild touch of the wind in summer. Nine entire poems are devoted to a conscious celebration of the wind: **"The West Wind," "Summer Wind," "After a Tempest," "The Hurricane," "The Evening Wind," "The Winds," "The Voice of Autumn," "The Wind and Stream," "May Evening"**; and in most of his other poems the wind is a prominent theme. **"Green River"** opens characteristically, "When breezes are soft." More than in anything else, he found the healing power of nature in the wind:

> . . . The sweet breeze
> That makes the green leaves dance, shall waft a balm
> To thy sick heart.

He meditates on this balm in two entire poems, **"The Evening Wind"** and **"May Evening."** Bird song, the music of brooks, "and soft caress of the fresh sylvan air," he writes of his boyhood days, raised his love spirits and invited him to lose himself in daydreams and in **"Autumn Woods"** he exclaims:

> Ah 'twere a lot too blest
> Forever in thy colored shades to stray;
> Amid the kisses of the soft southwest
> To roam and dream for aye.

The sensuousness of such writing may lack the passion and fine excess of the European romanticists of his time, but it is surely pronounced enough to make us modify our conception of Bryant as a "cold" elemental poet. The usual effect of the caress of the wind, it should be added, was not the longing "to dream for aye," but pleasure and refreshment in the "flowing air" regarded as the token of life.

"Oh Life! I breathe thee in the breeze," is almost as typical of his poetry as the view of nature as "the great tomb of man." Poet of death and the grave, he is also a poet of life and of the unending motion, of the illimitable air. If anything in nature is endowed by Bryant with spirituality, it is the wind—"heaven's life-breathing wind," "the breath of God."

In his accuracy in the details of external nature, Bryant is of the nineteenth century; in his sensuousness, which, though not negligible, lacked the abandon characteristic of latter-day poetry, he is rather of the age of Cowper; in his general attitude toward life and nature, he is still less modern—is, indeed, Puritan. (pp. 9-13)

Puritanism, rather than Wordsworth, makes fundamental contributions to the writing that follows **"Thanatopsis."** In such a poem as **"A Forest Hymn"** all the leading influences on Bryant's view of nature are plainly at work. There is the graveyard conception of nature:

> Lo! all grow old and die—but see again,
> How on the faltering footsteps of decay
> Youth presses . . .

There is the Puritan and deistic conception of nature as a revelation of the divine, which runs through the entire poem:

> . . . Grandeur, strength, and grace
> Are here to speak of thee.
>
> (pp. 16-17)

This is the essential Bryant, the belated voice of New England Puritanism, clear and firm as the morning. Puritanism freed from its excessive Hebraizing, and finding, in poetry and nature, an incentive to a new expression. The rapt adoration of the Puritan in the deeper hours, his passionate vision of God and the ineffable loveliness and magnificence, no poet of the nineteenth century could well have; instead Bryant gazed with joy and awe upon the spectacle of God's work, nature. The Puritan's horrible fear of hell, of the unendurable, unending tortures which sinners (that in mankind, with a few exceptions) were certain to suffer at the hands of an angry God, this likewise no poet of the nineteenth century could well have; instead, Bryant meditated, with a morbidness that owes more to his forbears than to eighteenth-century sentimentalism, on the "never-ending Flood of Years," the pitiless call of the grave. For the spiritual aspiration of the Puritan divines he substituted an awed regard for nature; for their emphasis on the terrors of hell he substituted the somber certainty of the grave. The substitutions are important, it is true, marking both losses and gains; but they do not involve an essential shift in temper. More distinctly than any other of the greater American poets, Bryant brings into our literature the Puritan bent. (pp. 18-19)

Norman Foerster, "Nature in Bryant's Poetry," in South Atlantic Quarterly *(reprinted by permission of the Publisher; copyright © 1918 by Duke University Press, Durham, North Carolina), Vol. XVII, No. 1, January, 1918 (and reprinted in an abridged form as "Bryant," in his* Nature in American Literature: Studies in the Modern View of Nature, *Russell & Russell, 1958, pp. 1-19).*

FRED LEWIS PATTEE (essay date 1922)

[*An American literary historian, critic, poet, and novelist, Pattee was a pioneer in the study of American literature. He believed that literature is the popular expression of a people, rather than the result of the work of an elite. Pattee reputedly held the first chair in American literature at a United States university. Discussing Bryant's link with eighteenth-century literature, Pattee concludes that Bryant was at his best when "he forgot his eighteenth-century manners and cried from his heart." Though Bryant's influence on American poetry was slight because it was "swal-*lowed up" by English and German Romantic influence, his poetry "is the poetic monument to our early Puritan origins," Pattee asserts. In a later piece (see excerpt below, 1923), Pattee examines Bryant's tale, "Medfield," and suggests that its theme, if better handled, "would have made it one of the select few tales in American literature."*]

Only half-heartedly was [Bryant] a child of the nineteenth century. He was of the classicists, law-bound as by iron, self-contained, reticent. (p. 319)

Anything like self-revelation he shrank from. He would not republish from "The North American Review" his really beautiful **"Lines to a Friend on his Marriage,"** but he could cherish as if it were gold the undistinctive translation from Simonides which had appeared in the same number. He aimed at the intellect of his reader, and he leaves him cold. Like all other New Englanders, he preached constantly, but it was with the calm, contemplative voice of Watts rather than with the passion of Wesley.

But cold though he was, we may not say that the emotional within him was atrophied. It is only because it was not that he lives to-day. We make a list of the few poems where for a moment he forgot his eighteenth century manners and cried from his heart, and as we study them we wake to the realization that we have duplicated the little list upon which his fame must depend. **"The Waterfowl"** is a cry from a soul deeply stirred, and so are **"Green River"** and **"I Cannot Forget,"** and the **"Death of the Flowers." "The Hymn to Death"** . . . contains a bit of unconscious self-revealing that throws a flood of light upon the poet. The first two thirds of it is in the stately Bryant manner, a contemplative treatise upon Death, as detached and as brilliantly conventional as Pope's "Essay on Man," a cold argument just as one argues upon politics, but before the poet had finished, his father died and the poem turned suddenly into a cry from a man's soul.

> Alas! I little thought that the stern power
> Whose fearful praise I sang, would try me thus
> Before the strain was ended. It must cease—
> For he is in his grave who taught my youth
> The art of verse, and in the bud of life
> Offered me to the muses. Oh, cut off
> Untimely!

In his treatment of nature he was influenced by Wordsworth, but not fundamentally. In spirit he was of the eighteenth century even here. There is little in him of the democratic and the social. His is the soul of a Wharton and a Logan who would retire to the woods for their own pleasure and profit. His ideal is the Puritan one of self-realization, self-improvement, self-salvation. He would retire from the "haunts of men" as often as possible to repurify himself, to forget amid the beauties of nature the misery of the crowd, to revive the visions of his boyhood spent amid the solitudes, and to get nearer to God whom, in the jostling crowd, he could not feel. His are the poems of a solitary soul intent upon contemplation of the deeper problems, a soul that escapes now and then into the silences for itself alone. (pp. 320-22)

His real contribution to American poetry came from his personality rather than from his message; that majestic, solemn individuality that wrought itself without effort into all that he did during the brief period of his inspiration. There is a bardic ring to his song that one finds in no other modern poet. (p. 323)

His blank verse, solemn and resonant, like the reverberations of organ tones down the aisles of a cathedral, is one of the glories of American literature. He did but little, but that little is permanent. American poetry began as the American nation began, with a tremendous note of seriousness, with a broadness of view commensurate with the continent, with the voice of primeval forests and boundless prairies, yea, even with "**The Song of the Stars**" and "**The Firmament.**"

And though he learned his art of eighteenth century England he is nevertheless our own; last voice of our earlier traditions, first voice of our larger visions as a new nation under the sun. He used the materials of the western world; the native water-fowl, the yellow violet, the primitive forests. Not wholly in his turns of phrase is he free of Pope and his century—he can call fishes "the scaly herds" and he can advise Dana to change his "The Dying Crow" to "The Dying Raven"—yet most marvelously is he American if one reads him in comparison with his contemporaries. He draws his figures and illustrations from the life about him. Even in his essay on "**Trisyllabic Feet,**" in which he remarks that Young imitated Pope to his own disadvantage, he will use a native comparison: "It was like setting the Mississippi to spout little *jets d'eau* and turn children's waterwheels."

And it was no narrowly localized America that he sang; no little provincial area glorified, no New England insulated and made a *new* England. The freshness and broadness of the western world are in his song. The first unquestioned poet in America was the first all-*American* poet. Our literature opens with a note that is a worthy prelude to all that may be in the centuries to come.

The influence of Bryant upon the New England group that arose in the thirties was peculiar. His success as a poet and the chaste beauty of his nature lyrics stimulated nearly all of them to their first efforts, but his distinctive note was echoed by few of them. He led them undoubtedly to native themes, but he imparted to none his classic soul. The influx of transcendentalism and of romanticism quickly overcame his influence and swallowed him up. Wordsworth, Byron, Shelley, Keats, Tennyson, and the German romanticists ruled the mid-years of the century until the early pioneer classicist was forgotten. His "**Thanatopsis**" and his solemn contemplations of death may for a time have prolonged our period of sadness and sentiment, that adolescent growing period in America. . . . (pp. 324-26)

He is a lone, cold peak on the horizon of our poetry, grand and solemn in the morning twilight of American song. He did but little, but that little is unlike anything else in the range of our literature. He is the poetic monument of our early Puritan origins, the mark upon the border-line between the old passing order and the new world that was to be. (p. 326)

> *Fred Lewis Pattee, "The Centenary of Bryant's Poetry," in his* Side-Lights on American Literature *(copyright, 1922, by The Century Co.; copyright renewed © 1949 by Fred Lewis Pattee; reprinted by permission of E. P. Dutton, Inc.), Century, 1922, pp. 293-326.*

FRED LEWIS PATTEE   (essay date 1923)

Bryant's tale, "**Medfield,**" . . . [has] a theme which, had it been better handled, would have made it one of the select few tales in American literature. It was also the precursor of Maupassant's "Le Hula" and Bierce's "The Real Thing." The author prepares his reader by scientific exegesis after the manner Poe was to use in later years. . . . (p. 44)

The failures of the story come at the points where most of the other tales of the period fail. The materials are excellent, but they are not handled with effect. The narrative is wordy; the introduction is too long and it is not skillfully joined to the second part. Despite the scientific approach, there is lack of verisimilitude. It does not strike the reader as a real experience: it does not grip and convince as a story of the kind must do if it is to be believed at all. The flood of horror that would surge over one who sees such a hand upon his arm should be communicated to the reader, but the reader of "**Medfield**" does not shudder; on the contrary, when there enter the two skeletons, hired, doubtless, by the wife on account of their superior strength, he is inclined to smile. Then suddenly at the close comes the suspicion, one cannot explain why, that the final intent of the story is ethical, that it is a craftily concealed sermon. (p. 45)

> *Fred Lewis Pattee, "The Arrival of the Annuals," in his* The Development of the American Short Story: An Historical Survey *(copyright, 1923 by Harper & Row, Publishers, Inc.; copyright renewed © 1950 by Fred Lewis Pattee; reprinted by permission of Harper & Row, Publishers, Inc.), Harper & Brothers, 1923, pp. 27-51.**

WILLIAM LYON PHELPS   (essay date 1924)

[Bryant's poetry] at its warmest never reached the boiling point. This may partly have been owing to the fact that when he was a child, his parents, becoming alarmed at the unnaturally large size of his head, used to soak it in cold water, sometimes breaking the ice to do so. Bryant never quite got this chill out of his style. (p. 14)

The fact that Bryant, in his early years, wrote so much about death, and that his masterpiece, *Thanatopsis,* deals wholly with death both in its title and in its theme, is not in itself a sign of gloom or of religious training or of Puritanism. Nor do I believe that any particular event or the influence of any other poem is responsible for his dwelling so much on thoughts of the tomb. When a young man writes about death, it is not an indication of morbidity, but rather of normalcy. (p. 15)

Although Bryant was a devout Christian, it is rather surprising that there is nothing Christian, nothing indeed religious, to be found in *Thanatopsis*. It is purely pagan. It is no more Christian than it is American. It might have been written by any poet of any nationality or of any century. We are advised to go to Nature for counsel; she comforts us with the thought of her eternal calm, in contrast to the transitory and feverish existence of man. She teaches us the democracy of death. (p. 16)

Bryant's position in American literature is similar to that of Wordsworth in English literature. Bryant wrote about one hundred and sixty poems of which more than one hundred have Nature as a theme. He is our first nature-poet, and in some aspects has never been surpassed by his countrymen. Emerson is more minute, more intimate; but in the large manner, and in the philosophy of peace derived from the contemplation of natural objects, Bryant is as distinctly first with us as Wordsworth is in Britain.

Bryant is the poet of Autumn, as Whittier if of Winter, and Lowell of June. And while Bryant occasionally gives us faithful pictures of autumnal scenery, it is, curiously enough, not the American, but the *English* Autumn that he most characteristically portrays. It would seem almost as if, instead of using his eyes, he had followed literary conventions. (p. 19)

Bryant resembles Wordsworth in his austerity. He could not let himself go; his poetry lacks warmth of expression. His ode to his sweetheart [*Oh, Fairest of the Rural Maids*] shows no *desire*. He calls her a "rural maid," and speaks of her calm eyes and the "holy peace" in her breast. I cannot believe that she liked this poem.

But when Bryant leaves human nature alone, and talks of Nature, he is at his best. His poetry of the woods and mountains, plains and seas has the austerity of grandeur. The more impersonal his subject, the better was his treatment of it. The complexity of the human heart was either beyond his capacity, or he was not really interested. Can you imagine Bryant writing a stage-play?

So far as I can make out, Bryant's poetry shows a sonorous bass voice, but not an interesting mind. He had no whimsies. His imagination was under perfect control.

Like Wordsworth, he had no humour. But this limitation did not produce the disasters so regrettable in the Englishman, because Bryant knew he was not funny, and never tried to be. (pp. 25-6)

Nor is there any doubt-struggle in him; no agony of despair; no self-conflict; no seventh chapter of Romans. His battles were all won.

There is something depressing about Bryant's lack of doubt, lack of passion, lack of temptation, lack of conviviality. Let it be granted that water is the best and most healthful of beverages; even so, for poetical purposes, for convivial songs, it lacks inspiration. The following line from Bryant is both anti-climactic and discouraging:

Fill up the bowl from the brook that glides.

Bryant belongs to Classicism in the best sense of the word. His poems are not paintings—they are statues. He was a great sculptor; he cultivated the lapidary style. He has the purely classical qualities of reserve, restraint, self-suppression, purity of line, objectivity. His literary manner was Greek, his character Roman.

There is little original thought in Bryant. He was meditative rather than thoughtful. He was not pithy, challenging, paradoxical, like Donne or Browning. He does not illuminate a subject, as Goethe invariably did. You cannot imagine him the hero of any such book as [Goethe's] Conversations with Eckermann. His themes are conventional.

Perhaps, for the reasons just stated, his poetic career was not a development. *Thanatopsis* written in his youth, *The Flood of Years* written after he was eighty, are similar in style, movement, and manner. Bryant's career had no beginning, no fruition, no decline. The best work written in his twenties shows no sign of youth, and the latest no sign of age. There is no juvenility in one, and no decay in the other. He is ever the same. The source of the river is as large as its mouth.

When he was an old man, he translated the *Iliad* and the *Odyssey*. In literalness, simplicity, and dignity, his translation is adequate; but Homer had many qualities that were beyond the reach of Bryant. The flexibility of Homer's style is hardly suggested in the English; the multitudinous seas of the Greek poetry, Homer's rippling verse, its charming ease and grace, are not rendered; Bryant's translation is too rigid and monotonous. (pp. 27-9)

Bryant was once thought to be not only our first poet in time but also in degree; to-day it is clear that two such different men as Poe and Emerson have both surpassed him. Bryant is little read to-day, although a few of his pieces are imperishable. But his place in American literature is secure, for the following reasons: He is the Father of American Poetry: He is preeminently our poet of Nature: He is a master of blank verse: He is a teacher of peace and rest.

There is an elemental quality in his work, that is lacking often in more brilliant writers. His poetry is clear and cold like a mountain lake, and seems to come from an inexhaustible source. There are times when we find him colourless, for he will never satisfy the love of excitement. But in certain moods, when we are weary of doubt and struggle, weary of passion and despair, weary also of cant, affectation, and the straining for paradox— then there is a pleasure in his pathless woods. His calm, cool, silent forests are a refreshing shelter. Some of us, like Hamlet, are too much in the sun; Bryant is a shadowed retreat. (pp. 29-30)

> *William Lyon Phelps, "Bryant," in his* Howells, James, Bryant and Other Essays, *The Macmillan Company, 1924, pp. 1-30.*

VERNON LOUIS PARRINGTON (essay date 1927)

[*An American historian, biographer, and critic, Parrington is best known for his unfinished literary history of the United States,* Main Currents in American Thought. *Though modern scholars now disagree with many of his conclusions, they view Parrington's work as a significant first attempt at fashioning an intellectual history of America based on a broad interpretive thesis. Written from the point of view of a Jeffersonian liberal,* Main Currents in American Thought *has proven a widely influential work in American criticism. Parrington here defends Bryant's reputation from "a serious injustice . . . done him by the critics." Placing particular emphasis on Bryant's journalistic career, Parrington praises him as the father of nineteenth-century poetry and journalism in America. In writing that Bryant "turned his back on all middle-class temptations," Parrington is in sharp contrast to Harriet Monroe, who asserted that Bryant was ruined as a poet because of his middle-class inclinations (see Additional Bibliography).*]

Since [Bryant's] death a serious injustice has been done him by the critics, who have dwelt too exclusively on his work in the field of verse to the neglect of other work in fields perhaps quite as significant. The journalist has been forgotten in the poet, the later democrat who spoke for American liberalism has been displaced by the youthful versifier who described American scenery. For this our bellettristic historians, who are impatient of any incursions into matter of fact, are to blame. Yet to ignore so much of Bryant results in underestimating him, and this serves to explain the thin and shadowy quality of his present reputation. He was a much larger man and more significant than the critics have made him out to be. His active and many-sided life is very inadequately expressed in the slender volume of his verse, excellent as much of that is. The journalist and critic who for fifty years sat in judgment on matters political and economic as well as cultural, who reflected in the *Evening Post* a refinement of taste and dignity of character before unequaled in American journalism, was of service to America quite apart from his contribution to our incipient poetry. He was the father of nineteenth-century American journalism as well as the father of nineteenth-century American poetry. In the columns of the *Evening Post* the best liberalism of the times found a place, inspired and guided by

Bryant's clear intelligence. The lucidity of his comment and the keenness of his humanitarian criticism set the editor apart from shriller contemporaries, and made him a power for sanity in a scurrilous generation. (pp. 238-39)

The narrow but real genius of Bryant is peculiarly elusive. His was essentially a self-pollenizing nature that needed few contacts with other minds. He lived within himself, little swayed by modes of thought, slowly maturing the native fruit of his speculation. The very tenacity and persistence of his intellectual life, the rigid integrity of his thinking, suggest the confidence of one who drew his nourishment from within, whose life was an organic growth. It is impossible to mistake his origins. The roots go down to deep substrata of Puritan seriousness and Puritan austerity. . . . There is no pagan luxuriance, no riot of color or scent. The ethical idealism of New England is given stately form if not rendered altogether lovely; the passion for righteousness is held in restraint but it retains much of its tempered acidity. (pp. 239-40)

In politics and religion, as in poetry, he was a man of few ideas, but those ideas were creative, and determined all his thinking. (p. 241)

He turned his back on all middle-class temptations, refusing to speculate, not grasping at unearned increment, believing that America had a nobler destiny in store than could be measured by exploitation. An old-fashioned liberal, he set himself resolutely against the exploitative spirit that was clamoring for internal improvements, a protective tariff, speculative profits. The bitter struggle over the Bank and the American System, in which he was drawn to Jackson by principle as well as by admiration for his courage, laid the emphasis in his mind on financial and industrial problems and made him the outstanding journalistic opponent of Henry Clay. From first to last Bryant was anti-Whig. (p. 243)

[The *Evening Post* under Bryant] had been brought close upon financial breakers by its attack on the money-interests. The working classes read it eagerly, but their indorsement could not make good the loss of advertising and patronage by the wealthy; yet even in such straits Bryant remained true to his liberalism and joined his associates in upholding the proletarian cause. (p. 245)

From defending the rights of free labor to defending the rights of free speech, was an easy step. . . .

A trenchant critic of the rising capitalism, delighting in exposing the fallacies of the new economics and in pricking the bladders of political reputations, . . . Bryant was perhaps the most distinguished of the liberals created by the revolutions that were enthroning the middle class in power. The simplicity of his *laissez-faire* philosophy . . . may seem somewhat old-fashioned today; but his ingrained democracy, his sturdy defense of the rights of free men, his championship of unpopular causes, his tolerance and fairness and keen sense of justice, ought not to seem old-fashioned. He may not have been a great poet, but he was a great American. (p. 246)

Vernon Louis Parrington, "Some Contributions of New England," in his Main Currents in American Thought, an Interpretation of American Literature from the Beginnings to 1920: The Romantic Revolution in America, 1800-1860, Vol. 2 *(copyright 1927 by Harcourt Brace Jovanovich, Inc.; renewed 1955 by Vernon L. Parrington, Jr., Louise P. Tucker, Elizabeth P. Thomas; reprinted by permission of the publisher),* Harcourt Brace Jovanovich, 1927 *(and reprinted by Harcourt Brace Jovanovich, 1958), pp. 238-70.**

TREMAINE McDOWELL   (essay date 1935)

[*McDowell was one of the earliest critics to provide a full-scale critical study of Bryant's work. He asserts that "Bryant was a pioneer interpreter of Romance literatures in America." In support of his view of Bryant as a Romantic writer, McDowell points to Bryant's treatment in his poetry of the savage, pioneers, history, and legend.*]

Of the Romantic themes favored by Bryant, one of the earliest to emerge in his verse was the noble savage. Occasionally he portrayed Indians as barbarians, either "roaming hunter tribes, warlike and fierce," or warrior clans who laid up glory "for many an age to last." . . . More frequently he envisioned red heroes gifted with unsurpassed endurance and valor, "a noble race!" An Indian of this generous mould was ever master of the elements and ruler of forest and stream:

> In many a flood to madness tossed,
>   In many a storm has been his path;
> He hid him not from heat or frost,
>   But met them, and defied their wrath.
>
> Then they were kind—the forests here,
>   Rivers, and stiller waters, paid
> A tribute to the net and spear
>   Of the red ruler of the shade.

This superiority of the savage lay, Bryant believed with the Primitivists, in his lack of artificial culture and his nearness to the Creator. . . . [But it] is clear that Bryant dealt, not with realities of Indian atrocities or the squalor of aboriginal life, but with creations of romantic fancy.

The prairie and its pioneers likewise had for Bryant a lasting fascination. Early and sentimentally he rhymed of hunters of the West who go "in depths of woods to seek the deer" and who serenade their loved ones with songs of swans and nightsparrows, mistletoe, and "jessamine." In his prose fiction [for example, his short story **"The Skeleton's Cave,"**] written apparently in emulation of Cooper, he portrayed more virile and yet picturesque frontiersmen, of whom Le Moire is representative: a dark-faced and long-haired hunter, clad in a "blue frock-coat trimmed with yellow fringe and bound by a sash at the waist," deerskin pantaloons, and deerskin moccasins. . . . After Bryant came face to face with authentic plainsmen and their families, in his prose he no longer romanticized the frock-coated pioneer. Rather, he recorded the actualities of his dreary life: his wretched dwelling, its single room half filled with beds and cribs on which lay a sick man and several children all brown with dirt; his sweaty wife and daughter who cooked greasy meals in a huge fireplace; and the stifling air, the whimperings and whinings, and the offensive odors of the place, which prevented Bryant from sleeping. (pp. xlv-xlviii)

Bryant's concern with the past was often unromantic, particularly when he wrote in didactic mood. His treatment of the history and the legends of his own country, however, was commonly both nationalistic and emotional. His commemoration of Indian and pioneer has already been discussed. To the Pilgrims he paid high tribute and likewise to the heroes of the American Revolution. Particularly Romantic was his treatment of the past in a group of little-known tales and sketches, not to be found in his collected works: **"A Pennsylvania Legend," "A Border Tradition," "The Cascade of Melsingah,"**

"**The Legend of the Devil's Pulpit**," two series of "**Reminiscences of New-York**," and "**Medfield**." Here, perhaps stimulated by the vogue of Irving's stories, Bryant soberly recorded picturesque anecdotes and supernatural legends. . . . But Bryant's touch was too heavy for such fanciful narratives; they became dull and diffuse in his hands.

With tradition and superstition, he often associated grotesque horror. When discussing death in relation to members of his family or to himself, he found its claims too serious to be romanticized. But when he wrote ballads on the tragic fate of Indians and hunters, travellers and robbers, the element of terror appeared. Versifying the details of a murder among the Berkshires, he fancied that when the dreadful deed was done,

> The mountain wolf and wild-cat stole
> To banquet on the dead. . . .

Bryant's first visit to Germany further encouraged him to dabble in blood. There, for example, he wrote seriously and with no thought of burlesque his remarkable tale of handsome Albert, led into the forest by a dark-haired enchantress.

> Next day, within a mossy glen, 'mid mouldering trunks
>   were found
> The fragments of a human form upon the bloody
>   ground;
> White bones from which the flesh was torn, and locks
>   of glossy hair;
> They laid them in the place of graves, yet wist not
>   whose they were.
>
> And whether famished evening wolves had mangled
>   Albert so
> Or that strange dame so gay and fair were some
>   mysterious foe
> Or whether to that forest-lodge, beyond the mountain
>   blue,
> He went to dwell with her, the friends who mourned
>   him never knew.

Returning to America, he versified a tragic German legend and translated Romantic poems by Uhland, Müller, and Chamisso. Meanwhile, he was writing prose tales of terror: "**An Adventure in the East Indies**," "**Story of the Island of Cuba**," "**The Indian Spring**," and "**The Skeleton's Cave**." In the last story, he permitted himself one particularly grotesque touch: three characters, entombed with a mouldering skeleton, are so hard pressed by starvation that one of the group finally suggests that his companions devour him. "Look at my veins," he begs, "they are full yet, and the muscles have not shrunk away from my limbs; would you not both live the longer, if I were to die?"

Bryant's Romantic liking for the languages and literatures of France, Italy, and particularly Spain developed during his early years in New York City. Here a family of French Catholics caught his interest and apparently led him to improve his knowledge of the French language. Then, in the midst of his heavy toil as a magazine editor, he learned to read Italian, Spanish, and Portuguese. The first result of this activity was a review of a sixteenth-century work on the Provençal poets, in which Bryant recounted sentimental legends and rhapsodized over the golden age of the troubadours. . . . (pp. xlix-liii)

Then followed another review; a tale of Spanish life in Cuba and one of French life in North America; and essays, enlivened by colorful anecdotes, on Spanish customs, Moorish ballads, and female troubadours. Even more notable was Bryant's delight in the physical beauty of Granada and all southern Spain, revealed before Irving had published his Spanish sketches and before Bryant had visited Europe. Most notable of all were the verse translations from European poets which he made during these years—translations from the Provençal of Bernard Rascas and Peire Vidal, from the Portuguese of Belchio Manuel Curvo Semedo, from the Spanish of anonymous balladists and song writers, of Leonardo de Argensola, Fernand Ruiz de Villegas, Louis Ponce de Leon, Pedro de Castro y Añaya, and José Iglesias de la Casa. Writing before Longfellow had left college or Lowell had left dame school Bryant was a pioneer interpreter of Romance literatures to America. (pp. liii-liv)

> *Tremaine McDowell, "Introduction" (copyright, 1935, by American Book Company; copyright renewed © by Dimmes McDowell Bishop; reprinted by permission of D. C. Heath & Company), in* William Cullen Bryant: Representative Selections *by William Cullen Bryant, edited by Tremaine McDowell, American Book Company, 1935, pp. xiii-lxviii.*

GEORGE ARMS (essay date 1949)

[*In contrast to William Ellery Leonard, who viewed the simplicity of diction and philosophy in Bryant's work as a unifying feature (1917), Arms maintains that the "thinness" of thought and diction "does his poetry harm." Thoroughly analyzing themes and imagery in the poems, Arms eventually focuses on dramatization in Bryant's verse—a feature which, Arms suggests, provides a "richness which compensates for the generally naive single-mindedness of Bryant's thought."*]

In religion, Bryant was a Unitarian who regularly worshipped in a Presbyterian church. In politics, he was a laissez-faire liberal who helped found the Republican party. In philosophy, he affirmed natural goodness but not the goodness of natural man. Such inconsistencies, which are common enough, should not cause dismay. But more completely than seems possible in a man of intelligence, Bryant was not only unconcerned by the difficulties of his position but was oblivious of them. And this lack of complexity does his poetry harm.

Though a brooding sympathy helps to clothe the bareness of thought, sentimentalism too often marks sympathy that lacks texture. Perhaps "**The Greek Boy**" shows best how much complexity is needed. The poet addresses a Greek youth brought to this country to be educated and envisages in him the revival of classical culture. But a note in the collected poems suggests that the boy was being educated to be a missionary. Nearly fifty years after the poem was published he sent Bryant a letter largely confined to telling of its writer's debt to Christianity: "My country is free and I am free, and what is more, I am a believer in Christ, thanks to those who taught me." Here then is the vivifying circumstance that the poem lacks; and without insisting that Bryant should have used *this* circumstance in his poem, I do hold that the constant evasion of *this kind* of circumstance makes much of Bryant's poetry as flaccid as a gift annual.

Thinness of thought is closely related to thinness of diction. A part of this further disappointment is peculiar to the demands of readers today. Used to the sharp bite of colloquialism in our poetry, we can hardly understand how a contemporary reviewer would dare to call Bryant's language "idiomatic and racy—the language of people of this world such as they use when they utter home-bred feelings in conversation with one another around the fireside or the festive board." A phrase in "**The Ages**" when America is described as "lifter-up of proud sky-mingling mountains'' is perhaps the happiest; but even here the raciness is of a literary rather than colloquial sort.

The language does have a justness about it, a justness that reminds us of the eighteenth-century tradition at its best. Not infrequently the niceties are too unpretentious for the dulled sense of today's reader, yet as I hope to show when we examine certain poems later on, those niceties do exist. (pp. 215-16)

The diction is just and it has dignity, and it lends itself to a satisfactory if not unique rhythm. But the diction is often trite and clumsy, too. Beginning at his first poems, we can end up with a crammed bagful of clichés when we reach **"A Lifetime,"** which is almost solidly built up of trite phrasing. Frequently also Bryant depends upon the assumption that his words must be dignified just because they are his words, and we get such outrages as ''On the infant's little bed, wet at its planting with maternal tears.'' Partly he suffered from a static view of language. . . . Even though he elsewhere fought against being weakly imitative, his diction is often outworn.

Bryant may also have suffered from being put into a false position by what he thought were the proper conventions of his time, as is suggested by descriptions of him in his old age when he appears to have returned to a boyhood rusticity of manners and diction. ''He had a strange fondness for talking with queer and common people—farmers, woodmen, and stage-drivers,'' an early acquaintance remembered. The dichotomy of artificial and natural speech emerges from an examination of the humorous poetry. . . . But his own familiar poems that depend upon verbal wit are notably poor. He is more successful when as in **"Robert of Lincoln"** and **"The Planting of the Apple-Tree"** he makes use of colloquial situations, depending only slightly for development upon vocabulary.

Bryant's critical writing makes clear that his faults in ideas and diction are not fortuitous but basic. Although his criticism is not to be despised, parts of it give uneasy pause. Poetry, he believed, differs from prose ''by excluding all that disgusts, all that tasks and fatigues the understanding, and all matters which are too trivial and common to excite any emotion whatever.'' . . . Bryant's goal was less the functional simplicity of a great building than the homely simpleness of a one-room cabin. (pp. 216-17)

Even more relevant to his practice in imagery are Bryant's remarks on imagination in his 1826 lecture **"On the Nature of Poetry."** He begins the lecture by challenging the principle of mimesis. ''Instead of a visible and tangible imitation,'' poetry employs ''arbitrary symbols, as unlike as possible to the things with which it deals.'' Still, as he goes on, he subordinates imagination to feelings and understanding. . . .

Bryant's own poems largely reflect this ultimate indecisiveness of theory. If the image of his poem is in relatively small compass, it is apt to lack vigor. . . . [When Bryant] attempts sharp images, they are often unintentionally gauche. The final lines of **"Oh Fairest of the Rural Maids"** are ludicrous if image is realized as image. They come too close to the Morlay-Cooglerian couplet for comfort:

> My feet so tired, they must have rest;
> I'll pillow them on a maiden's breast.

When the image is neither short nor sharp, when it rather consists in the event of the poem . . . Bryant achieves success. Sometimes the fundamental metaphors become badly scrambled ones, as in **"The Past."** Bryant prided himself upon this poem, and he may have consciously juxtaposed his two figures

of the past as prison and as womb. But if he knew what he was doing, he still did not work out the relationship upon as full terms as he ought to have. . . . In other poems, as in **"The Flood of Years,"** there is a looseness in handling metaphors similar to that of **"The Past,"** but the closeness of pattern in other respects and the largeness of vision assist in our acceptance.

A worse indictment against the poems is that frequently they have no image at all when an image seems to be demanded. In **"The Poet,"** for instance, I judge that Bryant allowed the metaphor of weaving to languish because he could not come to terms with it. Yet it is hard to reduce a poet's practice to generality without exception, as one stanza in this same poem shows. The sudden shift to the image of the sea from that of a dusty street (recalled by ''windless'') could hardly be more happily handled:

> Yet let no empty gust
>   Of passion find an utterance in thy lay,
> A blast that whirls the dust
>   Along the howling street and dies away;
> But feelings of calm power and mighty sweep,
> Like currents journeying through the windless deep.

Here, as elsewhere, Bryant produces poetry of a high order. In another poem, **"Green River,"** the dual use of the river as a symbol of peacefulness and of poetry makes for a fine structural intensity. . . . [In] the last couplet the poem is brought into focus in a manner perhaps forced by the words ''image'' and ''greener,'' but also with dazzling clarity.

Those poems which contain the image in the event are also likely to be poems with a dramatized occasion. Even in **"Green River"** the poet is there (''I steal . . . I often come'') in a series of scenes. His presence lends vigor to the meditation. This aspect of **"Green River,"** partially realized as it is, may serve to introduce one of the two great virtues of our poet. As we shall see, dramatization is frequently indirect, often so indirect as to make its presence doubtful in a single poem. But a reading of all the poems assures us that Bryant worked dramatically more often than not. (pp. 218-19)

The obliqueness of Bryant's dramatization serves his purpose better than a full and direct presentation of scene and character. He was apparently unable to achieve complete objectivity. Thus his better work results either from self-dramatization or dramatization of nature, for unconsciously he may have recognized the danger of too obviously posing or too flagrantly personifying. He must also have realized his inability to characterize others, either through examining his own poetry or through reading reviews unfavorable to this aspect of his work. . . . But in practice he fell short, for those poems in which Bryant made a direct dramatization of characters other than himself are his worst. Among the best known of this group are **"The Indian Girl's Lament"** and **"Song of Marion's Men,"** and similarly wooden displays make up a solid bulk of his poetry.

At its most successful, the method is dramatization of self or of nature, as I have said. The two familiar instances of the latter are **"Thanatopsis"** and **"Inscription for the Entrance to a Wood."** About both of these early poems this fact is notable: Bryant reached his final dramatic form only after revision. The available evidence shows only one redraft of **"Inscription,"** but the changes are significant. As it originally appeared in the *North American Review*, the poem was entitled **"A Fragment"** and lacked the last three lines of the final version. These lines enforce the sense of a particular occasion, of which the final title (traditional as it is in concept) gives the scene.

With "**Thanatopsis**" we have several drafts, which show that Bryant could not decide whether to make the major part of the poem the voice of his better genius or the meditation of the author or the voice of nature. . . . [Does] the poet play no part other than that of introducing nature's words? I should like to suggest that the poet resumes with his own voice in the didactic close, beginning "So live, that when thy summons comes to join." Bryant first added the closing lines when he returned to the dramatic introduction of the "better genius," and he revised them when he finally settled upon the "still voice" of nature. In their final form (separated by spacing only after several editions) they do not destroy either the poem's symmetry or nature's objectivity if they are regarded as balancing lines 1-17. In those earlier lines the poet gives general promise of gladness, beauty, and sympathy. But when nature speaks, she offers at best cold comfort. . . . (pp. 219-20)

In spite of the term "self-dramatization" the poems of which it is used have their own integrity and do not depend upon Bryant's life for their effectiveness. We have as poet a man like Bryant, but a man who is presented to us independently in a poem. By using detail from outside, drama may be diminished rather than heightened. (p. 220)

In "**The Prairies**" Bryant again [as in "**Hymn to Death**"] dramatizes an event recognizably from his own life. Again, also, the presentation is obliquely dramatic. . . . From [the heart and sight] duality he achieves his symbol, as he stands between two worlds. The present uncultivated plain heralds through the bees a new civilization, which Bryant elegiacally hints will perish like the older civilization which the prairies had known. Out of such dramatization comes a richness which compensates for the generally naïve single-mindedness of Bryant's thought, and sometimes gives complexity to the thought itself.

In his better poems Bryant also achieves intensity by structure. His technique may well remind us of his close connection with the eighteenth century, and it helps to make him available to the twentieth. But we often overlook it in Bryant because of the same historical stock response, additionally complicated by the poet's smooth vocabulary, that has made us blind to his use of drama. Yet indubitably Bryant has structure, not only as any poet must have it, but as one of his two major ways of achieving poetry. (p. 221)

We have already seen closely patterned verse in such poems as "**Green River**" and "**Hymn to Death**." Two more poems, both of which likewise make use of image and drama, may be examined as further examples. These are "**To a Waterfowl**" and "**The Evening Wind**."

During Bryant's lifetime "**To a Waterfowl**" was regarded as one of his greatest achievements, but both then and now the didactic ending has caused uneasiness. . . . No one, indeed, has troubled to point out that in "**To a Waterfowl**" there is not merely one didactic passage, but two, and that the relation of the first to the second and the gradual growth toward the second statement make that statement inhere in the poem. The symmetrical placing of two "morals" (one in the fourth stanza and the other in the eighth) gives in itself a pleasing framework. But more subtle is their interrelation. The first statement reads, "There is a Power whose care / Teaches thy way along that pathless coast," and by natural expansion what is taught by God in the fourth stanza gives its lesson to the poet in the

eighth. Other anticipations lead into the final statement with a technical nicety that surely contributes to less tangible emotions. Immediately following the first statement the poet calls our attention to the air (through "pathless coast" he has led into it from lake, river, and ocean of stanza three), and he follows this scene with a reference to land (line 19). When we come to the "moral" of the last stanza, we find it predicated upon the same contrast. Tonally indeed "sky" and "steps" (especially "steps") receive major emphasis in their lines. Here too the poem reaches its moment of dramatic revelation: it is just before the line in which the maligned lesson is announced that the first reference to the poet is made—"on *my* heart, / Deeply hath sunk the lesson." And not until we are at the climax of the lesson itself does the poet use "I," revealing himself upon the scene at the same moment that he voices his final idea. This idea is bound up to the scene as much emotionally as the poet is bound to the idea dramatically.

Though the number of Bryant's poems which have moral pendants are relatively few in his total work, most readers think otherwise. Because of this false impression, it is appropriate to turn from "**Waterfowl**" to "**The Evening Wind**," which concludes not with a moral but a picture. "**The Evening Wind**" also differs from "**To a Waterfowl**" in that it begins with the poet ("Spirit that breathest through *my* lattice") and after the first stanza deals with material beyond his direct vision. The idea of the poem is recurrent in Bryant, that of the wind as a part of the "elemental harmony" (a phrase Bryant used in translating a part of Boethius), bringing life to men and nature. The wind comes to the poet from the sea; from him it goes into "the vast inland stretched beyond the sight"; finally it returns to the sea with an announcement, merging idea and form, of "the circle of eternal change." With a technical deftness Bryant reinforces the concept of the circle by using detail of an earlier stanza in the last line of his end-note:

> Sweet odors in the sea-air, sweet and strange,
>   Shall tell the homesick mariner of the shore;
> And, listening to thy murmur, he shall deem
>   He hears the rustling leaf and running stream.

Highly wrought structure, while not present in all of Bryant's poems, occurs in many. The preparation in "**Monument Mountain**," though inept, is at least meticulous. In "**Autumn Woods**" and "**The Death of the Flowers**" careful cross-reference helps to control excesses in sentimentalism and moralizing. When in other poems there is no deficiency lurking in these, Bryant's consciousness of form brings a certain greatness. The syllogistic structure of "**An Evening Revery**" produces a competent poem; in conjunction with oblique dramatization and an ironical interplay of thought, it yields a poem that belongs with Bryant's best. In the sonnet "**October**" we find a neat joining of octave and sestet, and the introduction of a new figure in the final couplet gives the power of appropriate variety to the smooth unity of what has gone before.

In spite of manifest deficiencies in Bryant, there are then compensating merits. He had the merit essential to poetic success, a sense of form; and his deficiency in ideas, diction, and imagery are somewhat less important than they might otherwise be because of a highly personal yet valid means of dramatization. Certainly, as do most poets of any time and as did nearly all poets of the nineteenth century, Bryant wrote much that is worthless. . . . But if we go to the best of his poetry and use a taste critically fastidious but tolerant to older fashions, we can regard Bryant with both respect and pleasure. (pp. 221-23)

George Arms, "American Literature Re-Examined: William Cullen Bryant," in The University of Kansas City Review, *Vol. XV, No. 1, Spring, 1949, pp. 215-23.*

DONALD DAVIE (essay date 1955)

It is convenient to point to the sixth stanza [of **"To a Waterfowl"**] as the point at which we feel a more than usual honesty in [Bryant]. 'And scream among thy fellows . . .' Screaming, with its connotations of rage and terror, seems not at all appropriate to Bryant's intention in this place, where 'rest' in the line before, and 'sheltered' in the following line, carry the idea of earned repose, wings folding, and the fall to rest. But the moment is beautifully controlled; for the implications of earned repose are there, but qualified and sharpened by the word 'scream'. We are only too ready to lapse with the bird into shelter, into the arms of a comfortable Providence; but Bryant will not allow it, demanding that we remain alert, aware of the bird in itself as a foreign creation, not only as a text for the poet's discourse. How easy, and how dishonest, would have been the word 'cry', falling fitly into place with the tired lapse upon the lap of nature. But in that case it would have been a tired child that lapsed upon a mother's lap, the lap of 'mother Nature' or a maternal God. And the cry would not have been what it purports to be, the cry of a bird, but a human cry, or a bird's cry treated as if human. Water-fowl *do* scream. Yet it is not true that the word denotes only. It carries connotations, though not the ones expected. It connotes the bird's 'beastliness', its otherness, its existence in and for itself, as well as in the eyes of man. There is no question of our entering into this otherness by an effort of sympathy. We are only to remember that a bird is not a man. So we are not invited to identify ourselves with the bird, only, while keeping our distance, to take it for a sign. 'Summer home' has the same effect.

This is enough to show Bryant disowning the indulgence of the neo-Georgian poet. It is just as important to notice how he avoids the self-indulgence of another kind of poet, how the surprising word draws no attention to itself, how the temptingly *recherché* epithet is avoided, so that the momentary pungency does not halt the exposition. So I said that it is convenient to regard this point as the one at which our attention is forced to be close. It is convenient so to regard it. But in fact there is no forcing here or anywhere else. The demand for attention does not assert itself. It is easy to read this poem carelessly and pass it off as merely creditable or even dull.

One could for instance equally well take the last line of the fourth stanza, 'Lone wandering, but not lost'. If we look back on this from the end of the poem, we perceive that 'lost' is something not far short of a pun. Here the word has the homely tang of 'Lost in a wood'; but after the rest of the poem has been read, it takes on also the other meanings or the other shades of meaning represented by 'the lost tribes', or even by 'lost' = 'damned'. For the moment what is pleasing is the approach to popular idiom in a poem up to this point couched in rather literary diction. The word demands once again an alertness in the reader, a keeping of one's wits about one, a refusal to go all the way after the easily cheapened emotional appeal of 'lone'. And on the other hand the pun or near-pun is submerged, refusing the opposite temptation to stand and preen upon a slick smartness. The poet can have it both ways.

It may be here, then, that the careful reader first becomes aware of having to deal with something more than a didactic set-

piece. Certainly the first stanzas seem to promise no more, if even so much. 'Rosy depths' is weak, and so is 'crimson sky', while it is only the vagueness of the second line which prevents the reader from asking whether 'steps' is the right word for a progress which leaves a glow. At this point we do not know what we are in for, and later, when we realize that it is no part of the poet's intention to be vivid or 'concrete', our objections to 'rosy depths', for instance, may disappear. . . . Still, the language of the first two stanzas is no more than tolerable at best. And 'Thy figure floats along' is perhaps unacceptable on any terms. 'Falling dew' may be called artificial, in the sense that it does not appeal to sense-experience (no one sees the dew falling) but to deductions from that experience. 'Thy figure floats along' is artificial in another and less excusable sense. It does not appeal beyond experience to a known fact. It does not appeal to experience, for 'floating' does not adequately represent the experience of seeing a bird in flight; it is as vague as 'figure'. Still less, on the other hand, does it appeal to a known fact, belying experience, about the flight of a bird. The appearance is of ease, the fact is effort. But neither ease nor effort is represented by 'floats'. Moreover there is the disagreeable association of the 'Gothick' heroine seen as a floating form down a perspective of dank arches. This precariousness has its own charm; but it is charming not to the reader of poetry but to the antiquarian amateur. And the image causes discomfort. (pp. 130-32)

["**To a Waterfowl**"] exists in a sort of hiatus between two traditions [of Classicism and Romanticism] and in a makeshift convention compounded of elements from both. This is the secret of that precariousness which manifests itself in such uneasy locutions as 'Thy figure floats along'; and it is this that makes the right reading of the poem such an exacting test of taste, difficult but also salutary.

'Weedy lake', for instance, goes along with the 'falling dew' of the first line. It appeals beyond sense-experience in just the same way. 'Rushy' or 'reedy' would have been the Romantic word. And bullrushes are weeds. But to call them so shuts out Sabrina and Midas and their whispering, and places them firmly in the vegetable kingdom, where, for this poet as for the botanist, they belong. 'Chafed' does just the same. The chafing of land by the sea is not an observed fact, but a deduction from many observed facts. 'Chafed' is a dry, merely descriptive word. 'Weedy' and 'chafed', then, belong to one convention, as the appropriate diction of an age concerned not so much with experience as with the lessons to be drawn from it. 'Plashy', on the other hand, and 'marge', familiar archaisms, seem to invite just those legendary and literary associations that the other epithets so sternly suppressed. These are not *dry* words at all; they yearn out at the reader, asking him to colour with inarticulate feeling the things to which they refer. They thus appeal to quite another convention. Some readers may feel this betwixt-and-between air unsettling; others may think the poet deserves credit for bringing the two conventions into harmony. I will say only that the harmony, if it is achieved, is precarious, in the sense that while the poet may sustain it throughout his poem (and the reader feels that it is touch and go with him all the way), his success will not help him with the next poem he writes—he is as far as ever from perfecting a style that he can trust, a reliable tool. He is even further from himself contributing to a tradition in the shape of a heritable body of techniques; no later poet will be able to take his procedure as a model. (p. 133)

Poet and reader alike begin to move with more assurance in the fourth stanza. Here, for the first time in the poem, we encounter something in the nature of [ambiguity]. . . . For 'teaches thy way' appears as an impurity, an awkward construction forced upon the poet by the exigencies of metre and rhyme, until we remember the usage 'teaching the way to do'. And this, once remembered, gives to the phrase the sense not only of guiding along a navigated track, but of teaching wings how to fly. In the same way, the sea-coast is not pathless, but only the coast imagined as duplicated at the altitude of the bird's flight. And once the idea of altitude is introduced, there is the merest hint, no more, of that other 'coast' which comes with 'coasting', so obviously a better word for the flight of a bird than that 'floating' of six lines before.

Only now can the point of the pun on 'lost' be properly taken. For in the third line of this stanza the equable flow and the subdued tone are abandoned. 'The desert and illimitable air'— a reverberation, a powerful élan; and fine, but at once controlled and valued by the earthy and quaint tang of the colloquial 'lost'. The Miltonic blast has been worked for, and is paid for; at the same time it asserts magnificently the importance and the glory of what the poet has in hand. And so it is possible to talk in a heightened tone, to move into 'that far height, the cold thin atmosphere', and for the wings to grow into sails, into a dragon's vans, 'fanning' the air. So the subsidence is effected upon several different levels. First the movement subsides after the beautiful break at 'weary'. Second, the flight subsides to the nest. Third, the vaulting human thought subsides, to a need for shelter. And finally, with 'scream among thy fellows', the bird subsides, from a dragon or an angel, fanning the wheat from the chaff in lofty speculation, to being, precisely, once more a bird, a brute creature.

Thus, when,

> Thou'rt gone, the abyss of heaven
> Hath swallowed up thy form,

not only is the flying bird lost to sight, but the symbol too is lost to the eye of the mind. The abyss is not only the blue depth, but also the profundity of paradox in which the questions of destiny evade answer. Only so, having realized the incomplete and arbitrary nature of the 'lessons' given, can Bryant's certainty ('And shall not soon depart') appear heroic and admirable, more than a windy gesture. The certainty of conviction impresses the more, not because of the uncertainty of the revelation, but because of the poet's acknowledgment of what in it would seem uncertain to others.

Or so we might have said, were it not for the last stanza. It is difficult to be fair to this. The moral is thumped home very pat indeed, but I think we deceive ourselves if we suppose that this is what offends us. We should not mind the certainty if the moral itself were more acceptable. Perhaps most readers will agree with me in thinking the migratory instinct in birds is no just analogy for the provisions made by divine solicitude for the guidance of the human pilgrim. And Bryant seems to assert something closer than analogy. In fact he seems now, at the end, to approach that identification of himself with the bird, that earlier he took care to avoid. Yet we cannot but think that the human being has a margin of choice for good and evil, that a bird has not. Hence divine guidance in the human soul must work in a way very different from the automatic and undeviating operation of instinct in migratory birds. To think otherwise is to cheapen alike the idea of Providence and the idea of human dignity—a dignity which depends, by the traditional paradox, upon the possibility of human depravity. (pp. 134-35)

[If] the lesson to be drawn is as straightforward as this, if supernatural guidance in human life is no more of a mystery than the migratory instinct in waterfowl (mysterious as that is), then 'the abyss of heaven' is surely not deep enough. It is no longer the profundity of paradox, only those 'rosy depths' of the first stanza, which have grown, in the interim, no ruddier and hardly any deeper. 'Abyss' now comes to seem a pretentious word, too effusive, making promises that cannot be redeemed.

Thus the piece is seriously flawed both first and last. It is not a great poem, it is only just, perhaps, a good one. Just for that reason it demands very careful reading. When a poet's achievement is precarious at best, he requires in especial degree the co-operation of his readers. Not that he should be repeatedly given the benefit of the doubt; that would be not co-operation but indulgence. Rather it is a question of permitting the poem to establish its own convention; and where a poet is himself uncertain about the convention he is writing in (having perhaps to express something for which the established conventions are inadequate, yet lacking the energy to break wholly free of them), the reader has to be patient while the poet feels his way towards the convention he wants. Bryant feels his way through three or four stanzas. (p. 136)

[In] periods such as our own, or Bryant's, when the genres are being reshuffled so that they are no longer mutually exclusive, the poet finds it much harder, not just to hold, but to direct the reader's attention, so that he shall know what to look for, what not to expect. Even in these cases, however, the poem establishes a convention for itself by, in effect, challenging comparison with certain poems and not with others. We begin to get somewhere with Bryant's poem only when he brings it home to us (and perhaps to himself) that, although this poem could never have been written in the eighteenth century, yet it belongs, and is to be taken, along with an eighteenth century poem such as Gray's 'On the Spring', not with Shelley's 'To a Skylark'. (pp. 136-37)

> *Donald Davie, "Bryant: 'To a Waterfowl'" (reprinted by permission of the author), in* Interpretations: Essays on Twelve English Poems, *edited by John Wain, Routledge & Kegan Paul, 1955, pp. 129-37.*

ALBERT F. McLEAN, JR.   (essay date 1964)

[*McLean is the author of the only book-length study of Bryant's work to date. He limits discussion to Bryant's poetry alone, proposing that "it is in the poems themselves that Bryant stands revealed." In this excerpt, McLean explores Bryant's treatment of themes such as natural man, nature, woman, sexuality, and mutability. He concludes that "rational abstractions" provide "a firm, credible foundation for the highly personal superstructure" of Bryant's poems. McLean also briefly touches upon the political context of some of Bryant's poems.*]

"The Prairies" is a very convincing and compelling work, not because it is the springing to life of a hypothesis—the greatness and promise of America—in an appropriately spontaneous fashion, but because it is a complete realization by the poetic intelligence of what it means to entertain this hypothesis. Bryant was not, as Whitman was to be, temperamentally or intellectually ready to take the optimistic plunge into the benevolent cosmos. His dream must break, leaving him "in the wilderness alone." But this is the source of the poem's strength, even though it may be a source of philosophical confusion. If the sublime esthetics of the national spirit were one order of truth which the poet could express through the medium of natural imagery, there was another order of truth which placed man, as an autonomous consciousness, apart and isolated from the natural phenomena which he perceived. **"The Prairies"** does not reconcile these truths, but it forcefully expresses the dilemma of the romantic sensibility as it sought political conviction in a dream of America, the Beautiful. (pp. 43-4)

Simple emotions were not Bryant's forte. The almost prosaic language of his verses and the general clarity of the dramatic situations of the poems are too often deceptive. Even his little verses on flowers, unpretentious and subdued as they appear, are not pure expressions of delight and admiration. Inhibiting the emotional impulse which brings the poet to the exquisite and delicate subject matter of violets, gentians, and windflowers is not only the artist's sense of form but also an intelligence alert to physical and moral relationships. Instead of simplicity, these poems contain an involvement and intricacy which is their real merit. And furthermore, what they may lose in lyrical power is often compensated for by the poet's insight into the fullness of his experience.

That these poems can be read—and too often are—as polite sketches with appended moral sentiments is unfortunate; and yet such misinterpretations reflect Bryant's own dilemma in the face of natural beauty. Does Nature, after all, unite beauty and moral truth within the same discernible objects, or are there two quite distinct orders of value? At times Bryant writes as though beauty necessarily entails some sort of certitude and has its own authority; but the more successful poems . . . , imply that it is the imagination of the poet and the human capacity to formulate experiences into art which ultimately unifies value with perception, truth with beauty. (pp. 46-7)

[The subject of women in Romantic poetry] is shrouded in conflicting ideas and emotions, but the poet finds in this very ambiguity the kind of material his imagination requires. Here is a more profoundly ethical poetry than that of "the land" or that of floral beauty. Using his proper tools of imagery, structure, and rhythm, the poet sifts the values and feelings relating to romance in the modern world. Out of his own divided feelings about natural man (*Is there a natural woman also?*), about chastity (*Is it of God and Nature?*), and about the involvement of love with passion (*Can the higher be reached without the lower?*), Bryant fashioned his lyrics of young maidens in Nature.

Representative of one extreme position, and widely anthologized, is **"Oh Fairest of the Rural Maids,"** a rather polite and unambitious piece of flattery . . . : The association of the "sylvan wild" with feminine beauty passes unquestioned in this poem. No instance of Nature more violent than the playful wind or the quiet spring arises to shatter the pretty comparison. But perhaps there is a lingering doubt—at least the concluding stanza takes pains to relate the untraveled forest to the young woman's innocence:

> The forest depths, by foot unpressed,
> Are not more sinless than thy breast;
> The holy peace, that fills the air
> Of those calm solitudes, is there.

Thus, the compatibility of natural beauty and moral purity are upheld through bland assertion. There is, however, a trace of equivocation in the awkward expression "Are not more sinless," and a straining for the image in "foot unpressed," by which the undefiled quality of the female breast is described.

Other poems partially retract this absurd commitment to the absolute sinlessness of the female sex. The children of nature in **"An Indian Story," "Monument Mountain,"** and **"The Strange Lady"**—all Indian maidens—are plagued by terror and guilt as no flaxen-haired, blue-eyed rural maids could ever be. In portraying the stirrings of passion within these female characters, Bryant seems to have drawn, especially in **"The Strange Lady,"** upon the romantic stereotype described by Mario Praz as *La Belle Dame Sans Merci* [Fatal Woman]. For the most part, however, these Indian characters, although subject to the pains of passion, are devoid of malignance and cruelty.

The poem in which Bryant's matured treatment of Nature and sexuality occurs is **"Monument Mountain,"** a fine work in several ways. Although there are imitative elements in it, the poem is remarkably vivid in its setting, consistent in its synthesis of human and natural elements, and of an almost classical deliberateness in its movement toward the fatal close. The tale, which gives the poem its structure, is simply that of an Indian maiden, "bright-eyed / with a wealth of maiden tresses."

> She loved her cousin; such a love was deemed,
> By the morality of those stern tribes,
> Incestuous, and she struggled hard and long
> Against her love, and reasoned with her heart,
> As simple Indian maiden might.

> (pp. 51-2)

It is a tale with Hawthorne's darkness about it; and, like Melville's novel, *Pierre*, which it may well have inspired, **"Monument Mountain"** treats the subject of incest in such a way that innocence itself is made the source of grief and guilt. Also, like the major works of Hawthorne and Melville, this poem is unified by a dominant central symbol: the mountain which derives its name from the monument of rough stones placed there by the mourning tribes. The mountain symbolizes Nature, not only, as we might expect, in its permanence and immensity, but also in those qualities of beauty and savagery as they are paradoxically combined in natural objects: "Thou who wouldst see the lovely and the wild / Mingled in harmony on Nature's face, / Ascend our rocky mountains."

And what is true of Nature, is also by implication true of natural man. Though the climber of the mountain may achieve an "expanding heart," "a kindred with a loftier world," and "The enlargement of . . . vision," the experience is not one of tranquility but an imposing mixture of peace and terror, loveliness and wildness. Even while the eye takes in "white villages, and tilth and herd," it also sees "bare old cliffs," seared by the elements to "chalky whiteness":

>   . . . It is a fearful thing
> To stand upon the beetling verge, and see
> Where storm and lightning, from that huge gray wall,
> Have tumbled down vast blocks, and at the base
> Dashed them in fragments, and to lay thine ear
> Over the dizzy depth, and hear the sound
> Of winds, that struggle with the woods below,
> Come up like ocean murmurs.

The sensibility, nourished by these contradictory aspects of the scene before it, turns to the tale—the "sad tradition of unhappy love" to find a relevance to human experience.

The poem develops dramatically from this point, tracing the impact of the outlawed desires of the maiden upon her body and her spirit. . . . The natural passion of the innocent has, as she herself recognizes, become unnatural. Only through death can she return to a state of harmony with Nature. Only death restores the balance between her beauty and her wildness. (pp. 52-4)

Much later in his career, Bryant reworked the theme of lost innocence into a fantasy, **"Sella."** . . . However, this thinly veiled story of sexual awakening, also hinting of an incestuous relationship, comes to a happier conclusion than **"Monument Mountain."** (p. 54)

The contrast between **"Monument Mountain"** and **"Sella"** does not reflect any substantial shift in Bryant's treatment of sexuality. In both poems the metaphor of ascent (the Indian maiden climbs the mountain, while Sella emerges from the fantasy world of the sea) indicates the capacity of human beings to transcend their limitations, either self-imposed, as in Sella's case, or instilled in the conscience through tribal mores. In both poems the emphasis is upon the moral and emotional conflicts within the individual rather than upon any romantic or sexual contact between the girl and her lover. Indeed, the implication of these two poems is that sexuality is almost entirely an intimate, personal problem in which the loved one or society at large has little stake. Chastity is not glorified as a social ideal but as a personal standard gleaned from some contact by the uncorrupted innocent with the spiritual laws governing the universe. (p. 55)

[Poems] such as **"A Forest Hymn," "Inscription for the Entrance to a Wood,"** and **"A Summer Ramble"** [are] confessions rather than credos. They are, after all, neither statements of faith nor philosophical treatises; they are accounts of an individual as he faces Nature in search of religious illumination. The philosophical framework is just that—a framework—for within it mood, reflection, and speculation play in a highly unpredictable fashion.

The synthesizing process by which Bryant created these poems is most evident in **"A Forest Hymn."** Fundamentally a reasoned statement in verse about the appropriateness of worshiping God in natural surroundings, this poem gathers a particular drive of its own as it develops; and it soon discards argumentation as its structural device.

The rational abstractions serve their purpose, however, in providing a firm, credible foundation for the highly personal superstructure. (pp. 58-9)

[It] is in the diction of this poem, rather than in its structured argument that feeling brims with precision and intensity. Particularly in the second division of the poem, immediately following the lines on "the boast of our vain race," the poet breaks from his moralistic moorings to address a God directly perceived; the poem moves from a hymn to the First Cause to a lyric prayer to the personal deity of the poet:

> . . . But thou art here—thou fill'st
> The solitude. Thou art in the soft winds
> That run along the summit of these trees
> In music; thou art in the cooler breath
> That from the inmost darkness of the place
> Comes, scarcely felt; the barky trunks, the ground,
> The fresh moist ground, are all instinct with thee.

It is with the "barky trees" that observation sharpens; and, in the phrases reflecting the process of contemplation itself—"the ground, / The fresh moist ground"—the accumulation of natural fact begins. In rapid succession follow a bird, herbs, the spring, an oak, each absorbed into the generalization regarding God's presence, but also recreating the experience of private

communion with Nature. The last lines of this division press to its ultimate bound the poet's apprehension of the spiritual reality of the occurrence within the forest scene:

> That delicate forest flower,
> With scented breath and look so like a smile,
> Seems, as it issues from the shapeless mould,
> An emanation of the indwelling Life,
> A visible token of the upholding Love,
> That are the soul of this great universe.

This is the core of piety in a poem which might otherwise have been merely conventionally religious. This is the momentary baring of the vital center of the religious life. That the doctrine of immanence runs counter to the poet's rational convictions regarding the order of the universe and the status of natural objects as "tokens" of the Creator's power and goodness signifies the imaginative vitality of the poem. (pp. 59-60)

If Nature poetry was to draw much of its power from religious experience, however, it faced the great dilemma well known to the saints and mystics of the West. Subsequent to the tidal flow of illumination must come the slow ebbing of grace. What has been lived can only be remembered, not relived; the poet, like the saint, must seek his inspiration in time as best he can. Bryant revealed, in passages, a partial recognition of such a waning sensitivity. Both **The Old Man's Counsel** and **"Among the Trees"** have rather fine lines recognizing the pathos of this loss. (p. 62)

[To] the difficulties already inherent in Bryant's creative process, the theme of death added philosophical and artistic problems of a much wider scope than he encountered in his other poems. Only in **"Thanatopsis"** was he able to rise above the involvements and contradictions posed by this theme. Only in **"Thanatopsis"** was he able to adapt the dialogue and the loose associationism of his blank verse to a structured, consistent discourse. The other poems about death, as the subsequent discussion shall point out, were fragmentary, equivocal, or, at best, evasive in their handling of this theme. (pp. 65-6)

Throughout [**"Thanatopsis"** the] emphasis upon the differences between "forms" and some sort of transcendent reality reoccurs. The "pale form" of line 20 and the "fair forms" of line 36 both refer to the material remains—the corpse of the poet. The sufferings of a dying man are, as conceived by the poet, "sad images." In line 64 human beings are described in terms which connote the illusory quality of life: ". . . and each one as before will chase / His favorite phantom. . . ." And the concluding statement of the poem, which occurs only in the final draft, defines decisively the limited role of visual perceptions, whether they be "forms," "images," "phantoms," or, as in this case, "pleasant dreams": ". . . approach thy grave, / Like one who wraps the drapery of his couch / About him, and lies down to pleasant dreams."

In contrast to the aberrations of sight, however, are the verities of sound. Not the sounds of sense perception, it is true, but the mysterious words which the Old Testament prophets had heard emerging out of the burning bushes and whirlwinds of their symbolic surroundings. Like Grey before him and Tennyson after, Bryant seized upon the provocative paradox of the "still voice," and in the context of **"Thanatopsis"** made it a credible source of his consolations for death. For the poet as listener, in contrast to the poet as seeker or visionary, was all that the poem needed. The dialogue was maintained, albeit somewhat onesidedly; and the vastness of Nature was not diminished through a trivial metaphor. Bryant could have his visual imagery, yet deny it, too, as the very lines in which the still voice occurs demonstrate:

> Go forth, under the open sky, and list
> To Nature's teachings, while from all around—
> Earth and her waters, and the depths of air—
> Comes a still voice—

The power and meaning of **"Thanatopsis"** hang by this slender thread. Rational consciousness and natural piety are both satisfied by this simple, allusive device. The dialogue, seemingly threatened by the absorption of consciousness into the perpetual cycle of Nature, has been restored on a deeper level of understanding than that implied by the other poems of Nature. For the assumption upon which all of the consolations of the poem are based is that the faculty of human reason—while it may operate independently of Nature and achieve a degree of self-realization—can never enter into a dialogue with Nature on equal terms. That Nature speaks to man through forms—including his own "pale form"—and with a "various language" indicates the limitations of human understanding. Indeed, it is this insight, with its suggestion of Hebraic prophecy, which motivates the entire development of the theme of **"Thanatopsis."** The human reason is gently persuaded to abandon its presumptuous claims to uniqueness and autonomy. Death is to be recognized as a fulfillment of the life of partial knowledge—not as the termination of an absolute consciousness. The dialogue no longer assumes that the voice of man is capable of bouncing echoes off an objective mountain; it proceeds in the understanding that the very images, words, sounds, and ideas projected by man are merely chips and slivers from a monumental wholeness and truth. Although the dialogue is still functional in the poem, the poet at last has been awed into a tentative silence while the "still voice" of universal wisdom has its say.

However, this reversal—or inversion—of the customary direction of the dialogue posed formal problems even while it solved intellectual ones. The blank verse could no longer drift on the currents of the poet's revery. . . . [The] formal requirements were, first, a clear progression of ideas toward a definitive conclusion; second, a calm, authoritative voice which spoke not merely to the poet in his privacy but to all receptive men; and third, a language which would apply universal truth to the commonplace.

Each of these requirements had been met by a rhetorical style which Bryant, throughout his youth, had encountered Sabbath after Sabbath. The old "plain style," imported to New England by the earliest settlers, had been preserved in the small towns of white clapboard houses through nearly two centuries of theological strife. . . . Although Bryant may not have been aware that the plain-style sermon was the form he sought, its applicability was clear enough. Consciously or not, **"Thanatopsis"** became a Romantic sermon. (pp. 76-9)

This simple, sturdy form—which had brought a vigorous clarity into the religious life of American Protestantism—instilled into **"Thanatopsis"** its own rugged genius. The indigenous culture of Bryant's native land had contributed, in a fashion unsuspected by either his admirers or his detractors, to the formation of a poetic masterpiece, the first created since the founding of the Republic. (p. 79)

A recognition of the broad outlines of the Puritan sermon in **"Thanatopsis"** does more, however, than reveal a subliminal means for achieving this unity in the poem; it defines the specific intent of each of the three sections. The initial passage,

as we have seen, introduces the philosophical premises of the poem, as well as the major problem to be resolved. The central section, however, drops from the level of meditation to that of debate. The third and final passage once more elevates the discourse by its direct assault on the moral behavior of man. (p. 80)

Nearly one fifth of the poems composed by William Cullen Bryant make reference, if only in passing, to political ideas or events. . . . To a lesser extent, perhaps, than in his poems on Nature or death, his poems of progress still reveal the responses of the private self to the experience of the world. The powerful visions which he had of human history and of natural processes are brought forward to make their comments on the "issues" before him and to contribute toward these integrated and balanced complexes of feelings and ideas that are works of art. (p. 85)

[In **"The Fountain"**] Bryant boldly combined his vision of Nature and his conception of human progress. Something of the "happy land" lingers in his description of the agrarian society which evolves by the "fountain" (a woodland spring), but far mightier forces are at work in the poem than those which make and overthrow mere empires. No longer is the rise of a national republic central to the cosmic enterprise, for framing the poem is a terrifying conception of the mysterious subterranean forces which have created the spring and which shall, in the due course of time, destroy it. The optimism of Bryant's early faith in human progress is thus drastically qualified by the discovery of geological change.

"The Fountain" is a complex poem, and the symbolic use of the fountain—both as a structural device and as a means for synthesizing ideas—is one of Bryant's finest achievements. Starting with a simple and prosaic analogy between the emergence of clear, cool water from "red mould and slimy roots of earth" and the mysterious ways of God, who brings "from the dark and foul, the pure and bright," the poet moves quickly into his personal response to the fountain. His observation of the wild-vine, the spice-bush, the viburnum, and the chipping sparrow conjures up scenes from the long history of the fountain: first before the intrusion of man, and then the "histories that stir the heart / With deeper feeling," the days of barbarism, savage warfare, and hunting. (pp. 99-100)

With the ascent of civilization, however, the fountain—like Nature itself—becomes less significant to the surrounding life. Eventually it is merely an isolated watering spot for the less established members of the community—the woodsman, the hunter, the soldier—and a place for children to play. (p. 100)

This "eternal change" which the poet, as well as the sage, recognized, destroys even as it creates. Although no mention is made of the future for the secure rural community which had grown up near the spring, the concluding lines cryptically imply a dark prophecy. Just as the dynamic processes which had brought clear water out of the bowels of the earth had also given rise to a higher state of culture, so these same processes, which can choke off the water at its source or pollute it in passage, can also demolish the "happy land." This conclusion is left unstated, and the conjectures of the poet are intentionally tentative. (p. 101)

"The Fountain" is notable for its subtle avoidance of these issues, and for its use of the theory for imaginative rather than for polemical purposes. (p. 102)

Albert F. McLean, Jr., in his William Cullen Bryant
(copyright © 1964 by Twayne Publishers; reprinted

with the permission of Twayne Publishers, a Division of G. K. Hall & Co., Boston), Twayne, 1964, 159 p.

ROY HARVEY PEARCE (essay date 1965)

[In this brief discussion of Bryant's poetic theory, Pearce focuses on Bryant's belief that "poetry mediated between the contemplative and the active life," and terms his theory "cautionary" and "conservative." Pearce does credit Bryant's "truly patriarchal significance for the Fireside Poets."]

[For William Cullen Bryant, poetry] mediated between the contemplative and the active life. This doctrine teetered on the edge of the essentially radical thinking of Emerson: that in poetry, and only in poetry, man could come to know himself, so as then to make of himself what he would. But Bryant, attending always to the actual conditions of American life, searching always for some ultimate orthodoxy, could scarcely go so far. Here, for all his love of Wordsworth and his kind, his essential rationalism took over. The ground of the moral sentiment lay not in man but in Nature—Nature *apart* from man. In the end, poems about Nature were lessons learned, not experiences lived through. The teacher was God; and the poet went to this greatest of teachers in His classroom of Nature so that he himself could become a teacher. In the midst of all his liberal political activities, in all his bravery and nobility as a person, Bryant could only assure his readers—who were students of Nature too, only less advanced than he—that whatever was was somehow right because [it was] somehow in the nature of Nature. He sought to read the lesson of history as the lesson of progress. Yet he read it only in Nature, where even as it was exemplified, expounded, and confirmed, it was given a certain stability and balance; so that his poems again and again are, in effect, exercises which rationalize the fate of Americans and their culture. He interprets the American dream—inevitably set in natural surroundings—in a way intended to strengthen the character of the dreamers.

His revisions of **"Thanatopsis"**—which put its death-theme under the dispensation of the order of Nature—are well known. The young Bryant gave himself over in powerful and particularized verses to evoking the blank finality of death; the slightly older Bryant, mindful of his responsibilities to make sense out of even the senseless, surrounded the earlier poem with explanatory material, so that he could advise his reader nobly to

> approach thy grave,
> Like one who wraps the drapery of his couch
> About him, and lies down to pleasant dreams.

The poet reasons his way to a happy ending. Now the reader can "live." Bryant has left behind even the *frissons* of the British Graveyard Poets who were his models and of the fanciful Freneau in his "House of Night." Bryant was, however, not "catering" to his readers' dubieties, for their dubieties were his own. He could assure them as a father, even a young one, assures his children, still mindful of his own childish fears. Bryant wanted above all to be at once a teacher and a family man. His nation was at once his class and his family.

Thus his way with history too. Again and again—the best-known examples are **"The Ages," "The Past," "The Prairies," "The Antiquity of Freedom,"** and **"The Flood of Years"**; but there are others—he surveyed human history, put it into natural, cosmic perspective, and concluded that Americans and their institutions were its heirs; that all of man's suffering pointed to the triumph of such institutions. He was much too

honest to imply that suffering was over once and for all and that American society was not itself only one link in the sublime chain of infinite being. He only wanted to say that it was all right, that it had to be, that we have survived and are the better for it, that living through it we have helped make it all right. (pp. 206-08)

In a sense, Bryant was so assured in his theory of poetry (and all that it implied for his role and that of his readers) that he had to concern himself only with matters of technique and form. His critical essays are quite commonplace when they deal with the nature of poetry in his world and quite interesting when they deal with making poems: problems of the authority of traditional forms, allowable variations in metrics, and the like. Yet on the whole, like his poetry, they are cautionary, reminding the poet (speaking on behalf of his readers) that if he were to be true to his vocation, he had to be above all expert in its methods. That the methods are as conservative as Bryant's larger theory of poetry testifies only to the pervasiveness of his essential conservatism as poet. Herein lies Bryant's truly patriarchal significance for the Fireside Poets. Whatever his political and social views and whatever theirs, in seeking a poetry of the people, he and they perforce sought a poetry which would reinforce the people's opinions and prejudices, show that their dreams (we call them fantasies) did not challenge the nature of the "real" world in which they lived, but rather confirmed it. Bryant's understanding of the poet's peculiar American vocation, expressed early in his life, is at one with the kind of poetry he produced through that life. (p. 209)

Roy Harvey Pearce, "American Renaissance (2): The Poet and the People," in his The Continuity of American Poetry *(copyright © 1961 by Princeton University Press; excerpts reprinted by permission of Princeton University Press), revised edition, Princeton University Press, 1965, pp. 192-252.**

HOWARD MUMFORD JONES (essay date 1967)

Bryant is a poet of process—of an eternal movement, sometimes thought of as cyclical, sometimes as spiral, which he finds in the universe and which he usually thinks of as divinely directed, though the director is only sparsely a Christian God. In many important pieces by Bryant the poem goes no farther than stating or implying that the universe means largely and means well. Christianity becomes more often a symbol of process than the cause of it; and for that reason, though the man Bryant may have passed from the stoic into the Christian, the poetry follows no such uniform development.

Stoicism, like Christianity, is a word of many meanings and as a philosophy alters from age to age. I think, however, it is generally true of the stoic point of view, first that knowledge of the cosmos is realized by virtuous action; second, that all existence is probably within the knowable universe; third, that God, or the gods, or the world soul is to the universe what the soul is to man; fourth, that justice is a general, not a local concept; and fifth, that the stoic has a deep conviction of the weakness and misery of man, of the ineluctability of evil, and of the vanity of life, but that he tries to attain resignation to the course of things because the course of things is somehow supremely directed, probably by divinity. . . . It seems to me that Bryant combines, from his reading of classical antiquity, the melancholy and the grandeur of the Virgilian sense for history and the stoic's belief that there is an intelligible purpose in the universe, even if man cannot wholly comprehend that purpose. All this he tried to fuse with Christianity, but I think it true that Bryant was not so much the poet of nature or of death or of Christian principles as he was a premature existentialist. These ideas are not incompatible. Bryant's constant cry is that man is alone in a cosmos too vast for his comprehending except as process, some imperfect glimpse of which he may attain. (pp. 31-2)

Bryant is the poet of elemental forces—death and life, the seasons, storm and calm, the sea, the wind, the snow, but he is not a Christian "nature poet" as Whittier or Longfellow is. Indeed, if one is to save this melancholy spirit for Christian poetry, one is almost tempted to define him as a Christian who fell into the heresy of Manichaeism—that the struggle between darkness and light, between tragedy and calm, between good and evil, is his central reading of the Christian faith. It is unorthodox to say so, but I feel, in studying Bryant, that his Christianity was a piece of personal sincerity that cannot be questioned, and that so far as his world view is concerned, Christianity is for him an outward and modern symbol of an ancient and more primitive faith. . . . Whether one thinks . . . that Bryant's questing ends in piety (in the Christian sense), or with me that it goes back to a more primitive and persistent philosophy of stoicism, one thing is clear: Bryant's verse demands a more searching analysis than it has received. We have passed beyond the bias of the nineteenth century in reading him, but we have not as yet plucked out the heart of his mystery. (pp. 37-9)

Howard Mumford Jones, "Landscape As Religion: Irving, Bryant, Cooper," in his Belief and Disbelief in American Literature *(reprinted by permission of the Literary Estate of Howard Mumford Jones; © 1967 by the Frank L. Weil Institute), University of Chicago Press, 1967, pp. 24-47.***

DONALD A. RINGE (essay date 1971)

[*In his book* The Pictorial Mode: Space & Time in the Art of Bryant, Irving & Cooper, *Ringe deals with the artistic uses of space and time in American literature. In the following excerpt, he demonstrates how Bryant's moral themes are revealed in his particular handling of spatial and temporal imagery. Bryant manipulates these two variables, according to Ringe, to convey themes such as historical change and repetition, and progress. Ringe argues that Bryant understands time "as both cyclical and linear," but that ultimately Bryant believes that "time moves forward toward an unlimited freedom and progress for all men."*]

Since the moral theme in Bryant and Cooper hinges upon the physical contrast between the smallness of man and the vast expanse of the universe, those aspects of the natural scene which most clearly reveal the contrast can express the theme with the least danger of misinterpretation. From this point of view, it is well to consider first the use that Bryant and Cooper make of cosmic space, for no other element in the external world can suggest so well the smallness of the human being. In Bryant, the device appears quite early, for it is one of the means he used to develop the theme of **"Thanatopsis."** In the central section of the poem among a group of images designed to expand the context in both space and time, he includes the lines:

> The golden sun,
> The planets, all the infinite host of heaven,
> Are shining on the sad abodes of death,
> Through the still lapse of ages. . . .

Like most of the figures in the poem, the image is well designed to place the concept of death in so broad a framework that the idea of one's physical end shrinks almost to insignificance by comparison.

In other poems, too, the endless reaches of space are designed to illuminate the contrast. Thus, in **"To a Waterfowl,"** the poet develops a large part of his poem through images that connote the expanse of limitless space. The flight of the bird "far, through [the] rosy depths" of the evening sky, the vast distance he is to cover as he makes his way through "the desert and illimitable air," and his final disappearance into "the abyss of heaven"—all suggest so great a sense of space that man, in gazing into it, should become aware of the greatness of the God who created the world and who cares for its creatures. . . . Perception of this relation, then, should fill him with faith and help him put aside all petty cares for self and worry over the future. In a similar fashion, the "beautiful, boundless" sky, "bright vault, and sapphire wall" in **"The Firmament"** connote the vastness, grandeur, and beauty of God's creation, toward which one should turn, when tired of the empty mirth of men, to find a place "of innocence and rest." . . . It is only through a perception of one's true relation to the boundless universe, the poet seems to say, that one can maintain his sense of proportion in life—a conclusion that the imagery of these poems is designed to encourage.

A related idea is expressed, but more obliquely, in **"A Song of the Stars."** In this highly imaginative poem, Bryant envisions the stars coming into being in the first dawn of creation when

> the world in the smile of God awoke,
> And the empty realms of darkness and death
> Were moved through their depths by his mighty breath,
> And orbs of beauty and spheres of flame
> From the void abyss by the myriads came. . . .

The succeeding stanzas, quoting the stars' song, are consistently developed through numerous images of light and space to suggest the size and grandeur of the newly created cosmos, and the lines move with a joyous sweep well suited to the idea the poet is expressing. But in the concluding stanza, he reminds the reader that, boundless and beautiful though the stars may be, they are, in comparison with their Creator, but dim lamps. The effect that this reversal of the image is intended to have is obvious. If the stars shrink to such insignificance when seen in relation to God, how much more the human being who can hardly comprehend the distant reaches of cosmic space! (pp. 31-3)

The poems of Bryant provide perhaps the best example of the use of detail to reveal the poet's fundamental attitude toward nature and man. Basic to Bryant's poetry is the view of the world as the harmonious creation of God, innocent in itself and instructive of only good to men. As he wrote in his **"Lectures on Poetry"**: "There are a purity and innocence in the appearances of Nature that make them refuse to be allied to the suggestions of guilty emotion. We discern no sin in her grander operations and vicissitudes, and no lessons of immorality are to be learned from them, as there are from the examples of the world. They cannot be studied without inducing the love, if they fail of giving the habit, of virtue." Bryant was well aware of the obvious presence of evil in life and had of necessity to come to grips with the basic question of its nature and origin. Consistently in his verse, he attributes evil to the passionate nature of fallen man, who is the disruptive element in an otherwise ordered creation.

To suggest the idea, therefore, that men are responsible for the disharmony so apparent in the world, Bryant sometimes turned to the use of sharp and unexpected detail. By including only one appropriate detail in a typical, harmoniously presented landscape, he was able to suggest his basic philosophic position to his readers. Thus, in "The Ages," he uses Edenic imagery in his landscape description, depicting the "youthful paradise" of untouched America at the time of the discovery. At the end of the passage, however, he includes one striking image to carry the weight of his meaning.

> There stood the Indian hamlet, there the lake
> Spread its blue sheet that flashed with many an oar,
> Where the brown otter plunged him from the brake,
> And the deer drank: as the light gale flew o'er,
> The twinkling maize-field rustled on the shore;
> And while that spot, so wild, and lone, and fair,
> A look of glad and guiltless beauty wore,
> And peace was on the earth and in the air,
> The warrior lit the pile, and bound his captive there. . . .

The single detail enables the poet to convey his point with strict economy and telling effect.

The device need not always be so starkly melodramatic. A group of contrasting details, suitably juxtaposed, could embody a similar meaning. Thus, in "The Fountain," Bryant plays one detail against another to suggest essentially the same theme. In one part of the poem, he includes both the deeply wooded, untouched landscape and a dying Indian, struck by an unseen hand in the forest depths, who crawls from the woods to "slake his death-thirst" at the fountain. In the lines that immediately follow, a "quick fierce cry"—the Indian war whoop—"rends the utter silence," and a violent conflict ensues. Its ultimate significance, however, is suggested by the varied details that Bryant includes:

> Fierce the fight and short,
> As is the whirlwind. Soon the conquerors
> And conquered vanish, and the dead remain
> Mangled by tomahawks. The mighty woods
> Are still again, the frighted bird comes back
> And plumes her wings; but thy sweet waters run
> Crimson with blood. Then, as the sun goes down,
> Amid the deepening twilight I descry
> Figures of men that crouch and creep unheard,
> And bear away the dead. The next day's shower
> Shall wash the tokens of the fight away. . . .

The violence of passionate men and the transience of their willful acts are both implied by the series of briefly detailed images through which the episode is presented. (pp. 70-2)

The concept of an ordered nature expressed in the works of [American] writers formed the philosophic basis for a similar concept of order in human society, where change was even more apparent than in the natural processes of the external world. In both the broad sweep of history and the more narrow range of contemporary society, time brought incessant change that the writers had of necessity to deal with if they were not to surrender completely to the vision of a disordered social world. (p. 174)

The cyclical theory of history found frequent expression in their prose and verse. In Bryant's "The Prairies," the poet wrote an imaginative account of the American past, stressing the successive cultures of Mound Builders and Indians, which, he conceived, had risen, flourished, and faded in the American

West, to be succeeded at last by the civilization of the white man. In "The Ages," moreover, . . . he details the whole sweep of Western history. . . . Implicit in the whole development is the concept of the cyclical theory of history. Civilizations rise and flourish, only to decay and be eventually succeeded by others which recapitulate the same process. At one level, then, Bryant reconciles the problem of historical change in terms of an ever-recurring cycle, a view that would seem to imply that history is simply the endless repetition of an inevitable social process.

Such a conclusion is justified in part by the analogy to nature that Bryant draws early in the poem. He begins "The Ages" with a serious question of the meaning of change in human life. When the good man dies, he writes, does goodness die with him? Will succeeding ages see a falling off in virtue? This view would seem to imply that a principle of deterioration operates in the historical process. Bryant does not accept this conclusion. Rather, drawing an analogy to the natural scene, he observes that nature, for all the change that it must undergo, does not seem to fade. Thus, he writes,

> Look on this beautiful world, and read the truth
> In her fair page; see, every season brings
> New change, to her, of everlasting youth;
> Still the green soil, with joyous living things,
> Swarms, the wide air is full of joyous wings,
> And myriads, still, are happy in the sleep
> Of ocean's azure gulfs, and where he flings
> The restless surge. Eternal Love doth keep,
> In his complacent arms, the earth, the air, the deep. . . .

If change in nature is ordered and controlled by the power of a beneficent God, so also, the logic of the analogy would have it, will change in the social world be contained by his will.

Bryant, however, does not end here. To do so would imply that history has no meaning but the recurring cycle itself, that time goes on in an ordered pattern without cumulative loss or gain. To Bryant's mind, the study of history should not lead one to this conclusion, for, he argues, many "cheerful omens" suggest that better days are coming.

> He who has tamed the elements, shall not live
> The slave of his own passions; he whose eye
> Unwinds the eternal dances of the sky,
> And in the abyss of brightness dares to span
> The sun's broad circle, rising yet more high,
> In God's magnificent works his will shall scan—
> And love and peace shall make their paradise with
>   man. . . .

Human reason, instilled in man by his Creator, will lead the race toward a Golden Age in the future. "Sit at the feet of History," Bryant goes on to say, and you will perceive the truth of this interpretation. You will learn of the gradual progress that has been made as successive cultures rise above the ones that went before. The light of reason leads men forward to truth, which, surviving the onslaughts of error, cannot be destroyed on earth. It remains undaunted after error has been put to flight.

The culmination of this process is, as one might expect, the United States of America. Here the white man supplants the Indian, the woods recede as "towns shoot up," and the earth is turned into farms. The march of civilization is now toward the western ocean, a process that Bryant sees, in this poem at least, as leading to good.

> Here the free spirit of mankind, at length,
> Throws its last fetters off; and who shall place
> A limit to the giant's unchained strength,
> Or curb his swiftness in the forward race?
> On, like the comet's way through infinite space,
> Stretches the long untravelled path of light,
> Into the depths of ages; we may trace,
> Afar, the brightening glory of its flight,
> Till the receding rays are lost to human sight. . . .

In Bryant's view, therefore, historical time must be seen as both cyclical and linear. Though the history of the past clearly indicates that all civilizations must perish—a view that sometimes gives pause to his own optimism about America's future—nonetheless the broad movement of time is linear. Beginning at the dawn of history, time moves forward toward an ultimate goal of unlimited freedom and progress for all men. (pp. 175-77)

So important is [the concept of time and space] in Bryant's verse that most of his major poems stress the enormous dimensions of the universe he envisions. Consider, for example, the middle section of **"Thanatopsis."** This part of the poem, designed to reconcile the reader to the thought of death, places the concept of individual mortality in a context of such vast space and time as truly to suggest the universality of death. He begins the section with a temporal image, reminding the reader that at his death, he will "lie down / With patriarchs of the infant world," and with "hoary seers of ages past." He then turns immediately to a spatial development, describing,

> the hills
> Rock-ribbed and ancient as the sun,—the vales
> Stretching in pensive quietness between;
> The venerable woods—rivers that move
> In majesty, and the complaining brooks
> That make the meadows green. . . .

By juxtaposing the temporal and spatial images in this way, Bryant suggests the breadth of the time-space dimension necessary for the development of his theme.

The spatial images, however, as so far developed, are not of the same order as the temporal. Bryant has evoked a range of time stretching back to the dawn of history, but has described a generalized scene that could simply be western Massachusetts. One suspects that this choice was deliberate, for in the lines that immediately follow, the scene suddenly expands to enormous proportions, almost as if Bryant, determined to impress the reader with the breadth of his vision, forces him to participate in an enlarging awareness of space. Thus, he expands the description first to continental size with the suggestion that surrounding all this pleasant landscape lies "old Ocean's gray and melancholy waste," and then enlarges the dimensions further to include the entire cosmos.

> The golden sun,
> The planets, all the infinite host of heaven,
> Are shining on the sad abodes of death,
> Through the still lapse of ages. . . .

Thus, he evokes an image of space of truly vast proportions and closes with an image of time that enlarges upon the one with which he began. Indeed, even the rhythm of the final line suggests the glacial movement of cosmic time.

Other poems by Bryant make use of similar devices to project their quite different themes. **"To a Waterfowl,"** for example, clearly suggests an enormously spacious world both in the "rosy depths" of sky and "the desert and illimitable air" against which the bird is seen, and in "the abyss of heaven" which swallows up his form in the last stanza. Yet the poem also contains a clear, if somewhat underplayed, movement in time. From the very first word—"whither"—we are made aware that the bird is not stationary, but moves constantly through the enormous reaches of space that Bryant suggests with his spatial diction. . . . Though less explicit, certainly, than **"Thanatopsis,"** this poem too is developed in terms of the complex relations of space and time.

"A Forest Hymn" provides yet another example of Bryant's use of space and time in the development of his moral themes. The size of the trees in the virgin forest set the scale for the human observer, for the poet, standing beside the "immovable stem" of a "mighty oak" feels "almost annihilated" by the comparison. . . . The temporal dimension, on the other hand, is suggested by "the century-living crow" that, born in the tops of the trees, "grew old and died / Among their branches." . . . Beyond these points for measurement, however, the mind perceives a scale that far transcends the human, for man, in the presence of these woods, feels his spirit bowed "with the thought of boundless power / And inaccessible majesty." . . . Contemplation of the natural scene, especially in the space-time dimension, turns the observer's thoughts toward the Deity, whose "grandeur, strength, and grace" are suggested by the similar qualities the poet perceives in the forest giants, and whose eternity is suggested by the recurring cycle of ever-renewing life to be seen in successive generations of forest trees. . . . And with this perception comes the spirit of humility that the poet always sees as the appropriate end of man's contemplation of God's wonderful works in nature.

The best example of Bryant's use of the technique, however, is probably **"The Prairies,"** for in this poem the concepts of space and time firmly control both structure and meaning. From the very first lines of the poem, where words like "boundless," "encircling vastness," and "far away" suggest the dominant effect, Bryant develops his vision of an enormously spacious world. Like many another writer of the time, he compares the prairie to the open sea and suggests both size and movement in the patterns of light and shadow he describes as wind and cloud sweep over the prairies to make the surface roll and fluctuate like waves on the ocean. . . . As in **"Thanatopsis,"** he expands his vision to continental proportions by including in his description of the Illinois prairies the winds that have played

> Among the palms of Mexico and vines
> Of Texas, and have crisped the limpid brooks
> That from the fountains of Sonora glide
> Into the calm Pacific. . . .

Indeed, he even employs a single detail in "the prairie-hawk that, poised on high, / Flaps his broad wings, yet moves not" . . . to intensify, as in the **"Waterfowl,"** the infinite reaches of space.

All of this is preparation for the middle section of the poem that develops the temporal aspects of the theme. This enormous space has been the stage on which has been enacted a drama of vast proportions, beginning in the distant past

> while yet the Greek
> Was hewing the Pentelicus to forms
> Of symmetry, and rearing on its rock
> The glittering Parthenon . . .

and projecting forward into the future, when, he foresees, an "advancing multitude" will "fill these deserts." . . . Within this sweep of time, innumerable changes have occurred. Mound Builders have yielded to Indians, and they in turn to the white men. Beaver and bison have gone, the bee, forerunner of the white men in the movement across the continent, has already arrived, and the herds of cattle that will one day graze on the prairies are still to come. The breathtaking sweep of time that Bryant envisions here is the temporal counterpart of the broad reaches of space he evokes in the opening section. Together, they project a vision of reality truly majestic in its vast dimensions.

Most important, however, is the significance of this vision for man. Bryant was deeply affected by his view of the Illinois prairies, and this poem is the result of that experience. His "heart swells" and his sight dilates, he tells us, as he observes "the encircling vastness," . . . and his thoughts are turned toward the God who has

> smoothed these verdant swells, and sown their slopes
> With herbage, planted them with island groves,
> And hedged them round with forests. . . .

Contemplation of space, therefore, as in **"A Forest Hymn,"** turns the mind of the observer to the greatness of God, who has performed such magnificent works. Contemplation of time, on the other hand, makes one aware of the mutability of all terrestrial things. "Thus change the forms of being," Bryant writes,

> thus arise
> Races of living things, glorious in strength,
> And perish, as the quickening breath of God
> Fills them, or is withdrawn. . . .

The evocation of space and time thus suggests the infinity and eternity of God, the Creator, and brings home to the observer his own smallness in relation to so great a Being. This awareness of self as existing in an enormous world of space and time is especially emphasized in the closing lines of the poem, when the poet's imaginative vision is swept away and he becomes aware once again that he is "in the wilderness alone." . . . (pp. 213-17)

Not all Bryant's poems reveal so clearly the fundamental nature of his view of reality nor the philosophical implications that his vision had for him. At times he would simply concentrate on one small aspect of the natural world, as in poems like **"The Yellow Violet"** or **"To the Fringed Gentian,"** and develop his theme through the analogy he perceived between the natural phenomenon and the truths of the moral world. At times, too, he would turn to allegory, as he did in **"The Flood of Years"** or **"Waiting by the Gate,"** to develop his themes. But many of his poems—and these are among his best ones—evoke the sense of space and time that we have examined here. In these, Bryant reveals his cosmic view and the moral vision of life he derived from it. For him, the natural world must be seen as existing in vast reaches of both space and time. The thinking man must perceive this fact, approach his Creator with deep humility, still his violent passions, and arrange his life in accord with the rational order he perceives in the natural world. In such a universe, Bryant insists, concern with self is the rankest form of pride and desire for material gain the sheerest folly. (pp. 217-18)

> *Donald A. Ringe, in his* The Pictorial Mode: Space & Time in the Art of Bryant, Irving & Cooper *(copyright © 1971 by The University Press of Kentucky), University Press of Kentucky, 1971, 244 p.**

ADDITIONAL BIBLIOGRAPHY

Allen, Gay Wilson. "William Cullen Bryant." In his *American Prosody,* pp. 27-55. New York: American Book Co., 1935.
>A technical analysis of Bryant's poetic theory and practice, finding Bryant "eminently important in the history of American versification because his technique was finished, effective, and truly artistic."

Bigelow, John. *William Cullen Bryant.* Boston, New York: Houghton Mifflin Co., 1890, 355 p.
>Biography of Bryant by a man who was his friend, associate, and the co-owner of the *New York Evening Post.* Bigelow concludes that Bryant was "essentially an ethical poet," and that as a journalist he was mainly interested in "wrongs to be repaired."

Boynton, Percy H. "Early Metropolitans: William Cullen Bryant." In his *Literature and American Life,* pp. 273-83. Boston: Ginn and Co., 1936.
>Discusses Bryant's divided allegiance to journalism and poetry. Boynton asserts that even though Bryant played "the role of the urban satirist" when he relocated to New York, he was still the rural moralist in inclination.

Brooks, Van Wyck. "Our Poets." In his *America's Coming-of-Age,* pp. 39-105. New York: B. W. Huebsch, 1924.*
>Criticizes Bryant for his moral endings and for his lack of flexibility as a wordsmith. Brooks writes that Bryant "was as bald, as plain, as immovable, so to say, as an old settee."

Brown, Charles H. *William Cullen Bryant.* New York: Charles Scribner's Sons, 1971, 576 p.
>The definitive modern biography.

Cairns, William B. *British Criticisms of American Writings, 1815-1833.* University of Wisconsin Studies in Language and Literature, no. 14. Madison: University of Wisconsin Press, 1922, 319 p.*
>Summary of early English periodical criticism of Bryant's work.

Callow, James T. *Kindred Spirits: Knickerbocker Writers and American Artists, 1807-1855.* Chapel Hill: The University of North Carolina Press, 1967, 288 p.*
>Discusses Bryant's friendships with other writers and artists of the Knickerbocker school in New York. Callow finds that Bryant and his artist friends mutually influenced one another, especially in their treatment of landscape.

Conner, Frederick William. "Bryant, Longfellow, and Lowell: Rejection, Indifference, Discomfort." In his *Cosmic Optimism: A Study of the Interpretation of Evolution by American Poets from Emerson to Robinson,* pp. 167-90. Gainesville: University of Florida Press, 1949.*
>Commentary about Bryant's "cosmic optimism" and his disagreement with Darwinism. Conner stresses that Bryant could not believe in evolution because he felt that "it deprived the soul of its independent, supernatural character."

Duffey, Bernard. "Romantic Coherence and Romantic Incoherence in American Poetry." *The Centennial Review* VII, No. 4 (Fall 1963): 219-36.*

Briefly examines Bryant's work in the context of American Romanticism. Duffey posits that Bryant's attitude toward nature is that of a "celebrant of a holy communion and its blessings."

Duffey, Bernard. "The Idyllic Imagination: 'Snow-Bound', Bryant, Emerson, Longfellow, Holmes, Whittier." In his *Poetry in America: Expression and Its Values in the Times of Bryant, Whitman, and Pound,* pp. 43-60. Durham, N.C.: Duke University Press, 1978.*
 An expanded and more detailed version of Duffey's 1963 article (see annotation above).

Free, William J. "William Cullen Bryant on Nationalism, Imitation, and Originality in Poetry." *Studies in Philology* LXVI, No. 4 (July 1969): 672-87.
 Examines the importance of Bryant's critical tenets to the development of poetry in nineteenth-century America. Free concludes that Bryant's aesthetic was a coherent one, and that he "deserves credit for being able to posit a workable relationship between tradition and individual talent" during an emotionally difficult time in American history.

Glicksberg, Charles I. "Bryant, the Poet of Humor." *Americana* XXIX, No. 3 (July 1935): 364-74.
 Attempts to prove that Bryant is not a "consistently gloomy" and didactic poet. Glicksberg cites Bryant's occasional poems, parodies, and satires as examples of pieces "composed in a rollicking, carefree spirit, the meter clattering at a jolly clip."

Godwin, Parke. *A Biography of William Cullen Bryant.* 2 vols. New York: D. Appleton and Co., 1883.
 An extensive biography of Bryant by his son-in-law. Godwin particularly applauds Bryant for being aware of his powers and limitations and for never being "tempted to go outside of the sphere in which he had achieved success."

Herrick, Marvin T. "Rhetoric and Poetry in Bryant." *American Literature* 7, No. 2 (May 1935): 188-94.
 Concludes that Bryant's poetry often lacks spontaneity and passion because of his preoccupation with the rhetorical aspects of poetry.

Johnson, Curtiss S. *Politics and a Belly-full: The Journalistic Career of William Cullen Bryant.* New York: Vantage Press, 1962, 209 p.
 A complete account of Bryant's journalistic career.

Monroe, Harriet. "Aere Perennius." *Poetry* VI, No. IV (July 1915): 197-200.
 Accuses Bryant of having lived "downward rather than upward" after his early poetic successes. Monroe cautions that Bryant does not deserve respect as an artist because he "sacrificed the muse, not to those violent enemies, the flesh and the devil, but to that more insidious one, the world."

Nevins, Allan. *The Evening Post: A Century of Journalism.* New York: Boni and Liveright, 1922, 590 p.*
 A history of the *New York Evening Post.* Nevins considers Bryant's editorship in the context of the history of the newspaper.

Phair, Judith Turner. *A Bibliography of William Cullen Bryant and His Critics: 1808-1972.* Troy, N.Y.: The Whitston Publishing Co., 1975, 188 p.
 A research guide containing an introduction, listing of books and articles on Bryant, book reviews of Bryant's works, and a section on foreign references.

Pritchard, John Paul. "William Cullen Bryant." In his *Return to the Fountains: Some Classical Sources of American Criticism,* pp. 13-25. Durham, N.C.: Duke University Press, 1942.
 Traces classical influence in Bryant's poetry. Pritchard acknowledges Bryant's acquaintance with neoclassical writers, as well as with Aristotle and Horace, and determines that "neoclassicism and romanticism are the two forces which exert strong influence upon Bryant."

Pritchard, John Paul. *Literary Wise Men of Gotham: Criticism in New York, 1815-1860.* Baton Rouge: Louisiana State University Press, 1963, 200 p.*
 Places Bryant's lectures on poetry in the context of nineteenth-century New York intellectual life. Bryant's lectures of 1826, Pritchard writes, "are the *locus classicus* for American claims to originality."

Quinn, Arthur H[obson]. "The Frontiers of Life and Death." In *The Literature of the American People: An Historical and Critical Survey,* edited by Arthur Hobson Quinn, pp. 248-61. New York: Appleton-Century-Crofts, 1951.*
 A general discussion of Bryant's poetry. Quinn especially singles out the characteristics of "nobility" and "loftiness" in Bryant's poetry and considers him a figure "difficult to overestimate" in American literature.

Sanford, Charles L. "The Concept of the Sublime in the Works of Thomas Cole and William Cullen Bryant." *American Literature* 28 (January 1957): 434-48.*
 A look at Cole's treatment of the sublime in his landscape paintings and Bryant's treatment of the same in his poetry. Influenced by Edmund Burke's theory of the sublime, both men "turned to nature as a symbol of permanence amidst change and as a refuge from a crass, materialistic civilization."

Spencer, Benjamin T. "Bryant: The Melancholy Progressive." *Emerson Society Quarterly* (II Quarter 1966): 99-103.
 Concludes that Bryant was not essentially a Utopian poet. According to Spencer, Bryant viewed life as a trial and regarded it with melancholy, though he tempered his attitude with the hope of a final reward.

Stoddard, Richard Henry. "A Memoir of Bryant." In *Chronologies of the Life and Writings of William Cullen Bryant,* by Henry C. Sturges, pp. vii-xxx. Burt Franklin Bibliography and Reference Series, no. 164. 1903. Reprint. New York: Burt Franklin, 1968.
 A brief general appraisal of Bryant's poetic achievement, written by a friend. Stoddard praises Bryant's continued growth as a poet, despite early success, and his "unrivalled skill" in portraying American natural scenery.

Williams, Stanley T. "William Cullen Bryant." In his *The Spanish Background of American Literature, Vol. II,* pp. 122-51. New Haven: Yale University Press, 1955.
 Discusses Bryant's interest in Spanish literature and life as reflected in his travels, his writings, and his "prolonged devotion to Cervantes and to Spanish religious poetry." Williams feels that "Bryant's place as a Hispanophile is inadequately recognized."

Wilson, James Grant. *Bryant and His Friends: Some Reminiscences of the Knickerbocker Writers.* New York: Fords, Howard, & Hulbert, 1886, 443 p.*
 Largely biographical treatment of Bryant and his circle in New York.

Lydia Maria Child

1802-1880

(Born Lydia Maria Francis) American novelist, essayist, short story writer, editor, and poet.

Child is remembered today primarily for her abolitionist and humanitarian writings. Her *Appeal in Favor of That Class of Americans Called Africans,* one of the first anti-slavery volumes published in the United States, helped advance the abolitionist cause. She further expressed her humanitarianism in *Letters from New-York,* a popular collection of essays which describes the city's social and political conditions, and in *History of the Condition of Women in Various Ages and Nations,* one of the earliest American feminist treatises. Child's popularity, however, came largely from her juvenile and domestic writings. She was the editor of the children's periodical, *Juvenile Miscellany,* and contributed most of the stories and poems that appeared in it. Her poem, "Boy's Thanksgiving," which contains the lines "over the river and through the woods, to grandfather's house we go . . ." remains well known. Child's widely-read handbooks *The Frugal Housewife* and *The Mother's Book* provided advice on economical housekeeping and child-rearing.

The youngest of six children, Child was born in Medford, Massachusetts to a successful baker and his wife. The couple stressed the importance of frugality and compassion to the family and demonstrated their own charity by feeding the poor and helping runaway slaves. Child briefly attended Medford's village school and seminary, but her elder brother Convers Francis, a noted Unitarian minister and historian, was primarily responsible for her education. Convers shared his sister's intellectual interests and provided her with books on philosophy, art, literature, and theology. As a young girl, Child could knowledgeably discuss such authors as Homer and John Milton.

When Child was twelve, her mother died and she was sent to live with a married sister. Ten years later she moved to Watertown, Massachusetts and joined her brother's household and his intellectual circle, which included such noted New England Transcendentalists as Ralph Waldo Emerson and Margaret Fuller. There Child wrote her first novel, *Hobomok: A Tale of Early Times,* which after a poor critical reception became a popular success. Concerned with the then-scandalous topic of interracial marriage, the novel depicts Salem during colonial times. Her next novel, *The Rebels; or, Boston before the Revolution,* brought Child wide literary acceptance. In 1826, she founded the *Juvenile Miscellany,* which became popular with both children and adults.

In 1828, Child married David Lee Child, a prominent Massachusetts lawyer and legislator who was well known for his outspoken political beliefs. Encouraged by her husband, Child became interested in the abolitionist movement. After David gave up his law career to devote himself exclusively to abolitionist activities, Child wrote prolifically to support their household. She was concerned, however, because her fictional and domestic writings did little to further the abolitionist cause, and she began work on *Appeal in Favor of That Class of Americans Called Africans.* This lengthy essay, though welcomed by

Courtesy of Prints and Photographs Division, Library of Congress

her fellow abolitionists, outraged most of Child's readers. The public boycotted her fiction, her friends abandoned her, and subscriptions to the *Juvenile Miscellany* dropped so drastically that the magazine was eventually discontinued.

Ostracized by social and literary groups and facing financial ruin, Child continued with what she called her "mission of humanity." She moved to New York and assumed the editorship of William Lloyd Garrison's *National Anti-Slavery Standard.* During this time, Child composed *Letters from New-York,* which was one of the most popular American books of the 1840s. After returning to her farm in Wayland, Massachusetts, Child published, among other works, her well-received novel, *Philothea: A Grecian Romance,* and *The Progress of Religious Ideas through Successive Ages,* a comparative study of religions.

Nineteenth-century critics generally considered Child's novels to be important for their historical, rather than literary interest. Noted in her time for her elaborate and colorful representations of character and scene, Child is criticized today for her flamboyant, undisciplined style and weak characterization and plot. Modern critics do recognize Child's flair for description, but most agree that she was popular primarily for her sentimentality, sincerity, and compassion. Child's nonfiction prose is often regarded as her most enduring contribution. Modern critics cite *Letters from New-York* in particular for its logical, systematic construction and forceful style.

Though her works are dated by their subject matter and sentimental tone, Child is still valued for her contribution to American popular literature and for her dedication to humanitarian concerns. While her writings on abolition, feminism, and religion have been superseded by more scholarly studies, she is respected as a pioneer in those fields.

(See also *Dictionary of Literary Biography*, Vol. 1: *The American Renaissance in New England*.)

PRINCIPAL WORKS

Hobomok: A Tale of Early Times (novel) 1824

The Rebels; or, Boston before the Revolution (novel) 1825

The Frugal Housewife (handbook) 1829; also published as *The American Frugal Housewife*, 1829

The Mother's Book (handbook) 1831

*The Ladies' Family Library. 5 vols. (biographies) 1832-35

Appeal in Favor of That Class of Americans Called Africans (essay) 1833

Philothea: A Grecian Romance (novel) 1836

Letters from New-York (essays) 1843

**Flowers for Children. 3 vols. (short stories and poetry) 1844-55

Letters from New-York, Second Series (essays) 1845

The Progress of Religious Ideas through Successive Ages (essay) 1865

A Romance of the Republic (novel) 1867

Letters of Lydia Maria Child (letters) 1883

*This work includes *Biographies of Lady Russell and Madame Guion*, *Biographies of Madame de Staël and Madame Roland*, *Married Women; or, Biographies of Good Wives*, and *History of the Condition of Women in Various Ages and Nations*.

**This work includes the poem ''Boy's Thanksgiving.''

THE NORTH AMERICAN REVIEW (essay date 1824)

[*Hobomok*] displays considerable talent, which we hope will be again called into exercise. . . . The principal characters, some of which are historical, as Governor Endicott, Lady Arabella Johnson and her husband, are generally very well conceived and supported; the sketches of society and manners are drawn with a faithful hand; the incidents are detailed with a truth and spirit, which give animation and interest to the story. The author has an eye for the beautiful and sublime of external nature, and a heart for the tender and generous traits of the human character.

In many respects this little work is calculated deeply to engage the feelings, and in some parts it possesses considerable pathos. We regard it, however, rather as an earnest [example] of what the author can do, than as a performance from which he can promise himself much reputation. With all its merits it has defects, which prevent it from leaving, upon the whole, a favorable or a pleasing impression. We think it a fault in the plan of so short a work, that it introduces so many characters

and incidents not immediately connected with the main object; they do not sufficiently bear upon that which is the principal business of the piece; they do not contribute to advance the action, but rather divert the mind, and weaken the interest by multiplying the objects of the attention. It spreads over too wide a field; it consumes, if we may use such an expression, too much historical material for a tale of this kind. We are presuaded the author of *Hobomok* would have succeeded better had he made it entirely a work of fancy, so far as characters and incidents are concerned, and merely attempted to illustrate the circumstances, situation, and manners of our forefathers and the aborigines, and the scenery of our country. As it is, there is a want of unity, which prevents a sustained and continued interest. There is a great number of particular passages, which by themselves have every requisite of a fine novel, but they fail as parts of a whole. In general, we believe, it will be found that the most interesting narrations are those, which are minute in the detail of events and conversation, and which embrace but a small portion of time; those in which all the circumstances cluster around a few characters, producing a single and concentrated interest.

To our minds there is a very considerable objection to the catastrophe of this story. . . . [The] train of events not only unnatural, but revolting, we conceive, to every feeling of delicacy in man or woman.

We may appear perhaps to have found more to blame than praise in this tale; we do not wish to leave this impression. Its excellencies outweigh its faults. We have been more particular in speaking of the latter, because we hope to hear again from the author, and feel assured that they are only the results of inexperience in this kind of writing; that the author may amend them and at the same time retain all the other qualifications for a good writer, which are here exhibited. (pp. 262-63)

> *A review of "Hobomok, a Tale of Early Times," in* The North American Review, *Vol. XIX, No. XLIV, July, 1824, pp. 262-63.*

[JARED SPARKS] (essay date 1825)

[Hobomok *first attracted brief, generally unfavorable notice (see excerpt above from* The North American Review, *1824). As a result, sales of the novel were limited. Hoping to increase sales, Child submitted the novel to Jared Sparks, the editor of* The North American Review *and a friend of her brother, Convers, and asked him to review it more extensively. This review provided the impetus necessary for* Hobomok's *subsequent acceptance and popularity.*]

There can be, we believe, but one opinion respecting [*Hobomok*]; it is in very bad taste, to say the least, and leaves upon the mind a disagreeable impression. Still it should be remembered, in respect to its probability, that if our ancestors were more sternly virtuous, they were certainly without much of the delicacy and refinement of the present generation.

The characters in this novel . . . are too numerous, and the interest is lessened by being divided among so many. But they are drawn, in most instances, with great discrimination, as well those which are borrowed from history, as those which are purely fictitious. The strange mixture of good sense, piety, fanaticism, and intolerance, which distinguished our puritan ancestors, varied in different individuals, by the different degrees of natural talent, or education, is displayed with great ingenuity and power. The death bed scenes of the Ladies, Mary

Conant and Arabella Johnson, are described with feeling and pathos, and varied with considerable skill. (p. 87)

[The] principal beauties in this work are to be found in the delineations of the Indian character. We have seldom met with more successful efforts in this way, than the descriptions of the characters and language of Hobomok and Corbitant. We are only sorry that the author's plan did not admit of their more frequent appearance. (p. 90)

The tone of the work is generally sombre, and accords well with our associations with the early history of New England, and the days of sickness, sorrow, privation, and religious austerity. We never read the records of those times without a sensation of melancholy and pity, mingled with respect and national pride, and the author of **Hobomok** seems to feel and inspire a similar sensation.

We think this book has suffered much from the general prejudice against the catastrophe of the story, and that its animated descriptions of scenes and persons, its agreeable style, and the acquaintance with the history and spirit of the times which it evinces, have not received the credit due to them. But we doubt not, that it will one day be regarded with greater favor, and that it is by no means of the same ephemeral class, with some others of our American novels. It will stand the test of repeated readings, and it will obtain them. (pp. 94-5)

> *[Jared Sparks], in a review of "Hobomok," in* The North American Review, *n.s. Vol. XII, No. XXIII, July, 1825, pp. 86-95.*

THE AMERICAN MONTHLY REVIEW   (essay date 1832)

[In *The Biographies of Madame de Staël, and Madame Roland,* Mrs. Child] has mingled with remarkably good judgment her own reflections with the biographical narrative, and has given a due proportion of her pages and of her strength to the history of the childhood and youth of Madame de Staël, as influenced by the character and opinions of her parents, by her education, and by the society to which she was exposed. (p. 231)

[She] has ably traced the history of Madame de Staël's literary and political career, of her persecutions, and of her more private life. As a politician, no one, we think, can withhold from her the praise of remarkable moral courage and consistency. If in any thing Mrs. Child has indulged too freely in panegyric, which one is very apt to do, who becomes enamored of a subject long near at heart, she generally shows great discrimination; and if we make any abatements from the eulogy with which she closes the life of Madame de Staël, we cannot fail to appreciate its eloquence and sincerity. (p. 232)

We look forward with great expectations to Mrs. Child's continuation of her labors, and congratulate her, in this age of literary projects, upon her successful choice of subjects. (p. 235)

> *"Mrs. Child's 'Biographies',"* in The American Monthly Review, *Vol. II, No. III, September, 1832, pp. 230-35.*

MRS. [LYDIA MARIA] CHILD   (essay date 1833)

[*In the following preface to her* Appeal in Favor of That Class of Americans Called Africans, *Child anticipates a hostile reaction to the work. Stating that she is on a "mission of humanity," Child defends her decision to speak out in favor of what many Americans considered a "vulgar" cause.*]

Reader, I beseech you not to throw down this volume as soon as you have glanced at the title. Read it, if your prejudices will allow, for the very truth's sake:—If I have the most trifling claims upon your good will, for an hour's amusement to yourself, or benefit to your children, read it for *my* sake:—Read it, if it be merely to find fresh occasion to sneer at the vulgarity of the cause:—Read it, from sheer curiosity to see what a woman (who had much better attend to her household concerns) will say upon such a subject:—Read it, on *any* terms, and my purpose will be gained.

The subject I have chosen admits of no encomiums on my country; but as I generally make it an object to supply what is most needed, this circumstance is unimportant; the market is so glutted with flattery, that a little truth may be acceptable, were it only for its rarity.

I am fully aware of the unpopularity of the task I have undertaken; but though I *expect* ridicule and censure, I cannot *fear* them.

A few years hence, the opinion of the world will be a matter in which I have not even the most transient interest; but this book will be abroad on its mission of humanity, long after the hand that wrote it is mingling with the dust.

Should it be the means of advancing, even one single hour, the inevitable progress of truth and justice, I would not exchange the consciousness for all Rothchild's wealth, or Sir [Walter Scott's] fame.

> *Mrs. [Lydia Maria] Child, in a preface to her* An Appeal in Favor of That Class of Americans Called Africans, *Allen and Ticknor, 1833, p. v.*

[G. MELLEN]   (essay date 1833)

[We] are not sure that any woman in our country would outrank Mrs. Child. This lady has long been before the public as an author, with much success. And she well deserves it,—for in all her work—we think that nothing can be found, which does not commend itself by its tone of healthy morality, and generally by its good sense. . . . We have long watched the course of Mrs. Child, and in general, with satisfaction. Sometimes we have been more than satisfied,—we have admired her.

[Mrs. Child began] as a novelist. . . . [On] the whole she succeeded. To us this appears the more singular, and the more a subject for self-congratulation with the author, as the work she began with was an Indian story. We are stern unbelievers in Indian tales. We are tired of them,—and were so before Mrs. Child [wrote **Hobomok**].

Mrs. Child drew her savage very well,—though not so well as [Charles Brockden] Brown. Still there was an evident inclination to throw more of civilized life and conversation into the portraiture than is admissible; and though she had too much tact not to avoid the gross inconsistencies into which some who preceded and many who have followed her, have fallen, still **Hobomok** cannot be reckoned by any means faultless, and belongs to the second class of Mrs. Child's productions. (pp. 139-40)

We have no very particular recollection of [the plot of **The Rebels**]. . . . We remember, however, being pleased by the narrative,—by the drawing of some of the characters, and the management of some of the scenes. Some of the witty portions, or what were intended as such, struck us as not particularly happy. The old jokes of Dr. Byles were rather heavily introduced, and were also not the best which he is said to have committed. Puns, unless they are very good,—that is, very bad ones,—for the worse they are the better,—are a poor material for the pages of a work like the one referred to. The Doctor had wit, but Mrs. Child had done better by us, had she given us some of her own description in the place of these specimens of reverend humor. (p. 140)

In becoming the editor of the *Juvenile Miscellany,* Mrs. Child conferred a favor on parents and children alike; especially on the moral and religious portion of the community. This little work is admitted on all hands to be singularly excellent in its way. Its design and execution are both admirable. To one who has thought little of these things, it may appear an easy matter to make a book of this kind; so didactic and simple. But it is this very simplicity, that makes it a difficult work. (p. 141)

The power alone of producing such a series of short instructive stories as the *Miscellany* presents, so well calculated to captivate the youthful attention, and to fix youthful sympathy, argues a remarkable power of invention. In fact, it is one of the best proofs of the author's capacity for higher things. In the instance of Mrs. Child, this fertility is uncommon,—and we should all hold ourselves happy that we have a genius who comes to all our hearths, giving token of holding out so well, from the fund she has shown us already. (pp. 141-42)

[*The Frugal Housewife*] is a more revolutionary book than any other that Mrs. Child has written,—more so even than [*The Rebels*]; for the revolution with which this busies itself, extends all over our houses. It operates like a health committee, or a committee of vigilance. No woman will plead ignorance of its texts, and no daughter who looks to an establishment will dare own herself without it. (p. 142)

The Girl's Book and *The Mother's Book* were but parts of the general plan which our author appears to have laid out, of designating, in a simple way, the reciprocal duties of parent and child, and showing to both, by example and precept, the importance of the several relations in which they stand to each other. At least these good lessons are derivable from both the works, whether there was any particular intention of inculcating them or not. . . . The observations upon marriage struck us as particularly sensible. They are in good season for all the world,—and would have been, a century ago. They would form an excellent tract for the continent, and in England especially would they be of pungent application. Alas! even republican America must come in for her share of the reproof which these remarks embody. (p. 143)

The works we have thus noticed, with the exception of the novels, are those of Mrs. Child's collection that particularly aim to be useful,—we mean useful in the most direct and simple forms of usefulness. It is not one person in a generation, though endowed with all the talent to do it, who will undertake to perform the service to society which has been done by this lady. (pp. 143-44)

Though she calls [the miscellaneous pieces of *The Coronal*] the 'airy nothings' of the mind, Mrs. Child and all who are in the habit of thinking with her on this subject, may be assured that such nothings are frequently our pleasantest literary substance, and find 'a local habitation' in the bosoms of men,—and sensible men too,—where graver matters in octavo are permitted to subside into forgetfulness. . . . [The tales that make up this volume] are good specimens of the class of writings to which they belong,—the graceful, gay effusions that redeem our magazines and Annuals.

It would be wrong to pass by the poetry, of which the volume furnishes a few short pieces. We know not that Mrs. Child makes pretensions to poetic distinction, but we freely say that she might lay claim to excellence in this particular, and that with a good degree of success. (p. 146)

Of [Mrs. Child's *The Ladies' Library*], three volumes have already appeared,—excellent specimens,—and constituting so many of a series that our author intends to give to the public, from time to time. The first [containing the lives of Madame de Staël and Madame Roland] will prove, perhaps, as interesting as any one to most readers, as well from the subject as the style. . . . The manner of her story is clear, simple, sometimes eloquent, and always in good taste. This is fortunate, where so peculiar a strain is required. In a work that contains a mixture of the biographical with the historical, we might expect some departure from the tone appropriate to both, and an appearance of effort in the writer, to keep up to the spirit of each department. But there is nothing like this. The style is sustained throughout, and sufficiently easy to keep the reader always interested,—just as we are interested by the conversation of a person who talks fluently, to the point, and in full possession of his subject. We are glad to see these leading volumes of a collection that bids fair to be so valuable. It is not enough to hear about eminent men or eminent women, day after day, from eulogists,—or to see them in their works merely. We want the speaking portrait. (p. 148)

In her *Biographies of Good Wives,* . . . Mrs. Child has given us some excellent pictures of women. . . . The book is calculated to be interesting to intelligent young readers; and though most of the lives are familiar in their leading incidents to the general reader, there will still be something found in the volume new and pleasing even to children of an older growth. There is no portrait in the gallery here opened to us, to which we can point with particular emphasis, as containing anything very extraordinary in its lineaments or execution. It is enough to say that there are many fine heads, and that the management of the coloring is generally judicious. (p. 158)

[It] cannot but have struck the reader of this volume, that if Mrs. Child merely intended it to set forth the biographies of good wives, she has done more than was 'set down in the bond.' She has given us here the lives of good husbands as well as of good wives,—and that in so many instances, that it would warrant a change of the title. In some cases, it must be allowed that the wife plays but a second part in the story, and we are constrained to say, that on one or two occasions, the lady was in so dim a distance that we could hardly discern her. But these are trifles. The writer is true to her main object, in the leading portraits. (p. 162)

We trust that Mrs. Child will continue her useful labors, and have no doubt that they will be received with constantly increasing favor. We would not have her desert fiction altogether. This would be needless severity of construction, in determining what was useful. High and beautiful lessons may be inculcated by a good story, and as good a rule in morals *deduced*, as *laid down*. We are in favor of the employment of efficient mind in the realms of fancy. We want works of imagination that shall do us honor and good at the same time; and these we can have. (p. 163)

[*G. Mellen*], *"Works of Mrs. Child,"* in The North American Review, *Vol. XXXVII, No. LXXX, July, 1833, pp. 138-64.*

THE AMERICAN MONTHLY REVIEW (essay date 1833)

[*Because* Appeal in Favor of That Class of Americans Called Africans *addressed such a controversial subject, few journals reviewed the book. While admitting that Child "has treated the subject of slavery . . . with much more temperance, with far less prejudice, and with greater ability" than others, the author of the following review expresses regret that a writer who had previously "done so much credit to herself and her sex" with her domestic and children's writings should venture "on such a troubled sea."*]

[We] have never been so fortunate as to meet with . . . from an abolitionist [what Mrs. Child termed "mild and candid discussions"] till we read [*An Appeal in Favor of That Class of Americans Called Africans*]. Those that we have seen before, are more like the discussions of demoniacs than of rational thinking men. (p. 297)

We feel in duty bound to say that Mrs. Child has treated the subject of slavery, and of the collisions between the Colonization and Anti-Slavery Societies, with much more temperance, with far less prejudice, and with greater ability, than [other authors on that subject]. Her **"Appeal"** is written with the affections of a woman and the strength of a man. But we deeply regret that a lady, who by her writings has done so much credit to herself and her sex, so much for the improvement of her countrywomen, and of mankind, should venture with her bark on such a troubled sea, upon a voyage of discovery, with such pilots as she would seem to confide in. (p. 298)

> "African Colonization," in The American Monthly Review, Vol. IV, No. IV, October, 1833, pp. 282-98.*

MRS. [LYDIA MARIA] CHILD (essay date 1836)

[*In the following preface to her novel,* Philothea: A Grecian Romance, *Child defends her decision to write what she anticipates many readers will find "utterly useless." She explains that* Philothea *is an opportunity to "bid adieu to the substantial fields of utility, to float on the clouds of romance."*]

This volume is purely romance; and most readers will consider it romance of the wildest kind. A few kindred spirits, prone to people space "with life and mystical predominance," will perceive a light *within* the Grecian Temple.

For such I have written it. To minds of different mould, who may think an apology necessary for what they will deem so utterly useless, I have nothing better to offer than the simple fact that I found delight in doing it.

The work has been four or five years in its progress; for the practical tendencies of the [era] and particularly of the country in which I lived, have so continually forced me into the actual, that my mind has seldom obtained freedom to rise into the ideal.

The hope of extended usefulness has hitherto induced a strong effort to throw myself into the spirit of the times; which is prone to neglect beautiful and fragrant flowers, unless their roots answer for vegetables, and their leaves for herbs. But there have been seasons when my soul felt restless in this bondage,—like the Pegasus of German fable, chained to a plodding ox, and offered in the market; and as that rash steed, when he caught a glimpse of the far blue sky, snapped the chain that bound him, spread his wings, and left the earth

beneath him—so I, for awhile, bid adieu to the substantial fields of utility, to float on the clouds of romance. (pp. vi-vii)

> Mrs. [Lydia Maria] Child, in a preface to her Philothea: A Romance, Otis, Broaders & Co., 1836, pp. vi-viii.

[EDGAR ALLAN POE] (essay date 1836)

[*A prominent American poet and short story writer, Poe is generally considered to be the most outstanding early-nineteenth-century American critic. In the following brief review of* Philothea, *Poe describes the novel as a "signal triumph for our countrywomen," noting that its "purity of thought and lofty morality are unexceptionable."*]

Mrs. Child is well known as the author of **"Hobomok," "The American Frugal Housewife,"** and the **"Mother's Book."** She is also the editor of a "Juvenile Miscellany." The work before us is of a character very distinct from that of any of these publications, and places the fair writer in a new and most favorable light. **"Philothea"** is of that class of works of which the Telemachus of Fenelon, and the Anarcharsis of Barthelemi, are the most favorable specimens. (p. 659)

The plot of **"Philothea,"** like that of the Telemachus, and of the Anarcharsis, should be regarded . . . as the mere vehicle for bringing forth the antique "manners, costume, habits, and modes of thought," which . . . [are] at variance with a popular interest to-day. Regarding it in this, its only proper light, we shall be justified in declaring the book an honor to our country, and a signal triumph for our country-women.

"Philothea" might be introduced advantageously into our female academies. Its purity of thought and lofty morality are unexceptionable. It would prove an effectual aid in the study of Greek antiquity, with whose spirit it is wonderfully imbued. We say wonderfully—for when we know that the fair authoress disclaims all knowledge of the ancient languages, we are inclined to consider her performance as even wonderful. There are some points, to be sure, at which a scholar might cavil—some perversions of the character of Pericles—of the philosophy of Anaxagoras—the trial of Aspasia and her friends for blasphemy, should have been held before the Areopagus, and not the people—and we can well believe that an erudite acquaintance of ours would storm at more than one discrepancy in the arrangement of the symposium at the house of Aspasia. But the many egregious blunders of Barthelemi are still fresh in our remembrance, and the difficulty of avoiding errors in similar writings, even by the professed scholar, cannot readily be conceived by the merely general reader.

On the other hand, these discrepancies are exceedingly few in **"Philothea"** while there is much evidence on every page of a long acquaintance with the genius of the times, places, and people depicted. As a mere tale, too, the work has merit of no common order—and its purity of language should especially recommend it to the attention of teachers. (p. 662)

> [Edgar Allan Poe], in a review of "Philothea," in The Southern Literary Messenger, Vol. II, No. 10, September, 1836, pp. 659-62.

[C. C. FELTON] (essay date 1837)

The early writings of Mrs. Child gave brilliant promise of future eminence in the path of imaginative literature. The little tale of **"Hobomok"** contains passages of pathos and power, which are certainly extraordinary, coming from so young and untried an hand. Notwithstanding some serious defects in the plot, the numerous excellences of the work, its copious, vigorous, and eloquent style, and the rare descriptive talent it manifested, placed its gifted and youthful authoress, at once, among our most promising writers of fiction. . . . [The] same vigorous expression, lively fancy, and copious eloquence, which charmed the readers of "Hobomok," were undeniably exhibited [in "The Rebels"]. . . . (p. 77)

["**Philothea**"], as its title indicates, is an attempt to paint the manners and life of Grecian classical times. The attempt is a bold one. (p. 78)

Mrs. Child has some intellectual traits, which are well suited to success in this field of literary enterprise. She has a vigorous and exuberant imagination, and an accurate eye for beauty of form. She understands the harmonious construction of language, and can describe both nature and society with liveliness and truth. Her style, in its general character, is rich and eloquent; abounding in brilliant turns and fanciful illustrations. It is generally simple, energetic, and impressive, but sometimes it is too dazzling. In fact, the copiousness of her imagination, and the ardor of her feelings, which lend such power to her enthusiastic eloquence, in a measure injure her style for classical novel-writing. It is deficient in *repose;* we must use that word for want of a better. Classical scholars feel that ancient literature is deeply impressed with the peculiar quality, which can be described in its effect by that word alone. The study of the best classics soothes and solemnizes the mind like the contemplation of nature, or the presence of a gallery of ancient statues, standing before us in the marble stillness of centuries; and our imagination craves the same impressive effect in a work that essays to recall the spirit of classical times. In this point of view, it appears to us that Mrs. Child has not been entirely successful. She has not gone out of her peculiar feelings and opinions far enough to give us something thoroughly Greek. We trace distinctly enough certain ways of thinking, that belong, not merely to modern times, but to Mrs. Child herself. Through the whole work, we are threading the mazes of an imaginative faith, and a transcendental philosophy, partly Platonic, partly Swedenborgian. This influence has guided her in forming the leading characters, and in constructing the discourses and dialogues, in which their peculiarities are unfolded. (p. 79)

[Mrs. Child] has introduced upon her canvass the figures of mighty historical characters, who will task all the vigor of her pencil. How has she succeeded? We have already spoken in general terms of her style. In ["**Philothea**"] it has all its characteristic beauty and force. It is musical and significant. The glories of Athens are described in language fresh and sparkling, like the radiant forms of art, which filled the proud city. The imagery she draws around her scenes, and the associations she awakens, are in strict keeping with the time, the character, and the place. She has mastered all the learning requisite to the preserving of the outward proprieties, and the allusions and scenery are fastidiously correct. Indeed, it may justly be said, that she is too laboriously classical in minute details; in her Atticism, she is hyper-Attic, and might be known for a foreigner on classic ground, as Theophrastus was hailed "O Stranger" by a fishwoman of Athens, in consequence of the elaborate finish of his pronunciation. The general idea of each of her historical characters seems to us historically correct; but the details are not always so. The picture of the age is in the main truly colored; yet there are many features, in the character of the times, which are not sufficiently brought out. (p. 83)

The two characters on which Mrs. Child has expended the most care and labor, are evidently those of Plato and Philothea. So far as her portrait of the philosopher goes, it is unquestionably correct; but, led by some elective affinity, she has selected a few of Plato's philosophical doctrines, and represented his character only through their medium. The consequence is, that the Sage of the Academy appears but in one light. He is for ever the mystic and the moralizer, with a dash of sentiment that almost unmans him. . . .

[This] is a partial view of Plato's character; true as far as it goes, and false in its general effect. The themes he is made to touch upon exclusively, he *did* discuss occasionally; they formed a part, but not the whole of his philosophy. . . . [We] think that our author has not given a full and complete view, or even a justly proportioned view, of his intellectual constitution.

Philothea is a beautiful creation. A woman of great personal loveliness, educated in the midst of all the influences that can refine the imagination, deeply imbued with the more spiritual part of the Platonic philosophy, in daily communion with all of wit and genius that the best portion of Athenian society could offer; she rises before us, a being of such pure beauty, that we think of her not as of a daughter of this world, but as a child of the skies. The character is drawn with a delicate perception of the minutest proprieties and the finest shades. No discordant act breaks the harmony of her being; no harsh or violent sentiment, no wild passion, mingles with the gentle tone of her daily thoughts. The supernatural incidents that occur after her death, are a beautiful finale to the rich music of her life. But can we realize the character? does it belong to human life, and Attic life? No. It is a lovely dream of Mrs. Child's imagination. (pp. 83-5)

["**Philothea**"] will take a permanent place in our elegant literature; for, though deficient in some points of execution, it has the vital qualities that will save it from the common doom. Every page of it breathes the inspiration of genius, and shows a highly cultivated taste, in literature and art. The structure of its style is such as belongs only to a mind of fresh and vigorous powers; and the greatest fault of its plot,—its tendency to an excessive idealism,—will perhaps scarcely abate its popularity. (p. 85)

> [C. C. Felton], "Mrs. Child's 'Philothea'," in The North American Review, Vol. XLIV, No. XCIV, January, 1837, pp. 77-90.

[D. G. MITCHELL] (essay date 1845)

Letters are not to be read in a crowd, but by one's self, and late into the evening or at dusk. Nor must they be read aloud, but softly and quietly, with the mind free and the heart open. With these thoughts uppermost turn we again to the title before us:—"**Letters—from New York.**" A bold preface of the place. A good letter should have a blurred post-mark "we canna weel mak out," leaving us doubtful till our wishing eyes catch the first glimpse of the friendly hand running along the top-line in characters, how much plainer than print—New York. And then what—in the matter before us? No address—no kindly word—. . . no half-line? No, surely these of Mrs. Child's are no real letters. They have only one requisite—a careless freeness, how little without the rest! (p. 61)

[There] are numerous stories, and anecdotes, . . . scattered up and down throughout the volume, interesting enough for a book of much greater pretension; and subtracting somewhat from them, as in courtesy due to [Mrs. Child's] very active fancy, they are very reliable stories, and safe to be read. . . .

And of places, and histories around New York, are these true daguerreotypes and transcripts, such as we would put into the hands of a fresh country cousin, even in lieu of a pocket map. (p. 65)

[We] wish that the writer, in place of her meek dissent and quiet ridicule, had employed every allusion that her memory would justify, and every figure of speech her rhetoric could command, to satirize the dogmas of fashionable life. In such work we would bid her, earnestly and in good faith, God-speed; adding thereto, whatever of mockery our feeble language could promote, to throw the foulest odium on those puppets of their own fashion, who prescribe modes and orders for social intercourse. Any severity of remark, any bitterness of ridicule, would be mild weapons wherewith to controvert that growing spirit of stupid formalism which prevails through all the ranks of city life. . . . (p. 69)

Written, as ["Letters—from New York"] seems to have been, at different times, and without comparison of the parts, there is of necessity frequent repetition of some opinions and phrases. Many things are for the like reason carelessly said—some un-prettily said; and her illustrations, though fanciful, are many of them crude and undigested. But there is little that is common-place in the volume. This is praise; better praise than we wish we could give parts of it, which seem to us objectionable in sentiment. Moreover, there is a vivacious naturalness about the book, compassing even its oddities, covering up its minor defects of rhetoric, that to one like ourselves, tired with the heat and dust of this dry September, is refreshing as an April shower. At times, too, there are scattered up and down over the letters little eloquent apostrophes, which, if we liken its general vivacity to a shower, may in sequence be likened to an iced draught of the pure element. We have not even now said what we might say, that there is an extravagant tone per-vading the whole, which being at once natural and graceful in the writer, we can by no means condemn; but the same being strange and unsuited to a running comment upon practical mat-ters, and such occasionally are sublimed by the writer's touch, we cannot wholly praise. Mrs. C. should have written "Letters from the Country." How redolent would they have been of fresh air and springing verdure! . . . As it is, we see everyday scenes when we see them at all—for it is wonderful how the writer, living in a city, has found extrinsic sources of interest—through a prism. . . .

["Letters—from New York"] is, in short, a book for a steam-boat ride, but not upon the Hudson; to relieve a sick chamber, but the patient must not be nervous; to engage a man after business hours, but he must avow the Woman's Rights. It is a book for you, indulgent reader, to run through after this hasty comment, and say if you will be most her friend or our friend—or, better, friend to both.

One word more, and a kind one, to Mrs. Child. We wish not to lessen one iota the amount of your influence, which we believe to be considerable; and so believing, we implore you, by your hatred of formalism and cant, of ostentation and pride—by your sympathy with human want, and your hearty relish for all that is natural and noble in thought and in action, to direct that influence against the crying evils of social life. Your energies misdirected will avail less than those of a weak man; rightly directed, they will avail more than those of the strongest. (p. 74)

[*D. G. Mitchell*], "Notes upon Letters," in The American Review, *Vol. I, No. I, January, 1845, pp. 60-74.*

RUFUS WILMOT GRISWOLD   (essay date 1847)

[*Griswold was an anthologist, magazine editor, and an advocate of "Americanism" in literature. In the following brief survey of Child's works, he remarks that the author's writings abound "in bright pictures and fanciful thoughts," and that she has "shown that fine perception of the mysterious analogy which exists be-tween the physical and moral world."*]

Except Mr. Ware's *Zenobia* and *Probus*, **Philothea** is the only classical romance deserving any consideration that has been produced in this country, and it is worthy to be ranked with those admirable works. The scenery is purely Grecian; all the externals are in keeping; the narrative is interesting and clearly defined; and the style is elevated and chaste, abounding in unlooked-for turns and spontaneous beauties. But the author seems hardly to have caught the antique spirit: the philosophical tone of Philothea reminds us quite as much of Boston as of Athens. . . .

[*Fact and Fiction*] is a collection of tales, of various kinds, but all characteristic and excellent, which [Mrs. Child] had previously published in the periodicals. **"The Children of Mount Ida,"** and **"A Legend of the Apostle John,"** relate to classical times, and have the marble polish and chasteness of her Phil-othea. To another, **"Hilda Silfverling,"** a fantasy, she has imparted the interest and imagery that belong to Scandinavian manners and scenery. But perhaps those which have most of her own individuality are **"The Neighbour-in-Law,"** an ad-mirable illustration of the power of kindness in softening and moulding natures beyond all other influences, and the **"Beloved Tune,"** an expression of mental experiences, resembling some of the fine pieces of imagination interspersed with the second series of her *Letters from New York.*

Mrs. Child has a large acquaintance with common life, which she describes with a genial sympathy and fidelity,—a generous love of freedom, extreme susceptibility of impressions of beauty, and an imagination which bodies forth her feelings in forms of peculiar distinctness and freshness. Her works abound in bright pictures and fanciful thoughts, which seem to be of the atmosphere in which she lives. She transfuses into them some-thing of her own spirit, which, though meditative and some-what mystical, is always cheerful and radiant. In her revelations on music, illustrations of the doctrine of correspondences, and all the more speculative parts of her various writings, she has shown that fine perception of the mysterious analogy which exists between the physical and moral world, and of the mode in which the warp and woof of life are mingling, which is among the first attributes of the true poet. (p. 427)

Rufus Wilmot Griswold, "Lydia M. Child," in his The Prose Writers of America: With a Survey of the History, Condition, and Prospects of American Lit-erature, *Carey and Hart, 1847, pp. 426-33.*

[JAMES RUSSELL LOWELL]   (poem date 1849)

[*Lowell was a celebrated nineteenth-century American poet, critic, essayist, and editor. He was sympathetic with Child's political views, being himself an abolitionist and a contributor to the Na-*

tional Anti-Slavery Standard, *which Child coedited. In the following excerpt from* A Fable for Critics, *his book-length poem featuring witty critical portraits of his contemporaries, Lowell stresses Child's humanitarianism, equating her with the idealized heroine Philothea, from her novel of the same name. Lowell's biographer, Martin Duberman, noted that Lowell's friendship with Child "led him to extravagantly inflate [her] talent and importance."]*

There comes Philothea, her face all a-glow,
She has just been dividing some poor creature's woe
And can't tell which pleases her most, to relieve
His want, or his story to hear and believe;
No doubt against many deep griefs she prevails,
For her ear is the refuge of destitute tales;
She knows well that silence is sorrow's best food,
And that talking draws off from the heart its black
    blood,
So she'll listen with patience and let you unfold
Your bundle of rags as 'twere pure cloth of gold,
Which, indeed, it all turns to as soon as she's touched
    it,
And, (to borrow a phrase from the nursery), *muched* it,
She has such a musical taste, she will go
Any distance to hear one who draws a long bow;
She will swallow a wonder by mere might and main
And thinks it geometry's fault if she's fain
To consider things flat, inasmuch as they're plain;
Facts with her are accomplished, as Frenchmen would
    say,
They will prove all she wishes them to—either way,
And, as fact lies on this side or that, we must try,
If we're seeking the truth, to find where it don't
    lie. . . .

                                            (p. 61)

The pole, science tells us, the magnet controls
But she is a magnet to emigrant Poles,
And folks with a mission that nobody knows,
Throng thickly about her as bees round a rose;
She can fill up the *carets* in such, make their scope
Converge to some focus of rational hope,
And, with sympathies fresh as the morning, their gall
Can transmute into honey,—but this is not all;
Not only for those she has solace, oh, say,
Vice's desperate nursling adrift in Broadway,
Who clingest, with all that is left of thee human,
To the last slender spar from the wreck of the woman,
Hast thou not found one shore where those tired
    drooping feet
Could reach firm mother-earth, one full heart on whose
    beat
The soothed head in silence reposing could hear
The chimes of far childhood throb thick on the ear?
Ah, there's many a beam from the fountain of day
That to reach us unclouded, must pass, on its way,
Through the soul of a woman, and hers is wide ope
To the influence of Heaven as the blue eyes of Hope;
Yes, a great soul is hers, one that dares to go in
To the prison, the slave-hut, the alleys of sin,
And to bring into each, or to find there, some line
Of the never completely out-trampled divine;
If her heart at high floods swamps her brain now and
    then,
'Tis but richer for that when the tide ebbs agen,
As, after old Nile has subsided, his plain
Overflows with a second broad deluge of grain;

What a wealth would it bring to the narrow and sour
Could they be as a Child but for one little hour!

                                            (pp. 64-5)

[James Russell Lowell], in his A Fable for Critics: A Glance at a Few of Our Literary Progenies, *second edition, G. P. Putnam, 1849, 80 p.**

WENDELL PHILLIPS (eulogy date 1880)

[Phillips, a noted nineteenth-century abolitionist, claimed he was recruited to the anti-slavery cause by Child's Appeal in Favor of That Class of Americans Called Africans. *One of Child's most loyal supporters, he expresses his admiration for her in the following eulogy.]*

Mrs. Child's character was one of rare elements, and their combination in one person rarer still. She was the outgrowth of New England theology, traditions, and habits—the finest fruit of these: but she could have been born and bred nowhere but in New England. . . .

Lavishly endowed, her gifts were not so remarkable as the admirable conscientiousness with which she used them. Indeed, an earnest purpose, vigilant conscientiousness, were the keys to her whole life and its best explanation. (p. 263)

Her **"Progress of Religious Ideas"** was no mere intellectual effort. It was the natural utterance of a deep, kindly, and respectful sympathy with each [creed]. There was no foolish tenderness, no weak sentimentality about her. She held every one, as she did herself, strictly to the sternest responsibility. (p. 265)

What variety of gifts! everything but poet. Narrative, fiction, journalism, history, sketches of daily city life, ethics, consolation for the evening of life, ennobling our nature by showing how, under all error, there lives the right purpose and principle. And she had nothing of the scholar's disease, timidity and selfishness. Her hand was always ready for any drudgery of service. (p. 267)

Wendell Phillips, "Appendix: Remarks of Wendell Phillips at the Funeral of Mrs. Child" (1880), in Letters of Lydia Maria Child *by Lydia Maria Child, edited by Harriet Winslow Sewall, Houghton Mifflin and Company, 1883, pp. 263-68.*

THE ATLANTIC MONTHLY (essay date 1882)

[Mrs. Child's] novels were not her most successful works. They had a reputation at the time when they were published, but it was due largely to the meagre supply of native fiction. Miss Sedgwick was a truer artist. Indeed, it was not on the artistic side that Mrs. Child's contributions to literature were strongest. She was a moralist and reformer, and used literature for the purpose of accomplishing special objects; her best stories were short narratives which she was impelled to give in the warmth of her interest for some unfortunate or victim, as the pathetic story which she tells of the Umbrella Girl in her **"Letters from New York."** (p. 840)

The terrors of slavery are laid bare in many effective passages in these letters, and the book is thus in many ways a harrowing and distressing one, but there are reliefs in incidents which are sometimes exciting and stirring, and sometimes humorous. The picture of the escape of George Thompson is very graphic, and one is not disposed to look too closely into the supposed conspiracy against his life. Then there are glimpses of prominent actors in the scenes, which help to vivify the times. (pp. 842-43)

Mrs. Child's character . . . is disclosed in these letters. Beyond this, the book has a genuine value as a transcript in glowing language of a period of our national life when a woman's sympathy was a powerful lever in the great upheaval which followed. (p. 844)

"Lydia Maria Child," in The Atlantic Monthly, *Vol. L, No. CCCII, December, 1882, pp. 839-44.*

JOHN GREENLEAF WHITTIER (essay date 1883)

[*A poet, reformer, journalist, and critic, Whittier is considered one of the most influential nineteenth-century American literary figures. Whittier and Child shared many political and social conerns, and their friendship spanned several decades. After her death, Whittier compiled a selective volume of Child's correspondence, to which he contributed a eulogistic poem (see excerpt below, 1883) as well as the following introduction. Here Whittier characterizes Child as "a practical philanthropist" who "from the first was no mere closet moralist, or sentimental bewailer of the woes of humanity. She was the Samaritan stooping over the wounded Jew."*]

It is not too much to say that half a century ago [Mrs. Child] was the most popular literary woman in the United States. She had published historical novels of unquestioned power of description and characterization, and was widely and favorably known as the editor of the "Juvenile Miscellany," which was probably the first periodical in the English tongue devoted exclusively to children, and to which she was by far the largest contributor. Some of the tales and poems from her pen were extensively copied and greatly admired. (p. vii)

It is quite impossible for any one of the present generation to imagine the popular surprise and indignation which ["**Appeal in behalf of that Class of Americans called Africans**"] called forth, or how entirely its author cut herself off from the favor and sympathy of a large number of those who had previously delighted to do her honor. Social and literary circles, which had been proud of her presence, closed their doors against her. The sale of her books, the subscriptions to her magazine, fell off to a ruinous extent. She knew all she was hazarding, and made the great sacrifice, prepared for all the consequences which followed. (p. ix)

A practical philanthropist, she had the courage of her convictions, and from the first was no mere closet moralist, or sentimental bewailer of the woes of humanity. She was the Samaritan stooping over the wounded Jew. She calmly and unflinchingly took her place by the side of the despised slave and free man of color, and in word and act protested against the cruel prejudice which shut out its victims from the rights and privileges of American citizens. (p. x)

[Her] charming Greek romance of "**Philothea**" and her "**Lives of Madame Roland and the Baronness de Staël**" proved that her literary ability had lost nothing of its strength, and that the hand which penned such terrible rebukes [as "**Appeal in behalf of that Class of Americans called Africans**"] had still kept its delicate touch, and gracefully yielded to the inspiration of fancy and art. While engaged with her husband in the editorial supervision of the "**Anti-Slavery Standard**," she wrote her admirable "**Letters from New York;**" humorous, eloquent, and picturesque, but still humanitarian in tone, which extorted the praise of even a pro-slavery community. Her great work, in

three octavo volumes, "**The Progress of Religious Ideas,**" belongs, in part, to that period. It is an attempt to represent in a candid, unprejudiced manner the rise and progress of the great religions of the world, and their ethical relations to each other. She availed herself of, and carefully studied, the authorities at that time accessible, and the result is creditable to her scholarship, industry, and conscientiousness. If, in her desire to do justice to the religions of Buddha and Mohammed . . . , she seems at times to dwell upon the best and overlook the darker features of those systems, her concluding reflections should vindicate her from the charge of undervaluing the Christian faith, or of lack of reverent appreciation of its founder. (pp. xi-xii)

"**A Romance of the Republic,**" a story of the days of slavery, [is] powerful in its delineation of some of the saddest as well as the most dramatic conditions of master and slave in the Southern States. . . .

The introduction to ["**Aspirations of the World**"], occupying fifty pages, shows, at three-score and ten, her mental vigor unabated, and is remarkable for its wise, philosophic tone and felicity of diction. It has the broad liberality of her more elaborate work on the same subject, and in the mellow light of life's sunset her words seem touched with a tender pathos and beauty. (p. xix)

John Greenleaf Whittier, in an introduction to Letters of Lydia Maria Child *by Lydia Maria Child, edited by Harriet Winslow Sewall, Houghton Mifflin and Company, 1883, pp. v-xxv.*

JOHN GREENLEAF WHITTIER (poem date 1883)

We sat together, last May-day, and talked
　　Of the dear friends who walked
Beside us, sharers of the hopes and fears
　　Of five and forty years

Since first we met in Freedom's hope forlorn,
　　And heard her battle-horn
Sound through the valleys of the sleeping North,
　　Calling her children forth.

And youth pressed forward with hope-lighted eyes,
　　And age, with forecast wise
Of the long strife before the triumph won,
　　Girded his armor on.

Sadly, as name by name we called the roll,
　　We heard the dead-bells toll
For the unanswering many, and we knew
　　The living were the few.

And we, who waited our own call before
　　The inevitable door,
Listened and looked, as all have done, to win
　　Some token from within.

No sign we saw, we heard no voices call;
　　The impenetrable wall
Cast down its shadow, like an awful doubt,
　　On all who sat without.

Of many a hint of life beyond the veil,
　　And many a ghostly tale
Wherewith the ages spanned the gulf between
　　The seen and the unseen,

Seeking from omen, trance, and dream to gain
  Solace to doubtful pain,
And touch, with groping hands, the garment hem
  Of truth sufficing them,

We talked; and, turning from the sore unrest
  Of an all-baffling quest,
We thought of holy lives that from us passed
  Hopeful unto the last,

As if they saw beyond the river of death,
  Like Him of Nazareth,
The many mansions of the Eternal days
  Lift up their gates of praise.

And, hushed to silence by a reverent awe,
  Methought, O friend, I saw
In thy true life of word, and work, and thought,
  The proof of all we sought.

Did we not witness in the life of thee
  Immortal prophecy?
And feel, when with thee, that thy footsteps trod
  An everlasting road?

Not for brief days thy generous sympathies,
  Thy scorn of selfish ease;
Not for the poor prize of an earthly goal
  Thy strong uplift of soul.

Than thine was never turned a fonder heart
  To nature and to art
In fair-formed Hellas in her golden prime,
  Thy Philothea's time.

Yet, loving beauty, thou couldst pass it by,
  And for the poor deny
Thyself, and see thy fresh, sweet flower of fame
  Wither in blight and blame.

Sharing His love who holds in His embrace
  The lowliest of our race,
Sure the Divine economy must be
  Conservative of thee!

For truth must live with truth, self-sacrifice
  Seek out its great allies;
Good must find good by gravitation sure,
  And love with love endure.

And so, since thou hast passed within the gate
  Whereby awhile I wait,
I give blind grief and blinder sense the lie:
  Thou hast not lived to die!

                              (pp. 269-71)

John Greenleaf Whittier, "Within the Gate," in Letters of Lydia Maria Child by Lydia Maria Child, edited by Harriet Winslow Sewell, Houghton Mifflin and Company, 1883, pp. 269-71.

THOMAS WENTWORTH HIGGINSON (essay date 1899)

In judging of ["**Hobomok**"], it is to be remembered that it marked the very dawn of American imaginative literature. . . . "**Hobomok**" now seems very crude in execution, very improbable in plot; and is redeemed only by a certain earnestness which carries the reader along, and by a sincere attempt after local coloring. It is an Indian [version of Alfred Tennyson's] "Enoch Arden," with important modifications, which unfor-

tunately all tend away from probability. Instead of the original lover who heroically yields his place, it is to him that the place is given up. The hero of this self-sacrifice is an Indian, a man of high and noble character, whose wife the heroine had consented to become, at a time when she had been almost stunned with the false tidings of her lover's death. The least artistic things in the book are these sudden nuptials, and the equally sudden resolution of Hobomok to abandon his wife and child on the reappearance of the original betrothed. (p. 114)

["**The Rebels; or, Boston before the Revolution**"] was a great advance on its predecessor, with more vigor, more variety, more picturesque grouping, and more animation of style. The historical point was well chosen, and the series of public and private events well combined, with something of that tendency to the over-tragic which is common with young authors,—it is so much easier to kill off superfluous characters than to do anything else with them. (p. 115)

[In her "**History of Woman**," Mrs. Child] aimed at a popular, not a profound, treatment. She was, perhaps, too good a compiler, showing in such work the traits of her brother's mind, and carefully excluding all those airy flights and bold speculations which afterwards seemed her favorite element. The "**History of Woman**," . . . was a mere assemblage of facts, beginning and ending abruptly, and with no glimpse of any leading thought or general philosophy. It was, however, the first American storehouse of information upon that whole question, and no doubt helped the agitation [of women's rights] along. (p. 120)

The name ["**Appeal for that Class of Americans called Africans**"] was rather cumbrous, like all attempts to include an epigram in the title-page, but the theme and the word "**Appeal**" were enough. (p. 121)

The tone [of the "**Appeal**"] is calm and strong, the treatment systematic, the points well put, the statements well guarded. The successive chapters treat of the history of slavery, its comparative aspect in different ages and nations, its influence on politics, the profitableness of emancipation, the evils of the colonization scheme, the intellect of negroes, their morals, the feeling against them, and the duties of the community in their behalf. As it was the first anti-slavery work ever printed in America in book form, so I have always thought it the ablest; that is, it covered the whole ground better than any other. (p. 123)

I well remember the admiration with which ["**Philothea**"] was hailed; and for me personally it was one of those delights of boyhood which the criticism of maturity cannot disturb. What mattered it if she brought Anaxagoras and Plato on the stage together, whereas in truth the one died about the year when the other was born? What mattered it if in her book the classic themes were treated in a romantic spirit? That is the fate of almost all such attempts. . . . (pp. 124-5)

["**Isaac T. Hopper; a True Life**"] gave another new sensation to the public, for [Mrs. Child's] books never seemed to repeat each other, and belonged to almost as many different departments as there were volumes. The critics complained that this memoir was a little fragmentary, a series of interesting stories without sufficient method or unity of conception. Perhaps it would have been hard to make it otherwise. Certainly, as the book stands, it . . . serves as an encyclopaedia of daring and noble charities. (pp. 130-31)

["**A Romance of the Republic**"] was received with great cordiality, and is in some respects [Mrs. Child's] best fictitious work. The scenes are laid chiefly at the South, where she has given the local coloring in a way really remarkable for one who never visited that region, while the results of slavery are painted with the thorough knowledge of one who had devoted a lifetime to their study. The leading characters are of that type which has since become rather common in fiction, because American society affords none whose situation is so dramatic,—young quadroons educated to a high grade of culture, and sold as slaves after all. All the scenes are handled in a broad spirit of humanity, and betray no trace of that subtle sentiment of caste which runs through and through some novels written ostensibly to oppose caste. The characterization is good, and the events interesting and vigorously handled. The defect of the book is a common one,—too large a framework, too many *vertebrae* to the plot. Even the established climax of a wedding is a safer experiment than to prolong the history into the second generation, as here. The first two thirds of the story would have been more effective without the conclusion. (pp. 137-38)

[Mrs. Child] was one of those prominent instances in our literature of persons born for the pursuits of pure intellect, whose intellects were yet balanced by their hearts, both being absorbed in the great moral agitations of the age. . . . In a community of artists, she would have belonged to that class, for she had that instinct in her soul. But she was placed where there was as yet no exacting literary standard; she wrote better than most of her contemporaries, and well enough for her public. She did not, therefore, win that intellectual immortality which only the very best writers command, and which few Americans have attained. (pp. 140-41)

Thomas Wentworth Higginson, "Lydia Maria Child," in his Contemporaries, *Houghton Mifflin and Company, 1899, pp. 108-41.*

ALEXANDER COWIE   (essay date 1948)

[*A noted authority on American fiction, Cowie is also an esteemed historian, biographer, and critic. His* The Rise of the American Novel *and* American Writers Today *are studies which trace the evolution of the American novel by studying the artistic development of the novelists themselves. In his study of Child, Cowie concludes that "fiction was not her forte," and stresses that although her reconstruction of history is accurate, Child's characterization is not so successful. He calls* The Rebels; or, Boston Before the Revolution "unnecessarily complex" *and states that* Philothea *shows literary promise, but "its merits are [still] not sufficient to lift it above the level of mediocre fiction." Letters from New-York "is probably Mrs. Child's most valuable legacy"; she undertook a sociological study which proved her pen "equal to the description of devastating contrasts." As a whole, Cowie finds that Child "never quite worked out a plan whereby her social studies could be used to nourish her art as a novelist."*]

Hobomok: A Tale of Early Times is interesting by reason of its early position among historical romances treating of the American Indian in relationship to seventeenth-century life in Massachusetts. (p. 178)

It is obvious that *Hobomok* contains strong elements of reader-interest—the theme of [Tennyson's] Enoch Arden in the main plot, a love affair among secondary characters which anticipates Longfellow's "Speak for yourself" scene in "The Courtship of Miles Standish," and the problem of miscegenation. The marriage of a white girl to an Indian, however "civilized," was a move to be taken only with the greatest caution by a novelist. . . . Accordingly Mrs. Child did well, from the point

of view of romance, to send her noble Indian back to the forest. In any case, he will not really suffer much, for he is but a lay figure, artificial in language and action. The whole action of the book is pretty much askew anyway. The love affair of Sally Oldham (who tells her suitor to speak for himself) is treated at first as if it were to form an important part of the story, but Sally is practically ignored by the author thereafter. Sally is a pretty good character, though, with plenty of sparkle in her eye and pepper on her tongue. She can talk like a person instead of a copybook—as when she says with monosyllabic fervor: "Folks who have the least to do with love are the best off." But Sally is an exception, and Mary is accorded those rhetorical flourishes that are the unhappy rule in most early novels. Mary's appearance must remind the reader of "a Parian statue, or one of those fair visions which fancy gives to slumber," and when it is her lot to see Charles go away on his shipwreck assignment, she is described as "a lily weighed down by the pitiless pelting of the storm; a violet shedding its soft, rich perfume on bleakness and desolation . . ." She becomes a vessel of sentimentality and in many ways she anticipates the pallid, neurotic heroines of the school of Edna Earl in Mrs. Wilson's *St. Elmo*. The imaginative reconstruction of early Salem and Plymouth days, though on a slight scale, is rather better than the characterization. The details of domestic life among well-to-do people are well suggested and due attention is given to religion in the lives of the early settlers. The author roguishly exposes the local minister as quite willing to give "a sly look and word" to Sally if "his good-woman was out of the way." Yet in general the Puritan community is viewed favorably. . . . (pp. 179-80)

[*The Rebels, or Boston Before the Revolution*] was inferior to *Hobomok*. Although the author in part lived up to her promise that she would write "the domestic annals" of the period, . . . the major narrative events of the book are unnecessarily complex, and the style is over-wrought and over-allusive. The turgid political discussion arising out of the national emergency (emphasis is on the Stamp Tax crisis) reveals the author's youthful limitations. Again the most effective elements are the details of everyday life and the sprightly treatment of female characters. There is variety (if not subtlety) in the author's portrait of Miss Sandford—a spinster who looks like "an antediluvian image," speaks in "the squeaking tones of antiquated coquetry," and conducts herself in such fashion as to elicit Dr. Mather Byles's query: "Has Aunt Sandford been backbiting her neighbours till her double teeth ache?" But lively, brash phrasing could not save *The Rebels* from rather harsh treatment [from contemporary critics]. . . . (p. 180)

[*Philothea*] shows greater ability in novel-construction than Mrs. Child's earlier stories, but its merits are not sufficient to lift it above the level of mediocre fiction which was prolifically produced in the thirties. It constitutes, however, one of the early signs of a vogue for novels laid in early eras—whether Greek or Roman or early Christian. *Philothea* is a tale of Greek life—mainly a love story—in the days of Pericles. Its subject-matter enabled Mrs. Child to capitalize her respectable knowledge of antiquity, but the author erred in her artistry by grafting New England morality upon Greek life. It is superior to the earlier novels in its style. . . . *A Romance of the Republic*, . . . should logically have been her best fiction, for its theme was that which had dominated the active middle years of her life, namely, abolition. But a new disadvantage rose to prevent her from reaching high distinction as novelist, and this time it was the hampering grip of propaganda. Interested in political and civil freedom for humanity, she could not emancipate her fictional characters from ideological bondage. Her quadroons are hardly more than one-quarter real. The book finally fails to achieve authenticity. Mrs. Child knew slavery as an institution, but she did not know the South intimately and she had to resort to artificial coloring of the local scene. Moreover her narrative suffers from having "too large a framework, too many *vertebrae* to the plot" [see excerpt above by Thomas Wentworth Higginson, 1899]. (pp. 181-82)

[Mrs. Child was] recognized as one of the most able women of her generation. But fiction was not her forte. Her brave little attempts at the historical romance it now seems a folly to compare with Cooper's brilliant enterprises. Yet she had a great deal of force as a writer of nonfiction and at one or two points her ideas on social problems converged with those of Cooper. She saw and deplored some of the same conditions that Cooper energetically denounced upon his return from Europe, particularly the unfortunate conditions under which young folk grew up in commercial New York. These ideas she expressed in various places, notably in **Letters From New York** . . . , a work which, from the point of view of the general student of literary history, is probably Mrs. Child's most valuable legacy. Like Cooper, she was disheartened by America's tendency to ape European ways and to establish unwholesome class cleavages on the basis of money. Her pen was quite equal to the description of devastating contrasts:

> Rapid approximation to the European style of living is more and more observable in this city. The number of servants in livery visibly increases every season. Foreign artistic upholsterers assert that there will soon be more houses in New-York furnished according to the fortune and taste of noblemen, than there are either in Paris or London; and this prophecy may well be believed, when the fact is considered that it is already not very uncommon to order furniture for a single room, at the cost of ten thousand dollars. There would be no reason to regret this lavishness, if the convenience and beauty of social environment were really increased in proportion to the expenditure, and if there were a progressive tendency to equality in this distribution. But, alas, a few moments' walk from saloons superbly furnished in the style of Louis 14th, brings us to Loafers' Hall, a dreary desolate apartment, where shivering little urchins pay a cent apiece, for the privilege of keeping out of watchmen's hands, by sleeping on boards arranged in tiers.

(pp. 182-83)

Mrs. Child saw many of the same symptoms of an ailing society that Cooper saw, but her diagnosis was different. Whereas Cooper was inclined to ascribe many socio-economic evils to a corrupt press and to political causes (the waning prestige of landed proprietors, etc.), Mrs. Child, who was a social worker, came to grips with evil as she saw it on the Bowery and on Blackwell's Island. She did not look at the problem of general social amelioration from a political angle or from, what was just as frequent in her day, a religious angle. She took a sociological stand. She felt that poverty was the greatest menace to society: "If we can abolish *poverty*, we shall have taken the greatest step toward the abolition of crime." . . . The problem, she grants, is a difficult one, but she sees most hope in an educational program with respect to correctional media: society

must not merely punish criminals but must educate them and provide economic opportunity for them. Here was a line of thought which Cooper never followed, for he almost never met the lower classes, excepting his own servants, at close range. Sooner or later, novelists would have to reckon with underprivileged folk. The domestic sentimentalists of the fifties and sixties would finger some of the issues delicately for a Victorian public, but the real battle for social security would not be waged by novelists until after the Civil War. As for Mrs. Child, perhaps at first she instinctively recoiled from trying to express deeply felt social lessons in the artificial medium of the novel. At any rate she never quite worked out a plan whereby her social studies could be used to nourish her art as a novelist. Her short stories occasionally traversed ground that their author had known in actuality, but the stories she left untold or told only in the form of treatise or tract were the more numerous. She had, as Lowell said, a "great heart," but not a great gift as a fiction-writer. (p. 184)

Alexander Cowie, "Contemporaries and Immediate Followers of Cooper, I," in his The Rise of the American Novel, *American Book Company, 1948 (and reprinted by American Book Company, 1951), pp. 165-227.**

GAIL PARKER (essay date 1972)

[Lydia Maria Child] never found perfect repose within her art. She was fascinated by Swedenborg's belief in the existence of precise correspondences between nature and the spirit, and more specifically, by the possibility that the correspondence between Fourier's plan of society and Swedenborg's description of life among the angels meant that Fourier had been sent to earth "to answer the prayer, 'Thy kingdom come on earth as it is in heaven.'" Yet while she was intrigued by the prospect of social reorganization, she was even more charmed by the effect a lively sense of correspondence had on her perceptions here and now. "There *was* a time," she wrote in the first of her **Letters from New York,** when the blind beggar sitting before the mansion of the slave trader, when street cries and horse carts

> would have passed me by like the flitting figures of the magic lantern, or the changing scenery of a theatre, sufficient for the amusement of the hour. But now I have lost the power of looking merely on the surface. Everything seems to me to come from the Infinite, to be filled with the Infinite, to be tending toward the Infinite.

In short, Swedenborg's philosophy gave Mrs. Child a way to justify her own overwhelming interest in the contemporary scene. She could concentrate on local color only when she knew that her observations could be translated into spiritual terms on a moment's notice. For example, after praising the public gardens in New York, she goes on to point out "that in this worst emporium of poverty and crime, there are, *morally* speaking, some flowery nooks, and 'sunny spots of greenery.'" (pp. 20-1)

To Mrs. Child's way of thinking, no individual was so vicious that he could not be saved by maternal influence, or the influence of a maternal surrogate such as the Genius of Temperance—or the Virgin Mary. (p. 21)

Mrs. Child's scorn for intellect must be read as the climax of a sustained defense of the downtrodden. Actually her allegiance to impulse was more ambiguous. The elaborate ways in which she worked out the doctrine of correspondence suggest how important it was to her to have a sense of intellectual mastery. Yet sometimes even Swedenborg's formulations were not enough, action not analysis was called for, and Mrs. Child was left face to face with her sympathetic energies. (p. 22)

For all her sympathy with the generous Irish, and Africans, and those women of whom the best that could be said was that they were affectionate, Mrs. Child was no egalitarian. Underlying her broadmindedness was a firm conviction that she, and women like her, were in the vanguard of spiritual evolution. She could tolerate Tom, Dick, and Harry in the faith that exposure to literature, music, flowers, and virtuous women would transform them into "Mr. Thomas, Richard, and Henry. In all these things," she lectured her audience, "the refined should think of what they can *impart,* not of what they can *receive.*"

Lydia Child's praise for the single standard was of a piece with this elitism; as far as she was concerned men were in sad need of all the virtues commonly prescribed for women. (p. 23)

Mrs. Child's **Letters** were a species of free association; she wandered from observation to interpretation and back again. Yet when her meanderings are charted they have a logic of their own. Her account of [a] temperance parade is first supplemented by a short treatise on the domestic affections. Then she has a vision of John the Baptist preparing a pathway through the wilderness. And, finally, she comes back to the parade to work out its correspondences. (p. 24)

[As] long as women like Lydia Maria Child . . . clung to the vocabulary of religious struggle they were never without a cause to focus their energies. Sin was everywhere. (p. 25)

> *Gail Parker, in an introduction to* The Oven Birds: American Women on Womanhood, 1820-1920, *edited by Gail Parker (copyright © 1972 by Gail Thain Parker; reprinted by permission of Doubleday & Company, Inc.), Anchor Press, 1972, pp. 1-56.**

WILLIAM S. OSBORNE   (essay date 1980)

[*Although he notes that Child exhibits skill in characterization and historical depiction, Osborne cites a major flaw in* Hobomok. *The depiction of the marriage of a white woman to an Indian is "disturbing" to the reader, according to Osborne, and her attempt to "make [Hobomok] white" is even less excusable. In spite of this flaw, Osborne remarks,* Hobomok "*can be safely compared with any work of fiction which had been produced in America." Osborne agrees with Cowie (1941) regarding Child's other works, however. He concludes that while* A Romance of the Republic *is "well-paced" and* Philothea *is "skillfully composed," Child's "talent is largely undisciplined: her most effective writing was charged with an emotional fervor. . . . [Her] strongest appeal," Osborne continues, "may well rest with her nonfiction of the workaday world . . . where real problems are dealt with in clear, hard-hitting, energetic prose. . . ."*]

Hobomok is not [a] first-rate fiction . . . ; it was too hastily written, uneven in development, immature in style. Yet there is remarkable skill in creating characters and in depicting the times, and Mrs. Child's earnestness in telling the story carries the reader along. (p. 39)

New England's past provides the framework for Mrs. Child's story, but **Hobomok** is a romance. Undoubtedly, the novel is wrongly named, for it is more a tale of the Salem villagers than it is a story about the Indians. (p. 46)

Sally is loyal to her friend, Mary, even when the Salem villagers—and Mary herself—are shocked by her "error in judgment," her marriage to Hobomok. She tells Mary in all sincerity: "I always thought he was the best Indian I ever knew; and within these three years he has altered so much, that he seems almost like an Englishman. After all, I believe matches are foreordained." If there is a bit of bewilderment in Sally's remark, she is attempting to rationalize an incredible situation—the marriage of a white woman to the manor born to an Indian primitive. Although the unlikely union speaks well for Mrs. Child's liberal mind, her treatment of the circumstances leading to the marriage is the feeble effort of an inexperienced novelist working out the details of her plot. Nor does any trait in Mary's character suggest the possibility of such a marriage. In fact, at one point in the story, Sally, who is prattling about marriage and the scarcity of young men in the village, remarks that the only "chance a body has for a husband" it to "pick up some stray Narragansett." "'O, don't name such a thing,' said Mary shuddering." And in the ensuing conversation the young women even suggest that they, like their Salem neighbors, regard the Indians as agents of the devil. (pp. 48-9)

As a tale of New England, as social history of a seventeenth-century village—which matter constitutes two-thirds of the narrative, incidentally—**Hobomok** satisfies the reader. Mrs. Child justifies the tale with an intimate knowledge of the Puritans' conduct and thought; she comprehends their theological concerns, their fears and apprehensions; she captures through history and legend the spirit of the times. However, the marriage of Mary Conant and Hobomok, so crudely grafted onto the narrative, disturbs the reader.

Hobomok figures in the novel as a character of secondary importance; and as a character of secondary importance, the reader is duly informed about him. Conant and Oldham, Mary and Sally reveal themselves to the reader, through their conversations and through their actions. Mrs. Child speaks for Hobomok; she also reports his activities. There are conversations between Mary and her lover which the reader is privy to, reinforcing the romance that obviously exists. The reader is told that Hobomok has loved Mary from a distance, ever since that day when "Mary had administered cordials to his sick mother, which restored her to life after the most skilful [sic] of their priests had pronounced her hopeless; and ever since that time, he had looked upon her with reverence, which almost amounted to adoration." (p. 49)

Since love "deep and intense" for a white woman has struck the redman, Mrs. Child, to forestall her readers' protests over miscegenation, uncolors him. She makes him white. She apologizes for his Indianness. Here, for the modern reader, is "the very bad taste."

No longer a character in his own right, Hobomok becomes the novelist's pawn. Hobomok, "cast in nature's noblest mould . . . clever . . . and comely withal," is Indian in name only. To make him an acceptable suitor, she alienates him from his brothers. (p. 50)

Hobomok is now a white man in thought and emotion, in deed and association. The transformation is unforgivable. Ironically, Mrs.Child has made him one of our literature's earliest alienated heroes. (p. 51)

In Mrs. Child's day it was no doubt the miscegenation which may have embarrassed her readers; today it is Mrs. Child's denial of Hobomok as an Indian—a denial Mrs. Child herself would quickly repent. . . . The fault can best be explained by the inexperience of the writer.

When the fault is set aside, *Hobomok* as a social history of seventeenth-century New England is sensitively done. The details of the Puritan way of life are solidly sketched, the pastimes and anxieties of the Salem villagers are animatedly described, the characters are remarkably alive. The pathos is sometimes overwrought, and the style is often pretentious; yet what novel written in the same period is free from such affectation.

Mrs. Child clearly makes her point about the excess of religious zeal, how it warps individuals and erodes the church—a remarkably liberal view to express in a society not yet aware of Emerson's opinion of organized religion. In this respect *Hobomok* is seen in sharper focus by the modern reader, and Mrs. Child herself is seen in a way typical of her own character. "Nature's noblest mould" is not so much the primitive savage, already familiar to readers of fiction in her day, but the man of conscience—capable of rising above forms and ceremonies, above the restraints imposed by society, and capable of exercising a freedom which guarantees the happiness of his fellow human being. Society limits man's nobler nature, often debases him. Conant is not a free agent because his religion, imposed by society, will not allow him freedom. Hobomok, "whose nature was unwarped by the artifices of civilized life," can stoically renounce personal happiness for the happiness of others. (pp. 53-4)

As important as *Hobomok* is in affirming Mrs. Child's own principles, the novel . . .—in spite of its flaw—can safely be compared favorably with any work of fiction which had been produced in America—no mean accomplishment for a novice. (p. 54)

The Rebels, or Boston before the Revolution, Mrs. Child's second effort to create fiction out of New England's past, is largely a failure for her reader and for the modern reader: a complicated plot, principal characters who are clearly borrowed from the sentimental tales in vogue with readers a generation before, token descriptions of the social pageant, and an inflated style far more precious than that in *Hobomok.* . . .

Unlike *Hobomok,* which is indeed a chapter of New England's past, *The Rebels* lacks similar structure because Mrs. Child has no clear focus. The title suggests an historical novel, yet there are only two scenes—admittedly, dramatically written—that echo the history of the times: the sacking of the governor's mansion by an unruly mob angered over the recent imposts levied by the Crown and the fervent appeals of the patriots Samuel Adams and James Otis to let conscience and conduct be the guide to the citizens' resistance to the policies of Parliament. (p. 55)

Unlike *Hobomok,* the novel does not catch the spirit of the times. Although the Puritans were believable, the principals in *The Rebels* are dull. . . . The minor characters are better: the sprightly spinster aunt Miss Sandford and the appallingly egocentric Rev. Mather Byles drawn from life. The two groups of lovers—with the possible exception of the profligate Mrs. Child may have recalled from reading a novel like [Hanna Foster's] *The Coquette*—are inanimate. . . . They deliver set speeches in parlor English, greet calamity with grave composure and good fortune with magnanimous sentiment. They are paragons of propriety who possess, according to the author, "deep wisdom . . . passive courage . . . unyielding firmness." The reader questions their plausibility.

Moreover, the plot is unbelievably complicated by baby-snatchings, concealed identities and clouded ancestries, hidden documents and death-bed confessions which reduce an heiress to pauperism. Individual scenes are badly managed; one in particular, a midnight visit to the tomb of a dead mistress by the bereaved lover, is the kind of grisly horror that better belongs in the verse of the graveyard poets. And none too skillfully does Mrs. Child lead the characters, and the reader, through the morass. . . . *Hobomok* may have been flawed, but a second novel ought to show improvement. (pp. 56-7)

[The style of *The Rebels*] strikes the modern reader as flamboyant and turgid. In all that she writes Mrs. Child could never be called an accomplished stylist, but *The Rebels* suffers more noticeably than any other piece of her writing from an effusive style.

If *The Rebels* is not an historical novel and is not social history, what is it?. . . [There are] several domestic scenes played out in parlors or bedchambers or libraries and in strolls on the Common where pride and prejudice alternately play their parts, all faintly reminiscent of a Jane Austen novel. *The Rebels,* which defies close calling, suggests a novel of manners, yet recalls the sentimental tale, and anticipates the domestic romance so popular with women readers in the 1850s. Thus the novel is a vehicle for Mrs. Child's tale of Boston, where the course of true love never runs smoothly, where appearances are deceptive, where sacrifice is the epitome of virtue, and where disappointments are stoically managed. It is a sentimental tale. (p. 57)

With the fictional characters in [*Philothea*] Mrs. Child works her fantasy; with the historical personages she exercises the novelist's prerogative to heighten a trait of character or to ignore another, selecting in the portrait of the principals their particular idiosyncrasy which satisfies her demands for the romance. (p. 74)

Philothea's character is delicately, sensitively, wrought; nothing discordant interrupts the harmony of her being—no harsh sentiment, no wild passion, no unlovely thing. She is the ideal. She is not Greek, and she is not human; she is the dream-creation of Mrs. Child's rich imagination. Nevertheless, she seems far more sensitive a character of fiction than Mary Conant or Grace Osborne and Lucretia Fitzherbert. (pp. 88-9)

Philothea is sheer romance, gossamerlike. The pages of the book unfold the glory of the age Mrs. Child is so imaginatively creating. Athens—its temples and villas, its altars and statues—glows in refulgent light. Its history, customs, legends, and routine of daily life come alive before the reader. The style complements the story, musical and metaphorical, glittering like the radiant forms of art which fill the ancient city. The imagery, the allusions, the associations she awakens, and the scenes she paints all invoke the glorious age. (p. 89)

As a novel [*Philothea*] is far more skillfully composed than *Hobomok* and *The Rebels.* Some years hence Hawthorne will write a definition of the romance, yet Mrs. Child has written a romance largely along the lines Hawthorne will suggest, "to present truth under circumstances, to a great extent, of the writer's own choosing or creation . . . so [to] manage his atmospherical medium as to bring out or mellow the lights and deepen and enrich the shadows of the picture." The plot of *Philothea* is simple, the structure is tight, the style is rich, the background is carefully sketched in, the characters are substantial, and the themes are artfully worked out. If it is true, as Mark Van Doren said of Hawthorne, that a writer's genius is reflected in one book, then *Philothea* is Mrs. Child's. She never equaled her accomplishment again. "The flowers of the field are unlike," Philothea tells Eudora, "but each has a beauty of its own." *Philothea* has its unique beauty. (p. 90)

[*A Romance of the Republic*] was drawn from real-life incidents "which [grew] out of slavery"; yet in the words of one of the characters in the novel, Mrs. Child's "too fertile imagination" made that reality "strange and romantic." Not content with telling a simple story, she improved upon real life with an elaborate tale of intrigue. . . .

It is somewhat surprising that a woman of Mrs. Child's intellect did not adapt her "novel-making" to the current literary tastes. The material for a realistic story was present in Mrs. Child's novel; however, she chose to package it in sentiment and suspense. Apparently friends warned her, suggesting that she tell her story squarely; the plight of mulattoes in American society was real enough for truly dramatic effort. But she preferred to embellish real life, thereby magnifiying the story out of proportion. (p. 145)

The long novel is astonishingly well paced, which comes as a surprise to wary readers; and it concludes happily, which is no surprise to readers accustomed to living vicariously the agony and the ecstasy of the heroines' dilemmas. (p. 146)

Romance is written with a rather steady hand—the characters themselves supplying the dramatic focus for the story. And for the first time Mrs. Child creates truly believable characters, and the reader becomes attached to them. Rosa and Flora are far more real than Mary Conant, Lucretia Fitzherbert, and the lovely but idealized Philothea. The girls because of the "false position in which they were placed by the unreasoning prejudice of society" immediately engage the reader's sympathy; unlike their quadroon mother. . . . (p. 151)

[Mrs. Child's] talent was largely undisciplined: her most effective writing was charged with an emotional fervor of the moment, like the *Appeal;* or was written under the pressure of deadlines, like the essays in the *Letters;* or was found in a novel like *Philothea,* some four or five years in progress. Like Cooper she wrote too much, and like Cooper she did not revise. Style in her nonfiction is homely and appropriate; style in her fiction is often tedious and effusive. *Philothea* seems the exception. . . .

[For] the modern reader Mrs. Child's strongest appeal may well rest with her nonfiction of the workaday world—the domestic manuals, the *Appeal,* and the *Letters,* where real problems are dealt with in clear, hard-hitting, energetic prose. . . . Although one may question the nearsightedness of her viewing the world through New England eyes, that world was nevertheless in her impressionable years a land of prophets and doers who spoke of the ideal and also of the real life. Mrs. Child

tried in her writing and in her service to others to extend her readers' "unboundable empire" and to make them aware of their capacity. (p. 163)

> *William S. Osborne, in his* Lydia Maria Child *(copyright © 1980 by Twayne Publishers; reprinted with the permission of Twayne Publishers, a Division of G. K. Hall & Co., Boston), Twayne, 1980, 196 p.*

ADDITIONAL BIBLIOGRAPHY

Baer, Helene G. *The Heart is Like Heaven: The Life of Lydia Maria Child.* Philadelphia: University of Pennsylvania Press, 1964, 339 p.
> A popular biography of Child, written for young readers.

Beach, Seth Curtis, "Lydia Maria Child: 1802-1880." In his *Daughters of the Puritans: A Group of Brief Biographies,* pp. 79-119. Boston: American Unitarian Association, 1905.
> An excellent summary of Child's life. Beach provides little critical analysis, but comments on the political and social forces that prevailed during Child's lifetime.

Edwards, Herbert. "Lydia M. Child's *The Frugal Housewife." The New England Quarterly* XXVI, No. 2 (June 1953): 243-49.
> A general discussion of Child's *The Frugal Housewife.* Edwards elaborates on the work's initial impact, and assesses its literary value.

Karcher, Carolyn L. "Lydia Maria Child and the *Juvenile Miscellany.*" In *Research about Nineteenth-Century Children and Books: Portrait Studies,* edited by Selma K. Richardson, pp. 67-84. Urbana, Ill., Champaign, Ill.: University of Illinois Graduate School of Library Science, 1980.
> A valuable source of information on Child's involvement with the *Juvenile Miscellany.* Karcher outlines the periodical's development and describes the social forces that influenced its popularity. Karcher cites Child's abolitionism as the cause of the magazine's eventual collapse.

Meltzer, Milton. *Tongue of Flame: The Life of Lydia Maria Child.* New York: Thomas Y. Crowell Co., 1965, 210 p.
> A biography written for a juvenile audience. Based on Child's correspondence, the work recreates her adolescence, traces her literary career, and briefly discusses each of her publications.

Taylor, Lloyd C., Jr. "Lydia Maria Child: Biographer." *The New England Quarterly* XXXIV, No. 2 (June 1961): 211-27.
> An assessment of Child's ability as a biographer. Taylor asserts that "much of [Child's] work lacks literary distinction" and suggests that her biographies are of more historical than literary value.

Ware, Ethel K. "Lydia Maria Child and Anti-Slavery: Parts I and II." *The Boston Public Library Quarterly* III, No. 4 (October 1951): 251-75; IV, No. 1 (January 1952): 34-49.
> Explores Child's participation in the anti-slavery movement. Ware discusses Child's editorial stance in the *National Anti-Slavery Standard,* and reviews her later abolitionist writings.

(Henri) Benjamin Constant (de Rebecque)

1767-1830

Swiss-born French novelist, essayist, diarist, journalist, autobiographer, and translator.

Renowned during his lifetime as a statesman and political writer, Constant is remembered today for his novel, *Adolphe*. Commonly thought to be based on Constant's romance with the French writer Mme. de Staël, the novel recounts the affair of an egocentric young man and a married woman who dies when she realizes the insincerity of her lover's feelings. Critics particularly praise Constant's keen analysis of the title character, who is caught in the conflict between passion and reason and helpless in the face of what Paul Bourget described as "the continual destruction of the love in [his] heart by the action of his mind." Praised as strikingly modern in its theme and analytical nature, *Adolphe* is admired equally for its spare prose style. Constant's precise, unadorned language is considered extraordinarily evocative, and many critics echo Martin Turnell's statement that Constant "possessed the great French masters' power of seizing the obscurest feelings at the moment of their formation and translating them into exact language."

Constant was born in Lausanne, Switzerland. His mother died two weeks after his birth, and his father placed the boy first in the care of relatives, then with a governess, and finally with a succession of eccentric and difficult tutors. At thirteen Constant was taken to England to enroll at Oxford University, but was turned away because of his age. He subsequently studied at the University of Erlangen in Germany and at Edinburgh University in Scotland. In 1787 Constant initiated the first of a series of notable love affairs when he became involved with Mme. de Charrière, a woman of letters twenty-seven years his senior. In spite of his marriage in 1789, Constant maintained his relationship with Charrière until approximately 1795, when he became enamored of the noted intellectual and author Staël. Although both were married, Constant and Staël had a daughter together and were involved until 1811.

It was during his liaison with Staël that Constant became active in French politics. A supporter of Barras throughout the period of the Directory, Constant was elected to the tribunate, but, opposing the Bonaparte regime, lost his post in 1802 and a year later followed Staël into exile. During the next several years Constant alternated between Switzerland and Weimar, Germany, where he came in contact with the primary forces behind the German Romantic movement: August Wilhelm von Schlegel, Friedrich von Schlegel, Johann Wolfgang von Goethe, and Johann Christoph Friedrich von Schiller, whose drama *Wallenstein* Constant translated into French. Constant was productive during this period, working on his *De la religion considérée dans sa source, ses formes, et ses developpements*, a historical consideration of religion that was to be a lifelong project. In addition, Constant composed political essays advancing his strong liberal theories, notably *De l'esprit de conquête et de l'usurpation dans leurs rapports avec la civilisation européenne*, an indictment of Napoleon's regime. Constant subsequently came under criticism by reconciling with the Empire of the Hundred Days, but conditions had stabilized by 1819 so that he was able to win election to the Chamber of Deputies.

Until the time of his death Constant served with distinction in various government positions in addition to writing numerous political pamphlets and contributing political articles to newspapers.

Of his literary endeavors, Constant reportedly took the most pride in his *De la religion considérée dans sa source, ses formes, et ses développements*. Although it was received well in its time, later critics often overlook the work. George Brandes offered a partial explanation for the lack of critical interest in *De la religion* in his statement in 1872 that the work had grown "old-fashioned" and was "merely of historical interest as typical of the halfheartedness and indecision of the period in which it was written." Constant's political works, too, are seldom treated by English-language critics. Perhaps because they help to illuminate *Adolphe*, somewhat more critical attention has been granted Constant's autobiographical writings. The *Journal intime de Benjamin Constant et lettres à sa famille et à ses amis*, which incorporates his diary and selected letters, is generally valued by critics for the revelations it provides into Constant's mind and personality. *Le cahier rouge de Benjamin Constant* is considered a charming, picaresque account of Constant's youthful travels. Of the autobiographical writings, critics most often comment on the novel fragment *Cécile*, which was not discovered until the 1950s. Like *Adolphe*, this unfinished fiction is regarded as a thinly-veiled account of Constant's own life and experience, in this case his relationship with Charlotte von Hardenberg, his second wife.

If there is a common thread running through Constant criticism in recent years, it is a reaction against the strictly biographical interpretation of his works, including *Cécile*, but most notably *Adolphe*. Among critics who believe that such an approach diminishes Constant's artistic achievement are Turnell, Edward D. Sullivan, and William W. Holdheim, who wrote: "We must reject an interpretation which in effect equates literary form with psychological structure, denies the creative process by affirming its coincidence with self-observation, and thus establishes a too simple relationship between life and art." The major link between commentators on *Adolphe* is their praise for the novel's penetrating character analysis, austere style, and expression of modern sensibility. The majority of critics join David Cecil in ranking it confidently "among the supreme masterpieces of prose fiction."

PRINCIPAL WORKS

Des effets de la terreur (essay) 1797

Des réactions politiques (essay) 1797

Wallstein [translator; from the drama *Wallenstein* by Johann Christoph Friedrich von Schiller] (drama) 1809

De l'esprit de conquête et de l'usurpation dans leurs rapports avec la civilisation européenne (essay) 1814

Réflexions sur les constitutions, la distribution, et les garanties dans une monarchie constitutionelle (essay) 1814

De la responsabilité des ministres (essay) 1815
  ["On the Responsibility of Ministers" published in journal *Pamphleteer*, 1815]

Adolphe: Anecdote trouvée dans les papiers d'un inconnu et publiée par M. B. de Constant (novel) 1816
  [*Adolphe: An Anecdote Found among the Papers of an Unknown Person and Published by M. Benjamin de Constant*, 1817]

Mémoires sur les Cent-Jours en forme de lettres. 2 vols. (letters) 1820-22

De la religion considérée dans sa source, ses formes, et ses développements (essay) 1824-31

Mélanges de littérature et de politique (essay) 1829

"Réflexions sur la tragédie" (essay) 1829; published in journal *Revue de Paris*

Lettres de Benjamin Constant à Madame de Récamier, 1807-1830 (letters) 1882

Journal intime de Benjamin Constant et lettres à sa famille et à ses amis (journal and letters) 1895

Le cahier rouge de Benjamin Constant (autobiography) 1907

Cécile (unfinished novel) 1951

Journaux intimes (journals) 1952

Benjamin Constant: Oeuvres (novel, unfinished novel, autobiography, journals, essays, and speeches) 1967

SISMONDO CARLO LEONARDO SISMONDI (letter date 1816)

[*A Swiss historian and scholar, Sismondi frequented the same social and literary circles as did Constant. In the following letter,* *Sismondi gives his enthusiastic reaction to* Adolphe *and compares Constant with his fictional hero.*]

[I have read] *Adolphe* twice over; you will think this overmuch for a work you attach little importance to, and wherein, indeed, one does not feel a very lively interest in any of the personages. But [Constant's] analysis of every sentiment of the human heart is so admirable, there is so much truth in the hero's weakness, such insight in his observations, such purity and vigour in the style, that the book gives infinite pleasure in the reading. I am the more sensible of it, I well believe, because I recognize the writer in every page, and never did a confession present a more striking likeness to my eyes. He explains all his faults, but he does not excuse them, and he seems to have had no thought of making them amiable. It is quite possible that he was, at an earlier day, more capable of real love than he shows himself in his book; but, when I knew him, he was what Adolphe is, and, with just as little of love in his composition; not less tempestuous, not less given first to soothe and then from some notion of kindness to deceive afresh the woman whose heart he had rent asunder.

> *Sismondo Carlo Leonardo Sismondi, in a letter to Countess d'Albany in 1816, in* The Latin Genius *by Anatole France, translated by Wilfrid S. Jackson (copyright, 1924, by Dodd, Mead and Company, Inc.; originally published as* Le génie latin, *A. Lemerre, 1913), Dodd, Mead, 1924, p. 259.*

STENDHAL [PSEUDONYM OF HENRI BEYLE] (essay date 1825)

[*Stendhal is considered one of France's greatest novelists, and his masterpiece,* The Red and the Black, *is regarded as a significant contribution to the development of the modern psychological novel. In the following excerpt, Stendhal briefly reviews one of Constant's political speeches, praising Constant's persuasive use of irony, humor, and wit and his strategy in advancing his ideas.*]

The most remarkable volume which has appeared this month is, beyond any doubt, the one containing three speeches by M. Benjamin Constant, General Foy and M. de Girardin protesting against the projected law by which the returned *émigrés* hope to pocket the equivalent of more than forty million pounds sterling. (p. 196)

If . . . , in this competition for pre-eminence between three men of the highest talent, M. Benjamin Constant finally carried off the palm, this may be attributed to his having adopted a tone suited to his audience. Addressing both the Chamber and the nation by whom his speech would be read the following day, he succeeded in making the partisans of the bill *swallow contempt* in all its forms. . . . M. Constant succeeded, with consummate art and skill, in covering with ridicule the three hundred and seventy wigged heads which decide the destiny of France. To complete his triumph, the triumph of the subtlest wit and most adroit strategy which have been seen anywhere for a good many years, M. Constant never once allowed his opponents time to interrupt him. They would begin to understand the bitter irony of one sentence, only when the orator was in the middle of the next. . . . [The speech contains] a faithful account of M. Constant's terrible reply to the *émigrés'* constant boast of heroic fidelity. He demonstrates, with the utmost clarity . . . , that, after returning under Bonaparte in 1801, after crowding into his ante-chamber and after swearing allegiance to him, they can scarcely boast of their fidelity and still less of their heroism; simply of their prudence. This passage, which it is impossible to read without laughing . . . , is unquestionably equal to the finest passages in Pascal's *Lettres Provinciales*. It would be to the advantage both of the public and of M. Constant himself if his own works on religion were written with the same fervour and the same talent. (pp. 197-98)

> Stendhal [pseudonym of Henri Beyle], "Benjamin Constant in the Chamber of Deputies" (originally published as "Letters from Paris by Grimm's Grandson, No. IV," in The London Magazine, n.s. Vol. I, No. IV, April, 1825), in his Selected Journalism from the English Reviews, edited by Geoffrey Strickland, John Calder Ltd, 1959, pp. 196-202.

GEORGE RIPLEY (essay date 1838)

[Ripley, an American critic affiliated with the New England Transcendentalists, was a founder of the Transcendentalist journal, the Dial, and a chief supporter of that group's Brook Farm community. He here assesses Constant's "character as a writer." Ripley stresses the "truth to himself" that marks Constant's writings and praises the "reconciling tendency" of his mind. In addition, Ripley notes the contrasting schools of literary thought that influenced Constant: the contemporary French writers such as François Marie de Voltaire on one hand, and the German Weimar circle, including August Wilhelm von Schlegel, on the other.]

Various as were the pursuits of Benjamin Constant, large as was the compass of action and thought, in which he has gained a brilliant reputation and bestowed durable benefits upon his race, his character as a writer presents an example of consummate unity, that is no less rare than it is attractive. He was always the same man, always possessed with the same dominant ideas, always devoted to the same interests, always looking to the same objects, whether in the sphere of politics, of elegant literature, of historical investigation or of philosophical discussion. His opinions, of course, like those of every honest and thinking man, were not unfrequently modified; his views on some points, indeed, underwent a thorough revolution; and the practical measures, which he supported may not in every case have the appearance of perfect consistency; but still, we find the same distinct and strongly marked impression of individuality under all circumstances; we recognize in every change of costume or of position, the same peculiar mental endowments and tendencies, which were brought to our notice upon our first acquaintance with the man. (pp. 63-4)

[Constant] could not bind down his free thoughts to the opinions of any sect or corporation. He was unwilling to make his own ideas the gauge of another man's intellect; or to be measured himself by any arbitrary standard which might be proposed. He valued truth above all things, and independence as the condition of obtaining truth. Accordingly, he could not be made the victim of any of the partial and limited tendencies of the day. He refused to be shackled by devotion to the favorite theories or projects which were everywhere springing up. The realization of his principles were deemed by him to be of greater consequence than the success of his plans. We therefore find that though acting with others, he always acted out himself; though a lover of sympathy, he never courted it, at the expense of his convictions. Fearful of unwise extremes,—in consequence of the soundness of his mind, and never of paltry timidity,—he exercised a healing, reconciling influence over the conflicting views, which came within his province. He ac-

cordingly holds an eminent rank among those who may be honored as the true mediators of society. (pp. 64-5)

The history of Benjamin Constant, as a literary man, exhibits the reconciling tendency which has been pointed out, as the peculiar characteristic of his mind. Born at a period when the literature of France was at the summit of its glory and seemed to fill the eye of the world, he was not seduced into the unqualified admiration which was claimed for it as its due; but was impressed, from the beginning, with the pure and lofty promise of a more substantial literature which was just rising from an opposite quarter of the heavens. He had been accustomed to look up to Bayle, Voltaire and Montesquieu, as the masters of his mind; but he was not so strongly bound by the spell of their names, as to be indifferent to the new and glorious manifestations of thought which were bursting forth from such men as Lessing and Herder, Wieland and Göthe, though beyond the Rhine.

His mode of thinking accordingly betrays nothing of the polished but cold exclusiveness which characterized the fastidious literature of France, during the latter part of the last century. He perceived that the violation of dainty forms is oft-times more than atoned for, by the fresh and gushing life which breaks through them; and that a strict observance of conventional canons is easily made the refuge of imitators and the shield of stupidity. He would not withhold his sympathy from the spirit of beauty, though appearing in an unauthorized shape; and hence refused to worship the reigning idols of the public taste. He scorned to narrow his mind to the petty limits of artificial restrictions; and thus was enabled to enrich the literature, to which he might have been denounced as a traitor. After leaving, for a season, the path which was prescribed by the prevailing taste of the day, he returned from his wanderings through a land of fragrant wild-flowers, with noble offerings for his native shrine. We perceive from the earliest display of his powers, a broader foundation of logical strength, a higher degree of robust action, and a more daring boldness of expression in his style, than had hitherto been usually exhibited by the most popular writers. (pp. 67-8)

At the same time that he refused to acknowledge the canons of taste, by which thought was then restrained in the reigning fashion of French Literature, he cultivated a true classical purity of expression, free from the affectation of foreign combinations, presenting no trace of the imitation of favorite authors, clothing unwonted thoughts in the genuine forms of the mother tongue, and though embodying the most profound ideas, transparent as the day. His native clearness of mind, his inborn sense of the Beautiful and the True, and his sharp logical acuteness, prevented him from falling into the obscurity and extravagance which are usually found in the first growth of a strong and luxuriant literature, and no less in the writing of those who are so enamored of its freshness and bloom, as to lose their self-subsistence and waste the very pith of life in foolish imitations. If he sometimes approaches by the exceeding fineness of his views and the airy subtilty of his distinctions, to the confines of Teutonic mysticism, he is soon drawn back by the precision of French taste and the balanced action of his own mind, to the regions of daylight and common sense. He thus presents a beautiful example of the healthful influence of one literature upon another. Combining the pointedness and rapid movement of the French writers, with the depth and solidity of the German, he exhibits the excellent effects of discarding the precise formulas of a pedantic school and indulging the mind with the freest and most varied culture, which it can gain. His wit is not unfrequently no less salient and biting than that of Voltaire, while his reverence for all that is truly venerable, his sympathy with the higher feelings and holier aspirations of our nature, indicate the spiritual and religious direction, which he was compelled by the force of light, the supremacy of thought, to adopt as the only natural and just path for a being like man.

The influence of Benjamin Constant was combined with that of August Wilhelm Schlegel and Madame de Staël to promote a better understanding between the literary men of France and Germany; and to reveal the treasures of the latter country to the students and thinkers of the former. His own translation of Schiller's *Wallenstein* [*Wallstein*] was made with the view of adapting it for representation on the French stage; and hence, it is easy to conceive that it must have failed of doing anything like justice to the magnificent original. . . . Benjamin Constant himself acknowledges in a singularly candid criticism on his own production . . . that by a too strict adherence to the rules of the French theatre, he destroyed much of its dramatic effect. But however this may be, it served to awaken attention to the masters of German poetry and to increase the general interest in a literature which has since done so much for the refreshment of France. Among the miscellaneous writings of Benjamin Constant we find the critical essay on this drama, to which I have just alluded. It presents an accurate delineation of its chief characteristics, and a true conception of its spirit, while it breathes a warm sympathy with its fine moral portraitures. The description of Thecla is scarcely surpassed by any thing that I know of in modern French prose; and I cannot but regard the whole piece as an admirable specimen of discriminating, philosophical criticism. Its concluding passage is [an] expressive . . . summary of the literary principles of the author. . . . (pp. 68-70)

> *George Ripley, "Benjamin Constant" (originally published as an introduction to his* Philosophical Miscellanies, Vol. 2, *Hilliard, Gray and Company, 1838), in* American Literary Criticism, *edited by William Morton Payne, Longmans, Green, and Co., 1904 (and reprinted by Books for Libraries Press, 1968; distributed by Arno Press, Inc.), pp. 63-70.*

GEORGE BRANDES (essay date 1872)

[*Brandes, a Danish literary critic and biographer, was the principal leader of the intellectual movement that helped bring an end to Scandinavian cultural isolation. He believed that literature should reflect the spirit and problems of its time, and that it must be understood within its social and aesthetic context. Brandes's major critical work,* Main Currents in Nineteenth-Century Literature, *won him admiration for his ability to view literary movements within the broader context of European literature. The following excerpt from* Main Currents *begins with a brief discussion of Constant's religious writings. Brandes then compares* Adolphe *with Johann von Goethe's novel* The Sorrows of Young Werther, *noting that the books, "taken together, form a double picture of the pope-like power of society to bind and loose" lovers. Constant's analysis of love in the novel, Brandes suggests, is so thorough that he ultimately works against himself, presenting the psychology of love rather than its poetry. Brandes also proposes that* Adolphe *is* Werther *from a woman's point of view. He praises the "conscious intelligence" of Eléonore, identifying her type of character as a first step toward the appearance in literature of women of genius.*]

The title character of [*Adolphe*] is less brilliant than René [from the novel *René* by François René de Chateaubriand], less mel-

ancholy than Obermann [from the novel *Obermann* by Étienne Privert de Sénancour], but he is a representative of the same restless and unsatisfied generation. He too is related to Werther, but, like René, he is the child of the age of disillusionment. It was not until after the fall of the Empire that the book appeared, but it was written, or at any rate projected, in the first years of the century. Like those other books which on their emotional side are in touch with Rousseau, and which perpetuate his tradition, it conflicted sharply with the prevailing sentiments of the day. In Paris figures and the sword held sway, in literature the classic ode and science were in vogue, whereas in Constant's book emotions and psychical analysis predominated. (p. 63)

[*De la religion considérée dans sa source, ses formes, et ses développements*], planned at the close of the century to effect the same object from a Protestant standpoint that Chateaubriand aimed at from a Catholic [in his *Le génie du christianisme; ou, Beautés de la religion chrétienne*], namely, the revival of the religious spirit in France, had originally a very different character from that which it finally acquired. If the first part were published as it was originally written, entirely in the eighteenth-century manner, it would indicate in its author exactly the stage of mental development indicated in Chateaubriand by his book on the Revolutions [*Essai historique, politique et moral sur les révolutions anciennes et modernes considérées dans leurs rapports avec la révolution française*]. In the form in which it has taken its place in French literature the work is remarkable for its calm, passionless style, its unprejudiced views, and an erudition not common at that period. Its weaknesses are its total lack of warmth and the general indecision of its principles. (p. 66)

Constant regards religion as progressive; he starts from the premise that the religious feeling is a fundamental element of the human soul, that it is only the forms it assumes which differ, and that these are capable of ever-increasing perfection. . . . [He] imagines that in his *sentiment religieux* he has discovered a kind of spiritual primary element, incapable of further resolution, an element which is unalterable and universal, *i.e.* diffused over the whole earth and unaffected by time; and upon this theory, which is incompatible with the data of psychology, he bases his whole conservative system. As far as possible he evades troublesome questions: he refuses, for example, to decide whether mankind came into being in a savage or in a paradisaically perfect condition; and he expressly states that he begins with a delineation of the lowest fetish worship only for the sake of order, that he by no means denies that this pitiable stage may have been the result of a fall, this hypothesis, indeed, seeming to him a very probable one.— Few books have more rapidly grown old-fashioned than this of Constant's, which is now merely of historical interest as typical of the half-heartedness and indecision of the period in which it was written. (pp. 67-8)

Adolphe is a love story which, in its presentment of the relations of the individual to society, takes a quite different point of view from *Werther*. In *Werther* outward, and, by reason of these, also inward, obstacles prevent the union of a couple obviously made for each other. In *Adolphe* outward, and because of them, also inward, reasons part two beings who are united. *Werther* represents the power of society, and of once-accepted social responsibilities, to hinder a love match. *Adolphe* describes the power of society and of public opinion to absolve from accepted personal responsibilities and to sever a long-united pair. The books, taken together, form a double picture of the pope-like power of society to bind and loose. But whereas *Werther* depicts the feelings of the pre-revolutionary, enthusiastic, energetic generation to which its author belonged, the feelings described in *Adolphe* are those of the first French generation of the new century.

Unlike former love stories, *Adolphe* does not delineate love only in its first awakening in the dawn of delusive hopes, but follows it through its whole existence, depicts its growth, its strength, its decay, its death, and even pursues it to the other side of the grave and shows the feelings into which it is transformed. Hence *Adolphe,* even more than *René*, is the story of the individual's rude awakening from delusion, the representation of the anguish of disappointment. It is the flower of life which is here stripped of its petals one by one and carefully dissected. In this point, too, the book is a great contrast to *Werther*. *Werther* is naïve in comparison. It is the same flower, the perfume of which is a deadly poison to Werther, that is calmly dissected by Adolphe. The change is expressed in the very costume; the blue coat and yellow waistcoat have made way for our dull, funereal black.

But the flame which is extinguished in the man's breast now burns in the woman's. *Adolphe* is woman's *Werther*. The passion and melancholy of the new age have advanced another step; they have spread to the other sex. In *Werther* it was the man who loved, suffered, stormed, and despaired; in comparison with him the woman was sound, strong, and unharmed—perhaps a trifle cold and insignificant. But now it is her turn, now it is she who loves and despairs. In *Werther* it was the woman who submitted to the laws of society, in *Adolphe* it is the man who does so. The selfsame war waged by Werther in the name of his love is now waged by Eléonore, and with equally tragic result.

It is scarcely an exaggeration to call this romance the prototype of a whole new species of fiction, namely that which occupies itself with psychical analysis. It is its treatment of love that is new. (pp. 73-4)

An attempt had [previously] been made to explain the attraction to which we give the name of love by instituting a parallel between it and the attraction with which we are familiar in inanimate nature. But there was yet another step to be taken, namely, to dissociate love from everything with which it had hitherto been connected, and analyse it. This task fell to the lot of the unsettled, unsatisfied generation to which Constant belongs. However much men had differed in their conception of love, its causes and its consequences, they had all agreed in accepting the emotion itself as something understood, something simple. They now for the first time began to treat it as something composite, and to attempt to resolve it into its elements. In *Adolphe,* and the fiction which follows in its steps, an accurate calculation is made of how many parts, how many grains, of friendship, how many of devotion, of vanity, ambition, admiration, respect, sensual attraction, hope, imagination, disappointment, hatred, weariness, enthusiasm, calculation, &c. on the part of each, go to make up the compound which the two concerned call their love. With all this analysis the emotion lost its supernatural character, and the worship of it ceased. Instead of its poetry, its psychology was offered to the reader. (p. 75)

It is the question of the conditions of constancy which is treated of in *Adolphe*—under what conditions is passion lasting or otherwise? And it is the answer to this question which is really an impeachment of society. For it is maintained that while

society, in this case represented by public opinion, upholds those unions which are of its own institution, it at the same time basely strives to destroy all possibilities of faithfulness in any union it has not sanctioned, even if that union be to the full as honourable, to the full as unselfish, as any of those which it fences round and supports.

Constant prefers his accusation in a story which could hardly be less pretentious. It contains but two characters, no scenery, and there is not a single fortuitous incident in the whole course of its action. Everything occurs according to the natural laws indicated by the relations of the couple to each other and to society in general. The reader follows this history of two souls to its close much as a student of chemistry watches the fermentation of two substances in an inexplosible phial and observes the results. (pp. 76-7)

[Eléonore] is in reality an entirely new female type . . . , a type which many years later Balzac appropriates, styles ''la femme de trente ans'' [a woman of thirty, as in Balzac's novel of the same name], and varies with such genius that he may be said to be its second creator, and which George Sand too developed and embellished in a whole series of her novels. Under the treatment of these two authors this type proved to be a whole, hitherto unknown, world, in which every feeling, passion, and thought was infinitely stronger than in the world of the girlish heart. (p. 80)

The fact that the type, and with it the conflict of woman with society, appears in literature so long before George Sand, is to be explained by the circumstance that Eléonore is modelled from the strongest woman of the day, the woman who ventured to oppose Napoleon himself—Mme. de Staël. (p. 82)

A sharp contrast [to the German female characters of Goethe] confronts us in the new type of Frenchwoman; instead of sweetness, clinging affection, naturalness, we have passion, will, energy, and conscious intelligence. For it was in the most remarkable and intellectual woman of the day, a woman who had given up country, peace, and prosperity, rather than submit to the petty tyranny with which Napoleon's despotism pursued the unsubmissive, that Constant found the new type.

The appearance of woman in literature as conscious intelligence is a first step towards her appearance as genius. We already see Mme. de Staël's turban appearing on the horizon. The woman who shares man's passions and struggles will soon share his genius and his renown. Yet a little while and the struggle ends in victory, the same woman who succumbs under the name of Eléonore is crowned at the Capitol as Corinne [the protagonist in Mme. de Staël's novel, *Corinne; ou, L'Italie*]. (p. 84)

George Brandes, ''Constant: 'On Religion'—'Adolphe','' in his Main Currents in Nineteenth Century Literature: The Emigrant Literature, *Vol. I, translated by Diana White and Mary Morison (originally published as* Hovedstrømninger i det 19de aarhundredes litteratur: Emigrantlitteraturen, *1872), William Heinemann, 1901 (and reprinted by Heinemann, 1923), pp. 63-88.*

THE ECLECTIC MAGAZINE   (essay date 1882)

[Nothing] can exceed the naïveté of the letters of Benjamin Constant [to Madame Récamier in *Lettres de Benjamin Constant à Madame Récamier*]. The gamut of hopeless passion is probably limited, and therefore somewhat monotonous; and the lovesick statesman strikes the usual notes in the usual manner. It must be allowed, however, that he omits none; and he appeals to the obdurate heart of Madame Récamier by all the conventional considerations with which we are familiar. . . . One might suppose, to listen to his language, that the fate of Europe, nay the permanent welfare of mankind, depended upon his softening her heart. (p. 813)

We might fill pages upon pages with extracts from his letters; but they would be merely [repetitious]. No gleam of poetry, no novelty of sentiment, no sparkle of wit, ever relieves the steadfast monotony of despairing passion. (p. 815)

> *"A Statesman's Love Letters,"* in The Eclectic Magazine, *n.s. Vol. XXXV, No. VI, June, 1882, pp. 811-17.*

THE SATURDAY REVIEW, LONDON (essay date 1895)

The **"Journal Intime"** of Benjamin Constant . . . is one of the most curious and instructive human documents that have been provided for the surprise and enlightenment of the student of souls. . . . [There] was not a single interest, out of the many that occupied [Constant's] life, which he did not destroy by some inconsequence of action, for no reason in the world, apparently, except some irrational necessity of doing exactly the opposite of what he ought to have done, of what he wanted to do. . . . Love, political power, and literary fame were the three main interests of his life; and it was the caprice of his nature, in regard to all three, to build with one hand while he pulled down his own work with the other. How well he knew his own weakness, this Journal shows us on every page. . . .

[Constant] was never tired of listening to himself, and the acute interest of this Journal consists in the absolute sincerity of its confessions, and at the same time the scrutinizing self-consciousness of every word that is written down. . . . [He] is very real, with that distressing kind of reality which afflicts the artist, and out of which, after he has duly suffered for it, he creates his art, as Benjamin Constant created **"Adolphe."** **"Adolphe,"** a masterpiece of psychological narrative, from which the modern novel of analysis may be said to have arisen, is simply a human document, in which Benjamin Constant has told the story of his liaison with Mme. de Staël. (p. 267)

> *"Benjamin Constant,"* in The Saturday Review, *London, Vol. LXXX, No. 2079, August 31, 1895, pp. 267-68.*

[A. INNES SHAND] (essay date 1895)

Benjamin Constant presents one of the most curious and complicated of psychological and intellectual studies, and if his journals [*Journal intime de Benjamin Constant et lettres à sa famille et à ses amis*] do not solve the problem to our satisfaction, assuredly we cannot complain of any lack of candour. . . . Naturally we compare Constant with Pepys, but they only resemble each other in their absolute unreserve. Pepys reveals his foibles and petty vanities, either unconsciously or with childlike simplicity. Constant does not condescend to trifle with such minute details as the cut of a coat or the items of a tavern-bill. But, on the other hand, in his sensitive self-searching, he ruthlessly submits himself to an unsparing course of the probe and the scalpel. Anxious to understand the secrets of his own moral mechanism, to the last he can never come to definite conclusions; but in trying all possible methods of getting at the truth, he takes us entirely into his confidence.

In his extreme unreserve as to his sentimental relations with the softer sex, he resembles Rousseau. But whereas—to put it bluntly—we never know whether Rousseau is lying or no, we always have the conviction borne in upon us that Constant is strictly honest and veracious. At the same time, in fairness we are bound to add that such honesty was one of the very few sterling qualities to which he could lay claim; and, moreover, the honesty was chiefly displayed when he was confessing himself in private for his personal satisfaction. . . . Constant was absolutely destitute of a moral sense. He was a brilliant failure, and he might have been a more brilliant success had he persuaded himself that honesty was the wisest policy. Most politicians who have no fixed principles go astray through perverted ambition or self-seeking. Constant perversely shifted his ground, and changed his opinions, at the times when a change was sure to be prejudicial: in other words, he always ratted at the wrong moment. The explanation was, that he was a waif of the world, drifting upon the tide of his passions and caprices. (pp. 341-42)

Much of the piquancy of these journals is to be sought in the fact that this exceptionally shrewd man of the world was keenly alive to the snares that beset him, and nevertheless habitually walked into them. He learned no practical lessons in the course of a checkered life, and never profited by his bitter experiences. He is ever longing for the repose that always eludes him; yet he knows he could attain it by an effort of the will. A confirmed sceptic, if not an actual atheist, he would have willingly rested on the rock of Christianity, but he could not reason himself into the beliefs that he envied. . . .

[Constant] was an Epicurean fatalist, who strove to fancy himself a predestinarian, because it spared him the worries of continued conflict. (p. 342)

[He] was a remarkable example of the possible endurance of an overtasked brain against prolonged and excessive strain. (p. 343)

In this miscellany of matter, all suggested by the meditations or incidents of the moment, we come sometimes on pieces of criticism which are . . . acute and original. So that, whether we are disposed to agree or dissent, the journals are invariably suggesting subjects for reflection. (p. 345)

Unfortunately, with a heart and a brain always beating at fever-heat, [Constant] was lacking alike in conscience and in backbone. After a troubled life of ceaseless activity, he died discredited, if not actually disgraced; and as for the philosophical and political treatises on which he chiefly valued himself, they were soon ignored, and are now forgotten. If his literary fame survives, save in vague impressions, it is in his once popular romance of '**Adolphe**,' and we doubt whether even the name of that novel is known to a score of the literary men on this side of the Channel. (p. 350)

> *[A. Innes Shand], "Benjamin Constant,"* in Blackwood's Edinburgh Magazine, *Vol. CLVIII, No. DCCCCLIX, September, 1895, pp. 341-50.*

ANATOLE FRANCE (essay date 1913)

[*A French novelist and critic, France is valued for the artistic clarity and control of his prose style and the ironic tone that dominates his creative and critical works. In the following, France attributes* Adolphe's *artistic success to the fact that Adolphe, the "scoundrel-hero," is depicted so honestly that the reader identifies—and ultimately sympathizes—with him.*]

It is now nearly a century since *Adolphe* appeared, and changing generations in succession have scarcely altered in attitude towards this singular work. The book has retained their admiration; its hero has always been visited with every severity of criticism. For a hundred years Adolphe's hardness of heart, his unfeelingness, his ingratitude, as contrasted with the devotion of the incomparable Ellénore, have never ceased to raise indignation in noble hearts. How comes it then, as we reread this tale of love, we are filled with profound pity for this alleged butcher of hearts, and that he should seem to us to be the most pitiable of victims? Can it be that we are inspired by some perverse illusion, or that there has been some strange misconception of a character whose lively sensibility and endless scruples put him at the mercy of an imperious and passionately selfish woman? Poor, poor Adolphe, who threw away his life and youth and peace of mind as so many morsels for an insatiable mistress to devour! She loves him, no doubt, but with what a ferocious, implacable, and unendurable love. How little resignation, how little shame or discretion, how little of the pride "which fears to be importunate" in this faded heroine, who forces herself on him, obstinate and furious, unwitting that love has wings, and will not go down on its knees to recite a lesson it no longer heeds. (pp. 261-62)

How remote is all this from the eighteenth century, and its pleasant ways, its lightness of touch, its elegance and its scepticism! (p. 262)

After having made the wretched Adolphe drink the cup of bitterness and humiliation to the dregs, Ellénore decided to die, in order to endow him with eternal remorse. Benjamin Constant, who was a brave man, has done the thing handsomely; he has sacrificed himself, and left the limelight to his heroine. But sometimes his impatience, and his resentment, have been too strong for him: they keep revealing themselves. For in this troublous soul, swept by many a parching breath, and where no fruit would ripen more, lived one virtue still—sincerity. This man, whom the wretchedness of his life led into unceasing deception, never deceives himself. He passes judgment on himself without weakness or mercy, nor does he display any of that complacent self-pity that is so much the fashion nowadays. He tells us his faults, and that without fatuousness: he does not present his case as unique, his sufferings as anything extraordinary or beautiful, his lapses from virtue as psychological rarities for the enjoyment of lovers of such matters. He is very simple, and very severe on himself; and therefore one is tempted to be indulgent to him. Yes, doubtless, Adolphe's was a weak soul, eager to grasp at happiness, unable to keep it. An ardent but sterile soul, whose visions withered as soon as seen. Obstacles increased and sharpened his desire: attainment left him lassitude and disgust. But his chief victim was ever himself, and the cold cruelty of the libertine was never his, nor the still crueller indifference of the lover whose dream is fled. He is filled with anguish, he is racked with remorse, and the grief of the woman he loves no longer vibrates in him and puts him to torture.

We repeat: this lover whose heart is dead within him, this unhappy prisoner standing amid a love laid in ashes, appears to us a very martyr to his compassion and patience, and our undivided pity is for him and not for the tyrannical figure that stifles and oppresses him. (pp. 263-64)

[Certainly] no soul, in its shifts and confusion, seems more calculated than his to disconcert the observer. Its every trait seems passing and contradictory, and on the wing. Passion breaks forth, but calculation is at its side. (p. 264)

Still, the soul that is the theatre of such diverse conflicting sentiments is watched by a mind that is sagacious, and penetrating, and not to be bought off. In this distracted and murky soul, the mind remains intact; and it would seem as though a double spirit were struggling in the man; that standing where the centuries meet, he is subjected to their contrary currents; that he keeps a scepticism beneath his passion, and can never be sincerely moved, nor coldly sceptical. (pp. 264-65)

Such a nature [as Adolphe's] is too complex to be embraced in any one formula, too supple and too shifting to take an exact outline, too agitated always to be consistent. (p. 265)

Adolphe, unlike René, his illustrious contemporary [from François René de Chateaubriand's novel, *René*], did not know how to practise the art of make-believe, and treat himself to a wondrous comedy; he was without the wonder-working genius, the lyric power of the author of *Atala* and the *Natchez* but his taste was more unfailing, he had a clearer sense, a sincerer conscience. The Abbé Morellet, the last representative of the old French good taste, would have found nothing to quarrel with in the irreproachable pages of *Adolphe.* . . .

From the point of view of literature, *Adolphe* is still a masterpiece. Its form is limpid, alive, and delicate; it does not smell of the lamp; the subtlety of its thought never weighs on the simplicity of the style. And the man of letters never reveals his hand, and that is a delight to us in itself. For, even if the literary man be a genius, he is subdued to what he works in, and his work will show the dye. (p. 266)

> *Anatole France, "Benjamin Constant," in his* The Latin Genius, *translated by Wilfrid S. Jackson (copyright, 1924, by Dodd, Mead and Company, Inc.; originally published as* Le génie latin, *A. Lemerre, 1913), Dodd, Mead, 1924, pp. 258-66.*

DAVID CECIL   (essay date 1949)

[*Cecil, an important modern British literary critic who has written extensively on eighteenth and nineteenth century authors, is highly acclaimed for his work on the Victorian era. Cecil does not follow any school of criticism; rather, his literary method has been described as appreciative and impressionistic. His essays are characterized by their lucid style, profound understanding, and conscientious scholarship. In the following excerpt, Cecil praises the austerity and economy of Constant's art. He declares that* Adolphe *deserves a place "among the supreme masterpieces of fiction" because it expresses "the universal predicament of mankind."*]

Adolphe has never been much read in England. It is too French. For all that the author happened to be a Swiss, his book is a typical French classic: and the French and English classic conceptions of fiction are poles apart. . . . The French classical novel . . . is out, not so much to entertain, as to illuminate. It is, first of all, a serious study of the principles governing human action. And its characteristics are logic, concentration, intellectual force. (p. 141)

[*Adolphe* is a] story of inaction, not action; and it is told with an austere concentration. Not an episode, not a comment but refers to the main theme; no characters but the hero and heroine are described in more than bare outline; and even they are described almost exclusively in relation to the central situation. We are told far more about their intellectual and emotional make-up, than about their appearance or demeanour or tricks of speech. Indeed they do not speak much. Adolphe, it is true, tells the story himself: but he doesn't reproduce his conversations with others in dramatic form; he just tells us the matter of what was said and the effect it had on him, with a running analytic commentary. There is a brief, brilliant account of his relations with his father—his father is the only other sharply individualised character in the story—but for the most part we see Adolphe only in relation to himself and Ellénore, and Ellénore only in relation to Adolphe. Further, the drama has no background. The lovers move from Germany to Bohemia, from Bohemia to Poland, but we are shown nothing of these countries. Adolphe and Ellénore are always, as it were, alone together in a small, featureless sitting-room.

It is interesting that Constant should have limited himself in this way; for there are signs that he could describe background very well if he wanted. Almost at the end of the story, when both the lovers have been forced to realise the true position, and when Ellénore is already sinking to death, they go for a short walk with one another: and for once Constant does indicate the landscape behind them. "It was," he says, "one of those winter days when the sun shines sadly over the greyish landscape as if it looked with pity on an earth which it had ceased to warm. . . . The sky was serene, the trees were leafless; not a breath stirred in the air, not a bird crossed it: everything was motionless and the only sound that made itself heard was that of the frozen grasses as they broke beneath our feet." These brief sentences show an acute sensibility to the physical scene, a sharp perception of physical detail. Constant has included them, however, not for their own sake but because they symbolise the mood of the hero and heroine. This mood is calm, there is even a tinge of tenderness in it. But it is a hopeless tenderness—like that of the sun shining without heat on the dead earth. Nowhere else in the story, we must suppose, did the author conceive the landscape background as being capable of thus enforcing the emotional significance of his drama. For nowhere else does he make use of his sense of landscape.

A similar deliberate severity shows itself in the style of the book. Just once or twice Constant allows himself an image: and then it is always extraordinarily brilliant and arresting. Ellénore, when Adolphe first meets her, fiery, sombre, fitful, troubled, makes an effect like that of a beautiful storm, "un bel orage"—the expression is almost untranslatable—Adolphe's last passages of untroubled love, faint reflections of the past, resemble "those pale faded leaves . . . that grow languidly on the branches of an uprooted tree". But for the most part the style is as plain and uncoloured as it can well be. Constant is deliberately out to create the illusion that he is not composing a literary work at all, but just giving us a bare exact record of fact.

Indeed, his is the most austere kind of art. This is appropriate to his subject. Frustration is a bleak distressing theme. And Constant puts in nothing to soften its painfulness. Nobody could read *Adolphe,* surely, to satisfy their wish-fulfilment dreams, or as a means of escape from the harsh facts of ordinary life. Always in it we are in the presence of reality, if not at its ugliest, yet at its saddest and most disillusioning. All the same, this monotonous, painful little tale of failure and futility is enthralling. . . . As successfully as Jane Austen and Turgenev, Constant solves the chief technical problem facing the writer of fiction; he satisfies equally the claims of life and art. Perhaps his achievement in this respect is not quite so extraordinary as theirs, for he does not try to impose unity on so diverse and complex a scene. The French ideal of form did not let him. Forced as he is to concentrate rigidly and exclusively on his drama, he cannot make use of the material by

which Jane Austen and Turgenev suggest the presence and movement of the rest of the world surrounding it, which they contrive so wonderfully to incorporate into their pattern. But, within its narrower scope, *Adolphe* is just as realistically convincing as any of their books, and just as shapely. . . . The end comes to us as inevitable as the final chord of a Bach fugue. Yet though the book is so logical, it never seems artificial. The development is so true to experience as to seem quite free and spontaneous; we seem to be watching something happening in real life, not staged for us in the theatre of art. (pp. 142-45)

The fluctuating phases of the . . . [drama are portrayed with] insight and subtlety: all its complex movement of quarrel and reconciliation, jealousy and remorse, false hope and final disillusionment. (p. 147)

[Consider the passage of analysis at the point] in the drama where Ellénore has tried flirting with other men as a means of reviving Adolphe's love.

> She thought of re-animating my love by rousing my jealousy; this was only to stir ashes which nothing could rekindle. Perhaps too, without realising it, a little feminine vanity mingled with her calculation. She was wounded by my coldness, so she wished to prove to herself she still had the power of pleasing someone. And, finally, perhaps in the loneliness of heart, where I had left her, she found a kind of consolation in hearing someone else repeat to her those words of love, which from me she heard no longer.

How subtle this is and how economical! A twisted, complex knot of mixed motives disentangled in four brief sentences. Most novelists would have taken ten pages over it and then failed to make it clear. This economy is an outstanding characteristic of Constant's art. Again and again we come on a sentence which, like a stone thrown into a pool, sets our thoughts expanding in ever-growing circles of significance. Listen to this:

> Man's sentiments are mixed and confused; they are made up of a multitude of varied impressions which escape exact observation; and words, always too crude and too general, can serve to indicate but never to define them.

(pp. 147-48)

Such sentences set our reflections wandering far beyond the drama of Adolphe and Ellénore. Here we come to what sets *Adolphe* among the supreme masterpieces of fiction, to what makes it, not only a good, but a great book. It has a universal application. Constant has envisaged his story with such profound penetration that he reveals it as a particular instance of a universal law. Adolphe's tragedy is in a sense a particular one; it is largely due to that peculiar weakness of will, which is his characteristic sin. But as we contemplate it, the question strikes us, is this the fundamental cause? Is there not something fatal in the very nature of the passion in which he is involved? His history is only one instance of a situation which must always arise as long as the passion of love agitates the hearts of men and women; that false position which comes when two people, outwardly bound to each other, are inwardly at war; because one loves more than the other, and therefore demands something that the other cannot give. . . . Everywhere there are Ellénores and Adolphes to be found; and nowhere in literature will they find their predicament portrayed with so concentrated a truth as in the pages of Constant. The tragedy of Adolphe's weakness is also the tragedy of all unequal love. (pp. 149-50)

As the drama mounts to its disastrous climax, and Adolphe begins to review and look back on its long disillusioning course, he begins to see it in relation to his general situation as a human being. In this new perspective, it looks different. Why should he mind so much if his life and talents are unfulfilled? What does fulfilment mean? Helpless, ignorant and feeble, man is cast into the world for a few brief years, to struggle as he can, till death comes to cast him once more into darkness. (p. 150)

[In the passage where Adolphe watches Ellénore receive the last rites of the church on her death bed,] Adolphe's helplessness is revealed to us as only one example of that helplessness which is the common characteristic of humanity; his predicament illustrates the universal predicament of mankind, as Constant conceived it. It is a peculiarly depressing conception, one must admit. For it stirs in us nothing of the sense of glory born in the midst of suffering, which we get from the more heroic types of tragedy. . . . Disaster does not intensify or exalt Adolphe's personality; it merely deflates it. His is a purely regrettable story of slow dreary defeat; and Constant compels us to savour every bitter drop of disillusionment and mortification which this defeat implies. However, this is not a fault. On the contrary, it is the ruthless though restrained consistency with which Constant is true to his grey vision that makes his achievement unique. Here, expressed once and for all—in faultless and imperishable form—is a picture of human existence, as seen by a spirit, honest, intelligent, sensitive; but without faith, without hope. (pp. 151-52)

> *David Cecil, " 'Adolphe'," in his* Poets and Story-Tellers: A Book of Critical Essays, Constable, 1949, *pp. 139-52.*

MARTIN TURNELL   (essay date 1950)

[*Turnell is a noted critic who has written extensively on French literature. In his discussion of* Adolphe, *he praises Constant's spare, exact style and singles out his "power of enclosing in a complete image feelings which seem to lie just beyond language." He also analyzes the complexity of Adolphe's personal drama and Constant's skillful construction of the action. While Turnell allows* Adolphe *an "immense stature among modern novels," he cautions that Constant's influence on the modern novel is not as extensive as it may first appear to be. According to Turnell, the development of society and man has imposed a certain method on the novelist, and Constant is merely one of its first—though most eminent—practitioners.*]

Adolphe is the perfect example of the solitary destructive analysis of the nineteenth-century novelists. The words, [that part of us which is observing the other], shows to what lengths the ravages of self-consciousness had already gone. Racine's characters are destroyed by a violent conflict, those of the nineteenth-century novelists by a process of gradual corrosion, a paralysis which spreads over their minds and reduces them to complete impotence.

'No one', said Rudler, 'would read *Adolphe* if it were a novel in three volumes.' Its brevity is, indeed, an essential part of its greatness. Constant uses an ingenious adaptation of the method of Racine to present a nineteenth-century situation. The events which he describes extend over a period of four years, but by deliberately telescoping them, by compressing

his story into a *récit* [narrative] of less than a hundred pages, he achieves the same intense concentration of emotion, the same density that we find in Racine instead of the slow diffusion of emotion that we find in [Gustave Flaubert's] *L'Éducation sentimentale*. It is this which makes his experience so overwhelming, and sometimes so revolting.

The difficulties and dangers of the method are immense. It needs intellectual integrity and clear-sightedness amounting to genius. For one of the principal dangers is that the mind, speculating about its own processes in retrospect, will end by distorting and falsifying the *données*. It is the temptation to which Rousseau succumbed. The other great danger is that the novel will cease to be a work of art at all and will degenerate into a psychologist's case-book. This, it seems to me, is what sometimes happens in the later volumes of [Marcel Proust's] *A la Recherche du temps perdu* and in [Jules Romains's] *Les Hommes de bonne volonté*.

Constant succeeded brilliantly where most of his successors failed. (pp. 101-02)

[His] attitude is one of extreme circumspection. He is determined to separate illusion from reality, false feelings from true, the feelings themselves from the interpretation which the mind automatically places on them to protect itself. It is not simply that he possessed that *vue directe*—that luminous glance—into the complexity of the human heart . . . ; it is that we perceive the feeling and the moral judgment as separate and distinct. We do more than that. We perceive the simultaneous existence of different levels of feeling, . . . 'the need of his heart for love and of his vanity for success'. The *impuissances* and *faiblesses* [impotences and weaknesses] are never converted into *calculs* and *systèmes* [calculations and plans].

When this method is turned on Adolphe the results are impressive. He is not merely the pivot of the book; he is, strictly speaking, the only character in the book. Everything is rigorously subordinated to a single aim—to illuminating the deepest and unexplored places of the personality. In reading *Adolphe* I am sometimes reminded of an X-ray photograph, but an X-ray photograph in which one sees the blood flowing and the nerves throbbing. There are four main factors in his make-up: an intense vitality, an extreme shyness derived from his father, a deep-seated pessimism and, most important of all, what he calls *un besoin de sensibilité* [a want of feelings]. (p. 103)

A large part of the book is devoted to the elucidation and analysis of this *besoin de sensibilité* which was undreamed of in the psychology of the seventeenth-century writers and which bears no relation to the *froideur* and the *indifférence* [coldness and indifference] that their characters display towards one another. What is disconcerting about Adolphe is that he is at once almost unbearably sensitive and insensible to the point of brutality, that he possesses great reserves of emotion but gives the impression of complete aridity. While it is true that his life is continually disrupted by gusts of violent feelings, these feelings are indeterminate and unattached. The intellect is incapable of directing them towards any useful end and they can never be *adequate* substitutes . . . for other feelings that he does not possess. For the clue to the contradictions of Adolphe's character lies in the fact that he did not possess certain feelings which a normal person must be expected to possess. He is perpetually trying to create the missing feelings, to convince himself that he does possess them, that he is reacting normally to a particular situation. The strain gives the first part of the novel its restless, destructive movement. (p. 105)

The movement of *Adolphe* is a twofold one. There are sudden élans, sudden expansions of feeling, but intimately connected with them is the reverse movement—the sudden contraction which deflates the feeling of fullness like a bubble and leaves only a desperate sense of emptiness and exhaustion. The 'Charme de l'amour' [charm of love] is followed almost immediately by . . .

> Ellénore was undoubtedly a source of keen pleasure in my life, but she no longer represented a goal: she had become a bond.

The theory of the 'goal' [*but*] and the 'bond' [*lien*] dominated Constant's personal life as it dominates the life of his hero. The intellect proposes the wrong 'goal', directs the violent but indeterminate feelings into the wrong channels, or at any rate allows them to flow into the wrong channels. (p. 108)

[All Adolphe's] nervous energy is converted into 'suffering', into that personal and highly original suffering which springs from the perception of his own incompleteness and which inhibits action. . . .

The 'charm of love' may be unpaintable, but the disenchantment which follows the disappearance of an illusion is not and produces some of Constant's most striking pages. The eighteenth-century antithesis, often so clumsy, is moulded to his purpose and becomes an exact instrument for measuring the fluctuations of feeling, for registering the stages of his disenchantment. The contrast between the *but* and the *lien* is one example and there are others: . . .

> Tired by her love, I was, so to speak, basking in the indifference of others.
>
> We lived thus for four months in a forced intimacy which was sometimes sweet, but never completely free. We found pleasure in it but no more charm. . . .
>
> (p. 109)

Paul Bourget once declared that the whole drama of *Adolphe* lies in 'the continued destruction of love in the young man's heart by the action of his mind, and his mistress's continual effort to rebuild by passion and tenderness the feeling which she sees crumbling away'.

This view cannot be accepted without reservations. . . . [Both] Adolphe and Ellénore up to a point mistake the shadow for the substance, and in the last part of the book she tries ironically to reconstruct an illusion. For *Adolphe* has three phases. The first is the pursuit of the 'goal'—the conquest and seduction of Ellénore. The second is the period of disenchantment—the discovery that there is no 'goal'. In the third, the 'goal' is the rupture with Ellénore.

In the last phase there is a new alignment of forces and Adolphe, in spite of himself, makes common cause with his father and the Baron de T—— in the destruction of his mistress. (p. 111)

The drama is more complex than at first appeared. The outer conflict between father and son, between the individual and society is reflected in the inner conflict in Adolphe's mind. The voices of the father and the Baron are like the chorus in a Greek tragedy. Whatever their shortcomings, they represent a norm. . . .

> Ah, had heaven granted me a woman whom social conventions permitted me to acknowledge and whom my father would not have been

ashamed to admit as his daughter, then, making her happy would have been a source of infinite happiness to me.

> (p. 113)

[This passage reveals] the extent to which Adolphe has compromised with society. The attitude that he displays is not held up to admiration. His father's disapproval of the connection with Ellénore is understandable, but there is no genuine *moral conviction* behind this disapproval. . . . It has not been sufficiently remarked that [*Adolphe*] contains a number of general statements which read for all the world like maxims lifted from the pages of the seventeenth-century moralists: . . .

> There are things one does not say for a long time, but, once they are said, one never stops repeating them.
>
> It is a fearful misfortune not to be loved when you love; but it is a very great misfortune to be loved passionately when you love no longer.
>
> (pp. 113-14)

They are not abstractions or conclusions which are imposed on experience from without. They are statements of general validity which emerge logically from [Adolphe's] experience. They are always dramatically appropriate . . . and fall into their appointed places, carrying in each case the revelation of Adolphe to himself a stage further. They provide a background of sanity which places Adolphe's disordered feelings . . . in their true perspective. It is this that gives the whole book its incomparable poise and maturity which make it almost unique in nineteenth-century literature.

The more one studies the text of *Adolphe,* the more impressed one is by the skill with which it is constructed, with which the diverse strands are woven into the pattern. The inner and outer conflicts revolve like concentric circles. Phrases and words are constantly echoing and answering one another. (pp. 114-15)

[Images] dovetail into one another, but the connection between them is so close that it would be more exact to call them sections of a single expanded image. Ellénore's attempt to break down Adolphe's opposition to her provokes a contrary movement which is expressed in the third or final section of the image: . . .

> 'Let me hear no cruel word from you,' she said. 'I make no further demands. I oppose nothing; but that voice I loved so much, that voice which moved my heart, do not, I pray, let it penetrate to my heart to rend it.'

Although the 'storms' described in the closing chapters remind us of the bitter encounters between Racine's characters, the resemblance is a superficial one. They are the signs of nervous exasperation and their function is to reveal an interior, subterranean process of dissolution. . . .

> We were living, so to speak, on memories of our hearts which were sufficiently strong to make the idea of separation painful to us, but too weak to permit us to find happiness in being united. . . . I should have liked to give Ellénore proof of my feelings which would make her happy; sometimes, I used afresh the language of love; but these emotions and this language resembled those pale and faded leaves which, amongst some remaining funereal vegetation,

grow languidly on the branches of an uprooted tree.

This passage is constructed out of simple materials which seem at first to give it a literary flavour; but when we look into it, we see how effective the first sentence is in describing the atmosphere of gradual dissolution. The ['remaining funereal vegetation,' and] the ['pale and faded leaves'] . . . convey not merely the dissolution of an attachment, but the disappearance of all feeling. It is characteristic of Constant's images that they nearly all lead back to the speaker. It is Adolphe himself who is [an 'uprooted tree']. (pp. 116-17)

These images are not numerous—it is this that makes them stand out with such power—but each one leads logically to the next and marks a further stage in the process of decay. The sections of the landscape image are as closely linked as those of the image of the *sanctuaire intime* [intimate sanctuary] and the separate strands of the images winding in and out of one another give the book its rich complexity. . . . (p. 117)

Constant's experience is never merely personal. The autumnal imagery, with its emphasis on death and decay, faithfully reflects the mood of the age which produced it. The change from autumn to winter, too, has its point. It marks the beginning of the final phase in their relationship. The barren beauty of the scene, the pale sunshine which no longer warms the earth and the sigh of resignation leave an almost painful sensation of life running to waste. Adolphe's dilemma is not less painful. What feeling persists stiffens, becomes hard and brittle as a frozen immobility steals over it. (pp. 117-18)

In spite of its brevity, *Adolphe* gives us an extraordinary, an oppressive sense of time passing. The young man whom we meet in Chapter I has no 'past'. The starting point is the *impressions primitives et fougueuses* [primitive and passionate feelings], the spontaneous overflow of a genuine, unattached vitality. This vitality attaches itself to Ellénore. . . . When we look back, we see that the whole book is a logical progression from the *impressions primitives et fougueuses* to the frozen winter scene, from youth to middle age, from middle age to death. Ellénore may seem, on account of her violence, to stand for life, but she is really a death-symbol. (p. 118)

It has been said that Constant was lacking in imagination and unfavourable comparisons between his style and Chateaubriand's were sometimes made by nineteenth-century critics. . . . [Instead] of writing a poetical prose in the manner of the Romantics with their large and blurred effects, Constant confines himself strictly to the prose use of language. His genius, like Racine's, is the genius of the French language. In English and German literature there is often an unanalysed residue in the feelings presented. We are conscious of intimate stresses and frustrations beating behind a wall of words, and this makes a whole poem or a whole novel vague and blurred. In Constant's prose there is no vagueness and no blur. He possessed the great French masters' power of seizing the obscurest feelings at the moment of their formation and translating them into exact language. Not a shade, not a tremor escapes him. This is not all. What is striking about his style is the number of different notes that he succeeded in extracting from his instrument. It ranges from passages of precise analysis and adaptions of the seventeenth-century moralists to passages like 'Charme de l'amour' and the autumnal imagery of the closing chapters which reveals his exceptional delicacy in rendering the shift and change of mood, his power of enclosing in a concrete image feelings which seem to lie just beyond language. (p. 119)

Adolphe is in a sense the allegory of the rootless cosmopolitan who belongs nowhere, can settle down nowhere. He chooses Ellénore as a protection against a hostile world, as a shield which enables him to evade problems which he is unable to face. His life with her is unsatisfactory, but there is a masochistic element in the way in which she is struck down. He destroys the object of his affections, destroys the protector in response to an unconscious urge to continue his wanderings, to a torturing need to feel that he is in fact 'étranger pour tout le monde'. Yet this does not detract from the unique value of *Adolphe*. It is an account of a man who achieved emotional freedom which at the same time freed the novel from the domination of an outworn psychology. (pp. 121-22)

The interior void, the feeling of life ebbing into the sand, which is at the heart of *Adolphe,* is something new in European literature. It is different from Pascal's *angoisse métaphysique* [metaphysical anguish] and from the sense of emptiness and waste that we feel in *l'Education sentimentale.*

When we compare Constant's novel with the productions of our own time, we may easily conclude that its direct influence has been considerable. This is almost certainly a mistake. It is rather that the way in which man and society have developed has imposed a certain method on the novelist. Constant was the first representative of a fresh situation and his novel is an eminent example of the new technique.

Constant's maturity and the way in which his moral experience is an integral part of his emotional experience give *Adolphe* its immense stature among modern novels, make it a standard by which other writers can be tested. Far from being merely a personal confession, it is a record, as all great art must be, of something that happened to human nature. It records the disintegration of the unity of the individual in a hostile environment. All Adolphe's best faculties—his magnificent intelligence, his nervous vitality—are at odds with one another and contribute to the work of destruction; and this makes him the ancestor of the heroes of innumerable modern novels. Constant's unerring sense of moral values is one of his outstanding merits, but it is clear that his hold on them is precarious, that humanity is turning its back on them and moving in the other direction. (p. 122)

Martin Turnell, ''Benjamin Constant and 'Adolphe','' in his The Novel in France: Mme. de la Fayette, Laclos, Constant, Stendhal, Balzac, Flaubert, Proust *(copyright 1950 by Martin Turnell; reprinted by permission of the Literary Estate of Martin Turnell), Hamish Hamilton, 1950, pp. 79-122.*

EDWARD D. SULLIVAN   (essay date 1959)

[*Sullivan suggests that Constant's primary concerns in* Adolphe *are expressed by three key words that recur in the novel and throughout Constant's writings: goal, bond, and constraint. Sullivan theorizes that, while Constant examined these questions from the point of view of the individual in* Adolphe, *in his religious and historical writings he addressed the same problems taking all of society into consideration.*]

Benjamin Constant's *Adolphe,* so briefly compact and so elegantly precise, suggests a tightly-coiled spring possessing an enormous power of expansion. Some of that power has been concealed by our excessive preoccupation with Constant's biography. . . . (p. 293)

Adolphe, taken by itself, is a singularly sober tale, sparingly written and studded with maxims of general wisdom brilliantly expressed; it is, indeed, "classical" in its form, avoids particularities of setting and lacks both local color and a sense of historical moment. The form of the work pushes toward the universal, removes us at once and irrevocably from the contingencies of history and the distractions of details. Where Balzac immerses his characters in a specific historical context, displays them against the world of objects, and achieves his general meaning by going beyond them, Constant moves at once into the realm of the unparticularized human problem, a position from which he is dislodged only because his notebooks and letters supply the personal particulars he so deliberately left out of his work. *Les Liaisons dangereuses* of Laclos is strikingly similar to *Adolphe* in its absence of picturesque detail and in its fondness for analysis; but it is saved from the restrictive fate of being called a "personal" novel only because we know so little about Laclos, and because what we *do* know about the man reveals so little about his motives for writing the book. As a result, when we read *Les Liaisons dangereuses* we concentrate on Valmont and Madame de Merteuil, on their analysis of others, on the strategy and tactics of domination; but when we read *Adolphe,* we concentrate on Benjamin Constant's difficulties with Madame de Staël and other women in his life.

If we cut *Adolphe* loose from its autobiographical moorings for a time . . . we may be able to see it as a work that deals, sometimes indirectly but always incisively, with psychological, social, and moral questions that remain peculiarly relevant in our own time.

The deep sense of what Constant is writing about in *Adolphe* is revealed not so much by his journals as by his vocabulary: his central preoccupations are reflected in his obsessive use of certain words that recur at the most critical moments. Such key-words provide useful instruments for measuring the power of expansion of this singularly compressed book. . . . I should like to suggest three [words] . . . which take us from the particular situation of the two lovers out toward a wider range of problems. The words that I find most highly-charged and suggestive are: *but, lien,* and *contrainte* [goal, bond, and constraint], words that are curiously echoed not only in *Adolphe* but elsewhere in Constant's writings, both in his diaries and in his political essays. (pp. 293-94)

[Constant] is engaged, of course, in a study of a variety of the *mal du siècle,* of the man unable to find a meaningful role for himself in life. But, where René [from Chateaubriand's novel *René*] and his brethren express their melancholy lyrically without attempting to get to the bottom of it, Adolphe gets what consolation he can, not in rhetoric but in analysis. His analysis, however, is not the analysis of love, as is sometimes too glibly stated. It is directed very precisely at an assessment of the effects of the absence of love in a situation that is meaningless without it. . . .

Two of the three key-words that I mentioned, *le but* and *le lien* describe the subject and trace out the action of this tale of a man's efforts to leave a woman whom he does not love. (p. 295)

Adolphe, in the story, begins and ends as a young man who has no clear conception of his role or purpose in life. Ellénore, obviously, provides no answer to his problem, and the question that underlies all his preoccupations, "Quel est mon but?" [What is my purpose?] is only an aspect of the vaster question

that is put indirectly: What is man's goal, his purpose? The question of purpose is raised from the individual level to the general when, at the end, Adolphe's uncertainty evokes a somber picture of the human condition, of man's need to cling to some support, to grasp at any form of belief: ". . . dans la nuit épaisse qui nous entoure, est-il une lueur que nous puissions repousser? Au milieu du torrent qui nous entraîne, est-il une branche à laquelle nous osions refuser de nous retenir?" . . . [In the darkness that surrounds us can we afford to reject a single dream? In the torrent which sweeps us away is there a single branch that we can dare not to grasp?] The voice is that of Constant the life-long student of religion and author of *De la Religion considérée dans sa source, ses formes et ses développements.* (p. 296)

Adolphe's search for a *but* and his efforts to rid himself of the false goal that had become a *lien* are marked by an obsessive reliance on the most important key-word of all, *la contrainte,* which introduces a curious psychological complexity and widens the range of the moral drama. It is a concept that Adolphe invokes with great frequency as a justification of his conduct, using it in two rather different senses, both of which involve an abdication of will. First of all, it is an index of Adolphe's apathy that his actions are invariably the result of outside pressures, *une contrainte,* and his responses are simply to react against them. If social forces or individual advice (from his father or from the ambassador) urge him in one direction, he recognizes the constraint and goes in the opposite. His feeling for Ellénore is made up largely of his opposition to efforts by others to remove her; *la contrainte* revives his love and resolution, but his will depends for its energy on an exterior stimulus. Secondly, Adolphe calls upon the idea of *la contrainte* as an excuse for whatever he does, as well as what he fails to do. He denies his own moral responsibility and puts all the blame, both for his loving Ellénore and for not loving her, on forces stronger than himself. (p. 297)

[According to Adolphe,] man's will and feelings are powerless before the combined onslaught of destiny, the laws of society, and just plain circumstances; and all that man's reason can do is to recognize the situation, that is, yield by that most irrational of surrenders which, both in French and in English, is described as "listening to reason."

What is at issue here is not simply a young man's rather ill-advised behavior in an affair with a young woman, but rather an approach to the fundamental question of a man's responsibility for his own actions. The same excuse is offered in the "Lettre à l'éditeur" at the end of the story, as if to support Adolphe's denial of responsibility:

> Le malheur d'Ellénore, *wrote the commentator,* prouve que le sentiment le plus passionné ne saurait lutter contre l'ordre des choses. La société est trop puissante, elle se reproduit sous trop de formes, elle mêle trop d'amertume à l'amour qu'elle n'a pas sanctionné. . . .
>
> [The tragedy of Ellénore proves that the most passionate sentiment cannot struggle against the order of things. Society is too powerful, too protean, it mixes too much bittersweetness with a love it does not sanction. . . .]

But the reply of the *éditeur* with which Constant ends his story is a sternly worded indictment of those who like Adolphe, put the blame always on some one or something outside themselves, and who use analysis as a substitute for repentance:

''Je hais cette faiblesse qui s'en prend toujours aux autres de sa propre impuissance, et qui ne voit pas que le mal n'est point dans ses alentours, mais qu'il est en elle.'' . . . [I detest the weakness which always blames others for its own impotence, and does not see that evil is not in its surroundings, but in itself]. Constant refuses to admit the argument that makes a snug refuge out of overwhelming circumstances. . . . (pp. 297-98)

Benjamin Constant, as a political observer, was peculiarly conscious of the connotations of the word liberty and recognized that liberty involves responsibility. The conclusion of *Adolphe* leads us directly to Constant's political writings, in which this advocate of liberty deals with the same fundamental questions. One page in his essay, *De l'Esprit de conquête* provides a strong link to *Adolphe* and projects us toward [the] thorny problems of authority and obedience, of free decision and military constraint, of the responsibility for tyranny. . . . Adolphe's abdication of responsibility in the personal sphere is strikingly illuminated by a transference of the same problem to a political context. If you resign yourself to your fate, if you accept the *contrainte* of circumstances, if you yield and put all the blame on the superior force that threatens you, the consequences are most serious in the area of government. Constant summons all those who have accepted the rule of a conqueror, of a dictator, to examine their consciences; not to rebel necessarily, but to see clearly their moral position, and to judge themselves. A people that is subject to a dictator can always blame the fortunes of war, withdraw from action, like Adolphe, in the name of a capricious destiny; but if analysis probes deeply enough it can speak with the voice of conscience. . . . (p. 298)

Adolphe began as the cry of a suffering individual, of a single exasperated human. It developed as the probing analysis of a peculiar individual relationship, but it is by no means limited to the particulars of Ellénore and Adolphe, nor should it be restricted by our concern for Benjamin and his models. . . . For all the lack of specific historical or local detail, for all the lack of references to a particular time or place, fundamental forces are present in the book. We are deeply involved, not in the underbrush but in the very roots of the social organism, and Adolphe moves not only in the realm of individual psychology, but in the social and moral domains as well. His bewilderment as to his *but* (and man's general purpose on earth) finds elaborate extension in the vast stretches of Constant's writings on the history of religions; his use of *contrainte* as both motive and excuse moves us at once into the area of choice and responsibility, involves Adolphe in decisions and indecisions that find their counterparts in the political sphere in Constant's preoccupation with usurpation, conquest, and the nature of political liberty. Ellénore and her pathetic story are simply a *lien;* but *lien* has, happily, two meanings, and what was a restrictive *bond* for Adolphe, the character, can serve us as a connecting *link* to a large and vital domain. (p. 299)

Edward D. Sullivan, ''Constraint and Expansion in Benjamin Constant's 'Adolphe','' in The French Review *(copyright 1959 by the American Association of Teachers of French), Vol. XXXII, No. 3, February, 1959, pp. 293-99.*

WILLIAM W. HOLDHEIM (essay date 1961)

[*The following excerpt is from Holdheim's full-length survey of Constant's writings. He examines Constant's autobiographical works, regarding* Le cahier rouge *and* Cécile *particularly in light of the question of autobiography versus artistic creation, and he describes Constant's methods in* Journal intime *as ''not analysis, but book-keeping,'' and as moving ''towards an algebra of the soul.'' In addition, Holdheim discusses Constant as a literary critic, asserting that while not a major figure in the history of criticism, he is ''brilliant and sensitive.'' Finally, Holdheim touches upon Constant's political writings and concludes that over all, Constant was most striking in the modernity of his outlook.*]

To put it bluntly, there was, and still is, a widespread belief that Constant was not really a *creative novelist.* (p. 28)

We must reject [, however,] an interpretation which in effect equates literary form with psychological structure, denies the creative process by affirming its coincidence with self-observation, and thus establishes a too simple relationship between life and art. (p. 29)

[Constant's] writings, valuable as they are for a knowledge of the man, cannot be identified with his life, and the critic should insist on their primarily *literary* character. But Constant's repeated experiments with autobiography do reveal some of the problems inherent in this genre and clarify the relationship between literature and life, the complexity of which cannot be grasped by a ''biographical'' approach. (pp. 29-30)

[In the *Cahier rouge,*] Constant tells about his youthful follies without complacency or self-indulgence, with an inimitable irony not entirely free from sadness. Of course there can be no question of noting everything, since the very process of narration naturally imposes a choice, But even beyond such necessary omissions this autobiography is strongly and deliberately stylized. (p. 30)

Misunderstanding caused by overpowering timidity is the common characteristic of [the book's] delightful adolescent adventures. An . . . extreme episode of this kind is the description of the famous meeting between Constant and his father in Bois-le-Duc, near the end of the book. Benjamin returns from his illicit English escapade, trembling in expectation of the paternal ire, but Juste Constant does not even refer to the matter. Benjamin, on his part, is incapable of uttering his carefully prepared apologies, despite the sincerity of his remorse. The relationship between the father and his son is poisoned at the core by the unconquerable timidity of both. The significance of this incident goes far beyond its obvious psychological interest, for in the framework of the *Cahier rouge* timidity is much more than a psychological problem: it is the very image and principle of the ultimate impossibility of communication between men. Expressing the essence of all the other misunderstandings, the scene between Juste and Benjamin assumes symbolic proportions. This episode is no longer humorous. Briefly but clearly it reveals a tragic note which is *secretly* present throughout the book: the realization of man's inescapable loneliness.

The amusing events can usually hide this aspect of the book, for misunderstanding can be seen in two perspectives. Viewed in a *subjective* context, it exemplifies the breakdown of human communication. Seen from the outside, however, from the point of view of ''objective reality'', it is a distorted picture of the true state of affairs. The novelist can detach himself from his subject, even if it is his own life, and occupy this objective point of vantage. In the *Cahier rouge* the essential tragedy of contorted communication is absorbed by the comedy of errors, in which reality is dissolved in the workings of caprice. Misunderstanding becomes just one expression of a pervasive insubstantiality of the real, which is the dominant note of the entire work. With consummate skill Constant conjures up a world where events, even though the protagonist is floating at their mercy, have a basic lack of solidity. Somehow reality seems to have lost the power of gravity. The climax is the fantastic Odyssey through England, which defines all the laws of common sense.

Benjamin's vagabondage through England is distinctly pica-resque in both tone and content, and indeed the *Cahier rouge* as a whole is very much a picaresque novel. Perhaps there is an even closer parallel with Voltaire's ''philosophical'' adventure story, notably *Candide,* which is itself largely pica-resque in technique. There is the same sober precision and rapidity of style, the same contraction of time. Above all, the novelistic world shows the same weightlessness which para-doxically enables a hero who is buffeted by the vicissitudes of fortune to move about as if he were not subject to the resistance of matter. This is a world where anything may happen and where nothing seems to be irrevocably serious. We see that the *Cahier rouge* is firmly grounded in the literary tradition of the eighteenth century. (pp. 32-4)

[The] story has an additional dimension: that of memory. Con-stant wrote his book near the end of the Napoleonic era, and the air of unreality it exhales is *also* that of an historical epoch which has passed away, together with his youth. This note of nostalgia for the past already belongs to the nineteenth century. The very intensity of the problem of human communication is also a modern element. But both nostalgia and loneliness, both depth in time and subjective intensity, are absorbed by the picaresque technique: a specifically modern content is mastered by an older form. In this subtle way Constant's autobiography is a novel of transition. (p. 35)

No doubt [in the *Cahier rouge*] Constant set out to write the story of his *entire* life, but in his hands the material acquired novelistic structure and was transformed into literature. It is reasonable to assume that aesthetic considerations played a major role in determining the interruption of the work. Sooner or later the inner logic of narration will clash with the data of biography. (p. 36)

The subject [of the unfinished autobiographical novel *Cecile*] requires an almost dramatic concentration, an elimination of all elements that do not contribute to the unfolding of the crucial theme. Thus time and action are entirely governed by one central line of development, and in the deforming mirror of this ''autobiography'', Constant's whole life appears as a grad-ual but certain progress towards the fated union with Cécile. (p. 37)

The almost exclusive concentration on the three principal char-acters underlines the dramatic quality of the narrative. The rapidly sketched characterization of Madame de Malbée, with her strangely indefinable charm, is a literary portrait in the tradition of French classicism. As the story develops, her au-thoritative, masculine side prevails and the heroine is clearly depicted as her polar opposite. Appropriately, Cécile's picture is vaguer than that of her more positive rival. Less a woman than a symbol of femininity, moving in an all-pervading aura of gentleness, Cécile is surely even sweeter and more angel-ically patient than the historical Charlotte [Constant's second wife, who provided the model for Cécile]. She is very much the passive, innocently victimized heroine of pre-romantic lit-erature, one of the numerous successors of Richardson's Cla-rissa Harlowe. The man who hurts her is as weak as the real Constant, and certainly even more cynical. The weak hero is another stock character in the novels of that period, but the narrator of *Cécile* can boast an additional dimension of odious-

ness. His hidden motives, generally disreputable, are com-pletely transparent to his own scrutiny, and his matter-of-fact report of his actions is interwoven with an equally dispassionate disclosure of their secret mechanism. As in the *Cahier rouge,* self-judgment takes the indirect form of irony. But the irony of the *Cahier rouge* is a kind of perpetual amusement, light and devoid of bitterness. The tone of *Cécile,* however, is sar-donic, and we gain the impression that the narrator views him-self with detached and imperturbable disgust. . . . The dom-inant tone of [the hero's] irony is a detached and impersonal contempt which, pointing beyond the hero of *Cécile,* is directed at every man's basic egoism. Thus the tone of the novel ac-quires a certain stateliness. (pp. 38-40)

For its human interest alone, Constant's [*Journaux intimes*] would be an outstanding specimen of this type of [introspective] literature. Moreover, the authentic personal flavour, coupled with Constant's habitual brilliance and clarity of style, makes its reading a rewarding experience. It is rarely a cheerful doc-ument: the reader senses Constant's eternal fear of causing pain, his awareness of the passing of time, his obsession with death, and his tormenting indecision. The judgments on people, events, and works of literature and scholarship, penetrating and often spiced with delightful irony, again and again crys-tallize into those pithy and perfectly formulated *aperçus* which make Constant a successor of the seventeenth century French moralists. (p. 50)

It is commonly assumed that Constant's journal is a classic document of self-analysis. This view is based on the reputation of the man and on certain preconceived ideas about the genre (for in a journal, after all, one is supposed to ''analyze one-self''), but is not supported by a careful reading of the text. . . . What is truly surprising in Constant's diary is the fact that his quest for self involves only a bare minimum of real self-ex-ploration. There is some, but very little of that eternal ques-tioning (centering on the query ''Who am I?'') which is so striking in the journals of Amiel or Gide. The inner tendency of this diary, excepting the early *Amélie et Germaine* episode [which forms the first volume of the four *Journaux*], increas-ingly moves towards the simple statement of fact. ''I must *record* . . .'', ''I *register* my sorrows . . .''—the terminology is revealing: this is not analysis, but book-keeping. (pp. 51-2)

The abbreviated sections of the diary are of cardinal importance because they represent the ideal limit of this tendency. Desire for secrecy or lack of time cannot completely account for these abridgements. . . . Already in his full-length *Journal* Constant declares that he does not want to re-live his impressions, but only to remember *that* he experienced them. The abridged version tends to eliminate all subjective elements and to reduce biography to a succession of bare facts. Its ideal limit is the statement in its pure form. As an example, here is the entry for 25 May 1805: ''4. 2. Dinner with Hochet. Evening at Mme Gay's. Letter from Mme de Staël. 2. 2. 2. 2. 2. 2. 12. 12. 12. 1.'' Fortunately for us, Constant has left the key to the code. *1* stands for physical pleasure, *2* for the wish to break with Madame de Staël, while *4* and *12* mean, respectively, ''work'' and ''love for Madame Dutertre''. Altogether there are seventeen such figures, and among others their meanings include the temporary revival of affection for Madame de Staël, marriage plans, hesitations concerning Madame Dutertre, and uncertainty about everything. Thus emotions are not com-pletely eliminated from the *Journal abrégé* [the journal's third section], but are maintained in the form of symbols which endow them with statistical coldness and objectivity. Even where symbols do not replace words, linguistic expression is stripped and reduced to a minimum. The numerical code is the final step, for it transcends language towards an algebra of the soul.

All linguistic formulation entails a falsification, for it constitutes an intervention of the writer. Here we touch upon the intrinsic paradox of self-description. The writer changes in the very act of observing and describing himself, even if he shuns the more active intervention of self-analysis and the subjectivism of emotion. In moving away from language, Constant's journal seeks the precision and objectivity of mathematical formulation. In the very act of observing himself Constant paradoxically tries to eliminate himself as an observer. It is as if he hoped that the abridged form, so easy to survey, will *by itself* unveil the inner pattern of his life. He has written the journal *par excellence,* which illuminates the paradox inherent in this genre. The logic of the journal, as an instrument of self-exploration, ultimately leads to the rejection of language: it is the literary genre which must try to cancel itself.

But this anti-literary, anti-subjective trend, which ultimately tends to reduce individual experience to a succession of quantitatively measurable symbols, cannot be consistently maintained. Thus the incursion of passion (first for Charlotte, later for Madame Récamier) always changes the character of this diary, plunging it again into the subjectivism of linguistic expression: the sentences become longer, the rhythm fuller, the tone emotional. At such times Constant's desire for "theoretical" self-knowledge is overpowered by his need of emotional catharsis. Therefore the consciously anti-literary tendency of the later journals rarely reaches its extreme limit. (pp. 52-4)

In both *Adolphe* and *Cécile* . . . the seemingly factual account of actions and events always conceals their analysis: the "statement of fact" is a hidden interpretation. The narrator can create the illusion of perfect objectivity, although he tells the story of his own life, because he is also the author of a novel and shares the author's fictional detachment. A diarist who analyzes himself remains plunged in life, in the stream of *becoming,* where nothing is ever finished. His questioning is perpetual and the answer will always elude him. But in *Adolphe* and *Cécile* the narrator is like a god who hovers above a realm which *is what it is,* "objectively" and for all times, a world where everything is clear and defined. It is a world of *fiction,* no matter how much it may resemble the author's life. (pp. 55-6)

In *Adolphe* and *Cécile* [the author] turns into the uncommitted, omniscient observer and recorder of a story which may be full of anguish and division, but which has the harmony, unattainable in life, of a thing closed in itself, finished and explained. The "explanation" belongs to the sphere of literature, not to the sphere of cognition: Constant has transcended not only his life, but also his urge to elucidate his life, by integrating both in the realm of fiction. In writing his novels he found catharsis rather than truth. (pp. 56-7)

Many critics have praised Constant's "sincerity" in his novels, while others have called it in question. Both judgments are equally beside the point. In the domain of the novel, "falsifications" are not vices but literary transpositions. Sincerity itself is not an ethical but an aesthetic quality which serves to endow the work with an additional dimension. The atmosphere of "veracity" which characterizes Constant's autobiographical novels is not a virtue, but an artistic device. (p. 57)

Constant, versatile as he was, also wrote some literary criticism. Though his place in the history of criticism is not par-

ticularly important, his contribution is more significant than would appear at first sight. Most of his critical writings are collected in the [*Mélanges de littérature et de politique*].

As a critic Constant may be considered a transitional figure. Although he expresses the beginnings of a liberation from traditional classicist standards of judgment, he is basically still a classicist in taste, as appears from his essay **"De la littérature dans ses rapports avec la liberté",** in which he duly deplores the "coarse expressions" in Sallust's and Lucretius' works. . . . The elegance and aesthetic purity of the classical Augustan period remain Constant's criterion of excellence, and he sees the subsequent evolution of Roman literature as a process of degeneration. (pp. 58-9)

Constant played a part in the revolt against the constraints imposed upon French tragedy, that chief bastion of classicist doctrinaire thinking. In 1809 he published an unsuccessful adaptation of Schiller's historical drama *Wallenstein* for the French stage. In the preface to his **Wallstein** he warned against the threatening asphyxiation of French tragedy through the tyranny of antiquated rules, condemning above all the crippling demand for unity of time and place. This manifesto, in which Constant was more or less the spokesman for the Coppet group, became an important landmark in French criticism. However, it was not really revolutionary: the eighteenth-century *philosophe* Diderot had already attacked the unities of time and place. (p. 60)

Occasionally Constant likes to relate literary works to their sociological context. Here again he is no pioneer: the trend comes from the Montesquieu tradition, and the eighteenth-century writer Marmontel had engaged in this type of criticism. Madame de Staël had done the same in her books *De la littérature* and *De l'Allemagne,* and Constant's article on literature in relation to liberty is in effect a more erudite treatment of a problem she had taken up in the latter work. But Constant uses the sociological approach with moderation and never in any systematic way. It serves him to clarify some aspects of a writer but never leads to the sweeping generalizations in which Madame de Staël loved to indulge, or to the levelling relativism of the later nineteenth century. Constant was too perceptive a connoisseur of literature, he stood too close to the aesthetic essence of a work, to succumb to these temptations. (pp. 61-2)

In an otherwise unimportant essay on Madame de Staël and her novel *Corinne,* Constant declares that the contemplation of beauty detaches the observer from himself. This is clearly an echo of the Kantian theory which defines the aesthetic emotion as "disinterested pleasure". Constant's familiarity with the German language, his profound understanding of contemporary developments in German thought and letters, account for numerous traces of German influence in his writings on literature. (p. 62)

All this makes Constant the critic a brilliant and sensitive dilettante who was exposed to the currents of his time, but not a major force in the history of criticism. His one work which shows truly powerful originality was ignored and completely forgotten for more than a century. I am referring to the **"Réflexions sur la tragédie",** which appeared in the *Revue de Paris* in 1829 and was not republished until recently. This important essay contains nothing less than a re-examination of the concept of tragedy. . . . Constant contends that both . . . [the idea of tragedy through character and tragedy in social condition] have exhausted their resources and that the individual can no longer be primary in a period in which the masses have become conscious of their existence. The drama of the future is the "tragedy of society". In the plays of the past, society has never been more than a framework, but now it must come to occupy the central place. The depiction of a complex social system of laws, institutions, and interrelations which oppresses and finally crushes the individual offers new dramatic possibilities.

The **"Réflexions sur la tragédie"** appeared when the romantic movement was in process of capturing the French stage. No wonder that the essay found no echo! Constant is too far ahead of the romantic individualism of his time. . . . [His] dramatic theory definitely foreshadows the naturalist drama of the late nineteenth century. (pp. 63-4)

De l'esprit de Conquête et de l'Usurpation [is] the most remarkable of [Constant's] political writings from our present-day point of view. This brief work of 1813 is much more than an anti-Napoleonic tract. With rare penetration Constant analyzes certain ominous developments of French society under Napoleon, but he does not stop there: pushing these trends to their conclusion, he arrives at a prophetic prognosis of some of the most negative aspects of modern life. (p. 94)

The varied elements of Constant's political thought, his vacillations on the question of property, the aristocratic components of his liberalism—these are factors which have led to the view that Constant, as a political thinker, marks the transition between the eighteenth and the nineteenth century. Without being false, this perspective is limited and fails to bring out the inner consistency of his thought. It has been said that Constant is still very much (too much) a man of the eighteenth century, since he attaches exaggerated value to general definitions and abstract principles. This type of criticism comes from the later nineteenth century, at times too triumphant about its pet discovery: the principle of historical relativity. But Constant's definitions, his principles of government, the legal forms on which he places such emphasis—they are not comparable to the general truths by which a certain eighteenth-century tradition wished to reconstruct reality according to universal reason and common sense. They are principles of legality, purely protective and defensive, desperate attempts to exorcise and master the chaotic flux of events by means of reason.

Constant knew much about the tragic cruelty of history. We may compare him to a coastal dweller, engaged in building dykes against the onrushing waves. He had a nightmarish vision of the future and recognized the forces which had been let loose. The *Esprit de Conquête* is one of the first penetrating cultural diagnoses of a very pessimistic and very lucid nineteenth-century tradition and its author deserves to be named as a precursor of such theorists as Burckhardt and Tocqueville. (pp. 101-02)

Benjamin Constant, though one of the first intellects of his time, was not really great, and yet he is more living now than most of his contemporaries. In fact, it is the timeliness of Constant, his *modernity,* which is his most striking characteristic. (p. 111)

Constant verbalized some of the primary themes which were to run through nineteenth-century thought—preoccupations that are with us even now. He clearly saw and felt the rift between man and the universe and between the individual and society, and he knew that man was alienated from himself. Constant understood the temptation of solving this dilemma on the sociopolitical plane, but he rejected it. . . . The truth is, Constant has no cure for the dividedness of modern man, neither a political nor, like Schiller, an aesthetic one: his nostalgic re-

ligious solution is singularly unconvincing. But the very insight into the problem, and its clear formulation, is no mediocre achievement.

Even Constant's self-exploration should be placed in this wider context, for it is much more than the narcissism of a mere egomaniac. If Constant grappled with the problem of "sincerity", it was also because he felt that nothing was certain any more, and that man himself had become questionable. . . . What Constant faced was nothing less than the spectre of *dehumanization.* (pp. 111-12)

The world which Constant both describes and represents is one where nothing is fixed and indubitable and where being and seeming, truth and make-believe are inextricably intermingled and often indistinguishable. Who is to say what is fake and what is "genuine", and who can draw the line between originality and imitation? (pp. 115-16)

Is Benjamin Constant an unauthentic "individual"? We probably must answer yes, only to add that this judgment is of limited scope and beside the point. Constant's real "authenticity" lies in his urge to understand and clarify problems, and in the inner consistency of his thought. He never overcame his fragmentation, but though the completeness and integration which he sought was denied him in his life, he realized it in literature in the perfect articulation of the world of *Adolphe,* where everything seems translucent to reason. (p. 116)

> *William W. Holdheim, in his* Benjamin Constant *(© William Holdheim 1961; reprinted by permission of Humanities Press Inc., Atlantic Highlands, NJ 07716), Hillary House Publishers, Ltd, 1961, 126 p.*

ALISON FAIRLIE (essay date 1966)

The concentration and complexity of Constant's *Adolphe,* and its relation to a particularly stimulating biographical background, have meant that critical attention has been focussed on the main character. The minor characters have generally been considered as simply a means of externalising his inner dilemma. Ellénore, more developed, is yet seen mainly as a foil: either a patchwork of reminiscences from different real women, therefore criticised as shifting too suddenly from the tender to the shrewish; or a composite abstraction, presenting the essentials of Constant's reactions to many women, but hardly an individual in her own right. . . . Because Constant draws so largely on personal material, it has been taken for granted that he lacks creative imagination in the treatment of any character other than his own. . . .

Perhaps in fact it is precisely because the most essential factor in Adolphe's character is his hypersensitivity to the hurts or the judgments of other human beings . . . [that the other characters] appear in the novel not just as abstractions, foils or pivots, but, however briefly, as people in their own right. In the present article I shall be concerned primarily not with their origins in reality, but with the degree of coherence, conviction and individuality to be found in them if one simply reads the text as it stands. (p. 28)

Ellénore is neither incoherently composite adjunct nor lifeless schematic abstraction. . . . She is a character in her own right, created from the beginning to have those qualities which will with ineluctable logic destroy her by slow stages, as well as those which will create the tension between exasperation and tenderness in Adolphe. Those qualities, too, which will enable two characters of equal stature most closely to understand, and most blindly to misinterpret, each other, as each in turn hopes against hope for a solution, or lucidly realises the tragic impossibility.

Ellénore's development throughout the novel will be influenced by three sides: her basic nature as a woman, her social position as caused by the circumstances of her past, and her individual temperament. The dramatic complexities which these may cause have been deliberately suggested from the start. Her central quality is that *dévouement* [self-sacrifice] which Constant sees as the focus of woman's energy, denied other outlets. . . . [Ellénore's] capacity for devotion will both attract and weary Adolphe. . . . (p. 29)

As to her intelligence, the famous phrase 'Ellénore n'avait qu'un esprit ordinarie' [Ellénore's intellect was not extraordinary] . . . , often assumed to be a sop to prevent Mme de Staël recognizing herself, might better be seen as an integral part of the tragic pattern. That she is not the exceptional or superior rebel against society, with inner resources in her own originality, intensifies her dependence on Adolphe and his sense of guilt at the prospect of abandoning her. Yet she is given 'idées justes . . . expressions, toujours simples . . . quelquefois frappantes par la noblesse et l'élévation de ses sentiments' [just ideas, and her clear expression of them was sometimes striking because of the nobility and elevation of her feelings] . . . which will lead to her destructive lucidity in laying bare Adolphe's later efforts to console and placate. An additional touch conveys the charm of her way of speech, as a foreigner: attracting Adolphe because it breaks through the trite or affected formulae of convention, giving something live, graceful, novel.

In every detail from the beginning she is presented not as the meek ideal who will later inexplicably change, but as a complex character where each potentiality for the future is sharply delineated. From the very outset we are shown 'la fierté qui faisait une partie très remarquable de son caractère' [the pride which was so remarkable in her character] . . . , and the word *fierté* [pride] is taken up throughout the book. Her pride and her lack of rebellious intellect make her long for a place within the stability of an accepted social and religious code; her long years of devotion to the Comte de P. have won only a precarious condescension. . . . Her intense but troubled relationship with her children is characterized. Her anxiety at an hour's absence from them will be transposed to her feeling for Adolphe in Ch. IV. The difference in age between herself and Adolphe needs only the slightest allusion at the start, and brief, cruel mention by le Baron de T. in Chapter VIII; Constant need not make explicit the undertones of fear, effort to placate, gratitude and suppressed resentment that will follow in the woman who has risked everything for a younger lover.

It is therefore no sudden change owed to some different 'model' that takes place in Ellénore; but the implacable workings of an ironical logic within a deliberately constructed character. Her firm efforts at dignified resistance gradually give way to the joy of conferring happiness on another, in keeping with the two factors of pride and devotion picked out from the start. Faced by the fear of loss (ironically brought about by the overintensity of these very qualities) her pride and devotion become possessive and domineering, and, when driven to despair, shrewish and tormenting. . . . [She] is made yet more desperate by the knowledge of how Adolphe's lack of response is forcing her into harshness. This crescendo is constantly punctuated by the tender or terrified submissiveness and inherent gentleness which lead to the resignation of the final scenes.

Each sacrifice adds to his irritation, each sign of irritation to his remorse and her bitterness. However diverse the origins of individual incidents, there is no patchwork here. Constant has given Ellénore precisely the details of mind, feeling and situation which will best intensify a logical and insoluble dilemma for both his characters.

To show the conscious and coherent construction of Ellénore's character, three particular examples from among many might be more closely examined—taken from beginning, middle and end of novel. First, there is the skill with which every detail (planned and unplanned) of Adolphe's campaign to win her (Chs. II & III) works insidiously on precisely those qualities which most matter to her individual nature. He appeals to her pity for suffering and her startled gratitude at an eloquent expression of a devotion very different from the condescending, practical attitude of the Comte de P.; he calls on her sense of justice . . . , he doubly bears on her desire for unblemished reputation by threatening an outbreak in public if she will not see him in private, and by wounding her through the accusation of frivolity; he shifts suddenly into the tender evocation of what their hidden friendship could offer; above all, in every detail of their relationship, he brings home to her the pride and peace she finds in preventing another's pain or making another happy. . . . Ironically, in the second half of the book, it will be the desire to spare pain, give happiness and avoid scandal which will motivate Adolphe in turn.

The example from the middle of the novel I have taken as one among many proofs that Constant, far from being exclusively concerned with the self-analysis of Adolphe, investigates with understanding and through Adolphe's own imaginative sympathy, the motives behind other individual conduct. In Ch. VIII . . . Ellénore will attempt to provoke jealousy in Adolphe. Briefly and pointedly there is given a suggestive insight into three motives that contribute to her allowing the attention of others. The main cause is the effort, undertaken too late, at a planned provocation to Adolphe's feeling. Here all the components of her character as seen in Ch. II are deliberately taken up: 'fierté' [pride] and 'inquiétude' [anxiety], 'impétuosité' [impetuosity], determination to be respected in society and the combination of 'esprit ordinaire' [ordinary intellect] with 'idées justes' [just ideas], so that the miscalculation of her plans is now motivated and understood in a few phrases. . . . The second motive, unrecognized by herself, is 'quelque vanité de femme' [some feminine vanity] . . . in a deeply wounded and ageing woman. . . . Third, and most suggestive, there is the need for the reassurance of those words which habit had made so intimate a part of lost experience:

> Peut-être enfin . . . trouvait-elle une sorte de consolation à s'entendre répéter des expressions d'amour que depuis longtemps je ne prononçais plus.
>
> [Perhaps, too, . . . she found a sort of consolation in hearing the language of love which I had long ceased to speak.]

The insight into Ellénore stems also from applying to her, with logic, irony and sympathy, the same laws of human behaviour which have activated Adolphe. The galvanism by the obstacle has often been at the centre of his hurt or his actions: he sees all too clearly how, once he begins to move away from Ellénore, she in turn will be caught in the same mechanism. . . . (pp. 29-32)

There is, I think, nothing incoherent, shadowy or subsidiary in this portrait. It is perhaps rare for a novel written in the first person to give such equal status, such compassionate and detailed understanding, to the figure who is the source of the narrator's tragedy. In the double tragedy of Adolphe and Ellénore, the other characters are of course secondary. Yet what is surprising in so brief and concentrated a narrative is how often they are brought alive in that flash of individuality which goes beyond any schematic function as foils to self-revelation, pivots to narrative, or mere symbolic pawns.

Adolphe's father serves primarily to explain in depth the origin of impulses and inhibitions in the central figure, but a suggestive understanding of the father's individual nature is created in careful touches and with deliberate progression. High expectations and unsystematic indulgence educate an 'infant prodigy' into ambition for renown (to which Ellénore is to prove an obstacle) and into irresponsibility. . . . The father's conviction of the unimportance of the passing love-affair contributes to Adolphe's initial involvement in feelings which cannot so easily be cast aside; his sense of the seriousness of marriage will be part of the background to Adolphe's struggle. But what comes most individually alive is the analysis of how the cold, caustic, ironical surface covers a deep affection rendered incommunicable by that most stifling form of timidity, family inarticulacy: the inability, within the close and awkward relationship, to express feelings, so that they are distorted into dry or biting phrases. Here as always it is the combination of abstract analysis and live detail which succeeds. (p. 35)

The novel gives persuasive detail not simply to [the father's] fruitless efforts to guide his son, whether by advice which leaves Adolphe free, or by one sudden moment of compulsion, but also to the theme of deep affection frustrated by the problem of expression. In Ch. IV his permissiveness is merely briefly stated. In Ch. V two hard, constrained sentences announce a decision, followed by a gesture refusing further discussion. This strangled conversation contrasts with the relatively long direct quotation from a letter in Ch. VI, combining pride in his son's capacities, insight into his nature, will to practical help and firm warnings, with the personal bitterness insinuated in a passing phrase. . . . [It] is through his letters to the Baron de T., not those directly to his son, that he is able to express, and that Adolphe finally realises, the extent of his father's [distress]. . . . If it is his effect on Adolphe (provoking rebellion and affection, cynicism and remorse, respect and mistrust for accepted values) which is his central function, yet he comes alive in his own right through minimal but carefully varied means, as a sharply delineated character.

The Comte de P. plays his necessary part in the narrative through his matter-of-fact appreciation of Ellénore's past devotion, his efforts to have her accepted socially, so that he welcomes Adolphe in his salon, yet his coldness of nature which strengthens her joy in Adolphe's early worship. But even this thumbnail-sketch of a character is given his moment where he moves beyond the mere necessities of plot to be seen in an individual flash from within. In Ch. IV he stands by the fireside discussing Adolphe's approaching departure, and lets fall one of those remarks about 'some people' provoked by bitter resentment:

> Au reste, ajouta-t-il en regardant Ellénore, tout le monde peut-être ne pense pas ici comme moi.
>
> [Besides, he added, looking at Ellenore, perhaps not everybody here thinks as I do.] . . .

One might look further at the old woman in Chapter I, necessary as an influence on Adolphe's early sense of the vanity of things,

but aphoristically characterized in a way which goes beyond this necessity, or the tiny moments when Ellénore's children are shown in puzzled surprise before the passions of adults, or even the undertones as regards the friend of Ellénore in whom Adolphe confides in Ch. VIII. But the most triumphant study of a secondary character is certainly that of the Baron de T. in the last chapters. To dismiss him as an exteriorisation of Adolphe's inner desires is to miss the savour of a quiet but virulent analysis.

This is the skilful diplomat, used to manoeuvres on a large scale, now exercising the same talents on the minor task of inculcating conventional commonsense into the erring son of an old friend. His mixture of apparent frankness, professional eloquence, and exact timing of each stage of the campaign is conveyed in the detail of ideas, letters, speech and gestures. He manoeuvres, deflates, flatters and appeals, saying never a word too much, but leaving these words to echo at planned intervals. . . . Once confidence has been established [with Adolphe], he encourages veiled discussion of the possessiveness of women, or drops a remark about those who cannot be received in society. After the preparation of intimate dinners, he arranges the climax of a larger reception, first leaving Adolphe to the horrors of public gossip tattling and whispering around him, then at the strategic moment taking him under his wing to show what power a respected reputation can exercise. Briefly he draws the moral at the end of the evening, appealing in crescendo to the essentials of reputation, family affection and, above all, Adolphe's inability to make Ellénore happy whatever his sacrifices. Finally, when even this persuasion cannot break through Adolphe's indecision, he sees with the practised eye of the diplomat the devastating use that can be made of the partly false implication of the documents in the case. (pp. 35-7)

The outer observer, however penetrating, sees only a simplified part of the real experience, ignores one dimension of it. If this is true of the Baron de T., it is still more so of the whole cloud of anonymous witnesses who form the background. In this novel of only a hundred pages, it is astonishing how the irony of constant misjudgments or piercing half-truths is given range and variety, not as abstract statement or as diatribe against society, but in the detail of everyday life. The respectable judge complacently or maliciously; the scandal-mongers rejoice in any fragment of gossip; the 'sensible' see easy solutions; the would-be seducers seek to profit from the situation; well-meaning friends by their sympathy falsify the real issue. Each change in the relationship between Adolphe and Ellénore gives more sharply pointed instances: two relatives of the Count who had been forced by him to live on good terms with Ellénore are, once she turns to Adolphe, able to use moral principles as a cloak for their spiteful joy in breaking with her; her children provide another stimulus to conventional judgment; the men who frequent her salon become insultingly familiar. . . . Drawing-room or death-bed are ringed round by the pressing presence of others, giving in flashes of detail the sense of convention, criticism, mistaken sympathy, or surmise. (p. 38)

Through the interplay between his central characters and their relationships with counsellors or observers, [Constant] has modified, re-defined, or simply questioned preconceptions around such subjects as love, vanity, ambition, devotion, giving the insight of a *moraliste* [skilled analyst] into their complex components, part self-sacrifice, part self-seeking, part self-deception. But he is novelist as well as *moraliste*: his characters, within his concise and selective technique, are 'incarnés dans chaque détail' [embodiments of each detail]. (pp. 38-9)

Alison Fairlie, "The Art of Constant's 'Adolphe': II. Creation of Character" (copyright ©1966 by Forum for Modern Language Studies *and Alison Fairlie; reprinted by permission of the editors and publishers), in* Forum for Modern Language Studies, *Vol. II, No. 3, July, 1966 (and reprinted in her* Imagination and Language: Collected Essays on Constant, Baudelaire, Nerval, and Flaubert, *edited by Malcolm Bowie, Cambridge University Press, 1981, pp. 28-39).*

R. V. CASSILL (essay date 1971)

[*Adolphe*] is a sentimental novel and a period piece. The emotions and the situation are unmistakably those of the very early part of the nineteenth century—and that for most of us is a brandy that has aged too long and lost flavor and sting. Subject to psychological analysis it yields fluently—and rather trivially. Adolphe is lazy, insecure, oversubtle, and equivocal in his intents. Ellenore is compulsive and self-deluding. There is hostility as well as love in the feelings of each for the other. All this has been much more deeply explored since Benjamin Constant wrote. (pp. 39-40)

[Clearly,] in the turning of the plot to make a statement about the nature and fate of the human pair, [*Adolphe*] is a prototype for *Anna Karenina, Madame Bovary* [respectively by Leo Tolstoy and Gustave Flaubert], and very many other stories of the century in which much of the question of human freedom was found in the riddles of adultery. But since it is so stripped, compact and epigrammatic, so lacking in furniture, scene, and complication compared to the novels of Flaubert and Tolstoy, why does *Adolphe* seem so necessary when we have *them*? I don't mean necessary to a literary historian, but to the all-out reader. . . . (pp. 40-1)

For my part, it seems all the more necessary and moving *because* we have those other, larger—more *novelistic*—expansions of a story essentially the same. It is as true to say that *Anna Karenina* prepares us to read *Adolphe* as to put the proposition the other way around. (p. 41)

It does not matter how we rank *Adolphe* or *Anna Karenina* as long as we perceive that the former, by its epigrammatic voice and a structure honed, worn, and fitted to an epigrammatic simplicity, holds the timeless quandaries about love and responsibility, liberty and choice, up to a different light. It may be that the epigrammatic novel reminds us that not all the soul's truth is rendered by representations of the visible world or by psychic response. There are agonies and exaltations more plainly revealed by and to the rational intellect than to the dumb, suffering body or the yearnings of emotion. There are existential contradictions in the human condition as well as the contradictions of intent dear to psychological therapists. . . . And it may be we seek purposely for emotional torments and the sexual disequilibriums guaranteed to provoke them in order to be diverted from the agony of the soul confronting its mortal condition. The pain and nobility of the contradictions perceptible to the intellect alone are the signal substance Constant isolates within the appearances of his sentimental tale. For this task the stark and epigrammatic manner is exactly suited. It is the weapon of choice for the ironic mind in its war with the ironies of the Creator.

And the most gallant submission. For irony is an assurance against victory. It armors the spirit, and makes it doubly vulnerable; offers intellectual haven from the shocks of contradiction and contingency—and exposes the primal flaw of con-

tradition in our mortality. It reconciles us to the equivocation of heaven by surrendering our deep hunger for simplicity and assurance.

O man, what will you have? Different kinds of irony? Fine. There are different kinds, and they *war* in this novel.

Adolphe's disapproving father writes to him: "I can only feel pity that with your spirit of independence you invariably do what you do not want to do." Plainly this is the voice of irony in its mocking aspect. In what we generally call its classic aspect. The experienced man wishes to warn and instruct his errant son by a satirical appropriation of irony. . . . Pluck out thine eye and be whole, urges the classic spirit of satire. Lie on the Procrustean bed. "Keep it in your pants."

This is not, we feel, necessarily superior wisdom; nor is it the theme of *Adolphe,* which, though it is certainly a didactic novel, is not facile in its prescription. . . . [Constant] would not have bothered with Adolphe only to let him be outsmarted by a satirical older party. (pp. 41-2)

The novel offers no period or moment of relief in [its] sexual agony. The pacing of the story (which is often confused by indifferent readers with a question of whether something gaudy happens on each page, but which truly has to do with the way interest is compounded in the central issue) is like the tightening of a bowstring when the bow is drawn. It is, literally, awful. (p. 43)

There is no . . . mercy in Constant's novel. Only the icy geometry of fate, exacting anguish at every moment as the price of youthful persistence in the face of impossibility. No English tolerance. Only the braying of desire in the stony vessel of the law.

The psychology of the main character is lucid enough—even rather trivially schematic, as I said before—until one locks with the mystery of why one who understands so well that he is headed for despair nevertheless persists on his course. Against common sense and then against the mocking that succeeds it, he goes on, deeper and deeper. It is not an inferior wisdom that makes him persist. He hopes, however ingenuously, that the contradictions which he recognizes so sharply can be traversed. Hold fast an hour longer, drive an inch or a mile farther, and daylight will appear. Equivocation and contradiction cannot be denied or overcome by the unvanquished spirit, but perhaps, just perhaps, they can be transfigured. Hope as well as satiric mockery is an ironic response to the conditions of mortality. Hope is irony in its tragic aspect. (p. 44)

I have wondered, not quite voluntarily—perhaps even subverbally among those operations of cognition where words and things are not perfectly distinguishable from each other—if the paradigmatic form of *Adolphe* is not simply that of the common genital sexual act. Is this unsynchronizable exchange of stimulations not so deeply embedded in the biological forms of male and female that it must always show itself in long, short, and intermediate intercourse? And if this is so, does it not mean that fate is flesh and all act is thought?

I review a contemporary novel and—not quite voluntarily—transpose its scenes and dramatic development into epigrammatic patterns and syllogisms like those which show so plainly on the surface of *Adolphe*. It is not quite certain that the art of the novel, or of reading novels, is a constant engagement with concreteness, or with things *realized*, in the Jamesian phrase. Our grasp of the kind of realities fiction has to deal with can never be accomplished without the kind of generalization Constant handled so brilliantly. (p. 45)

I think about *Adolphe* and *Don Quixote* [by Miguel de Cervantes]. The note and the values in *Quixote*, essentially Christian, are close enough for comparison, but not the same. The knight's mortal defeat is, in itself, transfigured. In renunciation he claims. By yielding affirms. There is a transfiguration in *Adolphe*, but it has nothing to do with the outcome of the story. Spirit and flesh, and their destiny, are more nearly integrated. There is no "other-worldliness" about it. The heights and the depths are closer home.

I remember being in love and wanting to be adequate to it. That is a way of thinking about *Adolphe*—as the novel in turn, with all its associations in literature and memory, is a way of thinking about this necessarily hopeful, necessarily desperate condition. (p. 46)

> *R. V. Cassill, "Benjamin Constant's 'Adolphe'" (© 1971 by Crown Publishers, Inc.; reprinted by permission of R. V. Cassill and David Madden), in* Rediscoveries: Informal Essays in Which Well-Known Novelists Rediscover Neglected Works of Fiction by One of Their Favorite Authors, *edited by David Madden, Crown, 1971, pp. 38-46.*

ADDITIONAL BIBLIOGRAPHY

Bowman, Frank. "Benjamin Constant: Humor and Self-Awareness." *Yale French Studies*, No. 23 (Summer 1959): 100-04.
    Proposes that Constant employed two types of humor in his writing. The first, according to Bowman, is a humor of "both attack and defense" by which Constant attempts to create a heroic persona. The second is a wit using "verbal resources" such as parody and understatement. Bowman asserts that this verbal humor is devoted to reconciling Constant's heroic persona "with his consciousness of his tragic plight."

Cruickshank, John. *Benjamin Constant*. New York: Twayne Publishers, 1974, 170 p.
    A general survey of Constant's fictional works and of his main writings on politics and religion. Proceeding from the belief that readers tend to consider Constant as only the author of *Adolphe*, Cruickshank devotes liberal space to Constant's political, religious, and critical writings so that the general reader will gain a more comprehensive understanding of Constant's intellectual abilities. As Cruickshank notes, this work relies on the work of previous Constant scholars.

Dodge, Guy Howard. *Benjamin Constant's Philosophy of Liberalism: A Study in Politics and Religion*. Chapel Hill: The University of North Carolina Press, 1980, 194 p.
    The only full-length study in English of Constant's political philosophy. Dodge examines Constant's contribution to liberalism and analyzes his political theory. Included is a complete bibliography on Constant's political writings and thought.

Fink, Beatrice C. "Benjamin Constant and the Enlightenment." In *Racism in the Eighteenth Century*, edited by Harold E. Pagliaro, pp. 67-81. Studies in Eighteenth-Century Culture, vol. 3. Cleveland, London: Press of Case Western Reserve University, 1973.
    Detailed essay assessing the impact of eighteenth-century thought, particularly teleological historicism, on Constant's theoretical writings.

France, Anatole. "Benjamin Constant's *Journal*." In his *On Life and Letters*, first series, translated by A. W. Evans, pp. 51-62. London: John Lane The Bodley Head; New York: Dodd, Mead and Co., 1924.
    Biographical sketch stressing Constant's misanthropy, solitariness, and unhappiness. France writes: "We may judge [Constant] severely, but there is one greatness which we cannot deny him: he was very unhappy, and that is not the lot of a mean soul."

Hawk, Affable [pseudonym of Desmond MacCarthy]. "Review of *Le cahier rouge*." *The New Statesman* XVI, No. 403 (1 January 1921): 393.
    Review of *Le cahier rouge* noting the book's ability to make "an unforgettable impression of truthfulness."

Heck, Francis S. "Benjamin Constant." In his *Spiritual Isolation in French Literature from Benjamin Constant and Sénancour*, pp. 19-80. Madrid: Dos Continentes, 1971.
    Examines the growth of Constant's feeling of spiritual isolation: its genesis in his ancestry and childhood, its development in his thwarted search for love and his first political phase, and its culmination in the latter part of his life. The critic quotes frequently from Constant's letters, journal entries, and other writings in order to illustrate the malaise that Constant experienced.

Higonnet, Margaret, and Higonnet, Patrice. "On the Side of Disinterestedness." *Times Literary Supplement* (10 October 1980): 1123-25.
    A review of several new editions of Constant's political writings and an examination of his present-day reputation. The Higonnets term Constant "the most thoughtful *litterateur* between Diderot and Stendhal," and the "most thoughtful *politique* between Rousseau and Tocqueville."

Murry, John Middleton. *The Conquest of Death*. New York, London: Peter Nevill Limited, 1951, 306 p.
    A "consideration of the problem of love and death" consisting of a translation of *Adolphe* and a lengthy commentary on the novel. The latter, which fills nearly two hundred pages, is a highly evocative and personal meditation on death and love which Murry describes as an "assertation of the reality of 'revelation.'" Murry uses *Adolphe* as a springboard for his essay because, he states, the novel "is, or contains, a 'revelation,' in the religious sense of the word."

Nicolson, Harold. *Benjamin Constant*. London: Constable Publishers, 1949, 290 p.
    A biographical study. As Nicolson notes, the book is "not a work of original research"; rather, it is useful as a survey of Constant's life, work, and reputation.

Oliver, W. Andrew, ed. *Adolphe: Anecdote trouvee dans les papiers d'un inconnu*, by Benjamin Constant. New York: St. Martin's Press: Macmillan, 1968, 153 p.
    An edition of *Adolphe* containing six brief essays written by the editor concerning the genesis, autobiographical content, and tragic elements of *Adolphe*. Oliver also traces Constant's literary background, his conception of tragedy, and his art. The volume also includes selections from *Cécile*.

Schermerhorn, Elizabeth W. *Benjamin Constant: His Private Life and His Contribution to the Cause of Liberal Government in France, 1767-1830*. London: William Heinemann Ltd., 424 p.
    A comprehensive biography particularly detailing Constant's political activity.

Scott, Geoffrey. *The Portrait of Zélide*. New York: Charles Scribner's Sons, 1927, 276 p.
    A biography of Mme. de Charrière that details her friendship and correspondence with Constant. In addition, the 1927 edition includes an essay, "Postscript on Benjamin Constant," that recounts the events of his life following the termination of his relationship with Mme. de Charrière in 1795.

Stendhal [pseudonym of Henri Beyle]. *Selected Journalism from the English Reviews, with Translations of Other Critical Writings*, edited by Geoffrey Strickland. New York: Grove Press, 1959, 337 p.
    Contains two brief articles on *Adolphe* and an article discussing Constant as a politician entitled "Benjamin Constant in the Chamber of Deputies," which is excerpted above, 1825.

Sidney Lanier

1842-1881

American poet, critic, essayist, novelist, editor, and travel writer.

In his position as the foremost poet of the Reconstruction South and as a leading proponent of temporal prosody, Lanier is a significant, if embattled, figure in American literature. "The Symphony" and "The Marshes of Glynn," his best-known poems, exemplify Lanier's passionately-held—and controversial—conviction that verse is governed by the laws of music. For the strong musical orientation of his prosodic theory and practice, Lanier has been hailed as one of the "first princes of American song," but dismissed by others as a mere verbalist. His views on the social and economic issues affecting the South have proven to be equally divisive, for commentators have variously promoted and repudiated Lanier as a spokesperson for his native region.

Born and raised in Macon, Georgia, Lanier mastered numerous musical instruments as a child and read the chivalric romances of Sir Thomas Malory and the medieval chronicles of Jean Froissart. Matriculating at Oglethorpe University, a local Presbyterian institution, in 1857, he came under the tutelage of Professor James Woodrow. A natural scientist educated at the University of Heidelberg, Germany, Woodrow encouraged his protegé's interest in the German Romantic writers, and he engendered in Lanier an enthusiasm for nature and science that would inform his poetry and criticism. Lanier enlisted in the Confederate Army shortly after he graduated from Oglethorpe. The hardships that he endured during the Civil War permanently undermined his health: he returned to Macon in 1865 afflicted with tuberculosis. Lanier remained in the South until 1873 and made several tentative attempts to establish himself as a writer. He published the novel *Tiger-Lilies,* an unlikely amalgam of German romance and Civil War intrigue, contributed minor poems to periodicals, and continued to work on "The Jacquerie," a lengthy narrative poem based on a popular insurrection in medieval France.

In 1873, concerned that his life would be shortened by illness and convinced that, for aspiring writers in the South, "the whole of life had been merely not dying," Lanier resolved to move to the North and dedicate his life to music and literature. He went to Baltimore and thereafter enjoyed the greatest recognition of his career. The Peabody Orchestra hired Lanier as their first flutist, and in 1875 he received national attention for his poems "Corn" and "The Symphony." In the following year he was commissioned to write the text for a cantata to be composed by Dudley Buck and performed at the opening of the national Centennial Exposition at Philadelphia. While the performance seems to have vindicated the work as a suitable text for music, many critics objected that *The Centennial Meditation of Columbia* was unacceptable as verse. Despite this setback, *Lippincott's Magazine* featured another commissioned work, the "Psalm of the West," in its centennial issue, and in 1877 ten of his verses, including "Corn," "The Symphony," and the "Psalm of the West," were published in his first volume of *Poems.* Many critics believe that Lanier reached his poetic acme in later works such as "Sunrise," "Individuality," "Sunset," and "The Marshes of Glynn" (subse-

quently collected as "Hymns of the Marshes" in the *Poems of Sidney Lanier*). Unfortunately, financial pressures repeatedly called Lanier away from his verse. Compelled earlier in his career to support himself by writing potboilers such as the travel guide *Florida: Its Scenery, Climate, and History,* he turned in the last years of his life to academic lectures and literary hackwork for additional income. In 1878-81 Lanier edited four boys' books—popular redactions of works by Malory, Froissart, and other writers. In addition he delivered two series of lectures later published as *Shakspere and His Forerunners: Studies in Elizabethan Poetry and Its Development from Early English* and lectured on the English novel at Johns Hopkins University in Baltimore. He wrote *The Science of English Verse* and the posthumously published *The English Novel and the Principle of Its Development,* his major critical works, in connection with the Johns Hopkins lectureship. In August 1881, seeking relief from his hectic activities and his recurring attacks of tuberculosis, Lanier retreated to Lynn, North Carolina, where he died.

As a prosodist and poet, Lanier was enthralled with sound and melody. In *The Science of English Verse* he defined poetry as a succession of sounds and silences regulated by the temporal laws of music, and he employed musical notation to illustrate his scansion. He also devoted a significant portion of his treatise to the analysis of the tonal qualities of language and their application in verse. Most of his own verse is deliberately, if not predominantly, musical. In "The Symphony," he used his favorite devices of onomatopoeia, alliteration, run-on lines, metrical substitution and internal rhyming to simulate the "voices" of various orchestral instruments. "The Marshes of Glynn," Lanier's rhapsodical hymn to the transcendent spirit within nature, and his highly-praised poem "Sunrise" have, according to Edwin Mims, "a cosmic rhythm that is like unto the rhythmic beating of the heart of God." In addition to musicality, Lanier invested many of his poems with elaborate imagery that has been overwhelmingly decried as vague and superficial.

Lanier neglected the idea-content of poetry in *The Science of English Verse*, a weakness that critics often detect in his verse, but the themes expressed throughout his works reflect his belief in the didactic mission of the artist. Many of Lanier's concerns were topical. In the 1880 essay "The New South," he addressed the issue of Southern cultural autonomy, repeating the argument advanced in his poem "Corn" that crop diversification was essential to Southern economic independence. His *The Centennial Meditation of Columbia*, and "Psalm of the West" are regarded as post-Civil War affirmations of national unity. But Lanier, who founded his literary criticism in *The English Novel* on his belief in the ascendancy of spiritual values in life and literature, is best known for his preoccupation with large abstractions such as love and beauty. In "The Symphony," for example, Lanier protested against the materialism of his age by denouncing the inhumanity of commercialism and promoting the beneficent forces of love. While Lanier's detractors often cite the final line of the poem, "Music is Love in search of a word," as conclusive evidence of his essential vagueness, his admirers regard the sentiment as the key to Lanier's high-minded philosophy of life and art.

Lanier unwittingly established the standard for his early critical reputation when he asserted that "I *know* through the fiercest tests of life, that I am in soul and shall be in life and utterance a great poet." Although most early commentators felt that Lanier's musical predilections and inflated metaphors and similes compromised his claim to poetic genius, they consistently exalted him as one of the truest men of letters America had produced because of his lofty sentiments and artistic dedication. This view prevailed into the 1930s, when the Agrarian critics Allen Tate, Robert Penn Warren, and John Crowe Ransom, in reaction to Aubrey Harrison Starke's biographical study of Lanier, denied that Lanier had any special significance for American literature. Exposing the vagueness of Lanier's theories and poetic images and scorning his critical judgments as eccentricities, the Agrarians characterized Lanier as a blind poet whose Romantic egoism vitiated almost every aspect of his thought and work. They also rejected Lanier as an advocate of Southern interests and perceived the nationalism embodied in the "Psalm of the West" and other works to be an implicit defense of the Northern industrial program that threatened Southern economic autonomy following the Civil War. Subsequent critics have agreed with many of the Agrarians's strictures, but they have been less willing to gainsay Lanier's achievements and significance. In 1954 Jay B. Hubbell stated that, despite his limitations, Lanier was "beyond question the most important American poet to emerge in the later nineteenth century" after Walt Whitman and Emily Dickinson. His reputation was further enhanced in the 1970s by the criticism of Jack De Bellis and Louis D. Rubin, Jr., who agreed that Lanier was ultimately the master—not the servant—of his mellifluous meters.

While few critics have defended Lanier's greatness as a poet, many have conceded that, at best, he was a genuine artist endowed with a distinctive voice and an original style. Given these qualities and his eminence over his Southern contemporaries, it is likely that Lanier will retain his position as a significant if minor figure in American literature. His reputation as a prosodist is more formidable, for modern metrists generally concur with Karl Shapiro's opinion that *The Science of English Verse* "remains one of the best expositions of its theory in the literature of metrics."

(See also *Something about the Author*, Vol. 18.)

PRINCIPAL WORKS

Tiger-Lilies (novel) 1867
Florida: Its Scenery, Climate, and History (travel handbook) 1875
The Centennial Meditation of Columbia (poetry) 1876
Poems (poetry) 1877
"The Marshes of Glynn" (poetry) 1878; published in *A Masque of Poets*
"The New South" (essay) 1880; published in journal *Scribner's Monthly*
The Science of English Verse (criticism) 1880
The English Novel and the Principle of Its Development (criticism) 1883
Poems of Sidney Lanier (poetry) 1884, 1891, 1916
Letters of Sidney Lanier: Selections from His Correspondence, 1866-1881 (letters) 1899
Shakspere and His Forerunners: Studies in Elizabethan Poetry and Its Development from Early English (criticism) 1902
The Centennial Edition of the Works of Sidney Lanier (poetry, poem outlines, criticism, essays, travel handbook, and letters) 1945

THE ROUND TABLE (essay date 1867)

[We have] seldom read a first book more pregnant with promise [than Mr. Lanier's *Tiger Lilies*,] or fuller of the faults which, more surely than precocious perfection, betoken talent. We take it for granted that Mr. Lanier is young; on that assumption we have chiefly based our praise. His errors seem to us to be entirely errors of youth and in the right direction. If we have to complain that Mr. Lanier sometimes forgets he is writing prose, that his characters garnish their talk with more tropes and metaphors than is usual in this workaday world, that his dialogue reads too often like a *catalogue raisonné* [descriptive catalog] of his library, that he offers us only frothy fancies where we look for substantial thoughts, it is still pleasant to find in these vagaries traces of a scholarly and poetic taste. Exuberance is more easily corrected than sterility; and time, which chastens and purifies the imagination, can scarcely supply its want. When Mr. Lanier learns to "bridle in his struggling muse" with whatever pain it may cost him, or at least to confine her curvetings to her legitimate province of verse, we hope to have from his pen a better novel than *Tiger Lilies*— a better one, in fact, than any Southern writer has hitherto blest us with. . . .

Most readers will find the ending [of *Tiger Lilies*] rather abrupt, but it is not inartistic. There are some superfluous characters in the book whose business seems mainly to show the poetic and linguistic attainments of the Southern warrior, and no very original ones. There is, too, in the style a straining after novelty and an affectation of quaintness so marked as to be often unpleasant. But with all its faults the book has uncommon merit; there is a freshness in the treatment, a vivacity and vigor, and in the prison scene, especially, a sense of humor which gives it an honorable distinction from the mass of recent Southern literature. If Mr. Lanier will only remember that Mr. Charles Reade is an author whose faults are so much more easily acquired than his excellences as to make him, for a young writer, the worst possible model, and that long abstract disquisitions on metaphysics and music do not enhance the interest of a work of fiction, we do not hesitate to say that his next book will justify our prophecy of success.

A review of "Tiger Lilies: A Novel," in The Round Table, *Vol. VI, No. 151, December 14, 1867, p. 396.*

THE ATLANTIC MONTHLY (essay date 1868)

[*In its ironic review of* Tiger-Lilies, *The Atlantic Monthly reflects the critical consensus that the novel is an unsuccessful and perhaps ill-advised attempt to combine a tale of Southern intrigue and Civil War combat with the traditions of German romance. Garland Greever tempers this estimate in his fuller treatment of the novel (1945).*]

It is plain that Mr. Lanier has taken more Jean Paul [Richter] than is good for him. He is saturated with Richter, and redolent of him; and, worse still, he has touches of the musical madness which has in these times afflicted persons of sensibility. . . . Conceive of a pleasant Southern gentleman who builds a country-seat in a cove of the Tennessee River, and calls it Thalberg! Naturally, there comes to live near him, in great seclusion, among the mountains, Ottilie, a German lady who has been betrayed by John Cranston, an American, then visiting the master of Thalberg. At the same time, Rübetsahl, formerly Ottilie's betrothed, arrives. Surprises, discoveries, developments; a duel between Rübetsahl and Cranston at a masked ball for love of Felix Sterling of Thalberg, and for revenge of Ottilie. The war of secession occurs at this period; and all our friends go into the Southern army except wicked John Cranston, who becomes a Federal major. The lord and lady of Thalberg are shot at their own window by a deserter from the Southern army, and Felix and Rübetsahl are finally united at the capitol gates in Richmond, after the Confederates have abandoned the city. It is rather uncertain about Ottilie and Philip Sterling. Cranston goes vaguely to the deuce.

The story is full of the best intentions and some very good performance. The author has a genuine feeling for Southern character, and we see some original poetry and natural traits in his people, in spite of Richter and music. But as a whole **"Tiger-Lilies"** will not do, though we are not sure that Mr. Lanier will not succeed better in time. There is every element of romance in the life of the South, and he has a clear field before him. There are rogues at the North, too, and he need never be at a loss for villains. If only he will write us a good novel, he may paint us as black as he likes.

A review of "Tiger-Lilies," in The Atlantic Monthly, *Vol. XXI, No. CXXV, March, 1868, p. 382.*

THE NATION (essay date 1875)

The most noticeable poem in the magazines for June, after Mr. Lowell's ["Ode read at the Concord Centennial"], is a long piece called **"The Symphony,"** by Sidney Lanier, which appears in *Lippincott*. It is fluent, fanciful, and sweet, not oversensible, and hurt by mannerisms both of expression and sentiment, some of which seem to be original and some caught in Mr. Morris's school. But it is better than most magazine verse, and is worth reading for the sake of the fancy it displays.

A review of "The Symphony," in The Nation, *Vol. XX, No. 517, May 27, 1875, p. 362.*

THE NATION (essay date 1875)

Mr. Lanier's poetical licenses in prose are . . . fewer than usual [in his paper on **"St. Augustine in April"**]. He has an agreeable style when it is not surcharged with imagery. Even here his rhetorical-poetical foible of seeing "God in everything" displays itself once too often, in the passage where he speaks of "a morning which mingles infinite repose with infinite glittering, as if God should smile in his sleep." In a former paper of his, also on Florida, similes like this occurred several times, if we remember rightly.

A review of "St. Augustine in April," in The Nation, *Vol. XXI, No. 539, October 28, 1875, p. 277.*

THE NATION (essay date 1876)

[*Lanier wrote* The Centennial Meditation of Columbia *as the text for a cantata that was performed at the opening of the national Centennial Exposition at Philadelphia in 1876. Published prior to the performance without composer Dudley Buck's musical score, the work was ridiculed in* The Nation *and other publications for its incoherence. Lanier subsequently issued a lengthy philosophical defense of his* Centennial Cantata *(1876), arguing that a musical text must be written and judged as the servitor of the music for which it is composed.*]

An injury has, we fear, been inflicted on the Centennial celebration by the acceptance, as a portion of the opening ceremonies, of a "Cantata" written by Mr. Sidney Lanier. . . . It is entitled the **"Centennial Meditation of Columbia,"** and the personification of the universal Yankee nation is represented as indulging in reflections such as—

> Humbler smiles and lordlier tears
> Shine and fall, shine and fall,
> While old voices rise and call
> Yonder where the to-and-fro
> Weltering of my Long-Ago
> Moves about the moveless base
> Far below my resting-place

and much more which reads like a communication from the spirit of Nat Lee, rendered through a Bedlamite medium. In one sense, perhaps, it is suitable to a commemoration of the Declaration of Independence, as it is a practical assertion of emancipation from the ordinary laws of sense and sound, melody and prosody. Seriously, but that the music is already composed for it, we should hope it was not too late to save American letters from the humiliation of presenting to the assembled world such a farrago as this as their choicest product.

A review of "Centennial Meditation of Columbia," in The Nation, *Vol. XXII, No. 563, April 13, 1876, p. 247.*

SIDNEY LANIER (essay date 1876)

[*In his response to the critics of his* Centennial Cantata, *excerpted below, Lanier emphasizes that a poem written for an orchestral composition must be technically adaptable to orchestral interpretation. His principal contentions, that the poem should only express general conceptions, and that it need not be "perfectly clear, smooth, and natural," were vigorously disputed by* The Nation (1876) *and* The Atlantic Monthly (1876).]

Probably there are not five English-speaking persons who have ever given an hour's systematic thought to the following question: What changes have been made in the relations of Poetry to Music by the prodigious modern development of the orchestra? (p. 266)

[The] attitude of American criticism toward a recent poem of the author's known as the **Centennial Cantata** . . . has clearly revealed the circumstance that the fundamental question herein mooted has not even occurred to more than one or two either of those who blamed or those who praised, though it would seem that not only a discussion but some definite solution of that question must necessarily precede anything like an intelligent judgment of the poem. (p. 267)

In any poem offered by a poet to a modern musical composer, the central idea, as well as every important subordinate idea, should be drawn only from that class of intellectual conceptions which is capable of being adequately expressed by orchestral instruments. . . . [The gigantic illustrations of Richard Wagner have] widened the province of orchestral effects to such a magnificent horizon that every modern musical composer, whether consciously Wagnerite or not, is necessarily surrounded with a new atmosphere, which compels him to write for the whole orchestra, and not for the human voice as a solo instrument and for the orchestra as a subsidiary one. This principle *(a)* would therefore seem to be self-evident, inasmuch as every part of the text which does not conform to it is manifestly not available for the musical composer, and so much waste matter *quoad* [as regards] music.

(b) Inasmuch as only general conceptions are capable of such interpretation, a poem for (say) a cantata should consist of one general idea, animating the whole; besides this, it should be composed of subordinate related ideas; each of these subordinate ideas should be the central idea of a separate stanza, or movement; each stanza should be boldly contrasted in sentiment with its neighbor stanzas, in order to permit those broad outlines of tone-color which constitute the only means known to music for differentiating ideas and movements from each other; and, finally, the separate central ideas of these subordinate stanzas, or movements, should not run into each other, but begin and end abruptly.

An attentive consideration of this principle *(b)* will go far toward effecting a complete reversal of the generally-received opinion that a poem for musical representation ought necessarily to be perfectly clear, smooth, and natural. For [such conceptions as can be reproduced in music] . . . are necessarily always large, always general, always abruptly outlined when in juxtaposition. An illustration drawn from the art of painting will at once make this plain. The illuminating power of music . . . is, when compared with that of the non-musical inflections of the human voice in pronouncing words, about as moonlight when compared with sunlight. Now fancy that a capricious sovereign should order his court-painter to execute a picture which was to be looked at only by moonlight; what would be the artist's procedure? In the first place he would choose a

mystical subject: for moonlight, with its vague and dreamy suggestions, would be favorable to its treatment. He would next select gigantic figures, for the same reason; and while these figures would have to be even harshly outlined in order to make them distinct, the painter would permit himself indefinite liberty as to the background and as to the spaces between separate figures, in order to fill these as far as possible with the same vague and dreamy subtleties appropriate to moonlight.

The poet, called on to write a cantata-text for music, is precisely in the position of a painter called on to paint a picture for moonlight; and the author desires that this illustration should be kept in mind when he comes to show presently how this parallel course has been followed.

(c) When a poetic text is to be furnished for an orchestra in which the human voices greatly outnumber the instrumental voices, the words of the poem ought to be selected carefully with reference to such quality of tone as they will elicit when sung. For example, when a language consists, as ours, mainly of the two classes of Saxon and Latin derivations, and when the nature of the orchestral effect desired is that of a big, manly, yet restrained jubilation, I think the poem ought to be mainly of Saxon words rather than the smoother-sounding Latin forms of our language. At any rate, I tried this experiment in the poem alluded to. . . . (pp. 268-70)

Having thus announced—let it here be said, with all disclaimer of dogma and with all the timidity which every pioneer should preserve—these meagre outlines of principles, I come to the second part of my task, which is to verify them by inquiring which kind of ideas or poems have been selected by the greatest musical masters of modern times for orchestral representation. . . .

[Berlioz's *Opium Dream of an Artist*] immediately occurs, in support of the position that a text for music should present gigantic figures, broadly outlined and even abruptly so sometimes, but giving backgrounds and spaces of vagueness which the artist leaves to the hearer's imagination to fill up. . . . Passing from Berlioz to Liszt, I instance the latter's nobler translation into music of Lamartine's *Meditation upon Death*.

This immediately suggests the very striking tone-picture which Saint-Saëns has made of a French verse describing a dance of skeletons; indeed, the first line of the verse itself if pure gibberish, being only "Zig, zig, zig." (p. 270)

When the author received his very unexpected appointment from the Centennial Commission to write the text for a cantata which was to be interpreted by an orchestra of one hundred and fifty instruments and a chorus of eight hundred voices, it immediately suggested itself to him that the principal matter upon which the citizens of the United States could legitimately felicitate themselves at this time was the fact that after a hundred years of the largest liberty ever enjoyed by mortals they had still a republic unimpaired. The idea, then, of the Triumph of the Republic over the opposing powers of nature and of man immediately suggested itself as logically proper to be the central idea of the poem; and inasmuch as the general idea of triumph over opposition is considered reproducible by well-known orchestral effects, it was made at once the logical and musical Refrain of the work, nature and man shouting several times, "No! thou shalt not be!" and the Land finally exclaiming in triumph, "I was, am, and I shall be." Thus was satisfied the principle above marked *(a)*. In accordance with principle *(b)* the poem was constructed in eight different metred stanzas, each of which was informed by its own sentiment, and was differentiated from its neighbor by making that sentiment such as required strong musical contrasts as compared with the sentiment preceding or following it. For example, the first stanza of ten lines was to be interpreted by sober, firm, and measured progressions of chords, representing a colossal figure in meditation; the next (Mayflower) stanza contrasted this with an *agitato* sea movement . . . ; the next (Jamestown) movement contrasted this with a cold and ghostly tone-color, the author having filled the stanza with long *e* vocables in order to bring out a certain bassoon quality of tone from the human voices on the "thee, thee," "ye," and the like, and having made the stanza itself a gaunt and bony one in metre and form, to type the trials of the early colonists as they rose before the meditative eye of Columbia out of the weltering sea of the Past. . . . (pp. 271-72)

Finally, to conclude these illustrations drawn from the *Cantata*—the author desiring to experiment upon the quality of tone given out by choral voices when enunciating Saxon words, as compared with that from smoother Latin derivatives, wrote his poem almost entirely in the former. . . . The result was a complete vindication. The manner in which the short, sharp, vigorous Saxon words broke, rather than fell, from the lips of the chorus, and a certain suggestion of big manliness produced by the voices themselves in enunciating these abrupt vocables, will probably never be forgotten by any unprejudiced person who was in hearing of the chorus on the opening day of the International Exhibition.

In closing this paper, the author begs to remind the reader that all herein said of his cantata-text has reference solely to its technical adaptability to musical interpretation, and that when he had thought out the principles herein announced his task had but begun; for it still remained to evolve out of these materials anything possessing such unity as might entitle it to the name of poem. In point of fact, the course pursued was simply to saturate his mind with these ideas and then wait for the poem to come. (pp. 272-73)

Since, taking the meanest possible view of [the author's] cantata-text, it was at all events a faithful attempt to embody the status of poetry with regard to the most advanced musical thought of the time, made upon carefully evolved laws and with clear artistic purposes, which is more worthy of his countrymen's acceptance, that, or the far other endeavor of certain newspapers to belittle the largest anniversary's celebration of our country by the treatment of one of its constituent features in a manner which evinced not only a profound unconsciousness of principles, even preliminary to the possibility of any right judgment in the matter, but also a more inexcusable disregard for the proprieties of a dignified occasion and for the laws of respectable behavior? (p. 273)

> Sidney Lanier, "Essays on Music: 'The Centennial Cantata'" (originally published under a different title in New York Herald Tribune, May 20, 1876), in his The Centennial Edition of the Works of Sidney Lanier: "The Science of English Verse" and Essays on Music, Vol. II, edited by Paull Franklin Baum, The Johns Hopkins University Press, 1945, pp. 266-73.

THE NATION   (essay date 1876)

[*The Nation reacted sharply to Lanier's defense of his "Centennial Cantata" (1876). The periodical's criticism of Lanier's* vagueness of expression and lack of intellectual discipline anticipates the views of Allen Tate (1933) and Robert Penn Warren (1933). Its suggestion that Lanier misjudged the ideational powers of music and sound relations also informs the criticism of Edd Winfield Parks (1936).]

[Mr. Sidney Lanier] has printed a long letter in the *Tribune* to show that his ['**Centennial Cantata**'] was "at all events a faithful attempt to embody the status of poetry with regard to the most advanced musical thought of the time, made upon carefully evolved laws, and with clear artistic purposes." This statement of his object indicates the defect alike of his poem and of his letter. No one accustomed to use words with precise and definite meaning could speak of a poem as an attempt to embody the status of poetry with regard to musical thought or anything else. Mr. Lanier's poetic sensibility and serious purpose cannot make up for the lack of clear expression in his writing. This lack is the evidence not so much of want of practice in composition as of discipline in thought. His letter contains much that is interesting in regard to the extension of the capacity of the modern orchestra, to the relation of the voice as a solo instrument to the other instruments of the orchestra, and to the nature of musical interpretation. But the most important part of it is vitiated by a fallacy prevalent at the present time among loose thinkers concerning music. He affirms that the ideas in every poem intended for a musical accompaniment should belong only "to that class of intellectual conceptions which is capable of being adequately expressed by orchestral instruments." But music is not capable of adequately expressing any strictly intellectual conceptions. . . . At its best, it can do nothing to express ideas; it can but arouse emotions in harmony with certain broad, intellectual conceptions. . . . Mr. Lanier has at least succeeded in showing that the difficulties of writing a good poem for musical accompaniment have been increased by the vast development of the powers of the orchestra, and that, with all his good will, careful legality, and artistic purpose, he did not succeed in writing one that is universally approved.

> *A review of "Centennial Cantata," in* The Nation, *Vol. XXII, No. 569, May 25, 1876, p. 336.*

THE ATLANTIC MONTHLY   (essay date 1876)

[*Like* The Nation (1876), The Atlantic Monthly *took issue with Lanier's defense of his "Centennial Cantata" (1876). The critic disputes Lanier's view that musical texts need not be "perfectly clear, smooth, and natural" and deprecates his reliance on theory in composing the poem. Edmund Clarence Stedman (1888), Edd Winfield Parks (1936), and other critics also maintained that Lanier's preoccupation with theory detracted from his poetry.*]

The greater part of Mr. Lanier's poem [for Mr. Buck's "Centennial Cantata"], apart from all considerations of its intrinsic poetical worth or unworth is suitable to musical treatment in the dramatic, declamatory, Liszt-Wagner style, but is very ill adapted to musical treatment in the purely musical style in which Mr. Buck [the composer] is so gracefully at home. (p. 123)

Mr. Lanier recently wrote a newspaper letter in which he defended at great length his choice of method in composing this cantata-text. He there lays down three principles which, in his view, constitute the *a, b, c* of the matter. . . . We have nothing to object to the sincerity of Mr. Lanier's convictions, and, as we have intimated, we think he produced various phrases and movements well adapted to dramatic musical arrangement; but we feel bound to oppose his theory that poetry written for music need no longer be "perfectly clear, smooth, and natural." There are critics quite as competent as Mr. Lanier who do not believe that the poorness of Wagner's texts for his own operas is at all essential to their musical splendor. And what does Mr. Lanier say to Schiller's ode, "An die Freude," so magnificently set by Beethoven in his Ninth Symphony? We know of no text, either, which might so well inspire a musician of the modern school as Coleridge's "Ancient Mariner," . . . a poem largely made up of clear and precise narrative. . . . Mr. Lanier's fundamental error appears in a simile to which he confidently calls our attention, namely, that a poet asked to write a cantata-text is in precisely the predicament of a painter whimsically required to paint a picture that shall be viewed only by moonlight. This is as ludicrous as it is loose in its analogy. Mr. Lanier himself points out in one case the power of music to invest unmeaning syllables with great effect; and this alone shows that music is not an indistinct medium for the transmission of impressions, comparing with the power of non-musical vocal inflections "as moonlight . . . with sunlight." The syllables "zig, zig, zig" cannot possibly be made impressive in non-musical utterance. So that the idea that music, as contrasted with simple elocution, enfeebles and makes vague, falls to the ground. And even granting that it does make things vague, we should say that the poet, instead of adding to the dimness and mysticism of musical expression, ought to throw into his words a compensating clearness. In either case, then, Mr. Lanier is at fault. He has been misled by a simile, and has gone astray by reason of that peculiar and excessive roominess which an uncertain grasp of principles is apt to create in the mind. His law of the prevailing general idea and of the related subordinate ideas is quite correct, but not at all new; his choice of Saxon words is highly commendable; but his rejection of clearness and intelligibility is a lamentable error. It is quite possible that fine things may be produced in a mystical and indefinite vein, but no art can ever achieve greatly which sets out with forethought to be mystical and vague. Mr. Lanier says that he saturated his mind with a theory, and then waited for the poem to come. He would have done better to keep his mind more clear from theories, and to have gone ardently and without prejudice in search of his poem. As it is, in expounding the alphabet of a new poetic-musical art, he has forgotten that it must have a grammar also. And though undoubtedly revolutionary forces have been at work in music, and are now at work in poetry, which the general public may not appreciate, yet the criticisms which the Centennial cantata-text has met represent a healthy and instinctively correct popular protest against what is really a hasty and defective attempt to overthrow artistic order. (pp. 123-24)

> *A review of "The Centennial Meditation of Columbia," in* The Atlantic Monthly, *Vol. XXXVIII, No. CCXXV, July, 1876, pp. 122-24.*

THE NEW YORK TIMES (essay date 1876)

[The following critiques Lanier's Poems, *which, while dated 1877, appeared in autumn 1876.]*

Mr. Lanier became suddenly famous this year as the author of a cantata which was sung at the opening of the Centennial Exhibition. It exhibited so strong a leaning to the music to which it was set, it was so much of a libretto composed to accompany the music, that people who value the independence of literature from other forms of art were not much pleased with the performance. The ordinary libretto of an opera is often absurd enough, but at least it tells a story more clearly, more comprehensibly to the non-musical mind, than the opera music itself. But Mr. Lanier, with perhaps too great a care for the difficulties before the composer of the cantata's music, seemed to have tried to do part of his work. . . . [In *Poems* we have] **"The Symphony,"** in which people who like the mixture [of poetry and music] will find the two arts agreeably wedded, and almost everybody can admire the portions that allude to nature. Leaving aside the setting of this poem, the various musical instruments that speak one after another, as in an orchestral piece, the spirit that breathes through it all is pure and refined. If one divests himself of the impression made by many versifications the reverse of happy, the thought Mr. Lanier is presenting appears a noble one. It may not be conceived from the broadest standpoint, but as far as it goes it speaks well for him. Not unnaturally, since he is of Southern origin, trade appears to him in the darkest colors, and anything like bargaining in love calls for the severest indignation on his part; his poem, therefore, becomes a sermon directed against the material, trafficking character of the age and the country.

"Corn" is even better than **"The Symphony."** It is more distinctly Southern; takes hold more directly on human life, and, moreover, tells a little tragic story without undue tragedy in the telling of it. . . .

[The] story begins:

> Upon that generous rounding side,
>   With gullies scarified,
>   Where keen neglect his lash hath piled,
> Dwelt one I knew of old, who played at toil,
> And gave to coquette Cotton soul and soil,
>   Scorning the slow reward of patient grain,
>   He sowed his heart with hopes of swifter gain,
>   Then sat him down and waited for the rain.
> He sailed in borrowed ships of usury—
>   A foolish Jason on a treacherous sea,
>   Seeking the Fleece and finding misery.

This will give an idea of Mr. Lanier's virtues and failings. He has seized the relation between cotton and corn, and makes his Georgian planter gamble in the one instead of living sturdily by the other. He has touched on the Southern habit of borrowing and repudiating, and neither makes an apology for it nor is violent against it. This is all good. The spirit is excellent, the idea well conceived, and the execution in some respects far from bad. But there is a straining after effect in adjectives and phrases. "Neglect" is called "keen," and is personified as holding a lash. Surely, that is not fine. There is a flavor about "coquette" as an adjective which is hardly pleasing; nor, after a man has sowed his heart, can he sit down and wait for the rain without being the victim of a common fault in writers—namely, the putting of the strongest position first, so that the reader descends to the climax of the passage.

What remains of this slender volume cannot come in for praise. Mr. Lanier is vague, and in the love poems here given, cold. He seems to have read Swinburne too much, and to have caught unconsciously some of his outside characteristics. Readers of "Erectheus" will remember how monotonous Swinburne becomes with his lines beginning each one with, "And the"—"And the"—"And the." One is tempted to exclaim over these supplementary poems: Here is a clever man who thinks he has something to say, but he has nothing.

> *A review of "Poems by Sidney Lanier," in* The New York Times, *December 2, 1876, p. 3.*

THE NATION   (essay date 1877)

[*In this review of his 1877 volume of* Poems, The Nation *characterizes Lanier as a "bizarre" poet and rues the fact that he seems to have influenced the verse of another poet, Mr. V. Voldo.*]

It must be sorrowfully owned that Mr. Lanier, who has by nature a thin vein of real poetic sentiment, shows no symptom of relaxing that convulsive and startling mode of utterance which amazed the nation in his Fourth-of-July ode. In his volume called '**Poems**' . . . there is a genuine feeling for nature—in some passages of "**Corn**," for instance—and there are some really dramatic touches in the soliloquy of Columbus. But the entire absence of simplicity spoils everything; and the worst of it is that he has a disciple [in Mr. V. Voldo]. Just as Thackeray declared that there was no Irishman in London so out-at-elbows but he had some subordinate Irishman to attend upon him, so the more *bizarre* a poet is, the more sure he is of an imitator.

> *A review of "Poems," in* The Nation, *Vol. XXIV, No. 601, January 4, 1877, p. 16.*

HARPER'S NEW MONTHLY MAGAZINE   (essay date 1877)

The *Poems* of Sidney Lanier . . . show genuine poetic genius. There is exhibited in them a real insight into nature—the true poetic gift—and the author sometimes puts a deal of philosophy in a single word or phrase, as "the matted miracles of grass." They are worth a second reading, and some of them require it to get their full benefit. (pp. 617-18)

> *A review of "Poems," in* Harper's New Monthly Magazine, *Vol. LIV, No. CCCXXII, March, 1877, pp. 617-18.*

THE SPECTATOR   (essay date 1879)

"**The Marshes of Glynn**" . . . [shows] signs of power; it has an air of youth about it,—and we should recommend the writer to beware of adjectives; let his substantives be strong, his adjectives few and quiet, and he will gain in effectiveness. (p. 248)

> *"A Masque of Transatlantic Poets," in* The Spectator, *No. 2643, February 22, 1879, pp. 247-48.**

SCRIBNER'S MONTHLY   (essay date 1881)

[*Along with the work of Frances Hodgson Burnett, George W. Cable, and Joel Chandler Harris,* Scribner's *cited Lanier's poetry as evidence of the growing strength and legitimacy of Southern literature. The periodical's emphasis on Lanier's "fine nature" and "varied culture" was also the keynote of Edwin Mims (1905) and other early critics.*]

Sidney Lanier is a rare genius. No finer nature than his has America produced. His work is not popular, nor is it likely to become so, for his mind is of an unusual cast and his work is of an exceptional character. He is a man of more varied culture, perhaps, than any one of those [Southern writers] we have mentioned. The world of American letters will unite with us in the hope that the delicacy of his health will not interfere with the full unfolding and expression of his power. (p. 786)

> *"Southern Literature," in* Scribner's Monthly, *Vol. XXII, No. 5, September, 1881, pp. 785-86.**

THE CRITIC, NEW YORK   (essay date 1885)

[As a whole, Sidney Lanier's poems, which are now published in the ***Poems of Sidney Lanier,***] are so entirely unlike the poems of the day, that one has no standard to judge them by. They recall Swinburne, but only in the astonishing manipulation of metre and cadence and involution. We seem to hear through them the susurrus of the flute which the poet handled so magically; they are set to a music, they are wedded to an imagery, of their own; forceful, plaintive at times, intellectual to a degree that reminds one of the Emersonian manner without the Emersonian tartness. In them the old sentimental love-sick South is no more; there is a new juice and sap, a vivid but controlled imagination, unknown to the grasshopper-songsters of twenty years ago. The old coleopter has died, and in its stead has come a thing Psyche-winged and fair, full of music and longing. [The ***Poems of Sidney Lanier***] is not so much a lament—a Linos-song—for departing summer, as a prophecy of impending springtime. Since Poe, the South has had no such singer. (pp. 3-4)

> *"Sidney Lanier," in* The Critic, *New York, n.s. Vol. III, January 3, 1885, pp. 3-4.*

EDMUND CLARENCE STEDMAN   (essay date 1885)

[*A major nineteenth-century American critic and anthologist, Stedman gained wide critical influence as the author of* Victorian Poets *(1875) and* Poets of America *(1885). In conjunction with his popular* American Anthology *(1900), the latter work helped to establish a greater interest in and appreciation for American literature. A foe of the "heresy of the didactic," Stedman wrote criticism which is often informed by his belief that "a prosaic moral is injurious to virtue by making it repulsive." Stedman established a precedent in Lanier criticism by discussing Lanier's poetic achievement in the context of his musical predilections. Like Aubrey Harrison Starke (1933) and Edd Winfield Parks (1936), Stedman felt that Lanier's absorption with music-based prosodic theory spoiled the natural, inherently musical utterance evident in his "spontaneous" verse.*]

[Lanier's] difficulties were explained by the very traits which made his genius unique. His musical faculty was compulsive; it inclined him to override Lessing's law of the distinctions of art, and to essay in language feats that only the gamut can render possible. For all this, one now sees clearly that he was a poet, and bent upon no middle flight. He magnified his office, and took a prophetic view of its restored supremacy. The juvenile pieces . . . have little in common with ordinary verse of the time. "**Nirvâna**," "**Resurrection**," and the songs for "**The Jacquerie**," are such as herald a new voice; and later efforts of the kind also show his gift unadulterated by meditations on rhythmical structure. Among these are the "**Song of the Chattahoochee**," almost as haunting as [Edgar Allan Poe's] "Ulalume," "**The Revenge of Hamish**,"—than which there are few stronger ballads,—"**The Mocking Bird**," "**Tampa Robins**," "**The Stirrup-Cup**," "**The Bee**," and "**The Ship of Earth**." But turn to the productions which he deemed far more significant, in view of their composition upon a new and symphonic method. In time he doubtless might have wrought out something to which these would seem but preliminary experiments. "**The Centennial Cantata**" was written to be sung, and when rendered accordingly no longer appeared grotesque. We may surmise that the adaptation not of melody alone, but also of harmony and counterpoint, to the uses of the poet, was Lanier's ultimate design. Nor is it safe to gainsay the belief that he would have accomplished this more nearly, but for his early death and the hindrances of sickness and embarrassment that long preceded it. Compositions suggestive and reverberant as "Sunrise" and "The Marshes of Glynn" go far toward vindicating his method. Yet even in these there is a surplusage, and an occasional failure to make not only outlines but impressions decidedly clear. "The Symphony," "Corn," and other over-praised ventures on the same plan, seem to me nebulous, and often mere recitative. The danger of too curious speculation is suggested by the strained effect of several ambitious failures, contrasted with the beauty of his unstudied work. An old foe, didacticism, creeps in by stealth when work upon a theoretical system is attempted. Let critics deduce what laws they may; it is not for the poet deliberately to set about illustrating them. The formulas devised by Poe and others often are found to suit, designedly or not, their inventor's personal capabilities. Lanier's movement to enlarge the scope of verse was directly in the line of his own endowment; he has left hints for successors who may avoid his chief mistake—that of wandering along in improvisation like some facile, dreamy master of the key board. That remarkable piece of analysis, *The Science of English Verse,* serves little purpose except, like Coleridge's metaphysics, to give us further respect for its author's intellectual powers. (pp. 449-51)

> Edmund Clarence Stedman, "The Outlook," in his Poets of America, *Houghton Mifflin Company, 1885 (and reprinted by Houghton Mifflin, 1913), pp. 435-76.**

EDMUND GOSSE (essay date 1888)

[*A distinguished English literary historian, critic, and biographer, Gosse wrote extensively on seventeenth- and eighteenth-century English literature. His commentary in* Seventeenth-Century Studies *(1883),* A History of Eighteenth Century Literature *(1889),* Questions at Issue *(1893), and other works is generally regarded as sound and suggestive, and he is also credited with introducing the works of the Norwegian dramatist Henrik Ibsen and other Scandinavian writers to English readers. Gosse was convinced that Lanier was not an authentic poet. With some vigor, he directly challenges the contemporary "idolatry" of Lanier in his essay "Has America Produced a Poet?" Gosse's allusions to Baltimore refer to Johns Hopkins University, where Lanier had worked as a lecturer.*]

When I was in Baltimore . . . the only crumple in my rose-leaf was the difficulty of preserving a correct attitude toward the local deity. When you enter the gates of Johns Hopkins, the question that is asked is, "What think you of Lanier?" The writer of the *Marshes of Glynn* had passed away before I visited Baltimore, but I heard so much about him that I feel as though I had seen him. The delicately-moulded ivory features, the profuse and silken beard, the wonderful eyes waxing and waning during the feverish action of lecturing, surely I have witnessed the fascination which these exercised? Baltimore would not have been Baltimore . . . if it had not welcomed with enthusiasm this beautiful, pathetic Southern stranger. But I am amazed to find that this pardonable idolatry is still on the increase. . . . (pp. 78-9)

From Baltimore drunk with loyalty and pity I appeal to Baltimore sober. What are really the characteristics of this amazing and unparalleled poetry of Lanier? Reading it again, and with every possible inclination to be pleased, I find a painful effort, a strain and rage, the most prominent qualities in everything he wrote. Never simple, never easy, never in one single lyric natural and spontaneous for more than one stanza, always forc-

ing the note, always concealing his barrenness and tameness by grotesque violence of image and preposterous storm of sound, Lanier appears to me to be as conclusively not a poet of genius as any ambitious man who ever lived, laboured, and failed. I will judge him by nothing less than those poems which his warmest admirers point to as his masterpieces; I take *Corn, Sunrise,* and *The Marshes of Glynn.* I persist in thinking that these are elaborate and learned experiments by an exceedingly clever man, and one who had read so much and felt so much that he could simulate poetical expression with extraordinary skill. But of the real thing, of the genuine traditional article, not a trace.

> I hear faint bridal-sighs of brown and green
> Dying to silent hints of kisses keen
> As far lights fringe into a pleasant sheen. . . .

This exemplifies the sort of English, the sort of imagination, the sort of style which [Lanier's admirers contend] are to make Keats and Shelley—who have found Bryant and Landor, Rossetti and Emerson, unworthy of their company—comfortable with a mate at last. If these vapid and eccentric lines were exceptional, if they were even supported by a minority of sane and original verse, if Lanier were ever simple or genuine, I would seize on those exceptions and gladly forget the rest; but I find him on all occasions substituting vague, cloudy rhetoric for passion, and tortured fancy for imagination, always striving, against the grain, to say something prophetic and unparalleled, always grinding away with infinite labor and the sweat of his brow to get that expressed which a real poet murmurs, almost unconsciously, between a sigh and a whisper. . . . Lanier must have been a charming man, and one who exercised a great fascination over those who knew him. But no reasonable critic can turn from what has been written about Lanier to what Lanier actually wrote, and still assert that he was the Great American Poet. (pp. 79-81)

> Edmund Gosse, "Has America Produced a Poet?" *(originally published in* The Forum, *Vol. VI, October, 1888), and reprinted in his* Questions at Issue, *William Heinemann, 1893, pp. 69-90.**

CHARLES W. KENT (essay date 1892)

[*In contrast to Edmund Clarence Stedman (1885), Kent generally regards Lanier's application of his prosodic theories as a positive influence on his verse. Lauding Lanier's masterful use of tone colors in his later poems, Kent asserts that Lanier's musicality and "high sense of beauty" place him among the ranks of the great poets.*]

Lanier's earliest poems were conventional in form and largely so in sentiment. His first published poem was, "To—" (. . . 1863); the measure was according to usual notation Iambic tetrameter or, to use his own notation, it was three-rhythm and the metre consisted of four bars. . . . The "Wedding Hymn" (. . . 1865) in the rhythm of the first poem, is uneven and somewhat flat. The "Last Words of Stonewall Jackson" (. . . 1865) consists of six verses of four lines each, three lines being of five bars and the fourth of three. In the same rhythm and without material variation from these forms are: the full-vowelled, sonorous "Night" (. . . 1866), with end-stopped lines; the freer poem "To Wilhelmina" (. . . 1866) with run-on lines; the musical "Birthday Song" (. . . 1866); the faintly poetic, "Night and Day" (. . . 1866). . . .

In the long poem, the "Jacquerie" . . . , which bears the date 1868 but which was written probably at different times, we have several indications of his later skill. It begins with heroic verse in rhyme couplets but soon drops into heroic blank verse with occasional internal rhyme. There are numerous examples of repeated run-on lines while the words of the lines begin to be knit together by phonetic syzygy; onomatopoeia is now used to good effect and alliteration becomes frequent. This poem is sometimes faulty in narration but it is very dramatic . . . and nobly expressed. (p. 48)

In **"Nirvâna"** (. . . 1869) the liquid sounds prevail, giving to this yearning melody a peculiar smoothness, while the same smoothness due to liquids and sibilants aided by alternate rhyme is present in **"Resurrection"** (. . . 1868). (p. 49)

The movement of [**"Corn,"** written in 1874,] is, in type, iambic, of five bars, but the metre is irregular. The rhyme is at first in triplets, later in couplets and then without fixed order. The rhymes bright: opposite, fall: whimsical are to be noted. The poem abounds in alliteration and phonetic syzygy; liquids and sibilants are freely used. In spite of the commonplace theme and an even more commonplace application in the latter part, the poem seems to me not only full of thought and fine feeling, but no less full of poetical parts and impressive lines. The poem lacks artistic unity and it is truth, but not what Arnold in Aristotle's term would call "high truth." (p. 50)

The years 1874, 1875, 1876 were very rich in poems from Lanier, varying in merit from unsuccessful ventures to a rarely equalled artistic perfection. Of the latter class was **"My Springs"** . . . , a beautiful lover-like tribute to his wife's eyes. The poem is full of tender feeling, and the grace with which the poem is bound together by answering letters and related consonants is worthy of great praise. (p. 51)

Of peculiar interest is the poem **"Special Pleading,"** . . . because the author of it says:

> In this little song I have begun to dare to give myself some freedom in my own peculiar style, and have allowed myself to treat words, similes, and metres with such freedom as I desired. The result convinces me that I can do so now safely.

The result is not so convincing to others. By freedom in the use of words he meant no doubt such compounds as 'heartbreak,' 'times-to-come,' 'Now-time,' 'Lonesome-tree,' 'dusk-modestly,' 'star-consummate,' 'rose-complete,' 'dusk-time.' By freedom in similes such as the following:

> Poor Now-time sits in The Lonesome-tree
> And broods as gray as any dove, etc.

> When Day and Night as rhyme and rhyme
> Set lip to lip dusk-modestly, etc.

Indeed all the similes are indistinct, and almost impossible to realize in pictures.—The movement is iambic, but the time is somewhat irregular or equalized by pauses, insertion of extra short syllables, etc. The whole poem shows a freedom, that limited by good taste and a sensitive ear, as Lanier generally curbed license, could lead to admirable results, but left uncurbed or unregulated, as here, detracted greatly from the poem. The sentiment is too unclear to be strong.

The long poem **"Symphony"** . . . is in all essential respects more artistic and its defects are of a different nature. (p. 52)

[**"Symphony"**] shows, perhaps, a greater freedom than the poem **"Special Pleading"** but it is a wiser freedom, a freedom conscious of itself and well in hand. Only in the flute song is there confusion and then it is the multitudinous music of unnumbered flute notes. This seems to me the most successful of Lanier's long poems. It is rich in thought and word, surpassingly musical in method, and with the unity of a masterly composition. Lanier's [music and poetry] are here indissolubly interwoven.

The next long poem **"Psalm of the West"** . . . , bolder in design and more difficult in conception, lends itself to very easy division into separate parts. In fact it is far more a number of related pictures placed near each other than one picture with many parts. (p. 53)

In continuity it stretches from a remote past to an unknown future, but the poem is not an organic whole and it leaves no idea of completeness. In spite of the beautiful lines, the quotable phrases, and the well-told stories, it remains as evidence of our author's failure to write as *aus einem Guss*—with one moulding. The poem is strong in its parts but, like the young Adam it describes, it lacks equal and rounded development.

I confess that I feel a pleasure in turning from this effort to interpret a nation's life, to the **"Waving of the Corn"** . . . wherein nature's life is so beautifully interpreted. This poem is particularly happy in the lines in which, not inferences but facts, are simply and unaffectedly recorded. (p. 54)

[From Lanier's experiences in Florida and Georgia in 1877,] we have several additional examples of how much he saw in nature. . . . [**"Tampa Robins"** is] a gaily colored grove painting with "sunlight song and orange blossoms" in profusion. Its spirit, as its coloring, is bright and hopeful. . . . The **"Mocking Bird"** . . . , a legitimate sonnet, is poetic in thought but restrained and formal in expression. Freer far in movement, and far more irregular in metre, is the graceful and suggestive poem, the **"Bee."** . . . In the music of this poem and in the masterly use of alliteration and syzygy, this poem is an adequate prelude, if not a fair companion piece to one of the most musical of English poems, the **"Song of the Chattahooche."** . . . The music of a song easily eludes all analysis and may be dissipated by a critic's breath, but let us try to catch the means by which the effect is in part produced. In five stanzas of ten lines each, alliteration occurs in all save twelve lines. In eleven of these twelve lines internal rhyme occurs, sometimes joining the parts of a line, sometimes uniting successive lines. Syzygy is used for the same purpose. Of the letters occurring in the poem about one-fifth are liquids and about one-twelfth are sibilants. The effect of the whole is musical beyond description. It sings itself and yet nowhere sacrifices the thought. Poe's "Ulalume" and Tennyson's "Brook," or whatever other poem you may choose with which to compare this highest achievement of our artist's musical art, will find in this a fair and unyielding competitor. (pp. 55-6)

To the **"Hymns of the Marshes"** belong the three: **"Individuality," "At Sunset"** and the **"Marshes of Glynn."** Of these **"Individuality,"** (. . . 1878-79) exhibits a growing boldness in run on lines, which now become run-on stanzas. . . . [**"At Sunset"** (1879-80)] is original in rhyme order and poetical in effect but it lacks distinctness of meaning. The **"Marshes of Glynn"** (. . . 1878) is extremely beautiful, filled as it is with soft sounds. Alliteration is very frequent while the verse structure becomes more and more free and is clearly based on time. (pp. 56-7)

The swansong of our poet is **"Sunrise"** (. . . 1880). . . . It is a fitting climax of a progressive genius, not that it represents the best that he wrote, or that it suggests the limit of his art, but in that it shows a clearer conception than ever of quantity as the basis of verse and an unreserved allegiance to this theory. (p. 57)

[Lanier's] poems preserving as they do, almost universally the beloved three rhythm, illustrate, particularly in his later days, full recognition of the time element and an utter disregard of fitting lines for mechanical scansion. [His theory of poetic rhythm] in its application seems to have all the flexibility of the sister art of music and to leave the poet utterly untrammeled, responsible to his own genius alone, and to be judged only by his power of making himself understood in song. (pp. 58-9)

[No] poet seems to have recognized more fully the colors of verse and how the colors were to be attained. Other poets may have succeeded almost or fully as well in producing the effects, but Lanier examined the reasons and used the means with clear purpose. In his opinion the music of poetry, or rather poetry as music, could use and must use all available means to impart to itself the true and desired color of tones. Rhyme wherever occurring, the judicious and pleasing arrangement of sonorous vowels, the selection of consonants that would lend the quality appropriate to the theme, that would not clog with awkward combinations of letters the easy flow of vocables, the union of parts of lines by similarity of initial sounds—all these were not for him accidental phenomena but the essential attributes of color—effects in word painting. (p. 59)

For the musical composer of English verse there seem to be no clogs of established form or fixed principles, in this far-reaching and suggestive theory of verse. Let him find the tune with all its accompaniments of appropriate color and suit it to a typic rhythm and naught but his own power and taste, naught but his hearer's capacity and ear stand in the way of a perfect poem. To overcome these difficulties are, however, present tasks of sufficient gravity to command the attention of the poetic mind. The dangers, however, are as potent as the possibility of achievement is clear.

First, until our ear is trained to catch the subtleties of these rhythmic forms, or until the poet reads full well the power of his hearer, elaborate form may seem but formlessness. This formlessness, which I think I discover in several places in Lanier's poems, is due in every case, I believe, to the exactions of his musical conception. He had no sympathy with that formlessness which is the "lawlessness of art." His formlessness was that of a composer, the music of whose soul cannot be forced into a formal score or rendered on the ordinary instrument of language.

The second danger is a tendency to strain for form effects and leave the substance unexpressed. If I mistake not this fault is present, too, in our author. Yet he had no sympathy with that perfection of form, wherein no substance is found. Lanier was a poet as well as an artist, and if at times his artistic temperament seemed to eclipse his poetic thought, grant that to the poet mind the very manner of expression may indicate the thought that lies beneath, while to the duller ear the thought must come in completed form.

These two seem to me to be the faults natural to Lanier's theory, and faults which he did not escape. (p. 60)

I believe that [certain faults noted by Stedman and other critics] must stand unanswered, but I would read over against them these merits of [Lanier's] verse that seem to supplement his faults. It is true that his musical faculty made him attempt that

which as yet seems impossible for poetry, but his attempts to remove this impossibility and to clothe his thoughts in a garb of music, gave us such poems as **"Tampa Robins,"** the **"Mocking Bird,"** the **"Song of the Chattahoochee."** This same keen appreciation of thought and word in music wedded, make him in numerous passages like Chaucer or Keats in his "divine fluidity of diction," like Swinburne in his picturing words; like Ruskin in his artistic finish; like Milton in his rhythmic movement. We must acknowledge that parts of some of his poems do sometimes seem the ready utterance of an unrestrained imagination, but these very parts impress us with the richness, the luxuriance of an imagination that sometimes tangles thought in a net work of ideas. True, he does seem to improvise, but this proves him far more than a mere skilful artisan in metre and rhyme. It shows the natural utterance of his overfull soul—the spontaneity of his poet-spirit. We must bear in mind that Lanier complained, and complained earnestly, "that in poetry criticism was without a scientific basis for even the most elementary of its judgments"; that Lanier, who conceived his art as a divine gift and knew no higher aim than the pursuit of truth, set to work to seek the foundation and the laws of versification. . . . He believed in his own genius, he was . . . confident that he had mastered the science [of English versification]. His fidelity to truth left him no alternative. He must apply it. Lanier's mistake, I believe with Stedman, was his attempt to illustrate laws. He was sometimes under the sway of a theory, when he might have been free; he was now and then constrained when he might have been natural. Perhaps this was didacticism, as Stedman suggests, but Lanier seems to me to be didactic in another sense. The poet becomes too often an avowed teacher of morals—the sermons were no less valuable because in pleasing verse, but the poetry was too often burdened with the lesson it must teach. The moral purpose is not only inferred but it too often proclaimed itself.

The quality that ranks Lanier by the side of the great poets is his "high sense of beauty." His loftiness of mind, the serenity of his soul, the high aim of his living, his deep and firmly rooted love transmuted the "beauty of holiness" into the "holiness of beauty" and unsealed his eyes so that he recognized this divine stamp of beauty in creator and creature alike. But if his sense of beauty made him a peer of our great poets, it was the heavenly gift of music that distinguished him from them. Milton, it is true, whom he most resembles in this respect, had a knowledge of music, but not the same passion for it. Milton's music was more a recreation, an accompaniment of reverie; Lanier's was a fiery zeal, a yearning love, a chosen and adequate form of expression of his soul's deepest feeling. Combined with this passion for music was his technical knowledge of the art, and these combined formed at once the foundation and the framework of his poetry. He seems literally to have sung his poems, they are essentially musical, tuneful, and melodious. Surcharged with music he overflows in mellifluous numbers. Here, then, Lanier stands out differentiated in the choir of poets and here we find that distinctive quality which is the very flavor of his writing. (pp. 61-2)

[I] believe in Lanier's own words that in soul he was a great poet. I ask . . . in conclusion, "was he a great poet in utterance?" I answer, yes. Certainly not the greatest because of his limitation of subject-matter and of form. Limitations, it is true, that he might have overcome, but . . . he died too young to have fixed beyond controversy his own place. . . . [In] the decade since his death his fame has spread beyond the confines of south, of north, of America and [he] is now heralded by many ardent admirers across the waters. May the circle of his readers continually grow, and the praise of his real admirers be unstifled, for naught but good can come of knowing him, and naught but loftier living can come of loving him. (pp. 62-3)

Charles W. Kent, ''A Study of Lanier's Poems,'' in PMLA, 7, Vol. VII, No. 2, April-June, 1892, pp. 33-63.

RICHARD Le GALLIENNE (essay date 1900)

[*Le Gallienne was an English poet, critic, essayist, and novelist. Best known for his literary activities during the 1890s, he was closely associated with the* fin de siècle *figures Aubrey Beardsley and Oscar Wilde. In the excerpt below, Le Gallienne records his admiration of the ecstatic quality of Lanier's* ''Hymns of the Marshes,'' *describing those poems as his supreme achievement. He expressed less enthusiasm for* The Science of English Verse, *remarking that* ''all the metrical training a poet needs is birched into him at school.'']

[Had Sidney Lanier] written all his other poems, and missed writing [**''Sunrise''** and the **''Marshes of Glynn,''** two of his **''Hymns of the Marshes''**] (striking, suggestive, and finelined as those other poems often are), he could hardly have been said to succeed in his high poetic ambition—as by these two poems I think he must be allowed to succeed. In the other poems you see many of the qualities, perhaps all the qualities, which strike you in the [**''Hymns of the Marshes''**]—the impassioned observation of nature, the Donne-like ''metaphysical'' fancy, the religious and somewhat mystic elevation of feeling, expressed often in terms of a deep imaginative understanding of modern scientific conceptions; in fact, you find all save the important quality of that ecstasy which in the **''Hymns''** fuses all into one splendid flame of adoration upon the altar of the visible universe. The ecstasy of modern man as he stands and beholds the sunrise or the coming of the stars, or any such superb, elemental glory, has, perhaps, never been more keenly translated into verse. Those who heard Lanier play remarked upon ''the strange violin effects which he conquered from the flute.'' Is it fanciful to feel that in these long, sweeping, and heart-breakingly sensitive lines, Lanier equally cheated his father, who . . . ''feared for him the fascination of the violin''? (pp. 346-47)

Anyone who pleases may find little literary faults [in Lanier's verse in the **''Hymns''**]. Even I could do that. But if only I could praise it as it deserves! Those who should imagine that Lanier wrote in this apparently ''loose'' Atlantic-roller metre from metrical ignorance are, of course, very much mistaken. On the contrary, he was a very learned metrist, as those who have grappled with his book on *The Science of English Verse* will know. In that book the inherited music in him came out once more as theory, his contention being that metrical law must be based on musical law. Personally, I have no opinion on the subject; and, however valuable in its province Lanier's treatise may be, I can only wish he had spent the precious six weeks it took to write it . . . in writing another of his **''Hymns of the Marshes.''**

I wonder whom these learned treatises on metre benefit. Not the poets, I am thinking. . . . It is to be feared that poetry comes by nature—and there is no poetry without a musical ear—and that all the metrical training a poet needs is birched into him at school. Indeed, I think most poets take lessons in metre after they are famous; for fear of awkward questions. The only training in metre a poet needs is the reading of great

poets; not anatomically, but just—naturally. The study of metre is the study of skeletons. The study of skeletons never yet helped a man to dance. (pp. 348-50)

Richard Le Gallienne, ''Sidney Lanier'' (reprinted by permission of The Society of Authors as the literary representative of the Estate of Richard Le Gallienne), in The Academy, Vol. LVIII, No. 1450, February 17, 1900 (and reprinted in his Attitudes and Avowals: With Some Retrospective Reviews, John Lane Company, 1910, pp. 342-50).

L. W. PAYNE, JR. (essay date 1903)

[With] all his intense application and wide reading . . . , one must see that it is not as a technical scholar that Lanier is to find his place among American critics, but rather as an inspiring writer and lecturer on poetry. As a judge of what is best in literature and as a natural appreciative critic on poetry and life, he yields to none who has written on this side of the water. His appreciation and criticism were not second-hand nor in any sense servile. He went back to the original sources and read the poets, not about them, and his utterances were the natural and spontaneous expression of his own emotions and judgments. He was a discoverer and revealer of the beauties of poetry yet unappreciated and of poets who had long lain neglected, and his discoveries will to a great degree stand the accumulated judgment of time.

It is true that Lanier, with his Southern temperament, was an enthusiast; but his taste was so pure and his judgment so sure that he rarely allowed himself to be betrayed by the ruling passions of his life into statements too excessive and dogmatic. This intense enthusiasm is one of the characteristics that make his lectures so entertaining and inspiring. In the lectures . . . [published in **''Shakspere and His Forerunners''**] he naturally excluded all the dry-as-dust criticism characteristic of the German school; and yet he did not despise the results to be obtained from the patient examination and collection of facts, especially when they are applicable to the deeper significance of the personality and growth of art and character in any given author. (p. 453)

[Two chapters of **''Shakspere and His Forerunners''**] are devoted to Shakespeare's pronunciation. . . . Of course it is of interest to know how Shakespeare and his contemporaries actually talked; but such uncertain quantities as the shades of tone of vowels and consonants, which can hardly be determined and recorded in our own days even with the help of electrical appliances, become still more matters of speculation and conjecture when an attempt is made to reproduce the exact pronunciation of any past age. When Lanier enters this field of investigation he is not authoritative, and naturally it is here that he is least interesting and convincing. (p. 456)

[In his discussion of the music of the Elizabethan period], however, our author gets into a field in which he had made original investigations and one in which he could speak with more authority. No one, perhaps, was better prepared to speak on the ''Music of Shakespeare's Times'' than the poet-musician. He had examined the music and the musical history of this period as carefully and as fully as it was possible for him to do, and the results of his investigations are worthy of respectful consideration and study. . . . [The] whole historical development of music, from the Gregorian chants to Queen Elizabeth's Virginial Book are presented in the most delightful manner. (pp. 456-57)

[The author's lectures on the Elizabethan] historical setting would doubtless have been very much extended had he lived. Still we have quite a satisfactory if not an adequate presentation in these volumes. (p. 457)

Like Lowell, and with a skill almost if not quite equal to that of this eminent epigrammatic critic, Lanier had the faculty of coining a happy phrase to crystallize the sum and substance of an author and his work. . . . Of Swinburne he says: "He invited me to eat; the service was silver and gold, but no food therein save pepper and salt." Of William Morris: "He caught a crystal cupful of the yellow light of sunset, and, persuading himself to dream it wine, he drank it down with a sort of smile." (pp. 459-60)

It is needless to say that the gleam of the poet's imagination is often seen in a flash of brilliancy through the rich foliage of the lecturer's prose. The translations of the excerpts of Old English poetry are some of them particularly noteworthy, and the style throughout is lighted up by the ground-glass glow of poetic thought and ornament. (p. 460)

Of course, if the author had edited the work . . . , we might have had a more perfectly unified series, a compacter treatment, and on the whole a more artistic presentation of the ideal of the master poet which the author had so nobly conceived. But we should have lost something of the personality of the lecturer, something of the man, and we much prefer to have the lectures just as the poet left them rather than lose anything of his charming personality. . . . In judging the content of the work one should remember that the material was prepared almost twenty-five years ago, and in criticising the form one should bear in mind the purpose for which the lectures were intended and the absence of the author's pruning hand in the editing. Even in the face of the great strides made in critical methods during the last quarter of a century, it is my opinion that students and lecturers on English literature of the period of which the book treats will get much suggestion and information, as well as pleasure and inspiration, from these volumes. (pp. 461-62)

> *L. W. Payne, Jr., "Sidney Lanier's Lectures," in*
> The Sewanee Review *(reprinted by permission of the editor; published 1903 by The University of the South), Vol. XI, No. 4, October, 1903, pp. 452-62.*

RICHARD WEBB (essay date 1903)

[*Webb characterizes Lanier as a potentially great poet whose high promise was undermined by time limitations, failure to discipline his imagination, and the influence of his theory of verse. Nonetheless, he finds Lanier to be one of America's truest nature poets and men of letters, maintaining that "his is certainly the greatest contribution any one man from the South has made to the stock of our national literature." Webb's study, presented at Yale University in 1903, was published in 1941.*]

With the purpose of encouraging his wife at a time when he was misunderstood and severely criticized, [Lanier] wrote the following sacred confession, not boastfully, but humbly and sincerely:

> This—dimly felt while I was doubtful of my own vocation and powers—is clear as the sun to me now that I *know,* through the fiercest tests of life, that I am in soul, and shall be in life and utterance, a great poet.

In soul he was undoubtedly a great poet. It is in utterance that he fails. When we contemplate the sublime faith of the man, and the essential nobility of his character, it seems a profanation to criticize adversely the work put forth by his hands. But when we do judge his works, as we must do, and apply to them world standards,—and the very fact that they demand such measurement is a tribute to their greatness,—we must realize that somewhere between the splendid poetic equipment and the product it gives forth, there is something lacking—the product does not reach the standard we had a right to expect. This failure, we believe, is largely a failure of utterance, and three general causes seem responsible for it: (1) cramped external circumstances; (2) a failure to restrict at all times his extremely active imagination; and (3) the influence of his theory of verse. (pp. 31-2)

Little time was left [Lanier] from his effort to gain food in which to perfect his poems, and the continual strain did not leave him in a mood conducive to the production of great poems. . . . In some of the poems he did write out at such times are signs of hurry and incompleteness.

Some of Lanier's ardent admirers have made the mistake of comparing him with Tennyson. Nothing could be more unjust to Lanier. . . . Tennyson was a professional poet whose business was his art, Lanier a professional musician, writing his poetry between hackwork stints, orchestra practice, and hemorrhages of the lungs. (pp. 33-5)

It cannot be stated dogmatically that if Lanier had lived eighty years free from any sickness, he would have revised [his poetry] and given it a clearness and simplicity which it lacks. It is fair to give him the value of the doubt, and to believe that the cramping conditions under which he wrote and the shortness of time he had in which to perfect his work militated against clearness of expression and a free and simple utterance. (p. 36)

The accusation is [often made] that Lanier's over-luxuriant imagination was teeming with too many schemes, would not content itself with simplified thoughts, and inveigled its possessor into believing a thing clear when it was clear to himself however obscure it might be to others. A better psychological statement would be that he lacked will power to compel himself to stick to one work till he had given it perfect form. (p. 38)

Lanier had the keenest sensibilities for beauty, a strong, acute intellect, a very active imagination, and for practical purposes a strong will, as instanced in his determination to live and do his work in spite of overwhelming odds. It is doubtful whether his will is sufficiently in evidence in his poems. . . . [All] great art must have will in its making, and must have it regnant in the product, so that the art shall not give the percipient a sense of vapid beauty. . . . Much of Lanier's work is deficient in this quality. Ruskin makes absolute command over passion a necessary quality of the highest poetry. Lanier fails in this sometimes, but more often his failure is not having his imagination under the control of regulative reason. (pp. 38-9)

The last cause which makes against perfection in his work, one which has often been suggested, but never clearly demonstrated, and which is of the greatest importance, is that his intense love of music and his consequent theory of verse on a musical basis, have led him to give more attention to the science of verse than to its artless spontaneity, and to care more for tone-color than for a "noble naturalness" of expression. (p. 39)

[The influence of Lanier's theory of versification] is constantly seen in his poems. It was utterly impossible that he should write verse and not write it with some idea of his theory in mind. This is a very potent reason why his work often gives evidence of strain, labored effect, affectation.

Fortunately we have two poems which will at once show the truth of this statement. . . .

[Lanier stated that when he wrote **"My Springs"** he tried to conform to the "tyrannies" of conventional versifications. It] is one of his best, smoothest poems. It maintains a high excellence throughout, with an evenness that is rare in his longer poems. His usual faults of turbidness, obscurity, strain after effects in sound to the detriment of the sense, are largely wanting. There is a simplicity of faith and of utterance, a sweetness of thought in fitting expression that he hardly ever surpasses. The poem is not so ambitious as some of his symphonies in verse, and is pitched on a comparatively low key, over which he has the mastery. He is simply attempting to express to his wife the appreciation he has for her beneficent influence over his life. He does this with some attention to the smoothness, "the smugness of modern verse," of which he complains:

> In the heart of the Hills of Life, I know
> Two springs that with unbroken flow
> Forever pour their lucent streams
> Into my soul's far Lake of Dreams.
>
> .   .   .
>
> Always when Faith with stifling stress
> Of grief hath died in bitterness,
> I gaze in my two springs and see
> A Faith that smiles immortally.
>
> .   .   .
>
> O Love, O Wife, thine eyes are they,
> —My springs from out whose shining gray
> Issue the sweet celestial streams
> That feed my life's bright Lake of Dreams.

The whole poem is built on a conceit worthy of Donne and his metaphysicals, but it is so smoothly and beautifully handled that, far from being disgusting, it pleases immensely. (pp. 46-7)

Now compare with this the **"Special Pleading,"** of which he has the following to say:

> In this little song I have begun to dare to give
> myself some freedom in my own peculiar style,
> and have allowed myself to treat words, sim-
> iles, and metres with such freedom as I desired.
> The result convinces me that I can do so now
> safely.

Unfortunately, **"Special Pleading"** gives too evident signs of the presence of his theory. It is not nearly so simple, so graceful, so direct in its appeal as **"My Springs."**

> Time, hurry my Love to me:
> Haste, haste! Lov'st not good company?
>   Here's but a heart-break sandy waste
> 'Twixt Now and Then. Why, killing haste
> Were best, dear Time, for thee, for thee!
>
> Oh, would that I might divine
> Thy name beyond the zodiac sign
>   Wherefrom our times-to-come descend.
>   He called thee *Sometime.* Change it, friend:
> *Now-time* sounds so much more fine!

> Sweet Sometime, fly fast to me:
> Poor Now-time sits in the Lonesome-tree
>   And broods as gray as any dove,
>   And calls, *When wilt thou come,* O Love?
> And pleads across the waste to thee.

Comment is hardly needed. Three or four readings are required to get an inkling of what it is all about. We have here all the obscurity of Browning, with none of his solid thought to make it worth while ferreting out its meaning. We see here how sadly lacking in controlling reason the man might be on occasions. The affected personification of *Now* and *Then,* and the fanciful conceit of Now-time sitting on a Lonesome-tree brooding like a dove, are simply abominable, and ought to have been suppressed by all means. If this poem is a fair example of the freedom of expression for which he pleaded, we would all prefer to take our Walt Whitman straight. If the line, "Now-time sounds so much more fine," is the result of freedom in versification, we pray to be delivered from it. (pp. 48-9)

[**"Individuality,"** written about the time his theory of verse was taking form, provides additional evidence of the influence of his theory. Let us] take the first three stanzas of **"Individuality:"**

> Sail on, sail on, fair cousin Cloud:
> Oh loiter hither from the sea.
>   Still-eyed and shadow-brow'd,
> Steal off from yon far-drifting crowd,
> And come and brood upon the marsh with me.
>
> Yon laboring low horizon-smoke,
> Yon stringent sail, toil not for thee
>   Nor me; did heaven's stroke
> The whole deep with drown'd commerce choke,
> No pitiless tease of risk or bottomry
>
> Would to thy rainy office close
> Thy will, or lock mine eyes from tears,
>   Part wept for traders'-woes,
> Part for that ventures mean as those
> In issue bind such sovereign hopes and fears.

The first stanza is admirable. It has a mystic air and a pleasant melody that are delightful. Its fine rhythm is gained by causing the accent to fall on naturally stressed syllables, and by having exactly the right number of syllables:

> Sail on, sail on, fair cousin Cloud; etc.

In the other two stanzas he demands freedom from the bondage of accents, and throws in gratuitous syllables that mar the rhythm as ordinarily read. In the second stanza is an extra syllable in the first, fourth, and fifth lines. "Deep," in the fourth line, the most important word in the line, receives no accent, while the unimportant "with" gets one. A more unwieldly line can hardly be found. In the third stanza "to" in the first line, and "for" in the fourth, are further examples of unimportant words accented. . . . [Lanier's] trouble is that in trying to win freedom in versification, he runs into license. It is good to vary monotonous regularity with an occasional departure, but it is bad art to make the departures so prominent as is done here. We believe that the time-basis *is* the right *Basis* in theory, and that accent is dependent on stress, but for this very reason words or syllables which are naturally stressed should receive the rhythmic accent as the rule, and departures should be the occasional exceptions. (pp. 51-2)

In his very latest and best poems occur blighting signs of his ever-present attempt to convey the richness of musical tones and tunes into verse. . . . In the first stanza of **"Sunrise"** we have this statement:

> Up-breathed from the marshes, a message of range and
>   of sweep,
> Interwoven with waftures of wild sea-liberties, drifting,
>
>   Came through the lapped leaves sifting, sifting,
>   Came to the gates of sleep.

This is wonderfully musical. The last two lines are magical in their melody. But when we come to analyze it, we feel that Tennyson would not have endured the forced "waftures of wild sea-liberties," in spite of its alliteration and fine vowel sequences. It required a mind of a very fanciful turn to conceive of a message as *sifting* through lapped leaves, before the days of wireless telegraphy. Two stanzas below a tree is the "burly-bark'd, man-bodied Tree." His imagination has become riotous, and has conceived the tree as a living person.

Later he calls passionately upon the leaves:

> Teach me the terms of silence,—preach me
> The passion of patience,—sift me,—impeach me,—

It is at least doubtful whether patience would be a passion if the alliteration were less pleasing. It is difficult for a matter-of-fact person to understand how leaves are to sift him and impeach him. "Impeach me" makes a fascinating double rhyme with "preach me," and this accounts for its use. (pp. 53-4)

The ear may be surfeited with rich sounds, as the taste with sweets, and this not infrequently happens in reading [Lanier's] poems. Such repetitions of similar sounds as the following soon weary the ear of anyone, and, for some readers, have a disgusting effect:

> Emerald twilights,—
> Virginal shy lights,

Or:

> The tide is at its highest height:
> And it is night. . . .

In this way his words often become as ineffective as tinkling cymbals and sounding brass. (p. 55)

Lanier was not all defects. . . . In treating of subjects very dear to him inspiration would sometimes snatch him above the trammels which bound him down, and he would pour forth melodious verse which incontestably demonstrates his right to rank as a true poet. Nature more often than other subjects aroused his emotion and imagination to the white heat necessary to fuse and mold his matter into fit form. . . . The large forms of nature gave him a sense of freedom, and revealed to him the greatness of the world and the greatness of God. This effect is magnificently described in **"The Marshes of Glynn."** In this poem he makes his only successful attempt at the grand style. There is something about the sweep of the thought and the roll of some of the verse which reminds us somewhat of Milton, though his frequent lapses into shorter lyric expressions break the sonorous flow. (pp. 57-8)

The gentler forms of nature he knows as intimately as old-time friends. He converses with the leaves and the flowers, and almost identifies himself with them. . . . (p. 59)

Crashaw is the type of the mystic poet who is rapt in ecstasies by religious fervor. Lanier had much the same spirit, but the mystic was more fully developed in him by his love of nature. **"A Ballad of Trees and the Master"** has an exquisite pathos and mellow music, which make its mysticism wonderfully appealing. (pp. 59-60)

He did not care to write poems on conventional nature subjects. His poems are on phases of nature little sung in verse before. . . . Many people had gazed on the stagnant waters of the Marshes of Glynn before Lanier's day, no doubt, but no one had thought them a fit subject for a poem. The nature-poet gazed upon them, and to his large imagination they offered manifold beauties which inspired his greatest creation. His "fieldward faring eyes" fell on a commonplace corn-field, and out of that glance came one of his most characteristic poems. . . . He gives to the mocking bird in one of his finest lyrics the homage which English poets have always given the lark. He sings the song of the **"Tampa Robins"** with the bird's own lilt. . . . (pp. 60-1)

All in all, Lanier has one of the truest and richest nature-notes in American poetry. Indeed, so intimate and personal was his treatment of nature that it is a question whether his obscurity is not partly due to the fact that few readers can appreciate nature as he did, and so find his poems meaningless. Wordsworth suffered before him from the same cause, and he can afford to dwell in such noble company where he may have "fit audience though few." (p. 61)

The criticism has often been brought against Wordsworth that in his eager pursuit of inanimate nature he omitted man, the most important of all nature's manifestations, from his scheme. With all his appreciation for nature, Lanier elevates man infinitely above her in importance and gives him the station of honor in his poems. . . . This human element finds frequent expression in the notes of hope and love. . . . In **"The Symphony"** his spiritual, artistic nature cries out in righteous indignation against a mercenary age which tramples the poor ruthlessly under its heels, and buys the purity of women as indifferently as it does any other merchandise. This indictment of Trade is sharper, deeper, more passionate than Tennyson's in "Locksley Hall," but it is saved from the personal bitterness which Tennyson has put into his by a larger note of love which pervades the whole. His chivalrous love of women has found beautiful expression here in the prayer of the true knight to his true lady, which he makes the clarionet sing. He cannot bear to close the poem with anything but a hopeful note:

> And yet shall Love himself be heard,
> Though long deferred, though long deferred:
> O'er the modern waste a dove hath whirred:
> Music is Love in search of a word. . . .

Through all his poems runs this shining strand of hope, with never the signs of bitterness and disgust with the world which we might expect from a man who had suffered as he had. . . . [Lanier's] strongest appeal is to the heart. With the violin in **"The Symphony"** he cries, "The Time needs Heart." As few men have, he devoted himself with all unselfishness to fulfilling this need. His best poems are permeated with the warmth and glow of the South and have in a marked degree the final test of all art—emotional appeal. In poems like **"Sunrise"** and **"The Marshes of Glynn"** the great deeps of the soul are touched. Love is the ruling passion of his life. . . . (pp. 62-4)

His strong, attractive personality, animated with love, breathes through his poems, and comes to the heart of his hearers like a balmy, soothing breeze from his own Southland.

From such ideality in life, we naturally expect Romanticism in his art. . . . We find little of the clear, simple grandeur of Greek art, but much of the suggestiveness of the Romanticists, especially in his nature treatment. He has been compared with Keats, not always with a clear distinction of his inferiority to that poet. . . . He is unquestionably very like Keats in his sensitiveness to all kinds of delicate beauty, and in his tendency toward the Romantic, but he fails utterly to reach the pure Greek simplicity of expression which Keats attains in his best works.

Because he was naturally lyric in his qualities, . . . we may look to his songs for some of his best products. The songs written for **"The Jacquerie,"** an early unrevised poem . . . , are bubbling over with vigor and music, but are rough and unpolished. In some of his later songs, notably in **"A Song of Eternity in Time"** and **"A Song of the Future,"** we find a rich melody, joined to a smoothness of expression not often found in his long poems. (pp. 64-5)

Tennyson, Poe, and other poets have done some striking things in the line of onomatopoeia, but to Lanier belongs the honor of the pioneer in his effort to make a poem do the work of a symphony and a poem at the same time. . . . The most concise definition of art is unity in variety. Surely **"The Symphony"** admirably fulfils that definition. There is a great variety in the subject matter: a severe condemnation of trade with a plea for the poor, by the violin; the beauties of nature, sung by the flute; a searching denunciation of man's inhumanity to woman, by the clarionet; an offer of knightly service to women, by the horn; a plea for innocence in life, by the hautboys; and a final paean of victory for love, by the bassoons. All this variety of subject is given with the varying effects of the different instruments, now fast in short, snappy lines, now slow, stately, sonorous in long full lines, now in the depths of despair and misery, now on the heights of faith and love. The thread of unity in it all is the common attack on Trade and the plea for heart and love in life. It is by no means perfect in execution, and fails in many points in diction and in rhythm, but as a whole it is a wonderful poem in the greatness of its idea and the adequacy and fitness with which it is carried out, and the wonderful harmony that it contains, to say nothing of individual lines of striking beauty in thought and melody. It is furthermore very significant in its suggestion as to the possibilities of poetry in the future. (pp. 66-7)

Considering all things, we believe we have evidences enough in [Lanier's] work to declare that he was a genuine poet, though not a great genius. As to his final rank in American poetry, only Time can decide that. His is certainly the greatest contribution any one man from the South has made to the stock of our national literature. It is also equally certain that he was one of the truest men of letters America has produced, not one of the greatest, because his work is too small in compass and too full of obvious defects, but certainly one of the truest in his ideals and in his aspirations; one of the sincerest in his hatred for the low and vulgar; and one of the most unselfishly earnest in his desire to teach people to love and admire the greatest things of life. (pp. 69-70)

Richard Webb, "Sidney Lanier, Poet and Prosodist" (1903), in Sidney Lanier: Poet and Prosodist by Richard Webb and Edwin R. Coulson, University of Georgia Press, 1941, pp. 3-70.

EDWIN MIMS   (essay date 1905)

[Mims was Lanier's first critical biographer. In his Sidney Lanier, *excerpted below, he attempts to provide a "judicial" estimate of*

Lanier's overall achievement. He finds that Lanier's reputation as a prose writer suffered unduly from the publication of unrevised material; as a critic, that he lacked catholicity of judgment, but frequently exhibited penetration and subtlety; as a prosodist, that his theory of verse, important for its emphasis on form, could not be applied to actual poetic rhythms. Mims also maintains that, as a poet, Lanier occasionally eschewed ornate rhetoric and fancy, united sound and sense, and created works that are unique, original, and enduring. His views on Lanier's relationship to the New South became an issue in the criticism of Aubrey Harrison Starke (1933 and 1934), Allen Tate (1933), Robert Penn Warren (1933), and John Crowe Ransom (1934).]

[Lanier had qualities of mind and ideals of life] which have been too rare in his native section. He was a severe critic of some phases of its life. From this standpoint his career and his personality should never lose their influence in the South. There had been men and women who had loved music; but Lanier was the first Southerner to appreciate adequately its significance in the modern world, and to feel the inspiration of the most recent composers. There had been some fine things done in literature; but he was the first to realize the transcendent dignity and worth of the poet and his work. . . . Compared with other writers of the New South, Lanier was a man of broader culture and of finer scholarship. He did not have the power to create character as some of the writers of fiction, but he was a far better representative of the man of letters. The key to his intellectual life may be found in the fact that he read Wordsworth and Keats rather than Scott, George Eliot rather than Thackeray, German literature as well as French. He was national rather than provincial, open-minded not prejudiced, modern and not mediaeval. His characteristics . . . are all in direct contrast with those of the conservative Southerner. There have been other Southerners . . . who have had his spirit, and have worked with heroism toward the accomplishment of enduring results. There have been none, however, who have wrought out in their lives and expressed in their writings higher ideals. He therefore makes his appeal to every man who is to-day working for the betterment of industrial, educational, and literary conditions in the South. There will never be a time when such men will not look to him as the man of letters who, after the war, struck out along lines which meant most in the intellectual awakening of this section. He was a pioneer worker in buiding up what he liked to speak of as the New South:—

> The South whose gaze is cast
> No more upon the past,
> But whose bright eyes the skies of promise sweep,
> Whose feet in paths of progress swiftly leap;
> And whose fresh thoughts, like cheerful rivers, run
> Through odorous ways to meet the morning sun!
> (pp. 298-99)

Speculations as to what Lanier might have done with fewer limitations and with a longer span of years inevitably arise in the mind of any one who studies his life. If, like the late Theodore Thomas, he had at an early age been able to develop his talent for music in the musical circles of New York; . . . if, like Lowell, he could have given attention to literary subjects and lectured in a university without teaching classes of immature students or without resorting to "potboilers" . . . ; if, like Poe, he could have struck some one vein and worked it for all it was worth,—if, in a word, the varied activity of his life could have given way to a certain definiteness of purpose and concentration of effort, what might have been the difference! . . . And yet one feels that if Lanier had had time and health to work out all these diverse interests and all his varied experiences into a unity, if scholarship and music and poetry could have been developed simultaneously over a long stretch of time, there would have resulted, perhaps, a more many-sided man and a finer poetry than we have yet had in America. (pp. 340-41)

The lines of Robert Browning's poems in which he sets forth the glory of the life of aspiration—aspiration independent of any achievement—ring in one's ears, as he reads the story of Lanier's life. . . . The imperfect poems, the unfinished poems, the sheaves unharvested, . . . are suggestive of one of the finest aspects of romantic art. "I would rather fail at some things I wot of than succeed at others," said Lanier. There are moods when the imperfection of Lanier pleases more than the perfection of Poe—even from the artistic standpoint. What he aspired to be enters into one's whole thought about his life and his art. (pp. 341-42)

But the time comes when none of these considerations . . . should interfere with a judicial estimate of what he really achieved. . . . One has the authority of Lanier's writings about other men and his letters about his own poems for judging him only by the highest standards. Did he in aiming at a million miss a unit? Was he blinded by the very excess of light? . . . [Will] there be enough inherent worth in his work to keep his fame alive? These are questions that one has a right to ask.

And, first, as to Lanier's prose work. He has suffered from the fact that so many of his unrevised works have been published; . . . some of them are disappointing. If, instead of ten volumes of prose, there could be selected his best work from all of them, there would still be a residue of writing that would establish Lanier's place among the prose writers of America. There is no better illustration of his development than that seen in comparing his early prose—the war letters and **"Tiger Lilies,"** for instance, or such essays as **"Retrospects and Prospects"**— with that of his maturer years. I doubt if justice has been done to Lanier's best style, its clearness, fluency, and eloquence. It may be claimed without dispute that he was a rare good letter-writer; perhaps only Lowell's letters are more interesting. The faults of his poetry are not always seen in his best letters. In them there is a playfulness, a richness of humor, an exuberance of spirits, animated talk about himself and his work, and withal a distinct style, that ought to keep them alive. There might be selected, too, a volume of essays, including **"From Bacon to Beethoven," "The Orchestra of To-Day," "San Antonio de Bexar," "The Confederate Memorial Address," "The New South,"** and others. (pp. 342-44)

It goes without saying that Lanier was not a great critic. He did not have the learning requisite for one. One might turn [to] the words of his criticism of Poe and say that he needed to know more. . . . [While] he read French and German literature to some extent, he did not go into them as Lowell did. Homer, Dante, and Goethe were but little more than names to him. Furthermore, his criticism is often marked by a tendency to indulge in hasty generalizations, due to the fact that he had not sufficient facts to draw upon. An illustration is his preference of the Elizabethan sonnets to the English sonnets written on the Italian model, or his discussion of personality as found in the Greek drama. His generalizations are often either patently obvious or far-fetched. He was too eager to "bring together people and books that never dreamed of being side by side." His tendency to fancy, so marked in his poetry, is seen also in his criticism, as for instance, his comparison of a sonnet to a little drama, or his statement that every poem has a plot, a crisis, and a hero. He had De Quincey's habit of digressing

from the main theme. . . . This is especially seen in his lectures on the English Novel, where he is often carried far afield from the general theme. In his lectures on **"Shakspere and His Forerunners,"** he was so often troubled with an embarrassment of riches that he did not endeavor to follow a rigidly formed plan.

A more serious defect, however, was his lack of catholicity of judgment. He had all of Carlyle's distaste for the eighteenth century; his dislike of Pope was often expressed, and he went so far as to wish that the novels of Fielding and Richardson might be "blotted from the face of the earth." His characterization of Thackeray as a "low-pitched artist" is wide of the mark. . . . [He] over-praised many men. When he says, for instance, that Bartholomew Griffin "will yet obtain a high and immortal place in English literature," or that William Drummond of Hawthornden is one of "the chief glories of the English tongue," . . . one wonders to what extent the "pleasant peril of enthusiasm" will carry a man. One may be an admirer of George Eliot and yet feel that Lanier has overstated her merits as compared with other English novelists, and that his praise of "Daniel Deronda" is excessive. (pp. 344-46)

Without very great learning and with strong prejudices in some directions, Lanier yet had remarkable insight into literature. Lowell's saying that he was "a man of genius with a rare gift for the happy word" is especially true of some of his critical writing. Examples are his well-known characterizations of great men [such as Buddha, William Langley, Ralph Waldo Emerson, and Alfred Tennyson] in **"The Crystal."** . . .

There are scattered throughout his prose works criticisms of writers that are at once penetrating and subtle. (p. 347)

Lanier's enthusiasm for Chaucer is typical of much of his critical writing. He was a generous praiser of the best literature, and generally his praise was right. "Lyrics of criticism" would be a good title for many of his passages. There was nothing of indifferentism in him. . . . [He had] enthusiasm for many of the periods and many of the authors of English literature. It is a distinction for him as a critic that he has set forth in so many passages his conception of the mission of poetry,—passages that are in the line of succession of defenses of poetry by Sidney, Hazlitt, and Shelley.

There is enough good criticism in the Shakespeare lectures and in the **"English Novel,"** in the prefaces of the boy's books and in his letters, to make a volume of interest and importance. Suppose we . . . select from [the Shakespeare lectures and the **"English Novel"**] such passages as the discussion of personality, the relation of music, science, and the novel, the criticism of Whitman's theory of art, the discussion of the relation of morals to art, the best passages on Anglo-Saxon poetry and the Elizabethan sonneteers, and the finer passages on Shakespeare's growth as a man and as a dramatist. Such a volume would, I believe, confirm one in the opinion that Lanier belongs by right among the best American critics. Certainly, the **"Science of English Verse"** entitles him to that distinction. (pp. 350-52)

There is little objection to Parts II and III of the **"Science of English Verse."** . . . It is with the main thesis of the first part that many disagree—the author's insistence that the laws of music and of verse are identical. . . . Lanier believed that . . . the basis of rhythm [in verse] is time and not accent. Every line is made up of bars of equal time value. (pp. 354-55)

Lanier's theory is a good one in so far as it applies to the ideal rhythm, for the melody of verse does approximate that of music. If one considers actual rhythm, however, he is forced to come to the conclusion that no such mathematical relation exists between the syllables of a foot of verse as that existing between the notes of a musical bar. In poetry another element enters in to interfere with the ideal rhythm of music, and that is what Mr. More has called "the normal unrhythmical enunciation of the language." The result is a compromise shifting toward one extreme or another. . . . Unquestionably, the lyrics and choruses of the Greek drama were thoroughly musical; Sophocles and Æschylus were both teachers of the chorus. Many of the lyrics of the Elizabethan age were written especially for music. . . . Who will say that Coleridge's "Christabel" and "Kubla Khan" are not disembodied music? . . . Tennyson realized the musical effect of "Paradise Lost" when he spoke of Milton as "England's God-gifted organ-voice;" and he himself in such lyrics as those in the "Princess" and the eighty-sixth canto of "In Memoriam" wrought musical effects with verse. . . . The theory will not hold, however, in much dramatic verse, or in meditative blank verse, as used by Wordsworth. Much of the poetry of Byron, Browning, Keats, and Shakespeare, while supremely great from the standpoint of color, or dramatic power, or picturesqueness, or thought, is not musical. To bring some poems within the limit of musical notation would be impossible.

While then one must modify Lanier's theory, the book emphasizes a point that needs constantly to be emphasized, both by poets and by students of poetry. Followed too closely by minor poets, it will tend to develop artisans rather than artists. Followed by the greater poets,—consciously or unconsciously,—it may prove to be one of the surest signs of poetry. This phase of poetical work needed to be emphasized in America, where poetry, with the exception of Poe's, has been deficient in this very element. Whatever else one may say of Emerson, Bryant, Whittier, or Longfellow, he must find that their poetry as a whole is singularly lacking in melody. Moreover, the poet who was the most dominant figure in American literature at the time when Lanier was writing [Walt Whitman], prided himself on violating every law of form, using rhythm, if at all, in a certain elementary or oriental sense. . . . One may be thoroughly just to Whitman and grant the worth of his work in American literature, and yet see the value of Lanier's contention that the study of the formal element in poetry will lead to a much finer poetry than we have yet had in this country. (pp. 356-59)

[Lanier] has, in many other places, given his ideas of the poet's character and his work in the world. . . . He had an exalted sense of what poetry means in the redemption of mankind. He had little patience with the cry, "Art for art's sake," or with the justification so often made for the immorality of the artist's life. Milton himself did not believe more ardently that a poet's life ought to be a true poem. (pp. 359-60)

Lanier believed that he was, or would be, a great poet. . . . [He] hoped that he would accomplish something different from the popular poetry of the period. . . . His characterizations of contemporary poetry are strikingly like those of Walt Whitman. Different as they were in nearly every respect, the two poets were yet alike in their idea that there should be a reaction against the conventional and artificial poetry of their time,— the difference being, that Whitman's reaction took the direction of formlessness, while Lanier's was concerned about the extension and revival of poetic forms. In both poets there is a range and sweep, both of conception and of utterance, that sharply differentiates them from all other poets since the Civil War.

The question then is, whether Lanier, with his lofty conception of the poet's work, and with his faith in himself, succeeded in writing poetry that will stand the test of time. He undoubtedly had some of the necessary qualities of a poet. He had, first of all, a sense of melody that found vent primarily in music and then in words which moved with a certain rhythmic cadence. . . . His best poems move to the cadence of a tune. . . . Sometimes there was a lilt like the singing of a bird, and sometimes the lyric cry, and yet again the music of the orchestra. . . . Sometimes, as in the **"Marshes of Glynn"** and in the best parts of **"Sunrise,"** there is a cosmic rhythm that is like unto the rhythmic beating of the heart of God, of which Poe and Lanier have written eloquently.

Besides this melody that was temperamental, Lanier had ideas. He was alive to the problems of his age and to the beauties of nature. . . . He wrote of religion, social questions, science, philosophy, nature, love. . . . So he is in no sense a "jingle man." There is a note of healthy mysticism in his poetry that makes him akin to Wordsworth and Emerson. A series of poems might be selected that would entitle him to the praise of being "the friend and aider of those who would live in the spirit."

With the spiritual endowment of a poet and an unusual sense of melody, where was he lacking in what makes a great poet? In power of expression. He never attained, except in a few poems, that union of sound and sense which is characteristic of the best poetry. The touch of finality is not in his words; the subtle charm of verse outside of the melody and the meaning is not his—he failed to get the last "touches of vitalizing force." He did not, as Lowell said of Keats, "rediscover the delight and wonder that lay enchanted in the dictionary." He did not attain to "the perfection and the precision of the instantaneous line." Take his poem **"Remonstrance,"** for instance. It is a strong utterance against tyranny and intolerance and bigotry, hot from his soul; but the expression is not worthy of his feeling. A few lines of Lowell's "Fable for Critics" about freedom are better. The same may be said of his attack on agnosticism in **"Acknowledgment." "Corn"** while representing an extremely poetical situation, leaves one with the feeling of incompleteness: the ideas are not adequately or felicitously expressed. There is melody in the **"Marsh Song at Sunset,"** but the poem is not clear. Or take what many consider his masterpiece, **"Sunrise."** There is one of the most imaginative situations a poet could have,—the ecstasy of the poet's soul as he rises from his bed to go to the forest, the silence of the night, the mystery of the deep green woods, the coming of "my lord, the Sun." There is nothing in American poetry that goes beyond the sweep and range of this conception. But look at the words; with the exception of the first stanza and those that describe the dawn, there is a nervousness of style, a strain of expression. If one compare even the best parts with the "Evening of Extraordinary Splendor and Beauty" by Wordsworth, he sees the difference in the art of expression. There is in Wordsworth's poem the romantic mood,—the same uplift of soul in the presence of the greater phenomena of nature,—but there is a classic restraint of form; it is "emotion recollected in tranquillity."

What, then, is the explanation of this defect in Lanier? Undoubtedly lack of time to revise his work is one cause. . . . The revision of **"Corn"** [and other poems] . . . shows conclusively that he had the power of improving his work. With more time he might have achieved with all of his poems some of the results attained by such careful workmen as Tennyson and Poe.

But lack of time for revision will not explain all. There were certain temperamental defects in Lanier as poet. There was a lack of spontaneous utterance. . . . This is not to say that Lanier simulated poetic expression, but his words are not inevitable enough. He often lacked simplicity.

Furthermore, he suffered from a tendency to indulge in fancies, ''sucking sweet similes out of the most diverse objects.'' He was inoculated with the ''conceit virus'' of the seventeenth century. . . . He did not restrain his luxuriant imagination. The poem **''Clover''** is almost spoiled by the conceit of the ox representing the ''Course-of-things'' and trampling upon the souls (the clover-blossoms) of the poets. **''Sunrise''** is marred by the figure of the bee-hive from which the ''star-fed Bee, the build-fire Bee, . . . the great Sun-Bee,'' emerges in the morning. (pp. 360-67)

Lanier was undoubtedly hampered, too, by his theory of verse. The very poem **''Special Pleading,''** in which he said that he began to work out his theory, is a failure. Alliteration, assonance, compound words, personifications, are greatly overused. Some of the rhymes are as grotesque as Browning's. Instead of the perfect union of sound and sense, there is often a mere chanting of words.

It is futile to deny these tendencies in Lanier. They vitiate more than half his poems, and are defects even in some of the best. Sometimes, in his very highest flight, he seems to have been winged by one of these arrows. But it is equally futile to deny that he frequently rises above all these limitations and does work that is absolutely unique, and original, and enduring. Distinction must be made, as in the case of every other man who has marked qualities of style, between his good work and his bad work. He has done enough good work to entitle him to a place among the genuine poets of America. (pp. 367-68)

Indeed, if one had to rely upon one poem to keep alive the fame of Lanier, he could single out **''The Marshes of Glynn''** with assurance that there is something so individual and original about it, and that, at the same time, there is such a roll and range of verse in it, that it will surely live not only in American poetry but in English. Here the imagination has taken the place of fancy, the effort to do great things ends in victory, and the melody of the poem corresponds to the exalted thought. It has all the strong points of **''Sunrise,''** with but few of its limitations. There is something of Whitman's virile imagination and Emerson's high spirituality combined with the haunting melody of Poe's best work. Written . . . when Lanier was in the full exercise of all his powers, it is the best expression of his genius and one of the few great American poems. (p. 371)

Edwin Mims, in his Sidney Lanier *(Copyright 1905 by Edwin Mims. Reprinted by permission of Houghton Mifflin Company), Houghton Mifflin, 1905, 386 p.*

JOHN MACY (essay date 1913)

[*Macy regards Lanier as a metrical virtuoso and praises his works lavishly. Departing from the view that Lanier's theory of verse interfered with his poetry, Macy held rather that Lanier's theory followed his art. The volume of poetry to which Macy refers is probably the 1891 edition of Lanier's* Poems.]

Three volumes of unimpeachable poetry have been written in America: ''Leaves of Grass,'' the thin volume of Poe, and the poetry of Sidney Lanier. (p. 309)

When he died at thirty-nine . . . he was the unapproachably best American poet of his generation. If ever there was a born genius since Keats, it was Lanier. . . . [There] may well be a cry of pain for the unfinished **''Hymns of the Marshes.''** His voice was growing greater when he ceased to sing, and, like Keats,

> his angel's tongue
> Lost half the sweetest song was ever sung.
>
> (p. 312)

Yet it is not for what he might have done but for what he did that the impartial assessment of time will sum his merits. It is humane to remember that he wrote **''Sunrise''** . . . when he was too ill to eat and his temperature was at 104; then it is well to remove all the cross lights of biography and stand face to face with his **''Sunrise,''** a poem magnificent in conception, perfect in workmanship, ultimate poetry. (pp. 313-14)

[**''Sunrise''** and Francis Thompson's ''Ode to the Setting Sun'' have much in common:] opulence, splendour of metaphor and an amazing virtuosity in metrical matters which in turn allies them with Swinburne. . . . (p. 315)

One other resemblance resides in their work, in their convictions, the fresh vigour they have given to the symbols of Christianity which had well nigh perished out of modern poetry. . . . And both [Lanier and Thompson] use the symbols rather for their beauty than for their religious import.

To say at once the worst that can be said of either of them, both Thompson and Lanier are subject to the same temptation, or they are driven to the brink of the same danger, and both triumphantly avoid falling into the abyss where poetry ceases and mere ''metricism'' begins. They are both so abundant in fancy and overflooded with metaphors, and withal so adept at playing with measures, that now and again their exuberance and nimbleness almost betray them; but because they are both austere artists and passionately intend what they say, they are saved. It is a danger merely and they tremble on the verge of it. One would gladly strike out of Thompson the too visibly crafty rhymes . . . , and one would as gladly prune out some of Lanier's internal rhyming and obvious assonances. . . . However, they sin but little and—this is the all-immortalizing distinction—they sin as poets, not as versifiers.

That Lanier was a musician as well as a poet . . . , and that he expressed his theory in **''The Science of English Verse,''** are facts caught at too eagerly by those who would account for some of his most evidently musical arrangements of words. The truth about him, as about all artists, is that his theory followed his art; he was a poet first and a student, or, rather, a professor, of technic afterward. His theory of verse merely codifies . . . the fact which all poets instinctively know and all true poetry exemplifies, that poetry is, in half its nature, music, and that it consists not of spoken words but of chanted words. . . . There is only one law for all music and for all poetry (independent of the explicit meaning necessarily resident in human words), and that law is: if it sounds right, it is right. The counting of feet is superfluous. If they are to be counted at all, Lanier's way is the way to count. . . . Lanier's verse, being true to English poetry, to the effects of English words on the ear, would probably have been what it is if he had never been an instructor and a technically capable musician and had never expounded his principles. (pp. 316-18)

Lanier was in a sense a fresh unschooled discoverer of the poets. They did not become stale with class-room familiarity while he was young; he loved them as part of nature, as Keats discovered and loved Chapman and Spenser. How far he was from abject worship of his poet-heroes is shown in **"The Crystal,"** in which is wrought out, with telling phrases that are marvels of criticism, the bold and refreshing idea that all the masters of song, Shakespeare, Homer, Dante, have much to be forgiven. That is a great poem in which a poet adequately praises another, in which he does not droop upon a greater strength, but stands, for one song's duration at least, the equal of his adored. Such poem is that **"To Our Mocking-Bird,"** where the bird and Keats are identified and the Cat and Death are rebuked together.

Lanier, like all his race of poets, sang praises to his fathers in melody. Yet he does not smell of the library. He is a poet of nature and of things, of the meaning of central present things that harry and strengthen the heart of man. In **"Corn"** for once an American poet strode into our splendid native golden fields and sang what his eyes saw, and deeper, what the harvests of the fields can be for man. **"The Symphony"** . . . is no mere interplay of melodies, but the cry of the old-new spirit of brotherhood against the debauchery of trade. By it Lanier becomes one of the goodly band of modern men dissatisfied with man's violations of man, and his voice is strong enough to admit him to the still smaller band of poets who are the voices of the present life, of these very times—with Morris and Whitman. . . . Oddly enough, he, the devotee of pure music, dared the historic theme which so many Americans have tried, . . . and in the **"Psalm of the West"** he did make a chant of America and Freedom which has in its short compass something like epic vision and is, if not the noblest of Lanier, far above most patriotic verse, and artistically excellent.

Lanier stands alone in that era of American poetry which is chiefly marked by a false post-Tennysonism, an era of nicely made lyrics that have neither passion nor an individual sense of beauty. . . . If Lanier had no equal contemporaries, he may have successors, for when an age is shuddering on its first gray verge and its day-facts lie in the future, it is permitted to be hopeful for it. (pp. 320-22)

> *John Macy, "Lanier," in his* The Spirit of American Literature *(copyright 1913 by Doubleday & Company, Inc.; copyright renewed 1940 by William M. Rockwell, as literary executor to the Estate of John Macy; reprinted by permission of Doubleday & Company, Inc.), Doubleday, Page & Company, 1913, pp. 309-23.*

HOWARD MUMFORD JONES   (essay date 1918)

[*A distinguished twentieth-century American critic, humanist, and literary scholar, Jones is noted for his illuminating commentary on the development of American culture and literature. For him, Lanier's work represents the outpourings of an "abnormally spiritual man" whose ascetic temperament cut him off from vital sources of poetic inspiration. Citing elaborate conceits and lack of spontaneity as his greatest technical faults, he nonetheless finds merit in a number of Lanier's productions, especially the "Hymns of the Marshes," which he describes as "masterpieces." Jones allows Lanier a relatively modest place in literature as one of the "most interesting" minor American poets.*]

[There] comes with such purity as Lanier's a certain softness, a fastidiousness, a kind of unconscious and perfectly irreproachable intolerance. Lanier was the last man in the world to repeat the Pharisee's prayer, or to die of a rose in aromatic pain, but he could withdraw from the sweat of life completely.

Chastity of spirit is sometimes narrow. Hence, the white flame of Lanier's spirit burnt always in a prism; the hammer of his exaltation rose and fell monotonously on the same themes—music and art, soul and love, art and music, love and spirit. One longs at times for a human flaw in the crystal of such perfection. The reader tires of Lanier's continual excitement of spirit, misses in **"The Symphony"** the hearty humanness of "Abt Vogler," or of so humble a piece as "Gaspar Becerra," and in the hush and incense of his love poetry pines for an honest country smack.

There are two remarkable instances of this narrowness in Lanier's work. **"The Crystal"** is the best single example; its criticisms of Homer, Socrates, Buddha, Dante and others, some of them just, have the fastidious air of a spiritual amateur, and the manner with which he forgives each in turn (Socrates for a "year worn cloak," Milton for the wars of "Paradise Lost" and Æschylus that he never "learned to look where Love stands shining") is full of syrupy patronage; one is reminded of a very young clergyman.

Lanier served throughout the war. He was young and certainly impressionable, and his military experience embraced the Seven Days, lonely work in the signal corps, and the foulness of a federal prison. Longfellow, who was not in the conflict, gave us "Killed at the Ford"; Lowell, with greater reason, wrung a cry out of the depths in "The Washers of the Shroud," and even Whittier, a Quaker, wrote the war's most quoted ballad, "Barbara Frietchie." Whitman, unlike these, toiled among the wounded; out of the sweat and agony came "The Wound Dresser," and such unforgettable pictures as "Cavalry Crossing a Ford," and a phrase that sums up the horror of the hospitals, blood "dripping horribly in the pail." When we turn to Lanier we get in **"Tiger Lilies"** a literary conceit which fantastically pictures North and South as two planters cultivating a flower, and in **"The Psalm of the West"** the prettified figure of a tournament between "Heart" and "Brain." "Heart" is "a youth in crimson and gold," "Brain" is "steel-armored, glittering, cold"; naturally, he runs Heart down, whereupon Heart somewhat fatuously remarks, "My love to my beloved" and expires.

We must allow much for Lanier's bad health. This, like his temperament, cut him off from human nature's daily food to brood on questions of art and music. Thus he wrote, quite wrongly, in **"To Bayard Taylor,"** of

> The artist's pain—to walk his blood-stained ways,
>   A special soul, yet judged as general—
> *The endless grief of art,* the sneer that slays,
>   The war, the wound, the groan, the funeral pall.

Emerson, or Poe, or Longfellow, does not talk that way about art. The famous and eminently false line with which he ended **"The Symphony"**

> Music is love in search of a word

is not the utterance of a large and healthy spirit; it is the reflection of an abnormally spiritual man. (pp. 671-72)

Out of this brooding, then, on art and the workmanship of art spring Lanier's two great faults—his elaborate conceits (with these go his excessive personifications) and his lack of spontaneity. Instances of the first mar even his best work. The most curious example is an early poem, **"Clover,"** inscribed to the memory of Keats, which is full of strained fancies. The poet lies down in a clover field and utters these far-fetched lines:

> Now, Cousin Clover, tell me in mine ear:
> Go'st thou to market with thy pink and green?
>
> . . . .
>
> Three Leaves, instruct me! I am sick of price.

Then he holds up two clover-stems to frame his face, the clover-field becomes the "Up-and-Down of Time," the clover-blossoms are the heads of his favorites in art—"Raphael, Lucretius, Omar, Angelo" (the list is reminiscent of the World's Best Books)—when presently

> Comes the Course-of-things shaped like an ox,
> Slow browsing, o'er my hillside, ponderously—
> That hath his grass, if earth be round or flat.
> . . . . . . This cool, unasking ox
> Comes browsing o'er my hills and vales of Time,
> And thrusts me out his tongue, and curls it, sharp,
> And twists them in all—Dante, Keats, Chopin,
> Raphael, Lucretius, Omar, Angelo . . . .
> . . . and champs and chews,
> With slantly-churning jaws and swallows down.

This is the very parody of poetry; it recalls Carew, and Fletcher's "The Purple Island." . . . Sometimes [Lanier's] conceits are pretty and ingenious, but they are not great poetry, or even good poetry, and [those] admirers who try to place him among the great American poets are merely doing him a grave injustice.

It cannot be denied that much of his work lacks spontaneity. He had a new, and, as he thought, epoch-making idea of verse-technique, which led him to prefer great irregularities in line and stanza structure. But, unfortunately, Lanier's verse does not follow the only plan which such verse can properly follow; it does not conform to the contour of the thought, it is shaped according to a complex pattern of phrases, bars, and time-values which have their place in another art. A comparison with Lowell's odes points the difference:

> Who now shall sneer?
> Who dares again to say we trace
> Our lines to a plebeian race?
> Roundhead and Cavalier!
> Dumb are those names erstwhile in battle loud;
> Dream-footed as the shadow of a cloud
> They flit across the ear,

owes its shape to the laws of language as they express thought, but

> Gleams of the live-oaks, beautiful, braided and woven
> With intricate shades of the vines that myriad-cloven
> Clamber the fork of the multiform boughs—
> Emerald twilights
> Virginal skylights
> Wrought of the leaves to allure to the whisper of vows,

owes it shape to nothing but caprice and a mistaken attempt to do with language what belongs to music. With Lowell, form and thought were fused together; with Lanier, the entire process was conscious and sophisticated; he tries to load every rift with ore until the lines swing across the brain without making any impression. Indeed, it is probable that many of those who read Lanier do so because they have a sense, as Lowell said of Emerson, that something beautiful passed by; they do not have to consider what it was, and could not tell if they were asked.

Great poets keep the faculties awake, they wrestle with the mind, as Lanier seldom does. (pp. 672-74)

Many of his faults he could not escape, even if he had been a more virile writer than he was; they were inherent in the age. (p. 674)

If Lanier turned in disgust from

> the vigorous tale
> Of bill for coin and box for bale,

he did no more than Taylor, Aldrich, E. R. Sill, Simms, and Stoddard. One searches in vain in the poetry of Lanier's period for the earnestness and fire of Whittier or Lowell; the nation was apparently flatulent, stertorous, corrupt, and contented; and, as in all such periods, there was a tremendous preoccupation with art and technique and very little interest in ideas and issues. We were living (as in Emerson's prime) in the trough between two great moral issues.

If we turn from this consideration of Lanier's shortcomings to the noble pleasure of praising, we find that he has given us two forceful ballads, **"The Revenge of Hamish"** and **"The Song of the Chattahoochee,"** and lyrics like **"Life and Song," "The Stirrup Cup," "Evening Song," "Marsh Song,"** and **"The Ballad of Trees and The Master,"** which, though some of them are obviously bookish, are quaint, direct and melodious. **"How Love Looked for Hell"** is a piquant poem; it will have the same admiration that Donne has in English literature. Of the longer pieces, **"The Symphony"** has immortal stuff in it, though some parts of it, notably the "horn solo," are tainted with sentimentality. The **"Psalm of the West"** fails as a whole, but it contains the sonnets on Columbus which are masculine, like **"Hamish"** and better art. There remain the **"Hymns of the Marshes"** as Lanier's typical work. These are masterpieces; the music of parts of them is unparalleled in American song, and such a passage as the one beginning

> As the marsh-hen secretly builds on the watery sod,
> Behold, I will build me a nest on the greatness of God.

is better than Whittier; it has the toughness and spiritual resiliency of William Vaughn Moody. In these hymns all is melody, there is little painting or sculpture, and if the sense is often drowned in a flood of vowels, at its best the movement is bold, free and original.

If we try to put all this together, we shall find that Lanier is not what has been claimed for him, one of the great American poets, but rather one of the most interesting of our minor writers. His genius, admirable as it was, was something handicapped by his temperament and his time. He was further handicapped by a theory of technique which crippled his spontaneity, and by manners which are idiosyncrasies and not style. Lanier was, in short, rather a lover of things beautiful than a creator; a brave soldier riding on the quests of a spiritual knighthood, but of a knighthood, like its earthly prototype, which left an inextensive structure behind it, quaint and courtly, but not great, and filled with the memory of the word as it never was. (pp. 674-75)

Howard Mumford Jones, "Critical Comments: Sidney Lanier," in American Poetry, *edited by Percy H. Boynton with Howard M. Jones, George W. Sherburn, and Frank M. Webster (reprinted with permission of Charles Scribner's Sons), Charles Scribner's Sons, 1918 (and reprinted by Granger Books, 1978), pp. 670-75.*

T. S. OMOND (essay date 1921)

[In his English Metrists, *a seminal history of English prosody, Omond discusses the significance of Lanier's* The Science of English Verse. *While he criticizes Lanier's contention that English verse is predominantly three-beat in rhythm and questions individual scansions in the book, Omond credits Lanier with advancing the scientific study of prosody and establishing temporal relations as an essential element of verse. Harriet Monroe generally concurred with Omond's assessment (1941 and Additional Bibliography); George Saintsbury disputed it (1923).]*

If I cannot, with some of his American admirers, think that Lanier has spoken the last word about English verse [in *The Science of English Verse*], I gladly join them in proclaiming the importance of his book, which to many people came as a revelation. (p. 195)

[In his consideration of 3-rhythm, Lanier] traces its prevalence from "our father Caedmon" down to Morris and Swinburne, and finds identity of movement where most people feel diversity. Criticism which asserts sameness of structure in the metres of ["The Battle of Maldon" and the "Ormulum," the "Cuckoo Song" and the "Canterbury Tales," the "Song of Ever and Never" and Hamlet's soliloquy] . . . seems to me to miss its mark. Even were fundamental rhythm the same in all these, their differences would outweigh that sameness. The gulf that separates Langland's verse from that of Chaucer . . . is not bridged by saying that both wrote in 3-rhythm, or even that one is "ancient heroic measure" and the other "modern." . . . Of course Lanier knew this well, indeed he states it himself . . . ; but this does not suggest to him any doubt. It does not prevent his declaring . . . that the overwhelming bulk of English poetry since the 14th Century is written in 3-rhythm. (p. 200)

It will be seen that it is for principles rather than conclusions that I hold Lanier's book valuable. Particular scansions often seem to me quite erroneous, as when he makes consist of trisyllablic feet the poem beginning "Agincourt, Agincourt" . . . ; and his habit of letting accents come irregularly in successive feet seems to me destructive of true analysis. And, though he fully recognised *rests,* he does not in my opinion make nearly enough use of them. . . . His musical preconceptions, I think, led him too much to make syllables embody rhythm . . . ; and I doubt if he sufficiently realised that suspensions of sound may occur when in no way dictated by meaning or sentential rhythm. . . . But criticism must yield to praise so far as fundamentals are concerned. It is Lanier's glory to have brought these finally to light. Temporal relations are shown by him essential to verse; whether or no we accept his reading of these matters comparatively little. The "new prosody" takes in his book a step which can never be retraced. I have said that to many the book came as a revelation; its reading first showed myself how far prosodic science had advanced during the eighth decade of last Century. The name of Sidney Lanier is imperishably associated with that advance; he led its triumphant attack upon the fortresses of prejudice and superstition. If he made mistakes, they may well be forgotten in view of his great achievement. He showed, once for all, where the foundations of true prosody lie. . . . (pp. 201-02)

> *T. S. Omond, "The New Prosody: 1850-1900," in his* English Metrists: Being a Sketch of English Prosodical Criticism from Elizabethan Times to the Present Day *(reprinted by permission of Oxford University Press), Oxford at the Clarendon Press, Oxford, 1921 (and reprinted by Phaeton Press, 1968), pp. 166-236.* *

H. L. MENCKEN (essay date 1922)

[Mencken was one of the most influential social and literary critics in the United States from the eve of World War I until the early years of the Great Depression. A redoubtable individualist and iconoclast who encouraged contemporary American writers to practice realism and shun the anglophilic, moralistic bent of nineteenth-century writers, Mencken once wrote: "All my work, barring a few obvious burlesques, is based upon three fundamental ideas. 1. That knowledge is better than ignorance; 2. That it is better to tell the truth than to lie; and 3. That it is better to be free than to be a slave." In Mencken's opinion, The Science of English Verse *was "the first intelligent work ever published upon the nature and structure of the sensuous content of English poetry." Notwithstanding this praise, he rues Lanier's neglect of the clang-tint of words and the ideational content of poetry.]*

[Sidney Lanier was the first to show] the dependence of poetry upon music. He had little to say, unfortunately, about the clang-tint of words; what concerned him almost exclusively was rhythm. In **"The Science of English Verse,"** he showed that the charm of this rhythm could be explained in the technical terms of music—that all the old gabble about dactyls and spondees was no more than a dog Latin invented by men who were fundamentally ignorant of the thing they discussed. Lanier's book was the first intelligent work ever published upon the nature and structure of the sensuous content of English poetry. He struck out into such new and far paths that the professors of prosody still lag behind him after forty years, quite unable to understand a poet who was also a shrewd critic and a first-rate musician. But if, so deeply concerned with rhythm, he marred his treatise by forgetting clang-tint, he marred it still more by forgetting content. Poetry that is all music is obviously relatively rare, for only a poet who is also a natural musician can write it, and natural musicians are much rarer in the world than poets. Ordinary poetry, average poetry, thus depends in part upon its ideational material, and perhaps even chiefly. It is the *idea* expressed in a poem, and not the mellifluousness of the words used to express it, that arrests and enchants the average connoisseur. (pp. 152-53)

> *H. L. Mencken, "The Poet and His Art," in his* Prejudices, *third series (copyright 1922 by Alfred A. Knopf, Inc.; copyright renewed © 1949 by H. L. Mencken; reprinted by permission of the publisher), Knopf, 1922 (and reprinted by Knopf, 1924), pp. 146-70.* *

GEORGE SAINTSBURY (essay date 1923)

[Saintsbury was a prominent English literary historian and critic in the late nineteenth and early twentieth centuries. A prolific writer, he composed a number of histories of English and European literature as well as several critical works on individual authors, styles, and periods. In Saintsbury's opinion, Lanier violated an "apparently immutable law" by intermixing prosody and music. Taking issue with T. S. Omond's praise of The Science of English Verse *(1921), he assails Lanier's views on tone color and the role of "three-time" and accent in English poetry.]*

Although Mr. Omond sees numerous faults of detail in . . . [Sidney Lanier's *The Science of English Verse*], he hails him as, on the whole sound in principle; and American prosodists generally seem to regard him as a prosodic Moses who *was* allowed actually to lead others to the Promised Land. For my part, I can only chose my visor, put lance in rest, and loosen sword in scabbard. On no terms can I accept Mr. Lanier here. To begin with, he does not merely, like Steele . . . , use musical analogies and parallel explanations, but he interprets prosody wholly and exclusively in terms of music, and uses no other symbols than musical notes. Now this I am bound to pronounce something like impertinence, in the worse as well as in the less bad sense of the word. If I ask a man to translate some Greek for me into English, and he translates it into Spanish, I have a right to retort something less than courteously. His Spanish translation may or may not be correct. I may know Spanish enough to make it intelligible to me, or I may not. The impertinence remains. Secondly, I cannot understand how such a student as Mr. Omond can credit Lanier with having, in the year 187-something, "finally established temporal relations as essential to verse," "brought fundamentals to light," and so on. I cannot see that he did anything of the kind; and I am quite sure that, if he did, he was doing nothing new. Every one who ever used the words "long" and "short," and who did not go a-wandering after accentualism, had always known the temporal character of our rhythms. But, as always, I bring Mr. Lanier to the trial of the pyx, *in particulars*. It may be that English iambic verse is in "3-time" from some crotchet-and-quaver point of view—it is not from any other; and if it were, the whole beauty of *actual* "3-time" substitution would disappear. However keen his musical ear may have been, his prosodic one must have been pretty dull; for his individual scansions are often atrocious, and he sees identity where there is at once the widest and the subtlest diversity. But one citation shall serve for a thousand. *Paradise Lost* "is written in the *same* typic form of 3-rhythm as Shakespeare's plays." Oh, very like a whale indeed, Mr. Lanier—quite remarkably like a whale!

Of course I know I shall be told that it is my Philistine indifference to "pitch" and "tone-colour," and things of that sort, which makes me insensible of Lanier's merit. "Hippocleides does not care" much. In fact, when Hippocleides finds, not Lanier, but a pupil of his, declaring that such a sound as "oo" in "gloom" is "peculiarly adapted to express horror, solemnity, awe, deep grief, slowness of motion, darkness, and extreme or oppressive greatness of size," he feels inclined to send for his table, and indulge in a few gesticulations. Change *g* for *b*, and "bloom," in flesh and flower, expresses "horror, etc., etc.," admirably, does it not? (pp. 493-95)

Without irreverence one may say that Lanier is but another instance of the apparently immutable law, that music and prosody *must* be kept apart, great as they both are, and near as they come to each other.

Let it, however, be granted that a writer with such a sponsor as Mr. Omond, and with so fair a herd of disciples, deserves more serious treatment than this. He shall have it. At the very opening . . . of his preface Lanier remarks that the doctrine that accent makes a syllable long is "unaccountable *to the musician*." Perhaps; but this of itself is evidence that "the musician" is not at the point of view; for this doctrine is certainly not "unaccountable" even to those prosodists, such as Mr. Omond himself, who think it wrong. The fact . . . that accent has no place in music at once shows that music and prosody cannot be on all fours. . . . [To] rule accent altogether out of English prosody would be, to me, absurd. You must keep it in its place, and take care that that place is a minor or subsidiary one—that of a caterer, valet, or some such official; but a place it must have.

Again, Lanier's doctrine that "verse deals purely with sounds" is *dolosa*. It does; but *with what kind of sounds*? He lays down in parallel statements (typographically ordered so as to indicate their importance), as his base-doctrines, the propositions that

"the exact co-ordinations which the ear perceives as rhythm, time, and tone-colour, suggested to it by musical sounds, are music," and that the ditto ditto suggested by spoken words are verse. This, or rather the inferences from it, I deny. In the first place, an unknown language produces a quite different effect from music. In the second, the *variation*, and, above all, the *composition*, of spoken (or rather read) sounds is very different from, and infinitely more complex than, that of music. You cannot get out of this by juggling about "tone-colour," and by arguing that different instruments vary the same note, and different performers the same notes on the same instrument. There is no analogy here to the subtlety of verse. (pp. 495-96)

From this initial confusion we should be prepared for another; and it duly follows. Even Mr. Omond is staggered by the facility with which Lanier discovers his favourite "three-rhythm" alike in Anglo-Saxon verse and the Cuckoo-song, in Langland and in Chaucer. The fact is, of course, that, by the usual processes of slur and shake, you can get almost any rhythm into any other *musically*. . . . You cannot do that on any sound system of prosody.

In fact Lanier shows eminently what all his kind show more or less. They and the accentualists distribute—to speak with no irreverence—a breach of one of the laws of the Athanasian Creed between them. By neglecting all but stressed syllables, and casting loose the others, the accentualists "divide the substance" of feet. By their promiscuous valuations of possibly equivalent, but actually different, foot-forms, the musicalists "confound the persons." Only by recognising the independent personality of different feet can the true nature of English verse be understood; and, when you once leave that citadel of strength, you enter upon a labyrinth, the outlets of which are beset by Guest on one side and Lanier on the other, in the same fashion and position in which Gibbon long ago established Cerinthus and Apollinaris, but *not* in the double "twilight of sense and heresy." (pp. 496-97)

George Saintsbury, "American Poets and Prosodists," in his A History of English Prosody from the Twelfth Century to the Present Day: From Blake to Mr. Swinburne, *Vol. III, second edition, Macmillan and Co., Limited, London, 1923 (and reprinted by Russell & Russell, 1961), pp. 480-505.**

AUBREY HARRISON STARKE (essay date 1933)

[*In his biography* Sidney Lanier, *excerpted below, Starke portrayed Lanier as a writer of uneven accomplishments who yet "appeals to posterity" because of the fineness of character revealed in his life and works. Concerned that Edwin Mims (1905) had identified Lanier exclusively with the South, Starke also promoted Lanier as a poet of national interest and appeal. Starke's commentary, particularly his championing of Lanier's "nationalism" and his status as "a man we all should know," elicited pointed rebuttals from Allen Tate (1933) and Robert Penn Warren (1933).*]

"The Symphony" is the first of the truly national poems that Lanier wrote, for his protest here is not against the evils in southern life, or in Georgia life, but in the national life—against, indeed, the whole spirit of the age in which he lived. With its fierce denunciation of industrial enslavement it suggests Mrs. Browning's "Cry of the Children" and Hood's "Song of the Shirt," but the protest is against no particular evil, in behalf of no one group. Lanier shows, as the English poets did not, the far reaching effects of industrial ills not merely on the industrial slaves but on the industrial slaveholders, the undermining of the whole society by a social evil. . . .

The Trade of the poem is modern capitalism, which prevents harmony in national life. The voices of protest are the voices of orchestral instruments, which should be played in harmony, in a perfect symphony; the figure used is one Lanier loved and one particularly appropriate to the kind of national life of which he dreamed. (p. 205)

The final definition [of the poem, "Music is Love in search of a Word",] is a spiritual gloss on Mme. De Staël's famous definition, which Lanier had read as a youth: "Music is love's only interpreter"; . . . but it is religious as well. . . . [It recalls] the declaration of Felix Sterling, in *Tiger-Lilies,* that "Music means harmony, harmony means love, and love means—God!" This is the core of Lanier's philosophy, and **"The Symphony,"** though certainly not the most effective nor the most beautiful of Lanier's poems, is, for the revelation it makes of his philosophy, without doubt the most significant.

Undeniably there are defects in **"The Symphony,"** phrases that jar as badly as anything in **"Corn,"** an exaggerated use of compound words—more than seventy different ones, whole lines that one would wish omitted, epithets that are ridiculous, but **"The Symphony"** possesses a music more varied and more beautiful than that of **"Corn,"** and a richness of imagery that comes from a close observation of nature unsurpassed by that of Marlowe or Shakspere or Keats for accuracy. Furthermore, [as Walter Page noted,] in this poem Lanier "achieved the amazing *tour de force* of making real poetry out of the money question," and poetry that is truly symphonic. Even so, **"The Symphony"** is less important as poetry than as protest, the first full-voiced protest of an able poet against the economic tyranny that still keeps politically freed men enslaved. With its evidence of Lanier's reaction against gross materialism and too pure transcendentalism, and his attempt to direct the attention of poetry to the practical problems of the world, it is the most succinct evidence we possess of Lanier's concern with the predominant movement of his century, the industiral revolution as social fact and as philosophic ideal. And in spite of its emphasis on spiritual values, Lanier's poem, it may be justly insisted, presents an intelligible program for social amelioration. (pp. 209-10)

[Lanier's] respect for science led him naturally to seek to discover—if such existed—laws of poetical construction. . . . In his investigation he was successful, and his proposition that time is the basis of rhythm has become accepted as the fundamental law of metrical and poetical structure. One may wish that the book [*The Science of English Verse*] in which he set forth the principles of his investigations and his conclusions were a more finished piece of work, like Harvey's book on the circulation of the blood and Darwin's on the origin of species, at once a literary and a scientific classic, but the final triumph and vindication of his conclusions is the vindication of his work. . . .

It was as a scientist, of course, analyzing and dissecting, discovering adherence to or deviation from natural laws, that Lanier undertook his work as a critic. In this he was particularly successful, for to power of analysis was added in him the intuition of the artist; and his acute critical judgments, happily expressed in memorable phrases, are little masterpieces of their kind. (p. 440)

With time to work out critical principles, to fill in the gaps in his knowledge, to correct by study and research his hasty generalizations and mistaken assertions, he might have become a critic of prominence and importance. Actually he made amazing mistakes, which give one every right to speak of [what a reviewer in *Literary World* in 1883 termed] the "calm bigotry" of his attitude; but his characterization of Thackeray as a "low-pitched satirist" is no more mistaken than Thackeray's famous estimate of Swift; and important critics have gone wrong in betting on less important novelists than George Eliot. Lanier's published lectures are filled with admirable passages of criticism, so fine that they more than make up for other passages which as criticism are only unlicensed enthusiasm. On the whole they are acute and suggestive, as are most of his essays. And in at least one of the essays in which Lanier attempted a formal critical analysis of the work of one man, the essay on **"Paul H. Hayne's Poetry,"** he produced criticism which, no matter how enlarged or amplified, must remain in principle unchallenged.

Lanier's defects as a critic are enthusiasm, lack of catholicity of judgment, and didacticism. Enthusiasm is of course a quality in a critic not to be despised, a quality that has often done notable work in turning appreciation toward a neglected writer. If enthusiasm led Lanier frequently to unbalanced judgments, it thus led most of his contemporary critics, for romantic criticism, knowing no fixed criteria, does not always achieve sound conclusions; as in the work of Pater, romantic criticism of art often becomes worthy art without being important criticism. (p. 441)

Lack of catholicity of judgment is a more serious defect in a critic, but catholicity is often a mark of uncertainty, and Lanier knew what he knew, knew what was true and what was to be preached in the gospel of beauty it was given him to deliver. He is to be more admired for his honesty in voicing his dislike of the novels of Fielding and Richardson—his contempt for "this muck of the classics"—than other critics who, with insipid and pious references to classics, seek to ignore or justify much that is truly foul and vulgar. If Lanier erred, he erred on the side of righteousness. That he could be fair, that he could praise for one quality what he must condemn for another and could find beauty where ugliness and vulgarity are also present, is proved by the earnest, impartial discussion of Whitman in *The English Novel.*

Lanier's chief defect as a critic is his didacticism. . . . Believing passionately in the holiness of beauty, and that the artist's equipment is God-given, free though the artist is to do with it as he will, and convinced that his business in life, the thing that justified his existence, was to make poems, Lanier could not have been other than a religious poet. . . . [Nor could he] judge the work of others by any other standard than that by which he worked and by which he judged his own work. . . . If he postulated moral earnestness in the work of others, he himself labored in the most sincere, unselfish spirit of revealing the good and reviling the evil, singing God's praises and doing God's work.

The misfortune is not, therefore, that Lanier's work as a critic was characterized by such qualities—for critics of all sorts are needed and critics of Lanier's type fulfill a useful function—but that his work as a poet should possess the same characteristics. Intoxicated by enthusiasm, he . . . made such outpourings of the thoughts in his soul that many lines he wrote are almost embarrassing to read. Such entire lack of reserve in spiritual matters, such frank disclosures of sacred intimacies in his uxorious life with nature, affect the reader as Whitman's frankness and lack of reserve in physical matters affected his first readers; it is like the unguarded candor of adolescence, which arouses our sympathy without enlisting our respect: one sympathizes for Lanier rather than with him. . . . (pp. 442-43)

Lack of catholicity of judgment led him, moreover, to persist in his own way of writing, contrary to the advice of even the most friendly critics. . . . If it could be said with justice [by a reviewer in the *Nation*] in 1888 that "to some he seems like a poet of another age discoursing on modern themes," with how much more justice may this be repeated now. By the language of even his best verse Lanier is dated, dated—in spite of the persisting modernness of his essential ideas—as belonging to an era for which we of today have little sympathy. His poetry is Victorian poetry, for the language is the lush language of sentimentalism, and sentimentalism combined with didacticism is an almost inescapable blight to any poem.

Much of the didacticism in his poetry, like the enthusiasm of his criticism, may be traced, however, to his state of health. Cut off by it rather than by temperament or by desire from the conventional activity of daily life, he lived so exclusively in a world of artistic speculation and scientific questioning that things spiritual came to be more familiar to him than things material, and moral facts to be taken for granted as much as physical facts are. And though he did consciously work in an attitude of moral earnestness, many of the didactic statements are as undeliberate as breathing. He was, Professor H. M. Jones asserts, and one must agree with him, "an abnormally spiritual man" [see excerpt above, 1918], but because he was it is unfair and unprofitable to judge his works by canons that deny the essential healthiness of spirituality. (pp. 443-44)

Fortunately, however, Lanier, with the inconsistency of men of genius, often produced poetry—not the major portion of his poetry, but much of it—marred neither by superabundance of enthusiasm, nor verbal conceits and awkwardnesses, nor by strained fancies, nor by a didacticism offensive to the average reader. The contemplation of nature endowed him—if only temporarily—with something of the largeness and beauty of nature, so that his best work is what we call natural—simple and easy and spontaneous. Tortuous though the sentences may appear in **"The Marshes of Glynn,"** the tortuousness is that of forest patterns; the sentences are as unstudied as the subject is original and unborrowed. Nor is the exquisite simplicity of his several descriptions of sunset a studied simplicity. It is as if Lanier, in the presence of nature, lost his own identity and became only an instrument on which nature played, an instrument capable of the most precise rendition of nature's harmonies. (p. 444)

[Lanier believed] that great music is but the rhythm of a great personality, one living in accordance with the laws of nature, or . . . one living as the greatest of poets, the crystal Christ, the poet of conduct, has shown us how to live.

It is for his life, therefore, more than for his poetry, and for his poetry as a revelation of his life, that Lanier has appealed and must appeal to posterity. It is as impossible to dissociate Lanier and his best verse as it is to dissociate Wordsworth and "The Prelude," or Mrs. Browning and the "Sonnets from the Portuguese," or Francis Thompson and "The Hound of Heaven," or Whitman and the "Song of Myself." It is highly personal poetry, the more enjoyable for being so. We are all at heart hero-worshippers, and we need nothing more than contact with heroes—with great men. For hero-worship is good for the soul of the worshipper; it transfers to him something

of the quality of the hero, and aids his moral growth as a man. The more carefully we study Lanier's life, . . . the more valuable does the revelation that he made of himself in his poetry become.

We cannot, however, ignore the fact that in emphasizing Lanier's fineness of spirit and nobility of utterance, praising a few poems and overlooking many, we are being timid and refusing to answer the question, Was Lanier a great poet? . . . [Does] Lanier appear in the body of his work a true poet, an authentic *vates* [bard]? (pp. 445-46)

[Gamaliel Bradford says that Lanier] chose the most promising, the most poetical subjects, but the battling spirit so characteristic of the man, so evident in the letters and the lectures, is not in his poetry [see Additional Bibliography]. And Bradford is right: what Lanier achieved he achieved all too seldom: there is in his poetry so little of the natural magic that is the supreme felicity of great poets, though so much in his work just fails of achieving this magic, this poetic perfection—as if Pegasus leapt but could not soar. (p. 446)

A clew to Lanier's failure to achieve the unfailing spontaneity of utterance which distinguishes good poetry from bad . . . is afforded by certain of [Lanier's] so-called poem outlines, which examination proves to be very literally that. . . . [Some of them] are so much like prose summaries of poems made as an academic exercise that one is forced to the conclusion that they are just the reverse—drafts for poems, sketched in exact detail. . . . Though a musician with an instinctive feeling for rhythm, Lanier seems to have lacked the lyrical ability capable of sustained utterance: he did not . . . think his poetical thoughts in appropriate verse form, save in such an unusual case as that of **"A Ballad of Trees and the Master."** The fact that so many of his poems seem to be the distillation of passages of his prose, seems also to suggest the necessity of thinking his work out for content before putting it down in form.

It is not, then, that Lanier . . . lacked the time to revise his work; the defect lies in the fact that he should have had to revise as much as he did. . . . [We] have in his letters ample evidence of the care Lanier expended upon his poems. The result of this care . . . is too often a studied effect; the poetry, for all the rich qualities Lanier's irradiating imagination gave it, is more epigrammatical than truly lyrical.

This tendency toward epigrammatic writing, finding expression in fancies and similes, spoils such poems as **"The Bee"** and **"Clover,"** poems nobly conceived and not lacking in high poetic lines. The tendency, become a fixed habit, manifests itself even in **"Sunrise,"** in the figure of the beehive from which the "star-fed Bee, the build-fire Bee, . . . the great Sun-Bee," emerges each morning. Had music and poetry been truly wedded, so that their offspring were the child of love and not of chance, or had Lanier been more of the artist and less of the scientist, such lines as those which mar the very climax of **"Sunrise"** would never have been written.

Another clew to the reason for Lanier's failure . . . remains for the psychologist to develop. Lanier in 1861, at the age of nineteen, . . . looked forward to several years of study in a German university and then to such an academic and literary career in America as Longfellow, after studying in Germany, was already enjoying, and to a life darkened by no financial cares. When the Confederacy was established his future seemed even brighter, for now it would be closely identified with the brilliant future that seemed certain for his native Georgia and for the new nation. War at first meant no end to his dream. (pp. 446-48)

Then events took another turn. . . . [Lanier] went into battle, into prison. He came out broken in health. The Confederacy collapsed, and with it his dreams. From one point of view the rest of Lanier's life, coinciding as it did with a period of political reconstruction, was spent in an attempted spiritual and physical reconstruction, a vain effort to regain health and to achieve . . . the success and the rewards that the future offered in 1861. He did not altogether fail in the attempt, but what he achieved is far different from what he sought. If we contrast, for instance, **"The Tournament: Joust the First,"** written possibly in 1862, at the latest in 1867, and at either date before he had awakened to complete realization of the wreck of his hope, with almost any poem of the last years save the **"Evening Song"** and **"A Ballad of Trees and the Master,"** we see what effect the years of reconstruction had on his work: the early poems so smooth and easy in versification, so simply and beautifully lyrical, the later poems so rarely simple and lyrical, so often involved in thought and meter, in language and in metaphor—and between them days and nights of painful effort to justify by theory what he did by instinct. We are reminded inevitably of the apologetic literature that came from the pens of southern political and military leaders during this same period. (p. 448)

The poet's career, especially in Lanier's conception of it, must be a social one, and to Lanier society became a symbol of the opposite of God, and he found genuine happiness only in nature and in art. But his hectic joy in his abandonment to nature and to music is one of his weaknesses: these masters . . . took payment, as it were, for their gift in shutting him off from the understanding, the appreciation, and the sympathy, of the majority of his fellow men. Viewed thus, his career as a poet appears but the wreck of a career, though a career of unusual promise.

He was, we must admit, no more a great poet than Georgia, or any other southern state, was a great state, or the United States a great nation during the period in which Lanier lived. That he did write some great poetry is no more to be wondered at than that the United States produced some great art, arrived at noteworthy achievements in the sciences, during the same period. And greatness we cannot deny to the best of Lanier's poetry. . . . Lanier possessed if only to a limited extent the poet's natural endowment of melody . . . . He had, moreover, a splendid intellect, one which if frustrated in fullest development was yet alive to the problems of his age and his country, of man and nature, and of man in nature. And he had deep compassion, deeper than that of any other American poet. . . . The songs that are his best—**"Sunrise," "The Marshes of Glynn," "Corn,"** and a few others, the **"Evening Song," "Opposition," "A Ballad of Trees and the Master," "The Stirrup-Cup,"** and **"The Revenge of Hamish"**—have the enduring qualities of originality and of his rare endowment, and the perfection that the true artist, not out of his knowledge but out of the wisdom that comes of pain, gives to his creation.

There is of course more melody, more perfect rhythmical beauty in his early master, Poe, more vigor and strength in Whitman, but no more magic in either, and no more of the ecstasy that all true poets must know. . . . Longfellow's poetry is more learned and more finished, more carefully thought out and better executed; Emerson's often possesses a simplicity which limitation of skill gave him and which the confusion of talents too frequently denied Lanier. But Lanier's poetry often reveals a depth that Longfellow's never reveals, and a beauty that Emerson—whom in ethical qualities Lanier was most like—never achieved. If his flight was less sustained than that of either Longfellow or Emerson, his ability to soar less certain, he did nevertheless fly higher. He knew the high poetic heavens that Poe and Whitman knew, and that these three alone among American poets have known.

Compared with British poets Lanier seems of course much less great. . . . [In] spite of the largeness of his themes and his proneness to grapple with intellectual problems, there is not in Lanier much similarity to Tennyson, with whom he has been most often compared, nor, in spite of the beauty and the unconventionality of his verse, with Swinburne, who loved musical meters as passionately as he; nor is there much resemblance between his bright, sunlit poetry and the lovely melancholy verse of Keats. The only British poets with whose work that of Lanier seems to have a great deal in common are poets of a lower order, such poets as D. M. Dolben and Francis Thompson. . . . (pp. 449-50)

Such a comparison is, however, unnecessary and, when made, a little ridiculous. Just as Whitman is different from Wordsworth, and Emerson from Carlyle, so is Lanier different from any English poet with whom comparison might be made. The difference is in the essentially American quality of his poetry. In the marsh hymns he introduced a new theme to our literature, revealing the beauty of the apparently drab and colorless marshes. . . . It is a great joy—for no quieter phrase will describe it—that the lover of our forest and sea-shores, our hills and our marshes, finds in reading Lanier's poetry. (pp. 450-51)

[An] American quality in **"The Symphony"** may be difficult to define and impossible to illustrate by quotation, but it is there, as inescapably there as it is in **"The Psalm of the West,"** where it is more apparent. It is this American quality that will perhaps prevent any very general appreciation of Lanier's poetry abroad, for his poetry is at once less descriptive of America—and therefore less easily appreciated—than that of Whitman, and more distinctly American than that of Poe. His appeal must ever be to those who love America, love the bright warmth of the sun on her broad fields, and understand the American spirit. One may well paraphrase the song of the good angel in his **"Centennial Cantata"** and say that so long as we shall love true love, and truth, and justice, and freedom, and God, and our fellow men, admire bold criticisms and hold brave hope in good to come, no matter how dark the present may be, the name of Lanier—in whose poetry these virtues are manifest—shall shine, and his fame glow.

For his best prose less can be claimed than for his best poetry. . . . [There] are not among Lanier's essays—even if we consider the separate lectures as essays—enough successful ones on subjects of enduring interest to make up a volume of separate, self-contained pieces of finished work, a volume that would measure up to Lanier's own ideal of a scholarly book. And so all of Lanier's prose, the good and the bad, the finished and the unfinished essays, . . . must survive together for the light they throw on his life. . . . (pp. 451-52)

But even as a revelation of the man, Lanier's formal prose will never take the place of his personal letters. For Lanier was an excellent letter writer and, except in the letters to his wife and his brother, where he let himself go completely, the faults of his poetry are for the most part absent, as are the faults of his other prose. In them—especially in the letters written after

1869—is to be found Lanier's prose style at its best, with its clearness, fluency, eloquence, beauty, reflecting well the resiliency of his mind. And in them also is to be found what all too often is missing in the more formal prose, a delightful playfulness, humor not made up entirely of puns, animated, excited talk about himself and his work, and an unconscious delineation of his character more complete than any a biographer might produce. . . .

[Indeed, a volume of his best letters,] with its revelation of a character as beautiful as its type is rare, of the genuinely poetic temperament illustrated in a man who with Promethean spirit defied discouragements, might achieve a fame and circulation independent of any interest in Lanier's poetry, as Johnson is known through Boswell's biography, Gibbon through his autobiography, Saint Augustine through his confessions, Amiel through his journal, to many who have not read and will never read the formal writings of the same men. (p. 452)

[We] need to know [Lanier], and so long as he becomes known to us for what he was, so long as he becomes known not merely to some but to all who love and cherish the American spirit and our great men, it matters little whether we find him in his poetry or in his letters, or in the tradition that lingers. . . . It is only essential that we come to know him: until we have, discussion of his final rank as a poet is somewhat futile, and after we have, it appears unnecessary. We shall forgive him then, as he forgave others, the more or less, the ''little mole of defect'' in even his best work, and we shall elevate him from the rank of the uncertainly talented, in which he as a poet remains, to companionship with the great, the great not merely for what they did, but for what they became—and for what they have the power to do for others. (p. 454)

Aubrey Harrison Starke, in his Sidney Lanier: A Biographical and Critical Study, *University of North Carolina Press, 1933, 525 p.*

ALLEN TATE   (essay date 1933)

[*In the essay ''A Southern Romantic,'' excerpted below, Tate treats Aubrey Harrison Starke's commentary (1933) as a specimen of the prevailing ''uncritical'' approach to Lanier's work. Applying the principles of the New Critics, with whom he was associated, Tate closely analyzes Lanier's symbols, exposing their vagueness and detecting in these and other shortcomings the ''general weakness of the romantic sensibility.'' A member of the Agrarians, a group of writers dedicated to preserving the Southern way of life and Southern values, Tate viewed Northern industrial capitalism as a threat to the traditional Southern farming economy. Like the Agrarian critics Robert Penn Warren (1933) and John Crowe Ransom (1934), Tate interprets Lanier's ''nationalism'' as an endorsement of Reconstruction-era Northern industrial capitalism and a betrayal of the South.*]

Lanier made the literal attempt to transform poetry into a branch of music. It is to this fallacy that most of Lanier's critics have ascribed the defects of his verse. It explains his more obvious failures. But his chief limitation is probably due to the general weakness of the romantic sensibility. It is likely that had he never studied music his poetry would have been in principle the same.

From the time of his death until the Great War his reputation grew. For two reasons, I believe, it is declining. His poetry has little to say to this century either in substance or in technique. And it has never received any very precise critical evaluations. It became generally understood at the end of the last century—in the best anthological circles—that Lanier was the chief poet of the South, if Poe was not Southern; superior to his contemporary, Hayne, and to his earlier contemporary, Henry Timrod. It is time, if one found it interesting enough, to dispute at least the latter half of that judgment, and time, also, to remember a name that the generation after Lanier forgot: Thomas Holley Chivers. It is the desire to give Lanier a ''rank'' and to worry his poetry into some kind of ''social significance,'' rather than the critical impulse to estimate the exact quality of his work, that has kept him from being justly placed in American letters. (p. 67)

[Mr. Aubrey Harrison Starke] makes tedious a false issue that Professor Mims (see excerpt above, 1905) discussed at sufficient length. Now that the euphemisms of *fin de siècle* nationalism have served their purpose, and the trusts and mergers have had their way, the innocent social beliefs of Professor Mims' ''nationalism'' are no longer necessary. So Mr. Starke takes higher ground: Lanier was a figure on the model of Christ. . . . Professor Mims is a less suggestive critic [than Starke]:

> [Lanier] was inoculated with the conceit virus of the seventeenth century. . . . He did not restrain his luxuriant imagination. The poem **''Clover''** is almost spoiled by the conceit of the ox representing the ''Course-of-things'' and trampling upon the souls (the clover-blossoms) of the poets. . . .

[''Clover''] is a model of what poetry should not be; it is one of the worst pieces of writing in nineteenth-century American verse. But is its defect that of the seventeenth-century conceit?

Lanier believed that he employed the seventeenth-century conceit, and his critics have believed it after him. . . . But Lanier was mistaken, and Professor Mims, I believe, was misled. The mistake assumes that any unsuccessful figure of speech is conceit, and therefore bad. The allegory of the ox is execrable, but it is not conceit. It is a symbol. (pp. 67-8)

The trouble with the ox is not that he is a conceit, but that he is not. The conceit does not *represent* anything. . . . [It is] only illustrative. . . . But it is characteristic of a symbol, like the Cross, that it represents with a high degree of constancy the same emotions and ideas. The ox is a bad symbol for Lanier's purpose because it represents nothing but a confused abstraction that never reaches visible connection with the clover-like souls. All effort to perceive the relation in exact images ends in ludicrous failure. The symbol is a humorless and pretentious failure of sentimentality.

It has been necessary to labor the point in order to understand its implications. The habit of Lanier's critics is to approach his poetry after his biography, to see his verse as the ''interpretation'' of social and moral ideas implicit in the general course of his career: he is a poet with a social point of view. It is my purpose here, however, to look at the poetry first, the final test of the poet's clarity and depth, of the value of what he said to his age. . . .

Of [his poetic output] there are perhaps five pieces that entitle Lanier to a place among the minor writers of the Gilded Age. **''From the Flats,''** in which he achieves his greatest precision of statement; **''A Ballad of Trees and the Master,''** his most successful experiment in rhythm; and **''Tampa Robins''**—these three poems are largely free from the extravagant vices of the poet's vocabulary. They add nothing to the long tradition of

English verse; they are the super-magazine poetry of a commonplace and confused mind, which for the moment escapes from the romantic ego and fixes itself upon *objects perceived*. (p. 68)

Of the two most ambitious poems ["**Sunrise**" and "**The Marshes of Glyn**" (*sic*),] "**The Marshes of Glyn**" is the better. It has two distinct features: a mechanical versification superimposed for its own "musical" value upon the subject; a muddled handling of the images, a fault concealed by the use of semi-symbolic abstractions and moralistic ideas. It is probably correct to assume that Lanier's whole theory of verse, greatly spun out with incidental truths in "**The Science of English Verse**," is a rationalization of his incapacity to set forth a clear image: the theory holds that "all ideas may be abolished out of a poem without disturbing its effect on the ear as verse." The results of the theory in Lanier's work are the two defects of "**The Marshes of Glyn**." . . .

The theory of an absolute metrics is possible only in an age that takes an irresponsible view of the subject-matter of poetry; and this, in spite of the high moral tone habitual with Lanier, is precisely what he did. His way of "abolishing out of a poem" all its ideas is to write from an incoherent center, and to put the ideas in at random. The moral relations implied by his general terms are not mastered; this inexactness of his statement invalidates his moral point of view.

It is the great weakness of the humanitarian-romantic movement in literature. Take the famous lines from "**The Marshes of Glyn**":

> Inward and outward to northward and southward the
>   beach-lines linger and curl
> As a silver-wrought garment clings to and follows
>   the firm sweet limbs of a girl.

The intention is a simple simile, but to write it concisely and accurately was too difficult for Lanier. There is not, in all his work, sufficient insight into his own romantic sensibility to permit him to carry it to its logical conclusion. While his French contemporaries were consciously protesting against the consequences of romanticism in literature, and of its social counterpart, industrial capitalism; while they were consciously mixing their metaphors so as to create a precise image of spiritual damnation—Lanier remained the dupe of his own assumptions, and to the end of his life misunderstood the implication of his position.

In evasion of the most arduous labor of the poet, he sprinkled his poems with meaningless didacticisms. . . .

In 1876, a critic in *The Nation* [see excerpt above] wrote: "Mr. Lanier's poetic sensibility and serious purpose cannot make up for a lack of clear expression in his writing. This lack is the evidence not so much of want of practice in composition as of discipline of thought." Lanier's comment on this criticism, a judgment which applies to his whole career as well as to the question under controversy in *The Nation*, was written in a letter to his brother; it is of great interest:

> . . . it has naturally caused me to make a merciless arraignment and trial of my artistic purposes; and an unspeakable content arises out of the revelation that they come from an ordeal confirmed in innocence and clearly defined in their relations to all things. I do not hate people who have so cruelly maltreated me; they knew not what they did. . . .

The passage deserves study; it contains the whole explanation of Sidney Lanier. Its intellectual insincerity is, I believe, inextricably bound up with a kind of moral insincerity inseparable from the mentality of Victorian romanticism in America. The self-reverence echoing the words of Christ; the evasion of intellectual responsibility by means of the pseudo-mystical belief in the innocence of his ego; the perverse determination to protect the ego from reality—all this is familiar in the naturalistic tradition. We have seen the effects of that attitude in his poetry—the incapacity to write precisely, and the rationalization of the defect with confused allegory. It is a fundamental quality of his entire moral and intellectual outlook. (p. 69)

Given the formula upon which his poetry was written—a formula that we have examined—we may deduce his general intellectual procedure. As he failed to present one clear image in his verse, so he failed to see through a single leading idea of his age. And this failure, as in the case of his poetry, betrayed him into large abstractions with moral names; he identified with "truth" those political notions, those public movements, those theories of art, which promised success to his career. For the self-reverent romantic, having only an ego, has only, for the world, the extension of that ego which is a career.

Lanier's prose no less than his verse is a mass of disorderly ideas. The spirit of his critical writings is optimism and easy analogy. For one thing, he shared with his age the delusion that the function of applied science is to make men at home in nature. The political direction of that scientific age was taking man out of nature in the religious sense, and enslaving him to a naturalistic order. This "materialism" Lanier denounced throughout his career, but because his alternative to it was only a "faith" that it would eventually prove beneficial to society, he based his career upon its more respectable vulgarities. Having convinced himself, in an essay called "**The New South**," that the South would become, after the break-up of the plantations, a region of securely rooted small farmers, he was at liberty to misunderstand the social and economic significance of the Civil War, and to flatter the industrial capitalism of the North in a long poem, "**Psalm of the West**," a typical expression of Reconstruction imperialism. "There is nothing sectional," writes Mr. Starke, "in this chant of the glory of freedom." On the contrary it is all sectional—with Northern sectionalism, which becomes the "nationalism" of the Southern liberals in the generation of Harris, Grady and Lanier. In Lanier's poem it is a nationalism of complimentary allusion to Massachusetts and of large personifications that could mean almost anything to a poet who had not grappled with the inner spirit of his age; a poet to whom the first reality is the inviolability of his own personality.

The trouble with the age, thought Lanier, was that Trade had crushed Chivalry. Having said that, in several allegories, he proceeded, in terms that made the issue seem different, to flatter Trade. He believed that the searing blast of art should be tempered to the shorn and public lamb; that he must defer to the public taste, consciously, in order the better at some later time to instruct it. No one who has studied his career will deny that he did both; though one must admit that his instruction could have been better than it was. On the whole one must confess that Sidney Lanier was a prophet foretelling only the blessings of our own age. His refusal to look for a fundamental alternative to the beliefs of the Reconstruction era, and his acceleration of those beliefs under the illusion that he was correcting them, are in the intellectual tradition of our time. He was a nineteenth-century leader who helped to make us what we are today. (pp. 69-70)

Allen Tate, "A Southern Romantic," in The New Republic, Vol. LXXVI, No. 978, August 30, 1933, pp. 67-70.

ROBERT PENN WARREN (essay date 1933)

[*A confrere of Allen Tate (1933) and John Crowe Ransom (1934) in the Agrarian and New Criticism movements, Warren took the publication of Aubrey Harrison Starke's* Sidney Lanier *(1933) as the occasion to characterize Lanier as "The Blind Poet." According to Warren, Lanier's oeuvre is beset with vagueness, contradiction, abstraction, and sentimentality, defects which he ultimately attributes to Lanier's "basic bewilderment."*]

The German Romantics, we are told, and the English Romantics with their Victorian brethren for that matter, defined the demesne that was always to remain Lanier's "spiritual home". . . . From the spiritual abode he brought a message which, according to Mr. Starke, is "particularly worth listening to in the present period of economic and social unrest". The message appears in varying forms, in the poems and in the several volumes of collected prose. It is a message sometimes contradictory or vague, as a communication from the realm of spirits is apt to sound in perverse mundane ears. (p. 31)

[Lanier's theory of etherealization, propounded in **Retrospects and Prospects**,] is a sort of text for Lanier's work. . . . (p. 32)

For man this etherealization seems to correspond to the development of "personality", which since the Renaissance has assumed three characteristic new relations. . . . And all of these new relations, which find their characteristic expressions in Music, the Novel, and Science, respectively, are rooted in Love. (pp. 32-3)

The important thing is this: where did [this theory] guide Lanier? In literature it led him to prefer Tennyson to Milton, because Tennyson is "more spiritual" and has purged himself of Milton's "purely physical accessories". He preferred George Eliot to Fielding, that "muck of the classics", and, incidentally, to Shakespeare, presumably because she "shows man what he may be, in terms of what he is". In architecture it led him to regard the rapidity and lightness of commercial construction as an indication of "the veritable etherealizing change which it has undergone". (p. 33)

[Lanier's] nationalism represented, I surmise, an "etherealization". . . . The basis of such new etherealized relations, it is worthy of recollection, is Love—that "key to Lanier's philosophy". The Civil War, recently concluded, had been the great single step toward the achievement of the new nationalism. The Civil War, we may infer, was, if not itself an act of love, a step toward a loving synthesis. (pp. 33-4)

Lanier was not realistic. He wrote as a poet of the new nationalism, and at the same time he protested (although he once found it in his heart to approve big corporations because they were "needed") against the domination of Trade, by which he meant, apparently, commerce and industry. . . . Specifically, as in the **Symphony**, his objection is that Trade dries up the springs of Love, that its ethics are those of war, that it does not permit the labourer to recline "where Art and Nature sing and smile". Mr. Starke submits that the **Symphony** "presents an intelligible program for social amelioration". This program is Love, and the instrument of its execution is music. . . . But what Mr. Starke fails to see, as Lanier failed, is that the nationalism mystically embodied in the **Psalm of the West** was a nationalism of Trade. *Amor vincit omnia* [love conquers all]—even the contradiction.

Lanier's evangelical concern with science meant a similar contradiction, or rather a two-edged one, as related to art and to society. Science, along with the nature-metaphor, he regarded as an indication of the Love of Nature . . . the new *rapport* between Man and Nature. "We found", he said to his audience in Baltimore, "that science and poetry had been developing alongside each other ever since early in the seventeenth century; inquiring into the general effect of this long contact, we could only find that it was to make our general poetry greatly richer in substance and finer in form." It is, probably, a defect of taste to prefer "darling Tennyson" to Milton; it is a defect of another order to confound science with art, the abstract with the concrete, the practical with the contemplative. . . . It is no wonder that Lanier likewise failed to perceive that the science he adored was the handmaid of the industrial system he detested. (pp. 34-6)

Now all of Lanier's judgements on the arts, as judgements, are devoid of interest except such interest as is felt in eccentricity. His social judgements in themselves are interesting only in so far as they illustrate the peculiar and sometimes irresponsible confusion into which the Southern liberal lapsed. The artistic judgements, to put it bluntly, simply mean that Lanier, despite his professions of extreme sensitivity, was really lacking in capacity for aesthetic perception. He did not *see* anything. He was a doctrinaire; that is, he appreciated a work of art to the degree in which it supported his especial theory of progress. But that very theory of progress, and his particular social applications of it, mean that he did not think except in obvious and incomplete analogy. These various judgements are worthy of discussion at all only because they may clarify, to some extent, the properties of his poetry.

Lanier's fame depends on his poetry. If he had not written the poems, he would now be a scarcely remembered flute-player with liberal views and a handsome head. His personality, Mr. Starke to the contrary, would not command us.

Lanier's conception of himself, of the poet's rôle, was a paradoxical one, but one characteristic of the century in which he lived. . . . [The] poet is not only a special soul set apart, but a social prophet. That is, the business of the poet is two-fold: he must "express" his own etherealizing personality and must reform the personalities of other people. Or perhaps it was not as paradoxical as it seems; the egotist imposes himself.

The difficulty, for Lanier, was insoluble. No poem of his represents a single vision, for the fatal self-consciousness intervenes. The obvious criticism is that he is didactic. But, more fundamentally, the trouble was that he never understood the function of idea in art. He regularly performed an arbitrary disjunction, both in creation and in criticism, between the idea and the form in which it might be embodied. Painting etherealizes by freeing itself of the "purely material load of colour". *The Princess* is superior to *Paradise Lost*. Or religion etherealizes by losing its "material props", by which, I suppose, he meant dogma, ritual, and, finally, the Church itself. Lanier's poetry, by consequence, was intellectual in a bad sense—in the sense that Browning or Tennyson, or better, Elizabeth Browning, all better poets, were frequently intellectual. The idea is never realized; it remains abstract; it does not achieve the status of experience.

Lanier's imagery, in this respect, is instructive. Early in his poetical career he wrote to his father: "I have frequently noticed in myself a tendency to a diffuse style; a disposition to push my metaphors too far, employing a multitude of words to heighten the patness of the image and so making of it a *conceit. . . .*'' This self-criticism has been almost consistently echoed by writers on Lanier, such as Professor Howard Mumford Jones [see excerpt above, 1918], with the assumption that the conceit is necessarily bad. Lanier occasionally did employ images that might be termed conceits, but they were bad conceits, ''yoked by violence''. (pp. 36-9)

But more generally, in the attempt to communicate a poetic idea, Lanier resorted to something that is more like a fragmentary allegory than like the conceit. The conceit . . . affords more than one point of contact between the two elements involved in the image, more than one term of comparison. . . . Now an allegory seems to be a system of assigned equivalents. Such a system is comprised by the Ox representing the ''Course-of-Things'' and the heads of clover representing the poets in *Clover* . . . or by the ''young Adam of the West'' representing America in *Psalm of the West*. . . . [In *Marsh Song*, Lanier uses] literary allusion with allegorical implication. I shall only quote the first stanza:

> Over the monstrous shambling sea,
>   Over the Caliban sea,
> Bright Ariel-cloud, thou lingerest:
> Oh wait, oh wait, in the warm red West,—
>   Thy Prospero I'll be.

Except for the first line this stanza conveys no perception, and even the literal, the intellectual meaning is dependent on a knowledge of [William Shakespeare's] *The Tempest* for comprehensibility. The allegory, even, is second-hand. This is perfectly arbitrary, arbitrary in the same way that the assignment to various instruments of different attitudes in regard to Trade is arbitrary in the *Symphony*. It is but another example of Lanier's failure to realize an idea poetically.

Lanier was right, however, when he commented on his tendency to diffuseness, a fault which arose from vagueness of perception. (pp. 39-41)

Much of Lanier's imagery, much that has been excessively admired, reduces to nothing more than verbalism. (p. 42)

[Lanier's abstractness is expressed in his] fondness for adjectives like *dear, sweet, adorable,* and *thrilling,* and for lines like

> Of the dim sweet woods, of the dear dark woods . . .

This abstractness, it seems, derives from Lanier's sentimentality, a property quite as common and offensive in his prose as in his verse. (''That adorable sonnet'', ''our adorable John Keats''.) That is, Lanier insists on an emotional attitude for which he can provide no stimulus; the reader is asked to accept the poet's experience on trust, the one thing a reader declines to do, unless he, like the poet, is a sentimentalist.

This sentimentality is not confined to detail, but appears, naturally enough, at the very root of Lanier's inspiration. It is a result of his basic bewilderment. The general theme of all his poetry, the critics say, is Love, which apparently was the name he bestowed on any emotional disturbance. . . . [When] he tried to define his attitudes in presumably sober prose, he merely resolved a confusion or contradiction by appeal to that term. In poetry his theme is most commonly manifested in what has been called his ''nature-worship''. . . . Despite the fact that he has been frequently praised as an observer of Nature, . . .

he exhibited a remarkably feeble capacity for seeing anything; his use of imagery makes that clear. He referred to Nature as a vague embodiment of his private agitations, his desire for marriage with the All. (pp. 43-4)

As with all sentimentalists, Lanier's emotionalism was a species of self-indulgence, which probably accounts for the fact that he was able to communicate nothing. It was a species of self-indulgence both sensual and effeminate, as his relaxed rhythmic effects often imply. But rhythm is not the only evidence. The glades in the marshes are

> Cells for the passionate pleasure of prayer to the soul
>   that grieves. . . .

And he could commit himself to these lines:

> Tell me, sweet burly-barked, man-bodied Tree
> That mine arms in the dark are embracing, dost know
> From what fount are these tears at thy feet which flow?

The most charitable pronouncement on this, as on much of Lanier's poetry, is that it is absurd.

Lanier has only a doubtful importance for us. What he had to say has been said by better men in a better way: Wordsworth, Coleridge, Tennyson, Shelley, Emerson, Carlyle, Browning, Longfellow, Ruskin, Swinburne. Lanier merely recapitulated in a vulgar and naïve version what today may appear as their fallacies and confusions, the unsatisfying quality of their work. He was the final product of all that was dangerous in Romanticism: his theory of personality, his delusion of prophecy, his aesthetic premise, his uninformed admiration of science, his nationalism, his passion for synthesis, his theory of progress. What was valuable in his century passed him by. He was admired because, as Tennyson to England, he spoke to America, and tardily to the South, in the accent of its dearest anticipations:

> Now the glittering Western land
> Twins the day-lit Eastern Strand;
> Now white Freedom's sea-bird wing
> Roams the Sea of Everything;
> Now the freemen to and fro
> Bind the tyrant sand and snow,
> Snatching Death's hot bolt ere hurled,
> Flash new life around the world,
> Sun the secrets of the hills,
> Shame the gods' slow-grinding mills,
> Prison Yesterday in Print,
> Read To-morrow's weather-hint,
> Haste before the halting Time,
> Try new virtue and new crime,
> Mould new faiths, devise new creeds,
> Run each road that frontward leads,
> Driven by an Onward-ache,
> Scorning souls that circles make.

After all, Mr. Starke may be right. Perhaps we should know Lanier. He may help us to assess our heritage. (pp. 44-5)

Robert Penn Warren, ''The Blind Poet: Sidney Lanier,'' in The American Review, *Vol. 2, No. 1, November, 1933, pp. 27-45.*

AUBREY STARKE   (essay date 1934)

[*Starke responded to the Agrarians' criticism of Lanier's ''nationalism'' in the essay ''The Agrarians Deny a Leader,'' ex-*

cerpted below. He defends Lanier's "nationalism" as an attempt to reconcile North and South on traditional, non-economic grounds and charges the Agrarians with critical hindsight in expecting Lanier to anticipate future industrial evils. Noting the correspondence between the principles articulated in the Agrarian manifesto I'll Take My Stand and Lanier's essay "The New South," Starke concludes his essay by claiming that Lanier was in fact a model agrarian. John Crowe Ransom considered the merits of Starke's claim in the essay "Hearts and Heads" (1934).]

[Mr. Tate and Mr. Warren make numerous charges against Lanier in their recent essays (see excerpts above, 1933 and 1933).] It is with the charge that Lanier was blind to the defects of his age, and that instead of understanding and championing a Southern way of life (that of the Agrarians!) he flattered Northern industrialism and celebrated the Northern way, that we are here most concerned.

It may, however, be remarked that it is unfair to accuse Lanier [as Mr. Tate did] of tempering "the searing blast of art . . . to the shorn and public lamb",. . . . Lanier was compelled by necessity to "defer to public taste, consciously", in order not merely that he might "at some later time . . . instruct it" but that he might keep his body and soul together until that later time (which he failed, however, in doing). If that he did so is not to his credit, it is certainly not, from any reasonable point of view, to his shame. (pp. 537-38)

His desire to speak out boldly in criticism of his times, if not apparent in such poems as **"Corn"** and **"The Symphony"**, is certainly manifest in the . . . commencement address delivered in Americus, Georgia, in 1869, and in . . . [the poem **"Remonstrance."**] Much of the work Lanier did see published, and most of his work that has been published since his death, is mere literary hack-work. As such it is not often surprisingly good, but it is often—for a product of the "Brown Decades"—surprisingly outspoken, and denunciatory.

To call Lanier's nationalism a left-handed acceptance of Northern industrialism is to label him as something of a Benedict Arnold of the Southern way of life. [In a letter recently published in *The New Republic* (see Additional Bibliography)], Mr. Tate explains his reference to Lanier's "flattery" of the industrial capitalism of the North thus: "**'The Psalm of the West'** is praise of 'nationalism', *argal* of Northern sectionalism, *argal* of industrialism. I hope this is not too esoteric in its logic."

Esoteric it is, however. . . . [Lanier] did not see that the triumph of the North meant the triumph of industrialism, and could not have seen it. He was no prophet, as his attempts at prophecy (as in his discussion of the "etherialization" which he thought was taking place in all orders of social activity) prove. It is an easy thing in 1934 to say what the Northern victory in 1865 brought about in the succeeding sixty-nine years, but it would have been remarkable if anyone dying in 1881 could have foretold the course of industrial capitalism for the next fifty-three years (especially the bond-servant it was to make of science) and the depression that began in 1929, in a land of plenty.

The Northern victory to Lanier meant the shattering of his dream that the new (agrarian!) Confederacy was to inaugurate an era of artistic and intellectual splendour, rivalling that of the Athens of Pericles. It meant the loss of health, of opportunities for intellectual advancement, and of any chance of living the peaceful, ordered life the New Agrarians celebrate. (pp. 538-39)

Lanier however neither sought refuge in another land nor comfort in any adopted attitude. He accepted defeat, admitted it, and proceeded to forget it, in every way that was possible but also noble and dignified, and that he did so seems to me greatly to his credit. He did not embrace a nationalism that was really nothing more than Northern sectionalism, but he tried to be a reconciling influence between North and South and to recover, for himself and for those who would hear him, the old ideals of nationalism known to Washington and Jefferson and Adams. . . . In **"The Psalm of the West"** the best passages, poetically, are those which ascribe to Columbus emotions—dreams for the land of his discovery—which Columbus surely never felt. It was no thought of the United States under the presidency of Grant that inspired Lanier but a vision of America as a land of promise still, in spite of Civil War, and Reconstruction, and Civil Rights Bills, and of corruption that touched the White House.

And if, in that Centennial Ode (for **"The Psalm of the West"** was commissioned for publication in *Lippincott's Magazine* for July, 1876) Lanier describes the Civil War "unrealistically", as Mr. Warren says, as a chivalrous joust between two knights, Heart (the South) and Brain (the North), he was in doing that being a little more clear than Mr. Warren is willing to admit. (pp. 540-41)

What Lanier said under guise of the allegory of Heart and Brain (written possibly as early as 1862, and merely re-used in 1876) was true then as it is now. A cultured Southern lady who knew Lanier . . . wrote recently in reference to the removal of a young Northerner—Sidney Lanier's grandson!—to the South, to make his home there: "He will not be disappointed if he comes prepared to find less *head* but perhaps more *heart* here than in New England." She was surprised later, upon rereading **"The Psalm of the West"**, to find that Lanier himself had expressed so clearly what she meant. Lanier's statement of a truth is courteous, and generous. That it is "unrealistic" as an account of the Civil War is beside the point: a realistic description would have been out of place in a centennial ode as a matter of taste and of tact. (p. 542)

When it came to fighting a battle in behalf of a cause that was, for Lanier as for us, a living cause, and not one already lost, he too could be brutally frank and realistic. . . . The late Vernon Louis Parrington observed that Lanier was "the first of our poets to cry out against [industrialism] as a deadly blight on life and civilization.". . . He who could write

> Does business mean, *Die, you—live, I?*
> Then "Trade is trade" but sings a lie:
> 'Tis only war grown miserly.
> If business is battle, name it so:
> War-crimes less will shame it so:
> And widows less will blame it so.

was not one ever to flatter industrialism, even indirectly, or by implication. (pp. 542-43)

Lanier distrusted industrialism, because he hated social injustice, and he saw that capitalistic industrialism produced it. If Lanier accepted science, hailed excitedly the new scientific discoveries of his age, and the application of science to inventions that should make living more agreeable instead of more sordid and unendurable (as Mr. Andrew Nelson Lytle has convincingly demonstrated in his contribution to *I'll Take My Stand*), it was because Lanier, even in the 1870's, had faith enough to believe that science, which seemed a divine gift, could not be used for man's debasement. (pp. 543-44)

[Lanier] had acquired . . . a knowledge of practical agriculture, and he had from first to last a deep concern for it. (p. 544)

His little-known but effective early dialect poems are—with a single exception—all descriptive of farmers, and are pleas in behalf of diversification of crops. They are in a sense a poetic counterpart of the editorials of Mr. Joseph Clisby, editor of the Macon *Telegraph and Messenger* (referred to by name in one of the poems), urging the planting of more corn and less cotton, and—as such—propaganda. Lanier's vision of a South economically ruined by over-production of cotton but redeemed by the production of corn . . . is expressed in **"Corn"**, a poem indigenous to a Georgia corn-field.

But the agrarian *ideal* is not one of one-crop agriculture. **"Corn"** suggests an immediate solution for a present evil; it is not a programme for a continuous social development. Proof that Lanier was a wise agrarian must be sought elsewhere. I find it in the very essay, **"The New South"**, that Mr. Tate seems to think so little of. (pp. 544-45)

The New South, Lanier was careful to state, meant—in distinction from the old—small farming, the development of which "during the last twenty years becomes the notable circumstance of the period". If successful small farming, with each farm thoroughly self-sustaining, is not the agrarian ideal at its purest and best, as stated even in the symposium *I'll Take My Stand*, I know not how to label it. (p. 545)

Indeed, Lanier's essay on the New South would not be out of place in the Agrarian symposium. Certainly it is the ideal of the Agrarians that he expresses in his statement that "on the large farm [with its seasonal over-turn of labour] is no abiding-place; the labourer must move on; life cannot stand still, to settle and clarify". *Settle and clarify!* It is the settled and clarified life, surely, that Mr. Stark Young praises as the aristocratic; and it is the Southern way of life, whether it be agrarian or industrial.

It is something I still fail, after considerable effort, to understand that Mr. Allen Tate could ever once have read **"The New South"** and stated: "Having convinced himself [in this essay] that the South would become . . . a region of securely rooted small farmers, [Lanier] was at liberty to misunderstand the social and economic significance of the Civil War, and to flatter the industrial capitalism of the North in . . . **'[The] Psalm of the West'**." The poem, of course, antedates the essay by four years, though Mr. Tate ignores that. He ignores also, and more regrettably, that in the essay Lanier characterizes large farming as manufacturing, points out the evils of it, and expresses his fine "indignation" against it.

Mr. Warren finds inconsistency in Lanier's protest against the domination of Trade and the fact that "he once found it in his heart to approve big corporations because they were 'needed'". What Lanier actually wrote was: "Our republic vitally needs the corporation for the mighty works which only the corporation can do, while it as vitally needs the small farmer for the pure substance of individual and self-reliant manhood which he digs out of the ground, and which, the experience of all peoples would seem to show, must primarily come that way and no other." In their prefatory "Statement of Principles" the contributors to *I'll Take My Stand* declare:

> An agrarian society is hardly one that has no use at all for industries. . . . An agrarian society is one in which agriculture is the leading vocation . . . that becomes the model to which

the other forms approach as well as they may. . . . An agrarian régime will be secured readily enough where the superfluous industries are not allowed to rise against it.

(pp. 546-47)

In matters touching national problems and affairs, Lanier refused to be sectional (in the derogatory sense of the world). . . . But Lanier loved the South. He was proud that he was a Southerner. He rejoiced that he was chosen to write the **"Centennial Cantata"** "as representative of our dear South". He never lost touch with the South, and specifically with Georgia, whose hills, rivers and marshes he described in his best and best-known poems. (p. 548)

In [Lanier's poem **"The Homestead"**] the State of Georgia speaks, announcing fundamental principles of social living of which New Agrarians and New Dealers alike must approve.

> I will no man shall homeless be,
> I will no weeping wife shall flee
> From shadow of her own roof-tree
>   Forth driven by hard neighbor.
>
> I know the large sweet sanctities
> That grow in homes, and unto these
> I add the might of my decrees
>   To make the home-strength stronger;
>
> To foster the confirm the place
> Where Birth hath glory, Life hath grace
> And Death hath smiles upon his face
>   When Life has grace no longer.

Instructions are then given for the planting of various fruits, grains, vines, and vegetables, because

> Lean Hunger starves with plenteous fright;
> Want dies, death-stricken with delight;
> And Crime slinks back into his night;
>   Where Plenty rides proud prancing.

For Southern agrarians, for even two of them, to attack Lanier as a poet (and by poet I do not here mean versifier but, in Lanier's own conception of the poet's function, leader of men) is one of the curious, unexpected things that happen to disturb one's sense of a settled and clarified order. (p. 550)

That Mr. Tate and Mr. Warren should have revealed so unpredictable an attitude toward Lanier—chief glory, in poetry, of the South they celebrate—is to be explained, if we grant them sincerity in their attitude, by their failure to realize that the problems of the 1930's and of the 1870's are not identical. Their excessive and defiant sectionalism drives them, though by curious, precious, and tenuous illogicality, to the conclusion that Lanier, striving to be national in the large and important sense of the word, could not have remained Southern, and that in praising nationalism he was actually praising Northern capitalistic industrialism. Lanier repeatedly pointed out the evils and dangers inherent in capitalistic industrialism. Messrs. Warren and Tate, seeing the destruction these evils have accomplished, condemn Lanier for not rejecting industrialism absolutely . . . *before the evils had proved themselves not merely inherent but potent.* As well condemn him for advocating small farming because, as Mr. John Crowe Ransom regretfully states, the small farms into which the Southern plantations were often broken after the war "have yielded less and less of a living". (pp. 550-51)

[In his essay in *I'll Take My Stand*, Herman Clarence Nixon, professor of economics at Tulane] quotes Lanier's definition that "The New South" means small farming with approval, at least with approval of the definition as a statement of historic fact in 1880—which is all one can properly ask that it be; and he points out that Lanier's use of the phrase, "New South", was different both from that of Henry Grady and that of W. D. Kelley, and in no wise meant an industrialized South. One feels that Professor Nixon, at least, recognizes Lanier's one ambitious excursion into the field of economic investigation as sound and conclusive, however, Mr. Tate and Mr. Warren—poets *primo,* not economists—may feel about it.

So we come to the conclusion that Mr. Tate and Mr. Warren are poor critics of the social order, as being unable to recognize correct social interpretation or to hear sympathetically a social plea so nearly their own. . . . (pp. 551-52)

And if a body of doctrine is to be judged by its leaders, we reject, accordingly, the new Southern agrarianism, the expounders of which reject so boldly, so boastingly, the courteous, vigorous plea of a leader of a half-century ago. But agrarianism, as a way of life, is superior to and distinct from the shortcomings of any would-be exemplifiers of it, as it is superior to sectional interpretation of it. Mr. Tate calls Lanier's "a commonplace and confused mind" and his poetry "muddy, pretentious, and false". Mr. Warren calls Lanier blind, his poetry "a vulgar and naïve version" of the poetry of the earlier romantics and the contemporary Victorians. An impartial, open-minded examination of his works and his life should convince one, however, that these are harsh and unfair adjectives to apply to Lanier.

If a civilization is to be judged by its embodiment in individuals, individuals, in turn, are to be judged in respect to their appreciation—their relization and their revelation—of the civilization which nurtured them. . . . [Lanier's] appreciations, in verse and prose, of America—"dear land of all my love"—and of Georgia—"my Georgia"—are generous, sincere, and moving, and reveal in the singer a character of tremendous appeal. They entitle him, moreover, to the respect and courteous consideration of all who love the American spirit, in its larger national manifestations, or in its narrower sectional manifestations—especially its manifestation as life settled and clarified, lived graciously in an aristocratically provincial agrarian society. (pp. 552-53)

Aubrey Starke, "The Agrarians Deny a Leader," in The American Review, *Vol. 2, No. 5, March, 1934, pp. 534-53.*

JOHN CROWE RANSOM (essay date 1934)

[*An American critic, poet, and editor, Ransom is considered one of the most influential literary theorists of the twentieth century. He is best known as a prominent spokesperson for the Fugitive, Agrarian, and New Criticism movements in American literature. Ransom's essay "Hearts and Heads," excerpted below, represents the final exchange in the critical debate sparked by Aubrey Harrison Starke's* Sidney Lanier *(see excerpts above by Starke, 1933 and 1934, Allen Tate, 1933, and Robert Penn Warren, 1933). In considering Starke's claim that Lanier was a model agrarian, Ransom concedes that Lanier showed a "correct apprehension of some of the obvious evils of industrial capitalism, and some of the benefits of agrarian farming." However, he concurs with his fellow Agrarians Tate and Warren in maintaining that Lanier "failed strategically" in overlooking the inimical re-*

lationship that existed between Reconstruction-era nationalism and agrarianism.]

Lanier was a Georgian; he fought on the Confederate side in the Civil War, and lived just through Reconstruction; and his attitude to the war, to the enemy, to the nation, to the Southern poet's function, was frequently lacking in critical intelligence and in dignity. (p. 555)

What was the war about? It was popularly thought to be about slavery, but Lanier had no particular interest in slavery pro or con. He was temperamentally one of the Platonists, in love with big abstract ideas, and he was probably on the point of conceiving a grand attachment for the nation—for he did conceive one a little later under the most unfavourable circumstances—and was disturbed at the thought of disunion. But when Alexander Stephens joined the Confederate Government it was all the evidence he needed; he joined the Confederate army. He was the perfect private, without a thought of his own. (pp. 555-56)

[When] the war was ended he still had no opinions about it, nor in the course of subsequent years did he seem to acquire any. . . . His resistance was over. He was not sustained by the sense that there was still a fight to make, a community of effort to share. . . . What he wanted was to play the flute and write verses, but there was little chance for the troubadour in the South then. He wrote characteristically to a Northern friend in 1866: "You are all so alive, up there, and we are all so dead, down here." Dead to the things he liked to do. But that is too petulant to be mistaken for the language in which the leader refers to his people. He would not have accepted agrarians like Mr. Tate and Mr. Warren; why should they accept him? (p. 556)

He did not remain in the South; he got out as soon as he could. He pursued acquaintance and friendship in Philadelphia, Baltimore, New York, among the Brahmins of Cambridge; . . . he constantly sought publication in Philadelphia and New York. It is impossible to escape the impression that throughout his life he was much too eager for the friendship and praise of the persons he admired; inordinately concerned with seeing his work printed, in the first place, and well received, in the second. He was dependent, like some vaudeville artist, upon the sympathy of an immediate audience, and without the iron that we suppose in the predestinate poet. If he had real creative genius—and he had at least a constant artistic predilection, and a talent, which for Americans of that period ought to count as genius—he paid for it by his temperamental defects. And yet this consideration need not arise if we were permitted to regard him simply as a poet; so that is seems a pity that Mr. Starke insists upon our seeing him also as a strong personality, as a Southern and agrarian leader.

Now it may be that Mr. Tate and Mr. Warren, in their strict examination of his verses, do not give Lanier the full benefit of their historical sense. As an American poet of 1875 he could hardly be expected to know as much about poetry as may be known by intelligent poets now, for there have come in our time a vast experimentation and a body of criticism to which he had no access. Furthermore, they may be wrong in asking of him as an occasional economist an understanding of the drift of industrial capitalism equal to that acquired painfully by our own post-War generation; Mr. Starke urges this point against them. But as for Lanier's disinterest in the contemporary realities of his section the case is exactly reversed. It cannot be counted a moral derelication today if a Southerner, or any American, is content in his attachment to the abstract nation, no longer needs his own roof-tree, and flits easily from place to place within the Union; there is at the most a question of philosophical intuition, or of taste. But the detachment of Lanier, a Southerner under Reconstruction, suggests the obtuseness which is moral. Nationalism had not begun to be one of the stereotyped liberal virtues in Lanier's South, and had no business being one, and Mr. Starke does not realize what a simple anachronism he commits in ascribing it pridefully to his hero.

Lanier discovered in himself, and undoubtedly in many Southerners, a certain softness of attitude which may be admired, perhaps, so long as it does not become too determining. It was "love"; at its highest a very fancy Platonic attitude, metaphysical, close to the religious essence, and rising into a rapport with nature and man; but in practice a temper that found it too painful to cherish resentment, and a poor thing for the South when its interest lay in maintaining against tyranny its own particularity. (pp. 557-58)

The South had lost its national voice, but it was still itself, . . . and it could not trifle with the risk of disintegration by crumbling. There was the fact that the South was being forcibly reconstructed politically. Behind that was the fact that the South, if and as it should be allowed a normal self-determination within the Union again, would have to fortify its economic and cultural patterns . . . through the most continuous and self-conscious effort. Nationalism was not an attitude which was open to the South at the moment, and it would be open, when peace did come, only with very steady reservations. But Lanier early became a burning nationalist, asking of the sections not that they, not even that his own, be anything in particular, but only that they be bound together in brotherly love.

Lanier did not have in him a normal degree of the sense of being placed or rooted anywhere. And yet it must be said that there is in him at any moment a natural piety in one sense; a love (nostalgia it amounts to when he is gone from it) for the specific physical nature of his own region. But there is an insufficient sense of the cause of this love: the specific way of living, in the provincial Georgia country. I hope, like Mr. Tate, that this is not too esoteric; I am saying that sensibility to nature is an acquired faculty, and depends on having the right working relation with nature, the right economy, rather than on having tours and picnics.

In his **Centennial Ode of 1876** Lanier interpolated a little poem which he had written years before, representing the Civil War as a joust between two noble knights, Heart and Brain. They fight, and Heart is beaten down, but Brain raises him up. The passage ends:

> Heart and Brain! no more be twain;
> Throb and think, one flesh again!
> Lo! they weep, they turn, they run;
> Lo! they kiss: Love, thou art one!

This little poem is interesting in more ways than one. If it was written, as Mr. Starke shows is possible, as early as 1862, it was not written like a soldier. And given to the world as late as 1876, it was still anticipatory rather than descriptive. Between the war and the Centennial was a long interval in which no reconciliation had occurred; on the contrary, Brain had filled the interval with humiliations for Heart; and Heart had been very surly. If the Centennial anniversary must not pass without some poet's making chivalry out of that disreputable span of history, it was doubly ironical that the burden had to be assumed by a Southern poet, by poor Lanier. Mr. Warren says of these

pretty verses that they are not realistic. I do not imagine he means by the word to criticize the representation of ugly modern warfare by a mediaeval tourney, as Mr. Starke seems to think. Poets may prefer the Ptolemaic sword to the Copernican rifle, without altering also the spirit of the occasion; but if they do that, they may be blamed for unrealism, to the extent that the occasion can no longer be identified.

But the two combatants also cannot quite be identified under the symbols of the head and the heart. I judge it was an aspiration of Lanier's that the South should lead the Union in the power of love, and that he should be its poet. As an offset to that claim, or even as a matter of fact, he was probably prepared for the North to lead in brain-power. Whatever may be said about the first of these identifications, the latter, that of the North with brain, is a concession that nobody in the Union today, I imagine, would be so cruel as to exact of a Southerner.

It might be strongly argued, and documented, that Lanier had no great opinion of the comparative Southern intelligence. There was perhaps in him something of a "defeatist complex". . . . It appeared in his self-exile from the South. . . . It appears also in his many admirations of the marvels of applied science, which were scarcely to be observed in the Southern heavens. It does not appear anywhere, so far as I can see, that he admired the Southern life for any unique merit. Possibly there was none, and in that event he is absolved. But I suspect his credentials. To him the South must have seemed "backward", to use a more recent phrase; but for his part he always looked forward.

And as to a South pre-eminent in love, and Southerners peculiarly perfected in that virtue, the identification is invidious to the North, and on the whole absurd. . . . At the moment when the expansive Sidney Lanier was seeking friends in the North, and loving them as hard as they would allow him, many other Southerners were still at home indulging in the only postwar luxury that is given to all the vanquished: hatred. They should have found something better to do. But it was not incumbent upon them to do what he was doing; the Northern friends were scarcely doing that. Students in moral philosophy find no prettier puzzle to work at than the question of what would remain to human life if it were actuated by perfect altruism. But it is only an academic puzzle, for the most part; biology does not permit us to victimize ourselves as much as we might like. Love could not solve the problems of the South in Lanier's day; no more than its problems today.

Mr. Starke, in the article, makes it his chief contention that Lanier was a good agrarian, in the sense in which Mr. Tate and Mr. Warren are publicly known to be agrarians, in the sense in which Mr. Starke intimates that he himself is an agrarian. (pp. 559-63)

There is something invincible in the champion of a poet who, not assenting to the unfavourable report that has been received upon his poetry, demands that he be examined upon his agrarianism. But it can be easily done. Things were different in this poet's time from what they are today, as Mr. Starke reminds us, and we could hardly expect him to know the answers that we would like. But it may be readily said that Lanier showed at one time or another a correct apprehension of some of the obvious evil of industrial capitalism, and of some of the benefit of agrarian farming.

"He was the first of our poets to cry out against [industrialism] as a deadly blight on life and civilization." The statement is incontrovertible and impressive. And what was the precise trouble with industrialism, or "Trade", as he liked to call it for its greater ignominy? There is this sort of thing in the **"Symphony"**:

> And ever Love hears the poor-folks' crying,
> And ever Love hears the women's sighing . . .

and this sort of thing, with more specification:

> But, oh, the poor! the poor! the poor!
> That stand by the inward-opening door
> Trade's hand doth tighten ever more,
> And sigh their monstrous foul-air sigh
> For the outside hills of Liberty,
> Where Nature spreads her wild blue sky
> For Art to make into melody!

And there is this from a letter about the novel which he never lived to write, defining its central thesis:

> . . . it is *now* the *gentleman* who must arise and overthrow *Trade*. That Chivalry . . . which does not depend upon birth but which is revelation from God, of justice, of fair dealing, of scorn of mean advantages; which contemns the selling of stock which one *knows* is going to fall to a man who *believes* it is going to rise as much as it would contemn any other form of rascality or of injustice or of manners:—it is this which must in these latter days organize its insurrections and burn up every one of the cunning moral castles from which Trade sends out its forays upon the conscience of modern society.

These passages are typical of Lanier on the industrial society, and the touch is only that of the moralist in economics. We gather that Trade is the enemy of chivalry and even of common honesty; and that the great fortunes, as they are acquired under the forms of capitalistic organization, entail at the other end of the line great destitution; two sound objections, neither an agrarian one. It was doubtless too early to see that dangerous, or possibly that fatal, flaw in the capitalistic system that we have recognized though not cured: its expansive principle, which does not permit of stability, and which secretes idle capital and idle labour at such a rate that periodic breakdowns are inevitable. Lanier was a long way behind the modern critics of industrial capitalism, but he was also a long way behind Marx. His objections are not precisely economic ones.

And what did he propose to do about these evils? If he were more explicit in his reflections upon the factory scene in the second bit above, or had other passages on this kind of scene in which he was explicit, the reader would be inclined to construe the argument thus: That the poor should never have entered the inward-opening door to earn a wage but should have remained on the outside hills and farmed them. He does not actually say it; and I believe that it does not occur to him, but that he is saying rather awkwardly that Trade, instead of tightening the door to keep them in for longer hours at smaller pay, should let them out early to go and picnic over the hills, or spend their leisure time in cultural pursuits, et cetera, et cetera. And the grand insurrection which is to rise against Trade in the projected novel is not endowed with any physical character, and is only intended to enforce reforms on the order of "fair play" and "social justice", reforms of the heart rather than of the constitution; obviously a proposition of the sort that today we would call "liberalism", meaning nothing very ef-

fectual, and certainly nothing agrarian; an activity for the debating society.

Lanier does not appear to object to the factory system as such; as one that subtracts the dignity from human labour and the aesthetic value from the product. In this respect he is behind Ruskin and Morris, his English analogues; behind them in his economic thought, and far behind them in his uneducated taste. He was a man impressed unduly by mechanical products and the new applications of science. The taste for the mechanical is a taste for the abstract, but the philosophical status of agrarianism is that it is opposed to abstraction, and as an artist Lanier should have seen that his love of the Platonic abstraction was destructive to his poetry.

And how does he represent the life of the land, which is the positive pole in any agrarianism? Many citations might be made from his verse, but . . . they would not distinguish him. The first subject of poetry is nature, and most poets are agrarians in feeling, and it is useless to attach a doctrinal importance to his songs of the land, or even his song about corn. But here is, in prose, his **"New South"**, upon which Mr. Starke banks heavily, and even a little poem or so with an economic thesis. Lanier had . . . [admired] the first reform step taken in the agriculture of the cotton belt: diversification, the substitution of corn for cotton. . . . In Lanier's time it meant principally for a long period that a farmer could get more money for his corn than for his cotton; and that is not exactly agrarianism, though agrarians would be sympathetic. But it must be added that at least once, and perhaps we might say occasionally, he put with the idea of corn the idea of subsistence farming, and there we have agrarianism beyond a doubt, perhaps its most pointed essence. Mr. Tate and Mr. Warren should not have overlooked this, though the total exhibit is slight. But subsistence farming was common enough on Southern farms, on small farms generally, in Lanier's time; if it had not been he would have made more of a show with it in the poems. It was the big Western farm which was really revolutionary, with its one money crop and its migrant workers, and it is pleasant to know that Lanier did not approve it. (pp. 564-68)

Lanier's influence upon Southern agriculture must have been small, and it was certainly, though not consciously, self-contradicting. He wrote admiringly of Georgia landscape and Georgia small farmers, but the example he set was that of leaving Georgia. He was also an uncritical nationalist. . . . There was a very definite relation between agrariansim and nationalism, which Lanier did not even suspect. And Mr. Starke seems to confess that he too does not grasp the connection even today. (pp. 568-69)

Sidney Lanier, though he might have devoted his life to the elucidation of pure agrarian theory, must have failed strategically for not being able to tell its friends from it enemies. (p. 571)

> *John Crowe Ransom, "Hearts and Heads," in* The American Review, *Vol. 2, No. 5, March, 1934, pp. 554-71.*

GAY WILSON ALLEN (essay date 1935)

[Lanier's fundamental assumption in *The Science of English Verse* is] that "there is absolutely no difference between the sound-relations used in music and those used in verse." This concept is based on a confusion of *song* and *poetry*. It is generally believed that poetry originated as song, and poems

today are frequently written to be sung. . . . [But] the articulation (which of course includes ''sound-relations'') of words
spoken or read and of those which are sung is distinctly different. The time relations between spoken English syllables
are very complicated and precarious . . . ; whereas in singing,
the time relations are fixed by the musical composition, the
voice modulating the pronunciation to fit the music. . . . (pp.
278-79)

Lanier's desire to explain English versification by the principles
of music lead him astray, however, when he takes the stand
(which is logical after his first fundamental but erroneous assumption) that *time* is the only important element in the rhythm
of verse. (p. 279)

That the pronunciation of syllables does consume units of time
and that, therefore, time is one important element in verse is
so obvious that it is trite; but laboratory experiments have
shown that the actual time covered in the pronunciation of
syllables in English verse varies so greatly that it is impossible
either to write or read (naturally) a passage so that the series
of sounds are even proportionately equal. Thus accent . . . is
the *only* element in English verse which is sufficiently rhythmical for us to measure outside the laboratories of the physicist
and the applied psychologist.

Lanier speaks frequently of his own laboratory experiments at
Johns Hopkins, but such a theory of English prosody as he
held was based on an hypothesis *ad hoc.* And it is essentially
the same as Poe's, despite Lanier's belief that he disagreed
with Poe. For one of the cardinal doctrines of [Poe's] *The
Rationale of Verse* is that every foot is equal in time to every
other foot in the line of verse. (p. 280)

Lanier tried out his ''system'' [of musical analysis and nota-
tion] extensively on Anglo-Saxon verse, which contains usually
four accented syllables to the line but an indefinite number of
unaccented ones. By giving a time value to pauses and silences,
he demonstrated that the Anglo-Saxon line can be read with
equivalent duration for each bar [i.e., foot]. (p. 281)

There is no doubt that Anglo-Saxon verse can be sung (and
possibly was) in this manner. But whether modern poetry,
based only partly on Anglo-Saxon traditions and usually not
intended to be sung, should be *read* to such a scheme . . . is
a different matter. (p. 282)

Probably not one person in one hundred, reading naturally,
will ''time'' the ''bars''—even proportionately—as . . . [Lan-
ier's musical] notations demand. It is the artificiality of the
system which is objectionable. (p. 283)

In summing up Lanier's contribution to the *science* of American
prosody, we must emphasize his intentions more than his actual
accomplishments though one great tribute to his actual accomplishments is the fact that metrists still find his treatise useful.
Yet he deserves great credit for approaching his subject scientifically, and (as part of the scientific method) experimen-
tally. That his experiments were not sufficiently extensive and
complete is of course true, and his own musical talent and
predilections caused him to set up an untenable major hypothesis, but a great part of his treatise is scientifically correct, and
all of it is challenging and suggestive. (pp. 284-85)

[It] is doubtful whether any other prosodist has presented the
quantity argument with so much clarity and force as we find
in *The Science of English Verse.* (p. 285)

Gay Wilson Allen, ''Sidney Lanier,'' in his American
Prosody, *American Book Company, 1935, pp. 277-
306.*

EDD WINFIELD PARKS   (essay date 1936)

[*In his introduction to* Southern Poets, *excerpted below, Parks
assesses Lanier's achievement as a prosodist and as a poet. He
criticizes Lanier for confusing poetry with music in* The Science
of English Verse, *echoing H. L. Mencken's belief that Lanier had
neglected the idea-content of poetry in his prosodic theory (1922).
While Parks claims that the majority of Lanier's poems are spoiled
by didacticism, he maintains that Lanier ''approached greatness''
when he wrote spontaneously.*]

The title alone [of *The Science of English Verse*] reveals one
fundamental misconception: there is an art of poetry, a technique of versification—but a *science of verse* is a contradiction
of terms. The second fundamental error is Lanier's confusion
of art-forms, his belief in the identity of music and poetry:
''The art of sound must always be regarded the genus, and
music and verse its two species. Prose, scientifically considered, is a wild variety of verse. . . . When we hear verse, we
hear a set of relations between sounds; when we silently read
verse, we *see* that which brings to us a set of relations between
sounds; when we imagine verse, we *imagine* a set of relations
between sounds.'' (p. lxxiii)

With these and similar statements Lanier dismisses the vital
element of intellectual content. That, one may say, he took for
granted, although this supposition will, of itself, damage his
theory considerably. . . . Less obvious but equally important
is another factor which weakens his theory: although words
and music may, as Richard Wagner observed, complement
each other, one can never replace the other. In attempting that
replacement, which necessarily required an identity between
the two forms, Lanier failed. . . . (pp. lxxiii-lxxiv)

[Lanier] concluded his volume with a one-page chapter which
says that his science consists only of hints, not laws; that ''For
the artist in verse there is no law: the perception and love of
beauty constitute the whole outfit; and what is herein set forth
is to be taken merely as enlarging that perception and exalting
that love. In all cases, the appeal is to the ear. . . .'' Of what
value, ultimately, is this platitude? Is the body of the study as
valueless as its hypothesis and its conclusion? When all the
false and worthless elements are stripped away, certain other
elements of value do remain, but they are suggestive hints on
the relation of melody and harmony to words, on the complementary nature of music and words. This value itself is not
what Lanier intended, for he considered the laws of these arts
as identical.

That Sidney Lanier was consciously aware of pictorial as well
as harmonic qualities in his verse is apparent from reading the
''Hymns of the Marshes,'' the **''Song of the Chattahoochee,''**
or half a dozen other of his poems. That he was in part a local
colorist can be discerned in his novel, *Tiger Lilies,* in *Florida,*
with its gorgeous word pictures, and in his dialect poems. . . .
''Thar's More in the Man Than Thar is in the Land'' is not
distinguished poetry, but it warrants the title of Lanier's most
popular poem, and it is a good example of local color poetry.
Essentially, however, Lanier wanted to get away from a section
where old values were rapidly disintegrating. . . . This is not
the mood of the local colorist, but of one who desires to be in
the vanguard of change. It is not surprising that Sidney Lan-

ier . . . never developed a theory of local color, never developed his beginnings in that field of writing. (pp. lxxv-lxxvii)

When as poet he attempted only to feel and to see, Lanier approached greatness. (p. cxvi)

[He] sometimes forgets his unassimilated reading, forgets his belief that the artist must be "afire with moral beauty just as with physical beauty," forgets his philosophy, and writes. Then he becomes the poet. Then he writes such valid and impressive poems as the artless and spontaneously spiritual **"Ballad of Trees and the Master"** and the quick-moving, brutal, uncharacteristic **"Revenge of Hamish."**

When one forgets the message intended for the brain and concentrates on the pictorial harmonies intended for eye and ear, one can find a definite beauty in **"Sunrise"** and **"Song of the Chattahoochee."** In this he excelled. With good reason have critics acclaimed **"The Marshes of Glynn"** his finest poem; the philosophical moral is bedded so deeply that the reader is hardly conscious of it, while the gorgeous sweep of scene is carried by an uneven melodious effect which weaves and twists through forest patterns, through the live-oaks and the marsh-grass, the marsh and the sea. The effect is hypnotic. . . . (p. cxvii)

In his spontaneous lyrics and his sensuous descriptive verse Lanier achieves striking and original effects. I do not refer to his virtuosity in such a poem as **"The Symphony"**. . . . That is only a clever experiment in technique by a dexterous artificer, which concentrates attention on the superficial form. In better and less obvious poems he skillfully used alliteration, tone color, vowel sounds, and mixed rhythms to give musical effects and pictorial values: the ultimate effect is that of a richly embroidered sensuosity, which, unlike Swinburne's, never shades into sensuality. Only when he neglects his philosophy does he write authentic poetry. For that reason it is impossible to agree with John Macy [see excerpt above, 1913] that only "three volumes of unimpeachable poetry have been written in America, 'Leaves of Grass,' the thin volume of Poe, and the poetry of Sidney Lanier" (there are, also, Emerson and Timrod and Emily Dickinson). In Lanier's case the elimination of bad poems must be too drastic. Yet, in the six or eight which remain, there is the distinctive mark of a poet who wrote far better than he knew, who achieved a limited but fine body of work which in the main is unlike that which greater poets have done. (pp. cxvii-cxviii)

> *Edd Winfield Parks, in an introduction to* Southern Poets, *edited by Edd Winfield Parks, American Book Company, 1936, pp. xvii-cxxix.*

CONRAD AIKEN   (letter date 1941)

> [*In an effort to assess Lanier's influence on modern writers, Edwin R. Coulson solicited the testimony of Aiken, an American poet, critic, and fiction writer. Aiken's comments, which downplay Lanier's influence, may be compared with the positive testimony of Edwin Harris (1941) and Harriet Monroe (1941).*]

I'm afraid I can't say that Lanier ever influenced me, nor was he ever among my enthusiasms. Nor do I think that he has had much or any influence on the modern poet—though of course I may be wrong. I hadn't thought of him for years—but I remember a time when I was an undergraduate at Harvard—1908 or so—when he became a momentary enthusiasm, if only because he was relatively obscure, and Southern. (pp. 76-7)

> *Conrad Aiken, in an extract from a letter to Edwin R. Coulson, in* Sidney Lanier: Poet and Prosodist *by Richard Webb and Edwin R. Coulson, University of Georgia Press, 1941, pp. 76-7.*

EDWARD HARRIS   (letter date 1941)

[Lanier] has long been my favorite American poet; perhaps my favorite of all, but Keats comes close in my affection. I believe Lanier has never received the recognition he deserves, mainly because of the War and because of the literary exile into which the South went after the War—whether voluntarily or not, the results were the same. I think Lanier had Poe's music and more; Poe always seemed to me a bit shoddy and a bit too French—a bit showy and "pretty." Besides, Lanier had ideas, perhaps ideas that time will prove as rich as any Emerson muddied up and a lot easier to grasp. (pp. 80-1)

> *Edward Harris, in an extract from a letter to Edwin R. Coulson in* Sidney Lanier: Poet and Prosodist *by Richard Webb and Edwin R. Coulson, University of Georgia Press, 1941, pp. 80-1.*

HARRIET MONROE   (letter date 1941)

> [*Monroe, the founding editor of* Poetry: A Magazine of Verse *and a poet in her own right, agreed with the principles Lanier set forth in* The Science of English Verse, *if not with his own use of them. In response to Edwin R. Coulson's query regarding Lanier's influence, she testifies that the treatise influenced her own poetic technique and all her thinking about poetic rhythms. Monroe's statement that* The Science of English Verse *"lays the foundation for a modern science of prosody" is in line with the criticism of T. S. Omond (1921). Monroe died in 1936; the above date reflects the first publication of her letter to Coulson.*]

When I was twenty or less I read with profound agreement Lanier's *Science of English Verse,* which I still think lays the foundation for a modern science of prosody. Prosody, as it is still usually taught, is as medieval and as absurdly confusing, in my opinion, as astrology; but astronomy has replaced astrology, whereas, the old absurd prosody is still taught.

No doubt Lanier's book influenced my own technique and all my thinking about poetic rhythms, but I never cared greatly for Lanier's own work in use.

> *Harriet Monroe, in an extract from a letter to Edwin R. Coulson, in* Sidney Lanier: Poet and Prosodist *by Richard Webb and Edwin R. Coulson (reprinted by permission of The University of Georgia Press; © 1941 by The University of Georgia Press), University of Georgia Press, 1941, p. 91.*

CLARENCE GOHDES   (essay date 1945)

> [*Like many of Lanier's critics, Gohdes primarily approaches* The English Novel *not as polished criticism, but as a collection of unrevised lectures. His remarks on Lanier's treatment of personality refer to Lanier's theory that the human personality has undergone a refining process of evolution, a historical development reflected in literature "from Aeschylus to George Eliot."*]

The reader who approaches [the lectures published in *The English Novel*] with the purpose of being informed about the English novelists will be inevitably disappointed. Chaotic, deficient in facts, they nevertheless present at least a toying with a number of literary topics of considerable importance. By all odds the chief of these is the evolution of a relatively "real-istic" psychology in the treatment of personality—a development which continues to mark the progress of the literature of the present century, especially the more intellectual novels. Here Lanier put his finger on one of the essential major characteristics of literature since the Renaissance. Here he really demonstrated a remarkable advance "from Aeschylus to George Eliot." It is interesting to observe that the psychology of personality is a subject to which Americans are especially devoted, and Lanier must be remembered as one of our first critics to project a lengthy application of it to the history of literature. He is also one of our earliest commentators on the principles of "naturalism" as set forth in Zola's *Le roman expérimental.*

In general, however, *The English Novel* should be viewed not as an incomplete trifling with certain important ideas or a pioneer effort in criticism, but as a series of "extension" lectures interspersed with a plethora of illustrative readings. As such, they are probably as good as the average run of similar performances. The world has surely outgrown the prudery of Lanier's day, and there is little wit or verbal felicity to redeem his critical opinions, but it is worthy of remark that most of the specimens which he selected for reading are still considered "good literature." Could one ask more from any "extension" course sixty years afterwards? (pp. x-xi)

> *Clarence Gohdes, in an introduction to* The Centennial Edition of the Works of Sidney Lanier: "The English Novel" and Essays on Literature, Vol. IV *by Sidney Lanier, edited by Clarence Gohdes and Kemp Malone (copyright 1945, The Johns Hopkins Press; copyright renewed © 1973 by Charles R. Anderson), The Johns Hopkins University Press, 1945, pp. vii-xi.*

GARLAND GREEVER (essay date 1945)

[*Greever provides what is perhaps the closest critical examination of* Tiger-Lilies. *While he concedes that the narrative is rife with defects, Greever compares the work favorably with other war fiction of the Civil War era and praises Lanier's realistic depiction of the character and dialect of the Pike County mountaineer.*]

Tiger-Lilies is not homogeneous in either matter or form. As a narrative it succeeds in spots, is a failure as a whole. Nobody ever read it through for the fiction's sake. (p. xv)

Certain incidents are sinewy and believable. Especially so are the deer hunt in Book I, and in Book II Cain's ruse for routing the marauders, his reaction (both emotional and verbal) to his brother's recreancy, Gorm's return to what had been home, the charge of the Confederate battleline, the prison scenes, and in general the life and talk of soldiers. These convince because of their closeness to reality. But the intervening atmosphere is remote and the movement sluggish. Outside of Book II the narrative nowhere really marches.

The characterization likewise is weak in the aggregate, though in several minor instances and two or three major ones original and promising. Percymmon, crass exponent of Trade, is a man of straw dangling in a void. The prisoners, on the contrary, if sometimes extravagantly limned, speak and act as a rule with homely verity. In the main plot are four categories of leading persons—cultured summer visitors, transcendental German exiles (with anguished memories), illiterate mountaineers, and villains. Their flesh and blood values vary in inverse ratio to their social standing. Only now and again do the visitors acquire any measure of vitality. The Germans are still more tenuously

connected with a recognizable world. The mountaineer Cain is unique in that he strides through three books as a human being. Gorm, mountaineer and villain, and the only other prominent character in Book II who apparently was not thought of til Book 1 was finished, is not given a sympathetic role—Lanier could not condone evasion of public duty—but has the understanding and even the sympathy due one who suffers because of the draft. Cranston, villain and representative of Bohemianism and Trade, attains self-realization, ceases to be a mere abstraction, and, like Gorm, comes partly alive. (pp. xvi-xvii)

[The] mood and effect of the volume are exuberant amateurism. That the author was a young man may be seen in the humor, in the intricacy of some of the craftsmanship, and in the lyrical strain.

The humor is abundant and somewhat varied, though frequently of a kind that has not worn well. Often it turns to far-fetched puns and practical jokes involving physical discomfort. Again, it pokes fun at somebody or something—through respectful gibes, as at John Sterling during the deer hunt; through burlesque, as of Mrs. Parven at the ball; through obvious satire, as of Percymmon; or once at least (in touches regarding the war-flower) through irony so detached and mordant as to bring [Jonathan Swift's] "A Modest Proposal" to mind. Yet again, and somewhere between its boisterous and its intellectual aspects, it is sheer glad-hearted response to the world's geniality, perhaps reveling in quirk of phrase or fancy, perhaps simply a-tingle with inner satisfaction.

The craftsmanship is too often indirect or oversubtle. In his poetry Lanier could deliberately scaffold his meaning about with ingenious carpentry. In his prose likewise he again and again could abandon forthrightness. With a native aptitude for detecting similarities, he filled—and overfilled—his works with comparisons, which he tended to expand into "anaconda conceits" or even into allegories. The image of the war-flower at the beginning of Book II makes that chapter the best known in the novel. But the figure may be deemed more clever than appropriate; a flower is too frail to symbolize adequately the destructiveness of war, especially when the comparison is sustained and elaborated.

The poetry springs from a young man's awareness of the immanence of beauty. Lanier saw loveliness everywhere. In presenting it to readers he pressed comparisons into service. Some of these . . . show artifice. Some are so protracted as to stifle narrative. But the best have a spontaneity and an unexpectedness hardly short of breath-taking. (pp. xvii-xviii)

[*Tiger-Lilies* is not primarily a war novel; but, had] Lanier set out to make it such, it should surpass everything in the field except [John William De Forest's] *Miss Ravenel's Conversion.* (p. xxviii)

Tiger-Lilies makes use of several conventions of war fiction in the South and of others of war fiction in the whole country. It savors the life of a cultivated household. It marshals youth accustomed to the genteel manner. It admits wandering ladies, not indeed to battlefields, but to the downfall of the Confederate capital. It pictures (in the Smallins) the house divided. It has a man from the North (Cranston) in love with a girl from the South (Felix). But it tempers these materials with a moderation foreign to most war novels. The youths are not too baronially exalted. Femininity is kept from the front until the hurried last scenes. Brother is pitted against brother naturally and effectively. Between Northern man and Southern girl is raised no barrier of sectionalism.

The novel differs from nearly all rivals in its closeness to the actualities of warfare. Though it is not fully or consistently realistic, . . . it has a preserving salt of realism. It catches the accent of soldier talk, the trials of the infantry, the hilarities and the hazards of scouting, the scarcity of food and clothing in the South in 1864, the loneliness of isolated civilians, the demoralizing effects of captivity, the moods of battle . . . , and other aspects of the time and milieu.

Yet it escapes the perturbation and the seething immediacy of many war novels. Its mood is emotion recollected in tranquillity. (pp. xxviii-xxix)

It carries no illusions about armed strife. Though appreciative of the self-sacrifices and heroisms, it is equally sensible of the "frauds and corruptions and thefts." It perceives that "a rich man's war" may be "a poor man's fight." So convinced has its author become, by the year following Appomattox, that conflict is futile that he takes his stand as an unqualified pacifist: "If war was ever right, then Christ was always wrong."

It is uniquely non-partisan. It neither proclaims nor intimates that this section or cause is superior to that. It is neither defiant nor abject at the outcome of the conflict. Nowhere does it boast. Nowhere does it apologize.

Finally, it radiates good will. (p. xxix)

The announced theme of *Tiger-Lilies* is love. That Lanier truly adheres to this theme, and exemplifies it, is a feat without parallel among the war novels of the era.

As portrayal of the mountaineer *Tiger-Lilies* relates itself to literary tendencies of the day and shows Lanier in rapport with the indigenous in American life. (p. xxx)

He does not render [mountain speech], to be sure, with entire consistency. He perhaps segregates it less rigorously than he might from other patois, as that of Georgia crackers in his subsequent poems. He may have mixed what his ears told him with what his eyes found in printed works like [William Tappan] Thompson's. But he is artistic and reasonably faithful in his use of the vernacular. The pungency of colloquialisms and the pith of idioms are in his lines, and for simple eloquence unfalteringly sustained Cain's rebuke to Gorm is the noblest passage in the volume.

In portraying his mountaineers he at times resorts to artifice. Cain's talk about the elephants, in Book I, Chapter II, has a forced, almost a freakish, note. Gorm's gaucherie and gluttony at the restaurant, in Book II, Chapter XI, accord with that stock device of the local colorists, the outlandish character in incongruous surroundings. Cain is foisted upon a squad of gentlemen for effect rather than from need.

But Lanier does not set the mountain folk, and above all the Smallins, before us as mere Pike County curiosities. He does not make them shiftless, taciturn, and queer, as their kind came to be represented. He portrays them as individuals. Cain, with the resinous smell of the mountains about him, is the most vital character in the novel. Gorm, repulsive and grotesque at first, becomes less abnormal as he returns to the haunts from which he was conscripted against his interests and his desire. When he stands by the ashes of his home and the grave of his wife he changes into a human being.

In the movement toward maturing realism [in American literature], *Tiger-Lilies* has its place. It is not one of the first works to delineate [the character of the Pike County Man] or employ local color. It is, however, one of the very first to exhibit these tendencies, not in sketches or stories, but in a novel. It may be classed with the earlier ventures through its emphasis on regionalism, through its riotous farce, through its artistic unripeness, and through its sharing in the sudden expansion and rapid development in the use of dialect. It differs from the earlier ventures in here and there merging its melodrama into drama, in levying somewhat extensively upon the actual, and in advancing as far as it does toward realism. More nearly than these tentative, pioneer works it spans the major aspects of the movement as a whole. (pp. xxxi-xxxii)

> *Garland Greever, in an introduction to* The Centennial Edition of the Works of Sidney Lanier: "Tiger-Lillies" and Southern Prose, Vol. V *by Sidney Lanier, edited by Garland Greever with Cecil Abernethy (copyright 1945, The Johns Hopkins Press), The Johns Hopkins University Press, 1945, pp. vii-lx.*

LEWIS LEARY   (essay date 1947)

[*In his review of* The Centennial Edition of the Works of Sidney Lanier, *excerpted below, Leary departs from Allen Tate (1933), Robert Penn Warren (1933), and John Crowe Ransom (1934) by refusing to consider Lanier an "embarrassment" to Southern letters. Although he acknowledges that Lanier never succeeded in articulating his transcendent vision of existence, he maintains that "none need be ashamed" that he attempted to do so.*]

[Lanier's] head was forever among the stars, and he seems never to have learned enough of language or himself to translate what he found of vision there into other than conventional generalities. His *Tiger-Lilies* is unreadable, not so much because of bad models in Novalis and Longfellow, but because it never succeeds in saying what Lanier must have meant it to say. It is a young man's headful of ideas, allowed to churn meaninglessly because the words he had learned got in the way of his expression. So the pieces gathered as **"Southern Prose"** . . . also represent Lanier at his loquacious and inarticulate worst. His models seem often the grandfathers of Senator Claghorn, and the tight-clenched sincerity of what he meant cannot, even in tolerance, gainsay such things as his approval of photography as an "etherealization" of painting because it portrays "little ones saying prayers at mothers' knees" rather than "bloody heeled conquerors soiling the plains", . . . or the funeral oration in which, after picturing partners, colleagues, brethren of the bar, admirers, and friends glorifying the tomb of the deceased with floral offerings, Lanier portrays himself as one who "steals in modestly and quietly, and as it were in secret lets fall his humble violet from the woods upon the glorious pile of homage, dropping thereon his unobtrusive tear." Surely, the English language and sincerity of grief have seldom been more unfeelingly profaned. (pp. 266-67)

[The] honeyed tone and heightened phrase become as much a part of Lanier's personality as his straight, black beard and his deep-set, consumptive's eyes. His own words seem to have acted on Lanier much as did the playing of sweet music, suggestive of meaning never expressed. . . . [They] served as an opiate which allowed him to escape the traps of poverty, obscurity, and disease which mortality had laid for him, to soar for a moment to a pure atmosphere of his own making, where love ruled as kindly despot and where coughs and the ugly noise of trade had no place. Such luxurance of expression . . .

became his natural idiom . . . , the best he could find to communicate the warm glow of understanding with which the words themselves transfused him.

But our rational generation would make a thinker out of each of its prophets. And Lanier presents himself as a man of very few thoughts. He did draw both the evolutionary doctrines of the late nineteenth century and an earlier romantic perfectionism into his tolerant embrace to explain what he called the "etherealization" of all things from gross to spiritual manifestations, but his exposition could have convinced few, even of his generation, except as it reinforced their desire to believe that all things work together toward good. His reaction against trade and his championship of love as a panacea for earthly ills was certainly less intellectual than emotional. Even his theories of art, specifically his analogies between music and poetry, grew from his attempt to transfer to words the exquisitely sweet feelings which music induced and were the results of feeling rather than thought. Like most of us, Lanier seems to have been an enthusiastic rationalizer of what he believed to be true. (pp. 267-68)

[Lanier's letters] bring us as close as we have probably ever been brought to the day-by-day workings of an artist's mind. Lanier writes with no audience in view except the person to whom he is writing. Now he is the poet misunderstood, . . . ridiculing the "tobacco-sodden bosh such as Southern editors are prone to eject." Now he brags: whatever the world's estimate, he had "never yet failed to win favor with an artist." We, more properly schooled in reticence, may be embarrassed by the unrestrained outpourings of his love for Mary Day Lanier or by his proudly innocent flirtations with other women. We may be repelled by his intensity throughout. But the man finally revealed is—we must borrow his favorite words to describe him—infinitely sweet and courageous, to the point that we are again tempted to agree that Lanier's life was incomparably his greatest poem. (p. 268)

[Many critics have maintained that Lanier] was first and spontaneously a musician, only secondly and more artificially a poet. However this may be, the possibility of Lanier's ever having attained breadth of achievement as a creative musician . . . must be discounted by his critical attitude toward music. His approach to it was literary. He expected it to say things. It did say things to him, of cavaliers and fair ladies, of huntsmen and wooded glens, of flirtations and minuets. As Edwin Mims has said, "He saw music as he heard poetry." And he felt music, as "a great, pure, unanalyzable yearning after God." Music was thus the matrix, not only of Lanier's personality and profound religious belief, but of his artistic creed: "Language is a species of music." The poet expressed the unexpressable, so that "every poet worthy of that name must in his essential utterance belong to the School of David." He is the "Forlorn Hope that marches ahead of mankind," singing even truths which are belied by appearances. (p. 270)

It was not only, as Lanier said of Poe, that he did not know enough. . . . [He died] without opportunity ever to mold what he did know into forms which more than suggested his meaning. . . . [He] was allowed neither time nor tranquillity properly to examine himself or the words to which he intrusted his interpretation of what Virginia Woolf called the "luminous halo" which surrounds existence.

Another way of expressing much the same thing might be to say that Lanier simply never matured, or, better, that amid the febrile business of his life, he never allowed himself oppor-

tunity for maturity. His reach so far exceeded his grasp that the [*Centennial Edition of the Works of Sidney Lanier*] may seem, as someone has said, a cumbersomely large pedestal for a very small statue. But Lanier's acknowledgment of literary debts to Emerson, Whitman, Poe, and Hayne, and the ample suggestions offered [in the *Centennial Edition*] and elsewhere that he has spoken in our generation to Vachel Lindsay, Carl Sandburg, Harriet Munroe [*sic*], perhaps to Robert Frost, place him unequivocally within the main current of American poetry. He knew, as did Walter Pater, that "all art constantly aspires." And he knew, as Milton knew, that only very great men write great poems. It is not difficult to pick him apart, to expose, as he exposed better than any commentator, his grievous deficiencies. He stood for a moment breathlessly on tiptoe to see beyond sectional, beyond national boundaries to a world of spirit, which all men might enter. Though the mysterious regions he dared explore with such meager equipment yielded him few poems which measure to his standards or ours, none need be ashamed of Sidney Lanier, or embarrassed that his was a forlorn hope. He knew, as W. H. Auden said many decades after him, that "we must love one another or die." And he knew, most surely, that "beauty dieth not, and the heart that needs it will find it." (pp. 270-71)

Lewis Leary, "The Forlorn Hope of Sidney Lanier," in South Atlantic Quarterly *(reprinted by permission of the Publisher; copyright © 1947, copyright renewed © 1974, by Duke University Press, Durham, North Carolina), Vol. XLVI, No. 2, April, 1947, pp. 263-71.*

JOHN GOULD FLETCHER (essay date 1949)

[*An American poet and prose writer, Fletcher won recognition early in the twentieth century as an Imagist poet and innovator of polyphonic prose. Subsequently at the forefront of the Agrarian movement, which he left in 1947, Fletcher was awarded the Pulitzer Prize for Poetry in 1939 for his* Selected Prose. *Fletcher felt that, by dismissing him as a "confused romantic," Lanier's modern critics were overlooking his achievements. In the following essay, he compares Lanier favorably with several prominent nineteenth-century poets and praises him as an insightful prosodist. Himself the author of several symphonic compositions in verse, Fletcher agrees with Lanier's fundamental analogy between music and poetry.*]

[Just what Lanier achieved in his poems] might best be stated if we attempt to compare his work mentally with that of Gerald Manley Hopkins who was so largely his contemporary. . . . Hopkins, like Lanier, felt he had two vocations, as poet and painter, but unlike Lanier, his occasional devotion to another art only aided and abetted his poetry. Not only this, but Hopkins early acquired a body of philosophical ideas from Thomas Aquinas and Duns Scotus which did valiant service in defining and limiting and clarifying his own tendency toward romantic pantheism. In the case of Lanier, in the two unquestioned masterpieces of his art, the **"Sunrise"** and **"The Marshes of Glynn,"** there is no final religious creed to be found but that of complete pantheism, an entire surrender of man to nature:

Ye lispers, whisperers, singers in storms,
Ye consciences murmuring faiths under forms,
Ye ministers meet for each passion that grieves,
Friendly, sisterly, sweetheart leaves.
Oh, rain me down from your darks that contain me,
Wisdom ye winnow from winds that pain me—

This recalls, though in a more elaborate way, Swinburne's constant substitution of sound for sense. . . . Lanier was a poet hallucinated by sound alone, to an even greater extent than Swinburne had been. This fact limits, and defines as well, the quality of his thinking—always inferior to his power of sensation.

The **"Marshes of Glynn"** has the same hypnotic and rhapsodic quality that carries us quite away from definite ideas, to a realm where sensation is more than thought—and in addition it has perhaps an even clearer, because a more visual, quality in its presentation:

> Sinuous southward and sinuous northward the
>   shimmering band
> Of the sand-beach fastens the fringe of the marsh to the
>   folds of the land.
> Inward and outward to northward and southward the
>   beachlines linger and curl
> As a silver-wrought garment that clings to and follows
>   the firm sweet limbs of a girl.
> Vanishing, swerving, evermore curving again into sight,
> Softly the sand-beach wavers away to a dim gray
>   looping of light.

The skill with which vowel sounds are here combined with consonants is certainly not inferior to that displayed anywhere by Swinburne. In fact, for their more subtle variations of metrical effect, I am inclined to think these lines (along with several others by the American poet) are better than anything done by the English one. If we prefer Hopkins to either Swinburne or Lanier, it is not because Hopkins was a better craftsman, but because his poems gain a heightened effect from the sheer hazardous beauty by which the English Jesuit leaps from natural pantheism to Christian dogma and back again. Neither Swinburne nor Lanier had this degree of *mental* intensity and dexterity.

"The Symphony" . . . must be counted as a failure, for two reasons. In the first place, as Calvin S. Brown has pointed out [see Additional Bibliography] . . . , Lanier nowhere suggests a progression from theme to theme: after a good general introduction, and several interpolated instrumental solos, the single movement lapses not into a fugue, built up of contrasting and amplified themes, but into Lanier's bland statement that "life" is a "sea fugue writ from east to west"—a statement not overburdened with any concreteness. This leads up to the second fault of the **"Symphony"**: the substitution of abstract ideas for definite and concrete conceptions. (pp. 98-9)

[**"The Psalm of the West"**] is shot through and through with . . . abstractions, and is a monument of misplaced ingenuity. Unfortunately, one realizes while reading it (it is very nearly unreadable) that Lanier was, despite all his hatred of commercialism, all his worship of knightly chivalry, a moralistic Puritan to the core—always denying the direct appeal of experience upon the senses, out of which his best poetry came; and always substituting for it the Platonic Ideal. His poetry, for just that reason, has lost its appeal to the moderns. . . . Had Lanier been either more realistic, "hankering, gross, mystical, nude," in the sense of Whitman, or more definitely cross-grained and theological as Hopkins was, he would have made, altogether, a greater poet.

"Corn," however, seems to me an unqualified success, though many of Lanier's critics have not agreed with me. There is just enough plot and contrast of theme, between the flourishing corn-field described and the deserted hillside field, now gullied-

out and wasted, where cotton once reigned supreme, to make this poem one of Lanier's finest achievements. (p. 100)

"The Revenge of Hamish," with its direct and savage forcefulness of narrative, is certainly among Lanier's finest poems—and with its burden of tragic irony, reveals that he might have been a somewhat greater narrative poet than Longfellow ever was, either in "Hiawatha," or in "Evangeline" or "Tales of the Wayside Inn." . . . [It] is a miracle of modern and modulated versification, according to the principles which its author dealt with so lovingly in *The Science of English Verse*. The whole underlying idea of Hopkins' later innovations in "sprung rhythm" is set out by the last stanza, in unmistakable terms:

> And gazed hungrily o'er, and the blood from his back
>   drip-dripped in the brine,
> And a sea-hawk flung down a skeleton fish as he flew;
> And the mother stared white on the waste of blue,
> And the wind drove a cloud to seaward, and the sun
>   began to shine.

Each of these lines is *temporally* equivalent to the others, though no one would know this fact by measuring feet, or counting syllables; since the rhythm shifts from a furious presto pace to a slow lento adagio. Truly no better example could be cited of what Lanier was capable of by way of variation in his own verses. (pp. 100-01)

[Lanier's early poem **"The Jacquerie"**] contains several fine lyrics and represents him at his most romantic. There are strange, beautiful passages in it, akin in nightmare quality to Poe, and also not unlike the Shelley who wrote "The Sensitive Plant" and the "Triumph of Life." I myself rank it rather higher than do most of Lanier's critics. Its place in his poetry recalls somewhat that of "Hyperion" in Keats' production. It is unfinished—and it is full of suggestive ideas.

All this would indicate that Lanier ranks rather higher as a poet than most judges of poetry today would admit. (p. 101)

[Lanier's *The Science of English Verse* is a] final and irrefutable challenge to all who, like George Saintsbury [see excerpt above, 1923] and the Academics in general, scan poetry by the stress and the foot alone. . . . [Lanier's] chief arguments that verse is at one and the same time a set of specially related sounds, rhythm ("series of sounds and silences with primary reference to their duration"), tune, and tone-color are altogether unanswerable. . . .

If the moderns would but read this poetic testament, then all the dry dessications of irony, and the tortured ingenuities of idea evident in so much modern poetry would tend to disappear. T. S. Eliot himself, if we are to judge his achievement on the basis of "Ash Wednesday" and the "Four Quartets," seems to be perfectly aware that the basic structure of poetry is—as Lanier contended—musical; and Eliot uses his ideas and symbols in musical development, repetition, and progression in temporal (not formal) sequence in these two works. Nor need we deny the early objection that Frost seems to have felt, that Lanier's handling of the language is artificial, and that he paid but little attention to normal conversational speech rhythm. . . . It is a strange fact about poetry, that while the rhetoric of one day and age passes and is altered, the poetry—in its highest essence—always remains. This is truly the case with Sidney Lanier, who has had one reader for every ten who have mistakenly supposed that Longfellow, Lowell and Holmes wrote better poetry. Unlike these, he was not totally bound by the conventions of Victorian verse. His revolt may have been more emotional than reasoned; but a revolt it was—and he remains a figure pathetic, but also challenging—a poet who had barely worked out a new and possible *method* before death took all away. (p. 102)

                    John Gould Fletcher, "Sidney Lanier," in The University of Kansas City Review, *Vol. XVI, No. 2,*
                    Winter, 1949, pp. 97-102.

JAY B. HUBBELL (essay date 1954)

[Hubbell's remarks appear at the conclusion of his lengthy discussion of Lanier's poetic career in The South in American Literature. *In part, the criticism excerpted below reflects his preceding depiction of Lanier as a poet vainly struggling to support himself in an age that valued prose.]*

In spite of the obstacles which confronted [Lanier], he did manage to produce a handful of poems which give him a secure place among the American poets. (p. 770)

[He had really begun his poetic career only seven years before his death.] In that time he had written **"The Revenge of Hamish," "A Ballad of Trees and the Master," "The Song of the Chattahoochee,"** and **"The Marshes of Glynn"** and its companion poems, which for many readers added a new beauty to the Georgia coast country so unlike anything else celebrated in American poetry. In his Macon period he had written **"Life and Song"** and **"Nirvâna,"** which are as good as all but the best of his later poems. He is not as great a poet as Whitman, whose background and methods were so different, or Emily Dickinson, whose name he probably never heard; but if we leave aside these two, Lanier was beyond question the most important American poet to emerge in the later nineteenth century.

One cannot help admiring the man Lanier and sympathizing with him in his struggle to be the great poet he felt he might become; and yet regretfully one concludes that he never fully understood his own endowment and his limitations. . . . In spite of his study of the English classics and of the technique of verse, he remained fundamentally an improviser, a poet of impressive fragments, not an expert craftsman like Poe tirelessly revising a poem until it became the perfect embodiment of a thought. His feverish reading in science, fiction, and poetry had no great effect upon the poems he composed. He believed in the prophetic function of the poet, but what most impresses those who read his verses is not his message but the word music and the magical pictures of the Georgia coast country. It is a hard thing to say, but one feels in some of Lanier's poems the strained language and the tumult of emotions in the breast of a sick and harried man. He might have written as Melville wrote of his own difficulties to Hawthorne: "The calm, the coolness, the silent grass-growing mood in which a man *ought* always to compose,—that, I fear, can seldom be mine. Dollars damn me; and the malicious Devil is forever grinning in upon me, holding the door ajar. . . . What I feel most moved to write, that is banned,—it will not pay. " (pp. 770-71)

                    Jay B. Hubbell, "The New South, 1865-1900: Sidney
                    Lanier," in his The South in American Literature:
                    1607-1900, *Duke University Press, 1954, pp. 758-*
                    76.

ROBERT H. ROSS (essay date 1961)

[In his essay on "The Marshes of Glynn," Ross explores what he perceives as flaws in the poem's structure, syntax, symbols,

and "message." *Like Hyatt H. Waggoner (1968), he suggests that Lanier did not come to terms with the philosophical implications of his conception of nature.]*

"The Marshes of Glynn" is Lanier's finest nature hymn. . . . [It] is the one poem in which, as Professor Charles Anderson demonstrates, almost all the major intellectual and aesthetic forces in Lanier's life came to a focus [see Additional Bibliography] . . . .

Even after its many excellences have been conceded, however, **"The Marshes of Glynn"** reveals several shortcomings which have never been explored in sufficient detail. (p. 404)

Among the more conspicuous flaws in **"The Marshes of Glynn"** one can point first to a lack of structural balance. The poem contains three basic images, the woods, the marsh, and the sea. The central experience to be conveyed is a moment of transcendental oneness with nature, a moment in which, as the poet says, "belief overmasters doubt, and I know that I know." The experience is induced in the poet primarily, as the title implies, by the marsh. One might expect, then, that the marsh image would necessarily be central. But only at lines 47-48, just slightly less than halfway through the poem, is the poet prepared to step out onto the beach . . . and undertake the central experience of his poem. In terms of the whole poem he has dallied too long in his dappled woods hypnotized by the incidental wealth of images he has been able to evoke from them. Thought progression and structural balance suffer while he dallies.

This fundamental lack of focus in **"The Marshes of Glynn"** appears in yet another distressing way: the suspended constructions which require a reader to thread his way through an incredibly dense thicket of rhetorical underbrush in order to arrive, exhausted, at the essential predication of a sentence. Perhaps Lanier's often deplored "verbalism" arises more from his predilection for the suspended construction than from any other single source. Finite verbs and independent constructions are relatively few in **"The Marshes of Glynn."** In the first line of the poem, for instance, the poet addresses himself, presumably in the vocative, to the woods, the "Glooms of the live-oaks." The following nineteen lines are only, syntactically speaking, a series of parallel constructions describing the woods; not until line 20 is the final, independent predication achieved as the reader learns that the "glooms" . . . "held me fast in your heart and I held you fast in mine." (p. 405)

[Lines] 19-36 comprise another unit of thought which again exemplifies the technique of suspended predication. . . . In the first thirty-six lines of the poem precisely two independent predications appear.

One notes, too, in **"The Marshes of Glynn"** those characteristic adjectives and verbs which betray Lanier's addiction to the pathetic fallacy and to the sentimental view of nature which it implies. . . . The marshes "publish" themselves "to the sky" and "offer" themselves "to the sea"; the "tolerant plains . . . suffer the sea and the rains and the sun" (ll. 66-67). The "visage of space" in line 36 is . . . "sweet"; and the "limbs" of the girl in line 52 are both "firm" and "sweet." Lanier never quite escapes the implications of that typical adjective "sweet."

Another flaw in **"The Marshes of Glynn,"** at least to the modern eye, is the didactic method by which the poet first describes natural phenomena and then abstracts and expatiates on their "meaning" or "lesson." The result is at best an artificial division between form and idea and at the worst tiresome didacticism. Although in "**The Marshes of Glynn**" Lanier escapes most of Longfellow's more obvious homiletics—partly perhaps because of his very obscurity—he makes use of Longfellow's method at several points. Lines 49-60, for example, are pure evocative, descriptive poetry. Having just stepped from the canopied, shady woods, the poet uses [in lines 49-52] two suggestive (though slightly ornate) figures of speech to describe his feeling of freedom as he contemplates the expanse of the beach. . . . [And in lines 56-62], as the poet describes the amplitude of the marsh, there is still no hint of the didactic method. . . .

But in lines 61-78 comes the almost inevitable abstraction and the application of the "meaning" of the marsh and beach images to the realm of the "I" of the poem. The method becomes particularly bald in lines 71-78, where the poet compares his own activities in the world of the spirit to the mundane activities of the marsh hen:

As the marsh-hen secretly builds on the watery sod,
Behold I will build me a nest on the greatness of God:
I will fly in the greatness of God as the marsh-hen flies
In the freedom that fills all the space 'twixt the marsh
    and the skies.

(pp. 405-07)

By this kind of technique the experience which the reader is called upon to create is not conveyed intrinsically by the tone, texture, metaphors, and images of the poem itself; it is rather abstracted, tagged, and described in passages which, in spite of their rolling cadences, are essentially prosaic. (pp. 407-08)

Even more distressing than . . . [these shortcomings] in "**The Marshes of Glynn**" is another defect. The three major nature symbols of the poem are fuzzy; their implications are ambiguous and, sometimes, contradictory. If the poem is to achieve "the status of experience" [see excerpt above by Robert Penn Warren, 1933] then that experience must rest fundamentally on the poet's development of the woods, the marsh, and the sea as symbols. They must emerge crystal clear and consistent if the reader's understanding of the poet's experience is not to be vitiated. That they emerge something less than clear is demonstrable.

The woods as symbol seem to stand for several things, depending upon which section of the poem one chooses to examine. . . . [In lines 18-34 the] woods emerge as representative of the conventional romantic concept of nature as the benign healer of man's troubled spirit. "Now," says the poet, because his soul "all day hath drunken the soul of the oak," his heart

    is at ease from men, and the wearisome sound
        of the stroke
Of the scythe of time and the trowel of trade is low,
And belief overmasters doubt, and I know that I know.

(ll. 26-28)

There is nothing startling in that; it is a conventional and, on its own terms, acceptable symbol. The difficulty arises in lines 29-48, where the woods suddenly begin to assume another set of overtones. Here they begin to symbolize not only the healing power of nature—the power, that is, which helps the poet resolve his struggle between faith and doubt—but also the doubt itself. Indeed, the woods almost inevitably have to become a symbol of doubt which the poet leaves behind, for he has to step out of them to reach a position on the beach where his final mystical resolution is possible. . . .

The poet's insistent juxtaposition of the images of the woods and the marsh adds to the obscurity. The entire description of the woods conveys the feeling of being enclosed, covered over. . . . The marsh is described in terms precisely opposite: it is characterized by the words "length," "breadth," and "sweep"; it is "candid and simple and nothing-withholding and free." One can scarcely suppose, in a poet who uses parallelism and antithesis so habitually as Lanier, that such a juxtaposition is anything but studied and deliberate. The very openness and spaciousness of the marsh, indeed, make it a particularly apt symbol for much that poets found disturbing in nineteenth-century science. . . . [The] concept of the unimaginable immensity of cosmic space, with the consequent diminution of the world and man, was equally as desolating to some poetic temperaments as the mechanistic implications of the doctrine of natural selection or survival of the fittest. It is not stretching the point too far, in fact, to suggest that in the very sweep and immensity of his marsh Lanier saw a natural symbol for many of the profoundly disquieting doubts raised by mechanistic science. The suggestion is borne out by the poem. Before the mystical experience described in "**The Marshes of Glynn**" had occurred, it was precisely the "length and the breadth and the sweep" of the marshes which had terrorized the poet: their "length was fatigue," their "breadth was bitterness sore"; and "terror and shrinking and dreary unnamable pain / Drew over me out of the merciless miles of the plain." At the moment of the experience described in the poem, however, Lanier discovers that because nature has taken on a new transcendental spirituality for him, space is no longer fearsome. (pp. 409-10)

If this reading is justified, several interesting questions of logic and consistency arise. In the first place, is there any essential distinction between the woods and the marsh as symbols? Lanier apparently intended that there should be. But each seems to represent, at some point, the principle of cosmic doubt, the woods *after* the poet is standing on the beach, the marsh *before* the central experience of the poem had occurred. It is not clear, then, why the poet should take such pains to establish woods and marsh as symbolic antitheses, so deliberately stressing the covert quality of the woods as opposed to the openness and amplitude of the marsh. Or again, if a reading leads one to conclude that during the time consumed by the experience of the poem the marsh is transformed from a symbol of the poet's doubt to a symbol of his new-found faith in the spirituality of nature, then it would seem that the woods, as antithesis to the marsh, must become the symbol of the "doubt" which the poet has "overmastered." . . . But where, in the first thirty-four lines of the poem, then, has one received any clear intimation that the woods were Lanier's *selva oscura* of doubt? Rather, in those lines they seemed to be his spiritual comforter and healer. Surely there is an inherent inconsistency in the proposition that Lanier's woods can simultaneously symbolize the cosmic doubts inferred, say, from Darwin or Lyell and the characteristic Wordsworthian concept of nature as healer. The poet cannot have it both ways; his woods may well symbolize either idea separately, but in the first seventy lines of "**The Marshes of Glynn**" two antithetical concepts are confusingly intermixed. Perhaps not even Emerson can fuse Darwin with Wordsworth. (pp. 410-11)

The marsh image presents further complications. Even if, by the time he reaches line 70, a reader is prepared to accept the marsh as symbolic opposite of the woods in spite of the ambiguous implications of both images, in lines 71-78 Lanier suddenly introduces another concept altogether. Not content to let his images alone communicate his experience, the poet performs his "arbitrary disjunction" between form and idea [see excerpt above by Robert Penn Warren, 1933] and attempts to explain the "lesson" which he has derived from his experience. . . . [In] elucidating the "meaning" he has found in the marshes, the poet once again falls victim to ambiguity. As the marsh hen builds "on the watery sod," so he will build his nest "*on* the greatness of God"; as the marsh grass sends its roots into the sod, so the poet will lay hold "*on* the greatness of God." The comparisons, put into parallel construction by the force of the prepositions "in" and "on," do not quite come off because of a shift in point of view in the final two lines of the passage. The shift is from metaphor to simile, and logical consistency is shattered as the poet claims: "*like to the* greatness of God is the greatness within / the range of the marshes, the liberal marshes of Glynn."

The third major image of the poem, the sea, is also obscure. For sheer picture, lines 81-98 can scarcely be surpassed. The orchestral effect of Lanier's verse emerges at its best in these lines with their simple, climactic coda: "The tide is at its highest height: And it is night." With this statement the experience of the poem ends. Unfortunately, the poem goes on. Again Lanier separates idea from form and tries to elucidate the "meaning" of his descriptive passages. This time he confuses the reader thoroughly, once and for all. In an implied comparison, as the tide rolls in from the sea over the marsh, so the "waters of sleep" will roll in "from the Vast of the Lord" over the "souls of men." The "Vast of the Lord" is presumably Lanier's poetic equivalent of the Emersonian concept of the oversoul. One does not quarrel with Lanier's transcendentalism; it is impossible, however, to overlook the question of content: how can the poet's comparison of the tide to the "waters of sleep" be considered relevant to this particular poem in this particular context? Even more confusing is the elucidation of the "meaning" of the "waters of sleep" metaphor in the lines which follow and with which the poem ends:

> But who will reveal to our waking ken
> The forms that swim and the shapes that creep
> Under the waters of sleep?
> And I would I could know what swimmeth below when
>   the tide comes in
> On the length and the breadth of the marvelous
>   marshes of Glynn. . . .

[One] can only remark the apparent incongruity and irrelevance of these last seven lines of the poem. Surely their almost macabre tone is out of keeping with the tone of sober exaltation which the poet maintains throughout the second half of his nature hymn. Moreover, one has not been prepared for the "waters of sleep" metaphor. To be sure, a thread of time runs through the entire poem. As the poet lingered in the woods it was noon; as he stepped out onto the beach it was evening; and at the end, as the tide comes full, "it is night." Night surely is the time for sleep. And so perhaps one should take Lanier's "waters of sleep" metaphor as merely a piece of decorated literalness: now that night has fallen the poet can go to sleep. Such a reading seems decidedly lame, for it fails to explain the apparent irrelevance of the next question:

> But who will reveal to our waking ken
> The forms that swim and the shapes that creep
> Under the waters of sleep?

Viewed in their relationship to the whole poem, the final seven lines seem to be a logical and aesthetic non-sequitur.

It is possible to suggest at least one reason why symbolic ambiguity should have occurred in **"The Marshes of Glynn,"** for in Lanier one recognizes again the lineaments of an intellectual and spiritual problem common to many poets in the middle and late nineteenth century. **"The Marshes of Glynn"** is a nature poem, but at the time he wrote it Lanier had not reasoned out a consistent philosophy of nature. . . . Like many poets of his age, as Professor Anderson points out, Lanier had been "brought up in the romantic school of nature worship," but by the seventies he had been deeply perturbed by the implications of the new science. . . . It was the Darwinian theory of evolution . . .—and particularly its implication of nature as an impersonal, amoral force—which disturbed him more profoundly than any other scientific revelation of his age. . . . (pp. 412-14)

Like other thoughtful men of his time, he was beset by the claims of both heart and head; and like others he temporized, trying to maintain in uneasy suspension the best of both worlds. If he could not fail to recognize the validity of the claim made upon his intellect by nineteenth-century scientific rationalism, neither could he ever entirely shake off the emotional claims of his inherent romantic nature worship.

The would-be catalyst to the unstable compound of Wordsworth-*cum*-Darwin was Emerson. . . . Emerson's transcendental view of nature gave Lanier fresh insight into the "vast spiritual background of the sensuous world and the essential kinship of each and all." . . . [His] discovery of Emerson served to strengthen Lanier's romantic view of nature, for Emerson lent respectable philosophical sanction to what Lanier's heart longed to believe. (p. 415)

One inevitably wonders whether the transcendental view of nature was wholly convincing for Lanier and whether it enabled him to resolve all his doubts about nature's beneficence. . . . The tone and "message" of **"The Marshes of Glynn"** would argue for an affirmative answer: traditional interpretation correctly regards the poem as a sustained hymn to the transcendent spirit within nature. But the ambiguity and the contradictory implications of its nature symbols lead one to suggest that although the intensity of Lanier's struggle toward a consistent and intellectually respectable attitude toward nature had perhaps been allayed by his contact with Emerson, Lanier had not yet reached a wholly satisfactory resolution to the perennial late nineteenth-century problem. It is doubtful that he ever did. In any case . . . when he composed **"The Marshes of Glynn,"** Lanier, like Matthew Arnold some thirty years before, seems to have been *in utrumque paratus* [prepared for either event]. (pp. 415-16)

Robert H. Ross, " 'The Marshes of Glynn': A Study in Symbolic Obscurity," in American Literature *(reprinted by permission of the Publisher; copyright © 1961 by Duke University Press, Durham, North Carolina), Vol. 32, No. 4, January, 1961, pp. 403-16.*

EDMUND WILSON   (essay date 1962)

[Wilson is generally considered America's foremost man of letters in the twentieth century. A prolific reviewer, creative writer, and social and literary critic endowed with formidable intellectual powers, he exercised his greatest literary influence as the author of Axel's Castle *(1931), a seminal study of literary symbolism, and as the author of widely-read reviews and essays in which he introduced the best works of modern literature to the reading public. In* Patriotic Gore, *a study of the literature of the American Civil War period, Wilson characterizes Lanier's work as the epit-*

*ome of Southern chivalric idealism. His critical reaction to La-
nier's writing, excerpted below, is both censorious and sympathetic: insipid, prudish, humorless, and "sometimes a little stupid,"
Lanier is yet to be admired, according to Wilson, as a rare and
true man of letters whose later work showed increasing artistic
accomplishment.*]

If one reads very much of Lanier, one is tempted in the long
run to lose patience with him. He is at once insipid and florid.
He is noble, to be sure, but his nobility is boring; his eloquence
comes to seem empty. . . . [And] though we may sympathize
with his scorn for commercial ideals, we may find him rather
tiresome about it. . . . (p. 460)

Lanier's purity is also prudish. Despite the wicked burst of
passion in *Tiger-Lilies,* the Puritan subdues the Romantic. When
Lanier attempts to deal with the English novel in a series of
lectures at Johns Hopkins, we discover that all the classic
novelists from Fielding and Smollett to Thackeray are offensive
to his moral sense, . . . and that he can only fully approve of
George Eliot, to whom he devotes a disproportionate amount
of space. But it was not merely prudery no doubt which made
him dislike these authors. The dream of Arthurian chivalry to
which he was so much addicted must have made them all seem
to him vulgar, and it excluded a sense of humor. . . . Though
sensitive, Lanier is limited, sometimes a little stupid.

And yet there was in Sidney Lanier something that commands
our respect, even our admiration. In his life he was, in a real
sense, heroic; his passion for the arts was intense . . . ; and
the work that he was doing at the time of his death seems to
show that he was becoming a first-rate artist. The closer one
gets to him, the more one is disposed to agree with the opinion
of Barrett Wendell, in his *A Literary History of America,* that
Lanier "was among the truest men of letters that our country
has produced." (pp. 461-62)

The early poems of Sidney Lanier had suffered somewhat from
peculiarities of style which were not at all characteristic of the
facile American verse of the period: a stiffening of the lines
with consonants that bristle, impede and deaden and that recall
the Anglo-Saxon poetry which Lanier had been at pains to
study and the German of his early addiction. Though he had
thoroughly mastered music—and perhaps for this very reason—it was precisely in verbal music that his poetry had always
been deficient. . . . But—very late in the day to be sure: in
1878—Lanier began producing . . . the sequence of *Hymns of
the Marshes,* of which he lived to finish only a few. In these
he displays rather suddenly new colors and new rhythms and,
for Lanier, a new way of experiencing life. He has hitherto
dealt almost exclusively in imagery of a conventional romantic
kind and in allegories and moral abstractions. But now at last,
in his relation to the outer world, he is beginning to explore
real landscapes and in the inner one to deal with the psychology
of emotion. The "high-minded" early Lanier, who has seemed
rather remote and monotonous, is turning here into a man and
a poet; and his stockade of dental and palatal consonants seems
in process of becoming fluidified with the flooding of the Marshes
of Glynn. (pp. 464-65)

*Edmund Wilson, "The Myth of the Old South, Sidney
Lanier, the Poetry of the Civil War, 'Sut Lovin-
good'," in his* Patriotic Gore: Studies in the Literature of the American Civil War *(reprinted by permission of Farrar, Straus and Giroux, Inc.; copyright
© 1962 by Edmund Wilson), Oxford University Press,
New York, 1962, pp. 438-528.**

HYATT H. WAGGONER (essay date 1968)

[*Waggoner discounts Lanier's reputation as a distinguished poet
and prosodist; his scepticism derives from his belief that Lanier's
prosodic theory is totally misguided and that his poems are emotionally and prosodically abstract. Despite Harriet Monroe's claim
that* The Science of English Verse *influenced her poetic technique
(1941), Waggoner states that "no American poet, with the exception of John Gould Fletcher (1949), in his last pathetic period,
has yet been influenced by Lanier, either by his theory or his
practice."*]

Sidney Lanier, it seems to be universally conceded, was the
best of the poets produced by the South in the last half of the
century, as Poe was the region's foremost poet in the first half.
But it might be more expressive to turn this statement around
and say that he was the least bad of them. Henry Timrod and
P. H. Hayne are the other two in this regional category, and
their work is so bathetic that to call Lanier's *better* is not to
say anything absolutely positive. (p. 235)

His poetry is full of intense feelings about Nature and God; of
elaborately euphonious patterns of sound, including sounds that
are intended to remind us of the sounds of musical instruments;
and of personal bravery. But the feelings tend to float freely
around in a misty atmosphere, unanchored to any palpable
earth; the sound patterns have little relation to what Eliot would
later call the only "music" proper to poetry; and the bravery
is felt only as a quality of the man, not as a quality of the
verse.

How standard and unanchored the feelings are can be illustrated
by two brief passages from . . . **"The Marshes of Glynn."**
(p. 236)

[In a passage describing the marshes, the woods are referred
to as "dim," "sweet," "dear," and "dark."] Shortly after
this we learn why the woods have been called "dim" and
"sweet" and "dear" and "dark": They provide "Cells for
the passionate pleasure of prayer to the soul that grieves."
They provide refuge from "the scythe of time and the trowel
of trade." In the marshes, the speaker tells us, "belief overmasters doubt, and I know that I know." It will no doubt seem
terribly crass and unfeeling to note that the poem does not tell
us, in this passage or anywhere else, very much about how the
marshes support and strengthen the speaker's religious faith.

Late in the poem the speaker resolves to remain close to God,
as he has felt himself close while in the marshes. . . . Wishing
to be like "the catholic man who hath mightily won / God out
of knowledge and good out of infinite pain / And sight out of
blindness and purity out of a strain," he decides to imitate the
marsh-hen:

As the marsh-hen secretly builds on the watery sod,
Behold I will build me a nest on the greatness of God;
I will fly in the greatness of God as the marsh-hen flies
In the freedom that fills all the space 'twist the marsh
    and the skies;
By so many roots as the marsh-grass sends in the sod
I will heartily lay me a-hold on the greatness of God;
Oh, like to the greatness of God is the greatness within
The range of the marshes, the liberal marshes of Glynn.

When Emerson had found God in his experience, in moments
of exceptional and unpredictable readiness. . . . he had understood the experience as made possible by a rare inward harmony
and alertness—body-sense, instinct, emotion, conscience, intellect, imagination, all working together. He had felt himself
suddenly *one* with nature, and through nature with God, be-

cause he had been one with himself. Perfect wholeness was the condition of such an experience and of the insights it yielded. The scene itself did not have to be especially beautiful or sublime, vast, dim, or ethereal. And the God Emerson found this way was not the God of the New Testament.

But Lanier was hoping to move "through Nature to God" . . . without keeping, as Emerson had counseled, *all* his "faculties alert." There is a good deal of emotion in his poem, and a good deal of imagination, of a sort, but no suggestion of a bodily or instinctive response to the sensuous or tactile quality of the marshes, and only the flimsiest sort of analogies to represent intellection. A marsh is water and mud and grasses and sand; but the sand on the beach never gets into Lanier's shoes or blows in his eyes. Instead, it is seen only at a distance, and not *felt* at all. It is presented as what he knows is on the beach, and would know, even if he had never seen a beach; and the beach itself as it curves away into the distance reminds him of "a silver-wrought garment that clings to and follows the firm sweet limbs of a girl."

By this time we are pretty far from the sandiness of sand. (pp. 236-38)

As for intellection, Lanier seems not to realize, what Emerson had realized so long before, that to take nature as a sufficient revelation of God required among other things keeping oneself open to the possibility of having to redefine what one *meant* by "God." . . . "If design govern in a thing so small," then the open-minded thinker ought to consider not just the apparently Providential way in which the marsh seems planned for marsh-hens to build their nests on, but the predators that find the marsh-hens Providentially provided for them as food. One could as easily infer from the marsh, as it exists in Lanier's poem, a "design of darkness to appall" as one could a loving personal God. Somewhat more easily perhaps. The diminished, wistful ghost of Bishop Paley, that great rationalistic theologian of the beginning of the century, hovers over the poem, holding in one spectral hand the "evidences of the existence and attributes of the Deity, collected from the appearances of nature." Lanier writes as though Emerson, Thoreau, Hawthorne, and Melville, in their several ways, had not made it impossible for the thoughtful late-nineteenth-century poet to be completely satisfied by the good bishop's version of the argument from design. (pp. 238-39)

["**The Symphony**," Lanier's] attempt to unify the arts of music and poetry, was misguided from the start. . . . [Sound] and sense fight it out with no decisive victory. And surely, without the title and the several clues thrown out in the poem to guide our reading, we would never guess that we were supposed to be listening to the sounds of flutes, violins, and so on. (p. 239)

The best that can be said for [*The Science of English Verse*] is that it makes a courageous attempt to do what Lanier was not equipped by either temperament or study to do—to explore the whole history of English verse and deduce from it the laws that govern what he calls "tune" in poetry.

There is of course no "tune," that is, no melodic line as we find it in music, in poetry, so that no matter how learned Lanier had been, no matter how incisively clear-thinking a scholar he might have been, he could not possibly have succeeded in his effort. . . . [As] Eliot, among others, has said, the "music" of poetry is a radically different kind of "music" from the "music" of music. If that were not so, then the most "musical" poetry ought to be composed in sounds that were not words, that had no *semantic* value. Fortunately, no American

poet, with the exception of John Gould Fletcher in his last pathetic period, has yet been influenced by Lanier, either by his theory or by his practice. I say "fortunately" not just because the theory is unsound and Lanier's practice not such as any later poet, up to now at least, could imitate successfully, but even more because if it were *possible* to apply the theory to the creation of an actual poem, the result would be such very poor and thin and uninteresting "music"—like whistling the Brandenburg Concerto, or playing Handel's Water Music on a Jew's harp. (pp. 239-40)

> *Hyatt H. Waggoner, "Some Lesser Figures," in his* American Poets: From the Puritans to the Present *(reprinted by permission of Louisiana State University Press; copyright © 1968 by Hyatt H. Waggoner), Houghton Mifflin Company, 1968, pp. 225-61* [and to be published in a revised edition by Louisiana State University Press (new material, copyright © 1984)].*

JACK DE BELLIS (essay date 1972)

[*De Bellis's analysis of "The Symphony" reflects his belief that Lanier attempted to use his art to educate the emotions of his rationalistic age. In maintaining that Lanier successfully advances his didactic aims in "The Symphony" by skillful manipulation of metrical effects and musical analogy, De Bellis challenges critics such as Robert Penn Warren (1933), who held that in his poetry, Lanier "regularly performed an arbitrary disjunction . . . between the idea and the form in which it might be embodied."*]

[When Lanier wrote "**The Symphony**," he envisioned that] musical verse would etherealize poetic sentiments, and both arts would reveal the errors of reason and thus ameliorate the sources of social injustice. If "Music is Love in search of a word" states a didactic program of moral education, the music of his poem demonstrates the value of pure emotion as the sounds of the words create responses in advance of intellectual understanding, as is often the case in Walt Whitman, Algernon Swinburne, Paul Verlaine, and Dylan Thomas. . . .

[Although a musical style in poetry could raise the verbal level and etherealize it,] content could not be entirely disowned, for Lanier was afraid his awareness of the education of feelings would be misunderstood if he relied totally on the musicality of verse. And so "**The Symphony**," a daring and original experiment in musical verse, is also an orchestration of many specific themes of morality, chivalry, protest and accommodation. (p. 77)

Social correction in art often produces propaganda and thus simplicity and stereotyping—enemies of creative art. Lanier had other ideas about how society could be changed, ideas involving an ingenious manipulation of poetic images and, above all, poetic music. . . .

In "**The Symphony**" he was not interested in pinpointing specific social problems so that he could offer what Starke has called "an intelligible program of social amelioration" [see excerpt above, 1933] . . . [He] wished to examine a more general condition of injustice: the loss of love, which required a new education of feelings. And so it is the music, within the style and form of the poem, which must be understood to be Lanier's way of evaluating the human condition. (p. 80)

The structure of the poem may be called "stichic" since there are no stanzaic divisions and, in addition, no sectional ones. But, instead of promoting diffusiveness, Lanier has carefully distinguished major and minor sections of the poem for specific effects. (p. 81)

The over-all sections of the poem are clearly four—given to the strings, flute, clarinet and horn, oboe and bassoon. The first section can be divided into three parts: in the first part, lines 1-12, the violins attack Trade, and a five-line "bridge" shows the entrance of the "mightier strings"; in the second part, lines 29-50, the strings first generalize about economic exploitation and imitate the voices of the poor; in the third part, lines 54-68, a four-line bridge introduces the relation between Trade and war.

The first dozen lines convincingly demonstrate a special tone color that distinguished the sound of the strings:

"O Trade! O Trade! Would thou wert dead!
The Time needs heart—'tis tired of head:
We're all for love," the violins said.
4   "Of what avail the rigorous tale
Of bill for coin and box for bale?
Grant thee, O Trade! thine uttermost hope:
Level red gold with blue sky-slope,
8   And base it deep as devils grope:
When all's done, what hast thou won
Of the only sweet that's under the sun?
Ay, canst thou buy a single sigh
12   Of true love's least, least ecstasy?"

These lines are tetrameter triplets with frequent substitution . . . and little end-stopping, giving a sense of movement toward the rhetorical questions. The monosyllabic terseness is well suited to social protest. (p. 82)

Though Lanier uses triplets mainly, he does employ couplets or groups of couplets; and in [Paul Fussell, Jr.'s,] view the couplet "is likely to be lean and clean, spare and logical . . . a texture supremely appropriate to sarcasm or solid virile reasoning." Yet triplet rhyme, a hallmark of most of the section, "tends to produce fatiguing and sometimes comic or bizarre effects." Therefore, Lanier's prosody is composed of conflicting elements, just as his intention balanced social protest against etherealized poetry. These conflicts in conception and prosody may help to explain the uneven effect of the poem, for Lanier was still in his apprenticeship and unable to follow his ideas to their logical conclusions. (pp. 82-3)

Within twelve lines Lanier alters the rhyme scheme from triplet to couplet twice, a characteristic aspect of the strings, as is the unusual way in which the rhyme is varied. Line four introduces a medial rhyme with the final rhyme ("avail"-"tale"); and, when the rhyme changes in line six, the rhyme word again chimes with internal words ("O"-"most"-"hope"). . . . This pattern becomes evident: when the rhyme sound changes, a word usually in the medial foot anticipates the rhyme. But Lanier varies the pattern the second or third time that the rhyme appears in order to prevent monotony. He gives unity to these dozen lines by beginning and ending with repeated words: 1: "Trade"-"Trade"; 12: "least"-"least." . . .

Lanier uses alliteration in some striking ways to bind his most important words together and to establish the specific musicality of the violins. Lines 1 and 2 show alliterations not only on *t*s and *w*s but also on *tr* clusters from line to line, sometimes disguised ("tired") and sometimes by concealed alliteration. Kenneth Burke has proposed that sounds of the same phonetic group are related by concealed alliterations. . . . Burke has also suggested the term "colliteration" for a similarity of final consonant sounds, and we notice concealed colliteration between the words tra*de* and lea*st*. (p. 83)

In the first two lines other sound relations besides alliterative ones are felt. In line 1, "Would thou wert dead" sounds effective because the *d-t-d-* colliterate and the *th-d* alliterate. In line 2, the same key sounds are used: in "The Time needs heart—'tis tired of head" the *n* takes its place in the concealed alliteration, while the aspirated *h* in the medial foot (heart) works with the *h* of "head" to produce a sense of strain and urgency. . . . [We also note that] the *tr-d* of "Trade" is changed to *r-t-d* of "wert dead"; and also *r-t-t-* of "heart—'tis." The original pattern is reinstated in "tired" with t-r-d. As for the last couplet, lines 11-12, the alliteration of *s* in 11 and *l* in 12 is apparent. . . . In line 11, Lanier uses *st* (can*st*) which is repeated with variation in "lea*st*, lea*st*, ec*st*asy." The proliferation of this kind of tone color in these twelve lines creates a sound recognized as belonging to the strings, but the recognition may not be a very conscious one. (p. 84)

The second part of the string section opens with an echo of the violins' fourth line, as if picking up a theme for development presented in the "introduction" section of this "movement."

18   Yea, what avail the endless tale
Of gain by cunning and plus by sale?
Look up the land, look down the land—
The poor, the poor, the poor, they stand
Wedged by the pressing of Trade's hand
Against an inward-opening door
24   That pressure tightens evermore:
They sigh a monstrous foul-air sigh
For the outside leagues of liberty,
Where Art, sweet lark, translates the sky
28   Into a heavenly melody.

The repetition re-establishes the pattern of assonance anticipation, for the first and second rhymes have internal rhyme the first time they appear. Though the third rhyme does not, the fourth returns to the pattern with the repeated word "sigh." . . . [The] repeated words are the new tone color which the violins developed to accompany the new themes, or the developed themes.

The strings' imitations of the poor folks' protest brings in another kind of sound duplication:

29   'Each day, all day' (these poor folks say),
'In the same old year-long, drear-long way,
We weave in the mills and heave in the kilns,
We sieve mine-meshes under the hills,
And thieve much gold from the Devil's bank tills,
To relieve, O God, what manner of ills?

Aside from word repetitions, line 30 contains the first incidence of double internal rhyme. And it creates a perpendicular rhyme: "weave"-"thieve"-"relieve". . . . Following the plea of the poor, Lanier drops his sound devices one by one, altering the rhyme pattern and meter instead. Lines 35-40 rhyme six consecutive lines, and lines 40-47 shift rhyme only slightly from "tone"-"alone"-"Throne" to "so"-"No"-"know"-"Go." Lines 44 and 45 have two feet, and the striking line "Trade is trade," line 50, is headless and is echoed in form later in the flute section and inverted in the clarinet-horn section. (pp. 85-6)

The closing part of the violin section uses devices from all previous parts but expands the internal rhymes:

58   Does business mean, *Die, you—live, I?*
Then 'Trade is trade' but sings a lie:
'Tis only war grown miserly.

61   If business is battle, name it so:
        War-crimes less with shame it so,
        And widows less will blame it so.
        Alas: for the poor to have some part
        In yon sweet living lands of Art,
66   Makes problem not for head, but heart.
        Vainly might Plato's brain revolve it:
        Plainly the heart of a child could solve it.

The most striking feature of these lines is the five-word rhyme of lines 62-63. It brings the use of feminine rhyme in the poem to its peak and marks the first time the rhyme word for two or more lines is the same. The result is chantlike, and it is intensified by the closing couplet which begins and ends with feminine double rhymes.

Unquestionably, the poem is a tour de force of the musicality of verse. . . . This analysis of only 20 percent of the poem shows that Lanier had found unending possibilities for etherealizing poetry, though we might decide, of course, that he neglected to let the sound echo to the sense; but I think additional study of the poem reveals otherwise. (pp. 86-7)

Some of the finest imagery and most musical phrases Lanier ever created are in the flute's section. Near "pistils, and petals crystalline," fly "film-winged things." The Jay "hints tragedies" with "sparklings of small beady eyes." When merged to sound devices, the lines reach a summit of Lanier's power:

153   Each dial-marked leaf and flower-bell
        Wherewith in every lonesome dell
        Time to himself his hours doth tell;
156   All tree-sounds, rustlings of pine-cones,
        Wind-sighings, doves' melodious moans,
158   And night's unearthly under-tones:

This passage shows unobtrusive but effective weavings of the *M* group (*m-n-p-b-f-v*) and the *N* group. The diction is specific and the rhyme words chosen to link together words of the sounds of nature. (p. 88)

The flute section is the longest and the most seductive, but it creates doubt about its organic function in the poem. For the first theme sounded in the poem was social injustice, and the flute has withdrawn into nature; but, ironically, instead of discovering Transcendental insights, it recovers the theme of the violins. The flute first explores Lanier's notion that man at last is a brother to nature, using the violins' "All for love" as a point of departure. This idea of the etherealized relation of nature to man leads associatively to the theme of man's inhumanity to man. With form following sense, the iambic pentameter of the etherealization passage dissolves and is replaced by a loosened iambic tetrameter which repeats with variations lines 21-28:

191   But oh, the poor! the poor! the poor!
        That stand by the inward-opening door
        Trade's hand doth tighten ever more,
        And sigh their monstrous foul-air sigh
195   For the outside hills of liberty,
        Where Nature spreads her wild blue sky
        For Art to make into melody!

By imitating the music as well as the images of the violins, Lanier binds the flute section to the strings section and shows that withdrawal into nature is only a brief respite for future battles with the enemy. The flute's final lines echo the opening theme of the strings and its "coda":

205   Trade! is thy heart all dead, all dead?
        And hast thou nothing but a head?
        I'm all for heart," the flute-voice said.

After opening with a variation in the usual meter of the poem, altering the length of feet from one to five feet, rhyming uneven feet, and using phrases to suggest rhythmic groupings, the flute has returned to the rhythmic starting point and disappeared. Lanier was now faced with the problem of sustaining the reader's interest without becoming mannered or boring, and a partial solution was to repeat the scheme of the first two movements with the variety offered by duos of instruments, rather than single voices. And thus he could make smaller divisions of his last two "movements" and partly overcome the disadvantages of the large form he had chosen. (pp. 88-9)

In [the clarinet and horn] section Lanier uses alliteration and vowel chiasmus to accentuate through cacophony the horror of the misuse of women. Reiterating the theme of the violins, the clarinet also wishes Trade would die because of the "shameful ways" of women "At the beckoning of Trade's golden rod!" Such exploitation will naturally move to destroy nature next:

225   Alas when sighs are traders' lies,
        And heart's-ease eyes and violet eyes
        Are merchandise!

The unfortunate preciosity of these lines is offset by the atypical congestion of assonances and consonances. . . . The result is a contrived phonetic log jam, a Browningesque dissonance to underscore the outrage of the abused lady.

In [a "bridge" passage in] section one, the bridegroom strings came quickly to the violins' aid; now the French horn defends the clarinet from Trade. Lanier had claimed in **"The Orchestra of Today"** that no one could fail to detect the "peculiarly feminine character" of the clarinet's higher registers and, riding out of **"The Jacquerie,"** the French horn responds to the clarinet by fitting its strength of character to the strongest form in the poem, the ballad, . . . ending with a refrain "Fair lady," . . . Chivalry lives . . . and the decadent institution is transformed. The horn, like the "mightier strings" opposes Trade with a Christian manliness. (pp. 89-90)

The horn pledges his undying chivalry while fighting in the "patient modern way" (poetry and song?), but it is never clear how love can be asserted in an unjust world or why the horn imagines his "modern way" can contend with modern Trade. In terms of the immediate context, Lanier very likely wants to suggest that, without lady worship, the exploitation of women is inevitable. Apparently the horn vanquishes his foe through his music, having etherealized Trade, for spiritualization is in fact the modern way. Lanier has acted out his notion that, in the cyclic nature of things, Chivalry must rise to overthrow Trade through the leadership of a great man. (pp. 90-1)

By now it is clear that the "great man" . . . has appeared in the disguise of all the instruments of **"The Symphony."** In the third section, he emerges as a knight, but he now takes the form of the prophet, personified by the bassoon. The bassoons' paradoxical images create a mystical vision of "the coming reign of beauty and art." . . . Since love unites opposites, it is fitting that the bassoon opens with descriptions of contrasts in the image of the pulsating sea:

341   Bright-waved gain, gray waved loss,
      The sea of all doth lash and toss,
      One wave forward and one across:
      But now 'twas trough, now 'tis crest,
      And worst doth foam and flash to best,
        And curst to blest.

                              (pp. 91-2)

The sea's spin-drift moods have prepared for the musical metaphor which leads directly to the mystical vision:

347   Life Life! thou sea-fugue, writ from east to west,
      Love, Love alone can pore
      On thy dissolving score
      Of harsh half-phrasings,
        Blotted ere writ,
      And double erasings
        Of chords most fit.
      Yea, Love, sole music-master blest,
      May read thy weltering palimpsest.
      To follow Time's dying melodies through,
      And never to lose the old in the new,
      And ever to solve the discords true—
        Love alone can do.

The meter now fluctuates rapidly varying the phrasings and fitting music to sense as conflicting discords match resolving chords. Love supplies the other half of the "harsh half-phrasings" to create a tonic chord. And Love is the main theme of the orchestra because it unifies the many voices and styles of the instruments; they are literally "all for love." Love unites the old and new, and it reads through a vertical view of life the core of tensions that have always characterized the human condition. What had begun in social protest now ends by describing the spiritual discord and the spiritual wasteland created by "Reconstructed" but unregenerate men.

The bassoon has used the feminine double rhymes of the "bridges," the varied meter of the flute, and the alliterative and assonantal devices of the strings. Now it uses the chant of the violins:

360   And ever Love hears the poor-folks' crying,
      And ever Love hears the women's sighing,
      And ever sweet knighthood's death-defying,
      And ever wise childhood's deep implying,
364   But never a trader's glozing and lying.

The many participle rhymes hint that the spiritual descent is at hand.

Since love had been unable to hear Trade, perhaps because this musical tribute, Lanier's **"Symphony,"** had overcome its dissonance, one guesses that Trade simply and spontaneously etherealizes in its presence. The poem could end here, but the bassoons provide an epilogue that is a coda to the symphony and the poem:

365   And yet shall Love himself be heard,
      Though long deferred, though long deferred:
      O'er the modern waste a dove hath whirred:
      Music is Love in search of a word."

The lower case *h* of "himself" does not distract us from recognizing the advent of Christ and the Second Coming. The instruments have made all varieties of love their theme; and Love himself, the Great man, has responded. In Lanier's poem, as in his metaphysics, not only is God Love, but Love is God.

Lanier had often used the dove as a bird of prophecy. . . . All the other birds—ravens, pigeons, falcons, jays, mudhens, larks—in some ways share the spiritual connotations of the dove. But only the dove has the most important religious meanings: peace (Genesis 8:8-12); gentleness (Matthew 10:16); and the Holy Ghost (Leviticus 14:22). As Noah's dove sought land and found it through God's mercy, so does the religious word that man accepts on faith become concretized in an image of a rainbow. For Lanier, the image is that of the dove; for, like the rainbow, the dove assures Lanier that the modern waste will not destroy itself. The dove is, therefore, a sign that the theme of **"The Symphony"** will be realized, giving purpose and rationale to Lanier's complex esthetic procedures in creating a musical verse. (pp. 92-4)

Lanier had written in **"Retrospects and Prospects"** that music's "two dove's-wings" would carry "a whole world-full of people to Heaven!" In **"The Symphony,"** he had demonstrated the morality of feeling through the interaction of musical instruments and God's instrument; through the manipulation of music metaphors; and, above all, through the employment of a rich musical poetry. The error of the age had deafened man to his own intuitive recognition of the place of love in his life, but future poetry exemplified by this poem, would restore the proper sense of true spiritual harmony. In recovering man's capacity to love, Lanier had found his poetic voice. (p. 94)

    Jack De Bellis, in his Sidney Lanier *(copyright ©*
    1972 by Twayne Publishers; reprinted with the per-
    mission of Twayne Publishers, a Division of G. K.
    Hall & Co., Boston), Twayne, 1972, 169 p.

LOUIS D. RUBIN, JR. **(essay date 1975)**

[*Rubin describes Lanier's literary career as a long process of self-education in which he gradually discarded restrictive conventional verse forms and adopted the distinctive prosodic techniques required to express his exalted view of the world. Lewis Leary (1947) had earlier maintained that Lanier never succeeded in articulating his vision of existence.*]

If one had to characterize the personality of Sidney Lanier, the word that would probably come to mind is *intensity.* (p. 107)

[For] Lanier it seemed necessary that everything about life be exalted to the utmost degree; he wrote, played music, studied, and loved with a degree of emotional intensity that, when not held rigorously in check by the discipline of a form, was often embarrassing. The famous concluding line of his later poem **"The Symphony"**—"Music is Love in search of a word"—however vague its poetic meaning, is almost a paradigm of his own mental attitude: all his life he seemed to be seeking a way to transcend the boundaries of human life and the material world and attain a unified, visionary celebration of pure essence, without knowing exactly how to go about it. (p. 108)

Tiger-Lilies is a bizarre novel, a preposterous combination of German transcendentalist philosophizing, after the manner of Novalis and Jean Paul Richter. The opening sections take place in a Tennessee mountain retreat named Thalberg, inhabited by heroes, villains, philosophers, and musicians from several continents; there is also a melodramatic revenge plot and some Civil War scenes, including several interesting army episodes. It is largely the last-named that elevate the novel above the level of Augusta Evans Wilson's *St. Elmo* and *Macaria,* which otherwise it resembles in technique. On the other hand, there is an element of exuberance in *Tiger-Lilies,* a ferocity of expressiveness that gives the work, in its very failure, a dignity of sorts. One has the feeling about it, for all its clumsiness, its amateurish handling of plot and characterization, its undigested (and in the form presented, undigestible) pudding of ideas, that the person who wrote it was no mere hack, no journeyman romancer, but an intellect of potentially formidable powers. (pp. 109-10)

What would have been needed for Lanier to write a good novel was never to happen: a much more sophisticated and intelligent tutelage in the form of fiction than he was ever to receive. He had no idea at all of what it was possible to achieve in fiction, or how to achieve it. . . . (p. 110)

Lanier's ideal for the novel would have been a work of which there is no evidence that he ever heard: Melville's *Moby-Dick*. But so disorganized, so undisciplined, and so romantic was Sidney Lanier's intellect that he could never have managed the profound exploration into motive and meaning that Melville offers. Lanier was really not, as Edmund Wilson declares, "sometimes a little stupid" [see excerpt above, 1962]. Instead, he was very poorly educated . . . and also *mis*educated, in that the sentimental romanticism that passed for intellectual currents in western society of the mid-nineteenth century prevented him from examining and coming to terms with the life around him and his own relationship to it. Nothing could be further separated than the occasional realistic dialogue and humorous satire in *Tiger-Lilies* and the overriding romanticism, sentimentality, and empty ideality of the novel. Lanier had no notion of how to bring them together; for his puritan theology prevented him from making any exploration into psychology. The result was that he attempted to etherealize everything; in particular the strong sexual element in his makeup went completely unrecognized—for he had been taught to ignore the body—and instead was diffused in wild, ungrounded, latently pantheistic ideality.

During this period Lanier was writing and publishing some poetry. None of it is noteworthy, for the idiom in which he wrote and the conventions that he knew were most unsuitable to his talents and alien to his temperament. He was trying to write the abstract, bloodless, formally regular poetry of ideality, as practiced by his friend Paul Hamilton Hayne, by Longfellow, and by the other poets of the genteel school. What Lanier needed was a poetic convention that would permit him to develop and combine images, not arrange them separately in isolated units; and he needed an approach to language that would bring him closer to the representation of the things of his experience, not one that drew him away from a saving grounding in actuality and toward abstract summary. (pp. 111-12)

[It was in **"Corn"** that he first produced a poem in which,] instead of using language merely to fill out conventional stanzaic forms, he began to shape metrical patterns toward an overall tonal effect, with words chosen toward that goal.

The most notable feature of **"Corn"** is the way in which, using the model of the Cowleyan ode with its lines of irregular lengths and its diverse patterning, Lanier begins to break away from the singsong repetition of conventional lyric verse. . . . [He] allowed himself to interpolate dactyls and trochees into the dominant iambic meter, and the resulting freedom made it possible for him to choose words that could provide tonal effects of alliteration and consonance. He began, for almost the first time, to place the premium on language texture, and the result was that he found himself doing what so much of the poetry of his time did not manage: selecting words for their

sensuous associations as much as for their denotative use in the thought content of the poem. Poe, whose work Lanier's sometimes resembled, had placed a similar importance upon the sound effect of language, but had done so crudely and mechanically, achieving for the most part only a vulgar, repetitive excess that often clashed with the content. Lanier, however, was able, in certain lines and stanzas of his new poem, to create rhythms and images that genuinely blended sound with meaning and achieved subtle formal effects. . . . [In addition, there] is an attentiveness to overall pattern—a marshaling of rhyme, sound, texture, and sense, with each line given a distinctive role in its own right as well as in the total development of the poem—that is not only new for Lanier but otherwise largely missing from the American poetry being written during his time. The movement is *orchestral*: it is as if, at last, Lanier was not merely concentrating his entire effort on a single theme, but was adapting the idea he was developing in the poem to the total performance, seeing to it that the texture of the language, the weight of the individual words, images, and lines, the advancing rhythm of the whole—all functioned in unison. (pp. 117-18)

[One] has the feeling that somehow the experience of playing as first flutist in the Peabody Orchestra was more than incidentally involved in the new development in poetry. . . . [It] seems evident that the experience of having had to discipline his flute so that it became part of a larger and more complex musical utterance was making itself felt in the richness and massed complexity of the new poetic technique. Until then, Lanier had never as a poet been able to harness and control the intense, lavish exuberance of emotion and idea that dominated his consciousness; now, by moving to give his poetry an orchestral tone rather than to perform as a solo instrument, he was beginning to find the formal control he needed to express himself.

This is not to say, however, that **"Corn"** is a successful poem, or even, all in all, a particularly good one. Not only is there still far too much abstract ideality and poeticizing, but the overall thought content of the poem is hackneyed and trite. The personification of the corn as "the poet-soul sublime" is all too farfetched:

> Soul calm, like thee, yet fain, like thee, to grow
> By double increment, above, below . . .
>
>   Yea, standing smiling in thy future grave,
>   Serene and brave,
>   With unremitting breath
>   Inhaling life from death,
> Thine epitaph writ fair in fruitage eloquent,
>   Thyself thy monument.

This is a bit much to make even of a very Wordsworthian stalk of corn. And when Lanier gets to the comparison of corn farmer with cotton farmer, he loses control of the overall movement and imagery of his poem in the interests of delivering his economic message. The result at that point resembles nothing so much as third-rate eighteenth-century programmatic verse, or perhaps Wordsworth at his more simplistic, as when the poor cotton farmer-speculator "mourned his fate unkind":

>   In dust, in rain, with might and main,
>   He nursed his cotton, cursed his grain,
>   Fretted for news that made him fret again,
> Snatched at each telegram of Future Sale,
> And thrilled with Bulls' or Bears' alternate wail—

It is difficult to conceive of either a bull or a bear wailing, much less in alternation; and the use of capital letters to signify that the stock exchange is meant, rather than the stockyard, especially when appearing in a poem about rural life, only makes the figure more artificial. **"Corn"** is, finally, withered by its message; the ideological argument, so simplistic and so tendentious, comes as an appalling anticlimax to the description of the natural scene, and even the dignity and music of the final stanza, which is one of Lanier's best, cannot salvage it. (pp. 118-20)

[**"The Symphony"** is as contrived in effect as it is in design.] Not only is the personification of the instruments as singers inveighing against trade a very strained device, but the theme of the poem, as developed by Lanier, is sentimental and insubstantial. . . . If **"The Symphony"** is compared with a work such as Thoreau's *Walden,* its sentimentality is all too obvious. For Thoreau utilized the rhythms of the seasons and developed the exploration of nature and consciousness as both rebuke and counterforce to industrialism and the accumulative instinct, and posited the organic vitality and simplicity of life and growth against the sterility and specialization of modern urban society. Lanier has no such counterforce and no such vital, explorative metaphor to oppose to trade; the best he can manage is all-too-repetitiously to inveigh against it, in the name of "love," without any metaphoric embodiment of a way that love is to go about overcoming its enemy. He has his flute propose the spirit of nature as alternative, but does not offer any hint of a method whereby the opposition is to be mounted. . . . Thus the protest remains abstract and unspecific, disembodied and, because without any grounding in the actual conditions of human needs and possibilities, sentimental. (pp. 121-22)

[Lanier's hostility to the commercial society of his time] never really becomes anything beyond an emotion: strongly held, constantly felt, but not ever critically examined or made the occasion for a searching analysis of the underlying premises of the society. . . . Certainly the Agrarians—Robert Penn Warren, Allen Tate, and John Crowe Ransom—were quite correct when they pointed out that in paradoxically championing an expansive American nationalism while decrying the commercial spirit that sinewed it, Lanier was failing to realize that the two were mutually interdependent. . . . (pp. 124-25)

The Agrarians were just a little unfair. Lanier's views on industrialism and the commercial ethos, and their incompatibility with the artistic impulse, were closer to those of the Agrarians than they cared to admit, and Lanier's attitudes were like theirs, importantly an outgrowth of southern origins. (p. 125)

Be that as it may, when the Agrarians objected . . . to the didacticism and the crude, emotional, polemical statement of theme in **"The Symphony,"** they were on firm ground. Edd Winfield Parks's verdict on the poem—"a clever experiment in technique by a dexterous artificer, which concentrates attention on the superficial form"—is the best that can be said for it [see excerpt above, 1936]. Yet though as a poem it is a failure, once again the failure is of a different order and scale than what most of Lanier's contemporaries were managing. . . . The poem lacks the richness and concrete texture of the rural descriptions in **"Corn,"** but Lanier does develop the specific metaphor of the orchestra throughout. Thus **"The Symphony,"** for all its vagueness of argument and its contrived form, does to an extent create its own context rather than merely refer to one based on ideas, as the general run of poetry of the period is wont to do, and it possesses a clumsy and rather diffused but genuine vigor. (p. 126)

[The] rather dubious last line of **"The Symphony"**—"Music is Love in search of a word"—is by no means so obscure in meaning if we read it as a way of expressing the poet's own passionate quest to write poetry that could have the emotional and . . . spiritual impact of music. Lanier wanted very much to compose verse that would create the ravishing *effect* that music had on his own sensibility. But as long as he attempted to do this through so-called noble and beautiful ideas, . . . the result was abstraction—*i.e.,* the content of the line "Music is Love in search of a word," with the emotion dissolving into sentimental excess.

But when . . . [in the late 1870's he read the Anglo-Saxon and Middle English poets,] he came upon poems originally meant to be chanted rhythmically . . . and with a prosody designed to guide the response to the chant. Such poetry seemed to him to possess, in its mechanics, precisely the virtues and techniques of music-making: a measure based on time intervals and not metric feet, with duration as the guide to syllabic stress, and sound combinations used for emotional coloring. To be sure, the same was true of later poetry, but the dominance of the iambic foot in the verse of his own time had impeded, for him, the perception of the nature of that relationship. When he thought of poetry in terms of iambic meter, he had thought in terms of its idea content, so automatic was the conventional iambic rhythm. Reading the older poetry broke up the usual expectations and made him conscious of what it was possible to do with language in terms of duration, stress, combinations of sound, and pitch. (pp. 128-29)

[Lanier propounded his theory of the musical basis of poetry in *The Science of English Verse*. This work] has its flaws, yet is altogether a distinguished production. It represents what Lanier was capable of as an analytical thinker when his subject was precisely defined and his terms of reference were specific and limited. . . . [There] can be no doubt that he provided a method of accounting for the way that verse is structured that helped notably toward freeing the theory of prosody in English from the straitjacket of an outmoded, too mechanical system of metrical form.

Where he went wrong was in his disinclination to recognize the essential difference between the rhythm of verse and that of music. . . . [The] rhythm of poetry is achieved in language and serves the purpose, along with the connotative associations of words, of fusing emotion and idea into a larger unit of meaning. The words of a poem both *denote* experience and also, along with sound, rhythm, rhyme, and imagery, *connote* it; and the total meaning of the poem cannot be perceived through musical relationships alone, any more than through a prose paraphrase of the ideas denoted therein. Music, by contrast, does not serve to represent ideas; it develops sustains, and explores emotional states, and its rhythms and patterns are not subject to any such denotative function. Thus when Lanier says that "the term 'verse' denotes a set of specially related sounds," and builds his theory upon determining the relationships between sounds, he views the rhythmic and tonal relationships of verse as a mathematical absolute, rather than as one very important functional device of a more complex overall objective.

For Lanier's future as a poet, it was not so much the actual writing of *The Science of English Verse* as his thinking about the subject and his involvement in the older, noniambic forms of English poetry that were significant. One immediate and observable result was a ballad entitled **"The Revenge of Ham-**

ish,'' which Lanier apparently wrote in 1878 as an experiment in the use of logaoedic dactyls. (pp. 130-31)

What is . . . interesting, I think, is what the writing of the poem shows about Lanier as poet. By deliberately selecting an incident presumably out of Scottish history, and setting it as a narrative in order to illustrate the use of an ancient poetic rhythm, Lanier was subjecting his muse to an arbitrary formal discipline not only of rhythm and pattern but of content as well. He was all but eliminating his usual didactic stance; there could be little or no philosophizing about love versus trade, the beauty of truth, and the unity of love, music, and language, in a narrative poem designed to accomplish so precise an objective. The result is, as poetry, quite satisfying. (pp. 132-33)

He needed distancing, the discipline of a formal pattern and also of a concrete, externalized content, if he was to break loose from the idealized abstractions of the poetry of his time and create in language. . . . But in **''The Revenge of Hamish''** the pattern and content were ultimately *too* formal, *too* external; he was unable to get his own passionate concerns into it at all; the first-person utterance of lyric poetry would be required for that. (p. 133)

''The Marshes of Glynn'' is by no means a perfect poem— nothing that Sidney Lanier wrote ever approached that status. He is, as always, too willing to settle for sound at the price of appropriateness, as in his too precious rhyming, ''emerald twilights'' with ''virginal shy lights.'' In his famous strophe to the marsh hen . . . there remains, alas, a slight taint of the ludicrous, the marsh hen not being a notably religious fowl in its nest-building activities. On the other hand there is a distinct gain in the fact that he *is* writing about marsh hens, marsh grass, watery sod, live oaks, and other items of his experience of coastal Georgia. . . . For **''The Marshes of Glynn''** is the poem in which, emboldened by the emphasis upon nature he learned from Emerson and the language-use he learned from Whitman and the older English poets, Lanier for the first time draws deeply and amply on the specificalities of his own locale, without trying to translate them into terms of a more abstract, literary reference. The poem is *about* the coast of Georgia, and the language is bent to the purpose of describing it. . . . The language, in syntax and word-tone, is full of movement, allowing Lanier to make his point by accumulation, with the long sentences and the linking constructions designed to lead the reader's attention onward rather than to fragment the experience into separate parts. This is what Whitman had shown him, and this is what he needed if he were going to communicate his own view of the world. For as we have seen, what he had always wanted to do was to release passion into affective language, to find words to express and give form to the emotion that he experienced in playing and listening to music. His art and his temperament were not suited for analytical discrimination or working out of complex relationships; what he had to offer was expansiveness of feeling, the passionate fullness of an affirmative, romantic response to a multiplicity and variety of experience. Long lines, alliteration and assonance that built one association upon another, internal rhymes that joined the images within a line together, end-rhymes that brought the long strings of images and associations into cumulative relationship, and an irregular pattern of verse that did not strive to force a too fixed, too intricate form upon the experience but only keep it controlled and moving forward—this was the proper prosody for Lanier.

His youthful Calvinism had become pantheism now—or rather, a kind of enthusiastic yea-saying, a delighted affirmation of

God, whose kingdom was nature, and who, however theologically undiscriminated, was worshipped in passionate praise for His creation. (pp. 136-38)

The poem ends, as is proper for a poem in which the religious experience of nature and the day and night are fused into a kind of emotional, sexual fulfillment, with an image of release into mystery, in which the themes of marsh, sea, night, and God are joined into one final statement, the marshland in darkness:

And now from the Vast of the Lord will the waters of sleep
   Roll on in the souls of men,
   But who will reveal to our waking ken
   The forms that swim and the shapes that creep
   Under the waters of sleep?
And I would I could know what swimmeth below when the
                                                   tide
      comes in
On the length and the breadth of the marvellous marshes
   of Glynn.

Thus concludes Sidney Lanier's best poem and, I think, one of the two or three most distinguished of all poems written by nineteenth-century southern poets. It comes as culmination of a long process of education, in which Lanier had not only to learn much, but also to unlearn even more. The poem is very much in the long tradition of southern poetry, in that it emphasizes formal texture, sound, rhetorical ornament, rather than direct personal statement, content, meter-making argument. . . . [For] all the intensity that went into its making, it is formal, essentially impersonal, public. It is characteristically southern, too, in its strong emphasis on place. (pp. 138-39)

But there is one element of the poem that represents a distinct break with Lanier's southern origins. If one compares **''The Marshes of Glynn''** with such poems as Simms's ''The Edge of the Swamp'' or Timrod's ''Spring'' or, for that matter, with a twentieth-century poem such as Robert Penn Warren's ''Bearded Oaks,'' it becomes obvious that Lanier is doing what the others cannot or will not do: he is directly identifying his situation with nature, and declaring not only that man may learn *in* nature but that his true image of himself is *as* natural rather than social being. The other southern poets will not proceed that far; however beautiful they may find nature, they tend always to see it as separate from man and finally aloof from him. But Lanier, tutored by Emerson, ventures beyond that. Viewing the edge of the marsh and the sea, he declares,

   Somehow my soul seems suddenly free
From the weighing of fate and the sad discussion of sin,
By the length and the breadth and the sweep of the marshes
   of Glynn . . .

which is farther into nature by a crucial step than the southern writer has usually been willing to go. Lanier in his best poem has joined Emerson, Thoreau, Bryant, Whittier, and, intermittently, Emily Dickinson in a transcendent view of nature that erases the barrier between it and man and places man at home in nature as refuge from society. (pp. 139-40)

Sidney Lanier, I think, was potentially a major poet; and the tragedy is that it was only in the final years of his short life that he was exposed to the conditions that could enable him to develop his abilities. Lanier required what Mark Twain . . . possessed: the experience of distancing from his origins that could give him the perspective and the contrast of social attitudes and values that in Mark Twain's instance resulted in several great works of fiction. Historically, socially, Lanier was closely bound to the South; temperamentally, emotionally, he was at odds with many of its attitudes and qualities. Thus his ways of thinking about conduct, decorum, the social ideal prevented him from following the lead which his temperament and his intellect suggested, which was along the same paths as an Emerson, a Whitman, or an Emily Dickinson. Temperamentally, emotionally, he was a pantheist, a naturalist; but as a product of the southern social and cultural community he drew back. From the evidence of his several major poems of the late 1870s and 1880s, it seems obvious that he was breaking away from what for him were frustrating restraints. Had he been able to begin the process sooner, the break would have become more crucial for him, and the creative tension between the two antithetical modes of thought and feeling might well have produced just the kind of dialectic of head and heart that, embodied in language, could result in major poetic achievement. All the elements for such a struggle, and its potential artistic resolution, were there, but they came into focus too tardily and too briefly. (pp. 141-42)

The body of Lanier's poetic work is small, and of that, very little is of first importance. Indeed, the total quantity of Lanier's poetry that merits the attention of later generations might be safely contained in several dozen printed pages. But in a poem such as **"The Marshes of Glynn"** we can see what he might have been as poet. At his best he was quite original, and full of a kind of powerful, passionate sincerity that breaks out of the morass of contrived pieties and warmed-over ideality in language and attitude that characterizes the poetry of his time. Certainly he wrote a handful of poems that are better by far than anything written by the so-called leaders of American poetry of the period: nothing by Stedman, Taylor, Boker, Stoddard, or Aldrich is of the order of **"The Marshes of Glynn,"** **"Sunrise,"** or even **"Corn."** Emily Dickinson and Whitman are another matter; but in Lanier's time the one was utterly unknown and the other considered neither respectable nor poetic. Lanier's achievement, desperately won, is that even while paying his respects to the outward forms of the poetry of the dominant genteel tradition, he stretched them to new limits and actually managed to force new vigor and life into them. It could not endure; and a new literary generation would find it necessary to break with them entirely. When that day came, however, it could finally be recognized what this former Confederate soldier, adherent to the attitudes and values of his time and forced by dint of his origins and circumstance to contend against appalling odds, came close to doing. Not for half a century after his death would there be another southern poet worthy to stand alongside him. (p. 144)

> *Louis D. Rubin, Jr., "The Passion of Sidney Lanier," in his* William Elliott Shoots a Bear: Essays on the Southern Literary Imagination *(reprinted by permission of Louisiana State University Press; copyright © 1975 by Louisiana State University Press), Louisiana State University Press, 1975, pp. 107-44.*

ADDITIONAL BIBLIOGRAPHY

Allen, Gay Wilson. "Sidney Lanier As a Literary Critic." *Philological Quarterly* XVII, No. 2 (April 1938): 121-38.
  Identifies and elucidates the central tenets of Lanier's critical doctrines. Allen concludes his essay with a brief discussion of Lanier's pronouncements on individual works and authors and provides an estimate of Lanier's contribution to the field of literary criticism.

Andersen, Johannes C. "Poetry and Music." In his *The Laws of Verse,* pp. 172-82. Cambridge: Cambridge University Press, 1928.*
  Maintains that much of Lanier's prosodic theory is untenable because fixed time values cannot properly be assigned to spoken syllables.

Baskervill, William Malone. "Sidney Lanier." In his *Southern Writers, Vol. I,* pp. 137-298. 1897. Reprint. New York: Gordian Press, 1970.
  An early study of Lanier's life and works. Reverence is the keynote of Baskervill's essay, which was superceded in 1905 by Edwin Mims's critical biography, *Sidney Lanier* (see excerpt above).

Bradford, Gamaliel. "Sidney Lanier." In his *American Portraits: 1875-1900,* pp. 61-83. Boston, New York: Houghton Mifflin Co., 1922.
  An ingenuous examination of Lanier's inner life as revealed in his letters, biography, and poems. Bradford ultimately expresses disappointment that Lanier did not "put his soul" into his poetry.

Brooks, Van Wyck. "Sidney Lanier." In his *A Chilmark Miscellany,* pp. 297-303. New York: E. P. Dutton & Co., 1948.
  Discusses Lanier's contributions to American literature. While he comments on the originality of Lanier's experiments in verse form, Brooks notes that Lanier "struck one in later times as more important in the role of a personage and thinker than he was as a poet."

Brown, Calvin S. "Sonata Form." In his *Music and Literature: A Comparison of the Arts,* pp. 161-77. Athens, Ga.: The University of Georgia Press, 1948.*
  Examines Lanier's adaptation of symphonic form in "The Symphony." Brown feels that the symphonic structure of Lanier's poem disintegrates after the flute solo, and he suggests that concern for "poetic" considerations prevented Lanier from pursuing the musical analogy further.

Introductions to *The Centennial Edition of the Works of Sidney Lanier, Vols. I-X,* edited by Charles R. Anderson. Baltimore: The Johns Hopkins Press, 1945.
  Thorough, scholarly introductions to Lanier's works and letters by such critics as Charles R. Anderson, Paull Franklin Baum, Philip Graham, Garland Greever, Cecil Abernethy, Kemp Malone, Clarence Gohdes, and Aubrey H. Starke. (See excerpts above by Gohdes and Greever, 1945).

Commager, Henry Steele. "A 'Gallant and Heroic Figure'." *The New York Times Book Review* XCVI, No. 32,411 (20 October 1946): 6, 38, 40.
  A review of *The Centennial Edition of the Works of Sidney Lanier.* For Commager, who avers that "a dozen or a score of Lanier's best poems are destined for immortality," the principal effect of the volumes is to reveal Lanier's courage, magnanimity, and consecrated devotion to art.

Coulson, Edwin R. "Lanier's Place as American Poet and Prosodist." In *Sidney Lanier: Poet and Prosodist,* by Richard Webb and Edwin R. Coulson, pp. 73-103. Athens, Ga.: The University of Georgia Press, 1941.
  A survey of modern critical opinion regarding Lanier's influence and stature as a poet and prosodist. Coulson's study features original commentary by Harriet Monroe, Edward Harris, Robert Hillyer, Conrad Aiken, and other writers. (See excerpts above by Monroe, Harris, and Aiken, 1941.)

Dabney, J. P. Preface to his *The Musical Basis of Verse: A Scientific Study of the Principles of Poetic Composition,* pp. viii-x. New York: Longmans, Green, and Co., 1901.
  Praises Lanier's principle of using musical notation to analyze verse, but questions some of his judgments as a practitioner. Dabney suggests that many of Lanier's verse notations represent a misguided attempt to reconcile quantity with accent, and he disagrees with Lanier's conception of three-beat measure.

De Bellis, Jack. "Sidney Lanier." In his *Sidney Lanier, Henry Timrod, and Paul Hamilton Hayne: A Reference Guide*, pp. 1-105. Reference Publications in Literature, edited by Joseph Katz. Boston: G. K. Hall & Co., 1978.

> An extensive annotated bibliography on Lanier's life and works published from 1868 through 1976.

Garland, Hamlin. "The Verse of Sidney Lanier." In his *Roadside Meetings*, pp. 144-53. New York: The Macmillan Co., 1930.

> Recalls Lanier as one of his early literary enthusiasms. Garland remarks on the powerful personal appeal of Lanier's altruism and "exquisite" sensibility to nature, and he testifies that Lanier's free conception of verse form taught him "freedom within law" in poetry.

Graham, Philip. "Lanier and Science." *American Literature* 4, No. 3 (November 1932): 288-92.

> Proposes that Lanier's interest in modern science enriched his art. While many critics argue that the conflicting claims between scientific advancement and social and spiritual ideals undermined the philosophical integrity of Lanier's work, Graham contends that this conflict "brought the spark of life to his poetry" and inspired his best poems.

Harman, Henry E. "A Study of Sidney Lanier's 'The Symphony'." *The South Atlantic Quarterly* XVII, No. 1 (January 1918): 32-9.

> A consideration of "The Symphony" as Lanier's poetic masterpiece.

Monroe, Harriet. "Rhythms of English Verse." In her *Poets and Their Art*, pp. 268-84. New York: The Macmillan Co., 1926.*

> Credits Lanier with providing conclusive proof that time is the basis of rhythm in English verse. Monroe's exposition of the temporal foundations of rhythm is similar to Lanier's, for she uses musical notation to indicate time relations and identifies three-time as the dominant rhythm in English poetry.

Parks, Edd Winfield. *Sidney Lanier: The Man, the Poet, the Critic*. Athens, Ga.: University of Georgia Press, 1968, 108 p.

> A tripartite, primarily descriptive account of Lanier's life, poetry, and critical views.

Pearce, Roy Harvey. "American Renaissance (2), The Poet and the People: Timrod and Lanier." In his *The Continuity of American Poetry*, pp. 236-46. Princeton: Princeton University Press, 1961.*

> Depicts Lanier as a poet who unsuccessfully attempted to move away from the domain of public, occasional poetry—his "major

literary heritage" as a Southern writer—to the realm of private, personal verse.

Petry, Alice Hall. "Death as Etherealization in the Poetry of Sidney Lanier." *South Dakota Review* 17, No. 1 (Spring 1979): 46-55.

> Observes that while Lanier omits death from his discussion of etherealization in the essay "Retrospects and Prospects," he treats it as a microcosm of etherealization in his poetry.

Shapiro, Karl. *A Bibliography of Modern Prosody*. Baltimore: The Johns Hopkins Press, 1948, 36. p.*

> A brief, annotated bibliography of modern prosody. In his annotation for *The Science of English Verse*, Shapiro describes the work as "one of the best expositions of its theory in the literature of metrics."

Starke, A. H. "More about Lanier." *The New Republic* LXXVI, No. 987 (1 November, 1933): 337-38.

> In a letter to the editor, Starke responds to Allen Tate's commentary on his *Sidney Lanier* (see excerpts above by Starke and Tate, 1933). Starke corrects several "misstatements" made by Tate, and he defends Lanier as an earnest critic of industrialism.

Stedman, Edmund Clarence. "Sidney Lanier." In his *Genius and Other Essays*, pp. 250-53. New York: Moffat, Yard, and Co., 1911.

> A eulogistic tribute originally presented at an 1881 memorial gathering for Sidney Lanier. While Stedman recalls Lanier as the poet/artist, he also suggests that his absorption with prosodic theory inhibited spontaneity in his verse.

Tate, Allen. "More about Lanier," *The New Republic* LXXVI, No. 987 (1 November, 1933): 338.

> In a letter to the editor, Tate issues a rejoinder to Aubrey H. Starke's response to his commentary on Starke's *Sidney Lanier*. Tate agrees with Starke's statement that "The Symphony" is an indictment of industrialism, but he points out that "'The Psalm of the West' is praise of industrialism, for this simple reason: it is praise of 'nationalism,' *argal* of Northern sectionalism, *argal* of industrialism."

Ward, William Hayes. "Memorial." In *Poems of Sidney Lanier*, edited by Mary D. Lanier, pp. xi-xli. New York: Charles Scribner's Sons, 1884.

> The first authorized biographical portrait of Sidney Lanier, edited by his wife.

John Gibson Lockhart

1794-1854

(Also wrote under the pseudonyms of Dr. Peter Morris, Z, and Mordecai Mullion) Scottish biographer, critic, essayist, editor, poet, novelist, and translator.

Lockhart is primarily remembered for his biography of Sir Walter Scott, *Memoirs of the Life of Sir Walter Scott, Bart.*, and his critical contributions to *Blackwood's Edinburgh Magazine* and the *Quarterly Review*. The *Life of Scott* is considered by many to be inferior only to James Boswell's *The Life of Samuel Johnson* among biographies in the English language. As a critic, Lockhart helped to ensure the success of *Blackwood's*, and his trenchant wit earned him the nickname of "The Scorpion." Later, as editor of the British *Quarterly*, he influenced the literary tastes of the British public for over a quarter of a century.

The son of a Presbyterian minister, Lockhart was born in Cambusnethan, Lanarkshire, Scotland and raised in Glasgow. He entered the University of Glasgow where his proficiency in classical literature won him a scholarship to Balliol College, Oxford. At Oxford, he not only excelled in the classics, but also developed an interest in Spanish and German literature and became fluent in several languages. Throughout his schooling, Lockhart enjoyed drawing caricatures of his classmates and teachers. His keen sense of the ludicrous, evident in these early caricatures, was later exhibited in his contributions to *Blackwood's*, as well as in *Peter's Letters to His Kinsfolk*, a lampoon of Edinburgh society.

The "mischievous Oxford puppy," as James Hogg referred to him, graduated from Balliol College in 1813 and returned to Glasgow to study law. He was admitted to the Scottish bar in 1816, but never practiced law. In 1817, inspired by his appreciation of German literature, he traveled to Weimar, Germany, where he met Johann Wolfgang von Goethe, whom he considered the greatest living poet. Lockhart's trip was financed by the publisher William Blackwood, with the agreement that Lockhart would translate into English Friedrich Schlegel's *Lectures on the History of Literature*.

Many critics note the influence of German thought on Lockhart's work. Some attribute the melodramatic tone of his fiction to a fascination with the themes of early nineteenth-century German novels. As a critic, he is often credited with promoting German literature in England before the influence of essayist Thomas Carlyle.

Shortly after his return from Germany, Lockhart became a principal contributor to *Blackwood's*, a Tory periodical founded in 1817 to counter the popular Whig journal *The Edinburgh Review*. In October, 1817, he coauthored the notorious "Translation from an Ancient Chaldee Manuscript," in which prominent members of Edinburgh society are satirized in biblical language. Written by Lockhart, Hogg, John Wilson, and William Maginn, the composition created such a stir that it was quickly suppressed by Blackwood. This controversial piece set the tone for the magazine. In the same issue also appeared "On the Cockney School of Poetry," the first of a series of scathing essays written between 1817 and 1825 under the pseudonym of Z, in which he assailed John Keats and Leigh

Hunt for their political beliefs and, indirectly, for their inferior education and upbringing. Although pseudonyms were used interchangeably by various authors in the early days of *Blackwood's*, most critics attribute the articles on the "Cockney School" to Lockhart, who is often castigated for his unfair treatment of Keats and Hunt. Virginia Woolf, for example, notes that Lockhart "rushed to his doom" by allowing personal prejudices to influence his negative review of Keats, which she describes as an attempt "to snuff out between finger and thumb one of the immortal lights of English literature."

In 1820, Lockhart married Sophia Scott, the daughter of Sir Walter Scott. The following year he became involved in a dispute with John Scott, the editor of *Baldwin's London Magazine*. Scott's magazine had been the subject of bitter invective in *Blackwood's*. In three essays in *Baldwin's*, Scott mistakenly named Lockhart as author of the slur against his magazine and rebuked him for denying that he was the editor of *Blackwood's*. The lengthy debate culminated in a duel between Scott and John Christie, Lockhart's lawyer, in which Scott was killed. Lockhart continued to write for *Blackwood's*, but even though he was less active in the campaign against the Whigs, his reputation was severely damaged by the scandal.

In addition to critical essays, Lockhart occasionally contributed poetry to *Blackwood's*. Of his verses, which remain uncollected, "Captain Paton's Lament" and "Mad Banker of Amsterdam" are most often praised for their flowing rhythm. Lockhart is best known as a poet for his *Ancient Spanish Ballads, Historical and Romantic*, a volume of poems translated freely from Spanish, which critics agree preserves and, in some instances, heightens the beauty of the original ballads.

While writing for *Blackwood's*, Lockhart produced several novels in quick succession. The first of these, *Peter's Letters to His Kinsfolk*, consists of sketches of Edinburgh society in the form of letters. In several of the sketches, Lockhart ridiculed leading Edinburgh Whigs, and the novel, when first published, contributed to the rivalry between *Blackwood's* and *The Edinburgh Review*. Whig reviewers condemned *Peter's Letters* as libelous but acknowledged Lockhart's abilities as a satirist. In his biography of Scott, Lockhart apologized for *Peter's Letters*, commenting that "nobody but a very young and thoughtless person could have dreamt of putting forth such a book." Later critics, however, find little in Lockhart's criticism of Edinburgh life to warrant the initial harsh reception of *Peter's Letters*.

Of the novels that followed *Peter's Letters*, critics have judged *Some Passages in the Life of Mr. Adam Blair, Minister of the Gospel at Cross-Meikle* most favorably. Based on a true story, *Adam Blair* is the tragic account of a minister's sin of fornication and his subsequent punishment. Some early reviewers found the subject matter offensive, but many modern critics praise *Adam Blair* for its examination of eighteenth-century Scottish morals. Henry James declared that the moral questions examined in *Adam Blair* justify its comparison with Nathaniel Hawthorne's novel *The Scarlet Letter* and remarked that "they deal alike with the manners of a rigidly theological society." Many critics consider Lockhart's examination of his character in *Adam Blair* important to the development of the psychological novel. His last novel, *The History of Matthew Wald*, is also noted by later critics for its psychological elements. In general, Lockhart was not successful as a novelist. Most critics agree with George Saintsbury's statement that "Lockhart had every faculty for writing novels, except the faculty of novel-writing."

From 1825 to 1853, Lockhart was editor of the *Quarterly Review*. He wrote over one hundred articles for the magazine, many of which are still considered entertaining, if not always insightful. During his years at the *Quarterly*, Lockhart was less inclined to allow party politics to determine his critical judgments. Despite his aversion to their political principles, Lockhart acknowledged the works of William Wordsworth, Samuel Taylor Coleridge, and Percy Bysshe Shelley. His somewhat erratic criticism of fiction has been attributed by Woolf to his tendency to overestimate the importance of novelists whose subject matter closely resembles the themes of his own novels. Lockhart's derogatory review of Alfred, Lord Tennyson's 1832 volume of poetry is singled out by early reviewers, along with his attacks on Keats and Hunt, as evidence of his contentiousness. Modern critics, however, maintain that the review was not undeserved, and point out that Tennyson himself respected Lockhart's opinion so much that in a later edition of the volume he altered or omitted the passages Lockhart had censured.

Critics unanimously agree that as a biographer Lockhart has few rivals. He first showed his talent for the form in brief biographies of Napoleon Bonaparte and Theodore Hook. His *Life of Robert Burns* is distinguished by its sympathetic unpatronizing insight into Burns's character. Critics consistently praise Lockhart's masterpiece, the *Life of Scott*, for its unity and proportion. He is especially admired for underplaying his own role in the biography, in spite of his close relationship with Scott. M. Clive Hildyard, Sir Herbert Grierson, and Saintsbury consider Lockhart's dignified presentation of Scott's death in the closing pages of the *Life of Scott* one of his greatest achievements. When it was first published, some reviewers objected to Lockhart's frank discussion of Scott's financial downfall and complained that he emphasized Scott's faults; however, more recent critics view the *Life of Scott* as an idealization of its subject. Lockhart's method of compiling Scott's vast correspondence—his frequent combination of letters or deletion of portions of them without indicating textual omissions—has received much critical attention in the twentieth century. His detractors argue that this practice is deceptive and misleading; others feel it is an artistic device which makes the biography more cohesive.

Lockhart's years at the *Quarterly* were darkened by the deaths of his wife, his two sons, and Scott. In 1853, he resigned as editor, and he died a year later. While he has always been acclaimed as a biographer, Lockhart's reputation as a critic declined in the nineteenth century because of his association with *Blackwood's*. The first biography of Lockhart, Andrew Lang's *The Life and Letters of John Gibson Lockhart*, published in 1897, did much to improve his image. With the publication in 1931 of *Lockhart's Literary Criticism*, edited by Hildyard, twentieth-century commentators began to reassess Lockhart's contribution. Modern critics tend to ignore Lockhart's youthful indiscretions and comment that it was his reserve, which was often interpreted as aloofness, as much as his biting wit, that caused his criticism to be judged unfairly in his own lifetime. He is regarded as a versatile, if somewhat severe critic whose opinions of his contemporaries, though lacking depth, are generally considered accurate when not distorted by political animosities.

PRINCIPAL WORKS

Peter's Letters to His Kinsfolk [as Dr. Peter Morris] (epistolary novel) 1819
Valerius: A Roman Story (novel) 1820
Some Passages in the Life of Mr. Adam Blair, Minister of the Gospel at Cross-Meikle (novel) 1822
Ancient Spanish Ballads, Historical and Romantic [translator] (poetry) 1823
Reginald Dalton (novel) 1823
The History of Matthew Wald (novel) 1824
Life of Robert Burns (biography) 1828
Memoirs of the Life of Sir Walter Scott, Bart. 7 vols. (biography) 1837-38
Lockhart's Literary Criticism (criticism) 1931

M. M. [MORDECAI MULLION, PSEUDONYM OF JOHN GIBSON LOCKHART] (essay date 1819)

[*Lockhart wrote the following laudatory review of* Peter's Letters to His Kinsfolk *before he had finished the novel, in order to encourage interest in the book. It was not until several months after this review appeared in* Blackwood's Edinburgh Magazine *that* Peter's Letters *was first published. Lockhart praises* Peter's Letters *for its sincerity and absence of prejudice, and he extols the novel as a "graphical and trustworthy" sketch of Scottish society. More importantly, Lockhart defends his use of satire in* Peter's Letters *by commenting that he "does not . . . bestow his cuts except where they are pretty well merited." Lockhart again promoted his own work in an anonymous review of* The History of Matthew Wald *that was published in* Blackwood's *(1824).]*

Though it is said on the title-page [of **"Peter's Letters to His Kinsfolk"**] that these volumes are sold by all the booksellers, yet, strange to tell, a single copy is not to be found among all the bibliopoles of Edinburgh. These gentlemen are really very remiss—and seem not to know their own interest. (p. 612)

Dr [Peter] Morris (for he is the author) . . . has given to the world two very amusing volumes. He performed his journey from Aberystwith, where, we understand, he is in very extensive practice as a medical man, in a shandry-dan of his own invention, of which, by the bye, we hear the rather too much—it being evidently the Doctor's hobby. (pp. 613-14)

[Peter] devotes two long letters to the state of education in Edinburgh, and though we have detected some errors in his account of the course of study pursued in our university, and can by no means concur with him in some of his very severe strictures on not a few of the professors, yet it is wonderful with what acuteness he has penetrated into the spirit of the system. (p. 616)

When we consider how difficult a thing it is to get rid of national prejudices of any kind, and more particularly, how deep-rooted those prejudices are which men educated at Oxford commonly bear towards the very name of Presbyterianism, we cannot refuse to Dr Morris the praise of having overcome his prejudices in a way that does equal honour to the perspicacity of his intellect, and the goodness of his heart. We trust the liberal and manly style in which he expresses these sentiments, may produce some effect on those for whose benefit he appears to have thrown them out. (p. 617)

His book is a valuable present to the people of England and Wales for it furnishes the only graphical and trustworthy sketches of the present manners and society of Scotland which they have it in their power to peruse. . . . He is singularly free from that passion for fine writing which infects most modern tourists. He never goes about the bush for a phrase, but seems resolved to express his meaning in the most brief, and direct, and precise manner. His compliments have an air of sincerity about them which must additionally endear the Doctor to those who had the pleasure of knowing him personally during his stay among us. . . . The Doctor is a keen satirist too, but as, in general, he does not seem to bestow his cuts except where they are pretty well merited, we, for our parts, are very willing to pass over this little failing. . . . (p. 621)

> *M. M. [Mordecai Mullion, pseudonym of John Gibson Lockhart], "Observations on 'Peter's Letters to His Kinsfolk',' in* Blackwood's Edinburgh Magazine, *Vol. IV, No. XXIII, February, 1819, pp. 612-21.*

WALTER SCOTT   (letter date 1819)

[Scott was a Scottish novelist, poet, historian, biographer, and critic of the Romantic period who is best known for his historical novels, which were a great popular success. The following generous assessment of Peter's Letters to His Kinsfolk *is drawn from a letter that Scott wrote to Lockhart prior to Lockhart's marriage to Scott's daughter, Sophia. Scott's comment that Lockhart presented a "too favourable" view of Edinburgh society in* Peter's Letters *contrasts sharply with the opinion of most early reviewers of the novel who, in the words of Lockhart, "denounced [it] as a mere string of libels."]*

I think the Doctor [in **Peter's Letters to His Kinsfolk**] has got over his ground admirably;—only the general turn of the book is perhaps too favourable, both to the state of our public society, and of individual character. . . . But it was, in every point of view, right to take this more favourable tone, and to throw a Claude Lorraine tint over our northern landscape. We cannot bear the actual bare truth, either in conversation, or that which approaches nearest to conversation, in a work like the Doctor's, published within the circle to which it refers.

For the rest, the Doctor has fully maintained his high character for force of expression, both serious and comic, and for acuteness of observation, . . . and his scalpel has not been idle, though his lenient hand has cut sharp and clean, and poured balm into the wound. What an acquisition it would have been to our general information to have had such a work written, I do not say fifty, but even five-and-twenty years ago; and how much of grave and gay might then have been preserved, as it were, in amber, which have now mouldered away. When I think that at an age not much younger than yours I knew Black, Ferguson, Robertson, Erskine, Adam Smith, John Home, &c. &c., and at least saw Burns, I can appreciate better than any one the value of a work which, like this, would have handed them down to posterity in their living colours. Dr Morris ought . . . to revive every half century, to record the fleeting manners of the age, and the interesting features of those who will be only known to posterity by their works. If I am very partial to the Doctor, which I am not inclined to deny, remember I have been bribed by his kind and delicate account of his visit to [my home at] Abbotsford. (p. 404)

> *Walter Scott, in a letter to J. G. Lockhart on July 19, 1819, in* Memoirs of the Life of Sir Walter Scott, Bart. *by J. G. Lockhart, R. Cadell, 1837-1838 (and reprinted in* The Life of Sir Walter Scott, Bart.: 1771-1832 *by J. G. Lockhart, revised edition, Adam & Charles Black, 1893, pp. 404-05).*

THE MONTHLY REVIEW, LONDON   (essay date 1819)

[The author of this essay correctly assumes that Dr. Peter Morris, the author of Peter's Letters to His Kinsfolk, *is an imaginary figure. However, the essayist mistakenly conjectures that* Peter's Letters *is the joint production of John Wilson and Lockhart, arguing that inconsistencies in Dr. Morris's character can be resolved if the novel is attributed to both Lockhart and Wilson. Although the critic finds* Peter's Letters *entertaining, he dismisses the book as a "satirical" and "ill meaning publication," and he censures the authors for encroaching upon the privacy of Edinburgh's citizens. This essay typifies contemporary response to* Peter's Letters.]*

Though the plan [of **Peter's Letters to His Kinsfolk**] is by no means novel, as we are in possession of numerous letters in this style both from the *dead and the living,* and the very title is almost a plagiarism on Mr. Walter Scott's work, *Paul's Letters to His Kinsfolk,* yet few have exceeded these young authors (as we believe them to be) in the management of the device. . . . It is always difficult to look on familiar things with the eye of a stranger; and it requires a strong imagination, capable of divesting itself of those particulars which would betray a local acquaintance. For our part, we cannot admit that Dr. Morris is one of this sort of visitors, and therefore the movers of the machinery are by no means fortunate in preserving the *probability* of this part of their drama. His particular descriptions of characters and scenery are far too perfect and minute for the casual eye of a mere traveller; while the warmth and vividness of his language partake little of the sobriety of so old a gentleman as Dr. Morris is represented to be. There is a want of keeping in the picture . . . , supposing it to be drawn by the hand of a Welsh tourist; while, if we attribute it to the united genius of Mr. L— and Mr. J. W—, its inconsistences will vanish, and the various groupes of figures will appear in their true light and position. (pp. 309-10)

[The authors are themselves barristers, scholars, orators, and critics, and thus] we have lawyers, poets, and critics, represented in every attitude; while they do not allow *the Doctor* even once to hint at the gentlemen of his own profession. Yet to have been consistent, they should not only have permitted him to descant on physic, but, as he is stated to be an elderly gentleman, and a great admirer of antiquity, he should have exhibited a little more of the Roman spirit of Fabricius when he suddenly beheld the elephant of Pyrrhus; and not have started back with surprize and delight when the curtain was drawn from the literary monster, and Edinburgh flashed on his bewildered view. If he had likewise consulted Horace, as much as he appears to be acquainted with the doctrine of Epicurus . . . , the Welsh physician would have appeared more in character. . . . With such exceptions, however, the *chief* author is really an entertaining and enlightened traveller, apparently an agreeable companion, and by no means a despicable poet, as his letters frequently evince by bold imagery, lively descriptions, and ridiculously happy delineations of events. A strain of good humour, cleverness, and even occasional wit, is also manifested, which is well adapted to delineate the peculiar character and manners of a people like the Scotch; and, though not to be compared to our masters in this line, Cervantes, Le Sage, Montesquieu's Chinese Letters, Voltaire's Novels, or even (Southey's) Espriella's Letters of a Spaniard from England, the pseudo-doctor has given a portrait which is the best that we have seen for some time. Those who love enthusiasm in describing the characters and customs of a country, or who venerate the "*amor patria*" [love of fatherland] reduced to the finest *threads* of distinction, will here find ample materials for thought and entertainment; and, though we consider this method of trumpeting forth the modern names and honors of a nation as neither extremely judicious nor perfectly warrantable, it is one great source of the amusement of which we are sensible while we peruse the work. . . . (pp. 310-11)

Certainly, however, Mr. L— and Mr. J. W— have taken too much liberty with the private life of their countrymen; among whom, we are persuaded, many celebrated names would by no means wish to join in this sort of "literary patriotism" of the north. . . .

A lowering system would certainly be attended with benefit, in reducing that boisterous flow of animal spirits which is continually displayed in over-wrought and enthusiastic language, and exhausting itself in praises of every northern object that it meets. Though we may suppose the Doctor to have fixed on this *laudatory system* in order to make himself agreeable to his hosts, and to proceed more comfortably on his tour, yet he has something too ostentatious in his manner and conversation; too affected a grasp of powerful intellect, too fine and even minute a discernment of taste. (p. 311)

[His] splendid descriptions, both of persons and places, are often not only imaginary and unfounded, but when he has roused the expectations of his readers, he concludes in trifling local details, which are quite out of the province of a stranger, and must be by no means interesting to his 'kinsfolk' at home. In this spirit, he descants too minutely on the visages, qualifications, and respective practice of the lawyers. . . . The spouting clubs, periodical works, colleges, and *conversazioni* [conversations], and in fact every thing with which we may suppose the souls of young authors to be smitten, are described in detail in the same manner; while the good *Doctor* is made a cat's paw, and obliged to lend his authority to their boyish tricks, to the exclusion of all acquaintance with medical men and more serious pursuits. He is thus obliged, rather inconsistently for an elderly gentleman, to write in a *jovial* and youthful strain. . . . [The Doctor] is evidently biassed by a national enthusiasm, which is continually leading him into extremes either of praise or blame; and which has the unfortunate effect of turning the former into ridicule, and disarming the latter of its sting. (p. 312)

We cannot think that the Doctor has properly divested himself of the prejudices of 'a political creed,' in his estimation and representation of literary characters: for he too plainly betrays an intention (however vain) of throwing ridicule on some whom at the same time he pretends to admire. . . . [The] work is not only a satirical but an ill meaning publication, and has faults which all its genius, shrewdness, and amusing anecdote would vainly attempt to redeem. . . . [We] wish it had been confined [to the consideration of matters more generally pleasing], instead of taking the unauthorized freedom of forging names and incidents in order to give it an air of popularity. It would then have been an entertaining and unexceptionable production, and a happy delineation of the scenes and manners of the northern metropolis. Indeed, the lighter subjects are treated in a more masterly style than the serious and profound; and the description, for instance, of Edinburgh amusements, particularly dancing, is [good]. . . . (pp. 318-19)

In conclusion, we would observe that this production is written in much too violent a strain both of eulogy and satire. . . . Allowing for the faults of youthful writers, however, and regarding it as the joint composition of the before mentioned Mr. L and Mr. J. W, we must admit that the intellectual portion of the work is honourable to their talents. If they would divest themselves of the shackles of party, the littlenesses of local prejudice, and that love of ridicule which is not wit, and finally exchange the spirit of literary animosity in which they began for a disinterested love of literature itself, we should peruse with more pleasure any future series of their letters; which may exhibit as much ingenuity, united with knowledge of the world, and be unblemished by the faults of the present volumes. (p. 321)

> *A review of "Peter's Letters to His Kinsfolk," in* The Monthly Review, *London, Vol. XL, November, 1819, pp. 308-21.*

THE LONDON MAGAZINE (essay date 1822)

We have been entreated by several soft readers, to walk, as a short cut to the temple of pure feeling, through [*Some Passages in the Life of Mr. Adam Blair, Minister of the Gospel at Cross-Meikle*];—and we have at length yielded to these intreaties, and tried this literary *halfpenny hatch* leading through the gardens of sensibility and the flowers of morality to the temple itself. The dust (we use the mildest word)—the gloom,—the tediousness of these "passages" have been to us so offensive, that we have determined upon running our critical broom through them, to make the way clearer, and the darker turns lighter, for all future travellers in the tender line.

The title of this book would lead all simple hearted Christians into the belief that it treated of struggles of the spirit,—that it contained heart-searching admonitions,—fearless and patient controversies,—lonely and pious meditations—reasonings,—exhortations,—prayers! Let such readers put up the little swindler on the shelf again, and return to some old favourite and assured author; for Mr. Adam Blair is not the man for their money. If there *be* any controversies, they arise between Mr. Adam the minister, and the husband of his "adored Charlotte;" if any meditations exist, they are the meditations of a couple of holy and young Scotch creatures, who make love in a moonlight churchyard, on the tombstone of the deceased and buried Mrs. Blair. If there be any heart-searching admonitions, they are merely uttered by the young clergyman, to reprove the fallen wife for the errors into which he had helped her. In short, the lovers of Tillotsop, and South, and Taylor, and of those who have breathed consolation to the miserable, and spoken quiet happiness to the good,—must stand aside, and turn a *deaf eye* to the present discourse. (p. 485)

[We] cannot dismiss the volume without seriously and earnestly protesting against this parody on feeling; this mockery of pathos; this mad and wicked brawl of intemperate and unnatural passion. We know not what real and pure interest can be excited, by this filthy betrayal of vice in characters and in situations to which we are accustomed to look for the decencies, the virtues, and the white enjoyments of life!—For what worthy end religion is thus to be stained and insulted we cannot conjecture. . . . Is it absolutely necessary that crime should be prepared as a *dram* for the world;—that women should be wives before their seduction; and that the adulterers . . . should be in holy orders!—That a man should woo a woman at the tomb of his dead wife,—and that prayer and religion should be made the panders to immorality? Having shown the book in its true colours, and spoken strongly of it as we feel,—we hurl it aside;—and rejoice that it is not from the English press, that so dirty and helpless a volume has issued. (p. 490)

> *A review of "Some Passages in the Life of Mr. Adam Blair, Minister of the Gospel at Cross-Meikle," in* The London Magazine, *Vol. V, No. XXIX, May, 1822, pp. 485-90.*

[FRANCIS JEFFREY]   (essay date 1823)

[*Jeffrey was a founder and editor of the* Edinburgh Review, *one of the most influential magazines in early nineteenth-century England. A liberal Whig, Jeffrey often allowed his political beliefs to color his critical opinions. In the following essay, Jeffrey complains that, with the exception of* Valerius: A Roman Story, *the novels of John Galt, John Wilson, and Lockhart are inferior imitations of Sir Walter Scott's works. Jeffrey praises* Valerius *for its originality and power but concludes that the novel fails because its subject matter is of little interest to contemporary readers.*]

In the arduous task of imitating [Sir Walter Scott] the great novelist, [John Galt, John Wison, and John Gibson Lockhart] have apparently found it necessary to resort to the great principle of division of labour; and yet they have not come near to equal the work of [Scott's] single hand. (p. 160)

[Wilson and Lockhart] have formed themselves . . . upon the poetical, reflective, and pathetic parts of their common model. . . . Though far better skilled than [Galt] in the art of

composition, and chargeable, perhaps, with less direct imitation, we cannot but regard [Wilson and Lockhart] as much less original, and as having performed, upon the whole, a far easier task. They have no variety of style, and but little of invention,—and are *mannerists* in the strongest sense of that term. Though unquestionably pathetic in a very powerful degree, they are pathetic, for the most part, by the common recipes, which enable any one almost to draw tears who will condescend to employ them. They are mighty religious too,—but apparently on the same principle; and, while their laboured attacks on our sympathies are felt, at last, to be somewhat importunate and puerile, their devotional orthodoxies seem to tend, every now and then, a little towards cant. This is perhaps too harshly said; and is more, we confess, the result of the second reading than the first, and suggested rather by a comparison with their great original, than an impression of their own independent merits. (p. 161)

['**Valerius**', however, is] original in conception and design. . . . It is a work to be excepted certainly from our general remark, that the productions [of Galt, Wilson, and Lockhart] were imitations of the celebrated novels [of Sir Walter Scott], and their authors disciples of that great school. Such as it is, '**Valerius**' is undoubtedly original; or at least owes nothing to [Scott]. It would be more plausible to say, that the author had borrowed something from the travels of Anacharsis, or the ancient romance of Heliodorus and Chariclea—or the later effusions of M. Chateaubriand. In the main, however, it is original; and is written with very considerable power and boldness. But we cannot, on the whole, say that it has been successful; and even greater powers could not have ensured success for such an undertaking. We must know the daily life and ordinary habits of the people in whose domestic adventures we take an interest:—and we know nothing of the life and habits of the ancient Romans and primitive Christians. We may patch together [information] . . . out of old books, and pretend that it exhibits a view of their manners and conversation; but the truth is, that all that is authentic in such a compilation can amount only to a few fragments of such a picture; and that any thing like a complete and living portrait must be made up by conjecture, and inferences drawn at hazard. Accordingly, the work before us consists alternately of enlarged transcripts of particular acts and usages, of which accounts have been accidentally transmitted to us, and details of dialogue and observation in which there is nothing antique or Roman but the names,—and in reference to which, the assumed time and place of the action is felt as a mere embarrassment and absurdity. To avoid or disguise this awkwardness, the only resource seems to be, to take shelter in a vague generality of talk and description,—and to save the detection of the modern in his masquerade of antiquity, by abstaining from any thing that is truly characteristic either of the one age or the other, and consequently from any thing by which either character or manners can be effectually delineated or distinguished. The very style of ['**Valerius**'] affords a curious example of the necessity of this timid indefiniteness under such circumstances, and of its awkward effect. To exclude the tone of modern times, it is without idiom, without familiarity, without any of those natural marks by which alone either individuality of character, or the stamp and pressure of the time, can possibly be conveyed,—and runs on, even in the gay and satirical passages, in a rumbling, roundabout, rhetorical measure, like a translation from solemn Latin, or some academical exercitation. It is an attempt, in short, which, though creditable to the spirit and talents of the author, we think he has done wisely in not seeking to repeat,—and which, though it has not failed through any deficiency of his, has been prevented, we think, from succeeding by the very nature of the subject. (pp. 179-80)

['**Adam Blair**'] is a story of great power and interest, though neither very pleasing, nor very moral, nor very intelligible. (p. 185)

There is no great merit in the design of this story, and there are many things both absurd and revolting in its details; but there is no ordinary power in the execution; and there is a spirit and richness in the writing. . . . (p. 186)

> [*Francis Jeffrey*], "*Secondary Scottish Novels*," in The Edinburgh Review, *Vol. XXXIX, No. LXXVII, October, 1823, pp. 158-96.**

C. N. [CHRISTOPHER NORTH, PSEUDONYM OF JOHN WILSON] (essay date 1824)

> [*A Scottish critic, essayist, novelist, poet, and short story writer, Wilson is best known as Christopher North, the name he assumed when writing for* Blackwood's Edinburgh Magazine, *to which he contributed for over twenty-five years. Wilson and Lockhart became close friends through their association with* Blackwood's. *It is generally agreed that Wilson's rollicking humor and eloquence, combined with Lockhart's biting wit, were responsible for the early success of the magazine. Here, Wilson proclaims* Reginald Dalton *a "work of genius" and praises Lockhart's forceful, vigorous style and vivid delineations of character; Wilson's assessment, however, is qualified. He complains that Lockhart frequently treats serious subjects with undue levity and, ironically, to illustrate this point, he comments that* Reginald Dalton *too often resembles "Christopher North, in the gown of an undergraduate." Furthermore, Wilson objects to Lockhart's "unaccountable" use of "ugly and vulgar expressions."*]

The author of "**Reginald Dalton**"] is a man of a singularly powerful and original mind, widely versed in literature and book-knowledge, and keenly observant of human nature, as displayed on the stage of the world. There is a force and vigour in his style of thinking and writing, not excelled by any man of this age; and often, too, an elegance, a gracefulness, and a beauty, that come charmingly in among his more forceful delineations, and shew that he could, if he would, be equally effective in the touching and pathetic. He pours out all his thoughts, feelings, observations, remarks, fancies, whims, caprices, follies, sarcasms, and jocularities, with the same easy, we had almost said careless, spirit of lavish profusion. He seldom remains long on one key, but he strikes it strongly, till the corresponding chord in the heart vibrates to its centre. He rarely seems anxious to work up any effect, but seizes the main interest of the feeling or incident which he is dealing with; and having brought it out boldly, he proceeds forthwith on his career, and hurries forwards with a free, and sometimes impatient consciousness of strength, among new scenes, new emotions, and new characters. Accordingly, he is never wearisome nor languid; never exhausts a passion either in himself, the agents in his history, or his readers, but, by a constant succession of various feelings springing out of each other, keeps the scene busy, and the imagination on the alert, infusing life, spirit, bustle, and vivacity throughout the work during its whole progress, and almost always becoming, when he ceases to be impressive and impassioned, excessively amusing and entertaining,—and when he leaves the deeper feelings of our nature, almost always glancing over the surface of life with a truly engaging spirit of youthful elasticity, and a beaming freshness of youthful enjoyment that inspires cheerful sympathy, and makes one in love with the everyday world. It is evident

that the volumes are written by one who, in the strength and prime of manhood, has not yet lost the animation and lightheartedness of youth. There is nothing young in the opinions, the reflections, the views of human life, when the writer addresses himself seriously and solemnly to the stronger and permanent principles of action in our nature, but there is much that is delightfully juvenile—puerile, if you will—in the byplay, the under-plot, the inferior incidents, and the depicting of the various auxiliary characters,—and the gravest and most formal personage that ever wore gown or wig, at bar, in pulpit, or in bench, must surely relax the sternness of his physiognomy at many of the ludicrous details of occurrences . . . that permeate the book almost from beginning to end, and alternate most effectively with matters of very serious import. . . . (p. 102)

Now, it is pretty obvious, that in a book written on such principles, and by such an author, various faults of considerable magnitude, and of no unfrequent recurrence, will be found. For, in the first place, it is not always possible to escape in good time from the extreme levity, and the joyful absurdities of reckless boyhood or youth; and in indulging, *con amore*, in such strains of description, a writer, with a keen sense of the frolicsome, the ludicrous, and the piquant, must be in perpetual danger of offending, either by the untimely introduction of such mirthful topics, or by their undue prolongation, or by "a certain spice" of them remaining behind, even after a serious, solemn, or affecting appeal has been made to the better and higher feelings. This, we think, frequently happens throughout these volumes. The current of deeper emotion is too often checked or diverted; and although the book may not, on that account, be a less true picture of human life, nevertheless we expect human life, in all its varieties, to be something different, in a work of imagination, from what it is in reality. This author occasionally destroys his most complete and powerful illusions, as if he did do so, either on purpose to startle and perplex, or because he himself really felt less at the time, than the reader, over whom his genius prevailed, and were more indifferent than they ever could be to the beings of his own creation.

But farther—the humour—the wit—the fun and frolic—the grotesque and the ludicrous—are sometimes not only out of place, but not very good in themselves, or if very good, yet not of a kind precisely which one is in the habit of meeting with in handsomely printed works in three thick volumes. Ever and anon our author waxeth facetious on other authors alive and merry like himself, deals out little biting and pinching quips modest, right and left, apparently without malice or meditation, but in mere *gaieté du coeur* [light heartedness]. When he is in such moods, whatever comes uppermost, out it goes, so that more than once we thought we were reading [*Blackwood's Edinburgh Magazine*], and that Reginald Dalton was no other than Christopher North, in the gown of an undergraduate. Perhaps the names of about twenty living persons of eminence occur in a work which is one of mere fiction, and it is impossible to tell how strange is the effect of these flesh-and-blood gentlemen dining or drinking, or sitting on coach-boxes, or being introduced to Reginald Dalton and his fellow-phantoms. Instead of throwing an air of reality, and truth, and good faith over the narrative, it breaks the spell most teasingly, and more than once we have laid down our volume with a "says a frown to a smile," rather angry at being bammed and trotted by this capricious, wayward, and incurable quizzer.

To be done, for the present, with our enumeration of faults, we must take the liberty of hinting to this author, that, in the midst of his powerful, eloquent, and idiomatic English, he, too often, lets slip words, phrases, epithets, and modes of expression, that border upon the coarse and vulgar—grate upon the ear at least, if not upon the mind, and occasionally impair, in some measure, the beauty of his most overwhelming or exquisite descriptions. Perhaps something of this is unavoidable in a style so natural, bold, and flowing; but the tendency to it may at least be controlled. . . . (pp. 102-03)

Reginald is undoubtedly a fine youth . . . , and [his father's] appearance, manner, conversation, pursuits, and character, are revealed to us by the touches of a master's hand. There is something earnestly, calmly, and yet deeply affecting in the elegant and still seclusion of the life of the melancholy scholar and gentleman, over whom hangs the shadow of solicitude and fear for an only son just about to leave him for the first time. . . . An air of pensive elegance breathes over the beautiful vicarage of Llanwell, and, without effort of any kind, the author has succeeded in making most pathetic and affecting the yearning affection of the pious and widowed father, and the reverential love of his yet unstained and innocent son. (p. 104)

[The] merit of this book is not in the story, but in the sentiments, the situations, the descriptions, and the characters. (p. 105)

[In the first place], "**Reginald Dalton**" will be universally acknowledged to be a *work of genius*. The conception of it is both poetical and philosophical. It is, on the whole, a fine and a bold illustration of a segment of life's circle. It is a living moving picture—a sort of peristrephic panorama.

In the second place, the main object of the work, namely, a delineation of the youth of a given individual, is attained. . . .

In the third place, a great deal of talent is shewn in the sketches of character throughout the three volumes, and for the most part they are true to nature. . . .

And, lastly, there is throughout, such a power of writing, beautifully, gracefully, vigorously, sarcastically, and wittily, at will, as will puzzle most of our acquaintances to equal. . . .

Now for the demerits.

In the first place, the deep and vital interest of the history ceases with the conclusion of the second volume. The third, although we are involved in the curious and exciting progress of an uncommon and ingenious denouement, is to us frequently teazing and bothering. Let us, if possible, have no more wills and title-deeds, and cursed parchments of all sorts fluttering and creaking in novels. They are becoming a perfect nuisance.

In the second place, there is not a due proportion preserved between the sad, serious, solemn, pathetic, and impassioned, and the light, airy, frolicsome, and absurd. There is rather too much of the latter. They sometimes seem to be the principal and prevailing character of the work. This is a pity, and obviously happened because the author wrote away without any very regular plan. . . .

In the third place, not a few of the incidents are in themselves baddish. (p. 120)

In the fourth place, the author feels apparently the highest pleasure, and often puts out his highest powers, in describing characters, which to us are by no means agreeable to look upon or converse with—their absence would be good company. . . .

Finally, although this author generally writes with most extraordinary power, and also with extreme elegance, he not seldom falls into ugly and vulgar expressions, in a way to us unaccountable. We have been told the book is full of Scotti-

cisms, but we know nothing about Scotticisms, and have no doubt that they are most excellent things. We allude to lowish— or slang-whanging phrases—or hard-favoured or mean-gaited words intruding themselves; or, what is worse, seemingly being introduced on purpose into the company of all that is graceful and accomplished. (p. 121)

> C. N. [*Christopher North, pseudonym of John Wilson*], *in a review of "Reginald Dalton," in* Blackwood's Edinburgh Magazine, *Vol. XV, No. LXXXV, January, 1824, pp. 102-24.*

[J. G. LOCKHART] (essay date 1824)

Mr. Matthew Wald [tells] his own story, in the remarkable [*The History of Matthew Wald*], and every person who reads it must admit that it is a story eminently unfit for being told by any one but its hero. It is indeed a story, not only abounding in, but overflowing with, variety of highly interesting incident and adventure; but throughout the whole of its tenor, everything is decidedly and entirely subordinate to the minute and anxious, although easy and unaffected, anatomy of one man's mind. . . . The chief sympathies which he excites are placed far beyond the reach of any external accidents whatever. (pp. 568-69)

Under any modification of form and circumstance, such a tale must have been both interesting and instructive; but it is much the more interesting without question, because, from its being written in the first person, we are reminded at every step, or rather, to speak more accurately, we are kept continually impressed with the sense, that he, of whose fortunes we are reading, possessed not only a powerful intellect, but a high and imaginative genius. . . . (p. 569)

This narrative will be universally a favourite with all who are capable of appreciating strength and originality of conception— as to incident, and still more as to character—and a very extraordinary command of language. This volume is written throughout with a commanding vigour and energy, and whenever the subject demands it, the author rises into the most genuine eloquence of passion—and yet, with but a few trifling exceptions, nothing, it appears to us, can be more simple, easy, and graceful, than the whole tone of expression. The work is, moreover, rich in shrewd, sagacious, home-thrusting remarks upon human life and manners; and altogether **Matthew Wald** affords indubitable evidence of the rapid progress which its author had made in the knowledge of mankind, since he first appeared in the field of romance, and also in the art of composition. No one who ever read any one of his books, could deny to him the possession of intense energy, both of thought and expression. The style of **Matthew Wald** exhibits prodigious improvement as to harmony of tone: it is quite free from the faults of prolixity and turgidity, and bears the impress not merely of great but of uniform power. (p. 572)

> [*J. G. Lockhart], "Remarks on the Novel of Matthew Wald," in* Blackwood's Edinburgh Magazine, *Vol. XV, No. LXXXVIII, May, 1824, pp. 568-79.*

THE MONTHLY REVIEW, LONDON (essay date 1824)

[*The History of Matthew Wald*] is well written, and sometimes exhibits symptoms of high and successful daring: while the sketches of Scotish scenery, Scotish dialogue, and Scotish manners, are pleasingly interposed, and carry with them a strong air of verisimilitude. Yet the general effect of the tale is far from pleasing, and seems to have been conceived in a mood of deep-seated misanthropy,—a spirit of dark and gloomy resentment against human nature. This has evidently betrayed the author into that sentimental raving which was first introduced, we are inclined to think, by the Vicomte de Chateaubriand; in which the warmth and enthusiasm of the phrase so far transcend the usual course of human feeling, that we immediately suspect the whole to be hypocrisy instead of sentiment;—a system of vulgar horror and exaggeration, in which emotions are pushed into madness, and the incoherent dreams of phrenzy are absurdly attempted to be shaped and modified into description. (pp. 382-83)

Yet all is not in this manner; for there are several exquisite touches in the narrative of *Matthew Wald,* which shew that the author's excellence lies in softer and more mellowed tints of delineation. (p. 384)

There is something aukward and inartificial in the winding up of this most spirited narrative. We do not see exactly why the author judged it necessary to tinge the mind of [Wald's wife] Joanne with methodistical notions:—the circumstance has no influence over her fortunes or those of Wald himself;—and the placing of Katherine [the companion and friend of Wald's youth], who had been deserted by her husband, in the very next house to that which was occupied by Matthew, has too much the appearance of a forced contrivance.

On the whole, however, we think that this . . . is a story of great interest. The moral, indeed, if it has any, is not to be discerned through ordinary glasses: but the great example of [Sir Walter Scott] shews that pleasing fictions may be written without any moral purpose, and therefore we stifle an objection that was ready to start from our pen. . . . [If] the fable be not well designed, the richness and vivacity of the composition bespeak the hand of no ordinary artist. (pp. 388-89)

> *A review of "The History of Matthew Wald," in* The Monthly Review, *London, Vol. CIV, August, 1824, pp. 382-89.*

WALTER SCOTT   (letter date 1825)

[*The following is taken from a letter that Scott wrote to John Murray, the publisher of the* Quarterly Review, *shortly after Murray invited Lockhart to become the* Quarterly's *editor. Scott defends Lockhart against his detractors, who consider him unfit for the position as editor because of his reputation as a critical "Scorpion." He speaks highly of Lockhart's qualifications for the post and dismisses the younger man's early, caustic essays in* Blackwood's Edinburgh Magazine *as youthful "follies."*]

I was much surprised to-day to learn from Lockhart by letter that some scruples were in circulation among some of the respectable among the supporters of the *Quarterly Review* concerning his capacity to undertake that highly responsible task. (p. 220)

It seems extremely hard (though not perhaps to be wondered at) that the follies of three- or four-and-twenty should be remembered against a man of thirty, who has abstained during the interval from giving the least cause of offence. There are few men of any rank in letters who have not at some time or other been guilty of some abuse of their satirical powers, and very few who have not seen reason to wish that they had restrained their vein of pleasantry. Thinking over Lockhart's offences with my own, and other men's whom either politics or literary controversy has led into such effusions, I cannot help thinking that five years' proscription ought to obtain a

full immunity on their account. There were none of them which could be ascribed to any worse motive than a wicked wit, and many of the individuals against whom they were directed were worthy of more severe chastisement. . . . Of [Lockhart's] general talents I will not presume to speak, but they are generally allowed to be of the first order. This, however, I *will* say, that I have known the most able men of my time, and I never met any one who had such ready command of his own mind, or possessed in a greater degree the power of making his talents available upon the shortest notice, and upon any subject. . . . Speaking upon my honour as a gentleman and my credit as a man of letters, I do not know a person so well qualified for the very difficult and responsible task he has undertaken, and I think the distinct testimony of one who must know the individual well ought to bear weight against all vague rumours, whether arising from idle squibs he may have been guilty of when he came from College—and I know none of these which indicate a bad heart in the jester—or, as is much more likely, from those which have been rashly and falsely ascribed to him. (pp. 221-22)

Those who are interested in the matter may be well assured that with whatever prejudice they may receive Lockhart at first, all who have candour enough to wait till he can afford them the means of judging will be of opinion that they have got a person possibly as well situated for the duties of such an office as any man that England could afford them. (p. 223)

> *Walter Scott, in a letter to John Murray on November 17, 1825, in* Memoir and Correspondence of the Late John Murray, Vol. II, *edited by Samuel Smiles, John Murray, 1891, pp. 220-24.*

THOMAS CARLYLE   (essay date 1837)

[*Carlyle was a noted nineteenth-century Scottish critic and historian. His discussion of* Memoirs of the Life of Sir Walter Scott, Bart. *is respectful, but cautious. While he admires Lockhart's thoroughness in collecting his materials for the* Life of Scott, *he considers the biography "not so much a composition" as a "compilation well done." In response to critics of the biography who complained that Lockhart had marred Scott's reputation by revealing too much information about his financial troubles, Carlyle praises Lockhart's candor and attests to his loyalty towards Scott. Carlyle's comment that Lockhart's conception of the biography was not "very elevated" is disputed by Saintsbury (1884).*]

Our verdict [on *Memoirs of the Life of Sir Walter Scott, Baronet*] in general would be, that [Mr. Lockhart] has accomplished the work he schemed for himself in a creditable workmanlike manner. It is true, his notion of what the work was, does not seem to have been very elevated. To picture-forth the life of Scott according to any rules of art or composition, so that a reader, on adequately examining it, might say to himself, "There is Scott, there is the physiognomy and meaning of Scott's appearance and transit on this earth; such was he by nature, so did the world act on him, so he on the world, with such result and significance for himself and us:" this was by no manner of means Mr. Lockhart's plan. A plan which, it is rashly said, should preside over every biography! (p. 189)

[In *Life of Scott,* seven] biographical volumes are given where one had been better. . . . (pp. 190-91)

Mr. Lockhart's aim, we take it, was not that of producing [a highflown work of art] . . . : or indeed to do much other than to print, intelligibly bound together by order of time, and by some requisite intercalary exposition, all such letters, documents and notices about Scott as he found lying suitable, and as it seemed likely the world would undertake to read. His Work, accordingly, is not so much a composition, as what we may call a compilation well done. Neither is this a task of no difficulty. . . . Let us take the Seven Volumes, and be thankful that they are genuine in their kind. Nay, as to that of their being seven and not one, it is right to say that the public so required it. To have done other, would have shown little policy in an author. Had Mr. Lockhart laboriously compressed himself, and instead of well-done compilation, brought out the well-done composition, in one volume instead of seven, which not many men in England are better qualified to do, there can be no doubt but his readers for the time had been immeasurably fewer. If the praise of magnanimity be denied him, that of prudence must be conceded, which perhaps he values more.

The truth is, the work, done in this manner too, was good to have: Scott's Biography, if uncomposed, lies printed and indestructible here, in the elementary state, and can at any time be composed, if necessary, by whosoever has a call to that. As it is, as it was meant to be, we repeat, the work is vigorously done. Sagacity, decision, candour, diligence, good manners, good sense: these qualities are throughout observable. The dates, calculations, statements, we suppose to be all accurate; much laborious inquiry, some of it impossible for another man, has been gone into, the results of which are imparted with due brevity. Scott's letters, not interesting generally, yet never absolutely without interest, are copiously given; copiously, but with selection; the answers to them still more select. Narrative, delineation, and at length personal reminiscences, occasionally of much merit, of a certain rough force, sincerity and picturesqueness, duly intervene. The scattered members of Scott's Life do lie here, and could be disentangled. In a word, this compilation is the work of a manful, clear-seeing, conclusive man, and has been executed with the faculty and combination of faculties the public had a right to expect from the name attached to it.

One thing we hear greatly blamed in Mr. Lockhart: that he has been too communicative, indiscreet, and has recorded much that ought to have lain suppressed. Persons are mentioned, and circumstances, not always of an ornamental sort. . . . The English biographer has long felt that if in writing his Man's Biography, he wrote down anything that could by possibility offend any man, he had written wrong. (pp. 191-92)

Probably it was Mr. Lockhart's feeling of what the great public would approve, that led him, open-eyed, into this offence against the small criticising public: we joyfully accept the omen.

Perhaps then, of all the praises copiously bestowed on his Work, there is none in reality so creditable to him as this same censure, which has also been pretty copious. It is a censure better than a good many praises. . . . For our part, we hope all manner of biographies that are written in England will henceforth be written so. (pp. 193-94)

As to the accuracy or error of [the] statements about the Ballantynes and other persons aggrieved, which are questions much mooted at present in some places, we know nothing at all. . . . We can only say, these things carry no look of inaccuracy on the face of them; neither is anywhere the smallest trace of ill-will or unjust feeling discernible. Decidedly the probabilities are, and till better evidence arise, the fair conclusion is, that this matter stands very much as it ought to do. Let the clatter of censure, therefore, propagate itself as far as it can. For Mr. Lockhart it virtually amounts to this very considerable

praise, that, standing full in the face of the public, he has set at naught, and been among the first to do it, a public piece of cant; one of the commonest we have, and closely allied to many others of the fellest sort, as smooth as it looks.

The other censure, of Scott being made unheroic, springs from the same stem; and is, perhaps, a still more wonderful flower of it. . . . But connected with this, there is a hypothesis now current . . . : That Mr. Lockhart at heart has a dislike to Scott, and has done his best in an underhand treacherous manner to dishero him!. . . [If] Mr. Lockhart is fairly chargeable with any radical defect, if on any side his insight entirely fails him, it seems even to be in this, that Scott is altogether lovely to him; that Scott's greatness spreads out for him on all hands beyond reach of eye; that his very faults become beautiful, his vulgar worldlinesses are solid prudences, proprieties; and of his worth there is no measure. (pp. 195-96)

And so in sum, with regard to *Lockhart's Life of Scott,* readers that believe in us shall read it with the feeling that a man of talent, decision and insight wrote it; wrote it in seven volumes, not in one, because the public would pay for it better in that state; but wrote it with courage, with frankness, sincerity; on the whole, in a very readable, recommendable manner, as things go. Whosoever needs it can purchase it, or purchase the loan of it, with assurance more than usual that he has ware for his money. (p. 196)

> *Thomas Carlyle, "Sir Walter Scott" (originally published as "'Memoirs of the Life of Sir Walter Scott, Baronet',"* in London and Westminster Review, *No. 12, 1837), in his* Critical and Miscellaneous Essays: Collected and Republished, *Vol. IV,* Brown and Taggard, *1860, pp. 185-251.**

J. G. LOCKHART   (essay date 1838?)

[*In the following essay, which is drawn from* Memoirs of the Life of Sir Walter Scott, Bart., *Lockhart discourages comparisons between the* Life of Scott *and James Boswell's* The Life of Samuel Johnson *by insisting that he never intended to "Boswellize Scott" by giving a detailed account of Scott's conversation.*]

I never thought it lawful to keep a journal of what passes in private society, so that no one need expect from the sequel of [*The Life of Scott*] any detailed record of Scott's familiar talk. What fragments of it have happened to adhere to a tolerably retentive memory, and may be put into black and white without wounding any feelings which my friend, were he alive, would have wished to spare, I . . . introduce as the occasion suggests or serves. But I disclaim . . . anything more than this; and I also wish to enter a protest once for all against the general fidelity of several literary gentlemen who have kindly forwarded to me private lucubrations of theirs, designed to *Boswellize* Scott, and which they may probably publish hereafter. To report conversations fairly, it is a necessary prerequisite that we should be completely familiar with all the interlocutors, and understand thoroughly all their minutest relations, and points of common knowledge and common feeling, with each other. He who does not, must be perpetually in danger of misinterpreting sportive allusion into serious statement; and the man who was only recalling, by some jocular phrase or half-phrase, to an old companion, some trivial reminiscence of their boyhood or youth, may be represented as expressing, upon some person or incident casually tabled, an opinion which he had never framed, or if he had, would never have given words to in any mixed assemblage—not even among what the world calls *friends* at his own board. In proportion as a man is witty and humorous, there will always be about him and his a widening maze and wilderness of cues and catchwords, which the uninitiated will, if they are bold enough to try interpretation, construe, ever and anon, egregiously amiss—not seldom into arrant falsity. For this one reason, to say nothing of many others, I consider no man justified in journalizing what he sees and hears in a domestic circle where he is not thoroughly at home; and I think there are still higher and better reasons why he should not do so where he is. (p. 369)

> *J. G. Lockhart, in a chapter in his* Memoirs of the Life of Sir Walter Scott, Bart., *R. Cadell, 1837-38 (and reprinted in his* The Life of Sir Walter Scott, Bart.: 1771-1832, *revised edition, Adam & Charles Black, 1893, pp. 367-76).*

R. F. [R. F. FORD]   (essay date 1840)

[*Ancient Spanish Ballads, Historical and Romantic*] was one of [Lockhart's] first productions, and gave the high promise of excellence which his subsequent productions (too few) have so well verified. He evidently entered on the subject *con amore*. . . . Perfectly acquainted with the genius and feeling of his original, Mr Lockhart has never thought it necessary to adhere to every part, particle, and iota of his text, but has rather desired to put forth a Spanish book in the form which would be the most acceptable to an English reader: with this object in view he has, like a skilful artist, selected and dwelt only on those leading features which fix character, and confer identity and reality; he has rejected the ordinary and condensed the diffuse, while at other times he has engrafted on the Spanish olive some healthy scions of our English oak; and has dovetailed in his mosaic work with such curious felicity, that nothing but a close collation with the Spanish text will enable the reader to distinguish the additional from the original work. This power of passing into the spirit of a foreign composition, and of blending new matter into another composition, as it is the most difficult, so is it one of the greatest triumphs of the highest class of translation. It requires patience, tact, and genius; and becomes trying in proportion as the translator is himself a poet, and thus compelled to rein in his aspirations to another pace. . . . (pp. 305-06)

> *R. F. [R. F. Ford], in a review of "Ancient Spanish Ballads, Historical and Romantic," in* The London and Westminster Review, *Vol. XXXIII, No. 2, March, 1840, pp. 302-24.*

SIR NATHANIEL   (essay date 1854)

The characters engaged in the action [of "**Valerius**"] present a fair diversity of types of society in [Rome], but for the most part lacking individuality and life. Valerius himself is too much of the faultless walking gentleman, though his betrothed, the high-hearted and deep-hearted Athanasia, is some removes beyond the standard walking lady. (p. 58)

Jeffrey's fling at Mr. Lockhart, as being "mighty religious too," and as obtruding a "devotional orthodoxy" with a tendency, "every now and then, a little towards cant" [see excerpt above, 1823],—which, however, had reference to his Scotch novels (in common with those of Professor Wilson)—finds no justification, so far as it is a sneer, in the instance of "**Valerius.**" The author has even exercised a reserve and restraint, in the face of strong temptations (from the nature of his agitating theme) to an opposite treatment, which to many appear

forbiddingly cold and fatally apathetic. It cannot be alleged that his heathens are all painted black, and his Christians white. . . . The keen-scented editor of the *Edinburgh* [Jeffrey], must have been keen-scented beyond human or even canine parallel, could he have sniffed the odour of sanctity, in "devotional orthodoxy" power, and in the rankness of a tendency to "cant," in the too dispassionate and so far uncharacteristic colloquies of Mr. Lockhart's Roman Christians. They are, in fact, unreal from their very failing to speak out: not that they would, or ought to, speak out when to do so would be unseasonable and fruitless—but that where they would, and ought to, they do not. . . . The book seems to have been flung off at a heat—not of enthusiasm; there is indeed little in its composition, whether we regard the story or the accessories, to belie the assertion that it took but three weeks to write. . . . (pp. 59-60)

Maiden aunts and uninitiated papas must have formed horrible notions of Oxford, if they had within reach no corrective or alternative, to restrain and tone down the effect of "**Reginald Dalton**'s" revelations—which are certainly open to the charge of giving an *einseitig* [biased] and exaggerated picture of Alma Mater-ia. But the picture won eager albeit shocked gazers, by its broad strokes and its high colouring—and may, we suspect, have tended . . . to induce anxious "governors" to send their boys to [the University of Edinburgh]. . . . The hero's university course is only an episode; but to it the leading interest of the work attaches, and upon it the novelist has expended the best of his power and pains. Reginald's subsequent experiences in London and elsewhere are dull, and loosely put together. The table-talk—wine-table, breakfast-table, supper-table, or what not—so profusely detailed, is too frequently of the veriest weak tea-table sort: weak enough, mawkish and vapid enough, to make one almost incredulous of its coming from the trenchant pen of the editor of the *Quarterly*, and the manly, vigorous, forcible biographer of Sir Walter Scott. The humourous parts of "**Valerius**" were flat, nor are those of this tale of modern life much more potent—though there is certainly some pungent satirical writing, and a plentiful seasoning of caustic wit. (pp. 60-2)

The "dark grief" that tabernacles with "the guilty," and the "various passions" that agitate the bosom of frail humanity, were impressively delineated in the two Scotch novelets, "**Adam Blair**" and "**Matthew Wald.**" . . . ["**Adam Blair**"] is not improved in moral tone, however it may be heightened in melodramatic colouring, by the evident influence exercised on the author's mind by his familiarity with German fictions; to the morbid characteristics of which, he too nearly adapted his own story. . . . In "**Matthew Wald**" there are some powerful bits of tragic, or rather perhaps of melodramatic writing. . . . (pp. 62-3)

We reckon it blessing rather than bane that our limits defy us to be prosy about that glorious piece of biography, the "**Life of Scott.**" It is far too interesting and valuable to be a present text of controversy, about the Ballantines "and a' that." . . . "**The Life of Burns,**" again, is a pleasant compilation—vigorous in narrative, and set off with fit reflections, the germ of other and deeper ones, in the essays of Wilson and Carlyle. (p. 63)

> *Sir Nathaniel, "John Gibson Lockhart," in* The New Monthly Magazine, *Vol. CI, No. CCCCI, May, 1854, pp. 56-64.*

THE SOUTHERN LITERARY MESSENGER (essay date 1855)

[In] literature, Lockhart was guilty of injustice to his own surpassing powers. With all his passion for letters, with all the ambition for literary fame which burnt in his youthful mind, there was still his shyness, fastidiousness, reserve. No doubt he might have taken a higher place as a poet than by the *Spanish Ballads,* as a writer of fiction than by his novels. These seem to have been thrown off by a sudden uncontrollable impulse to relieve the mind of its fulness, rather than as works of finished art or mature study. . . . They were the flashes of a genius which would not be suppressed. . . . [His] exuberant spirits, his joyous humour, his satiric vigour, his vehement fun, when the curb was once loosened, ran away with him, he himself could hardly see whither. (p. 175)

Lockhart is only known as a poet . . . by his *Spanish Ballads.* Those ballads (the unanswerable proof of excellence in ballads) caught at once, and live in the general ear. They have every characteristic beauty of ballads—life, rapidity, picturesqueness, suddenness, grace, quaintness, simplicity without baldness, energy without effort. We will not vouch for their fidelity to the original poems, but they have a better fidelity to the spirit of the wild, romantic, and chivalrous times, when Moor and Christian met on the borders to fight and make love. They are Spanish to the very heart.

Of his novels, two, in their different ways, are of a very high order. . . . *Valerius* contains as much knowledge of its period, and that knowledge as accurate, as would furnish out a long elaborate German treatise on a martyr and his times. It is as true, as lively, as poetical as Chateaubriand's boasted *Martyrs* is dull, artificial, false. Lockhart did not read up the times to write *Valerius;* but being full, from his enjoyment of the authors, of the times, dashed out *Valerius* boldly, freely, seemingly without study. It is, in our judgment, incomparably the best work of fiction founded on classical manners. (pp. 175-76)

[Lockhart's] strength lay in biography; his best papers in the *Quarterly Review* were full and rapid condensations of widespun volumes on the lives and works of authors or statesmen. But while his relation and singular qualifications gave him unrivalled advantages for [his *Life of Scott*], they involved him in no less serious and peculiar difficulties. (p. 176)

Lockhart resolved boldly, fairly, to reveal the whole; for Scott's fame we think he judged wisely, even though the book may have been in some degree weighed down. If there were those who suffered by the exposure, we cannot but think they deserved to suffer. All that was sordid and grasping in [book] trading speculation seemed to fall off from the majestic image of Scott; he rose like a hero in the old Greek tragedy, doing battle to the last with destiny, nobler in his sad and tragic end than at the height of his glory. All this must have been in the keen and far-sighted view of Lockhart; and must redound to his praise as a wise, as well as faithful and masterly biographer. (pp. 176-77)

There was one thing which set Lockhart far above common critics: high over every other consideration predominated the genial love of letters. Whatever might be the fate of those of more doubtful pretensions . . . , if any great work of genius appeared, Trojan or Tyrian, it was one to him—his kindred spirit was kindled at once, his admiration and sympathy threw off all trammels. We have known, where he has resisted rebuke, remonstrance, to do justice to the works of political antagonists,—that impartial homage was at once freely, boldly,

lavishly paid. We sincerely believe that Lockhart had no greater delight or satisfaction than in conferring well-merited praise, hailing the uprising of any new star, and doing just honour to those whom after ages will recognize as the leaders of letters in our day. (p. 177)

> *"The Late John Lockhart," in* The Southern Literary Messenger, *Vol. XXI, No. 3, March, 1855, pp. 173-77.*

[G. R. GLEIG] (essay date 1864)

[The] editor, whose privilege it may one day be to exhibit Lockhart as he was in the dawn of his literary reputation, will best do so by reproducing portions from such scholarly papers as **'The Greek Drama,'** the **'Horae Germanicae,'** with snatches of songs, such as **'The Lament for Captain Paton,'** or **'The Clydesdale Yeoman's Return,'** and a stanza here and there taken from the extravaganza **'The Mad Banker of Amsterdam.'** It is in these and in his hearty criticisms upon Wordsworth, Coleridge, Bowles, and Sir Walter Scott, that Lockhart comes forth in his true colours. How full of manly geniality and of spirit (less discernible in the originals) are the **'Spanish Ballads'** . . . ! Their bold movement and fine rhythm, unless we mistake, have given valuable hints to more modern poets. (p. 456)

[Why] the good people of Edinburgh should have been so excessively angry with [**'Peter's Letters to His Kinsfolk'**] and with its author it would be difficult to explain. Looking at the performance after an interval of forty-five years, we can discover no single expression which ought to have rankled in the most sensitive of Scottish minds. The manners of the age are delineated, lightly, perhaps, but surely not untruly—the ludicrous preponderating in all cases, whether individuals sit for their portraits, or the General Assembly passes under review. But when the worst is said that can be said of such a performance, it seems impossible to treat it as anything more serious than a very clever and sagacious though perhaps somewhat lengthy *jeu d'esprit.* (p. 461)

'Valerius, a Roman Story,' is beautifully written; stately and grave in style as becomes the subject; describing life and manners in the ancient capital of the world as only a scholar brimming over with knowledge could do. Everybody admitted, when it first came out, that the book was perfect in its way, and no one, we presume, will now dispute the justice of the verdict. . . . The truth is, that **'Valerius'** belongs to that class of novels which scholars hardly care to take up, and which mere readers of fiction cannot appreciate. There is little story in it, properly so called, and what there is touches but indifferently modern tastes and sympathies. The loves of Sextus and Sempronia interest nobody; even Valerius and Athanasia take scarcely any hold upon us; and Dromo the slave and the pedagogues Xerophrastes and Parmeno are considerable bores. Still the general effect is grand. The scene in the dungeon where Tisias is confined, the combat of the gladiators, and the execution of the Christian martyr, are masterpieces of wordpainting. We feel that there was great originality in the conception of the whole plot, and the skill displayed in working it out is extraordinary. Yet the results undeniably disappoint us. We soon weary of pageants, however gorgeous, which neither excite our feelings nor appeal to our memories.

As the machinery of **'Valerius'** had been made use of to exhibit the author's acquaintance with Roman manners and customs in the reign of Trajan, so it appears as if in **'Reginald Dalton'**

Lockhart's chief aim had been to describe undergraduate life as it was at Oxford during the earlier terms of his own academical career. If such were really his intention, he succeeded with just as much of exaggeration as was necessary to throw an air of romance over very commonplace incidents, but with an adherence to truth and a manliness of expression. . . . Even of 'Reginald Dalton,' however, we are constrained to admit that the conception is superior to the execution. Admirable bits occur here and there, some even of surpassing beauty; but, taken as a whole, it falls undeniably short of what the talents and genius of the author might have justified us in expecting. Lockhart's strength did not lie in the direction of novel-writing. He could tell a story admirably; he could not write a novel. In corroboration of this assumption we may observe that the tales which followed 'Reginald Dalton' come as near to perfection as works of the sort can well do. But then they are composed upon a plan essentially different from that either of 'Valerius' or of 'Reginald Dalton.' ['Adam Blair' and 'Matthew Wald'] are tales of passion, told vigorously yet simply, and with little or no effort at dramatic effect. . . . There is prodigious power in both stories; great vigour of narrative, great beauty of expression, great depth of pathos; but they are not the productions of a man whom Nature designed to take his place in the foremost rank of the masters of fiction. (pp. 463-65)

[As editor of the 'Quarterly Review,' Lockhart] could by a few touches add grace and point to the best written papers— . . . he could throw off superfluous matter, develop a half-expressed thought, disentangle a complicated sentence, and give life and spirit to the solid sense of a heavy article, as the sculptor animates the shapeless stone. (p. 466)

His intellect exercised for many years an acknowledged, and, we think, a most salutary influence over the literary tastes of a great nation. *This* was the way in which his genius made itself felt. Nor could we recall, in his generation, a mind fitter for the work. . . . No man could have produced so good an English dictionary or an edition of some great English classic; no man could judge better of the compositions of others, or could write in purer style himself. He was not only critic but author, and had imagination as well as judgment; he was kind and considerate towards unpretending merit, ready to recognise and welcome real talent in friend or foe, and severe only where presumption went hand in hand with ignorance. . . . He could write on Greek literature—on the origin of the Latin language—on novels—on any subject, from poetry to dry-rot; but his biographical articles bear the palm. Many of them contain the liveliest and truest sketches that exist, of the characters to which they are devoted, with many a wise and eloquent discussion of points of social morality, and here and there an amusing half-involuntary revelation of Lockhart's own opinions and experiences. Some of his shorter and more fragmentary productions appeal so directly to our hearts and understandings that we accept them without hesitation as the productions of a man of striking ability. Take, for example, his well-known delineation of Theodore Hook. We are not acquainted with anything of the kind in any language, ancient or modern, which holds the reader's attention with a more iron grasp, whether to his entertainment or his agony.

Of his great work, the 'Life of Scott,' though thrown off in the scanty leisure of a too busy life . . . , it is not too much to say that there are very few pieces of biography in the language worthy to be compared with it. (pp. 480-81)

[G. R. Gleig], "Life of Lockhart," in The Quarterly Review, Vol. CXVI, No. CCXXXII, October, 1864, pp. 439-82.

HENRY JAMES, JR.   (essay date 1879)

[*James was an American-born English novelist, short story writer, critic, essayist, and playwright who is considered one of the greatest novelists in the English language. Although best known for his novels, James is also admired as a lucid and insightful critic. Here, he asserts that Lockhart's examination of a minister's moral dilemma in* Some Passages in the Life of Mr. Adam Blair, Minister of the Gospel at Cross-Meikle *justifies the novel's comparison with Nathaniel Hawthorne's* The Scarlet Letter. *James, however, finds that the stories differ greatly in tone; although he considers* Adam Blair *an "excellent second-rate" novel rather than a masterpiece like* The Scarlet Letter, *he notes that Lockhart's "warm and straightforward" treatment of his subject makes Hawthorne's novel seem "passionless" by comparison. James here presages the approach of such later critics as David Craig, Francis Russell Hart, and Thomas C. Richardson (1963, 1978, 1979), who consider* Adam Blair *an important study of the morals of a rigidly religious society in eighteenth-century Scotland.*]

I was made to feel [the] want of reality, [the] over-ingenuity, of *The Scarlet Letter,* by chancing not long since upon a novel which was read fifty years ago much more than to-day, but which is still worth reading—the story of *Adam Blair,* by John Gibson Lockhart. This interesting and powerful little tale has a great deal of analogy with Hawthorne's novel—quite enough, at least, to suggest a comparison between them; and the comparison is a very interesting one to make, for it speedily leads us to larger considerations than simple resemblances and divergences of plot. (p. 111)

I confess that a large portion of the interest of *Adam Blair,* to my mind, when once I had perceived that it would repeat in a great measure the situation of *The Scarlet Letter,* lay in noting its difference of tone. It threw into relief the passionless quality of Hawthorne's novel, its element of cold and ingenious fantasy, its elaborate imaginative delicacy. . . . [The] absence of a certain something warm and straightforward, a trifle more grossly human and vulgarly natural, which one finds in *Adam Blair,* will always make Hawthorne's tale less touching to a large number of even very intelligent readers, than a love-story told with the robust, synthetic pathos which served Lockhart so well. His novel is not of the first rank (I should call it an excellent second-rate one), but it borrows a charm from the fact that his vigorous, but not strongly imaginative, mind was impregnated with the reality of his subject. He did not always succeed in rendering this reality; the expression is sometimes awkward and poor. But the reader feels that his vision was clear, and his feeling about the matter very strong and rich. . . . Lockhart, by means much more vulgar [than Hawthorne], produces at moments a greater illusion, and satisfies our inevitable desire for something, in the people in whom it is sought to interest us, that shall be of the same pitch and the same continuity with ourselves. Above all, it is interesting to see how the same subject appears to two men of a thoroughly different cast of mind and of a different race. Lockhart was struck with the warmth of the subject that offered itself to him, and Hawthorne with its coldness; the one with its glow, its sentimental interest—the other with its shadow, its moral interest. Lockhart's story is as decent, as severely draped, as *The Scarlet Letter;* but the author has a more vivid sense than appears to have imposed itself upon Hawthorne, of some of the incidents of the situation he describes; his tempted man and tempting woman are more actual and personal; his heroine in especial, though not in the least a delicate or a subtle conception, has a sort of credible, visible, palpable property, a vulgar roundness and relief, which are lacking to the dim and chastened image of Hester Prynne. But I am going too far; I am comparing simplicity with subtlety, the usual with the refined. Each man wrote as his turn of mind impelled him, but each expressed something more than himself. Lockhart was a dense, substantial Briton, with a taste for the concrete, and Hawthorne was a thin New Englander, with a miasmatic conscience. (pp. 112-13)

> Henry James, Jr., ''The Three American Novels,'' in his Hawthorne, *Macmillan and Co., London, 1879, (and reprinted by Harper & Brothers, Publishers, 1880, pp. 102-41).**

[A. INNES SHAND]   (essay date 1882)

[To] do justice to [Lockhart's] rare versatility; to the refinements of his style and the facility of his execution; to the extent of his acquaintance with literature in all its branches, ancient and modern, English and foreign,—he should be judged by the masses of articles he furnished to 'Maga' ['Blackwood's Edinburgh Magazine'] and the 'Quarterly.' (p. 116)

[For] freshness and vigour, he never surpassed some of the very first articles he contributed to 'Maga.' Nor would it be easy to select a happier specimen of those than the first of a series of papers on **'Greek Tragedy,'** which appeared in the first number. It is as remarkable for taste as for fire, and shows all the confidence given by a firm grasp of the subject; although we see signs of literary inexperience in certain defects of artistic construction. In the good old style, to which some of the writers for our contemporary periodicals might nevertheless incline with advantage, he dashes at his subject somewhat boldly; but we are charmed afterwards by a compactness which is at once lucid, pregnant, and methodical. (p. 120)

It would have been well for Lockhart, as even in his hot youth he was ready enough to admit, had he been content to be brilliant without being stinging, and playful without being personal. But even those who smarted from sharp personalities, or who condemned them, were compelled, by such scholarly articles as the **'Greek Tragedy,'** to admit that the satirists were men of attainments, and writers of no ordinary skill. (p. 121)

[We] must remember that the dangerous weapons [Lockhart] sometimes abused in his youth, were habitually turned in his maturity to nobler purposes. But it is pleasanter to turn to his poetry in 'Maga,' which varies as much in the style as the measures. The best known, if not the best, of his numerous shorter pieces, is his **'Captain Paton's Lament.'** . . . [**'Mad Banker of Amsterdam'**] is a poem of tremendous promise and decidedly remarkable performance. . . . It is not only that he exhibits wonderful command of the metre [in his poetry], weaving easily into his flowing stanzas the most uncompromising phrases, which he has the knack of making flexible—that he works up his rhymes with the dexterity of a jackdaw out of materials he pillages from both dead and living languages—but he suggests an endless succession of grotesque ideas and allusions from what seems to be precisely the most humorous point of view; and he dashes off a series of most ludicrous Dutch sketches, with all the character and minute drollery of an Ostade or Jan Steen. (p. 123)

We must not dismiss Lockhart's poetry without adverting to his [**'Spanish Ballads'**]. . . . To say nothing of the martial fire and chivalrous spirit of the original, which are admirably preserved, they are a wonderful combination of literary taste with graceful scholarship. And the introduction, by the way, well deserves reading, as throwing lights, that were in those days

original, on the deterioration of the Spanish character since the middle ages, and on the manners of the Spanish Moors. . . . It is seldom, indeed, that a translator has thrown himself so absolutely into the spirit of his subjects, while following so closely the letter of his original. Yet if Lockhart fetters himself, he carries his shackles with such ease that he almost seems to wear them as ornaments, changing a harsh jangle into harmonious music. (p. 125)

[In **'Peter's Letters,'** a] limited provincial society, with its cliques and circles, found a ''chiel amang them taking notes,'' and the chiel was a master of comic portraiture, whether with the pen or the pencil. . . . [We] should do very grave injustice to the book were we to characterise it as chiefly a satirical performance. It is true that there is a vein of piquant subacidity in it; but, generally speaking, the vigorous portrait-painting is executed with a generosity that places in the most favourable light the most striking features of the subject. (pp. 126-27)

[Though Lockhart's novels] show his talents, and were fairly successful at the time, . . . he cannot be said to have shone in fiction. He could conceive a powerful plot, and tell a story admirably; but the very qualities that made the excellence of his brilliant social sketches were inimical to the proportions and the completeness that are essential to the highest fiction. His novels abound in spirited pieces of description, and are enlivened by telling scenes; but the author's favourite bents are perpetually diverting him into side paths, and the interest naturally grows languid as attention is distracted from the characters. Thus the characters in his **'Valerius'** seem mere lay figures, galvanised into life after their sleep of centuries, in the midst of an exceedingly vivid reproduction of Rome and Roman manners in the reign of Trajan. . . . Lockhart has made a creditable display of his taste and scholarship [in **'Valerius'**], but it must be confessed that his fancy failed him; and though some of his most moving scenes are magnificently painted, the story makes but slight impression on the feelings. And **'Reginald Dalton'** may be very similarly criticised, although the subject might seem to have recommended itself to his especial genius, and though he described the troubles and humours of undergraduate life at Oxford from recent and personal experiences. And it is to be remarked that . . . the vivacious and satirical Lockhart was disposed to luxuriate in gloom. . . . **'Adam Blair'** is the most melancholy of all, [but] it is also the most artistically successful; for it is successful because the author has proved his power by enlisting our feelings profoundly in favour of the minister. (pp. 128-29)

Lockhart's biographical abilities were altogether *hors de ligne* [first rate], although, undoubtedly, he was exceptionally fortunate in his subjects. He had the memory and the minute observation of a Boswell, with a nature altogether antipathetical to that of [Samuel Johnson's] obsequious shadow. He was never dazzled by the brilliant sparkle of genius, and he was keenly alive to defects. He could arrange his materials as happily as he selected them. He could grasp characters as he grouped facts and incidents picturesquely round his central figure; his knowledge of character and of human nature quickened his intuitive gifts of perception; and, satirist as he was, he had the kindly sympathies which showed the object of his affections in their most engaging lights, while passing judgment on their faults and foibles with the tolerance of a man of the world. (p. 129)

[The **'Life of Scott'**] is no unworthy memorial of the illustrious writer whose career has been depicted sympathetically and admiringly, yet with an absolute sincerity that does equal honour to Sir Walter and his son-in-law.

Lockhart's work in the 'Quarterly' . . . marks, of course, the maturity of his literary experience. Yet we may be forgiven for expressing the opinion, that in independence of thought, as in inimitable vigour and freshness of style, the early papers in 'Maga,' such as those on **'Greek Tragedy,'** . . . will compare with it by no means unfavourably. Necessarily, what strikes us first is . . . the extraordinary range of most incongruous subjects which he handles with all the knowledge of an expert; while they are remarkable enough as mere proofs of the industry of a man who mixed much in the world, and had always many irons in the fire. Next, since the knowledge is never ostentatiously paraded, we only gradually awaken to the extent of his literary attainments, and in that respect the advance is very visible. His political information is become accurate and practical; he writes in an intimate acquaintance with public men and their probable lines of conduct in particular circumstances; he makes the most of exceptional sources of information; while he judges political opponents with almost cynical tolerance, and his impressions have ripened with experience into convictions. That he was an admirable editor we cannot doubt. (p. 130)

Lockhart's case is a proof . . . of the precariousness of the tenure of literary reputations. His character as a writer stands high, no doubt; but adequate justice has never been done to him, and the life of one of the most brilliant of biographers remains unwritten. (p. 131)

> [A. Innes Shand], "The Lights of 'Maga'—II: The Heroes of the 'Noctes'," in Blackwood's Edinburgh Magazine, *Vol. CXXXII, No. DCCCI, July, 1882, pp. 116-31.*

GEORGE SAINTSBURY (essay date 1884)

[Saintsbury was an English literary historian and critic who wrote during the late nineteenth and early twentieth centuries. A prolific author, Saintsbury composed a number of histories of English and European literature as well as several critical works on individual authors, styles, and periods. In his appreciative survey of Lockhart's works, Saintsbury singles out Lockhart as a "special example" of a nineteenth-century author who missed his "due meed of fame." Although Saintsbury dismisses Lockhart's novels, he credits him with "considerable poetical faculty" and asserts that, as a critic, Lockhart was impartial and versatile, as well as one of the first English commentators to unite criticism of various art forms. Saintsbury argues that Lockhart's greatest achievement was as a biographer. He praises Lockhart's biographies for their objectivity and proportion and, in contrast to Thomas Carlyle's assessment of Memoirs of the Life of Sir Walter Scott, Bart. as a "compilation" rather than a "composition" (1837), he remarks that Lockhart's biographies "have the peculiarity of being full of facts without presenting an undigested appearance."]

In every age there are certain writers who seem to miss their due meed of fame, and this is most naturally and unavoidably the case in ages which see a great deal of what may be called occasional literature. There is, as it seems to me, a special example of this general proposition in the nineteenth century, and that example is [Lockhart]. . . . [There] is no collected edition of his works; his sober, sound, scholarly, admirably witty, and, with some very few exceptions, admirably catholic literary criticism, is rarely quoted; and to add to this, there is a curious prepossession against him, which, though nearly a generation has passed since his death, has by no means disappeared. . . . [While] the work of many of Lockhart's con-

temporaries, famous at the time, distinctly loses by re-reading, his for the most part does not; and it happens to display exactly the characteristics which are most wanting in criticism, biographical and literary, at the present day. . . . [Those characteristics are] sobriety of style and reserve of feeling, coupled with delicacy of intellectual appreciation and aesthetic sympathy, a strong and firm creed in matters political and literary, not excluding that catholicity of judgment which men of strong belief frequently lack, and, above all, the faculty of writing like a gentleman without writing like a mere gentleman. No one can charge Lockhart with dilettantism: no one certainly can charge him with feebleness of intellect, or insufficient equipment of culture, or lack of humour and wit. (pp. 1-3)

"The scorpion which delighteth to sting the faces of men," as he or Wilson describes himself in the **Chaldee Manuscript** . . . , certainly justified the description. . . . [The **Chaldee Manuscript**] is capital journalism; and the exuberance of its wit, if it be only wit of the undergraduate kind . . . , is refreshing enough. . . . [**Peter's Letters to His Kinsfolk**] is one of the most careful examples of literary hoaxing to be found. . . . [Many of the descriptions] are admirable; and there is a charming sketch of Oxford undergraduate life, less exaggerated than that in **Reginald Dalton,** probably because the subject was fresher in the author's memory. (pp. 4-5)

[No] one but a very clever person, whether young or old, could have written it, though it is too long and has occasional faults of a specially youthful kind. (p. 5)

[Lockhart's] novels, though containing much that is very remarkable, are not his strongest work; indeed, any critic who speaks with knowledge must admit that Lockhart had every faculty for writing novels, except the faculty of novel-writing. **Valerius** . . . is, like everything of its author's, admirably written, but, like every classical novel . . . , it somehow rings false and faint, though not, perhaps, so faint or so false as most of its fellows. **Adam Blair** . . . is unquestionably Lockhart's masterpiece in this kind. It is full of passion, full of force, and the characters of Charlotte Campbell and Adam Blair himself are perfectly conceived. But the story-gift is still wanting. The reader finds himself outside: wondering why the people do these things, and whether in real life they would have done them, instead of following the story with absorption, and asking himself no questions at all. The same, in a different way, is the case with Lockhart's longest book, **Reginald Dalton;** and this has the additional disadvantage that neither hero nor heroine are much more than lay-figures, while in **Adam Blair** both are flesh and blood. The Oxford scenes are amusing but exaggerated—the obvious work of a man who supplies the defects of a ten years' memory by deepening the strokes where he does remember. **Matthew Wald** . . . has excellent passages, but is conventional and wooden as a whole. . . . [Not] many things are more indicative of his literary ability than that, after a bare three years' practice, he left a field [novel writing] which certainly was not his. (pp. 7-8)

[It] is evident that [Lockhart] had very considerable poetical faculty. The charming piece, **"When youthful hope is fled"** . . . ; the well-known **"Captain Paton's Lament"** . . . ; and the monorhymed epitaph on **"Bright broken Maginn"** . . . , which really is a masterpiece of humorous pathos, are all in very different styles, and are all excellent each in its style. But these things are mere waifs, separated from each other in widely different publications; and until they are put together no general impression of the author's poetical talent, except a vaguely favourable one, can be derived from them. The **Spanish Ballads** form something like a substantive work, and one of nearly as great merit as is possible to poetical translations of poetry. I believe opinions differ as to their fidelity to the original. Here and there, it is said, the author has exchanged a vivid and characteristic touch for a conventional and feeble one. . . . But such things will happen to translators. . . . [Certainly] no one can fail to enjoy the *Ballads* as they stand in English. The **"Wandering Knight's Song"** has always seemed to me a gem without flaw, especially the last stanza. Few men . . . manage the long "fourteener" with middle rhyme better than Lockhart, though he is less happy with the anapaest, and has not fully mastered the very difficult trochaic measure of **"The Death of Don Pedro."** In **"The Count Arnaldos,"** wherein, indeed, the subject lends itself better to that cadence, the result is more satisfactory. The merits, however, of these *Ballads* are not technical merely, or rather, the technical merits are well subordinated to the production of the general effect. . . . The ballad effect is . . . the simplest and most primitive of all poetical effects; it is Lockhart's merit that he seldom fails to produce it. The simplicity and spontaneity of his verse may, to some people, be surprising in a writer so thoroughly and intensely literary; but Lockhart's character was as complex as his verse is simple, and the verse itself is not the least valuable guide to it. (pp. 9-10)

[Lockhart's *Life of Burns* and *Life of Scott*], with the sketch of Theodore Hook written for the *Quarterly* in 1843, . . . make three very remarkable examples of literary biography on very different scales, dealing with very different subjects, and, by comparison of their uniform excellence, showing that the author had an almost unique genius for this kind of composition. . . . [They] are all equally well-proportioned in themselves and to their subjects; they all exhibit the same complete grasp of the secret of biography; and they all have the peculiarity of being full of facts without presenting an undigested appearance. . . . [Lockhart's biographies belong equally] . . . to the literature of knowledge and the literature of power. They are storehouses of information; but they are, at the same time, works of art, and of very great art. The earliest of the three, the *Life of Burns,* is to this day by far the best book on the subject. . . . Lockhart was a decided Tory, and Burns, during the later part of his life at any rate, had permitted himself manifestations of political opinion which Whigs themselves admitted to be imprudent freaks, and which even a good-natured Tory might be excused for regarding as something very much worse. But the biographer's treatment of both these subjects is perfectly tolerant, judicious, and fair, and the same may be said of his whole account of Burns. Indeed, the main characteristic of Lockhart's criticism, a robust and quiet sanity, fitted him admirably for the task of biography. He is never in extremes, and he never avoids extremes by the common expedient of see-sawing between two sides, two parties, or two views of a man's character. He holds aloof equally from *engouement* [infatuation] and from depreciation, and if, as a necessary consequence, he failed, and fails, to please fanatics on either side, he cannot fail to please those who know what criticism really means.

These good qualities were shown even to better advantage in a pleasanter but, at the same time, far more difficult task, the famous *Life of Scott.* The extraordinary interest of the subject, and the fashion, no less skilful than modest, in which the biographer keeps himself in the background, and seems constantly to be merely editing Scott's words, have perhaps obscured the literary value of the book to some readers. Of the perpetual comparison with Boswell, it may be said, once for

all, that it is a comparison of matter merely; and that from the properly literary point of view, the point of view of workmanship and form, it does not exist. Perhaps the most surprising thing is that, even in moments of personal irritation, any one should have been found to accuse Lockhart of softening Scott's faults. . . . [In] fact, Lockhart, considering his relationship to Scott, and considering Scott's greatness, could hardly have spoken more plainly as to the grave fault of judgment which made a man of letters and a member of a learned profession mix himself up secretly, and almost clandestinely, with commercial speculations. On this point the biographer does not attempt to mince matters; and on no other point was it necessary for him to be equally candid, for this, grave as it is, is almost the only fault to be found with Scott's character. This candour, however, is only one of the merits of the book. The wonderfully skilful arrangement of so vast and heterogeneous a mass of materials, the way in which the writer's own work and his quoted matter dovetail into one another, the completeness of the picture given of Scott's character and life, have never been equalled in any similar book. Not a few minor touches, moreover, which are very apt to escape notice, enhance its merit. Lockhart was a man of all men least given to wear his heart upon his sleeve, yet no one has dealt with such pitiful subjects as his later volumes involve, at once with such total absence of "gush" and with such noble and pathetic appreciation. . . . I do not think that, as an example of absolute and perfect good taste, the account of Scott's death can be surpassed in literature. The same quality exhibits itself in another matter. No biographer can be less anxious to display his own personality than Lockhart; and though for six years he was a constant, and for much longer an occasional, spectator of the events he describes, he never introduces himself except when it is necessary. Yet, on the other hand, when Scott himself makes complimentary references to him . . . , he neither omits the passage nor stoops to the missish *minauderie* [mincing manners], too common in such cases, of translating "spare my blushes" into some kind of annotation. (pp. 11-14)

The head and front of Lockhart's offending, in a purely literary view, seems to be the famous *Quarterly* article on Lord Tennyson's volume of 1832. . . . Now I do not think I yield to any man living in admiration of Lord Tennyson, but I am unable to think much the worse, or, indeed, any the worse, of Lockhart because of this article. In the first place, it is extremely clever, being, perhaps, the very best example of politely cruel criticism in existence. In the second, most, if not all, of the criticism is perfectly just. . . . The best justification of Lockhart's verdict on the volume of 1832 is what Lord Tennyson himself did do with the volume of 1832. Far more than half the passages objected to have since been excised or altered. But there are other excuses. In the first place, Mr Tennyson, as he then was, represented a further development of schools of poetry against which the *Quarterly* had always, rightly or wrongly, set its face, and a certain loyalty to the principles of his paper is, after all, not the worst fault of a critic. In the second, no one can fairly deny that some points in Mr Tennyson's early, if not in his later, manner must have been highly and rightly disgustful to a critic who, like Lockhart, was above all things masculine and abhorrent of "gush." In the third, it is, unfortunately, not given to all critics to admire all styles alike. (pp. 21-2)

Lockhart, within his own range, and it was for the time a very wide one, was certainly not a narrow critic, just as he certainly was not a feeble one. In . . . *Peter's Letters* (which, with all its faults, is one of his best, and particularly one of his most spontaneous and characteristic works) the denunciation of the "facetious and rejoicing ignorance" which enabled contemporary critics to pooh-pooh Wordsworth, Charles Lamb, and Coleridge is excellent. . . . Another point in which Lockhart made a great advance was that he was one of the first (Lamb himself is, in England, his only important forerunner) to unite and combine criticism of different branches of art. He never has the disgusting technical jargon, or the undisciplined fluency, of the mere art critic, any more than he has the gabble of the mere connoisseur. But it is constantly evident that he has a knowledge of and a feeling for the art of line and colour as well as of words. Nothing can be better than the fragments of criticism which are interspersed in the Scott book. . . . It is, moreover, characteristic of Lockhart as a critic that he is, as has been noted, always manly and robust. He was never false to his own early protest against "the banishing from the mind of a reverence for feeling, as abstracted from mere questions of immediate and obvious utility." But he never allowed that reverence to get the better of him and drag him into the deplorable excesses of gush into which, from his day to ours, criticism has more and more had a tendency to fall. If he makes no parade of definite aesthetic principles, it is clear that throughout he had such principles, and that they were principles of a very good kind. He had a wide knowledge of foreign literature without any taint of "Xenomania," sufficient scholarship . . . in the older languages, and a thorough knowledge and love of English literature. His style is, to me at any rate, peculiarly attractive. Contrasted with the more brightly coloured and fantastically-shaped styles, of which, in his own day, De Quincey, Wilson, Macaulay, and Carlyle set the fashion, it may possibly seem tame to those who are not satisfied with proportion in form and harmony in tint; it will certainly not seem so to those who are more fortunately gifted. Indeed, compared [with] Wilson's welter of words, now bombastic, now gushing, now horse-playful . . . , it is infinitely preferable. (pp. 22-4)

[There] is no doubt that though Lockhart was an admirable critic merely as such, a poet, or at least a song-writer, of singular ability and charm within certain limits, and a master of sharp light raillery that never missed its mark and never lumbered on the way, his most unique and highest merit is that of biographer. Carlyle . . . does not allow this, and complains that Lockhart's conception of his task was "not very elevated" [see excerpt above, 1837]. . . . Lockhart's plan was not, it seems, in the case of his *Scott*, very elevated, because it was not "to show Scott as he was by nature, as the world acted on him, as he acted on the world," and so forth. Now, unfortunately, this is exactly what it seems to me that Lockhart, whether he meant to do it or not, has done in the very book which Carlyle was criticising. And it seems to me, further, that he always does this in all his biographical efforts. Sometimes he appears . . . to quote and extract from other and much inferior writers to an extent rather surprising in so excellent a penman, especially when it is remembered that, except to a dunce, the extraction and stringing together of quotations is far more troublesome than original writing. But even then the extracts are always luminous. With ninety-nine out of a hundred biographies the total impression which Carlyle demands, and very properly demands, is, in fact, a total absence of impression. The reader's mind is as dark, though it may be as full, as a cellar when the coals have been shot into it. Now this is never the case with Lockhart's biographies, whether they are books in half a dozen volumes, or essays in half a hundred pages. He subordinates what even Carlyle allowed to be his "clear nervous forcible style" so entirely to the task of representing his subject, he has such a perfect general conception

of that subject, that only a very dense reader can fail to perceive the presentment. (pp. 24-5)

He was an eminent example, perhaps one of the most eminent, of a "gentleman of the press." He did a great many kinds of literary work, and he did all of them well; novel-writing, perhaps, . . . least well. But he does not seem to have felt any very strong or peculiar call to any particular class of original literary work, and his one great and substantive book may be fairly taken to have been much more decided by accident and his relationship to Scott than by deliberate choice. He was, in fact, eminently a journalist, and it is very much to be wished that there were more journalists like him. For from the two great reproaches of the craft to which so many of us belong, . . . he was conspicuously free. He never did work slovenly in form, and he never did work that was not in one way or other consistent with a decided set of literary and political principles. . . . [All of his works have] the same careful though unostentatious distinction of style, the same admirable faculty of sarcasm, wherever sarcasm is required, the same depth of feeling, wherever feeling is called for, the same refusal to make a parade of feeling even where it is shown. Never trivial, never vulgar, never feeble, never stilted, never diffuse, Lockhart is one of the very best recent specimens of that class of writers of all work, which since Dryden's time has continually increased, is increasing, and does not seem likely to diminish. The growth may or may not be matter for regret. . . . But if the office is to exist, let it at least be the object of those who hold it to perform its duties with that hatred of commonplace and cant and the *popularis aura* [popular regard], with, as nearly as may be in each case, that conscience and thoroughness of workmanship, which Lockhart's writings uniformly display. (pp. 26-7)

George Saintsbury, "Lockhart" (originally published as "John Gibson Lockhart," in The National Review, *London, Vol. III, No. 18, August, 1884), in his* The Collected Essays and Papers of George Saintsbury: 1875-1920, Vol. II, *J. M. Dent & Sons Ltd, 1923 (and reprinted by Johnson Reprint Corporation, 1969), pp. 1-27.*

M. CLIVE HILDYARD (essay date 1931)

[*The following essay is drawn from Hildyard's introduction to Lockhart's* Literary Criticism, *a work that prompted twentieth-century commentators to reassess Lockhart's abilities as a critic. In her appreciative survey of Lockhart's literary criticism, Hildyard singles out Lockhart's commentaries on Percy Bysshe Shelley, Samuel Taylor Coleridge, Lord Byron, and William Cobbett as evidence of his critical acumen. While Hildyard regards Lockhart as a critic of the first rank, she does not consider his judgments infallible; she voices a commonly expressed opinion which holds that Lockhart unjustly attacked Leigh Hunt and John Keats for their political beliefs and, indirectly, for their inferior education and upbringing.*]

[Lockhart] was branded as the "Scorpion" in the early days of his career and the real value of his critical position has not been generally recognised. As a biographer he stands admittedly in the first rank, but as a critic, too, he has high claims. A man of wide and generous enthusiasms to whom literature was the passion and solace of life, he was well suited to the task, and combined in an unusual degree the attributes of the scholar and the connoisseur. He was "literary" in the highest sense of the word. He was himself a master of pure English; his judgment was tempered with imagination, and he had a delicate taste.

He had, too, not a little of the essayist's versatility and could write agreeably on Greek literature, Deer Stalking, German Watering Places and Dry Rot. . . . (p. 1)

Lockhart's task as editor of the *Quarterly* proved exacting. . . . [He] never hesitated to use his editorial powers, and would sometimes even interpolate passages of his own. The skill with which he effected this unusual operation seems occasionally to have mitigated the offence. (pp. 3-4)

The Lockhart of the *Quarterly* was clearly not the Lockhart of *Blackwood's*. (p. 4)

The apparent change, however, was merely due to a rigorous self-restraint, and the careful reader might still detect the feline touch as well as the feline grace. (p. 5)

The outstanding feature of Lockhart's critical work is its extreme reticence. In the majority of his articles in the *Quarterly* it would be infinitely more interesting to have his extended critical views and fewer pages of extracts. It is the same effacement that meets us in his *Life of Scott.* He believed strenuously in the author's right to plead his own cause. It was a generous belief but English criticism is the poorer for it. (pp. 5-6)

It can be claimed for Lockhart's reviews that they are, almost without exception, well worth re-reading to-day, and are not to be mistaken for ephemeral journalism. Even when he is criticising forgotten novels . . . , he contrives to make his criticism readable and entertaining in spite of the dullness of his material. In all his work he shows sound literary appreciation and catholicity of taste and judgment. On religious matters he was broad-minded and tolerant; politically, he sympathized strongly with Carlyle in later years. . . . On all subjects he writes clearly, trying to keep before him . . . Voltaire's rule of always being sure before you write anything that you have a perfectly clear idea of what you want to say. He is never careless and never extravagant. Quick to discover real merit, he hated every kind of pretension and presumption. His feelings he held in very strong reserve, but those who knew him best testify that he was not only singularly unaffected but as sensitively sympathetic as he was intellectually keen. (p. 6)

In considering Lockhart's criticism of *Keats* we must remember that it was an age of personalities, when "the author was nothing—the Reviewer everything," and when political antagonism ran so high that the critic assailed the individual rather than the party and succumbed to bias and personal prejudice. . . . In a private letter Lockhart was capable of writing sympathetically of Keats and hoping that he would get over his illness and live to be a merry fellow, but as a critic he followed the bias of his age, and would neither acknowledge the real promise shown in Keats's early work nor show any enthusiasm for the great odes, the merit of which he can hardly have failed to recognise. (pp. 7-8)

For Lockhart, there was a very special cause of offence in the work of Keats. A classical scholar himself, he regarded the classics, in much the same way as the University Wits of an earlier age, as the scholar's prerogative, and it irritated him that Keats, knowing no Greek, should go to Greek mythology for the subject of his verse. Nevertheless, Lockhart never denied that Keats had the making of a real poet, if he would but forswear Cockneyism and Mr. Leigh Hunt. We can only regret that he did not allow his better judgment to overrule his political bias. . . . (pp. 8-9)

Lockhart's estimate of *Leigh Hunt,* whom he regarded as the king of the Cockneys and responsible for the literary crimes of his followers, cannot be regarded as a fair one. It is an estimate which emphasises all his faults and ignores his merits. (p. 9)

While he detested his principles, Lockhart was fully alive to the beauties of *Shelley's* poetry, and wrote with unbounded admiration of the magnificent opening scene of his "Prometheus Unbound." And in writing of *Wordsworth* and *Coleridge* Lockhart is at his very best. He was one of Wordsworth's earliest admirers. . . . [After] having read the "Excursion," he says: "He strikes me as having more about him of that sort of sober, mild sunset kind of gentleness, which is so dear to me from the recollections of Euripides and the tender parts of the Odyssey, than any English poet ever possessed, save Shakespeare, the possessor of all,"—a criticism which deserves to rank, in penetration and in felicity of phrase, with the greatest eulogies of Wordsworth.

His entire treatment of Coleridge is one of Lockhart's happiest critical achievements. His appreciation of his subtle melodies is equalled by his admiration for his critical gifts. In his review of Coleridge's *Table-Talk,* he calls him a "beautiful poet," an "exquisite metaphysician," a "universal scholar" and a "profound theologian." . . . "In almost every other point of view as unlike Dr. Johnson as one man of great faculties and great virtues can be to one another, Mr. Coleridge must be allowed to have been his legitimate successor as the great literary talker of England. . . ." (pp. 9-10)

This praise reveals the true critic. In coupling Coleridge's name with that of Johnson, he is unconsciously suggesting an ideal combination for the criticism of Shakespeare, a blend of Coleridge's subtle intuition and Johnson's sound common-sense. His general estimate of Coleridge has been approved by a century of criticism. . . .

On the other hand, Lockhart's estimate of *Campbell* is a striking instance of the fallibility of contemporary criticism, since he based his praise almost entirely on Campbell's longer poems. But Lockhart was not alone in this opinion. It was the popular view of the time, and was heartily endorsed by Byron. . . .

As early as 1813 we find Lockhart anticipating a critical dictum of Matthew Arnold's. . . . [In] praise of *Byron's* "Lara" [he] says: "I delight in all the great poets of our day, and am willing to put Wordsworth and Byron at the top." He took an extremely sane and, for his day, courageous view of *Don Juan.* He saw its "great" qualities and was willing to overlook its excesses, which, as he rightly points out, were no worse than much that had been accepted and praised in the work of earlier writers. (p. 11)

Of the thirty poems in [Tennyson's] 1833 volume reviewed by Lockhart, seven were omitted in future editions of Tennyson's works, and almost every line with which the critic found fault was either omitted or re-written. This is in itself a tribute to the soundness of Lockhart's criticism in spite of the fact that his remarks were undoubtedly written in a vein of mockery. . . . "The Lady of Shalott," to which Lockhart was particularly unsympathetic and the beauties of which he has been blamed for not seeing, was drastically changed. Indeed there is not only some excuse for Lockhart's criticism but a distinct justification for it when one realises that the poem as he read it was in a form radically different from that which now everyone acclaims. . . . Similar justification might be offered for Lockhart's criticism of "The Lotus-eaters," though here one is inclined to be less indulgent to the critic, since the opening verses, in which the Spenserian stanza is wedded to an ideal subject, were unchanged but for a single line. The last part of the Choric Song, however, was considerably altered, and the lines which Lockhart quoted were subsequently removed.

One may agree that the pleasantries in which Lockhart indulged in this review were somewhat unworthy of his maturer judgment, but it cannot be said that the jibes were wholly unmerited. They were, at least, entirely beneficial in their result, and inspired the poet to some of his happiest revisions. (pp. 13-15)

Lockhart's estimate of *Cobbett* is one of the most impressive instances of his acumen and impartiality. After long neglect, Cobbett has come to be recognised generally as a master of English and a writer of great, simple prose. But his most perfervid admirer at the present time could add little of moment to Lockhart's discriminating eulogy.

In his treatment of contemporary fiction Lockhart, himself a minor novelist of distinction, proves at once his acuteness and his fallibility. Of the scope of the novel he took a wide and liberal view. While insisting on human nature as the main source of the novelist's material, he admits the legitimacy of imaginative and supernatural elements, and maintains the horrible to be as valid an ingredient as the pathetic or the ludicrous. (pp. 15-16)

In his particular judgments we find the usual mixture of hits and misses characteristic of contemporary criticism in every age. He had a high estimate of Godwin, and in respect of his drawing of female characters was prepared to set him above Scott himself. The conclusion of [William Godwin's] *Mandeville* he considered to be the most powerful description of madness since Lear. Marryat he thought "a capital writer," considering him as far above the then belauded Fenimore Cooper and, as a master of circumstantial detail, worthy to be mentioned with Defoe. The extravagances of the Dandiacal School naturally invited the attentions of the Scorpion, and Lockhart had dealt faithfully with Bulwer before [Thomas Carlyle's] *Sartor Resartus* astonished the readers of 'Maga's' [*Blackwood's Edinburgh Magazine's*] London descendant, *Fraser's Magazine*. Of Borrow and Morier he wrote with enthusiasm, and if he failed badly over [William Makepeace Thackeray's] *Esmond*, he went far to repair his mistake by his generous admiration for *Vanity Fair*. It is, rather oddly, with the novels of Theodore Hook, a writer whom one might think little likely to attract him, that the criticism of Lockhart most nearly approaches excess. For he discerned in Hook the potentialities of another Smollett or Le Sage and confidently predicted the resuscitation of his fame. While admitting her ability, Lockhart shrewdly detected the radical weakness in Mrs. Radcliffe's use of the supernatural and emphasised the greater subtlety of Maturin. The women novelists, however, mostly received generous treatment at Lockhart's hands, and he shared Scott's admiration for Maria Edgeworth, Susan Ferrier and Jane Austen. His appreciation of [Charlotte Brontë's] *Jane Eyre* . . . is one of his critical triumphs, but its brilliance is obscured by his failure to detect the genius of Emily Brontë.

Nowhere do we more regret the desultoriness and brevity of Lockhart's critical work than in his infrequent treatment of biography. For the little that he does give us fulfils our natural expectation. He does justice to Prior's *Life of Goldsmith,* which was certainly not superseded by Forster's, and calls attention to the distorted and green-eyed view of Goldsmith revealed in

the references of Boswell. And while commending Prior's happy industry in the collecting of Goldsmith's letters, he does not fail to indicate the literary charm of the letters themselves. . . . Excellent also is Lockhart's theory of the happy consequences of Boswell's nationality. For it is plain, argues Lockhart, that "much about Johnson, which would have been passed over as too familiar for special notice, by any Englishman, was quite new, and being Johnsonian, of grand importance" to Boswell, while Johnson, on the other hand, was led to discourse on a thousand topics on which he would have thought it superfluous to comment to an Englishman.

It was Lockhart's enviable fortune to be the biographer of the two greatest writers of his country. The *Life of Burns* has naturally been overshadowed by . . . [the *Life of Scott*], and has itself been followed by many biographical essays on Burns which have had the benefit of the results of later research. Yet, it may be doubted whether Lockhart has left any clearer proof of his literary competence, sound judgment and good taste than this short biography which in many respects is still the best. Lockhart's attitude to his subject is typical of the man, and not at all in accordance with what might be expected from the prevalent misconceptions of his character. There is no word here of academic patronage for a peasant poet, just as there is naturally no complacent apologising for his vices as with an earlier biographer or a striving after startling paradoxes as with a later. (pp. 16-18)

In writing of Burns, whom he had never seen or known, Lockhart revealed a remarkable sympathy and understanding. When he essayed the far greater task of recording the life of Scott, he had to contend not only with the vast amplitude of his materials but with the uncritical promptings of a filial loyalty and devotion. The triumphant success with which he overcame the one difficulty and resisted the other is the abiding proof of Lockhart's artistry. (p. 19)

[From] beginning to end of [Scott's *Waverley*] series, Lockhart was able to describe with the authority and the ardour of an eye-witness the triumphal progress of the Great Unknown. It was, however, part of his theory that the biographer should be the historian rather than the critic, and while he duly records the fluctuations in critical opinion regarding the *Waverley* Novels, he is himself tantalisingly reticent. Thus it happens that the great biography adds surprisingly little to the body of Lockhart's critical work. On particular novels his comments may not agree with general later opinion, but on the larger issues he is expectedly sound. The European celebrity of *Ivanhoe* did not blind Lockhart to the truth that the highest reach of Scott's genius is to be found only in the novels dealing with Scottish life and character. And from these he unerringly singled out for special praise [*Nigel*]. (pp. 19-20)

In his early days, in *Peter's Letters to his Kinsfolk,* when only *Waverley, The Antiquary* and *The Heart of Midlothian* had yet appeared, Lockhart with quick intuition apprehended the greatness of Scott's achievement and boldly claimed for him that he had done for the most interesting times in the annals of Scotland what Shakespeare and Clarendon had done for two great periods of English history. That opinion his maturer judgment endorsed, and he emphasised, eloquently and unanswerably, the magnitude of the services that Scott had rendered both to Scottish and to Romantic literature generally. (p. 20)

The closing pages of the *Life of Scott* are Lockhart's highest achievement. He finished a task of great magnitude and difficulty with consummate dignity and tact. To all but a few of his contemporaries Lockhart's habitual reticence concealed the greatness of his powers and the emotional depth of his character, just as the fragmentary nature of so much of his writing has stood in the way of later appreciation of his criticism. . . . Lockhart had many of the critic's most invaluable gifts, of which not the least was a style of great clarity and strength. He employed no meretricious aids, but wrote with a scholarly precision and restraint. Emotion breaking through and colouring an habitual reserve has often been productive of magical effects. As it was with Johnson, so was it with Lockhart. The long and studied repression at last yielded to emotion, and the closing scene at Abbotsford is portrayed for ever in one of the most haunting passages of English prose. (p. 21)

> *M. Clive Hildyard, in an introduction to* Lockhart's Literary Criticism *by John Gibson Lockhart, edited by M. Clive Hildyard, Basil Blackwell, 1931, pp. 1-21.*

VIRGINIA WOOLF   (essay date 1931)

[*A discerning and influential English critic and essayist as well as a novelist, Woolf is one of the most prominent literary figures of the twentieth century. In her insightful analysis of Lockhart's literary criticism, she discusses Lockhart's personality and delineates the reasons for his failure as a critic.*]

Lockhart was not an ambitious man, and, for all his powers, he was, save in one instance, rather careless in the use he made of them. . . . [He] held no very exalted view of his mission [as a reviewer]. The business of reviewers, he said, was "to think not of themselves, but of their author. . . . This excludes all chance of formal, original, or would-be original disquisition on the part of the journalist." Hence, though Lockhart must have filled volume upon volume with his reviews, very little of Lockhart is to be found embedded in them. (p. 69)

Yet the work was well worth doing, both because Lockhart had a bold, vivacious mind which leaked into his reviews in spite of his theories, and then again, though Miss Hildyard rates him too highly as a critic [see excerpt above, 1931], he is a fine sample of a reviewer and serves to show the nature and function of those curious creatures whose lives, if they are as gay and giddy as a gnat's, are also as short. . . . His most necessary quality, it would seem, must be that which in other walks of life would be called, respectfully enough, courage. A new and unknown writer is a very dangerous person. . . . When Lockhart, we have to remember, saw ranged on his table the usual new books, their names conveyed nothing to him. Keats, Hook, Godwin, Shelley, Brontë, Tennyson—who were they? . . . It was for him to make the trial and decide the question. . . . The public who paid to be told what to read would be justly annoyed if they were told to read the wrong things.

Lockhart was well qualified for the business. . . . [But] there were drawbacks. The Lockharts were an old Scottish family; and when you add an Oxford education to a young man of an old Scottish family you are making it very difficult for him to be just to apothecaries, for example, who think they can write poetry, or to Cockneys who have the temerity to talk about the Greeks. Moreover, Lockhart was one of those quick-witted indolent people who, as Sir Walter complained, feel the attractions of "the gown and slipper garb of life, and live with funny, easy companions" gossiping and telling stories instead of attending to the serious business of life and making a name for themselves. The doors and windows of his study let in

rumours, prejudices, odds and ends of unsubstantiated gossip. . . . Keats, Lockhart knew, was a friend of Leigh Hunt, and therefore presumably a Liberal, a Cockney. He knew vaguely that his father had kept livery stables. It was impossible, then, that he should be a gentleman and a scholar. All Lockhart's prejudices were roused and he rushed to his doom—the worst that can befall a reviewer. He committed himself violently, he betrayed himself completely. He tried to snuff out between finger and thumb one of the immortal lights of English literature. For that failure he has been gibbeted ever since. (pp. 69-71)

[To] write about a new book the moment it comes out is a very different matter from writing about it fifty years afterwards. (p. 72)

But even so, Lockhart was not so far out as might be expected; in other words, he was very often of the same opinion as we are. He saw the importance of Wordsworth and Coleridge; he welcomed Borrow and Beckford; he placed [Charlotte Brontë's] *Jane Eyre,* in spite of its coarseness, very high. It is true that he predicted a long life for *Zohrab the Hostage,* who has had a short one. Probably because he was a novelist himself his criticism of fiction was erratic, and his enthusiasm for the novels of Godwin and Hook seems to show that they excited his own creative power and thus deflected his critical judgment. Tennyson he bullied with unchastened insolence, but, as Tennyson proved by accepting some of his criticism, not without acuteness. In short, the case of Lockhart would seem to show that a good reviewer of contemporary work will get the proportions roughly right, but the detail wrong. He will single out from a number of unknown writers those who are going to prove men of substance, but he cannot be certain what qualities are theirs in particular, or how the importance of one compares with the importance of another.

One may regret, since this is so, that Lockhart fixed his mind so much upon contemporaries and did not give himself the benefit of a wider perspective. He might have written with far greater safety and perhaps with far greater authority upon the dead. . . . A reviewer can skim the surface, but there are "matters of such moment, that it is absolutely impossible to be a great critic while the mind remains unsettled in regard to them." Because he was aware of this, Lockhart was a good reviewer, and content to remain one. But he was too sceptical, too diffident, too handsome and well bred perhaps; he lived too much under the shadow of Sir Walter Scott, he had too many worries and sorrows and dined out too often to push on into those calm and austere regions where the mind settles down to think things out and has its dwelling in a mood of gentle and universal contemplation. So he was content to go on knocking off articles, and cutting out quotations and leaving them to moulder where they lay. But if his reviews show by their power, their insolence, their very lack of ambition, that he had it in him to do better, they also remind us that there is a virtue in familiarity. We lose something when we have ceased to be able to talk naturally to Johnny Keats, to regret the "early death of this unfortunate and misguided gentleman" Mr. Shelley. A little of the irreverence with which Lockhart treated the living would do no harm to our more sober estimates of the dead. (pp. 72-4)

> *Virginia Woolf, "Lockhart's Criticism" (1931), in her* The Moment and Other Essays *(copyright 1948 by Harcourt Brace Jovanovich, Inc.; renewed 1976 by Harcourt Brace Jovanovich, Inc. and Marjorie T. Parsons; reprinted by permission of the publisher; in Canada by the Author's Literary Estate and The*

Hogarth Press Ltd.), Harcourt Brace Jovanovich, 1948, pp. 69-74.

GILBERT MacBETH (essay date 1931)

[*The following essay is drawn from Macbeth's* John Gibson Lockhart, *the first full-length critical study of Lockhart's work. Macbeth's analysis is considered one of the most important efforts to define Lockhart's critical importance. Macbeth finds that Lockhart exerted a noteworthy influence on the development of nineteenth-century literature. Although Macbeth does not consider Lockhart's novels as significant in themselves, he regards them as indicative of trends in later nineteenth-century fiction. As a critic, Macbeth asserts, Lockhart is of interest primarily as a proponent of German ideas in England, particularly through his dissemination of Friedrich Schlegel's historical theory of literature. Macbeth concludes that Lockhart exerted his greatest influence through his role as editor of the* Quarterly Review; *he remarks that by virtue of his success in "guiding the reader through the new maze of publications, pointing out the nature or tendency of the various works, and judging what is worth reading and what is not," Lockhart should not "be disregarded in a study of the transition in English literature between 1825 and 1850."*]

[The] relation of *Valerius* to Scott's historical novels is perfectly plain. It tries to do what none of the earlier classical romances attempted; it endeavors to draw a picture of the manners and external aspects of the times in which the action takes place. Lockhart was a good classical scholar—what could be more natural than for him to wish to use his classical learning as Scott had used his mediaeval lore? . . . No better evidence of Lockhart's familiarity with the late Roman classics, such as the younger Pliny, Juvenal, and Martial, could be wanted than what is found in *Valerius*. (pp. 15-16)

Particularly noteworthy is the impartiality shown by Lockhart in his treatment of Christian and pagan characters and customs. The pagan characters are as human and as likeable as the Christians, and there is no effort to represent the pagan world as sunk in the darkness of vice and despair, to be relieved only by the coming of Christianity. The pure motives and the humanity of the Romans in their opposition to the new religion are fairly given. . . . But a novel, in the end, must be judged as a novel; and as a novel Lockhart's *Valerius* is a failure. The action is slow; the dialogue is diffuse, stilted, and hopelessly unnatural. The personages, too, do not live. The fundamental gift of the novelist, the faculty for creating convincing characters, is lacking. It follows that there is no successful analysis of the inner life of the characters. In the course of the story the hero makes the momentous change from paganism to Christianity; but we learn scarcely anything of the internal conflict that would be expected in such a crisis. The story is one of superficial incident and detail. (pp. 16-17)

[In *Valerius*, Lockhart's] eye for external detail is given full scope; in the three later [novels] his interest in internal developments in his characters appears in greater or lesser degree. *Adam Blair, Reginald Dalton,* and *Matthew Wald* are, each in its own way, psychological. (p. 17)

It would hardly be possible to develop such a story [as *Adam Blair*] without giving a good deal of attention to the psychological elements, but Lockhart's treatment places even more emphasis upon these than is demanded, perhaps, by the nature of the matter. . . . [Lockhart's] psychological point of view is not confined to certain pages and chapters; he is engaged throughout in turning the eyes of the reader towards the inner life of Adam Blair. . . . Blair's uncertainty as to his own mo-

tives, not to be cleared for him until the critical moment actually arrives, is portrayed with some care. Not so much attention is given to the internal aspects of Charlotte's share in the action. . . . (pp. 23-4)

It is not difficult to decide to what tradition this novel belongs. Though its background is in Scotland, with some scenes picturing Scotch character and habits, and though a Scotch clergyman is its leading personage, the work is in no essential way an imitation of [Scott's] *Waverley* or its successors. The strain of strong feeling that runs throughout the story is something that Scott seldom attempted. *Adam Blair,* by reason of its great concern with the presentation of emotional states of people who are passing through racking and crucial experiences, has much more in common with the novels of Mackenzie, Godwin, C. B. Brown, and the Germans. . . . [*Adam Blair* is] strongly reminiscent of the German manner in its frank handling of passion. A deliberate attempt is made to create for the reader the dangerously seductive atmosphere that surrounds the innocently unaware minister after the arrival of Charlotte at his home; and the climax of the story is narrated with considerable daring for the time when Lockhart was writing.

Adam Blair is Lockhart's best novel. It has great power in some respects, and it shows Lockhart groping towards a deeper and more honest interpretation of life than was to be ordinarily found in English fiction in his day. Yet, as a novel, it is not really a success. It is a tremendous advance over Lockhart's first effort at fiction, *Valerius,* particularly in its representation of the inner life of its characters; but it nevertheless falls short of creating the illusion of reality for the reader. The fault is not in Lockhart's vision or in his conception of what is required of the novelist; it is in his inability to reproduce the reality which he sees. (pp. 24-5)

[In *Reginald Dalton*] Lockhart manifests the same general interest in the inner life of his characters that was visible in *Adam Blair*. . . . But the focus of attention is not upon the character of Reginald so much as upon its clash and reaction with the world as he experiences the formative events that prepare him for active life. This process of finding oneself, of orientation in the world and in society, was a favorite theme of the German novelists, and Lockhart may well have had some of their treatments in mind when he wrote *Reginald Dalton.* The greatest example of the *Bildungsroman,* or the apprentice novel, was, of course, Goethe's *Wilhelm Meister;* but there were other outstanding works of the sort. . . . In all these there is a conscious attempt on the part of the hero to adapt himself to life or to arrive at a philosophy of life. Since Reginald's profiting from his experiences is of the passive kind, perhaps Lockhart's novel is more accurately described as an *Entwicklungsroman* [a novel emphasizing the development of the principal character], a term which does not imply a deliberate purpose and conscious goal in the hero's journey through life. It is nevertheless clear that Lockhart intended to do something else than merely to recount a series of youthful adventures, such as is found in [Henry Fielding's] *Tom Jones* or [William Makepeace Thackeray's] *Pendennis*. It must be admitted that his intention is not carried out in a definite and thorough fashion; and his purpose seems at times quite uncertain. Reginald's encounter with the world is not always kept before the reader; and in the last volume the theme is lost almost entirely, while Lockhart relies upon the more obvious but less abiding interest of plot.

There are a number of interesting aspects of *Reginald Dalton,* such as the autobiographical, sentimental, Wordsworthian, and realistic elements, about which a good deal could be said; but they can only be mentioned. (pp. 27-8)

[*The History of Matthew Wald*] carries to an extreme the psychological tendencies that Lockhart displays in his earlier fiction. (p. 28)

The story has the smell of the grave about it, and the incidents and descriptions possess the vividness of an ugly dream. The gruesomeness of the atmosphere is heightened by the addition of episodes and details whose introduction could be justified on no other grounds. The influence of Godwin is visibly strong; like several of Godwin's novels, *Matthew Wald* is a study of mental aberration. It is particularly reminiscent of [William Godwin's] *Mandeville,* which likewise describes the effects upon a man's conduct of a persecution- and hate-obsession, culminating in an insane attack upon the supposed persecutor and object of hatred. In *Matthew Wald* Lockhart entered the field of abnormal psychology. (p. 29)

It is a matter for regret that [Lockhart] did not continue in the field [of novel-writing]. True, he was not a born story-teller like Scott; but there have surely been successful novelists who were not "to the manner born," who had to learn their trade. . . . It is clear that he had not yet found himself when he wrote [*Matthew Wald*]; the fact that no two of the novels are in the same vein indicates that he had not discovered his true field. *Reginald Dalton* leans, perhaps, the other way from *Matthew Wald,* to the outer life rather than the inner; *Adam Blair* must be regarded as best maintaining the balance of Lockhart's sane and penetrative insight into the body and the soul of the world in which we live. If he had persevered, it is possible that his art would have perfected itself; and he may have been an influential figure in the history of the novel during the transition to the Victorian period. He had ideas about the possibilities of this literary type that would have been of the greatest moment had they been adequately embodied in creative forms; but these ideas remained largely in the shadow, because Lockhart lacked the power of execution. The task was left for other writers. The Brontës, Mrs. Gaskell, George Eliot, Meredith, in England, and Hawthorne in America, traveled by separate paths in the general direction pointed out by the novels of Lockhart; that is, in the direction of a more complete realization and a more profound interpretation of life. Lockhart's novels, as they stand, are worthy of perusal for their isolation of certain literary currents that were soon to blend indistinguishably with the main stream of nineteenth century fiction. (pp. 30-1)

Lockhart was by reason of his critical background peculiarly qualified to pass sympathetic judgments upon his leading contemporaries. From his university days he had read with enthusiasm the modern literatures of Europe, and the recent literature of Germany in particular. But what is really important is that he had assimilated . . . the ideas of the new school of criticism arising in Germany; he had grasped the historical idea of literature. . . . [The] historical method, by reason of its fundamental concept of literature as the expression of aspects in the life of the group out of which it springs, argues against the setting up of any one body of literature as ideal, and conduces to a sympathetic appreciation of the literature of all ages and nations. (pp. 84-5)

Lockhart, then, was a critic who regularly viewed any piece of literature as a mirror of the age, as a manifestation of forces current in the civilization that produced it, and therefore to be evaluated in relation to such forces, without reference to alien standards. We should not expect a critic with such principles

to experience any great difficulty in accepting the leading writers of the early nineteenth century. . . . Without a doubt Lockhart realized that he was living in a great epoch of English literature, and that the chief writers of his times were all united by common characteristics, being the expression of certain elements in the life of the times. . . . It is unlikely that many critics of the time of Lockhart perceived with such clearness the working of the *Zeitgeist* [spirit of the age] in the poets then writing. (pp. 85-6)

Up to the beginning of the nineteenth century, critics had been prone to regard poetry as an imitation or an embellishment rather than as something more vital and essential. But a new conception of poetry had arisen with the rise of the Romantics; for them it was no superficial decorative art, but a representation of emotional and imaginative experience, an interpretation of the deepest feelings of man. The critical outlook that Lockhart had derived from Germany made it almost inevitable that he should share this view of poetry. Believing as he did that literature is an expression of the spirit of the age, he would naturally think of poetry as primarily a matter of feeling. The high value that he placed upon the *feelings* of nationalism and religion in literature, in keeping with the theories . . . of Friedrich Schlegel, is alone a strong indication of how he regarded poetry. Other signs pointing in the same direction are not hard to come upon. His own creative work in the field of the novel, and his semi-creative translations of the Spanish ballads, in one way reveal his tendency. (pp. 86-7)

There was one factor, unfortunately, which militated against the superior performance as a critic that we should otherwise have a right to expect of Lockhart. . . . [Schlegel] rated very highly the elements of national and religious tradition in literature, and . . . Lockhart followed him in this respect. . . . Lockhart's adoption of Schlegel's special point of view had, at any rate, some unhappy consequences. In addition to being in revolt against the literary conventions of the preceding century, certain of the Romantics were in revolt against religious and political traditions. A critic with Lockhart's sense of the importance of such traditions, even with the most liberal views on literature, such as Lockhart possessed, would be handicapped in the appraisal of writers of this class. More unfortunate still, and perhaps as a consequence of his Schlegelian convictions, Lockhart chose to affiliate himself with periodicals which were the mouthpieces of highly conservative elements in politics and religion, with the result that he had every inducement to go to extremes in the application of this special phase of his critical theory. (pp. 87-8)

[Lockhart] was an upholder of critical principles, of which the historical idea was fundamental, which permitted him, with some qualifications, not only to view with sympathy the writings of his great contemporaries, but to do full justice to them. As a consequence, he was in the advance of many of the periodical critics of his time in his recognition of the genius of such writers as Wordsworth, Coleridge, Shelley, and Lamb. His failures, notably in regard to Keats and Hazlitt, were due partly to his critical principles and partly to circumstances [such as Blackwood's offensive against the "Cockney School" of poetry], but do not constitute a serious reflection on his critical sense. His tolerance and universality in literature impress us as unusual. (p. 128)

Notwithstanding the importance in his eyes of national and traditional ideals in literature, he was not narrow in his politics. He was ordinarily moderate and fair enough in his Toryism not to be prejudiced against a writer for his liberalism or his radicalism. He showed himself superior to party considerations in his estimates of Byron and Shelley. His position in regard to Hunt, Keats, and Hazlitt was partially dictated by political considerations, it is true, but under very special circumstances. In his reviews in the *Quarterly* he usually manifests a freedom from political bias when dealing with *belles-lettres*. . . . [When] everything is weighed, we must believe that Lockhart did not fall very far short of the ideal impartiality he had marked out for himself at the outset of his career, in the essay in *Blackwood's* deploring the prevalence of political narrowness and prejudice in contemporary periodical criticism. The question of religious bias in Lockhart's criticism is bound up with that of his political bias. . . . [He placed much stress] upon religious elements in literature; this point of view could conceivably result in an emphasis of a particular creed. At the same time his liberality in respect to Roman Catholicism in his early years would argue the presence of a general breadth in matters of religious differences. . . . [As] editor of a conservative periodical whose policies he had to further, his views naturally narrowed; but there is no discovered instance in his reviews of unfairness to a writer on account of religion or race.

Lockhart is perhaps more vulnerable to the accusation of permitting certain other motives to color his attitude towards the writers receiving judgment before his tribunal. His position in regard to Keats was determined to some extent by the fact of Keats's lack of social prestige. The very term "Cockney School," which Lockhart originated, has an unpleasantly snobbish implication. . . . [Keats and Hunt] were twitted for their provincialisms of language, such as the dropping of the letter *r*, and their deficient education, while the fact of their low birth was expressly or implicitly introduced. Lockhart possessed a haughtiness and a pride that sometimes degenerated into an objectionable sense of superiority; but, except in the instance of the "Cockney School," there is no important place in his literary criticism where this fault appears. On the contrary, he is more than likely to show a particular friendliness towards a writer of humble origin. In his biography of Burns he shows how he can sympathize with one of low birth and circumstances, and elsewhere he demonstrates his good will towards such writers generally. He is sometimes found actually helping along by encouragement and more material aids struggling and unknown authors. (pp. 128-30)

All in all, Lockhart had no reason to feel ashamed of the record of the *Quarterly Review* during the twenty-five and more years that he was at the helm. But the achievement of the periodical he edited is not in itself a sufficient measure of his own achievement. What he actually accomplished as editor can never be satisfactorily estimated. The extent to which he determined in advance the nature of the reviews in the *Quarterly,* the extent to which he modified them after the reviewer had done, can in most instances only be guessed at. We know that he had a certain degree of freedom in so determining and modifying the reviews, and that on occasion he exercised his power. . . . That his influence was in the main for the good is something that only the most skeptical can question.

The one really disappointing thing about Lockhart's career with the *Quarterly* is his failure to choose more permanent works for the subjects of his own reviews. Only about one-fourth of them were of the purely literary sort, and only a portion of these possessed an obvious claim to remembrance. The larger part of his reviews had to do with biography and books of travel. (pp. 134-35)

A point of the greatest interest in connection with Lockhart's entire career as a critic of literature is his possible influence as a propagator of German critical ideas. His constant employment of the historical approach to literature in *Blackwood's* and elsewhere in his early writings must have had an effect not only upon his immediate associates but upon the public. . . . In an account of the rise of historical criticism in the nineteenth century in England the name of Lockhart should play a no insignificant part. By means of the historical idea Lockhart was enabled to provide a critical basis for the literature of the Romantic period, including its harking back to earlier times—to the primitive ballad and to the middle ages. His interest, moreover, in tradition, an interest which was an outgrowth of his historical point of view, led to an insistence upon traditional or conventional morality, which appears in his writings from the beginning of his career, and which accentuated itself as he passed to the editorship of the *Quarterly Review.* Not only his own work but everything in the *Quarterly* is imbued with a very strong tincture of the ethical bias which to-day is called Victorian. Lockhart in this respect forms a link between the Romantic and the Victorian ideals. His Romantic theory of literature originated in him a salient characteristic of Victorianism. Lockhart as editor of the *Quarterly Review* should not be disregarded in a study of the transition in English literature between 1825 and 1850. (pp. 136-37)

[Lockhart] is by no means to be regarded as a great critic, for he had little of the genius for conveying his aesthetic reactions to the reader, a faculty that constituted the excellence of writers like Lamb, Hazlitt, and De Quincey. But the function of the reviewer is not so much that, as the more humble but just as essential task of guiding the reader through the maze of new publications, pointing out the nature or tendency of the various works, and judging what is worth reading and what is not. In the performance of this labor Lockhart was, with but very few major exceptions, eminently successful; and by virtue of his skill in this work he was also a successful editor. It is likely that his most powerful influence as a critic was exerted not through his own writings but indirectly as editor of the *Quarterly Review.* (p. 137)

Lockhart's genius was primarily intellectual. The clarity of his mental operations is visible in his very style, in the precision and the crystal clearness with which he expressed his perfectly defined thoughts. Even when the diction or the syntax of his sentences is defective, as it sometimes is in his hastily composed letters and periodical pieces, the ideas themselves seldom fail to stand out for the reader. He did not have the imagination of a creative writer. The best intrinsically of his creative work is found in his translations of the Spanish ballads, which, though translations, are truly creative in a restricted sense. The success with which Lockhart caught and refined the spirit of the originals of these ballads proves that he was in no way deficient in aesthetic sensitiveness and the capacity for *feeling* poetry; that his own verse is insignificant is because he lacked either originality of feeling or the ability or disposition to embody his sensations adequately in words. (p. 206)

In the summing up of Lockhart's career, one aspect of it is sure to attract the notice of the reader—the contrast between his early promise and his actual achievement. His biographical work, of course, must be given the highest praise; but as a youth he showed signs of attaining distinction both in the creative sphere and in the province of literary criticism. Apart from biography, his literary history practically comes to an end at about the age of thirty, an age at which many writers, and critics in particular, are just beginning to find themselves. (pp. 207-08)

Gilbert MacBeth, in his John Gibson Lockhart *(reprinted by permission of the University of Illinois Press; originally a thesis presented at The University of Illinois in 1931), University of Illinois Press, 1935, 229 p.*

ROBERT RAIT   (lecture date 1933)

[Rait is one of the first twentieth-century critics to comment on Lockhart's method of presenting Scott's vast correspondence in Memoirs of the Life of Sir Walter Scott, Bart. *Rait argues that Lockhart's manipulation of Scott's letters is an artistic device that contributes to the biography's cohesiveness. His opinion is challenged by Herbert Grierson but echoed by Francis R. Hart (1933, 1971).]*

Nothing in English biography will compare with the tender dignity and restraint of [the closing chapters of the **'Life of Scott'**]; no more moving pages were ever penned than those which describe Sir Walter's last illness.

On the other hand, recent investigation has revealed a flaw in Lockhart's work. . . . It has been shown that Lockhart's transcripts were careless; he altered the text; and he ran letters together without indicating the circumstance. (p. 121)

I [believe] that Lockhart regarded the letters, not as texts, but simply as material for the **'Life.'** They were very numerous and the book was long. Scott often wrote to different friends on the same day letters which varied only in special passages. To Lockhart himself he wrote on different days letters, portions of which, when strung together, gave a continuous statement. Such letters Lockhart worked into his narrative, altering them in detail where necessary. . . . The method which he employed was not the method of modern editors, but Lockhart was writing a biography, not printing a collection of letters. A modern full-dress biography would have given the letters textually or with marks of omission, and would have produced a better quarry for future investigators. But modern full-dress biographies are rarely read. The burden of material, conscientiously printed in order that the reader may form his own judgment, is so great that the reader, if any there be, generally forms no judgment at all. Lockhart's book was read. It was also a work of art, and I believe it was read because it was a work of art. Look at the way in which he introduces the letters. He never throws them at you with a "he wrote" or similar phrases. They are always illustrations of his theme, artistically woven into the narrative. Faithful transcription and exact reproduction do not fit in with such a scheme. Art is deliberate, and no subject of a biography ever chose the topics of his letters to suit the exigencies of his future biographer. . . . There can be no doubt that if we want Scott's letters—and I for one want them very much—they must be printed and edited. But I am not sure that Lockhart erred. He certainly did not err as an artist, and I do not know that we can hold him to our own conception of the necessity of literal accuracy, so long as he cannot be shown to have been guilty of misrepresentation. He produced a bad compilation; he wrote a great book. (pp. 125-27)

Robert Rait, "Boswell and Lockhart" (originally a speech read before the Royal Society of Literature of the United Kingdom on February 8, 1933), in Essays by Divers Hands, *n.s. Vol. XII, 1933, pp. 105-27.**

HERBERT GRIERSON   (lecture date 1933)

[The] **Life of Scott** is a great work of art, a biography which just as a work of art is rivalled only by Boswell's *Johnson*, and Froude's *Carlyle*, while it has pages which in beauty of feeling and style rise to a higher level than anything in these works. Such is the account of Scott's last illness and death, to which the only parallel I can recall is Walton's narrative of John Donne's last days and death. (pp. 132-33)

Lockhart quite justifiably conceived it to be his main task to present and do justice to the greater and better, the essential Scott, and not to darken the picture by too constant insistence on the reverse side of the canvas. . . . (p. 139)

Lockhart's methods in biography [can be considered] . . . under two heads—his treatment of the letters, and his dramatic descriptions of persons and incidents, the method which he had used for imaginary scenes in **Peter's Letters** and in the **Noctes Ambrosianae**. The term which Lockhart applied to his manner of printing the letters is "manipulation"; and some such manipulation seems to me legitimate for one who is not editing the letters as such, but weaving them into a biography. . . . But Lockhart's manipulation goes at times beyond what is legitimate. . . . His dealing with the letters may be described under one or two heads. The text is seldom quite accurate, though the changes are often trifling. He condenses letters. He corrects Scott's Scotticisms and errors in expression, sometimes in fact. . . . He omits portions of letters, necessarily; but he does this in two different ways, and thus produces what may at least be described as a *suggestio falsi* [misrepresentation]. In some cases he inserts stars to indicate omissions, but as often as not he gives no such indication. But if some omissions are marked, then the absence of marks leads the reader to assume that there are no omissions. This is his method not only in the **Life** but in the **Ballantyne Humbug Handled**. . . . Lockhart also "telescopes" letters, makes one letter out of what are really two or more. Even this might be done in a legitimate manner, if nothing actually misleading were introduced, though I think our modern standards of accuracy would hardly allow of such manipulation. (pp. 139-40)

Some of [the] omissions in letters, and Lockhart's silence about episodes in Scott's life and experience, are readily explicable by another difficulty which the biographer had to overcome, besides his desire to do justice to the best and most attractive aspect of his hero. Lockhart was bound to consider the feelings of many persons still alive, or whose relatives were among his own friends. (p. 141)

One wishes that Lockhart had used a little of the same self-restraint and discretion with regard to the Ballantynes and Constable; but on these he let himself go in the dramatic, satirical manner of **Peter's Letters** and the **Noctes** and **Blackwood** and **Fraser**. We owe to this, certainly, some of the most piquant pages in the **Life**—descriptions of James [Ballantyne] proposing "the Author of *Waverley*" at printing-house banquets, and of Jocund Johnnie [Ballantyne] "rattling down the Newhaven Road with two high-mettled steeds prancing tandem before him and most probably—especially if he was on his way to the races at Musselburgh—with some 'sweet singer of Israel' flaming with all her feathers beside him". Such touches as these are clever, yet not in the best of taste, for obviously if a man is known by his associates such a vivid portrayal of the Ballantynes somewhat detracts from the picture of Scott which Lockhart wished to present. (p. 142)

Moreover, one's dislike of these satiric anecdotes about the Ballantynes and Constable is heightened by some distrust of their strict veracity. One suspects that he has allowed prejudice and later feelings to colour his account of past events. Lockhart, quite like the modern biographer, allowed himself to dramatize scenes, and I can see no great harm in that. Boswell did the same, though Boswell's dramatization seldom goes beyond a record of conversation . . . . [Furthermore] Boswell's account of conversations give an unmistakable impression of veracity, while for his vivid descriptions of incidents, Lockhart, it would appear, drew a good deal upon his imagination. The result is often delightful, as for example the narrative of his first visit to Abbotsford along with Wilson. . . . But there are some of them which it is difficult to accept at their face value because they will not fit in with dates and other evidence. (p. 143)

What one is to think of these various problems is difficult to decide, and I should prefer at present to keep them *sub judice* [under judgment]—and that is indeed where I must leave Lockhart himself. Some of the incidents do no violence to the general character of the picture he is presenting, but others seem to me to be coloured by prejudices conceived at a later time. It is also possible that for each of them there may have been some actual happening which either Lockhart's memory distorted or which he allowed himself to dress up dramatically. . . . Allowance . . . must be made for the difficulties with which he had found himself faced when all the undercurrents of Scott's life were revealed to him. He could not but wish to show him in the most favourable, which is also ultimately the most just, light. Lockhart acknowledged Scott's faults, but could not resist the temptation to divert attention to some extent from these by what one might call a covering attack upon the Ballantynes and Constable. (pp. 150-51)

> *Herbert Grierson, "Lang, Lockhart, and Biography" (originally a lecture given at the University of St. Andrews in 1933), in his* Essays and Addresses *(reprinted by permission of the author's Literary Estate and Chatto & Windus), Chatto & Windus, 1940, pp. 119-52.**

DAVID CRAIG (essay date 1963)

[The] source of Lockhart's material was that pre-industrial Scotland in which almost every value, belief, and social drive took a religious form and operated inside the framework of the Kirk. . . . During his early days in Edinburgh, the quickening movement of the mass of the people into the towns, to a life of crammed streets and tenements, factory work, and political agitation, was transforming life and literature. (pp. v-vi)

Rapid social change made itself felt in literature as romanticism—the sensibility that feels experience as a flux of emotions. *Adam Blair,* for all its dutiful references to the old framework, nevertheless makes us feel the stir of a new feeling for life. The book is emotional in its essence. We do not mainly remember from it a scene with solidly real surroundings, a variety of people distinct in all their traits, a wider society visible, so to speak, close at hand. Rather we remember the distinctive emotional *timbre*—anguished bereavement dulled into quiet submissiveness, passion distraught because it has to fight with its own inhibitions, the sentiments of reverence, desire, remorse: all given in the eloquent abstractions of early Romantic prose, rather than in precise evocation of behaviour itself. Over this whole a colouring is thrown in the form of 'atmosphere': dark nights, which lend themselves to strange suggestions, are more typical of the book than daylight. (pp. vi-vii)

[*Adam Blair* is] one of the first pieces of Scottish literature in which we feel that the author is as much at home in the general British cultural climate as in the Scottish. (p. vii)

Nevertheless the novel does belong (though in a new form) to the main Scottish tradition, for it shows a minister as the centre of gravity in his community. . . . This is what accounts for the psychological core of the novel and the matters that many of us must find hardest to enter into imaginatively—the appalling consequences that follow on Adam's adultery, the fatal and near-fatal illness, the utter social ostracism that descends on Adam and ruins his daughter's life. (pp. vii-viii)

[Lockhart] did not deal with [his material] *via* the painstaking description of 'manners' that had been the method of his immediate seniors in Scottish fiction, Walter Scott [and John Galt]. . . . Scott's *Waverley* had appeared. . . . By this time, too, Galt's *Annals of the Parish* . . . had appeared, and the vein of fiction-as-social-history must have seemed nearly worked out, especially to a young writer anxious to make his distinctive mark. By the 1820's the Romantic poetry will have sunk deeply into his sensibility, with the result that when he came to tell his old Scottish story, he did so in a manner vibrant with emotion.

The modern reader is bound to feel that the novelist's manner from Chapters XIII-XIX is hectically melodramatic, and these are the chapters in which Adam and Charlotte sleep together and dree the weird of it. No sooner have they sinned than Lockhart plunges them into a nightmare train of sufferings. Devils creep round them, they hesitate on the brink of suicide, hector each other quite in the manner of grand opera . . . , and finally fall into the inevitable romantic prostration—fever, coma, and for one of them death. If Lockhart's readers did not query the plausibility of these consequences, it was because they were so attuned to the code which regarded the least 'irregularity,' or extra-marital passion, as an unspeakable crime. The trouble is that it remains literally unspeakable in the novel—their love is never either shown or acknowledged—their 'fall' is followed in the first edition by a couplet of poetry and two rows of asterisks. Lockhart even has to make the pair drunk, as though to avoid facing the possibility that an unmarried couple might in all sanity have intercourse.

I am not implying that a novelist at that period should, or could, have presented love-making in the open modern way, or even with the brutal candour of the 18th century. What one expects is that the novelist should be perfectly clear-sighted about what he is presenting. Lockhart has brought his couple to the point of consummated passion, while suggesting scarcely one step in the growth of this strong feeling. In Chapter XII where Adam thinks over all that Charlotte has meant to him . . . there is no word of anything even verging on acknowledged passion. This, it could be argued, is to present a man without enough self-knowledge to realise the feelings gathering force inside himself. But, as we read through the novel, it affects us rather as a sheer gap—a withholding of essentials on the part of the author. (pp. xi-xiv)

If there is evasion here, it has its counterpart in the direct suppressions that follow Adam's confession and penance. He is utterly humbled. . . . His former friends never come near him, [his daughter] Sarah never marries although she has 'ripened into womanhood' and become 'the most beautiful girl in that part of the country'. It is not that such an outcome is inconceivable in itself. Our most serious criticism is rather that Lockhart presents this outcome, in all confidence that his readers will approve, as the perfection of goodness and a supremely just moral consummation.

This kind of morals, setting the highest value on self-abnegation, repression, and self-sacrifice, is at the core of work after work as the 19th century goes on; think of Charlotte Brontë's *Jane Eyre* . . . , Nathaniel Hawthorne's *The Scarlet Letter* . . . , or George Eliot's 'Janet's Repentance' from *Scenes of Clerical Life*. . . . (p. xv)

[What D. H. Lawrence later opposed was] submission to a principle that we have to will ourselves to believe—that does not emerge from the real needs of our natures. This to my mind is a key problem in **Adam Blair**. Adam, raised . . . to the ministry, has to rebuke penitent sinners from the pulpit, 'but he never failed to commence his address to the penitent before him, by reminding him, and all present, of his own sin and its consequences.' One is driven to wonder how such self-mortification was humanly possible. Could a man be so subdued as to act as a living object-lesson his whole life long, meek and uncomplaining? Would the ego not revolt at all, through some kind of self-hatred or hatred of the community? (pp. xviii-xx)

[What Lockhart, Hawthorne, Brontë, and Eliot] as a group seem to represent . . . is moral conscience that has hypertrophied and become so over-susceptible that it is forced compulsively into the most harrowing ordeals. I suggest that this is indeed what was happening; conscience was the strongest element surviving from the old religious culture, now that the less tenable things (Calvinist predestination, the literal truth of the Bible, the unquestioned authority of minister and Kirk Session, superstition of various kinds . . .) were losing their power over the freer minds. (p. xxi)

Lockhart's own generation was notable for a drift away from formal religion. . . . But the mental habit of anxiously weighing and testing one's actions in the light of an 'ultimate' value long outlived the religious cult with which it had originally been bound up. The peculiar quality of **Adam Blair**—its raw material rooted in old Presbyterian Scotland but the doing of it permeated with the rather worried emotionality of the Romantic frame of mind—is due, I suggest, to its position at this stage in the re-absorption of religious feelings and ideas into the general atmosphere of our culture. (p. xxii)

Lockhart scarcely had the deep current of imaginative power that makes a man work as an artist to the end of his days. Yet **Adam Blair** and **Matthew Wald** are sufficiently charged with life to make us regret the works that 'might' have come. . . . [He] was pulled south on that cultural drift which emptied Scotland of every kind of talent—craftsmanly and technical, intellectual, political—in his and the succeeding generations. Is he yet another case . . . of an artist who could have continued to tap his most personal, imaginatively fruitful levels of experience only if he had stayed close to its native sources? (p. xxv)

> *David Craig, in an introduction to* Some Passages in the Life of Mr. Adam Blair, Minister of the Gospel at Cross-Meikle *by J. G. Lockhart (© Edinburgh University Press 1963), Edinburgh University Press, 1963, pp. v-xxv.*

FRANCIS R. HART (essay date 1971)

[*Francis R. Hart's* Lockhart As Romantic Biographer *is the most exhaustive study of Lockhart's biographies, which he considers central to a historical understanding of the genre. According to Hart, Lockhart was the "greatest of Romantic biographers," whose artistic commitment to organic narrative and insistence on a cultural view of his subject signaled a reaction against the Enlightenment conception of biography which, Hart states, is best represented by James Boswell's* The Life of Samuel Johnson. *For Hart's discussion of Lockhart's novels, see excerpt below (1978).*]

Lockhart objected to the historiographer's 'custom of drawing a man's character at full length, when he first introduces him'. The alternative—the autobiographical mode—is to allow the character to present himself, and it is this alternative Lockhart claims for the **Life of Scott:**

> It was my wish to let the character develop itself: and conscious that I have wilfully withheld nothing that might assist the mature reader to arrive at just conclusions, I am by no means desirous of drawing out a detailed statement of my own.

But this would seem precisely the justification Boswell offers for delaying the collection 'into one view' of Johnson's 'capital and distinguishing features'. The terms are identical: 'The character of SAMUEL JOHNSON has, I trust, been so developed in the course of this work, that they who have honoured it with a perusal, may be considered as well acquainted with him'. Are the great biographers of Enlightenment and Romanticism in fact indistinguishable? If not, then such similarities must be more apparent than real; and this is the case. Both Boswell and Lockhart aspired to copious particularity, and both were subjected to charges of confusing the essential and the trivial. . . . [For] the Enlightenment biographer, the particular truth was an illustration of essential character; for the Romantic, it was an organic symbol in the unfolding of personality. Likewise, both biographers aspired to autobiographical directness; but for one the ideal was dramatic and the character static, while for the other the ideal was narrative and the character dynamic. (pp. 9-10)

[The immediate origin of Lockhart's narrative craft is easy] to find. Lockhart became a biographer largely by chance; from his earliest literary aspirations, he was a novelist by choice. . . . It is no accident he is charged with 'fictionalizing' [the **Life of Scott**]. Like those of Carlyle, another novelist turned biographer-historian, Lockhart's ideas of narrative form, effect, and even 'truth' are governed by the norms of the novel and not, like Boswell's, by those of the forensic dramatist. Lockhart's theory of fiction is richer than his theory of biography, and it is there that we find his fullest conceptions of narrative 'character', 'development', and form. (p. 14)

[The characteristics of his novels, which include the] imaginative rendition of milieu and cultural type, dominated by a cultural view of history and morality, [mark] Lockhart as Romantic novelist and theorist of fiction. . . . If Lockhart differs from the Enlightenment biographer in his anti-analytic preference for organic narrative revelation, he differs as basically in his cultural conception of biographical subject and milieu. And when the novelist crosses the thin line between genres to become the biographer, the same conception of historical authenticity controls biographical recreation. For him, the genres overlap in their fidelity to cultural truth. (p. 16)

Biographical theory in the half-century following Boswell seems to turn on a major paradox. On the one hand, the method of compendious compilation excludes the biographic personality; on the other, that personality is central and inviolate. In practice, the greatest of Romantic biographers, Lockhart, resolved the paradox; and his mode of doing so . . . accounts for his most controversial features as a biographer: the apparent fusion of formal naiveté and sophisticated editorial art; the application of fiction's methods and effects to an art of the irreducible fact;

the licentious use of documents, the freedom with which memoir, letter, and anecdote alike—prized as originals—are unobtrusively manipulated.

The Romantic biographer would not work without voluminous original materials, merely narrating and summarizing. Nor could he work with them, extracting, excerpting, destroying their personal integrity. The solution, then, was to work *through* them, selecting, manipulating, even 'contaminating', to make them accord more closely with his intuitive grasp of his subject. The solution was to Boswellize or Scottize his originals, and having by selection or revision made the self-revelation more true to the essential character than it always seemed in the originals, to arrange his materials, to cause them to evolve in an organic form which would reveal the life as the reticent biographer had conceived and experienced it.

Such a solution would account for some of Lockhart's insistence on the responsibility, ethical and aesthetic, of the editor of private papers. For that insistence demanded more than avoidance of unessential 'personality' and pain to the living, more than syntactical and organizational clarification and compression. Such a solution leads us to a fuller and more technical understanding of the term he uses for such procedures—'manipulation'—than present connotations allow. It reveals the painstaking art to which he refers by the humble word 'compilation'. (pp. 42-3)

[*Peter's Letters*] is biographical. Its biographical emphasis constitutes its significant deviation from its own genre; indeed, the generic transformation it represents is itself of major importance to biography. . . . [It calls attention to Lockhart's] early sceptical flirtation with a popular theory, a fad, of characterology. . . . [It] displays the creation and use of a complex biographical *persona,* capable of great tonal range from enthusiastic reverence to detached scientific acumen; nor is one *persona* enough, but a second is employed to allow biography by dialogue. The future biographer is present, too, in narrative and anecdotal style, in the power of significant description, in a sense of epistolary tact and of characterizing tone and manner in individual speech. He is present in architectonic power—the ability to organize the multiple details of Peter Morris's experience into a thematic unity, a comprehensive persuasion. He is present, too, in the controlling themes and in the biographical subjects who embody these themes, Burns and Scott. If Lockhart the cultural theorist preconceived his later biographical subjects, it is to *Peter's Letters* we must go for the preconceptions. Here, both are seen in the light of theoretic issues—the question of a national culture, the cultural value of literary genius—which dominate *Peter's Letters.* Here we see the literary biographer emerging from the theorist of literary culture. (p. 49)

[Lockhart's] imagination and rhetorical skill allowed him to sustain a multiplicity of *personae.* We are simultaneously confronting a young 'wit' with extraordinary 'adaptive power' in society. We shall be speaking of a man whose adult life was a sequence of strong fidelities to older and more rigid and dominant personalities—Wilson, Scott, Croker. . . . [His mode, biography, demanded] the projecting and rhetorical sustaining of such fidelities and their appropriate tones and perspectives. We see early a natural inclination which made Lockhart supreme as biographer. He could, while retaining a critical detachment, adopt an appropriate point of view and tone by rhetorical impulse. He could project and animate facets of his own complex sensibility, some of which strongly qualified or contradicted each other. (p. 51)

Peter's Letters gives actuality to a wholly fictitious observer, then dramatizes as his experience impressions from the experience of his creator, incidents illustrative of historic personages. But since Peter's experience, being fictitious, can be wholly shaped by preconceptions of the people encountered, Lockhart is free to reshape the data of his own experience in accordance with thematic interpretations of personality. The procedure is extreme in this early work; but behind such a theory of anecdote is the same 'unscientific' notion of historical truth which has caused charges of dishonesty to be levelled at his later full-scale biographies. (p. 65)

Peter's Letters is worth attention, not only because it reveals the attitudes and skills that made Lockhart a biographer and includes early perspectives on his future subjects, but also because it remains a singular achievement as a first book. (p. 75)

It is as a social phenomenon that the [*Life of Burns*] most emphatically presents [Burns], for Lockhart found in the problematical encounter of a brilliant, commanding, crude social presence and an Edinburgh gentility that lionized him with ruthless fickleness, the ideal matter of the literary form that always interested him most: the novel of manners, of complex social dynamics. Central to the encounter was the question of literary patronage. What permanent support did Burns receive from his lionizing countrymen, what did he deserve, how was the blame for relative neglect to be apportioned? The entire biography is a restrained but incisive exploration of these questions. In the pervasive presence of no other complex of questions is Lockhart's individual tone more evident. (p. 99)

But the central moral question in the book is not to be measured by a measuring of patronage or neglect. However willing to excuse Burns at the expense of his countrymen, Lockhart measures the man himself by the degree of his intellectual and spiritual transcendence over the circumstances of social caprice. The area of ultimate moral concern is not social but personal. Lockhart surveys and judges social irresponsibilities, but he consistently moves beyond them to consider Burns as a supreme member of a tradition of tragic genius. (pp. 99-100)

It is on Burns's conversation that Lockhart focuses his biography's most masterful section: the analytical sketch of Burns's uniquely problematical position in society. He is presented as the jealously self-assured genius and wit, overwhelming 'the most cultivated understandings of his time in discussion'. Foreseeing from the beginning of his triumph that none of it could last—this, too, is a testament to his 'gigantic understanding'. . . . [The] insistence on Burns's powerful understanding, the stress on his conversational brilliance, the emphasis on the social nature of his meteoric career—all are parts of the same thematic purpose. And in terms of the same purpose, one can best understand Lockhart's treatment of the poetry.

The provenance of the poetry is directly traced to actual experience—national, social, or personal. The process of composition is a swiftly spontaneous crystallization of the same wit and ardent eloquence which never deserted Burns under the circumstances of impromptu social discourse. There is little emphasis on the *inventive* aspect of Burns's genius. . . . His is not the poetry of private invention, but of an experience removed from the normal only by its picturesqueness and the intensity of feeling with which it is transmitted. Directly occasioned by social or personal experience, it remained a part of that experience, a direct index of sensibility and a moment in the history of a consciousness. Burns, Lockhart insists, was unusual in this respect. 'No man ever made his muse more completely the companion of his own individual life'. . . . (pp. 103-04)

From the outset Lockhart stresses [this] closeness by referring to biographical events and personalities in terms of the poetry with which they were associated. . . .

Emphasis placed on occasional provenance is responsible for what appears, in Lockhart's work, a foreshortening of the process of poetic composition. To be sure, the brevity of his narrative demanded compression. But it is clearly part of Lockhart's interpretation that for Burns, composition was a spontaneous act in close touch with occasioning circumstance. To incorporate this theme Lockhart had only to select and compress, for the legend of Burns's spontaneity and facility was very much alive. And though modern scholars are most sceptical of such anecdotes, they are unlikely to discover evidence on which to base substantial refutation. (p. 107)

Aware that his own opinions were remote by contrast with the testimony of biographical witnesses, Lockhart conceived his role as compiler-editor and, on occasion, jurist. (p. 123)

Though ostensibly he interferes little, he remains in control [in the *Life of Burns*], and what evolves is a symposium of voices, quietly dominated by a judicious moderator. He marshals witnesses with a pleader's skill; and in the shape of an expertly managed inquiry, his investigation seems to present itself as the inquirer-compiler sits modestly by. . . . [From] Lockhart we rarely detach ourselves, for in his inquiry we detect no intrusive personality, but simply a mode of presentation, a principle of orderly arrangement. The impression is augmented by his painstaking citation of sources, in a small popular book, for almost every bit of evidence. Such documentation is no footnote fetish, but an important part of the *persona,* the inquiring tone, and a means of achieving a far stronger sense of authenticity than the contemporary reconstructive biographer, with his dogged omission of scholarly apparatus and his glib redaction of original testimony, can ever achieve. The first-hand accounts presented are, however, compiled with such skill that, while they may supplement, illustrate, validate, qualify, or contradict each other, they never simply coexist. The witnesses are presented, allowed the full effect of their individual views before they are questioned, and critically collated with modest caution. (pp. 123-24)

Almost invariably, . . . units of inquiry and dialogue are carefully integrated into narrative sequence. The book is built in subject units which approximate chronological phases—units gathered around such centres as early home life, family, education, domestic labour, beginnings of poetry and early effects of his *penchant pour l'adorable moitié du genre humain* [taste for the attractive half of mankind]. In building such narrative units, Lockhart's usual procedure is to quote Burns's own account (from the Moore letter), then the account of one or more observers (Gilbert, Murdoch, Dugald Stewart), then to give his own understated summary and comment, to be followed when appropriate with an amplification (in documents) of a major topic, with a significant incident or dominant feature of personality, and with what appears a direct illustration from the poems themselves. (pp. 124-25)

The procedure appears simple enough, yet the unity and authenticity it effects are unique in early Burns biography. Unique, too, is the way Lockhart suggests major themes simply by grouping. . . . [It] is part of Lockhart's structural tact that he knows when and when not to generalize, when and when not

to set aside narrative limits for wider expository development. (p. 125)

As narrative art Lockhart's *Napoleon* is largely an independent work; its style and form are as responsible as its interpretative moderation for its survival as a popular biography.

In general, the demands of compression and coherence have dictated the character of syntax and diction, as well as the organization and location of narrative units. Initially Lockhart could eliminate much by excluding two types of composition responsible for the great length of Scott's and Hazlitt's works [on Napoleon]. . . . As jurist [Scott] felt compelled to collect and weigh every consideration, to expend pages on what might and should have been done, to adjudicate comprehensively among discordant viewpoints—in short, to lose the life's dramatic reality in commentary and judgement. Hazlitt's chief interest was in his 'speculative episodes'—in his efforts to bend every pliable incident to his thesis. . . . (p. 148)

Much cutting, then, was ready-made for Lockhart. But there remained the compression and manipulation, which a decade of editorial practice had taught him. . . . The results in Lockhart's 'brief' *Napoleon* are long but unified paragraphs which do the work of entire loosely constructed chapters in Scott, and sentences which, for all their syntactical complexity, are direct and even elastic. Diction, too, while necessarily compressed and formal, is more precise if only through the elimination of Scott's rhetorical figures. (p. 149)

[Often] Lockhart's narrative speeds on without pausing for specific scene or dialogue. Anecdotes involving minor figures are rare, and in scenes where they do appear, only Napoleon, as a general rule, is directly quoted. During the imperial middle years of Tilsit and Dresden, Lockhart scarcely pauses, not sharing Hazlitt's enjoyment of the imperial *parvenu* lording it over legitimate monarchs. The account of the Peninsular campaigns, properly subordinate in a biography of Napoleon, includes few scenes. These are artful decisions. Throughout the book composition controls style and interpretation, and Lockhart's is the structure, not of a political or military survey, but of an intensely dramatic career whose most striking segments are its rise and fall. (p. 155)

Memoirs of the Life of Sir Walter Scott seems largely a string of letters and journal extracts until one counts pages. Since Lockhart minimized his own contribution, one is surprised to find that correspondence, autobiographical fragment, diary, and Journal comprise just half of the finished work. The most abundant materials, Scott's letters, make up just over a fourth. Lockhart is responsible for the notion that the work is overwhelmingly autobiographical. . . . He calls the *Life* 'this compilation of his private correspondence' . . . and speaks of 'the copious and candid correspondence from which it has been throughout my object to extract and combine the scattered fragments of an autobiography'. . . . (p. 199)

The uses of this many-voiced correspondence are various. In a narrative structure the most obvious function is narrative: the letters are Scott's accounts of the events in his life. Occasionally Lockhart arranges letters in a simple chronological series to fill out the narrative of a year or a season. More generally, however, he conceives of the letters as illustrative materials, and several major uses derive from this conception.

As in the *Burns,* Lockhart's division of his narrative is not into simple chronological units, but rather into periods or phases characterized by major events or interests or locations. Correspondence is frequently selected, edited, and grouped . . . to illustrate a complex of interest and activity together with the predominant tone of mind and emotion at a certain period. The result has been well described by John Rycenga as 'a kind of epistolary mosaic in illustration of a complex series of events or personal attitudes'. Occasionally the period is focused on a single event. . . . At such points, chronological order is sacrificed to portray intensively Scott's evolving awareness of the particular event. Most important, letters are selected and arranged to illustrate the relationships which made up Scott's life as a social being and determined the various roles of his active personality. . . . (p. 201)

Excisions [of letters] are prompted . . . by a desire for compression and focus, for the avoidance of unimportant or irrelevant topics. . . . Occasionally such compressions prevent premature introduction of subjects or events to be emphasized later. In each case Lockhart seems to have decided whether the subject warrants postponement. If not, he leaves the passage intact and risks digression. (pp. 204-05)

Such [a device] for narrative organization would scarcely evoke criticism today if Lockhart were not judged as an editor of letters and if he or his publisher had not violated the later convention of signifying every textual omission and emendation. Less easily accepted is another, more extreme editorial device utilized for the same ends. . . . [It] is the device of amalgamating or telescoping extracts from separate letters into ostensibly single documents. Though not used generally throughout the *Life,* it proves a useful means of incorporating bits and pieces of otherwise insignificant or irrelevant letters. (p. 205)

Lockhart did not possess Boswell's positivistic passion for sheer verification. He held to the Wordsworthian distinction: 'Truth is not here, as in the sciences, and in natural philosophy, to be sought without scruple, and promulgated for its own sake, upon the mere chance of its being serviceable'. His own guiding sense of the truth of Scott's life—and to this truth there is surely no indifference—is in full conformity with the Romantic conception of symbolic fact. . . . His aims are profoundly different from those of Boswell: his ambiguous antecedent had sought the immediacy and authenticity of dramatic scene, while he worked for the significant organicism of panoramic narrative. He is, for better or worse, a Romantic biographer, in his method as in his epistemology. To base judgement, therefore, on the conventional comparison of his work with Boswell's is as misleading as to insist that Wordsworth be judged as an eighteenth-century loco-descriptive poet or Byron as an Augustan satirist. This much we can conclude from the uses Lockhart made of his materials. (pp. 236-37)

The anecdotes he gives as his own are as skilfully set as those attributed to others. More valuable—for the Lockhart enthusiast the most memorable passages of the entire work—are the panoramic reminiscences of Scott's later life. Such extended views, like chapters in the *Burns* and the *Napoleon,* are descriptive units adapted to narrative movement. Each opens with Scott observed at a specific time and place and then smoothly expands into a general but concrete panorama based on the observations of several years. . . . All are infused with the reflective sympathy that has been anticipated throughout the first half of the *Life,* and thus the rhetorical unification of the work is perfected. And all reveal the persistent and inter-related themes which unobtrusively form the entire narrative and thus define the personality of Lockhart's Scott.

The themes are all conditioned by a fact easily overlooked, one which marks an essential difference between *The Life of Scott* and its Boswellian antecedent. Lockhart's biography was a supplement to Scott's autobiographical introductions and notes. Lockhart knew—and he warns the reader—that such materials are not of absolute reliability. Nonetheless, they provide an indispensable link between the works of a powerful imagination and—Lockhart's continuation—a narrative of the growth of that imagination. Certain normative views of the creative process and of the sociology and ethics of the imaginative life assume thematic dominance. Scott's works become moments in the history of a uniquely imaginative life. (pp. 240-41)

The conclusion [of the *Life of Scott*] is, as a rhetorical action, . . . the most extraordinary manifestation of the complex relationship of Lockhart and Scott, for the understanding of which no brief comparisons with Boswell and Johnson will suffice. If it is true that Boswell's *Johnson* is inseparable from the autobiography of that enigmatic biographer, it is even more true of Lockhart's *Scott,* to the extent that Lockhart possessed profundities of intelligence and feeling unknown to Boswell. Rycenga appears right: 'Lockhart's *Scott* is not so personal a study as Boswell's *Johnson.*' But this is only because the intricately reticent Lockhart's personal involvement is assimilated so fully into the narrative form and method of his work. (p. 250)

In view of . . . the complex ways in which Scott was indeed the centre of his biographer's experience and self-knowledge, it is surprising that there was any judicial detachment at all in his *Life of Scott.*

The evidence of severity is undeniable. For the most part, though, apparently as an obligation he owed his better nature, and in conformity with his definably Romantic conception of biographical decorum, Lockhart allowed his fidelity to govern his detachment. The dominant tone in the *Life* remains closer to the elegiac than to the judicial. It is the tone of the lone survivor, the last of the retainers. And suitably, at Dryburgh Abbey, in the final tonal gesture of his great biographical creation, Lockhart had himself buried at the feet of his *ain deir lord* [Scott]. (p. 252)

Francis R. Hart, in his Lockhart As Romantic Biographer *(© Francis R. Hart 1971), Edinburgh University Press, 1971, 299 p.*

FRANCIS RUSSELL HART (essay date 1978)

The romantic discovery of time and place is more prominent in the four novels of John Gibson Lockhart, than in either Galt or Ferrier. Lockhart had a more varied critical sense of the possibilities of fiction than either, however, and his novels are four different experiments in mode and method. *Valerius* and *Matthew Wald* are first-person narratives—one a historical romance, the other a bitter Godwinian picaresque. *Adam Blair* and *Reginald Dalton* are omniscient third-person narratives, the first a restrained and compassionate brief narrative of tragic passion, the other a colorfully digressive, humorous romance of university life and mysterious inheritance. Lockhart, throughout his experiments, shares Galt's historical interest in provincial manners, as well as his concern for the "metaphysical anatomy" of his characters. But with Susan Ferrier he shares something more basic: the mixture of satiric vigor with a severe but compassionate piety, and a strong sympathy for presbyterian character and tradition. His peculiar artistic excellence as a novelist is a skillfully manipulated mobility of perspective and variety of tone. David Craig, for whom *Adam Blair* remains among the most significant of novels in the Scottish religious tradition, suggests that for Lockhart Galt's "vein of fiction-as-social-history must have seemed nearly worked out [see excerpt above, 1963]. The evidence confirms this view. Lockhart's many theoretical statements about the novel stress repeatedly that while the novelist has access as social historian to endless treasures, he must never forget his primary formal obligations as an artist. And Lockhart succeeded remarkably in practicing as he preached.

All four of his novels are rich surveys of local manners, or more than that, of the spirit or ethos of a milieu. . . . [All] are manners pieces of the same breadth, color, and economy as the great panoramic summaries in Lockhart's biographies. . . . Yet in Lockhart's novels an interest in manners is subordinated to fictional form and meaning. (pp. 68-70)

[In *Valerius* an] episodic plot keeps the sensitive, humane protagonist-observer almost constantly in motion; the facts of Roman place become the concrete impressions of personal experience. Unlike Scott, whose descriptions are set-pieces in the late eighteenth-century picturesque mode, Lockhart and his protagonist luxuriate in vivid local images that are suggestive of postromantic travel literature. The sensations of the stranger lost outside the Colliseum, the eyewitness impression of the passionate mob, particular faces in spiritual stress—all are nightmarishly vivid. . . . [Lockhart has an] ironic view of imperial spectacle. . . . Valerius's observations are always formed by the same contrast between melancholy superstition in the most "enlightened" and a tranquillity of countenance that suggests the mysterious transcendence of the Christian. Valerius's motive in summoning up images of his romantic voyage is part of his Christian character and experience, and essential as well to Lockhart's satiric intention. (p. 70)

Lockhart's exotic localism is controlled by a satiric perspective like that found in Galt and Ferrier. . . . In Rome [*Valerius*] encounters vain metropolitans mocking the pretensions of nouveau provincials and boasting of "the air of the Capital." But the truth of the air of the Capital is blood-thirsty folly and melancholy superstition. Roman philosophers are philosophers only in name. The supposed "enlightened" and "metropolitan" are alike narrow and irrational; real enlightenment is found in what metropolitan perspectives find provincial. Lockhart's satiric intention is identical with Ferrier's: to show that the enlightened piety of Christianity is the opposite of provinciality.

One technical criticism remains to be answered. . . . [Some] complain that Valerius's conversion is never made explicit [see excerpt above by Macbeth, 1931]. In fact, it is one of Lockhart's unique skills as a novelist that he can trace highly idiosyncratic subjective experience purely by implication—that he can objectify psychological process through a vivid impressionism. . . . Valerius's remembered impressions of Rome are formed into the implicit drama of his conversion. Every locale, incident, and character functions in this drama, not just as an external type, but also as a subjective symbol. The same is true of Adam Blair's adulterous passion and Matthew Wald's monomania.

The lively melodrama *Reginald Dalton* has its own similarities to the romance of *Valerius*. (p. 71)

The chief manners interest of the novel centers on undergraduate life at Oxford: a street fight between town and gown, college dinners, parties in "rooms," provincial ladies' teas,

rowing on the river—all done in the romance mode of *Valerius* but with a distinctive tone, and all in Lockhart's favorite manner of rapid impressionistic panorama. So skillful is the economy that at climactic points Lockhart can introduce a localized manners vignette without digressive effect. (p. 72)

Lockhart's narrative voices are so various and versatile that he can severely satirize worldly vulgarities and yet at the same time delineate with lively dramatic sympathy passionate scenes of juvenile abandon: drinking, fighting, hunting. Anticipating *Matthew Wald,* he seems able even to identify with feelings of violent, even brutal hatred. Yet, all of this is framed in and consistently controlled by a severe piety, a penetrating sense of the worldliness in the most admirable or gentle characters: Reginald's father the vicar is capable of romantic self-delusion and self-interest; Father Keith can momentarily be a snob and slightly drunk.

Lockhart delighted in a Scottish mixture of severe piety and boisterous animal spirits. His delight in the mixture gave him his dominant voice in the antics of early *Blackwood's;* and the narrator he evolved for *Reginald Dalton,* in his omniscience, his urbanity, and his extraordinary tonal range, is an identifiably Blackwoodian voice. He is garrulous and good-humored in his comments; some of them become colloquial essays that generalize action and character. His flexible omniscience allows character to achieve the ironic complexity we associate with such later English Victorians as Eliot and Trollope. Such mobility of viewpoint makes the book a remarkable conflation of brilliant surface and psychological intricacy. The conflation, like the tonal mixture of boisterous gusto and severe piety, belongs in the Ambrosian atmosphere of early *Blackwood's,* anticipates the biographer of Burns who valued equally the rantin dog and the Saturday night cottar, and in general suggests how a novel can be distinctively Scottish with little Scottish subject matter.

The novel belongs to the Blackwood group in its serious romance plot as well. . . . The inheritance romance recalls Galt's *Entail* and Ferrier's *The Inheritance.* . . . The dark places of the human heart are in all [of the three idolatrous fathers]; and all, in their struggles of conscience, discover the blindness of human pride and the emptiness of worldly idols. In Lockhart, as in Ferrier, the satiric and the severely pious are closely linked.

Dalton, a young man of feeling, finds Gothic exultation in destructive emotional conflict: "There was trouble, darkness, miserable darkness within; but there was burning ire too—indignation, and contempt, and steady scorn, and the hot thirst of blood; all these, strangely blended with the tender yearnings of a young and living love, and yet all shrouded and enveloped, more strangely still, in a profound feeling of weariness of life." . . . Wald, the manic disinherited picaro of Lockhart's fourth novel, is a more extreme form of the same collection of moods. . . . His early description of the step-uncle who has beaten him illustrates the close connection of satiric acuteness, wrathful vanity, and self-disgust:

> I had heard, I know not from whom, when Mather first came to the parish, that his father was a barber. Conceive how often this recurred to me now—conceive how I grinded my teeth, as I lay counting hour after hour through the night, upon the sweet idea that I was trodden under foot by the spawn of a village shaver—that he had whipped me—that I had borne the

marks of him on my back! . . . His fine large white teeth seemed to me as if they belonged to some overgrown unclean beast—some great monstrous rat. . . . What exquisite vulgarity did I not see in his broad flat nails, bitten to the quick! . . .

Wald's "intense perceptions" of exquisite vulgarity are our access to his world, as though a Smollettesque Heathcliff were to tell his own story. His choleric impressionism allows many vivid sketches, some grotesquely humorous, some poignantly lovely, momentary glimpses of transcendence, of pastoral peace. His intense perceptions are animated by a deeply divided self that he himself has fractured. . . . (pp. 72-4)

We depend on [Wald's] impulsive, anguished character engendered by . . . sin for our vision of his picaresque world. It is a grim and grotesque world in which character is almost always mysterious, surprising, the repository of secret pain and corruption. . . . [This] world's chief quality is moral surprise—the noblest man's capacity for meanness, the villain's capacity for moments of magnanimity. (p. 75)

[We] are left with [a] final gesture of Blackwoodian mystification, turned here to the service of Lockhart's perennial theme of character as dark mystery, to be judged only in humility and compassion, to be understood cautiously with an abiding sense of how complex and surprising it may be.

Lockhart's best novel is his third, **Adam Blair.** Lockhart's purpose in **Adam Blair** is a fusion of cultural description and moral persuasion; its truth is historical and normative. Like other Blackwoodians, he seeks to correct false cosmopolitan views of Scotland's "primitive peasantry" by showing the peasant's natural intelligence and traditional piety. With Ferrier's satire he shares the representation of enlightened sceptics chastened and in some measure restored to traditional local pieties. The urbane narrator's view of parochial piety is expressed in what would seem condescension were it not for the tone of quiet respect and tragic compassion. A distinction between characters of urbanity and characters of a regional typicality is suggested in the scenes where some speak Scots and some do not. . . . Scots is not used for intrinsic evocative value (as Galt and Moir use it), or for social or regional differentiation (as in Ferrier and Hogg). It is used to suggest a general character of traditional simplicities and pieties, and it is saved for characters who have them. (pp. 75-6)

Speech style has another dramatic function in the novel as well. . . . [Charlotte Campbell's] corrupt, worldly sympathy is carefully distinguished from the restrained and delicate compassion of [Blair's] presbyterian parish. Indeed, the parish's quiet and profound awareness makes it seem almost speechless. There is little dialogue. In **Adam Blair,** Lockhart seems to be opposing Galt's provincial community of traditional talkers to his own of quiet, respectful concern.

Like most of the people of the novel, the narrator has a solemn and modest respect for the privacy of individual character. He has Lockhart's view, as [seen in] **Matthew Wald,** of the sacred mystery of each human spirit, the difficulty of knowing or judging another. Often one character senses that another wishes to be alone and leaves him or remains at a quiet distance. The novel's silence is remarkably expressive. (pp. 76-7)

Some readers feel unprepared for Blair's overwhelming adulterous passion [see excerpts above by Saintsbury, 1884 and Craig, 1963]. There is no explicit psychologizing; the passion's

slow and inexorable growth is dramatized, in the way Lockhart the critic had so admired in Goethe's *Wilhelm Meister*. It is done by implication, at a respectful distance. . . . Two scenes bring [Blair and Charlotte] into highly emotional and ill-clad proximity. . . . The community is fully aware of the dangers of their situation—the bereaved, lonely husband and a houseguest with a shady past. We cannot miss the direction of the relationship, though Adam seems blind to it. We join the community in profound sympathy, but we share the narrator's characteristic acuteness and severity in detecting spiritual weakness.

This distanced yet penetrating sense of the minister's noble weakness makes Adam Blair seem a completely individualized character. Yet his individuality is generic. He is his peasant grandfather's descendant and his father's son, a parish minister of the Scottish southwest; he has a communal identity inseparable from milieu, role, and ancestry. The narrator repeatedly reminds us of those determinants of character. The truth of the story is itself offered as testimony to the valuable reality of such a recent past: in such a place to such a man a tragedy and its triumphant outcome could have occurred. The tale is generalized in reflections about the workings of nature. There is a pervasive hint of archetypal allusion in Adam's name, his fall, his deceptive Eden, his stormy night of sin and the horrors of remorse that follow. Yet even this universality is tied to cultural particularity: the shape of the tale illustrates the spiritual workings of a particular way of life.

The evocation of local setting is restrained and subordinate. There is none of the panoramic impressionism of **Valerius** and **Reginald Dalton.** . . . Rustic provinciality simply conceals the spiritual nobility and delicacy of the peasant. Lockhart is consciously a Wordsworthian pastoralist. Yet his moral compassion and severity are expressive of the specific milieu whose ethos he celebrates.

But like the narrator of **Reginald Dalton,** this narrator is capable of a sophisticated instinct for the signs of grace in fallen worldlings. Lockhart, like Ferrier and Galt (and, much later, Robin Jenkins and Muriel Spark), may be seen as a distinctively presbyterian satirist of worldliness. He treats Charlotte Campbell and her husband with urbane restraint, seeing their worldliness, yet allowing them their moments of grace. The realization of such characters is the major difference between **Adam Blair** and its oft-noted analogue, *The Scarlet Letter*. Charlotte is as complex a female character as can be found in nineteenth-century British fiction. She is . . . a mixture of self-indulgent weakness and self-sacrificial strength. . . . Her buoyant will to survive anticipates Becky Sharp [in William Makepeace Thackeray's *Vanity Fair*], but manifests a sexuality Becky lacks. . . . [Charlotte's husband's] brief, quiet confrontation with the convalescent Blair is the greatest scene in Lockhart's fiction. The vain, vulgar worldling forgives and protects the remorseful minister from exposure. His compassion is genuine, his delicacy remarkable. He transcends his cultural typicality, as Highland mercenary and Lowland minister meet in sorrow on the shore of a Highland loch. (pp. 78-80)

Francis Russell Hart, " 'The Other Blackwoodians':
Moir, Ferrier, Lockhart, Wilson," in his The Scot-
tish Novel: From Smollett to Spark (copyright ©
1978 by Francis Russell Hart; excerpted by permis-
sion of the President and Fellows of Harvard Col-
lege), Cambridge, Mass.: Harvard University Press,
1978, pp. 53-84.*

THOMAS C. RICHARDSON (essay date 1979)

[*Adam Blair*] was certainly something new and bold, a tale of human nature told with a force rarely achieved in Scottish novel writing. In his novel of Scottish life, Lockhart attempts to capture the feelings of the nation, to join Sir Walter Scott's accomplishments in filling a gap in the portrayal of character left by the eighteenth-century intellectuals. . . .

"We read no fiction twice", Lockhart [wrote], "that merely heaps description upon description, and weaves incident with incident, however cleverly. The imitating romancer shrinks at once into his proper dimensions when we ask—what new character has he given us?" Lockhart could answer his own question, of course, with Adam Blair. Adam Blair is a character who finds renewed life in generation after generation of us who are blind to our natures, to the varied and conflicting forces that shape our personalities. (p. 52)

The complete title of the novel, *Some Passages in the Life of Mr Adam Blair, Minister of the Gospel at Cross-Meikle,* is a significant indicator of the focus of the work, and substantially answers the critics who regard as shallow the characters of Sarah, Charlotte, Mrs Semple, Dr Muir, and John Maxwell. Lockhart's purpose in the novel is to reveal the character of Blair to the reader, to show through "some passages" in the life of the protagonist the universality of the conflict of natural passions and learned attitudes; all other characters exist in relation to Blair and for the purpose of developing this conflict. The structure of *Adam Blair* is more easily understood in the light of Lockhart's idea that the novel has replaced drama as a vehicle for character representation. Lockhart adopts the basic structure of the tragedy for *Adam Blair.* The rising action or conflict is set in motion by the death of Adam's wife, Isabel. The conflict builds through the relationship of Adam and Charlotte to the crisis, which occurs at the point of their adultery. The confession and resignation of Blair at the meeting of the Presbytery stimulate the catastasis. The catastrophe occurs, ironically, not with the death of the hero but with his restoration to his original position, minister of the parish of Cross-Meikle.

Adam Blair is a tragic tale of innocence and experience, the story of a man who moves from a comfortable state of "sinless" existence into the realm of experience and reality. It is tragic, however, not because Adam falls from his community pedestal as a result of a moral weakness in his character; it is tragic because Blair and the community fail to achieve a vision of reality from the experience. Blair, like Hawthorne's Young Goodman Brown, is compelled to have an experience that is a challenge to his established beliefs and representative of some confrontation with evil which emerges from within himself; however, he is complacent in his existence above sin, at least the public, black-and-white sins which can be witnessed by all members of the community, and thus he is blind to the necessity and the nature of the experience. . . . Adam Blair's life is characterised by a . . . self-righteous complacency, a self-satisfied existence in innocence, sheltered from temptation and evil by a loving wife, a family history of public righteousness, and a supportive community of people whose vision of reality corresponds exactly and who allow their minister to bear the burden of righteousness which relieves them from the responsibility of attaining a knowledge of good and evil beyond superficial social indiscretions. Blair, like Brown, when confronted with a challenge to his moral existence, fails to meet the challenge; he is unable to see the shortcomings in his own character.

Blair's self-righteousness and blindness to his nature derive from his recognition of his role as a minister in a Scottish community and an inherited family tradition. . . . The elder, John Maxwell, is the living tie of Blair to his ancestors and the attitudes of the parish. (pp. 55-6)

Maxwell functions on a second important level in the novel: he symbolically links Blair to natural passions and thus serves as a touchstone for Blair's conflict between the natural and the learned. Maxwell, a farmer, is a simple man, a man of natural goodness, a figure on the level of Wordsworth's Simon Lee or leech-gatherer, but one whose ties to the natural world have been somewhat impaired by his religious training. Maxwell represents a blend of the learned Presbyterian attitudes and the natural passions although, as becomes clear at the end of the novel, he is by no means an ideal model for the reconciliation of Blair's conflict. Maxwell's wife died when he, like Blair, was a relatively young man. Maxwell coped with his natural passions, particularly grief and sexual desire, by suppressing them through labour. (p. 57)

Blair, who by the end of the novel is blind to the characteristics of natural passion, turns to the life of peasant labour as a self-inflicted punishment for his sin. Nature, often a source of comfort and strength to Blair before his adultery (*e.g.* after the death of his wife), becomes a vehicle for humiliation and degradation. Lockhart thus underscores the shortsightedness of Blair's vision, his inability to see and understand that "human nature will have its way, and the soul cannot long shut itself against the impressions of the bodily senses." . . .

Lockhart gradually and carefully develops the tragedy of Adam Blair through the relationship of Charlotte and Adam following the death of Isabel. . . . [To] Blair, happiness and comfort were ultimately inextricably bound with a healthy relationship with his wife, which meant, as the novel implies, sexual satisfaction. . . . [As] Isabel's health declined, Blair experienced the mental, emotional and physical strain of the lack of female companionship. For a considerable time before the death of his wife Blair did not share the same bed with her. (p. 58)

When Charlotte comes to visit Blair, then, Blair is emotionally keyed for the development of an intimate relationship. Blair is attracted to Charlotte not only because she is an old friend and a mother figure to his daughter, he is physically attracted to her as well. The relationship is made easier by the fact that Charlotte, too, is emotionally and sexually frustrated. (p. 59)

[The ending of the novel implies that to] remember the family of Blairs is to remind oneself of the nature of man. To doubt that such things might have been is to open the way for the return of the self-righteousness and blindness to self that characterised the generations of Blairs. *Adam Blair,* like the tragedy, exists to give the reader an experience from which he can emerge with a heightened vision of life. (p. 60)

Thomas C. Richardson, "Character and Craft in Lockhart's 'Adam Blair'" (copyright © 1979 by Thomas C. Richardson), in Nineteenth-Century Scottish Fiction: Critical Essays, *edited by Ian Campbell, Carcanet New Press, 1979, pp. 51-67.*

ADDITIONAL BIBLIOGRAPHY

Carswell, Donald. "John Gibson Lockhart." In his *Sir Walter, A Four-Part Study in Biography: Scott, Hogg, Lockhart, Joanna Baillie,* pp. 209-61. London: John Murray, 1930.

A biographical sketch which focuses on the controversies and scandals caused by Lockhart's caustic essays in *Blackwood's Edinburgh Magazine*. Carswell applauds Sir Walter Scott for recognizing the folly of Lockhart's involvement with *Blackwood's* and sympathetically remarks that "by his association with *Blackwood's* [Lockhart] had brought opprobrium not only on himself but on the great man who had generously befriended him and taken him into his family."

Clive, John. "Peter and the Wallah: From Kinsfolk to Competition." In *History and Imagination: Essays in Honor of H. R. Trevor-Roper,* edited by Hugh Lloyd-Jones, Valerie Pearl, and Blair Worden, pp. 311-25. New York: Holmes & Meier Publishers, 1982.*
    Compares *Peter's Letters to His Kinsfolk* with George Otto Trevelyan's epistolary novel *The Competition Wallah.* Clive finds that "beneath [Lockhart and Trevelyan's] leisurely and often playful use of the epistolary genre lay serious concerns and polemical intentions."

Ewen, Frederic. "John Gibson Lockhart: Propagandist of German Literature." *Modern Language Notes* XLIX, No. 4 (April 1934): 260-65.
    Regards Lockhart as "significant in the dissemination of German literature in the years immediately preceding Carlyle's advent" and cites his "overpowering enthusiasm in the cause of Goethe" as the "central kernel" of his "inclusive" appreciation of German letters.

Gordon, [Mary]. *'Christopher North': A Memoir of John Wilson, Late Professor of Moral Philosophy in the University of Edinburgh.* New York: The H. W. Hagemann Publishing Co., 1894, 484 p.*
    A biography by one of John Wilson's daughters which includes correspondence between Wilson and Lockhart. Gordon presents Lockhart as a "cold, haughty, supercilious" man who discarded his Edinburgh friends when he became editor of the *Quarterly Review.* Gordon's account of her father's relationship with Lockhart is generally considered a misrepresentation of Lockhart's character.

Jack, Ian. "Two Biographers: Lockhart and Boswell." In *Johnson, Boswell, and Their Circle: Essays Presented to Lawrence Fitzroy Powell in Honour of His Eighty-fourth Birthday,* pp. 268-85. London: Oxford at the Clarendon Press, 1965.*
    An interesting comparison of Boswell and Lockhart's techniques in composing their famous biographies. Jack argues that the *Life of Scott* exhibits Lockhart's "indifference to the precise truth" and maintains that because of Boswell's insistence on accuracy, the *Life of Johnson* "makes even Lockhart's *Life of Scott* seem, by comparison, a work of the second rank."

Kestner, Joseph. "Defamiliarization in the Romantic Regional Novel: Maria Edgeworth, Walter Scott, John Gibson Lockhart, Susan Ferrier, and John Galt." *The Wordsworth Circle* X, No. 4 (Autumn 1979): 326-30.*
    Suggests that the recognition of political and social problems in Irish and Scottish Romantic regional literature prompted Thomas Carlyle to demand "speech and articulate inquiry about [the condition of England]" and presaged the writings of Elizabeth Gaskell, Charles Kingsley, and Benjamin Disraeli. Kestner asserts that the works of John Galt, Maria Edgeworth, Susan Ferrier, Sir Walter Scott, and Lockhart are studies in the technique of defamiliarization, "the central method by which the Romantic regionalists approach their 'condition of England'." In particular, Kestner discusses defamiliarization in *Adam Blair.*

Kestner, Joseph. "Lockhart's *Peter's Letters to His Kinsfolk* and the Epistolary Genre." *The Wordsworth Circle* XI, No. 4 (Autumn 1980): 228-32.
    Maintains that *Peter's Letters to His Kinsfolk* cannot be simply classified as an epistolary novel because, in addition to its epistolary characteristics, it displays the formal elements of the novel and the biography. Kestner argues that "*Peter's Letters* represents an unusual combination of genres, drawing on the letter for its conventions of sender, on the biography for its focus in individual letters, on the novel for its conception of its audience."

Lang, Andrew. *The Life and Letters of John Gibson Lockhart.* London: J. C. Nimmo; New York: Charles Scribner's Sons, 1897.
    The first, and most exhaustive, treatment of Lockhart's life.

Lochhead, Marion. *John Gibson Lockhart.* London: John Murray, 1954, 324 p.
    A sympathetic biography which attempts to eliminate the "stain" on Lockhart's reputation that persists as a result of his early labeling as "the Scorpion which delighteth to sting the faces of men."

Lochhead, Marion. "Coleridge and John Gibson Lockhart." In *New Approaches to Coleridge: Biographical and Critical Essays,* edited by Donald Sultana, pp. 61-79. Critical Studies Series, edited by Anne Smith. London: Vision; Totowa, N.J.: Barnes & Noble, 1981.*
    An account of the friendship between Lockhart and Samuel Taylor Coleridge based on Lockhart's defense of Coleridge's *Biographia Literaria* in *Peter's Letters to His Kinsfolk.*

Martin, Terence. "Adam Blair and Arthur Dimmesdale: A Lesson from the Master." *American Literature* 34, No. 2 (May 1962): 274-79.*
    Challenges the analogy between *Adam Blair* and Nathaniel Hawthorne's *The Scarlet Letter* which "with an assist from James [see excerpt above, 1879] . . . has been given institutional status." Martin argues that James based his comparison of the two works on a misinterpretation of *The Scarlet Letter.* According to Martin, James found that "a great deal of analogy" existed between the narratives because he viewed Arthur Dimmesdale, rather than the scarlet letter itself, as central to Hawthorne's novel.

Oliphant, [Margaret]. *Annals of a Publishing House: William Blackwood and His Sons, Their Magazine and Friends.* 2 vols. New York: Charles Scribner's Sons, 1897.*
    A detailed account of Lockhart's association with *Blackwood's Edinburgh Magazine* which includes correspondence between Lockhart and his editors. Oliphant devotes a chapter to Lockhart's involvement with the magazine, from his early collaborations with John Wilson to his frequent contributions from London.

Parker, W. M. "Lockhart's *Life of Scott:* A Plea for Revision." *The Times Literary Supplement,* No. 1833 (20 March 1937): 210.
    Finds that as a reference work the *Life of Scott* has little value because Lockhart "embroiders, exaggerates, or distorts, his statements of fact" and "'manipulates' . . . letters in a deceptive fashion."

Strout, Alan Lang. "John Gibson Lockhart: Lockhart and *Blackwood's Magazine.*" *Notes and Queries* CLXXV (15 October 1938): 275-79.
    Discredits the commonly-held belief that Lockhart was a critical "Scorpion." Strout points out that Lockhart, unlike John Wilson, never castigated personal friends nor did he continue to recklessly satirize his contemporaries later in his career. Furthermore, Strout notes that Lockhart publicly apologized for some of his early attacks on the "Cockney" poets.

Charles Robert Maturin

1780?-1824

(Also wrote under the pseudonym of Dennis Jasper Murphy)
Irish novelist and dramatist.

Maturin is remembered primarily for his novel *Melmoth the Wanderer*, which is considered among the finest examples of Gothic fiction in the English language. By virtue of its complicated revenge plot, seemingly supernatural phenomena, and use of landscape to create an atmosphere of horror and suspense, *Melmoth* is strongly reminiscent of the Gothic novels of Ann Radcliffe and Matthew Lewis. Critics distinguish it from the works of these earlier writers, however, by its attention to the psychology of despair and the torments of religious doubt. More popular in France than in England or Ireland, *Melmoth* exercised a great influence on nineteenth-century French writers. Maturin's most notable French admirer, Honoré de Balzac, was so impressed with the novel that he wrote a sequel to it entitled *Melmoth réconcilié*.

Maturin was born in Dublin, where he spent most of his life. He graduated from Trinity College in 1800 and in 1803 was ordained a minister of the Church of England. After a brief apprenticeship as curate of the county parish of Loughrea, Galway, where he became familiar with the Irish peasantry that he later wrote about in such novels as *The Wild Irish Boy* and *The Milesian Chief*, Maturin went to St. Peter's Church in Dublin, where he served as curate for the rest of his life. Although Maturin greatly preferred the fashionable St. Peter's to the rural parish in Loughrea, he found it impossible to support his wife and family on his meager salary. In order to supplement his income, he embarked on a literary career.

Fearful of jeopardizing his chances for advancement within the Church, Maturin published his first three novels, *Fatal Revenge; or, The Family of Montorio*, *The Wild Irish Boy*, and *The Milesian Chief*, under the pseudonym of Dennis Jasper Murphy. While critics consider Monk Lewis's influence evident in the abundance of horrible details in *Fatal Revenge*, they attribute the rational denouement of the story to Radcliffe's influence. Critics consistently complain that Maturin's attempt to "explain away" the miraculous events of the story results in a disproportion between cause and effect that gives the novel, in the words of the critic Niilo Idman, an "air of charlatanism." Nevertheless, *Fatal Revenge* is considered superior to *The Wild Irish Boy* and *The Milesian Chief*, which are seldom included in critical discussions of Maturin's works.

In 1814, Maturin sent Sir Walter Scott the manuscript of his first drama, *Bertram; or, The Castle of St. Aldobrand*, a play that unites the Byronic hero and the Gothic villain in a single character. Scott was so impressed with the play that he referred Maturin to Lord Byron, who belonged to the committee that selected plays for production at London's Drury Lane Theater. Through Byron's influence, Drury Lane produced *Bertram* in 1816. Although the play's immediate success prompted Maturin to drop the pseudonym he had used for his first three novels and identify himself, his newfound literary recognition ultimately proved a disaster for Maturin. Convinced that *Bertram* was the beginning of a brilliant dramatic career, he recklessly spent his profits and was plunged deeply

into debt. His subsequent plays, *Manuel* and *Fredolfo*, were dismal failures, and to add to his difficulties, *Bertram*'s irreverent sentiments were imputed by ecclesial officials to Maturin himself, and he lost any chance of being promoted within the Church.

Maturin resumed his career as a novelist with *Women; or, Pour et contre*, for which he temporarily abandoned the Gothic idiom. A satire on the religious views of a narrow middle-class Calvinist sect, *Women* reflects Maturin's opposition to religious fanaticism and is today considered an insightful analysis of Evangelicalism. Maturin returned to the Gothic form in his masterpiece, *Melmoth*. Based on the Wandering Jew and Faust legends, *Melmoth* tells the story of a seventeenth-century scholar who sells his soul to the devil in exchange for a prolonged life. The novel's structure is complex, consisting of five interlocking tales which one early reviewer compared to a "nest of Chinese boxes." Contemporary critical reaction to *Melmoth* was mixed: while some reviewers denounced Maturin's presentation of the diabolical Melmoth as impious, others praised the novel for its graphic descriptions of horror and suffering. Critics writing around the turn of the century applauded *Melmoth*'s emotional intensity, and modern commentators support this opinion. Robert Kiely and Coral Ann Howells argue that the impact of *Melmoth* derives primarily from Maturin's examination of human responses to terror and oppression. Douglas Grant calls

Maturin a "brilliant psychologist of the perverse" whose interest in extreme emotional states anticipated the psychological novels of Fedor Dostoevski and Franz Kafka. In addition to its investigation of human psychology, *Melmoth* is also admired for its analysis of the spiritual consequences of religious fanaticism. William F. Axton, for example, distinguishes *Melmoth* from earlier Gothic novels because of its "compelling statement of the grand theme of perverted faith." In Maturin's last novel, *The Albigenses*, he treats the theme of religious fanaticism in a historical romance modeled on the works of Scott.

With the exception of *Bertram*, none of Maturin's works was a critical or popular success. Contemporary critics generally considered Maturin a talented but injudicious writer, whose novels and plays were marred by excesses of horror. Later nineteenth-century commentators frequently attributed his lack of critical acclaim to the diminishing popularity of Gothic fiction. Twentieth century critics have focused largely on *Melmoth*, although some recent critics, including Robert E. Lougy and Robert Lee Woolf, assert that Maturin's reputation as a Gothic novelist has overshadowed his importance as a proponent of Irish regional literature. Today Maturin is generally regarded as the unjustly forgotten author of one of the finest Gothic novels in English. *Melmoth* is said to have influenced the work of such diverse writers as Balzac, Baudelaire, Alexander Pushkin, Nathaniel Hawthorne, Edgar Allan Poe, and Oscar Wilde. The breadth of the novel's appeal attests to its enduring interest.

PRINCIPAL WORKS

Fatal Revenge; or, The Family of Montorio [as Dennis Jasper Murphy]   (novel)   1807
The Wild Irish Boy [as Dennis Jasper Murphy]   (novel) 1808
The Milesian Chief [as Dennis Jasper Murphy]   (novel) 1812
Bertram; or, The Castle of St. Aldobrand   (verse drama) 1816
Manuel   (verse drama)   1817
Women; or, Pour et contre   (novel)   1818
Fredolfo   (verse drama)   1819
Melmoth the Wanderer   (novel)   1820
The Albigenses   (novel)   1824

[SIR WALTER SCOTT]   (essay date 1810)

[*Scott was a Scottish novelist, poet, historian, biographer, and critic of the Romantic period who is best known for his historical novels, which were a great popular success. Scott was unaware of the true identity of Dennis Jasper Murphy when he reviewed Maturin's first novel, which he erroneously refers to as* Fatal Revenge; or, The House of Montorio *rather than* The Family of Montorio. *Although Scott's review is an indictment of the Gothic novel in general, he expresses regard for Maturin's talents, commenting that* Fatal Revenge *is a "remarkable instance of genius degraded by the labor in which it is employed." In 1812, when Maturin discovered that Scott was the author of the review, he wrote him a grateful letter, which initiated a correspondence between the two that lasted until Maturin's death.*]

Amid [the] flat imitations of [Mrs. Radcliffe's] 'Castle of Udolpho' we lighted unexpectedly upon ['**Fatal Revenge; or, the House of Montorio**'], and, in defiance of the very bad taste in which it is composed, we found ourselves insensibly involved in the perusal, and at times impressed with no common degree of respect for the powers of the author. We have at no time more earnestly desired to extend our voice to a bewildered traveller, than towards this young man, whose taste is so inferior to his powers of imagination and expression, that we never saw a more remarkable instance of genius degraded by the labour in which it is employed. It is the resentment and regret which we experience at witnessing the abuse of these qualities, as well as the wish to hazard a few remarks upon the romantic novel in general, which has induced us . . . to offer our criticism on the ['**Fatal Revenge; or, the House of Montorio**']. (pp. 341-42)

In the first place, . . . we disapprove of the mode introduced by Mrs. Radcliffe, and followed by [Mr. Dennis Jasper Murphy] and her other imitators, of winding up their story with a solution by which all the incidents appearing to partake of the mystic and marvellous are resolved by very simple and natural causes. . . . [It] is as if the machinist, when the pantomime was over, should turn his scenes 'the seamy side without,' and expose the mechanical aids by which the delusions were accomplished. In one respect, indeed, it is worse management; because the understanding spectator might be in some degree gratified by the view of engines which, however rude, were well adapted to produce the effects which he had witnessed. But the machinery of the castle of Montorio, when exhibited, is wholly inadequate to the gigantic operations ascribed to it. There is a total and absolute disproportion between the cause and effect, which must disgust every reader much more than if he were left under the delusion of ascribing the whole to supernatural agency. This latter resource has indeed many disadvantages. . . . But it is an admitted expedient; appeals to the belief of all ages but our own; and still produces, when well managed, some effect even upon those who are most disposed to contemn its influence. We can therefore allow of supernatural agency to a certain extent and for an appropriate purpose, but we never can consent that the effect of such agency shall be finally attributed to natural causes totally inadequate to its production. . . . [We] fling back upon the Radcliffe school their flat and ridiculous explanations, and plainly tell them that they must either confine themselves to ordinary and natural events, or find adequate causes for those horrors and mysteries in which they love to involve us. (pp. 344-45)

In the second place, we are of opinion that the terrors of this class of novel writers are too accumulated and unremitting. The influence of fear—and here we extend our observations as well to those romances which actually ground it upon supernatural prodigy as to those which attempt a subsequent explanation—is indeed a faithful and legitimate key to unlock every source of fancy and of feeling. Mr. Murphy's introduction [to '**Fatal Revenge; or, the House of Montorio**'] is expressed with the spirit and animation which, though often misdirected, pervade his whole work.

> I question whether there be a source of emotion
> in the whole mental frame so powerful or uni-
> versal as *the fear arising from objects of invis-*
> *ible terror.* Perhaps there is no other that has
> been, at some period or other of life, the pre-
> dominant and indelible sensation of every mind,
> of every class, and under every circumstance.
> (pp. 345-46)

We grant there is much truth in this proposition taken generally. But the finest and deepest feelings are those which are most easily exhausted. The chord which vibrates and sounds at a touch, remains in silent tension under continued pressure. Besides, terror . . . will come and go; and few people can afford timidity enough for the writer's purpose who is determined on 'horrifying' them through [the novel's] three thick volumes. The vivacity of the emotion also depends greatly upon surprize, and surprize cannot be repeatedly excited during the perusal of the same work. It is said, respecting the cruel punishment of breaking alive upon the wheel, that the sufferer's nerves are so much jarred by the first blow, that he feels comparatively little pain from those which follow. There is something of this in moral feeling; nor do we see a better remedy for it than to recommend the cessation of these experiments upon the public, until their sensibility shall have recovered its original tone. The taste for the marvellous has been indeed compared to the habit of drinking ardent liquors. But it fortunately differs in having its limits: he upon whom one dram does not produce the effect, can attain the desired degree of inebriation by doubling the dose. But when we have ceased to start at one ghost, we are callous to the exhibition of a whole Pandemonium. In short, the sensation is generally as transient as it is powerful, and commonly depends upon some slight circumstances which cannot be repeated. (pp. 346-47)

These appear to us the great disadvantages under which any author must at present struggle, who chooses supernatural terror for his engine of moving the passions. We dare not call them insurmountable, for how shall we dare to limit the efforts of genius, or shut against its possessor any avenue to the human heart, or its passions? Mr. Murphy himself, for aught we know, may be destined to shew us the prudence of this qualification. He possesses a strong and vigorous fancy, with great command of language. He has indeed regulated his incidents upon those of others, and therefore added to the imperfections which we have pointed out, the want of originality. But his feeling and conception of character are his own, and from these we judge of his powers. In truth we rose from his strange chaotic novel romance as from a confused and feverish dream, unrefreshed, and unamused, yet strongly impressed by many of the ideas which had been so vaguely and wildly presented to our imagination. . . .

If the author of ['**Fatal Revenge; or, the House of Montorio**'] be indeed . . . young and inexperienced, without literary friend, or counsellor, we earnestly exhort him to seek one on whose taste and judgment he can rely. He is now, like an untutored colt, wasting his best vigour in irregular efforts without either grace or object; but there is much in these volumes which promises a career that may at some future time astonish the public. (p. 347)

> *[Sir Walter Scott], in a review of "Fatal Revenge; or, The Family of Montorio," in* The Quarterly Review, *Vol. III, No. VI, May, 1810, pp. 339-47.*

SIR WALTER SCOTT   (letter date 1812)

[The following commentary on Fatal Revenge *and* The Wild Irish Boy, *which is drawn from a letter to Maturin, echoes Scott's earlier remarks on* Fatal Revenge *(1810). He credits Maturin with "a powerful imagination and a very uncommon command of language" but objects to his frequent reliance on elements of horror in his novels.]*

My attention was indeed very strongly excited both by the *House of Montorio* and the Irish tale [*The Wild Irish Boy*] which it was impossible to confound with the usual stile of novels as they bear strong marks of a powerful imagination and a very uncommon command of language and excite upon the whole a very deep though painful interest. I have regretted if you will forgive me writing with so much freedom that the author had not in some respects rendered his fictions more generally acceptable by mitigating some of their horror. . . . But the redundancies of a powerful fancy can be brought within the rules of a more chastened taste and the lighter graces are usually within the attainment of those who can strike the higher tones of composition. (p. 7)

> *Sir Walter Scott, in a letter to Charles Robert Maturin on December 23? 1812, in* The Correspondence of Sir Walter Scott and Charles Robert Maturin *by Sir Walter Scott and Charles Robert Maturin (copyright, 1937 by The Board of Regents of The University of Texas), University of Texas Press, 1937, pp. 7-8.*

SIR WALTER SCOTT   (letter date 1814)

[In 1814, after Bertram *was rejected by a Dublin theater, Maturin sent a copy of the play to Scott. Scott was so impressed with* Bertram *that in 1815, he sent it to Lord Byron, a member of the Sub-Committee of Management at the Drury Lane Theater, where the play was eventually produced. In the following excerpt, which is drawn from a letter that Scott wrote to Maturin shortly after he received the play, Scott warmly praises* Bertram *and offers helpful suggestions about revising the drama for the stage.]*

In general I like [*Bertram*] very much indeed. . . . The character of Bertram is highly dramatic, well-got up and maintaind with a Satanic dignity which is often truly sublime—the Lady Imogine may be also considered as a master-piece, and the language throughout is beautiful even to redundance. In short I think if represented by adequate performers the piece cannot fail of success. . . . As a general remark I have observed that the language is somewhat redundant—not that I would wish it retrenched for the press—but upon the stage there is an impatience in the English audience for bustle & action which will not endure anything to be said or done that has not some immediate effect upon the progress of the piece. . . . I would leave no luxuriance, however beautiful, which tends to weaken the main growth of the tree. . . . I do not well know *what* to say about the Black Knight—it is at once a grand & terribly bold attempt to introduce upon the stage an agent of this nature & I wish your idea may be perfectly understood by the audience. Should they misconceive his nature or take it into their head that circumstances were not sufficiently explaind respecting him, it would have a bad effect upon the piece. . . . If you can bring out the same effect upon the stage as in the closet, I think the effect will be prodigious.

My last criticism is of a more decided cast & I entreat your particular attention to it. The incidents in the V. act, beautifully conceived & versified, will nevertheless have some chance of being heavy on the stage because the murder of Aldobrand being once committed, the catastrophé of the criminal lovers should be hurried forward with much greater rapidity [and] combination. . . . When the audience knows that the crime has been committed & the punishment is impending, they are impatient of delay and exact a rapid & simultaneous movement of all the branches of the plot to its final completion. . . . I would not hesitate to compress & remodel the two last acts—

the piece is long upon the whole and would bear such abridgement as might be necessary in so far as the watch is the critic. These are my observations upon a piece which I admire exceedingly and which does great credit to the richness of your imagination & the powers of expression you have employd—in fact you are in the happy predicament of needing only the pruning knife. (pp. 30-1)

> *Sir Walter Scott, in a letter to Charles Robert Maturin on October 8, 1814, in* The Correspondence of Sir Walter Scott and Charles Robert Maturin *by Sir Walter Scott and Charles Robert Maturin (copyright, 1937 by The Board of Regents of The University of Texas), University of Texas Press, 1937, pp. 29-31.*

[GEORGE GORDON (LORD)] BYRON   (letter date 1815)

[*An English poet, dramatist, and satirist, Byron is considered one of the most important poets of the nineteenth century. Because of the satiric nature of much of his work, Byron is difficult to place within the Romantic movement. His most notable contribution to Romanticism is the Byronic hero: a melancholy man, often with a dark past, who eschews societal and religious strictures, and seeks truth and happiness in an apparently meaningless universe. In 1815, Byron was nominated to the Sub-Committee of Management at the Drury Lane Theater. Along with George Lamb, a fellow committee member, he was influential in securing the production of* Bertram *at the Drury Lane Theater. The following is drawn from an encouraging letter that Byron wrote to Maturin shortly after he read* Bertram.]

[Mr. George Lamb] & myself have read [*Bertram*]:—he agrees with me in thinking it a very extraordinary production—of great & singular merit as a composition—& capable—we hope—with some alterations & omissions—of being adapted even to the *present* state of the Stage—which is not the most encouraging to men of talent.—What it seems to want for this purpose is *lowering* (in some of the Scenes)—& this for the sake of the physical powers of the actor—as well as to relieve the attention of an audience:—no performer could support the tone & effort of continual & sustained passion through five acts—the "dark Knight" must also be got rid of—and another catastrophe substituted—which might be done with no great difficulty. (p. 40)

> [*George Gordon (Lord)] Byron, in a letter to Charles Robert Maturin on December 22, 1815, in* The Correspondence of Sir Walter Scott and Charles Robert Maturin *by Sir Walter Scott and Charles Robert Maturin (copyright, 1937 by The Board of Regents of The University of Texas), University of Texas Press, 1937, pp. 39-41.*

GEORGE LAMB   (letter date 1816)

[*Lamb was a member of the Drury Lane Theater committee that selected* Bertram *for production. With Lord Byron and Sir Walter Scott, he was one of the most enthusiastic admirers of the play but, like them, he advised Maturin to rework the drama for a more powerful stage presentation. In the following, which is taken from a letter that Lamb wrote to Maturin several months before the play opened at the Drury Lane Theater, Lamb outlines his proposals for cuts and alterations in the play.*]

[The] strain of vehement passion is too unvaried throughout [*Bertram*], not merely for the feelings of the Audience, but for the powers of any Actor to support. The Characters of Bertram and Imogine are of such length, so constantly on the Stage, and never except in situations of agitation and passion; that

there are no performers whose physical strength would not sink under them before half the play was over. There is also too great a succession of long speeches, which however may be easily remedied by curtailment or breaks introduced.—The Dark Knight of the Forest and all relating to him should clearly be cut out: He is a personage who would be unintelligible to the majority of the audience, or if intelligible, offensive.—The omission of this character can be effected without the least violence to the plot or conduct of the piece.—The third Act is the weakest and least interesting, little progress in the plot is made by it. It is also precisely like the fourth in construction. . . . These two acts I think must be blended into one, and the little which the third act at present contributes to the forwarding of the plot, namely the disclosure of St. Aldobrand's designs against Bertram and the imparting of it to Bertram, might be effectually supplied by beginning the act with a scene between Bertram and the robbers in which they might communicate to him his danger from St. Aldobrand, the knowledge of which they may have acquired by spies or any underhand means. I think by this alteration the fourth act will be rendered most horribly striking. It is lucky that at present the two first acts are so long, that with some quieter scenes interpolated which I conceive imperatively necessary for the relief of the Audience not less than a respite to the Actors, they will easily be made into three acts of quite sufficient length. . . . The fifth act and the Catastrophe must be materially altered. . . . The first scene however must remain nearly as it is, and the finding of Bertram shut up with the dead body in the Castle.—The scene however of Bertram in the vault of the Convent must be omitted, and there must not be two scenes of Imogine's wanderings. The Death of the Child I am inclined to think will . . . be too much for the Audience. Of course the disappearance of Bertram must be done away with. . . . To this part of the alteration I would wish you particularly to dedicate your powerful pen. . . . I think there is a feeling already touched upon which might be finely worked up in a concluding scene. Namely, Bertram's remorse at finding that his crimes have driven Imogine, the only being he regards on earth, to distraction. His despair and self-accusing grief at seeing her might be finely contrasted with his dumb and hardened guilt in the prior scene with the Monks. . . . It is for you who have so finely conceived the character of Bertram, to point out a conclusion consistent with it, whether to fall by his own hand or sternly wait the blow of justice. It is the fifth act particularly in which your assistance will be wanted to complete your own Drama. (pp. 42-4)

> *George Lamb, in a letter to Charles Robert Maturin on January 2, 1816, in* The Correspondence of Sir Walter Scott and Charles Robert Maturin *by Sir Walter Scott and Charles Robert Maturin (copyright, 1937 by The Board of Regents of The University of Texas), University of Texas Press, 1937, pp. 41-5.*

[WILLIAM HAZLITT]   (essay date 1816)

[*An English critic and journalist, Hazlitt was one of the most important commentators of the Romantic age. He is best known for his descriptive criticism in which he stressed that no motives beyond judgment and analysis are necessary on the part of the critic. Though Hazlitt wrote on many diverse subjects, his most important critical achievements are his interpretation of William Shakespeare's characters as "pictures" of life, and his revival of such Elizabethan dramatists as John Webster, Thomas Haywood, and Thomas Dekker. In this review of* Bertram, *Hazlitt argues that the play typifies the faults of contemporary tragedies*] *and cites its lack of adherence to the Aristotelian rules of tragedy and its inaccurate representation of reality.*]

[The new tragedy of **Bertram**] has entirely succeeded, and it has sufficient merit to deserve the success it has met with. We had read it before we saw it, and it on the whole disappointed us in the representation. Its beauties are rather those of language and sentiment than of action or situation. The interest flags very much during the last act, where the whole plot is known and inevitable. What it has of stage-effect is scenic and extraneous, as the view of the sea in a storm, the chorus of knights, &c. instead of arising out of the business of the play. We also object to the trick of introducing the little child twice to untie the knot of the catastrophe. One of these fantoccini exhibitions in the course of a tragedy is quite enough. The general fault of this tragedy, and of other modern tragedies that we could mention, is, that it is a tragedy without business. Aristotle, we believe, defines tragedy to be the representation of a *serious notion*. Now here there is no action: there is neither cause nor effect. There is a want of that necessary connection between what happens, what is said, and what is done, in which we take the essence of dramatic invention to consist. It is a sentimental drama, it is a romantic drama, but it is not a tragedy, in the best sense of the word. That is to say, the passion described does not arise naturally out of the previous circumstances, nor lead necessarily to the consequences that follow. . . . As the opera is filled with a sort of singing people who translate every thing into music, the modern drama is filled with poets and their mistresses, who translate every thing into metaphor and sentiment. **Bertram** falls under this censure. It is [William Shakespeare's *Winter's Tale* or *A Midsummer Night's Dream*], but it is not [Shakespeare's] *Lear* or *Macbeth*. The poet does not describe what his characters would feel in given circumstances, but lends them his own thoughts and feelings out of his general reflections on human nature, or general observation of certain objects. In a word, we hold for a truth, that a thoroughly good tragedy is an impossibility in a state of manners and literature, where the poet and philosopher have got the better of the man; where the reality does not mould the imagination, but the imagination glosses over the reality; and where the unexpected stroke of true calamity, the biting edge of true passion, is blunted, sheathed, and lost, amidst the flowers of poetry strewed over unreal, unfelt distress, and the flimsy topics of artificial humanity, prepared beforehand for all occasions. (p. 313)

[In **Bertram** the] whole of the character of *Clotilda*, [*Imogine's*] confidante . . . is superfluous. She merely serves for the heroine to vent the moods of her own mind upon, and to break her enthusiastic soliloquies into the appearance of a dialogue. There is no reason in the world for the confidence thus reposed in *Clotilda*, with respect to her love for the outlawed *Bertram*, but the eternal desire of talking. Neither does she at all explain the grounds of her marriage to *Aldobrand*, who her father was, or how his distresses induced her to renounce her former lover. The whole is an effusion of tender sentiments, sometimes very good and fine, but of which we neither know the origin, the circumstances, nor the object. For her passion for *Bertram* does not lead to any thing but the promise of an interview to part forever, which promise is itself broken. . . .

That part of the play where the chief interest should lie, namely, in the scenes preceding the death of *Aldobrand*, is without any interest at all, from the nature of the plot; for there is nothing left either to hope or to fear; and not only is there no possibility of good, but there is not even a choice of evils. The struggle

of *Imogine* is a mere alternation of senseless exclamations. Her declaring of her husband,—"By heaven and all its hosts, he shall not perish," is downright rant. She has no power to prevent his death; she has no power even to will his safety, for he is armed with what she deems an unjust power over the life of *Bertram*, and the whole interest of the play centers in her love for this *Bertram*. Opposite interests destroy one another in the drama, like opposite forces in mechanics. (p. 314)

[William Hazlitt], in a review of "Bertram," in The Examiner, No. 438, May 19, 1816, pp. 313-15.

THE ECLECTIC REVIEW   (essay date 1816)

[**Bertram; or the Castle of St. Aldobrand**] has obtained, upon the stage, a popularity that would seem altogether undeserved. That the Author has strong powers no one can doubt; . . . the reader will find in the course of [**Bertram**], passages that prove him to have *very* strong powers. The piece might be objected to for its want of dramatic interest, for the bad taste of its poetry, but its principal fault, (in the absence of which objection indeed, we should quietly have left it to its fate,) is its vicious and abominable morality.

The foundation of the piece is love. We have no fault to find with this. (p. 379)

[However, if] the poet has not sufficient range among the varieties of pure and innocent love,—if guilty passion must be painted,—let it be painted at least according to nature. Let us see the modest charms of the innocent maiden, the mild eye, the healthy glow, changed for the bold front, the distempered flush of the prostitute; the gentle gaiety for an unfeminine laugh; the fond confiding love for a ranging lawless appetite. But no; it is too much the taste of the present day, to bring forward the guilty passion of a wife for her paramour,—and fouler abominations which we dare not even name,—not, indeed, with direct admiration, but in such a manner, and with such a mixture of virtuous remorse and high-toned feeling, that we cannot hate the crime. It is in vain to say the poet does his part, the crime meets its punishment;—the poet does not do his part; oh, he basely deserts his duty, he foully prostitutes his high talent, if he raises one thought in the reader's mind, that he dares not approve and cannot reprobate. We do not say—we are far from thinking, that any female shall be so led away by the example of this worthless Imogine, as forthwith to desert a true and noble husband, for a man without principle, of no feeling but for himself: but this we say, that the poet who throws around such a character the charm of strong feeling, of constancy in love, &c. does his best to deprive us of that abhorrence of sin which is our best preservative in the ways of virtue; and that in this sense 'the thought of wickedness is sin.' . . . (pp. 380-81)

[We] believe the immorality [of **Bertram**] to be nothing but a consequence of [its] bad taste,—a part of a wrong system, *the system of effect*. In this system, the consideration seems to be, not what is naturally pleasing, what, being according to nature, must continue to please, but what will produce a grand sensation;—no matter how, no matter what the sensation is, pleasing or unpleasing,—so that it is but strong enough, so that you can but take away the reader's breath, and make him stare, you have gained your point. . . . [The writer does not consider] that he is perpetually increasing the difficulty of writing on this system; that readers' nerves are hardening; that what will produce a pretty strong shock now, will, by dint of repetition, pass over without any effect at all. (pp. 384-85)

[This piece has deficiencies] as a drama. There are no characters of consequence but Bertram and Imogine. . . . [How] perfectly unnatural, and therefore, how perfectly undramatic they are. . . . There is scarcely any plot, any business: what is wanted here is made up in talk. The first two acts the reader may get through pretty well, spite of an old Prior who, at sight of a ship sinking, 'falls into the arms of the monks.' After this, he may read,—but, we imagine, he will hardly be able to feel any longer. (pp. 385-86)

> *A review of "Bertram; or, The Castle of St. Aldobrand," in* The Eclectic Review, *n.s. Vol. VI, October, 1816, pp. 379-86.*

CHARLES ROBERT MATURIN   (essay date 1818)

[In the following excerpt, which is taken from Maturin's preface to his novel Women, *Maturin discusses the popular reception of his novels.]*

"Montorio" (misnomed by the bookseller "The Fatal Revenge," a very book-selling appellation) had some share of popularity, but it was only the popularity of circulating libraries: it deserved no better; the date of that style of writing was out when I was a boy, and I had not powers to revive it. When I look over [my early prose works] now, I am not at all surprised at their failure; for, independent of their want of *external* interest, (the strongest interest that books can have, even in this reading age,) they seem to me to want *reality*, vraisemblance; the characters, situations, and language, are drawn merely from imagination; my limited acquaintance with life denied me any other resource. In ["Women; or, Pour et contre,"] perhaps there may be recognised some characters which experience will not disown. Some resemblance to common life may be traced in them. On this I rest for the most part the interest of the narrative. The paucity of characters and incidents (the absence of all that constitutes the interest of fictitious biography in general) excludes the hope of this work possessing any other interest. (pp. iii-v)

> *Charles Robert Maturin, in a preface to his* Women; or, Pour et Contre, *Vol. I, A. Constable, 1818 (and reprinted by Garland Publishing, Inc., 1979), pp. iii-v.*

[SIR WALTER SCOTT]   (essay date 1818)

[In this review of Women, *Scott repeats the critical points of his earlier commentaries on Maturin's works (1810, 1812, and 1814). He finds* Women *superior to Maturin's other works because it exhibits fewer supernatural horrors and less "luxuriance of language."]*

The faults of *Bertram* are those of an ardent and inexperienced author; but its beauties are undeniably of an high order; and the dramatist who has been successful in exciting pity and terror in audiences assembled to gape and stare at shows and processions, rather than to weep or tremble at the convulsions of human passion, has a title to the early and respectful attention of the critic. (p. 234)

[Women; or Pour et Contre: A Tale] is framed upon a different and more interesting model [than Mr. Maturin's earlier novels], pretending to the merit of describing the emotions of the human heart, rather than that of astonishing the reader by the accumulation of imaginary horrors, or the singular combinations of marvellous and perilous adventures. Accordingly, we think

we can perceive marks of greater care than Mr. Maturin has taken the trouble to bestow upon his former works of fiction. . . . (pp. 234-35)

[The] resemblance betwixt the character and fate of Zaira [in *Women*] and Corinne [in Madame de Staël's *Corinne; ou, L'Italie* is] a coincidence so near, as certainly to deprive Mr. Maturin of all claim to originality, so far as this brilliant and well painted character is concerned. In her accomplishments, in her beauty, in her talents, in her falling a victim to the passion of a fickle lover, Zaira closely resembles her distinguished prototype. Still, however, she is Corinne in Ireland, contrasted with other personages, and sustaining a different tone of feeling and conversation and argument; so that we pardon the want of originality of conception, in consideration of the new lights thrown upon this interesting female. . . . On the other hand, the full praise, both of invention and execution, must be allowed to Mr. Maturin's sketch of Eva. . . . [The character of De Courcy] is provokingly inconsistent; and we wish the ancient fashion of the Devil flying off with false-hearted lovers . . . had sustained no change in his favour.

Indeed, such a catastrophe would not have been alien to the genius of Mr. Maturin, who, in [*Women*] as well as in former publications, has shown some desire to wield the wand of the enchanter, and to call in the aid of supernatural horrors. (pp. 253-54)

[In *Women*] Mr. Maturin has put his genius under better regulation than in his former publications, and retrenched that luxuriance of language, and too copious use of ornament, which distinguishes the authors and orators of Ireland. . . . [It] is an error to suffer the weeds to rush up with the grain, though their appearance may prove the richness of the soil. There is a time when an author should refrain, like Job, 'even from good words—though it should be pain to him.'—And although we think Mr. Maturin has reformed that error indifferently well, in [*Women*], we do pray him, in his future compositions, to reform it altogether. (pp. 256-57)

> *[Sir Walter Scott], in a review of "Women; or, Pour et Contre: A Tale," in* The Edinburgh Review, *Vol. XXX, No. LIX, June, 1818, pp. 234-57.*

THE MONTHLY REVIEW, LONDON   (essay date 1818)

Women; or, Pour et Contre (a title of itself sufficient to impeach the good taste and good sense of the author,) is the worthy and legitimate successor of those faulty monsters, *Bertram* and *Manuel*. . . .

[In *Women*, to] expose the repellent and unsocial manners of [a Calvinistic] sect, who are called in derision, levelled at their own presumption, 'evangelical,' seems the main moral object of the writer; and we grant that his design, had it been executed judiciously and fairly, would have been praiseworthy: but it is obvious that, to attain this purpose of discountenancing spiritual pride and gloomy superstition, the author must not on the one hand grossly overcharge the picture which he wishes to hold up to reprobation; nor, on the other, must he omit to present a rational and amiable contrast, in the person of at least *one* specimen of pure and social Christianity. In both these points, Mr. Maturin has entirely failed. . . . Where is the exemplar of natural unaffected goodness, cheered and supported by religion, and accessible to all the sweet charities of life? We must assert that, when the excesses and perversions of piety form a principal feature in any picture, good judgment and honest feeling ought to enforce the necessity of introducing a *defence* which may counterbalance the *attack*. (p. 404)

The *seesaw* . . . attempted to be described [in **Women**], the play of contrasted character, cleverly kept up, might have afforded great delight: but it is so perfectly wild and unmanageable in the hands of its inventor, (if he may be so called,) that it loses all its force in diffusion, and all its delicacy in abruptness: for both diffuse and abrupt is this novelist, in alternate succession;—now passing over most interesting events, without an effort to do them justice; then at once plunging us into a sea of difficulties, out of which we may struggle at our leisure. (p. 405)

It may, indeed, be easy to discover the original cause . . . of many of the author's unsuccessful attempts. They are to be traced to the great success of some late *Scotish* novels; and in them we see the foundation not only of Zaira's *Irish-gypsey* mother, but of the general endeavour to delineate the harsh features of Calvinism. Mac Owen is but the faint echo of Mcsomebody, whose name we forget, but whose character we well remember, in [Sir Walter Scott's] *Old Mortality*. A fatal snare is laid for the efforts of inferior genius, by these bold and happy portraits of a first-rate master.

We would by no means deny considerable power to Mr. Maturin, as far as that power may be seen in the variety of his materials, although not in the accuracy of his knowledge; and in the rapidity, although not in the elegance, of his movements, as the historian of fictitious events. His pervading faults are too great suddenness of change in character, and too coarse a daubing of colours thrown over all his descriptions. His story is thus rendered improbable; and his language is debased by the grossest licence of construction and indistinctness of phraseology. His classical learning, also, is of the common kind, although manifestly dragged in for purposes of display; and, we are convinced, by several plain indications, that he has not a sufficient reverence for the great names of poetical antiquity. (pp. 406-07)

Among the grosser improbabilities of incident, we may mention the dream of Eva that she sees Zaira and De Courcy on a hill together, and that her lover tramples on her as he is getting into a carriage;—a dream that takes place at the very same time at which De Courcy fancies that he sees, with his eyes open, and broad-awake, exactly the same objects. This is not the only instance of such grotesque absurdity in these volumes. The delirious dreams of several of the sick persons are really too mad for pleasant perusal; and how any author can delight in this anatomical exhibition of human ravings, we are at a loss to conceive. People familiarly fancying themselves in Hell, and other horrors of this nature, ought not to be tolerated in the literature of a civilized nation. Indeed, a very indecent because a very familiar use, and on the most worldly occasions, is made of the texts of Scripture throughout the present work. . . . (p. 410)

Still, it would be unjust to conclude without acknowledging that this novel, in spite of all its glaring defects, is capable of *amusing* an idle hour, though we cannot discern any human *profit* likely to accrue from it.—We should add that it exhibits a Madame St. Maur, a Frenchwoman *à toute outrance* [of great extreme] yet, notwithstanding this universal sin of overcharging the colours of character, (a vice perhaps borrowed from stage-practice,) Madame St. Maur is one of the best supported personages in this prolonged exhibition of three tomes of romance. (p. 415)

"Maturin's 'Women, a Tale'," in The Monthly Review, *London, Vol. LXXXVI, August, 1818, pp. 403-15.*

T. D. [SIR THOMAS NOON TALFOURD] (essay date 1820)

The author of "**Montorio**" and of "**Bertram**" is unquestionably a person gifted with no ordinary powers. He has a quick sensibility—a penetrating and intuitive acuteness—and an unrivalled vigour and felicity of language, which enable him at one time to attain the happiest condensation of thought, and at others to pour forth a stream of eloquence, rich, flowing, and deep, checkered with images of delicate loveliness, or darkened by broad shadows cast from objects of stern and adamantine majesty. Yet, in common with many other potent spirits of the present time, he fails to excite within us any pure and lasting sympathy. We do not, on reading his works, feel that we have entered on a precious and imperishable treasure. They dazzle, they delight, they surprise, and they weary us— we lay them down with a vague admiration for the author, and try to shake off their influence as we do the impressions of a feverish dream. It is not thus that we receive the productions of genuine and holy bards—of Shakespeare, of Milton, of Spenser, or of Wordsworth—whose far-reaching imaginations come home to our hearts, who become the companions of our sweetest moods, and with whom we long to "set up our everlasting rest.". . .

[The works of Mr. Maturin] have no fibres in them which entwine with the heart-strings, and which keep their hold until the golden chords of our sensibility and imagination themselves are broken. They pass by us sometimes like gorgeous phantoms, sometimes like "horrible shadows and unreal mockeries," which seem to elude us because they are not of us. When we follow him closest, he introduces us into a region where all is unsatisfactory and unreal—the chaos of principles, fancies, and passions—where mightiest elements are yet floating without order, where appearances between substance and shadow perpetually harass us, where visionary forms beckon us through painful avenues, and, on approach, sink into despicable realities; and pillars which looked ponderous and immovable at a distance, melt at the touch into air, and are found to be only masses of vapour and of cloud. He neither raises us to the skies, nor "brings his angels down," but astonishes by a phantasmagoria of strange appearances, sometimes scarcely distinguishable in member, joint, or limb, but which, when most clearly defined, come not near us, nor claim kindred by a warm and living touch. This chill remoteness from humanity is attended by a general want of harmony and proportion in the whole—by a wild excursiveness of sensibility and thought— which add to its ungenial influence, and may be traced to the same causes.

If we were disposed to refer these defects to one general source, we should attribute them to the want of an imagination proportionate to sensibility and to mastery of language in the writer's mind, or to his comparative neglect of that most divine of human faculties. (p. 18)

[Mr. Maturin's] sensibility is so much more quick and subtle than his authority over his impressions is complete; the flow of his words so much more copious and facile than the throng of images on his mind; that he too often confounds us with unnumbered snatches and imperfect gleams of beauty, or astonishes us by an outpouring of eloquent bombast, instead of enriching our souls with distinct and vivid conceptions. Like many other writers of the present time—especially of his own country—he does not wait until the stream which young enthusiasm sets loose shall work itself clear, and calmly reflect the highest heavens. His creations bear any stamp but that of truth and soberness. He sees the glories of the external world, and the mightier wonders of man's moral and intellectual nature, with a quick sense, and feels them with an exquisite sympathy—but he gazes on them in "very drunkenness of heart," and becomes giddy with his own indistinct emotions, till all things seem confounded in a gay bacchanalian dance, and assume strange fantastic combinations; which, when transferred to his works, startle for a moment, but do not produce that "sober certainty of waking bliss" which real imagination assures. (p. 19)

Mr. Maturin gave decisive indications of a morbid sensibility and a passionate eloquence out-running his imaginative faculties, in the commencement of his literary career. His first romance, the **"Family of Montorio,"** is one of the wildest and strangest of all "false creations proceeding from the heat-oppressed brain." It is for the most part a tissue of magnificent yet unappalling horrors. Its great faults as a work of amusement, are the long and unrelieved series of its gloomy and marvellous scenes, and the unsatisfactory explanation of them all, as arising from mere human agency. This last error he borrowed from Mrs. Ratcliffe [sic], to whom he is far inferior in the economy of terrors, but whom he greatly transcends in the dark majesty of his style. As his events are far more wild and wondrous than hers, so his development is necessarily far more incredible and vexatious. . . . Great talent is, however, unquestionably exhibited in this singular story. A stern justice breathes solemnly through all the scenes in the devoted castle. "Fate sits on its dark battlements, and frowns." There is a spirit of deep philosophy in the tracing of the gradual influence of patricidal thoughts on the hearts of the brothers, which would finally exhibit the danger of dallying with evil fancies, if the subject were not removed so far from all ordinary temptations. Some of the scenes of horror, if they were not accumulated until they wear out their impression, would produce an effect inferior to none in the works of Ratcliffe or of Lewis. . . . The diction of the whole is rich and energetic—not, indeed, flowing in a calm beauty which may glide on for ever—but impetuous as a mountain torrent, which, though it speedily passes away, leaves behind it no common spoils. . . . (p. 20)

"The Wild Irish Boy" is, on the whole, inferior to **"Montorio,"** though it served to give a farther glimpse into the vast extent of the author's resources. **"The Milesian"** is, perhaps, the most extraordinary of his romances. There is a bleak and misty grandeur about it, which, in spite of its glaring defects, sustains for it an abiding-place in the soul. Yet never, perhaps, was there a more unequal production—alternately exhibiting the grossest plagiarism and the wildest originality, . . . [at times displaying] offensive bombast, and anon disclosing the simplest majesty of nature, fluctuating with inconstant ebb between the sublime and the ridiculous, the delicate and the revolting. **"Women, or Pour et Contre,"** is less unequal, but we think, on the whole, less interesting than the author's earlier productions. He should not venture, as in this work he has done, into the ordinary paths of existence. His persons, if not cast in a high and heroic mould, have no stamp of reality upon them. The reader of this work, though often dazzled and delighted, has a painful feeling that the characters are shadowy and unreal, like that which is experienced in dreams. They are unpleasant and tantalizing likenesses, approaching sufficiently near to the true to make us feel what they would be and lament

what they are. Eva, Zaira, the maniac mother, and the group of Calvinists, have all a resemblance to nature—and sometimes to nature at its most passionate or its sweetest—but they look as at a distance from us, as though between us and them there were some veil, or discolouring medium, to baffle and perplex us. Still the novel is a splendid work; and gives the feeling that its author has "riches fineless" in store, which might delight as well as astonish the world, if he would cease to be their slave, and become their master.

In the narrow boundaries of the Drama the redundancies of Mr. Maturin have been necessarily corrected. In this walk, indeed, there seems reason to believe that his genius would have grown purer, as it assumed a severer attitude; and that he would have sought to attain high and true passion, and lofty imagination, had he not been seduced by the admiration unhappily lavished on Lord Byron's writings. The feverish strength, the singular blending of good and evil, and the spirit of moral paradox, displayed in these works, were congenial with his tastes, and aroused in him the desire to imitate. **"Bertram,"** his first and most successful tragedy, is a fine piece of writing, wrought out of a nauseous tale, and rendered popular, not by its poetical beauties, but by the violence with which it jars on the sensibilities, and awakens the sluggish heart from its lethargy. **"Manuel,"** its successor, [is] feebler, though in the same style. . . . In **"Fredolpho,"** the author, as though he had resolved to sting the public into a sense of his power, crowded together characters of such matchless depravity, sentiments of such a demoniac cast, and events of such gratuitous horror, that the moral taste of the audience, injured as it had been by the success of similar works, felt the insult, and rose up indignantly against it. Yet in this piece were passages of a soft and mournful beauty, breathing a tender air of romance, which led us bitterly to regret that the poet chose to "embower the spirit of a fiend, in mortal paradise of such sweet" song.

We do not, however, despair even yet of the regeneration of our author's taste. There has always been something of humanity to redeem those works in which his genius has been most perverted. There is no deliberate sneering at the disinterested and the pure—no cold derision of human hopes—no deadness to the lonely and the loving, in his writings. His error is that of a hasty trusting to feverish impulses, not of a malignant design. There is far more of the soul of goodness in his evil things, than in those of the noble bard whose example has assisted to mislead him. He does not, indeed, know so well how to place his unnatural characters in imposing attitudes—to work up his morbid sensibilities for sale—or to "build the lofty rhyme" on shattered principles, and the melancholy fragments of hope. But his diction is more rich, his fancy is more fruitful, and his compass of thought and feeling more extensive. (pp. 20-1)

T. D. [Sir Thomas Noon Talfourd], "Maturin" (originally published as "On the Living Novelists—No. IV: Maturin," in The New Monthly Magazine, *Vol. XIV, No. LXXIX, August, 1820), in his* Critical and Miscellaneous Writings of T. Noon Talfourd, *second edition, A. Hart, 1850, pp. 18-21.*

BLACKWOOD'S EDINBURGH MAGAZINE (essay date 1820)

We do not envy those who are incapacitated by extreme delicacy of taste, or, we should rather perhaps say, by extreme indulgence in the habits of strict criticism, from enjoying such works as those of Mr. Maturin. They are all, prose and verse, full of faults so numerous, that it would be quite fatiguing—

so obvious, that it would be quite useless to point them out. . . . [There] is not one of them that has either beginning, or middle, or end. The author, in a very great proportion of every work he has written, has been contented with copying the worst faults of his predecessors and contemporaries, in the commonest walks of fictitious writing. In his best passages there is always a mixture of extravagance—in the whole of his works there is not, perhaps, to be found one page of perfectly natural thought, or perfectly elegant language. And yet, where is the lover of imaginative excitement, that ever laid down one of his books unfinished—or the man of candour and discrimination, who ever denied, after reading through any one of them, that Maturin is gifted with a genius as fervently powerful as it is distinctly original—that there is ever and anon a truth of true poetry diffused over the thickest chaos of his absurdities—and that he walks almost without a rival, dead or living, in many of the darkest, but, at the same time, the most majestic circles of romance?

Encouraged by praise at once so high and so universal, it is no wonder that a young author of the true Milesian breed should regard with very considerable indifference the cavils of the hypercritical;—nay, that he should be contented to go on ''sinning glorious sins''—a sort of applauded rebel against all the constituted authorities of the literary judgment-seat. But, nevertheless, it is a very great pity that such should be the continued course of his career. He should remember, that although his faults are not able to deprive him of the admiration of the present time, they may bid very fair to shut him out altogether, or nearly so, from the knowledge of posterity. He should remember, that it is one thing to be an English classic, and another to occupy ''ample room and verge enough'' in every circulating library throughout the land. We are far from saying that Mr. Maturin should write less—but we do say, that he should write a great deal more—observe a great deal more—and correct a great deal more. If he does not, he may depend upon it he will never fulfil the rich promise of his **''Montorio;''** for that . . . , we are quite sure, is the best of all his performances.

Next to **''Montorio,''** however, we have no hesitation in placing this new romance of **''Melmoth the Wanderer,''** which, whatever faults may be discovered or pointed out, either in its conception or in its execution, or in both of these, cannot fail to be read universally, and to please universally. It is infinitely better than **''Women, or Pour et Contre,''** or **''Fredolfo''** or **''Bertram''**—excellent as all these works are in their several ways—and one reason for this is, that it is infinitely more horrible—for in horror, there is no living author, out of Germany, that can be at all compared with Mr. Maturin.

The chief fault of the story is, that there is too much uniformity in the sources of its horror—and yet, there is nothing more admirable than the variety of application by which the same cause of horror is made to diffuse its shadow over so many different walks of life. The error and the beauty go hand in hand together in this respect—no very uncommon circumstance, by the way, in regard to the works of Mr. Maturin.

The truth is, however, that it is mere courtesy to call **''Melmoth''** ''a Romance;'' for [it contains] as many or more stories which, with the exception of the agency of one character common to them all [John Melmoth, the wanderer], have no sort of connexion with each other, their personages being otherwise quite different, and their scenes laid at different periods, and in quite different parts of the world. (pp. 161-62)

There is an infinite display of genius in the conception of all and each of [the] tales; they are all sketches, but they are all sketches that could not be executed but by the hand of a master; and no eye can look on any one of them, without being satisfied that the same hand *might* produce things no less perfect than powerful, were such the good will and pleasure of Mr. Maturin. Perhaps the finest design of the whole is that of the story of the Spanish Girl that has been wrecked, and preserved alone, upon an island of the Indian Sea. . . .

Another very fine story is that of a young Spaniard, whom the sins of his mother, and the weakness of his father, have condemned to the conventual life, and who . . . explores almost in vain every human resource of invention and boldness, in order to escape from its thraldom. The great merit of this tale lies in the Author's strenuous rejection of all those vulgar horrors by which the disciples of the Radcliffe School have been accustomed to deepen their portraitures of monastic misery. . . . (p. 163)

Mr. Maturin is, without question, one of the most genuine masters of the dark romance. He can make the most practised reader tremble as effectually as Mrs. Radcliffe, and what is better, he can make him think as deeply as Mr. Godwin. We cannot carry the commendation sought for by this species of exertion much higher than we do when we say, that in our opinion, a little more reflection and labour are all Mr. Maturin wants, in order to enable him to attain a permanent eminence. . . . (p. 168)

''Melmoth the Wanderer, &c.'' in Blackwood's
Edinburgh Magazine, *Vol. VIII, No. XLIV, November, 1820, pp. 161-68.*

THE QUARTERLY REVIEW (essay date 1821)

Mr. Maturin has contrived . . . to unite in [**'Melmoth'**] all the worst particularities of the worst modern novels. . . . We do not pronounce this judgment hastily, and we pronounce it with regret—we honour Mr. Maturin's profession even when he debases it, and if **'Melmoth'** had been only silly and tiresome, we should gladly have treated it with silent contempt; but it unfortunately variegates its stupidity with some characteristics of a more disgusting kind, which our respect for good manners and decency obliges us to denounce. Mr. Maturin means, we hope and are ready to believe, no harm—he seems, indeed, like the Pythia of old, to be but a very imperfect judge of the meaning of any thing which he utters in the fury of his inspirations; and he will, perhaps, be himself surprised to learn, that, during his convulsions, he makes the most violent assaults, not merely on common sense and the English tongue,— these are trifles—but on decency, and even religion:—whether Mr. Maturin be or be not conscious of what he is doing, it is equally our duty to endeavour to counteract the mischief of what he has done. (pp. 303-04)

[The stories in **'Melmoth'**] are contained one within another like a nest of Chinese boxes; but instead of being the effect of nice workmanship, Mr. Maturin's tales are involved and entangled in a clumsy confusion which disgraces the artist, and puzzles the observer. . . . [The] hero of all the stories is the DEVIL—*the Devil himself,* who, in the words of the sermon [on which **'Melmoth'** is based], 'traverses the earth,' with the kind offer of damnation to any one who may choose to accept of his obliging services. To the introduction of a fictitious devil . . . for the purposes of pleasantry, no one would object; but when he is brought forward in seriousness and sadness,

surrounded with his scriptural attributes, and employed in en-
snaring consciences and in propagating damnation, then we
must be allowed to say the matter becomes too solemn, too
tremendous for the handling of such 'weak masters' as Mr.
Maturin: and this miserable mixture of the most awful truths
with the most paltry fables, appears to us the work either of
impiety or insanity, of a mind either very loose in its principles,
or very wild in its operations.

But while we complain of the production of the Devil in this
shape, Mr. Maturin's countrymen will, with some reason, re-
monstrate against 'the local habitation and name' which, 'in
his fine frenzy,' he has conferred upon his incognito Satan.—
The Devil, it seems, is an Irish gentleman of respectable family,
who was born (as we guess) about the year 1640, and after
various adventures, died at Wexford, about the month of December, 1816, in the 177th year of his age. We shall not stop
to laugh at the meanness and manifest absurdities of such a
conception: we shall only say that Melmoth, (the incarnate
fiend,) during his peregrination of two centuries, does less
mischief than a clever mortal would have done; and indeed,
Mr. Maturin's devil seems to have known as little how to
interest or captivate mankind, as the reverend author himself.
(p. 304)

[Mr. Maturin's devil] neither tries by adversity, nor tempts by
prosperity; but, as far as we can discover, takes events as he
finds them, and acts as a mere man would probably do, if one
could imagine a man at once supremely wicked and supremely
stupid, with a heart to conceive all kinds of atrocity, and with
an intellect which could not guide him in robbing a hencoop.

Such is the *pauvre diable* [poor devil], the 'lubber fiend,' which
Mr. Maturin has produced from the unlimited materials at his
disposal—eternal youth—irresistible beauty—inexhaustible
wealth—ubiquity, omnipotence, and desperation! These are
Mr. Maturin's implements: and the squabbles of a convent,
picking up a girl in the streets, eloping with a merchant's
daughter, and frightening an old maid in a country churchyard,
are the glorious result of such a combination of magnificent
machinery!

[We] must in candour give the excuse which Mr. Maturin
makes for himself in the last sentence of his preface [to **'Melmoth'**].

> I cannot again appear before the public in so
> *unseemly* a character as that of a writer of ro-
> mances, without regretting the *necessity* that
> compels me to it. Did my profession furnish
> me with the means of subsistence, I should hold
> myself *culpable* indeed in having recourse to
> any other, but—am I allowed the choice? . . .

Mr. Maturin is well aware, it seems, that he appears in an
unseemly character, but pleads his necessities. . . . If he thought
he was doing nothing derogatory, nothing wrong, we might
pity Mr. Maturin's weakness of understanding; but when he
owns that he does wrong *knowingly*, but for *hire*, we add to
our contempt for his understanding, scorn of his principles;
and the sooner he wholly throws off a character which he
degrades by such *unseemly* and *culpable* practices, the better.
We, and all the world except Mr. Maturin, can see very good
reasons why his profession will not afford him *means of subsistence*—he designates himself as the *author of* **'Bertram,'** a
play; we hear of his sermons only as the foundation of an
unseemly novel, and then, forsooth, this labourer for the stage

and the circulating library, wonders that the Church does not
provide subsistence for him! (p. 311)

"Maturin—'Melmoth, the Wanderer'," *in* The Quarterly Review, *Vol. XXIV, No. XLVIII, January, 1821,
pp. 303-11.*

THE LONDON MAGAZINE   (essay date 1821)

[Undoubtedly] the same wild genius, which has flashed a splendour around the muse of **Bertram,** flits occasionally amid the
ruined abbeys and spectral creations of **Montorio.** It is impossible to read this last romance without being struck with the
powerful capabilities of its author. Full of incident, striking,
though incredible—fruitful in imagination, perverted, but magnificent, it covers its extravagance and its paradox with a robe
of eloquence sufficient to adorn, if not to hide, its manifold
infirmities. In the language of Mr. Maturin, indeed, many of
his errors find a species of redemption—it is clearly the phrase
of an informed mind, often elevated, but seldom inflated—
copious, and at times, perhaps, even redundant, but totally
divested of meagreness and vulgarity. It is at once classical
and natural, teeming with allusions which "smell of the lamp,"
and with graces to be acquired only in good society—it is the
diction of a man who has groped all day amid the dust of the
learned, and shaken it off at night on the threshold of the
drawing-room. His language, however, is almost the only
symptom which he deigns to give of ever having either studied,
or associated with, humanity. He glories in caverns—falls in
love with goblins—becomes naturalized amid ruins, and revels
in the grave. The Devil is a prodigious favourite with Mr.
Maturin. He is a principal figure in all his performances. . . .
(pp. 514-15)

[We] consider this as one of the author's most objectionable
propensities. There are some subjects too sacred, and some too
accursed, for familiarity. The name before which the world
bends, and the name at which the world shudders, are not the
legitimate topics of romance. Their interest is too awful for
contact—their mystery is too sublime for penetration—even
the veil that shadows them is too intensely bright for human
vision to gaze upon and live. Mr. Maturin, perhaps, imagines
that, because his hand is consecrated he may touch the ark;
but he should remember, that its possession was a trust, and
its home was the temple. There exists throughout his writings
a continual dalliance with other subjects of the same class,
though of less solemn import. The novel writer has world
enough without encroaching on these confines. (p. 515)

We object to [Mr. Maturin], that, in some instances, he is too
much the divine—in others, not enough so—that, when he is
not controverting, he is seducing—that he is alternately the
sectarian or the sensualist. (p. 516)

For his theological discussions, perhaps, excuses may be suggested—we can imagine, but do not admit them. . . . [A] novel
is no place for a polemical disquisition—the acerbities of sects,
and the subtleties of theologians, are quite opposed to the
levities of a romance—they are like the passing of a thunder
cloud, dark, and heavy, and death-fraught, athwart the tinted
sky of an autumnal evening. But, indeed, the author before us
is not so much argumentative as intolerant—he scarcely condescends to discuss—his weapon is sarcasm, and when he is
not sneering, he is denouncing.—This is sometimes carried so
far, that we have frequently been inclined to doubt which is
his real character, a sceptic or a zealot—a bigot or a philosopher. In his exposure, or rather, reproof, of some obnoxious

heresy, the primitive faith itself becomes endangered, and we have almost imagined we saw Voltaire in disguise, when we were undeceived by the bitter earnestness of the expostulation, or the animated and indignant sincerity of the invective. (pp. 516-17)

[There is] a terrible fidelity—a murderous consistency in [Mr. Maturin's delineations of character]—but they have no prototype except in his own brain—nature disowns them, and history holds up the monsters, whom every brow has frowned on, and every age abjured, as angels in the comparison. It is a serious fault, we had almost said crime, in Mr. Maturin, that he should not only body forth such creations, but inspire them with such potency of evil; that he should give them talent in proportion to their crimes, and energy commensurate with their malignant dispositions. By way of preserving their consistency, he not only fills them with demoniac propensities, but demoniac powers, and seizes upon every opportunity, to put both in ferocious and active operation. His manifold demons have a restlessness of mischief, which not even the author of all mischief could surpass, and genius quite adequate to their horrible ambition. To be sure, all this may be consistent. But why create such characters at all, and then, for the purpose of their foul consistency, collect all that infidelity has poured out against religion, all that desperate sophistry has urged for vice, and all that discontented depravity has flung upon the institutions of civilized society, and give them additional circulation and publicity through such perverted and culpable instrumentality. That those characters are contradistinguished from others, who endeavour to oppose and contravene their tenets, is no apology at all. There is no use in raising such disquisitions. The scaffold and the dungeon exhibit every day to crime the practical tendency of its doctrines; and if these and the pulpit are not sufficient, there can be no use in combating them through the medium of romances,—and not merely combating them, but taking care to provide them with weapons for the conflict, sufficient almost to endanger victory. There is a burning eloquence—a sarcastic bitterness—an insidious plausibility about all Mr. Maturin's murderers and demons which well might have been spared. The taunts against religion are too keen, the invectives against society too terrible, the spirit of malignant discontent against the order of things established, is too subtle, too ascetic, and too sustained, to be quite affected; and though we believe that this author, both in his heart and in his life, contradicts such doctrines, he may rest assured that the eloquence with which he enables his devils to enforce them must offend, though it cannot harm, the virtuous; and may, perhaps, but too fatally, mislead many who are as yet hesitating upon the Rubicon of crime. (pp. 517-18)

[*Melmoth*] is a most characteristic epitome of all his productions. Genius and extravagance—nature and prodigies—angels and devils—theology and libertinism, contest every line of every page of these volumes, and leave us in doubt, at last, whether we should most admire, or deplore, the perverted talent which they indisputably discover. The idea of the work, we are told in the preface, is taken from a passage in one of the author's *sermons.* . . . [Those] sacred truths which as the representative of Christ he has . . . promulgated from the pulpit, the moment he descends from it, are converted into the theme of a romance. We marvel much that he waited till he came down, and should marvel less if the congregation doubted what it was he was about to deliver when he went up. (p. 518)

We acquit Mr. Maturin, however, of every thing, except the affectation of this impiety. The novel is not taken from any

sermon, but from the Faustus of Goethe. . . . Melmoth is Doctor Faustus, under the title of the "Wanderer," and closely resembles him, not only in his life and fate, but in many of his adventures. It is a much closer imitation even than the Manfred of Lord Byron. . . . The hero of such a tale [as *Melmoth*] must manifestly be possessed of great advantages, which, we think, however, the author has surrendered, by dividing the narrative into several distinct stories, having no very obvious connection, and, of course, losing much of their interest. These stories are told by a Spaniard, who has been wrecked upon the coast of Ireland, and who has been saved by young Melmoth, a descendant—a *coeval* descendant—of the Wanderer. Before the appearance of the Spaniard, however, there is a terrible delineation of a miser's death-bed, drawn with great power, and with great local accuracy. It is a most faithful portraiture of Irish manners in low life, and an awful one of a departing spirit, frightfully struggling between the fascination of earth's crimes, and the horror of eternity's retribution.

The first of these stories is the Spaniard's own, which, the preface tells us, a *friend* has censured, as tending too much to revive the terror-striking school of Mrs. Radcliffe. He must, indeed, have been a *friend* who made the objection—a much more serious one was obvious. The tale is tainted throughout with the sins to which we have adverted, and contains descriptions sufficient to terrify a martyr. (pp. 518-19)

[The "**Tale of the Indians**"] is very fantastic, but parts of it are extremely beautiful. The whole sketch of Immalie, in her island—the worship of the peasantry—the innocence of her infancy, and the sad reverses of her maturity, are all finely and powerfully described. Such a being, to be sure, never was, nor can be; but improbability is not an objection to a romance, and, least of all, to a romance of Mr. Maturin's. (p. 523)

> *"On the Writings of Mr. Maturin, and More Particularly His 'Melmoth'," in* The London Magazine, *Vol. III, May, 1821, pp. 514-24.*

[P. G. PATMORE]   (essay date 1824)

We were a little disappointed in finding that Mr. Maturin's [*The Albigenses, a Romance*] is not of a character that either entitles or entices us to make it the occasion of a general examination of his literary pretensions. For we could not do this effectually, without adducing various examples of the faults and the good qualities that are peculiar to his writings; and it so happens, that the work now before us is almost entirely deficient in either of these. It is, perhaps, not very difficult to account for this. Mr. Maturin, though now a tolerably practised writer, is far from having acquired that command over the efforts of his pen which the time that he has exercised it would, under ordinary circumstances, have given him: for his mind is not one that will submit to be "constrained by mastery," either in its strengths or its weaknesses. It may be *led,* we sincerely believe, to perform very valuable services to the republic of letters; but it may not be *driven* to do either good or evil. And if it *be* driven, the results will be a something between the two, and bearing no distinctive character whatever. Now, we conceive the work before us to have proceeded from an artificial and ill-considered impetus. . . . Mr. Maturin has publicly stated, as an excuse (*that* is the form under which he most unnecessarily puts it) for writing Romances at all, that his necessities oblige him to do so; and yet all the Romances he has hitherto written have subjected him to the most virulent abuse from several of those critical tribunals, on whose fiat the popularity of works of this class mainly depends—or, at all events, by which that popularity can be greatly advanced, and still more greatly retarded. And this abuse, too, when it has descended to detail, has, in almost every instance, been levelled at precisely those portions of the works in question in which the author must have felt, and every one else must have admitted, that the beauties, if beauties the works contained, were to be found. What could a writer, but little acquainted with the nature of his own powers, and avowedly employing them with a view to present distinction, be expected to do under such circumstances, but resolutely set himself to avoid the errors that seemed to lay in the way of his object? And in doing so, what could be expected as the first result of this effort, but what we, in fact, meet with in [*The Albigenses*] . . .?—namely, a production in which all the most glaring faults that existed in his previous ones are in a great degree absent; and in which all the beauties which more than redeemed those faults, are absent too. The truth is, Mr. Maturin did not seek instruction from the right source. Instead of feeling contempt for those who expressed a contempt which they did *not* feel towards him, he flew to *them* for that counsel which he should have taken of his own good sense, and his own heart. If, instead of hastily putting forth his works in the crude and indigested state in which they were first thrown off from his rapid and heedless pen, he had taken time to consider of that respect which is due to the opinions, and that tenderness which should not be withheld even from the prejudices, of the world to which he was addressing himself, he would not have given any excuse, much less any reason, for those attacks which have been made upon him. But when they *were* made, if, instead of succumbing to them, as he appears in part to have done, he had determined to show only that due sense of their value which consisted in proving them to be unmerited (which he might easily have done), his present work would have been very different from what it now is; for almost every noticeable part of it gives evidence of his merely wishing to escape that censure which, with an equally small share of pains, he might have set at defiance. (pp. 551-52)

[The] author of *The Albigenses* has produced a tale which is very far from being equal in point of general interest to those of the same class which have before proceeded from his pen; and which, as we have before hinted, is almost entirely deficient in those detached passages of power, spirit, and tragic pathos which formed the most striking features of those works. The plot of the present tale is no less wild and unconcocted than that, for example, of *Melmoth;* while it wants all that interest (such as it was) which arose from the supernatural machinery of the latter.

Another great failure in the work before us, arises from an attempt in the author to depict historical characters, and to represent them in something like the circumstances in which they were actually engaged. To depict *character* at all is not Mr. Maturin's forte; and to construct a character which shall at once be consistent with itself and with human nature out of the fragments and hints (often contradictory) that occur in what is called history, requires a knowledge of human nature, and a delicacy of tact, that are rarely indeed to be met with. In this respect, as well as in some others, Mr. Maturin comes painfully in contact with his reader's ideas of his great contemporary [Sir Walter Scott], and the silent, and perhaps unconscious, comparisons they are compelled to make in consequence, render them less easily satisfied than they might otherwise be. The only character in this work, whether historical or fictitious, which is drawn with any thing like vigour and consistency, is

that of the bishop of Toulouse. And in his we have but a few striking and prominent points—none of those subtle and almost evanescent traits which escape the notice of the general observer, but on which half the truth and all the delicacy of the picture depend.

The other, and most crying and conspicuous general defects of this romance, are, the inordinate length to which the plot is spun out, and the consequent flaggings of the progressive interest on which so great a portion of the attraction, and therefore the merit, of a work like this depends; and the extremely unskilful manner in which the different portions of the plot are united with, or rather are disunited from, each other. This latter defect distracts and confuses the reader's attention, and causes the complication of the plot, which can be introduced for no other purpose than that of encreasing the interest, to produce a directly opposite effect.

The only positive defect that we shall notice in the detail of *The Albigenses,* is this: that the comic parts of it are all, without exception, totally bad. The marvellous appetite, and the mal-a-prop Latin of the abbot of Normoutier, are dull and dreary to the last degree; and the heavy trifling of Sir Ezzelin de Verac, is a mere impertinence. (pp. 552-53)

But we can confidently state, to the readers of works of this nature, that, with all its faults, they will find *The Albigenses* well worth a perusal. They will meet, in the first place, with a very vivid general picture of the manners, habits, and tones of feeling, of a most singular and interesting, if not a most enviable state of society—a picture, they may rest assured, very little if at all exaggerated, either in its individual features or its general effect. The relative conditions of the various classes of society—from the monarch on the throne down to the vassals of the soil—they will find depicted, generally speaking, with considerable truth, and the distinctions between each class preserved with due care. They will find the modes of warfare, which were of such paramount importance at that period, described with much occasional force and spirit; the prevalent religious and moral feelings, and the superstitions of the day, illustrated and brought into action in various ways, and in a very lively and effective manner; the scenery, as connected with the kind of dwellings that were rendered necessary by the then predatory modes of life, sketched with a vigorous, and tolerably faithful hand. And finally, they will meet with some very interesting and poetical pictures, consisting of groups and of single figures, painted with a degree of elegance, distinctness, and finish, which they will scarcely find in this author's previous works, and at the same time free from that overwrought and extravagant style of colouring, as well as of design, which greatly detracted from the effect of his other performances, in the eyes of all but those who prefer tawdry and meretricious ornament to the simple beauties of nature and truth. (pp. 553-54)

[P. G. Patmore], in a review of "The Albigenses," in The Westminster Review, *Vol. I, April, 1824, pp. 550-54.*

THE MONTHLY REVIEW, LONDON (essay date 1825)

[The four volumes of **"The Albigenses; a Romance"** are] the most pleasing and successful effort of the late Mr. Maturin's talents; and talents he must be allowed to have possessed, far above the common order. . . . [His talents, however], were not always most judiciously and happily directed, nor sufficiently under the control of good taste or chastised feeling; yet they displayed a degree of spirit, energy, and resources, calculated to interest a large portion of the admirers and readers of modern romance. Displaying abilities, perhaps, second only in this species of composition to the greatest writer of his age in that department [Sir Walter Scott], it is rather singular that he did not produce a more striking impression on the public mind and favor, than that he should have acquired the sort of celebrity which he has enjoyed. With less enthusiasm and extravagance, and a little more discretion and sound taste, he would doubtless have attained a higher station in the rank of his literary contemporaries; and a station which his genius, properly tempered and controlled, was well qualified to fill and adorn.

To the peculiar cast of that genius, may be added a studied eagerness after novelty and display; which, by overshooting its own mark, more frequently tended to weary or to revolt his readers, than to rivet them with fresh earnestness to his pages. In his love for the mysterious and the marvellous, Mr. Maturin knew no bounds; and he was apt to imagine that he was consummating the triumph of his art when revelling in all the luxuriance of his fancy, or passing the extreme bounds of nature and probability. Thus, in his dramatic as well as his romantic compositions, instead of attempting to restrain the exuberance of his feelings, his invention seemed to be always on the stretch; and, by coloring his pictures to an excessive degree, he injured much of their natural beauty and effect. He never seemed to know when he had done well, nor when he had achieved enough; and his incidents, personages, and descriptions, howsoever ably conceived and embodied, are all liable to the same error,— all overloaded, until he cloys us with the very scenes and characters in which we had become really interested. All his works contain rich and full materials, moulded with the hand of genius but not of judgment; abundant proofs of which deficiency are to be found in his **"Melmoth;"** fewer in his tale of **"Woman;"** and perhaps least of all in [**"The Albigenses."**] (pp. 170-71)

We believe that we may ascribe this superiority of good taste in [**"The Albigenses"**] chiefly to its historic character; which must have acted, in some degree, as a counterpoise to the usual wild and unfettered sallies of the writer's imagination. It certainly betrays a less wilful indulgence of his wonted mystery and extravagance: his descriptions, being confined to real scenery and manners, are less overwrought; the characters are more within keeping; and the whole tissue of the story and its adventures is less forced and unnatural. (p. 171)

[**"The Albigenses"**] undoubtedly, we think, discovers riper and more enlarged powers than any single one among his former productions; it displays wider views, with more information, reflection, and research; and it is directed to higher and more important objects, viz. the inculcation of religious toleration, humanity, and peace, than we find in many of our modern historical romances.

Thus his animated descriptions of the leading characters, the champions of the church in the thirteenth century,—of the growing splendor of its pontiffs,—of the feudal and chivalric spirit excited against the zeal and fanaticism of all who were termed heretics,—are interweaved with a regular and interesting story; and, in addition, we are presented with many able and judicious remarks on the policy, manners, and revolutions of the period described. The scene of course is placed in the somewhat hacknied and stale regions of Languedoc and Provence, and the chief actors are . . . very familiar and serviceable heroes to all romance writers. . . . It is therefore only to

the spirit and execution of his work that we are to attribute the author's success, which unites great variety of incident and information with no uninteresting fable. The story is formed wholly on a romantic, or we should say, chivalric basis; for its hero is not merely the pink of courtesy, . . . but a very grave, gentle, unassuming, and respectable young man. . . . (pp. 172-73)

Several of the more prominent characters, both traditional and fancied, stand forth in scarcely less powerful lights and bold relief than we discern in the more correct and masterly delineations of [Scott's] "Waverley." In the portraits, indeed, of one or two of the Huguenot preachers, the author appears to have held his great contemporary in his eye; though it is rather on the same views and principles of historic romance than in traces of peculiar and servile imitation, that the resemblance is to be discovered. (p. 174)

[There] is an earnestness, a stirring life and action, in the whole of the writer's incidents and descriptions, which conveys a vivid impression, and seems to transport the reader back into the scenes that are past. The same may be said of many of his characters, which are strongly drawn and well contrasted; though certainly too numerous, and too arbitrarily brought into notice. . . . [The characters] maintain their own peculiar traits throughout; and though many of the adventures and descriptions are carried beyond all probable bounds, the personages who figure in them are always distinct, natural, strong, and interesting. (pp. 176-77)

In the third and fourth volumes,—but there ought not to have been four, according to the plan and progress of the plot,— we begin to be sensible rather too early of the diminishing interest of the work; and the hand of a master is wanting as we approach nearer to its final development. All the heroes seem to possess a miraculous gift of life; for, when we are led to think that they are quietly laid in the earth, after having received wounds enough to "kill off" a regiment, we suddenly behold them figuring once more in the "tilted field," where they "fight all their battles o'er again," and "thrice they slay the slain." We are thus presented with the same incidents and characters, even to satiety; and we sigh to reach the *dénouement* of a story, which at the same time is but too easily foreseen. The most imminent danger which threatens the hero, Sir Paladour, ceases almost to excite commiseration, and the delicate situation and hair-breadth escapes of the Lady Isabelle do not impose on us for a moment. We perceive that they are both destined to triumph "over fate and time," and may safely defy the bitterest persecutions of a host of enemies; protected as they are by the shield of love and chivalry, whose miraculous power never deserts them until they are made finally happy. (p. 179)

"Maturin's 'Albigenses; a Romance'," *in* The Monthly Review, *London, Vol. CVI, February, 1825, pp. 170-79.*

THE IRISH QUARTERLY REVIEW   (essay date 1852)

Amongst the many Irishmen of undoubted genius, who have died within the past thirty years, there is not one whose memory is so much neglected, or whose works are so forgotten, as those of Charles Robert Maturin. . . . [He] gave up all the fair buoyant years of life to the service of poesy and literature, and the only blemish of his *early* novels, and the sole fault of his tragedies, is that which his own character, and the peculiar cast of his mind impressed upon them—they are too ideal. . . .

[Experience] shows that the first efforts in poetry and prose of some of our most admired writers, exhibited no traits of the bright excellence by which afterwards they were so gloriously distinguished. Amongst all the men of genius this century, Maturin is the one for whom most indulgences must be claimed; but whilst we claim them, we are not, for a moment, contending that a poet is to demand for himself, or his works, any peculiar exemption from these rules, which religion and society have set up as the guides for all men in the conduct of their lives. (pp. 141-42)

Charles Robert Maturin was essentially a poet. In his case . . . , the adoption of the church as a profession was a most grave mistake, and all through his chequered existence, genius incited him to one course of conduct, whilst duty imperatively commanded the adoption of another. The great misfortune of his life was, that in him, as in many other clever men, the intellectual faculty was so strong, that genius, and feeling, and impulse, ever drove him onward, and all the calm resolvings of reason and deliberation were forgotten, in the wild whirl of excited fancy. (p. 143)

["The Family of Montorio, or the Fatal Revenge"] is a work belonging to the school founded by Mrs. Ratcliffe [*sic*]—overladen with all kinds of horrors, trap doors, and unexpected apparitions. . . . ["The Wild Irish Boy" is] a romance displaying all the fancy and brilliancy of thought, which marked the earlier production, "Montorio," and exhibiting a depth of passionate feeling, wild and intense as that of [Johann Wolfgang von Goethe's] "Werther." (p. 147)

[In "The Milesian Chief" all] the beauties and all the defects of Maturin's genius and style are apparent, it is true, but, over all, there is so great a brilliancy of thought, and a mastery of language so perfect, that certain passages of the tale rise to the highest order of eloquence. But beautiful as [Maturin's] works are, we fear that very few of our readers, born within the present century, have even seen them. . . . This neglect in a great measure arises from the fact, that the stories are founded on a mixture of the supernatural and the real; the denouements are brought about by a series of events comprising all that is wild, and horrible, and unearthly. The taste for this species of composition had almost passed away when ["Montorio," "The Wild Irish Boy," and "The Milesian Chief"] were published, and we believe that to produce a successful romance of [Mrs. Ratcliffe's] "Mysteries of Udolpho" school, even at the period when "The Milesian Chief" was published . . . , the author should possess the mighty genius of Scott. (pp. 148-49)

[All] that can be asserted against ["Bertram, or the Castle of St. Aldobrand"] comes to this, that its plot is, in part, founded on the often performed tragedy, "Isabella, or the Fatal Marriage" [by Thomas Southern], and in part, on a now forgotten play, called "Percy," the production of that sublimely rigorous friend of virtue, Hannah More.

We are quite willing to admit, that in "Bertram" there is too much of the melodramatic tinge. Passion, human passion and feeling, may be too highly painted, but this is only to say that the tragedy is not perfect. If we look back through the pages of the old dramatists, we find this same fault appearing in the works of our tragic writers. . . . Maturin may have shown some want of taste, but it was a want common to other men of great genius. . . . (p. 157)

["Manuel"] undoubtedly was a failure, and a wretched one. In thought and language it was poetic, but its fault consisted in the number of underplots, which prevented the full and clear development of the main incident. (p. 161)

["Woman, or Pour et Contre" and "Melmoth the Wanderer"] prove that Maturin, as he advanced in experience, tamed down the wild love of romance and mystery which actuated him in earlier years. . . . (p. 164)

["The Albigenses"] is one of his best productions, and increases our regret that the grave should so soon afterwards have received him. (p. 166)

> *"Rev. Charles Robert Maturin," in* The Irish Quarterly Review, *Vol. II, No. V, March, 1852, pp. 141-70.*

THE SATURDAY REVIEW, LONDON   (essay date 1891)

The popularity of **Bertram,** and the admiration for it entertained by Byron and Scott [see excerpts above, 1815 and 1814], appear perhaps extraordinary to us. . . . [To] modern criticism it seems exaggerated and bombastic. (p. 437)

It is on account of [**Melmoth the Wanderer**] that Maturin deserves to be remembered. **Melmoth the Wanderer** and the *Frankenstein* of Mrs. Shelley are far the most powerful of the pseudo-romantic school of fiction—that school which attained its highest popularity in the novels of Monk Lewis and Ann Radcliffe, and which found its crudest expression in *The Castle of Otranto* of Horace Walpole. Neither *Frankenstein* nor **Melmoth,** however, although pre-eminent in scenes of horror, is a fair example of this kind of fiction. They contain pathos and psychological observation altogether foreign to it. Maturin furthermore possessed an antiquarian knowledge of demonology, and was steeped in the esoteric doctrines of diabolic mysticism. In literature also he achieved a difficult feat—he wrote a successful novel in a style that had already become jejune.

Again, in **Melmoth** Maturin avoids—as does Mrs. Shelley—the grave artistic fault of excessive *explanation*. In the terrific romances of that time, the author, having expended some skill and a deal of invention in order to frighten the reader with his ghosts and goblins, almost invariably gives away the truth, so to speak, at the end of the story—we come to be deceived and are only disillusioned. (pp. 437-38)

When **Melmoth** was published . . . , a better taste in English fiction had already set in; but its merit is independent of any prevailing taste or fashion. Several thrilling novels might be carved out of it. The excitement is kept up through four volumes; and, up to the last page, the reader can never guess what is about to happen. . . .

[Various entrancing narratives] are thrown together with little or no construction into this extraordinary production. In books of this period the peculiar mental tortures which attended incarceration in a Spanish convent are usually neglected for physical horrors; but Maturin deals as terribly and far more delicately with daily conventual life. He is not led into those puerilities into which prejudice and ignorance have led his contemporaries. Charles Lamb used to say that no one could read the murder scene in *Macbeth* at midnight without a feeling of fear. Though no other comparison is suggested, it may be as truly said of **Melmoth** that several scenes in it will produce the same effect at any hour. . . .

Maturin's other works are interesting chiefly because they were written by the author of **Melmoth.** In **Women** he deserted his usual style, and attempted elaborate characterization and social satire with some success. Dublin Dissenting society is minutely described, and the characters possess at least the merit of being alive. (p. 438)

"A Forgotten Writer," in The Saturday Review, *London, Vol. LXXI, No. 1850, April 11, 1891, pp. 437-38.*

THE ATHENAEUM   (essay date 1892)

['**Melmoth the Wanderer**'] may be welcomed . . . as a contribution towards the curiosities of literature. Distinctly the most remarkable of the British triumvirate which, in the early part of the century, won a momentary fame as the school of horror, Maturin is much less known to the readers of to-day than either Monk Lewis or Mrs. Radcliffe. (p. 560)

'**Melmoth the Wanderer**' is in parts very thrilling; its Elizabethan feast of horrors has a savour as of a lesser Tourneur. But it is interesting only in parts, and at its best it never comes near the effect which the great masters of the grotesque and terrible—Hoffmann, Poe, Villiers de l'Isle-Adam—have known how to produce. A freak of construction, which no artist could have been guilty of, sends us wandering from story to story in a very maze of underplots and episodes and interpolations. Six separate stories are told—all in parenthesis—and the greater part of the book is contained within inverted commas. What is fine in it is the vivid, feverish way in which, from time to time, some story of horror or mystery is forced home to one's sensations. It is the art of the nightmare, and it has none of the supremacy in that line of the 'Contes Drolatiques' of Balzac. But certain scenes in the monastery and in the prisons of the Inquisition—an attempted escape, a scene where an immured wretch fights the reptiles in the darkness—are full of a certain kind of power. That escape, for instance, with its consequences, is decidedly gruesome, decidedly exciting; but compare it with Dumas, with the escape of Monte Cristo. . . . [Where Dumas produces his] effect by a simple statement—a record of external events from which one realizes, as one could realize in no other way, all the emotions and sensations of the persons who were undergoing such experiences—Maturin seeks his effect, and produces it, but in a much lesser degree, by a sort of excited psychology, an exclamatory insistence on sensation and emotion. (p. 561)

A review of "Melmoth the Wanderer," in The Athenaeum, *No. 3366, April 30, 1892, pp. 560-61.*

THE TIMES LITERARY SUPPLEMENT   (essay date 1920)

There is scarcely any book of merit which has been so completely forgotten as "**Melmoth the Wanderer**," and few authors have been so soon neglected as Charles Robert Maturin. . . .

It is entirely on "**Melmoth the Wanderer**" that Maturin's reputation rests, and the book has a certain historical interest in the development of the novel. It is the culmination and crowning achievement of the novel of Terror and Wonder in England. . . .

In spite of all its defects of construction, no other novel conveys in a more real way the thrill of terror. That, indeed, is almost its sole interest. . . . Maturin builds up his efforts with a series of suggestive touches, those instinctive premonitions of something strange in even ordinary affairs; and he certainly describes powerfully and well; his descriptive power is, indeed, an essential feature of the secret of conveying his supernatural fear. . . .

[The defects of the book] are obvious. The construction especially is involved and clumsy. One may, however, remember Maturin's position when criticizing it. He was faced with the problem of finding some method which would introduce his hero in various centuries and many countries, and the tale within the tale had been a very definite expedient of eighteenth-century fiction. And even the very confusion of the kaleidoscopic plot may be said to help in conveying that feeling of unreality—the dream sense of not being able at any given moment to say whether we are in this world of reality or in some other—which is essential to the supernatural mood. A more serious artistic blemish is the lack of restraint, which shows itself at times in the rhetorical fustian of the style, but more often in the descriptions. He will spoil his best effects by going too far, passing from subtle psychological play to a riot of exaggerated physical horror.

"Maturin and the Novel of Terror," in The Times Literary Supplement, *No. 971, August 26, 1920, p. 548.*

EDITH BIRKHEAD   (essay date 1921)

[*Birkhead's* The Tale of Terror: A Study of the Gothic Romance *is regarded as an important twentieth-century study of the Gothic novel. In her discussion of Maturin's works, Birkhead focuses on* Fatal Revenge *and* Melmoth. *Birkhead notes Maturin's indebtedness to earlier Gothic novelists, but distinguishes him from his predecessors "by the powerful eloquence of his style and his ability to analyse emotion." Birkhead is one of the first twentieth-century critics to comment on the psychological insight displayed in* Melmoth. *Her essay presages the approach of such later critics as Douglas Grant (1968), Francis Russell Hart (1968), Robert Kiely (1972), and Coral Ann Howells (1978).*]

[In *The Family of Montorio*] we wander, bewildered, baffled and distracted through labyrinthine mazes. . . . We stumble along blind alleys desperately retracing our weary steps, and, after stumbling alone and unaided to the very end, reach the darkly concealed clue when it has ceased to be either of use or of interest to us. Many an adventurer must have lain down, dispirited and exhausted, without ever reaching his distant and elusive goal. . . . The impressive figure of Schemoli, with his unholy power of fascinating his reluctant accomplices [the brothers Annibal and Ippolito], lends to the book the only sort of unity it possesses. But even he fails to arouse a sense of fear strong enough to fix our attention to so wandering a story. Like the doomed brothers, we drift dejectedly through inexplicable terrors, and we re-echo with fervour Annibal's dolorous cry: "Why should I be shut up in this house of horrors to deal with spirits and damned things and the secrets of the infernal world while there are so many paths open to pleasure, the varieties of human intercourse and the enjoyment of life?"

Maturin, a disciple of Mrs. Radcliffe, feels it his duty to explain away the apparently miraculous incidents in his story, but he lacks the persevering ingenuity that partly compensates for her frauds. On a single page he calmly discloses secrets which have harassed us for four volumes, and his long-deferred explanations are paltry and incredible. The bleeding figures that wrought so painfully on the sensitive nerves of Ippolito are merely waxen images that spout blood automatically. Disappearances and reappearances, which seemed supernatural, are simply effected by private exits and entrances. Other startling phenomena are accounted for in the same trivial fashion.

Maturin seems to have crowded into his story nearly every character and incident that had been employed in earlier Gothic romances. Schemoli is a remarkably faithful portrait of Mrs. Radcliffe's Schedoni [in *The Italian*]. From beneath his cowl flash the piercing eyes, whose very glance will daunt the bravest heart; his sallow visage is furrowed with the traces of bygone passions; he shuns society, and is dreaded by his associates. The oppressed maiden, driven into a nunnery, drugged and immured, the ambitious countess, the devoted, loquacious servant, the inhuman abbess—all play their accustomed parts. The background shifts from the robber's den to the ruined chapel, from the castle vault to the dungeon of the Inquisition, each scene being admirably suited to the situation contrived, or the emotion displayed. Maturin had accurately inspected the passages and trap-doors of Otranto [in Horace Walpole's *The Castle of Otranto*]. No item, not a rusty lock, not a creaking hinge, had escaped his vigilant eye. He knew intimately every nook and cranny of Mrs. Radcliffe's Gothic abbeys. He had viewed with trepidation their blood-stained floors, their skeletons and corpses, and had carefully calculated the psychological effect of these properties. He had gazed with starting eye on the lurid horrors of "Monk" Lewis, and had carried away impressions so distinct that he, perhaps unwittingly, transferred them to the pages of his own story. But Maturin's reading was not strictly confined to the school of terror. He had studied Shakespeare's tragedies, and these may have suggested to him the idea of enhancing the interest of his story by dissecting human motive and describing passionate feeling. In depicting the remorse of the count and his wife Zenobia, who had committed a murder to gratify their ambition, and who are tormented by ugly dreams, Maturin inevitably draws from *Macbeth*. (pp. 84-5)

Maturin is distinguished from [incompetent romance writers] . . . by the powerful eloquence of his style and by his ability to analyse emotion, to write as if he himself were swayed by the feeling he describes. His insane extravagances have at least the virtue that they come flaming hot from an excited imagination. (p. 86)

Melmoth shows a distinct advance on *Montorio* in constructive power. Each separate story is perfectly clear and easy to follow, in spite of the elaborate interlacing. . . . The story of Immalee, who is visited on her desert island by the Wanderer in the guise of a lover as well as a tempter, forms the most memorable part of *Melmoth*. In the other stories the stranger has been a taciturn creature, relying on the lustre of his eyes rather than on his powers of eloquence to win over his victims. To Immalee he pours forth floods of rhetoric on the sins and follies of mankind. (pp. 88-9)

This extraordinary romance, like *Montorio*, clearly owes much to the novels of Mrs. Radcliffe, and "Monk" Lewis. Immalee, as her name implies, is but a glorified Emily [from Mrs. Radcliffe's *The Mysteries of Udolpho*] with a loxia on her shoulder instead of a lute in her hand. The monastic horrors are obviously a heritage from ["Monk" Lewis's] *The Monk*. The Rosicrucian legend, as handled in *St. Leon*, may have offered hints to Maturin, whose treatment is, however, far more imaginative and impressive than that of Godwin. . . . Marlowe's *Dr. Faustus* and the first part of Goethe's *Faust* left their impression on the story. The closing scenes inevitably remind us of the last act of Marlowe's tragedy. But, when all these debts are acknowledged they do but serve to enhance the success of Maturin, who out of these varied strands could weave so original a romance. *Melmoth* is not an ingenious patchwork of

previous stories. It is the outpouring of a morbid imagination that has long brooded on the fearful and the terrific. Imbued with the grandeur and solemnity of his theme, Maturin endeavours to write in dignified, stately language. There are frequent lapses into bombast, but occasionally his rhetoric is splendidly effective. . . . (pp. 91-2)

There are no quiet scenes or motionless figures in *Melmoth*. Everything is intensified, exaggerated, distorted. The very clouds fly rapidly across the sky, and the moon bursts forth with the "sudden and appalling effulgence of lightning." A shower of rain is perhaps "the most violent that was ever precipitated on the earth." When Melmoth stamps his foot "the reverberation of his steps on the hollow and loosened stones almost contended with the thunder." Maturin's use of words like "callosity," "induration," "defecated," "evanition," and his fondness for italics are other indications of his desire to force an impression by fair means or foul.

The gift of psychological insight that distinguishes *Montorio* reappears in a more highly developed form in *Melmoth the Wanderer*. "Emotions," Maturin declares, "are my events," and he excels in depicting mental as well as physical torture. The monotony of a "timeless day" is suggested with dreary reality in the scene where Monçada and his guide await the approach of night to effect their escape from the monastery. The gradual surrender of resolution before slight, reiterated assaults is cunningly described in the analysis of Isidora's state of mind, when a hateful marriage is forced upon her. Occasionally Maturin astonishes us by the subtlety of his thought:

> While people think it worth while to torment
> us we are never without some dignity, though
> painful and imaginary.

It is his faculty for describing intense, passionate feeling, his power of painting wild pictures of horror, his gifts for conveying his thoughts in rolling, rhythmical periods of eloquence, that make *Melmoth* a memory-haunting book. With all his faults Maturin was the greatest as well as the last of the Goths. (p. 93)

> *Edith Birkhead, "The Novel of Terror: Lewis and Maturin," in her* The Tale of Terror: A Study of the Gothic Romance, *Constable & Company Ltd., 1921, pp. 63-93.**

NIILO IDMAN (essay date 1923)

[*Idman's book-length study of Maturin focuses on the romantic aspects of his works. Idman faults Maturin for his poorly constructed plots but notes that in many of his works, the romantic atmosphere created by his rich, musical style makes this defect seem of secondary importance.*]

In *Montorio* the disproportion between cause and effect is nothing less than prodigious; and such elements as would actually be grand and imposing in the plan itself, are, in the course of execution, sadly affected by the air of charlatanism inseparable from a plot constructed in the Radcliffe manner. It would be different, and far more satisfactory, if the brothers were, for instance, represented as acting under a kind of hypnotic influence. As it is, the scheme of Orazio is, essentially, carried out by means of talking sheer nonsense to two full-grown people; and facilitated by accidents and singular coincidences which are as incredible as would be the appearance of all the legions of the supernatural world. The wonderful talents of Orazio, above all his capacity of swiftly covering great distances, become almost unnecessary, considering the never-ending maze of secret passages and subterranean recesses at his disposal; there are no two apartments, far or near, unconnected by these means of escape, if need be, and the strangest thing of all is that Orazio, after an absence of twenty years, still is the only person perfectly acquainted with them, wherever they are. For him there is no more difficulty in smuggling letters to Ippolito's room at Naples, than in suddenly turning up in the prison-cell of the Inquisition. Among other extraordinary circumstances contributing to the success of Orazio's enterprise, the occurrence of two earthquakes with the same issue, the liberation of a person from his prison by crushing its walls, is the most unfortunate. This repetition of an event which, even if introduced singly, makes unusual claims upon the reader's credulity, seriously cools his excitement even at the first perusal. . . . It is almost intolerable to re-read *Montorio*, from beginning to end, in spite of the many impressive passages it contains. However, as it is unavoidable in a story constructed in accordance with the principles of *Montorio,* that the elaborate fabric collapses at the final revelation of the 'truth' and the placing side by side of causes and effects, it must still be considered as a success in its kind if this does not happen too soon; and in *Montorio* the reader is, until the explanation of Orazio, really kept believing that the incidents related are of a preternatural character. Hence the 'passion of supernatural fear,' though capable of being inspired only once, is as genuine as that which any Gothic story is likely to create. (pp. 32-3)

[*The Wild Irish Boy*] shows inferior work to a degree truly astonishing. Were it not for certain episodes where genuine power is displayed, and for the fact that the book was entirely a work of imagination, without any hidden aims of personal import—it would not fall very short of that species of composition, the producers of which Maturin once characterized as 'infamous and ephemeral scribblers, who pander for the public lust after anecdote that vilify the great, debase the illustrious, and expose the unfortunate, under the titles of a Winter, a Month, or six Weeks at the metropolis or some place of public resort.' *The Wild Irish Boy* is brimful of august personages, lords and ladies, represented in a most unfavourable light, distorted and exaggerated by the feverish imagination of one who knew nothing of his subject. The fashionable world is condemned as sinful and utterly demoralizing, high life consists but of high vices, described and investigated from every side; while the kind of pure, old-fashioned, religious, home-like existence that is recommended as its contrast, is not found interesting enough to be illustrated otherwise than by very imperfect glimpses. Extravagant as the tone is, it becomes perfectly absurd when the moralist comes into conflict with the patriot. The author appears to have feared that the feelings of the public whose taste he is trying to gratify, might be offended by too much abuse of the British aristocracy—the pride of the nation!—and occasionally the tendency bursts into quite an opposite direction. The young fool of a hero—whose autobiography the book represents—has been painting the whole lot in the blackest of dyes, indulging in the grossest of dissipations and capable of the most contemptible baseness; yet once, seeing them all collected at a royal birth-day, he hits upon comparing them to the 'courtiers' of Napoleon—whom he has never beheld—with the result that he is 'elated with confidence, with exultation, with pride,' and feels satisfied that the English upper ten yet 'loved their king, and worshipped their God,' and, with many vices, 'yet were the first on earth in national virtues.' The sense of national superiority in the English public is flattered by a sweeping condemnation of everything foreign—it is clear that the glorification of *Ireland* must consequently be rather loose and rhapsodical—; espe-

cially are all Frenchmen and -women represented as monsters of malignity and immorality, and Voltaire and Rousseau mentioned with Puritan abhorrence. (pp. 47-9)

[*The Wild Irish Boy*] is diffuse and clumsily constructed; . . . it contains certain good suggestions that are not made the most of, and cleverly built-up situations which lead to platitudes or are forcibly and implausibly dissolved. . . . The autobiography does not attach itself quite naturally to the correspondence that precedes it, and the intrigue, when it once commences, is continually interrupted by discussions and episodes. (p. 56)

[The great bulk of the book] aspires to treat of modern life in higher circles, of which Maturin, at the time, knew little or nothing. The descriptions, consequently, lack all atmosphere of reality, nor does the characterization augment the value of the whole. The worst of it all is that the hero is so uninteresting, and does not in the least fulfil the expectations roused by the effusions of Elmaide St. Clair. . . . That the reader cannot feel sympathy for [Ormsby Bethel,] the hero, is of course in itself no fault in a book, but in this case it is only too evident that it is the author's intention he should.—The wholly imaginary character of Lady Montrevor is too superlative and violently exaggerated, and her wonderful accomplishments, of mind and body, are endlessly repeated in a most extravagant language. Her daughter Athanasia is more interesting; she is one of those delicate and ethereal beings Maturin always succeeded in designing. . . . (pp. 58-9)

The Milesian Chief could not be better characterized than Talfourd does in his much-quoted phrase: 'There is a bleak and misty grandeur about it which, in spite of its glaring defects, sustains for it an abiding place in the soul' [see excerpt above, 1820]. The defects are glaring indeed. The composition, here as always the blind side of Maturin, is anything but flawless. The development of the intrigue is sometimes primitive, sometimes rough and rhapsodical. Repetition occurs frequently in the adventures—the saving of lives especially is an actual habit with the brothers O'Morven; Connal's journey to Dublin is so long as to be a digression, and not particularly interesting; the end is forced and theatrical, and some of the characters are made nothing of. These faults were, at all times, counterpoised by plenty of good characterization and impressive narrative; but now, at a distance of a hundred years, they appear so unimportant just because the whole is wrapped up in that 'bleak and misty grandeur.' The absence of technical defects is, after all, but a negative merit which swiftly loses its charm, while the creations of a truly poetical imagination are never entirely defaced by the wear and tear of time. The romantic atmosphere about the best scenes in *The Milesian Chief,* in so far as such a thing can be defined, arises from a close affinity between the human emotions and the sombre scenery around, effected by the instrumentality of a suggestive, passionate, and musical style. In point of description *The Milesian Chief* shows a great advance from Maturin's earlier works; the nature of Western Ireland had, perhaps, never yet been depicted with a power and accuracy like this. (p. 94)

[*Manuel*] is, indeed, Maturin's weakest production. . . . (p. 135)

Throughout the four first acts the tragedy is well-nigh deprived of all dramatic vigour by incessant interruptions of the main plot. That consists, or ought to consist, in the development of the fate of Manuel until his madness—like Lear's [in William Shakespeare's *King Lear*]—breaks out after an accumulation of disappointments; but besides there being, in every act, plenty of dialogue to no purpose, the interest is divided among episodes very loosely connected with the intrigue. . . . Of the characters De Zelos is, upon the whole, the most interesting. . . . His lack of self-command, however, is so exaggerated and his nervousness so evident, that no one can be in doubt of his guilt, which is made only too clear by several incidents long before his name is read on the dagger. . . . The most depressing quality of *Manuel,* as a production of Maturin's, is that its poetry certainly is 'no great things.' There is nothing of the breath of romance which runs through several passages of *Bertram.* The language is, for the most part, uninspired, and stored with hackneyed phrases and vulgar exclamations. (pp. 137-39)

[The first two acts of *Fredolfo*] are, in every respect, the best part of the play. They have the character of an introduction containing the necessary premises for the catastrophe that follows, but they are well conceived and full of stirring life. In the very first scene the tragedy of Fredolfo is alluded to by an old attendant of his in a conversation with a minstrel, and the spectator thus becomes aware that a gloom is cast over the life of the hero. At the arrival of Berthold it becomes clear that he is the evil genius of the drama; he is received by the inmates of the castle with curses and maledictions, and when Urilda recovers from her swoon she shows equal horror and disgust at the sight of him. (pp. 183-84)

[What] raises the first two acts so far above the rest, is the romantic glamour shed over the persons and events, much of which fades away as the play advances. The figure of Adelmar is an exceedingly poetic one. He does not—like Bertram—belong to the typically 'Byronic' heroes; there is nothing demoniac or criminal about him. Yet he is not bloodless or commonplace; he has an air of romance and mystery of his own, and his speech is pervaded, as it were, by an echo from his native Alps. He never assumes any *pose,* for he can afford to do without one. (pp. 187-88)

Considering the inordinate length of *The Albigenses,* it must be admitted that the story is fairly well constructed, and the rich materials—although of little originality—not unskilfully arranged. In this respect there certainly can be detected a sort of improvement on Maturin's earlier romances; but it is a very poor compensation for the loss of their peculiar charm in style and description. In *The Albigenses* there is hardly a page which could not have been written by somebody else; the personal note in the diction, the keenness of psychological insight, and the characteristic boldness of imagination which distinguished *Women* and *Melmoth,* and even *The Milesian Chief,* have completely disappeared. (p. 293)

[Maturin wrote *The Albigenses*] without inspiration; and that is why the adventures and hair-breadth escapes fail to excite, and the characters appear so hopelessly conventional. The characterization is, in fact, the weakest side of *The Albigenses,* and that of the principal personages the least worthy of Maturin's powers. Paladour and Amirald simply possess every chivalrous virtue imaginable, neither being subject to any faults whatsoever, nor is there one single individual trait to distinguish them from others. The description of these two paragons is pervaded by a deadly seriousness and an unbroken solemnity, all the more causeless as both are destined to become perfectly happy in the end. The influence of Scott, which otherwise is perceptible throughout the story, in no instance extends itself to the treatment of the heroes. (p. 295)

Niilo Idman, in his Charles Robert Maturin: His Life and Works, *Constable & Co Ltd, 1923, 326 p.*

BERTRAND EVANS (essay date 1947)

[Critics during Byron's age immediately observed that both the character of Bertram and the play *Bertram*] were Byronic, and present examination sustains the observation. But . . . a view of both the character and the play against the background of the dramatic tradition . . . [beginning with Horace Walpole's] *The Mysterious Mother* in 1768 makes it apparent that their origins preceded Byron's birth; for both character and play are thoroughly in the Gothic tradition. To identify them with the Byronic is therefore to identify the typical Gothic protagonist and the dramatic type he dominated with the Byronic. (pp. 194-95)

[If the] testimonies of the age identify the play positively with the Byronic . . . , [the plot and settings identify] it as positively with the Gothic. In no materials or purposes does *Bertram* differ from the Gothic drama of the preceding half-century.

Just as the whole play is Gothic, so is its protagonist a Gothic villain transformed to a hero who retains the conventional marks of villainy. Bertram is consumed by an inexplicable torment. . . . What ails this Bertram whom contemporaries identified as Byronic? His villainous ancestors in past decades suffered for three reasons: because, born of a castle ruin, they were afflicted with its gloom; because star actors interpreted the villain's role, and agony was at once opportunity for histrionics and invitation to public sympathy; and because they had committed crime for which conscience—and the censor—demanded a show of remorse. It was through this suffering that the villain became a hero; consequently, as hero, he continued to suffer. The trait which transformed him naturally remained dominant—even though he no longer had a personal cause, or sometimes even a reasonable excuse for possessing it.

Bertram is an excellent exemplification of this fact. In the early scenes of the play, when the prior describes his "feverish tossings and deep-mutter'd groans," there is no source for his agony except his inheritance from his dramatic ancestry. The remorse of these villainous ancestors was at least ostensibly rooted in the dark crimes they had committed. But Bertram, before the early scenes which show him tormented, had committed no crime; and at the time his agony is most intense he does not even know that Imogine, from whom he had been separated, had married: his torture therefore cannot be ascribed to that cause. Bertram, then, if the foolish truth must be stated, suffers because he is the kind of hero who suffers.

The spectacle of a hero suffering remorse when he has committed no crime to cause it was an inevitable result of the transformation of villain to hero. As "villain," the character could be supposed to have committed foul crimes, and, because he had committed them, his most violent show of agony could be excused. As "hero," his reputation could no longer be blackened by crimes of such magnitude as would motivate that very agony which, by rendering him attractive, had made him a hero. *Bertram* shows little effort by Maturin to solve this vital riddle. Bertram suffers only because he was created in the tradition of the agonized protagonist.

Dark, grand, mysterious, lonely, defiant, and tormented, Bertram is the hero of the flashing eye, the proud nature, and the splendid physique. The attractive qualities of the old villains are assembled to make his bid for admiration, forgiveness, and tears. . . . [The] type of Bertram had been created as an object of terror; from Walpole's Isabella down through five and a half decades young ladies like Imogine and her attendant had fled in panic through haunted galleries and subterranean vaults, pursued by men like Bertram. Now the women confess an instant and utter fascination: the admiration for dark eyes and proud physique and the magnetic attraction of a great soul agonized have overcome all, and terror of the Gothic villain has become worship of the Byronic hero. (pp. 196-98)

Mere failure to relate **Bertram** to that large share of the eighteenth century represented by the Gothic tradition would perhaps not in itself be a grave matter. But this failure illustrates a general misconception which is important. To misjudge the relation of **Bertram** to the Gothic tradition is to misjudge the relation of the Byronic in general to that tradition. It is to suppose that the Byronic came into existence in 1812 with publication of *Childe Harold* and by 1816 had had only four years of expression in *The Giaour, The Bride of Abydos, The Corsair,* and *Lara*. As a matter of fact, these years and these poems were consummations, not beginnings. (p. 199)

> Bertrand Evans, *"Gothic Acting Drama, 1801-1816,"* in his Gothic Drama from Walpole to Shelley *(reprinted by permission of the University of California Press), University of California Press, 1947, pp. 177-99.**

MURIEL E. HAMMOND (essay date 1956)

[The] names of the principal Gothic novelists, with the exception of Horace Walpole, Mrs. Radcliffe, and Monk Lewis, are forgotten. . . . Most, perhaps, deserve the oblivion which has enveloped them, but a few are worthy of a better fate. Notable among these is the Irish clergyman, Charles Robert Maturin. . . . (p. 97)

Melmoth, the finest of his works—and he was never an incompetent writer—. . . is a book worthy to be judged on its own merits, and not just as a better than average product of a dubious literary movement. . . .

[The work] falls into five sections, set within a loose framework and linked by the figure of the Wanderer—part Faust, part Mephistopheles, the tempter, and part Wandering Jew. (p. 98)

The Spaniard's tale, while ostensibly an account of the circumstances which induced him to take his vows, of his misery in and ultimate escape from the monastery, is basically a treatise on Maturin's own views on Catholicism. The accounts of floggings and tortures, of imprisonments and faked miracles, may be accepted as part of the general paraphernalia of the Gothic novelist's convention, but the voice of Maturin, the Protestant clergyman, descendant of the persecuted Huguenots, rings out in blazing sincerity. (p. 100)

['**Guzman's Family**'] is a study in the horrors of starvation and extreme poverty. It is remarkable chiefly for the character of the courageous and dignified Ines, believed to be a portrait of Maturin's wife, and for the sympathetic figure of a priest. . . .

['**The Lovers' Tale**'] is singularly uneventful, considering the fact that it is told by Melmoth, and it is debatable whether it is in keeping with his character. It is often tedious, and the three main figures never become more than the stock characters of any romantic novel. . . .

One of the chief criticisms of *Melmoth* is that Maturin drew upon a number of easily recognizable sources, ranging from [Johann Wolfgang von Goethe's] *Faust* to [Lewis's] *The Monk*. . . . But [*Melmoth*] still remains a work of great individuality. All the Gothic writers borrowed from each other,

but not all were gifted with Maturin's ability to refurbish a well-tried theme. Throughout, with the possible exception of '**The Lovers' Tale**', the reader is swept along, believing all, devouring all—even the discourses on theology and sociology, from which it is easy to trace Maturin's success as a preacher. Later, one may stop to criticize: to say that the Immalee-Isidora history is too remote from reality; to wonder why Melmoth should waste his time tempting essentially good persons when he must have realized—since all knowledge was his—that he could only meet with failure; to argue that the boy Alonzo would not be able to reason like a professor of theology, or to complain of the too opportune discovery of the will in the Guzman tale. All such criticism is valid; but it is apparent only when the book has been laid down and the reader has returned to his normal powers of belief and judgement. Until then Maturin can hold him enthralled, arousing both fear and pity. Neglected and wellnigh forgotten, C. R. Maturin remains the finest of the Gothic novelists, and *Melmoth* the greatest of the tales of terror. (p. 101)

> Muriel E. Hammond, *"C. R. Maturin and 'Melmoth the Wanderer',"* in English, *Vol. XI, No. 63, Autumn, 1956, pp. 97-101.*

WILLIAM F. AXTON (essay date 1961)

[Axton asserts that Maturin's primary intent in Melmoth *is to expose the corruption engendered by religious authoritarianism. According to Axton,* Melmoth *is the "highest artistic achievement" of the Gothic genre because in it, "the Gothic mummery of the horror novel was brought to serve the uses of a profoundly tragic religious parable. . . ." Axton's emphasis on the theme of religious fanaticism in* Melmoth *is supported by the later comments of Robert Kiely (1972).]*

[Maturin's] playwriting experience had greatly increased his artistic mastery if not his money-making capacity, and during the [last] six years of his short life he produced his three finest works, including his masterpiece, *Melmoth the Wanderer*. In [*Women; or Pour et Contre, Melmoth,* and *The Albigenses*] Maturin examines the great theme of his imaginative life, the tragic human perversion of a religion of love into a means of self-torment and torture of others.

Women; or Pour et Contre . . . , a novel undeservedly forgotten, deals with the spiritual consequences of narrow middle-class Calvinism, the emotional starvation engendered by its gloomy rigorism, its substitution of prudential morality and self-righteousness for Christian charity, and its prostituted use as an instrument for economic aggrandizement. . . . To an extent the novel presents a symbolic opposition between the respective spiritual inadequacies of Catholicism, Calvinism, and free thought; but *Women* is also a parable of Maturin's inner struggle between religious faith and the life of the imagination, neither of which wholly satisfied his spirit and each of which was exclusive of the other under the social conditions then prevailing. In a larger sense *Women* concerns the entire tragic situation of the artist in middle-class industrial and commercial society, forced by a corrupt sectarianism into a fatal division between the religious and the imaginative halves of his being, unable to bridge the two worlds of faith and artistic creation as earlier writers in more unified societies had been able to do so successfully.

Maturin's last novel, *The Albigenses* . . . , treats of the cruelties that result from religious sectarianism joined with political factionalism. A historical novel clearly made in the pattern of

Maturin's friend and advisor, Scott, *The Albigenses* recounts the savage suppression of a heretical medieval cult with democratic and Protestant leanings by the combined forces of an international church and intrenched political despotism. (pp. xiii-xiv)

[*Melmoth* is] a brilliant culmination and fusion of the suggestive terrors of Mrs. Radcliffe, the lurid horrors of "Monk" Lewis, and Maturin's own profound psychological insight into torture and suffering. While *Melmoth* embraces all the conventional machinery of Gothic romance, it is lifted above the artistic level of the blood-and-thunder school by its compelling statement of the grand theme of perverted faith that so haunted Maturin's imagination in the last years of his life. (p. xiv)

Self-damned, possessed of supernatural powers, and strangely sympathetic, Melmoth is an epitome of the Gothic hero-villain. But he is more: however much he may delight in the tortures of others, he is raised to something very close to tragic stature by Maturin's sensitive presentation of his suffering. Melmoth becomes almost forgivable because of his tormented awareness of his own evil. The root of Melmoth's pain and damnation lies in his obsession with the perversion of the Christian doctrine of love by the depraved human spirit. To him all human institutions, all classes, factions, and sects, are at work corrupting religion into an instrument of tyranny, self-aggrandizement, and torment.

Melmoth the Wanderer's structure—a system of interpolated tales nested one within another like the boxes of a child's toy—is a conscious artistic device which serves several important functions. The tales are analogous in theme and pattern of action: each deals in differing terms with social or religious sadism. More important, the succession of narrative interpolations leads the reader, in the **"Tale of the Indians,"** directly but subtly into the heart of the author's themes. Finally, the deliberate variation in point of view and the multiplicity of narrators protect the author, who had already suffered by a false identification with the blasphemous opinions of his characters, from the pious reader's imputation of heterodoxy.

The nested tales, which serve to organize the novel around implicit analogies of character and action, are partially linked by a fairly consistent strain of imagery. Wherever the reader turns in *Melmoth,* he is confronted by some new variety of religious perversity, economic injustice, or political or social despotism. An omniscient third-person narrator's account of young John Melmoth's return to the deathbed of his miserly uncle gives way quickly to Biddy Brannigan's account of the Melmoth family's complicity in Cromwell's pitiless reduction of Ireland during the English civil wars and in the ruthless expropriation of Irish Catholics' lands by ambitious Roundheads. She also tells him the strange tale of an immortally young ancestor, the Wanderer. Thus from the beginning Melmoth is closely linked to the interrelated evils of sect and faction, and their exploitation by greedy and ambitious men. The next phase of the narration, the tale of Stanton, a Restoration Englishman whose story survives in a crumbling manuscript, carries these themes farther—in the character of a corrupt inquisitorial priest who has arrogated to himself the divine power of identifying evil, in the ironic contrast between the statue of a compassionate Virgin and a tapestry which depicts the cruelties practiced upon infidel Moors by a savage Christianity, and in the story of Stanton's unjust confinement in Bedlam by a greedy relative.

In Stanton's tale a paradigm of the action and religious theme is provided by the Bedlam sequence, a "nightmare" symbol-

ization of the insanity of factional and sectarian fanaticism that has turned the Christian world into a madhouse. . . . [This sequence] depicts the normal world of sectarian and factional violence as insane, and suggests the sense of horrified entrapment felt by a "mere honest man" in a world gone mad.

A brief return to an omniscient point of view allows Maturin to introduce Alonzo Monçada's autobiography, the **"Tale of the Spaniard,"** which from that point on provides the narrative framework for all but the last few pages of the novel. In Monçada's story the author continues to explore the corruption of Christian civilization; but now the object of attack has shifted to the sadism and masochism of Catholic institutional practices, a very common theme in the Gothic novel. . . . Of first importance is the implicit identification of Monçada's reactions to an enforced conventual life with Stanton's response to his confinement in Bedlam. The entrapment created by greed and the thirst for power in both secular and ecclesiastical society gives rise to insanity, perversion, and cruelty. The vision of a world imprisoned by the savage restraints of the old order is here again presented to the reader's gaze.

Maturin's condemnation of Catholic authoritarianism centers on what the author saw as universal Christian failings: unnatural restraints and self-discipline, vulnerable isolation from reality, narrow sectarian emphasis on minor doctrinal differences, and rigorous insistence on conformity to arbitrary norms of behavior. The effects of these evils lie in the suppression of the free play of the natural affections and the consequent blossoming of those vices whch another, later Gothic writer [Charles Baudelaire] was to call "les fleurs du mal" [the flowers of evil].

The parricide monk, narrator of a tale interpolated in Monçada's story, epitomizes the psychological damage resulting from ecclesiastical despotism in his sadism, his nihilism, his hypocrisy, and his complex hatred of the faith of others. Indeed the plot against Alonzo in which the parricide monk figures so prominently is itself the height of exquisite sadism in its cruel encouragement and unexpected frustration of Monçada's hope of freedom. Melmoth's presence as a member of the Inquisition sitting in judgment on Monçada indicates the perverse enjoyment of others' torment bred by a religious system based on the exaltation of suffering. And the parricide's murder at the hands of a mob prophesies the fate of an oppressively authoritarian religion and government before the pent-up outrage of a victimized populace.

Having escaped the terrors of the Inquisition and the temptation of Melmoth, Monçada finds refuge in the vaults of the Jew Adonijah, whose gentleness and compassion contrast ironically with a Christianity committed to his conversion by the sword. But the significance of this episode derives from the structural and thematic implications of the series of interpolated tales inside of the old patriarch's manuscript story of Immalee, itself a tale interpolated in Monçada's biography; for here are embodied all the narrative's motifs up to this point in a form that indicates their complex interrelationships.

The most famous and generally admired of these interpolated stories is the **"Tale of the Indians,"** relating the tragic love affair of Immalee and Melmoth, in which the issues of the entire novel are generalized and summarized and the character of Melmoth is most fully developed into symbol. In its broad outlines the story of Immalee's love for the doomed and depraved Wanderer is a tragic allegory of Christian history. A religion of love and compassion, represented by Immalee's innocent benevolence and by the selfless charity of her love for Melmoth, supplants an ancient and sadistic worship of Shiva, a deity who indirectly suggests the character of the Old Testament Jehovah. Immalee, isolated since infancy from the corrupting influences of civilized institutions, gives promise of redeeming the depraved human spirit of her tempter, Melmoth, whose evil consists in his cynical despair of human love and compassion. Ironically, this despair is the product of the very knowledge he had sold his soul to gain. The temptation he offers the girl is her infection with his own despair before the spectacle of the universal perversion of devotion into sadism. Displaying to Immalee a long perspective of the cruelty which has characterized the religious history of man, he follows it with a catalogue of the alternative compassionate ideals of Christianity, a vision which contrasts bitterly with the reality of this faith as pictured in earlier pages of the novel. To this nightmare of torment Melmoth adds an equally depressing survey of secular wrong: the colonial exploitation of subject peoples, the corruptions of urban life, economic and legal injustice, the tyranny of kings and oligarchs—all miseries of human invention piled atop the natural evils of disease, famine, and catastrophe to which mortal flesh is doomed.

When Immalee responds compassionately and without despair—and with growing love for the man she knows to be the worst of sinners—she opens for him the possibility of his redemption through belief in the reality of disinterested love. The Wanderer sets before us the image of theological despair: obsessed with the perversion of worship into an instrument of suffering, he is blinded to the vision of an ultimate, indestructible spiritual order and providence. Immalee (hardly a noble savage or a representative of natural goodness) is the living presence of the undefiled religious impulse in mankind. Melmoth's despair prompts the bargain he offers those brought to the verge of his own insane desperation by corrupt humanity. The bargain itself is their renunciation of belief in any ultimate moral order, their acceptance of the despairing madness which is Melmoth's torment and damnation. The relief the Wanderer seeks is the conquest of his hopelessness; and Immalee's essentially Christian love comes close to redeeming him.

Immalee's return to civilized Christian society foredooms the possibility of Melmoth's redemption. The combined forces of her mercenary father, her stupid and bigoted mother, her socially ambitious bourgeois brother, and a worldly priest destroy her marriage to Melmoth, the child born of their union, and Immalee herself—just as the linked powers of mercantile greed, aristocratic and middle-class rigidity, and sectarian corruption destroy the hope that the Christian spirit holds out to suffering mankind. The **"Tale of Guzman's Family"** and the **"Tale of the Lovers,"** which are introduced into the central narrative of Immalee and Melmoth, repeat this theme in different milieux, and prefigure the issue of the story of the girl and her demon lover.

The tragic irony in *Melmoth the Wanderer* as in Marlowe's *Faustus* arises from the fact that the protagonist is damned by his own inability to perceive the existence of ultimate goodness which is manifest all about him. Submerged in and by his own despair, Melmoth cannot see the little good that redeems all in the unselfish love of Walberg, Elinor, and Immalee and in the moral order implied by their unshaken faith. It is at once Melmoth's torment and the motive of his sadism that he cannot bring himself to believe in the ultimate reality of love's regenerative power, so obsessed is he by his vision of human perversion, so blinded by the glare of needless human suffering. It is indeed a madhouse world that Maturin projects, but the greatest insanity of all is Melmoth's despair of it.

Maturin's grand and melancholy theme achieves its final, compelling statement in the involuted narratives of Monçada, Immalee, the Walbergs, and the Mortimers; his protagonist's damnation comes with melodramatic swiftness and the novel ends upon a note of "wild surmise." In *Melmoth the Wanderer,* the Gothic mummery of the horror novel was brought to serve the uses of a profoundly tragic religious parable, the highest artistic achievement of the genre. In some sense a lost soul himself, Maturin, we may hope, has found at least a modest immortality in *Melmoth*'s fame. (pp. xiv-xviii)

> *William F. Axton, in an introduction to* Melmoth the Wanderer *by Charles Robert Maturin (reprinted by permission of University of Nebraska Press; © 1961 by the University of Nebraska Press), University of Nebraska Press, 1961, pp. vii-xviii.*

DOUGLAS GRANT (essay date 1968)

Maturin was at his weakest in narrative. Whether the action takes place in the south of Italy, or in the west of Ireland (the scenes of his first and two succeeding novels respectively), the sequence of events is equally confused, and must be followed with uncritical determination. The interest of the books lies not in the action, but in emotions and their effects upon personality. (pp. viii-ix)

Maturin's obsession with violent emotion is romantic, speaking generally; Byronic, referring to character. When Thomas Moore was attempting to explain the relation of Byron to the spirit of the age, at the time of the publication of the first cantos of *Childe Harold* (in 1812, the same year as the appearance of *The Milesian Chief*), he observed acutely that while it might be an exaggeration to claim that Byron was 'as much the child and representative of the Revolution, in poesy, as another great man of the age, Napoleon, was in statesmanship and warfare', it would have to be conceded that 'the free loose which had been given to all the passions and energies of the human mind, in the great struggle of that period, together with the constant spectacle of such astounding vicissitudes as were passing, almost daily, on the theatre of the world, had created in all minds, and in every walk of intellect, a taste for strong excitement, which the stimulants supplied from ordinary sources were insufficient to gratify'. Maturin reflected these forces as much as Byron, and Bryon himself recognized their kinship with each other. (p. ix)

None of Maturin's characters, not even Bertram, expressed the 'passions and energies' of the age in the way that Childe Harold characterized them; and if Maturin had died . . . after the appearance of *Women,* he would have been remembered as a talented but incoherent writer at the best, with one lucky success on the stage to his credit. But in *Melmoth the Wanderer,* written when his fortunes were in steady decline, if not yet at the bottom, he created a character that was to rival Childe Harold in significance, if not in popularity—Melmoth the Wanderer, a most 'Byronic' figure; a damned and fiery intelligence; the eternal outcast. (pp. ix-x)

Each of Melmoth's attempts to shift his burden on to someone else makes a separate story; a casual arrangement, which saves Maturin from exposing his weakness in the handling of plot. . . . The stories are in themselves generally clear enough and, once the governing idea is understood, the connection between them, however arbitrary, is at least acceptable. But the real interest of the book lies in the relations of Melmoth himself and his victims. 'Anything of intense and terrible resolution,' it is said about Melmoth, '—of feeling or action in extremity,—made harmony with the powerful but disordered chords of his soul.' He seeks out opportunities to gratify his craving for excitement and traps his victims where he can study them more fully, whether within the walls of a madhouse, or the confines of a monastery, or the conventions of a family, or within those mere cruel, insubstantial cells of hope and fear and innocence.

Maturin is a brilliant psychologist of the perverse. The monastery in which Alonzo Monçada is immured, in the longest of the stories, may seem the projection of a Protestant imagination tantalizing itself with scarlet notions of Rome, rather than a realistic description of a religious house, but Monçada's sickening persecution by his fellow monks, which is carried to criminal extremes, and the extravagant attempts of his younger brother Juan, his *alter ego,* to liberate him are coherent and compulsive. A reader does not easily forget Monçada's journey through the labyrinthine, narrowing subterranean passages, with a parricide monk as guide, to its despairing conclusion. The more delicious persecution of Immalee (or Isidora, as she is called on her return to Spain) probes the sexual fantasies that were to engage many of the later romantics, especially Edgar Allan Poe. . . . We are always aware in *Melmoth the Wanderer* that if it belongs to the Gothic novel of the past—to the world of Ann Radcliffe and 'Monk' Lewis—it anticipates the psychological, metaphysical novel of the future. Dostoevsky and Kafka are low on the horizon, in the ascendant. (pp. x-xi)

[*Melmoth the Wanderer* is] of its time in being a local and historical as well as a Gothic novel. The opening scenes on the west coast of Ireland are among the most interesting in the book, in their details of life and customs in those outlandish parts; and though it may appear at first that Maturin was prompted to take an interest in local colour by the example of Maria Edgeworth and Walter Scott, it is worth noticing in defence of his originality, that while he was clearly indebted to Miss Edgeworth, whose *Castle Rackrent* appeared in 1800, his own *The Wild Irish Boy* preceded the earliest of Scott's novels by several years. As a historical novelist concerned with the events of the seventeenth century, Maturin must be numbered among the legion inspired by Scott; but in his choice of period he again anticipated Scott, who had not yet turned his attention directly to the seventeenth century in England. . . . Maturin often seems, in his hesitant originality, to resemble the prospector who strikes a lode but fails to follow it to its wealthy conclusion.

Maturin criticized his early novels as lacking in reality [see excerpt above, 1818], and *Melmoth the Wanderer* itself would have to be classed as fantastic rather than realistic if it were to be judged by its settings—a madhouse on the outskirts of seventeenth-century London, the cells of the Spanish Inquisition, an isle in the Indian Ocean. But the ideological and political unrest of the Commonwealth seemed to Maturin's contemporaries to anticipate their own revolutionary era; the factious turmoil in devastated Spain, which had inspired Goya's terrible etchings, illustrated in its most extreme form the political and moral instability that followed upon the Napoleonic wars; and the satanic review of the gruesome religious customs of India reflected the age's fascination with the exotic and remote. As an Irishman, Maturin knew the cruel effects of religious bigotry and political intolerance and, in the footnotes in which he remarks on recent brutalities in Ireland, he betrays the domestic origin of his obsessions. The temper of *Melmoth the Wanderer* is violent and modern: the world of the midnight arrest, the trumped-up charge, the third degree, and the concentration camp waits darkly upon revelation.

Maturin is a careless, but a fine writer. He has particularly a strong sense of pictorial effects and many of his scenes resemble pictures in their deliberate composition—especially and significantly those of Fuseli, a fellow master of the outrageous and macabre. Lady Montrevor, in *The Wild Irish Boy,* directly recalls the artist when she exclaims: 'I saw your father—saw him with that cruel smile which I yet see, and which you may see any day in Fuseli's picture of the serpent and Eve.' He can use a telling detail, based upon close observation. When Old Melmoth lies dying at the beginning of the story, it is noted that his hands 'lay extended on the bed like the claws of some bird that had died of hunger,—so meagre, so yellow, so spread'.

Maturin is often too lushly poetical in his descriptions, a common fault in the prose of the time, but he can capture, admirably and frighteningly, moments of intense fear and despair. The scene where the parricide monk is torn to pieces by the mob and Monçada, who is viewing and involuntarily participating in the grisly scene from his place of hiding, betrays himself to the searching gaze of Melmoth is an instance of his power. (Significantly, the scene is inspired by reminiscences of street violence in Dublin.) Maturin also excels in rhetoric, as one would expect from an accomplished and popular preacher, and the character of Melmoth stands out convincingly because his speeches ring true, whatever their exaggerations and incoherencies, and make his motives comprehensible. . . . (pp. xii-xiii)

> *Douglas Grant, "Introduction" (introduction, notes, select bibliography, and chronology © Oxford University Press 1968; reprinted by permission of Oxford University Press), in* Melmoth the Wanderer: A Tale *by Charles Robert Maturin, edited by Douglas Grant, Oxford University Press, London, 1968, pp. vii-xiv.*

FRANCIS RUSSELL HART (essay date 1968)

The experience of the enlightened person feeling haunted by some demonic self: this is the center of [Gothic] fiction. What manner of being is this? (p. 94)

The central question [exists] in Maturin's *Melmoth the Wanderer.* This seemingly immortal wanderer who offers earthly sufferers release in return for their souls—is he demon or man? is he really different from other men? The prisoner Stanton, the victim of avaricious relatives, accosts his tempter with "You, demon!" Melmoth's answer is a recurrent theme: "Demon!—Harsh words!—Was it a demon or a human being placed you here?" Other sufferers in the book are thrilled with the horrible suspicion that they are tormented by demons; Melmoth wrestles with the knowledge that he is *possessed* by one—a "demon of superhuman misanthropy"—and counters with the terrible possibility that all men are—or can be—agents of the devil, demonic at their most noble, demonic for those they love most. (pp. 95-6)

In Melmoth's case, the psychologizing is . . . undeniable. For his world Melmoth has become an inscrutable being of supernatural powers, eternally roaming the earth. But his habitat is graphically localized first and last in rural Ireland; . . . he is a "Cain of the moral world"—we would say a Cain psychologized. He has entered the realm of myth; he has become a legendary scourge, a reality remote from human imagining, yet it is to his humanizing, his de-mythologizing, that we attend throughout. Far from seeing character transformed into symbol or myth, we see myth psychologized into explicable character. From within we see the natural humanity of Melmoth striving to liberate itself from its fated demonic role: "with all his diabolical heartlessness, he *did* feel some relentings of his human nature"; but alas! "the habitual character of his dark and fiendish pursuit, rushed back on him." It is the distinction of [Matthew Lewis's] *The Monk* over again: nature struggles with the artificial but "habitual character" affixed by his demonic role. In his full humanity, Melmoth is pathetically aware of the struggle. He marvels in horror at the "demoniacal character" he has acquired: "the world could show him no greater marvel than his own existence." But it is no marvel of a Faustian folk superstition; his diabolism, he well knows, is of another kind, and to those who look upon him with naïve superstition his enlightened answer is the book's reiterated theme. Diabolism is in every man:

> I tell you, whenever you indulged one brutal passion, one sordid desire, one impure imagination—whenever you uttered one word that wrung the heart, or embittered the spirit of your fellow creature . . . whenever you have done this, you have been ten times more an agent of the enemy of man than all the wretches whom terror, enfeebled nerves, or visionary credulity, has forced into the confession of an incredible compact with the author of evil.

His demonism, he insists, is inseparable from the humanity of an explicable natural world—and we believe him because his own human torments are fully analyzed before our eyes. The "Cain," the figure of Faustian legend, is transformed into a character in a novel, and demands appropriate credence. (pp. 101-02)

> *Francis Russell Hart, "The Experience of Character in the English Gothic Novel," in* Experience in the Novel: Selected Papers from the English Institute, *edited by Roy Harvey Pearce (copyright © 1968 Columbia University Press; reprinted by permission of the publisher), Columbia University Press, 1968, pp. 83-105.**

ROBERT KIELY (essay date 1972)

[*Like William F. Axton (1961), Kiely distinguishes* Melmoth *from earlier Gothic novels because of its depiction of the repressive practices of the Roman Catholic church and authoritarian political systems. Kiely, however, views* Melmoth *as important primarily for its explorations into "the dark side of the human mind." He asserts that the separate tales in* Melmoth *are united by the theme of human misery and that Maturin's examination of the effects of pain on the human personality "illustrates a whole phase of romantic psychology and the creative process."*]

[*Melmoth the Wanderer*'s] thematic and stylistic links with Walpole, Radcliffe, and Lewis are not difficult to see, yet it is a wilder, more complicated, and, in many ways, a more daring work than most of its predecessors. In the first place, it is one of the rare works of Gothic fiction which dwells on the trappings of religion and is at the same time informed by a deep religious feeling. Living in southern Ireland as a Protestant minister, Charles Robert Maturin had a stronger and more lively emotional involvement with—if not a clearer understanding of—Roman Catholicism than did those English writers for whom "abbey" meant an ivy-covered ruin. Most of the properties of earlier Gothic fiction—the narrow cells, the dark cowls, the labyrinthine vaults—remain, but the attitude expressed toward them has little of antiquarian fondness or hesitant irony about it. On one level, *Melmoth the Wanderer*

is a belated work of the Reformation, a roar of outrage against the bigotry, superstition, sadism, and hypocrisy which had infested the Roman Church.

Secondly, there is a good deal more authentic republican spirit in Maturin's novel than in those of many of his predecessors despite their conventional odes to liberty and denunciations of despotic rule. There is a genuine distaste for authoritarian political systems, especially as they are linked with religious tyranny, and an insistence upon the right of the individual to determine his destiny on earth as well as to make his appeals to God without priestly interference. (pp. 189-90)

But however serious the religious and political levels of the book may be, *Melmoth the Wanderer* has as its main subject the dark side of the human mind. . . . [Like Lewis, Maturin] was fascinated by extremes of freedom and repression and the various kinds of anguish which they caused body and mind. But even more than was the case for Lewis . . . , painful subjects seemed to have stimulated [Maturin's] imagination into an extraordinary state of productivity. According to one of his own characters, "in situations of peril, the imagination is unhappily fertile." This seems to have been true of Maturin's imagination, which initiates "peril" and then divides and multiplies it like a Shakespearian pun. The structure of *Melmoth the Wanderer,* a series of narrations within narrations—often compared with a nest of Chinese boxes—defies conventional chronological sequence and replaces it with obsessive variations on the single theme of human misery. It is like a gruesome contest among the suffering to tell the worst tale of woe. Though the speakers are different, their narratives are given unity by a common pattern of torment and by the presence of the wraith-like Melmoth, who usually enters at a critical moment to tempt the sufferer into despair.

Though none of the main characters does yield to despair, almost all seem to enjoy lingering close to the edge and analyzing the various moods, emotions, and thoughts produced by enduring the nearly unendurable. While Maturin has his narrators discuss the effects of pain on the human personality, he implicitly suggests much about its uses as a subject for the artist. One of the points first and most often made is that extreme suffering reduces human nature to its essential character, undisguised by artifice and convention. . . . [That] pain provides a release from conventional life [Maturin] appears to acknowledge. It frees the artist from having to portray his characters in terms of their orientation to external custom, but it challenges him too, because it tests whether or not he has the power to portray anything else. (pp. 190-91)

Again and again, Maturin brings his characters into focus by showing them in an almost bestial state. And, in so doing, he not only separates them from social convention and abstract concepts, like the soul, but he shows them in a moment of intense and undivided vitality. For the artist, then, pain becomes an instrument by which life at an uncomplicated but nonetheless real level can be reached. The creature which the romantic novelist wanted to reach was the one who reacts to sight and sound and touch before it reacts to reason and custom. If Maturin assumed that it existed somewhere in everyone, it also seemed to him, writing in the second decade of the nineteenth century, that only a very sharp edge would bring it out.

But Maturin was not a romantic primitivist nor a mere sadist content to reduce his characters to palpitating flesh. The emergence of the purely physical character, like the shattering of conventions, is a preparatory phase in the experiment with pain.

As the victim's suffering is prolonged, he becomes, once again, a thinking and complicated being, but his mind is no longer a register filled with approved and familiar ideas, but a new world shaped by and shaping the misery it encounters. As he traces in each of the narratives the history of a mind newly made by misery, Maturin illustrates a whole phase of romantic psychology and the creative process. After being forced into a state of keen sensuous awareness, the victim begins to defend himself from the full impact of the painful stimulus by automatically breaking it down into minute details. He thus becomes a sharp if not rationally selective observer, giving emphasis to particles not because of their relevance to a preconceived pattern, but because of their physical proximity to him at a certain moment and in a certain place. (pp. 192-93)

By means of first person narratives, Maturin attempts to explore the minds of his victimized characters, tracing their course from a state of physical sensation, to a keen but highly subjective observation of detail, to an increasingly distorted sense of external reality, and finally to a point of inventiveness which recreates an imaginary world more distinct and affective than the world of objective reality. Shut away from the light of day and the routine of men, Monçada tries to invent his own time in order to escape the seemingly eternal blankness of his confinement:

> So I sat and counted sixty; a doubt always occurred to me, that I was counting them faster than the clock. Then I wished to be the clock that I might have no feeling, no motive for hurrying on the approach of time. Then I reckoned slower.

Monçada's problem is the opposite of that of the dying old monk who compares himself with a clock. Confined and suffering, even on the verge of lunacy, Monçada is the least mechanical of beings, sharply aware of himself, all the more painfully human in his incapacity to attain mathematical regularity. Through the perceptions of his imprisoned, isolated, or exiled narrators—as well as by means of the peculiar structure of the whole novel—Maturin unhinges fiction from clock and calendar chronology and makes time another projection of the individual imagination. (pp. 193-94)

In terms of physical action, **Melmoth the Wanderer** is a surprisingly static novel, though it gives an impression of continuous and frantic movement. One character is trapped in a madhouse, another in a monastery, another left ashore on an uninhabited island. A Protestant family is immobilized by poverty, religion and language in Spain; an orphaned English girl lives a life of quiet retirement in a country castle. There are, of course, attempts at escape, but it is perfectly true that chronological time has almost stopped for most of these characters and has given way to the less regular, more interesting rhythm of their emotions and imaginings. One character might be speaking for all when he explains that "events which would make a life-lasting impression on others, pass like shadows before me, while thoughts appear like substances. *Emotions are my events*." And it is just at this point in the victim's suffering, physically immobilized but mentally and emotionally excited, that he becomes inventive, even artistic, spinning out anecdotes, constructing scenery, describing gestures, remembering the past, anticipating the future, giving shape even to darkness.

For Maturin, as for Lewis, the artist is associated with the victim who unexpectedly finds himself inflicting confinement

and deprivation on others. He sacrifices physical movement in time to the intense emotion of a moment. (p. 194)

As one who imposes his own limits on the fluidity of life, the artist is, in Maturin's view, like an agent of death. Moreover, when the artist is most nearly the pure aesthetician—concerned with his response to composition, color, shape—he is least the compassionate man who is able to enter into the joys and sufferings of those he observes. However much they may have suffered themselves, Maturin's narrators can rarely resist expressing the peculiar aesthetic pleasure derived from watching the suffering of others. For all but the most depraved, this is not a prolonged form of sadism, but a momentary response usually followed by an onrush of sympathy and occasionally an attempt to be of help. Yet the instant exists when emotion has no moral consequence, but is an artistic medium which traces the outline of beauty. Beautiful objects, in the world of Maturin, do not derive their beauty primarily from proportion but from their strange milieu. They are the early buds of *les fleurs du mal* [the flowers of evil], forms emerging from or receding into darkness and filth.

Beauty is best recognized when placed against that which it is not. Thus the painters Maturin invokes are those best known for their treatment of light and shade, and the scenes during which he calls them forth are often the most gruesome or melancholy in the book. A novice tormented by his superiors provides Monçada with a typical analogy:

> I turned, and saw a group worthy of Murillo. A more perfect human form never existed than that of this unfortunate youth. He stood in an attitude of despair—he was streaming with blood. The monks with their lights, their scourges, and their dark habits, seemed like a group of demons who had made prey of a wandering angel,—the group resembled the infernal furies pursuing a mad Orestes. And, indeed, no ancient sculptor ever designed a figure more exquisite and perfect than they had so barbarously mangled.

It is obvious that Maturin is writing about and repudiating the perversion of human feelings in the name of religion. What complicates the scene is that the narrator relishes, with an artist's eye, precisely what the monks seem to enjoy doing to the beautiful novice. . . . As artist, the speaker is with the victimizers, even if, as moralist, he disapproves of them. Maturin demonstrates how moments of vivid pleasure mixed with pain can explode in lives of habitual repression. But who, one might ask, has been repressed and who is supposed to be pleased? Heterosexuality is treated as repressively in the novel as homosexuality. In fact, most sensual pleasure is shown somehow as blighted or obscured, not merely transient but inhibited and damaged at the core.

Maturin blames much repression on particular religious and political institutions, but a distrust of the senses seems to be so deeply rooted in his own mind as to color his entire concept of beauty. (pp. 194-96)

Maturin takes it for granted that some pleasures—perhaps the deepest sort—can be experienced only if the senses are curbed. The feeling of mystery, the straining to see what cannot be fully seen, contribute to the "power" of the moment. The island nearly overwhelmed by darkness or the flesh struggling against the inhibitions of the mind suggest the conditions of a peculiar beauty. Hence, one kind of "realistic" artist must dwell on that which his eye can never fully illuminate. (p. 196)

Beauty becomes, then, an unfulfilled promise, a hint of something beyond man's power to embody or the artist's power to convey. In most of the "picturesque" scenes in the novel, the characters portrayed are literally threatened by death as well as half-obscured by shadow; the central figures are what Maturin calls "heroes of submission," shown in helpless confrontation with a force stronger than they.

Maturin's carefully grouped portraits are not the mere whims of a warped aesthete, but a romantic vision of man's fallen state as emblemized by his incapacity to maintain stability and proportion in a life encircled by pain and death. If Maturin created new images of beauty in his dark art, they were images created in sorrow and longing for a beauty classically defined; an ideal lost, not rejected.

There is never any serious doubt in Maturin's works that the highly subjective and inventive state of mind brought about by extreme suffering is a form of insanity. Maturin projects, in the phrase of William F. Axton, a "madhouse world," and he knows it. In *Bertram,* Imogine nearly goes mad by closing her senses to immediate reality and indulging her mind with images of her absent lover. . . . Such madness may have its own compensations, even its own pleasures, but it is nonetheless a deviation from a remembered norm, a state of being in which man could still reach outside himself for communication, balance, support. The lovely Imalee [in *Melmoth the Wanderer*], living alone on a tropical island, with only the trees and birds as friends, embodies life in perfect harmony with Edenic nature. . . . But Maturin's other characters, having been deprived of innocent nature by original sin and alienated from one another by the corruptions of civilization, spin myths in their isolation, tell incoherent tales nourished by imperfect memory, myopic vision, and a sensation of chronic pain. The novelist who writes of misery in fragmented episodes, like the artist who paints figures half-swallowed by shadow, is not on a romantic holiday from classical restraint. He sees himself in the same dilemma as his subjects, confronted by a hostile obscurity which he has not the vision to penetrate or the power to change. (pp. 197-98)

Maturin, the Christian minister, provides narrative within narrative, layer within layer, probing always deeper and deeper, and coming up with a rearrangement of the same basic phenomena: isolation, the brief pain of knowledge, and the long, long madness which separates memory from oblivion. The lesson he tries to teach—which is not to despair—is all the more moving because his vision of man and nature gives so much to despair about. Maturin's Christian hope in God's mercy is shaped and intensified by his Calvinistic disbelief in man's ability to help himself. The most positive thing one can do is to keep faith in the Lord. That is the way to avoid ultimate despair, but it is based upon an attitude toward man and nature which leaves hope nowhere to go but heavenward.

Along with his institutional quarrel with Roman Catholicism, Maturin had serious theological objections to what he considered the Church's cavalier attitude toward human nature and especially its insistence on man's ability to participate, through good works, in his own redemption. *Melmoth the Wanderer* is filled with satirical jibes at the Catholic preoccupation with active charity and the competitive means by which Catholics try to attain heaven. Priests and pious ladies compare the wretchedness of the beggars they have helped and keep count of the sick they have visited. Maturin's point—certainly a familiar Protestant one—is that, even in his acts of apparent charity, man shows himself to be a corrupt creature motivated by self-interest.

The reformist's wish for a purging of worldly distractions is one of the controlling ideas of the novel. When the innocent Imalee comes to Spain from her tropical island, she speaks of hearing of a religion "so beautiful and pure" that in a Christian land she expected to find all Christians and was disappointed instead to find "only Catholics." Her idea of perfection is Christian virtue practiced in a natural, uncivilized setting like that of her island. The world of Catholic Spain is all restraint and contortion, "intelligence and luxury," while her natural paradise with its shores of "beauty and blessedness," is a place where birds fly freely and do not "break their bills against gilded wires."

If the scenes of monastery life narrated by Monçada show the perversity of Catholic asceticism, the long section in the Spanish household of Imalee's (Isadora's) parents demonstrates the hypocrisy of Catholic worldliness. Some of Maturin's best satire is directed against Imalee's mother, Donna Clara, who can shift her attention from a fine point of conscience to the dressing of her hair without a pause:

> She [would] fret about the family clock not chiming synchronically with the bells of the neighboring church where she performed her devotions . . . She fretted about everything, from the fattening of the 'pullen,' and the preparation for the olio, up to the increasing feuds between the Molinists and Jansenists . . . and the deadly dispute between the Dominican and Franciscan orders, relative to the habit in which it was most effective to salvation for the dying body of the sinner to be wrapped. So between her kitchen and her oratory,—her prayers to the saints, and her scoldings to her servants,—her devotion and her anger,—Donna Clara continued to keep herself and domestics in a perpetual state of interesting occupation and gentle excitement.

One can imagine the benevolent gusto with which Chaucer might have drawn such a character, or the stinging wit with which Pope would have coupled these incongruities. In the context of *Melmoth the Wanderer,* however, there is no gusto, and wit quickly gives way to wrath. The elements of this portrait are shown to be the vicious traits of a self-indulgent, superstitious, and arrogant bigot who disgusts the artist who has created her. For Maturin, the oratory and the kitchen do not belong together, and to mingle them in one's thoughts is not merely silly but sinful. In fact, man's tendency to think so much of things—whether food or shrouds—diverts him from the one true object of hope, the spirit of God.

Despite Imalee's dreams of a natural, almost primitive, Christianity, most of the evidence in *Melmoth the Wanderer* suggests that Maturin found the natural world as much of an obstacle to salvation as man's fallen human nature. Storms, lightning blasts, turbulent seas, and black nights may force man to turn in fear to God, but they are hardly the emanations of his benevolent power or the direct channels through which he may be reached. God is not in nature, he provides an alternative to it. (pp. 204-06)

[Goodness] is defined by Maturin in an almost totally negative way as that which is purified of physical life. . . . It follows that God would be conceived of as purity itself, an alternative to man just as he is an alternative to nature. The Incarnation, with its insistence on flesh and blood, must have been unpalatable to Maturin since he often writes as though it never occurred. His characteristic image of God is not the loving Christ, the son and brother of man, but "the great Contriver." Despite his earnest and holy war against despair, Maturin's peculiar combination of Calvinism and Deism is very like a religious system which undoes the work of the Nativity. It places man beneath contempt and God beyond human reach. (pp. 206-07)

The reader of *Melmoth the Wanderer* is witness to a tormented debate which seems to be taking place across a canyon. Empty space absorbs arguments and images before they ever reach the other side. The worst of all possible worlds and the most barren of pure heavens drift together into coherence and . . . give equal cause to despair. (p. 207)

> Robert Kiely, "'Melmoth the Wanderer': Charles Robert Maturin," in his The Romantic Novel in England (copyright © 1972 by the President and Fellows of Harvard College; excerpted by permission), Cambridge, Mass.: Harvard University Press, 1972, pp. 189-207.

ROBERT E. LOUGY (essay date 1975)

[*In his detailed survey of Maturin's works, Lougy concentrates on several recurring motifs in Maturin's writings, including the Wandering Jew and Faust legends, the psychology of evil, religious fanaticism, sexual repression, homosexual love, and Irish nationalism. According to Lougy, "Maturin's fascination with the unknown and taboo realms of human experience" resulted in a tension between his artistic vision and his clerical profession, which is "most apparent in the incongruity that often appears between the professed moral purpose of his writings and the writings themselves."*]

The plot is one of the weaker aspects of *The Family of Montorio*. Maturin devotes two of the three volumes to developing the figure of Father Schemoli as a supernatural being, in commerce with diabolic agents and capable of transcending both space and time, and then in the third volume, attempts a naturalistic account of the deeds and powers he possesses. . . . [It] is inconceivable that a mere man could be in so many places at exactly the right time and wield such psychological and physical power as Father Schemoli; but by the third volume we have already accepted him in these terms and feel somewhat deceived when Maturin tries to explain away all of these superhuman qualities. In his later works, such as *Bertram* and *Melmoth*, Maturin allows the supernatural to remain unencumbered by rational and quasi-scientific explanations. But as a young clergyman writing his first novel, Maturin understandably did not want to stretch the unorthodox in the work any more than necessary.

The Family of Montorio is, when compared to works such as *Women* and *Melmoth*, clearly inferior in terms of design and conception of character; but it contains some powerful and imaginative writing, suggesting Maturin's latent genius, and also possesses most of the major themes that were to occupy Maturin throughout his literary career. Within it we also see how well acquainted Maturin was with the nature of the gothic world and the gothic landscape. . . . (pp. 17-18)

The landscape of *The Family of Montorio* is primarily psychological, one structured to enhance the moods of terror, fear,

and suspense. There is only a perfunctory attempt to depict topography realistically. There exists, in fact, a disproportionate relationship between the number of words expended to define the terrain and the imprecise and vague notion we have of it. But the landscape is for the most part an externalization of the inner conflict of the characters. It also functions—at times, in an almost mechanical fashion—to further advance and heighten the plot: oceans exist for the purpose of creating tidal waves and storms, mountains for showing the disastrous consequences of earthquakes, and rivers for flooding and for carrying the characters from one place to another.

Like the physical landscape, the psychological landscape—of which the former is often but a projection—is also of a circumscribed nature. Certain emotions such as laughter, light wit, tranquility, and simple contentment are outside such a world; emotions, like the violent natural elements, must themselves be strong, violent, and rending. Consequently, the dialogue becomes the vehicle of emotions of fear, passionate hate, equally passionate (though often passionless) love, and heartbreaking sorrow. People never just talk—they plead, coerce, bribe, threaten, adore, whisper, intimidate. In a novel filled with many strengths and the promise of even better writing to come, it is with dialogue that Maturin has the most trouble, especially when he is trying to convey the more tender emotions. In dialogue conveying hate, fear, contempt, Maturin is much stronger. (pp. 19-20)

In contrast to the lame prose we find in some of his dialogues, when he is describing the emotions of horror and fear and the realm of the unknown and supernatural that give rise to these emotions, his language is strong, fast-moving and imaginative. (p. 20)

One of the most vividly realized passages in the novel is that in which Father Schemoli tells Annibal that he, Father Schemoli, is the spirit of a man who has been dead for over twenty years. During his description of "death" and the descent into hell, we see evidence of an imaginative genius in Maturin, beside which the best that Radcliffe and Walpole can offer grows pale by comparison. . . . Irish literature had to wait for more than a hundred years, until Joyce's *Portrait of the Artist as a Young Man*, before another writer would equal in vividness and grotesqueness Maturin's imaginative rendering of the horrors of Hell. (pp. 20-1)

In his first novel Maturin tentatively develops several motifs that become the major focal points of his later work. The first, for which he is perhaps most famous, is the theme of the Wandering Jew, the man separated either because of a great crime or great guilt from the rest of mankind. . . . [Not until *Melmoth*] does Maturin elevate such a figure into the realm of myth and symbol, but in *Montorio* he clearly has the possibilities of such a character in mind, for Father Schemoli himself is the classic example of such a figure, a predecessor of Melmoth the Wanderer. And as in the case of Melmoth, we see in Schemoli Maturin's wedding together of two legends, that of the Wandering Jew and that of Faust—a man cut off and elevated above mankind by virtue of a knowledge forbidden to ordinary men, a knowledge that is the source of his great power, his great suffering, and his violent end. But Maturin also provides an ironic twist to these legends in that Schemoli and Melmoth are destroyed as much by ignorance as by excessive knowledge.

The final motif in *Montorio* is that of sexual repression and sublimation manifested in religious fanaticism, in erotic fanaticism, and in an excessively idealized concept of love. Such fanaticism, as Maturin sees it, results in cruelty and aggression, directed either toward others or toward oneself. This motif is the major theme of *Women: or Pour et Contre* and is significant in both *Melmoth* and Maturin's last novel, *The Albigenses*. As an Anglican minister, Maturin shared with others a fear of the Roman Catholic Church, viewing it as a bulwark of the reactionary political forces of the time. It is in part for this reason that his explorations of religious fanaticism often center on it; but in *Women: or Pour et Contre,* he is equally critical of Calvinistic Evangelicalism. In much of his fiction, women especially are victimized by a religious and social code that demands sexual repression since they, unlike men, did not have access to harlots and brothels for release of sexual passions. It is more than coincidental that several of Maturin's central male characters, for example Ippolito in *Montorio* and Ormsby Bethel in *The Wild Irish Boy,* find their way to gaming-houses or brothels during times of emotional anguish or turmoil. A good part of *Montorio* is devoted to the journal of a young woman, Rosolia di Valozzi, which is a fascinating study of the agonies of a young woman who discovers that the desires of her body and the nature of her dreams do not correspond to the idea of Love she has been taught. In her attempts to deny or repress these "wayward" feelings, she tries to divert her passions into a love for God and nature, and thus her religious poetry and descriptions of Nature consequently assume erotic overtones. (pp. 21-3)

[Unlike *Montorio, The Wild Irish Boy*] seems to have arisen less from Maturin's desire to explore human nature than from his wish to make money. . . . That rough and crude, but powerful genius that Sir Walter Scott recognized [see excerpt above, 1810] is almost smothered here by Maturin's attempt to satisfy the public's taste.

The hero of the novel is Ormsby Bethel, a young man of mysterious background and origin who only at the end of the novel is reunited with his father. In this respect, the novel is a *Bildungsroman* [a portrait of the youthful development of a central character], but the possibilities inherent in the story of a young man's quest for identity never materialize. Maturin rather clumsily handles the problem of point of view and never seems sure of the novel's thematic focus. (pp. 23-4)

But this is also the first novel where Maturin chooses Ireland and its people as his subjects. . . . The only character [however] who speaks anti-English sentiments is DeLacey, a rich, old Milesian, who is throughout the novel an admirable and noble man, but nevertheless an anachronism. He has some strong things to say about the treatment of Ireland by the English, "those who have desolated the country, and razed every mark of power or of resistance from the face of it. . . ."

Although it might seem reasonable to suppose that Maturin, an Irishman who strongly identified with Ireland's history and fate, harbored sentiments similar to those uttered by DeLacey, one has to remember that Maturin was also, of course, a Protestant minister and that he puts some glowing comments about the English in the mouth of Corbett, the novel's most favorable character, who "knew the liberal and public spirit of many of the English nobility" and that such men "were . . . intent on cultivating the morals and minds of the lower orders, and providing for the temporal and spiritual comforts of the poor. . . ." Maturin seems here to take with one hand what he has given with the other and consequently creates a kind of obsequious tone not at all flattering to himself. This may be in part due to fear of offending the very people he hoped would buy his

book; but it probably also arises from the simultaneous love and hate that he, like Yeats and Joyce, seemed to feel toward Ireland. (pp. 24-5)

A more interesting and important aspect of a novel that fails to face Ireland and its problems directly, is the relationship Maturin depicts between Ormsby and Lady Montrevor. . . . The love of a young man for an older married woman is not so unusual, and if this were the only aspect of the relationship Maturin had developed, it would need little commentary. But not only is Lady Montrevor considerably older than Ormsby; she is also a former love of his father and will, at the novel's conclusion, become Ormsby's stepmother. In light of Maturin's first novel, in which two sons kill a man they think is their own father, this relationship becomes even more interesting as another example of Maturin skirting the edge of areas of relationships that are a repressed part of the psychic life of man. In each case, however, Maturin employs a technique corresponding closely to what Freud in his discussion of dreams and art has called "displacement"—Maturin treats the theme of the desire of the son to kill his father and to sleep with his mother; in each case, much of the underlying resonance and strength of his novels arise from the presence of these themes, but because he cannot treat these matters directly, he displaces the father in his fiction by making him an uncle and the mother by making her unrelated by blood.

There are other examples of this technique. For example, in the relationship between Cyprian and Ippolito in *Montorio,* there are strong overtones of homosexuality. . . . The fact that, at the novel's conclusion, we learn that Cyprian is really Rosolia di Valozzi in disguise does not mitigate the homosexual overtones of the relationship. It is simply another version of the technique of displacement: depict homosexual love, but displace one of the males by a female. These incidents from Maturin's first two novels are too numerous to be simply coincidental. They are deliberately created, and all deal with taboos; in each case, either the revelation of true identity or a premature death extricated Maturin from having to fulfill the terms of the experiences he has presented. . . . In both the gothic and the taboo, Maturin deals with the twilight regions of human life, between waking and sleeping, between the conscious and unconscious. Both represent the demonic and the irrational, those repressed but real fascinations we feel toward horror and fear. (pp. 26-8)

To write as Maturin did was to indulge in what is pleasurable in so far as it stands opposed to the painful reality of the present moment, no matter how horrible or grotesque the indulgence's form might be. In Maturin's case, it assumes primarily the form of exploring those aspects of human life that were far outside his ordinary circles. And as Maturin's literary career progresses, we see this cycle in operation—an ever increasing fascination that must explore deeper and deeper into the "midnight darkness of the soul," until finally one wonders whether Maturin finds himself, in a work such as *Melmoth,* pulled asunder not only from religious excesses, but from the very concept of orthodox religion, whatever its form.

This tension between Maturin's artistic vision and his clerical profession appears in much of his writing. It is, perhaps, most apparent in the incongruity that often appears between the professed moral purpose of his writings and the writings themselves—between the didactic meanings imposed by Maturin the clergyman upon a work that cannot accommodate such a meaning. His imagination and fascinations seem too strongly impelled toward those very things which, if we are to accept the moral purpose of the work, we are to shun. Although *Montorio* has such a purpose, it is expressed in fairly broad terms; however, in *The Wild Irish Boy,* the moral or didactic purpose is explicitly that "the more terrible consequences of practical deviation may be inferred and deprecated from their display." Fortunately, Maturin himself seems to have forgotten this moral purpose for the most part. The real strength of this novel is seen when Maturin moves farthest away from the conventions of the sentimental romance and allows his imagination the freedom to roam uninhibited through scenes with a strange mixture of corruption and innocence, insanity and sanity, death and sexuality, lust and religion. These scenes are purely gratuitous, having no integral relationship to the main plot line, and function, like some of Maturin's interpolated tales and poems, to give vent to an aspect of his imagination that must have felt constrained by the didactic and the sentimental. (pp. 29-30)

[Not] only does *The Milesian Chief* represent Maturin's attempt to synthesize the strongest aspects of his first two novels; it also represents a further advancement of his style and technique in exploring what he calls "the obscure recesses of the human heart." In his first novel, Maturin used the conventions of a genre which, as he was later to admit [see excerpt above, 1818], had already passed its zenith. Although he returns to the gothic techniques again in works such as *Bertram* and, of course, *Melmoth,* he does so only after exploring in *The Milesian Chief* the possibilities of touching those realms of our psychic life most affected by the gothic genre without actually employing the machinery of the gothic. He still employs some of the devices of the gothic, but he consciously downplays such devices. . . . In *Montorio* he had explored the fears, anxieties, and desires of man as he projects them outside of him; he now turns to the source of the projections itself, a region "equally obscure," if not more so. (pp. 32-3)

If *The Milesian Chief* shares some aspects of plot and character in common with Maturin's first two novels, it is quite different in the use he makes of these similarities. First of all, it is much more successful in its discussion of Ireland and its people. Whereas in *The Wild Irish Boy* one has the feeling that the setting was for the most part tacked on to the plot line, in this novel both the historical and the geographical setting contribute to the novel's theme. . . . Maturin is one of the first writers to explore the nature of the contradiction between the stereotype Irishman—wild, hard-drinking, fun-loving—and the sorrow and poverty concealed by it.

Placing the action of the novel after the Rebellion of 1798, Maturin has the opportunity to deal directly with the political and social tensions of the time. In setting brother against brother, he tries to find a symbol to convey the nature of the conflicts created by civil war, and although Desmond and Connal never engage in direct combat, the dissension within the families that frequently exists in civil war is artistically realized by Maturin. Connal is the novel's most romantic figure and his exploits and his endurance sometimes go beyond credibility, yet Maturin clearly shows him to be as much a victim of time and circumstance as the rest of the novel's characters. (pp. 35-6)

Maturin creates in the two brothers potential figures of romance, but at the same time suggests the danger of allowing romantic illusion to gain control of one's vision. War in the abstract is heroic and noble; but in the concrete, it results in death, mutilation, and agony. Connal does not see war as heroic and ennobling, and he makes it clear that time and circumstance rather than personal inclination have made him a rebel. Maturin

develops this conflict within Connal in a decisive manner and shows considerable improvement in character development since *The Wild Irish Boy.* In Connal we also see the elaboration of one of Maturin's favorite themes—the danger of abstracting or idealizing virtues to such an extent that we use them to rationalize or conceal evil deeds and motives. One of the most fascinating aspects of Connal is his recognition of the disparity between words and the deeds we commit in their names and his simultaneous awareness that he must act, in spite of this recognition.

If patriotism and religion are often employed by the human mind to justify agony and pain on a grand scale, it is love that most often causes pain on the personal level. Maturin's treatment of love is one of his most interesting—and most enigmatic—aspects, primarily because one is never quite sure of his perspective toward his material. Sometimes he is clearly outside of and critical toward the relationships he depicts; at other times, he seems to participate in the very attitudes of which he has elsewhere shown the dangers. The character of Armida is perhaps the most clearly realized and developed in [*The Milesian Chief*]. Quite early, it is observed that "her talents are real, but her character is artificial." The rest of the novel is devoted to creating in her a woman who slowly and painfully realizes her true character through her love for Connal. She is one of Maturin's most beautifully drawn women and her courage, her resentments, her vacillations, and her gradual recognition of self come forth vividly.

However, other themes are responsible for the perplexity one feels when trying to discover a consistent pattern in Maturin's attitudes toward love. In so far as he shows both the destructive and the ennobling qualities of love, Maturin is within a tradition running from Plato to Shakespeare. But in order to understand why he so often views love as a force leading to death or insanity, we have to consider his strong Calvinistic leanings. . . . [His] scathing critique of the Calvinistic temperament in *Women* not withstanding, he maintains throughout his writings a strong Calvinistic outlook. The world for him is an abode that constantly tempts and threatens its inhabitants. Madness, sickness, and death seem to be its predominant characteristics, and happiness is most often a fleeting and transient gossamer that few succeed in capturing. Analogous to this world view is his vision of man aspiring to the spiritual and transcendent, whether through love or religion, yet forever victimized by a body filled with errant emotions and passions. (pp. 36-8)

Maturin frequently writes of the dangers of trying to sublimate or repress one's sexuality and of how fanaticism, cruelty, and loss of human feelings can result from such attempts; but at the same time, there is in his writings a strong fear of the body and disgust of sensuality. The love that humans, as opposed to angels, experience must necessarily involve the physical as well as the spiritual and this alone is enough to make love in Maturin's fiction inherently destructive. Men and women are doomed not by their faults and weaknesses so much as by the unavoidable fact that they are human. It is in this respect that Maturin seems closest to his contemporary, Lord Byron. In both, we see the affirmation of love's redemptive powers coupled with a sense that by falling in love one repeats man's original fall from paradise; in both we see an attraction and a repulsion by the human body. In Maturin the sensualist is barely held in check by the Calvinist, but the check is always there. (pp. 38-9)

Maturin's recurrent treatment of homosexual love can only partially be explained by his fascination with the unknown and taboo realms of human experience; he also uses homosexual love to explore the nature of heterosexual love. It is for him at once a more etherealized and transcendent love and also a love more filled with passion, guilt, and danger. In this respect, homosexual love is a surrogate for heterosexual love in the extreme. Maturin's fear of the body and of sexuality is, as it were, legitimized by locating the fear within a taboo topic. The homosexual love he depicts is a love that is always potential and never fulfilled, one more fraught with peril than the love between man and woman, but also one in which both internal and external pressures provide a check to prevent a complete commitment. In one place [in **The Milesian Chief**], Desmond can refer to his love for Endymion as "a love passing that of women" while simultaneously being racked by the guilt he feels for such a love. This is very much the case of Maturin's own attitude toward love in his art: he speaks of it as ennobling and rewarding but shows it to be an emotion generating the forces of its own destruction and the destruction of those who yield to it. (p. 40)

In **Women**, Maturin finds for the first time a perfect combination for all of his talents as a novelist and creates a work which, though preeminently a psychological novel within a realistic framework, contains elements of the historical novel, the romance, and the gothic. And in his portrayal of the two heroines, Eva and Zaira, Maturin is so skillful that a number of years would pass before novelists would treat with comparable sensitivity and insight the themes he pursues. . . . [**Women**] is a biting and perceptive analysis of Evangelicalism—of the increasing power and wealth of the Evangelicals, of the ways in which they used the Sabbath School system to proselytize their beliefs and of the various societies they established. Particularly in the figure of Mr. Wentworth, Maturin captures that mixture of worldliness and piety, of capitalistic initiative and Calvinistic ardor, of secular goals "justified" by divine providence.

But although it contains an indictment of Evangelicalism and the hypocrisy it engendered, **Women** is primarily Maturin's further exploration of the psychological and physical nature of love as experienced by its three central characters, Charles De Courcy, Eva Wentworth, and Zaira Dalmatiani, and as such, it is one of Maturin's masterpieces. (pp. 51-2)

[It] is obvious that Maturin is not writing a conventional love story. Maturin chooses a setting that contains, as he states in his preface, "a paucity of characters and incidents" [see excerpt above, 1818], and thereby gives himself freedom to explore more fully the various aspects of love. When we first meet Eva, she is young, innocent, and deeply committed to the faith of her family. In Maturin's description of her "ethereal lightness and purity, a visible sanctity," we see shades of Byron's Haidee and Maturin's own Immalee. Contrasted to her is Zaira, sensuous, dark-haired, older, and already experienced in life, having been seduced and married at the age of fifteen. But they are each vulnerable to love's destructive passions.

In this novel, as in **The Milesian Chief,** Maturin's depiction of love is complex and double-edged. On the one hand, he is critical of the unnaturalness of denying one's physicality and aware of the painful consequences of trying to sublimate all traces of human love into religious devotion. For all of her innocence, Eva is as much the destroyer as the destroyed. In one place, Charles, rebuffed by Eva, stops visiting her, "for he felt he could no longer support the sight of the face whose every glance seemed to be drinking up his blood." The image

of Eva as vampire is quite appropriate, for in her unearthliness she demands of Charles more than is humanly possible to give, and in escaping from her, he simply affirms through action that he must recognize his physical as well as spiritual needs. Similarly, Maturin shows how Eva's sexuality, though consciously denied, is nevertheless sublimely present in a religion charged with passionate and erotic undertones.

Maturin realized that sexual asceticism is not limited to women alone, for Charles is entrapped as much by his idealization of woman as by his passions. Attracted to Eva and experiencing strange and unaccountable emotions for the first time, Charles views these new emotions as sacrilege against Eva as well as against the pure concept of love he had previously held. For both of them, the guilt that arises from the violation of previously held ideals manifests itself in suffering: in Eva's case, in a self-imposed isolation during which she tries, through penance and suffering, to rarify her love for Charles into a love exclusively for Christ; and for Charles, in a physical sickness and deterioration brought about by the strong and irreconcilable conflicts within him. Again, we see a conflict in Maturin as well. For the most part, he is clearly critical of the sexual repression, but at the same time he seems implicitly to share some of the attitudes of his characters, or at least he creates a world view that supports their validity. In one respect, the story of the love between Eva and Charles (and between Zaira and Charles) is the story of a love that could perhaps have been happily resolved had they been able to free themselves from those demands that seem to invariably destroy any chance for a satisfactory relationship. But in another respect, it is not so much personal inadequacies that bring about sorrow and suffering as it is the nature of love itself. Love carries the seed of its own destruction, and when man falls in love, the force is released that will inevitably cause pain. Man is born into a fallen world and, since only innocence can assure felicity, the fact that innocence must be lost guarantees the omnipresence of suffering. (pp. 52-4)

[**Women**] is Maturin's fullest attempt to work within a realistic framework and to account for the actions of the characters not in terms of a larger system imposed upon them, but in terms of their own weakness and strengths. The motivations and behavior of the three central characters are depicted with a strength and a self-confidence that Maturin only possesses when he is writing according to his own artistic desires. . . . Maturin's analysis of Zaira's anguish contains some of his most astute psychological insights. Prefiguring some later nineteenth-century female characters, such as Flaubert's Emma Bovary and Hardy's Sue Bridehead, Zaira interprets the pain she suffers as arising from a personal transgression and consequently turns to religion in hopes of doing penance and alleviating her inner sense of guilt. This analysis of Zaira's religious anguish, of the spiritual and sensuous vying for power within her, stands almost by itself among nineteenth-century British novels, since the depiction of religious experiences was traditionally left to poetry, confession and tract. (p. 55)

[**Fredolfo**] is not great drama—the stage was not the proper medium for Maturin's particular talents—but on the other hand it is a much better play than the eminently successful **Bertram**. (p. 58)

[**Fredolfo**] contains much violence, but none of the violence is gratuitous. . . . Maturin does a superb job of introducing quickly and dramatically the major characters and setting the mood of tension. But what makes this drama superior to his first two plays is the skill with which he probes into the nature of guilt, violence, and evil. It is the aspect of *Fredolfo* that most clearly prefigures *Melmoth* and, like that work, *Fredolfo* has to be understood primarily in psychological terms. . . . [Berthold] is the play's pivotal character, not only illuminating our understanding of the other major characters, especially Fredolfo and Wallenberg, but also himself moving toward a symbolic role as the embodiment of evil and the demonic. However, Berthold is also a man and his human dimensions are dramatically conveyed by Maturin, for we see both his anguish and his frustrated tenderness. . . . [He] asks for our sympathy because of his suffering and arouses our fear because of the violence that this suffering can provoke. Incapable of creating or sharing pleasure, he uses his power to convert the world around him into an arena of pain in which the anguish of others serves to diminish his own isolation.

It is in his capacity as inflictor of pain and punishment that Berthold approaches a symbolic role. For, in spite of his weakness and deformity, Berthold exerts a control over Fredolfo from which he cannot escape; in fact, Berthold is the play's moral agent, and it is in relation to him that we judge the actions of the other characters. He is not, of course, a moral agent in terms of the good that he might perpetrate, but in the evil he evokes from others. . . . In *Bertram* Maturin had wanted to explore the demonic through the Dark Knight; in *Fredolfo,* by using the figure of a grotesque and misshapen human, Maturin is able to do so, and, at the same time, succeed in keeping his play intact. As the play advances, the relationship of Fredolfo and Berthold is powerfully delineated, and Berthold, in his ugliness and great capacity for violence, comes to symbolize the subrational and the nonpublic part of Fredolfo. . . . (pp. 58-60)

If Berthold represents the demonic counterpart of Fredolfo, he also represents the human counterpart of Wallenberg. . . . In Wallenberg's character, Maturin probes the sources of rage and evil and, in doing so, suggests that Wallenberg is but a Berthold without the physical deformity. However, his character is not so fully developed as Berthold's in that there does not seem to be adequate motivation for his rage and fury. In Berthold's case, our compassion is stirred by a man who, despite his twisted body and deranged mind, does possess traces of gentleness and love and who could have been capable of tenderness. Wallenberg gives no indication of tender feelings. . . . [In] his characterization of Wallenberg, Maturin is not interested in conventional causality, but in a psychological study of evil. (p. 61)

[*Fredolfo*] is, in many respects, his best constructed and strongest piece of dramatic writing. His drama is strongest in those scenes in which he can reveal his characters at a moment of heightened emotional intensity either through soliloquy or monologue; but for the most part, Maturin's writing depends upon his creation of mood and of a physical and psychological setting that he could not sufficiently realize within the constraints of drama. He is strongest in his descriptive narrative and in his often detailed analysis of motives and hidden fears and hates, and weakest when writing dialogue. In fiction he was able to use various techniques—letters, manuscripts, diaries, and a fictional narrator—in order to compensate for his weakness in creating credible dialogue. But in spite of the limitations the dramatic form created for Maturin, there are some scenes within *Fredolfo* in which character, action, and language seem perfectly welded together. (pp. 62-3)

> *Robert E. Lougy, in his* Charles Robert Maturin *(© 1975 by Associated Presses, Inc.), Bucknell University Press, 1975, 89 p.*

CORAL ANN HOWELLS (essay date 1978)

[*Like Robert Kiely (1972), Howells argues that the impact of* Melmoth *derives from Maturin's examination of human responses to terror and oppression. According to Howells, Maturin transforms suffering "into a literary aesthetic, so that in his hands it becomes nothing less than the raw material for psychological enquiry." Howells maintains that* Melmoth *must be read as Maturin's commentary on the paradoxical nature of the human condition, where the individual is both victim and tormentor.*]

The fascination of that distinctively Gothic knot of feelings, Love, Mystery, and Misery, survived all its ardent exponents and vigorous detractors to find its most powerful imaginative treatment in *Melmoth the Wanderer.* . . . *Melmoth* gives the fullest expression to that obsession with intense private experience that characterises Gothic fiction and relates it to the wider currents of Romanticism. In Maturin's dark imagination all the Gothic neuroses are exacerbated: crises of suffering are embodied in a romance which marks the high point of extravagant Gothic rhetoric. . . . Maturin rationalised his concern with pain and suffering by claiming that it was the only sure means to spiritual growth, though the exclusiveness of his preoccupation with the 'dark abyss' as he calls it, argues for a very peculiar sensibility indeed. We must call his fiction Gothic, but it is Gothic energised by the pathological intensity of its explorations into the darkest regions of human consciousness and presented in language that is wholly in keeping with the hyperintensity and resonance of the writer's psychological perceptions. (p. 131)

Maturin's fascination with the supernatural and his consistent preoccupation with dread, fear and terror would make him a Gothic writer by any definition, but the imaginative range of his psychological speculations and the minutiae of his emotional analyses give him a superiority over those novelists who used the techniques of sensationalism with no other purpose than to shock and frighten their readers. As a practitioner of the craft, Maturin was perfectly aware that the spell of Gothic fiction lay in its power to arouse certain feelings in its readers. . . . He used traditional Gothic techniques in a conscious attempt to stimulate his readers into a state of total empathy with his characters but he also used such techniques as instruments for exploration into hitherto uncharted areas of psychology. As in those other romantic novels, Mary Shelley's *Frankenstein* and James Hogg's *Confessions of a Justified Sinner,* Gothic machinery becomes in Maturin's hands a metaphorical language for describing new insights into human suffering and conflict. (p. 133)

In the extravaganza of its conception, *Melmoth* is a romance of epic proportions, for Maturin had an eclectic and imaginative view of history. We find episodes that enact the great myths of human history, like the Garden of Eden and the Fall, the sufferings of Satan and forebodings of the Day of Judgement, all woven into the texture of historical fact in the detailed accounts of Melmoth's experiences on earth from the early 1600s to 1816. As a historical novelist, Maturin has a great deal in common with Scott . . . ; both of them give life to their evocations of the past by minute historical detail, yet both of them believe in the need for history to be recreated in the crucible of the individual imagination. Such a creed provokes some of the most brilliant scenarios in the novel, such as the recreation of the panic caused by the Great Fire of London, or the animated decadence of the Restoration stage. However, the author's obsession with but a single area of feeling—as opposed to the many and varied historical settings—changes his romance into an allegory of a world where the chief preoccupations of man are guilt, suffering and care. Like its central figure, the novel wheels about free of the ties of time and place, thus missing the sustained grandeur of epic or tragedy, though it has hints of both. (p. 135)

[The] imaginative impact of the book comes . . . from the description of human responses to fear, terror and oppression. All Maturin's tales [in *Melmoth*] are about human beings struggling for survival in a world where man's rôle is that of a victim, tormented by external agents both human and supernatural, and always in danger of betrayal by his own passions and instincts. 'What is Man?', asks Maturin, fascinated by the duality of man's nature. . . . The paradox of the human condition is the real area of Maturin's exploration, which has as its starting-point a desperate faith in God's mercy as the only possible means of man's salvation. Given his tormented awareness, it is no wonder that his most powerful literary effects are those of terror and horror, and that the main character is the agent of moral chaos, himself a prey to monstrous spiritual despair.

Suffering for Maturin is more than a religious belief; it is an obsession which he transforms into a literary aesthetic, so that in his hands it becomes nothing less than the raw material for psychological enquiry. There is even the suggestion (made by one of the characters and italicised by the author) that a man may actually derive his sense of consequence from the sufferings inflicted on him: '*While people think it worth their while to torment us, we are never without some dignity, though painful and imaginary*'. . . . This surely is a psychological insight into the masochistic temperament rather than any religious truth. . . . Maturin pursues human beings to the extremes of their emotional, mental or physical endurance, in order to gaze intently on what remains as distinctively human when 'the tenth wave of suffering' is reached. The evidence recorded in *Melmoth* suggests that the 'varieties in moral botany far exceed the wildest anomalies in the natural [world]' . . . , a metaphor which aptly characterises Maturin's own genuinely scientific curiosity and the merciless precision of his dissections of human feelings. He isolates all his characters by pushing them beyond the normal range of sympathetic human comprehension into a dark inner world of which Melmoth's alienation is merely the most extreme example. From the depths of such experience emerge the products of the agonised imagination, the obsessions and the dangerously distorted dream worlds which form the substance of the novel. (pp. 137-38)

[We] can best appreciate Maturin's achievement if we see *Melmoth* as a document of its author's own pathological consciousness where everything—character, narrative design, feeling and style—is made to express that paradox which he saw as the central truth of the human condition. The description of his fictional method as 'a sort of excited psychology, an exclamatory insistence on sensation and emotion' [see excerpt above from *The Athenaeum*, 1892] is too impressionistic, but it does describe the sense of shock and emotional violence which the novel generates. It is Maturin's style as much as the events of his narrative that is responsible for this impression. . . . [The] language is remarkable in its physical concreteness and its poetic intensity. It is the language of romance—not romance in its vague dreamlike states but in its moments of preternatural clarity, unhinged from everyday modes of perception. It allows for a close scrutiny of the feelings of someone in a state of heightened awareness, at the extreme edge either of life or of sanity, when the mind as well as the

soul is 'trembling on the verge'. The style generates a sense of vertigo, as images of elemental conflict and apocalypse are hurled on top of one another, while minutely-observed psychological detail is carried in the breathlessly insistent rhythms of the prose. (pp. 138-39)

[For] Maturin anguish and suffering are the permanent features of the human condition, for which antithesis is the most appropriate expression; his characters' realisations are most frequently conveyed in paradoxes which disturb and energise in their exploration of extreme ranges of feeling. . . . (p. 139)

[The] pattern of paradox [operates] in every aspect of Maturin's creativity. . . . [Among these paradoxes are] the duality of man's nature as imagined in one individual, tragic love, the aesthetic appeal of horror, and a transcendent moment when tensions are resolved in an ecstasy of pure agony at the point of death.

By the very conditions of his existence Melmoth himself is a creature of paradox; in him the dual nature of personality is exaggerated into mythic dimensions of emotional and moral torment. Both man and devil, he exemplifies the conflict between human aspiration and the prohibitive forces of destiny. His existence is a living death both literally and metaphorically, where despair, misery and misanthropy are the direct results of a half-earthly, half-hellish being. (p. 140)

The love affair between Melmoth and Immalee explores the emotional aspects of Melmoth's cosmic despair, while at the same time translating tragic romantic love into an emblem of the spiritual condition of mankind. As a love 'begotten by despair upon impossibility', it is the longest and most strenuous demonstration in the novel of moral and emotional paradox. It has the strong imaginative appeal of myth, for Melmoth is literally a demon lover and Immalee, the innocent maiden on her Indian island, represents the lost ideal of the Edenic world, the only happy being in Maturin's fiction. . . . The structure of the conflict between good and evil in their love is continually drawn to our attention by authorial comments, by imagery, and by Melmoth's own repeatedly stated awareness of his role as destroyer. But the real interest lies not in the traditional moral fable but in the working out of a particular emotional relationship through a detailed analysis of the fantasies and frustrations contained within sexual love.

Like all Maturin's lovers, they are ill-fated, for he saw sexual passion as the supreme paradox of optimism and despair, the most exquisite form of suffering known to mankind. Lying at the conjunction of Man's finite nature with his infinite longings, love embodies the essential conflict between human desires and the prohibitive forces of destiny, so the condition of being in love inevitably precipitates a crisis of awareness where the lovers try to escape from human limitations by the only means available to them—fantasy or death. In common with other Gothic novelists, Maturin associated sexuality with fears of destruction, so great appeared to him the power released by instinctual urges; unlike the others he pushes this fear to its extreme, adding to the usual Gothic mixture of eroticism and guilt a dimension of metaphysical speculation. In his earlier novels, Maturin treated tragic love as an entirely human problem, investigating its confusion of anguish and delight and the romantic reasons for the death urge. . . . In *Melmoth,* tragic love goes beyond the strictly human situation into one which is fatal by definition. Melmoth is a phantom . . . ; he has already died one hundred and fifty years before he meets Immalee, and he constantly reminds her of the death-doomed quality of their love, 'Who can be mine and *live*?'. No real unity is possible for these lovers, locked as far apart as the worlds of life and death in a relationship which is based on the consequent emotional torment. It is to this context that the crises of fury and rapture belong and in which raging storms, a midnight wedding performed by a dead priest, and exotic tropical gardens are the imaginatively appropriate correlatives.

However their love is more than a darkly Romantic fantasy and it is worth noticing as symptomatic of Maturin's realistic if somewhat overdramatised psychology that there are real emotional reasons for the initial attraction between Melmoth and Immalee, just as there are reasons for the inevitable failure of their relationship. (pp. 144-46)

Every encounter between Melmoth and Immalee is a situation of conflict, made the more intense by the powerful sexual attraction between them and the inevitable failure of any impulse towards harmony and union. Melmoth's last visit to Immalee on her tropical island is typical of the crises which form the pattern of their relationship, where the inherent violence of frustrated passion gives Maturin the opportunity for the kind of sensational display of feeling in which he revelled. Melmoth's grand emotional assault lasts through a fierce tropical storm and is abandoned only when the girl, 'exhausted by emotion and terror', falls senseless at his feet. Maturin deploys all the standard Gothic visual techniques to create an immediate impact on his readers and to glamourise emotional violence. The tumult of the raging storm coincides with the rise and fall of their passions, and becomes not only the means by which feeling is amplified but a way of realising the emotional experience itself. (p. 147)

Melmoth's cosmic despair and [Maturin's] operatic mode of presentation heighten our awareness of the unreality of [Immalee and Melmoth's] love affair but through all the emotional violence there are glimpses of real feeling. The author manages to present the emotional effects of a breakdown of communication between two individuals where each is imprisoned in a private world of innocence or guilt. The failure of the relationship is shown to be psychologically as well as morally inevitable. (p. 151)

Maturin's analysis of the paradoxical nature of our response to terror and suffering extends from a contemplation of its victims to an interest in the feelings of its spectators. It is a disturbing truth that the spectacle of mental or physical agony can operate as a powerful imaginative stimulus, and the range of Maturin's speculations on this area of feeling is so wide as to establish it as a morally neutral fact about human psychology. It is an awareness shared by the most depraved and the most decent characters in the novel, and also exploited by the author as an essential part of his technique for stirring the feelings of his readers. (pp. 152-53)

It is an interesting comment on Maturin's psychological realism that he can make the most bizarre and horrible situations emotionally credible. *Melmoth* creates a world of subjective experience but it is far from the escapism of earlier Gothic novels; it is a world of nightmare not unlike the 'Nighttown' of Joyce's *Ulysses*, where anxieties and fears take on the exaggerated dimensions of obsessional fantasy. (pp. 154-55)

There is surely a contradiction in the author's own mind, caught as he is in a dilemma between his duty as a Christian moralist and the urges of his own dark Romantic sensibility. Whatever the rationale of his imposed religious framework, every situation develops its own momentum as an exploration of suf-

fering, conflict and frustration. Maturin makes some disturbing discoveries about man's emotional potential which give his own desperate faith in the possibility of man's salvation something of the aura of paradox in which he delighted. Because there are no rational or moral explanations for the psychological insights he records, the novel is a series of isolated *aperçus* into dream states, schizoid states and paranoic fantasy. *Melmoth* is full of the shocks of collision between emotional and moral opposites, between life and death, between the objective reality of fact and the subjective reality of feeling. It is as though the author can only create the sensation of being alive when poised on the very edge of experience where 'the soul [or the mind] trembles on the verge'. (pp. 157-58)

Coral Ann Howells, "C. R. Maturin, 'Melmoth the Wanderer'," *in her* Love, Mystery, and Misery: Feeling in Gothic Fiction (© *Coral Ann Howells 1978*), *The Athlone Press, 1978, pp. 131-58.*

ROBERT LEE WOLFF (essay date 1979)

The influence of Wordsworth's and Coleridge's *Lyrical Ballads* of 1798 is strongly visible [in *The Fatal Revenge; or, the Family of Montorio*]. Although *The Fatal Revenge* is not set in Ireland and does not deal directly with Irish subjects, its characters refer significantly to Ireland in their conversations. Praising Wordsworth and Coleridge as possessing a "spirit of simple appeal to the strong and common feelings of our nature," the hero of *The Fatal Revenge* also maintains that Irish poetry is "richer in its harmony and more melting" than that of these English Romantics. These apparently casual passages in *The Fatal Revenge* foreshadow Maturin's later contention—which underlay his Irish novels—that whereas England had subordinated nature to society, Ireland still lived close to nature. Thus the Irish had proper "natural emotions" suitable to a people still close to their ancient folk tradition. (pp. vii-viii)

[Maturin set *The Wild Irish Boy*] in Ireland, making the most of the double appeal of "national" tale and Gothic machinery, and combining both with a more explicit development of his own attitude towards Wordsworthian romanticism. (p. viii)

Nobody has ever thought of *The Wild Irish Boy* as a good novel. Its structure is loose, its plot improbable, its personages unconvincing even in its exotic framework. But as the vehicle for the earnestly held ideas of an Ascendancy clergyman about his native country it is nonetheless of extraordinary interest. (p. x)

A far better novel than *The Wild Irish Boy, The Milesian Chief* can be read as a commentary on the Irish rebellion of 1798, as viewed by a realistic, national-minded member of the Ascendancy who had been a full-grown youth of eighteen when the rebellion took place, and had learned its lessons. Among these was the unreliability of Irish peasant troops. Despite their courage, [the book's hero, Connal] O'Riordan believes, they easily get out of hand and terrify peaceable people. Even if his own rebellion should by any chance be successful, he knows that he and his forces will not be able to govern Ireland. Reluctantly he has come to the conclusion that Ireland cannot be truly independent. Either the French or the English must be relied upon to maintain order. . . . As for the peasantry, only a long period of education—and instruction in the Protestant doctrines of the Established Church—can save them from barbarism.

Ireland, Maturin wrote in his dedication to *The Milesian Chief,* is "the only country on earth, where, from the strange existing opposition of religion, politics, and manners, the extremes of refinement and barbarism are united, and the most wild and incredible situations of romantic story are hourly passing before modern eyes.'' The love affair between Armida and Connal—and that between Connal's brother and Armida's half sister—are both feverishly romantic in this especially Irish sense of the term as Maturin defined it. Connal hates and resents Armida, while all the time he loves her passionately. Armida simply cannot understand Ireland: one may conclude that despite her Italian cultivation, she is not a very intelligent girl. But this is not what Maturin intended to convey so much as the incompatibility between Connal's Gaelic culture and Armida's modern outlook. In ***The Milesian Chief***, readers will also find an ostensibly homosexual passion terrifying two innocent young men, one of whom is in fact a girl but does not know it. Besides, there are adulterous connections and sexually aggressive females. The novel is highly Byronic in the stormy quality of its characters. The wild landscape and the weather reflect the emotions of the personages. (pp. x-xii)

[***Fredolfo***] deals with Switzerland, crushed under the yoke of the Austrian invader. But it is clear that Maturin was thinking primarily of Ireland and the English invader. Just as in Thomas Moore's *Lalla Rookh* . . . , Irish problems are dealt with in disguise as the problems of what we might now call the Middle East, and just as in John Banim's *Damon and Pythias* . . . , Irish problems are discussed in the guise of those of classical Sicily, so Maturin's ***Fredolfo*** is in some sense an Irish play. . . . [The theme of national liberty] echoes Maturin's own *Milesian Chief* in a Swiss setting: when the population is ready to revolt to save him from captivity, Fredolfo, on his way to prison, adjures them not to make his cause their own. But these Irish references are by no means obvious. (pp. xiv-xv)

[***Women; or Pour et Contre***] is surely the most mature example of his fascination with his native country, yet it is also, perhaps primarily, an effort to understand feminine psychology. (p. xv)

The student of Ireland will be particularly interested in the Methodists, whose religious views, a relatively new feature of the Irish scene, are here satirized for the first time: a theme that in one form or another recurs in many later Irish novels. Maturin also attacks Catholicism and atheism. Confined to Dublin and its environs, the story nonetheless has its full share of romantic scenery and episodes: in the city a great fire, in the rugged nearby Wicklow hills a great storm, give Maturin full scope. The influence of Scott is more clearly seen in ***Women*** than in any of Maturin's earlier fiction. In the great ***Melmoth the Wanderer*** . . . the opening scenes take place once again in Wicklow and return briefly but effectively to Maturin's earlier interest in the Irish peasant. Obsessed, perhaps, with the problem of guilt, on which all of his fiction comments, whatever its central theme, and full of the strong Irish self-consciousness characteristic of the first two decades of the century, Maturin was, we realize, more than the last and one of the best of the Gothic novelists. He deserves to be rediscovered as a novelist of Ireland.

Maturin was a nationalist, who opposed the Act of Union. But he was deeply conscious of the miseries of his country and viewed them as a devout member of the Established Church. Not only his novels but also many passages in his published sermons enable a reader to estimate his attitudes towards his "deluded besotted country," as he once called it. (p. xvi)

To the ills of Ireland that Maturin resented he recognized the contribution of the Act of Union, with its unfortunate economic

consequences: emigration, unemployment, a flood of cheap English goods, the impoverishment of the cities, and even the weakening of national sentiment itself. Absenteeism and the irresponsibilities of rackrenting he understood and denounced. Beneath the romantic and the Gothic, these realities are present in Maturin's Irish novels. They serve to anchor the vision of reviving Gaelic nationalism—with its ruined towers and its active bards . . .—firmly in Irish reality and to make Maturin's novels highly important for the modern student of Ireland. (pp. xviii-xix)

> *Robert Lee Wolff, "The Irish Fiction of Charles Robert Maturin (1780-1824)" (introduction copyright © 1979 by Robert Lee Wolff), in* The Milesian Chief, *Vol. I by Charles Robert Maturin, Garland Publishing, Inc., 1979, pp. v-xix.*

ADDITIONAL BIBLIOGRAPHY

"'Christabel', &c.; and *Bertram, a Tragedy*." *The British Review and London Critical Journal* VIII (August 1816): 64-81.*

> A comparison of Samuel Taylor Coleridge's "Christabel" and *Bertram*. The critic dismisses Coleridge's poem as a "weak and singularly nonsensical and affected performance" while praising Maturin's play as "a production of undoubted genius." Some critics hypothesize that Coleridge's derogatory review of *Bertram* [see annotation below] was inspired in part by this essay.

Coleridge, S. T. "Chapter XXIII." In his *Biographia Literaria, Vol. II*, edited by J. Shawcross, pp. 180-207. 1907. Reprint. London: Oxford University Press, 1962.*

> A sarcastic, disparaging review of *Bertram* that first appeared in the *Courier* in 1816. Coleridge uses the play to illustrate his objections to "Jacobinical" drama, which he defines as a type of drama that excites misdirected sympathies in the audience. He cites Maturin's sympathetic presentation of his criminal hero as a striking example of the "confusion and subversion of the natural order of things" in Jacobinical drama.

Conger, Syndy M. "An Analysis of *Melmoth the Wanderer* and Its German Sources." In *Romantic Reassessment: Matthew G. Lewis, Charles Robert Maturin and the Germans, an Interpretative Study of the Influence of German Literature on Two Gothic Novels*, edited by James Hogg, pp. 160-255. Salzburg Studies in English Literature, edited by Erwin A. Stürzl, no. 67. Salzburg: Universität Salzburg, 1977.

> Discusses the nature and extent of Maturin's reliance on German sources for his presentation of Melmoth as part Faust, part Mephistopheles, and part Wandering Jew. According to Conger, "no Gothic novelist before Maturin had ever attempted such a portrait of villainy; and it was German legendary figures which helped him to do so successfully."

D'Amico, Diane. "Christina Rossetti: The Maturin Poems." *Victorian Poetry* 19, No. 2 (Summer 1981): 117-37.*

> Proposes that the themes and language of Maturin's novels, particularly of *Women*, provided the inspiration for Christina Rossetti's early poems. D'Amico finds the greatest evidence of Maturin's influence on Rossetti in the latter's extensive examination of the independent, heroic woman.

Dawson, Leven M. "*Melmoth the Wanderer*: Paradox and the Gothic Novel." *Studies in English Literature: 1500-1900* VIII, No. 4 (Autumn 1968): 621-32.

> Asserts that the paradoxical enjoyment of fear and the eroticism of terror are fundamental elements of the Gothic novel and that *Melmoth* is the most characteristic example of the use of paradox in Gothic fiction. Dawson demonstrates how the Gothic novelists' exploitation of paradox foreshadowed the Romantics' efforts to unify experience by a resolution of opposites and disparities.

Fairchild, Hoxie Neale. "The Child of Nature and the Noble Savage." In her *The Noble Savage: A Study in Romantic Naturalism*, pp. 365-85. New York: Russell & Russell, 1961.*

> Maintains that the character Immalee in *Melmoth* is the only figure in Gothic fiction who displays the qualities of the Noble Savage.

Goldstein, Jesse Sidney. "The Literary Source of Hawthorne's *Fanshawe*." *Modern Language Notes* LX, No. 1 (January 1945): 1-8.*

> Argues that Nathaniel Hawthorne patterned the plot elements and character portraits of *Fanshawe* on *Melmoth*.

Hayter, Alethea. "Coleridge, Maturin's *Bertram* and Drury Lane." In *New Approaches to Coleridge: Biographical and Critical Essays*, edited by Donald Sultana, pp. 17-37. Critical Studies Series, edited by Anne Smith. London: Vision; Totowa, N.J.: Barnes & Noble, 1981.*

> Explores Samuel Taylor Coleridge's motives for attacking *Bertram* [see annotation above].

Hennelly, Mark M., Jr. "*Melmoth the Wanderer* and Gothic Existentialism." *Studies in English Literature: 1500-1900* XXI, No. 4 (Autumn 1981): 665-79.

> Considers the Gothic novel a "prefiguration of modern existentialism" and identifies specific existential themes in *Melmoth*.

Hume, Robert D. "Exuberant Gloom, Existential Agony, and Heroic Despair: Three Varieties of Negative Romanticism." In *The Gothic Imagination: Essays in Dark Romanticism*, edited by G. R. Thompson, pp. 109-27. Pullman, Wash.: Washington State University Press, 1974.*

> Uses the terms "negative romanticism" and "dark romanticism" to describe the works of several authors, including William Beckford, Lord Byron, Matthew Lewis, Mary Shelley, and Maturin, who lack the optimism of such Romantic writers as William Wordsworth, William Blake, Percy Bysshe Shelley, and Samuel Taylor Coleridge. Hume analyzes the dark romantics' treatment of the theme of discontent in the Faust legend and concludes that in *Melmoth*, "the grandeur of pain and endeavour lend a tragic-heroic compensation" to the basic Faust myth.

Lévy, Maurice. Introduction to *The Fatal Revenge; or, The Family of Montorio*, by Charles Robert Maturin, pp. vii-xiv. New York: Arno Press, 1974.

> Laments that Maturin resorts to "mechanical and gratuitous devices" to explain the seemingly supernatural occurrences of *Fatal Revenge*. Nevertheless, Lévy finds Maturin superior to Gothic novelists who "extirpate the irrational in the end," because in *Fatal Revenge* Maturin's explanations "do not destroy the tale, or annihilate the mental anguish which is genuinely voiced in the rest of the book."

Null, Jack. "Structure and Theme in *Melmoth the Wanderer*." *Papers on Language and Literature: A Journal for Scholars and Critics of Language and Literature* 13, No. 2 (Spring 1977): 136-47.

> Argues that *Melmoth* derives its psychological intensity from its complex structure. Null contends that the fragmented structure of the novel reflects "organically the disorientation caused by the characters' loss of values."

Piper, H. W., and Jeffares, A. Norman. "Maturin the Innovator." *The Huntington Library Quarterly* XXI, No. 3 (May 1958): 261-84.

> Maintains that Maturin's reputation as a Gothic novelist has overshadowed his importance as a proponent of Irish regional literature. Piper and Jeffares assert that Maturin's novels are explorations of Irish culture in which he combined Irish nationalism with Wordsworthian Romanticism to contrast English and Irish culture as well as "natural" and cosmopolitan character. According to Piper and Jeffares, Maturin was "one of the earliest distillers of that blend of naturalism and Romanticism which was to be so potent in the nineteenth century."

Praz, Mario. "The Shadow of the 'Divine Marquis': Maturin and His *Melmoth*." In his *The Romantic Agony*, translated by Angus Davidson, pp. 116-20. 1933. Reprint. New York: Meridian Books, 1956.

> Explores the "predilection for cruel and terrifying spectacles" displayed by Maturin in *Melmoth*.

Prosper Mérimée

1803-1870

(Also wrote under pseudonym of Clara Gazul) French short story writer, dramatist, poet, critic, novelist, historian, and translator.

Mérimée is generally considered one of France's greatest short story writers. For his insightful depiction of human nature, he has been compared with both Stendhal and Gustave Flaubert. Like Stendhal, he exhibited emotional restraint in his prose; like Flaubert, he emphasized economy of language and psychological detail. Mérimée's prose style is perhaps best exhibited in *Carmen*, the passionate story that inspired Georges Bizet's famous opera of the same name. Though best-known for his short stories and novellas, Mérimée excelled in many genres. His novel *Chronique du temps de Charles IX (1572: A Chronicle of the Times of Charles the Ninth)* attests to his interest in history and his narrative skill and was called "the most artistic of historical novels" by the noted English critic Arthur Symons. Mérimée's plays, which are clever imitations of Spanish dramas, are considered by many to be more successful than their models. In addition to writing, Mérimée achieved renown as a statesman and translator of Russian literature. Though interest in his work has flagged in the twentieth century, critics continue to judge his various works as outstanding examples of their genres.

Born in Paris, Mérimée was raised among the artists, critics, and writers who attended his parents' literary salon. At the Lycée Napoléon, Mérimée excelled in his studies of languages and literature and upon graduation pursued law at the University of Paris. Instead of studying, however, he preferred to frequent literary salons, where he met Stendhal, who became a close friend. Stendhal encouraged Mérimée to write and introduced him to a number of influential authors. In 1824, Mérimée wrote articles on the Spanish theater for *Le Globe,* a Paris journal, and collaborated with Stendhal on a play which was never produced. The next year, Mérimée published *Théâtre de Clara Gazul (The Plays of Clara Gazul),* a volume of dramas that were presented as the work of Clara Gazul, a fictitious Spanish actress. Mérimée posed as a Spanish woman for the portrait of the authoress and even provided a false biography. Though intended as parodies, the plays were well received by an unsuspecting public, and critics pronounced them superior to other Spanish dramas of the period. Subsequently, Mérimée wrote *La guzla; ou, Choix de poésies illyriques,* a collection of ballads that were purportedly transcribed from Serbian by Hyacinthe Maglanovitch. Like *The Plays of Clara Gazul,* these ballads met with unanimous acclaim, and few doubted their authenticity. Later Mérimée said that he had written both *The Plays of Clara Gazul* and *La guzla* in order to display "the simplicity and basic absurdity of the use of local color."

Next Mérimée turned to the historical novel, and published *1572: A Chronicle of the Times of Charles the Ninth*. In an unusual twist, Mérimée failed to provide an ending for the book, and instead asked his readers to provide their own. Like his two earlier hoaxes, *1572: A Chronicle of the Times of Charles the Ninth* displays the cynical side of Mérimée's art. Shortly following the publication of his novel, Mérimée began a career

as a public official. He served in a number of government positions throughout his lifetime, including Inspector General of Monuments and senator. His travels as a statesman provided the inspiration for the stories he wrote for the *Révue de Paris* between 1829 and 1845. These tales were later collected and published as *Mosaïque*. Mérimée's first attempt at the short story form, "Mateo Falcone," established him as a master of the genre. "Mateo Falcone" and subsequent stories reveal Mérimée's ability to combine the passionate themes of Romanticism with the stylistic precision characteristic of Realism. *Columba*, the best known of Mérimée's longer stories, analyzes the many aspects of love and, like *Carmen*, is considered a masterpiece of narration. Both of these stories display Mérimée's artistic detachment, which critics consider to be among his greatest techniques. Following *Carmen*'s publication in 1845, Mérimée wrote little fiction until 1869, when he composed his final stories. Critics concur that these tales, published posthumously as *Dernières nouvelles*, indicate that over the years he had retained his storytelling ability.

Though critics primarily praise his short stories, Mérimée himself valued his historical writings most highly. Both *1572: A Chronicle of the Times of Charles the Ninth* and a later work, *Histoire de Don Pédre Ier*, are admired by many critics as masterpieces of scholarship and style. Mérimée especially enjoyed Russian history and literature. He began to study the

Russian language in 1848 and by 1849 had translated several tales of Alexander Pushkin, whose precise style of literary expression is similar to Mérimée's own. Later, Mérimée translated Nikolai Gogol's *The Inspector General* and *Dead Souls*. Little was known of Russian literature in France at this time, and Mérimée was its principal interpreter. Of all Mérimée's work, his correspondence best reveals his enigmatic personality. In 1831 Mérimée met Jenny Dacquin, a young girl who became his close friend and correspondent for forty years. His letters to her, published in 1873 as *Lettres à une inconnue* *(Letters to an Unknown)* vividly present the events and attitudes of his era. Written with wit and perception, his correspondence also reveals Mérimée as a kindly and loyal friend.

Carmen has remained popular throughout the twentieth century through the ballets, films, and new stagings of Bizet's opera that it has inspired. Mérimée's other works, however, are not widely read, although critics continue to judge them positively. Commentators as diverse as Henry James and George Brandes praised Mérimée's short stories and historical works, and more recent critics laud Mérimée's narrative skills and objective prose style. While scholars rarely fault Mérimée's work, some have asserted that his abilities are essentially technical and that his work lacks emotion. However, most critics agree that Mérimée's enduring appeal lies in the objectivity and lucid precision of his prose. V. S. Pritchett perhaps best captured the essence of Mérimée's style when he termed it "crystalline, exact, apparent."

PRINCIPAL WORKS

Théâtre de Clara Gazul [as Clara Gazul]   (drama)   1825
  [*The Plays of Clara Gazul*, 1825]
La guzla; ou, Choix de poésies illyriques   (poetry)   1827
La jacquerie   (drama)   1828
Chronique du temps de Charles IX   (novel)   1829
  [*1572: A Chronicle of the Times of Charles the Ninth*, 1830]
Le carrosse de Sainte-Sacrement [as Clara Gazul; first publication]   (drama)   1830
L'occasion [as Clara Gazul; first publication]   (drama) 1830
*Mosaïque   (short stories)   1833
Columba   (novella)   1841
  [*Columba*, 1843]
La Vénus d'Ille   (short story)   1841
Carmen   (novella)   1845
  [*Carmen*, 1878]
Histoire de Don Pédre Ier   (history)   1848
  [*History of Peter the Cruel*, 1849]
**Nouvelles   (short stories)   1852
***Dernières nouvelles   (short stories)   1873
Lettres à une inconnue   (letters)   1874
  [*Prosper Mérimée's Letters to an Incognita*, 1874; also published as *Letters to an Unknown*, 1897]
The Writings of Prosper Mérimée   (poetry, drama, novellas, short stories, novel, and letters)   1905
Oeuvres. 12 vols.   (poetry, drama, novellas, short stories, novel, and letters)   1927-33

*This work includes the short stories "Mateo Falcone," "Vision de Charles XI," "L'enlèvement de la rédoute," "Tamango," "La perle de Toledo," "La partie de trictrac," "Le vase étrusque," and "Les mécontents."

**This work includes the short stories "Arsène Guillot" and "L'abbé Aubain."

***This work includes the short stories "Lokis," "Djoûmane," and "La chambre bleue."

THE MONTHLY REVIEW, London   (essay date 1827)

[*The following essay indicates the generally warm critical reception of* La guzla. *The critic does not question the authenticity of the ballads, but expresses regret that so little information is available about their anonymous collector and translator.*]

[*La Guzla; ou Choix de Poesies Illyriques,*] purports to be literal translations in the French, of some popular ballads from the Illyrian language, such as they are chaunted at this day by wandering minstrels, amidst the mountains south of the Danube, to the sounds of [an ancient instrument called] the gusle or guzla. (p. 375)

[*La Guzla*] is the work of an industrious and persevering stranger, who saw the minstrel, and listened to his strains; and who was guided in his selection of the traditionary songs of Illyria, by the impressions which they immediately left upon his own heart and imagination. (p. 376)

[Almost every composition in this volume] is marked by peculiar excellence. Bred up amidst those scenes of nature, which are ever most congenial to the poetic temperament, it would not have been surprising that the Illyrian bard should yield his fancy to the innocent illusions of contemplation. But this master of the guzla seems to have been more practically disposed. His lyrics are calculated for immediate effect; boldness of thought and energy of diction are their characteristics: they irritate, but do not soothe; they express the exultation of triumphant revenge, and the scorn of confident bravery. Sometimes, too, there intrudes a levity of expression, with which the strongest emotions of passion are by no means inconsistent. (pp. 378-79)

[This] little work is presented to the public in the most unpretending manner. Even the name of the possessor of so much industry, information, and taste, as this volume indicates, is suppressed, and with it, no doubt, a number of personal anecdotes, which would have thrown light on the poetical text. If, as we trust he will be encouraged to do, the collector will continue the publication of Illyrian Ballads, it is desirable that his illustrations should be given on a more extended and elaborate scale, than that on which they are furnished in the pages before us. (p. 384)

> "Illyrian Poetry," *in* The Monthly Review, *London, Vol. XXVII, November, 1827, pp. 375-84.*

[MARY SHELLEY]   (essay date 1829)

[*An English author best known for her novel,* Frankenstein, *Shelley was the wife of the poet Percy Bysshe Shelley. A frequent correspondent of Mérimée, she received his work enthusiastically and included several of her own translations from* La guzla *in the admiring review excerpted here.*]

[The **"Comedies de Clara Gazul"**] were, in every way, striking and interesting productions, possessing at once the faults and beauties of [Spanish drama], full of spirit, originality, and fire.

They were introduced by an account of their feigned authoress, which, as well as the dramas themselves, is remarkable for its utter freedom from affectation. There are to be found in them none of those defects, too generally attributed with justice to French imaginative works: there is no circumlocution, no parade, and their very hyperbole, as being common to the Spanish drama, is natural and in its place. . . . Energy is the characteristic of these pieces, mingled with a display of knowledge in the lighter touches of humanity; such as the sweet gracefulness of Iñez, and the struggles between a Catholic woman's religion and her love in **"Le Ciel et l'Enfer."** This drama is one of the best in the book; it is founded on the stormy passion of jealousy, the most terrible and selfish of human emotions, and the most interesting, from its being the most universal. As Clara Gazul was a Liberal, inquisitors and priests are attacked in her productions, and there reigns through all of them the spirit of freedom from political and religious servitude.

The author's next work was in a very different style, resembling the first in one particular only, that it is an imitation. It is entitled the **"Guzla,"** and imports to be a translation of a collection of Illyrian national poems. . . . We are introduced also to an imaginary person, Hyacinth Maglanovich, who is supposed to be the author of the greater number of the poems in the **["Guzla"].** They are warlike, pathetic, and amatory—and, above all, whatever is their theme, they are characterised by the utmost simplicity, while a vein of sweetness runs throughout, that lends to each a particular charm. By a strong effort of the imagination, the young Parisian [Mérimée] writes as if the mountains of Illyria had been the home of his childhood; the rustic and barbarous manners are not softened, nor the wild energy of the people tamed; and, if we trace any vestige of civilization, it merely arises from the absence of all that would shock our tastes or prejudices. (pp. 72-3)

The last production of this author, recently published, is now before us. It is ushered in as no imitative attempt. **"La Jaquerie"** consists of a series of dramatic scenes, developing the history of an insurrection in France, almost contemporary with those in our own country which occurred under Richard II. . . . The plan of the author of **"La Jaquerie"** is, to give a faithful picture of the manners of those times, bringing together under one point of view the many and successive scenes and personages that formed the then state of society. A history written with this view would develop a new and terrible page of human experience. To present this to us in the form of dialogue merely is a difficult undertaking; individual character is lost in the infinite variety of persons made to pass before us, and we have the ideal instead of the real being presented to us. We are introduced to the factious priest, murmuring because, in the choice of an abbot, the monks prefer the noble blood of another to his learning. We have the knights of France, whose very names awaken all the delusive associations of romance; the English captains of adventurers, whose trade was war; the burgess grasping and cowardly; the robber driven to outlawry by the cruelty of his superiors, and nourishing vengeance as a duty; the peasant first sinking beneath, and then rising to throw off oppression; and finally the lord of the castle, the feudal chief, the suzerain of the surrounding country, his daughter and her betrothed lover, and the baron's men at arms, who though, in the language of the day, a villain, joins the gifts of poetry to those of valour. (pp. 78-9)

We feel the want of one prominent character to concentrate the interest, without which a dramatic composition is never perfect. But the author has not aimed at a regular tragedy, and

he has succeeded in giving us in a series of interesting scenes, a forcible picture of the manners of our ancestors, and of the crimes and misfortunes resulting from the feudal system, from which our state of civilization preserves us.

To the **"Jaquerie"** is added a drama, entitled the **"Family of Carvajal."** This is a tremendous domestic tragedy. . . . In this production the author is no longer a painter of manners only, but he becomes a depictor of passion, an observer and a narrator of the secret motives that influence our nature, and the dread events that are the result of unlawful indulgence. It is a question whether certain combinations of circumstances, though it is allowed that they have existence, should be recalled to our memory and represented to our imaginations. But it is difficult for the author, whose impulse is a gift of his nature, whose talent is spontaneous, who can no more repress the yearning of his mind to trace the boundaries of the unknown intellectual world, than he can rule the pulsations of his heart; it is difficult for him to submit to rules imposed by those whose tamer thoughts never emerge from the narrow bounds of their personal experience; who repose in a windless atmosphere, and who fear to have their downy slumbers broken by the war of elements. Columbus, anticipating the discovery of the unknown shores that pale our western progress over the wild and distant waves of the Atlantic, felt the old world, extended in latitude and longitude so far and wide, a narrow prison—and thus the imaginative writer, who deems that beyond the usual track he may find a fresh and untried ground, courageously launches forth, leaving the dull every-day earth behind him. If his discoveries do not interest us, do not let us vituperate his adventurous spirit, and thus degrade ourselves to the level of all detractors from the fame attendant on intellectual enterprise. Let us remember that the poets of Greece, whose names are as a part of our religion, and the highly-gifted dramatists of our own country, have been prone to select as subjects for their tragedies, events grounded on the direst passions and the worst impulses.

The **"Family of Carvajal"** has given rise to these reflections: they may be received as applying to every similar production which seeks to interest by new and strange combinations, and which are vivid in their conception and strong in their delineation of what they only know through the innate force of the imagination. The author before us has shewn no lack of boldness in his treatment of the subject, while he has never overstepped those boundaries which must be observed for our tastes not to be shocked, instead of our interest excited. He has made the father and daughter equally impetuous and resolute, but one is the oppressor, the other the victim. The scene is laid in an unpopulated province of New Granada, and the father is represented as a despot over his wife, a cruel tyrant to his slaves, a man grown old in crime. His hapless daughter was brought up in a rustic semi-barbarous convent, and she returns home to find herself an associate of guilt, to which her proud heart refuses to yield, while love for another adds to her vehemence and misery. This meeting of two fierce natures in unnatural discord presents a new and terrible source for dramatic interest. Each scene transcends the one before in its appalling horror; and the last, in which the miserable girl poignards her father, completes the dark picture, spreading over the canvas the lurid hues of whirlwind and volcano. We turn trembling from the contemplation, while we confess the force of the genius that presents it to our eyes. (pp. 79-81)

[Mary Shelley], "Illyrian Poems—Feudal Scenes," in The Westminster Review, Vol. X, January, 1829, pp. 71-81.

JOHANN WOLFGANG VON GOETHE [CONVERSATION WITH JOHN PETER ECKERMANN] (conversation date 1830)

[A preeminent figure in German literature, Goethe was a shaping force in the major literary movements of the late eighteenth and early nineteenth centuries. He is best known for his drama Faust *and his early novel,* The Sorrows of Young Werther. *The following remarks on Mérimée were culled from the volume of conversations that were transcribed and collected by Goethe's secretary and companion the last decade of his life.]*

"It is surprising to me," remarked I, "that even Mérimée, who is one of your favourites, has entered upon this ultra-romantic path, through the horrible subjects of his '**Guzla.**'"

"Mérimée," returned Goethe, "has treated these things very differently from his fellow-authors. These poems certainly are not deficient in various horrible *motives*, such as churchyards, nightly crossways, ghosts and vampires; but the repulsive themes do not touch the intrinsic merit of the poet. On the contrary, he treats them from a certain objective distance, and, as it were, with irony. He goes to work with them like an artist, to whom it is an amusement to try anything of the sort. He has, as I have said before, quite renounced himself, nay, he has ever renounced the Frenchman, and that to such a degree, that at first these poems of Guzla were deemed real Illyrian popular poems, and thus little was wanting for the success of the imposition he had intended.

"Mérimée," continued Goethe, "is indeed a thorough fellow! Indeed, generally, more power and genius are required for the objective treatment of a subject than is supposed." (pp. 452-53)

> *Johann Wolfgang von Goethe, in a conversation with John Peter Eckermann on March 14, 1830, in his* Conversations of Goethe with Eckermann and Soret, *edited by John Peter Eckermann, translated by John Oxenford, revised edition, George Bell & Sons, 1883, pp. 450-57.* *

[FREDERICK HARDMAN] (essay date 1847)

Rarely, in these days of profuse and unscrupulous scribbling, do we find an author giving the essence, not a dilution, of his wit, learning, and imagination, dispensing his mental stores with frugal caution, instead of lavishing them with reckless prodigality. Such a one, when met with, should be made much of, as a model for sinners in a contrary sense, and as a bird of precious plumage. Of that feather is Monsieur Prosper Mérimée. He plays with literature, rather than professes it; it is his recreation, not his trade. . . . In two-and-twenty years he has written less than the average annual produce of many of his literary countrymen. In several paths of literature, he has essayed his steps and made good a footing; in not one has he continuously persevered, but, although cheered by applause, has quickly struck into another track, which, in its turn, has been capriciously deserted. His "**Studies of Roman History**" give him an honourable claim to the title of historian; his "**Notes of Archaeological Rambles**" are greatly esteemed; he has written plays; and his prose fictions, whether middle-age romance or novel of modern society, rank with the best of their class. (p. 711)

[He] has thrown off a number of tales and sketches. . . . They are all remarkable for grace of style and tact in management of subject. One of the longest, "**Colomba**," a tale of Corsican life, is better known in England than its author's name. It has been translated with accuracy and spirit. . . . The Corsican

Vendetta has been taken as the basis of more than one romantic story, but, handled by M. Mérimée, it has acquired new and fascinating interest; and he has enriched his little romance with a profusion of those small traits and artistical touches which exhibit the character and peculiarities of a people better than folios of dry description. "**La Double Méprise,**" another of his longer tales, is a clever *novelette* of Parisian life. According to English notions its subject is slippery, its main incident, and some of its minor details, improbable and unpleasant, although so neatly managed that one is less startled when reading them than shocked on after-reflection. . . . The plot is very slight; the tale scarcely depends on it, but is what the French call a *tableau de moeurs* [moral story], with less pretensions to the regular progress and catastrophe of a novel, than to be a mirror of everyday scenes and actors on the bustling stage of Paris life. The characters are well drawn, the dialogues witty and dramatic, the book abounds in sly bits and smart satire; but its bitterness of tone injured its popularity, and, unlike its author's other tales, it met little success. (p. 712)

We turn to another of M. Mérimée's books, in our opinion his best, an historical romance, entitled "**1572,**" a "**Chronicle of the Reign of Charles the Ninth.**" . . . [M. Mérimée has] been accused of adhering too closely to reality, to the detriment of the poetical character of his romance. He does not make his heroes and heroines sufficiently perfect, or his villains sufficiently atrocious, to suit the palate of some critics, but depicts them as he finds evidence of their having existed—their virtues obscured by the coarse manners and loose morality, their crimes palliated by the religious antipathies and stormy political passions of a semi-civilised age. He declines judging the men of the sixteenth century according to the ideas of the nineteenth. . . . Eschewing conventionality, and following his own judgment, and the guidance of the old chroniclers, in whose quaint records he delights, he has written one of the best existing French historical romances.

It would have been easy for a less able writer than M. Mérimée to have extended the "**Chronique**" ["**Chronicle**"] to thrice its present length. It is not a complete romance, but a desultory sketch of the events and manners of the time, with a few imaginary personages introduced. Novel readers who require a regular *denoûment* will be disappointed at its conclusion. There is not even a hint of a wedding from the first page to the last; and the only lady who plays a prominent part in the story, a certain countess Diane de Turgis, is little better than she should be. And yet, if we follow M. Mérimée's rule, and judge her according to the ideas and morals of the age she flourished in, she was rather an amiable and proper sort of person. (pp. 713-14)

By his countrymen, M. Mérimée's short tales are the most esteemed of his writings. . . . Once in eighteen months, or two years, he throws a few pages to the public, which, like a starved hound to whom a scanty meal is tossed, snaps eagerly at the gift whilst growling at the niggardliness of the giver. . . . A man of great erudition and extensive travel, he is thoroughly master of many languages, and, in writing about foreign countries and people, steers clear of the absurd blunders into which some of his contemporaries, of respectable talents and attainments, not unfrequently fall. His English officer and lady in "**Colomba**" are excellent; very different from the absurd caricatures of Englishmen one is accustomed to see in French novels. He is equally truthful in his Spanish characters. . . . Still we must hope there is some flaw in the glasses through which he has observed the gay world of Paris. The "**Vase**

Etrusque" is one of his sketches of modern French life, in the style of the **"Double Méprise,"** but better. It is a most amusing and spirited tale, but unnecessarily immoral. Had the heroine been virtuous, the interest of the story would in no way have suffered, so far as we can see; and that which attaches to her, as a charming and unhappy woman, would have been augmented. This opinion, however, would be scoffed at on the other side of the Channel, and set down as a piece of English prudery. . . . Fidelity to life in his scenes and characters is a high quality in an author, and one possessed in a high degree by M. Mérimée; but he has been sometimes too bold and cynical in the choice and treatment of his subjects. **"La Partie de Tric-trac,"** and **"L'Enlevement de la Redoute,"** are amongst his happiest efforts. Both are especially remarkable for their terse and vigorous style. (p. 723)

"Carmen" is a graceful and animated sketch, in style as brilliant as any thing by the same author—in the character of its incidents less strikingly original than some of his other tales. It is a story of Spanish life, not in cities and palaces, in court or camp, but in the barranca and the forest, the gipsy suburb of Seville, the woodland bivouac and smuggler's lair. . . .

"Carmen," related as the personal experience of the author during an archaeological tour in Andalusia in the autumn of 1830, is . . . graphic and fascinating. . . . (p. 726)

[*Frederick Hardman*], *"Prosper Mérimée," in* Blackwood's Edinburgh Magazine, *Vol. LXI, No. CCCLXXX, June, 1847, pp. 711-26.*

H[IPPOLYTE] TAINE (essay date 1873)

[*Taine was a French philosopher, critic, and historian whose theories involved the influence of environment and heredity on the development of human character. His well-known work,* Histoire de la littérature anglaise (History of English Literature) *analyzes literature through a study of race and milieu. Considered a Naturalist by most, Taine ascertains several Naturalist qualities in Mérimée's writing. Here Taine praises the brevity, sincerity, and action of Mérimée's novels.*]

[Mérimée] sought out types perverted, and types unsullied, "through an inexhaustible curiosity for every variety of the human species," and thus formed in his memory a gallery of living pictures inestimably more precious than any other kind; for those of books and of edifices are but empty shells, once tenanted, but whose structure may be known only by imagining the forms that dwelt therein, from the poems that have survived. By a sort of divination, keen, accurate, and swift, he made this mental reconstruction. In the *Chronicle of Charles IX,* in *The Experiments of an Adventurer,* and in the *Theater of Clara Gazul* it is evident that such was his involuntary method. His writings tend naturally to the demi-dreams of the artist, to scenic effect, and to romance which clothes the dead past with new life. (pp. xvii-xviii)

The bent of his mind led Mérimée to be suspicious, and suspicion carried to excess is harmful. To obtain from the study of any subject all that it is able to bestow, one must, I fancy, give oneself to it without reserve, be wedded to it, indeed, but not treat it as a mistress to whom one is devoted for two or three years, only to discard and take a new one. A man produces the best of which he is capable only when, after conceiving to himself some form of art, some method of science, in short some general idea of his subject, he becomes so enamoured that he finds it possessing attractions above all else—himself

especially—and worships it as a goddess, whom he is happy only in serving.

Mérimée, also, was capable of cherishing this affection and adoration, but after a time the critic within him awoke, bringing the goddess to trial, only to discover that she was not entirely divine. All our methods of science, all our forms of art, all our general ideas, have some weak spot; the inadequate, the uncertain, the expedient, the artificial, abound therein; only the illusion of love can find them perfect, and a sceptic does not remain long in love. He put on his magnifying glasses, and in the enchanting statue discovered a lack of poise, a vagueness and insincerity of construction, a modernity of attitude. Becoming disgusted, he turned away, not without reason, to be sure, and these reasons he explains in passing. He sees in our philosophy of history an element of speculation, in our mania for erudition the futility, inutility; he sees extravagance in our taste for the picturesque, and insipidity in our paintings of realism. (pp. xviii-xix)

Toward the end of his life, he avoided resolutely the acceptance of all theories; they were, in his opinion, good only to work on the credulity of philosophers and as a means of livelihood for professors. He accepted and repeated only anecdotes and small facts of observation in philology; for instance, the exact date when one ceases to meet in Old French the two cases derived from the Latin declension. By dint of his craving for certainty, knowledge came to be to him but a withered plant, a stalk devoid of blossoms. In no other way can we explain the lifelessness of his historical essays, *Don Pedro, The Cossacks, The False Demetrius, The Social War, The Conspiracy of Catiline,* studies vigorous, exhaustive, well-maintained and well-developed, but whose characters are not alive, probably because he did not care to give them life. For in another work, *The Experiments of an Adventurer,* he has caused the sap to return to the plant, so that it may be seen successively under its two aspects, dull and rigid in the historical herbarium, fresh and green in the work of art. In placing his Spaniards of the nineteenth century as the contemporaries of Sylla in this herbarium, they were as clearly seen by his inner vision, no doubt, as was his adventurer; at any rate, this would have been no more of a tax upon his mental retina. He was reluctant, however, to permit us to see them thus, conceding only facts which could bear the test of proof, refusing to give his own assumptions rather than authentic occurrences, critical to the impairment of his own work, severe to the point of suppressing the best part of himself, and of placing his imagination under the ban. (pp. xix-xx)

Certain gifts were his by nature which no amount of application can bestow, and which were never possessed by his master, Stendhal—the talent for scenic effect, for dialogue, for humorous situations. He knew the art of introducing two characters, and by their conversation alone of bringing them in strong relief before the vision of the reader. Like Stendhal, moreover, he understood personal peculiarities, and was a skilful story-teller. (p. xxi)

From the very first he had delighted in the Spanish drama, which is overflowing with vigour and action; and he borrowed a number of its situations to compose, under a fictitious name, some short pieces of deep purport and modern significance [*The Theater of Clara Gazul*]; and, a thing unique in the history of literature, many of these imitations—*The Crisis* and *Perichole,* for example—are superior to his original stories. Nowhere else do the characters stand out so distinctly and so energetically as in his comedies. In *The Conspirators,* and in

The Two Heirs, each personage . . . resembles one of those perfect watches of transparent crystal, in the face of which is visible, not only the exact time, but also the action of the entire interior mechanism. All the minutest details are burdened with significance.

It is the attribute of great masters of painting in five or six strokes of the crayon to sketch in a face which, once seen, can never be forgotten. Even in his less popular comedies—for example, in *The Spaniards in Denmark*—there are characters, like the Lieutenant Charles Leblanc and his mother, the spy, who will remain forever in the human memory. (pp. xxi-xxii)

Carmen, The Taking of the Redoubt, Colomba, Matteo Falcone, The Abbé Aubain, Arsène Guillot, The Venus of Ille, The Game of Backgammon, Tamango, even *The Etruscan Vase,* and *The Double Mistake,* are almost all little structures that stand now as firmly as the day they were erected. This is explained by the fact that they are built of carefully selected stone, not of stucco and other popular materials. Here we find none of those descriptions which pass out of fashion after half a century, and which to-day we consider so tiresome in the romances of Walter Scott; we see none of those reflections, disquisitions, inter-pretations, which we think so tedious in the novels of Fielding; nothing but action, and action never fails to be instructive. . . .

A second reason for their endurance is the brevity of these romances, the longest of them consuming but half a volume, while one is but six pages. All, however, stand out clearly and are carefully developed, the interest centred around a single action and a single purpose. (p. xxiii)

The types chosen by Mérimée were sincere, strong, and origi-nal. We may compare them to medallions of durable metal, in bold relief, set in an appropriate frame and amid harmonious surroundings; an officer's first battle, a Corsican vendetta, a slave-trader's last voyage, a slip from the path of integrity, the sacrifice of a son by his father, a secret tragedy in a modern salon. . . .

[Each] one is, in its little setting, a record of human nature, a record, complete and of far-reaching import, to which a phi-losopher, a moralist, may return year after year without ex-hausting its interest. (p. xxiv)

The wax taper of *Arsène Guillot* summarises many volumes concerning the religion of the common people and of the inmost feelings of courtesans. I know of no more scathing sermon against the blunders of credulity or of imagination than *The Double Mistake,* and *The Etruscan Vase.* In the year 2000 *The Game of Backgammon* will be read again, probably, to learn what it costs to cheat.

Notice, finally, that at no time does the author force himself on our notice that he may emphasise the lesson, but remains in the background, leaving us to draw our own conclusions. He effaces himself even deliberately so as to appear altogether absent. Future readers will show consideration for a host so polite, so graceful, so discreet in doing the honours of his own home. . . . Instead of exposing his knowledge, he conceals it; to listen to him, it would seem as if any one at all might have written his book. . . . If he wrote *The Experiments of an Ad-venturer,* it was because he had once, for a fortnight, had nothing better to do. . . . This resolution not to overestimate himself comes to be in the end an affectation. So great is his dread of appearing pedantic that he flies to the opposite ex-treme, and the result is his tone of flippancy, his unceremonious manner of the man of society.

The day may come when this will prove to be his vulnerable point, when it will be asked whether this perpetual air of irony is not intentional; whether he is justified in joking in the very midst of tragedy; whether his apparent callousness is not due to the fear of ridicule; whether his free-and-easy tone is not the effect of embarrassment; whether the gentleman has not been harmful to the author; whether his art was sufficiently dear to him. (pp. xxv-xxvi)

H[ippolyte] Taine, "Prosper Mérimée" (1873), in The Writings of Prosper Mérimée: Letters to an Un-known, Vol. 7 by Prosper Mérimée, translated by Olive Edwards Palmer (copyright, 1905 by George E. Croscup; originally published as his Lettres à une inconnue, 1874), Croscup & Holby Company, 1905, pp. v-xxviii.

HENRY JAMES   (essay date 1874)

[*James was an American-born English novelist, short story writer, critic, essayist, and playwright of the late nineteenth and early twentieth centuries who is considered one of the greatest novelists in the English language. Although best-known for his novels, James is also admired as a lucid and insightful critic. Here James indicates his admiration for Mérimée and calls his stories "chis-elled and polished little fictions." For a discussion of Mérimée's influence on James, see the P. R. Grover entry in the Additional Bibliography.*]

[We] confess that Mérimée's chiselled and polished little fic-tions, and indeed, the whole manner and system of the author, have always had a great fascination for us. He is, perhaps, the most striking modern example of zealous artistic conciseness—of the literary artist who works in detail, by the line, by the word. There have been poets who scanned their rhythm as narrowly as Mérimée, but we doubt whether there has ever been a prose writer. His effort was to compress as large an amount of dramatic substance as possible into a very narrow compass, and the result is that, though his stories are few and short, one may read them again and again, and perceive with each reading a greater force of meaning. Some of the earlier ones are most masterly in this pregnant brevity; the story seems to say its last word, as the reader lays it down, with a kind of magical after-resonance. We have often thought a selection might be made from [Mérimée's tales], and presented to young narrators as a sort of manual of their trade—a guide for the avoidance of prolixity. Mérimée's subjects are always of the romantic and picturesque order, dealing in action, not in sen-timent. They almost always hinge on a violent adventure or chain of adventures, and are strongly seasoned with bloodshed and general naughtiness. There are a great many sword-thrusts and pistol-shots, and a good deal of purely carnal love-making. At the beginning of his career the author had a great relish for Spanish local color, and several of his early works are richly charged with it. The **"Théâtre de Clara Gazul,"** written, we believe, before he was twenty-three, is a series of short tragic dramas on the picturesque cruelties and immoralities of Old Spain. One of his masterpieces, **"Carmen,"** published later, is the history of a wonderful *gitanilla*—a princess among the heroines who have dared much for love. With his brutal sub-jects and his cynical style, Mérimée is doubtless thoroughly disagreeable to such readers as are not fascinated by his artistic skill. To tell a terrible little story without flinching—without expressing a grain of reprobation for the clever rascal who escapes under cover of the scuffle in which his innocent rival has his brains blown out, or a grain of compassion for the poor guilty lady whose husband or father, brought upon the scene by the crack of pistols, condemns her to a convent cell for life; not to be sentimental, not to be moral, not to be rhetorical, but to have simply a sort of gentlemanly, epicurean relish for the bitterness of the general human lot, and to distil it into little polished silver cups—this was Mérimée's conscious effort, and this was his rare success.

Some of his best stories are those in which a fantastic or supernatural element is thrown into startling relief against a background of hard, smooth realism. An admirable success in this line is the **"Venus d'Ile"**—a version of the old legend of a love-pledge between a mortal and an effigy of the goddess. . . . Mérimée, making his heroine an antique brozen statue, disinterred in the garden of a little château in Gascony, and her victim the son of the old provincial antiquarian who discovered her, almost makes us believe in its actuality. . . . The first and much the best of the stories in [*Dernières Nouvelles*], **"Lokis,"** deals with a subject as picturesquely unnatural. A Polish lady is seized by a bear, and dragged for five minutes toward his hiding-place. She is rescued in time to save her life, but her reason has succumbed to her terror, and she remains for ever a monomaniac. A few months after her disaster she gives birth to a son. Mérimée tells us the son's story. We recommend it to readers not averse to a good stiff horror. . . . [We] strongly suspect that Mérimée's best things will be valued for many years to come. Among writers elaborately perfect in a somewhat narrow line he will hold a high place; he will always be admired by the votaries of "manner." Twenty years hence, doubtless, clever young men, reading him for the first time, will, in the flash of enthusiasm, be lending his volumes to appreciative female friends, and having them promptly returned, with the observation that they are "coarse." Whereupon, we suppose, the clever young men will fall to reading them over, and reflecting that it is quite right, after all, that men should have their distinctive pleasures, and that a good story by Mérimée is not the least of these. (pp. 170-72)

> Henry James, *"Mérimée's Last Tales"* (originally published in The Nation, *Vol. XVIII, No. 450, February 12, 1874), in his* Literary Reviews and Essays: On American, English, and French Literature, *edited by Albert Mordell, Twayne Publishers, 1957, pp. 169-72.*

[CAMILLE E. P. BARRÈRE] (essay date 1874)

[Mérimée's] historical works no one, not excluding himself probably, took a very great interest in; they are cold and stately—comparable for the matter, if the metaphor be permitted to us, to water contained in the finest Bohemian glass. As to his essays in fiction it is vastly different. When he has deigned to remain in his own time, and to pick out his personages and action from modern society, his productions have always been admirable both in matter and form. His process was much like Stendhal's. As he wrote for the select (if indeed he ever wrote for the edification of any one) he disdained the imbroglio of commonplace sentiments, the banalities of ordinary conversation; he obviously aimed at concentration and abridgment, at probing the acts of man by certain telling features of human nature, and, in fact, at leaving much for the reader to guess by suppressing what vulgarities are wearisome to the "profound few." This kind of work offers equal dangers and advantages; it excludes two thirds of the general readers who may be wanting in the quick sagacity requisite for the proper comprehension of the author's process, although in the main they may be qualified to appreciate the essence of his work; further,

it circumscribes the repute of a writer in a narrow circle, and, moreover, such style always tends to fall into obscurity and enigma. On the other hand, the omission of a great many strictly useless details preserves a work from the caprices of fashion and change of customs, and *Carmen* and *Colomba,* free as they are from descriptions of transient and superficial interest, and consisting solely of the condensed description of passions and impulses that are eternal, will be eternally useful, just as Shakspeare and Milton are. . . . [The literary merits of *Lettres à une Inconnue*] are of secondary consideration; suffice it to say . . . that their form, wit, and ingeniosity are paramount. As to the *Inconnue* [unknown woman], there is no need to inquire after her. What is thoroughly engrossing is the perusal between the lines of the desolate story of unhappiness the great sceptic relates. There are expressions for every disgust, words eloquent in their brevity expressive of deceptions, weariness, *ennui;* bitter estimations of men, impeachments of what he calls human imbecility; contemptuous allusions to his best friends, and topping all a clear disbelief in goodness, and those noble commonplaces, honour, love, chivalry, abnegation. It is worthy of special note that Mérimée is withal open to superstition, several instances of this being manifested in different letters; so strong is the yearning of every one towards a faith, whatever it may be. We have found but one good note in the two volumes of this correspondence; as to the harsh ones, they abound; on Frenchmen especially his satire never tarries. . . . Speaking of Englishmen, he says that individually they are stupid, but as a whole admirable. Few things, in fact, find grace in his eyes. (pp. 69-71)

Throughout [his correspondence] the emptiness of his life prevails. To sum up, he sifted languages, literatures, and characters; he studied his species in all parts of the globe; and, as a just retribution for spurning all subjects of study after devoting his attention to each, instead of drawing consequences from the synthesis of things, he sickened, and looked about him for something to love or to like. Failing in his endeavours, he . . . listlessly wandered through the drama of life, obviously without object, and certainly without desire. What was the use for him to apply his energy to some great work; to labour for a definite enterprise? He was a sceptic, and much of a cynic too; his soul was as well closed to narrow egotism as to a noble faith in the perfectibility of human attempts. Vanity he had none; he cared not a whit for glory. If he achieved a few masterpieces it was for his amusement, not for others—he despised others too much for that; and in his sometimes heroic contempt, the trace he would leave of his passage in this world troubled him but slightly. As most men who look upon the details of life too critically, he had lost sight of the good features of human nature only to give paramount importance to its vices. He commenced life on the defensive: suspicion bred bitterness; bitterness bred scepticism, scepticism bred the cynic. It is clear that such negative sentiments were not primarily in his heart, and that they derived their origin from mistaken notions. It is also clear that this singular man's heart never thrilled with love, and that a fatal distrust, on which we have commented, deprived him of a solace which might have made of him a far different individual from the polite, caustic, stoically desponding Mérimée, whom Renan gives as a type of a period. The "Unknown" was merely the recipient of those confidences which every mind has an irrepressible tendency to unfold; but that alone is no proof of amorous affection. Proud as he was, Mérimée doubtless selected her as the fittest person to preserve his secrets; and perhaps another deception might be added to the others, could he know that even this trust has been betrayed. Howbeit, the *Inconnue* was no more than a confidante. (pp. 72-3)

Two hours before breathing his last he wrote the note which closes the second volume of his correspondence. He was borne silently to the grave, momentarily forgotten. No doubt he would have approved of this oblivion and indifference. (p. 73)

[Camille E. P. Barrère], *"The Real Prosper Mérimée,"* in The Cornhill Magazine, *Vol. XXX, July, 1874, pp. 66-73.*

GEORGE BRANDES (essay date 1882)

[*Brandes was a Danish literary critic and biographer. In his major critical work,* Main Currents in Nineteenth-Century Literature, *Brandes viewed French, German, and English literary movements as a series of reactions against eighteenth-century thought. In the following, Brandes portrays Mérimée as an audacious and passionate author.*]

The critical temperament is above everything truthful; and Mérimée was remarkably so. His natural audacity, moreover, impelled him to say exactly what he thought, regardless of conventionalities. One sees from his letters how frank he was by nature, how inclined to speak the undisguised truth, and how impatient of conventional falsehoods and even of alleviating or embellishing circumlocutions. This is especially noticeable in the first volume of *Lettres à une inconnue.* Even in these love-letters Mérimée is almost rude when it seems to him that the object of his affections has expressed some merely conventional opinion. (p. 243)

Mérimée's earliest attitude as the dramatist and novelist is an attitude of literary aggressiveness. Although by nature an observer, he does not, like Balzac, set himself the task of representing, in all its breadth, the world he sees around him; neither is it his ambition that posterity shall study in his works the customs and ideas of his period; he desires to challenge a prevailing taste; and with the object of irritating and rousing his fellow-countrymen, he generally chooses themes which have as little connection as possible with modern civilised society. (p. 260)

Mérimée does not write for the "bourgeois," into whose eyes the slightest emotion brings tears; he addresses himself to people of stronger nerves, who require more violent shocks to move them. Therefore away with the regulation lengthy introductions, and all the preparations and omens of tragedy! (p. 261)

He is familiar with death. If the old designations were applicable in his case, we should call him a great tragic author; but Mérimée does not believe in what dogmatic upholders of Aristotelian principles call tragic expiation. . . .

Deepest down in his soul lies the love of strength. But he does not, like Balzac, love strength in the shape of strong desire, strong passions; he loves it in the form of original force of character and of stirring, decisive event; and therefore he naturally begins by feeling and reproducing the poetry of decisive event, long before he is mature enough to represent that of simple, strong character. Of all events, death is the most decisive; and hence it is that he falls in love with death—not, be it observed, with death as it is conceived of by spiritualists and believers, not with death as a purifying passage to another existence, but as a violent, sudden, bloody termination. (p. 262)

[In the *Théâtre de Clara Gazul*] it is amusing to observe the conflict of youth with the inveterate natural bias towards gloom and violence. Read superficially, the book produces the effect of a tolerably serious work. Professing to be written in the Spanish style, it nevertheless differs in many essential partic-

ulars from Spanish dramatic literature. The plays of which it is composed have no mutual resemblance; they do not, like the mantle-and-dagger tragedies, monotonously repeat the same types of character and the same situations, produced by jealousy and a touchy sense of honour; nor do they accept the extremely conventional ideas of morality current in the tragedies in question. Mérimée's characters have distinctly defined individualities; and instead of exhibiting superhuman self-control and resignation, they are carried blindly away by their passions and desires. (p. 263)

[*Clara Gazul* is] a merry book; the good lady who wrote it is no prude. But what a strange kind of mirth it is! Amongst its manifestations is the free use of the knife. If we try to find a parallel to it, nothing suggests itself but the sportive springs of a young tiger. Mérimée finds it almost impossible to end without killing all his principal characters, and one swordthrust succeeds the other almost automatically. But he amuses himself by destroying the illusion directly after the catastrophe; the actors rise, and one of them thanks the audience for their kind attention; the whole thing is turned into a jest. (p. 264)

His last tale, *Lokis,* is the story of a young Lithuanian count of mysterious descent, who from time to time is possessed by, or at least feels that he possesses, the instincts of a wild animal. He goes mad on his wedding-night and kills his bride by biting her throat. The count's character is drawn with delicate skill [and] the progress of his mental derangement is indicated by a few slight but graphic touches. . . . But the impression left by this vampire tale is one of disgust mingled with horror. The masterly treatment, the perfect style, the refined manner in which the loathsome subject is dealt with, remind us of the white kid gloves of the headsman. The story is only of interest to us as a proof of the strength retained by one of its author's original tendencies. (p. 265)

It is his passion for strength in its primitive nakedness which endows him with the historical sense. Hence the heroes of his historical works are always the wildest and most daring characters—Sulla, Catilina, Don Pedro the Cruel of Castile, the first pseudo-Demetrius, &c., &c. His conscientious accuracy and his distrust of the part played by imagination in science rob his historical works proper of life (he is most successful in *Don Pedro I.* and *Épisode de l'Histoire de la Russie*); but he at once imparts life to any period which he treats as the imaginative artist. (p. 268)

The separate personages in his *Chronique du Règne de Charles IX,* stand out . . . clearly from the background. They have strongly marked characteristics without on that account being modern . . . ; indeed Mérimée has bestowed such attention on details that each chapter in its graphic coherence forms a little whole, and the work in its entirety produces the effect of a mosaic design of character portraits and pictures of society. In the last of his semi-historical works, *Les Débuts d'un Aventurier,* we observe that what attracts him in the false Demetrius is the primitive cunning, the rough, vigorous Cossack character, and not those mental conflicts, ensuing on the fraud, which fascinated Schiller. Mérimée may be said to leave off where Schiller begins. The manners and customs of a definite group of human beings at a definite period are of far more interest to him than what these human beings have in common with universal humanity; hence here as elsewhere in his historical fiction, it is not the intellectual or emotional side of life which he shows us, but its character side—the results of strong, concentrated will-power. When he writes of modern times, he describes gipsy or brigand life, as in *Carmen,* a vendetta, as in *Colomba,* a horrible murder on the wedding-night, as in *La Vénus d'Ille* and *Lokis.* Or if he lays his plot within the pale of modern society proper, he either describes peculiarities of those classes which labour under social disadvantages—the bold language and irregular ideas of young ballet-dancers and actresses, the erotic temptations of Catholic priests; or contents himself with anything in the life of the upper classes that means character—a passionate love-affair terminated by a duel, a case of adultery which leads to the suicide of one of the parties concerned, any thoroughly scandalous story which it delights him to cast in the teeth of the effete, hypocritical society of the day. He feels himself in his element amidst merciless strokes of fate, terrible vicissitudes, violent passions which, when they are fortunate, override the conventions of society, and when unfortunate, are called crimes. Hence it was that modern Russian literature was so sympathetic to him. (pp. 269-70)

Two characteristic feelings lie at the root of Mérimée's disinclination to apprehend and treat the trenchant catastrophes in human life as tragic catastrophes; the one is a kind of fear that the trenchancy which he loves will lose its edge by the introduction of a reconciling element; the other is his disbelief in a greater, comprehensive whole, of which the single incident forms a part. When he produces, as he at times does, a genuinely tragic effect, it happens almost against his will, and is the result of a more mature and profound understanding of the human soul, and of a sympathy, growing with his growing experience of life, for cases in which there is a necessary connection between character and destiny. (p. 271)

In another little work of art, *La double Méprise,* Mérimée endeavours to represent the web of chance events, of conflicting and wrongly comprehended instincts, which make life so meaningless, and even what is saddest as foolish as it is sad and hideous; but as he unfolds the inner history of the painful incident, and as we by degrees learn that that which seemed foolish was inevitable, it ceases to be foolish. . . . Mérimée's art displays itself in [*La double Méprise*] in the calm assurance with which he takes his reader's hand and leads him through the labyrinth of all these ideas and emotions to a climax which is as inevitable as it is illogical. . . . Mérimée understood what a power, what a tragic motive force in human life, inevitable illusion or self-deception is. It is the source to which not only half of human happiness, but a considerable proportion of human misery may be traced.

But Mérimée approaches nearer than this to tragedy proper, where the fateful element sinks deep into the character, mingling with it as a poison mingles with the blood. Think of *Carmen.* From the day of José's first meeting with Carmen, the gipsy girl, the course of his life is changed; and he, the honest, good-hearted man, becomes of inevitable necessity, for her sake, a robber and a murderer. Nay, the author, whose aim as a young Romanticist was to hold as far aloof as possible from the poets who wrote tragedy in the ancient Greek style, approaches, in *Colomba,* with his modern Corsican heroine, nearer to Greek tragedy than any of his fellow-countrymen who hymned the fate of one or other of "Agamemnon's imperishable race." Not without reason has Colomba been compared to Elektra. Like Elektra, she broods, to the exclusion of every other thought, on the unavenged death of her father; like Elektra, she incites her brother to take a bloody revenge; and she is even less of the stereotyped tragedy heroine than Sophocles' young girl, for, clad though she is in the steel panoply of appalling prejudices, she bears herself simply and lovably. She is at once bloodthirsty and childlike, hard-hearted and girlish;

a fierce grace is her characteristic trait. It is easy for us now to see how much more nearly akin this fresh, vigorous daughter of a little southern island race is to the old Greek female characters than are all those princesses who walked the French stage in buskins, and borrowed the names of Elektra, Antigone, or Iphigenia. But she is perhaps still more nearly related to the heathen daughters of a far-away northern isle, the women of the Icelandic sagas, who brood with such passionate obstinacy over their family feuds, and force the unwilling men to take blood for blood. (pp. 271-73)

> *George Brandes, in his* Main Currents in Nineteenth Century Literature: The Romantic School in France, *Vol. V, translated by Diana White and Mary Morison (originally published as* Hovedstrømninger i det 19de aarhundredes litteratur: Den romantiske Skole i Frankrig, *1882), William Heinemann, 1904 (and reprinted by Heinemann, 1924), 391 p.**

WALTER PATER (essay date 1890)

[*Pater was a famed English critic and leader in the nineteenth-century revival of interest in Renaissance art and humanism. The following essay is considered one of the seminal studies of Mérimée and his work; Pater stresses Mérimée's ennui and the impersonality of his art.*]

In no century would Prosper Mérimée have been a theologian or metaphysician. But that sense of negation, of theoretic insecurity, was in the air, and conspiring with what was of like tendency in himself made of him a central type of disillusion. In him the passive *ennui* of [Étienne de Sénancour's] Obermann became a satiric, aggressive, almost angry conviction of the littleness of the world around; it was as if man's fatal limitations constituted a kind of stupidity in him, what the French call *bêtise.* . . . Almost everywhere he could detect the hollow ring of fundamental nothingness under the apparent surface of things. Irony surely, habitual irony, would be the proper complement thereto, on his part. In his infallible self-possession, you might even fancy him a mere man of the world, with a special aptitude for matters of fact. Though indifferent in politics, he rises to social, to political eminence; but all the while he is feeding all his scholarly curiosity, his imagination, the very eye, with the, to him ever delightful, relieving, reassuring spectacle, of those straightforward forces in human nature, which are also matters of fact. There is the formula of Mérimée! . . . What Mérimée gets around his singularly sculpturesque creations is neither more nor less than empty space.

So disparate are his writings that at first sight you might fancy them only the random efforts of a man of pleasure or affairs, who, turning to this or that for the relief of a vacant hour, discovers to his surprise a workable literary gift, of whose scope, however, he is not precisely aware. . . . [In] this age of novelists, it is as a writer of novels, and of fiction in the form of highly descriptive drama, that he will count for most:— *Colomba,* for instance, by its intellectual depth of motive, its firmly conceived structure, by the faultlessness of its execution, vindicating the function of the novel as no tawdry light literature, but in very deed a fine art. The *Chronique du Règne de Charles IX.* [*Chronicle of Charles the Ninth*], an unusually successful specimen of historical romance, links his imaginative work to the third group of Mérimée's writings, his historical essays. One resource of the disabused soul of our century . . . would be the empirical study of facts, the empirical science of nature and man, surviving all dead metaphysical philosophies. Mérimée, perhaps, may have had in him the making of a master of such science, disinterested, patient, exact: scalpel in hand, we may fancy, he would have penetrated far. But quite certainly he had something of genius for the exact study of history, for the pursuit of exact truth, with a keenness of scent as if that alone existed, in some special area of historic fact, to be determined by his own peculiar mental preferences. . . . Mérimée's style, simple and unconcerned, but with the eye ever on its object, lends itself perfectly to . . . an almost phlegmatic discovery of the facts, in all their crude natural colouring, as if he but held up to view, as a piece of evidence, some harshly dyed oriental carpet from the sumptuous floor of the Kremlin, on which blood had fallen.

A lover of ancient Rome, its great character and incident, Mérimée valued, as if it had been personal property of his, every extant relic of it in the art that had been most expressive of its genius—architecture. In that grandiose art of building, the most national, the most tenaciously rooted of all the arts in the stable conditions of life, there were historic documents hardly less clearly legible than the manuscript chronicle. . . . Structure, proportion, design, a sort of architectural coherency: that was the aim of his method in the art of literature, in that form of it, especially, which he will live by, in fiction.

As historian and archaeologist, as a man of erudition turned artist, he is well seen in the *Chronique du Règne de Charles IX.,* by which we pass naturally from Mérimée's critical or scientific work to the products of his imagination. What economy in the use of a large antiquarian knowledge! what an instinct amid a hundred details, for the detail that carries physiognomy in it, that really tells! And again what outline, what absolute clarity of outline! For the historian of that puzzling age which centres in the ''Eve of Saint Bartholomew,'' outward events themselves seem obscured by the vagueness of motive of the actors in them. But Mérimée, disposing of them as an artist, not in love with half-lights, compels events and actors alike to the clearness he desired; takes his side without hesitation; and makes his hero a Huguenot of pure blood, allowing its charm, in that charming youth, even to Huguenot piety. . . . The *Chronicle of Charles the Ninth* is like a series of masterly drawings in illustration of a period—the period in which two other masters of French fiction have found their opportunity, mainly by the development of its actual historic characters. Those characters—Catherine de Medicis and the rest—Mérimée, with significant irony and self-assertion, sets aside, preferring to think of them as essentially commonplace. For him the interest lies in the creatures of his own will, who carry in them, however, so lightly! a learning equal to Balzac's, greater than that of Dumas. He knows with like completeness the mere fashions of the time—how courtier and soldier dressed themselves, and the large movements of the desperate game which fate or chance was playing with those pretty pieces. Comparing that favourite century of the French Renaissance with our own, he notes a decadence of the more energetic passions in the interest of general tranquillity, and perhaps (only perhaps!) of general happiness. ''Assassination,'' he observes, as if with regret, ''is no longer a part of our manners.'' In fact, the duel, and the whole morality of the duel, which does but enforce a certain regularity on assassination, what has been well called *le sentiment du fer,* the sentiment of deadly steel, had then the disposition of refined existence. It was, indeed, very different, and *is,* in Mérimée's romance. In his gallant hero, Bernard de Mergy, all the promptings of the lad's virile goodness are in natural collusion with that *sentiment du fer.* . . . A winsome, yet withal serious and even piteous figure, he conveys his

pleasantness, in spite of its gloomy theme, into Mérimée's one quite cheerful book.

Cheerful, because, after all, the gloomy passions it presents are but the accidents of a particular age, and not like the mental conditions in which Mérimée was most apt to look for the spectacle of human power, allied to madness or disease in the individual. For him, at least, it was the office of fiction to carry one into a different if not a better world than that actually around us; and if the *Chronicle of Charles the Ninth* provided an escape from the tame circumstances of contemporary life into an impassioned past, *Colomba* is a measure of the resources for mental alteration which may be found even in the modern age. (pp. 13-22)

Crude in colour, sombre, taciturn, Corsica, as Mérimée here describes it, is like the national passion of the Corsican—that morbid personal pride, usurping the place even of grief for the dead, which centuries of traditional violence had concentrated into an all-absorbing passion for bloodshed, for bloody revenges, in collusion with the natural wildness, and the wild social condition of the island still unaffected even by the finer ethics of the duel. The supremacy of that passion is well indicated by the cry, put into the mouth of a young man in the presence of the corpse of his father deceased in the course of nature—a young man meant to be commonplace. ''Ah! Would thou hadst died *malamorte*—by violence! We might have avenged thee!'' In [the character of] Colomba, Mérimée's best known creation, it is united to a singularly wholesome type of personal beauty, a natural grace of manner which is irresistible, a cunning intellect patiently diverting every circumstance to its design; and presents itself as a kind of genius, allied to fatal disease of mind. (pp. 23-4)

Pity and terror, we know, go to the making of the essential tragic sense. In Mérimée, certainly, we have all its terror, but without the pity. . . . Seldom or never has the mere pen of a writer taken us so close to the cannon's mouth as in the *Taking of the Redoubt,* while *Matteo Falcone*—twenty-five short pages— is perhaps the cruellest story in the world.

Colomba, that strange, fanatic being, who has a code of action, of self-respect, a conscience, all to herself, who with all her virginal charm only does not make you hate her, is, in truth, the type of a sort of humanity Mérimée found it pleasant to dream of—a humanity as alien as the animals, with whose moral affinities to man his imaginative work is often directly concerned. . . . Stories that told of sudden freaks of gentle, polite natures, straight back, *not* into Paradise, were always welcome to men's fancies; and that could only be because they found a psychologic truth in them. With much success, with a credibility insured by his literary tact, Mérimée tried his own hand at such stories: unfrocked the bear in the amorous young Lithuanian noble, the wolf in the revolting peasant of the Middle Age. There were survivals surely in himself, in that stealthy presentment of his favourite themes, in his own art. You seem to find your hand on a serpent, in reading him. (pp. 27-9)

At the bottom of the true drama there is ever, logically at least, the ballad: the ballad dealing in a kind of short-hand (or, say! in grand, simple, universal outlines) with those passions, crimes, mistakes, which have a kind of fatality in them, a kind of necessity to come to the surface of the human *mind,* if not to the surface of our *experience,* as in the case of some frankly supernatural incidents which Mérimée re-handled. Whether human love or hatred has had most to do in shaping the universal fancy that the dead come back, I cannot say. Certainly that old ballad literature has instances in plenty, in which the voice, the hand, the brief visit from the grave, is a natural response to the cry of the human creature. That ghosts should return, as they do so often in Mérimée's fiction, is but a sort of natural justice. Only, in Mérimée's prose ballads, in those admirable, short, ballad-like stories, where every word tells, of which he was a master, almost the inventor, they are a kind of half-material ghosts—a vampire tribe—and never come to do people good; congruously with the mental constitution of the writer, which, alike in fact and fiction, could hardly have horror enough—theme after theme. Mérimée himself emphasises this almost constant motive of his fiction when he adds to one of his volumes of short stories some letters on a matter of fact—a Spanish bull-fight, in which those old Romans, he regretted, might seem, decadently, to have survived. It is as if you saw it. In truth, Mérimée was the unconscious parent of much we may think of dubious significance in later French literature. (pp. 30-1)

Mérimée, a literary artist, was not a man who used two words where one would do better, and he shines especially in those brief compositions which, like a minute intaglio, reveal at a glance his wonderful faculty of design and proportion in the treatment of his work, in which there is not a touch but counts. That is an art of which there are few examples in English; our somewhat diffuse, or slipshod, literary language hardly lending itself to the concentration of thought and expression, which are of the essence of such writing. It is otherwise in French, and if you wish to know what art of that kind can come to, read Mérimée's little romances; best of all, perhaps, *La Vénus d'Ille* and *Arsène Guillot*. The former is a modern version of the beautiful old story of the Ring given to Venus, given to her, in this case, by a somewhat sordid creature of the nineteenth century, whom she looks on with more than disdain. (pp. 31-2)

The intellectual charm of literary work so thoroughly designed as Mérimée's depends in part on the sense as you read, hastily perhaps, perhaps in need of patience, that you are dealing with a composition, the full secret of which is only to be attained in the last paragraph, that with the last word in mind you will retrace your steps, more than once (it may be) noting then the minuter structure, also the natural or wrought flowers by the way. Nowhere is such method better illustrated than by another of Mérimée's quintessential pieces, *Arsène Guillot,* and here for once with a conclusion ethically acceptable also. Mérimée loved surprises in human nature, but it is not often that he surprises us by tenderness or generosity of character. . . . It may be said, indeed, that only an essentially pitiful nature could have told the exquisitely cruel story of *Matteo Falcone* precisely as Mérimée has told it. . . . [*Lettres à une Inconnue* reveals a] reserved, sensitive, self-centred nature, a little pusillanimously in the power, at the disposition of another. For just there lies the interest, the psychological interest, of those letters. An amateur of power, of the spectacle of power and force, followed minutely but without sensibility on his part, with a kind of cynic pride rather for the mainspring of his method, both of thought and expression, you find him here taken by surprise at last, and somewhat humbled, by an unsuspected force of affection in himself. His correspondent, unknown but for these letters except just by name, figures in them as, in truth, a being only too much like himself, seen from one side; reflects his taciturnity, his touchiness, his incredulity except for self-torment. . . . Mérimée is always pleading, but always complaining that he gets only her second thoughts; the thoughts,

that is, of a reserved, self-limiting nature, well under the yoke of convention, like his own. (pp. 33-4)

The intimacy, the effusion, the so freely exposed personality of those letters does but emphasise the fact that *impersonality* was, in literary art, Mérimée's central aim. Personality *versus* impersonality in art:—how much or how little of one's self one may put into one's work: whether anything at all of it: whether one *can* put there anything else:—is clearly a far-reaching and complex question. Serviceable as the basis of a precautionary maxim towards the conduct of our work, self-effacement, or impersonality, in literary or artistic creation, is, perhaps, after all, as little possible as a strict realism. . . . Essentially unlike other people, he is always fastidiously in the fashion—an expert in all the little, half-contemptuous elegances of which it is capable. Mérimée's superb self-effacement, his impersonality, is itself but an effective personal trait, and, transferred to art, becomes a markedly peculiar quality of literary beauty. For, in truth, this creature of disillusion who had no care for half-lights, and, like his creations, had no atmosphere about him, gifted as he was with pure *mind,* with the quality which secures flawless literary structure, had, on the other hand, nothing of what we call *soul* in literature:—hence, also, that singular harshness in his ideal, as if, in theological language, he were incapable of grace. He has none of those subjectivities, colourings, peculiarities of mental refraction, which necessitate *varieties* of style—could we spare such?—and render the perfections of it no merely negative qualities. There are masters of French prose whose art has begun where the art of Mérimée leaves off. (pp. 35-7)

Walter Pater, ''Prosper Mérimée,'' in The Fortnightly Review, *n.s. Vol. XLVIII, No. CCLXXXVIII, December, 1890 (and reprinted in his* Miscellaneous Studies: A Series of Essays, *Macmillan and Co., Limited, 1895, Johnson Reprint Corporation, 1967, pp. 11-37).*

B. W. WELLS (essay date 1898)

Prosper Mérimée is a novelist whose place in the evolution of fiction it is difficult to fix, and therefore peculiarly interesting to study. It is customary, and not unjust, to regard him as the successor of Stendhal, but he had in him elements of closer relation to George Sand and others that suggest Balzac, while perhaps, after all, he will be found more closely allied to Flaubert than to any of his early contemporaries. . . . [Stendhal and Mérimée] shared in many sympathies and antipathies, especially in a contempt for the ethics of the bourgeoisie, which Mérimée expressed with an irony keener than Stendhal's and lighter than Flaubert's. The three were alike in their objectivity, and all excelled, though in different ways, in psychologic analysis. But in their romantic pessimism Mérimée and Flaubert part company with Stendhal, who never wholly threw off the rationalistic optimism of the eighteenth century, while Mérimée's cruel irony is more impassively indifferent than Flaubert's, having . . . little trace of the eighteenth century save in the audacious crudity and dry skepticism of his thought. With George Sand he shares the power of picturesque description, but he is too cynical to share her buoyancy. He has the somberness of Balzac, unrelieved by the latter's idealism; and he has Stendhal's morbid dread of being the dupe of his emotions, which in him showed itself in what none of these other four possessed—a high-bred, aristocratic, polished impassivity in his social bearing, and a corresponding pellucid but cold correctness in his style, where art hides art even more effectively than in Flaubert. His indifference goes so far as to suppress studiously all appearance of interest in his own work. . . . Until the rise of Flaubert he was the best, almost the only, representative in France of the strictly objective school in fiction. (pp. 167-68)

["**La Jacquerie**," Mérimée's first work in dramatic fiction, is] interesting chiefly because it showed at the outset all the qualities, except polish of diction, that were to mark his work to the close. These were an astonishing command of language, a remarkable power of conveying to the reader the spirit of a distant age and foreign scene. . . .

"**La Jacquerie**" was surpassed in all its qualities by "**Le Chronique du Règne de Charles IX.,**" whose central scene is the massacre of St. Bartholemew, which to him seems to illustrate the observation that all morality is relative, and suggests that "the decadence of energetic passion has been to the gain of tranquillity and, perhaps, of happiness." The story is told with great verve, and is full of adventure, of murder and blood; but there is shrewd historical analysis also, with picturesque scenes of bygone manners. The irony that runs through all Mérimée's fiction concentrates here its brightest flashes in the sermon of Père Lubin, and its most mordant bitterness in the spiritual brawl of priest and parson over the bed of the dying Voltairean Mergy, while the novel ends nonchalantly with a request to the reader to finish the story as best suits his fancy. As a whole, "**Le Chronique**" is a well-told story, but it lacks . . . [stylistic finish and intensity]. (p. 169)

[In "**Matéo Falcone**," Mérimée's] irony reaches the utmost pitch of its cruelty. Here is a man who has murdered his rival in love and yet has so Corsican a feeling of honor that he kills his son, a boy of ten, for failing in hospitality to a criminal, leaving the reader to conclude that, when civilization is stripped off, all moral action is the result of prejudice and of fatality. And yet one hesitates to accord "**Matéo Falcone**" the supreme touch of pessimistic irony when one reads the ghastly story of "**Tamango**." . . . Perhaps more bestial horror has never been crowded into so little room or recounted with such cold precision as in this story. (pp. 170-71)

In "**Le Vase Etrusque**," a story less well constructed than is usual with Mérimée, love and then jealousy seize on the else calm and clear mind of Saint-Clair and lead him with an inexorable fatality to destruction. In his proud nature, inclined to retrospect, ambitious, distraught, opinionated, and reserved, there seem many traits of Mérimée's self. (p. 171)

Always to some extent an enemy of the conventional, Mérimée was perhaps least so in "**La Double Méprise**" . . . , which seems rather in the manner of Bourget or of Prévost, a bit of pathological psychology. . . .

["**Les Ames du Purgatoire**"] is a development of the legend of Don Juan de Maraña, the incarnation of materialistic will trampling for his lusts on the honor of women, the lives of men, and the love of God, and then converted by a terrifying vision and turning his strong will toward furious penitence, as unspiritual at the last as at the first. . . . [Here] love is a tragic fatality, respecting neither law nor life. (p. 172)

Corsica is . . . the scene of "**Colomba**," in whose two hundred pages there is probably more exotic life than in any work of the French language. . . . The book is still, what it was from the beginning, by far the most popular work of its author, and, whether true or false in its local color, it certainly produces the illusion of reality. (p. 173)

["**Colomba**"] is the most cheerful, indeed, the only cheerful book of Mérimée. We pass through murder, but we come to marriage-bells, and the irony is less persistently sardonic. His pessimistic fancy habitually seeks escape from present conditions by creating a world of fiercer primordial passions, but he has never treated conventional society with such genial persiflage as in "**Colomba**." (p. 175)

"**La Chambre Bleue**," a mediocre piece of rather gruesome fooling in the manner of the last century, with more snickering in the irony than is usual in Mérimée, seems to reflect the influence of the imperial court and the evenings at Compiègne, but "**Lokis**" carries us once more to the weird lands of crime and passion, interweaving the vampire and werewolf superstitions of the past with modern theories of heredity. Here a son, whose mother before his birth had lost her reason in a bear's embrace, couples the nature of his noble ancestors with brute ferocity. The bears have an instinct that he shares their nature, and ghastly presentiments prepare us from the outset for the denouement where, in excess of love, he sucks the lifeblood of his spouse and escapes to the beasts of the forest. The tale is treated with admirable restraint. (pp. 178-79)

[Though] the imagination be romantic, the style . . . always is thoroughly realistic, and it is by this art that he succeeds in making "**Lokis**," "**Carmen**," or "**Colomba**" seem to us as natural to their environment as gloves and evening dress to our own. Thus he fascinates us by the extraordinary at the same time that he evokes our sympathy by the appearance of reality. This tends to give a certain malignity to his ironical skepticism. It has been said that he "despised" men too much to have faith in their progress. We shall not look for moral inspiration to one who could say of a drama, "The piece appears wearisome, although immoral;" nor can we look for intellectual inspiration to one who poses as a dilettante and is sure that to excel in any art "one must be a little *bête* [crazy]." No doubt Mérimée toyed with morality and no doubt his fiction contributed to the weakening of the will that characterized his generation. But as an artist his work has a refined distinction that is the more charming for its seeming lack of effort, hiding the most consummate art of limpid harmony. His work appeals only to a refined taste and to that it will appeal always for its restrained and delicate sense of proportion, so singularly lacking in his naturalistic successors. He is in the novel what Gautier is in poetry, the representative of art for art's sake. His style has been compared to a sheet of glass through which all that he wishes to show appears clear and distinct, while the medium itself leaves at the first reading no sensation. Yet if the critic concentrate his attention on this style, he will find that all in it has been subordinated to an esthetic purpose that produced its full effect of aristocratic daintiness and elegance, even while unrecognized. Among all French novelists he is preeminently the artist. (p. 179)

> B. W. Wells, "The Fiction of Prosper Mérimée," in
> The Sewanee Review, Vol. VI, No. 2, Spring, 1898,
> pp. 167-79.

ARTHUR SYMONS   (essay date 1901)

[*An English critic, poet, dramatist, short story writer, and editor, Symons initially gained notoriety as a decadent of the 1890s, and eventually established himself as one of the most important critics of the modern era. His sensitive translations of Paul Verlaine and Stéphane Mallarmé provided English poets with an introduction to the poetry of the French Symbolists. Though he was a gifted translator and linguist, it was as a critic that Symons made his most important contribution to literature. His* The Symbolist Movement in Literature *provided his English contemporaries with an appropriate vocabulary with which to define their new aesthetic—one that communicated their concern with dreamlike states, imagination, and a reality that exists beyond the boundaries of the senses. Symons finds in Mérimée a "union of curiosity with indifference." Like George Steiner (see excerpt below, 1963), Symons particularly notes the impersonality of Mérimée's style.]*

Mérimée realises a type which we are accustomed to associate almost exclusively with the eighteenth century, but of which our own time can offer us many obscure examples. It is the type of the *esprit fort* [strong spirit]: the learned man, the choice, narrow artist, who is at the same time the cultivated sensualist. To such a man the pursuit of women is part of his constant pursuit of human experience, and of the document, which is the summing up of human experience. To Mérimée history itself was a matter of detail. (p. 29)

[The **"Lettres à une Inconnue"**] have a delicately insincere sincerity which makes every letter a work of art, not because he tried to make it so, but because he could not help seeing the form simultaneously with the feeling, and writing genuine love-letters with an excellence almost as impersonal as that of his stories. He begins with curiosity, which passes with singular rapidity into a kind of self-willed passion; already in the eighth letter, long before he has seen her, he is speculating which of the two will know best how to torture the other: that is, as he views it, love best. (p. 31)

Perhaps of all love-letters, these of Mérimée show us love triumphing over the most carefully guarded personality. Here the obstacle is not duty, nor circumstance, nor a rival; but (on her side as on his, it would seem) a carefully trained natural coldness, in which action, and even for the most part feeling, are relinquished to the control of second thoughts. A habit of repressive irony goes deep: Mérimée might well have thought himself secure against the outbreak of an unconditional passion. Yet here we find passion betraying itself, often only by bitterness, together with a shy, surprising tenderness, in this curious lovers' itinerary, marked out with all the customary signposts, and leading, for all its wilful deviations, along the inevitable road.

It is commonly supposed that the artist, by the habit of his profession, has made for himself a sort of cuirass of phrases against the direct attack of emotion, and so will suffer less than most people if he should fall into love, and things should not go altogether well with him. Rather, he is the more laid open to attack, the more helplessly entangled when once the net has been cast over him. He lives through every passionate trouble, not merely with the daily emotions of the crowd, but with the whole of his imagination. Pain is multiplied to him by the force of that faculty by which he conceives delight. What is most torturing in every not quite fortunate love is memory, and the artist becomes an artist by his intensification of memory. Mérimée has himself defined art as exaggeration *à propos*. Well, to the artist his own life is an exaggeration not *à propos*, and every hour dramatises for him its own pain and pleasure, in a tragic comedy of which he is the author and actor and spectator. (pp. 32-3)

And so we find Mérimée, the most impersonal of artists, and one of those most critical of the caprices and violences of fate, giving in to an almost obvious temptation, an anonymous correspondence, a mysterious unknown woman, and passing from stage to stage of a finally very genuine love-affair, which kept him in a fluttering agitation for more than thirty years. It is curious to note that the little which we know of this *Inconnue* seems to mark her out as the realisation of a type which had always been Mérimée's type of woman. . . . Like so many artists, he has invented his ideal before he meets it, and must have seemed almost to have fallen in love with his own creation. (p. 33)

Mérimée as a writer belongs to the race of Laclos and of Stendhal, a race essentially French; and we find him representing, a little coldly, as it seemed, the claims of mere unimpassioned intellect, at work on passionate problems, among those people of the Romantic period to whom emotion, evident emotion, was everything. In his subjects he is as "Romantic" as Victor Hugo or Gautier; he adds, even, a peculiar flavour of cruelty to the Romantic ingredients. But he distinguishes sharply, as French writers before him had so well known how to do, between the passion one is recounting and the moved or unmoved way in which one chooses to tell it. To Mérimée art was a very formal thing, almost a part of learning; it was a thing to be done with a clear head, reflectively, with a calm mastery of even the most vivid material. . . . His own emotion, so far as it is roused, seems to him an extraneous thing, a thing to be concealed, if not a little ashamed of. It is the thing itself he wishes to give you, not his feelings about it; and his theory is that if the thing itself can only be made to stand and speak before the reader, the reader will supply for himself all the feeling that is needed, all the feeling that would be called out in nature by a perfectly clear sight of just such passions in action. It seems to him bad art to paint the picture, and to write a description of the picture as well. (pp. 34-5)

At a time when he had come to consider scholarly dexterity as the most important part of art, Mérimée tells us that **"La Vénus d'Ille"** seemed to him the best story he had ever written. He has often been taken at his word, but to take him at his word is to do him an injustice. **"La Vénus d'Ille"** is a modern setting of the old story of the Ring given to Venus, and Mérimée has been praised for the ingenuity with which he has obtained an effect of supernatural terror, while leaving the way open for a material explanation of the supernatural. What he has really done is to materialise a myth, by accepting in it precisely what might be a mere superstition, the form of the thing, and leaving out the spiritual meaning of which that form was no more than a temporary expression. (p. 35)

Mérimée had always delighted in mystifications; he was always on his guard against being mystified himself, either by nature or by his fellow-creatures. In the early "Romantic" days he had had a genuine passion for various things: "local colour," for instance. But even then he had invented it by a kind of trick, and, later on, he explains what a poor thing "local colour" is, since it can so easily be invented without leaving one's study. . . . Mérimée prized happiness, material comfort, the satisfaction of one's immediate desire, very highly, and it was his keen sense of life, of the pleasures of living, that gave him some of his keenness in the realisation of violent death, physical pain, whatever disturbs the equilibrium of things with unusual emphasis. Himself really selfish, he can distinguish the unhappiness of others with a kind of intuition which is not sympathy, but which selfish people often have: a dramatic consciousness of how painful pain must be, whoever feels it. (pp. 36-7)

And always in Mérimée there is [a] union of curiosity with indifference: the curiosity of the student, the indifference of the man of the world. Indifference, in him, as in the man of the world, is partly an attitude, adopted for its form, and influencing the temperament just so much as gesture always influences emotion. (p. 37)

Mérimée had an abstract interest in, almost an enthusiasm for, facts; facts for their meaning, the light they throw on psychology. He declines to consider psychology except through its expression in facts, with an impersonality far more real than that of Flaubert. The document, historical or social, must translate itself into sharp action before he can use it; not that he does not see, and appreciate better than most others, all there is of significance in the document itself; but his theory of art is inexorable. (p. 38)

Look, for instance, at his longest, far from his best work, **"La Chronique du Règne de Charles IX."** Like so much of his work, it has something of the air of a *tour de force*, not taken up entirely for its own sake. Mérimée drops into a fashion, half deprecatingly, as if he sees through it, and yet, as with merely mundane elegance, with a resolve to be more scrupulously exact than its devotees. "Belief," says some one in this book, as if speaking for Mérimée, "is a precious gift which has been denied me." Well, he will do better, without belief, than those who believe. Written under a title which suggests a work of actual history, it is more than possible that the first suggestion of this book really came, as he tells us in the preface, from the reading of "a large number of memoirs and pamphlets relating to the end of the sixteenth century." "I wished to make an epitome of my reading," he tells us, "and here is the epitome." . . . ["La Chronique du Règne de Charles IX"] is the most artistic, the most clean-cut, of historical novels; and yet this perfect neatness of method suggests a certain indifference on the part of the writer, as if he were more interested in doing the thing well than in doing it.

And that, in all but the very best of his stories (even, perhaps, in **"Arsène Guillot,"** only not in such perfect things as **"Carmen,"** as **"Mateo Falcone"**), is what Mérimée just lets us see, underneath an almost faultless skill of narrative. . . . Made out of elemental passions, hard, cruel, detached as it were from their own sentiments, the stories that he tells might in other hands become melodramas: **"Carmen,"** taken thoughtlessly out of his hands, has supplied the libretto to [Georges Bizet's *Carmen*,] the most popular of modern light operas. And yet, in his severe method of telling, mere outlines, it seems, told with an even stricter watch over what is significantly left out than over what is briefly allowed to be said in words, these stories sum up little separate pieces of the world, each a little world in itself. And each is a little world which he has made his own, with a labour at last its own reward, and taking life partly because he has put into it more of himself than the mere intention of doing it well. . . . In ["Carmen"] all the qualities of Mérimée come into agreement; the student of human passions, the traveller, the observer, the learned man, meet in harmony; and, in addition, there is the *aficionado*, the true *amateur*, in love with Spain and the Spaniards. (pp. 38-40)

> Arthur Symons, "Prosper Mérimée" (1901), in his *Studies in Prose and Verse, J M Dent & Sons Ltd, London, 1904, pp. 26-41.*

GEORGE SAINTSBURY   (essay date 1905)

[*Saintsbury was an English literary historian and critic of the late nineteenth century. A prolific writer, Saintsbury composed a number of histories of English and European literature, as well as several works on individual authors, styles, and periods. Saintsbury translated many of Mérimée's works into English. The fol-*

lowing, excerpted from his introduction to a collection of Mérimée's writings, surveys Mérimée's poetry, dramas, and letters, as well as his stories.]

It is noteworthy . . . that Mérimée's first exercises in [purely creative work], besides being hoaxes, were taken in paths which were not really his own. [His pseudonymous playwright] "Clara Gazul" writes things which at any rate look like plays. . . . Now, Mérimée certainly had not the dramatic, at least the theatrical, genius proper. . . . *La Guzla,* on the other hand, gives itself out as a translation of poetry; and affects the extremest poetic liberties of diction and of composition. And Mérimée . . . affected to care little, and did not probably care very much, for the form of verse. Yet both books have the most admirable literary quality—a quality so admirable as to make one heartily sorry that they are much more often spoken of as mere hoaxes than as anything else. (pp. xxxiii-xxxiv)

The "plays," under which head we may take not only *Clara Gazul* with the additions made to it later, but *La Famille Carvajal,* the *Jacquerie,* the more definitely dramatic volume entitled *Les Deux Héritages,* and the curious *Les Mécontents,* give us not merely a larger, but a more complicated and difficult subject. Authorities of the most diverse opinions have held that the connection between literature and drama is to a great extent fortuitous—that is to say, not, as it has been sometimes misunderstood, that a play may be thoroughly successful on the stage and have no literary qualities (which though true enough is immaterial), but that the qualities of literature as such, and the qualities of acted drama as such, are independent. Mérimée illustrates this remarkably from one side.

All [Mérimée's dramas] are literature, generally of a high and sometimes of quite the highest class. Scarcely one gives, as we read it, the idea of an actable drama, and not one that of a good actable drama. . . . Except that he employs the dramatic method of presentation *par personnages* [by characters] . . . instead of that of narration—except that he has side-headings of speakers' names, and stage-directions, and divisions of scenes—the whole thing is pure romance or pure novel. If there were not a great deal of pedantry in human nature I do not know why we should object to this. Some of the pieces, *Les Espagnols en Danemark,* for instance; *Les Deux Héritages* and some others would perhaps be better in narrative prose. *Le Carrosse du Saint Sacrement* might be. But I do not seem to see *Une Femme est un Diable,* or *L'Occasion,* or *Le Ciel et L'Enfer,* nearly so well in the continuous form; and when I compare *La Jacquerie* with *Charles IX,* I am by no means sure that the former would gain by adapting the shape of the latter. (pp. xxxv-xxxvi)

All this may be thought to show that Mérimée knew what he was about—a thing which perhaps happens more frequently than critics of great writers sometimes seem to perceive. His genius appears to have had what we may call its more concentrated and also its more desultory moments. In the former he wished to take a situation or set of situations, and put it, or them, with the utmost directness. . . . Then he wrote in plain narrative prose. At other times he wished rather to skirmish, to stroll about his subject and sketch it from various points of view; then he took the form by personages. This latter has resulted in some wonderful work. For the *Famille Carvajal,* I have, I confess, no great affection or admiration. Here only, perhaps, has Mérimée fallen into the mistake which originated in Early Romantic times and which has survived all the changes to the present day, that the revolting is the striking in itself. The "horrors" of *La Jacquerie* have, with the greater length, helped to make it more unpopular, but I think unjustly. They are not ubiquitous; the constant panoramic change of scene and subject is, except for persons whose power of attention is very feeble, rather fascinating; and the way in which the author manages not merely to paint manners but to insinuate character, is very masterly. (pp. xxxvii-xxxviii)

[*Une Femme est un Diable, L'Occasion, Le Ciel et L'Enfer, Le Carrosse du Saint Sacrement*] are so good in themselves that . . . they could not possibly have been told as well narratively. Three of the four are tragical; only one comic; but the mastery in either direction is practically indifferent.

Une Femme est un Diable is perhaps the weakest . . . , and the characters of the three inquisitors are somewhat conventional. But Mariquita, part victim, part almost unintentional temptress, is altogether admirable, and her various moods display a power of realisation and expression which the greatest masters of fiction have not surpassed. The pendant, for it is almost a pendant, *L'Occasion*, deserves at least the same praise and perhaps something higher still; for this is pure tragedy while the other is only sublimated melodrama. (pp. xxxviii-xxxix)

On the whole, however, *Le Ciel et L'Enfer,* which I think has not been a general favourite, seems to me the very best of the tragic pieces. The priest and the lover, though very good, are here purposely subordinated to Doña Urraca, the heroine; and once more her changes of mood, far deeper and more serious than Mariquita's, are a triumph. Coquetry, devotion, love, furious and almost murderous jealousy, love again and quite murderous repentance of the former act, all these drive over the soul of the heroine, and the scene of the story, like squalls and sunbursts on a stormy day—as suddenly, as irresistibly, as naturally. If Mérimée had written nothing else, he would have handed in his diploma-piece as a master with this.

He would have handed it as surely, though in another kind, if he had written nothing but *Le Carrosse du Saint Sacrement.* Here all is sunny enough; the spiteful tittle-tattle (whether it was quite false witness, one may be permitted to entertain the shadow of a doubt) of the secretary Martinez only gives the slight touch of dark needed to set off the brightness. The Viceroy, who allows himself to be fooled without being, in more than the very least degree, a fool, and who is wise enough not to quarrel with his own happiness; the Bishop, as wise in his generation yet not other than a very respectable child of light for all that; all the minor characters are capital. But the heroine, La Périchole, is something better. She is not only Mérimée's most amiable heroine, but what I trust I may be permitted to call, in deliberate flouting of a pedant objection, his "nicest." (pp. xxxix-xl)

Of course the not-quite-good heroine has great accommodations and great temptations for the novelist and the poet. . . . But it is quite unfair to take Carmen, who is probably his best known heroine, as his typical one. Colomba's eccentric ideas on the subject of murder were in the circumstances no blight on her general character, which is both stainless and amiable; anybody who could be quite certain of the absence of awkward points in his genealogy would be a fool not to marry Colomba if she would have him. La Périchole, . . . if not quite stainless, has not one unamiable fault. (pp. xli-xlii)

[It is generally agreed that Mérimée's] powers were not displayed at their very happiest in the *Chronique de Charles IX,* though Mérimée never did better things than the book contains. The demand for "unity" is sometimes thought a pedantic

one. . . . But to say "The Devil take all Unity" is as dangerous in literature as to say "The Devil take all Order" has often proved to be in war. . . . The *Chronique,* with all its brilliant sliding scenes, all its panorama as of a vivid dream, is certainly deficient in unity of any kind, whether of action, of character, or even that uncovenanted mercy the "Unity of Interest." . . . I am myself extremely fond of the *Chronique.* . . . But I can quite understand others failing to like it, and I can see that it has some positive defects.

I should be much less accommodating in the case of the shorter tales, from *L'Enlèvement de la Redoute* to *Colomba.* (p. xliii)

For myself, I have never known which to admire most—the variety of effect which Mérimée produces; the economy of means by which he produces it; or the absolute perfection of the effect produced. . . . *L'Enlèvement de la Redoute* has always been confessed to be a *ne plus ultra.* It is in race-horse condition; not an ounce of flesh on it that can hamper or drag its progress, not a muscle wanting in development to carry it at swiftest and surest toward the goal. The same is the case with what is perhaps its companion in general esteem, *Mateo Falcone.* But Mérimée, though never luxuriant, is not always thus ascetic. There is nothing of his that I myself prefer to the *Venus d'Ille.* . . . Mérimée's management of the supernatural is one of the most interesting points about him, and supplies another "note" to be carefully heeded in estimating his general character, literary and other. The blending [in the *Venus d'Ille*] of comedy with tragedy, of incident and suggestion, is unrivalled, or rivalled only by the other mixture of the voluptuous and the terrible. To call it, as it has been called, "a materialistic myth" is at least to suggest a gross misunderstanding. It is a resurrection of the flesh and blood from which all true myths have been originated. (pp. xlv-xlvi)

[And] who shall overpraise *Les Ames du Purgatoire*? I know no story of any writer to the style of which one of the hack words of criticism "limpid" applies so absolutely; and once more it has one of those extraordinary blends, antithesis, antinomies, which give such a savour to those who can savour them in literature. Mérimée is given out—perhaps gave himself out—as a professed unbeliever to an extent rather endangering his general reputation for restraint and "good form." Yet the religious tone which this story requires is infused neither in the least insufficiently nor with that ostentatious excess which is often visible in similar cases. And what is even more wonderful, it is kept in harmony with plenty of satiric touches; while the crisis-scene, where Don Juan is present at the last possible mass for his own soul, is almost unbelievably good. (pp. xlvi-xlvii)

Colomba and *Carmen*—the latter perhaps by the more adventitious and rather treacherous aid of music and acting than in itself, but still also in itself—are so much the best known things of their author that it is rather difficult to write of them; but they are also so much the most "considerable," in plenary combination of most of the senses of that word, that they can not be shirked. There can be no reasonable doubt that their author intended them as pendant studies of the South, and of the women of the South. As such, they could not—no such work from a man of Mérimée's age could—escape a slightly Byronic touch; but Mérimée's intense feeling for the absurd, the purity of his taste, and the detachment which it would be too complimentary to modernity to call modern in him, have completely kept off the rancid and the grotesque flavour and colour which usually mar Byronism. . . . I think Colomba was meant to be, and . . . I think she is, quite a good girl, and quite a ''nice'' though rather a formidable one. It is less a point of faith whether Mérimée has entirely freed her brother from the touch of comparative unmanliness which is almost inevitably suggested by such a Pallas-Diana of a sister. But the fact I think, is that Orso, Lydia, her father, the Prefect, the bandits, and all the rest are designedly, and in the case allowably, intended to be foils and sets-off to this Pallas-Diana herself. The pains which Mérimée has taken with her are extraordinary, and some of their results—the touch of literary interest in Dante, the *camaraderie* with the colonel and other things—may escape the careless; but they should not. (pp. xlvii-xlviii)

In *Carmen,* on the other hand, the interest is very much less centred in the heroine; indeed I am heretically inclined to think that the wicked gitana is much less really the heroine than José Navarro is the hero. She has a little too much of what I have just called her ''the wicked gitana'' in other words, of the type—that bane of French literature, which Mérimée, as a rule, has so successfully eluded or vanquished. Her hapless lover is much more of an individual, and it is more her office, baneful or not, to bring out his individuality than to display her own. It may even seem to some that the great chagrin of Mérimée's life—his jilting by an unlawful love of many years' standing—has reflected itself too closely for art in his delineation of Carmen's character. (pp. xlviii-xlix)

If, however, the character-painting on one side be a little ''out,'' it is flawless on the other; and the action, the description, and the rest throughout are incomparable. . . . Never was there a story which held the reader from beginning to end in so relentless and yet so delightful a grasp [as *Carmen*]; and seeing that it is not so very short this grip is even more remarkable than in mere ''moments'' of tale-telling like *Mateo Falcone* and the *Redoute.* Nor should we omit to notice the peculiar mastery of Mérimée's management of his rôle as narrator with a slight touch of actor as well. (pp. xlix-l)

[*Arsène Guillot*] is Mérimée's—that is almost as much as to say it has the easy mastery, the almost bewildering completeness and satisfaction of this master. But it displays these traits with an admixture of condescension to the weaker vessels and brethren,—to those who want something of impropriety in subject, something of conventional satire in treatment. Mérimée did sometimes condescend; and he has so condescended here. But he has not condescended very far and therefore, naturally, some say that he has not condescended far enough,—that Arsène is but a bread-and-butter Magdalen; Madame de Piennes a weakling ''beautiful-soul-with-temptations.'' . . . (pp. l-li)

L'Abbé Aubain, on the other hand, is a thoroughly delightful thing, and as masterly in reality as it is slight in appearance. Its interest is that of pure irony, though irony of the lightest and most delicate nature; and as all the great masters of irony know how to do, it is left by its author to make or miss its own way. (pp. li-lii)

As for the last fruits of [the wonderful tree of Mérimée's short stories], *La Chambre Bleue* and *Lokis,* the former has been carped at for its arrangement and the latter because we happen to know that Mérimée had at one time thought of making it more eccentric and more ''scabrous'' than it is now, at least on the surface. But this latter point of view is accidental and illegitimate; and we have nothing to do, as critics, with anything but the tales as they are actually submitted to us. And they are all but impeccable. The desideratum of a different ending or a different beginning or a different middle for *La*

Chambre Bleue is one of these critical ineptitudes for which there are two admirable proverbial phrases,—''Seeking noon at fourteen o'clock'' and ''Asking for better bread than is made of wheat.'' Mérimée, whose knowledge of life, if not coextensive with life itself (whose is?) was infallible where it extended, has taken two noted facts of life, the petty disappointment of great expectations, and the curious ''terrors of the night'' (for which in French there is an untranslatable word, *affres*) and has based his story on them. (pp. liii-liv)

Lokis aims higher. I should call it in all but the highest degree imaginative: few can refuse it the epithet of fanciful in all but the highest. In these highly pitched stories, the great difficulty is in the setting of the key at first, no doubt, but still more in the observation of it afterward. To my thinking, Mérimée has here ''kept the keeping,'' restrained his foot from ever stepping out of the enchanted circle, in a way that has never been surpassed. You could not have a better teller of such a story than the matter-of-fact but by no means milksop or merely pedantic hunter of Lithuanian irregular verbs; you could not put the setting better; you could not arrange a heroine more tempting and more provoking, or sketch an impossible-probable hero more convincingly. Every page of the history is a miracle. . . . (p. liv)

Finally, we have to turn on the results thus obtained the search-light of the *Letters.* Those to the *Inconnue* will sufficiently illustrate what is going to be said, for the average reader; the student really interested in Mérimée should not miss anything yet published, although the *Lettres à une Autre Inconnue* have the least really intimate note and add least of any kind to the others. (p. lv)

Some at least of the letters [of *Lettres à une Inconnue*] are among the most perfect love letters with which, in a pretty considerable acquaintance with the class of literature designated and so often misdesignated by that name, I have ever been able to acquaint myself. They are not, of course, extravagant, or lackadaisical; they have nothing of the stale *pot-pourri* odour about them, which seems to be so successful in sham collections of the kind, and which is perhaps not unknown in real ones. The spirit of them is passion, not sentiment, and long afterward, when (one does not quite know how) the passion has apparently subsided, the vestiges of the old flame flash and glow through the chit-chat and the commonplaces of age, nay, under the very shadow and chill of the wings of the Angel of Death. (p. lvii)

At any rate, here is the man ''in his habit as he lived'' in the one sense, as opposed to the writer in his habit as he seemed to so many, in the other. A man assuredly not perfect; nor a proper moral man by any means; not a religious one; not other things which the good man of the modern Stoics ought to be. A man with a fancy for some things which are not convenient; somewhat (though not when his friends were concerned) self-indulgent; by no means over-inclined to swim against the stream, though he could do this too; something of an epicurean, though not so much as he seemed to be; even less of a cynic, but a little somewhat of that too. Yet a man, who to very rare gifts of intellect added gifts not exactly common of heart and (I must ask indulgence for a minute) even of *soul;* a man who *could* (in the old Carlyle-Emerson sense) divine very much; who *knew* even more; and lastly, who *loved* more than all. (pp. lviii-lix)

George Saintsbury, in an introduction to The Writings of Prosper Mérimée: Carmen, Arsène Guillot, Abbé Aubain, *Vol. 1 by Prosper Mérimée, translated by Emily Mary Weller, The Lady Mary Loyd, and Edmund Burke Thompson, Croscup & Holby Company, 1905, pp. ix-lxv.*

V. S. PRITCHETT (essay date 1944)

[*Pritchett, a modern British writer, is respected for his mastery of the short story and for what critics describe as his judicious, reliable, and insightful literary criticism. He writes in the conversational tone of the familiar essay, and he approaches literature from the viewpoint of an informed but not overly scholarly reader. Here he expresses his admiration for Mérimée's "crystalline, exact, apparent" prose.*]

Repugnance certainly disturbs our admiration of [Prosper Mérimée's stories]; indeed, between Mérimée and the reader one might say that repugnances are exchanged like the names of seconds in a duel. We open **Colomba** or **Mateo Falcone** with the feeling that it is sunrise, that presently our infinitely accomplished adversary will come coolly through the woods and in a couple of minutes put a bullet through our lungs. We shall have died for God knows what, though Mérimée himself will suggest that our fate was an indifferent flash of the icy diamond of human life and passion. For Mérimée life is a campaign.

For us who have two wards in our blood such a writer has a peculiar interest. He can count on our repugnance and our attraction still. As a writer of *nouvelles* he is, without question, a master; and in stories of action or, perhaps one should say, in stories of the active and conscious man, he is inhumanly supreme. "I have spent my nights lately writing for posterity," he wrote in the **Lettres à Une Inconnue.** It is true. As bodies are preserved endlessly in ice, or the fly for ever printed flawlessly in amber, his stories appear new to the minds of every generation, so we cannot imagine a time when **Carmen** is forgotten or **Colomba** unreadable. The garments of the great encumber them; it is an effort to get at and read so many of the overwhelming figures of literature. But Mérimée remains crystalline, exact, apparent. The interesting thing is his refusal to be great. I mean his refusal to be a great man in the histrionic manner of the nineteenth century. Where his contemporaries in France and England seem to have gone to the wig-makers to dress for the character part of prophet, thinker and visionary, and to prepare the long oration of their careers, Mérimée steps back. Where they are positive and aggressive, he is negative and critical. They, in the manner of the century, are going to be great men. Their role and their audience will be everything to them. But when we look at Mérimée it appears to us that the sight of so many vibrant egotisms, warming up their engines and preparing to take off with a roar, must have produced in him a perverse decision, a decision without modesty, to stay isolated on the ground. And we know that it was his singular aim not to be a great man, but to be a scholar and a gentleman—an English gentleman, of all things, as romantic Frenchmen conceive that character to be. . . . He is not an aristocrat who inherits power in some sense as a trust; he is a middle-class man, the servant of aristocrats, who becomes the libertine of the will to power in human beings, pursuing it, inciting it, probing it, and in the story of **Colomba** exalting it. The themes of **Carmen,** of **Tamango,** of his superb historical novel, the **Chronicle of Charles IX,** of **Mateo Falcone** and even of that ironical little comedy of manners **L'Abbé Aubain,** are all alike in this respect: they are ruthless private wars, his people are goaded by pride or vanity to seek dominion. And when one side or the other has won, or when both have destroyed each other—what is left? For people whose lives play such a tune,

Mérimée is too honest an artist and too clear minded to suggest that anything can be left but the emptiness of conquest. . . . [In] general Mérimée leaves us abruptly and we see an empty stage where pity cannot tread. For pity has not been born.

In this attitude of mind Mérimée was prophetic. He foreshadowed one kind of writer who would succeed the prophets. His critical intelligence, the clear ring of an intellect unsheathed from the heart, evokes an echo in ourselves. He is the scholar, the artist, the poet of insensibility. He is—one hardly likes to breathe the suggestion—tough. . . .

And yet how refreshing Mérimée is! What brilliant uses may be made of an arrested development! The shock does not come, after all, until the ends of his stories: when the negro Tamango's broken glory fades into a Governor's anecdote, or when Carmen's death is merely a gloss on the customs of the gypsies. And that final shock is wiped out by the memory of the first shock we get when we begin a new story; the shock of pleasure and exhilaration in something new and strange. Mérimée is never boring. He writes like a gifted raconteur who is nonchalant, entirely at ease, but always alert in the presence of his circle. . . . One may resent a curtness which was the fruit of mistrust, and one may add that the man who is not duped has a fundamentally tiresome attitude to life; but the economy of Mérimée has another root. It lies in his rare gift of order, which I take to be the first essential of good narrative. It is Mérimée's gift of order which enables him to place his scenes, as Turvenev and Pushkin did, briefly but infallibly before our eyes; to know, in **Colomba,** for example, how much of Corsica to describe, how far to dilate on local custom, how far to build up his anecdotes about the vendetta until the main vendetta of the story looms over us like an iron cloud, impassable and momentous on a mountain road. A great part of the pleasure of reading his stories comes from our awareness of their construction. At each phrase we are conscious of being set free from the irrelevances by which other writers mystify the reader, and of being directed by a mind that knows how to eliminate. . . . He excels by his skill at rendering the depths by keeping to the surface, by attending to the beguiling and untrustworthy smile (?) of life. His own emotions abstain from the narrative and . . . we are free—that sense of freedom is the great gift of the Romantic tradition. With him we are free, also, of the Romantic burden. . . .

In their dissociation of power and energy and pride from the rest of life, Stendhal and Mérimée are prophetic of Fascism. And Mérimée added a predeliction for primitive types. He is saved from the complete accusation by his scholarship and by his detachment. . . . [Mérimée's] mind was sceptical. There is a clear statement of his scepticism in his historical novel **The Chronicle of Charles IX** where he extracts the utmost irony out of the religious wars and the massacres of St. Batholomew and detaches himself from the tale half-way through in order to explain his method of writing history to the reader. "This is not the last time brothers will kill each other in France," says the dying convert to his Huguenot brother; and Mérimée excels in describing the ambiguities of conscience in an age when professions of faith do violence to the soul. This novel set out to debunk the laden and stolid histories of Sir Walter Scott, and it reads as if it were written, not in the first half of the nineteenth century, but in the last twenty years. . . . And again we are struck by another aspect of Mérimée which brings him close to us: what he passes off as his belief in anecdote is really his perfunctory name for documentation. . . . He has the patience, the grace, the exactitude if he has also the perfunctoriness of the amateur. A writer might learn his art from him and dread the perfection he had learned.

> V. S. Pritchett, in a review of "Colomba," "Mateo Falcone," "Lettres à Une Inconnue," "Carmen," "Tamango," "Chronicle of Charles IX," and "L'Abbé Aubain," in The New Statesman & Nation (© 1944 The Statesman & Nation Publishing Co. Ltd.), Vol. XXVII, No. 675, January 29, 1944, p. 79.

ALBERT J. GEORGE (essay date 1955)

The strange unity of Mérimée's work can perhaps best be grasped from a knowledge of the man's personality. Certainly he was not an endearing person, a judgment on which everybody is unanimous. . . . This complete egoist never became anyone's disciple or dupe; he stood aloof to watch life roll by with disdainful tolerance. Mérimée viewed the world with jaundiced eyes. For him it was an unpleasant antheap, agitated by the superstitiously religious. . . . He preferred the aristocracy of a man on horseback like Napolean III to democracy, for he had no faith in the intelligence of the common man or any taste for his manners.

It is not surprising, therefore, that such an attitude colored his work, or that he approached the art of storytelling with a keen appreciation for irony. . . . A sharp awareness of the ridiculous tempered his choice of subjects, his exploitation of character, and his comments on the meaning of his stories. Hence, all types of irony can be found intermingled in his work: *verbal irony*, most often by understatement, as in *Colomba*, when he describes French bureaucracy or the English upper classes; *irony of manner*, a pretense of naïveté or open-eyed wonder, as in the Abbé Aubain; *dramatic irony*, that created by the twist of events, as in *Tamango* or the *Partie de trictrac*; and *cosmic* or *romantic irony*, the satire of frustration, of men's highest aspirations. This last constitutes one of Mérimée's most common techniques, evident in his better works, the *Double Méprise* or the *Vase étrusque*, both bitter comments on the destiny of man.

That Mérimée was not a professional writer makes it difficult to secure any very helpful information from him. Certainly he was not given to theorizing on the nature of his avocation. Writing was a side line for M. l'inspecteur général des monuments. He commented rarely on his art and these few instances are interlaced through a voluminous correspondence. Thus, the only way to uncover his aesthetics is to inqure how he put together his narratives and then poke amidst these findings for his notions of the brief tale and what, if any, contributions he made to its development.

The subject matter gives no help. The locales of the nineteen stories range from France, to Spain, to Corsica, Africa, Denmark, and Russia. Mérimée deals with the fantastic in the *Vénus d'Ille*, religion in *Fédérigo*, slavery in *Tamango*, and honor in *Colomba*. Such catholicity of taste reveals only a man close to romanticism who apparently exhibited little originality of background and theme. (pp. 29-30)

Similarly, most of the techniques he favored were also commonplace. The plots are shaped as sequential narration articulated by causality, though without any implication of determinism; they are told by a pseudo-author who occasionally interjects a caustic observation. These are presented as framework constructions, stories within stories (*Sorcières espagnoles, Il Viccolo di Madama Lucrezia*), with a goodly seasoning of

foreshadowing to titillate the reader (*Ames du Purgatoire*). Mérimée relies heavily on such exotic elements as distant lands, primitivism, dreams, visions and folklore. (p. 30)

Yet, closer observation shows that Mérimée offers more than just a resumé of the commonplaces of romanticism. Certainly he used all the themes in vogue, but, having learned his trade from Diderot and Sterne, he proffers them to the reader slightly out of focus, to create a universe in which only *his* will seems operative and beyond caprice. . . . The usual stock romantic plots were given strange twists. Mérimée delighted in ambiguous endings, leaving the reader to wonder whether the statue of Venus really crushed the boy or whether Charles XI actually did have a vision. Certainly the pure in heart will never understand *Lokis*. The Abbé Aubain resembles Jocelyn, but a clever and scheming one. Tamango may be a noble savage but his stupidity lands him in the kind of slavery which only an abolitionist British government could imagine. (pp. 30-1)

This kind of focus makes his work more interesting, perhaps, yet he deserves higher praise as a technician and a contributor to the development of short prose fiction. For all his mockery this satirist took his art seriously, and a close scrutiny of the variety of stories at which he tried his hand reveals a passion for experimentation which would enrich the medium he used. The short narrative he had chosen deliberately. He was not interested primarily in the development of incidents multiplied around a boy-girl entanglement—which would have led him to the romance; nor was he attracted by the possibility of creating fully-rounded characters by the slow erosion of cause-effect on a personality—which would have led him to the novel. Both these forms required settings spatially and temporally elongated. Rather he preferred to draw on the dramatic possibilities of life's ironies at given moments, to work with the explosive tensions which such compression made possible. This choice in essence limited him to the domain of the briefer narrative: the exploitation of a severely limited number of incidents, focussed to produce rapidly the maximum of effect; the development of character in a single situation. Both of these would further be restricted by considerations of time and space; the psychological time of the characters as well as the reader's sense of time, the space of the fable as well as the geography of the plot.

With a full appreciation of these boundaries, Mérimée experimented with the various problems involved in manipulating characters in limited time and space as he sought the frontiers of his medium. He would consequently write nineteen stories, no two of the same kind, and use a multiplicity of techniques to produce such divergent types of narrative as *Mateo Falcone*, the *Double Méprise, L'Enlèvement de la redoute* and *Colomba*.

Within these very short works his concern for psychological time caused Mérimée to treat incident variously, depending on the way in which he hoped to exploit it. Thus, the *Enlèvement de la redoute* occurs over a period of perhaps an hour, during which time Mérimée hoped to give a picture of people at a highly interesting moment. . . . On the other hand, in *Mateo Falcone* and the *Vénus d'Ille* everything is directed, in Poe-like fashion, toward the production of a single effect, concentrated, and stripped to barest essentials. All action is exteriorized, and passes in rapid tempo through a single crisis to explode in the climax, then decline in a brief dénouement.

The longer forms, too, include the same range of experimentation. The *Chronique* is an attempt to utilize Scott's technique of the romance, with its long historical background, and to weave through this extended setting a much shorter story than the romance called for. The focus was double, on both series of incidents. . . . [In] the *Vase étrusque* he marred the smoothness of his main plot by indulging in an ironic digression on the habits of the Jeune-France during a bachelor dinner. He was not now concerned with effect or exposition, but with revelation, with the portrayal of character, the psychological delineation of personality.

Thus a part-time writer made a major contribution to the history of the forms he practised. As a good romanticist he experimented, and this experimentation provided later men with an idea of how much could be expected from the medium of the short prose fiction. (pp. 31-3)

> Albert J. George, ''Prosper Mérimée and the Short Prose Narrative'' (originally a paper read at the MLA meeting in Chicago on December 26, 1955), in Symposium (copyright ©1956 by Syracuse University Press; reprinted by permission of Heldref Publications, a publication of the Helen Dwight Reid Educational Foundation), Vol. X, No. 1, Spring, 1956, pp. 25-33.

GEORGE STEINER (essay date 1963)

[*Steiner, a prominent American critic known for both literary and social studies, here examines the mystique of Mérimée's novella,* Carmen. *He discusses Mérimée's narrative technique of ''recounting events at secondhand,'' a device which Steiner finds somewhat arrogant, very elegant, and always compelling.*]

[Though] each period produces innumerable characters in art, poetry, or fiction, only a few have in them the spark of grace. Only a few can leap the gulf from momentary substance to lasting shadow. Of that number is Carmen.

Cigar girl, Gypsy, thief, tramp, seducer, victim, Carmen has secured her place in modern mythology. Sung in every opera house the world over, mimed in countless ballets, filmed, decked out in traditional or contemporary garb, as the Sevillian gitana or Carmen Jones, she has passed into the language. (p. 261)

At first glance it is not easy to say why Carmen should have blazed into such profusion of life. The fatal lady, the doomed temptress with the black, riveting eye, was a cliché of romantic fiction. Descended from the vampire women of the Gothic ballad, she had by the 1840's become a shopworn fixture of pulp and pathos. . . . No—the spell of *Carmen* lies deeper.

Carmen is an addict of freedom. She would rather die than yield a jot of her wanton sovereignty. ''Carmen will always be free'': that imperious claim to liberty resounds through [Mérimée's] novella, again and again, like fire crouching and leaping in the wind. Yet, at the same time, she recognizes the bondage of love. It is not a servitude she herself can long endure. Yielding so little of herself, Carmen glides from man to man with ironic ease. But she knows that in others love can be a lasting venom. She senses that José will kill her. Indeed, she acknowledges his right to do so. . . . When he strikes, she accepts the blow as if it were a gust of wind.

It is this lightness of death that gives the story its great force. Though she has read the imminence of doom in her fortune-teller's cards, though she sees murder writ large in star and coffee grounds, Carmen does nothing to evade José's knife. Freedom is stronger than love and stronger than fear. She goes toward death with somber yet amused majesty. . . . ''Death, where is thy sting?'' That is the meaning of the tale, and it plucks at one of the major, hidden chords of human subversion. In each of us there lurks, in some hour, the thought of mocking death, of showing up the summoner for what he is, a mere importunate scarecrow, a beggar at the door of our freedom. Shallow, exotic, frivolous as she may be, Carmen shares with other enduring fictions an essential trait: she speaks something of our own innermost meaning. Like all great characters in art, she is part mirror and part dream. (pp. 262-63)

[Mérimée] was both a master and a servant of history. His imagination leaned heavily on a scaffolding of antiquarian records or local historical circumstance. He used his own times with shrewd deference, expending on the past what wildness or secrecy of spirit he possessed. What is more important: Mérimée wrote, as it were, from a distance. Literature was to him an eminent craft, not an obsession or the whole of life. He looked on it as his mistress; his marriage lay on more solid ground. And it is precisely the virtues of a liaison rather than of a deepening commitment that we find in Mérimée's best work.

Even in his most ardent narratives there is a touch of arrogance, the self-mocking condescension of a gentleman who entertains his guests with an after-dinner tale. Mérimée's characteristic device, the assertion that he is recounting events at secondhand, that the story has been told to him by someone else, is both a literary convention and a piece of snobbery. Amid the tight, professional skein of his art, one comes across the *gaucheries* of an amateur. When he published *Carmen* in book form, Mérimée added a final chapter on the manners and language of Spanish Gypsies. The fierce climax is blighted by this pedantic epilogue. Only an amateur or a writer in whom there is some covert disdain for his own trade would have committed this error. (p. 264)

[Stendhal and Mérimée] incarnate the survival in the Romantic era of eighteenth-century ideals of irony, reserve, and nonchalance. There was in them a touch of the dandy. They were neither priests nor servants to literature, but lovers and familiars. But whereas Stendhal made of this attitude a mask for his genius, it became the actual guise of Mérimée's great talent. (pp. 264-65)

Mérimée is a virtuoso of the short sentence and the full stop. His eloquence consists in the unflagging progress of his narrative and in the bare, nervous immediacy of his dialogue, not in the music of words. Mérimée worked consciously against the Romantic trend, rejecting the poetic glitter and sonority of Chateaubriand and Victor Hugo. He stands in a classic lineage, in the tradition of Voltaire and Laclos. . . .

Little outside Poe or Dostoevsky rivals the malignity, the tangle of hatred and contempt, rendered in the last scene of *Colomba*. (p. 265)

Though nothing else in his work quite matches the incandescence of *Carmen* and *Colomba*, nearly all of Mérimée's tales show a comparable economy and strength. *The Storming of the Redoubt* is a memorable sketch. One does not easily forget the vision of the Russian grenadiers, motionless, arms primed, above the heads of their assailants. The entire account of the chaotic, brutal mauling is a model of clarity. In *The Etruscan Vase,* Mérimée writes in the vein of Pushkin, whom he in fact helped introduce to Western European readers. The story is slight, yet it casts a grim spell. It plays on the nervousness and frivolous heroics of the post-Napoleonic generation. Amid the morass of peace, these dandies and ex-soldiers seek in dueling the lost fervor of battle. *The Game of Backgammon* is a classic in a *genre* characteristic of the nineteenth century—the gambling tale. Again we note the curious mixture of casualness and reserve in Mérimée's style. At the very instant of its pathetic climax, the story is cut short by a trivial interruption.

There is no more stringent test of narrative than violent physical action. Whether it be in the nocturnal brawl of Don Juan, in his account of a naval battle, or in the extraordinary scene of the ambush in *Colomba,* Mérimée's control never falters. (p. 266)

I keep thinking that a ''natural'' novelist is a man capable of telling an impromptu story and holding spellbound the passengers of a second-class railway carriage on a hot day. It is a trial to which I should not want to expose too many of our present masters.

But Mérimée would emerge triumphant. Once that somewhat clipped, elegant voice has begun a tale, it becomes nearly impossible to turn away. (p. 268)

> *George Steiner, ''Mérimée'' (copyright © 1963, 1967 by George Steiner; reprinted with the permission of Atheneum Publishers, New York; originally published in* Carmen, Columba and Selected Stories *by Prosper Mérimée, New American Library, New York, 1963), in his* Language and Silence: Essays on Language, Literature and the Inhuman, *Atheneum, 1967, pp. 261-68.*

A. W. RAITT (essay date 1966)

[*Raitt is the author of* Prosper Mérimée, *the definitive biography in English (see Additional Bibliography). The following survey of Mérimée's tales is excerpted from Raitt's introduction to Mérimée's short stories.*]

At a time when his Romantic contemporaries were yielding all too easily to a demonstrative and lachrymose prolixity, Mérimée deliberately opted for a reserved, almost offhand style, for effects which were baldly stated or obliquely implied, but never exaggerated, for feelings which were always subjected to the scrutiny of a corrective irony. But at the same time, he was drawn to subjects of near-melodramatic intensity—the slaughter of a son by his father, the tragic fate of a cargo of Negro slaves, the senseless death of a lover at the height of his happiness, the eerie murder of a bridegroom by a statue. By using a simple, laconic style to recount events highly charged with passion, Mérimée produced tales of overpowering impact and created the prototypes of what we now recognize as the modern short story.

Mérimée's remarkable narrative efficiency has often led to the reproach of coldness. It has been said, time and again, that he possesses no qualities except impeccable technical dexterity. . . . It is certain that Mérimée never attempts anything beyond his capabilities and that he is always in complete control of his medium. Words are used with telling economy, description is unobtrusively integrated into the action, character is revealed by an admirable choice of gesture and dialogue, and the mechanism of each story functions with unerring precision. A tale like *Mateo Falcone* is a masterpiece not so much of understatement as of exact statement: every detail counts. . . . Even in a longer work like *The Venus of Ille* where he appears to adopt the discursive, conversational manner of an uninvolved observer, he uses none but the most essential notations. Not many writers have equalled him in packing an explosive content into a few deceptively casual lines.

But to infer from this that Mérimée stand aloof from normal human reactions is to ignore the undercurrents which swirl dangerously beneath the calm surface of his tales. (pp. vii-viii)

There are two ways in which the true depths of his sensibility are indicated by his tales: by his recurrent preoccupation with the brutality of primitive passions, and by his aggressive scepticism about the real nature of the seemingly more refined intercourse of civilized society. In the early stories especially, Mérimée appears fascinated by outbursts of often murderous instincts in simple, uneducated people—a Corsican peasant, an African savage, or, somewhat later, a Spanish gipsy. The same obsession with uninhibited, bloodthirsty lusts and hates is carried over into the learned works which Mérimée devoted to the most fevered and lawless periods of Roman, Spanish, Russian, and French history. Like Stendhal, he seems to have regarded the free expression of fierce passions as the natural prerogative of man, which had been repressed and stultified, and like Stendhal, he derived considerable pleasure from occasions when the mask of hypocrisy dropped to reveal the naked face of bestiality.

The corollary to this predilection for primitive violence is a strong reluctance to accept at its face value the coinage of polite social behaviour. Mérimée delights in demonstrating how vile, how selfish, how stupid his fellow men can be, for all their supposedly elevated motives and gracious manners. In *The Game of Backgammon,* Roger, a proud and courageous officer, commits a despicable crime, that of cheating at cards, not so much because he needs the money as out of sheer greed. . . . In *The Etruscan Vase,* Mérimée mercilessly exposes the idiocy to which a man in love can sink; Saint-Clair's jealousy is awakened by a chance word, appeased by a rose in his mistress's hair, aroused again by the sight of an Etruscan vase, and finally dissipated by the breaking of the vase. But in the meantime, he has insulted a friend in a fit of childish pique and dies in the ensuing duel. The tone of *The Abbé Aubain* is much lighter; there, a high-born lady, tempted by the scandal of making a young priest fall in love with her, is outwitted by the priest, whose only interest is in preferment. Perhaps Mérimée's most remarkable essays in psychological penetration are *The Double Misunderstanding* and *Arsène Guillot.* . . . In both of them, Mérimée devastatingly analyses the fallibility and uncertainty of human motives, in the one case those of a virtuous married woman who in a matter of hours succumbs to the blandishments of a callous philanderer whom she does not even love, in the other those of a charitable lady who befriends a lovelorn *grisette* [working girl], only to end by stealing her lover.

There is more in these tales than the sardonic misanthropy which apparently inspires them. Mérimée resolutely refuses to sentimentalize over Saint-Clair, yet one feels an unspoken compassion with the man whose reticence towards the woman he loved needlessly provoked his own death. . . . Even *The Double Misunderstanding,* superficially one of his most cynical works, ends on a note of sudden pathos, when he remarks that the two main characters might perhaps have found happiness in mutual love, if either had understood the other. These fleeting glimpses of tenderness reveal that Mérimée was not wholly the hardened sceptic that he would have us believe, but rather a man so bruised by disappointment that he could never afford to take any feeling too seriously lest it hurt him unbearably.

Admittedly, Mérimée's all-embracing scepticism came in the end to poison the sources of his art. Already in one or two of the early tales there are disconcerting moments when the author coolly negates the very effects he has been seeking to create. When in *The Game of Backgammon* the captain's story is interrupted by the sighting of a whale, one senses Mérimée turning his back on the tragic events he has been relating. In *The Venus of Ille*, if the narrator seems as much concerned about archaeological discoveries as about the fate of his host's son, it is because Mérimée, too, is becoming increasingly mistrustful of even the most basic human emotions. (pp. ix-xi)

From the outset of his career, he had been curious about the strange and the supernatural, and they had provided him with some of his most striking successes, notably *The Venus of Ille*. But his interest was purely external and never involved the slightest inclination to believe in anything beyond the world of the senses. . . . So tales like *The Vision of Charles XI* and *The Venus of Ille* are masterly exercises in the art of conquering the reader's disbelief, rather than manifestations of belief on Mérimée's part. However, by the time he wrote *Lokis,* he had lost the faculty of persuading himself that the fantastic was even theoretically possible, and though he labours to recreate the sinister atmosphere of *The Venus of Ille* (rather too visibly, since he repeats the tricks of the earlier tale—the donnish narrator, the marriage preparations, the presages of disaster, and the slaying on the wedding night), he fails because he makes the story turn, not on the intervention of a supernatural though credible force but on a scabrous physiological impossibility. Mérimée's last tales clothe his sexual obsessions in a specious narrative disguise; they lack any vestige of the inner life of the masterpieces of his youth. (pp. xii-xiii)

> *A. W. Raitt, in an introduction to* The Venus of Ille *and Other Stories by Prosper Mérimée, translated by Jean Kimber (English translation and introduction © Oxford University Press 1966; reprinted by permission of Oxford University Press), Oxford University Press, London, 1966, pp. vii-xiii.*

D. L. GOBERT   (essay date 1972)

[Literary] critics echo one another in their evocation of Mérimée's objectivity and ironic detachment, and of his art of story telling. His objectivity is characterized by a calm and detached manner. Rapidity, concision, and relief characterize the conteur's style. Has everything been said about the objectivity of Mérimée? We are told that his ojbectivity results from his refusal to openly analyze his characters' inner states. Analysis nonetheless results directly through dialogue, . . . or by means of a gesture, an exterior attitude which translates an inner state. These statements are true, but they do not exhaust a description of the objectivity of Mérimée.

The fact is that Mérimée does pitilessly analyze his characters directly, although those submitted to a direct psychological *dépouillement* [scrutiny] are those who, believing that they are directing the action, undergo it. Herein lies the ironic opposition which is not only basic to "objectivity," but which characterizes the disposition which Mérimée's inescapable subjectivity offered him to inform and structure the reality which he fictionalized.

Inexorably, Mérimée poses in each of his contes a victim and a *meneur de jeu* [agitator of the game]. The victim, with whom the reader is forced to identify, is subjected to a complete psychological dissection by the author; the *meneur* [agitator], on the other hand, is seen only from the exterior, and is Mérimée in disguise. The objective treatment of the victim results from his utter ignorance of his own plight. Mérimée's victims

are . . . self-deluded creatures who may or may not ever arrive at self-elucidation. A victim with an objective awareness of his dilemma implies the sympathy of the author as an expression of the author's subjectivity. Don José, the victim of Carmen, is one of those rare creatures in Mérimée. Even in his case, however, the subjectivity is checked because the reader is not interested in Don José—only in Carmen. (p. 128)

With few exceptions, every story, or short novel, is a trick which Mérimée is playing on the reader. When they are devoid of serious consequences, they are essentially examples of comic gesture, in which the author methodically prepares us for one thing, while finally, surreptitiously, he hands us the opposite. When the ludicrous element is absent, the stories are often tragically ironic, by virtue of the same equivocation in gesture. The victim appears quite often in the traditional role of the ridiculous character, while the *meneur* may play the comic role. The ironic view of the world does not take the tragic seriously, but does approach the comic with more seriousness. This neutralization is reflected in Mérimée's single approach to the *nouvelle* [short story], regardless of its outcome. (p. 129)

Typically, the victim makes his entrance in the narrative prior to the manifestation of the adverse force: Fortunato (*Mateo Falcone*), Charles XI (*La Vision de Charles XI*), the soldier (*L'Enlèvement de la Redoute*), Saint-Clair (*Le Vase étrusque*), Roger (*La Partie de Tric-Trac*), Julie de Chaverny (*La Double Méprise*), Captain Ledoux (*Tamango*), Don Juan (*Les Ames du Purgatoire*), the Peyrehorade family (*La Vénus d'Ille*), Miss Lydia and Orso (*Colomba*), Mme. de Piennes (*Arsène Guillot*), Don José (*Carmen*), Mme. de P. (*L'Abbé Aubain*), the narrator in *Il Viccolo di Madama Lucrezia*, Léon and his anonymous mistress (*La Chambre bleue*), Michel Szemioth (*Lokis*), the narrator in *Djoûmane*. From the beginning, the reader is Mérimée's dupe: we accept all the more readily identification with the character initially presented because he appears to be master of the situation, or simply because we are excessively in his point of view of the action.

If the victim enters first, the adverse force—whether it takes the form of an individual, a supernatural force, or of an individual as pretext for the realization of the victim's self-delusion—is named quite often in the *nouvelle's* title, but will make a belated entry, and tension is thereby increased. Mateo Falcone, in order to save his family's honor, finds himself obliged to punish by death his own son, Fortunato. Colomba first leads her brother to avenge his father's death, then brings about his union with Miss Lydia. . . . The victim's own fears or character flaws may be the cause of his dilemma: the callow recruit in the *Enlèvement* undergoes the fear and dread of his first battle, only to find himself ultimately one of the few survivors, and in command. An individual may appear as an instrument, more or less involved in collaboration with the supernatural or with the victim's fears: Mathilde's ambiguous nature seconds Saint-Clair's uncontrollable jealousy as the force which victimizes him. (pp. 129-30)

The complementary distribution which characterizes the victim-*meneur* portrayal emerges as the framework in which the struggle is waged for the characters, and in which the trick is perpetrated on the reader by Mérimée. The victim is relentlessly dissected, and his very energetic attempts to control the action, to direct the course of the combat contrast ironically with the "absence" or mistaken identity of the real *meneur*. In effect, the force gives the impression of nonparticipation either by virtue of its mysterious, supernatural and unknown nature, or by its silence, and by Mérimée's deliberate omission of the character's inner thoughts. . . .

Ultimately, Mérimée is the *meneur,* the reader the victim. The author puts us on the wrong track, and we are duped into pretending not to know what will happen, just as the victim does not know, or pretends not to know. The prestidigitator feigns intimacy, while maintaining his ironic distance from the victim, in order to achieve the opposite, disguised relationship with the *meneur*—doubling himself—and maintaining this illusion by imposing distance between the two.

[*Mateo Falcone* and *Colomba*] . . . typify the story wherein the *meneur* takes the form of an individual motivated by a strong "passion." In the former, the author prefaces the action with his assurance of its veracity and gives all necessary information on the *meneur,* Mateo Falcone. This is necessary since, when Mateo makes his dramatic appearance, no extraneous details should detract from his act of vengeance. We are even told in advance that Mérimée has seen Mateo after the event in question, and that Mateo has aged from great suffering. Skillfully, Mérimée has issued a warning by presenting a "before" and "after," whereas the latter can be appreciated only after the action has been narrated. (p. 131)

Rather than prefacing the action of *Colomba* with the necessary background of the heroine as he did in *Mateo,* Mérimée utilizes the *in medias res* technique, intervening in Chapter VI to inform the reader of the history of the family and the cause of the vengeance which will motivate Colomba. If any doubt remains, Orso himself supplies in Chapter VII the key to understanding of Colomba, as he explains to Miss Lydia. Thereafter, Mérimée may exclude all analysis of Colomba's inner states, limiting us to the victims' view of her actions, gestures, and facial expressions.

The first five chapters establish the would be *meneurs,* that is the real victims, Miss Lydia and Orso. They will play slightly ridiculous roles in that they will appear to be very active and energetic while being, in reality, the passive tools of Colomba. (p. 132)

[The] role of *meneuse* [female agitator] Colomba plays is greatly enhanced by a double victory. Mérimée has her follow quite a logical and recognizable route: he unites the victims, introduces the *meneuse,* separates the victims, and Colomba concentrates first on one, then on the other, so that in the end the victims are reunited and rewarded. (p. 135)

The four *nouvelles* in which Mérimée undertakes narration of a sentimental or psychological crisis with more seriousness, *Le Vase étrusque, La Partie de Tric-Trac, La Double Méprise,* and *Arsène Guillot* have in common a character who proves to be his own victim, although another individual will aid in materializing the force. Here, the author may utilize the *nouvelle* to "rewrite" reality to his own satisfaction, calling out for compassion by the sacrifice of Saint-Clair and attempting to exorcise thereby his own repressive tendency—punishing her who scorned him because of his poverty (Julie in *La Double Méprise*)—ridiculing her who through an excessive, misdirected piety and zeal in converting others is ultimately her own dupe (Mme de Piennes in *Arsène Guillot*), and inferior to a simple *fille* [girl].

Le Vase étrusque and *La Double Méprise* contrast, in that the victim and *meneur* of the former are treated more sympathetically than in the latter. This would seem to indicate that when Mérimée allows himself the indulgence of subjectivity, he is

able to cast either himself or the "other" as victim. *Arsène Guillot* indicates an even greater flexibility in approach in that the *meneuse,* Arsène, plays the double role of passive *meneuse* and victim. (pp. 135-36)

La Partie de Tric-Trac offers a more striking *pirouette* at its conclusion than do the *nouvelles* of identical theme and structure. . . . The narration is cast as a story within a story, and Mérimée avoids the dénouement by not permitting his narrator to complete it. The result is to empty the tragic tale of its seriousness. Mérimée appears to have been the dupe of his narrator, to "justify" his dupery of the reader. Roger, the victim whose story his friend the narrator relates, is *dépouillé* [scrutinized] by the author as he writhes in the throes of guilt, seeing himself as the cause of the death of a gambling partner whom he has cheated. (p. 139)

[*La Partie de Tric-Trac* is the first *nouvelle*] in which Mérimée delegates narration to a "witness." When he returns to the theme of "self-delusion" in 1844 with *Arsène Guillot,* however, he will utilize omniscient narration as he had done when treating that theme in 1830 and 1833 with *Le Vase* and *Méprise* respectively. It would appear then, that *La Partie de Tric-Trac* (1830), which treats tragedy "lightly," represents experimentation in technique. Thereafter, Mérimée will reserve "witness" narration for the supernatural, and will return to omniscience, or will utilize the antithesis of omniscience—autonomous confession by the victim—for the theme of self-delusion.

When the *meneur* takes the form of a supernatural agent, the outcome for the victim can be either fatal or of no consequence. Of course, that which presents itself as the supernatural may prove to be only a dream (*Djoûmane*), or indistinguishable from a guilty conscience (*Les Ames du Purgatoire*), or explained as a trick played on a hapless, disinterested party (*Il Viccolo di Madama Lucrezia*). In that event, the supernatural as *meneur* is no more than a variation on the theme of self-delusion. The "unknown" which has plagued the victim and the reader is ultimately explained, and it is here that the reader's role as dupe is most accentuated. The reader's warning as to the trick which awaits him is given by Mérimée's willingness to utilize a first person narration, amounting to an implicit but deceptive "I was the victim." For Mérimée accepts unintroduced first-person narrative point of view only when he will survive the adventure to relate it personally.

La Vénus d'Ille and *Lokis* present as *meneur* the supernatural. . . . *La Vénus* afforded the author an automatic means for complete objectivity in the presentation of the *meneur.* A statue as supernatural agent also permitted the natural exercise of Mérimée's ability to denote by exterior expressions inner, and here, supposed inner states. Our first view of the victims is afforded after we have been informed, in a cursory fashion, of the identity of the force. M Peyrehorade, whose son will be the object of the death-giving love-clasp of the statue, would aspire to the role of *meneur,* as he imposes on the statue his own interpretation of her meaning to the author. Similarly, we meet the son, Alphonse, before being presented to the statue. The author himself appears to join in with the others, to gain an ascendancy over the statue by sketching her, but his efforts are unsuccessful. . . . Mérimée's native tendency to structure the conflict espouses with ease the subject matter itself.

The narrative point of view adopted by Mérimée in *La Vénus* and in *Lokis* is first-person "I was a witness." As noted earlier, the author utilized "witness" narration in *La Partie* in order to escape the responsibility of ending the story. This point of view permits him to disavow responsibility for the veracity of the fantastic, but imposes certain limitations. A simple witness, he denies himself the omniscience of a narrator outside the story. In his description of the victims he must forego analysis, and he relies heavily therefore on gestures and facial movements as expressive of inner states and on direct speech as revelatory of character. The distance between the force and the reader is maintained not only by the mystery of the unknown but by conjectures about the statue's displacement, by second-hand reportages on alterations in its posture. At such points where the witness listens to a witness, we are back into the story-within-a-story of *La Partie.* The witness deprives himself of the proof which the other "appear" to have. Mérimée has perfected his equivocal position: he disguises his omniscience in the form of an on-the-spot, reliable witness, the very promise of elucidation, whose knowledge is nonetheless imperfect. Inasmuch as the Vénus has been betrayed, we are asked to justify her crime, and the presentation, bordering on antipathy, of Alphonse and his father would mitigate their own tragedy.

Lokis represents a further refinement in the attempt of the author to confer autonomy on his *nouvelle.* It is somewhat the reverse of the procedure of *L'Enlèvement,* for example, where the author vouches for a narrator whom he introduces, but who will narrate in the first person. (pp. 139-41)

Similarly to Arsène Guillot, Michel [in *Lokis*] at once plays the role of victim and *meneur:* having mysteriously "inherited" the curse of transformation into a sort of werewolf, he is a victim who will become the *meneur,* murderer of his own fiancée. The latter, cast in the role of the coquette, appears at first to exercise an ascendancy over Michel, or Lokis, as he is called in his transformed state. The Professor is a witness who is denied first-hand experience of the tragedy, as was the witness of the *Vénus.* He differs from the latter, however, in that he seems more involved and baffled by that which involves him, less superior to the situation than Mérimée's spokesman in the *Vénus.* The Professor explains to his listeners at the end of the story the meaning of Lokis, permitting Mérimée to engage in some philological pedantry. This gives the reader a token ascendancy over the Professor's listeners, since we have guessed what Lokis must mean. (p. 141)

Carmen offers another unique combination in narrative technique. The narrator is the victim, condemned to die, whose testimony therefore is creditable but whose point of view is limited. The *meneuse,* Carmen, will be seen only through his eyes, from the exterior, or in terms of his own perusals and conclusions. The preliminaries to the narration, however, are rather complex and constitute from the point of view of the initial narrator, Mérimée, almost a story in itself. Furthermore, the preliminaries also show the typical structuring: Don José "aspires" to be a *meneur,* in that he first appears to the author as a person to be feared, a dangerous bandit, whom the author befriends. As chance would have it, the author next meets a seemingly innocent girl, Carmen, and their rendezvous is interrupted by the arrival of the apparent *meneur,* Don José. As a means of exposition, the author has utilized the structure which ordinarily an entire *nouvelle* will take. The "dénouement" of the preliminaries is provided by the author's reunion with Don José, the latter appearing now definitively as the victim of the real force which has brought him to ruin, Carmen.

The victim's self-analysis is sincere and pitiable, and he is endowed with an acute awareness of his plight. The reader associates himself with Don José by reason of the intimate

confidence which is achieved, and, aware of the horrible reality of the imminent execution, finds his interest maintained not by any single denouement to be feared, but rather by an unbelievably exasperating enumeration of the perfidies of Carmen. *Carmen* is the only *nouvelle* whose narrator, the victim himself, suffers a tragic fate. (pp. 142-43)

Carmen's popularity is perhaps partially due to the serious straightforwardness which characterizes the narration of that fatal love which Carmen has inspired. . . . [It] follows *Arsène* and precedes *L'Abbé Aubain* by one year, contrasting with both in tone and manner of narration. The narrator of *Carmen* is the victim, which constitutes its uniqueness. . . . We are asked to identify with the victim and to appreciate the *meneuse* from his limited point of view. We relive, therefore, his tribulations at the mercy of the capricious Carmen. Don José reveals his innermost thoughts (just as Mérimée dissects his victims through omniscient narration), and we are constantly confronted by an exterior view of Carmen. (p. 144)

Mérimée ends his career as conteur with three stories—*La Chambre bleue [Lokis,* and *Djoûmane*]. . . . The first treats in a suspenseful way self-delusion, and it is narrated by omniscience. The second is a less successful tale of the supernatural, the narrator of which is a witness. The third is the familiar hoax, the false supernatural narrated by the victim himself.

The witness of *Lokis* has promised to tell us everything he has seen, but unfortunately, he did not actually see Lokis. The victim in *Djoûmane* was not really in danger, he was only dreaming, but this fact must be revealed at a given moment. The reader has believed that Léon has been endangered by the mysterious *meneur,* the Englishman. In reality, it has been Léon's own guilty conscience which has victimized us. By three different approaches, the author arrives at an identical feat—the entertainment of the reader at the reader's own expense. (p. 146)

> *D. L. Gobert, "Mérimée Revisited," in* Symposium *(copyright © 1972 by Syracuse University Press; reprinted by permission of Heldref Publications, a publication of the Helen Dwight Reid Educational Foundation), Vol. XXVI, No. 2, Summer, 1972, pp. 128-46.*

MICHAEL TILBY (essay date 1979)

That Mérimée, in his portrait of Carmen [*Carmen*], succeeded in creating one of the most memorable of literary "femmes fatales" is beyond question. But it is perhaps not surprising that there has been relatively little discussion of the power that Carmen wields over the male sex. For to submit her portrayal to rational analysis would seem to destroy the illusions upon which our pleasure as readers depends. Yet to refuse to do so is to subscribe to a myth, to accept without question the universal nature of her deadly attractions, and perhaps even to accept her as the instrument of the devil. If, on the other hand, we refuse to accept the category of the "femme fatale", and admit the possibility that this might be to some extent a compensatory myth, at least as far as the characters are concerned, it is, I think, possible to make some interesting observations about the nature of Carmen's appeal, and to go some way towards understanding why what is a somewhat incredible, and at times almost ridiculous, story can give rise to a coherent and highly satisfying narrative. (p. 255)

[There] are of course aspects of Carmen's behaviour that compel us to accept her as an exceptional woman. The violence of her feelings is beyond dispute, as is the indefatigable energy she deploys in her life of banditry. But once we start reflecting on her character beyond the realm of objective facts, it is difficult to know just what to conclude. Here, as so often in Mérimée's stories, the author seems to be attempting to make us believe in phenomena that would normally arouse considerable scepticism. We are, it seems, encouraged not only to believe in the notion of a "femme fatale" but also to accept that in this case Mérimée's gipsy owes her power over men to a knowledge of the occult. Yet of course, if we examine the text carefully, it soon becomes evident that Mérimée takes pains to avoid direct presentation of any powers of this kind. . . . Mérimée is content to surround his gipsy with *suggestions* of magic. And contrary to what we at first may have thought, it is clear that we are not meant to attribute Carmen's power over men to her use of magic. As if to direct our responses, the narrator indeed declares that although he once believed in such matters, he is now cured of them. Nonetheless, it has to be recognized that the residual poetic force of such beliefs can and does still operate, despite our rejection of their literal significance. The role of magic in the story is, then, ambiguous: we know that we must resist becoming dupes of such explanations but we may nonetheless feel that they are metaphors for something else, which, although difficult to define, is undoubtedly part of the emotional relationships between the characters.

Only in a very limited sense, then, does the theme of magic contribute directly to our acceptance of Carmen as a "femme fatale". Perhaps not surprisingly we are left to look elsewhere. Everything in fact points to the need to investigate not Carmen in isolation but the relationships of which she is part.

Let us begin with an obvious fact: what we are given in *Carmen* is not a point of view that we can equate with that of the author. Instead, we find two narrators, both of whom must in a number of ways be thought of as distinct from Mérimée himself. Not only is José separated from him by nationality, age and temperament, the narrator of the story's framework is presented very much as a self-parody. More important still is the fact that there is much here to cause us to question the "reliability" of the two narrators.

Both narrators are highly impressionable, not to say gullible. The events of the story are such that to demonstrate this with reference to José would seem superfluous. The case of the author-figure is perhaps less obvious. From the outset, however, he shows himself easily seduced. Thus, before his encounter with Carmen, we find him charmed by the beauty of his surroundings. . . . The narrator clearly enjoys all experiences that engage the workings of his Romantic imagination. We might expect therefore to be given through his eyes a highly coloured portrait of Carmen.

But it is above all the inability of either narrator to respond fully to the challenges of Carmen's sexuality that causes us to question the picture we receive of her. It is noteworthy that, at the beginning, José does not fall for her charm. This is partly the result of his upbringing. . . . As for the narrator, one of the codes structuring his character is clearly an asexual one. In Mérimée's stories, learned activities always situate a character at the antipodes of passion. (pp. 255-57)

As the story progresses, we find Carmen playing a role that emphasizes the inadequacy of the two male characters. José tells us, for example, of a request for money. . . . Significantly, the first stop on their shopping expedition had been . . .

where she had purchased a dozen oranges. Oranges had earlier in the story become associated with Carmen's sexuality. . . . [Oranges] continue to function as a symbolic device when, ironically, José is transformed into an orange-seller.

Moreover, if we look at two of the principal acts committed by Carmen—the stealing of the watch and the disfiguring of her fellow cigarette-girl—together with the consequences of a third act: her causing José to lose his stripes—it is possible to glimpse just what, symbolically, she represents in this story.

Both José and the narrator are . . . made to lose precious possessions. There is particular emphasis on the narrator's timepiece; it is closely bound up with the ritual of seduction. . . . The removal of the watch, and the loss of the stripes, are clear signs that Carmen is experienced as a castrating figure, a constant threat to the male sex. It is indeed consistent with this role that, in the argument with the cigarette-girl, she should be seen as the woman with the knife. Moreover, her impulsive use of the knife employed in the manufacture of cigars forms an ironic contrast with José's actions: his use of pointed weapons is almost apologetic. (pp. 257-58)

The Carmen we are presented with is, then, a version of her that is intimately related to the inadequacy of the male characters. But whether it is a question of their descriptions of her or the role that she so perceptively plays, it is difficult to avoid the conclusion that she is a "femme fatale" only insofar as they are prepared to subscribe to such a mythical role. It follows that we never really get to know Carmen. It is certainly not inconceivable that Carmen would appear differently in relationships with other men, and in a different light in their accounts of her. When she "cuckolds" José, it is, appropriately, with a bull-fighter. But this is not only a concrete, and witty, representation of *les cornes* [horns], it is surely also a suggestion that Carmen needs a virility greater than that offered by either José or the narrator. She may enjoy playing with them, but there would seem to be the hope that, as a result of her behaviour, a powerful man would be challenged to respond to her in the ways she wants. (p. 258)

What Mérimée shows in *Carmen* is the gulf that separates language understood as literary meanings, etymologies etc., and language as used by human beings to further their own aims and ambitions. A response to the potential of language clearly requires considerable creative talents: . . . Carmen uses language as a means of silencing others, of mystifying or duping them, as well as a means of telling them what they want to hear. Her language cannot be dismissed as a mere exercise in local colour. It is the instrument through which Carmen imposes herself, with great dexterity, as a "femme fatale". Responding to the hints she carefully provides, the characters complete their picture of her according to their own notions of stereotype. . . . Carmen is the embodiment of a lie—she lies because she is constantly, and most successfully, creating herself as a fiction. It is clear, therefore, that Carmen's skilful use of language makes her in many ways the analogue of the creative writer. Yet since what Carmen creates is a plausible version of herself, she can also be said to be the analogue of the text. She is "read" by the male characters, who, more or less willingly, enter into the fiction she is creating, and in so doing, at times even "read" themselves as fictional characters. . . . (p. 260)

Viewed dispassionately, [Carmen] reveals an emptiness at the heart of her appeal. She gives a dramatic performance designed to create an illusion. When this illusion is shattered—though of course since we, as readers of fiction, are keen to believe in the myth of the "femme fatale", it is perhaps never totally shattered—we are left with mere words. Similarly, the fictional text is, from one point of view, a lie, a creation that has emptiness at its centre. The text consists of structures that *ultimately* refer the text to its origin, rather than to an independent external reality. At the same time, the originating source, the writer's own self, is not recognizably present in the text. The text is thus a sleight of hand. Like Carmen, it poses as something of substance and as something that is true, whereas in fact they are both hypocritical. . . .

[The fictional text] is nothing but artifice, at its centre there is a void, but the sense of reality it produces can often be more compelling than our experience of non-literary phenomena.

Given the view of fiction implied by this [essay's] description of Carmen, it is entirely understandable that the fastidious Mérimée was unable to write fiction with complete ease. He certainly needed to undercut his creations with a liberal use of irony. Moreover, we find in his stories a profound suspicion of language, for language has an alarming tendency to spin fictions. Although he will frequently parody the pedantry of a scholar or the phlegm of the Englishman, there is no doubt that a degree of linguistic continence was, for him, a desirable habit. Nonetheless, the two categories to which characters in *Carmen* are often related, the garrulous and the taciturn, are both seen as extremes to be avoided. Mérimée's economic narrative, enlivened by irony, reveals his own ideal. For if he was aware of the pitfalls presented both by language and the imagination, he did clearly respond to the appeal of fiction. But his achievement in *Carmen* is considerably greater than a passing reference to irony can suggest. What he has done is to write a fiction in which the character of Carmen and the effect she has on José and the narrator mirror the relationship that exists between the reader and the fictional text. (p. 261)

[Despite] the strong impression we have of Carmen, she is in many ways an illusion. Although we must accept that she is an exceptional woman, we in fact possess scant knowledge of her personality. This is not a novel, and the reader is not given an intimate portrayal of her emotional life. Instead, Mérimée gives us relationships of an almost algebraic nature, in which Carmen has no existence beyond a myth that has its origins in the inadequacy of the male characters. As such, she is experienced as a role, an amalgam of symbolic devices, rather than as a personality. In the final analysis, the descriptions tell us more about the two narrators than they do about Carmen.

An unsympathetic reader would be bound to conclude that this story is gratuitous. Mérimée is not concerned to present the reader with matter for reflection. He has no message to communicate. He produces no moral problems for our consideration. Neither his descriptions of place nor those of character are designed for our instruction. But a fairer assessment would accept that what Mérimée has in fact given us is a dramatized account of the appeal of fiction and the various mechanisms that operate in the fiction-maker's seduction of the reader. For . . . Carmen is pure "textuality". Our experience as readers, therefore, can legitimately be calculated only in terms of pleasure. (pp. 261-62)

To accept Carmen as a "femme fatale", however, indicates only a partial understanding of Mérimée's text. For if the text dramatizes the very nature of fiction, this involves not merely illustrating its appeal as myth, but also, as we have seen, facing up to the emptiness at its centre. Thus, Mérimée encourages

not merely the seduction of the reader but also the latter's gradual realization of the ambiguity that is at the heart of the appeal of all fiction. The act of seduction is merely the initial stage in the reader's relationship with the text. It is the very ambiguity of the fictional text that becomes the source of the peculiar appeal of fiction. . . . We can recognize that the story is in many ways preposterous, but, strangely, this is no longer a matter for real concern. On the contrary, we delight in the fact that we have fallen victim to the fatal fascination of the text.

In *Carmen,* we are, then, brought face to face with a "pure" fiction, one that is not disguised by the various concerns with which novelists seek to justify their imaginative worlds. Mérimée's text is characterized by a total lack of incidental detail; each detail is conceived as a significant piece in a carefully designed mosaic. The result is a work that possesses a remarkably tight, but amazingly natural, organization; it is self-contained almost in the manner of a poem. But what is important above all else here is the way it is in every respect a self-reflexive fiction designed to give us an unadulterated experience of the fictional. We are used, when reading so-called "self-conscious" works of fiction, to being shown the workings of the text. Mérimée's originality is to have given us a work in which the subject itself is a poetic image of the fictional text. (pp. 262-63)

Michael Tilby, "Languages and Sexuality in Méri-mée's 'Carmen'" (copyright © by Forum for Modern Language Studies *and Michael Tilby), in* Forum for Modern Language Studies, *Vol. XV, No. 3, July, 1979, pp. 255-63.*

ADDITIONAL BIBLIOGRAPHY

Aldington, Richard. "Mérimée's Youth." In his *French Studies and Reviews*, pp. 172-79. London: George Allen & Unwin, 1926.
    An examination of the Romantic elements in Mérimée's work.

Bowman, Frank Paul. *Prosper Mérimée: Heroism, Pessimism, and Irony.* University of California Publications in Modern Philology, edited by E. S. Morby, V. A. Oswald, Jr., S. B. Puknat, R. N. Walpole, and M. A. Zeitlin, Vol. 66. Berkeley, Los Angeles: University of California Press, 1962, 205 p.
    A detailed analysis of Mérimée's heroes and his attitudes towards religion, politics, love, friendship, and death.

Dale, R. C. *The Poetics of Prosper Mérimée.* The Hague, Paris: Mouton & Co., 1966, 181 p.
    A study of the comments on literary theory found throughout Mérimée's letters and essays on Russian literature. Dale argues that Mérimée followed no preconceived doctrine and was not a member of any artistic movement.

France, Anatole. "Mérimée." In his *On Life and Letters, second series,* translated by A. W. Evans, pp. 44-51. London: John Lane The Bodley Head; New York: Dodd, Mead and Co., 1924.
    A biographical study that presents Mérimée as a trustful, affectionate, and charming man.

Grover, P. R. "Mérimée's Influence on Henry James." *The Modern Language Review* 63, No. 4 (October 1968): 810-17.*
    Examines Mérimée's influence on Henry James. Grover provides quotes from James's autobiography documenting James's assertion that Mérimée's narrative technique and thematic development influenced his writing.

Johnstone, G. H. *Prosper Mérimée: A Mask and a Face.* London: George Routledge & Sons, 1926, 282 p.

A consideration of Mérimée as a noted statesman and author. Johnstone finds Mérimée unjustly overlooked in the twentieth century.

Raitt, A. W. *Prosper Mérimée.* London: Eyre & Spottiswoode, 1970, 453 p.
    The definitive biography of Mérimée. Raitt states that he seeks to "present a chronological account of an unusually fascinating existence . . . and to give some insight into a complex, contradictory, but profoundly human character."

Thibaudet, Albert. "Mérimée." In his *French Literature from 1795 to Our Era,* translated by Charles Lam Markmann, pp. 185-89. New York: Funk & Wagnalls, 1967.
    A discussion of Mérimée's life and his important contribution to the development of the short story.

Thorold, Algar. "Prosper Mérimée." In his *Six Masters in Disillusion,* pp. 26-55. 1904. Reprint. London: Archibald Constable & Co., 1909.
    Calls Mérimée's writings "products of the leisure of an accomplished man of letters."

Ullmann, Stephen. "Some Romantic Experiments in Local Colour." In his *Style in the French Novel,* pp. 40-93. New York: Barnes & Noble, 1964.*
    A history of the usage of local color in French Romantic literature. Ullmann states that Mérimée, like other Romantics, employed local color because it fulfilled his interest in both the picturesque and the exotic.

Thomas Moore

1779-1852

(Also wrote under the pseudonyms of Thomas Little, Esq. and Thomas Brown the Younger) Irish poet, lyricist, satirist, biographer, novelist, translator, historian, and dramatist.

Moore achieved great popularity during his lifetime for his poignant lyrics in *The Irish Melodies* and his exotic epic poem, *Lalla Rookh*. Some believe that he was among the first to use the flexible, rhythmic verse employed by the Romantics and by such modern poets as William Butler Yeats and Edward Thomas. At a time in Irish history when the English language had almost entirely superseded Gaelic, Moore was the first nationalistic poet to write in English, and thus he reached a larger audience. In addition, Moore's interweaving of Irish history, folklore, and legend sparked an interest in Irish mythology among his readers.

Born in Dublin, Moore as a child exhibited a lively propensity for music, singing, reciting, and writing poetry. He attended Trinity College from 1795 to 1799, where he was one of the first Catholic students. Several of Moore's friends were killed during the United Irishmen Rebellion of 1798—foremost among them Robert Emmet, the subject of some of Moore's most highly-acclaimed lyrics. He himself was interrogated by British officers, but refused to testify against any of his acquaintances. The episode greatly influenced Moore, who often treated the struggle for Irish nationalism in his subsequent writings. In 1799, Moore moved to London to enter the Middle Temple, but his interest in literature triumphed over his interest in law when his translation, *Odes of Anacreon*, which he had begun as a Trinity undergraduate, was published. Moore became the toast of London, and Lord Byron christened him "Anacreon Moore."

In 1803, Moore was appointed Registrar of the Admiralty, and traveled to America. He satirized his experiences there in a series of letters included in *Epistles, Odes and Other Poems*, written in a scathing tone that he later regretted. The sensual imagery and frankly amorous themes of some of the poems caused critics to declare that Moore's works were immoral. While acknowledging the beauty of Moore's poetry, other critics complained of a surfeit of descriptive detail and some accused him of being merely stylish rather than artistic.

The Irish Melodies, published between 1808 and 1834, formed the cornerstone of Moore's career. Beloved among all segments of the Irish and English population, *The Irish Melodies* were collections of songs based on traditional Irish folk melodies, with music composed by Sir John Stevenson and lyrics written by Moore. Songs like "At the Mid-hour of Night" and "'Tis the Last Rose of Summer" are generally sentimental and tuneful, and describe love, loss, and Irish mythology. Because he often sang songs from *The Irish Melodies* at public performances, Moore earned the nickname "Melody Moore." Critics often state that Moore's lyrics demonstrate his exceptional technical mastery in choosing words that enhance melody and rhythm.

Moore's *Lalla Rookh* is a series of individual poems connected by a prose frame. The dense oriental detail, romantic motifs, and vivid characterization of the piece were widely imitated

by other writers of the period. Moore's only other volume of lyric poetry, *The Loves of the Angels*, also Eastern in mood, is set in a Moslem heaven and depicts fallen angels who recount their life stories.

Intercepted Letters; or, the Twopenny Post Bag, The Fudge Family In Paris, Fables for the Holy Alliance, and *The Fudges in England* are satires which were aimed at Lord Viscount Castlereagh, the British foreign secretary. Written in the form of verse correspondence between various characters, these satires were highly praised by Moore's contemporaries for their incisive wit. Moore's Irish nationalist consciousness was heightened in 1823 after a tour of the impoverished south of Ireland. His patriotic stance is reflected in *Memoirs of Captain Rock*, whose title character is an Irish Robin Hood figure, and in *The History of Ireland*, which was poorly received. His only novel, *The Epicurean*, was unsuccessful. Finally, Moore's biographies, including *Memoirs of the Life of the Right Honourable Richard Brinsley Sheridan* and *Letters and Journals of Lord Byron, with Notices of His Life*, reveal him to be a fair and perceptive observer of his subjects. Moore's biography of Lord Byron, considered by some critics to be his most important prose work, has been acclaimed for its sympathetic observation of the poet's character.

Moore's reputation has declined since his death. Critics from the early twentieth century onward agree, however, that although his works are dated, they are historically important. Moore was one of the most popular writers in London in his time. Contemporary critics praised his rapturous diction, his deft handling of rhythm, and compared his style with that of Sir Walter Scott, Lord Byron, Robert Southey, and Robert Burns. Their praise, though, was often countered by complaints that his style was excessively ornate. Francis Jeffrey found Moore's style immorally lush in the early poems, but pedantic in *Lalla Rookh*. In the United States, a writer in the *North American Review* claimed that "harlotry has found in him a bard to smooth her coarseness and veil her effrontery." William Hazlitt, Moore's most acrimonious critic, labeled his style superficial, and characterized *The Irish Melodies* as "converting the wild harp of Erin into a musical snuffbox." Later, Arthur Symons noted a lack of decorum in Moore's works, echoing in part the earliest reviewers of Moore's poetry. Stephen Gwynn, refuting Symons, extolled Moore's innovations in prosody.

The field of Moore criticism lay fallow until 1937, when studies by Howard Mumford Jones and L.A.G. Strong reintroduced Moore as a subject for serious critical debate. Jones portrayed Moore as the embodiment of the Romantic bard, and stressed his contributions to English Romanticism. Strong, in a groundbreaking study of *The Irish Melodies*, reminded the critical world that Moore's lyrics, which had been studied as poetry, ought to be examined instead as songs. Disputed by some critics, this view was expanded by Hoover H. Jordan in his technically detailed study of the work. H. O. Brogan's reassessment of Moore's satires and his controversial claim that Moore's purpose was to prick the English conscience opened an area seldom explored by Moore critics. Modern studies of Moore tend to be cursory and biographical, though Robert Welch has written an in-depth study of Moore's divided nature as reflected in his conflicting impulses toward art and politics.

Moore's name has been generally relegated to the list of minor English Romantic writers, but his contributions to nineteenth-century literature are significant. The critical concensus indicates that he is perhaps most appreciated today as a light satirist. In his own day, however, his verse was highly appreciated. Byron called him "the poet of all circles, and the idol of his own," and Percy Bysshe Shelley wrote of him in his *Adonais*:

> . . . from her wilds Ierne sent
>   The sweetest lyrist of her saddest wrong,
> And Love taught Grief to fall like music from his tongue.

PRINCIPAL WORKS

Odes of Anacreon [translator] (poetry) 1800
The Poetical Works of the Late Thomas Little, Esq. [as Thomas Little, Esq.] (poetry) 1801
Epistles, Odes and Other Poems (poetry) 1806
The Irish Melodies. 10 vols. (song lyrics) 1808-34
M. P.; or, The Blue-stocking (drama) 1811
Intercepted Letters; or, The Twopenny Post Bag [as Thomas Brown the Younger] (poetry) 1813
Lalla Rookh (poetry) 1817
The Fudge Family in Paris [as Thomas Brown the Younger] (poetry) 1818
Fables for the Holy Alliance [as Thomas Brown the Younger] (poetry) 1823
The Loves of the Angels (poetry) 1823
Memoirs of Captain Rock (novel) 1824

Memoirs of the Life of the Right Honourable Richard Brinsley Sheridan (biography) 1825
The Epicurean (novel) 1827
Letters and Journals of Lord Byron, with Notices of His Life (biography) 1830
The Life and Death of Lord Edward Fitzgerald (biography) 1830
Travels of an Irish Gentleman in Search of Religion (essays) 1833
The Fudges in England [as Thomas Brown the Younger] (poetry) 1835
The History of Ireland. 4 vols. (history) 1835-46
Memoirs, Journal, and Correspondence of Thomas Moore. 8 vols. (memoirs, journal, and letters) 1853-56
The Poetical Works of Thomas Moore (poetry) 1910

THE EDINBURGH REVIEW   (essay date 1803)

It was probably . . . confidence in his growing powers, that induced Mr Moore to undertake a new version of [the *Odes of Anacreon*,] a work already so often translated; for there does not appear to have been any other excitement to the task, but the hope of excelling his predecessors. (p. 463)

[Moore] has used so little discrimination in deciding what odes are genuine, and what falsely attributed to Anacreon, that the most opposite styles may be easily detected in the perusal of his volumes; and it would be impossible to fix upon any one trait pervading the whole, so as to characterize the poetry. That the odes translated by Mr Moore are all Anacreontic, in so far as they are Bacchanalian or amorous, we admit; but we cannot imagine that the translator himself, notwithstanding his professed disregard of the opinions of commentators, believed all that he has given, to be the productions of the same individual. Some of them he allows to be spurious, and we are persuaded that he must have suspected many more. (pp. 467-68)

Anacreon never detains long an amorous sentiment or voluptuous image which comes across him. He gives it frankly, and without reserve; but never dwells upon it, or wantons with its circumstances, or gloats upon it in detail. . . . We disagree, therefore, with Mr Moore, as to the tendency of the poetry, not so much because we are shocked by any gross violations of decency in particular instances, as that we disapprove of his constantly inculcating the absurdity of forethought, and teaching that to drink and to love are the only occupations worthy of our solicitude. (p. 470)

[We] cannot be expected to award to Mr Moore the praise of being a faithful interpreter. Anacreon . . . used scarcely any poetical diction; but Mr Moore employs one that is both very copious, and extremely ornamented. Anacreon is sparing, even to niggardliness, of epithets. Mr Moore pours them forth with profusion on all occasions. In Anacreon, they are all essential adjuncts: in Moore, they are for the most part circumstances merely accessory, used, like the tails of Homer's similes, not for illustration, but for the imagery which they incidentally suggest. . . . Anacreon is less metaphorical and figurative than any other poet; less so, indeed, than some prose writers of antiquity. Mr Moore's imagination is as fertile in figures, as his wit is ready in conceits. All the additions which he makes to his original, are combinations of epigram and trope.

Such is the plan on which the whole version seems to be conducted. To improve the ancient bard, by filling up his ideas, lending him new beauties, and bringing out his thoughts, is the main object of our translator. This method is pursued with various success, sometimes greatly embellishing the original, and, in other instances, completely flattening its spirit. It is used with advantage in a few odes that are descriptive; but we feel it cumbersome in many of the lighter pieces, and quite intolerable in those which hinge on a conceit, or partake of the manner of an epigram. It has very much increased the bulk of the book, and has spun out some odes, which were once but catches or glees, to almost the dreary length of [the medieval *Ballad of Chevy Chase*]. What the original has gained in elegance, it has lost in vivacity. It is no longer the ingenuity of the thought which strikes; it is the magic of the diction which pleases. But every writer who has a great command over the common-places and common phraseology of poetry, is at times in danger of imposing upon himself very unmeaning sentences. We think Mr Moore often answerable for this inanity—for this trick of cheating his reader with the mere semblance of thought. (pp. 470-71)

On the whole, we think Mr Moore has damped the fire of his [*Odes of Anacreon*] by a profusion of epithet; and that, had he broken the uniformity of his diction with some passages of greater simplicity, he would have heightened our pleasure, without materially violating his own plan of translation. That plan, however, we think, is constructed with so little judgment, that he has totally failed in the important point, of being faithful to the manner of his original. We lament Mr Moore's general want of success in copying the happy finishing we have so much admired in Anacreon. A delicate hint in the original, becomes a tame exposition in the translation; and, where the poet's art was shown in leaving a picture or an inference to the mind of the reader, Mr Moore generally helps us to understand it with a compassion somewhat officious. (pp. 471-72)

But none of the manifest changes which Mr Moore has made upon his original, are more exceptionable than his constant employment of glowing language and attractive imagery in portraying those simple ideas that border a little upon the wanton. Far from showing the least reluctance to render fully intelligible those *incorrect* passages, he eagerly seizes every opportunity of enlarging upon and embellishing the little symptoms of temperament which not unfrequently escape Anacreon. (pp. 473-74)

A style so wantonly voluptuous, is at once effeminate and childish; and it is as unlike the original, as it is unmanly in itself. But we believe Mr Moore's ambition is not pointed towards the chaster graces of poetical composition. . . .

After dwelling so long upon those instances, in which Mr Moore's additions and changes are, we think, equally illegitimate for a translation, and unhappy as original composition, we must now inform our readers, that he has been extremely felicitous in explaining and embellishing several of the odes which Anacreon had left meagre and unintelligible. (p. 474)

Of Mr Moore's language, it will not be necessary to say much . . . ; [he displays] the enviable command of an expression at once easy, copious, and variously elegant. From this he seldom deviates; and, however he may have mistaken Anacreon's style in other respects, he is almost always strictly faithful to him in the possession of classical purity and propriety. (p. 475)

''Moore's 'Translation of Anacreon','' *in* The Edinburgh Review, *Vol. II, No. IV, July, 1803, pp. 462-76.*

[FRANCIS JEFFREY]　(essay date 1806)

[*Jeffrey was a founder and editor (1803-1829) of the* Edinburgh Review, *one of the most influential magazines in early nineteenth-century England. In the following review of* Epistles, Odes and Other Poems, *he thoroughly criticizes Moore for his immorality and licentiousness. Moore was so incensed by this article that he challenged Jeffrey to a duel, but the altercation was stopped by police, and the two men eventually became friends. Jeffrey later changed his opinion about Moore's moral intent (see excerpt below, 1817), and even offered him the editorship of the* Edinburgh Review.]

A singular sweetness and melody of versification,—smooth, copious, and familiar diction,—with some brilliancy of fancy, and some show of classical erudition, might have raised Mr Moore to an innocent distinction among the song-writers and occasional poets of his day; but he is indebted, we fear, for the celebrity he actually enjoys to accomplishments of a different description; and may boast, if the boast can please him, of being the most licentious of modern versifiers, and the most poetical of those who, in our times, have devoted their talents to the propagation of immorality. We regard [*Epistles, Odes and Other Poems*], indeed, as a public nuisance. . . . (p. 456)

There is nothing, it will be allowed, more indefensible than a cold-blooded attempt to corrupt the purity of an innocent heart; and we can scarcely conceive any being more truly despicable, than he who, without the apology of unruly passion or tumultuous desires, sits down to ransack the impure places of his memory for inflammatory images and expressions, and commits them laboriously to writing, for the purpose of insinuating pollution into the minds of unknown and unsuspecting readers.

This is almost a new crime among us. While France has to blush for so many tomes of 'Poesies Erotiques' [erotic poems], we have little to answer for, but the coarse indecencies of Rochester and Dryden; and these, though sufficiently offensive to delicacy and good taste, can scarcely be regarded as dangerous. (pp. 456-57)

The immorality of Mr Moore is infinitely more insidious and malignant. It seems to be his aim to impose corruption upon his readers, by concealing it under the mask of refinement; to reconcile them imperceptibly to the most vile and vulgar sensuality, by blending its language with that of exalted feeling and tender emotion; and to steal impurity into their hearts, by gently perverting the most simple and generous of their affections. In the execution of this unworthy task, he labours with a perseverance at once ludicrous and detestable. He may be seen in every page running round the paltry circle of his seductions with incredible zeal and anxiety, and stimulating his jaded fancy for new images of impurity, with as much melancholy industry as ever outcast of the muses hunted for epithets or metre. (p. 457)

A poet of a luxuriant imagination may give too warm a colouring to the representation of innocent endearments, or be betrayed into indelicacies in delineating the allurements of some fair seducer, while it is obviously his general intention to give attraction to the picture of virtue, and to put the reader on his guard against the assault of temptation. Mr Moore has no such apology;—he takes care to intimate to us, in every page, that the raptures which he celebrates do not spring from the excesses of an innocent love, or the extravagance of a romantic attachment; but are the unhallowed fruits of cheap and vulgar prostitution, the inspiration of casual amours, and the chorus of habitual debauchery. He is at pains to let the world know that he is still fonder of roving, than of loving; and that all the Caras and the Fannys, with whom he holds dalliance in these pages, have had each a long series of preceding lovers, as highly favoured as their present poetical paramour: that they meet without any purpose of constancy, and do not think it necessary to grace their connexion with any professions of esteem or permanent attachment. The greater part of the book is filled with serious and elaborate descriptions of the ecstacies of such an intercourse, and with passionate exhortations to snatch the joys, which are thus abundantly poured forth from 'the fertile fount of sense.'

To us, indeed, the perpetual kissing, and twining, and panting of these amorous persons, is rather ludicrous than seductive; and their eternal sobbing and whining, raises no emotion in our bosoms, but those of disgust and contempt. (pp. 457-58)

On looking back to the volume, with a view to estimate its poetical merits impartially, as separated from its sins of morality, we were suprised to find how little praise it could lay claim to; and are more and more convinced, that its popularity is owing almost entirely to the seduction of the subjects on which it is employed. (p. 461)

[The author's style is] tawdry, affected, and finical. . . .

[Mr Moore] has favoured his readers with several fine specimens of sublimity, and made a splendid display of his erudition, in a variety of mythological hymns and epistles. The most superb, perhaps, is a dithyrambic on the fall of Hebe, which has the merit of being almost entirely unintelligible. . . . (p. 462)

The pieces which approach the nearest to common sense, are those which are conceived in the form of Epistles to the friends of the author. They are written in the ordinary heroic measure, and, along with the characteristic tawdriness of his usual style, display occasional point and vivacity, that, under a severer training, might entitle the author to the attention of the public. (p. 464)

Whatever may be thought of the poetry or the politics of [Mr Moore's passages on America], they are at least innocent in point of morality. But they bear but a small proportion to the objectionable contents of the volume, and cannot be allowed to atone for the demerits of a publication which we would wish to see consigned to universal reprobation. (p. 465)

> [*Francis Jeffrey*], ''Moore's 'Poems','' in The Edinburgh Review, *Vol. VIII, No. XVI, July, 1806, pp. 456-65.*

LEIGH HUNT   (essay date 1811)

[*An English poet and essayist, Hunt is remembered as a literary critic who encouraged and influenced several young Romantic poets, especially John Keats and Percy Bysshe Shelley. In the following review of* M. P.; or, The Blue-Stocking, *Hunt reveals his disappointment in Moore as a dramatist. He terms the drama ''an unambitious, undignified, and most unworthy compilation of pun, equivoque, and clap-trap!''*]

[Instead] of an opera worthy of its poet, [*M. P.; or, The Blue Stocking* is] a farce in three acts of the old complexion! A string of common-places, the more unsightly from the few pearls

mingled with them! An unambitious, undignified, and most unworthy compilation of pun, equivoque, and clap-trap! (p. 53)

There is evidently nothing in this story which surpasses the invention of one of our common dramatists, and the characters do not put it to the blush. . . . Of the humour it is quite lamentable to think, after the touches of real pleasantry and wit that are to be found in the author's works. . . . [There is] a great deal of a well-established sort of wit, something between equivoque and pun, which is founded on the application of the titles of books to particular characters or circumstances. Puns also are abundant, in all their naked dignity, the chief language of the M.P. consisting in applying technical parliamentary phrases to the common occurrences before him; and as to clap-traps, if there are not many, the few are not calculated to make us regret the deficiency. . . . With regard to the language, considered in its composition and sentiment, . . . it has two or three real touches of wit, which rank it at once high above the reach of . . . vulgar hands: but wherever it is serious, it is too florid; it is not good, unaffected, characteristic language, and seems to be decisive against the author's turn for the drama. The only part in which the hand of Mr. Moore can be said to be truly visible is in the songs—not in many of them indeed, for a general disease of common-place seems to have seized him in approaching the Theatre, and several of the serious ones, as well as *all* the humourous, are not above the pitch of Mr. Colman; but still there is enough of elegance and of poetry to awaken all our regret at the company in which they are found. (pp. 54-5))

Such are the beauties and the defects of a piece which so raised and has so disappointed expectation—the beauties much superior indeed to those of common operas, but far from being among the happiest efforts of the author, the defects precisely of the poor quality of those operas and utterly unworthy of him. (p. 57)

> *Leigh Hunt, in a review of ''M. P.; or, The Blue Stocking'' (originally published in* The Examiner, *No. 99, September 15, 1811), in his* Leigh Hunt's Dramatic Criticism: 1808-1831, *edited by Lawrence Huston Houtchens and Carolyn Washburn Houtchens, Columbia University Press, 1948, pp. 52-60.*

[FRANCIS JEFFREY]   (essay date 1817)

[*Jeffrey considers* Lalla Rookh *to be ''the finest orientalism we have had yet,'' but also faults the ''excessive finery'' of his style, that Moore ''would be richer for half his wealth.'' Revising his earlier opinion about Moore's licentiousness (see excerpt above, 1806), Jeffrey praises the moral tone of ''Paradise of the Peri,'' and describes Moore ''as the eloquent champion of purity, fidelity and delicacy, not less than of justice, liberty and honour.''*]

There is a great deal of our recent poetry derived from the East: But [*Lalla Rookh*] is the finest orientalism we have had yet. . . . It is amazing, indeed, how much at home Mr Moore seems to be in India, Persia, and Arabia; and how purely and strictly Asiatic all the colouring and imagery of his book appears. He is thoroughly embued with the character of the scenes to which he transports us; and yet the extent of his knowledge is less wonderful than the dexterity and apparent facility with which he had turned it to account in the elucidation and embellishment of his poetry. There is not a simile or description, a name, a trait of history, or allusion of romance which belongs to European experience; or does not indicate an entire familiarity with the life, nature, and learning of the East. Nor are these barbaric ornaments thinly scattered to make up a show. They are showered lavishly over all the work; and form, perhaps too much, the staple of the poetry—and the riches of that which is chiefly distinguished for its richness. We would confine this remark, however, to the descriptions of external objects, and the allusions to literature and history—to what may be termed the *materiel* of the poetry before us. The characters and sentiments are of a different order. They cannot, indeed, be said to be copies of European nature; but they are still less like that of any other region. They are, in truth, poetical imaginations;—but it is to the poetry of rational, honourable, considerate, and humane Europe, that they belong—and not to the childishness, cruelty, and profligacy of Asia. (pp. 1-2)

The style [of *Lalla Rookh*] is, on the whole, rather diffuse, and too unvaried in its character. But its greatest fault, in our eyes, is the uniformity of its brilliancy—the want of plainness, simplicity and repose. . . . [There] is too much ornament—too many insulated and independent beauties—and . . . the notice, and the very admiration they excite, hurt the interest of the general design; and not only withdraw our attention too importunately from it, but at last weary it out with their perpetual recurrence. (pp. 2-3)

[Mr Moore] is decidedly too lavish of his gems and sweets;— he labours under a plethora of wit and imagination—impairs his credit by the palpable exuberance of his possessions, and would be richer with half his wealth. His works are not only of rich materials and graceful design, but they are everywhere glistening with small beauties and transitory inspirations—sudden flashes of fancy, that blaze out and perish; like earth-born meteors that crackle in the lower sky, and unseasonably divert our eyes from the great and lofty bodies which pursue their harmonious courses in a serener region. (pp. 3-4)

In order to avoid the debasement of ordinary or familiar life, the author has soared to a region beyond the comprehension of most of his readers. All his personages are so very beautiful, and brave, and agonizing—so totally wrapt up in the exaltation of their vehement emotions, and withal so lofty in rank, and so sumptuous and magnificent in all that relates to their external condition, that the herd of ordinary mortals can scarcely venture to conceive of their proceedings, or to sympathize freely with their fortunes. The disasters to which they are exposed, and the designs in which they are engaged, are of the same ambitious and exaggerated character; and all are involved in so much pomp, and splendour, and luxury, and the description of their extreme grandeur and elegance forms so considerable a part of the whole work, that the less sublime portion of the species can with difficulty presume to judge of them, or to enter into the concernments of such very exquisite persons. The incidents, in like manner, are so prodigiously moving, so excessively improbable, and so terribly critical, that we have the same difficulty of raising our sentiments to the proper pitch for them;—and, finding it impossible to sympathize as we ought to do with such portentous occurrences, are sometimes tempted to withhold our sympathy altogether, and to seek for its objects among more familiar adventures. Scenes of voluptuous splendour and ecstasy alternate suddenly with agonizing separations, atrocious crimes, and tremendous sufferings;— battles, incredibly fierce and sanguinary, follow close on entertainments incredibly sumptuous and elegant;—terrific tempests are succeeded by delicious calms at sea: and the land scenes are divided between horrible chasms and precipices, and vales and gardens rich in eternal blooms, and glittering with palaces and temples—while the interest of the story is

maintained by instruments and agents of no less potency than insanity, blasphemy, poisonings, religious hatred, national antipathy, demoniacal misanthropy, and devoted love. (p. 4)

[But] it would be quite unjust to characterize [*Lalla Rookh*] by its faults, which are beyond all doubt less conspicuous than its beauties. There is not only a richness and brilliancy of diction and imagery spread over the whole work, that indicate the greatest activity and elegance of fancy in the author; but it is everywhere pervaded still more strikingly with a strain of tender and noble feeling, poured out with such warmth and abundance, as to steal insensibly on the heart of the reader, and gradually to overflow it with a tide of sympathetic emotion. There are passages indeed, and these neither few nor brief, over which the very Genius of poetry seems to have breathed his richest enchantment—where the melody of the verse and the beauty of the images conspire so harmoniously with the force and tenderness of the emotion, that the whole is blended into one deep and bright stream of sweetness and feeling, along which the spirit of the reader is borne passively away, through long reaches of delight. . . . And though it is certainly to be regretted that [Mr Moore] should so often have broken the measure with more frivolous strains, or filled up its intervals with a sort of brilliant *falsetto*, it should never be forgotten, that his excellences are at least as peculiar to himself as his faults, and, on the whole, perhaps more characteristic of his genius. (p. 8)

The whole story [of *Lalla Rookh*] is very sweetly and gaily told; and is adorned with many tender as well as lively passages. . . .

The first piece, which is entitled '**The Veiled Prophet of Khorassan**,' is the longest, we think, and certainly not the best, of the series. (p. 9)

[The] character of Mokanna, as well as his power and influence, is a mere distortion and extravagance: But the great blemish is the corruption of Zelica, and the insanity so gratuitously alleged by the poet in excuse of it. Nothing less, indeed, would in any way account for such a catastrophe; and, after all, it is painful and offensive to the imagination. But we really have nothing but the poet's word for the existence of this infirmity: for, except in the agony in which she breaks away from Azim, she conducts herself with perfect composure and consistency throughout. Indeed, the very supremacy she exercises in the Haram, and her selection to conduct a scheme of artful seduction, are irreconcileable with the idea of habitual frenzy. The bridal oath, pledged with blood among the festering bodies of the dead, is one of the overstrained theatrical horrors of the German school; and a great deal of the theorizing and argumentation which is intended to palliate or conceal those defects, is obscure and incomprehensible. Rich as it is, in short, in fancy and expression, and powerful in some of the scenes of passion, we should have had great doubts of the success of this volume, if it had all been of the same texture with the poem of which we are speaking. Yet, even there, there is a charm, almost irresistible, in the volume of sweet sounds and beautiful images, which are heaped together with luxurious profusion in the general texture of the style, and invest even the absurdities of the story with the graceful amplitude of their rich and figured veil. (p. 12)

[We] observe, that there are here and there in ['**The Veiled Prophet of Khorassan**'] . . . some traces of misplaced levity and familiarity of tone—of that poor commonplace smartness which sometimes passes for wit and gallantry with men of the world, but is absolutely offensive in a poem of tragic interest. . . . [There] are blemishes of haste and extreme facility . . . [which] detract less from the merit of the poem than the pleasure of its readers.

The next piece, which is entitled **'Paradise and the Peri,'** has none of these faults. It is full of spirit, elegance, and beauty; and, though slight enough in its structure, breathes throughout a most pure and engaging morality. It is, in truth, little more than a moral apologue, expanded and adorned by the exuberant fancy of the poet who recites it. (pp. 18-19)

'The Fire Worshippers' is the next in the series, and appears to us to be indisputably the finest and most powerful. With all the richness and beauty of diction that belong to the best parts of Mokanna, it has a far more interesting story; and is not liable to any of the objections we have been obliged to bring against the contrivance and structure of that leading poem. (p. 22)

The general tone of [the choral dirge which concludes **'The Fire Worshippers'** is, however,] certainly too much strained. It is over wrought throughout, and is too entirely made up of agonies and raptures;—but, in spite of all this, it is a work of great genius and beauty; and not only delights the fancy by its general brilliancy and spirit, but moves all the tender and noble feelings with a deep and powerful agitation.

The last piece, entitled **'The Light of the Haram,'** is the gayest of the whole; and is of a very slender fabric as to fable or invention. In truth, it has scarcely any story at all; but is made up almost entirely of beautiful songs and descriptions. . . . [The lady's song from this section] is written in a kind of rapture,—as if the author had breathed nothing but intoxicating gas during its composition. It is accordingly quite filled with lively images and splendid expressions, and all sorts of beauties,—except those of reserve or simplicity. (p. 30)

[*Lalla Rookh*'s] great fault certainly is its excessive finery— and its great charm the inexhaustible copiousness of its imagery—the sweetness and ease of its diction—and the beauty of the objects and sentiments with which it is concerned. Its finery, it should also be observed, is not the vulgar ostentation which so often disguises poverty or meanness—but the extravagance of excessive wealth. (p. 33)

Mr Moore, in the volume before us, reminds us oftener of Mr Southey and Lord Byron, than any other of his contemporaries. . . . Mr Moore is more lively [than Mr Southey]—his figures and images come more thickly—and his language is at once more familiar and more strengthened with points and antitheses. . . . It is in [Mr Moore's] descriptions of love, and of female loveliness, that there is the strongest resemblance to Lord Byron—at least to the larger poems of that Noble author. In the powerful and condensed expression of strong emotion, Mr Moore seems to us rather to have imitated the tone of some of his Lordship's smaller pieces—but imitated them as only an original genius could imitate—as Lord Byron himself may be said, in his later pieces, to have imitated those of an earlier date.—There is less to remind us of Scott, than we can very well account for, when we consider the great range and variety of that most fascinating and powerful writer; and we must say, that if Mr Moore could bring the resemblance a little closer, and exchange a portion of his superfluous images and ecstasies for an equivalent share of Mr Scott's gift of interesting and delighting us with pictures of familiar nature, and of that spirit and energy which never rises to extravagance, we think he would be a gainer by the exchange. (pp. 33-4)

In an early Number of this work, we reproved Mr Moore, perhaps with unnecessary severity, for what appeared to us the licentiousness of some of his youthful productions. We think it a duty to say, that he has long ago redeemed that error; and that in all his later works that have come under our observation, he appears as the eloquent champion of purity, fidelity and delicacy, not less than of justice, liberty and honour. . . . All his favourites, without exception, are dutiful, faithful, and self-denying; and no other example is ever set up for imitation. There is nothing approaching to indelicacy even in his description of the seductions by which they are tried; and they who object to his enchanting pictures of the beauty and pure attachment of the more prominent characters, would find fault, we suppose with the loveliness and the embraces of angels. (pp. 34-5)

[Francis Jeffrey], "Moore's 'Lalla Rookh'," in The Edinburgh Review, *Vol. XXIX, No. LVII, November, 1817, pp. 1-35.*

THE NORTH AMERICAN REVIEW   (essay date 1817)

Whatever may be Mr. Moore's rank, in this age of firm and healthy poetry, he has certainly contrived to make himself notorious and popular. As he has never stood in the way of his brethren, they have agreed very generally to live upon good terms with him—sometimes intimating, in a mincing way, that he is rather too much of a rake among the muses, but oftener extolling him for what he has achieved, and more especially for what he promises. Such an idolater of freedom, both within doors and without, could hardly fail to be a favourite with libertines and patriots. At carousals, he has been hailed as a sort of enchanter, who could mingle sentiment and enthusiasm with excesses, which heaven had made merely vulgar and sensual. Harlotry has found in him a bard to smooth her coarseness and veil her effrontery, to give her languor for modesty, and affectation for virtue. (p. 1)

[He] is thought by some to be a wild, luxurious bard, who is to pass through a generous and yet repressing culture, from the frolicks of blooming time, to a full, rich, and sober maturity . . . whose impurity has its redeeming graces,—whose errours deserve merciful allowances, because they are on the side of sentiment and greatness. . . .

[Mr. Moore's] poetry, hitherto appears to have been little more than a mixture of musick, conceit, and debauchery.

His voluptuousness appears to be the coldest thing in the world, as remote as possible from sudden and momentary fervour. It has not the spirit of wild, careless, social frolick, which burns and goes out in a night; the gay and passing frivolity of a mind in idleness. It is the business of his leisure and retirement, the creature and plaything of his imagination. He is at home and most heartily at work, when his subjects are licentious. His mind, instead of withering, seems freest and happiest in fine elaborations of impurity, in soiling what is fair, and then garnishing it. (p. 2)

Mr. Moore may be very adroit at this work—he may call it poetry if he pleases; but he must allow us to infer from the pleasure he takes in it, that his mind is not of the loftiest character, nor ever under the influence of genuine enthusiasm and rapture. (p. 4)

With the most graceful facility of expression, with verse that sparkles and warbles through volumes, [Mr. Moore] is always exact, and polished, never loose but in sentiment. A sort of verbal beauty, a poetry of sound is sustained throughout, let the thought be ever so poor, or vulgar, and almost any thing may find its way to the heart, that glides thither so musically. (pp. 4-5)

But are we insensible to Mr. Moore's fancy? Certainly not— a more ingenious and indefatigable one we are unacquainted with—such an array of tropes and images may have never before been marshalled, even by the most downright oriental, as he has so beautifully set in order. Still we have a feeling to subdue within us, that these, for the most part, are mere ornaments and appendages—any thing but illustration or a poetical embodying of thought. They do not yield a warm, living illumination, that mingles naturally with the scenes it falls on, and is perceived only by the gladness and distinctness which it sheds. They are sought and finished with apparent diligence and anxiety, and instead of taking a subordinate place, they stand apart for independent notice and admiration, and glitter as if in pride of their own beauty. In many cases, the thought seems to be introduced, and in a particular shape and relation, for no other purpose than to justify some beautiful comparison. (p. 5)

Mr. Moore has great ease and sprightliness of narrative, a graceful airiness in touching and leaving a subject, sufficient variety of thought, though too much sameness in the colouring, with verse that flows in perpetual song, and figures that scatter a sparkling brilliancy from beginning to end. . . . It appears to be his main object to do things elegantly, as if his readers were forever about him, and they too, perfectly fashionable and well drest. This disposition is especially manifest in his descriptions of external nature. The world is but dim and coarse in his eyes, and so he exhibits it in a sort of gay transparency, as if gairishness became it better than the vesture it received from its former, as if the array of the lily were not before all artificial glory. He delights in luxurious clusters of gorgeous, showy objects, upon which art has bestowed care and polish, more than in minute discriminations of nature in her simple, careless forms and colours and situations. He loves to tamper with creation and subdue it, even though he should make its serenity lifeless, its magnificence gaudy, and its wild grandeur trim and sedate. (pp. 6-7)

Perhaps we have gone so far in our censures, that we can hardly call [Mr. Moore] a poet now, or admit that he has a delicate perception of beauty, without falling into inconsistency. But he has certainly written enough fine poetry, to make one lament, that bad morals and taste should have drawn from him so much that is worthless. (p. 7)

[*Lalla Rookh*] gives a very pleasant story in prose. . . . (p. 8)

[In 'The Prophet of Khorassan,' Zelica's] delirious raptures are mingled the fire and glare of something unholy. The picture of her dishonoured beauty is mournful enough; but Mr. Moore hangs over it with too much complacency. (p. 10)

[Azim] has none of Timon's sad, vehement misanthropy, nor of Richard's malicious scorn and fine sarcasm, nor of Satan's proud vindictiveness and unguarded sorrow. He is . . . a sour Jacobin, some low, clamorous ruffian, suddenly grown up to be a gentleman. His character exhibits, for a time, with considerable clearness and consistency, a combination of vile and prosperous insolence with lust and malignity—no very tempting compound, we admit, either in life or poetry, though it might require some skill, to form and preserve it. But Mr. Moore was too delicate an artist to rest satisfied with the close truth of a low, vicious character. Because the prophet was vigorous, cunning and fearless, he must needs be invested with grandeur, and become a finished gallant, a subtle poisoner of

innocence and a sublime warrior. To render him still more poetical, Mr. Moore has made a desperate effort to give him the ferocious levity and deadly irony, which sometimes throw a gleam of frightful mirth over a dark and severe character, deepening its malignity and horrour, like the grim smile, that glares amidst the scowls and shadow, the solitude and midnight of the countenance. Mokanna, however, remains inflexibly vulgar, in spite of all that Mr. Moore can do to heighten or rather mar his character. We may observe here, that he rarely looks upon a character as an individual, or a consistent whole. He appears to have certain prominent abstract qualities, virtues or vices, in store, which he has determined to attach to the first poetical personage, that comes in his way. He only wants an opportunity to bring them forward—it is of no concern to him whether the character hangs well together, is governed by any single principle, in a word, whether it has individuality or not. This may account for the singular incongruity of some of his characters and the ostentatious insignificance of others. (pp. 11-12)

For Mr. Moore's sake, we hope this story is founded in fact. Human nature is much better able than he to bear the weight of its absurdity. This is, we believe, his first attempt at the violent and awful in poetry, and if it is a fair specimen of his talent that way, he cannot hurry back too fast to his marvellous ballads, where it is no sin to turn the terrible into the ridiculous. We need not try to soften this, by adding that the poem has powerful passages—we wish it had more, and that its materials, which are often fine, had been better wrought.

We have next [in *Lalla Rookh*] a short, unpretending, delicate poem, '**Paradise and the Peri**,' in which Mr. Moore is quite at his ease, as the matter itself is light, and the strong heroick verse, which tried him so sorely before, is here given up for the gay and varied measure in which he has rejoiced all his life. (pp. 17-18)

The description of Hafed's retreat on the mountain is novel and distinct. Mr. Moore rarely gives a picture that has so much of truth and originality, and takes such entire possession of the imagination. (pp. 18-19)

['**Light of the Haram**,'] is one of our old fashioned Aprils—rain and sunshine, cool tears and soft gayety. There is besides, much of Mr. Moore's peculiar luxury of description. But how is it, that he cannot bring love and nature together, without some wanton association? (p. 23)

There is some difficulty in plainly setting out Mr. Moore's failures, for the very reason that he is seldom *decidedly* bad. He wants the *unreserved* faults as well as excellences of a free and intrepid mind. The very elaboration, which mars his beauties, takes off their nativeness, and gives most of his pictures an artificial, unsatisfying sameness, serves also to soften or obscure his defects. Where the thought fails altogether, he attempts to make up for it by a sort of verbal stress, earnestness and flow—there are musical combinations of phrases in his merest expletives—he never has an undress for fine thoughts, nor any thing short of costly apparel for those which are everyday and common. It comes of this, no doubt, that we read him with so little variety of feeling, such an evenness of interest, without offence and without rapture. . . .

[We] are obliged to take an abrupt leave of our poet, . . . with a conviction, all along, that he might, but never will, do better. (p. 25)

A review of "Moore's 'Lalla Rookh'," in The North American Review, *Vol. VI, No. XVI, November, 1817, pp. 1-25.*

BARON VON LAUERWINKEL [PSEUDONYM OF JOHN LOCKHART] (essay date 1818)

[*Lockhart wrote several novels, but his fame rests on his biography of Sir Walter Scott and his critical contributions to* Blackwood's Edinburgh Magazine *and the* Quarterly Review. *He asserts in the following essay that, despite his "lively and graceful genius," Moore has failed to serve as the national poet of Ireland to the extent that Burns served as the national poet of Scotland.*]

I admire the lively and graceful genius of [Moore]:—I appreciate the amiable temperament and dispositions which lend a charm to his verses, more touching than any thing which liveliness, grace, and genius alone could confer; but I cannot consent for a moment to class Mr. Moore with the great poets of England—no more can I persuade myself that he is likely to go down to posterity as the national poet of Ireland.—Whatever the measure of his power may be, that man is unworthy to be a national poet, whose standard of moral purity and mental elevation falls below that of the people to which he would have his inspiration minister. . . . No one can be less inclined than I am to speak harshly of an elegant, accomplished, and, in his own person, virtuous man; but I must say that I should be very sorry to think so meanly of Ireland, as to imagine her deserving of no better poetry than Mr. Moore can furnish.—Before any man can become the poet of a nation he must do something very different from what has either been accomplished or promised in any of his productions. He must identify his own spirit with that of his people, by embodying in his verse those habitual and peculiar thoughts which constitute the essence of their nationality. I myself have never been in Ireland; but I strongly suspect that Moore has been silent with respect to every part of her nationality—except the name. Let us compare him for a moment with one whose position in many circumstances resembled his, and whose works have certainly obtained that power to which he aspire. Let us compare the poet whose songs have been so effectually embalmed in the heart of Scotland, with him who hopes to possess, in that of Ireland, a mausoleum no less august.—Mr. Moore has attempted to do for Ireland the same service which Burns rendered to Scotland; but although his genius is undoubted, he has failed to so do.—He writes for the dissipated fashionables of Dublin, and is himself the idol in the saloons of absentees; but he has never composed a single verse which I could imagine to be impressed upon the memory, nor brought together a single group of images calculated to ennoble the spirit of an Irish peasant. (pp. 99-100)

Baron von Lauerwinkel [pseudonym of John Lockhart], "Thomas Moore" (originally published as an unsigned essay entitled "Remarks on the Poetry of Thomas Moore" in Blackwood's Edinburgh Magazine, *Vol. IV, No. XIX, October, 1818), in his* Lockhart's Literary Criticism, *edited by M. Clive Hildyard, Basil Blackwell, 1931, pp. 99-100.*

WILLIAM HAZLITT (essay date 1819)

[*One of the most important commentators of the Romantic age, Hazlitt was an English critic and journalist. He was one of the first critics to acknowledge Moore's artistic and moral integrity. Here he especially praises the manner in which Moore employs in his verse satires "the arts of fiction, not to adorn the deformed,*

or disguise the false, but to make truth shine out the clearer, and beauty look more beautiful." Yet in a later review, Hazlitt found Moore's poetry "vitiated or immoral" (see excerpt below, 1825).]

[Mr. Moore] is neither a bubble nor a cheat. He makes it his business neither to hoodwink his own understanding, nor to blind or gag others. He is a man of wit and fancy, but he does not sharpen his wit on the edge of human agony, . . . nor strew the flowers of fancy . . . over the carcase of corruption, for he is a man not only of wit and fancy, but of common sense and common humanity. He sees for himself, and he feels for others. He employs the arts of fiction, not to adorn the deformed, or disguise the false, but to make truth shine out the clearer, and beauty look more beautiful. He does not make verse . . . the vehicle of lies, the bawd of Legitimacy, the pander of antiquated prejudices, and of vamped-up sophistry; but of truths, of home, heartfelt truths, as old as human nature and its wrongs. Mr. Moore calls things by their right names: he shews us kings as kings, priests as priests, knaves as knaves, and fools as fools. He makes us laugh at the ridiculous, and hate the odious. . . . In the *Epistles of the Fudge Family,* we see, as in a glass without a wrinkle, the mind and person of Royalty in full dress, up to the very throat, and we have a whole-length figure of [Lord Viscount Castlereagh], in the sweeping, serpentine line of beauty, down to his very feet. (p. 288)

Miss Biddy Fudge takes the account of poke-bonnets and love-adventures upon herself; Mr. Bob, the *patés,* jockey-boots, and high collars: Mr. Phil. Fudge addresses himself to the Lord Viscount Castlereagh; and Mr. Phelim, 'the sad historian of pensive Europe,' appeals, we confess, more effectually to us, in words

> As precious as the ruddy drops
> That visit our sad hearts.

(pp. 290-91)

We like the political part of this *jeu d'esprit* [consisting of letters by Phil Fudge and Phelim Connor] better, on the whole, than the merely comic and familiar [letters written by Bob and Biddy Fudge]. Bob Fudge is almost too suffocating a coxcomb, even in description, with his stays and *patés;* and Miss Biddy Fudge, with her *poke* bonnet and her princely lover, who turned out to be no better than a man-milliner, is not half so interesting as a certain Marchioness in [Moore's] *Twopenny Post Bag.* . . . In short, the Fudges abroad are not such fat subjects for ridicule as the Fudges at home. . . . [But] as far as they go, Mr. Brown, Junior, uses the dissecting knife with equal dexterity, and equally to the delight and edification of the byestanders. (p. 297)

William Hazlitt, "The Fudge Family in Paris," in his Political Essays, with Sketches of Public Characters, *W. Hone, 1819 (and reprinted in his* The Complete Works of William Hazlitt: Political Essays, with Sketches of Public Characters, Vol. 7, *edited by P. P. Howe, J. M. Dent and Sons, Ltd., 1932, pp. 287-97).*

THE ECLECTIC REVIEW (essay date 1823)

At the first view, [Moore's choice of subject in *The Loves of the Angels*] seems a seductive one. It is of that mixed, semi-ethereal character which comports with the sentimental Magdalen muse of our Irish David. The Poet seems, as it were, to hover between *Sacred Melodies* and *Anacreon;* and his poetry reminds us of those solemn, languishing, pious airs which have of late become fashionable under the misnomer of sacred music, in which the opera and devotion seem to meet half-way. . . . In representing angels otherwise than as Scripture teaches us to conceive of them, there is a violation . . . of poetical propriety. The moral incongruity is still more glaring and palpable. The Christian reader cannot forget that these imaginary loves of the angels are, according to the fable, the illicit amours of apostate spirits. The Poet, by making every angel 'tell his tale,' has aggravated this impropriety to the utmost. . . . Mr. Moore has given us, in fact, under the disguise of a better title, 'Dialogues of Devils.' At least, if we have no authority for using that appellation in a plural form, these angels are, on the Poet's own shewing, fallen angels; and if fallen, they must be impure, evil, malignant intelligences. They are represented, however, in the poem as most amiable and interesting demons. The arch-tempter himself could not wish to have his portrait sketched by a more accommodating limner than Mr. Moore. (pp. 210-11)

[What] contradiction and absurdity are involved in the very notion which forms the ground-work of the poem! These angels are neither good enough for sinless spirits, nor depraved enough for sinful ones. They have all the mixed character of humanity in circumstances with which that character ill accords. They are neither in a state of perfection, nor of penal suffering, nor of probation. They are neither Mahommedan angels, nor Christian angels, nor Miltonic angels, but a nondescript order, fit for neither heaven, nor earth, nor hell, but, if there were a Purgatory, fit subjects for that central Penitentiary.

The most forcible objection to the poem is, after all, its profaneness. We do not say, its impiety. . . . We have no hesitation in acquitting Mr. Moore of the charge of intentional impiety. He is evidently anxious to protect himself from such an imputation, although, in some places, he has put into the mouths of his angels highly exceptionable and dangerous language. But profaneness is the inseparable and pervading quality of the poem. It is altogether a tampering with sacred things; a burlesque, how undesigned soever, of the Scripture doctrine of angels, and an indirect apology for angelic sinners. The constant references to the Supreme Being are essentially and distressingly profane; because Mr. Moore has suffered himself to adopt in many cases a phraseology so nearly Christian as to remind us continually of those awful truths which are too sacred to be made the playthings of fiction . . . . The extravagance of Oriental bombast is less exceptionable in its tendency than the infidel sentimentalism couched in such language as this:—

> But is it thus, dread Providence—
> *Can* it, indeed, be thus, that she,
> Who, but for one proud, fond offence,
>   Had *honoured* heaven itself, should be
> Now doom'd—I cannot speak it—no,
> Merciful God, it *is* not so—
>
>   (p. 212)

[We] are sorry that [Mr. Moore] should affect to be religious. He may do quite as much harm to religion in this way, as he has done formerly to morals. He may be guilty of almost as gross impropriety with angels for his theme, as when he was emulating Catullus in his amatory verses to courtesans. We beseech him for his own sake as well as that of the public, to leave theology alone, at least in his poetry. Let him, as Junius said of Garrick, 'keep to his pantomimes.' No poet in the present day—we will not except Campbell—can rival the Author of *Irish Melodies* in song-writing. In sweetness and in compass, in tenderness and pathos, in the genuine inspiration of nationality, and in a perfect command of all the fantastic

anomalies of rhythm and metre, Moore is the first lyric poet of his day, and scarcely inferior to those of any other day. Gleams and snatches of this talent frequently burst upon the reader in [*The Loves of the Angels*]; but there is abundantly too much of flowers, and rays, and wreaths, and wings; every thing is bright, and sparkling, and aromatic to excess, till the eye aches for relief, and the senses grow sick with the perfumery. Had Erin been the scene instead of Eden or its confines, and the lads of the Shillala been the lovers, instead of angels, we should have had something far better. (pp. 213-14)

> "Moore's 'Loves of The Angels'," in The Eclectic Review, n.s. Vol. XIX, March, 1823, pp. 210-17.

WILLIAM HAZLITT   (essay date 1825)

[*Though originally a great admirer of Moore's style (see excerpt above, 1819), Hazlitt came to criticize what he saw as Moore's tendency "to pander to the artificial taste of the age." Moore's "is the poetry of the bath, of the toilette, of the saloon, of the fashionable world," Hazlitt writes. He severely reprimands Moore for his style, which he describes as "florid to excess," and for his "dissipated, fulsome, painted patch-work" descriptions which do not, Hazlitt feels, win Moore "a passport to Immortality." Hazlitt does, however, except Moore's satires from his objections.*]

[Mr. Moore's] verse is like a shower of beauty, a dance of images, a stream of music, or like the spray of the water-fall, tinged by the morning-beam with rosy light. The characteristic distinction of our author's style is this continuous and incessant flow of voluptuous thoughts and shining allusions. He ought to write with a crystal pen on silver paper. His subject is set off by a dazzling veil of poetic diction, like a wreath of flowers gemmed with innumerous dew-drops, that weep, tremble and glitter in liquid softness and pearly light, while the song of birds ravishes the ear, and languid odours breathe around. (p. 250)

Mr. Moore's strictest economy is 'wasteful and superfluous excess': he is always liberal and never at a loss; for sooner than not stimulate and delight the reader, he is willing to be tawdry, or superficial, or common-place. His Muse must be fine at any rate, though she should paint, and wear cast-off decorations. Rather than have any lack of excitement, he repeats himself. . . . It has been too much our author's object to pander to the artificial taste of the age; and his productions, however brilliant and agreeable, are in consequence somewhat meretricious and effeminate. (p. 251)

Mr. Moore's poetry is vitiated or immoral: it seduces the taste and enervates the imagination. It creates a false standard of reference, and inverts or decompounds the natural order of association, in which objects strike the thoughts and feelings. His is the poetry of the bath, of the toilette, of the saloon, of the fashionable world: not the poetry of nature, of the heart, or of human life. He stunts and enfeebles equally the growth of the imagination and the affections by not taking the seed of poetry and sowing it in the ground of truth. . . . [Instead] he anticipates and defeats his own object by plucking flowers and blossoms from the stem, and setting them in the ground of idleness and folly, or in a cap of his own vanity, where they soon wither and disappear, 'dying or ere they sicken!' This is but a sort of child's play, a short-sighted ambition. (p. 252)

His volumes present us with 'a perpetual feast of nectar'd sweets'; but we cannot add, 'where no crude surfeit reigns.' He indeed cloys with sweetness; he obscures with splendour;

he fatigues with gaiety. We are stifled on beds of roses. We literally lie 'on the rack of restless ecstasy.' His flowery fancy 'looks so fair and smells so sweet, that the sense aches at it.' His verse droops and languishes under a load of beauty, like a bough laden with fruit. His gorgeous style is like 'another morn risen on mid-noon.' There is no passage that is not made up of blushing lines, no line that is not enriched with a sparkling metaphor, no image that is left unadorned with a double epithet. All his verbs, nouns, adjectives, are equally glossy, smooth and beautiful. Every stanza is transparent with light, perfumed with odours, floating with liquid harmony, melting in luxurious, evanescent delights. His Muse is never contented with an offering from one sense alone, but brings another rifled charm to match it, and revels in a fairy round of pleasure. The interest is not dramatic, but melo-dramatic: it is a mixture of painting, poetry, and music, of the natural and preternatural, of obvious sentiment and romantic costume. . . . (pp. 252-53)

Mr. Moore has a little mistaken the art of poetry for the *cosmetic art*. He does not compose an historic group or work out a single figure, but throws a variety of elementary sensations, of vivid impressions, together, and calls it a description. He makes out an inventory of beauty: the smile on the lips, the dimple on the cheeks, *item*, golden locks, *item*, a pair of blue wings, *item*, a silver sound, with breathing fragrance and radiant light, and thinks it a character or a story. He gets together a number of fine things and fine names, and thinks that, flung on heaps, they make up a fine poem. This dissipated, fulsome, painted patch-work style may succeed in the levity and languor of the *boudoir*, or might have been adapted to the Pavilions of royalty; but it is not the style of Parnassus, nor a passport to Immortality. (p. 253)

Mr. Moore ought not to contend with serious difficulties or with entire subjects. He can write verses, not a poem. There is no principle of massing or of continuity in his productions, neither height nor breadth nor depth of capacity. There is no truth of representation, no strong internal feeling, but a continual flutter and display of affected airs and graces. (p. 255)

All is flimsy, all is florid to excess. His imagination may dally with insect beauties, with Rosicrucian spells: may describe a butterfly's wing, a flower-pot, a fan; but it should not attempt to span the great outlines of nature, or keep pace with the sounding march of events, or grapple with the strong fibres of the human heart. The great becomes turgid in his hands, the pathetic insipid. . . . [Mr. Moore] would transform a magician's fortress in the Himalaya (stripped of its mysterious gloom and frowning horrors) into a jeweller's toy, to be set upon a lady's toilette. . . . The descriptions of Mokanna in the fight, though it has spirit and grandeur of effect, has still a great alloy of the mock-heroic in it. The route of blood and death, which is otherwise well-marked, is infested with a swarm of 'fire-fly' fancies.

> In vain Mokanna, 'midst the general flight,
> Stands, like the red moon, in some stormy night,
> Among the fugitive clouds, that hurrying by,
> Leave only her unshaken in the sky.

This simile is fine, and would have been perfect, but that the moon is not red, and that she seems to hurry by the clouds, not they by her.

The description of the warrior's youthful adversary,

> —Whose coming seems
> A light, a glory, such as breaks in dreams—

is fantastic and enervated: a field of battle has nothing to do with dreams. And again, the two lines immediately after,

> And every sword, true as o'er billows dim
> The needle tracks the load-star, following him—

are a mere piece of enigmatical ingenuity and scientific *mimminee-pimminee*.

We cannot except the **Irish Melodies** from the same censure. If these national airs do indeed express the soul of impassioned feeling in his countrymen, the case of Ireland is hopeless. If these prettinesses pass for patriotism, if a country can heave from its heart's core only these vapid, varnished sentiments, lip-deep, and let its tears of blood evaporate in an empty conceit, let it be governed as it has been. There are here no tones to waken Liberty, to console Humanity. Mr. Moore converts the wild harp of Erin into a musical snuff-box!

We *do* except from this censure the author's political squibs and the [**Twopenny Post-bag**]. These are essences, are 'nests of spicery,' bitter and sweet, honey and gall together. No one can so well describe the set speech of a dull formalist or the flowing locks of a Dowager [as Mr. Moore]. . . . (pp. 256-57)

His light, agreeable, polished style pierces through the body of the court, hits off the faded graces of 'an Adonis of fifty,' weighs the vanity of fashion in tremulous scales, mimics the grimace of affectation and folly, shows up the littleness of the great, and spears a phalanx of statesmen with its glittering point as with a diamond brooch.

> In choosing songs the Regent named,
> "Had I a heart for falsehood fram'd":
> While gentle Hertford begg'd and pray'd
> For "Young I am, and sore afraid."

Nothing in Pope or Prior ever surpassed the delicate insinuation and adroit satire of these lines and hundreds more of our author's composition. . . . The **'Fudge Family'** is in the same spirit, but with a little falling-off. There is too great a mixture of undisguised Jacobinism and fashionable *slang*. The 'divine Fanny Bias' and 'the mountains *à la Russe*' [in the Russian style] figure in somewhat quaintly with Buonaparte and the Bourbons. . . . The poet also launches the lightning of political indignation; but it rather plays round and illumines his own pen than reaches the devoted heads at which it is aimed! (pp. 257-58)

> *William Hazlitt, "Mr. T. Moore—Mr. Leigh Hunt,"*
> *in his* The Spirit of the Age; or, Contemporary Portraits, *H. Colburn, 1825 (and reprinted by Oxford University Press, 1947, pp. 250-61).**

[THOMAS LOVE PEACOCK]   (essay date 1827)

[*An Englishman renowned for his wit and erudition, Peacock contributed to the literature of the nineteenth century as a novelist, poet, and critic. In his review of* The Epicurean, *he terms it the work "of an author aiming at popularity," and though he considers it to be flawed, he states that the book "commits no sins on the score of knowledge which the audience it is made for is likely to detect." Peacock himself, however, detects many "sins": insufficient philosophy, implausible plot, and "total absence of any moral purpose."*]

[**"The Epicurean"**] will, no doubt, be infinitely acceptable to the ladies "who make the fortune of new books." Love, very intense; mystery, somewhat recondite; piety, very profound;

and philosophy sufficiently shallow; . . . strung together with an infinity of brilliant and flowery fancies, present a combination eminently calculated to delight this very numerous class of readers. (p. 351)

Mr. Moore has helped himself liberally [to details from Terrason's Romance of "Sethos"]; and by turning the absurd into the monstrous, and the improbable into the impossible, he passes his hero [Alciphron] through a process of half-burning, half-drowning, and half-hanging, from which his life is only saved by availing himself, on each occasion, of a fantastical means of escape which a single moment would have placed beyond his grasp, and his apprehension of which is nothing less than a miracle. He is landed from the three several elements in which he has escaped the several perils of suspension, combustion, and submersion, in a sunless Paradise—a subterranean garden lighted by a composition of golden moonlight, and some other light (gas perhaps), where he finds shrubs and flowers, and, amongst other marvels, verdant turf.

We recommend Mr. Moore to try the experiment of growing a pot of grass in his cellar before he again amuses the public with similar fantasies. (pp. 363-64)

Mr. Moore has misrepresented the Epicurean philosophy, and the character of the later Epicureans. He has drawn an Epicurean according to the vulgar notion entertained of that character by persons who know nothing about the matter. (p. 373)

The language of Mr. Moore's hero shows as little trace of any knowledge of the principles of [Epicurean] philosophy, as his conduct of any practical obedience to its precepts. (p. 376)

[Knowing] what we know of the Epicureans, both in respect of their theories and their practice, we must say, that there never was a more outrageous speculation on the extent of public ignorance, than to send the chief of the sect, [Alciphron] on such an errand as the quest of immortality in obedience to such a counsellor as an old man in a dream.

The hero's violent and exclusive passion, which is the mainspring of the entire narrative, is as much out of character as the motives of his visit to Egypt; and not a whit less so are many of the minor circumstances. He is influenced by omens as well as by dreams. He is scared by a skeleton, and awed by a mummy. He has no more morality than any ordinary "gay deceiver," and makes a substitute for it out of a chivalrous feeling. . . . (p. 377)

["The Epicurean"] is evidently [the work] of an author aiming at popularity. Every page, every sentence, is written manifestly *ad captandum* [for the sake of pleasing]. We always see the actor with his eye on the audience. . . . The book reads on lightly and pleasantly. It commits no sins on the score of knowledge, which the audience it is made for is likely to detect; it commits no material offence, except against what was thought good taste in Athens, and against the doctrines and memories of all that is most illustrious in the Pagan world; and, if that be an error, it is a pious one, and the author is to be the better loved for it. (p. 379)

Even if ["The Epicurean"] had merits of any kind, poetical, descriptive, narrative, or dramatic, much higher than any which it, in our judgment, possesses, they would scarcely reconcile us to the total absence of any moral purpose in a work of so much pretension. Still less, of course, can we consider its merits, such as they are, . . . as affording any compensation for the heavy delinquency of misrepresenting the Athenians, traducing the noblest philosophy of antiquity, and setting forth the impotence of philosophical education in the formation of moral character. (p. 384)

> *[Thomas Love Peacock], "Moore's 'Epicurean',"* in The Westminster Review, *Vol. VIII, No. 16, October, 1827, pp. 351-84.*

JOHN GREENLEAF WHITTIER (essay date 1831)

[*A noted poet, reformer, journalist, and critic, Whittier is considered to be one of the most influential nineteenth-century American literary figures. He finds Moore's biography of Byron profane, even though Moore had excised and destroyed before the book's publication much of what would have been considered obscene from Byron's personal papers. Whittier expresses concern that Byron's posthumous reputation will suffer because Moore has exposed Byron's vices "with the most unscrupulous fidelity."*]

[*Letters and Journals of Lord Byron, with Notices of His Life*] is little calculated to induce a favorable opinion of the illustrious individual whose life and private writings it has laid open to public scrutiny. It is we fear pernicious—eminently so—in its tendency. The low licentiousness—the vulgarity, obscenity, and profanity, which distinguish his private correspondence should never have been cast thus profusely before the public. We would not for our right hand read this book before a sister—we would not shock the ears of aged piety by a revelation of its unpardonable and impious language. It is strange that Thomas Moore should have given such a volume to the world. It will be read indeed with interest—for it relates to one of the world's great spirits—but it will add no wreaths to the fame of its author; and it will only cast a deeper shadow upon the reputation of the illustrious dead. It will check the warm flow of that sympathy, which the melancholy strains of the poet, and the glorious death of the man, were so well calculated to call forth. (p. 70)

Moore has exposed the dark errors and moral corruption of his friend [Byron], with the most unscrupulous fidelity. We are sorry for it—it was an unkind deed—and in our opinion, an unnecessary one. We would not willingly look upon such a picture of lofty genius and low depravity, as he has presented in the character of his illustrious subject. (p. 71)

> *John Greenleaf Whittier, "Moore's 'Life of Byron'"* (originally published in New England Weekly Review, *February 14, 1831), in his* Whittier on Writers and Writing: The Uncollected Critical Writings of John Greenleaf Whittier, *edited by Edwin Harrison Cady and Harry Hayden Clark, Syracuse University Press, 1950, pp. 70-1.*

EDGAR ALLAN POE (essay date 1840)

[*Considered to be one of America's outstanding authors, Poe was a poet, novelist, essayist, journalist, short story writer, editor, and critic. In the following discussion of "Alciphron," he asserts that Moore's style has some imaginative characteristics, although his "popular voice and . . . popular heart" generally deny him the quality of imagination, which Poe considers to be the artist's supreme gift. He praises Moore's "easy and ordinary prose manner, ornamented into poetry," as well as his "epigrammatic spirit," "fine taste," "vivacity," and "musical ear." Poe concludes that he "could not point out a poem in any language which, as a whole greatly excels ['Alciphron']."*]

[While] discussing the topic of Moore's station in the poetic world [critics experience] that hesitation with which we are obliged to refuse him the loftiest rank among the most noble.

The popular voice, and the popular heart, have denied him that happiest quality—imagination—and here the popular voice (*because* for once it has gone with the popular heart) is right, but yet only relatively so. Imagination is not the leading feature of the poetry of Moore; but he possesses it in no little degree. (p. 82)

It is the suggestive force [of imagination] which exalts and etherealizes the [following passages from Moore's "**Alciphron**"].

> Or is it that there lurks, indeed,
> Some truth in man's prevailing creed,
> And that our guardians from on high
>   Come, in that pause from toil and sin,
> To put the senses' curtain by,
> And on the wakeful soul look in!

Again—

> The eternal pyramids of Memphis burst
> Awfully on my sight—standing sublime
> 'Twixt earth and heaven, the watch-towers of time,
> From whose lone summit, when his reign hath past,
> From earth for ever, he will look his last.
>
> (p. 83)

Such lines as these, we must admit, however, are not of frequent occurrence in the poem, the sum of whose great beauty is composed of the several sums of a world of minor excellences.

Moore has always been renowned for the number and appositeness, as well as novelty, of his similes; and the renown thus acquired is strongly indicial of his deficiency in that nobler merit—the noblest of them all. No poet thus distinguished was ever richly ideal. . . . [Similes] are never, in our opinion, strictly in good taste, whatever may be said to the contrary, and certainly can never be made to accord with other high qualities, except when naturally arising from the subject in the way of illustration—and, when thus arising, they have seldom the merit of novelty. . . .

["**Alciphron**"] is distinguished throughout by a very happy facility which has never been mentioned in connection with [Moore], but which has much to do with the reputation he has obtained. We allude to the facility with which he recounts a poetical story in a *prosaic* way. By this is meant that he preserves the tone and method of arrangement of a prose relation, and thus obtains great advantages over his more stilted compeers. His is no poetical *style* (such, for example, as the French have—a distinct style for a distinct purpose) but an easy and ordinary prose manner, *ornamented into poetry*. By means of this he is enabled to enter, with ease, into details which would baffle any other versifier of the age, and at which Lamartine would stand aghast. For anything that we see to the contrary, Moore might solve a cubic equation in verse or go through with the three several demonstrations of the binomial theorem, one after the other, or indeed all at the same time. His facility in this respect is truly admirable, and is, no doubt, the result of long practice after mature deliberation. (p. 84)

In general dexterity and melody of versification the author of "**Lalla Rookh**" is unrivalled; but he is by no means at all times accurate, falling occasionally into the common foible of throwing accent upon syllables too unimportant to sustain it. Thus,

in the lines which follow, where we have italicized the weak syllables:—

> And mark 'tis nigh; already *the* sun bids,
> While hark from all the temples *a* rich swell,
> I rush in*to* the cool night-air.

He also too frequently draws out the word Heaven into two syllables—a protraction which it *never* will support.

His English is now and then objectionable, as . . . where he speaks of—

> lighted barks
> That down Syene's cataract *shoots,*

making *shoots* rhyme with flutes, below; also [in several instances], the word *none* has improperly a singular, instead of a plural force. But such criticism as this is somewhat captious, for in general he is most highly polished. (p. 85)

[The] exceeding beauty of "**Alciphron**" has bewildered and detained us. We could not point out a poem in any language which, as a whole greatly excels it. It is far superior to "**Lalla Rookh.**" While Moore does not reach, except in rare snatches, the height of the loftiest qualities . . . , yet he has written finer poems than any, of equal length, by the greatest of his rivals. His radiance, not always as bright as some flashes from other pens, is yet a radiance of equable glow, whose total amount of light exceeds, by very much, we think, that total amount in the case of any contemporary writer whatsoever. A vivid fancy, an epigrammatic spirit, a fine taste, vivacity, dexterity, and a musical ear have made him very easily what he is, the most popular poet now living—if not the most popular that ever lived—and, perhaps, a slight modification at birth of that which phrenologists have agreed to term *temperament*, might have made him the truest and noblest votary of the muse of any age or clime. As it is, we have only casual glimpses of that *mens divinior* [prophetic mind] which is assuredly enshrined within him. (pp. 85-6)

Edgar Allan Poe, "Thomas Moore: The Imagination and the Mystical in Poetry" (originally published as an unsigned review of "Alciphron, a Poem," in Burton's Gentleman's Magazine, *Vol. VI, No. 1, January, 1840), in his* Literary Criticism of Edgar Allan Poe, *edited by Robert L. Hough, University of Nebraska Press, 1965, pp. 78-86.*

H. R. MONTGOMERY (essay date 1860)

[*Montgomery, the author of the first full length biographical and critical study of Moore, asserts that Moore "must be pre-eminently regarded" as a national lyrist. He extolls the diction and imagery and the "surpassingly musical and luscious" flow of verse in* Lalla Rookh. *Yet he identifies the very lushness of imagery in the poem as its "great fault," stating that the reader feels "the want of plainness and repose as a relief to the mind." Montgomery adds that* The Loves of the Angels *strikes one as profane because "the improbability of the situations and incidents is too glaring to admit of our sympathizing in the catastrophe."*]

[It] is in his character as a national lyrist that [Moore] must ever be pre-eminently regarded. . . . Moore's musical talent contributed very materially to his success as a lyric poet [in *Irish Melodies*]. As it is found that few can write successful dramas for representation without an intimate knowledge of stage affairs, so it may be asserted that no poet could have written these *Melodies* who had not himself a musical genius. The successful adaption of the words both to the sentiment and the movement of the air is indeed wonderful, and not the least of his triumphs. In his mind, indeed, music and poetry were inseparable, and he regarded his own poetry as the offspring of his passion for music seeking expression in words. In general, lyric poetry, considered solely as poetry, labours under this serious disadvantage—that it can seldom stand alone. Indeed . . . we can seldom hear, without a feeling of disappointment, words alone which we have been accustomed to hear with music. It is the great merit of Moore's poetry that it will bear this hard test. Indeed, it is almost music in itself. . . . (pp. 57-8)

Any elaborate criticism of these exquisite lyrics is fortunately needless. The language of panegyric might be exhausted without exceeding their merits. . . . [Few] have not glowed with their fervour, been melted with their pathos, dazzled by their sparkling brilliancy, felt elevated by their lofty tone, or had their spirits stirred by their patriotic strains. Defects may no doubt be found. All [the *Irish Melodies*] are not pitched upon the same lofty key. . . . There may, perhaps, be too much conventionality—too much small gallantry—too much of the atmosphere of the saloons of fashion; and, even in expression, simplicity may too often be sacrificed to an irresistible tendency to epigrammatic point, and the indulgence of the ever-restless play of a fancy luxuriating in the prodigal display of its exuberant wealth of illustration; these, however, are but as the specks in the sun, inseparable, perhaps, from [Moore's] excessive brightness.

In the writings of the elder poets—Suckling, Lovelace, Herrick, Carew, or Waller—an occasional sweet song was a rare gem, and prized accordingly; and so of the beautiful lyrics occurring in Shakespeare; but the prolific fancy of Moore scatters its sparkling stores about with a profusion resembling the good genius of the fairy tale. Indeed, the more we consider the number, variety, and beauty of these glittering and glowing effusions, the more must our amazement grow at the riches of the apparently inexhaustible fountain from which they flowed so lavishly. (pp. 61-3)

Critics had not been wanting, who, wishing to depreciate [Moore's] genius, professed to doubt if the epigrammatic point and exquisite finish of his lyric productions were compatible with the capability for a wider field and longer flight. Such cavillers were silenced for ever. In *Lalla Rookh,* as in some splendid gothic temple, while the proportions of the whole structure were commanding, every point on which the eye fell displayed the same delicate tracery and finish that had characterized the smaller gems that had previously come from his hand. The diction of the poem is rich and glowing, as befits the sunny scenes it pourtrays; the imagery gorgeous, the illustration exuberant, and drawn, with the marvellous facility of an exquisite and restless fancy, from every source of eastern allusion; while the flow of the verse is surpassingly musical and luscious. . . . (pp. 74-5)

The whole is indeed, like some work of enchantment, and the reader is borne along, floating on a sea of more than earthly music, through bowers redolent of more than earthly perfume, through halls of more than princely luxury, with the sound of falling waters lulling the ear, and forms of more than earthly beauty dazzling the eye—till he sinks down exhausted from the very excess of rapture. This is, indeed, the great fault, if fault it must be called, of the work. It is too continuously brilliant and gorgeous—we feel the want of plainness and repose as a relief to the mind, just as one does under the constant glare of a tropical sun, and would often be glad to exchange

for it the grayest and dullest of his native skies. We feel, when exhausted with the constant strain upon our attention, as if we should like a little of the painting done in plain colours, with less vermilion. The poet has been too profuse and lavish of his treasures, and half the beauties, always exquisite in themselves, are actually overlooked from their excessive abundance; the mind not having time to rest on them, so incessant and constantly recurring are the claims upon its admiration. (p. 75)

"Paradise and the Peri" [one of the series of poems which constitutes *Lalla Rookh*] is a beautiful conception exquisitely executed. It is perfect in its way, and breathes throughout a moral tone of the highest and purest kind. (p. 81)

"The Fire-worshippers," however, is by far the noblest poem of the series. The story possesses more of human interest than any of the others, and intensely and powerfully engages the best sympathies and highest human passions of our nature. (p. 86)

Consider the subject as an allegory or what we may, . . . it is almost impossible that [*The Loves of the Angels*] should be . . . treated as to do away with the feeling of profaneness. Comparisons have, in consequence, been made to Moore's disadvantage, between his angels and those of Milton—but the fault was not in him—it was in his subject, and unavoidably so. On the whole, notwithstanding the exquisite polish of the verse, of the chaste beauty of the whole poem, the reader is apt to be cloyed with such excessive and continuous sweetness, unbroken by the workings of the sterner passions. It appears to want human interest. . . . The allegory or moral is not kept constantly, if at all, before the reader's mind, and literally the improbability of the situations and incidents is too glaring to admit of our sympathizing in the catastrophe. To make comparisons between Moore's angels and those of Milton . . . is manifestly unjust; they must be judged by what they profess to be—in fact, no angels at all. But therein lies a great necessary defect in the whole plot. We could conceive of bona-fide angels, but we have no conception of beings holding a middle place, with all the attributes of angelic natures and the frailties of humanity—such as the allegory assumes. They are quite different even from his own delightful Peris [angels in the Moslem heaven depicted in *The Loves of the Angels*], which we feel to be purely poetical creations. (pp. 109-10)

> *H. R. Montgomery, in his* Thomas Moore: His Life, Writings, and Contemporaries, *Thomas Cautley Newby, Publisher, 1860, 208 p.*

GEORG BRANDES   (essay date 1875)

[*Brandes was a Danish literary critic and biographer. His major critical work,* Main Currents in Nineteenth-Century Literature, *traces the development of European literature in terms of writers' reaction to eighteenth-century thought. In the following essay, Brandes credits Moore with being "the first to rouse English poetry from its engrossed preoccupation with nature, to impress it into the service of liberty, and to give the start to political poetry." The Irish Melodies, in Brandes's judgment, are "Moore's title-deed to immortality."*]

[Thomas Moore] was the first to rouse English poetry from its engrossed preoccupation with nature, to impress it into the service of liberty, and to give the start to political poetry. (p. 151)

[*Epistles, Odes, and Other Poems*] contain descriptions of nature as remarkable for their correctness as for their wealth of glowing colour. With his genuine English Naturalism, he was, however, more anxious to be truthful than to be brilliant, and was very proud of the many testimonies he received both from natives and travellers as to the correct impression he conveyed of [the American] country and people. (p. 164)

[*Irish Melodies*] is Moore's title-deed to immortality. Everything that his unfortunate country had felt and suffered during the long years of her ignominy—her agonies and sighs, her ardent struggles, her martial spirit, the smile shining through her tears—we have them all here, scattered about in songs which are written in a mood of half-gay, half-mournful levity and amourousness. It was a wreath this, woven of grief, enthusiasm, and tenderness, a fragrant wreath, such as one binds in honour of the dead, which Moore placed on his country's brow. Not that Ireland is often mentioned; there are as few names as possible in these poems—it was not safe to print Irish names. . . . [As] in the old Christian allegorical hymns, the mysticism increased in poetic effect. (pp. 165-66)

[In] everything that Moore wrote, there is a remembrance of Ireland. . . . [In *Lalla Rookh*, there] is not an image, not a description, or name, or historical incident of reference, which has any connection with Europe. Everything, without exception, bears witness to the familiarity of the author with the life and nature of the East. Nevertheless we know that the subject did not begin to interest him until he saw a possibility of making the struggle between the Fire-worshippers and the Mohammedans a pretext for preaching tolerance. . . . And the interest of the reader, too, is not really awakened until he begins to divine Ireland and the Irish under these Ghebers and their strange surroundings. Hence it is that *The Fire-Worshippers* is the only entirely successful part of the poem. The very names Iran and Erin melt into each other in the reader's ear. (p. 177)

[The political satire in *Fables for the Holy Alliance* and *The Fudge Family in Paris*] sounds very bad and very dangerous; the distance separating such a writer from the older generation of poets strikes us as great; it seems but a step from this to Shelley and Byron. But as a matter of fact, it is a long way; for all these attacks are not quite so seriously meant as one would imagine. . . . With all his apparent unrestraint, Moore kept within the bounds prescribed by the society in which he lived. The Whig leaders had, when he came to London, received him with open arms, and Moore became and remained the Whig poet, who in a long series of playfully sarcastic letters—rhymed feuilletons one might call them—treated the public questions and Parliamentary events of the day with sparkling wit and drawing-room humour of the best style, in the spirit of the Whig party. (pp. 180-81)

> *Georg Brandes, "The Poetry of Irish Opposition and Revolt," in his* Main Currents in Nineteenth Century Literature: Naturalism in England, *Vol. IV, translated by Mary Morison (originally published as* Hovedstrømninger i det 19de aarhundredes litteratur: Naturalism i England, *1875), William Heinemann, 1905 (and reprinted as* Naturalism in Nineteenth Century English Literature *by Georg Brandes, Russell & Russell, 1957, pp. 148-81).*

GEORGE SAINTSBURY   (essay date 1888)

[*Saintsbury was an English literary historian and critic. Offering relatively high praise of Moore's works, Saintsbury states that* The Irish Melodies *are indeed worthy of being called poetry rather than merely "musically melodious." Saintsbury defends Moore from charges of shallowness, commenting that "his note of feel-*

ing, if not full and deep, is true and real." However, he ranks Moore "only with those poets who have expressed easily and acceptably the likings and passions and thoughts and fancies of the average man."*]

["**Poems of the late Thomas Little**" put up Moore's] fame and rather put down his character.

In later editions Thomas Little has been so much subjected to the fig-leaf and knife that we have known readers who wondered why on earth anyone should ever have objected to him. He was a good deal more uncastrated originally, but there never was much harm in him. . . . There is not much guilt in Little, but there is certainly not much innocence. He knows that a certain amount of not too gross indecency will raise a snigger, and like Voltaire and Sterne himself he goes and does it. (p. 340)

["**Lalla Rookh**"] seems to me a very respectable poem indeed of the second rank. Of course it is artificial. The parade of second, or third, or twentieth-hand learning in the notes makes one smile, and the whole reminds one . . . of a harp of the period with the gilt a little tarnished, the ribbons more than a little faded, and the silk stool on which the young woman in ringlets used to sit much worn. . . . But much remains to "**Lalla**" if not to [the narrator] Feramorz. The prose interludes have lost none of their airy grace. . . . "**Paradise and the Peri**" is perhaps the prettiest purely sentimental poem that English or any other language can show. "**The Fire Worshippers**" are rather long, but there is a famous fight—more than one indeed—in them to relieve the monotony. For "**The Light of the Harem**" alone I have never been able to get up much enthusiasm: but even "**The Light of the Harem**" is a great deal better than Moore's subsequent attempt in the style of "**Lalla Rookh**," or something like it, "**The Loves of the Angels**." (p. 343)

As "**Lalla Rookh**" is far the most important of Moore's serious poems, so "**The Fudge Family in Paris**" is far the best of his humorous poems. I do not forget "**The Two-Penny Postbag**," nor many capital later verses of the same kind, the best of which perhaps is the "**Epistle from Henry of Exeter to John of Tehume**." But "**The Fudge Family**" has all the merits of these with a scheme and framework of dramatic character which they lack. Miss Biddy and her vanities, Master Bob and his guttling, the eminent turncoat Phil Fudge, Esq., himself with his politics, are all excellent. But I avow that Phelim Connor is to me the most delightful, though he has always been rather a puzzle. If he is intended to be a satire on the class now represented by the O'Briens and the McCarthays he is exquisite, and it is small wonder that Young Ireland has never loved Moore much. . . . [These] lighter poems of Moore are great fun, and it is no small misfortune that the younger generation of readers pays so little attention to them. For they are full of acute observation of manners, politics, and society by an accomplished man of the world, put into pointed and notable form by an accomplished man of letters. (pp. 343-44)

The singular musical melody of ["**Irish Melodies, National Airs, Sacred Songs, Ballads and Songs**"] has never been seriously denied by any one, but it seems to be thought, especially now-a-days, that because they are musically melodious they are not poetical. . . . It is acknowledged that [Moore's special virtue] consists partly in marrying music most happily to verse; but what is not so fully acknowledged as it ought to be is that it also consists in marrying music not merely to verse but to poetry. . . . It never seems to have mattered to him whether he wrote the words for the air or altered the air to suit the words. The two fit like a glove, and if, as is sometimes the case, the same or a similar poetical measure is heard set to another air than Moore's, this other always seems intrusive and wrong. He draws attention in one case to the extraordinary irregularity of his own metre (an irregularity to which the average pindaric is a mere jog-trot), yet the air fits it exactly. Of course the two feet which most naturally go to music, the anapaest and the trochee, are commonest with him; but the point is that he seems to find no more difficulty, if he does not take so much pleasure, in setting combinations of a very different kind. Nor is this peculiar gift by any means unimportant from the purely poetical side, the side on which the verse is looked at without any regard to air or accompaniment. For the great drawback to "songs to be sung" in general since Elizabethan days . . . has been the constant tendency of the verse writer to sacrifice to his musical necessities either meaning or poetic sound or both. . . . Now Moore is quite free from this blame. He may not have the highest and rarest strokes of poetic expression; but at any rate he seldom or never sins against either reason or poetry for the sake of rhythm and rhyme. He is always the master not the servant, the artist not the clumsy craftsman. (pp. 344-45)

To my fancy the three best of Moore's songs, and three of the finest songs in any language, are **"Oft in the stilly Night,"** **"When in Death I shall calm recline,"** and **"I saw from the Beach."** They all exemplify what has been pointed out above, the complete adaptation of words to music and music to words, coupled with a decidedly high quality of poetical merit in the verse, quite apart form the mere music. (p. 345)

[Moore's position is not equal to that] of Scott or Byron or Shelley or Wordsworth, but still a position high enough and singularly isolated at its height. Viewed from the point of strictly poetical criticism, he no doubt ranks only with those poets who have expressed easily and acceptably the likings and passions and thoughts and fancies of the average man, and who have expressed these with no extraordinary cunning or witchery. . . . If he does not always ring true, a much smaller part of him rings false than happens with far more pretentious poets. Again, he has that all-saving touch of humour which enables him, sentimentalist as he is, to be an admirable comedian as well. . . . [He] has the two qualities which one must demand of a poet who is a poet, and not a mere maker of rhymes. His note of feeling, if not full or deep, is true and real. His faculty of expression is not only considerable, but it is also distinguished: it is a faculty which in the same measure and degree nobody else has possessed. . . . The true poets and even the true satirists abide, and both as a poet and a satirist Thomas Moore abides and will abide with them. (pp. 347-48)

George Saintsbury, "Thomas Moore," in Macmillan's Magazine, Vol. LVII, No. 341, March, 1888, pp. 337-48.

ARTHUR SYMONS   (essay date 1905)

[*An English critic, poet, dramatist, short story writer, and editor, Symons initially gained notoriety as an English decadent in the 1890s, and he eventually established himself as one of the most important critics of the modern era. In the following, Symons refutes Stephen Gwynn's claim that Moore is primarily "an artist of metre" (1905), and posits that "it is the voice of the mob, prettily refined, sweetened, and set to a tune, which we hear in his songs." He also accuses Moore of lacking seriousness in his ideas, emotions, and even in his verse, which Symons terms "trot, gallop, and jingle."*]

Moore as a poet is the Irishman as the Englishman imagines him to be, and he represents a part of the Irish temperament; but not the part which makes for poetry. All the Irish quicksilver is in him; he registers change with every shift in the weather. He has the spirits of a Dublin mob; and it is the voice of the mob, prettily refined, sweetened, set to a tune, which we hear in his songs. But the voice of the peasant is not in him; there is in him nothing of that uneasy, listening conscience which watches the earth for signs, and is never alone in solitude. He is without imagination, and his fun and his fancy are but the rising and sinking of the quicksilver, and mean no more than a change in the weather. (p. 681)

He pleased by his songs and by his singing of them; how is it that the songs to-day seem to us like last season's fashions, melancholy in their faded prettiness? He gave pleasure, but the quality of that pleasure must be considered, and it will be seen that it was not the quality of poetic pleasure. (pp. 682-83)

It is to the Cavalier Lyrics, no doubt, that Moore at his best comes nearest; never within recognisable distance of any Elizabethan work, and never near enough to good work of the Restoration for the comparison to be seriously made. He has their fluency, but none of their gentlemanly restraint; touches of their crudity, but none of their straightforwardness; and of their fine taste, nothing, and nothing of the quality of mind which lurks under all their disguises. In Moore's songs there is no "fundamental brain-work"; they have no base in serious idea or in fine emotion. The sensations they render are trivial in themselves, or become so in the rendering; there is a continual effervescence, but no meditation, and no ecstasy. Between this faint local heat of the senses and the true lyric rapture there is a great gulf. Moore brims over with feeling, and his feeling is quick, honest, and generous. But he never broods over his feeling until he has found his way down to its roots: the song strikes off from the surface like the spurt of a match; there is no deep fire or steady flame. He never realised the dignity of song or of the passions. In his verse he was amorous, but a foolish lover; shrewd, but without wisdom; honest, but without nobility; a breeder of easy tears and quick laughter. He sang for his evening, not his day; and he had his reward, but most go without the day's wages. (pp. 683-84)

There is an **"Irish Melody"** of Moore which begins:—

Oh! had we some bright little isle of our own,
In a blue summer ocean, far off and alone,
Where a leaf never dies in the still blooming bowers,
And the bee banquets on through a whole year of flowers.

The idea has been repeated by another Irishman, Mr. Yeats, and his poem begins:—

I will arise and go now, and go to Innisfree,
And a small cabin build there, of clay and wattles made;
Nine bean-rows will I have there, a hive for the honey-bee,
And live alone in the bee-loud glade.

No two poems could be more exactly comparable; the resemblances are as striking as the differences; and the differences might teach in one lesson all that distinguishes what is poetry from what is not poetry.

And further, if you will compare the versification of these two poems, or indeed any other poems of the two writers, you will see how cheap, for the most part, were Moore's rhythmical effects, how continually he sacrificed the accent of the sense to the accent of the rhythm, and how little he made even out of those rhythms which he is believed to have introduced into

English. Those who still claim for Moore some recognition as a poet claim it mainly on account of his skill in metre, and on account of his tact in writing words for singing. . . . With a good poet, good music can make good songs; with a bad poet, the best of all music cannot do as much, and Moore, in putting words to his **"Irish Melodies,"** did not always give the tunes a chance. . . . [Mr. Gwynn tells us (see excerpt below, 1905)]: "He based his work upon Irish tunes, composed in the primitive manner, before poetry was divorced from music. One may say, virtually, that in fitting words to these tunes, he reproduced in English the rhythms of Irish folk-song." But we are told further, and then the case is altered: "The thing was not done completely: for instance, in the first number of the **'Melodies,'** the song, **'Erin, the tear and the smile in thine eye,'** is to the tune of 'Eileen Aroon,' and the Irish words . . . do not correspond in metre with Moore's. He has varied the tune, and is consequently using a different stanza." If, further, one may judge from Dr. Hyde's translations in his beautiful book, *The Love Songs of Connacht,* Moore has come very far short of having "reproduced in English the rhythms of Irish folk-song." Certain cadences he has caught, like that cadence of

At the mid hour of night, when the stars were weeping, I fly,

which we are told is "a metrical effect wholly new in English." To have introduced a new cadence into English is quite a creditable thing to have done, even without writing a good poem by its aid. And, though the poem beginning with this line may be "the most beautiful lyric that Moore ever wrote," I do not think it can be accepted as really a good poem. (pp. 684-86)

Moore's trot, gallop, and jingle of verse has, no doubt, its skill and its merit; but its skill is not seldom that of the circus-rider, and its merit no more than to have gone the due number of times round the ring without slackening speed. It entertains the most legitimately when it carries mere folly on its back. But Moore had ideals and ideas, and only the same trained nag to carry them. . . . Gradually he gave up writing verse, and wrote prose, controversial prose, and was looked upon as "the champion of the liberties of Ireland." It is significant of the whole man, and of how small a segment of him was an artist, that for Moore to become really serious meant giving up verse. Only in prose could he conceive of people being quite serious, and writing nobly. (p. 686)

Arthur Symons, "The Poetry of Thomas Moore," in The Fortnightly Review *(reprinted by permission of Contemporary Review Company Limited), n.s. Vol. CCCCLX, April 1, 1905, pp. 681-86.*

STEPHEN GWYNN (essay date 1905)

[*Gwynn stresses that "Moore's great distinction [is] that he brought into English verse something of the variety and multiplicity of musical rhythms," especially the rhythms of the Irish folk song. In addition, Gwynn believes that "there is no poet in English except Goldsmith who appeals to simple people so much as Moore." According to Gwynn, Moore holds an important place in the history of English poetry as an "artist of metre."*]

The last century has been one of increasing virtuosity in the management of lyric metres. From Cowper and Crabbe to Mr. Swinburne, is a strange distance; and it has not been sufficiently realised that Moore is very largely responsible for the advance. Many critics have noted the change from the strictly syllabic scansion of Pope's school to metres like those of Tennyson's *Maud,* and a hundred later poems, in which syllabic measure-

ment is wholly discarded. It has been noted also that, even in the freer metres of the sixteenth and seventeenth centuries, lyric writers confined themselves to variations of the trochee or iambic, and that an anapaestic or dactylic measure is hardly found before Waller. But it has hardly been recognised that till Moore began to use these triple feet, no poet used them with dexterity and confidence. (pp. 175-76)

Going back . . . to the seventeenth century for his inspiration in style, Moore began by using only the trochaic and iambic measures. In the *Epistles and Odes,* we find one epistle (that to Atkinson) written in well managed anapaests, but more notable is the very delicate rhythm of the **"Canadian Boat Song"**—inspired by a tune. It is Moore's great distinction that he brought into English verse something of the variety and multiplicity of musical rhythms. When the *Irish Melodies* began to appear, it is no wonder that readers should have been dazzled by the skill with which a profusion of metres were handled; and the poet showed himself even more inventive in rhythms than in stanzas.

The most curious part of the matter is that Moore was really importing into English poetry some of the characteristics of a literature which he did not know. He had not a word of Gaelic, and . . . desired to see it die out. . . . But he based his work upon Irish tunes, composed in the primitive manner, before music was divorced from poetry. One may say, virtually, that in fitting words to these tunes, he reproduced in English the rhythms of Irish folk song.

The thing was not done completely: for instance, in the first number of the *Melodies,* the song **"Erin, the smile and the tear in thine eye,"** is to the tune of "Eileen Aroon," and the Irish words . . . do not correspond in metre with Moore's. He has varied the tune, and is consequently using a different stanza, which corresponds with the Irish only in the last three lines of the refrain. In the other instance, that of **"O blame not the bard,"** there is a general correspondence in metre, but here the Irish metre is one not very different from an ordinary English stanza—though, as usual in Irish folk-poetry, the line is measured by time and not by syllables.

The need for fitting metre to music forced Moore into employing a wide variety of stanzas; and his example was of service in a day which had been little used to anything but the couplet and quatrain of three or four well-worn types. (pp. 176-77)

The peculiarity of [the metres in verses such as "The dream of those days when first I sung thee is o'er"]—the dragging, wavering, cadence that half baulks the ear—is the distinctive characteristic of Irish verse. No English poet, so far as I know, has caught it; but Mangan gave this character to some of his finest renderings from the Irish, and in our own day Mr. Yeats has shown an increasing tendency towards this subtle and evasive beauty.

It is I think mainly as an artist in metre that Moore still holds an importance in the history of English poetry; and any one considering [his] poems . . . will see how individual and original were his achievements. But the admirable qualities in his verse by which he impressed his contemporaries were rather those of lightness and swiftness: its sweetness, of which much was made, is a good deal less admirable. For this, however, the nature of his best lyric work was largely responsible.

He wrote songs to be sung; and the best verse is not that which sings best. Language has to be softened down for singing, as it need not be for speech; and this softening approaches to emasculation. The habit of writing for music injured Moore's versification even when he wrote narrative verse; and we have the result in the excessive smoothness of *Lalla Rookh.* (pp. 179-80)

[What] is sung can never be caught so easily as what is spoken. [Moore] was led, therefore, to use a strict economy of ideas; to expand rather than condense his meaning. (p. 180)

[It] is noticeable in the *Melodies* how often the whole song is merely the skilful and deliberate evolution of a single metaphor—an art akin to the rhetorician's. (p. 181)

Moore's lyrics are verse written for public utterance, designed to produce their impression instantly, and not to sink slowly into the mind: and it is useless to compare them with the packed thought of Shakespeare's sonnets, Wordsworth's odes, or whatever else is in the highest category of lyric poetry.

There is, however, a class of verse to which hardly anything can be preferred, and in it are not only the songs of Shakespeare, but some of Scott's and many of Burns's; music as simple as a bird's, dealing in the simplest emotions, free from all taint of rhetoric. In that class I do not think that anything of Moore's can be placed. (pp. 181-82)

[In one category, however, he] must be pronounced the equal of any man who ever lived. The lighter numbers breathe the very spirit of gaiety, united to a real distinction of style:—

> Drink to her, who long
>   Hath waked the poet's sigh,
> The girl who gave to song
>   —What gold could never buy.

Still more characteristic perhaps is another, so melodious and so roguish:—

> The young May moon is beaming, love,
> The glow-worm's lamp is gleaming, love,
>   How sweet to rove
>   Through Morna's grove,
> When the drowsy world is dreaming, love!

(p. 182)

Neither Prior nor Praed, nor any other master of the lighter lyric, has equalled these. . . . (p. 183)

There is of course a fashion in verse as in anything else, and Moore's excellences are precisely the least congenial to the current taste in criticism. There is a fashion for nakedness of expression, and Moore always shrank from brutality; there is a fashion for strained uses of language, and Moore was always studiously accurate and lucid. But it may be questioned whether, setting aside the opinion of professed and professional critics, Moore's poetry would not be found to retain a vigorous life. He was never, and never wished to be, in the least esoteric; his object was to be understood by all. A poet who insists upon this aim must perhaps sacrifice something, but he may also achieve something not common. Oddly enough, there is no poet in English except Goldsmith who appeals to simple people so much as Moore. These two can often bring poetry home in triumph where even Shakespeare would never find an entrance.

But Moore's importance in the history of literature lies in his connection not with English but with Irish literature. . . . [Ireland] heard for the first time in the *Irish Melodies* a song that came from the heart of Ireland, uttered in a language which nine out of every ten Irishmen could understand. . . . The other Irishmen who had shown great literary talent—Burke, Gold-

smith, and Sheridan—belonged body and soul to English letters. Moore's case was different. . . . He had given a voice to Ireland; he had put into her mouth a song of her own.

Standing apart now, from the times and circumstances in which Moore wrote, we can see that what Ireland got from him was not all gain. The literature produced so profusely in the days of Young Ireland, and modelled mainly upon him, echoes only too faithfully his declamatory tone; and worse than that, it is flooded by the exuberance of sentiment, which was Moore's besetting weakness. Other models, and, it is to be hoped, better ones, now are rapidly replacing those of Moore and his followers; with the younger generation, even in Ireland, he has lost his hold. (pp. 187-89)

[But] certainly it is no small title to fame for a poet that he was in his own country for at least three generations the delight and consolation of the poor. Tattered and thumbed copies of his poems, broadcast through Ireland, represent better his claim to the interest of posterity than whatever comely and autographed editions may be found among the possessions of Bowood and Holland House. (pp. 189-90)

Stephen Gwynn, in his Thomas Moore *(copyright in the United States of America, 1904; reprinted by permission of Macmillan, London and Basingstoke), Macmillan, 1905, 205 p.*

PADRAIC COLUM   (essay date 1937)

[*An Irish poet, dramatist, editor, and critic, Colum was one of the major writers of the Irish Literary Renaissance. In the following, he acknowledges Moore's contribution to both the ''Catholic Emancipation and the revival of the Irish spirit.'' But though Moore ''was the first poet of a national awakening,'' Colum comments, his poetry is ''mediocre,'' and ''should have been eclipsed in the generation that followed his or the generation after by a poet who would be more definitely Irish.'' Colum does cite several poems by Moore which, he believes, are examples of poetry rather than mere ''song-writer's art.''*]

Thomas Moore was the first in English-speaking Ireland to put himself forward as an Irish national writer; he was the first spokesman of the emerging Catholic community. . . . Ireland would be ungrateful if she did not acknowledge how much his devotion effected, both as regards Catholic Emancipation and the revival of the Irish spirit: no writer at the time could have done more than Moore did for both of these causes.

To appraise certain of his lyrics is difficult, for they are so associated with deeply loved music that their intrinsic character is not apparent. As verse the bulk is mediocre. Moore was concerned with writing words that would take the shape and keep the rhythm of a tune, and not with expressing a mood that was deeply personal. But many times he transcended the limit of the song-writer's art and wrote poetry: "**At the mid-hour of night when stars are weeping I fly**" is, no matter from what side we regard it, a memorable lyric; "**The Harp that once through Tara's Halls**" is not only a great song, but a poem that brings to us something that is very rare in poetry, the dignity of a nation's utterance; a fine poem, too, is "**Silent O Moyle**," with its unique assonantal music, and so is . . . "**How oft the banshee cried**"; if the three poems on Robert Emmett's [*sic*] fate—"**O breathe not his name**," "**When he who adores thee**," "**She is far from the land**"—were printed together we would see that Moore has written a noble threnody. (pp. 124-25)

He was the first poet of a national awakening; he fell heir to the music of his country, to the curiosity about Celtic past . . . ; to the romantic movement with its interest in national expression. His devotion to the Irish cause gave strength to part of his work. Moore's achievement should have been eclipsed in the generation that followed his or the generation after by a poet who would be more definitely Irish, who could bring into the new national expression the intensity of Gaelic feeling. But the dire conditions of the country prevented the emergence of such a poet from the only class that could have given him the proper endowment, the disinherited Catholic peasantry. (p. 125)

> *Padraic Colum, "The Irish Melodist," in* Commonweal *(copyright © 1937 Commonweal Publishing Co., Inc.; reprinted by permission of Commonweal Publishing Co., Inc.), Vol. XXVII, No. 5, November 26, 1937, pp. 123-25.*

HOWARD MUMFORD JONES (essay date 1937)

[*Jones wrote the first full-scale critical overview of Moore's works. Positing that "Moore's historic mission was to restore music to English verse as the romantics understood verbal music," he praises Moore's "fresh and individual" style. In addition, Jones suggests that Moore "embodied what no other poet of the age embodied—that mythical ideal of the romanticists, the national bard"; he emphasizes that Moore "did not merely 'belong' to the romantic movement; he incarnated it." Jones praises Moore's "sheer craftsmanship" in technique and the purity of his poetic style. Though he considers* Intercepted Letters; or, The Twopenny Post-Bag *to be "one of the most brilliant bits of rollicking light satire in the history of English verse," Jones regards Moore's biography of Byron as his "unforgettable achievement" and "the one book by which Moore really lives today."*]

[Despite] the skillful and easy versification—perhaps because of it—[*Odes of Anacreon*] leaves on the modern reader an impression of lush monotony.

In 1800, however, the romantic movement was yet young. . . . Poetry was stagnating in a Sargasso Sea of weedy rhetoric.

Moore's historic mission was to restore music to English verse as the romantics understood verbal music. Opening the volume at random, one finds the liquid movement of the lines admirable in their kind, even when the passage does not rise above the dead level of lusciousness. . . . There had been nothing like [Moore's poetry] since the seventeenth century. Readers found it strange, intoxicating, and sweet. Granted that to our taste this is vicious writing—vicious because the sense is drowned in the sound—it has yet that "luxury" in which Keats was to delight. Indeed, it is curious how *Anacreon* anticipates the styles of greater men. Byron, of course, went to school to Moore in his handling of octosyllables, but it is startling to find the movement of Shelley's "Lines Written Among the Euganean Hills" foretold in [Moore's translation **"Ode III"**]

> Listen to the Muse's Lyre,
> Master of the pencil's fire!
> Sketch'd in painting's bold display,
> Many a city first portray;
> Many a city, revelling free,
> Warm with loose festivity.
>
> (pp. 54-5)

Presumably the fashionable world of readers cared little for [his] astonishing revival of Cavalier beauty, but it certainly warmed to the delicate artifice of Moore's fusion of eroticism, wine, roses, and elegance. . . . Few poets upon their first entrance into English literature have sounded so fresh and individual a note. (p. 56)

[Moreover, the] *Odes of Anacreon* helped to give [an impulse] to the literary revival of Hellenism which forms an important living element in the romantic movement. For the Augustan age antiquity had been Roman or, when it was Greek, Greek in the fashion of Johnson's *Irene*. Now antiquity was becoming warm, colorful, and Hellenistic. (p. 57)

Moore's position in the romantic movement is not quite that obscure niche to which the Wordsworthians and the Coleridgeans, the Shelley specialists and the Keats enthusiasts have rather blindly consigned him. When he sang, calling forth laughter and tears, enthusiasm and sentiment, he embodied what no other poet of the age embodied—that mythical ideal of the romanticists, the national bard. Composing his own songs to airs of his own choosing, singing the glories and misfortunes of his race, asking from great lords and ladies only the reward and recognition of his art, Moore presented in his small person the union of music and verse, of folk tradition and courtly accomplishment of which the age had read in Ossian, in Scott, in novel and historical romance. In a sense Moore did not merely "belong" to the romantic movement; he incarnated it. He sang at one and the same time the rights of the people and the glories of ancient kings, the pangs of romantic love and the sympathy of nature. Hundreds who turned a deaf ear to Wordsworth listened, enraptured, to Moore; thousands to whom Shelley was a filthy atheist learned of tyranny and nationalism from the persuasive Irishman. The curse of Cain might rest on Byron's marble brow, but Moore's insinuating presence inspired neither shudder nor regret. (p. 110)

It must be said that no special pleading can ever raise Moore to the stature of a great genius. . . . The faults of the *Irish Melodies* are patent: they are too facile, too shallow—to sum it up in a word—too commercial. Yet, though it is unfair to judge them apart from the music (this is, however, the only critical judgment they have ever had!), even as poems they are more various, more truly lyrical, more cunningly fingered, and more soundly built than careless reading knows. . . . [His] sheer craftsmanship must place Moore on a plane with Shelley and Coleridge and Keats in technique, and . . . [his] management of pause and metrical fingering within the line, sometimes go beyond anything that any other romanticist has to show. The better parts of the *Melodies* are rich in verbal music. (pp. 110-11)

[*M.P., or, The Bluestocking*] has small "literary" merit, and Moore was right in not reprinting it among his collected poems; but in stage terms it was an effective and amusing musical comedy. . . . The plot is not more artificial than that of most musical comedies, and the characterization of certain parts— Sir Charles Canvas, the corrupt member of Parliament, Leatherhead the bookseller, and Lady Bab Blue, the blue-stocking— is adroit within the conventions of the genre. The love plot and the domestic scenes are bathed in sentimental diction— but in what musical comedy are they not? The satire on political corruption has not lost its sting, and though the wit of the piece suffers from the persistent search for puns, beloved of that age, some of the lines and some of the songs have a Gilbertian deftness. (p. 132)

[*Intercepted Letters, or the Twopenny Post-Bag*] set the style for a small regiment of imitators, and became . . . the talk of the town. To the modern reader unversed in the minutiae of Regency politics, the "point" of many of the digs is unfortunately obscured by a cloud of unfamiliar names revealed in the consonants and hidden in the vowels, but even a superficial acquaintance with the period makes it clear that the volume is in truth one of the most brilliant bits of rollicking light satire in the history of English verse. (p. 145)

No amount of special pleading will make *Lalla Rookh* a great poem, and yet the laudatory adjectives [applied to it in Moore's lifetime] were not all mistaken. It is curious to inquire into the reasons of [its] neglect, which are, briefly, that Moore shared the defects of his time and in this poem lacked its virtues. For the two grand faults of the romantic school were bookishness and rhetoric. (p. 172)

Lalla Rookh is undeniably bookish, the verse carrying a train of footnotes and an appendix of annotations as long as the countless lamps which Azim saw in the halls of the veiled prophet. . . .

The footnotes, however, are a venial sin; deeper lies the fatal failure of the poem imaginatively to fuse the results of all [Moore's] hard reading into a credible poetic world. [W. Beckford's novel] *Vathek* is twice as successful because it labors only half as hard. Moore's perfumed Orient discovers always a lurking odor of old leather bindings. (p. 175)

To point out the faults in [*Lalla Rookh*] is easy; it is a more interesting critical task to dwell upon some of its merits. For one thing, though Moore occasionally falls into the parliamentary manner . . . , his style is in the main pure. It may lack intensity; it may sink into bathos; its liquidity may cloy; but it is not gummy with archaic "beauties" nor clogged with superfluous ornamental rhetoric. Take, for instance, a passage describing carnage in "The Fire-Worshippers"; it is as swift and lurid as anything in Scott:

> . . . listless from each crimson hand
>   The sword hangs, clogg'd with massacre.
> Never was horde of tyrants met
> With bloodier welcome—never yet
> To patriot vengeance hath the sword
> More terrible libations pour'd! . . .

This, to be sure, is melodrama, but carnage is usually melodramatic, and this is melodrama in which every word tells. Yet the same work which contains these bloody horrors also contains so Shelleyan a lyric as that which begins:

> A Spirit there is, whose fragrant sigh
> Is burning now through earth and air,
> Where cheeks are blushing, the Spirit is nigh,
> Where lips are meeting, the Spirit is there! . . .

Place this beside Shelley's "Indian Serenade," and Moore's poem perhaps sinks to a secondary order of lyricism; and yet who, before Moore, had wrung quite this music out of English words, or who, before him, had attained this cool, luscious beauty? (pp. 177-78)

[The interludes containing Fadladeen's ironical comments] are amusing, but the difficulty is that they are in a different key from that of the rest of the work, and that Moore's resort to prose indicates a poverty of poetical resource. (p. 178)

["The Veiled Prophet of Khorassom" section of *Lalla Rookh*] lies halfway between the Gothic romance of Mrs. Radcliffe and romantic opera, and a fable so absurd could be made believable only by the burning imagination of a Shelley. This Moore did not possess. Nevertheless the narrative does move; and as the reader makes his way through [its] incredibilities,

he perceives that it is not the absurd events but their larger significance which is important. This tale of religious fanaticism, this story of whole peoples led astray by a cynical demagogue is recited for its modern application; and it seems clear that in "The Veiled Prophet of Khorassan" Moore intended some glancing reference to the Catholic question in Ireland. It is not that Mokanna is Daniel O'Connell, but rather the danger inherent in a situation which allows a demagogue to play upon the religious prejudices of an ignorant people—this is what Moore has in view. In an even larger sense the poem is a product of that disillusion which the French Revolution and the Napoleonic regime produced in many sensitive minds. (pp. 179-80)

"The Fire-Worshippers" [is] much the best thing in *Lalla Rookh*. . . . The inevitable love affair between Hafed and Hinda, daughter of the Moslem emir, mixes romantic tragedy with political struggle, and there is, among the little Persian band, a traitor who sells out to the conqueror. The overtones are unmistakably those of Irish rebellion, particularly the Robert Emmet episode. Moore hymns the doomed patriots and goes out of his way to excoriate the wretch who betrayed their cause. . . . [The] suggestion that Hafed is a Persian Robert Emmet, Hinda, Sarah Curran [his fiancé], and the traitor a composite portrait of government spies, is irresistible. "The Fire-Worshippers" has a vigor rare in Moore, an energy which patriotism and the detestation of treachery have breathed into the poem. . . . (p. 181)

[In *The Loves of the Angels*, Moore] abandoned the pentameter couplet (which had done for *Lalla Rookh*) as well as his characteristic anapaests, for an octosyllabic line. The verse is woven with a creamy consistency of texture which certainly evokes atmosphere, but which leaves the personages and events rather vague; and if the rococo ornamentation of *Lalla Rookh* is happily absent, the dreamy indefiniteness of time and place, the lack of something concrete to envision in the events make *The Loves of the Angles* a weaker production. (p. 218)

Moore's [*Letters and Journals of Lord Byron, with Notices of His Life*] remains one of the four or five great literary biographies in the English language. . . . To have written the life of the most discussed personality in England, and to have written it so well that all subsequent biographers have had to return to its estimate; to have moved tactfully among the thorny problems of Byron's career, among his friends with their frequently clashing views, and among his family with their reticences and their hostilities; to have discussed with reasonable accuracy the political and social problems, both national and international, which the tracing of Byron's career involved; and to have left on the reader after almost fifteen hundred pages of print an indelible impression of so complex a being—this, in sum, is Moore's unforgettable achievement. (pp. 273-74)

Like other great nineteenth-century biographies—Lockhart's *Scott* and Forster's *Dickens* are cases in point—Moore's *Byron* has required, and received, correction in the century which has elapsed since it appeared. This is inevitable; but it does not mean that the small triumphs of subsequent investigators in pointing out Moore's errors invalidate the book as a whole. That he took a sympathetic view of Byron and tended to exculpate or soften certain episodes which later biographers have condemned is natural and necessary—had he not been *en rapport* with his subject he would not have written a great book. Probably the two most serious defects in the study are Moore's failure in handling the problem of Byron's relations to his half-sister, and his failure in what today we consider elementary editorial honesty. (pp. 274-75)

But when all is said, the fact remains that Byron lives and moves and has his faulty being in Moore's pages in so vivid a manner that the discussion of that fascinating personality has ever since followed the lines (in the main) which the biographer laid down. Moore's triumph is owing principally to three considerations. In the first place, it is evident that the book is written *con amore*; that Moore, though he loved Byron, was fortunately sufficiently remote from him to achieve something like objectivity, yet sufficiently close to him to write sympathetically. In the second place, Moore's prose is, for once, lucent and easy; gone are the similes, the rococo decoration, the false oratorical style; as a consequence, we look *through* the style, and not *at* it. And in the third place, by adopting the "letters and journal" method Moore sacrificed the vanity of authorship to a triumph of art. Tommy was vain enough in small ways; but he was in this instance wise and humble enough to realize that no one could speak for Byron as Byron could speak for himself. The result is that, almost everywhere in the book, we feel we are in contact with one of the most vital and electric spirits in the whole range of English literature. Moore does this so easily that we are not conscious of his extraordinary management of the materials at his command. . . . [The] result was the one book by which Moore really lives today. (pp. 275-76)

> *Howard Mumford Jones, in his* The Harp that Once—A Chronicle of the Life of Thomas Moore *(copyright © 1937 by Henry Holt and Company; copyright renewed © 1964 by Howard Mumford Jones; reprinted by permission of the Literary Estate of Howard Mumford Jones), Holt, 1937, 365 p.*

L.A.G. STRONG   (essay date 1937)

[In his critical biography of Moore, Strong asserts that Moore's poetry should be considered in conjunction with its accompanying music. According to Strong, having to condense his poetry for music forced Moore to "prune" his rhetorical extravagance. Hoover H. Jordan (1962) expands on Strong's idea in a more detailed and technical analysis of Moore's verse in relation to music.]

[The *Irish Melodies*] are the pinnacle of Moore's work, his title to immortality: and nine-tenths of the criticism of them that has appeared has been on a wrong basis.

The essential point about the *Melodies* is that Moore intended them to reach his audience *through the mouth of a singer*. Words and music are indivisible. The lyric for each Melody is a lyric, not a poem: that is to say, it is the words of a song. Moore was writing for the voice, primarily for his own voice. He tested each one out himself, again and again, and his first care was to find words which *(a)* fitted the air, and *(b)* were singable. . . . To print by themselves the words of any of the *Melodies,* and judge them as a poem, is to put them to a test for which they were not meant. Moore never envisaged the printing of the words without the music, and only gave his consent, very reluctantly, when he found that a pirated edition, full of errors, was already on the market.

That some of the words stand very well by themselves—as poems—is beside the point. They can never so achieve a fraction of their full effect. (pp. 121-22)

Naturally, it was by a poetic technique that Moore secured his effects, but this was, in the *Melodies,* subordinated always to

the end in view, and used side by side with his feeling for music and his personal skill with his voice. Of the limitations his task imposed on him as a poet he was well aware. . . . Happily, they were limitations which did his poetic ability little, if any, harm. He was too flowery, and all the better for pruning. Even so, the floweriness would burgeon out unsuitably. (pp. 123-24)

Of sheer surface verse technique Moore had plenty. . . . [He] knew a thing or two about sound and rhythm and the craft of verse in general. In the *Melodies,* he was concerned with sound and rhythm only. His arrangement of vowel sounds is primarily a singer's, but some of the verses are very good to speak. The management of [vowel and consonant sounds] . . . shows a skill, a sheer knowledge of the business, that earns the respect of anyone who has realized that such problems exist. It must be admitted that his concentration on sound led Moore to write many things that look loose and silly in verse alone. . . . [But] we cannot, without injustice and stultification, consider the words apart from the air. (pp. 124-25)

[The *Irish Melodies*] are some of the most purely vocal lines ever set down. The voice cannot help singing them. Moore always flatters one's voice. . . .

As music, the phrases alone are not too easy to sing, but Moore has transformed them. First of all, his lines have an astonishing foward flow, an impulse running right through from the first word to the last. The placing of the consonants at the accented parts is beyond praise. (p. 126)

Moore brought to his task a musical ear, a voice, a high metrical skill, and a mysterious quality of which he himself knew nothing—the power to articulate, in his mannered, feminine way, the soul of a country. (p. 127)

One other quality of Moore's is brought out by the *Melodies,* and that is his excellence as a writer of light verse. Not all the airs on which he sought to "bestow the gift of articulation" were melancholy, and to the gayer of them he worthily responded. The metrical variety to which the airs compelled him was here shown at its happiest. . . . In its kind, there is nothing better [than Moore's light verse] in the language. . . . These lighter lyrics, while best in company with the airs to which they were written, can stand very happily by themselves. (pp. 136-37)

[After 1860 the *Irish Melodies*] spread everywhere, and retained their hold for more than fifty years, during which Moore was the musical voice of Ireland.

It was not only the plagency of the songs, their nostalgic melancholy, their insistence on the Gael's lost heritage, that so took hold on the Irish people. (p. 140)

> *L.A.G. Strong, in his* The Minstrel Boy: A Portrait of Tom Moore *(copyright 1937 by L.A.G. Strong and renewed 1965 by Sylvia Strong; reprinted by permission of Alfred A. Knopf, Inc.; in Canada by A D Peters & Co Ltd), Knopf, 1937, 317 p.*

HOWARD O. BROGAN   (essay date 1945)

[Brogan, in an essay focusing on Moore's satires, concludes that the satires "are much better than the romantic narratives which have given so unfortunately saccharine a flavor to his reputation."]

Moore's satires divide naturally into three parts: the early Juvenalian satires in heroic couplets; the Horatian satires written in lyric measures, chiefly during the middle period of his life; and the late prose satires. . . .

All these satires show classical moderation imposed upon a strong spirit of Irish independence. Moore was a cautious patriot, an enlightened Catholic, and a moderate Whig. His partisan prejudices, though strong, were subject to deflection by his individual beliefs or to modification by his common sense.

Love of moderation probably produced that independence of judgment which marks his first important satires [*Epistles, Odes and Other Poems*]. These, astonishingly enough, are directed at the United States. (p. 255)

In exposing the pretensions of the American character Moore shows shrewd observation, for he attacks at points which still attract the interest of novelists and historians. He begins by denouncing our inordinate love of wealth. . . . The hypocrisy of our pretended love of freedom is made evident by the presence of slavery in America. . . . And, finally . . . he is struck, as Hamlin Garland and Sinclair Lewis are, "by the constrast between the grandeur of the land and the meanness of the society . . ." Though he is not able to give very memorable expression to his indictments, Moore does show a capacity to recognize real weaknesses in the American character and a determination to tell the truth even when it contradicts his preconceptions. (pp. 255-56)

[He] thrusts his satire on the follies of [President Jefferson] into the obscurity of footnotes, and in the body of his poem repeats a palpable Federalist slander that Jefferson is a slave-beater and the keeper of a black mistress. He assails the President at an invulnerable spot and fails to exploit the real weaknesses of his victim. However, in venturing to attack Jefferson, who as author of the Declaration of Independence was idolized by the liberals of the world, Moore clearly reveals the moderate limits and ingrained independence of his own peculiar brand of liberalism. (p. 257)

[In his "philosophic satire," *The Sceptic*, he] writes isolated couplets worthy of Dryden or Pope, and the poems remain notable for their expression of the philosophic moderation and Irish independence of the poet. But his emotions were insufficiently aroused to carry his indignation home to the reader. He needed a subject which really moved him, and he has yet to find his proper technique.

The occasion which finally awakened both his wrath and his risibilities was the forsaking of the Whigs by the Prince Regent in 1812. (p. 259)

His attack was all the more devastating this time for being Horatian mockery than Juvenalian diatribe. The new manner was no doubt the natural expression of Moore's matured personality, but it was in part dictated by the nature of his victim and by the requirements of his medium of [newspaper] publication. . . . [Journalistic satire] came perfected to Moore's hand and found him already prepared by his society verse and his comic opera, the *M.P.* to become its master performer. When he began to empty the vials of his wrath and ridicule into the pages of the *Morning Chronicle,* it was apparent that satiric genius was again at large in England.

What then happened was an outpouring of some of the best light political satire in the language, bright shafts of arrowy laughter discharged, it is true, upon the whole Tory ministry and glancing ubiquitously through the stolid ranks of England's self-complacent, yet focused with a burning intensity—never adequately evaluated by Moore's biographers and critics—upon

the sins and follies, the absurd weaknesses and preposterous pretensions of that symbol of European legitimacy, the Prince Regent. (pp. 259-60)

The best satire in [*The Twopenny Post-Bag*] is on a subject incapable of serious treatment, the foppery of the Prince. (p. 262)

The obesity of the Prince is [also] made to appear most laughable. . . . The corpulence of the Prince, being the result of gross living, was a more legitimate subject for satire than are most physical defects; but we must not suppose that the gaiety of these verses could prevent them from being painful to the Regent. Nevertheless, had Moore written only these poems, his reputation as the best-humored of satirists would be justified. (p. 263)

The emphasis of Moore's satire [gradually shifted] from the foibles of the Regent to the follies of Tory leaders and Tory principles, and the shift was accompanied by a marked reduction of acerbity. In *The Fudge Family in Paris* . . . , the role of the Prince is strictly subordinated, and in *Fables for the Holy Alliance* . . . he is reduced to a shadowy background figure. His retreat is the signal for the release of a naturally exuberant good humor, only occasionally touched with bitterness, irreverent, irresistible, but not unkindly. (p. 267)

The Fudge family represent the more vulgar of the British tourists whom Moore found swarming in Paris, and the work has a perennial interest as a satire on the type. . . . [Bob Fudge and his sister Biddy] write in the frivolous anapaests of which Moore was so perfect a master. But the Fudges are not merely typical British tourists but are also Irish renegades, the father, Phil, being an apostate Catholic in the pay of Castlereagh, to whom he addresses his iambic tetrameter couplets. . . . In bold relief to the frivolity of Bob's and Biddy's letters and to the servile sycophancy of Phil's is the bold rebellion expressed in the heroic epistles written by Phelim Connor, Catholic tutor to the Fudges. Here Moore definitely becomes the keeper of the English conscience. A complete foreigner could not denounce "perfidious Albion" in stronger language. . . . The giddy naïveté of the children and the conscienceless cunning of their father "stick fiery off indeed" against the passionate sentiments and elevated rhetoric of the young tutor. The result is that one of the most readable satires in English becomes a moving condemnation, not without contemporary significance, of all those who attempt to justify the triumph of force instead of justice. (pp. 267-69)

Moore's achievement in light satire was brought to a peak by the novelty of the foreign travel and enforced residence abroad which produced *The Fudge Family in Paris* and the [*Fables for the Holy Alliance*]. His view of political events was enlarged, his outlook raised from the insignificance of the Regent to the general welfare of mankind. In tone he mellowed from fierce, personal indignation to irresistible good humor, set off occasionally by continued deep anger over the lot of his native country. But even though Moore never again produced quite the same caliber of sustained light satire, he continued almost to the end of his life to do what has been rightly described as the work of a political caricaturist. Seldom has work of this sort maintained such a level of excellence. Sometimes his satire is just as effective today as it ever was. . . . (p. 271)

[With *Memoirs of Captain Rock*] Moore's great satiric effort . . . had passed into prose. . . . The book is written with a fierce indignation reminiscent of Swift; but Moore does not have Swift's capacity for sustained irony. By degrees he forgets that Captain Rock is supposed to approve the tyrannous policy which has made his family great. Though Moore frequently rises to memorable heights of vituperation and invective, the book as a whole . . . is on the level rather of excellent propaganda than of real satire. It has not held its place as a classic of Irish agitation because of the implied condemnation of the popular political leaders of the Irish. (p. 273)

[In *Travels of an Irish Gentleman in Search of a Religion*] the irony fails to be sustained, for the method fluctuates uncertainly from insinuation to overt attack. Moreover, part of the argument, especially that attempting to dispose of the critical study of the Bible, has been definitely superseded. (p. 274)

These prose works are ably done and they add substantially to our opinion of Moore's abilities, but in his prose, as well as in his Juvenalian satires, he clearly falls short of the highest rank. For his Horatian satires, however, he must take a high position, with Gay and Prior as his only real rivals in English literature. . . . The quality of [his satiric production], considering that for the most part it is occasional verse, is astonishing. The wide range of interests and of lyric rhythms, the diversity of mood and manner—from exuberant gaiety, through trenchancy, to the larger dignity of a scornful contempt for all that is mean and little in human nature, and above all the integrity, the independence, and the clear sanity, all these traits command respect. No doubt Moore will continue to live chiefly in his songs, which hold a deathlike grip on the people; however they may fare with the critics. But the satires are much better than the romantic narratives which have given so unfortuntely saccaharine a flavor to his reputation, and as we lose our late Victorian prejudice against satire as a form of literature, the general opinion of Moore may very well be enhanced. (pp. 274-275)

Howard O. Brogan, "Thomas Moore, Irish Satirist and Keeper of the English Conscience," in Philological Quarterly, Vol. XXIV, No. 3, July, 1945, pp. 255-76.

ROBERT BIRLEY (lecture date 1961)

I do not suppose that it can be proved that [Moore] had read Beckford's *Vathek* before he wrote *Lalla Rookh*. He had certainly read it later in his life and it must be probable that he had done so as a young man. . . . Certainly Moore could not achieve the horrors of the hall of Eblis and his characterisation is far weaker than Beckford's. But he showed himself able to do what Beckford had done and combine the two romantic traditions of the eighteenth century. And there are other echoes too. For the mocking tone, which one hears at times, mocking himself and his readers, recalls the poems of a greater writer than Beckford.

> So let him—Eblis! grant this crowning curse,
> But keep him what he is, no Hell were worse!

Byron might have written those lines. (pp. 154-55)

[At the conclusion of *Lalla Rookh*] Moore holds out his hand to countless Victorian novelists to come.

This may help us to understand why *Lalla Rookh* was so popular. Only about twenty years before it was published, English literature had suddenly produced a new genre, the verse story. When one remembers Chaucer, Gower and Lydgate, and [George Ferrers's and William Baldwin's] *The Mirror for Magistrates*, it may seem strange that for two centuries it had been so neglected. No doubt the rise of the novel helped to revive it.

This new mould for poetry was used by all the leading poets of the early nineteenth century. Moore, then, wrote in a poetic form which was still quite new, but had already proved its popularity. At the same time readers found its setting and the oriental allusions exciting. He had one obvious precursor. Even Byron had to admit that 'Southey's unsaleables' came from the East. One might imagine that his *Thalaba* and *The Curse of Kehama* were one of Moore's sources of inspiration, but he does not seem to have been in the least interested in them. And there is a world of difference between Southey's portentously solemn poems and the lines that floated out of Moore's 'sparkling, anacreontic mouth'. (pp. 168-69)

As a period piece—and I do not think that our generation can regard it as anything else—[*Lalla Rookh*] is worth reading. Perhaps the time will come when [Edward Fitzgerald's] *Omar Khayyam* and [Edward Fitzgerald's] *Hassan* have been forgotten so long that they will not longer trouble us, and then, provided that the demands we make of poetry are not too high, *Lalla Rookh* may be found to have some rights of its own. (p. 171)

Robert Birley, "Thomas Moore: 'Lalla Rookh'," in his Sunk without Trace: Some Forgotten Masterpieces Reconsidered (originally a series of lectures given at Trinity College, Cambridge, between 1960 and 1961; © Robert Birley 1962; reprinted by permission of Granada Publishing Limited), Rupert Hart-Davis, 1962, pp. 136-71.

HOOVER H. JORDAN (essay date 1962)

[*Like Stephen Gwynn (1905) and L.A.G. Strong (1937), Jordan applies the techniques of musical analysis to Moore's poetry. He contends that Moore's lyrics have been underrated because they have been judged solely as poetry. According to Jordan, a close analysis of "the rise and fall of melody" and the "tone quality of vowel and consonant" reveals Moore's poetic craftsmanship more clearly and accurately than a strictly literary approach.*]

The inevitable consequence of [of judging Moore's lyrics as poetry] has been an undue denigration of Moore and an unfortunate ignorance about his talents. The rediscovery of his lyrics as part of the total song pattern may bring a realization that here is something distinctive, and as native to Moore's talents as *Don Juan* is to Byron's or "The Solitary Reaper" to Wordsworth's. (p. 407)

[From] the rise and fall of melody comes the total pattern of the song. The commonest musical pattern of the *Irish Melodies*—AABA—means among other things that the same general pitch relationships have been thrice repeated with one variation after the second musical phrase. The first two A repetitions, however, are often left in some suspension, resolved only by the final A statement. For the lyrist this assertion, suspension, and resolution means that the first half of the song pattern forms a unit with the two A phrases, the second half a balancing and concluding counterpart. The very simplest execution is illustrated by "**I saw from the beach.**" (p. 412)

The AABA musical pattern is somewhat more complex in songs like "**Oh! had we some bright little isle of our own,**" in which a couplet represents each A phrase and an alternate rhyme the B phrase. . . .

The *Irish Melodies,* of course, are composed of many musical patterns: AABB, ABBA, AABC, and so on. To suit words to this variety of patterns, Moore like most lyrists found rime essential for organizing his thought and did not experience the uneasiness about its use which is rather widespread in our time. (p. 413)

The musical pattern [of **"Let Erin remember the days of old"**] . . . is AABB. With the AA phrases Moore has used the alternating rime *abab*. Of especial interest is that he has been able to suit the musical note and the rime tone exactly: the *aa* rime (*old, gold*) is each time sung to B; the *bb* rime (*betray'd her, invader*), being a double rime, is set to G followed by F. The same principle is observed with the *cdcd* rime in the BB musical phrases: the *c* rime (*unfurl'd, world*) is set to C; the *d* rime (*stranger, danger*) to F, with an interesting variation at the end of the song (the first syllable of *stranger* falls on G which returns to F on the second syllable, a variation which gives a stronger finality to the closing musical pattern). (p. 416)

The rime sounds also accord with the general sentiment of the music, as Moore understands it. The musical pitch is ascending in all but the completing phrases of the BB pattern; it has, therefore, vigor relaxing toward the end, or, as the musical direction reads, it is "grand and spirited." Moore uses the long *o* and long *a* as the principal rime vowels, consistent with grandeur; the chief consonant in the rime is *d*, a stop consonant giving a firm check and vigor to each rime word up to the quiet close, which is effected by the *dz* sound of *g* and the terminal *r*. Rime is so useful to Moore throughout the song that for him to succeed without it is almost unthinkable. (pp. 416-17)

The lyrical weaknesses [of **"'Tis the last rose of summer"**] are evident enough. The "pathetic fallacy" is indulged to the point of sentimentality—the roses blush, give sighs, pine on the stem. Trite, stock phraseology, such as "Love's shining circle," "friendships decay," and "The gems drop away," are too patly taken from eighteenth-century verse to have freshness or force. The unfortunate possessive "Love's" throws an already vapid phrase into abstraction rather than producing the concreteness personification ought to render, while simultaneously it raises a grammatical question about the legitimacy of this use of the possessive case. Furthermore, stanza two may seem an excessively prolonged amplification of stanza one and sentimentally weak in depicting the speaker in the poem as extending kindness by scattering leaves over the garden.

Granted all this, which seems obvious enough, why has the song survived? . . . Clearly something must be said in its favor.

In the first place Moore was fortunate in finding words to capture the spirit of the music. (pp. 432-33)

The AABA music pattern of the melody is also well expressed by the lyric. The AA portion of stanza one is designated by the off-rime line endings *alone* and *gone;* the musical variation B is then happily left in suspension by two unresolved phrases: "No flower of her kindred, / No rosebud is nigh." This musical and linguistic pause is then resolved by the completing A phrase. An easy, natural ebb and flow of both words and music is thus attained.

The lyric next is apt in presenting its thought in three, easy, forward stages, one stanza for each, without unwarranted compression or undue diffusion. Even the laxness of stanza two is not in itself a vacuous diffusion, but simply a weakness of conception; Moore is unduly languid in thought. The pace of the stanza is none the less appropriate for a song. The basic image—a rose as the symbol of beauty, and the death of such beauty with the coming of cold weather—is quite satisfactory for a short poem. The symbol is also perfectly adequate for

expression of the human experience broached in stanza three. . . . (p. 433)

In tone quality of vowel and consonant Moore has achieved great success. Continuity of tone throughout ["**'Tis the last rose of summer**"] comes from a deft use of assonance. The low-pitched, prolonged *o* weaves somberly in and out—*rose, lone, no, no, rose* in stanza one; *lone, go, o'er* in stanza two; so, *follow, flown,* and *oh,* in stanza three. In contrast the high-pitched long *i* lightens the tone of stanza two—*I, pine, kindly, thy, thy, I, lie*—which carry over the sound from the final rime of stanza one—*nigh-sigh.* Additionally the long *e* of *leave, thee, sleeping, sleep, leaves,* and *bleak* offers a further long vowel repetition. While not so conspicuous as the long vowels, the short *e*, especially in stanza two with its higher tone, is helpful; the rime words—*stem, them; bed, dead*—are assonantal and contain the *e* picked up by *den, scent,* and *less.* Assisting the flow of the melodic line are not only the long vowels but also the semivowels *'tis, rose, summer, left, blooming, alone, all, her, lovely, companions, are, gone,* and so on in great abundance. The blend of these manifold liquids with the vowels gives the easy forward motion a deftness and lightness hard to achieve in our tongue. Their effect is well seen by the contrast which the harsh sounds of *bleak* provide in the final stanza. Frequent alliterations also assist the effects of consonance and assonance, as in *last, lone, lovely* or *stem, sleep, scatter, scentless.* The craftsmanship of Moore is considerable here; a close texture of verse is woven with such ease and naturalness that a clearly perceptible effect results without the obtrusions of rococo decoration. It is of the same genre as the superbly quiet effects of Wordsworth in the Lucy poems or "The Solitary Reaper." (p. 434)

Though close analysis of songs may seem tedious, in hardly any other way can the achievements of Moore be rightly esteemed. Ultimately about these achievements it should be said that among the early nineteenth-century poets he has a unique talent. It is not of the highest kind; it does not stir mind and emotion with a sense of the depth and extent of human life. But, let us remember, not many poets of any era have possessed this touch of greatness. To deny Moore an honored place among the minor but none the less genuine creative artists seems niggling. The *Irish Melodies* and many of his other songs provide a rich and moving experience that not just Ireland but all the English-speaking world can cherish as a real contribution to the human heritage. Appreciation, however, can result only when the words are joined with their lovely music. (pp. 439-40)

Hoover H. Jordan, "Thomas Moore: Artistry in the Song Lyric," in Studies in English Literature, 1500-1900 *(© 1962 William Marsh Rice University), Vol. II, No. 4, Autumn, 1962, pp. 403-40.*

ROBERT WELCH   (essay date 1980)

[*Welch detects "a fundamental uncertainty" in* The Irish Melodies, *which he believes derives from two contradictory impulses in Moore, the first "towards the creation of lovely verbal patterns," and the second "towards the writing of political songs, that would stir up political feeling through remembrance of the past." Welch asserts that "Moore did not achieve a synthesis of the two impulses," and that they eventually separated into "the ornamental, the fantastical precious" on one hand, and satire on the other. Moore's unsuccessful attempt to resolve the dichotomy, Welch suggests, turned* The Irish Melodies *into "a poetry of non-encounter, a flight from the self, and finally of irresponsibility towards the medium, at a time when that kind of irresponsibility was lethal to the future health of Irish poetry.'' Welsh concludes that ''Moore's elaboration of aural effect at the expense of sense contributed to the markedly rhetorical and sentimental quality of a great deal of nineteenth-century Irish poetry.''*]

[The] *Melodies* themselves constitute an interesting achievement, both in themselves and as a starting point for an Anglo-Irish poetry now fully conscious (one might say *self*-conscious) of its Irishness.

There are two points to be dealt with before considering the *Melodies* themselves; firstly, can they be thought of not just as songs, but as poems in their own right; secondly, to what sort of audience did Moore address them? It has often been maintained, most forcibly by L.A.G. Strong, that it is an injustice to the *Melodies* to subject them to any sort of rigorous analysis as verbal constructs. . . . This view has merit, of course, but it limits the discussion of the *Melodies* in the context of nineteenth century Anglo-Irish poetry. Much can be revealed about the sort of sensibility Moore typifies and about the sorts of difficulties Irish writing in English had to face up to in the nineteenth century by looking closely at what the words do (or do not do) on the page. Furthermore, we have Moore's own testimony that though his verses for the Melodies are to be sung rather than read, and that he can 'answer for their sound with somewhat more confidence than for their sense', yet he does say, in a preface to the third number of the *Melodies* (1810), that 'it would be affectation to deny that I have given much attention to the task.' (pp. 23-4)

[The verses in the *Melodies*] are lyrics then, where according to Moore's own disclaimer, the sound can be vouched for with more confidence than the sense. And yet, the sense is not so hopelessly wrapped in sweet concords as to decontaminate it, politically. From one point of view the lyrics are beautiful patterns of intricate interwoven sound, verbalisations of music's unutterable verities. From another point of view, though, the poems are political statements with designs upon a vaguely defined, but possibly powerful readership. In other words, Moore wants it both ways; he wants the songs to be political and yet he does not. Here there is an uneasy alliance, an ambiguity of intention, an uncertainty about the medium itself and what it is supposed to be doing that underlies many of the tensions, ambiguities, and stylistic difficulties of the *Melodies* themselves and much subsequent Anglo-Irish poetry. (p. 25)

In the 'War Song' . . . , the second poem in the first number of the *Melodies,* the remote medieval past of Brien Boru and the recent past of the '98 rebellion are drawn together. Recent events recall ancestral memories, and the ancestral memories give the recent events a touch of mythic significance. Moore's syntax, alluring and suggestive, is the perfect medium for joining the two pasts and for the emotional conjuring of a mood for the present. The two pasts mingle with a present that may flame up into violent intensity. The song toys with this exciting possibility:

> Remember the glories of Brien the brave,
>   Though the days of the hero are o'er;
> Though lost to Mononia, and cold in the grave,
>   He returns to Kinkora no more!
> That star of the field, which so often hath poured
>   Its beam on the battle, is set;
> But enough of its glory remains on each sword
>   To light us to victory yet.

Though verse of this sort (and there is much of it in Irish writing past and present) tends towards a static non-progressive

grace, a kind of musical suspension of the proper activity of the intelligence, nevertheless a metaphor persists, and the metaphor is one of light, a light that stays, a 'star of the field'. The glory has not faded entirely, and it may shine out again now, in the present. (p. 26)

Initially the poem maintains that enough glory is left to light the warriors of the present to a new victory, but in the second stanza that light is doomed to darkness. This contradiction is not surprising considering the emotional irresolution underlying the piece. On the one hand it is a political document inciting to heroism in the present; on the other it is a piece of aural excitement, owing much of its power to vague allusions to a dim past. It remains transfixed by the beauty of its own verbal movements, trapped by its own evocative music. What need is there of exact meaning, of reference to the actual, when words can create such elegant harmonies? It is enough to gesture towards some undefined heroism that happened once, and may happen again. But even if it does happen, the sun, symbol of liberty, will return to darkness, as ever. So the heroism is doomed before it can begin. This kind of poetry does not really engage with the issue it ostensibly presents. Rather does it create and elaborate a mood of melancholy dwelling on past glory. In the creation of such a mood ordinary thought sequences may easily get mislaid, the poem or song may unwittingly contradict itself.

This is certainly the mood created in **"Oh! Breathe not His Name'**. . . . Moore's song tries to do the impossible. It is a poem about Emmet's burial, and, being a construction of words, thereby undertakes to say something. Yet it also wishes to obey his command, seeing that Ireland has not yet been freed, and keep faithful silence. Moore would write and yet not write his dead friend's epitaph, again wanting to have it both ways. Silence becomes a virtue, something to be praised. Grief remains dumb, constrained, under strict instructions from the dead. Word-music, evocation is all. The song is a lyrical epiphany, a framing of grief in beautiful static concords, that are static in the sense that the words do not go inwards: they explore themselves, the medium, and by so doing, the subject itself. . . . (pp. 27-8)

Throughout the *Melodies* the verse is drawn to the necessity and inevitability of silence, darkness, death. The harp, that once 'shed' the soul of music (and thus, for Moore, of Ireland) through Tara's halls now hangs mute on the walls. . . . (p. 29)

He uses rhythm [in 'The Harp That Once'] to suggest what it was once like to experience that identity, placing and emphasising the word 'thrill' with its slender consonants in a sharp yet quiet relief against the broad, open vowels of the rest of the line. Unquestionably Moore is a master of evocative plangent suggestion.

In the second stanza of the poem Moore imagines the harp making one last sound in an environ of silence and death. The bright and glittering audience responds no more to its swelling tones. . . .

> No more to chiefs and ladies bright
>   The harp of Tara swells;
> The chord alone, that breaks at night
>   Its tale of ruin tells.
> Thus Freedom now so seldom wakes,
>   The only sound she gives
> Is when some heart indignant breaks
>   To show that still she lives!

The context of that twangling, dissonant chord, when the strings break, is silence, a desolation all the more complete because of the colour and vitality that once surrounded it. In the same way the desire for 'Freedom' when it rises in a man's heart suffers similar isolation. It too is a dissonant twangling in a desert bereft of human feeling. The heart breaks indignantly, just as the strings do, because it lacks a context, a context, it can only be, where action is possible. But action is not possible, so the heart that would hope for freedom must keep silence, and keep faith, under similar injunctions as the mourners are in **'Oh! Breathe not His Name'**. Its 'tale of ruin' is mere frustrated jangling in the night air. And yet, ironically, there is no dissonance in the piece itself: a poem which has for theme a broken ancient music is itself poised and exquisite, each syllable structured to the smooth iambic flow. The mood of melancholy weariness, of silent, repressed grief, predominates over the idea in the fourth line that the soul of this music is *not* dead, and by the time the poem closes this hope has been snowed under by the force of the impeccably rhythmic lament for a time and feeling lost beyond all recovery. The faint hope that briefly makes a shy entrance is overwhelmed by the sweep of the word-music that bemoans its passing. Once again the poem concludes with silence, darkness, death—easier, more effortless themes to deal with than those that would have arisen had Moore explored the tensions between nationalist hopes and sentimental lament for a Gaelic world. Instead, masterful proficiency takes over, dissolving the encounter with a living language (which a poem *should* be) in melancholy evocation of a past that never existed. The encounter with a living language, with the implications of the words used, is inevitably an encounter with the present state of the self. This may lead to difficulties, but language remains human, in contact with its deepest sources of strength, and in the long run it retains its health. Moore left the psyche unexplored. His rhythms suggest a mood rather than subtly delineating the contour of an inner state of being, as Wordsworth's do in *The Prelude* completed in 1805. Moore's words wash over his unease about Irish nationalism, about the dead men of '98.

The first number of the *Melodies* set the tone and manner of the remainder: an idealised and distant Gaelic world, faint hints that the glory associated with that world might once again reactivate itself (Tory reviewers felt Moore's verse to be bordering on sedition), and a magnificent diction and rhythmic power that tended to overwhelm all else. Not infrequently, the coy 'Anacreontic' note intruded, bringing to the *Melodies* an adolescent attitudinising. It could be said, perhaps, that the intoxications of lamenting words in the *Melodies* are a natural extension into an Irish context of the doctrine of Anacreontic indulgence, set forth in the *Odes* of 1800. In **'The Legacy'** in the second number of the *Melodies* . . . we have a curious mixture of a Regency version of ancient Ireland—bardic harps, ancient halls and so on—and an equally Regency version of the Greece of the voluptuary—foaming cups, the balmy drop of the red grape and such like.

More characteristic however, are **'Let Erin Remember the Days of Old'**, and **'The Song of Fionnuala'**, both also from the second number. In **'Let Erin Remember'** we have the familiar evocation of Gaelic Ireland before the days of the 'proud invader', her pristine green unsullied and untouched, not just an emerald in a stranger's crown. In the second stanza, however, Moore attempts to construct an image series which will convey how Gaelic Ireland impinges upon the present. (pp. 29-31)

'On Music' gives a good deal of insight into Moore's conception of his art, and also throws some light on Moore's conception of his medium. **'On Music'** is an important piece in the context of the *Melodies*, when we remind ourselves that music for Moore was an expression of the national identity, and was also indissolubly linked with the fundamental imaginative processes.

Music, as Moore understands it in **'On Music'**, is an art of memory, of evocation of the past in a present that has become faded. Music is an equivalent to and a celebration of the death of intensity. . . . Language, words, betray, because they lead one into denotation. One has to say things, to struggle with meaning, to be careful, too, of giving offence. Music creates no such problem, it denotes nothing, it simply is. A note is not something that can be argued about. But this poem also attempts to suggest, in a medium which it denies, that there are feelings lying too deep for words and that these, through inappropriate words, may be betrayed. Silence therefore, is the best answer; failing that, music, which is a disembodied medium, free of denotation and all its betrayals; and failing that, song, where words and rhythm can be brought to a fineness of movement and elegance suggestive of music itself, and ultimately of silence. To sum up, here is a poem on the impossibility of writing about anything of real significance. An evocation of music's power, it is also a confession of failure in the chosen medium. It is a curiously honest poem, and forthright in its own roundabout way. (pp. 36-8)

From the third and fourth numbers onwards, the political content of the *Melodies* becomes increasingly muted. Although from time to time touches of political passion do inflame them. Moore's political energies went increasingly into his Whig satires, the *Melodies* become more and more mere pleasant concatenations of sound, with a faintly Hibernian feel. From now on he seems to have lost interest in the enterprise. . . . (p. 39)

At this point Moore's imagination seems to move in two directions; one is towards satire. . . .

The other direction Moore's imaginative powers took could be regarded as the obverse of the satirical: they moved towards the fanciful, the ornamental, the fantastically precious, typified for us now by that extraordinary production, *Lallah Rookh*. . . . (p. 40)

This kind of fantastical decorativeness is an extension of the taste for sheer verbal pattern to be found in the *Melodies*. The delight in the remote past we find celebrated there translates into the geographical remoteness of *Lallah Rookh;* the Grecian attitudinising of some of the *Melodies* becomes a sensuous delight in exotic descriptive detail. (p. 41)

At the end of the sixth number . . . [of the *Melodies*], which was to have been the last, he bids farewell to his harp, employing the well-worn image of the harp of Aeolus. . . . Although a conventional image, the Aeolian harp acquires a somewhat more pointed overtone in the context of the *Irish Melodies*. Here, at the planned end of the series, Moore does a poetic vanishing act, disavowing the self entirely. He was the wind that stirred the strings, having no personality, no self. Such a degree of 'negative capability' is humanly impossible, but the fiction of it here, at this point, shows us again that Moore's *Melodies* are a poetry of non-encounter, of flight from the self, and finally of irresponsibility towards the medium, at a time when that kind of irresponsibility was lethal to the future health of Irish poetry. (pp. 42-3)

[From] the point of view of Anglo-Irish poetic tradition, which was in bad need of an Irish voice in English at this time, the

Melodies offered too much technical proficiency, too little verbal seriousness. In other words Moore showed nineteenth century Irish poetry a great deal about the exterior effects of rhythm, but very little about taking those rhythms into the psyche. Generalised moods are created in the long, expansive rhythms, but states of feeling are not delineated. We are given no sense of what the words felt like inside Moore's head. Moore built, right over the real deposits, a Celtic-looking fabrication, with dark turrets, winding stairways and gloomy interiors, where white-skinned maidens played on harps with golden strings. He built a shaky romantic edifice when what was needed was excavation. The excavators, the poetic archaeologists, were to come later, and they mostly came from the North, from Ulster men such as Ferguson and Allingham. Moore's elaboration of aural effect at the expense of sense contributed to the markedly rhetorical and sentimental quality of a great deal of nineteenth century Irish poetry.

Moore's was an impressionistic version of ancient Ireland, based on loose bits of information gathered here and there and presented in a language dripping with sensibility. He belongs to the tradition of Macpherson. He differs, though, in that his images of Gaelic Ireland are sometimes designed to carry contemporary political overtones, wheras the fascination of Macpherson's imaginings lay in the fact that his reckless barbarism was entirely irrelevant. Macpherson was the ultimate in emotional aesthetics. There was a good deal of emotional aestheticism in Moore too, but he does give the contemporary situation some weight, if only obliquely. Moore's emblems, the harp, the shamrock, the round tower, became the insignia of nineteenth century nationalism, trite emblems of political energy.

There is a fundamental uncertainty about the *Melodies,* an uncertainty deriving from two impulses, which in Moore were contradictory. The first impulse was towards the creation of lovely verbal patterns, suggestive of the moods the Irish airs evoked; the second was towards the writing of political songs, that would stir up political feeling through remembrance of the past. Moore did not achieve a synthesis of the two impulses; they separate in his later work, into ornamentation on the one hand and satire on the other. What he did achieve was a rich opaque musical medium that allowed a tense if often unsatisfactory interaction between the two; a medium full of hesitation, implication and images of inarticulacy, of grief struck dumb, of the faithful keeping of silence. Despite this jumble of themes and images, the atmosphere of the *Melodies,* conveyed through the fluid word-music, was very strong, creating in Irish poetry a tendency towards rhetorical ornament, obliqueness, and beneath the obliqueness, sentimental sedition. (pp. 44-5)

> *Robert Welch, "Thomas Moore: An Elegiac Silence," in his* Irish Poetry from Moore to Yeats *(copyright © 1980 Colin Smythe Ltd.), Smythe, 1980, pp. 17-45.*

ADDITIONAL BIBLIOGRAPHY

Brown, Wallace Cable. "Thomas Moore and English Interest in the East." *Studies in Philology* XXXIV, No. 4 (October 1937): 576-88.
   A detailed examination of Moore's Eastern sources for *Lalla Rookh, The Epicurean,* and *The Loves of the Angels.* Brown concludes that Moore's use of Eastern materials in these works is superficial and mainly decorative.

Byron, George Gordon, Lord. "To Thomas Moore: 'My Boat Is on the Shore'." In *Byron: Poetical Works,* 3d. ed., edited by Frederick Page, p. 102. London: Oxford University Press, 1970.
   A poem commemorating the close friendship of Byron and Moore.

De Ford, Miriam Allen. *Thomas Moore.* New York: Twayne Publishers, 1967, 128 p.
   A brief introduction to the life and works of Moore. De Ford supplements biographical and critical information with a selected bibliography of Moore's works and an annotated bibliography of critical writings on Moore.

Dowden, Wilfred S. "'Let Erin Remember': A Re-Examination of the Journal of Thomas Moore." *Rice University Studies: Studies in English* 61, No. 1 (Winter 1975): 39-50.
   Discusses a recently discovered manuscript of Moore's journal. Dowden proves that Lord John Russell expurgated many passages from the journal "for reasons of Victorian propriety." According to Dowden, many passages, especially those concerning the personal lives of Moore, Lord Byron, and Richard Brinsley Sheridan, were altered or distorted.

"Tom Moore in America." *Harper's New Monthly Magazine* LV, No. CCCXXVIII (September 1877): 537-41.
   An account of Moore's visit to America and his satirical treatment of it in his *Epistles, Odes and Other Poems.* The article recounts Moore's meeting with an inhospitable Thomas Jefferson and discusses Moore's subsequent lampoons of Jefferson.

Hawthorne, Mark D. "Thomas Moore's *The Epicurean:* The Anacreontic Poet in Search of Eternity." *Studies in Romanticism* 14, No. 3 (Summer 1975): 249-72.
   Traces the dichotomy in Moore's creative personality between lyricism and satire as it is reflected in "Alciphron" and *The Epicurean.* Hawthorne believes that the two works aid "our understanding of the crucial split in [Moore's] personality that revealed itself in the double role he played as lyricist and satirist, dreamer and realist."

Jordan, Hoover H. "Thomas Moore." In *The English Romantic Poets and Essayists: A Review of Research and Criticism,* edited by Carolyn Washburn Houtchens and Lawrence Huston Houtchens, pp. 202-27. New York: The Modern Language Association of America, 1957.
   A useful bibliographic essay which includes information on bibliographies, biographies, and editions of Moore's works, in addition to a survey of major trends in the criticism of Moore's works.

Jordan, Hoover H. *Romantic Reassessment: Bolt Upright, The Life of Thomas Moore.* Edited by James Hogg. Salzburg Studies in English Literature, edited by Erwin A. Stürzl, No. 38, 2 vols. Salzburg: Universität Salzburg, 1975, 666 p.
   An exhaustive biography of Moore. Jordan treats all phases of Moore's life and career in great detail, but his section on influences upon Moore's style, as well as sections which survey critical response to his works, are especially helpful.

Mackey, Herbert O. *The Life of Thomas Moore, Ireland's National Poet.* 2d. ed. Dublin: The Apollo Press, 1951, 39 p.
   A biographical study of Moore written from a strongly nationalistic viewpoint. Mackey emphasizes Moore's role as a serious "teacher of world values," and as a writer interested in "teaching his countrymen the glorious traditions of their race."

Mortimer, Raymond. "Thomas Moore." *The Living Age* 313, No. 4058 (April 15, 1922): 174-80.
   A brief review of *The Irish Melodies.* Mortimer finds a few of the poems to be marked by a "distinctive Irish rhythm" which is also present in the works of later poets William Butler Yeats and Edward Thomas.

Pollin, Burton R. "Light on 'Shadow' and Other Pieces by Poe; Or, More of Thomas Moore." *ESQ: A Journal of the American Renaissance* 18, No. 3 (3rd Quarter 1972): 166-73.*
   A study of Moore's influence on the works of Edgar Allan Poe. Pollin documents ways in which Poe used his knowledge of Moore's

poetry, prose, and satire in several short stories and in the poem ''The City in the Sea.''

White, Terence de Vere. *Tom Moore: The Irish Poet*. London: Hamish Hamilton, 1977, 281 p.
    A concise account of Moore's life and career. White refers to ''the tacit conspiracy to denigrate Moore's patriotism and confine his activity to drawing-room singing.''

Wickens, G.M. ''*Lalla Rookh* and the Romantic Tradition of Islamic Literature in English.'' *Yearbook of Comparative and General Literature* 20 (1971): 61-6.
    Considers *Lalla Rookh* to be the culmination of English interest in Eastern literary themes and motifs. Wickens attributes the decline of *Lalla Rookh's* popularity to the satiation of the public's taste for oriental subjects, not disenchantment with Moore as a writer.

Ann (Ward) Radcliffe

1764-1823

(Born Ann Ward) English novelist, poet, and journal writer.

Considered the most important writer of the English Gothic school, Radcliffe transformed the Gothic novel from a mere vehicle for the depiction of terror into an instrument for exploring the psychology of fear and suspense. Her emphasis on emotion, perception, and the relationship between atmosphere and sensibility helped pave the way for the Romantic movement in England. Radcliffe's best-known novel, *The Mysteries of Udolpho*, ranks as one of the chief exemplars of the Gothic genre.

Radcliffe was born in London. A shy child afflicted with asthma, she read widely. Though she was given a typical nineteenth-century young lady's education—private instruction in the classics, literature, painting, and drawing—Radcliffe received little encouragement from her parents to continue her studies. As a young woman, Radcliffe associated with the ''bluestockings'' Lady Mary Wortley Montagu and Hester Lynch Piozzi, who, biographers believe, provided her with inspiration and intellectual stimulation. In 1787 she married William Radcliffe, later the editor of the *English Chronicle*, who recognized her talent and encouraged her to begin writing novels.

Although Radcliffe was the most popular English novelist of her generation, she managed to avoid publicity almost entirely. In fact, when Christina Rossetti attempted to write a biography of Radcliffe in 1883, she was forced to abandon the project because of the lack of available information. For unknown reasons Mrs. Radcliffe withdrew entirely from public life in 1817 at the peak of her fame. Her absence triggered a series of rumors, the most widespread being that she had suffered a nervous breakdown brought on by the terrors described in her own works. Sir Walter Scott speculated that she stopped writing because she abhorred the manner in which her imitators had cheapened and sentimentalized the Gothic novel. Obituaries appeared in newspapers on the supposition that Radcliffe had died. Also in circulation were legends that Radcliffe had died in an insane asylum and that her ghost returned to haunt her imitators.

Radcliffe's first novel, *The Castles of Athlin and Dunbayne: A Highland Story*, made a negligible impression upon readers and reviewers alike. A historical romance set in Scotland, the novel abounds in the picturesque description and dark atmosphere that was to become Radcliffe's trademark. Yet it was criticized for its abundance of anachronisms, especially imposing upon feudal heroines a distinctively nineteenth-century sensibility. *A Sicilian Romance*, Radcliffe's next work, established her reputation as the preeminent Gothic novelist. Here the distinctive features of Radcliffe's style emerge more fully: the use of landscape to create a mood of terror, mystery, and suspense, intricacy of plot, a lyrical prose style, and a focus on individual psychology. *The Romance of the Forest*, and *The Mysteries of Udolpho*, her first signed work, strengthened her popularity and made her a best-selling author in England, the United States, and Europe. *A Journey Made in the Summer of 1794 through Holland and the Western Frontier of Germany* detailed her first trip outside of England. The

Italian; or, The Confessional of the Black Penitents, a Gothic mystery which is considered by some to be Radcliffe's best novel, traces the machinations of the monk Schedoni, who became a prototypical Gothic hero—brooding, mysterious, and fascinating. *Gaston de Blondeville; or, The Court of Henry III. Keeping Festival in Ardenne*, published posthumously, is a historical romance that Radcliffe presented as derived from ancient chronicles, which has never enjoyed much success. *St. Alban's Abbey*, a metrical romance set in medieval England, has attracted little notice. Though Radcliffe's poetry is generally considered inferior to her novels, it features the same lush, exotic descriptions as her novels.

Critics have speculated on the various influences upon Radcliffe's style, noting the similarities between her landscapes and the paintings of the Neapolitan painter and poet Salvator Rosa and the French landscape painter Claude Lorrain. Critics also note that her linking of terror and beauty corresponds with Edmund Burke's philosophy of the sublime and that her poetry resembles that of William Collins, James Thomson, Thomas Gray, and James Macpherson. In addition, Radcliffe's motif of the heroine in distress indicates a knowledge of sentimental novelists such as Charlotte Smith, although her works most often appear to be modeled upon the works of Horace Walpole. The primary distinguishing feature of Radcliffe's style is her explained endings. After elaborately setting up a mystery, planting the seeds of supernatural agency, and piquing the reader's curiosity, Radcliffe invariably resolves her plots in a rational and orderly way, finding reasoned explanations for seemingly supernatural events. Whether they praise or criticize her for this practice, critics cite it as Radcliffe's distinctive contribution to the development of the English novel.

Early critical response to Radcliffe's novels was mixed: while Samuel Taylor Coleridge attacked her explained endings for their inadequacy in satisfying the expectations of the reader, Sir Walter Scott called her ''the first poetess of romantic fiction'' for her natural descriptions. Other contemporary critics found her explanations tedious, her dialogue wooden, and her characters flat, though still others praised her brilliant rhetorical style, her examination of fear, and her affirmation of moral order at the conclusion of each novel. Thomas Noon Talfourd attributed Radcliffe's anticlimactic endings to her obedience to the conventions of the Gothic novel. He proposed that she felt the conventions of romance did not allow for supernatural agency, and that she therefore felt bound to explain it away. At the turn of the century, Walter Raleigh enlarged the popular understanding of Radcliffe by noting her role as a predecessor of the Romantic movement in England. Virginia Woolf disputed Talfourd by asserting that Radcliffe's novels were remarkably free from convention. Wylie Sypher's Marxist analysis delineated the novels' simultaneously bourgeois and anti-bourgeois tendencies, which he considered hypocritical. On the whole, however, Radcliffe's works received very little critical attention until the late 1950s, when Devendra P. Varma's overview of her novels again spurred curiosity about her work. The 1960s and 1970s reflected this surge of renewed interest. Varma, J.M.S. Tompkins, and Lynne Epstein have pursued new approaches to defining the role of description in Radcliffe's works; the extent and intent of her preoccupation with the realm of irrational behavior have been debated extensively by such critics as Nelson C. Smith, Robert Kiely, and Gary Kelly. Feminist studies on Radcliffe's heroines by Ellen Moers and Coral Ann Howells have further widened the scope of critical interpretation of her novels.

Today Radcliffe is generally regarded as a minor but influential author. Such writers as William Wordsworth, Coleridge, Percy Bysshe Shelley, John Keats, Anne and Emily Brontë, Matthew Gregory Lewis, Robert Louis Stevenson, and Lord Byron (who used Schedoni as the model for the Byronic hero), found her exploration of extreme emotional states intriguing and borrowed freely from her techniques. William Hazlitt wrote that "in harrowing up the soul with imaginary terrors, and making the flesh creep, and the nerves thrill with fond hopes and fears, she is unrivalled among her countrymen." Most critics now view Radcliffe as a key figure in the movement that freed the imagination from conventional and rational constraints and ushered in English Romanticism.

PRINCIPAL WORKS

The Castles of Athlin and Dunbayne: A Highland Story
    (novel) 1789
A Sicilian Romance (novel) 1790
The Romance of the Forest (novel) 1791
The Mysteries of Udolpho (novel) 1794
A Journey Made in the Summer of 1794 through Holland
    and the Western Frontier of Germany (journal) 1795
The Italian; or, The Confessional of the Black Penitents
    (novel) 1797
The Poems of A. Radcliffe (poetry) 1815
The Novels of Ann Radcliffe. 10 vols. (novels) 1821-24
Gaston de Blondeville; or, The Court of Henry III. Keeping
    Festival in Ardenne. St. Alban's Abbey: A Metrical
    Tale, with Some Poetical Pieces (novel and poetry)
    1826

THE MONTHLY REVIEW, LONDON **(essay date 1789)**

To those who are delighted with the *marvellous*, whom wonders, and wonders only, can charm, [*The Castles of Athlin and Dunbayne*] will afford a considerable degree of amusement. This kind of entertainment, however, can be little relished but by the young and unformed mind. To men who have passed, or even attained, the meridian of life, a series of events, which seem not to have their foundation in nature, will ever be insipid, if not disgustful. The author of this performance appears to have written on the principle of Mr. Bayes, to *elevate and surprise.* By means of *trap-doors, false pannels, subterranean passages,* &c. &c. this purpose is effected: and all this, as was before intimated, will possibly have its admirers. But though we are not of the number of such readers, we must honestly confess, that this little work is to be commended for its moral; as also for the good sentiments and reflections which occasionally occur in it.

A. B., in a review of ''The Castles of Athlin and Dunbayne,'' in The Monthly Review, *London, Vol. LXXI, December, 1789, p. 563.*

THE MONTHLY REVIEW, LONDON **(essay date 1792)**

The days of chivalry and romance being (ALAS! as Mr. Burke says,) for ever past, we must hear no more of enchanted forests and castles, giants, dragons, walls of fire, and other ''monstrous and prodigious things;''—yet still forests and castles remain, and it is still within the province of fiction, without overstepping the limits of nature, to make use of them for the purpose of creating surprise. By the aid of an inventive genius, much may still be done, even in this philosophical age, to fill the fancy with marvellous images, and to ''quell the soul with grateful terrors.''

In this way, the authoress of the ***Romance of the Forest*** is no mean performer. (p. 82)

The principal personage of the romance, Adeline, is a highly-interesting character, whom the writer conducts through a series of alarming situations, and hair-breadth escapes, in which she has very skilfully contrived to hold the reader's curiosity continually in suspense, and at the same time to keep his feelings in a state of perpetual agitation. Through the whole of the first two volumes, all is business, hazard, and alarm. Several characters, marked with different degrees of folly or criminality, are drawn with bold and decisive strokes; and these are contrasted with others, whose amiable qualities relieve the horrors of the scene, and render the picture, on the whole, pleasing. In the third volume, after Adeline has been tost on the stormy sea of misfortune, with scarcely a moment's respite, when her spirit is almost broken down with distress, she finds a calm retreat, in which she enjoys a long interval of sweet repose, and of which the reader gladly partakes; till at length new scenes of surprize, distress, and joy, are opened; through which it is impossible for a reader, not totally devoid of sensibility, to accompany her without strong emotions. (pp. 82-3)

[A] very considerable part of the merit of this work consists in the happy manner in which the authoress has concealed the termination of the plot till the last *éclaircissement.* . . . [We] have seldom met with a fiction which has more forcibly fixed the attention, or more agreeably interested the feelings, throughout the whole narrative. (p. 83)

''Mrs. Radcliffe's 'Romance of the Forest','' in The Monthly Review, *London, Vol. VIII, May, 1792, pp. 82-7.*

SAMUEL TAYLOR COLERIDGE (essay date 1794)

[*An English poet and critic, Coleridge and his poetry were central to the English Romantic movement. He is considered one of the greatest literary critics in the English language. Besides his poetry, his most important contributions include his formulation of Romantic theory, his introduction of the ideas of the German Romantics to England, and his Shakespearean criticism, which overthrew the last remnants of the Neoclassical approach to Shakespeare and focused on Shakespeare as a portrayer of human character. In this review of* The Mysteries of Udolpho, *Coleridge criticizes Radcliffe for her tendency to ''forget what is natural,'' her use of ''artificial contrivance,'' and the lack of unity in the novel; yet he praises Radcliffe's ability to sustain the reader's curiosity.*]

[*The Mysteries of Udolpho* does not] require the name of its author to ascertain that it comes from the same hand [that produced *The Romance of the Forest*]. The same powers of description are displayed, the same predilection is discovered for the wonderful and the gloomy—the same mysterious terrors are continually exciting in the mind the idea of a supernatural appearance, keeping us, as it were, upon the very edge and confines of the world of spirits, and yet are ingeniously explained by familiar causes; curiosity is kept upon the stretch from page to page, and from volume to volume, and the secret, which the reader thinks himself every instant on the point of penetrating, flies like a phantom before him, and eludes his eagerness till the very last moment of protracted expectation. This art of escaping the guesses of the reader has been improved and brought to perfection along with the reader's sagacity. . . . In this contest of curiosity on one side, and invention on the other, Mrs. Radcliffe has certainly the advantage. She delights in concealing her plan with the most artificial contrivance, and seems to amuse herself with saying, at every turn and doubling of the story, 'Now you think you have me, but I shall take care to disappoint you.' This method is, however, liable to the following inconvenience, that in the search of what is new, an author is apt to forget what is natural; and, in rejecting the more obvious conclusions, to take those which are less satisfactory. The trite and the extravagant are the Scylla and Charybdis of writers who deal in fiction. With regard to the work before us, while we acknowledge the extraordinary powers of Mrs. Radcliffe, some readers will be inclined to doubt whether they have been exerted in the present work with equal effect as in the *Romance of the Forest.* Four volumes cannot depend entirely on terrific incidents and intricacy of story. They require character, unity of design, a delineation of the scenes of real life, and the variety of well supported contrast. *The Mysteries of Udolpho* are indeed relieved by much elegant description and picturesque scenery; but in the descriptions there is too much of sameness: the pine and the larch tree wave, and the full moon pours its lustre through almost every chapter. Curiosity is raised oftener than it is gratified; or rather, it is raised so high that no adequate gratification can be given it; the interest is completely dissolved when once the adventure is finished, and the reader, when he is got to the end of the work, looks about in vain for the spell which had bound him so strongly to it. There are other little defects, which impartiality obliges us to notice. The manners do not sufficiently correspond with the aera the author has chosen. . . . The character of Annette, a talkative waiting-maid, is much worn, and that of the aunt, madame Cheron, is too low and selfish to excite any degree of interest, or justify the dangers her niece exposes herself to for her sake. We must likewise observe, that the adventures do not sufficiently point to one centre. . . . (pp. 355-57)

These volumes are interspersed with many pieces of poetry, some beautiful, all pleasing, but rather monotonous. . . . [Poetical] beauties have not a fair chance of being attended to, amidst the stronger interest inspired by such a series of adventures. The love of poetry is a taste; curiosity is a kind of appetite, and hurries headlong on, impatient for its complete gratification. (p. 366)

If, in consequence of the criticisms impartiality has obliged us to make upon this novel, the author should feel disposed to ask us, Who will write a better? we boldly answer her, *Yourself;* when no longer disposed to sacrifice excellence to quantity, and lengthen out a story for the sake of filling an additional volume. (pp. 369-70)

Samuel Taylor Coleridge, in a review of "The Mysteries of Udolpho" (originally published as " 'The Mysteries of Udolpho,' a Romance," in The Critical Review, *n.s. Vol. II, August, 1794), in his* Coleridge's Miscellaneous Criticism, *edited by Thomas Middleton Raysor, Cambridge, Mass.: Harvard University Press, 1936, pp. 355-70.*

THE MONTHLY REVIEW, LONDON (essay date 1794)

If the merit of fictitious narratives may be estimated by their power of pleasing, Mrs. Radcliffe's romances will be entitled to rank highly in the scale of literary excellence. There are, we believe, few readers of novels who have not been delighted with her *Romance of the Forest;* and we incur little risque in predicting that the *Mysteries of Udolpho* will be perused with equal pleasure.

The works of this ingenious writer not only possess, in common with many other productions of the same class, the agreeable qualities of correctness of sentiment and elegance of style, but are also distinguished by a rich vein of invention, which supplies an endless variety of incidents to fill the imagination of the reader; by an admirable ingenuity of contrivance to awaken his curiosity, and to bind him in the chains of suspense; and by a vigour of conception and a delicacy of feeling which are capable of producing the strongest sympathetic emotions, whether of pity or terror. Both these passions are excited in the present romance, but chiefly the latter; and we admire the enchanting power with which the author at her pleasure seizes and detains them. We are no less pleased with the proofs of sound judgment, which appear in the selection of proper circumstances to produce a distinct and full exhibition, before the reader's fancy, both of persons and events; and, still more, in the care which has been taken to preserve his mind in one uniform tone of sentiment, by presenting to it a long continued train of scenes and incidents, which harmonize with each other.

Through the whole of the first volume [of the *Mysteries of Udolpho*], the emotions which the writer intends to excite are entirely of the tender kind. Emily, the heroine of the tale, early becomes familiar with sorrow, through the death of her parents; yet not before the reader is made acquainted with their characters and manners, and has accompanied them through a number of interesting circumstances, sufficient to dispose him to the exercise of tender sympathy. At the same time, her heart receives, by slow and imperceptible degrees, the soft impressions of love; and the reader is permitted, without the introduction of any dissonant feelings, to enjoy the luxury of observing the rise and progress of this passion, and of sympathising with the lovers in every diversity of sentiment, which an uncommon vicissitude of events could produce; till, at last, Emily is separated from her Valancourt, to experience a sad variety of woe. With the interesting narrative of this volume, are frequently interwoven descriptions of nature in the rich and beautiful country of the South of France, which are perfectly in unison with the story; at the same time that they display, in a favourable light, the writer's powers of fancy and of language, and afford no small addition to the reader's gratification. We should have great pleasure, would our limits permit, in giving to our readers some specimens of these descriptions.

Something of the marvellous is introduced in the first volume, sufficient to throw an interesting air of *mystery* over the story; and the reader feels the pleasing agitation of uncertainty concerning several circumstances, of which the writer has had the address not to give a glance of explanation till toward the close of the work. In the remaining volumes, however, her genius is employed to raise up forms which chill the soul with horror. . . . (pp. 278-80)

Without introducing into her narrative any thing really supernatural, Mrs. Radcliffe has contrived to produce as powerful an effect as if the invisible world had been obedient to her magic spell; and the reader experiences in perfection the strange luxury of artificial terror, without being obliged for a moment to hoodwink his reason, or to yield to the weakness of superstitious credulity. We shall not forestall his pleasure by detailing the particulars: but we will not hesitate to say, in general, that, within the limits of nature and probability, a story so well contrived to hold curiosity in pleasing suspense, and at the same time to agitate the soul with strong emotions of sympathetic terror, has seldom been produced.

Another part of the merit of this novel must not be overlooked. The characters are drawn with uncommon distinctness, propriety, and boldness. (p. 280)

The numerous mysteries of the plot are fully disclosed in the conclusion, and the reader is perfectly satisfied at finding villainy punished, and steady virtue and persevering affection rewarded. If there be any part of the story which lies open to material objection, it is that which makes Valancourt, Emily's lover, fall into disgraceful indiscretions during her absence, and into a temporary alienation of affection. This, in a young man of noble principles and exalted sentiments, after such a long intimacy, and such a series of incidents tending to give permanency to his passion and stability to his character, we must think *unnatural*. The performance would in our opinion have been more perfect, as well as more pleasing, if Du Pont, Emily's unsuccessful admirer, had never appeared; and if Valancourt had been, as Emily expected, her deliverer from the Castle of Udolpho. The story, we apprehend, might have been easily brought to its present termination on this supposition.

The embellishments of the work are highly finished. The descriptions are rich, glowing, and varied: they discover a vigorous imagination, and an uncommon command of language; and many of them would furnish admirable subjects for the pencil of the painter. If the reader, in the eagerness of curiosity, should be tempted to pass over any of them for the sake of proceeding more rapidly with the story, he will do both himself and the author injustice. They recur, however, too frequently; and, consequently, a similarity of expression is often perceptible. Several of the pieces of poetry are elegant performances, but they would have appeared with more advantage as a separate publication. (p. 281)

> "Mrs. Radcliffe's 'Mysteries of Udolpho'," in The Monthly Review, London, Vol. XV, November, 1794, pp. 278-83.

SAMUEL TAYLOR COLERIDGE   (essay date 1798)

[*As in his review of* The Mysteries of Udolpho *(1794), Coleridge derides the Gothic novel form for its "attempt to please by what is unnatural." Though he feels that description in* The Italian *is "prolix," Coleridge finds the novel, on the whole, "an ingenious performance."*]

It was not difficult to foresee that the *modern romance*, even supported by the skill of the most ingenious of its votaries [Mrs. Radcliffe], would soon experience the fate of every attempt to please by what is unnatural, and by a departure from that observance of real life, which has placed the works of

Fielding, Smollett, and some other writers, among the permanent sources of amusement. It might for a time afford an acceptable variety to persons whose reading is confined to works of fiction, and who would, perhaps, be glad to exchange dullness for extravagance; but it was probable that, as its constitution (if we may so speak) was maintained only by the passion of terror, and that excited by trick, and as it was not conversant in incidents and characters of a natural complexion, it would degenerate into repetition, and would disappoint curiosity. So many cries 'that the wolf is coming,' must at last lose their effect. In reviewing the *Mysteries of Udolpho,* we hazarded an opinion, that, if a better production could appear, it must come only from the pen of Mrs. Radcliffe [see excerpt above, 1794]; but we were not totally blind to the difficulties which even she would have to encounter, in order to keep up the interest she had created in that work, and in the *Romance of the Forest;* and the present publication confirms our suspicions. *The Mysteries of Udolpho* fell short of the *Romance of the Forest,* by the tedious protraction of events, and by a redundancy of description: the *Italian* falls short of the *Mysteries of Udolpho,* by reminding us of the same characters and the same scenes; and, although the descriptive part is less prolix, the author has had recourse to it in various instances, in which it has no natural connexion with the story. There are, however, some scenes that powerfully seize the imagination, and interest the passions. Among these we prefer the interview between the marchesa and Schedoni in the church, and the discovery made by Schedoni that Ellena was his daughter. (pp. 378-79)

Among those parts of the romance which we disapprove, we may reckon the examination before the court of inquisition: it is so improbable, that we should rather have attributed it to one of Mrs. Radcliffe's numerous imitators.

But, notwithstanding occasional objections, the **Italian** may justly be considered as an ingenious performance; and many persons will read it with great pleasure and satisfaction. (p. 382)

> *Samuel Taylor Coleridge, in a review of "The Italian; or, The Confessional of the Black Penitents" (originally published as an unsigned essay in* The Critical Review, n.s. *Vol. XXIII, June, 1798), in* Coleridge's Miscellaneous Criticism, *edited by Thomas Middleton Raysor, Cambridge, Mass.: Harvard University Press, 1936, pp. 378-82.*

SIR WALTER SCOTT   (essay date 1824)

[*Scott was a Scottish novelist, poet, historian, biographer, and critic of the Romantic period who is best known for his novels, which were a great popular success. In this positive assessment of Radcliffe's novels, Scott hails her as "the first poetess of romantic fiction." Like Samuel Taylor Coleridge (1794), Scott is critical of Radcliffe's explained endings and notes that she is occasionally less successful in giving interest and dignity to her story than in "exciting interest and apprehension." However, he applauds the "force and vividness" of her descriptions and deems Radcliffe "a mistress of the art of exciting curiosity."*]

[*The Castles of Athlin and Dunbayne* gave] but moderate intimation of [Mrs. Radcliffe's] eminent powers. The scene is laid in Scotland, during the dark ages, but without any attempt to trace either the peculiar manners or scenery of the country; and although, in reading the work with that express purpose, we can now trace some germs of that taste and talent for the wild, romantic, and mysterious, which the authoress afterwards employed with such effect, we cannot consider it, on the whole, as by any means worthy of her pen. It is nevertheless curious to compare this sketch with Mrs. Radcliffe's more esteemed productions, since it is of consequence to the history of human genius to preserve its earlier efforts, that we may trace, if possible, how the oak at length germinates from the unmarked acorn.

Mrs. Radcliffe's genius was more advantageously displayed in the *Sicilian Romance*. . . . This work displays the exuberance and fertility of imagination, which was the author's principal characteristic. Adventures heaped on adventures, in quick and brilliant succession, with all the hair-breadth charms of escape or capture, hurry the reader along with them, and the imagery and scenery by which the action is relieved, are like those of a splendid Oriental tale. Still this work had marked traces of the defects natural to an unpractised author. The scenes were inartificially connected, and the characters hastily sketched, without any attempt at individual distinctions; being cast in the usual mould of ardent lovers, tyrannical parents, with domestic ruffians, guards, and others, who had wept or stormed through the chapters of romance, without much alteration in their family habits or features, for a quarter of a century before Mrs. Radcliffe's time. Nevertheless, the *Sicilian Romance* attracted much notice among the novel-readers of the day, as far excelling the ordinary meagreness of stale and uninteresting incident with which they were at that time regaled from the Leadenhall press. Indeed, the praise may be claimed for Mrs. Radcliffe, of having been the first to introduce into her prose fictions a beautiful and fanciful tone of natural description and impressive narrative, which had hitherto been exclusively applied to poetry. Fielding, Richardson, Smollett, even Walpole, though writing upon an imaginative subject are decidedly prose authors. Mrs. Radcliffe has a title to be considered as the first poetess of romantic fiction, that is, if actual rhythm shall not be deemed essential to poetry.

The Romance of the Forest, . . . placed the authoress at once in that rank, and pre-eminence in her own particular style of composition, which her works have ever since maintained. Her fancy, in this new effort, was more regulated, and subjected to the fetters of a regular story. The persons, too, although perhaps there is nothing very original in the conception, were depicted with skill far superior to that which the author had hitherto displayed, and the work attracted the public attention in proportion. That of La Motte, indeed, is sketched with particular talent, and most part of the interest of the piece depends upon the vacillations of a character, who, though upon the whole we may rather term him weak and vicious, than villanous, is, nevertheless, at every moment on the point of becoming an agent in atrocities which his heart disapproves of. (pp. 102-03)

The heroine, . . . wearing the usual costume of innocence, purity, and simplicity, as proper to heroines as white gowns are to the sex in general, has some pleasant touches of originality. Her grateful affection for the La Motte family—her reliance on their truth and honour, when the wife had become unkind, and the father treacherous towards her, is an interesting and individual trait in her character.

But although undoubtedly the talents of Mrs. Radcliffe, in the important point of drawing and finishing the characters of her narrative, were greatly improved since her earlier attempts, and manifested sufficient power to raise her far above the common crowd of novelists, this was not the department of art on which her popularity rested. The public were chiefly aroused, or rather fascinated, by the wonderful conduct of a story, in which the author so successfully called out the feelings

of mystery and of awe, while chapter after chapter, and incident after incident, maintained the thrilling attraction of awakened curiosity and suspended interest. . . . The tale was the more striking, because varied and relieved by descriptions of the ruined mansion, and the forest with which it is surrounded, under so many different points of view, now pleasing and serene, now gloomy, now terrible—scenes which could only have been drawn by one to whom nature had given the eye of a painter, with the spirit of a poet. (pp. 103-04)

[In *The Mysteries of Udolpho,* Mrs. Radcliffe] judiciously used a spell of broader and more potent command. The situation and distresses of the heroines, have here, and in *The Romance of the Forest,* a general aspect of similarity. Both are divided from the object of their attachment by the gloomy influence of unfaithful and oppressive guardians, and both become inhabitants of time-stricken towers, and witnesses of scenes now bordering on the supernatural, and now upon the horrible. But this general resemblance is only such as we love to recognize in pictures which have been painted by the same hand, and as companions for each other. Every thing in *The Mysteries of Udolpho* is on a larger and more sublime scale, than in *The Romance of the Forest;* the interest is of a more agitating and tremendous nature; the scenery of a wilder and more terrific description; the characters distinguished by fiercer and more gigantic features. Montoni, a lofty-souled desperado, and Captain of Condottieri, stands beside La Motte and his Marquis, like one of Milton's fiends beside a witch's familiar. Adeline is confined within a ruined manor-house, but her sister heroine, Emily, is imprisoned in a huge castle, like those of feudal times; the one is attacked and defended by bands of armed banditti, the other only threatened by a visit from constables and thief-takers. The scale of the landscape is equally different; the quiet and limited woodland scenery of the one work forming a contrast with the splendid and high-wrought descriptions of Italian mountain grandeur which occur in the other. (pp. 105-06)

[In *The Italian,* Mrs. Radcliffe] selected the new and powerful machinery afforded her by the Popish religion, when established in its paramount superiority, and thereby had at her disposal, monks, spies, dungeons, the mute obedience of the bigot, the dark and dominating spirit of the crafty priest,—all the thunders of the Vatican, and all the terrors of the Inquisition. This fortunate adoption placed in the hands of the authoress a powerful set of agents, who were at once supplied with means and motives for bringing forward scenes of horror; and thus a tinge of probability was thrown over even those parts of the story, which are most inconsistent with the ordinary train of human events.

Most writers of romance have been desirous to introduce their narrative to the reader, in some manner which might at once excite interest, and prepare his mind for the species of excitation which it was the author's object to produce. In *The Italian,* this has been achieved by Mrs. Radcliffe with an uncommon degree of felicity. . . . (pp. 106-07)

[The] introductory passage, which, for the references which it bears to the story, and the anxious curiosity it excites in the reader's mind, may be compared to the dark and vaulted gateway of an ancient castle, is followed by a tale of corresponding mystery and terror; in detailing which, the art of Mrs. Radcliffe, who was so great a mistress of throwing her narrative into mystery, affording half intimations of veiled and secret horrors, is used perhaps to the very uttermost. And yet, though our reason ultimately presents us with this criticism, we believe she generally suspends her remonstrance till the perusal is ended; and it is not until the last page is read, and the last volume closed, that we feel ourselves disposed to censure that which has so keenly interested us. We become then at length aware, that there is no uncommon merit in the general contrivance of the story; that many of the incidents are improbable, and some of the mysteries left unexplained; yet the impression of general delight which we have received from the perusal, remains unabated, for it is founded on recollection of the powerful emotions of wonder, curiosity, even fear, to which we have been subjected during the currency of the narrative. (p. 107)

On reconsidering the narrative, we indeed discover that many of the incidents are imperfectly explained, and that we can distinguish points upon which the authoress had doubtless intended to lay the foundation of something which she afterwards forgot or omitted. Of the first class, is the astonishment testified by the Grand Inquisitor with such striking effect, when a strange voice was heard, even in the awful presence of that stern tribunal, to assume the task of interrogation proper to its judges. The incident in itself is most impressive. As Vivaldi is blindfolded, and bound upon the rack, the voice of a mysterious agent, who had repeatedly crossed his path, and always eluded his search, is heard to mingle in his examination, and strikes the whole assembly with consternation. . . .

This is all unquestionably very impressive; but no other explanation of the intruder's character is given, than that he is an officer of the Inquisition; a circumstance which may explain his being present at Vivaldi's examination, but by no means his interference with it, against the pleasure of the Grand Inquisitor. (p. 108)

We may notice an instance of even greater negligence, in the passages respecting the ruined palace of the Baron di Cambrusca, where the imperfect tale of horror hinted at by a peasant, the guide of Schedoni, appears to jar upon the galled conscience of the monk, and induces the reader to expect a train of important consequences. Unquestionably, the ingenious authoress had meant this half-told tale to correspond with some particulars in the proposed developement of the story, which having been finished more hastily, or in a different manner from what she intended, she had, like a careless knitter, neglected to take up her 'loose stitches'. It is, however, a balking of the reader's imagination, which authors in this department would do well to guard against. (p. 109)

Mrs. Radcliffe, as an author, has the most decided claim to take her place among the favoured few, who have been distinguished as the founders of a class, or school. She led the way in a peculiar style of composition, affecting powerfully the mind of the reader, which has since been attempted by many, but in which no one has attained or approached the excellences of the original inventor, unless perhaps the author of *The Family of Montorio* [Charles Maturin]. . . .

The species of romance which Mrs. Radcliffe introduced, bears nearly the same relation to the novel that the modern anomaly entitled a melo-drame does to the proper drama. It does not appeal to the judgment by deep delineations of human feeling, or stir the passions by scenes of deep pathos, or awaken the fancy by tracing out, with spirit and vivacity, the lighter marks of life and manners, or excite mirth by strong representations of the ludicrous or humorous. In other words, it attains its interest neither by the path of comedy nor of tragedy; and yet it has, notwithstanding, a deep, decided, and powerful effect, gained by means independent of both—by an appeal, in one

word, to the passion of fear, whether excited by natural dangers, or by the suggestions of superstition. The force, therefore, of the production, lies in the delineation of external incident, while the characters of the agents, like the figures in many landscapes, are entirely subordinate to the scenes in which they are placed; and are only distinguished by such outlines as make them seem appropriate to the rocks and trees, which have been the artist's principal objects. The persons introduced—and here also the correspondence holds betwixt the melo-drame and the romantic novel—bear the features, not of individuals, but of the class to which they belong. A dark and tyrannical count; an aged crone of a housekeeper, the depositary of many a family legend; a garrulous waiting-maid; a gay and light-hearted valet; a villain or two of all work; and a heroine, fulfilled with all perfections, and subjected to all manner of hazards, form the stock-in-trade of a romancer or a melo-dramatist; and if these personages be dressed in the proper costume, and converse in language sufficiently appropriate to their stations and qualities, it is not expected that the audience shall shake their sides at the humour of the dialogue, or weep over its pathos.

On the other hand, it is necessary that these characters, though not delineated with individual features, should be truly and forcibly sketched in the outline; that their dress and general appearance should correspond with and support the trick of the scene; and that their language and demeanour should either enhance the terrors amongst which they move, or form, as the action may demand, a strong and vivid contrast to them. Mrs. Radcliffe's powers of fancy were particularly happy in depicting such personages, in throwing upon them and their actions just enough of that dubious light which mystery requires, and in supplying them with language and manners which correspond with their situation and business upon the scene. (pp. 110-11)

[Critics] were disposed to detract from the genius of the author, on account of the supposed facility of her task. Art or talent, they said, was not required to produce that sort of interest and emotion, which is perhaps, after all, more strongly excited by a vulgar legend of a village ghost, than by the high painting and laboured descriptions of Mrs. Radcliffe. . . . The feelings of suspense and awful attention which she excites, are awakened by means of springs which lie open, indeed, to the first touch, but which are peculiarly liable to be worn out by repeated pressure. The public soon, like Macbeth, become satiated with horrors, and indifferent to the strongest *stimuli* of that kind. It shows, therefore, the excellence and power of Mrs. Radcliffe's genius, that she was able three times to bring back her readers with fresh appetite to a banquet of the same description; while of her numerous imitators, who rang the changes upon old castles and forests, and 'antres dire,' scarcely one attracted attention, until Mr. Lewis published his *Monk*, several years after she had resigned her pen.

The materials of [her] celebrated romances, and the means employed in conducting the narrative, are all selected with a view to the author's primary object, of moving the reader by ideas of impending danger, hidden guilt, supernatural visitings—by all that is terrible, in short, combined with much that is wonderful. (pp. 113-14)

In working upon the sensations of natural and superstitious fear, Mrs. Radcliffe has made much use of obscurity and suspense, the most fertile source, perhaps, of sublime emotion; for there are few dangers that do not become familiar to the firm mind, if they are presented to consideration as certainties, and in all their open and declared character; whilst, on the other hand, the bravest have shrunk from the dark and the doubtful. To break off the narrative, when it seemed at the point of becoming most interesting—to extinguish a lamp, just when a parchment containing some hideous secret ought to have been read—to exhibit shadowy forms and half-heard sounds of woe, are resources which Mrs. Radcliffe has employed with more effect than any other writer of romance. It must be confessed, that in order to bring about these situations, some art or contrivance, on the part of the author, is rather too visible. Her heroines voluntarily expose themselves to situations, which in nature a lonely female would certainly have avoided. They are too apt to choose the midnight hour for investigating the mysteries of a deserted chamber or secret passage, and generally are only supplied with an expiring lamp, when about to read the most interesting documents. The simplicity of the tale is thus somewhat injured—it is as if we witnessed a dressing up of the very phantom by which we are to be startled; and the imperfection, though redeemed by many beauties, did not escape the censure of criticism.

A principal characteristic of Mrs. Radcliffe's romances, is the rule which the author imposed upon herself, that all the circumstances of her narrative, however mysterious, and apparently superhuman, were to be accounted for on natural principles, at the winding up of the story. It must be allowed, that this has not been done with uniform success, and that the author has been occasionally more successful in exciting interest and apprehension, than in giving either interest or dignity of explanation to the means she has made use of. (pp. 114-15)

[Mrs. Radcliffe's] heroines often sustain the agony of fear, and her readers that of suspense, from incidents which, when explained, appear of an ordinary and trivial nature; and in this we do not greatly applaud her art. A stealthy step behind the arras, may doubtless, in some situations, and when the nerves are tuned to a certain pitch, have no small influence upon the imagination; but if the conscious listener discovers it to be only the noise made by the cat, the solemnity of the feeling is gone, and the visionary is at once angry with his senses for having been cheated, and with his reason for having acquiesced in the deception. We fear that some such feeling of disappointment and displeasure attends most readers, when they read for the first time the unsatisfactory solution of the mysteries of the black pall and the wax figure, which has been adjourned from chapter to chapter, like something suppressed, because too horrible for the ear.

There is a separate inconvenience attending a narrative where the imagination has been long kept in suspense, and is at length imperfectly gratified by an explanation falling short of what the reader has expected; for, in such a case, the interest terminates on the first reading of the volumes, and cannot, so far as it rests upon a high degree of excitation, be recalled upon a second perusal. A plan of narrative, happily complicated and ingeniously resolved, continues to please after many readings; for, although the interest of eager curiosity is no more, it is supplied by the rational pleasure, which admires the author's art, and traces a thousand minute passages, which render the catastrophe probable, yet escape notice in the eagerness of a first perusal. But it is otherwise, when some inadequate cause is assigned for a strong emotion; the reader feels tricked, and as in the case of a child who has once seen the scenes of a theatre too nearly, the idea of pasteboard, cords, and pullies, destroys for ever the illusion with which they were first seen from the proper point of view. Such are the difficulties and dilemmas which attend the path of the professed story-teller,

who, while it is expected of him that his narrative should be interesting and extraordinary, is neither permitted to explain its wonders, by referring them to ordinary causes, on account of their triteness, nor to supernatural agency, because of its incredibility. It is no wonder that, hemmed in by rules so strict, Mrs. Radcliffe, a mistress of the art of exciting curiosity, has not been uniformly fortunate in the mode of gratifying it.

The best and most admired specimen of her art is the mysterious disappearance of Ludovico [the servant in *The Mysteries of Udolpho*], after having undertaken to watch for a night in a haunted apartment; and the mind of the reader is finely wound up for some strange catastrophe, by the admirable ghost-story which he is represented as perusing to amuse his solitude, as the scene closes upon him. Neither can it be denied, that the explanation afforded of this mysterious incident is as probable as romance requires, and in itself completely satisfactory. As this is perhaps the most favourable example of Mrs. Radcliffe's peculiar skill in composition, the incidents of the black veil and the waxen figure, may be considered as instances where the explanation falls short of expectation, and disappoints the reader entirely. (pp. 117-18)

Mrs. Radcliffe's powers, both of language and description, have been justly estimated very highly. They bear, at the same time, considerable marks of that warm, and somewhat exuberant imagination, which dictated her works. Some artists are distinguished by precision and correctness of outline, others by the force and vividness of their colouring; and it is to the latter class that this author belongs. The landscapes of Mrs. Radcliffe are far from equal in accuracy and truth to those of her contemporary, Mrs. Charlotte Smith, whose sketches are so very graphical, that an artist would find little difficulty in actually painting from them. Those of Mrs. Radcliffe, on the contrary, while they would supply the most noble and vigorous ideas, for producing a general effect, would leave the task of tracing a distinct and accurate outline to the imagination of the painter. As her story is usually enveloped in mystery, so there is, as it were, a haze over her landscapes, softening indeed the whole, and adding interest and dignity to particular parts, and thereby producing every effect which the author desired, but without communicating any absolutely precise or individual image to the reader. The beautiful description of the Castle of Udolpho, upon Emily's first approach to it, is of this character. It affords a noble subject for the pencil: but were six artists to attempt to embody it upon canvass, they would probably produce six drawings entirely dissimilar to each other, yet all of them equally authorized by the printed description. . . . (pp. 118-19)

It may be true, that Mrs. Radcliffe rather walks in fairy-land than in the region of realities, and that she has neither displayed the command of the human passions, nor the insight into the human heart, nor the observation of life and manners, which recommend other authors in the same line. But she has taken the lead in a line of composition, appealing to those powerful and general sources of interest, a latent sense of supernatural awe, and curiosity concerning whatever is hidden and mysterious; and if she has been ever nearly approached in this walk, which we should hesitate to affirm, it is at least certain, that she has never been excelled or even equalled. (p. 119)

Sir Walter Scott, in an introduction to The Novels of Ann Radcliffe *by Ann Radcliffe, Ballantyne Publishers, 1824 (and reprinted as "Ann Radcliffe," in his* On Novels and Novelists, *edited by Ioan Williams, Routledge & Kegan Paul, 1968, pp. 102-19).*

MRS. RADCLIFFE   (essay date 1826)

[The following excerpt from a fictional conversation between two travelers, Mr. S—— and W——, sets forth Radcliffe's famous distinction between horror and terror.]

[Said W——:] "Terror and horror are so far opposite, that the first expands the soul, and awakens the faculties to a high degree of life; the other contracts, freezes, and nearly annihilates them. I apprehend, that neither Shakspeare nor Milton by their fictions, nor Mr. Burke by his reasoning, anywhere looked to positive horror as a source of the sublime, though they all agree that terror is a very high one; and where lies the great difference between horror and terror, but in the uncertainty and obscurity, that accompany the [latter] . . . , respecting the dreaded evil?" (pp. 149-50)

"How can any thing be indistinct and not confused?" said Mr. S——. . . .

[Replied W——: "Obscurity,] or indistinctness, is only a negative, which leaves the imagination to act upon the few hints that truth reveals to it; confusion is a thing as positive as distinctness, though not necessarily so palpable; and it may, by mingling and confounding one image with another, absolutely counteract the imagination, instead of exciting it. Obscurity leaves something for the imagination to exaggerate; confusion, by blurring one image into another, leaves only a chaos in which the mind can find nothing to be magnificent, nothing to nourish its fears or doubts, or to act upon in any way; yet confusion and obscurity are terms used indiscriminately by those, who would prove, that Shakspeare and Milton were wrong when they employed obscurity as a cause of the sublime, that Mr. Burke was equally mistaken in his reasoning upon the subject, and that mankind have been equally in error, as to the nature of their own feelings, when they were acted upon by the illusions of those great masters of the imagination, at whose so potent bidding, the passions have been awakened from their sleep, and by whose magic a crowded Theatre has been changed to a lonely shore, to a witch's cave, to an enchanted island, to a murderer's castle, to the ramparts of an usurper, to the battle, to the midnight carousal of the camp or the tavern, to every various scene of the living world." (p. 150)

> *Mrs. Radcliffe, "On the Supernatural in Poetry,"* in The New Monthly Magazine, *Vol. XVI, No. LXI, January 1, 1826, pp. 145-52.*

[THOMAS NOON TALFOURD]   (essay date 1826)

[Prefixed to the posthumously published Gaston de Blondeville, *Talfourd's memoir was the first ever written about Radcliffe. Talfourd echos Sir Walter Scott's comments (see excerpt above, 1824) when he calls Radcliffe "the inventor of a new style of romance." He also praises her "daring economy" in employing "instruments of fear," and her excellent portrayal of scenery, but acknowledges her shortcomings in the area of characterization. Like Samuel Taylor Coleridge (1794), Talfourd considers Radcliffe's final explanations a "harassing expedient." Yet he defends this practice by dismissing it as a bow to "some established canon of romance."]*

[*The Castles of Athlin and Dunbayne,*] with a goodly number of old towers, dungeon keeps, subterraneous passages and hair-breadth escapes, has little of reality, or life; as if [Mrs. Radcliffe] had caught a glimpse of the regions of romance from afar, and formed a sort of dreamy acquaintance with its recesses and glooms. In her next work, the *Sicilian Romance,* she seems to obtain a bird's-eye view of all the surface of that delightful region—she places its winding vales and delicious bowers and summer seas before the eye of the mind—but is as yet unable to introduce the reader individually into the midst of the scene, to surround him with its luxurious air, and compel him to shudder at its terrors. In *The Romance of the Forest,* she approaches and takes up her very residence in the pleasant borders of the enchanted land; the sphere she chooses is small and the persons limited; but here she exercises clear dominion, and realizes every thing to the fancy. *The Mysteries of Udolpho* is the work of one, who has entered and possessed a mighty portion of that enchanted land; who is familiar with its massive towers and solemn glooms;—and who presents its objects of beauty, or horror, through a certain haze, which sometimes magnifies and sometimes veils their true proportions. In *The Italian,* she occupies a less space; but, shining in golden light, her figures have the distinctness of terrible pictures; and her scenes, though perhaps less astounding in the aggregate, are singly more thrilling and vivid. (pp. x-xi)

Mrs. Radcliffe may fairly be considered as the inventor of a new style of romance; equally distinct from the old tales of chivalry and magic, and from modern representations of credible incidents and living manners. Her works partially exhibit the charms of each species of composition; interweaving the miraculous with the probable, in consistent narrative, and breathing of tenderness and beauty peculiarly her own. The poetical marvels of the first fill the imagination, but take no hold on the sympathies, to which they have become alien: the vicissitudes of the last awaken our curiosity, without transporting us beyond the sphere of ordinary life. But it was reserved for Mrs. Radcliffe to infuse the wondrous in the credible; to animate rich description with stirring adventure; and to impart a portion of human interest to the progress of romantic fiction. She occupied that middle region between the mighty dreams of the heroic ages and the realities of our own, which remained to be possessed; filled it with goodly imagery; and made it resonant with awful voices. (pp. cv-cvi)

The principal means, which Mrs. Radcliffe employed to raise up her enchantments on the borders of truth, are, first, her faculty of awakening emotions allied to superstitious fear; and, secondly, her skill in selecting and describing scenes and figures precisely adapted to the feelings she sought to enkindle. (pp. cvi-cvii)

[Mrs. Radcliffe] purposes to influence the mind directly from without, instead of leaving it, after receiving a certain clue, to its own workings. In this style, up to the point where Mrs. Radcliffe chooses to pause and explain, she has no rival. She knows the string of feeling she must touch, and exactly proportions her means to her design. She invariably succeeds not by the quantity but the quality of her terrors. Instead of exhibiting a succession of magnificent glooms, which only darken the imagination, she whispers some mysterious suggestion to the soul, and exhibits only just enough of her picture to prolong the throbbings she has excited. In nothing is her supremacy so clearly shown, as in the wise and daring economy, with which she has employed the instruments of fear. A low groan issuing from distant vaults; a voice heard among an assembly from an unknown speaker; a little track of blood seen by the uncertain light of a lamp on a castle staircase; a wild strain of music floating over moonlight woods; as introduced by her, affect the mind more deeply than terrible incantations, or accumulated butcheries. . . . Her faculty . . . , which has been represented as melo-dramatic, is akin to the very essence of tragic power, which is felt not merely in the greatness of the actions, or sorrows, which it exhibits, but in its nice application to the inmost sources of terror and of pity.

It is extraordinary, that a writer thus gifted should, in all her works intended for publication, studiously resolve the circumstances, by which she has excited superstitious apprehensions, into mere physical causes. She seems to have acted on a notion, that some established canon of romance obliged her to reject real supernatural agency; for it is impossible to believe she would have adopted this harassing expedient if she had felt at liberty to obey the promptings of her own genius. So absolute was her respect for every species of authority, that it is probable she would rather have sacrificed all her productions, than have transgressed any arbitrary law of taste, or criticism. . . . [But such] impotent conclusions injure the romances as works of art, and jar on the nerves of the reader, which are tuned for grand wonders, not paltry discoveries. This very error, however, which injures the effect of Mrs. Radcliffe's works, especially on a second perusal, sets off, in the strongest light, the wizard power of her genius. Even when she has dissolved mystery after mystery, and abjured spell after spell, the impression survives, and the reader is still eager to attend again, and be again deluded. (pp. cxvi-cxvii)

Mrs. Radcliffe's faculties of describing and picturing scenes and appropriate figures was of the highest order. Her accurate observation of inanimate nature, prompted by an intense love of all its varieties, supplied the materials for those richly coloured representations, which her genius presented. Without this perception of the true, the liveliest fancy will only produce a chaos of beautiful images, like the remembered fragments of a gorgeous dream. How singularly capable Mrs. Radcliffe was of painting the external world, in its naked grandeur, her published tour among the English Lakes, and, perhaps still more, the notes made on her journeys for her own amusement, abundantly prove. . . . She seems the very chronicler and secretary of nature; makes us feel the freshness of the air; and listen to the gentlest sounds. Not only does she keep each scene distinct from all others, however similar in general character; but discriminates its shifting aspects with the most delicate exactness. No aerial tint of a fleecy cloud is too evanescent to be imaged in her transparent style. Perhaps no writer in prose, or verse, has been so happy in describing the varied effects of light in winged words. It is true, that there is not equal discrimination in the views of natural scenery, which she presents in her romances. In them she writes of places, which she has not visited; and, like a true lover, invests absent nature with imaginary loveliness. She looks at the grandeurs and beauties of creation through a soft and tender medium, in which its graces are heightened, but some of its delicate varieties are lost. Still it is nature that we see, though touched with the hues of romance, and which could only be thus presented by one who had known, and studied its simple charms.

In the estimate of Mrs. Radcliffe's pictorial powers, we must include her persons as well as her scenes. It must be admitted that, with scarcely an exception, they are figures rather than characters. No writer ever produced so powerful an effect, without the aid of sympathy. Her machinery acts directly on her readers, and makes them tremble and weep, not for others, but for themselves. Adeline, Emily, Vivaldi, and Ellena, are nothing to us, except as filling up the scene; but it is we ourselves, who discover the manuscript in the deserted abbey; we, who are prisoners in the castle of Udolpho; we, who are inmates of Spalatro's cottage; we, who stand before the secret tribunal of the Inquisition, and even there are startled by the

mysterious voice deepening its horrors. The whole is prodigious painting, so entire as to surround us with illusion; so cunningly arranged as to harrow up the soul; and the presence of a real person would spoil its completeness. As figures, all the persons are adapted with peculiar skill to the scenes in which they appear;—the more, as they are part of one entire conception. Schedoni is the most individual and fearful; but through all the earlier parts of [*The Italian*], he stalks like a being not of this world; and works out his purposes by that which, for the time at least, we feel to be superhuman agency. But when, after glaring out upon us so long as a present demon; or felt, when unseen, as directing the whole by his awful energies; he is brought within the range of human emotion by the discovery of his supposed daughter, and an anxiety for her safety and marriage; the spell is broken. We feel the incongruity; as if a spectre should weep. To develope character was not within the scope of Mrs. Radcliffe's plan, nor compatible with her style. (pp. cxvii-cxx)

As the absence of discriminated feeling and character was necessary to the completeness of the effect Mrs. Radcliffe sought to produce, so she was rather assisted by manners peculiarly straight-laced and timorous. A deep vein of sentiment would have suggested thoughts and emotions inconsistent with that "wise passiveness," in which the mind should listen to the soft murmur of her "most musical, most melancholy" spells. A moral paradox could not co-exist with a haunted tower in the mind of her readers. The exceeding coldness and prudence of her heroines do not abstract them from the scenes of loveliness and terror through which we desire to follow them. If her scrupulous sense of propriety had not restrained her comic powers, Mrs. Radcliffe would probably have displayed considerable talent for the humorous. But her talkative servants are all very guarded in their loquacity; and even Annette, quaintly and pleasantly depicted, fairly belongs to the scene. Her old-fashioned primness of thought, which with her was a part of conscience, with all its cumbrous accompaniments, serves at once to render definite, and to set off, her fanciful creations. Romance, as exhibited by her, "tricked in antique ruff and bonnet," has yet eyes of youth; and the beauty is not diminished by the folds of the brocade, or the stiffness of the damask stomacher.

These remarks apply, in their fullest effect, only to *The Mysteries of Udolpho,* and *The Italian,* in which alone the chief peculiarities of Mrs. Radcliffe's genius are decidedly marked. In her first work, *The Castles of Athlin and Dunbayne,* it is scarcely possible to discover their germ. . . . Those, who complain of the minuteness of Mrs. Radcliffe's descriptions, should read this work, where every thing passes with headlong rapidity, and be convinced of their error. In some few instances, perhaps, in *The Mysteries of Udolpho,* the descriptions of external scenery may occur too often; but her best style is essentially pictorial; and a slow developement of events was, therefore, necessary to her success.

The *Sicilian Romance* is a work of much more "mark and likelihood." . . . In tender and luxurious description of natural scenery, it is surpassed by none of Mrs. Radcliffe's productions. The flight of her heroine is like a strain of "lengthened sweetness long drawn out;"—as one series of delicious valleys opens on us after another; and the purple light of love is shed over all. Still she had not yet acquired a mastery over her own power of presenting terrific incidents and scenes to the eye of the mind, and awakening the throbs of suspense by mysterious suggestions. The light seen through the closed windows of the deserted rooms—the confession of Vincent stopped by death—the groans heard from beneath Ferdinand's prison—and the figure perceived stealing among the vaults, are not introduced with sufficient earnestness, and lose all claim to belief, by the utter incredibility of the incidents, with which they are surrounded. Escapes, recaptions, encounters with fathers and banditti, surprising partings, and more surprising meetings, follow each other as quickly as the changes of a pantomime, and with almost as little of intelligible connexion. . . . There are, in [the *Sicilian Romance*], incidents enough for two such works as *The Mysteries of Udolpho,* where, as in that great romance, they should not only be told, but painted; and where reality and grandeur should be given to their terrors.

In *The Romance of the Forest,* Mrs. Radcliffe, who, since the dawn of her powers, had been as one "moving about in worlds unrealized," first exhibited the faculty of controlling and fixing the wild images which floated around her, and of stamping on them the impress of consistency and truth. This work is, as a whole, the most faultless of all her productions; but it is of an inferior order to *The Mysteries of Udolpho* and *The Italian;* and can only be preferred by those, who think the absence of error of more importance than original excellence. There is a just proportion between all its parts; its mysteries are adequately explained; it excites and gratifies a very pleasant degree of curiosity; but it does not seem to dilate the imagination, nor does it curdle the blood. . . . The closing chapters of the work are inferior in themselves to its commencement; but they gratify by affording a worthy solution of the intricacies of a plot, which has excited so deep an interest in its progress.

The Mysteries of Udolpho is by far the most popular of Mrs. Radcliffe's works. To this preeminence it is, we think, justly entitled; for, although *The Italian* may display more purely intellectual power, it is far less enchanting. Of all the romances in the world, this is perhaps the most romantic. Its outline is noble, it is filled with majestic or beautiful imagery; and it is touched throughout with a dreamy softness, which harmonizes all its scenes, and renders its fascination irresistible. It rises from the gentlest beauty by just gradations to the terrific and the sublime. . . . The ideas of extent, of massiveness, and austere grandeur, conveyed in the description of the castle, have matchless force and distinctness, and prepare the mind for the crimes and wonders, of which it is the silent witness. . . . Not only the mysterious appearances and sounds appal us, but the rushing wind, a rustling curtain, the lonely watch-word on the terrace, have power to startle, and keep curiosity awake. . . . Such are some among the many striking features of this romance; its defects are great and obvious. Its mysteries are not only resolved into natural causes, but are explained by circumstances provokingly trivial. (pp. cxx-cxxix)

The Italian has more unity of plan than *The Mysteries of Udolpho;* and its pictures are more individual and distinct; but it has far less tenderness and beauty. Its very introduction, unlike the gentle opening of the former romance, impresses the reader with awe. Its chief agent, Schedoni, is most vividly painted; and yet the author contrives to invest him with a mystery, which leads us to believe, that even her image is inadequate to the reality. . . . The dreary horrors of the fisherman's cottage are admirably painted; but the effort to produce a great theatrical effect is very imperfectly concealed; and we cannot help being somewhat dissatisfied with the process of bringing a helpless orphan to such a distance, merely that she may be murdered with eclat; with the equally unaccountable delay in performing the deed; the strange relentings of the ruffian; and

the long preparation, which precedes the attempt of Schedoni to strike the fatal blow. There is great art in the scene, to which all this is introductory; and the discovery of the portrait is a most striking *coup de theatre;* but the art is too palpable, and the contrast between the assassin and the father too violent—at least, for a second perusal. Not so, the graphic description of the vast prisons of the Inquisition; they are dim, prodigious, apparently eternal; and the style is solemn and weighty as the subject. Mrs. Radcliffe alone could have deepened the horror of this gloom by whispers of things yet more terrible; and suggest fears of the unseen, which should overcome the present apprehensions of bodily torture. (pp. cxxix-cxxxi)

In her own peculiar style of composition, Mrs. Radcliffe has never been approached. . . . She only, of all writers of romance, who have awed and affected the public mind, by hints of things unseen, has employed enchantments purely innocent; has forborne to raise one questionable throb, or call forth a momentary blush. This is the great test not only of moral feeling, but of intellectual power; and in this will be found her highest praise. (pp. cxxxi-cxxxii)

> [*Thomas Noon Talfourd*], "Memoir of the Life and Writings of Mrs. Radcliffe," in Gaston de Blondeville; or, The Court of Henry III, Vol. I by Ann Radcliffe, Henry Colburn, 1826 (and reprinted by Arno Press, Inc., 1972), pp. i-cxxxii.

THE EDINBURGH REVIEW   (essay date 1834)

Mrs Radcliffe was as truly an inventor, a great and original writer in the department she had struck out for herself—whether that department was of the highest kind or not—as the Richardsons, Fieldings, and Smolletts, whom she succeeded and for a time threw into the shade; or the Ariosto of the North [Sir Walter Scott], before whom her own star has paled its ineffectual fires. The passion of fear,—'the latent sense of supernatural awe, and curiosity concerning whatever is hidden and mysterious'—these were themes and sources of interest which, prior to the appearance of her tales, could scarcely be said to be touched on. [Horace Walpole's] *Castle of Otranto* was too obviously a mere caprice of imagination; its gigantic helmets, its pictures descending from their frames, its spectral figures dilating themselves in the moonlight to the height of the castle battlements—if they did not border on the ludicrous, no more impressed the mind with any feeling of awe, than the enchantments and talismans, the genii and peris, of the *Arabian Nights.* A nearer approach to the proper tone of feeling, was made in the *Old English Baron;* but while it must be admitted that Mrs Radcliffe's principle of composition was, to a certain degree, anticipated in that clever production, nothing can illustrate more strongly the superiority of her powers, the more poetical character of her mind, than a comparison of the way in which, in these different works, the principle is wrought out;—the comparative boldness and rudeness of Clara Reeve's modes of exciting superstitious emotions, as contrasted with the profound art, the multiplied resources, the dexterous display and concealment, the careful study of that class of emotions on which she was to operate, which Mrs Radcliffe displays in her supernatural machinery. Certainly never before or since did any one more accurately perceive the point to which imagination might be wrought up, by a series of hints, glimpses, or half-heard sounds, consistently at the same time with pleasurable emotion, and with the continuance of that very state of curiosity and awe which had been thus created. The clang of a distant door, a footfall on the stair, a half-effaced stain of blood, a strain of music floating over a wood, or round some decaying chateau—nay, a very 'rat behind the arras,' become in her hands invested with a mysterious dignity; so finely has the mind been attuned to sympathize with the terrors of the sufferer, by a train of minute details and artful contrasts, in which all sights and sounds combine to awaken and render the feeling more intense. Yet her art is even more visible in what she conceals than in what she displays. 'One shade the more, one ray the less,' would have left the picture in darkness; but to have let in any farther the garish light of day upon her mysteries, would have shown at once the hollowness and meanness of the puppet which alarmed us, and have broken the spell beyond the power of reclasping it. Hence, up to the moment when she chooses to do so herself, by those fatal *explanations* for which no reader will ever forgive her, she never loses her hold on the mind. The very economy with which she avails herself of the talisman of terror preserves its power to the last, undiminished, if not increased. She merely hints at some fearful thought, and leaves the excited fancy, surrounded by night and silence, to give it colour and form.

Of all the passions, that of Fear is the only one which Mrs Radcliffe can properly be said to have painted. The deeper mysteries of Love, her plummet has never sounded. More wearisome beings than her heroines, any thing more 'tolerable and not to be endured' than her love tales, Calprenede or Scudery never invented. As little have the stormier passions of jealousy or hatred, or the dark shades of envious and malignant feeling, formed the subjects of her analysis. Within the circle of these passions, indeed, she did not feel that she could walk with security; but her quick perception showed where there was still an opening in a region of obscurity and twilight, as yet all but untrodden. To that, as to the sphere pointed out to her by nature, she at once addressed herself; from that, as from a central point, she surveyed the provinces of passion and imagination, and was content if, without venturing into their labyrinths, she could render their leading and more palpable features available to set off and to brighten by their variety the solemnity and gloom of the department which she had chosen. For her purpose, . . . the preliminary agency of powerful passions was, no doubt, necessary. But it was quite sufficient to exhibit them in their results, and any minute analysis of their growth or action, any great anxiety to give individuality of character to the beings represented, would have been thrown away; if, indeed, it did not actually interfere with, and run counter to her object. The moral interest involved in the actual play of passion would, at the best, have imperfectly amalgamated with the state of restlessness and suspense occasioned by the investigation of a train of mysterious occurrences, or the thrilling sensations of the supernatural. Nothing, indeed, in her tales, indicates the possession of any power of character-drawing; nor would it, in our opinion, have very materially increased their fascination, if her personages had been discriminated by more characteristic traits. For her object it was quite sufficient, that as the representations of classes, their leading outlines should be sketched with a firm and spirited hand. . . . [Her characters are] well sketched, though with a hasty pencil; but it is the scenes through which they are led, the skill with which she scatters over them her light and shadow, the magnificence or terror of the backgrounds on which they are relieved, the variety of the situations in which they are placed, and the sweet transitions from danger and anxiety to tranquility and joy in which she delights, which give them their main hold on the imagination and the memory.

The truth is, as has been very beautifully remarked by a critic, that though Mrs Radcliffe's supernatural machinery is represented as influencing her characters, we tremble and weep not for others but for ourselves [see excerpt above by Thomas Noon Talfourd, 1826]. It is on us directly that it properly operates. (pp. 329-32)

[The] profusion of landscape painting with which Mrs Radcliffe has been reproached, and which most readers may have thought carried to excess, was probably adopted on system, as an element of effect. Even while it tires us, as suspending the interest of the story, it probably attunes the mind to sympathy with the coming events, and, like an overture, conveys hints and shadows of what is to follow. (p. 332)

Though any one might have naturally inferred, from the character of Mrs Radcliffe's mind, as exhibited in her romances, that she had little turn for the more meditative and reflective kinds of poetry, we should hardly have anticipated her total failure in a metrical romance. For this species of poetry, so purely objective, as our German neighbours call it,—requiring little beyond a picturesque eye, and graphic hand, or perhaps some ingenuity of plot, and exacting no study of character, and but little strictness of versification,—one would have thought her powers extremely well suited. There seem, however, to be some who are poets in prose, but whose poetry forsakes them the moment they attempt to embody their ideas in verse; and one of these undoubtedly was Mrs Radcliffe. . . . [Her *St. Alban's Abbey* is] so miserably told, so broken and confused by tedious descriptions, that though we have toiled through the ten cantos which compose the story, we have the most indistinct notion what the whole is about. (pp. 337-38)

[Of her other poems,] we are compelled to say, that their merits are inversely as their length. The longer pieces, *Stonehenge*, and *Edwy*, are very tiresome, though some pleasing moonlight scenes in Windsor Park, in some measure relieve the tedium of the latter. But in the shorter pieces which are scattered through the book, there is frequently a fine power of description, a pleasing though vague melancholy, and occasionally considerable happiness of expression. (p. 339)

> *"Mrs. Radcliffe's 'Poetical Works',"* in The Edinburgh Review, *Vol. LIX, No. CXX, July, 1834, pp. 327-41.*

ANDREW LANG   (essay date 1900)

[Mrs. Radcliffe] delighted in descriptions of scenery, the more romantic the better, and usually drawn entirely from her inner consciousness. Her heroines write sonnets (which never but once *are* sonnets) and other lyrics, on every occasion. With his usual generosity Scott praised her landscape and her lyrics [see excerpt above, 1824], but, indeed, they are, as Sir Walter said of Mrs. Hemans, 'too poetical,' and probably they were skipped, even by her contemporary devotees. . . .

Mrs. Radcliffe does not always keep on her highest level, but we must remember that her last romance, **'The Italian,'** is by far her best. (p. 24)

[The **'Sicilian Romance'**] has a treble attraction, for it contains the germ of [Jane Austen's] 'Northanger Abbey,' and the germ of [Charlotte Brontë's] 'Jane Eyre,' and—the germ of Byron! Like [Henry Fielding's] 'Joseph Andrews,' 'Northanger Abbey' began as a parody (of Mrs. Radcliffe) and developed into a real novel of character. So too Byron's gloomy scowling adventurers, with their darkling past, are mere repetitions in rhyme of Mrs. Radcliffe's Schedoni. This is so obvious that, when discussing Mrs. Radcliffe's Schedoni, Scott adds, in a note, parallel passages from Byron's 'Giaour.' Sir Walter did not mean to mock, he merely compared two kindred spirits. 'The noble poet' 'kept on the business still,' and broke into octosyllabics, borrowed from Scott, his descriptions of miscreants borrowed from Mrs. Radcliffe. (pp. 24-5)

Jealousy and revenge are clearly indicated [in the **'Sicilian Romance'**]. But, in chasing mysterious lights and figures through mouldering towers, Ferdinand gets into the very undesirable position of David Balfour, when he climbs, in the dark, the broken turret stair in his uncle's house of Shaws (in 'Kidnapped'). Here is a *fourth* author indebted to Mrs. Radcliffe: her disciples are Miss Austen, Byron, Miss Brontë, and Mr. Louis Stevenson! (p. 25)

[**'The Romance of the Forest'** is] a fiction in which character is subordinate to plot and incident. There is an attempt at character-drawing in La Motte, and in his wife; the hero and heroine are not distinguishable from Julia and Hippolitus [of the **'Sicilian Romance'**]. But Mrs. Radcliffe does not aim at psychological niceties, and we must not blame her for withholding what it was no part of her purpose to give. **'The Romance of the Forest'** was, so far, infinitely the most thrilling of modern English works of fiction. (p. 31)

The roof and crown of Mrs. Radcliffe's work is **'The Italian.'** (p. 32)

'The Italian' is an excellent novel. The Prelude, 'the dark and vaulted gateway,' is not unworthy of Hawthorne, who, I suspect, had studied Mrs. Radcliffe. The theme is more like a theme of this world than usual. The parents of a young noble might well try to prevent him from marrying an unknown and penniless girl. The Marchese Vivaldi only adopts the ordinary paternal measures; the Marchesa, and her confessor, the dark-souled Schedoni, go farther—as far as assassination. The casuistry by which Schedoni brings the lady to this pass, while representing *her* as the originator of the scheme, is really subtle, and the scenes between the pair show an extraordinary advance on Mrs. Radcliffe's earlier art. The mysterious Monk who counterworks Schedoni remains an unsolved mystery to me, but of that I do not complain. He is as good as the Dweller in the Catacombs who haunts Miriam in Hawthorne's 'Marble Faun.' (p. 33)

Following Horace Walpole in some degree, Mrs. Radcliffe paved the way for Scott, Byron, Maturin, Lewis, and Charlotte Brontë, just as Miss Burney filled the gap between Smollett and Miss Austen. Mrs. Radcliffe, in short, kept the Lamp of Romance burning much more steadily than the lamps which, in her novels, are always blown out, in the moment of excited apprehension, by the night wind walking in the dank corridors of haunted abbeys. (pp. 33-4)

Andrew Lang, "Mrs. Radcliffe's Novels," in The Cornhill Magazine, *n.s. Vol. IX, No. 49, July, 1900, pp. 23-34.*

WALTER RALEIGH (essay date 1911)

[*One of the first critics to view Radcliffe's works in a literary as well as historical context, Raleigh commends Radcliffe's handling of suspense, fine use of romance conventions, and effective manipulation of scenery and sensation. In exhibiting these characteristics in her prose, Raleigh maintains, she "anticipated and guided the poetry of the Romantic revival."*]

[One] of the greatest of the English Romantic School, Mrs. Radcliffe never succeeded in conquering her fear of the supernatural so far as to allow it a place in her novels. Yet her series of fictions, from *The Castles of Athlin and Dunbayne* [to *The Italian*] . . . , exercised so enormous a power on the new generation, and displayed so many decisive advances on previous romantic essays, as to earn her a foremost place among the earlier apostles of Romanticism. (p. 227)

Her ignorance of the world at the time when she wrote was complete and many-sided. Human character she knew, not from observation but from dreams. The landscapes for which she is so justly famous are pictures of countries she never saw. There is nothing in her books that she did not create. And it is a testimony to the power of her art that her fancy first conceived a type of character that subsequently passed from art into life. The man that Lord Byron tried to be was the invention of Mrs. Radcliffe.

The plots of her stories have often been censured for their timidity. With an unprecedented control over the secrets of terror, a power of awakening by a touch all the vague associations and suggestions of superstitious awe, she yet shrinks from following Walpole, and never plunges into the frankly supernatural. Further, and here perhaps lies her chief mistake, she does not allow the supernatural even as a possible refuge. The explanations whereby her multiplied mysteries are ultimately dissipated, run on such severely natural lines as to recall the simplicity of Snug the joiner [from William Shakespeare's *A Midsummer Night's Dream*], and the reader is almost ashamed of his terrors when he is confronted with the dull mechanic who has simulated a lion so marvellously.

To historical precision there is no pretence. In *The Mysteries of Udolpho* . . . , a story dealing with events of the year 1584, Parisian fashions, French opera, and French manners, are spoken of as dominating the world. (pp. 228-29)

The machinery as well as the characters of these novels became the commonplaces of later romancers. The secret corridors, sliding panels, echoing vaults, and hidden trapdoors, the mouldering manuscripts discovered in massive chests and read at night by the light of a flickering candle, are all expedients beloved of Mrs. Radcliffe. The manuscript device, occurring in the works of Walpole and Miss Reeve, became so common a convention as almost to demand classification among the possible modes of telling a story. Mrs. Radcliffe strains it almost to breaking point; her manuscripts invariably become illegible at the point where some dire secret is about to be revealed. (p. 230)

The absurdities of the renascent romance are many, and are to be found on the surface. The merits of Mrs. Radcliffe are less obvious to a generation for whom her devices are no longer new. Yet with her works the Romantic School sprang at once to maturity. The Romantic movement may be described, in one aspect, as an invasion of the realm of prose by the matter of poetry; and in this regard no bolder inroads are to be chronicled from first to last than those that she planned and executed.

She has a fine command over the world of association and suggestion, distinctively poetic, and "a significant and expressive uncertainty of strokes and colouring." She knows the value of the mere absence of definition, the power of vacuity, darkness, solitude, and silence. (p. 231)

Another cardinal expedient of Mrs. Radcliffe and the school at large consists in the isolation of sense impressions commonly associated. Sights without corresponding sounds, sounds without corresponding sights, a touch in the dark—whether of the clammy hand of a dead person, or of "the mealy and carious bones of a skeleton," these things are made to yield a nameless subtle horror. (pp. 231-32)

The remaining contribution made by Mrs. Radcliffe to romantic method is to be found in her employment of scenery. Nowhere but from the poets could she have borrowed this. . . . The essence of Mrs. Radcliffe's scenery is that it is fictitious, lending the richness and fulness of harmony to the thin wavering melody of the plot. In the power which she assigns to flood and fell, sunset and storm, over the moods and passions of her characters, she becomes at times almost Wordsworthian. And her scenery, although artificial, is not glaringly unreal; there are traces of observation of some real atmospheric effects, and her descriptions bear witness to the acuteness of her senses. Sights are not allowed to obscure sounds, and sensations of odour and respiration, all the vague organic impressions that count for so much in the effect of natural surroundings, find their record. But perhaps the most remarkable point in her treatment of nature is the breadth and unity of her pictures. She never forgets the whole in the parts; details are sparingly introduced and generally with telling effect. Her landscapes might be named after the particular emotions they are built to house—terror, regret, security, or melancholy—and they would be in perfect keeping.

Thus, in more than one way, the prose of Mrs. Radcliffe anticipated and guided the poetry of the Romantic revival. Prose like hers could not hope to remain prose long; but technical inaptitude and the precedent set by the novelists prevented her from writing in verse. The narrative poems of the next century owed much to her influence, while the novel proper pursued its course on independent lines. (pp. 232-33)

> Walter Raleigh, "The Revival of Romance," in his The English Novel: Being a Short Sketch of Its History from the Earliest Times to the Appearance of "Waverley," *fifth edition, Charles Scribner's Sons, 1911, pp. 216-52.*

GEORGE SAINTSBURY (essay date 1913)

[*Saintsbury was an English literary historian and critic of the late nineteenth and early twentieth centuries. A prolific writer, Saintsbury composed a number of histories of English and European literature as well as several critical works on individual authors, styles, and periods. Saintsbury notes Radcliffe's influence on Sir Walter Scott and Lord Byron, praises her descriptions, and states that her explained endings, though sometimes tiresome, are "really a marvel of patience and ingenuity."*]

[*A Sicilian Romance, The Romance of the Forest, The Mysteries of Udolpho,* and *The Italian*] owed their original attraction to the skill with which, by the use of a Defoe-like minuteness of detail, added to a pictorial faculty which Defoe had not, an atmosphere of terror is constantly diffused and kept up. Very little that is terrible actually happens: but [Mrs. Radcliffe] succeeds (so long as the trick has not become too familiar) in persuading you that something very terrible is *going* to happen, or has just happened. And so the delight of something "horrid," as the Catherines and Isabellas of the day put it, is given much more plentifully, and even much more excitingly, than it could be by a real horror now and then, with intervals of miscellaneous business. In one sense, indeed, the process will not stand even the slightest critical examination: for it is soon

seen to consist of a succession of serious mystifications and non-comic much-ados-about-nothing. But these "ados" are most cunningly made (her last book, *The Italian,* is, perhaps, the best place to look for them . . .), and Mrs. Radcliffe's great praise is that she induced her original readers to suspend their critical faculties sufficiently to enable them to take it all seriously. Scott, who undoubtedly owed her something, assigned her positive genius [see excerpt above, 1824]: and modern critics, while, perhaps, seldom experiencing much real delectation from her work, have discovered in it not a few positive and many more indirect and comparative merits. The influence on Scott is not the least of these: but there is even a more unquestionable asset of the same kind in the fact that the Byronic villain-hero, if not Byron himself, is Mrs. Radcliffe's work. Schedoni did much more than beget or pattern [Byron's] Lara: he *is* Lara, to all intents and purposes, in "first state" and before the final touch has been put by the greater master who took the plate in hand.

But there is more to be said for Mrs. Radcliffe than this. Her "explained supernatural," tiresome as it may be to some of us nowadays, is really a marvel of patience and ingenuity: and this same quality extends to her plots generally. The historical side of her novels (which she does to some extent attempt) is a failure, as everything of the kind was before Scott . . . But one important engine of the novelist she set to work in a fashion which had never been managed before, and that is elaborate description. She shows an early adaptation of that "picturesque," of which we see the beginnings in Gray, when she was in the nursery, which was being directly developed by Gilpin, but which, as we may see from her *Travels,* she had got not merely from books, but from her own observation. She applies it both within and without: at one moment giving pages on the scenery of the Apennines, at another paragraphs on the furniture of her abbeys and castles. The pine forests and the cataracts; the skyline of Udolpho bathed in sunset glow, while a "melancholy purple tint" steals up the slopes to its foundations—are all in the day's work now; but they were not so then, and it is fair to say that Mrs. Radcliffe does them well. The "high canopied tester of dark green damask" and the "counterpane of black velvet" which illustrate the introduction of the famous chapter of the Black Pall in Chateau le Blanc may be mere inventory goods now: but, once more, they were not so then. And this faculty of description (which, as noted above, could hardly have been, and pretty certainly was not, got from books, though it may have been, to some extent and quite legitimately, got from pictures) was applied in many minor ways—touches of really or supposedly horrible objects in the dark, faint suggestions of sound, or of appeals to the other senses—hints of all sorts, which were to become common tricks of the trade, but were then quite new.

At any rate, by these and other means she attained that great result of the novel which has been noted in Defoe, in Richardson, and in others—the result of what the French vividly call *enfisting* the reader—getting hold of his attention, absorbing him in a pleasant fashion. The mechanism was often too mechanical: taken with the author's steady and honest, but somewhat inartistic determination to explain everything it sometimes produces effects positively ridiculous to us. With the proviso of *valeat quanium* [for what it's worth], it is not quite unfair to dwell, as has often been dwelt, on the fact that the grand triumph of Mrs. Radcliffe's terrormongering—the famous incident of the Black Veil [from *The Mysteries of Udolpho*]—is produced by a piece of wax-work. But the result resulted—the effect *was* produced: and it was left to those who were clever enough to improve upon the means. (pp. 160-63)

George Saintsbury, ''The Minor and Later Eighteenth-Century Novel,'' in his The English Novel, *J. M. Dent & Sons Ltd.*, 1913, pp. 133-88.*

EDITH BIRKHEAD (essay date 1921)

[*Birkhead discusses Radcliffe's ability to convince the reader of improbable occurrences and her originality in creating the romantic villain. Birkhead also comments that Radcliffe's dialogue is ''stilted and unnatural,'' but concedes that the novelist's chief interest was in situation rather than style.*]

Considered historically, [*The Castles of Athlin and Dunbayne*] is full of interest, for, with the notable exception of the supernatural, it contains in embryo nearly all the elements of Mrs. Radcliffe's future novels. . . . [Yet, the] faintly pencilled outlines, the characterless figures, the nerveless structure, give little presage of the boldly effective scenery, the strong delineations and the dexterously managed plots of the later novels. The gradual, steady advance in skill and power is one of the most interesting features of Mrs. Radcliffe's work. Few could have guessed from the slight sketch of Baron Malcolm, a merely slavish copy of the traditional villain, that he was to be the ancestor of such picturesque and romantic creatures as Montoni and Schedoni. (pp. 39-41)

[The incidents of strange lights and groaning in *A Sicilian Romance*] plainly reveal that Mrs. Radcliffe has now discovered the peculiar vein of mystery towards which she was groping in *The Castles of Athlin and Dunbayne*. From the very first she explained away her marvels by natural means. If we scan her romances with a coldly critical eye—an almost criminal proceeding—obvious improbabilities start into view. For instance, the oppressed marchioness, who has not seen her daughter Julia since the age of two, recognises her without a moment's hesitation at the age of seventeen, and faints in a transport of joy. It is no small tribute to Mrs. Radcliffe's gifts that we often accept such incidents as these without demur. So unnerved are we by the lurking shadows, the flickering lights, the fluttering tapestry and the unaccountable groans with which she lowers our vitality, that we tremble and start at the wagging of a straw, and have not the spirit, once we are absorbed into the atmosphere of her romance, to dispute anything she would have us believe. The interest of the *Sicilian Romance,* which is far greater than that of her first novel, arises entirely out of the situations. There is no gradual unfolding of character and motive. The high-handed marquis, the jealous marchioness, the imprisoned wife, the vapid hero, the two virtuous sisters, the leader of the banditti, the respectable, prosy governess, are a set of dolls fitted ingeniously into the framework of the plot. They have more substance than the tenuous shadows that glide through the pages of Mrs. Radcliffe's first story, but they move only as she deftly pulls the strings that set them in motion.

In her third novel, *The Romance of the Forest*, . . . Mrs. Radcliffe makes more attempt to discuss motive and to trace the effect of circumstances on temperament. The opening chapter is so alluring that callous indeed would be the reader who felt no yearning to pluck out the heart of the mystery. (pp. 41-2)

Although *The Romance of the Forest* is considerably shorter than the later novels, the plot, which is full of ingenious complications, is unfolded in the most leisurely fashion. Mrs. Radcliffe's tantalising delays quicken our curiosity as effectively

as the deliberate calm of a *raconteur,* who, with a view to heightening his artistic effect, pauses to light a pipe at the very climax of his story. Suspense is the key-note of the romance. The characters are still subordinate to incident, but La Motte and his wife claim our interest because they are exhibited in varying moods. La Motte has his struggles and, like Macbeth, is haunted by compunctious visitings of nature. Unlike the thorough-paced villain, who glories in his misdeeds, he is worried and harassed, and takes no pleasure in his crimes. Madame La Motte is not a jealous woman from beginning to end like the marchioness in the *Sicilian Romance*. Her character is moulded to some extent by environment. She changes distinctly in her attitude to Adeline after she has reason to suspect her husband. Mrs. Radcliffe's psychology is neither subtle nor profound, but the fact that psychology is there in the most rudimentary form is a sign of her progress in the art of fiction. Theodore is as insipid as the rest of Mrs. Radcliffe's heroes, who are distinguishable from one another only by their names, and Adeline is perhaps a shade more emotional and passionless than Emily and Ellena in *The Mysteries of Udolpho* and *The Italian*. The lachrymose maiden in *The Castles of Athlin and Dunbayne,* who can assume at need ''an air of offended dignity,'' is a preliminary sketch of Julia, Emily and Ellena in the later novels. Mrs. Radcliffe's heroines resemble nothing more than a composite photograph in which all distinctive traits are merged into an expressionless ''type.'' They owe something no doubt to Richardson's *Clarissa Harlowe,* but their feelings are not so minutely analysed. Their lady-like accomplishments vary slightly. In reflective mood one may lightly throw off a sonnet to the sunset or to the nocturnal gale, while another may seek refuge in her water-colours or her lute. They are all dignified and resolute in the most distressing situations, yet they weep and faint with wearisome frequency. Their health and spirits are as precarious as their easily extinguished candles. Yet these exquisitely sensitive, well-bred heroines alienate our sympathy by their impregnable self-esteem, a disconcerting trait which would certainly have exasperated heroes less perfect and more human than Mrs. Radcliffe's Theodores and Valancourts. Their sorrows never rise to tragic heights, because they are only passive sufferers, and the sympathy they would win as pathetic figures is obliterated by their unfailing consciousness of their own rectitude. (pp. 45-6)

Fortunately the heroine is merely a figurehead in *The Mysteries of Udolpho*. . . . The change of title is significant. The two previous works have been romances, but it is now Mrs. Radcliffe's intention to let herself go further in the direction of wonder and suspense than she had hitherto ventured. . . . Yet Mrs. Radcliffe, at the opening of her story, is sparing in her use of supernatural elements. We live by faith, and are drawn forward by the hope of future mystifications. . . . The anticipation is half pleasurable, half fearful, as we shudder at the thought of what may befall us within [the castle] walls. At every turn something uncanny shakes our overwrought nerves. . . . So exhaustive—and exhausting—are the mysteries of Udolpho that it was a mistake to introduce another haunted castle, le Blanc, as an appendix.

Mrs. Radcliffe's long-deferred explanations of what is apparently supernatural have often been adversely criticised. Her method varies considerably. Sometimes we are enlightened almost immediately. (pp. 47-8)

[Yet, it] is seldom that the rude awakening comes . . . swiftly. More often we are left wondering uneasily and fearfully for a prolonged stretch of time. The extreme limit of human endurance is reached in the episode of the Black Veil [in *The Mysteries of Udolpho*]. (p. 49)

[The] explanation falls so ludicrously short of our expectations and is so improbable a possibility, that Mrs. Radcliffe would have been wise not to defraud Catherine Morland [in Jane Austen's *Northanger Abbey*] and other readers of the pleasure of guessing aright. Few enjoy being baffled and thwarted in so unexpected a fashion. . . . [Long] ere this disclosure, we have learnt by bitter experience to distrust Mrs. Radcliffe's secrets and to look for ultimate disillusionment. . . . She deliberately excites trembling apprehensions in order that she may show how absurd they are. We are befooled that she may enjoy a quietly malicious triumph. The result is that we become wary and cautious. . . . The idea of explaining away what is apparently supernatural may have occurred to Mrs. Radcliffe after reading Schiller's popular romance, *Der Geisterseher* (1789), in which the elaborately contrived marvels of the Armenian, who was modelled on Cagliostro, are but the feats of a juggler and have a physical cause. But more probably Mrs. Radcliffe's imagination was held in check by a sensitive conscience, which would not allow her to trade on the credulity of simple-minded readers.

It is noteworthy that Mrs. Radcliffe's last work—*The Italian*—. . . is more skilfully constructed, and possesses far greater unity and concentration than *The Mysteries of Udolpho*. The Inquisition scenes towards the end of the book are unduly prolonged, but the story is coherent and free from digressions. The theme is less fanciful and far-fetched than those of *The Romance of the Forest* and *Udolpho*. It seldom strays far beyond the bounds of the probable, nor overstrains our capacity for belief. . . . *The Italian* abounds in dramatic, haunting scenes. . . . The climax of the story when Schedoni, about to slay Ellena, is arrested in the very act by her beauty and innocence, and then by the glimpse of the portrait which leads him to believe she is his daughter, is finely conceived and finely executed. Afterwards, Ellena proves only to be his niece, but we have had our thrill and nothing can rob us of it. *The Italian* depends for its effect on natural terror, rather than on supernatural suggestions. The monk, who haunts the ruins of Paluzzi, and who reappears in the prison of the Inquisition, speaks and acts like a being from the world of spectres, but in the fulness of time Mrs. Radcliffe ruthlessly exposes his methods and kills him by slow poison. She never completely explains his behaviour in the halls of the Inquisition nor accounts satisfactorily for the ferocity of his hatred of Schedoni. We are unintentionally led on false trails.

The character of Schedoni is undeniably Mrs. Radcliffe's masterpiece. No one would claim that his character is subtle study, but in his interviews with the Marchesa, Mrs. Radcliffe reveals unexpected gifts for probing into human motives. He is an imposing figure, theatrical sometimes, but wrought of flesh and blood. In fiction, as in life, the villain has always existed, but it was Mrs. Radcliffe who first created the romantic villain, stained with the darkest crimes, yet dignified and impressive withal. . . . The sinister figures of Mrs. Radcliffe, with passion-lined faces and gleaming eyes, stalk—or, if occasion demand it, glide—through all her romances, and as she grows more familiar with the type, her delineations show increased power and vigour. When the villian enters, or shortly afterwards, a descriptive catalogue is displayed, setting forth, in a manner not unlike that of the popular *feuilleton* of to-day, the qualities to be expected, and with this he is let loose into the story to play his part and act up to his reputation. . . Montoni,

the desperate leader of the condottieri in *The Mysteries of Udolpho*, is endued with so vigorous a vitality that we always rejoice inwardly at his return to the forefront of the story. His abundant energy is refreshing after a long sojourn with his garrulous wife and tearful niece. (pp. 50-4)

The [Schedoni] type undoubtedly owes something to Milton's Satan. Like Lucifer, he is proud and ambitious, and like him he retains traces of his original grandeur. Hints from Shakespeare helped to fashion him. Like Cassius [in *Julius Caesar*], seldom he smiles. . . . By the enormity of his crimes he inspires horror and repulsion, but by his loneliness he appeals, for a moment, like the consummate villain Richard III., to our pity. . . . (pp. 54-5)

Among the direct progeny of these grandiose villains are to be included those of Lewis and Maturin, and the heroes of Scott and Byron. We know them by their world-weariness, as well as by their piercing eyes and passion-marked faces, their "verra wrinkles Gothic.". . . The feminine counterpart of these bold impersonations of evil is the tyrannical abbess who plays a part in *The Romance of the Forest* and in *The Italian,* and who was adopted and exaggerated by Lewis, but her crimes are petty and malicious, not daring and ambitious, like the schemes of Montoni and Schedoni. (pp. 55-6)

[In *Gaston de Blondeville,* Mrs. Radcliffe] ventures to make one or two startling innovations. Her hero is no longer a pale, romantic young man of gentle birth, but a stolid, worthy merchant. Here, at last, she indulges in a substantial spectre, who cannot be explained away as the figment of a disordered imagination, since he seriously alarms, not a solitary heroine or a scared lady's-maid, but Henry III. himself and his assembled barons. Yet apart from this daring escapade, it is timidity rather than the spirit of valorous enterprise that is urging Mrs. Radcliffe into new and untried paths. Her happy, courageous disregard for historical accuracy in describing far-off scenes and bygone ages has deserted her. She searches painfully in ancient records, instead of in her imagination, for mediaeval atmosphere. Her story is grievously overburdened with elaborate descriptions of customs and ceremonies, and she adds laborious notes, citing passages from learned authorities, such as Leland's *Collectanea*, Pegge's dissertation on the obsolete office of Esquire of the King's Body, Sir George Bulke's account of the coronation of Richard III., Mador's *History of the Exchequer*, etc. We are transported from the eighteenth century, not actually to mediaeval England, but to a carefully arranged pageant displaying mediaeval costumes, tournaments and banquets. The actors speak in antique language to accord with the picturesque background against which they stand. [Yet,] *Gaston de Blondeville* . . . is noteworthy as an early attempt to shadow forth the days of chivalry. . . . The story of *Gaston de Blondeville* is tedious, the characters are shadowy and unreal. . . , yet, regarded simply as a spectacular effect, it is not without indications of skill and power. (pp. 56-8)

Mrs. Radcliffe's style compares favourably with that of many of her contemporaries, with that of Mrs. Roche, for instance, who wrote *The Children of the Abbey* and an array of other forgotten romances, but she is too fond of long, imperfectly balanced sentences, with as many awkward twists and turns as the winding stairways of her ancient turrets. Nobody in the novels, except the talkative, comic servant, who is meant to be vulgar and ridiculous, ever condescends to use colloquial speech. Even in moments of extreme peril the heroines are very choice in their diction. Dialogue in Mrs. Radcliffe's world is as stilted and unnatural as that of prim, old-fashioned school books. In her earliest novel she uses very little conversation, clearly finding the indirect form of narrative easier. Sometimes, in the more highly wrought passages of description, she slips unawares into a more daring phrase, *e.g.* in *Udolpho,* the track of blood "glared" upon the stairs, where the word suggests not the actual appearance of the bloodstain, but rather its effect on Emily's inflamed and disordered imagination. . . . Her attention to style is mainly subconscious, her chief interest being in situation. (p. 59)

All her novels, except *The Italian* and *Gaston de Blondeville,* had been written before she went abroad, and in describing foreign scenery she relied on her imagination, aided perhaps by pictures and descriptions as well as by her recollections of English mountains and lakes. The attempt to blend into a single picture a landscape actually seen and a landscape only known at second-hand may perhaps account for the lack of distinctness in her pictures. Her descriptions of scenery are elaborate, and often prolix, but it is often difficult to form a clear image of the scene. In her novels she cares for landscape only as an effective background, and paints with the broad, careless sweep of the theatrical scene-painter. In the *Journeys,* where she depicts scenery for its own sake, her delineation is more definite and distinct. She reveals an unusual feeling for colour and for the lights and tones of a changing sea or sky. . . . (p. 60)

With all her limitations, Mrs. Radcliffe is a figure whom it is impossible to ignore in the history of the novel. Her influence was potent on Lewis and on Maturin as well as on a host of forgotten writers. Scott admired her works and probably owed something in his craftsmanship to his early study of them. She appeals most strongly in youth. (p. 61)

> Edith Birkhead, " 'The Novel of Suspense'. Mrs. Radcliffe," in her The Tale of Terror: A Study of the Gothic Romance, *Constable & Company Ltd., 1921 (and reprinted by Russell & Russell, Inc., 1963), pp. 38-62.*

VIRGINIA WOOLF   (essay date 1929)

[*A discerning and influential English critic and essayist as well as novelist, Woolf is one of the most prominent literary figures of the twentieth century. Disputing Thomas Noon Talfourd's claim that Radcliffe adhered strictly to romance conventions (1826), Woolf finds that Radcliffe "pushes the liberties of romance to the extreme." Woolf considers descriptive writing to be Radcliffe's greatest talent, but argues that, because she is incapable of creating in her readers a mood which would make the mysteries believable, Radcliffe's books are ultimately "stale, forced, unappetizing."*]

The Mysteries of Udolpho have been so much laughed at as the type of Gothic absurdity that it is difficult to come at the book with a fresh eye. We come, expecting to ridicule. Then, when we find beauty, as we do, we go to the other extreme and rhapsodize. But the beauty and the absurdity of romance are both present and the book is a good test of the romantic attitude, since Mrs. Radcliffe pushes the liberties of romance to the extreme. Where Scott will go back a hundred years to get the effect of distance, Mrs. Radcliffe will go back three hundred. With one stroke, she frees herself from a host of disagreeables and enjoys her freedom lavishly.

As a novelist, it is her desire to describe scenery and it is there that her great gift lies. Like every true writer, she shoulders her way past every obstacle to her goal. She brings us into a huge, empty, airy world. A few ladies and gentlemen, who

are purely eighteenth century in mind, manner, and speech, wander about in vast champaigns, listen to nightingales singing amorously in midnight woods; see the sun set over the lagoon of Venice; and watch the distant Alps turn pink and blue from the turrets of an Italian castle. These people, when they are well born, are of the same blood as Scott's gentry; attenuated and formal silhouettes who have the same curious power of being in themselves negligible and insipid but of merging harmoniously in the design. (pp. 107-08)

[We] feel the force which the romantic acquires by obliterating facts. With the sinking of the lights, the solidity of the foreground disappears, other shapes become apparent and other senses are roused. We become aware of the danger and darkness of our existence; comfortable reality has proved itself a phantom too. Outside our little shelter we hear the wind raging and the waves breaking. In this mood our senses are strained and apprehensive. Noises are audible which we should not hear normally. Curtains rustle. Something in the semi-darkness seems to move. Is it alive? And what is it? And what is it seeking here? Mrs. Radcliffe succeeds in making us feel all this, largely because she is able to make us aware of the landscape and, thus, induces a detached mood favourable to romance; but in her, more plainly than in Scott or Stevenson, the absurdity is evident, the wheels of the machine are visible and the grinding is heard. She lets us see more clearly than they do what demands the romantic writer makes upon us. (pp. 108-09)

[Mrs. Radcliffe,] having climbed to the top of her pinnacle, finds it impossible to come down. She tries to solace us with comic passages, put naturally into the mouths of Annette and Ludovico who are servants [in *The Mysteries of Udolpho*]. But the break is too steep for her limited and ladylike mind and she pieces out her high moments and her beautiful atmosphere with a pale reflection of romance which is more tedious than any ribaldry. Mysteries abound. Murdered bodies multiply; but she is incapable of creating the emotion to feel them by, with the result that they lie there, unbelieved in; hence, ridiculous. The veil is drawn; there is the concealed figure; there is the decayed face; there are the writhing worms—and we laugh.

Directly the power which lives in a book sinks, the whole fabric of the book, its sentences, the length and shape of them, its inflections, its mannerisms, all that it wore proudly and naturally under the impulse of a true emotion become stale, forced, unappetizing. Mrs. Radcliffe slips limply into the faded Scott manner and reels off page after page. . . .

And so it slips along and so we sink and drown in the pale tide. Nevertheless, Udolpho passes this test: it gives us an emotion which is both distinct and unique, however high or low we rate the emotion itself. (p. 109)

> Virginia Woolf, "Phases of Fiction" *(originally published in* The Bookman, *New York, Vol. LXIX, Nos. 2, 3, and 4, April, May, and June, 1929), in her* Granite and Rainbow: Essays *(© 1958 by Leonard Woolf; reprinted by permission of the Author's Literary Estate and The Hogarth Press Ltd), 1958, Hogarth Press, 1958, pp. 93-145.**

R. AUSTIN FREEMAN   (essay date 1931)

[*Freeman notes that* The Mysteries of Udolpho *is free of "prolixity" and "verbosity" despite its "somewhat heroic dimensions." In contrast to many previous critics of Radcliffe who disliked her "explained endings," Freeman argues that her con-*

clusions are "satisfying and conclusive," and praises her for not making her "path easy by recourse to the supernatural."]

The story [of **The Mysteries of Udolpho**] is good enough to stand on its own merits, independent alike of extrinsic graces or shortcomings.

Compared with the works of our own times, this is a book of somewhat heroic dimensions, containing some three hundred thousand words, and being, therefore, equal in length to three good-sized modern novels. Yet, in spite of its bulk, there is a total absence of any tendency to "padding." The narrative pursues its quiet, leisurely way, after the dignified fashion of the time, but without prolixity or verbosity. The persons and the scenes are duly introduced to the reader in the opening pages with a careful formality of detail that contrasts strongly with the way in which some modern authors blunder into the midst of what is to the reader an unknown environment. There is much more description, especially of scenery, than would be thought admissible in modern work. But it is excellent description, strictly relevant to the action, and designed to create the desired atmosphere; and in many instances—as, for example, in the fine descriptive passages which illustrate the thrilling adventures of the heroine and her friends among the smugglers and bandits in a pass of the Pyrenees—the description of the background of the action is essential to, and inseparable from, the action itself.

As to the "period" atmosphere, the reader must pass over it as lightly as the author has done. It is of little consequence, for this makes no claim to be an historical novel; it is a story of mystery and stirring incident. For some reason, the author made the period the late sixteenth century—the story opens in the year 1584—but she is at no trouble to insist on it. The heroine, Emily St. Aubert, is surprisingly like a young English lady of the late eighteenth or early nineteenth century, and the atmosphere in general is more like that of the eighteenth than the sixteenth century. There occur, too, certain little anachronisms in connection with the accessories, or "properties." But these, even if they do not pass unobserved, will not trouble the reader; nor will he be seriously disturbed by encountering nuns, companionably perambulating the corridors of monasteries, or by discovering a Father Superior and a Lady Abbess presiding over their respective departments in the same institution. (pp. vii-viii)

[In **The Mysteries of Udolpho**, the] mysteries, indeed, are calculated most thoroughly to puzzle the reader and arouse in him a lively curiosity. Some of the incidents appear to be totally incredible and outside the limits of natural possibility. Nevertheless, when the explanations are given, the reader is able at once to accept them as satisfying and conclusive. And it must be set down as greatly to the author's credit that, unlike some of her contemporaries, she resisted the temptation to make her path easy by recourse to the supernatural. Even the most wildly improbable of the events so vividly described are eventually seen to be in full accordance with the order of nature.

If we wished to be critical, we might, perhaps, demur to some of the methods by which the mystery is maintained; particularly to the practice of withholding from the reader what are admittedly observed facts, and permitting him only to perceive their emotional effects. . . .

This, one feels, is false construction. The convention of the mystery story assumes that whatever is consciously seen by the character is seen by the reader. It is for the author so to arrange matters that the thing seen shall give no more information than is intended. (p. ix)

Nevertheless, and this criticism notwithstanding, all the mysteries are, in the end, completely and convincingly cleared up, and the reader closes the book with the feeling that he has been honestly dealt with, and that all doubtful matters have been disposed of to his satisfaction. (p. x)

> *R. Austin Freeman, in an introduction to* The Mysteries of Udolpho, *Vol. I by Ann Radcliffe, J. M. Dent & Sons Ltd, 1931 (and reprinted by J. M. Dent & Sons Ltd, 1959), pp. v-xi.*

J.M.S. TOMPKINS   (essay date 1932)

[*Tompkins states that Radcliffe's novels are "unashamedly romantic, with no didactic intent." Tompkins stresses that Radcliffe contributed to the development of the psychological novel in her analyses of fear and adds that many of her prose passages are unmatched in eighteenth century fiction.*]

More and more one sees in [Mrs. Radcliffe] the focus of all the romantic tendencies of her time. She collected, combined and intensified them, harmonizing her work by picturesque beauty and quickening it with fear and awe. What in others had been timid and tentative, in her is bold and assured. Others had paddled toy-boats in the edge of the perilous seas; her great ship takes the tide with its flags floating and its mistress aboard; for she was unashamedly romantic, and did not pretend that she provided romance in the interests of instruction. Only Sophia Lee had dared such a voyage before, and she had sailed under the countenance of the long-suffering and much-abused muse of history.

The function of Mrs. Radcliffe's books was to exercise and recreate, in the first place, the mind of the writer and secondly that of the reader. They are the day-dreams of a mind at once fastidious and audacious, capable of energy and langour, responsive to beauty and to awe, and tremblingly sensitive to imaginative fear. They are also the work of a conscientious craftsman, whose technique is always respectable, and whose development in power and self-knowledge from the pallid *Castles of Athlin and Dunbayne* . . . to the assured romantic splendour of **The Italian** . . . is interesting to follow. Her audience was ready for her. Her themes were not new; but never had mountains and spectral music, defenceless beauty and the Inquisition, ruined manors, vaults, pilgrims and banditti been adorned with so much unfamiliar gorgeousness; never had there been such ample provision for the romantic mood, so pure in quality and so respectable in form. Here was romance that could be enjoyed by statesmen and head-masters without embarrassment. Here, moreover, was a novelty of technique which did effectively make of her books a new kind of fiction. . . . She excited in her readers, by combinations of suspense, mystery and surprise, the sort of interest that continually strains to the outcome of a scene. For the first time reading was an exercise to be undertaken with bated breath. . . . (pp. 248-50)

Her romances have a strong family resemblance. They play, for the most part, in glamorous southern lands and belong to a past which, although it is sometimes dated, would not be recognized by an historian. In all of them a beautiful and solitary girl is persecuted in picturesque surroundings, and, after many fluctuations of fortune, during which she seems again and again on the point of reaching safety, only to be thrust back into the midst of perils, is restored to her friends and marries the man of her choice. In all of them this simple theme is complicated by mystery and involved at some point in terrible, often supernatural, suggestions. It would be possible to classify all the ingredients of Mrs. Radcliffe's romances under the two headings of Beauty and Terror, and such a classification would have the advantage of keeping well in view the cause of her enormous popularity. . . . Beauty refines terror, connects it with dignified associations and prevents it from verging on disgust; terror in turn heightens beauty, like the thundercloud impendent over so many scenes in eighteenth-century engravings. Such a harmony is found in *The Italian* in the chapters that deal with Ellena's imprisonment in the mountain convent of San Stefano and her escape with Vivaldi. The magnificence of the mountain scenery; the rich pomp of the church and the tyranny it fails to conceal; the valiance of the lovers and their fear, culminating in the dreadful minutes spent waiting in the remote stone cell, where the straw mattress, seeming still to retain the pressure of a prisoner's body, forces the imagination to dally with the horrible, but never defined, doom with which Ellena is threatened; the momentary relief, soon quickened by renewed apprehension, when at last they begin their flight through the blazing moonlight;—these form an interwoven texture of beauty and terror, to which the reader's mind responds in fluctuations of anxiety and satisfaction. There had been nothing like it in the novel before. . . . (pp. 251-52)

The indispensable elements for producing such an effect were scenery, a Gothic building (or two, or three) and the sensitive mind of a girl, attuned to all the intimations, sublime or dreadful, that she can receive from her surroundings. It was this preponderance of atmosphere over passion, or, rather, this reduction of passion to be no more than a component part of the atmosphere, which, together with the fact that we never behold the naked form of terror, but always its image obscurely reflected in the victim's mind, differentiates Mrs. Radcliffe's books from Walpole's *Castle of Otranto,* to which her debt is otherwise capital and perfectly authenticated. . . . The *raison-d'être* of her books is not a story, nor a character, nor a moral truth, but a mood, the mood of a sensitive dreamer before Gothic buildings and picturesque scenery. Story and characters are evolved in illustration of this mood; and Emily at Udolpho and Adeline at Fontanville Abbey are, as it were, organs through which these grim places speak, placed there to receive and transmit the faint rumours that cling about them, comparable with their trembling sensibilities to Aeolian harps. When all is said, however, a novel is neither a picture nor a lyric, and something more than attitude went to Mrs. Radcliffe's figures. There is dramatic tension in the scene at Udolpho where, as Emily sits at dinner among the fierce guests, the poison rises hissing in Montoni's glass, and in a moment swords are out. Satire pleasantly ripples the romantic surface in the pictures of La Motte and Madame Cheron, and a touch like that of the elegant Marquis, swearing grossly at Adeline's escape, taking pleasure in inventing and expressing the foulest abuse, has a reality that cannot be reduced to the picturesque. For the rest, she provided sufficiently interesting variants of the beautiful and unprotected heroine, the "sensible" and gallant hero, the benevolent guardian and the Gothic tyrant, and filled up the background with soubrettes, brigands, ecclesiastics and faithful servants; and all these people develop, in her later books, a power of appropriate gesture and resonant phrase that carries them triumphantly through their strong scenes. It is not life, but it is coherent fantasy. (pp. 253-56)

She was herself a theorist. "To the warm imagination," she writes, "the forms which float half-veiled in darkness afford a higher delight than the most distinct scenery the sun can show." To describe is to limit and circumscribe the operations of the reader's fancy, but to suggest is to stimulate it by the intimation of a grandeur or a terror beyond the compass of words. This principle she carried as far as it would go. Her books are full of the half-revealed, of objects that are betrayed sufficiently to excite curiosity but not sufficiently to allay it, of hints and traces that lead the mind into a region of vague sublimity. Her heroine's beauty gleams through a veil and a slouched hat shadows her villain. The crowning grace of her landscapes is mist, and music, to exert its most delicious power, must be breathed invisibly on the air. Fontanville Abbey is first seen at twilight, when the desolate La Motte family shelter in the half-explored building; and, indeed, none of her Gothic edifices are ever fully known, even to their inhabitants, whose steps are always liable to stray, as in a dream, into unfamiliar apartments and down crumbling stairways. This deliberate recourse to suggestive obscurity is most noticeable and most important in her dealings with terror. . . . Briefly, Mrs. Radcliffe approached the terrible with all the tremors of a highly-strung nervous system. . . . She is the poet of apprehension. Her theme is not the dreadful happening—very often nothing dreadful happens—but the interval during which the menace takes shape and the mind of the victim is reluctantly shaken by its impendence. Sources of and parallels to her devices can be found in the Elizabethan drama, but the drama has no room for the slow subjection of the mind to terror. For that we must wait for the psychological novel, towards the development of which Mrs. Radcliffe made a contribution in her analysis of fear. . . . [In] tracing the growth of fear, Mrs. Radcliffe takes a few steps in the direction of that science that was to become the guiding light of fiction a hundred years hence. . . . Her study of abnormal mental states, however, is strictly limited by the bias of her own tastes and opinions. Of all the passions she studies only fear, and fear, through the intervention of her sense of dignity, never reaches such a pitch as to deprave the fearful. Her heroines are timid but steadfast. They have no enemy within; they are sure that innocence will be divinely shielded, and they never doubt their innocence. Those pits of agony into which Maturin cast a glance, where lie the souls of those who feel an involuntary pollution darkening their minds and dread lest their natures should conform to those of their persecutors, were beyond her scan. Under the pressure of fear Adeline, Emily and the lovers of *The Italian* remain devout, merciful and essentially courageous. Beyond this point terror ceases to be "a pleasing luxury," and dream passes into nightmare.

Terror does not play a large part in *The Romance of the Forest.* In this book Mrs. Radcliffe first reached her full strength, and to do so she retrenched on the exuberance of *A Sicilian Romance* and concentrated on a smaller field of incident. There is, as always, flight and pursuit, but her fancy lingers gladly with the lovely waif, Adeline, in the glades of Fontanville Forest and the mountains of Savoy, and the book was admired for its idyllic charm rather than its thrills. Darker threads, however, are woven into the fabric, and Adeline's finely-imagined dreams, when she is unwittingly brought near the room where her father was murdered, provide, with Vivaldi's dreams in the prison of the Inquisition, the only instances in the books published in Mrs. Radcliffe's lifetime in which the intimations from the twilight side of our nature are justified. The supernatural continually fascinated her imagination, but in most cases reason and prudence induced her to disown its promptings. In *The Mysteries of Udolpho* she devoted herself to elaborating at Udolpho and at Château-le-Blanc an atmosphere of supernatural awe. There is certainly too much of this, seeing that it is all a cheat, that Laurentini di Udolpho is still alive, and that smugglers were responsible for the disappearance of Lorenzo and the shaking of the black pall. She makes the mistake, as Coleridge pointed out in his review for the *Critical* [see excerpt above, 1794], of raising expectation so high that it cannot be satisfied. In *The Italian,* which is altogether better wrought than the more popular *Mysteries,* the supernatural suggestions are slight and fade away before the more substantial terror inspired by monastic tyranny and the Inquisition. On this ground also she preserved her delicacy of taste and her cult of obscure suggestion. Where precision would lacerate the imagination she is impressively vague, and Vivaldi in the dungeons of the Inquisition hears nothing but a distant groan, sees only some undefined "instruments," and though once stretched in preparation on the rack, never feels its strain. The secret of the effect of these slight touches on the reader lies, of course, in preparation. On the one hand, there is the picturesque elaboration of scenes appropriate to dreadful incidents—dungeons and caves and moonlit ruins; on the other, there is a skilful though too lavish employment of suspense. The mind is first disposed to contemplate the terrible, and then worked into a fever of fluctuating emotion. . . . Perils threaten and withdraw; lovers part and meet and part again; mysteries are suspected and explained, but the explanation is misleading; false trails are laid; confessions are interrupted—if only by the dinnerbell; sudden knocking alarms us—even if it is only the servant. The sophisticated reader soon finds these shocks tedious and refuses to answer to the cry of "Wolf, wolf," while even at the height of her fame, critics advised her to bridle her ingenuity; but it was just this sustained command of the reader's nerves that was new, at a time when even the best novels were short-breathed, and one recalls that Henry Tilney [in Jane Austen's *Northanger Abbey*] read *The Mysteries of Udolpho* in two days, his hair standing on end the whole time.

It is the vice of her method that scenes of raised excitement, where suspense is continually heightened by mystery and unexpected incidents, must be followed by patches of flat explanation. Her ingenious plotting was, however, on the whole, much admired. Like Walpole, though to a far greater degree, she roused, baffled and finally satisfied the detective interest in her readers. In *The Romance of the Forest* three mysteries are mooted, that of Adeline, that of the Abbey and that of La Motte, and in the end all three run together in the hand of the Marquis. Providence, however, is the elucidator, not the persevering ingenuity of man, and for a modern taste there is too much chance and too many futile mystifications in these books. Their appeal was not intellectual but emotional. The reader is not invited to unpick a knot, but to enjoy the emotion of mystery; the knot, indeed, is not unpicked at all; at the appointed hour an incantation is breathed over it, and it dissolves, for the methods of an enchantress are not those of Sherlock Holmes. (pp. 257-62)

Mrs. Radcliffe was certainly a poet, though her verses, with their confused colouring and lack of outline, are the least satisfactory expressions of her spirit, and even in prose her style is hardly supple enough to convey her emotion. The informal notes in her diary are more transparent, and occasionally in her novels she strikes out a phrase which by its concentrated imagery stands out from its context; such are the "gasping billows" of the storm in which Emily is wrecked, and Vivaldi's reproach to Ellena, when she weeps as she promises to marry him: "Should your tears fall on my heart now?" There are other passages where the lyrical quality is apparent in the feel-

ing, though often blunted in expression. Her sense of the transitoriness of human beauty and joy is poetic rather than didactic, and there is a passage in *The Italian* where Vivaldi, going to Ellena's house, is assailed by a sudden irrational fear that she is dead, which is parallel to one of Wordsworth's *Lucy* poems. The exultation of Ellena in her mountain prison, Valancour's [*sic*] dread lest he should forget the face of his beloved, Adeline in the Alps, walking, as it seems to her, over the ruins of the world, are passages to be matched in the poets, but not elsewhere in the prose fiction of the eighteenth century. She was indeed, as Scott called her, the first poetess of romantic fiction. She liberated fancy and quickened colour, and fancy and colour, thus restored, were not long confined to the Gothic Romance. She lived to read and admire the Waverley Novels, for which she had helped to prepare the way. (p. 264)

J.M.S. Tompkins, "The Gothic Romance," in his The Popular Novel in England: 1770-1800 *(reprinted by permission of University of Nebraska Press), Constable & Company, Ltd, 1932 (and reprinted by University of Nebraska Press, 1961), pp. 243-95.**

ERNEST A. BAKER   (essay date 1934)

[*Baker points out that Radcliffe's novels represent the "best phase" of the Gothic romance genre and that her lasting contribution to romance was her use of atmosphere. According to Baker, she used atmosphere consciously, as no other author before her had. Furthermore, Baker recognizes Radcliffe as "the last of the novelists of sensibility" in the tradition of Fanny Burney and Jane Austen.*]

The name of Mrs Radcliffe has become almost a synonym for Gothic romance, and her novels do represent the best phase of the genre, before it began to degenerate into the ghastliness of "Monk Lewis" and the elaborate terrorism of Maturin. (p. 192)

From beginning to end [of *A Sicilian Romance*] . . . it is not violent scenes of action, so much as nervous apprehension, vague foreboding, subjective feelings of suspense, in short, the morbid phenomena of sensibility, that torture the heroine and those who love her, and keep sympathetic readers on tenterhooks. The novel of suspense has definitely arrived. (p. 194)

The plot [of *The Romance of the Forest*] is intricate and ingenious; the main secret is well kept, and the disclosure comes with an adequate shock of surprise. But in detail it is mechanical, and improbable to the point of absurdity; the writer has neither the knowledge of life nor of history to produce more than a thin semblance of reality. Mrs Radcliffe seems to have been as ignorant of the ways of the world as her innocent heroines. Banditti are always lurking in the woods; she seems to regard them as a kind of local fauna. In themselves, the characters are null. She has no insight whatever into the mentality of her villains, who are simply dissolute, and therefore ambitious, rapacious, criminal. The good people are absurdly perfect. The heroine, here and elsewhere, is a prudish, stilted, over-refined creature, always blushing and fainting, always indelicately sensible of the proprieties; the heroine of the novel of sensibility further idealized. And the more exemplary characters of the other sex are an exact counterpart. (pp. 194-95)

Contemplation of the beauties of nature slides insensibly into longing for the simplicity and idyllic happiness of rural life. . . . Rousseau was, indeed, one of the influences that nourished and moulded the imagination of Mrs Radcliffe. . . . (pp. 195-96)

But her finest passages of descriptive prose are evidently attempts with words on paper to rival the painters whom she most admired, Poussin, Claude, Salvator Rosa, and, especially in the two later Italian romances, Guido Reni. (pp. 196-97)

In *The Mysteries of Udolpho*, long tours in quest of the picturesque alternate with exciting melodrama, and the two are skilfully harmonized by her sense of atmosphere. . . . [But her descriptions] remain vague and generalized, the effects depending on impressive adjectives used with a feeling for rhythm and sonorousness. . . . Mrs Radcliffe almost trespasses into the novel of personal relations, and almost achieves lifelikeness in the vulgar Madam Cheron, whose ambitions land her in such fearful disillusionment when she is married to the unscrupulous lord of Udolpho. But her genius is for something entirely different. The vast and gloomy and impossible castle frowning along the edge of a precipice in the Apennines is a magnificent stage for blood-curdling events; it reeks with terror, it thrills with suspense. . . . Mrs Radcliffe had as good a talent for grim interiors as for broad landscapes. (pp. 197-98)

As to the more sensational excitements, they are uniformly based by Mrs Radcliffe on the device of some shock of fright, horror, or perturbing mystery, the explanation of which is withheld. Often it is merely withheld from the reader; the actors in the drama are aware of it. . . . Would Mrs Radcliffe have been more impressive had she never explained away her mysteries? Sometimes it hardly matters, oftener it matters a good deal. The music haunting the woods round the castle, the face that glares from the bed-hangings, and the strange disappearance of Ludovico, lose their sorcery and their terror when we learn that the one was produced by the lover's lute, and the others were tricks of the pirates who had their headquarters in the French château. Sometimes the reader cannot help being annoyed when she gives him an unseasonable view of the sham background and the conjurer's bag of tricks, and the world of gramarye is abruptly exchanged for that of common sense and commonplace. In this very novel there is a discussion on ghosts, and Mrs Radcliffe refuses to take sides. She gives her readers their fill of trepidation without once standing convicted of supernaturalism, at any rate, until she wrote *Gaston de Blondeville*. (p. 200)

[In *The Italian*,] it is the unrelaxing tension of vague and inexplicable terror that is the master element, terror which as often as not arises from the terror-striking look of a place, a forest, a ruin, a mountain gorge, and by the writer's magic is wrought by a pen keeping time and tune with the incidents and the feelings into a harmony that enthralls. From the outset, the key is pitched high; the dialogue often rises into an artificial diction. . . . The rhetoric of the Inquisitors and their magnanimous victims in the sombre final scenes is yet more exalted; it is meant to reach the sublime. . . .

The great abbey [to which Ellena is carried away] with its church and cloisters, its labyrinthine vaults and corridors, its chanting priests and nuns, and hordes of pilgrims, is another Udolpho, and a fit theatre for the gloomy scenes and gloomier apprehensions that Mrs Radcliffe conjures up out of her antipathy to the Roman Catholics. (p. 201)

Gloom and terror are piled up in a grandiose climax; and with praiseworthy skill the revolution in Schedoni's mind at the discovery of his supposed child, and the deliverance of the lovers whom he now befriends, are interwoven with the revelations that lead to the conviction of the arch-criminal by the Inquisition. Nothing is hurried; hopes and fears and dread of the worst calamities are balanced on the razor-edge of suspense, until justice can be dramatically executed all round.

No doubt it is all very unreal. The pictures of convent life are a caricature to those who know anything about it. And Schedoni and the malignant priest who conspires with and then betrays him are stage figures, not human beings. Mrs Radcliffe was a quiet domestic lady who never had a narrow escape in her life; and her talk of banditti and condottieri, of stilettos, pistols, and trombones, the way they are handled and the wounds they deal, is patently and absurdly a pretence. The narrative of the escape from the convent of San Stefano will not beguile the most innocent mind if it stops to reflect. The reader now must with an effort do what the reader then did with the greatest ease, enter into Ellena's panic-stricken mind, or Vivaldi's, and be plunged into the chill current of dread and premonition. He must not resist the spell of the twilit caves and dungeons, the mellifluous incantation of the prose-poetry, the fascination of such tableaux as Schedoni's colloquy with the marchesa in the transept, or the pitiless judges and the masked agents of the Inquisition. He must submit and allow these visions to congeal the blood. Mrs Radcliffe knew that fear and even repulsion may, like pathos and tears, be pleasant ingredients in a sensational dish. But probably her most lasting contribution to romance was simply this which we call atmosphere. Landscapes, seascapes, picturesque ruins, skies and storms evoke it, and make the right psychical accompaniment to the emotional drama. It was not something absolutely new in fiction, but no one had used atmosphere before as a principal element, and no one had used it so consciously. (pp. 202-03)

[Mrs. Radcliffe's *Gaston de Blondeville*] brought a real ghost on the stage. . . . What makes the book her dullest, however, is less the unfortunate ghost than the tedious historical facts which she too conscientiously worked into it. Mrs Radcliffe had to make history conform to her own preconceptions, or else leave it alone. It may have been her consciousness of this that made her refrain from publishing it. . . . She was the last of the novelists of sensibility; it was her sensibility that responded so cordially to the dual appeal of romance and of natural scenery. Her stories are all sentimental dramas; the heroines—and her heroes are all heroines—are cast in one mould, sensitive, devoted, virtuous beings, of the well-known stamp. Propriety was her watchword as it was Fanny Burney's. . . . [Every] one of her novels provides a lesson, which is received and taken to heart through the impression upon our sensibilities. (pp. 203-04)

She was a firm believer in the sentimentalist doctrine that virtue never goes without its reward. (p. 204)

Ernest A. Baker, "The Gothic Novel," in his The History of the English Novel: The Novel of Sentiment and the Gothic Romance, *Vol. 5 (by permission of Barnes & Noble Books, a division of Littlefield, Adams & Co., Inc.), H. F. & G. Witherby, 1934 (and reprinted by Barnes & Noble, 1957), pp. 175-227.**

WYLIE SYPHER (essay date 1945)

[*Sypher detects beneath the surface of Radcliffe's work "a pattern of socio-economic contradictions, paradoxes, ambivalences, and ambiguity that affords some criteria of the greater romantics and of British romanticism generally." The principal ambiguity in* The Mysteries of Udolpho, *according to Sypher, lies between "aesthetic values and moral values."*]

If one can force himself to penetrate the obvious, there appears beneath the surface of Mrs. Radcliffe's gothic fabrications a pattern of socio-economic contradictions, paradoxes, ambivalences, and ambiguities that affords some criteria of the greater romantics and of British romanticism generally. Other romantics may be more consciously hostile to bourgeois morality, but Mrs. Radcliffe betrays herself more suggestively than the romantic intensely at discord with his environment. In her, one more readily comprehends the total situation—the bourgeois standards and the oblique negation of those standards. Mrs. Radcliffe has a complexity all her own.

Since her work is uneven, we may depend chiefly upon the novel that was and is her best known, *The Mysteries of Udolpho*. . . . (p. 51)

The customary historico-literary estimate of the *Mysteries* runs about as follows: that here are Beauty and Terror; that gothicism is apparent in Mrs. Radcliffe's mock-historical apparatus, in her naïve devices to effect "horror," in the obviously manipulated plot; that the sublimities of "nature" and the pantheistic rapture it inspires, the exoticism of the setting, and the pseudo-Byronic excitements are "romantic"; that the moralizing affixed to the preposterous story is a dull conventionality. From the psychological view there is additional interest because of the apprehension, suspense, and anatomy of sensibility.

From a socio-economic point of view Mrs. Radcliffe is more perplexing. Her actual performance may be artless to the degree of naïvete. This performance is possible, however, only by certain assumptions on the part of both Mrs. Radcliffe and her reader. These assumptions—the social context of the novel—form a scheme of ambivalence that amounts to paradox and indicates deep cross-fissures running through bourgeois-romantic consciousness itself, the result of a contradiction arising between the artist and society. What happens if one substitutes for the customary platitudes—gothicism, melodrama, sentimentality, mediaevalism, feeling for nature—another set of platitudes, an evaluation in terms of [the Russian Marxist philosopher] Plekhanov's dialectical materialism? According to the first system of platitudes the novel is simple; according to the second it is astonishingly equivocal. The disabilities inherent in Mrs. Radcliffe's bourgeois romanticism become very plain. Critically, the platitudes remain platitudes, of course; we are not concerned with them but with their implications, particularly in regard to the inherent "vulgarity" of an art that half retains, half rejects bourgeois standards. Mrs. Radcliffe, writing as a tradesman's daughter from the "quiet shade of domestic privacy," occupies personally a somewhat ambiguous position.

The thoroughgoing ambiguity in her novel lies between aesthetic values and moral values, the conservative or bourgeois values being moral, the aesthetic values being "romantic" and in a limited sense "revolutionary." Both orders of values are, ultimately, those of the bourgeoisie—the moral values in direct, the aesthetic values in inverse, relationship to that class. Insofar as the novel satisfies the bourgeois moral code, it is in danger of being aesthetically unattractive, and insofar as it succeeds in evoking its intended aesthetic responses, it is in peril of violating a bourgeois moral code. Possibly such an opposition can be resolved only in a non-bourgeois society.

Throughout the *Mysteries* the moral responsibility (one cannot call it gravity) of the author, of her characters, and of her readers stands opposed to their aesthetic irresponsibility (not to call it frivolity). So far as the characters—and the author

and reader—are morally exemplary, they embody or subscribe to bourgeois faculties for providence, caution, dependability, self-interest, discreet benevolence, and sexual reliability or "purity." So far as characters, author, and reader are regarded aesthetically, they embody or tolerate anti-bourgeois impulses toward improvidence, instability, imprudent benevolence, and, in the case of Valancourt, a sexual waywardness that amounts to vacillation rather than Byronic naughtiness. Mrs. Radcliffe viewed in the light of socio-economic relations is thus unintentionally subversive, unwittingly ambiguous—an implied priggishness is set against an implied bohemianism: caution/incaution, selfishness/generosity, purity/impurity, etc.

All such ambiguities are left as ambiguities, without being any further resolved than Tennyson resolved the ambiguities within "Locksley Hall" or than Gray did within the "Elegy." Historico-literary criticism, dwelling upon the mechanism and literary antecedents of the novel, is prone to ignore them. Nor do the ambiguities exist in any tension or any metaphysical balance or reconciliation of discordant qualities. (pp. 51-3)

Clearly Mrs. Radcliffe's romanticism differs from the Byronic, Shelleyan, or Wordsworthian one, since there is a mode of resolution in these poets, who consciously rebel against the bourgeoisie by contempt, utopianism, or retreat. Intuiting the bourgeois-romantic dilemmas—urban/pastoral, caution/incaution, selfishness/selflessness—they attempt a resolution by simplification; Wordsworth's resolution being pastoralism, Byron's incaution, and Shelley's selflessness. Such "revolutionary" romantics exist by their commitments, into which they are forced by reaction. Yet they remain only mirror-revolutionists, since their rebellion, lacking full awareness of the historical process and failing to adjust their ego to the external world, is superficial. Mrs. Radcliffe neither realizes her dilemmas nor commits herself to resolutions. Even a complete "literary" criticism should take account of her situation and discriminate on these grounds between her romanticism and the romanticism of the poets mentioned. Scott's novels would stand, perhaps, rather near those of Mrs. Radcliffe, and also other "romantic" works by Southey, Campbell, or Rogers.

The sentimental/unsentimental ambiguity underlies many other ambiguities in the *Mysteries,* and is determined by the opposition of aesthetic response/moral response. The basic aesthetic scale is one of sensibility in the eighteenth-century sense of the word. The basic moral scale is one of shrewdness. This essentially bourgeois dilemma . . . is resolved imperfectly by charity—benevolence. Yet benevolence itself is subject to prudential check. The novels of the later eighteenth century are forever insisting on the dangers of undiscriminating bounty. . . . Thus the novel is morally directed toward caution (enlightened self-interest) and a proper restraint of generosity while it is aesthetically directed toward an indulgence of sentiment to the degree of incaution. Socially this is an important matter, since, as Mrs. Radcliffe says elsewhere, conduct should be determined by principle, not feeling; and the application of principle to alleviating social distress leads to a program in which "to each according to his needs" is a materialistic morality motivated not by feeling but intelligence. (pp. 53-4)

Like all gothic romance, the *Mysteries* is projected into the past. It lacks the antiquarian mechanics of Scott's novels, though Scott exhibits the same sort of ambivalence that appears in Mrs. Radcliffe—writing upon different scales or levels of value, chronologically. . . . Prudential motives are transposed into a gothic *mise en scène*. As a historical novel the *Mysteries* cannot be taken seriously on any count. But we are not concerned with its failure as a historical novel. Socially this ambivalence is testimony of the alienation of the romantic artist. Mrs. Radcliffe, evidently unable to generate aesthetic values from her bourgeois environment, is forced to undertake what Ruskin or Carlyle or Morris undertook, to seek aesthetic gratification in the mediaeval, all the while maintaining, in whole or in part, prudential-acquisitive ethical standards. . . .

Associated with this chronological "fault" is Mrs. Radcliffe's amusing projection of British protestant, rationalist, bourgeois religious conviction into the atmosphere of mediaeval Catholicism. Nearly all her novels pass double judgment upon the conventual institutions so essential to the plots. Religiously Mrs. Radcliffe has no illusions about them: they are outmoded, benighted, and often wicked establishments that betoken superstition and popery. . . . Aesthetically the convent or monastery may represent quite different values. . . . (p. 55)

The question of what seems horrible to Mrs. Radcliffe raises a question of what is horrible in the whole gothic tradition of romanticism. . . . In her ingenuous way Mrs. Radcliffe specialized in horrors—confinement in charnel houses, the discovery of corpses in bizarre putrefaction, groans, worms, epitaphs, and all the graveyard goings-on that connote the "gothic." The social implications of such horror are not much examined. Authentic horror is horrible by its contexts. Psychologically, religiously, ethically the corpses in Mrs. Radcliffe do not signify. Death is a physically repulsive phenomenon. Death in the poetry of Donne or in Conrad's *Heart of Darkness* connotes a psychological horror of which Mrs. Radcliffe is barren. . . . In Mrs. Radcliffe and romantic writers proficient in the macabre, horror causes purely aesthetic reverberations so far as it is effective at all. . . . This sort of "decadence" is, in its extreme, a bourgeois effect. It signifies the ultimate alienation of the writer from society and attests an art socially and religiously bankrupt, one result of a system of "naked self-interest and callous cash payment." The situation can be accounted for by the ambiguity of Mrs. Radcliffe's moral/unmoral orientation. . . . [The closing platitudes in the *Mysteries*,] morally, have no bearing upon the aesthetic significance of the book—the specific aesthetic effect being that of horror. But the horror is extraneous to the morality, in a vacuum of "pure" horror. This customary bourgeois moral/unmoral dichotomy in art results in a morality without aesthetic import and aesthetic responses of limited moral significance; in other words, myth is deprived of its deepest, most human resources. (pp. 56-7)

Other ethical ambiguities are implicit in the *Mysteries,* notably the ambivalence of urban:bourgeois/pastoral:anti-bourgeois. The first terms condition the moral practices of the characters; the second terms condition their moral ideals. The bourgeois:urban virtues of diligence, poise, suavity, caution, calculation, sobriety are everywhere set against the anti-bourgeois:pastoral virtues of indolence, unsophistication, naive impulse, and the peasant-like innocence and improvidence transcendentally elevated by Wordsworth. (p. 57)

[The] arts themselves become otiose—testaments of leisure, and of the discord between art and society. In her room adjoining the greenhouse Emily kept "her books, her drawings, her musical instruments, with some favorite birds and plants. Here she usually exercised herself in elegant arts, cultivated only because they were congenial to her taste"—i.e., useless, and economically as insignificant as the arts really are in St. George's Guild or in the visionary society of Morris. St. Aubert and Valancourt read Homer, Horace, and Petrarch because a concern with Homer, Horace, and Petrarch is of no practical effect. The arts are thus a form of commodity-fetishism. (p. 58)

An especially "romantic" form of socio-economic callousness appears in the idyllic scenes of peasant life, and in Emily's insistence that "poverty cannot deprive us of intellectual delights—*so long as we are not in want of necessaries*"! . . . The pastoral response to peasants and starlight is actually an aesthetic one, although it implies social and religious attitudes. . . . [Further,] a bourgeois religious faith necessitates a God of reward and punishment, whereas Emily's pantheistic optimism gushes up from the simple Wordsworthian trust that nature never betrays the heart that loves her. Wordsworth, Shelley, Byron, Carlyle, Ruskin, Morris, along with eighteenth-century deists and men of feeling were victimized by the modern confusion of aesthetic with social and religious responses.

The superficiality of romantic rebellion betrays itself in the social:democratic/unsocial:undemocratic ambiguity that terminated in "romantic isolation"—Byron's protest that "to fly from, need not be to hate, mankind" because "all are not fit with them to stir and toil." The Byronic revolt is as inconclusive as that of St. Aubert who, disillusioned with bourgeois society, becomes a mirror-revolutionist. (pp. 58-9)

The most apparent schism between Mrs. Radcliffe's bourgeois sentimentality and bourgeois ethics occurs in her pages upon love and marriage. The aesthetic values of love, such as youth, sensitivity to nature, innocence, and distress . . . are counterpoised by concern for economic security, the proprietary gestures of the male, the "purity" of the female, and her helplessness. Adeline, in *The Romance of the Forest,* intimates the dilemma of the bourgeois heroine situated between (1) a wealthy but "immoral" marquis, and (2) Theodore, who ("Let us fly; a carriage waits to receive us") has rescued her from this same marquis. . . . The urban:bourgeois/pastoral:anti-bourgeois ambiguity is inherent in the relationship of all Mrs. Radcliffe's heroes and heroines. This ambiguity conditions, by attraction or repulsion, the nature of the Wordsworthian female growing in sun and shower, the Shelleyan sister:spouse, the Byronic victim:vixen, the Tennysonian *hausfrau*. Dimly understanding how "the bourgeois sees in his wife a mere instrument of production," the romantics protested by either sentimentalizing or emphatic unconventionality. Again, whatever romantic revolt occurs against proprietorship in woman is partial—a revolt by sensibility rather than by principle.

Now it is perfectly true that Scott, Byron, Wordsworth, Shelley, or Ruskin are often characterized by their differences from Mrs. Radcliffe. Yet their very differences are to be measured against the ambiguities implied in *The Mysteries of Udolpho.* The socio-economic milieu in which they thought and wrote was the same as hers. It was a milieu that subjected the writer, in England at least, to the necessity either of compromise (the escapist direction of romanticism is a form of compromise) or of intransigence. Mrs. Radcliffe is no intransigent, and her awareness of her predicament is so imperfect that she cannot be said to compromise. Her fiction is meaningful because it so inadequately conceals the naked contradictions intrinsic in bourgeois romanticism, a revolt so radically inhibited that it failed to be in a deep social sense creative. (pp. 59-60)

Wylie Sypher, "Social Ambiguity in a Gothic Novel," in Partisan Review *(copyright © 1945, copyright renewed © 1972, by* Partisan Review*), Vol. XII, No. 1, 1945, pp. 50-60.*

WILLIAM RUFF   (essay date 1949)

Ann Radcliffe liked to march her adjectives in pairs: in her works expressions are "artless and simple," her heroine remembers "in melancholy and dejection," and appearances are "forlorn and desolate." Women are either "tranquil and composed" or "disturbed and uneasy," and when they are uneasy they show it by "quitting the room instantly, their hands clasped in an agony of despair." I think Ann Radcliffe would have called her style one of "modest elegance," and she referred too often to "elegance and propriety of thought" to try anything novel in language. Her figures of speech were already dead when she used them, for her novels are the charnel house of the poetry popular in the eighteenth century, and if she occasionally uses a fresh image, time has killed its beauty, as time has ruined those situations which once "thrilled bosoms with a kind of pleasing dread."

What Scott reluctantly criticizes in Ann Radcliffe is her use of denouement [see excerpt above, 1824]. He says she cheats. . . . Actually he might have said that Ann Radcliffe was never sufficiently thrilling. She did not have enough gothic monasteries, not enough murders; her villains died too soon or reformed too easily; her castles have too few secret chambers, and even the Italian inquisition does not use enough torture; girls are pursued through wild forests but no one ever catches them; they are kidnaped but are returned intact; her heroes are sentenced to die but are reprieved before they reach the scaffold. In short, her novels do not have enough blood.

True, she might have tried to make what horrors she has more intense, but it would take an artist like Scott to do such a thing; Ann Radcliffe does not have the power. (pp. 185-86)

I am convinced that she thought of herself, not as a writer of "those improbable fictions that sometimes are exhibited in a romance," but as quite another sort, one who "writes books which elevate the mind, and interest the heart." She thought of her own mind as one "enriched with taste, enlightened by science, and enlarged by observation, a benevolent, mild, and contemplative mind adorned by elegant literature." (At least, whenever she praises the taste in literature of her heroines, it is in these words.)

She was, in brief, a lady writing for ladies and gentlemen. And the work she did best might well be called the novel of taste. (p. 186)

One must, however, be fair to Mrs. Radcliffe in [the] matter of words. It is true she writes a dead language, but it is a clear one. There is no mystery in any of her books, no voice at midnight, no burning spear, no frightening picture, which she is not capable of explaining neatly and clearly. Never again will there be Ann Radcliffe's combination in fiction of cool temper and exciting incidents, of a discussion of the romantic and mysterious carried on with such cheerful lucidity. In her frigid tales of terror, clarity and good sense go with correctness and elegance, qualities which, of course, can allow no room for the supernatural.

And if it is true that she does not always build her stories to an appropriate climax and punish the wicked as a modern thriller would do, again she has the justification of taste. For good taste means that the wicked are wicked only so long as the story demands it; when virtue is ready to triumph the villains are lightly dismissed. . . . Nothing to excess in an ending is Ann Radcliffe's rule, and it is a very ladylike one. (p. 189)

Like every writer of romance with an interest in correct manners, she warns us against that insidious form of fiction where readers are "resigned to the illusions of the page," and especially she dislikes "a sentimental novel on some fashionable system of philosophy." She furnishes her readers romance and sentimentality—with the warning that they are upsetting. "Don't eat sweets," she says as she hands over a five-pound box of chocolates. I think she was sincere in this distrust of novels for their effect on susceptible readers. She often talked of "the pure delights of literature," and she was not seduced into making them less pure. She disliked people or books with "qualities which throw a veil over folly, and soften the features of vice into smiles." And if no one in her time would write books denouncing such follies, she would supply the need herself.

Ann Radcliffe's fiction can be read today as the embodiment of good taste. Other novelists have talked about taste and elegance, but only Ann Radcliffe makes the two words so consistently the backbone of all her fiction. Even if she wrote gothic romances, the gothic trimmings interested her less than the moral principles she taught; she wanted to write in the grand tradition of eighteenth-century letters—and be a moralist.

The novel of taste, then, is Ann Radcliffe's contribution to English literature, for in three novels she has combined adventure with the most high-principled characters in fiction. She has made the best of all possible worlds; her subject is shocking and her morality flawless. No matter how often her story threatens to be about horrid deeds, her heroine stands in the foreground of her books, pure, tender-minded, elegant, and conscious of the etiquette each situation demands. (pp. 190-91)

William Ruff, "Ann Radcliffe; or, The Hand of Taste," in The Age of Johnson: Essays Presented to Chauncey Brewster Tinker, *edited by F. W. Hilles (copyright, 1949, by Yale University Press; copyright renewed © 1977 by Mrs. Frederick W. Hilles), Yale University Press, 1949, pp. 183-93.*

EDWARD WAGENKNECHT   (essay date 1954)

[Wagenknecht is an American literary historian, novelist, anthologist, and biographer. His best-known works are Calvacade of the English Novel *and* Calvacade of the American Novel, *literary histories of the development of the novel in England and America. Wagenknecht praises Radcliffe's talent for "developing suspense and terror against marvelously picturesque backgrounds." Her descriptions successfully intensify the moods of her characters, according to Wagenknecht. However, he believes that, aside from Schedoni, the hero of* The Italian, *she created no characters who could match her plots and that her attitude toward the supernatural is "unsatisfactory."]*

[Mrs. Radcliffe's] first book, *The Castles of Athlin and Dunbayne* . . . , is brief and unimportant. In *A Sicilian Romance* . . . , she begins to find herself, but the book is overplotted and crowded with hairbreadth escapes. *The Romance of the Forest* . . . is much better. As the title implies, it belongs to one of the loveliest traditions in English literature—The Robin Hood-*As You Like It* tradition. The deserted abbey in which the ruined, half-criminal La Motte and his family take refuge together with Adeline, the girl so strangely entrusted to their care, provides a splendid background, and while the love-story is conventional enough, the tortured La Motte himself is an interesting character.

Such was the success of *The Romance of the Forest* that Mrs. Radcliffe's next book was awaited with breathless interest. When *The Mysteries of Udolpho* appeared in 1794, it can hardly have disappointed many readers. The plot is loosely knit, but the atmospheric background against which the exciting story unwinds is wide and impressive, and the development of the terror-theme while Emily is virtually held prisoner in the Apennines is masterly.

Yet *The Mysteries of Udolpho* is not Mrs. Radcliffe's masterpiece. That honor was reserved for *The Italian*. . . . Like her other books, it deals with young lovers persecuted by entrenched wrong and terrified by nameless fears, but the malign monk, Schedoni, who pursues them relentlessly only to find his fate involved in theirs, is such a character as she had never achieved before. The posthumous *Gaston de Blondeville* . . . was distinctly an anticlimax.

Mrs. Radcliffe's historical coloring is of no importance. That is why her first novel, with its medieval setting, failed. She locates her castle on the "northeast coast of Scotland, in the most romantic part of the Highlands," she gives her characters a few Scottish names, and then she imagines she is through. Actually, no matter what her period, she never gets out of the eighteenth century. The past fired her imagination but she never took the trouble to acquire any information concerning it. She is much less the scholar even than Charlotte Smith, who was so proud of her knowledge that she paraded it in footnotes.

But when it comes to developing suspense and terror against marvelously picturesque backgrounds, then Mrs. Radcliffe need apologize to nobody. It is true that we can no longer believe, as we once believed, that no novelist ever had this feeling for background before her, nor yet that she evolved her pictures wholly from within, but that is not important. The point is rather that what she did was done with marvelous skill. And it is greatly to her credit as an artist that passionately as she loved scenery, she never described it for its own sake; we get it always as it inspires and as it intensifies the moods of her characters.

She had a psychological interest in terror, which she distinguished sharply from horror. The first, not the second, is the source of the sublime: it "expands the soul, and awakens the faculties to a high degree of life" [see excerpt above by Mrs. Radcliffe, 1826]. We have had a hundred and fifty years of experimentation along this line since Mrs. Radcliffe laid down her pen; no doubt the modern reader will feel that she sometimes lacks subtlety. (pp. 118-19)

One reason for Mrs. Radcliffe's immense popularity was that she gratified the current taste for terror without ever violating the gentility, the sensibility which the times prized. It is not what happens in her books that terrifies us but only the fear of what may be about to happen. All her heroines are variants of the same noble type; her favorite word to indicate conduct of which she disapproves is "coarse." When Emily is imprisoned at Udolpho her maid gets hungry, but Emily herself is much too refined to think of eating. Prudery actually inspires grandeur in Mrs. Radcliffe's heroines; they achieve an impressive severity whenever they find it necessary to oppose their superior delicacy to the comparative commonness of the pursuing male. And they have the habit of coyly pushing the indelicate suggestion of early marriage far away from them on the basis of wholly fantastic scruples, even when in so doing they let themselves in for much additional misery (and the reader for many more thrills). When in *The Romance of the Forest* Adeline thanks Theodore for his generosity, he replies frankly, "Ah! call it not generosity, it was love!" And the tone of the scene is so delicate that the reader is almost shocked.

Mrs. Radcliffe's extreme sensibility does not help her with the modern reader, but this is not her most serious defect. Her real trouble is that except for Schedoni she created no character who is good enough for her plots. Her dialogue is unnatural, "refined." (p. 120)

[Her] attitude toward the supernatural is unsatisfactory also. It is like her attitude toward the Roman Catholic Church, which fascinated her as an artist and repelled her as a woman. She must have supernaturalism; she cannot get her best effects without it. But since she is a cultured lady of the Enlightenment, she must attempt the impossible task of saving her cake and eating it too. In *A Sicilian Romance*, Madame de Menon does indeed discuss the whole psychic question in a scientific, open-minded way, but the same can hardly be said for Mrs. Radcliffe's own comments in *Udolpho*. Except for *Guy de Blondeville* [*sic*], where she does have a bona fide ghost, her aim seems to have been to follow the bad example of Smollett and Clara Reeve (not Walpole's good one), and to offer at the close of her book neat naturalistic explanations for all the wonders the reader has met. . . .

Even where no question of the supernatural is involved, Mrs. Radcliffe sometimes "manipulates" her materials too obviously. (p. 121)

It is at least a question whether she does not usurp special privileges . . . when (as in the case of the Black Veil or the two dreadful lines in the St. Aubert manuscript [in *The Mysteries of Udolpho*]) she withholds from the reader vital information which the characters are allowed to possess. At the end of [*The Mysteries of Udolpho*] we are told what it was that the Black Veil really concealed. It was a realistic wax effigy of a human body in a hideous state of decomposition. Emily's single glance left her with the impression that this was the actual corpse of a former inhabitant of the castle whom she suspected Montoni of having murdered. As a matter of fact, however, it was created for another person altogether to aid him in his penance! Thus the most famous incident in *The Mysteries of Udolpho* turns out a gratuitous thrill, entirely unconnected with the action of the book. (p. 122)

> Edward Wagenknecht, "The Renascence of Wonder," in his Cavalcade of the English Novel: From Elizabeth to George VI (*copyright © 1943, 1954 by Henry Holt and Company, Inc.; copyright renewed, 1971, by Edward Wagenknecht; reprinted by permission of the author*), Holt, Rinehart and Winston, 1943 (*and reprinted as his* Cavalcade of the English Novel, *revised edition, Henry Holt and Company, 1954, pp. 110-33*).*

DEVENDRA P. VARMA (essay date 1957)

[*In the most in-depth treatment of Radcliffe's works to date, Varma writes that, of all her novels, he values* The Mysteries of Udolpho *most highly. Though* The Italian "*is a stronger piece of work in plot and characterization and displays more purely intellectual powers,*" *and is* "*the high-water mark of her achievement,*" *it is, Varma thinks,* "*less enchanting and has not the same glamour of love and romance*" *as* The Mysteries of Udolpho. *Varma also discusses the manner in which Radcliffe's characters are subordinated to atmosphere and scenery and criticizes her explained endings. Arguing for Radcliffe's literary significance, Varma points out that "the inclinations of her poetic sensibility foreshadow the period of the coming Romantic Revival."*]

[*The Castles of Athlin and Dunbayne*] is of no great length and may be regarded as an essay, a first step; but, with the exception of the supernatural, it contains in embryo all notable elements of Mrs. Radcliffe's romances. The slight sketch of Baron Malcolm "mighty in injustice, cruel in power", was to be the ancestor of fierce, picturesque characters like Montoni and Schedoni. We can also trace in this work some germs of that taste and talent for the wild, mysterious, and romantic which she was to employ with such powerful effect. Although it is a wild tale with improbable, strained, disconnected, and confused incidents, where incredible events follow each other in quick succession, yet there is in its atmosphere a feeling for nature, a power of imagery which anticipates finer things to come. (p. 87)

The setting of this tale is "in the most romantic part of the Highlands of Scotland" during the dark ages, but there is no effort to describe either the manners or scenery of the country. However, the picture of the castle itself is striking. . . . The novelist does not name a specific period as the setting, but endeavours to maintain an atmosphere of feudalism and the Middle Ages, by constant references to fortified castle sieges, armed vassals, dank dungeons, and threats of arbitrary executions. In spite of the goodly number of old towers, dungeons, keeps, subterranean passages, and hairbreadth escapes, the story has little veracity; and it appears as if the author had caught a glimpse of the regions of romance from afar, and formed a dreamy acquaintance with its recesses and glooms. The story lacks historical accuracy, but then most of the descriptions evolve not from original sources in ancient documents, but from the author's own imagination.

Her characters are made sensitive to the influence of scenery, as when the imprisoned Earl finds the view of distant hills a "source of ideal pleasure". They dwell among picturesque landscapes bathed in faint moonlight and swept by tumultuous gusts of wind. A shipwreck occurs on the coast in the atmosphere of stormy blasts, broken clouds, white foam, and "deep resounding murmurs of distant surges" of which Mrs. Radcliffe was particularly fond. Nor do we miss the parting sun trembling on the tops of the mountain and the softer shades falling upon the distant countryside, or the sweet tranquillity of evening that throws an air of tender melancholy over the mind, hushing sorrows for a while. She strikes here a new note in romantic fiction, and appears to be undoubtedly influenced by the fashionable enthusiasm for Ossian.

Although Mrs. Radcliffe does not introduce either the supernatural agency or superstitious terror in this romance, yet she raises terror and anguish to romantic heights by "dreadful silence" and horrors of darkness and loneliness, by the prolonged fear of death and by harrowing descriptions of hairbreadth escapes, by alternate suffusions of hope and the chilly touch of fear. She maintains this atmosphere of sublimated fear by obvious devices: obstacles are multiplied in order to depict a further interval of despair, an additional thrill of hope; and the total impression is forceful. (pp. 87-8)

Her next work, *A Sicilian Romance* . . . , marks a notable advance in exuberance and fertility of imagination. . . . The descriptions are fanciful and the narrative impressive, and Mrs. Radcliffe obtains a bird's-eye view of all the surface of that delightful region of romance, picturing its winding vales, delicious bowers, and summer seas, but is unable to introduce

the reader individually into the midst of the scene, to surround him with its luxurious air, and compel him to shudder at its terrors. The softer blandishments of her style, which were scarcely perceptible in her first work, are now spread forth to captivate the fancy. Her genius, which felt cramped in the bleak atmosphere of the Highlands, in her first novel, now blossomed forth in the luxurious climate of the sweet south. Indeed, the title of this work evokes an atmosphere of idyllic "Sicilian fruitfulness". (pp. 88-9)

Suggestions and stray hints thrown out here and there show the novelist's first grasp of the masterly power of presenting terrific incidents and scenes in later works. . . . The author is gradually learning to awaken the throbs of suspense by mysterious suggestions, and makes powerful use of subterranean passages, trap-doors with flights of steps descending into darkness, Gothic windows that exclude the light, the sobbing wind, and the wild haunts of Sicilian banditti.

Adventures are heaped upon adventures in a quick and brilliant succession, and the reader is hurried from scene to scene, through stirring incidents, in a state of bewildered excitement and curiosity. The escapes, recaptures, encounters with banditti, appear to have no credible sequence. The work has distinct traces of defects natural to an unpractised author. (pp. 89-90)

[Yet, the] imagery and the scenery relieve the tension created by fast-moving action, and the total effect is like that of a splendid Oriental tale. (p. 90)

There is a gradual improvement in the novelist's technique: the sufferings endured are more prolonged; the escapes attended with more difficulty and consequent suspense. Poetic justice and moral virtue triumph as usual. Here she also employs superstitious terror, and introduces phenomena ostensibly supernatural, but later explained away, a device which becomes a distinguishing mark of her work. The mysterious lights and noises that disturbed the castle of Mazzini she traces to natural causes, the secret of which is skilfully kept unrevealed until almost the end of the tale. There is, also, in this romance, emotional background as in the first novel, with moonlit romantic scenes, of fearsome forests and caverns, of stones and long reverberating peals of thunder, as circumstances demand.

The Romance of the Forest . . . is a far better planned and regulated work, in which we are aware of the first dawn of her mature powers. She begins her conquest of the fanciful and enchanted land of romance, although her range is yet small, and her persons limited. She harnesses her fancy to the pattern of a regular tale, and all the time keeps a masterly grip upon the reins of the story. She concentrates on a smaller field of incident, and exhibits a skill in handling materials and introducing to the imagination her tissue of mystery and terror. She displays the faculty of controlling the wild images which float around her, and investing them with consistency and truth.

Our interest is awakened by the very first hurried midnight flight of La Motte and his family to an unknown destination; then sustained by incidents following in quick succession—the heroine introduced in extraordinary circumstances; the charming forest scenes surrounding the deserted abbey of St. Clair offering a delicious asylum to the persecuted outlaw; his fears of discovery, his clandestine visits to the tomb; the vast solitudes of Fontanville; its wood-walks and valley glades glistening with morning dew. Mrs. Radcliffe shows especially a greater skill in her presentation of the desolate abbey. She touches the imagination with descriptions of the decaying ruins of ancient grandeur which evoke the eerie aspects, the weird abode of "powers unseen, and mightier far than we". She seizes upon the popular taste for scenic description which Gray and Rousseau encouraged. The impressions of the sylvan scene are delineated in poetic language. Extremely beautiful are her descriptions of the luxuriant woods, the huge-girthed oaks, the romantic glades and avenues, the tangled mazes and far-stretching vistas, the rippling stream winding past the grassy lawns, the delightful flowers, and "the sweet melody of feathered songsters mingling with the music of the waters in one harmonious cadence". (pp. 91-2)

Although the narrative of *The Romance of the Forest* is well constructed, and the intricacies of the plot excite a deep interest in the story, this work is more admired for its idyllic charms than for its thrills. It does excite and gratify a pleasant curiosity, but fails to dilate the imagination or curdle the blood. Darker threads are, however, woven into the fabric. In plot and atmospheric suggestion this novel marks a great advance on the former two, but although perhaps faultless in execution, it remains an attempt of an inferior order to *The Mysteries of Udolpho* or *The Italian.*

The Mysteries of Udolpho . . . , the most popular of Mrs. Radcliffe's works, exhibits all the potent charms of this "mighty enchantress". . . . It is a book which it is impossible to read and forget. Its noble outline, its majestic and beautiful images harmonizing with the scenes exert an irresistible fascination. It gradually rises from the gentlest beauty towards the terrific and the sublime.

In *Udolpho* Mrs. Radcliffe works on a broader canvas, on a larger and more sublime scale, enriches the characteristic traits of her genius, and perfects all her peculiar machinery. She has now conquered the enchanted land of romance and appears quite familiar with its massive towers and solemn glooms. . . . She presents the objects of beauty and of horror through a haze, which sometimes magnifies and sometimes veils their true proportions. The story abounds with more frequent instances of mysterious and terrific appearances. The intrigue is elaborated in a vaster framework, the villains are darker and fiercer, the castles more gloomy, the mysteries more impenetrable, the terrors more dreadful, while the beautiful young heroine, virtuous and innocent, endures a persecution crueller than before. The events are more agitating, the scenery wilder and more terrific. The scale of the landscape is equally different; the quiet, limited, woodland scenery of *The Romance of the Forest* forms a contrast with the splendid, highly wrought descriptions of Italian mountain grandeur in *Udolpho.* . . . Even *The Italian,* her next romance, although it is a stronger piece of work in plot and characterization and displays more purely intellectual powers, is less enchanting and has not the same moonlit glamour of love and romance. (pp. 93-5)

There is a mystic vagueness about the lovely landscape setting of Udolpho seen for the first time. Its gloom at nightfall, the ominous picture of its sombre exterior and shadow-haunted halls prepare us for the worst when we enter its portals. Our anticipation is a queer mixture of pleasure and fear, as we shudder at the impending events within its walls. Mrs. Radcliffe prepares each tragic denouement by sketches and panoramic views, which provide a backcloth for the enactment of the awe-inspiring horrors that follow in quick succession at Udolpho. (p. 95)

The romance is rich in striking effects, but its shortcomings are many and obvious. Although the thread of mystery becomes more and more intricate, and the author admirably manipulates her effects, so that the solution is held back until the last moment, the superstitious horrors are assigned to apparently very simple causes, and explained away by circumstances provokingly trivial. Appearances of the most impressive kind continually present the idea of supernatural agency, but they are at length accounted for by natural means. . . .

None the less the pall that moves in the funeral chamber, or the curtain which no one dares draw, strongly evoke our interest, and we feel the quickest throbs of curiosity. We have been affected so repeatedly, the suspense has been so long protracted, and the expectation raised so high, that no explanation can satisfy, and no imagery of horrors can equal the vague shapings of our imagination. (p. 97)

[*The Italian*] is probably her finest work, the high-water mark of her achievement. The story is more skilfully constructed, has a greater unity of plan and concentration than *The Mysteries of Udolpho,* while her pictures are more individual and distinct, her figures more terrible, and her situations more thrilling and vivid. Although the Inquisition scenes during the later chapters are unduly prolonged, the story is coherent and free from digressions. Mrs. Radcliffe did not copy nor repeat herself. . . .

The story commences in an impressive manner; unlike the tender and beautiful beginning of *The Mysteries of Udolpho,* it at once excites anxious curiosity and inspires us with awe. (p. 98)

The story develops in a series of dramatic, haunting scenes, which stand out in bold relief. . . . (pp. 98-9)

The episodes in the vast prisons and dungeons of the Inquisition are fraught with fear of bodily torture almost eclipsed by an apprehension of the supernatural, and Mrs. Radcliffe deepens the horror of this gloom by a whisper of things yet more terrible and evokes fear of the unseen. The Monk, who haunts the ruins of Paluzzi, and who reappears in the prison of the Inquisition, speaks and acts like a being from the world of spectres. The circumstances are contrived with admirable effect to heighten, vary, and prolong the feeling of curiosity and terror. Apparently endless agony of physical torture in the dungeons of the Inquisition is awfully suggested by the author's solemn and weighty style. (pp. 99-100)

This novel added a unique portrait to the gallery of Gothic fiction: Schedoni, the masterly plotter and murderer. . . . He is a character agitated by passion and will, whose actions are the mainspring of the plot. The wooing of Ellena by Vivaldi, is overshadowed by this dark and mysterious character, an interesting study in psychology, whose dominating figure is invested with an air of mystery. His spirit and personality envelop the entire atmosphere of the tale. (p. 100)

The only merit of [*Gaston de Blondeville*] is that here Mrs. Radcliffe makes the first use of supernatural machinery. In this very romance she gratified herself by introducing a true spectre. And the manner in which the supernatural agency is conducted, deepens the general regret that she had not employed it in her longer and more elaborate productions. (p. 101)

Her ingenuity fostered a new style of romantic fiction distinct from the poetical marvels of conventional tales of magic and chivalry or the realistic manner of Richardson and Fielding. Yet the wondrous and the credible are both woven into her fabric: the gossamer dreams of bygone times across the grim realities of her own days. She had not the art of stimulating the fancy by deft, light sketches of life and manners. Her most powerful effects are gained by the passion of fear, and this base emotion is raised to the dignity of romance. In the silence of nature we listen to echoes from beyond the grave, and with a tremulous eagerness we follow the sequence of events. She fascinates and appals us at the same time, and stirs up those secret springs of mortal apprehension which join our earthly existence and our spiritual self. This art is not melodramatic, but is very similar to the essence of tragic power, "which is felt not merely in the greatness of the actions, or sorrows, which it exhibits, but in its nice application to the inmost sources of terror and pity".

She approached the terrible with all the tremors of a highly strung nervous system, by working upon the sensations of natural and superstitious fear and making artistic use of obscurity and suspense, which remain the most fertile sources of sublime emotion. She skilfully selected and described scenes and figures precisely tuned to the feelings she sought to awaken. (pp. 101-02)

She excited the imagination by supernatural apprehensions, by phantom effects and half-heard sounds. In her hands the gusts of wind, the creaking door, even the sound of a common footstep became sources of terror and mystery. The crude machinery of Walpole's story—secret trap-doors, sliding panels, spiral staircases, and subterranean vaults—in her hands became artistic instruments to evoke an atmosphere of suspense and beauty.

She was skilful in producing terror by awakening a sense of mystery. The sequence of her narrative is so managed that it moves our minds to a feeling of impending danger, and we hold our breath in suspense. Her vast, antique chambers have about them a sense of unearthly presences; where an ominous silence prevails; where echoing footsteps die away in prolonged gloom, and where phantoms lurk in dark corridors, and whispers come from behind the tapestry, as it flutters in the gusts of wind. . . .

Strange occurrences that seem not of this world's ordering surprise our prudence: she knows the chord of feeling she must touch. Instead of exhibiting a succession of magnificent glooms, which only darken the imagination, she whispers some mysterious suggestion to the soul; and in nothing is her supremacy so clearly shown as in the wise and daring economy with which she has employed the instruments of fear. . . . (p. 102)

Her artistic use of suspense was different and distinct from the method of Richardson and Fielding who shaped the incidents in their novels to fit into a general plan or design. Also, in the picaresque fiction, the novelist had introduced action for its own sake, but Mrs. Radcliffe used 'action' for complicating the tissues of plot and then resolving them. (p. 105)

It is perhaps the vice of her method that scenes of raised excitement, where suspense is continually heightened by mystery and unexpected incidents, are followed by patches of flat explanation. A variety of startling phenomena resolved into petty deceptions and gross improbabilities, disappoints the fancy and shocks the understanding of the reader. (pp. 105-06)

She would have gained artistically had she left its existence a possibility: the simplicity of her explanations destroys the mystery. The supernatural continually fascinates, but in the end is proved to be a cheat. (p. 106)

Her suggested mysterious terrors, and the feelings they arouse until the moment of explanation, make one feel the full impres-

sion of the world of shadows although she stops short of anything really supernatural. She may dismiss her alarming circumstances in a matter-of-fact way; nevertheless she sends a chill down our spine. (pp. 106-07)

[The] technique of suspense was refined by her pen. In the works of Richardson and Fielding the interest of the novel was geared to the chief character, while Mrs. Radcliffe developed suspense until it predominated over character and became the main motif of the story. . . .

Her passion for the mysterious, the weird and eerie, was intensified by her love of romantic scenery, and a romantic passion for night and solitude pervades her pages. Her vivid glimpses of such landscape are as impressive as her terrible agencies of dread.

Her quick and accurate eye with a masterly power of observation captured all the naked grandeur of the external world, and fixed ever in beautiful images and scenes the varying tints or fleeting shadows of nature, spreading before our vision lovely fairy prospects. She looked at scenes with the eye not of a philosopher, but a landscape painter. (p. 110)

Atmosphere and scenery provide the whole focus of interest in the novels of Radcliffe, while the characters, like the figures in a landscape, are subordinated to effective scenes. The function of characters is to focus and enhance the sentiment of the scene: they are distinguished only by such features as are appropriate to their setting of dark battlements or rocks and trees. The scenes reflect the emotions of her characters; the gloom darkens when the incidents move towards a tragic catastrophe, and a warm sunshine spreads with the moods of happiness and security. . . . The chief interest perhaps does not lie in the characters of Emily and Montoni, or in the conflicts of Vivaldi or Adeline; it is the southern landscape that enchants us, whose cumulative effect is heightened in the happy musings of lovers or in their terror-stricken flight. The castles and the convents remain complete expressions of the victim as well as the tyrant. (pp. 113-14)

[Mrs. Radcliffe] establishes thus a concord in literature between man's mood and the changing aspect of nature, and gives an appropriate setting not only to the evil emotions, but also to the feelings of joy or content or love. The love of landscape is reflected in all her heroines, who purify their souls in the beauty of frequent dawns and sunsets, and draw fortitude and patience from the divine order of nature. The dominating force of atmosphere over passion is the cumulative effect of the landscape. At times, terror is obscurely reflected in the victim's mind. Changes in the moods of nature harmonize with the terrors of the heroine. The savage wildness of the mountain scenery or the dim shades of unexplored forest vistas exclude human aid and darken solitude. (pp. 114-15)

[Mrs. Radcliffe's] passion for romantic scenery, and her poetic treatment of landscapes, opened up new resources to the art of the novelist. She enlarged the scope and domain of prose fiction by liberating fancy and quickening colour. . . . The inclinations of her poetic sensibility foreshadow the period of the coming Romantic Revival. (p. 117)

In Mrs. Radcliffe's work there is the finest flowering of the novels of Terror. She eclipsed for a while the geniuses of Richardson, Fielding, and Smollett, but her own star dimmed at the ascendancy of Walter Scott, the Ariosto of the North. (p. 128)

Devendra P. Varma, "Mrs. Ann Radcliffe: The Craft of Terror," in his The Gothic Flame *(reprinted by permission of the author), Arthur Barker Ltd, 1957, pp. 85-128.*

FREDERICK GARBER (essay date 1968)

[In Mrs. Radcliffe's novels] characters themselves, for the most part, occur again and again as stock figures in predictable relationships and thus in similar plots. When the young man with his precipitate passions meets his female counterpart, they immediately love; love has to happen quickly in these novels since the tight pattern of the Radcliffean mode cannot function without it. The conventions begin in the nearly unreadable *Castles of Athlin and Dunbayne* and accrete until they hit a peak in *The Mysteries of Udolpho*, though they change significantly in *The Italian*. With the invariable youthful innocence of the principal sympathetic figures, with their sufferings, temptations, and eventual painfully acquired knowledge, it becomes clear that Mrs. Radcliffe's novels fit comfortably into the form of the *Bildungsroman*, the novel of education. All of the naïve heroes in this form go through an apprenticeship and initiation into the facts of the world as the author sees them. To this extent Mrs. Radcliffe's moral comments are inevitable and necessary, since with all their paraphernalia and conventions her novels unquestionably present life as it appears to her. When she writes in *The Italian* of Ellena's 'generous heart and inexperienced mind', the phrase summarizes neatly not only what the heroine is like but, as we can well predict, what she will go through in order to become experienced. No matter how happy the heroes and heroines turn out to be at the end, they are always more than a little battle-scarred. Yet the final relation of Mrs. Radcliffe's world to its readers (especially those with more than a century and a half of distance) has nothing directly to do with any moral concerns or, for that matter, with anything so urgent as a concern. Nor, on the other hand, does our complex delight in her novels rest merely in the pleasure of excitement over what happens next, since, apart from wondering how the heroine is going to be extricated from *this* difficulty, we have no doubt as to what ultimately is going to happen.

The basic pleasure in Mrs. Radcliffe's romances comes from a suspension of disbelief that leads to an enjoyment of the world of her fiction in and for itself. Cheerfully anachronistic in the tastes and attitudes she bestows upon her heroines, Mrs. Radcliffe is equally inaccurate in her descriptions of monastic life, the historical surroundings, and, we are told by some critics, even in the landscapes she describes. But this annoys us no more than it would in a fairytale or an opera. In fact, the quite improbable poems her heroines come out with have their exact counterpart in operatic arias. Historical realism has as little relevance to her manner as would fully rounded characters, whose unpredictable activities would only get in the way of the total effect. Her fiction has other laws. Scott pointed out, quite correctly, that her characters are generalized members of a class, and remain subordinate to the scenes in which they appear [see excerpt above, 1824]. This is an autotelic world of high artifice, where neo-classical concerns with the imitation of nature have less importance than the combination of effects that produces a self-sufficient harmony. One might say that character, landscape, morality, and decorum combine with emotion and event to make up the tone or atmosphere that emerges as the essential quality of Mrs. Radcliffe's world, a quality most difficult to achieve and to hold in balance. She

herself could not always do it. But when she did, and was at her best, no one could rival her in capturing and sustaining that atmosphere.

Perhaps the closest generic analogy appears in the fairytale, where the parallels indicate the nature of other appeals that her work can still offer. Those same neat and arbitrary moral distinctions we see in the romance occur in the tales, where we never doubt as to the rightness or wrongness of either side. Both genres present beings in human form (the wicked witch and the abbess, the ogre and the villainous count) who are able to wield demonic powers and cause the innocent to suffer for a while. Evil, in romances and fairytales, comes about through jealousy, lust for absolute power, love of tyranny, or perhaps no other reason but joy in malevolence. (pp. ix-xi)

With [Schedoni] her blacks and whites became complicated and grey. Schedoni is a many-sided figure, the triumph of her imagination in a book that frames him beautifully.

As a whole, and not only in its villain, *The Italian* shows an interesting shift in Mrs. Radcliffe's ideas of the Gothic, though the shift is by no means a radical change. The plotting returns to the tightness of the earlier *Romance of the Forest,* while the effects depend less on conventional paraphernalia such as the grisly reproduction of a decaying corpse in *The Mysteries of Udolpho.* The allegedly supernatural plays almost no part here, and when it does it is used mainly to emphasize Vivaldi's personality. Mrs. Radcliffe puts more stress in this book on elements like dialogue which . . . serves here primarily to reveal character and advance the action. On the other hand, *The Italian* was not meant to be a conventional realistic novel: it is still recognizably in Mrs. Radcliffe's Gothic mould.

Her instincts led her to play down certain aspects in order to make the novel conform to the personality of its central character. Monastic life, naturally gloomy and severe to her sociable nature, combined with the half-explained mysteries of Catholicism and the barely glimpsed horrors of the Inquisition to create the atmosphere for an intense experience of the sublime. But these qualities, which had appeared sporadically in her other novels, do not wholly explain the tone of *The Italian.* The book itself is stark and bare in its outlines and lack of adornment, quite without the clutter and complications of her earlier novels. So is its villain. From the first page of the introduction (symbolic in its depiction of a murderer within the bosom of the Church), solemnity and restraint define the tone and thus the very nature of our experience of *The Italian.* Even the descriptions of landscape occur less frequently, and without extension. What defines the book is Schedoni's personality which, like his room, is more austere than one would expect of an ordinary monastic. His monasticism, in fact, only emphasizes further the basic qualities of his personality: unlike Montoni or the Marquis de Montalt, he is no luxuriant, self-indulgent nobleman, though he had, significantly, been so. The other villains one can understand; their horrors are clear. His are not, because they are more within himself than in what he does to other people. With a difference of this sort *The Italian* could not help but diverge from the patterns of the other novels.

The book has its weaknesses, of course, and some of the expected absurdities. But one should not, because of these, ignore the great scenes studded throughout it, where what could have been melodramatic becomes brilliantly dramatic: as several examples, the tortured discussions between Schedoni and the Marchesa, the scene in which Vivaldi rants while Schedoni stands staring at the floor, the ominous ballet on the beach where Schedoni and Ellena pass back and forth before each other like comets about to collide. Even the scenes of the Inquisition, garish as they sometimes are, have moments when the inexplicable and therefore horrifying omnipotence of the tribunal recalls nothing so much as Kafka's Joseph K. [in *The Trial*] standing before the court that is judging him. . . . Something more than a Gothic thriller, then, *The Italian* has within it the elements of tragedy; but Mrs. Radcliffe's imagination was of the kind to create a mood and not a tragic fall. . . . Schedoni's agonies are unlike those of his Gothic predecessors. He made possible for Mrs. Radcliffe a novel that goes beyond the artifices of Gothic towards other dimensions. (pp. xiii-xv)

> *Frederick Garber, "Introduction" (introduction, notes, bibliography, and chronology © Oxford University Press 1968; reprinted by permission of Oxford University Press), in* The Italian; or, The Confessional of the Black Penitents *by Ann Radcliffe, edited by Frederick Garber, Oxford University Press, London, 1968, pp. vii-xv.*

LYNNE EPSTEIN (essay date 1969)

[*Epstein explores the relationship between Radcliffe's depiction of landscape and her acquaintance with three seventeenth-century landscape painters: Salvator Rosa, an Italian, and the French artists Claude Lorrain and Nicolas Poussin. She concludes that in her landscape descriptions Radcliffe "strikes an exquisite balance between decorum and moral sense on the one hand, and sentiment, benevolence, and sublimity on the other," and that in being able to achieve this balance, she owes much to Claude, Rosa, and Poussin.*]

Mrs. Radcliffe could not draw her images of nature from her native England because the simple, quiescent English scenery she knew failed to meet her need for the exotic. She therefore turned to the effulgence of the south of Europe. For her, as it was to be later for Thomas Mann (*Death in Venice, Tonio Kroger*), the South became the favored clime for tumultuous human passions.

To Mrs. Radcliffe Nature was a cryptogram for Man. Her heroes are all "peculiarly susceptible to the beautiful and sublime in nature"; her villains embody the "triumph of art over nature," the predominance of specious and ephemeral values over real and enduring ones. At times, to be sure, the landscape seems to constitute a mere backcloth, but even this background scenery exists to feed the protagonist's sensibility, to "reanimate" her spirits, awaken her enthusiasm, and elevate "her mind to . . . sublime complacency." The purely descriptive passages, moreover, bespeak the "certainty of a present God" and "lift the soul to their Great Author." We "contemplate with a feeling almost too vast for humanity—the sublimity of His nature in the grandeur of His works." Not only are character and environment impregnated with each other, but Nature itself is often the real protagonist.

Mrs. Radcliffe's Nature inspires that terror which, according to Burke, was the foundation of the sublime, the astonishment which "is that state of the soul in which all its emotions are suspended, with some degree of horror." Burke converted the taste for terror into an aesthetic system which certainly conformed neatly with the increasingly sensational tastes of the age. Mrs. Radcliffe, as a true disciple of Burke, favored beauty "accompanied by such shapes of grandeur as verge upon the sublime," shapes of grandeur which are commensurate with Burke's elements of sublime terror (privation, vastness, infin-

ity, difficulty, light and darkness, noise). Her landscapes of "beauty sleeping in the lap of horror" excite in her characters "a sense of sublimity rising into terror—a suspension of mingled astonishment and awe," and the oxymoronic sense of "pleasing dread" and "exquisite misery." Furthermore, inasmuch as sublimity is contingent not only on qualities abiding in the natural object, but also upon psychological and even physiological causes in the observer, imagination is quite as important as direct observation itself. . . . In describing foreign scenery, however, in the works (*Romance of the Forest* and *The Mysteries of Udolpho*) which she wrote before she went abroad in 1794, she relied not only on her imagination but also on the paintings of Poussin, Claude, and Rosa, which were completely attuned to her own artistic sensibility.

In painting her melancholy evening landscapes, Mrs. Radcliffe was inspired by Claude Lorrain, who was preoccupied with achieving a subtle luminosity that pervades his landscapes. His minute analyses of the quality of light according to the season of the year and even the hour of the day, and his feeling for horizons and boundless space, enabled him to imbue the image of nature with an elegiac mood that must have had a direct appeal to Mrs. Radcliffe. (pp. 109-10)

Like Claude, Mrs. Radcliffe is particularly intrigued by sunrise and sunset on the wavelets of a lake. Claude discovered the richness of contemplation of an immensity of light and space, and Mrs. Radcliffe is awed by the "grandeur of the wide horizon," the "flood of light," and the "glories reflected on the polished surface of the waves." (p. 110)

Furthermore, just as Claude's landscapes, expansive and atmospheric, are filled with a light that permeates the forms and softens the outlines of trees and architecture, so the "innumerable tints and shades, some veil'd in blue mists, some tinged with rich purple, and others glittering in partial light," impart "luxurious and magical colouring" to Mrs. Radcliffe's scenes. The predominance of sunlight in Claude is reflected in the "saffron glow" that suffuses Mrs. Radcliffe's landscape. The distant mountains (e.g., in Claude's "Narcissus and Echo") captured in transparent, silvery, shimmering tones, are the counterpart of Mrs. Radcliffe's mountains enveloped in a lustre of haze.

Night for Mrs. Radcliffe is a source of beauty as well as terror, and the moon, like a theatrical spotlight, illuminates from behind "dark and tattered clouds" the grim pursuer swiftly overtaking the fleeing, trembling heroine. The "pitiless pelting" of storms which wrack the night threaten man, yet fill his mind with enthusiasm. . . . In the same spirit the lone soldiers in Rosa's "Landscape with Soldiers" seem paralyzed with awe by the sublime terror of a night storm.

The resemblance between her storm scenes and Poussin's "Landscape with Pyramus and Thisbe" (1651) is even more striking. . . . The turmoil and disorder of Poussin's storm is a counterpart to the sea tempest that nearly drowns Emily and her fellow travellers [in *The Mysteries of Udolpho*]. The swirls of dust are tantamount to the tossing white foam of the waves, and Mrs. Radcliffe's dark storm, like Poussin's, reveals the personalities of those involved. . . . In Poussin's famous "Landscape With a Snake" (1648), subtitled "The Effects of Terror," he dissects terror by demonstrating the contagion of fear and terror as they pass from the hideous death scene to each successive group of figures, . . . which parallel Mrs. Radcliffe's "pleasing dread" and "exquisite misery." Terror is intensified by nature's serenity. The unbroken stillness of the lake reflects buildings and mountains with almost frightening precision; the effulgence of nature and the calm glow of the mountains are unremittingly counterpoised against the chaos of death and of man's mind. The same contrast is found in Mrs. Radcliffe: "The contending elements seemed to have retired from their natural spheres, and to have collected themselves into the mind of man, for there alone the tempest reigned."

Mrs. Radcliffe's romances also embody a most sincere enthusiasm for the sea. Her sensitivity to its beauty—to the delicacy of its evanescent effects, its vagrant gleams of color, its interplay of light and darkness, and its quality of transparency and luminosity—evidences her indebtedness to the paintings of Claude and Rosa, for she herself never personally experienced its "vast expanse [of] rolling waters" until after she had written [*Romance of the Forest* and *The Mysteries of Udolpho*]. To neo-classicism uniformity and regularity were a necessary ideal; Mrs. Radcliffe's oceans are amorphous, romantic, tumultuous—foreshadowing the mystic, inscrutable waters of [Herman Melville's] *Moby Dick*. Bounded by a Rosian chaos of rocks and falling cliffs, the ocean invoked in her "a sensation of unmixed terror [which] superseded that of sublimity." Indeed, of all "the grand objects which nature had exhibited, the ocean inspired her with the most sublime admiration." (pp. 115-17)

The forest, "with all its grandeur and luxuriance" but with "nothing . . . that is formal," becomes a symbol of Mrs. Radcliffe's virtuous people, who, like Rousseau's Émile, are children of nature, "simple and grand, like the landscapes among which they moved." Their minds are "delicately sensible to the beauties of nature . . . unbiased by intercourse with the world." Her villains, on the other hand, are insensitive to nature and are associated with the unnatural ostentation of the formal garden. Emily's aunt [in *The Mysteries of Udolpho*], perverting Nature's "stile of elegant simplicity," cultivates a garden in which trees are decorated with "a profusion of lamps, disposed with taste and fancy." (pp. 117-18)

The quiet woodland scenery of *Romance of the Forest* is in striking relief to the "gloomy grandeur" of the Italian mountains of *The Mysteries of Udolpho*. (p. 118)

Scenes of terror derived from mountain landscapes which threaten destruction to man are drawn from Salvator Rosa, whose savage "land of fearful enchantment" was ever-present in Mrs. Radcliffe's mind. The trees in his "Landscape with a Cascade" and "Landscape with Two Figures" are groaning giants, twisting and turning, inextricably bound in the throttling embrace of the vines that wind around them. The forest is a veritable torture chamber in which Rosa stretches his arboreal bodies on granite racks. Nature casts a death-pale shadow on Rosa's men, and in his "Landscape with Two Figures" the trees, with tentacle boughs ominously reaching out to strangle the two dwarfed men, seem to protrude from the painting. Mrs. Radcliffe's descriptions are often prose reproductions of Rosa's paintings, and she declares, early in *The Mysteries of Udolpho*, that hers were scenes such "as Salvator would have chosen had he then existed, for his canvas."

The Romanticist of the Gothic novel, Mrs. Radcliffe walks rather in "fairyland than in regions of realities." Her characters are stylized and lack psychological depth precisely because the romancer presents not real people but types. For it is Nature who is the real protagonist who dons the faces of the grand, the sublime, the beautiful. We are interested in the places which Scott describes because we associate them with his characters;

Mrs. Radcliffe's people are significant because of the natural situation or the place in which they happen to be. And it is in her depiction of these "natural" scenes that Mrs. Radcliffe's consanguinity with the three landscape masters—Claude, Poussin, Rosa—is most apparent. (pp. 118-19)

Although *Romance of the Forest* and *The Mysteries of Udolpho* are encumbered with redundant natural descriptions and stilted rhetoric, although their heroes are often equally stylized, these novels represent Mrs. Radcliffe's significant contribution to literary tradition largely because of their landscapes. Her eighteenth-century reason strikes an exquisite balance between decorum and moral sense on the one hand, and sentiment, benevolence, and sublimity on the other. And it is in this balance that her indebtedness to the landscape artists Claude, Rosa, and Poussin plays so large a part. The gothic excesses of Rosian landscapes are tempered by the pastoral serenity and controlled beauty of Claudian nature. "Learned" Poussin, with the juxtaposition of sublime grandeur and terror in his landscapes with the immanent precision and decorum of his art, achieves the ideal which eighteenth-century art was later to define as "occult balance." (pp. 119-20)

> Lynne Epstein, "Mrs. Radcliffe's Landscapes: The Influence of Three Landscape Painters on Her Nature Descriptions," in Hartford Studies in Literature (copyright © 1969 by the University of Hartford), Vol. 1, No. 2, 1969, pp. 107-20.

ROBERT KIELY (essay date 1972)

[*Comparing Emily St. Aubert, the heroine of* The Mysteries of Udolpho, *with earlier heroines of the English novel, Kiely finds that Emily is unique because "both the moral and material aspects of her ordeal are subordinated to the struggle which takes place within her mind." Kiely argues that the achievement of the novel is "the projection of the nonrational mentality into a total environment"; in this, Kiely asserts, Radcliffe "has succeeded in doing something new for the novel."*]

Neither the originator of the Gothic novel nor its most daring advocate, [Mrs. Radcliffe] nevertheless produced works which have come to be counted, with Walpole's novel [*The Castle of Otranto*], among the ancestors of English romantic fiction. Her gently euphemistic prose, her fainting heroines, and explainable ghosts were reproduced by other writers so quickly and on such a large scale that they were clichés before they had time to become conventions. (p. 65)

Like *The Castle of Otranto, The Mysteries of Udolpho* . . . is set in the past, 1584, and in Catholic Europe, France and Italy; the plot is involved, events are extraordinary and often violent; the cast of characters includes sensitive gentry, talkative servants, and a band of swarthy outlaws; . . . and the central image and most commanding physical presence in the novel is a Gothic castle. (p. 66)

Although the architecture of the castle is described in considerable detail, one is more aware of it as a random assemblage of ramparts, arches, towers, galleries, and corridors than as an aesthetically unified whole. But what distinguishes Mrs. Radcliffe's castle (and therefore her book) from Walpole's is not merely the quantity of information, but the kind of information and the manner in which it is presented. The Castle of Udolpho, unlike the Castle of Otranto, is placed in a natural setting and seen primarily through the eyes of a single major character. Ann Radcliffe takes that middle realm of nightmare presented in such hermetic confusion by Walpole and tries to place it in relation to an objective reality and an individual point of view. The fading light of the sun and the fears of Emily St. Aubert give a shape to Udolpho which has little to do with architecture.

Critics have often pointed out that in the writings of Mrs. Radcliffe nature is a stationary backdrop before which pass sentimental heroines of the sort which can be found in a large number of earlier eighteenth-century novels. To some degree this is true. When introducing a place where a major character lives or even stops for a few hours, Mrs. Radcliffe is likely to present a guide-book description. The views, usually encompassing enormous distances, are presented with the distinctness of telescopic vision on an extraordinarily clear day. . . . Presumably, nature is dependable, logical, and it rewards investigation. In order to understand abrupt natural changes or seemingly mysterious phenomena, it is simply necessary to study, to learn from experience, to move in closer and examine in minute detail, as St. Aubert does by collecting various species of plants. In the fiction of Mrs. Radcliffe one is either very close to or very far away from nature; one either "botanizes" like St. Aubert, gaining practical wisdom, or one muses from afar, like his daughter, discovering images of order and harmony everywhere. Emily St. Aubert loves to contemplate mountains, but Mrs. Radcliffe rarely fails, especially in the early chapters of her book, to place "gloomy pine" and "tremendous precipices" in perfect balance with "soft green pastures" and "simple cottages." "On the whole," the author wrote in her travel journal, "I prefer rich beauty to wild beauty." Human beings may become wild, confused, and unbalanced, but nature, if seen from the proper perspective, does not.

In the first chapters of the novel there is a great deal of attention paid to the peaceful landscape of Gascony where Emily St. Aubert lives quietly with her parents. The country, we are told, gives comfort, consolation, and wisdom, while the city fatigues and corrupts. (pp. 66-8)

Despite the painstaking descriptions, [Mrs. Radcliffe] seems, in the main, to be adhering to a neoclassical tradition rather than introducing new ideals into fiction. But to stop here is to fail the novel by treating its descriptive parts as isolated romantic poems manqué rather than placing them in the context of the whole narrative. For, if Mrs. Radcliffe shows obvious neoclassical influence in subordinating concrete particulars to moral generalizations, she reveals an equally strong inclination in the major section of the novel to subordinate everything—natural vistas, moral lessons, and even art itself—to an individual state of mind.

Despite the conventional speeches about the grandeur of nature and its power to convey the presence of what Mrs. Radcliffe calls the "Deity," there are as the narrative progresses a gradually increasing number of instances which reveal the relative impotence of nature beside the projections of the human imagination. The countenance of nature may be improved or worsened by one's state of mind, but landscape itself, though pleasant to a mind in repose, has almost no power to change the temper of a mind already filled with its own sorrows or joys. (pp. 68-9)

Especially after the death of her parents, [Emily's] thoughts return again and again to death and *intrude upon* rather than derive superficially from scenes of natural beauty. A sunset viewed during a trip to Seaford, rather than inspiring admiration or serenity, creates anxiety in her and prompts a nervously hopeful prayer that "the Creator of that glorious sun, which never fails in its course, will not neglect us . . . nor suffer us to perish." (p. 69)

It is inaccurate to describe Mrs. Radcliffe's characters, especially her heroines, as passive creatures who merely react emotionally to their immediate environment. On the contrary, there are many environments, meticulously described by the author, to which they cannot react at all, and others, of a more obscure sort, to which they seem constantly to overreact. (pp. 69-70)

While all is relatively calm in her life and her mind, Emily can derive moral edification and a mild *frisson* from a contemplation of the sublime juxtaposed with the beautiful. . . . The real nightmare for Emily—the Radcliffean personification of "beauty"—is not that she will wake up and behold a beast, but that she will wake up to a chaotic landscape where the boundaries have become blurred, where the sublime and the beautiful have fused and the integrity of her own role cast into doubt. (p. 70)

Mrs. Radcliffe's heroines are not always the simpering puppets which critical tradition has held them to be. They can, at times, be obsessive, implacable, and morbidly excitable women whose moods often make difficult situations worse. One might argue that the ease with which they become frightened is merely a sign of their general silliness and ignorance of the world, or that they are excitable because they have a special faculty for sensing danger, an intuitive ability to pierce through surface reality. . . . She may preach prudence, moderation, and universal harmony, but the potential fertility of that irrational state remains the most original and convincing aspect of Mrs. Radcliffe's art.

In the early chapters of the novel, the human mind, like the natural landscape, is presented as being composed of contrasting, even opposing, parts. Ostensibly, the moral lesson which justifies the telling of Emily St. Aubert's adventures is that of balance: reason against passion, sense against sensibility. "All excess is vicious," says St. Aubert early in Chapter II, and this, in different words, is about all he has to say, though the length at which he expounds upon this simple philosophy casts some doubt on his ability to practice what he preaches. In fact, the incongruity between human behavior and moral principles which increases as the book progresses is strangely prefigured in Emily's philosophical father. . . . In Fielding or Sterne, such contradictions would have obvious satiric overtones, but there is no irony in the manner in which St. Aubert is presented, and comedy is, of course, restricted to the servants. St. Aubert's deviations from his own rules only show, as he himself points out, the constant need for self-control even on the part of the wisest and most disciplined of persons. He may seem to us a nervous and morbid old man, but that is only because we do not at first share Mrs. Radcliffe's assumptions about the emotional excesses or utter barrenness of feeling which he could give into if he let himself.

The path which Mrs. Radcliffe's virtuous characters must try to keep winds literally between the madhouse and the graveyard—that is, between chaotic emotional release and an inhuman absence of feeling. (pp. 70-2)

Emily St. Aubert, the virtuous and sensitive heroine held prisoner by a relentless male, has often been called a Clarissa in Gothic setting. [The critic here refers to the title character from Samuel Richardson's *Clarissa Harlowe.*] The parallel is striking in a general way, but the differences in detail are more than a matter of sensational effect. In the first place, though various of Montoni's cohorts have amorous designs on Emily and though she is regularly menaced by abduction or rape, Montoni himself appears even less interested in her as a mistress than as a murder victim. If anything, Montoni serves as a restraint on the passions of his associates. . . . [Imprisoned] in a castle full of assassins, rapists, and thieves, the provocatively beautiful Emily, lodged in a bedroom with a door that cannot be locked from within, is spared a fate worse than death. In fact, the preservation of her chastity is not the central issue of the novel simply because the reader is never for a moment allowed to believe that Emily could be raped.

Sexual possession is hardly more of a moral problem in *The Mysteries of Udolpho* than it is in [Daniel Defoe's] *Moll Flanders*. Both heroines are, in a sense, unravishable. Indeed, if Emily is Clarissa Harlowe's sentimental sister, she is also Moll Flanders' indestructible cousin. Mrs. Radcliffe often calls our attention to the practical means by which Emily gets through each day despite her excited emotional state. On the superficial narrative level, the mystery of *The Mysteries of Udolpho* is not whether Emily will or will not be raped, murdered, or morally destroyed, but whether she will manage to extricate herself from uncomfortable situations of an increasingly bizarre and complicated nature. What we wonder about is not her virginity but her ingenuity under stress. There is undeniable gratification in knowing how she finds her way around the darkest recesses of the castle in the middle of the night; how she heats up her damp room, barricades the unlockable door, gains the sympathy of the servants, eavesdrops on secret conversations, and dines on figs and wine after having gone hungry during two days of slaughter among Montoni's men.

But though she has traits of both the practical and sentimental eighteenth-century heroine, Emily St. Aubert differs from them in one important way: both the moral and material aspects of her ordeal are subordinated to the struggle which takes place within her mind. Neither Montoni and his surrogates who threaten her virtue nor the "world" and its possessions have as much substance to her or to the reader as her own fears. Montoni differs from Lovelace because Emily hardly exists for him but also because he exists only in a distant and dreamlike way for her. Barricaded in her chamber with her books, drawing instruments, and lute, sending servants on errands, venturing into the corridors at night to catch glimpses of horrible sights and snatches of mysterious conversation, Emily half-creates her own Udolpho. (pp. 72-4)

Both literally and metaphorically, Emily is unable to see exactly where she is or what is going on around her. Friendly servants are mistaken for villainous captors because all are "figures seen at a distance imperfectly through the dusk." During the long period of her heroine's confinement in Udolpho, Mrs. Radcliffe's imprecise prose becomes increasingly less specific and denotative. Everything seen through Emily's eyes is envisioned through a dim blur; walls are "massy," ceilings "lofty," faces "menacing," and the corners of rooms invariably "remote." . . . Montoni does not curse in any common or specific way; he utters "inhuman expressions." Curiously enough, these euphemistic fragments serve as accurate indications of the state of Emily's mind as well as of the limitations of her descriptive powers. (pp. 74-5)

The little she does see both repels and attracts her: she is suspended between contradictory emotions in a mental state which makes rational perception, already impeded by circumstance, almost impossible. (p. 75)

The ghosts and horrors of Emily's imprisonment in the male world of Udolpho, however "logically" explained by Mrs. Radcliffe at the end, are the projections of hysteria. Emily

wants and does not want to know exactly what is going on in the castle; she wants and does not want Montoni to take more notice of her; and she wants and does not want one of his swarthy surrogates to come in the night and possess her. Mrs. Radcliffe justifies Emily's continuously putting herself in harm's way by defining the "faint degree of terror" she feels as one which "occupies and expands the mind, and elevates it to high expectation, is purely sublime, and leads us, by a kind of fascination, to seek even the object from which we appear to shrink." Not only does Emily tend to open unlocked doors and follow mysterious passageways, but she repeatedly reminds Montoni of her presence by sending her servant with messages to him, visiting him herself, and, on one occasion, throwing her arms around his knees to implore mercy.

Mrs. Radcliffe tells us more than once that Emily found Montoni and one or two of his friends "uncommonly handsome" despite their dark complexions and cruel expressions. (pp. 75-6)

Nothing drastic happens to Emily, either physically or morally. She does not die a martyr's death nor become the whore of outlaws. Imprisoned midway between the two extremes, she suffers the fate of the prototypical romantic character: deprived of a cathartic experience, incapable of tragedy, she is periodically immobilized by the imperatives of an imagination which transforms the limitations of present reality into a limitless future. (p. 76)

Emily's constant quests and narrow escapes seem merely outlandish unless we judge the narrative not in an historical but in a psychological context in which everything is possible and nothing is achieved. As Mrs. Radcliffe points out several times, Emily's life in the castle "appeared like the dream of a distempered imagination." As long as the dream persists, everything must remain possible, that is, without fulfillment—and the heroine's pursuers must be frozen in permanent chase. Though the minds which produced them differed vastly, Emily St. Aubert and the "still unravished bride" of Keats's Grecian urn have one thing in common: both are heroines to whom something is forever about to happen.

Even Emily's occasional periods of activity do not dispel the general atmosphere of hysterical paralysis. True, in her moments of self-composure, the Moll Flanders in her emerges, and she goes cannily about the business of self-preservation; but for every such hour there are days of weeping, fainting, and incapacity to act, and there are nights of sleeplessness and visions of ghostly presences. The hysterical heroine was not an invention of Ann Radcliffe's, nor does hysterical behavior have a particular importance for Romanticism except insofar as it exemplifies the power of the mind over external reality. The achievement of *The Mysteries of Udolpho* is not, then, the mere introduction of Gothic effects into an otherwise conventional sentimental narrative, but the projection of a nonrational mentality into a total environment.

One by one, Emily St. Aubert loses those anchors to objective reality which her father recommends as the only steadying influences on a highly "susceptible" mind. Like all romantic heroes and heroines, she is gradually separated from the world and imprisoned within her own consciousness. . . . Emily never gives up her ideal love of nature, but as an effective influence in her life, as a counterbalance to self-absorption, it nearly ceases to exist during her confinement in Udolpho. Yet Emily's resources are not totally exhausted. Without human or natural support, she turns to music and literature for consolation and order, but even art eventually fails her. . . . (pp. 76-8)

Emily, then, has almost nothing and no one to lean on, except one or two faithful servants. She is a romantic heroine largely by default. Having removed the rationalistic and objective supports so carefully enumerated in the early chapters of the novel, Mrs. Radcliffe leaves her heroine to the devices of her own mind which, admittedly, turns out to be a fairly dark and empty place, save for the presence of a few lascivious-looking but impotent spectres. There is nothing salutary, creative, or formative about Emily's interior experience. She does not emerge from her captivity in Udolpho with a fuller comprehension of the complexities of human nature or sympathy for its weaknesses: she is willing to dismiss Valancourt from her life at the first hint that he had gambled and caroused during his stay in Paris and, in fact, becomes so hysterical at the thought, that the poor fellow can never attempt to explain himself without causing her to become faint. Her idea of nature does not change either: she does not find a deeper rapport or a greater incongruity between herself and her natural surroundings, but resumes in the last pages of the book her never-ending walks in search of melancholy vistas and moral edification.

It must be understood that for the Radcliffean heroine, the romantic experience is not a desired initiation into a new reality but a temporary deprivation. She is not pictured beholding herself and the world with a new and powerful vision, but as one blindfolded and sent into momentary panic. The phantoms conjured up out of the darkness may be more or less entertaining, but when the blindfold is removed, there is the same orderly universe, bright and clear as it had been before—mountains distinct from valleys, virtue undaunted by vice. Mrs. Radcliffe's explicit moral, despite her penchant for romantic atmosphere, is antiromantic. What her heroines must do during their ordeals is not simply preserve their lives and their virginity—that they would do so is taken so much for granted it is hardly at issue—but they must "hold fast" in every way, keep every old idea and emotion intact, prohibit the darkness from informing their view of the day. All the weeping and fainting and fantasying, then, are supposedly the signs of an endurance test which proves that a well-instructed young lady can sacrifice her nerves without losing her principles.

Although Jane Austen was not in the least convinced by such reasoning, Sir Walter Scott and others thought this an excellent moral justification for the exaggerations of romantic fiction. . . . One cannot, of course, deny Mrs. Radcliffe her moral intentions, but it would be as difficult to claim for her a major role in the literature of prudential prose as to argue that her influence on Lewis, DeQuincey, Maturin, and scores of other romantic writers was primarily of a didactic nature.

If Mrs. Radcliffe taught anything to later writers, it was that a region other than that presupposed by rationality and a middle-class moral code might be accessible to novelists without their having to resort to the irrelevancies of courtly romance. Today her ruined abbeys and menacing foreigners may seem nearly as absurd as the artifices of seventeenth-century romance, but in their own time they were exaggerations of a relatively new kind for the novel and, even more important, they were placed in juxtaposition to subject matter and character types which could be found in the realistic fiction of the day. (pp. 78-9)

Like Walpole, Radcliffe meant to combine the excitement of earlier narrative and dramatic literature with the authenticity of the realistic novel. Oddly enough, the excessive conscientiousness with which she constructs the reasonable world outside Udolpho serves to weaken one's confidence in the reli-

ability of that world. The more elaborately "logical" her explanations of mysterious apparitions, the more we find ourselves becoming skeptical, not so much of the ghosts as of the explanations. She has shown all too well that there are crucial moments when neither reason nor faith in cosmic order is the central factor in the experience of an individual.

In *The Mysteries of Udolpho* she dismantles her heroine's rationally ordered universe with breathtaking thoroughness. The stability of human relationships is challenged; the harmonizing power of nature is challenged; the efficacy of art is challenged; and, most significant of all, the clarity of routine sensory perception is challenged. Despite other doubts, the reader is perfectly willing to believe that Emily St. Aubert is bereft and frantic. To the degree that Mrs. Radcliffe convinces us of that and constructs a physical setting which corresponds to an aroused emotional state, she has succeeded in doing something new for the novel.

The ghostly sounds and, even more, the elaborate explanations which set everything right at the end may not in themselves be wholly convincing. But then the preliminaries of total irrational disruption have been so vigorously begun that one can hardly expect things to be creditably reconstructed at once. The more profound and creative works of romantic fiction were to come later, but Mrs. Radcliffe had done more for the form than Gothic needlework. In her dark forests, ruined convents, and haunted castles, she had prepared whole regions bereft of reasonable certainties—"silent, lonely, and sublime"—where later heroes and heroines, more complex than Emily St. Aubert, would encounter shadows more interesting and consequential than those cast by the ambiguous Montoni. (pp. 79-80)

> *Robert Kiely, "'The Mysteries of Udolpho': Ann Radcliffe," in his* The Romantic Novel in England *(copyright © 1972 by the President and Fellows of Harvard College; excerpted by permission), Cambridge, Mass.: Harvard University Press, 1972, pp. 65-80.*

NELSON C. SMITH (essay date 1973)

[Mrs. Radcliffe's] best novel, *The Mysteries of Udolpho,* stands as an attack on the cult of sensibility. Near the end of *Udolpho,* when the servant Ludovico has mysteriously disappeared from a locked room, Mrs. Radcliffe writes, "it was difficult to discover what connection there could possibly be between [the disappearance and the existence of ghosts], or to account for this effect otherwise than by supposing that the mystery attending Ludovico, by exciting awe and curiosity, reduced the mind to a state of sensibility, which rendered it more liable to the influence of superstition in general.

This passage is central to an understanding of the serious purpose of Mrs. Radcliffe's novels: far from being an advocate of sensibility, she, like Jane Austen two decades later, shows its weaknesses and flaws. Not the least of these weaknesses is the fact that it reduces the mind, leading the imagination astray, away from reason. And when one departs from the rational, he naturally becomes more susceptible to the irrational, to superstition. Thus the Gothic novel was a perfect vehicle by which to show the extreme effects of sensibility. Mrs. Radcliffe could take the heroines of the sentimental novels, expose them to the conventions of the Gothic novels, and thereby show the defects of the former. In doing so, she manages to have her novels both ways: she can evoke the (for her) pleasurable emotions of fear and terror and then expose the rational causes to show the weaknesses of the sensibility which had given in to those emotions. (pp. 577-78)

The works of Mrs. Radcliffe, Miss Austen, and Miss Edgeworth, among others, clearly show the eighteenth-century concept of sensibility. But the modern meaning differs from Mrs. Radcliffe's; at least it has become more strict. The current pejorative meaning is that of a release of emotion, even an excess of emotion, and the cult of sensibility involved people willing to give themselves up to emotion. . . .

But the late late eighteenth-century authors did not know that they were writing novels of sensibility . . . , and though the term existed, it was neither so strict nor in such low favor. (p. 578)

[Sensibility], in its contemporary usage of compassion, sympathy, and sensitivity, was not in itself a decadent or despicable attitude. . . . But the excess of sensibility, the exaggerated emotional responses to a scene or action, the enjoyment of the emotion for its own sake—such as the mass weeping scenes in [Richardson's] *Clarissa,* Sterne's *Sentimental Journey,* [Mackenzie's] *The Man of Feeling,* and hundreds of less successful novels—were open to criticism from the time of Henry Fielding through to that of Jane Austen. . . . Mrs. Radcliffe's criticisms of . . . luxuriating in emotion do not possess the humor or the genius of Fielding or Miss Austen; but they nevertheless are clear, direct, and perhaps even more interesting. For she takes the typical heroine of sentimental novels and, using the techniques of the Gothic novel, reveals how such a state of mind brings about many of the terrors which the heroine faces. The cure for such an attitude, Mrs. Radcliffe makes clear, lies in a return to common sense. (pp. 579-80)

Like those heroines of the sentimental novels, Mrs. Radcliffe's main characters are all young, beautiful, and persecuted sometime-poetesses. They share with their fictional antecedents propensities for fainting—Mary, in *The Castles of Athlin and Dunbayne* . . . , faints nine times in forty pages, including twice in one paragraph—and weeping copiously. Indeed, sustained weeping was the truest test of the person of refined sensibility. But Mrs. Radcliffe varies the formula to fit the character. Emily, in *Udolpho,* weeps over the deaths of her parents, but neither she nor Ellena, in *The Italian,* dissolves in tears very often. Only Adeline [in *The Romance of the Forest*] luxuriates in the emotions raised by her misfortunes. . . . Adeline continues to weep throughout the novel and nearly loses the reader's sympathy because of her excessive self-pity. Her grief has another effect as well: it keeps her from learning the identity of her lover Theodore La Luc. (p. 581)

Emily, on the other hand, eases her grief over her separation from Valancourt and various other misfortunes, by exploring Udolpho. She cries only upon the deaths of her mother, father, and aunt, and upon the reflection that she will probably never see her lover, Valancourt, again after Montoni removes her from France to Italy. The scene of parting from Valancourt, however, is lightened by the advice of her aunt, the intensely materialistic and pragmatic Madame Montoni, who functions in the novel not only as an object of satire, but also as someone who criticizes the excesses of sensibility. . . . Mrs. Radcliffe makes fun of the aunt's "penetration" of the obvious [in her advice to forget Valancourt], but the criticism, though perhaps unjust, causes Emily at least to make her grief private. (p. 582)

But only by the actual end of the novel, some four hundred pages later, does Emily become properly chastized and sensible, for Mrs. Radcliffe has her most effective tricks left for

the tempering of Emily's mind: she has all the conventions of the Gothic novel to bring to bear as examples of the results of a mind made too susceptible by sensibility. . . .

Emily's sensibility, imagination and self-delusion combine, throughout the book, to produce the mysteries and terrors that confront her. Many readers point out that for all the gloom and mystery of Udolpho, nothing very terrifying really happens there: strange figures, black veils and "things that go bump in the night" make up most of the terrors. All that happens, indeed, results from Emily's being a high-strung heroine susceptible to the dangers of sensibility. (p. 583)

With the exception of the one finely realized scene at Montoni's banquet, where his wine suddenly hisses and boils over with poison and an accusing voice comes from nowhere, Mrs. Radcliffe maintains her point of view consistently with Emily so that all the terrors become magnified by her own sensibility and imagination.

Mrs. Radcliffe criticizes this youthful imagination throughout all her books. In *Athlin and Dunbayne,* for example, Matilda worries about her two children, Mary and Osbert, who "were arrived at an age, dangerous from its tender susceptibility, and from the influence which imagination has at that time over the passions." Later, the author continues, "as we advance in life, imagination is compelled to relinquish a part of her sweet delirium; we are led reluctantly to truth through the paths of experience." . . . In *The Italian,* Schedoni explains to the hero, Vivaldi, why he uses the supernatural to try to frighten the young man away from Ellena's house: "I trusted more to the impression of awe, which the conduct and seeming foreknowledge of that [specter-like monk who appeared to Vivaldi] were adapted to inspire in a mind like yours; and I thus endeavoured to avail myself of your prevailing weakness." Such weakness, Schedoni explains, consists of "a susceptibility, which renders you especially liable to superstition." . . . Mrs. Radcliffe constantly sets up her ideals as older, experienced people, not youthful heroes and heroines as susceptible to imagination as Vivaldi and Emily. (pp. 584-85)

[Emily's] sensitive imagination not only makes her more susceptible to superstition, it also increases her sense of self-delusion; though her senses of hearing and seeing at night seem overly developed, she has considerable difficulty in seeing things clearly, literally and metaphorically. (p. 585)

That she [sees ghosts] constitutes perhaps Mrs. Radcliffe's strongest criticism of Emily and, thence, of the excess of sensibility in general. (p. 586)

This criticism, perhaps more than anything else, accounts for Mrs. Radcliffe's explanations of the supposedly supernatural events, explanations which most critics find disappointing. . . . Mrs. Radcliffe's interest lies not in discussing the supernatural, but rather in exposing it in order to temper and chastize her young heroes and heroines, and her readers. As a champion of common sense, she must explain away the horrific effects, so that when they hear the explanations at the end of the novel, they will be ashamed of their absurd feelings. (pp. 586-87)

Finally, again in *Udolpho,* Mrs. Radcliffe plays with the stock Gothic convention of a mysterious heritage. She uses the device seriously in her other novels, from the awkward "strawberry mark" to identify the true heir in *Athlin and Dunbayne* to the more complex identifications of the family trees of Adeline and Ellena, both of which for a while seem to include the villain as the heroine's father. . . . Emily St. Aubert turns out to be the daughter of Monsieur and Madame St. Aubert, something everyone knew at the beginning of [*The Mysteries of Udolpho*]. Thus Mrs. Radcliffe ironically invents another mystery, one which turns on a knowledge of the Gothic convention of a mysterious background. This technique, too, undercuts Emily's role as heroine by making her position as secure and unquestionable as, say, Catherine Morland's [in *Northanger Abbey*].

All Mrs. Radcliffe's "heroines of sensibility," then, deserve criticism—for their self-indulgence, excess of sensibility, or untempered imagination—and all receive it directly at their author's hands. In every case, the standard by which Mrs. Radcliffe judges her characters is that of common sense. Excesses of any kind, including sensibility and romanticism, must be tempered by common sense. . . . [It] seems hardly fair to assert, as Harrison Steeves does, that "Miss Austen was the first to reassert with effect the importance of finding and maintaining the balance between judgment and emotion—or, to use her own fine title, between 'sense and sensibility.'" Mrs. Radcliffe establishes the difference nearly two decades before Miss Austen's published work. (pp. 589-90)

> Nelson C. Smith, "Sense, Sensibility and Ann Radcliffe," in Studies in English Literature, 1500-1900 (© 1973 William Marsh Rice University), Vol. XIII, No. 4, Autumn, 1973, pp. 577-90.

ELLEN MOERS (essay date 1976)

> [*Moers emphasizes "a locus of heroinism" in Radcliffe's Gothic fantasies, which later women "have turned to feminist purposes." Like Nelson C. Smith (1973), Moers recognizes the theme of the dangers of sensibility in Radcliffe's work. She also compares Radcliffe with Fanny Burney, and notes similarities in their treatment of "the horrors of a woman's life."*]

Ann Radcliffe, the greatest practitioner of the Gothic novel, was the most popular writer of her day and, in her moral views, among the most conventional. She is surely the last of turn-of-the-century writers to whom we would look for the expression of feminist doctrine. Nevertheless, the Gothic fantasies of Mrs. Radcliffe are a locus of heroinism which, ever since, women have turned to feminist purposes. Feminism and heroinism can often be seen to touch in women's literature, but they are not the same.

Ann Radcliffe began to write fiction at almost the same moment as Mary Wollstonecraft, and she too had an idea of female selfhood. But it was not the thinking woman, not the loving woman, but the traveling woman: the woman who moves, who acts, who copes with vicissitude and adventure. For Mrs. Radcliffe, the Gothic novel was a device to send maidens on distant and exciting journeys without offending the proprieties. In the power of villains, her heroines are forced to do what they could never do alone, whatever their ambitions: scurry up the top of pasteboard Alps, spy out exotic vistas, penetrate bandit-infested forests. And indoors, inside Mrs. Radcliffe's castles, her heroines can scuttle miles along corridors, descend into dungeons, and explore secret chambers without a chaperone, because the Gothic castle, however much in ruins, is still an indoor and therefore freely female space. In Mrs. Radcliffe's hands, the Gothic novel became a feminine substitute for the picaresque, where heroines could enjoy all the adventures and alarms that masculine heroes had long experienced, far from home, in fiction. (p. 126)

[There is a] particular kind of heroism, traveling heroinism, in the Radcliffean Gothic.

The travel motif in women's literature seems, however, to require separating into its two distant kinds: indoor travel and outdoor travel. Outdoor travel is imaginary planetary travel of the kind familiar to someone like Mrs. Radcliffe from the old romances. (We would be justified in surmising, if she did not tell us herself, that a "favourite volume" in the "little library" that the heroine carries about with her in *The Mysteries of Udolpho* is Ariosto's *Orlando Furioso*.) For outdoor travel the Radcliffe heroine becomes, in [Charlotte] Brontë's phrase, "the enchanted lady in the fairy tale," who flies through the air independent of the laws of gravity, time, perspective, and, certainly, of real travel. So Emily in *Udolpho* "travels several leagues" in the whisk of a phrase; sleeps one night "in a town on the skirts of Languedoc" and the next morning "enters Gascony." Without apparent effort she "ascends the Apennines," and from their heights easily espies the waves of "the distant Mediterranean."

The naïveté of her landscape painting makes one of the lingering, mysterious charms of Mrs. Radcliffe's fiction, which we moderns welcome as a touch of the surreal. It originated, as does so much of value to the literary imagination, in ignorance and inexperience. (pp. 127-28)

Indoor travel . . . is a more serious affair [than outdoor travel], because more possible for women; and Mrs. Radcliffe's inventive use of the Gothic setting for indoor travel produced a richer literary tradition. For indoors, in the long, dark, twisting, haunted passageways of the Gothic castle, there is travel with danger, travel with exertion—a challenge to the heroine's enterprise, resolution, ingenuity, and physical strength. (pp. 128-29)

It was *only* indoors, in Mrs. Radcliffe's day, that the heroine of a novel could travel brave and free, and stay respectable. Today young women make headlines by hijacking planes and carrying machine guns to bank robberies, but quite impossible for the Emilys and Evelinas of early women's fiction were the moderately adventurous outdoor activities by which, say, a Tom Jones could establish himself as a hero: blacking an eye, climbing a tree, fighting a duel, joining a regiment, poaching, roistering, and tramping. For heroines, the mere walking was suspect. "Whither have you been rambling so early?" asks Emily's aunt of Emily in the garden, near the start of *The Mysteries of Udolpho*. "I don't approve of these solitary walks." (pp. 129-30)

The Victorian woman writer's interest in Mrs. Radcliffe, long after her kind of mannered and genteel Gothic fiction had vanished from the literary mainstream, is a minor but interesting sign that women's literature flourished on its own traditions. More significant is the whole thrust in women's writings toward physical heroics, toward risk-taking and courage-proving as a gauge of heroinism, long after male writers had succumbed to the prevailing antiheroic, quiescent temper of the bourgeois century, and admitted, with whatever degree of regret or despair, that adventure was no longer a possibility of modern life. (p. 131)

We shall never know exactly why Mrs. Radcliffe shaped the Gothic novel as a structure for heroinism, but how she did so is at least worth a closer look.

In her best-known work, *The Mysteries of Udolpho* . . . , the narrative as a whole is designed to accord with the rhythms of a woman's life. Little critical attention has been paid to this shaping aspect of her Gothic, because the critics' attention, like that of Mrs. Radcliffe's vast popular audience, has been distracted by the isolated episodes of terror that make up the bulk of her *Mysteries:* the black veil, the burned manuscript, the mysterious nun, the ghostly musician, the living corpse, and so on. But she blocks out the narrative in terms of female childhood, youth, and faded maturity. *Udolpho* begins as an idyl—somewhere out of England, sometime in the past—the details are nothing, only the atmosphere matters: a muted, gentle, or—Mrs. Radcliffe's favorite meaningless word—a pensive serenity full of groves, streams, and vistas.

Emily's birthplace is in the valley—called La Vallée—where, after her brothers have conveniently died in infancy, and her mother has conveniently slipped away into a pensive death, Emily is left an only child, alone with her father, the perfect man. . . . Emily's father also dies early in the novel, but his influence persists as a moral force forever. It is the father who first warns Emily against the *dangers* of sensibility, a theme which pervades all Mrs. Radcliffe's fiction, to the surprise of her readers—for what is her Gothic novel, with its groans, shrieks, and tremors, but a subspecies of sensibility fiction? It is sensibility, however, with a difference. "Above all, my dear Emily," says the father, "do not indulge in the pride of fine feeling, the romantic error of amiable minds. . . . Beware of priding yourself on the gracefulness of sensibility. . . . Always remember how much more valuable is the strength of sensibility." The strength of sensibility is in fact what Mrs. Radcliffe's heroinism is all about.

Emily's father returns to play an important negative role, I rather suspect, in the person of the villain Montoni—one of those sinister Italian gentlemen that Ann Radcliffe found in the writings of her favorite English author (Shakespeare) but that she transformed into what looks very like a shattered mirror image of the impossibly good father of her imagination. Thus she seems to provide Emily with a father who is at one moment gentle, kind, and indulgent, and the next moment is whisked off the stage to be replaced by the father who is severe, demanding, nasty, and perverse. Montoni is of course not officially Emily's father; he plays the bad father role in his capacity of uncle by marriage. (Schedoni, the most splendidly sinister of Radcliffe's villains, in *The Italian,* is related to the fatherless heroine there by closer ties: he is her father's wicked brother and her mother's dreadful second husband.)

One critic of Mrs. Radcliffe, William Ruff, is so strongly impressed by her feminine bias that he wonders whether she should be considered a Gothic novelist at all, but rather a novelist of taste; and much closer in attitude than we have suspected to her apparent satirist, Jane Austen [see excerpt above, 1949]. . . . Leaving Jane Austen aside for the moment, I would suggest that where Ann Radcliffe writes about the horrors of a woman's life with a woman's sense of decorum, there she is very close to Fanny Burney, whose career as a novelist began over ten years before and ended over ten years after Mrs. Radcliffe's.

Fanny Burney's principal gift, as diarist and novelist, was for comic dialogue, and Mrs. Radcliffe, as far as we know, never cracked a smile, yet the real relationship between them has emerged more clearly with the passage of time. This is not merely because *The Mysteries of Udolpho* reads much less frightening today, more down to earth (and, all unconsciously, much funnier); while *Evelina* (and *Cecilia* and *Camilla* as well) reads much less funny than Burney intended, much more strained,

extreme, fantastic, and even frightening in the impossible trials to which the heroine is subjected. The perils that threaten *A Young Lady's Entrance into the World* (the subtitle of *Evelina*) seem to issue from the same grim realities of eighteenth-century girlhood that inspired Mrs. Radcliffe's Gothic: the same unjust accusations and uncaused severities; the same feminine malice and masculine cruelty; the restraints on her freedom, all the way to actual imprisonment; the mysterious, unexplained social rituals; the terrible need always to appear, as well as always to be, virtuous; and, over all, the terrible danger of slippage from the respectable to the unrespectable class of womanhood. If Burney and Radcliffe both traffic in real female fears, there is however an important difference between them beyond the presence or absence of the comic spirit: that is, their different sense of a woman's main guarantee of her security in the respectable class. For Fanny Burney, that guarantee was the social circle in which the heroine fixed herself, through marriage or other means; while for Ann Radcliffe it was property.

Here I would differ with Professor Ruff, when he writes that "two-thirds" of *The Mysteries of Udolpho* "is about the course of true love and not about gothic horrors at all"—for property seems to loom larger than love in *Udolpho.* The end of Emily's childhood idyl in The Valley is not her father's death, but an event which precedes it: his ruin. . . . A lover is of course provided; his name is Valancourt; Emily will duly marry him at the distant end of all her trials. But property interests dominate the second half of the novel, and account for the curiously delayed end of the love story.

In chapter 29, the death of her aunt makes Emily an heiress; in most of the ensuing chapters, she is engaged gently, pensively, yet firmly in the consolidation of her property. Her struggle with the villain Montoni is essentially legalistic, concerns her property rights. . . . It is lovely of Emily to think of Valancourt; but she seems to enjoy her legal debates with Montoni, and certainly relishes "the day devoted entirely to business" that she spends in chapter 48, when at last she starts to play the châtelaine. (pp. 134-37)

If this hasty sketch of the heroine of *Udolpho* as a kind of Capability Emily sounds like a travesty of the familiar Gothic heroine, that is because of what was done with the figure by the male writers who followed Mrs. Radcliffe. For most of them—an interesting exception is the American novelist Charles Brockden Brown—the Gothic heroine was quintessentially a defenseless victim, a weakling, a whimpering, trembling, cowering little piece of propriety whose sufferings are the source of her erotic fascination. The Marquis de Sade, for example, is known to have admired Mrs. Radcliffe's work. But that the sadistic ramifications of the Gothic were not at all her intention emerges from the one piece of almost certain information that we have about her literary development. She seems to have been dismayed by Matthew Lewis's avowed imitation of her work in his shocking novel called *The Monk;* and in defense of her genre she then wrote *The Italian,* a work which is at once a borrowing from and a severe corrective to "Monk" Lewis's erotic fantasy. *The Italian* proved to be Mrs. Radcliffe's last novel, though she lived a quarter of a century after its publication in 1797. It contains her best villain and best writing; its heroine, who spends many of the early scenes as a genteel but self-supporting needlewoman, is somewhat closer to Frances, the little lace-mender in Charlotte Brontë's *The Professor,* than she is to the garroted, raped, and debauched ladies in Lewis and de Sade. Whatever use was made of her fiction, the erotic flame burned very feebly in Mrs. Radcliffe. (p. 137)

Stability and integrity are . . . the major resources of the Radcliffe heroine; her sensibility and her decorum never falter; and however rapid or perilous her journeys, the *lares* and *penates* of proper English girlhood travel with her. She always manages to pack up her books, her sketching materials, and her lute, no matter how swiftly she is abducted from, say, Venice to the Castle of Udolpho. Locked up in a gloomy, haunted chamber high in a castle tower, Emily "arranged her little library . . . took out her drawing utensils, and was tranquil enough to be pleased with the thought of sketching the sublime scenes beheld from her windows." No mean-minded, authoritarian older man (the source of most of Emily's troubles) can be a match for such a young lady. "She opposed his turbulence and indignation," writes Mrs. Radcliffe in a sentence that is my choice for Emily's epitaph, "only by the mild dignity of a superior mind, but the gentle firmness of her conduct served to exasperate still more his resentment, since it compelled him to feel his own inferiority."

No matter what happens, Emily is always correctly employed, correctly behaved, God knows correctly spoken—and of course correctly dressed. (p. 138)

There is something very English about Mrs. Radcliffe's doll heroines . . . ; and something of perhaps solider historical than literary significance. They remind us of all the British ladies who in point of fact did set sail for Canada and India and Africa, with their bonnets, veils, and gloves, their teacups and tea cozies—ill-equipped for vicissitudes of travel, climate, and native mutiny, but well-equipped to preserve their identity as proper Englishwomen. (pp. 138-39)

The domination of the English novel by women at the turn of the eighteenth century came to an end for a while at least when Walter Scott, rather late in life, put aside poetry for fiction. (p. 139)

In an important way, however, the Radcliffe heroine differs from the Scott hero: though stable in her identity, she changes in a woman's way, as Waverley does not. In a word, she ages. All those vicissitudes, transports, and perils of Emily's adventurous life take their toll. "The bloom of her countenance was somewhat faded," writes Mrs. Radcliffe, "but . . . it was rendered more interesting than ever, by the faint expression of melancholy that sometimes mingled with her smile." In fact, melancholy is closing in on Emily, and at the end the adjective "drooping" begins to replace "pensive" in Mrs. Radcliffe's favor. . . . [Images] from the end of *Udolpho* bring to mind the atmosphere of *Persuasion,* last and most autumnal of Jane Austen's novels, and, in its vista opening toward the sea and the sailor's life, also the most adventurous. It is perhaps in *Persuasion,* rather than in *Northanger Abbey,* that Radcliffe's influence on Austen can most clearly be perceived. At least the faded Anne Elliot, victim of a woman's life, is closer than that silly goose of a Catherine Morland to Emily in *The Mysteries of Udolpho.*

What is officially called a happy ending—that is, marriage—brings *Persuasion* to a close, as well as all the Radcliffe novels. But I don't think my reaction is eccentric when I sense a specially female melancholy and weariness toward the close of the books that women writers have structured around the heroinism of travel and adventure—from Radcliffe to Austen to Sand to Cather. (pp. 139-40)

> *Ellen Moers, "Traveling Heroinism: Gothic for Heroines," in* Literary Women *(copyright © 1963, 1972, 1973, 1974, 1975, 1976 by Ellen Moers; reprinted*

by permission of Doubleday & Company, Inc.), Doubleday, 1976, pp. 122-40.

CORAL ANN HOWELLS   (essay date 1978)

[*Howells analyzes the manner in which Radcliffe stimulates the imagination of her readers. According to Howells, Radcliffe uses her characters to reflect emotion and activate the reader's "pattern of emotional association." Further, Moers concludes that Radcliffe always remains a separate presence in control of her narrative so that she can always be "manipulating her readers' responses."*]

[Mrs. Radcliffe's] magic is obviously a verbal one, for her spells are made out of words dexterously woven into narrative webs which entangle her reader's feelings and imagination in a maze of dreadful uncertainty. To start untangling the web we would be wise to look closely at the way Mrs Radcliffe uses language to register and interpret experience; what we shall find is a curious interweaving of Love, Mystery, and Misery with strands of eighteenth-century rationalism and moral judgement which produces a new pattern in fiction, a pattern which challenges us by its ambiguity.

Mrs Radcliffe's world is a frightening one full of shifting perspectives where ways of seeing and judging are continually dissolving into uncertainty; it has all the contours of picturesque fantasy or dream in its timelessness, its placelessness, and its arbitrariness. Yet we are always aware that this world has an outer shell around it, that of the author's controlling judgement which places romance in a definite relationship to the everyday world. Unlike much fantasy literature, Mrs Radcliffe's fiction is always responsive to the hazards and problems of life, a quality which gives it a toughness lacking in many other Gothic novels, for though she may neglect the trivia of living, she never offends her reader's common sense by denying that it exists. Frustration, disappointment and inconvenience are all there, but they are made manageable by a deliberate change in emphasis from practical realities to emotional and imaginative experience, while the formal elegance of her prose lifts the narrative out of the real world into a distanced literary mode of existence. Her novels reflect the romantic tendency to escape from immediate pressures into a private world where difficulties instead of being limitations become stimuli for imaginative flight. At the same time a hard core of rationality insisted on by the author makes it impossible for her heroines or her readers to forget that life cannot be lived for very long as escapist fantasy. The Radcliffian atmosphere of 'dreadful uncertainty' makes for a suspenseful kind of entertainment, and more importantly it creates the conditions for a somewhat anxious investigation into the relative importance of emotion, intuition and reason in human understanding. I say 'somewhat anxious', partly because of the kinds of feeling which Mrs Radcliffe treats and partly because her world of Gothic romance is so evidently one of sublimation and repression. (pp. 28-9)

[The castle of Udolpho] is Mrs Radcliffe's Heart of Darkness, the centre of anarchy and tyrannical power where all those feelings subversive of rational judgement have free range: perplexity and anxious fear on the heroine's part and aggressive hostility on the villain's. Udolpho provides an imagined landscape whose mysteries relate more to the human personality than to the environment. It is a world apart from eighteenth-century social orthodoxy with its ideals of 'order, peace, honour, and beauty' (as Lionel Trilling formulated them to describe Jane Austen's ideals) though Mrs Radcliffe does remind us of their continuous existence by containing Udolpho and its mysteries within a framework of eighteenth-century manners and domestic harmony. As a novel *Udolpho* is decorous and leisurely, 'rising from the gentlest beauty by just gradations to the terrific and sublime' then returning at the end to a picture of peace and order in the next generation very like the one with which it opened. (pp. 29-30)

[A brief summary of *Udolpho*] inevitably shows how closely the novel keeps to sentimental romance narrative. What it does not show is the strangeness of Mrs Radcliffe's world or the peculiarly enigmatic quality of her story-telling methods. Her world is always at one remove from the actual, for she is deliberately creating an imaginary landscape with a France and an Italy decorated with palaces of the imagination or of nightmare, and peopled by characters who are themselves abstractions and who feel with curiously aestheticised emotions. . . . Everything is filtered through Mrs Radcliffe's imagination which operates like moonlight on a landscape transforming the distinct outlines of reality into obscure romantic shapes. (p. 31)

What Mrs Radcliffe aimed to provide was a stimulus to her reader's imagination freed from the restrictiveness of rational definition. (p. 32)

Mrs Radcliffe's method of presenting her material is a complex mixture of external and internal techniques. Sometimes she works entirely by externals, describing characters, situations and scenery to the reader so that we may react to a concrete series of images in the way we might react to paintings in a gallery. At the other extreme she may use her own modified version of indirect interior monologue, showing how a character's mind and emotions are interacting in the very process of registering experience and compelling the reader's imaginative participation by the intensity of focus on one point of view. More frequently she combines internal and external methods so that scenery or incidents arouse the reader's emotions while at the same time they reflect the feelings of characters involved and allow the author yet another voice, discreet yet distinctly evaluative. Mrs Radcliffe moves deftly from one point of view to another, stimulating and guiding her reader's expectations and responses, while managing to preserve the illusion of imaginative freedom.

The variety and subtlety of Mrs Radcliffe's technique can be seen most clearly in her scenic descriptions and especially in her treatment of architecture. The description of the castle of Udolpho is a typical example of Radcliffian Gothic. (pp. 32-3)

The first paragraph [which describes the castle] is one of the purple passages of Gothic scenic description, an imaginative recreation in prose of a typical Salvator Rosa painting, with the physical features of sublimity carefully arranged in a deliberately aesthetic description. . . . Mrs Radcliffe stresses the emotional power of the visual impression by a brief shift to Emily's point of view, 'it all exhibited a stronger image of grandeur than any Emily had yet seen'. (p. 34)

If we look carefully at the syntax we notice a very odd thing: the subject of every sentence and clause is non-human. It is a road, mountains, vistas, the sun, or indeed the castle—there are no human agents here at all. The environment is supreme and things have an active life of their own, imposing their own conditions upon the human beings who come there. This is more than the effect of impressionistic description; it is basic to the Gothic heroine's experience of the world.

Once, it is true, we have a reference to Emily 'seeing' and that is her only response, a passive private registration. (p. 35)

In the next paragraph there is a shift to Emily's point of view, but the quality of her gazing has been altered by her knowledge that Udolpho belongs to Montoni. . . . The adjectives and the personification of the castle show the curious fusion that has taken place in Emily's mind between the attributes of the edifice and its owner, so that by the time the light fades there is no separation between the outer world and Emily's inner world; the 'terrific images' of sublimity have multiplied and transformed themselves in her imagination so that she 'almost expected' to see banditti rise up as fearful presences in a nightmare landscape. Her fears may have had some rational basis in sixteenth-century Italy, but Emily's reaction is primarily an imaginative one, more likely based on an authorial memory of Salvator Rosa's paintings than on anything in actuality. Udolpho has become for her the symbol of dread and everything associated with it shares the attributes of danger, so that even the 'deep' tone of the portal bell increases her 'fearful emotions'. These fears are exaggerated to such a pitch that she sees her arrival at Udolpho as her entry into a prison. (p. 36)

As frequently happens in *Udolpho*, the heroine's feelings have been presented in such detail and the reader's identification with those feelings so encouraged that we find we are accepting something as fact which is, or could be, merely a projection of the character's imagination. The author's balanced comment at the end of the paragraph is likely to be missed, quietly stated as it is within the context of Emily's fears. I think this is intentional: Mrs Radcliffe wanted to exploit the emotional possibilities of the scene, but her rational comment is there too, posing the antithesis between the suggestions of imagination and the justifications of reason, implying that there may be other ways of judging than the one chosen by the heroine and unobtrusively keeping the way open for a return via commonsense to the familiar world. (pp. 36-7)

Mrs Radcliffe did not really have to coerce her readers into sympathising with Emily's reactions; all she had to do was to direct their predictable responses. What is remarkable about the passage is the interplay between visual and emotional perspectives: visual continuity is combined with a shift in point of view from authorial scenic description to the heroine's subjective and emotionalised view of the castle. The latter is in fact a projection of her own fears. What begins as an appeal to the reader's aesthetic sense becomes through Mrs Radcliffe's subtle persuasions a way of emotionally involving us with the heroine's predicament, by what Burke called 'the contagion of the passions'. (pp. 37-8)

[Mrs Radcliffe establishes] a direct link between the reader and the feeling generated by a scene, frequently by encouraging our sympathetic identification with an intensely focussed though totally one-sided point of view. With increased emotional involvement, a 'clear idea of things themselves' recedes as much for us as for the hypersensitive heroine. Curiously, the more we become involved in her self-enclosed world, the less clearly we see the heroine herself. She too dissolves as a personality and remains with us only as a sensibility, a sensitive refracting medium for our own feelings. (pp. 38-9)

[In her description of Madame Montoni's funeral,] Mrs Radcliffe catches our attention by showing us the very moment of burial, that time of extraordinary transformation from humanity to earth which spells 'deadness' in all its brutal realism. . . . If the description were only this it would be pure graveyard horror, but Mrs Radcliffe encourages her readers to use a wider variety of imaginative responses by introducing a deliberately aesthetic dimension. . . . Just as she had borrowed from the compositional techniques of landscape painting in her description of Udolpho, now Mrs Radcliffe adopts [the Bolognese painter] Domenichino's technique of arranging figures in strongly contrastive groups. She gives us a detailed study of forms, with the fierce *condottieri* [leaders of a band of mercenaries] bending over the open grave 'contrasted by' the monk in his black robe and the veiled Emily beside him, the perfect emblem of grief. (pp. 41-2)

In such a presentation the technique is closer to visual art than to the novel, where we are accustomed to find feeling linked directly to the experience of particular characters; here Mrs Radcliffe is working entirely outside her characters, using them like the objects in a picture to reflect emotion outwards in order to stimulate our own patterns of emotional association. The peculiar combination of graveyard gloom, religiosity and aesthetic treatment makes this passage absolutely seminal for Gothic fiction. Mrs Radcliffe quite consciously provides a model which urges readers to create their own morbid fantasies for themselves, and indeed this is exactly what other Gothic novelists did (for they were all, like Monk Lewis, readers of Gothic fiction too). We can see the pattern of Madame Montoni's funeral repeated with variations in much of the fiction and poetry about burials throughout the nineteenth century, extending through the graveyard horrors of Lewis and Shelley to the poetry of Rossetti.

If Mrs Radcliffe's skill as a writer shows itself undeniably in the way her descriptions play with surfaces and appearances, it is also apparent when she portrays the registering consciousness of one of her characters. Those characters whose minds she gets closest to are her heroines, especially when they are in solitude. We learn very little about these girls in public situations for their manners are so delicate that their response to other people is very stylised and formal; it is only when the heroines are alone that we get a freer play of mind and a kind of anxiety-ridden emotional reverie is revealed, made all the more intense by their own self-enclosure. Mrs Radcliffe registers the obsessive quality of such mental activity with a precision which comes very close to the technique of interior monologue, though the presentation is always indirect, allowing a subtle interplay between the points of view of character and author. An excellent example of the combination of inner action with authorial intervention occurs in the incident where Emily, a prisoner in Udolpho, hears mysterious music under her window at midnight and jumps to the conclusion that the unknown singer is her lover Valancourt whom she had left behind in France. . . . (pp. 42-3)

Here we see the interior monologue becoming a refined technique for arousing suspense, for not only does it enact Emily's doubts and uncertainties but it has all the trappings of sentimental mystery which encourages the reader to engage with her in her dilemma. The process of emotionalised logic is registered so intensely and so exclusively from Emily's point of view that we lose all sense of how feeling may be distorting judgement. From the beginning we are caught up in Emily's restlessness of mind and body as the lonely girl reacts to a familiar song in a very unfamiliar place. Nostalgia combined with her sense of isolation encourages her to try to identify the unknown singer, and Mrs Radcliffe minutely traces the stages by which Emily succeeds in creating an emotionally satisfying solution to an incomprehensible mystery. Her memory of the past and her sensations on hearing the song provide such a powerful stimulus to her feelings that Emily's judgement is very quickly dominated by emotion. (p. 45)

It is Mrs Radcliffe's intention to appeal to our curiosity and sentimental interest in the lovers' fate so as to secure our sympathetic involvement. As so often happens, the authorial doubt so slyly expressed at the end is passed over unnoticed, the reader being so close to Emily's thoughts. We shall probably be as disappointed as Emily when she later discovers that the singer was not Valancourt after all. We have been persuaded to accept as argument a structure of restless longings and memories, for all that has been dramatised is Emily's self-enclosed consciousness, intensely active but not really relating to the outside world at all. She cannot influence her environment in any way and indeed the outside world is unresponsive to her at very crucial times. It is from this sense of Emily's powerlessness that we derive our image of her as the victim of circumstances and perhaps it is her own awareness of it that generates her deep melancholy and frustration. This passage reveals the double point of view which is operating so much of the time in Mrs Radcliffe's fiction: Emily's emotionalised view and a more objective view which is the author's, for though quiet and self-effacing Mrs Radcliffe is a distinctively separate presence always in control of the movement of her narrative and always manipulating her readers' responses. (pp. 46-7)

Mrs Radcliffe is on the way to creating an Emma [from Jane Austen's *Emma*] in Emily, for she is interested in examining how a girl's mental and emotional isolation may breed fantasies. However, her romance form with its extravagant crises of action and feeling works against her. Too often what is shown is a correspondence rather than a contrast between imagined fears and the reality of the romance world. There is no opportunity for a coherent dramatisation of Emily's development; so what we have is the exploration of certain aspects of personality within a very limited emotional framework. Unlike Emma, Emily does not grow any wiser; in the end she is merely rescued from the world of Udolpho and brought back to ordered society. There is no more relatedness between her experiences at Udolpho and at La Vallée than there is between a nightmare and an awakening in the light of day. Mrs Radcliffe does not even stress what must surely be Emily's remarkable powers of recovery; after all, [Charlotte Brontë's] Jane Eyre remembered her terrible childhood experiences in the Red Room for the rest of her life. We are forced to conclude that Emily St Aubert is not a character of flesh and blood like Emma Woodhouse or Jane Eyre but only a linear series of responses to outlandish situations. Although balanced judgement triumphs at the end, it is not enacted by the heroine but belongs solely to the author's argument and to her manipulative skill in shaping her narrative.

Although it is true that we have no coherent sense of Emily as a personality, her sensibility does provide the focus for that emotional area where Mrs Radcliffe's own sensitivity and skill are most acute: in the detailed exploration of certain anxiety states which are identifiably feminine and closely associated with isolation, dependence and sexual fears. The pretence at setting the story in the late sixteenth century gives Mrs Radcliffe the freedom to choose forms which both embody and disguise contemporary neuroses, and as Emily pursues her elusive way through the terrors of a world of romance her adventures are very evidently an analogue for the predicament of the late eighteenth-century woman. Like the heroines of Richardson, Fanny Burney and Jane Austen, Emily is forced to meet a series of challenges which are social and moral in origin and in which the only guidance on how to act comes from her own feelings. (pp. 48-9)

Emily's own cast of sensibility is peculiarly melancholy. . . . [She] not only expects the worst at all times but . . . her most acute feelings are those of misery and fear. Everything in Emily's make-up is an exaggeration of those negative responses which were often the only ones available to the late eighteenth-century woman who wished to preserve her own individuality. The danger for such a woman was that any ability she might have to act positively and spontaneously was liable to be corrupted by constant opposition and resistance from those around her. In Emily's case the corruption takes the form of her own prudential fears exaggerated to the point of neuroticism, and so often getting the better of her. It is characteristic of Emily that she is much more susceptible to Montoni's image than to that of her own true love Valancourt. Indeed what she feels most acutely in her relationship with Valancourt are the miseries rather than the joys of love—the pains of forced separation and the dreadful desolation when later she rejects him. Indeed, at the end when Valancourt comes running into her lonely tower to claim her as his wife, Emily has no intuition whatever either of his approach or his intention. On the other hand she is obsessed by Montoni from the very first time she sees him. . . . The longer Emily is in his house the more she allows her imagination to magnify his power over her. In a curious way Emily and Montoni are counterparts to each other in the same fantasy: he with his will to power and his display of 'conscious superiority' has the ideal foil in Emily, filled as she is with admiration for his exceptional qualities and at the same time terrified by the mysteriousness of a temperament diametrically opposite to her own. . . . Mrs Radcliffe's language suggests that their antagonism finds its parallel in the aesthetic antithesis between the sublime and the beautiful. . . . (pp. 50-1)

Certainly the antagonism between Montoni and Emily has a sexual resonance as well, all the more neurotic for being treated so evasively and indirectly. All the time Emily is under Montoni's protection she is obsessed by ideas of vice, rape and murder, though Montoni himself hardly seems to be aware of her except as an object to be exploited economically. Sexuality comes to the surface only on one extraordinary occasion, with Count Morano's jealous accusation that Emily has refused him because she is in love with Montoni. However, there is no attempt either by Emily or by the author to explore the mixed feelings of instinctual attraction and exaggerated irrational fear that Emily has for Montoni. Indeed, there is no overt acknowledgement of sexual feeling in the novel at all; there is merely the recognition of a nameless power which is a frightening, potentially destructive force capable of assaulting both the body and the will. This fearful awareness is surely at the basis of the threats of rape and murder which pervade Gothic fiction but which for Mrs Radcliffe hover only as nightmarish forms to torment the innocent minds of her heroines as they 'recoil in horror' and 'shake with dread' at the prospect of the villain's 'remorseless vengeance'. (p. 52)

Mrs Radcliffe's explanations are perhaps due to her being very alive to the *dangers* of abandonment to intense feeling. She attempts to suggest that these intensities are fairytale, daydream or even madness, and that real life is something different and much more ordinary—all of which perhaps accounts for our dissatisfaction at the end when we are asked to accept 'real life' again, a life which possesses the solid virtues of rational happiness but none of the excitements of the world of Udolpho. We feel that with the passing of Montoni and Udolpho into the world of darkness all the excitement has gone from Emily's life. . . . (p. 56)

[At the conclusion of *The Mysteries of Udolpho*] Mrs Radcliffe pushes aside the uncomfortable psychological insights and moral problems raised so that at the end the emotional resonance is rather disappointingly reduced and decorum is reasserted in the bland authorial voice justifying her tale for its entertainment value and its moral worth. The joy she celebrates is her joy at the restoration of a civilised humane order and the moral message she states so judiciously (indeed judicially) is the orthodox one that the antithesis between good and bad shall be shown to be resolved in the triumph of innocence and patience. (p. 59)

The ending of *Udolpho* is very close to conventional eighteenth-century assumptions but this should not blind us to the very real ambivalence in Mrs Radcliffe's attitude and technique. She exploits almost continuously a double point of view: her heroine's and her own, that of the participant and of the objective observer, or that of the feelings and that of the rational judgement, points of view which lead to totally different conclusions. At best, this produces the controlled ambivalence and 'dreadful uncertainty' which is the distinctive Radcliffian manner; at worst, it produces contradictions and the feeling of disappointment which Scott and Coleridge registered [see excerpts above, 1794 and 1824] and which we feel at the end of *Udolpho*. The underlying design of her fiction rests on the contest between her imagination and her sense of reality and in the course of the narrative we sense the pull in opposite directions as her imagination rises and then sinks back again under more rational control. (pp. 59-60)

If Mrs Radcliffe is like Jane Austen in so many of her assumptions about the relationship between private feeling and public living, she is also like her contemporary Joanna Baillie who in her *Plays of the Passions* (First Series, 1798) attempted to delineate 'those great disturbers of the human mind' in order to evaluate their proper place in total experience. Both Miss Baillie and Mrs Radcliffe find themselves forced to acknowledge that the forces of love, sex, fear and death actually lie under the surface of civilised life but both of them fear the consequences of excessive feeling and finally insist on a mannered world of social relationships which allows no room for other more dangerous insights. Mrs Radcliffe's unease with this compromise is evident throughout her narratives in her ambiguous recording of experience and reinforced by the anxiety-ridden self-enclosure of her heroines. She cannot stop herself making positive claims for imagination and feeling, even if she has to hide behind a mask to do it. . . . (pp. 60-1)

> *Coral Ann Howells, "Ann Radcliffe, 'The Mysteries of Udolpho',"* in her Love, Mystery, and Misery: Feeling in Gothic Fiction *(© Coral Ann Howells 1978), The Athlone Press, 1978, pp. 28-61.*

GARY KELLY (essay date 1979)

Did Ann Radcliffe share Walpole's aims in fiction? The similarities between her first novel and Walpole's suggest that she did. But even here she began to alter Walpole's fictional rhetoric in significant ways, adding new elements, emphasizing others, and suppressing others again, thus creating a different system of devices and a different effect. In general, she loosens, relaxes, softens, and sentimentalizes what Walpole had done. . . . Radcliffe places less emphasis on the terrors arising from shock and surprise, and thus softens the "cross-cutting" effect of these shocks and makes the narrative seem less disjointed. The "rationalizing" and diminishing of the use of the supernatural—in most literary histories seen as the distinctive trait of Radcliffe's Gothicism—also helps to throw greater emphasis on the milder emotions, by defusing the terrors. Furthermore, Radcliffe tries to eliminate mimetic expressiveness from her accounts of emotional response, although in all of her novels there are a few examples of attempts to register suspense or shock by syntax or by typographical devices such as the dash and exclamation mark. Finally, she moralizes her descriptions of emotion to a much greater extent than Walpole. She places more emphasis on the moral quality of emotional conflicts, she adds explicit morals to her novels, and she introduces the theme of benevolence as an aspect of sensibility.

The most important result of Radcliffe's changes, however, was compositional. The extraordinary emphasis on shock, surprise, and narrative disjunction in *Otranto* was a distinctly limited principle of composition—limited by the law of diminishing returns. Shock and surprise rapidly exhaust their freshness, and it is hard to imagine *The Castle of Otranto* being any longer than it is. In contrast, Radcliffe could make each of her novels up to *Udolpho* precisely one volume longer than its predecessor. By lowering the emotional intensity, slowing the pace, distributing the shocks and surprises more widely, emphasizing milder feelings and adding emotions which were responses to nature and social sympathy, and by moving these emotions, embodied in a heroine, into the foreground, Radcliffe opened Walpole's form to almost indefinite expansion. With each successive novel she expanded her material and refined her treatment of it, while keeping to Walpole's principle of the perplexed or "braided" narrative—maintaining a "constant vicissitude of interesting passions."

Ann Radcliffe altered Walpole's "invention" so consistently and progressively through the thirteen volumes of her published fiction that one is led to ask what "idea" her own novels dramatize. I think it is clear even from her first novel that her fiction embodies a model of the human mind in which reason chastens the passions, restrains the imagination, and reconstructs experience, thus presiding over individual moral growth and ensuring eventual happiness. The novels are relatively uninterested in social values or experience except as they reveal or dramatize individual moral character, and yet the novels also care little for any "realistic" presentation of individuality because it is the emotions themselves which Radcliffe is interested in, not their embodiment in character. (pp. 48-50)

[Since] each novel attends primarily to a heroine rather than a hero, [the] group of emotions . . . associated with the feminine character for centuries and now part of the dominant values of the culture of sensibility, naturally comes to dominate Radcliffe's fictional rhetoric. In other words, from *Athlin and Dunbayne* to *Udolpho* that group of emotions associated with female sensibility gradually moves towards establishing itself as the norm.

But only "towards", for there is another system, present throughout these novels, and traditionally associated not with femininity and youth, but with a fully realized humanity and maturity. This system is associated with reason, continually struggles against the excesses of sensibility, and eventually, in *The Italian,* forms a proper union with it. The difference between perplexity, terror, and sensibility in Radcliffe's novels is that the first two overpower or baffle reason, while the last can join with it to form the fully human individual who is the result and the goal of the experiences which the novel describes. The natural compatibility of reason and sensibility can be seen in the emotions or states of mind associated with reason: certainty, patience, fortitude, resignation, respect—in a word,

tranquillity. Radcliffe's heroes and heroines do not on the whole use reason to arrive at knowledge; rather, they use reason to chasten emotion to a just response to the facts of experience and observation. Reason schools Sensibility and then marries her.

There is of course a dark version of this picture. The villains and villainesses fail to rule their passions with reason, and although they do not suffer the wide range of perplexities and terrors endured by the heroes and heroines, they are only plunged deeper into the passions of ambition, pride, hatred, and revenge, and the tumults of self-conflict. (pp. 51-2)

Such is the model of human nature and knowledge embodied in Ann Radcliffe's novels, but it is hardly original. What is original is the way she takes over, adapts, and combines certain features of the fictional rhetoric of the day in order to dramatize this model. The plots, for example, are as conventional as the themes and characters, and are all based on the standard romantic plot: cavalier meets damsel, they fall in love, they are separated by circumstances or the machinations of their foes, they overcome or survive separate strings of difficulties, are reunited, and marry. . . . There is no variation from this pattern; the variations are all concentrated in the obstacles and delays and mysteries which keep the lovers apart, and, as we have seen, these variations are all motivated by the necessity of presenting "a constant vicissitude of interesting passions" in the various characters, but especially in the heroine.

There is no essential difference, for example, between castles on the north-east coast of Scotland, another on the north coast of Sicily, a ruined abbey in Fontainville Forest in France, a chateau in Languedoc and a castle in northern Italy, or a convent in southern Italy and the prison of the Inquisition. All are more or less exotic settings where the requirements of conventional domestic realism can be ignored and where occasions of melancholy, mystery, and terror may credibly be contrived at will, for the reader could hardly know any better, and wouldn't care anyway. There is, too, no essential difference between the various sets of characters. . . . In Radcliffe's novels individual psychology does not exist, only set patterns of virtuous sensibility, human weakness, or unfeeling depravity. . . . The lack of individuality of course extends to dialogue, which is stilted and probably derived from the Heroic Dramas of the previous age. But once again, the flatness of technique here does serve a purpose: it forces attention on the general moral issues being discussed, rather than on the individualistic expressive styles of the speakers. . . . Finally, setting itself is presented in generalized and abstract terms, derived from books of travels, pressed into the categories of sublime and picturesque, coloured by paintings or prints of Claude, Rosa, and Poussin, and described from the point of view of the affected sensibilities of the heroine. This brief summary of the formal elements of Radcliffe's novels clearly indicates that every aspect of her fictional technique has been generalized, and any stylistic trait that could make a technique noticeable by drawing attention to itself has been eliminated, so that the descriptions of emotional responses may be unrivalled in their dominance in the whole fictional structure.

How then are these descriptions organized into a temporal sequence? Are they organized at all? The typology of emotional states which was outlined earlier is associative in nature, and thus lacks any principle of organization based on moral development or progress. Therefore a fiction embodying that typology will itself be unprogressive and repetitive in form. The only principles distinguishing the parts of the system are conflict and gradation: some emotions are opposed by others; some are stronger than others. The only progressive principle comes from the emotions' relation to reason: reason chastens the passions, and so refines, harmonizes, and "tranquilizes" them. In Radcliffe's novels, however, the passages of sensibility are a kind of ground to the passages of perplexity, and this does constitute a sort of organizing principle, though an unprogressive one, and as a result of it the perplexities bear the burden of the novel's argument about the relation of emotion and reason. . . . [All] aspects of the novel's formal technique are motivated by the need to create occasions of sensibility or perplexity, but even the descriptions of different kinds of sensibility can be seen as motivated by the need to highlight the perplexities. Here already is the principle of alternation in the overall temporal pattern of the novels, and it is in fact the only strong organizing principle present in any of Radcliffe's fictions. The alternation need not, as in the cruder kinds of Gothic, be between diametrical opposites, but only between differences, and so throughout the novel the heroine merely goes through a variety of emotional states in more or less rapid succession. In fact in her most fully developed novel, *The Mysteries of Udolpho*, Radcliffe is fond of delineating a movement through gradations of sensibility rather than the extreme oscillations between sensibility, perplexity, or terror characteristic of her earlier work. Another way of varying the pattern (thus using the same material twice over, a truly housewifely economy) is to switch back and forth from one character to another, a device Radcliffe uses in *The Italian*. The word "meanwhile" appears at the head of chapter after chapter as the narrative switches from the heroine Ellena to Vivaldi the hero. These kinds of alternations or "constant vicissitudes," then, form the basic unprogressive pattern of Radcliffe's novels, one which is itself a kind of perplexity, in the root sense.

However, this "braided" form, which organizes the descriptions of emotion, would hardly sustain interest for a novel longer than *Otranto* without assistance from other formal principles, and of course the most important of these is suspense. Suspense is normally discussed as an affective rather than a formal device, and in Gothic fiction it clearly does have the former function. But it also serves to organize the material into both large and small units. . . . Nevertheless, suspense used in this way contributes nothing to any progressive development of form or theme in the novel, and is largely assimilated to the repetitive quality of the form. (pp. 53-6)

The significance of the suspenseful situations is diminished even further by Radcliffe's tendency, much commented on from her day to this, to explain the various mysteries on rational grounds, often in a dry and abrupt fashion. In other words, the "concatenation" in Radcliffe's novels is negligible, and this fact only allows "the constant vicissitude of interesting passions" to dominate completely the structure of her novels. (pp. 57-8)

In *The Italian* this is no longer the case. The dominant characteristics developed in *The Romance of the Forest* and *The Mysteries of Udolpho* are still present, but they are joined to a more powerful governing mystery, embodied in the character and actions of Schedoni, and as a result the whole fictional system is altered. Nevertheless, the alterations are characteristic ones and revolve around the identity of Ellena and Schedoni. Along with this goes the greater attention and more complex character given to Schedoni. His identity is not kept entirely concealed, but his real relationship to Ellena is, as he is first her persecutor, and then, allowed to believe that she is his

daughter, he becomes her protector. This reversal, however melodramatic, gives at least a little more unity to the plot. (p. 58)

[It] is clear that Radcliffe's novels are essentially unprogressive, like eighteenth-century fiction in general. . . . The real unifying principle in all of the novels . . . is the internal coherence of the system of emotions outlined earlier. This system was imbedded as a convention in the ideology of people of Radcliffe's class and education; therefore she could rely upon her readers' knowledge of the system precisely because it was conventional. (pp. 59-60)

The prose style of Radcliffe's novels represents a model consciousness, the kind of integrated and unified consciousness towards which her heroines are supposed to strive. And so the resolution of the conflict of reason and sensibility is not in the plot or argument of the novel, not in the dramatized moral growth of individual characters, but in the narrative voice. But since this resolution has taken place before the novel even begins, in a sense there is no dramatic resolution in the novel itself. The narrative voice continues throughout the novel to describe "constant vicissitudes of interesting passions" without itself undergoing those vicissitudes. At the same time the narrative voice is not ironically detached from what it describes. Rather it regulates the vicissitudes, absorbs, tempers, and rationalizes them in the same way that a calm, rational observer will report another's declaration of anger, confession of perplexity, or melancholy complaint, stripping it of its expressiveness in the process of reporting it. The material is absorbed into the narrative voice, the narrative voice does not lend itself to the material. In fact, every aspect of Radcliffe's novels is deformed in the same way. The stereotyped characterization, the stilted formal dialogue (hardly varied even by the "comically" loquacious servants), the mysteries and terrors blandly explained away or perfunctorily dismissed, the eschewing of the erotic suggestiveness and Grand Guignol horrors practised by other Gothicists, the avoidance of any aspect of language which was so lively as to draw attention to itself— all these aspects of Radcliffe's novels represent the deformation of fictional technique to serve the higher cause of good taste. (pp. 61-2)

She intended [her novels] primarily to have a conventional moral function, to dramatize the opposition of reason and emotion and to show the supremacy of reason in her narrative style; her readers and her imitators ignored her intention and appreciated her novels for their affective function, for their Gothic terrors and trimmings; but the exhaustion of those terrors and trimmings by her imitators leaves us with no alternative but to read her work for its rhetorical function, for the way she embodied her ideas in narrative style and form. We read Ann Radcliffe's novels as documents in the history of the language of literary forms. (p. 62)

Gary Kelly, " 'A Constant Vicissitude of Interesting Passions': Radcliffe's Perplexed Narratives" (copyright © 1979 The Board of Governors, The University of Calgary; reprinted by permission of the publisher and the author), in Ariel, Vol. 10, No. 2, April, 1979, pp. 45-64.

DAVID DURANT (essay date 1982)

[*Unlike such critics as Walter Raleigh (1911) and Devendra P. Varma (1957), Durant insists that Radcliffe is not a forerunner of the Romantic movement in England. Her reactionary nature in the novels, Durant points out, can be seen in the way she rejected the chaos she perceived in contemporary life and advocated a return to the pastoral simplicity symbolized by the family circle.]*

Ann Radcliffe's place among gothic novelists has been consistently misunderstood because she was a conservative writer in what is now considered a revolutionary movement. . . . It is not because she is puerile . . . , but because she is philosophically traditional, that her novels fit modern definitions of the gothic so badly. She is not a forerunner of the romantic movement, but the staunch foe of its most salient characteristics. Her novels testify to her recognition of those aspects of her age which were to produce the romantic revolution, but she saw them as omens of the disintegration of a culture she cherished. Her novels picture the strength of the irrational, but rather than viewing it as the needed corrective for an over-rationalistic age, she saw it as monstrous. She repeatedly describes situations in which hierarchy breaks down, leaving a world of individuals. But instead of applauding that new freedom, she portrays the resultant world as one where people are cut off from one another in crippling isolation. And, while her novels depend upon the malevolence of figures who bear the earmarks of the villain-hero, she resolutely contradicts any impulse to bring out their heroism. For Mrs. Radcliffe, the true gothic terrors were not the black veils and spooky passages for which she is famous, but the winds of change, dissolution, and chaos which they represented.

The vehicle of Mrs. Radcliffe's world view is a mythic pattern which underlies the differing characters, settings, and techniques of her major novels. Individually, each of the works seems simply to repeat the time-honored formula of the sentimental love story, complete with standard gothic complications. But taken together, her major novels demonstrate an obsession with the single subject of the coming of age of the individual. . . .

Her novels all begin by sketching the pastoral Eden of safe family life; move to the presentation of a fallen world where a father-villain betrays and persecutes the heroine; and end back in the haven of a new family which duplicates the virtues of the initial one. This pattern contrasts a safe, hierarchical, reasonable, loving world of the family with a chaotic, irrational, and perverse world of the isolated. Its circular shape suggests that the only solution to the problems of adult existence lies in returning to traditional, conservative values. (pp. 519-20)

All of Mrs. Radcliffe's heroines carry into their adventures the memory of pastoral innocence, where a family protected them from harm. This combination of the pastoral and the familial clearly builds on the sentimental tradition, where the heroine's life follows the archetype of the fall in domesticated form. But the Radcliffe myth is even more familial than its sentimental prototype. In her novels, innocence is not simply lack of corrupting experience, but a factor of the protection of a conventional hierarchy. This is emphasized by the nature of the fall from innocence in the Radcliffe novels. Her heroines are not thrust into the world because of their resistance to their family's plans for their marriage, nor for any other sin of disobedience. They enter the fallen world simply because their protectors disappear. God finds no one eating the apple; He simply disappears, taking the garden with Him. Thus, even in *A Sicilian Romance,* where Mrs. Radcliffe is most indebted to the sentimental novel, she is at pains to assure her readers that the heroine's trials come from no fault of her own. And in the

later, less sentimental versions of her myth, it is even clearer that there was no sin in the fall. Mrs. Radcliffe's heroines remain constant in their innocent goodness; only the world around them changes. That makes Mrs. Radcliffe's myth more deterministic and unpleasant than the normal education novel, since there is no poetic justice in the trials the girls undergo.

Mrs. Radcliffe's obsession with the family is indicated by making the first step in her heroine's descent into the world of experience a meeting with new parents. (p. 521)

The contrast between the community of the initial family and the autonomy of the members of the pseudo-family establishes the novels' contention that the gothic world is one of adult isolation. All of the heroine's gothic adventures are the result of the heroine's lack of community. . . . The isolation of the heroine in the adult world is dramatized by Mrs. Radcliffe's insistence on the necessity of flight for the innocent. The heroine's instinct after the loss of her real family is to join others, since she has learned to expect loving protection. But when she finds that protection false, she replaces her natural desire for community with an instinctive reaction of flight. Mrs. Radcliffe's discovery of the chase as a mainstay of her plots came in *A Sicilian Romance,* where Julia flees from her father; from her older suitor; from an interpolated group chasing another pair of lovers who have little else to do with the novel; from bandits; from her father's forces again; and finally from still another desperado band. The three later novels are not as full of flights, but they retain the basic fact of life in the fallen world: those around the innocent are almost inevitably hostile.

Mrs. Radcliffe's repeated explanation of the isolation that her heroines suffer in the fallen world is the inability of adults to understand each other. While she still lived with her family, the ingénue could know with some surety the motives and inner natures of those around her. But thrown outside the known confines of the family, she is faced with people whose characters are masked. This is partly a method of suspense. Thus, in *The Romance of the Forest,* Mrs. Radcliffe shapes almost every incident so that it will whet the audience's curiosity by limiting the narrative perspective to that of a heroine ignorant by force of circumstances. (pp. 522-23)

Udolpho expands this theme of adult ignorance by emphasizing the arbitrary nature of wickedness. Madame Cheron permits Emily's engagement to Valancourt, then abruptly breaks it off. Montoni spends the novel herding his bride and the heroine from one part of Europe to another for reasons which are clear only to himself. The unsure world of experience begins to infect the happy memories of the innocent family, when Emily begins to suspect both her father and Valancourt of duplicity. By the time she wrote *The Italian,* Mrs. Radcliffe had come to focus most of her attention on the problems of masked identity. All of the villains of the novel hide their wickedness beneath attractive exteriors. For the first time in her career, she made her villain a priest, insisting upon the discrepancy between his pious demeanor and his vicious hidden nature. And the entire last half of the novel stresses the masks of the adult world by shaping itself as a detective story where all is at last uncovered. No matter what the form of the novels, each depicts the world of experience as one of mystery, where goodness is surrounded by forces it does not understand.

The nature of the fallen world is characterized as much by its landscape as by its action and characters. Following the gothic convention, Mrs. Radcliffe made her heroines discover a nightmare world beneath the pastoral, after they had been expelled from secure family life. Her underground is a world of chaos, where the forces of the supernatural and of the illicit hold full sway. The ruined castles and abbeys are graphic symbols of the disintegration of a stable civilization; their underground reaches are the hiding places for all those forces which cannot stand the light of day. *A Sicilian Romance* establishes the gothic geography. . . . The intrusion of the supernatural into the world of depravity allows Mrs. Radcliffe to explain its malevolence. In the fallen world, there are forces which reason cannot explain: the true authority of reason which had restrained vice has been lost. Once out of the family, the heroine finds that chaos is loosed.

The contrast between the true family and chaos is exemplified by Mrs. Radcliffe's use of a false father as villain. The innovation came in *A Sicilian Romance,* which involves a mutation of the usual sentimental struggle between a heroine's love and a father's authority. . . . But in both *The Romance of the Forest* and *The Italian,* the parental status of the villain is explicit. . . . There is more than a hint of incest in this formula, but the main focus lies on the definition of an adult world in which the normal, loving relationships of fathers and children are replaced by unnatural and unprovoked enmity by the father. To Mrs. Radcliffe, the world outside the family is utterly perverse in its villainy.

Mrs. Radcliffe's gothic underworld speaks for her pessimistic estimation of the modern world which it symbolizes: it is absolutely wicked and completely beyond the control of the innocent. Her heroines are not as spineless as many of their sentimental cousins, but they can find no way to carry the fight to the wicked. Instead, they are wholly concerned with refraining from the wicked actions the hostile world tempts them to and withstanding the wiles of evil by fortitude. The heroines are upheld by a knowledge of their own rectitude and the comforts of belief in God's providence, while the villains are frenetic in their machinations. The result is a picture of a world where to be active is to be depraved. Common sense tells all the heroines that the world is much too strong to be overcome. The father-villain and his henchmen know more than the heroine about the world and have all the powers that come from position, riches, and masculinity. And while the wicked may occasionally stand in awe of goodness, they never find it persuasive. There are no Mr. B.'s [as in Samuel Richardson's *Pamela*] in Mrs. Radcliffe's world, ready to be converted by the example of the heroines they terrify. The Radcliffe pattern, instead, is a steady growth of infamy in the villains; the novels' outcomes inevitably show that they were even worse than they had seemed. Their intransigence suggests that the innocent can only suffer in the world outside the family.

The best proof of Mrs. Radcliffe's abhorrence of the modern world lies in the inevitable happy endings of her novels. The terms of success for her heroines are inevitably those which deny any virtue to the revolutionary world of chaos. For her plots are circular. Her heroines do not progress from adolescent innocence to adult goodness through the trials they undergo. Rather, they preserve their innocence through the gothic adventures until they can revert to the hierarchical, reasonable, and safe world of the family. Her heroines devise no strategies by which to appreciate a chaotic world; no method to accept or penetrate the masked character of the adult; and no acceptance of the irrational as a positive force. Nor do they find some new powers by which to change the terms of the world. Rather, they stumble upon the lost family, whose powers are sufficient to erase all traces of the modern world. The family

is capable of solving all the problems of the world: it gives the heroine an established place in a traditional hierarchy; overcomes her sense of loss of her initial family; provides her with a community which solves her isolation; surrounds her with people who are not masked; ends her flights; and denies the existence of the supposed ghosts. The family provides a traditional world as the providential reward for the heroine's goodness.

The traditional terms of the heroine's success suggest that the problems of the gothic underworld are not solvable. For to give her heroines a happy ending, Mrs. Radcliffe had to deny the very existence of the problems which her novels had posed. (pp. 523-26)

The conclusions make no attempt to disprove the iniquity of the underworld, but prove that a good person neither can nor should deal with the world.

One of the main proofs that Mrs. Radcliffe's conclusions solve the problems of the novels by evading them lies in her final treatment of her villains. She can find no solution to their perversion of the family short of denying the existence of its wickedness: the conclusions insist that the father-villain was not the heroine's father after all. In both *The Romance of the Forest* and *The Italian,* the villains prove to be imposters who have killed the real fathers. (pp. 526-27)

The most important denial of the gothic underworld consists of the final claim that none of the irrational forces which had seemed potent were supernatural at all. Like the majority of gothic writers, Mrs. Radcliffe posits a geography which coincides with the twentieth-century schema of conscious and unconscious. But while her novels had seemed to force their heroines to descend to the unconscious depths of the irrational, their conclusions insist that there was no such site to descend to. To the heroine, outside of the hierarchical system of the family, there often seem to be forces which reason cannot explain. But once she has returned to her family's world, the horrors behind the black veil seem to have been only an ugly statue; the ghostly murmurs were only the wind, the voice of a friendly prisoner, or the sounds of servants feeding an imprisoned mother; the dimly lit charnel houses turn out to have been only burial vaults; and apparitions only dreams. That return to logic has long irritated Mrs. Radcliffe's critics, simply because it shows all too clearly that she rejects the revolutionary gothic. She insists that as soon as one fully understands one's place in the ordered world of the family, all else falls into place. (p. 527)

The final rejection of the definition of the real world as isolated, perverted, and irrational makes Mrs. Radcliffe's novels oppose the tradition of the education novel. She accepts its usual psychodrama, but rejects its solutions. The starting point is conventional: life begins for the heroine in the happy time when she and her parents were identical in aims and character. But just when she reaches the age when it would be natural for her to emerge from the confines of family life, her childhood parents "die." Suddenly they seem new people, who treat her as an adult by putting their own interests on a par with hers. Where before they had been authority figures, omnipotent in knowledge and disinterested in their love, they now seem to be individuals, masking their selfish interests. They no longer protect her from the adult world. With the advent of suitors, the mother becomes jealous and the father a competitor, threatening the loved one, separating him from the daughter, punishing her with isolation. The completion of the psycho-drama seems predictable. The heroine will win her new love and then, perhaps, be able to accept her parents in their new role as equals. Mrs. Radcliffe's novels are so interesting because they defeat those expectations. The heroines persist in their adolescent view and are proven correct. Those selfish adults were not her real parents, but vile imposters. She will never achieve equal status with her parents; instead, she will rediscover them as distant arbiters and absolute authorities. The adolescent will have to sacrifice any hope of adult status, ignore the real world, and live docilely as a child for all of her life. But it is worth it: the outside world is too fraught with perils to be endured.

Mrs. Radcliffe's rebellion against the formula of the education novel suggests the true distinction of the gothic genre from its predecessors, as well as her differences from the other gothic novelists. . . . Mrs. Radcliffe remains a fine spokesman for the gothic simply because her themes were as escapist as her genre. This is not to say that her novels ignore contemporary life, but that they reject it. If one accepts the gothic underworld as an apt symbolic description of her age, then one must also accept the proposition that Mrs. Radcliffe rejects both the modern and the gothic. She offers against the chaotic universe the lost world of the pastoral. Her ideal is much more pleasant than the gothic underworld or the modern world that it symbolizes: it is free of the irrational, the unconscious, the individualistic, the isolated, or the masked. Her ideal is a paradise of set values, hierarchy, and joyous openness; it pictures the redemption which follows a virtuous life in the fallen world. Her novels are, finally, otherworldly. They do not offer their readers ways of dealing with the mundane world, but escape from it. Mrs. Radcliffe looks forward to no utopia forged out of the new conditions around her, but backwards to the sanctuary of an Eden. (pp. 528-29)

Her novels are written to and embody the response of a civilization which seemed to be facing anarchy. The French Revolution and the attendant radical movements in England threatened the form of government, the class structure, and the way of life of her country. Mrs. Radcliffe spoke for all those who saw these conditions and longed for a simpler, better age. Her gothic underworld pictures an era so threatening in its newness that it seemed uninhabitable; her conclusions depict an ideal which finds its happiness in resolutely turning its back on modern life. Few of Mrs. Radcliffe's readers probably understood the gothic as a symbol of the French Revolution, especially as they desired a literature which had no such application. But her appeal probably did lie in the general conformity of her myth to a frightened, reactionary impulse. The world outside, her novels insist, is gothic, but there is still perfect safety in return to the older, cherished verities of home and family. (pp. 529-30)

David Durant, "Ann Radcliffe and the Conservative Gothic," in Studies in English Literature, 1500-1900 (© 1982 William Marsh Rice University), Vol. 22, No. 3, Summer, 1982, pp. 519-30.

DAVID MORSE (essay date 1982)

Innocence is still for Mrs Radcliffe, as it was not for Lewis, a meaningful and realisable value, but the opposition between innocence and madness is transposed into a contrast between innocence and hypocrisy. It is also important to note that Mrs Radcliffe's attitude towards reason undergoes some modification. Her earlier novels were concerned to show how crucial was the role of reason in the struggle against the forces of

oppression and irrational domination and such an emphasis continues to be felt in *The Italian*. It is important that Vivaldi, Ellena's lover, should have an understanding 'sufficiently clear and strong to teach him to detect many errors of opinion, that prevailed around him, as well as to despise the common superstitions of his country', and it is equally significant that Schedoni, the hypocritical monk and dominant figure in the novel, should be shown as alienated from truth, to which both reason and feeling should lead. But Schedoni also exemplifies the tortuousness of reason, its ability to become alienated from itself through the very complexity and deviousness of its own workings. . . . Here is a great paradox. The Gothic novel shows a new awareness of the intricacy of mental processes that represents one of its most significant claims on our attention, yet what it exhibits it also deplores. The truth is there, open and transparent, yet man in his perversity cuts himself off from it. The most crucial and fundamental moral issues become badly blurred. Schedoni criticises the Marchese, Vivaldi's father, on the grounds that he cannot distinguish virtue from vice at the very moment when he and the Marchese are discussing plans for the murder of Ellena, whom they regard as an unworthy object for the affections of Vivaldi. At which Mrs Radcliffe applies the same criticism to them. . . . Thus, in *The Italian* Mrs Radcliffe is more disposed to see evil in the world as connected with faults in human nature. She still criticises evils and injustices and is conscious of their social and institutional basis, but there is [a] notably greater element of pessimism in her work, which doubtless registers the impact on her of the Reign of Terror in France. In *The Italian* she is highly critical of the injustice, arbitrariness and antidemocratic mystifications of the procedures of the religious Inquisition, but it becomes for her an exemplification not simply of the corruptness of civilisation, but also of human irrationality. . . . The Inquisition is itself a form of perversity: it sanctions the most awful crimes in the name of reason. Instead of assuming that it is only through culture that man is alienated from nature, the possibility has to be faced that man himself becomes, or has become, alienated from the natural. Thus the notion of hypocrisy as the embodiment of a socially generated false consciousness begins to acquire an internal dynamic of its own: it opens up the prospect of perennially false sets of relations— a hall of mirrors, of distorting mirrors, from which it is impossible to escape.

Nevertheless, although influenced by the new mood of irrationalism, Mrs Radcliffe does remain faithful to her belief in the goodness of human nature and in the value of spontaneity. She contrasts the frankness, sincerity, love of justice and generosity of Vivaldi with Schedoni, who 'saw only evil in human nature'. To see only this evil is to be guilty of partiality and excessive despondency, to align oneself with the forces of death against the forces of life. In this respect Mrs Radcliffe shows herself influenced by the symbolic language of *The Monk*. Throughout *The Italian* she is conscious of the difference between those who 'render life a blessing or a burden'. This also appears as a contrast between the sacred and the secular, between those, such as Paulo, who love life and wish to enjoy themselves, and those, such as Schedoni, whose tortuous spirits prevent them from living in anything other than a negative and malignant fashion. In *The Italian* 'enthusiasm' is seen as the greatest of all virtues: a generosity of spirit that contrasts with the meanness and narrowness fostered by the church. (pp. 61-4)

In *The Italian* as in *The Mysteries of Udolpho* it is the natural world and the contemplation of scenery that is marked by sublimity and grandeur which constitutes a crucial and saving moral resource. In the first section of the novel Ellena is seized by unknown ruffians and taken on an obscure and frightening journey. . . . [As they pass through highly dramatic mountainous scenery, her] spirits are 'gradually revived and elevated by the grandeur of the images around her'. . . . But the Radcliffian sublime, unlike that of Burke, does *not* convince the spectator of his insignificance, but rather has a reassuring and tranquillising effect. . . . It is through descriptions such as this rather than through Austenian character analysis that the development of subjectivity is presented: the progressive revelation to Ellena of herself as a free and autonomous human being rather than a helpless and abject dependant. (pp. 66-7)

In contrast with Ellena, the evil characters in the novel are shown to be unresponsive to nature—indeed, it is precisely this fact that serves as a sign of their depravity. Schedoni's inability to respond to the beauty of nature indicates that he lacks a capacity for genuine or spontaneous feeling, that he is too much the narrow rationalist. . . . Schedoni, who feels nothing, becomes prototypical of the consciousness that becomes alienated from the real world through an obsession with distinctions constituted through language. . . . The only truthful responses are spontaneous and intuitive; an excess of ratiocination does not simply lead to error—it leads to a total disjuncture between the objective world and the mind that purportedly contemplates it. . . . The horror of the demonic is that it knows only itself. Subjectivity becomes a prison. Thus, in some sense, the crucial moral distinction in *The Italian* becomes the line of demarcation that separates good from bad subjectivity: one points towards freedom, the other towards oppression.

The phenomenology of *The Italian* is significantly constituted through the imagery of the cloak and of the veil—tokens of the way in which relations become obscured and mystified and of the destructive nature of the intervention of the church between man, the world and his own nature. The omnipresent and omnipotent figure of *The Italian* is that of a monk muffled in cloak or cowl with no clue as to his identity, his character or his intentions. . . . Veil and cowl alike are the signs of a world that has lost its transparency, where anything can be anything and where nothing is but what is not. (pp. 68-70)

The greatest mystery in the novel is connected with the character of Schedoni. Schedoni is an absent presence: he does not directly appear in large sections of the narrative, but he nevertheless figures as the point of imaginative focus for the reader. His gigantic stature, his apparent omnipresence and omniscience, his formidable memory, which permits him to memorise down to the last detail an official document of the Inquisition—all this suggests the Superman. But Schedoni is also imposing because he represents the complex, multifarious personality, as contrasted with the simple, unambiguous personality of Ellena and Vivaldi. Everything connected with Schedoni raises problems of identity. Is he identical with the cowled figure who warns Vivaldi not to go to the villa Altieri? Is he the same person whose agonising symptoms of guilt and remorse created a stir at the confessional of the Black Penitents? Is he Ellena's father? Is he Ferrando, Count di Bruno, and was Ferrando also the man who confessed? Schedoni has a multiplicity of doubles. His assumed identity as Schedoni makes him his own double, but there is also Spalatro, his evil minion, and Nicola di Zampari, who is many times confused with him. The difficulty of making all these connections, of ever really establishing anything for certain, is precisely what constitutes the nightmare of a world deprived of transparency. To nail

Schedoni down is extremely difficult, since he can be proved guilty only if all the identities can be clarified. (pp. 71-2)

Nevertheless, Schedoni is not altogether without redeeming features—for the Romantic mind the hypocrite must always be a figure of compassion, as well as an object of moral censure. Schedoni, though lost in the labyrinthine workings of his own mind, is not altogether bereft of the redeeming power of sympathy. . . . But Schedoni must be condemned because for him there is no path leading back to humanity: his actions have cut him off irrevocably from the world of the human—for the Romantics the most terrible punishment of all. Schedoni may be superhuman, but he is also less than human. By implication Mrs Radcliffe is also making a statement about authenticity: the novel suggests that once you have lost it there can be no going back. This also reflects intriguingly on Schedoni's indecisiveness at critical moments: a man possessed by bad faith, he lacks any genuine basis for action.

The figure of Schedoni, when taken in conjunction with the thematic doubling of the theme of oppression, through the alternation of the narrative from Ellena to Vivaldi, creates a richer and more complex novel than *The Mysteries of Udolpho*. It is structurally polycentric and allows us to see events from a number of different points of view. Nevertheless, it may be objected that Mrs Radcliffe draws back from the more interesting implications of her subject, by first raising the possibility that Schedoni may be Ellena's father, only subsequently to discount it in a manner that appears anticlimactic. However, this is to ignore the obvious but important point that *The Italian* is a novel written by a woman. The mysterious omnipotence of Schedoni signifies the fact that woman lives in a world of masculine domination and her attempts to develop her identity and personality are thwarted at every turn. In Ellena's struggle towards self-realisation, it is Schedoni who stands there blocking the path and impeding her progress at every step of the way. It is therefore indispensable that Schedoni, like Montoni in *Udolpho,* be stripped of the appearance of grandeur. The full significance of the attempted murder of Ellena by Schedoni is that, symbolically, it is an attempted rape, a violation of the last vestige of her independence. But his inability to go through with it produces a reversal of roles: now it is Ellena who is dominant, Schedoni who is abject. But Schedoni's claim to the paternity of Ellena must be repudiated by Mrs Radcliffe not simply because he is the kind of man he is, but also because a validation of it would also be a symbolic validation of male dominance and omnipotence. Ellena has lost not only a father but also a mother, and Mrs Radcliffe quite consciously stresses the importance of this relationship in the closing pages of the narrative. . . . The significance of the mother-daughter relationship in the novel is not that a daughter necessarily feels more affection for a mother than for a father, but primarily that a mother is supportive of the feminine role; she can provide a strong and clear sense of what it is to be a woman. . . . In a very real sense Ellena's task in *The Italian* is to lose a father and find a mother. (pp. 72-4)

David Morse, "The Transposition of Gothic," in his Romanticism: A Structural Analysis *(© David Morse 1982; by permission of Barnes & Noble Books, a Division of Littlefield, Adams & Co., Inc.), Barnes & Noble, 1982, pp. 50-103.**

ADDITIONAL BIBLIOGRAPHY

Allen, M. L. "The Black Veil: Three Versions of a Symbol." *English Studies* 47, Nos. 1-6 (1966): 286-89.*

Discusses the symbol of the black veil, "simple but effective symbol of 'mystery' itself," as it is used in two stories influenced by Radcliffe's *The Mysteries of Udolpho*: Charles Dickens's "The Black Veil," and Nathaniel Hawthorne's "The Minister's Black Veil."

Beaty, Frederick L. "Mrs. Radcliffe's Fading Gleam." *Philological Quarterly* XLII, No. 1 (January 1963): 126-29.*
Argues that Radcliffe's *The Mysteries of Udolpho* is a direct source for William Wordsworth's "Ode: Intimations of Immortality" and Samuel Taylor Coleridge's "Mad Monk."

Dobrée, Bonamy. Introduction to *The Mysteries of Udolpho*, by Ann Radcliffe, edited by Bonamy Dobrée, pp. vii-xvi. London: Oxford University Press, 1966.
Provides a brief overview of the development of Radcliffe's style throughout her career. Dobrée praises Radcliffe's handling of structure in *The Mysteries of Udolpho* and her use of "what might be called common sense to the sentimental side" in her novels.

Durant, David S. "Aesthetic Heroism in *The Mysteries of Udolpho*." *The Eighteenth Century: Theory and Interpretation* 22, No. 2 (Spring 1981): 175-88.
Asserts that *The Mysteries of Udolpho* offers a critique of the Gothic by urging "on its audience what it shows in its heroine: a powerful imagination which consistently takes appearance for reality." Durant believes that, like Emily, the reader is asked to sort out realistic from fictional experience in the novel.

Evans, Bertrand. "Ann Radcliffe and Gothic Drama." In his *Gothic Drama from Walpole to Shelley*, pp. 90-115. Berkeley, Los Angeles: University of California Press, 1947.
A survey of the many stage adaptations of Radcliffe's novels. Evans contrasts the adaptations with the novels themselves.

Frank, Frederick S. "A Bibliography of Writings about Ann Radcliffe." *Extrapolation* 17, No. 1 (December 1975): 54-62.
A bibliography of works on Radcliffe published since the Gothic revival of the 1950s and "concerned exclusively with her life, influence, literary accomplishments, and place in the Gothic spectrum."

Garber, Frederick. "Meaning and Mode in Gothic Fiction." In *Racism in the Eighteenth Century*, edited by Harold E. Pagliaro, pp. 155-69. Cleveland, London: The Press of Case Western Reserve University, 1973.*
Considers *The Italian* and *The Mysteries of Udolpho* to be Radcliffe's best works. Garber lauds Radcliffe's "exceptional skill at both drawing out and mitigating epiphany," and notes that the two novels mentioned above are "acts of an adroit imagination manipulating a moral and modal counterpoint."

"Anecdote of Mrs. Radcliffe." *Godey's Lady's Book* XLV (September 1852): 225-27.
Describes Radcliffe's alleged arrest as a spy in 1795, at the border between France and Switzerland. What was thought by authorities to be a spy document was, in fact, the manuscript of *The Italian*.

Grant, Aline. *Ann Radcliffe*. Denver: Alan Swallow, 1951, 153 p.
A sentimentalized biography of Radcliffe that includes fictional conversations. Grant notes that the instability inherent in Radcliffe's novels reflects the politically unstable society in which they were published.

Havens, Raymond D. "Ann Radcliffe's Nature Descriptions." *Modern Language Notes* 66 (April 1951): 251-55.
Compares Radcliffe's nature descriptions in her novels with those in her travel journals. Havens concludes from the differences he notes that Radcliffe's turbulent descriptions in the novels were "in part employed to secure suspense and terror."

Kahane, Claire. "Gothic Mirrors and Feminine Identity." *The Centennial Review* XXIV, No. 1 (Winter 1980): 43-64.*
Discusses *The Mysteries of Udolpho* in terms of the heroine's quest for identity, which comes from "discovering the boundary between self and the mother-image archaically conceived." The

castle, according to Kahane, is at once a type of the maternal body, a place to re-experience the "less inhibited pleasures of childhood," and a place in which the heroine is "seduced by the experience of terror."

Kooiman-Van Middendorp, Gerarda Maria. "Ann Radcliffe." In her *The Hero in the Feminine Novel*, pp. 35-8. Middelburg, Netherlands: Firma G. W. Den Boer, 1931.
A discussion about male protagonists in novels by women novelists. Kooiman-Van Middendorp traces a resemblance between Samuel Richardson's "paragon of manly virtue" and the character of Valancourt in *The Mysteries of Udolpho*.

Lewis, Paul. "Fearful Lessons: The Didacticism of the Early Gothic Novel." *CLA Journal* XXIII, No. 4 (June 1980): 470-84.*
Considers Radcliffe a didactic novelist. Lewis also posits that "the very symmetry and repetitiveness of Radcliffe's novels, the order at the center of chaos, trains readers to relax and enjoy the terror."

McIntyre, Clara Frances. *Ann Radcliffe in Relation to Her Time*. Yale Studies in English, vol. 62. 1920. Reprint. Hamden, Conn.: Archon Books, 1970, 104 p.
A study of Radcliffe in relation to the political, literary, philosophical, and cultural influences of her time. McIntyre stresses that Radcliffe's most important contributions to nineteenth-century literature were her use of natural scenery and her manipulation of structure for the purposes of plot development.

"Mrs. Radcliffe's Posthumous Works." *The Monthly Review*, London II, No. vii (July 1826): 280-93.
A review of *Gaston de Blondeville*. The critic denigrates Radcliffe's reliance on supernatural agency, but judges parts of the novel to be "picturesque and affecting."

Murray, E. B. *Ann Radcliffe*. New York: Twayne Publishers, 1972, 178 p.
A useful general introduction to Radcliffe's life and works. Murray devotes a full chapter to each of the major novels, includes a section on influence, and a selected bibliography. "Psychological suspense was Mrs. Radcliffe's major contribution to the development of the novel," Murray asserts.

Railo, Eino. *The Haunted Castle: A Study of the Elements of English Romanticism*. London: George Routledge & Sons; New York: E. P. Dutton & Co., 1927, 388 p.*
A study of the elements of English Romanticism, especially its Gothic manifestations. Although he believes that "Radcliffe's books . . . really succeed in awakening an atmosphere of suspense," Railo also observes of Radcliffe's natural dénouements that "the final impression they make is feeble."

Summers, Rev. Montague. "A Great Mistress of Romance: Ann Radcliffe 1764-1823." *Transactions of the Royal Society of Literature of the United Kingdom* 2d. s. XXXV (1917): 39-77.
A brief overview of Radcliffe's novels. Summers posits that *The Italian*, because of its unity of plan, and its "scenes depicted in the most impressive and romantic manner," is the finest of Radcliffe's works.

Thomas, Donald. "The First Poetess of Romantic Fiction: Ann Radcliffe, 1764-1823." *English* XV, No. 87 (Autumn 1964): 91-5.
Finds that Radcliffe's novels are essentially "studies of the characters and sufferings of persecuted heroines," and that the other characters in each novel "exist only in relation to the heroine." Thomas further argues that Radcliffe's novels were popular in part because they present realistic characters "living in a Gothic fairyland but still confronted by the domestic or personal problems of middle-class mothers and daughters of the 1790s or 1800s."

Varma, Devendra P. Introduction to *A Sicilian Romance*, by Ann Radcliffe, pp. vii-xxvi. New York: Arno Press, 1972.
A survey of technique in Radcliffe's major novels. Varma particularly praises Radcliffe's successful depictions of the romantic villain. Varma adds that "Radcliffe's aesthetic practice gave a new dimension to romantic fiction."

Ware, Malcolm. "Mrs. Radcliffe's 'Picturesque Embellishment'." *Tennessee Studies in Literature* V (1960): 67-71.

> Contends that Radcliffe used descriptions "to relieve tension and attain aesthetic distance." Ware believes that her technique of "picturesque embellishment" prevented her scenes of terror from degenerating into horror.

Ware, Malcolm. *Sublimity in the Novels of Ann Radcliffe.* Essays and Studies on American Language and Literature, edited by S. B. Liljegren, vol. XXV. Upsala, Sweden: A. B. Lundequistska Bokhandeln, 1963, 62 p.

> An application of Edmund Burke's concept of sublimity to Radcliffe's novels. Ware states that "terror generated by Mrs. Radcliffe in her Gothic romances . . . is firmly rooted in the concept of sublimity as it was defined by Edmund Burke." He then discusses Radcliffe's descriptions in the novels in terms of Burke's principles. Though she is, according to Ware, a "direct descendant of the novelists of sensibility and sentimentality," Radcliffe's "distinguishing characteristic . . . is her use of . . . extended descriptive passages."

Wieten, Alida Alberdina Sibbelina. *Mrs. Radcliffe: Her Relation towards Romanticism.* Amsterdam: H. J. Paris, 1926, 146 p.

> Considers Radcliffe "one of [the] first exponents" of Romanticism, primarily because of her response to the natural world. Wieten concludes that Radcliffe "shadows forth Wordsworth's and Tennyson's intense joy in nature as well as Shelley's and Swinburne's love of liberty and abhorrence of restraint."

Anthony Trollope

1815-1882

English novelist, autobiography and short story writer, dramatist, and essayist.

Although Trollope is considered a major Victorian novelist, the precise nature of his achievement has proved elusive for critics. In spite of conflicting interpretations, commentators tend to agree that his characterizations form the basis of his importance, and they generally consider his finest efforts to be his two series of novels, each of which comprises six volumes. The Barsetshire series portrays middle-class life in an English cathedral town, while the Palliser series, or political novels, centers on a single character, Plantagenet Palliser, and the political milieu of London.

Born in London, Trollope was raised in poverty. His father failed at law and farming before going bankrupt, and his mother began what eventually became a lucrative writing career to support the family. Shy, awkward, and unkempt, Trollope was ridiculed by his wealthier classmates at Harrow and Winchester. At the age of nineteen he found work as a junior clerk at the Post Office and seven years later was transferred to Ireland, where he lived until 1859 when he returned permanently to London. He continued to work for the Post Office until 1867.

Trollope's move to Ireland inaugurated a period of change: for the first time in his life he was successful in work, love, friendship, and financial matters, and he began to write. His first novel, *The Macdermots of Ballycloran*, received little critical attention, but recognition came with the publication of *The Warden*, the first of the Barsetshire novels. *Barchester Towers*, the second novel in the series, was a popular success, and many readers still regard it as the apogee of Trollope's achievement.

Framley Parsonage, the fourth novel in the Barsetshire series, was Trollope's first work to appear in serial form, a method of magazine publication which promised a wide readership and greater critical response. The Barsetshire series elicited several comments which were repeated throughout Trollope's lifetime. Above all, critics warmed to his characters and praised both Trollope's lively and readable style and his humorous portrayal of everyday life. They also noted his fidelity to the English character, particularly in his portraits of young girls, although some critics noted that he overused the plot scheme of a heroine vacillating between two suitors. Trollope's early critics attributed a number of his faults, including careless construction, grammatical errors, and insubstantial story lines, to the fact that Trollope wrote quickly, and they blamed the exigencies of serial publication for his overly episodic and fragmentary plots. In addition, many commentators found Trollope's technique of allowing the narrator to constantly comment on the action and characters to be irrelevant and distracting. Still, the Barsetshire series contains Trollope's best-known and best-loved works, and many readers and critics consider these novels, particularly *Barchester Towers* and *The Last Chronicle of Barset*, the standard against which all his other novels should be judged.

In the mid 1860s Trollope's focus shifted from the postal to the political world. In 1868, he unsuccessfully ran for a seat in Parliament; four years earlier he had written *Can You Forgive Her?*, the first novel of the Palliser series. This series traces Plantagenet Palliser evolution from the time of his marriage to Lady Glencora through the increasing political responsibilities that eventually lead to his position as prime minister of England. Despite their depiction of political activity, however, these novels resemble the Barsetshire series in their avoidance of political and social commentary in favor of perceptive character studies. Several characters reappear throughout the series, and critics praise their development from one novel to the next. In particular, critics repeatedly point to Plantagenet Palliser and Lady Glencora as Trollope's most intimate, subtle, and profound studies of character. Trollope concurred with this assessment of his work. In his *An Autobiography*, he wrote that of all his characters, he preferred the old duke of Omnium, Plantagenet Palliser, and Lady Glencora: "I look upon this string of characters . . . as the best work of my life. Taking him altogether, I think that Plantagenet Palliser stands more firmly on the ground than any other personage I have created." And yet the Palliser novels were not as well regarded by Trollope's contemporaries as the earlier Barsetshire series; readers apparently found the world of politics not nearly as familiar or as pleasant as the provincial life of Barset.

The 1870s witnessed a decline in Trollope's popularity as his writing style and focus changed. Although they may include subjects similar to those in his earlier works, Trollope's later novels are more cynical and pessimistic in tone: *He Knew He Was Right* examines marriage and finds jealousy and corruption; *The Way We Live Now* studies society and uncovers financial and moral corruption. Critics objected to what they considered the sordid realism of these works, charging that Trollope ignored the novelist's responsibility of providing solutions to the social problems he depicted. In addition, because he was so prolific, Trollope was accused of commercialism.

Trollope's popularity and reputation, already failing at his death in 1882, deteriorated considerably following the posthumous publication of *An Autobiography*. The work's self-effacing tone reflects Trollope's modest opinion of his own talent and accomplishments. In *An Autobiography* Trollope described his rigidly-maintained writing schedule and his belief that writing was a craft, like shoemaking, that required perseverance and diligence for success. He denied that inspiration was necessary to literary work and claimed that his stories sprung from his pen without imaginative effort. Trollope's views on literature opposed the developing aesthetic theories of fin de siècle critics, who valued a carefully-honed work of literature. Trollope's discussion of his work methods provided ammunition for many of his detractors. They viewed his unrelenting schedules as proof that he had written too much and cited his comparison of novel-writing to shoemaking as proof that he was a simple craftsman.

Henry James's essay, published in 1883, is considered the first modern interpretation of Trollope's work. James's warm praise for Trollope's perceptive, vital characterizations and "complete appreciation of the usual" has formed the basis for continuing critical debate. James subscribed to then-current opinion in placing Trollope below the first rank of Victorian novelists, maintaining that Trollope had written too much and that his writing had become mechanical. James also criticized Trollope's use of the omnipresent narrator, which he found intrusive.

Early twentieth-century critics agreed that although his accurate pictures of everyday life were noteworthy, Trollope lacked the genius and vision essential to the great creative artist. An adherent of this view, George Saintsbury wrote in 1895 that Trollope was "doomed to pass." Twenty-five years later, in a reappraisal, Saintsbury modified this stance and claimed for Trollope a permanent place among Victorian novelists. Like many of his contemporaries, Saintsbury preferred the happier early novels to the later, darker works.

In his biographical-critical study published in 1927, Michael Sadleir presented Trollope as a serious writer. Like Henry James, Sadleir considered Trollope's "acceptance and his profound understanding of ordinary life" his greatest achievement. However, later critics, notably Bradford A. Booth, have disputed Sadleir's claim that Trollope was "the supreme novelist of acquiescence."

Trollope's work has been granted steady critical interest since the 1940s. His popularity soared during World War II when a generation of English readers found solace in his works. In her 1947 drama, *Anthony Trollope: A New Judgement*, Elizabeth Bowen examined the reasons behind this sudden resurgence. Written in the form of two dialogues, one between a young soldier and his uncle and the other between the soldier and Trollope's ghost, the drama expresses the idea that Trollope's celebration of the ordinary offered hope in the face of war. In the same year, Chauncey Brewster Tinker defended Trollope's narrative technique. In opposition to Henry James, Tinker maintained that the omnipresent narrator provides an impartial commentary on the action and helps to establish a relationship between the author and reader. Edd Winfield Parks supported Tinker's argument, stating that the narrator creates a bond that heightens the reader's sense of participation in the novel.

In the 1950s, A.O.J. Cockshut provoked wide critical debate with his thesis that Trollope's literary life represented one long "progress toward pessimism" and his assertion that the novels written after 1867 were Trollope's greatest achievement. Bradford A. Booth, a respected Trollope scholar who worked extensively with Trollope's letters and memoirs, rejected Cockshut's interpretation. Although he highly praised *The Last Chronicle of Barset* and *Orley Farm*, Booth determined that even these works are flawed and concluded that Trollope "was not a man of transcendent genius but of extraordinary talent." Recent critics consider Trollope a significant novelist and praise the style and structure of his novels as well as his complex view of society. The majority of commentators, including Joseph A. Baker, Arthur Mizener, Jerome Thale, John E. Dustin, William Cadbury, and Ruth apRoberts, base their appreciation of Trollope on an increased awareness of his artistry.

Critics continue to dispute the nature of Trollope's achievement, and there is no general agreement on his rank among writers of fiction. Yet commentators universally applaud the quality of his characterizations and regard Mrs. Proudie and Reverend Crawley from the Barsetshire chronicles and Plantagenet Palliser and Lady Glencora from the Palliser series as great imaginative creations. Many believe that Trollope was able to paint characters of such consistency, veracity, and depth because of his profound insight into and sympathy for his creations. Trollope himself considered the ability to live with one's characters essential and defined the main work of the novelist as "the creation of human beings in whose existence one is forced to believe." Many critics would find in Trollope's statement an apt description of his finest achievement.

(See also *Something about the Author*, Vol. 22 and *Dictionary of Literary Biography*, Vol. 21: *Victorian Novelists Before 1885*.)

*PRINCIPAL WORKS

The Macdermots of Ballycloran　(novel)　1847
The Kellys and the O'Kellys; or, Landlords and Tenants
　(novel)　1848
**The Warden　(novel)　1855
***Barchester Towers*　(novel)　1857
**Doctor Thorne　(novel)　1858
The Three Clerks　(novel)　1858
The Bertrams　(novel)　1859
***Framley Parsonage*　(novel)　1861
Orley Farm　(novel)　1862
****Can You Forgive Her?*　(novel)　1864
***The Small House at Allington*　(novel)　1864
The Belton Estate　(novel)　1866
The Claverings　(novel)　1867
***The Last Chronicle of Barset*　(novel)　1867
He Knew He Was Right　(novel)　1869
****Phineas Finn, the Irish Member*　(novel)　1869
****The Eustace Diamonds*　(novel)　1873

***Phineas Redux*   (novel)   1874
The Way We Live Now   (novel)   1875
***The Prime Minister*   (novel)   1876
The American Senator   (novel)   1877
Is He Popinjoy?   (novel)   1878
***The Duke's Children*   (novel)   1880
Ayala's Angel   (novel)   1881
Dr. Wortle's School   (novel)   1881
An Autobiography   (autobiography)   1883
An Old Man's Love   (unfinished novel)   1884
The Letters of Anthony Trollope   (letters)   1951

*Most of Trollope's works were originally published in periodicals.

**These works are collectively referred to as the Barsetshire series.

***These works are collectively referred to as the Palliser series, or
political novels.

JOHN BULL   (essay date 1847)

[*The Macdermots of Ballycloran was not a popular or critical
success, yet this early reviewer identified the quality which later
critics considered Trollope's greatest gift: he was "an acute observer of nature."*]

Mr. Trollope has produced a work of rare and singular merit
[in *The Macdermots of Ballycloran*] for, with almost a single
incident of domestic life, and embracing a period of time not
exceeding twelve months, he has constructed a story of surpassing and increasing interest to its close. The scene is laid
in Ireland, in the County of Leitrim, and the events are made
to bring out all the peculiar features of Irish life among the
peasantry, with a fidelity of description and knowledge of character equal to anything in the writings of Miss Edgeworth.
There is no extravagance, no caricature, none of the hacknied
circumstances which raise a laugh at the expense of truth. The
reader lays down the work at the end with the impression that
he has visited Ireland, conversed with the individuals who are
introduced, witnessed the scenes in which they are engaged,
listened to their language, and watched the progress of their
actions. All the characters are admirably discriminated, and
some of them are portrayed with a dramatic power akin to that
which we find in Sir Walter Scott's novels. . . . Mr. Trollope
is not only well acquainted with the peculiarities of Irish character, but he knows how to seize upon those which most vividly
exhibit the social features of the people. He is, too, an acute
observer of human nature, and it is because he never violates
its genuine impulses that his work, from the first page to the
last, lays so firm a hold upon the sympathy of the reader.

> *A review of "The Macdermots of Ballycloran," in*
> John Bull, *Vol. XXVII, May 22, 1847 (and reprinted
> in* Trollope: The Critical Heritage, *edited by Donald
> Smalley, Routledge & Kegan Paul, 1969, p. 549).*

SHARPE'S LONDON MAGAZINE   (essay date 1848)

['**The Kellys and the O'Kellys**'] is, as far as we can see, a
book written merely to amuse the reader; it is entertaining, and
not instructive;—indeed, we will not pretend to say that we
have discovered any moral in the book at all. . . . Moreover,
there is a sad want of interesting characters. The reader has
no admiration for, or sympathy with, any person in the book.

They are all just as common-place as if you had sent for them
all haphazard out of the street, and you do not much care if
you never see them again. There is nothing elevated, nothing
touching or tender throughout. . . .

'**The Kellys and the O'Kellys**' is *remarkably easy to read*. The
style is lively, clever, and uniformly amusing. It might be more
polished, it might be more eloquent; but there is no wisdom
in the criticism which finds fault with a plum because it is not
a pine-apple.

> *An extract from a review of "The Kellys and the
> O'Kellys," in* Sharpe's London Magazine, *Vol. VII,
> August, 1848 (and reprinted in* Trollope: The Critical
> Heritage, *edited by Donald Smalley, Routledge &
> Kegan Paul, 1969, p. 556).*

THE LEADER   (essay date 1855)

[*The following review of* The Warden, *Trollope's first successful
novel, cautions against the excessive use of the intrusive narrator,
a criticism echoed frequently in subsequent commentary.*]

The Warden has the first great recommendation of being a story
based on a good and solid foundation. Mr. Trollope has a
subject which it is worth while to describe, if we can do so
briefly without damaging the legitimate interests of his plot.
He starts with the very recognisable fact of a public charity,
in a cathedral town, which has been fairly and admirably founded
in bygone times, and which is very dishonestly managed at the
(modern) period of the story. . . . Here, assuredly, is a new
and an excellent subject for a novel—a subject which Mr.
Trollope has, in some respects, treated very cleverly. The character of the Warden is delightfully drawn, with a delicacy and
truth to nature which deserves the highest praise. Equally good
in their way are the feeble old Bishop, his truculent and intensely clerical son, who has married the Warden's eldest
daughter, and the old men who live on the mismanaged funds
of the charity. The defective part of the book is the conclusion,
which seems to us careless and unsatisfactory—as if the author
had got tired of his subject before he had done with it. The
passing introduction too of living authors, under farcically fictitious names, for the sake of criticising their books is a mistake—Mr. Trollope is far too clever a man, and has far too
acute and discriminating an eye for character to descend successfully to such low literary work as that. . . .

[This novel] certainly promises well for the author's future, if
he gives us more books. Assuming and hoping that he has not
written his last novel yet, we will venture to point out to his
notice two defects in his manner as a writer which he may
easily remedy, and which, he may take our word for it, are
felt as serious faults, not by critics only, but by the general
public as well. The first of the defects is that Mr. Trollope
speaks far too much in his own person in the course of his
narrative. It is always the reader's business, never the author's,
to apostrophise characters. The "illusion of the scene" is invariably perilled, or lost altogether, when the writer harangues
in his own person on the behaviour of his characters, or gives
us, with an intrusive "I," his own experiences of the houses
in which he describes those characters as living. (p. 164)

The second defect of manner which we have noticed in Mr.
Trollope is a want of thorough earnestness in the treatment of
the more serious passages of his story. The mocking tone is
well enough where the clerical aristocracy, and the abuses on
which they live, form the subject for treatment. But where the

main interest touches on the domain of real feeling—as in the chapter which illustrates the filial affection of the Warden's daughter, and the struggle between love and duty in the heart of her reforming lover—it is vitally important to the true effect of the scene on the reader, that the author should at least appear to feel sincerely with his characters. This Mr. Trollope, in the case of the young lady especially, seems to avoid. He exposes the womanly weakness of some of her motives with an easy satirical pleasantry which convinces us that he was himself not in the least affected by his love scene while he was writing it. There are certain maxims in Horace's *Art of Poetry* (to refer to a classical example, this time) which will remain great critical truths to the end of the world. Mr. Trollope must know the maxims to which we refer very well, and he cannot do better than apply them to himself the next time he gives us a novel. *The Warden* abundantly shows that he has powers far above the average as a writer of fiction. (pp. 164-65)

A review of ''The Warden,'' in The Leader, Vol. VI, No. 256, February 17, 1855, pp. 164-65.

[GEORGE MEREDITH] (essay date 1857)

[*Meredith was a respected nineteenth-century British poet, novelist, and critic. His creative works, though they are considered to lack a philosophical framework, reflect the ideas of his age: they embody a profound belief in evolution and in the essential goodness of humanity. His critical approaches derive from intuition rather than a consistent literary theory.*]

[''**Barchester Towers**''] is decidedly the cleverest novel of the season, and one of the most masculine delineations of modern life in a special class of society that we have seen for many a day. Those who have read its dashing predecessor, ''**The Warden**,'' will be quite up to the style and the story, which are both continued vigorously in ''**Barchester Towers**,'' and with renewed interest. . . . [Mr. Trollope] has, without resorting to politics, or setting out as a social reformer, given us a novel that men can enjoy, and a satire so cleverly interwoven with the story, that every incident and development renders it more pointed and telling. In general our modern prose satirists spread their canvas for a common tale, out of which they start when the occasion suits, to harangue, exhort, and scold the world in person. Mr. Trollope entrusts all this to the individuals of his story. (p. 595)

Mr. Trollope seems wanting in certain of the higher elements that make a great novelist. He does not exhibit much sway over the emotional part of our nature: though fairer readers may think that the pretty passages between Eleanor and her baby-boy show a capacity for melting woman's heart, at least. He is also a little too sketchy; the scenes are efficient in repose and richness: but let us cut short our complaints, thankful that we have a caustic and vigorous writer, who can draw men and women, and tell a story that men and women can read. (p. 596)

[*George Meredith*], in a review of ''Barchester Towers,'' in The Westminster and Foreign Quarterly Review, Vol. LXVIII, October, 1857, pp. 594-96.

THE SATURDAY REVIEW, LONDON (essay date 1858)

[*The following review is typical of the period in its enumeration of Trollope's faults, which, according to the reviewer, result from his prolific literary output, or ''the rapid multiplication of his progeny.''*]

In one sense it is good news to the readers of novels that Mr. Trollope has given another proof of his fecundity [in *Doctor Thorne*]. What he writes is sure to be very much above the average of the nourishment to which they are accustomed; but those who care for the interests of literature, and wish to see Mr. Trollope take the position to which he is unquestionably capable of rising, cannot but feel a considerable degree of uneasiness at the rapid multiplication of his progeny. . . . We are very sorry to say that the results which might have been predicted are obviously following. Mr. Trollope is acquiring great mechanical skill in those parts of his art in which such skill can be acquired, but he is losing what constituted the value and the promise of his style. Here and there he is very clever indeed, and the story is better than most other novels, but it shows a diminution in the life and point which belonged to its author's first tales; and though it must certainly be rated above the *Three Clerks* as a whole, the striking pieces are less striking. There is nothing in *Dr. Thorne* so tiresome as the history of Charley Tudor's first novel; but, on the other hand, there is nothing so good as the cross-examination of Undy Scott (highly irregular as it was in point of law), and nothing that can be for a moment compared to Mr. Slope and Archdeacon Grantley. . . .

The plot is obviously as slight as anything can be; but it affords opportunities for a great deal of description which no one but Mr. Trollope could have written, but which he with proper pains might have written much better. The two young ladies, Mary Thorne and Beatrice Gresham, are, we think, better drawn than any of his former female characters. There is nothing vulgar about them. Instead of boxing the ears of mercenary or heartless admirers in their proper persons, they leave that task to their brother and to the cook. . . .

The fault of the book throughout is its carelessness. The story is languid. Whenever a difficulty arises, Mr. Trollope tries to cut it instead of solving it. He turns to his reader, points out the difficulty, and coolly passes it over. In the second chapter of the first volume, which makes two separate starts, each dating twenty years before the main story, Mr. Trollope observes—''I quite feel that an apology is due for beginning a novel with two long dull chapters full of description . . . but twist it as I will, I cannot do otherwise.'' It was his business to do otherwise, and not to publish the book till he had succeeded. Mr. Trollope must know that nothing in this world is more provoking than a breach of duty urged by way of apology for another breach of duty. . . . The contract of the writer with the reader is to create and maintain a reasonably perfect illusion as to the reality of the events which he relates, and he breaks that contract if he wantonly points out the difficulties of his task, and says that there is a way out of them, but that he does not choose to take the trouble to find it. (p. 618)

A review of ''Doctor Thorne,'' in The Saturday Review, London, Vol. V, No. 137, June 12, 1858, pp. 618-19.

[E. S. DALLAS] (essay date 1859)

[Mr. Trollope is] the most fertile, the most popular, the most successful author—that is to say, of the circulating library sort. We believe there are persons who would rather not receive such praise, and who hold a circulating library success in great contempt, but they labour under a misapprehension. It is true that books which circulate without being cherished, which we read once and do not care to read a second time, which people borrow but never think of buying, are not the best of all books, and certainly are not the product of that mysterious something which we call genius. But genius is not everything in this world, and the presence of a few comets in the literary firmament need not make us blind to the existence of a good many stars. There are people who find Mr. Thackeray too thoughtful and Mr. Dickens too minute, who are tired of dainty fare and curious wines, who have had enough of the heavenly manna, and who long for the flesh-pots of Egypt. Mr. Trollope is the very man for them. There is no pretence about him, no shamming, no effort. He is always clever, often amusing, sometimes even great, or very near being great, but his predominating faculty is good sense. Belonging to the circulating library, Mr. Trollope's novels are free from those faults which we naturally associate with the circulating library—extravagance, trickery, false sentiment, morbid pictures. His style is the very opposite of melodramatic; it is plain and straightforward, utterly devoid of clap-trap. It is the style of a man who has a good deal to say, who can afford to say it simply, who does not attempt to astonish, and who is content to give his readers innocent and rational amusement. These novels are healthy and manly. . . . (p. 104)

Perhaps Mr. Trollope carries his aversion from everything melodramatic to an extreme, and though he errs on the right side, still he errs. The essence of melodrama is surprise. The situations are unexpected; the characters are doing things for which we were not prepared; passions are evoked which are not justified by the facts, and sentiments are expressed which have no relation to the circumstances. Everything, in short, is a surprise. Mr. Trollope, on the other hand, has vowed that there shall be no surprises in his novels. The characters shall be naturally evolved; the incidents shall grow out of each other; the passion shall not be exaggerated, and the sentiment shall veritably belong to the event. But in determining thus to show cause for every effect, and a sufficient motive for every act and word, Mr. Trollope seems at times to be too anxious to avoid startling results; afraid lest the reader should be taken unawares, he lets out his secret too soon, and long before he has laid down his lines of action he forewarns us of what is to happen—what is to be the joyous consummation or the dismal catastrophe which is the intended result of all his plans. At the first mention of his heroine's name he says, ostentatiously, 'Now, this is to be my *prima donna*—the lady you must all love, the lady I am going to pet, the lady whom fortune is to favour, the lady who is to get the prime husband at the end of the third volume.' Here the story is at once told, all suspense is removed, and when we see the heroine afterwards under a cloud we know that the cloud means nothing, or is intended but to make the sunshine which afterwards bursts forth more bright. So of another personage, we are informed that his character is unsound and must inevitably end in misery and ruin. This is a sure way to prevent our being surprised when misery and ruin overtake the poor wretch; but it is also a method apt to damp our interest in the event, and to destroy all the excitement of suspense. It is the expression of a manly aversion to melodramatic art with which we cordially sympathize, but it is also an appeal to sources of interest which are more welcome to the student of philosophy than to the reader of novels. Mr. Trollope says virtually, 'I will do what novelists never yet have done; I will begin with the end of the story; I will have no secrets; I will sacrifice all the interest of cunningly devised situations and mysterious occurrences; I will, not perhaps formally, but virtually, give my readers the action of the piece as an accomplished fact, and if I cannot amuse them with what else remains—namely, with the rational pleasure of following

the story in its details, tracing the gradual rise and progress of events, and describing the attendant circumstances,—then I may as well throw aside my pen altogether.' In making this resolve Mr. Trollope throws away, needlessly we think, some of the resources of his art; while, on the other hand, he wins our respect, and proves that a success which has not been purchased by vulgar methods must be due to merits of a sterling kind. (pp. 104-05)

> *[E. S. Dallas], in a review of "The Bertrams," in* The Times, *London (© Times Newspapers Limited 1859), May 23, 1859 (and reprinted in* Trollope: The Critical Heritage, *edited by Donald Smalley, Routledge & Kegan Paul, 1969, pp. 103-09).*

NATHANIEL HAWTHORNE (letter date 1860)

[Hawthorne is considered to be one of the greatest American fiction writers. His The Scarlet Letter, *with its balanced structure, simple, expressive language, and superb use of symbols, is a recognized classic of American literature. The following comment, one of the most frequently quoted appraisals in all of Trollope criticism, is universally hailed as a succinct and accurate summary of the nature of Trollope's art. Trollope himself, in* An Autobiography, *praised Hawthorne's astuteness: "The criticism, whether just or unjust, describes with wonderful accuracy the purport that I have ever had in view of my writing."]*

[It is odd enough] that my own individual taste is for quite another class of works than those which I myself am able to write. If I were to meet with such books as mine by another writer, I don't believe I should be able to get through them. Have you ever read the novels of Anthony Trollope? They precisely suit my taste,—solid and substantial, written on the strength of beef and through the inspiration of ale, and just as real as if some giant had hewn a great lump out of the earth and put it under a glass case, with all its inhabitants going about their daily business, and not suspecting that they were being made a show of. And these books are just as English as a beef-steak. Have they ever been tried in America? It needs an English residence to make them thoroughly comprehensible; but still I should think that human nature would give them success anywhere. (pp. 122-23)

> *Nathaniel Hawthorne, in an extract from a letter to Joseph M. Field on February 11, 1860, in* An Autobiography *by Anthony Trollope, Harper & Brothers, 1883 (and reprinted by University of California Press, 1947, pp. 122-23).*

THE SATURDAY REVIEW, LONDON (essay date 1861)

[Mr. Anthony] Trollope himself nowhere pretends to do more than to write down what he sees going on around him. He paints from the outside. This does not make his painting for all ordinary purposes the less real. What we know of most people that we meet is the way they dress, their fortune, their manners in the world, their aims, the general tenor of their lives, and the kind of remarks that they make when they are talking to their acquaintances. Mr. Anthony Trollope tells us all this about his heroes and heroines, and tells it [to] us with a strong dash of cleverness and fun. His business is simply to catch folly and fashions as they fly. We see Lady Lufton and Mrs. Grantley in the book just as we should see them if we were their neighbours in Barsetshire. We get tired of them as soon as, and no sooner than, we should get tired of Lady Lufton and Mrs. Grantley in real life, if they kept on calling once a month. We like to be amused, and we like to come across the characters that amuse us. . . .

[*Framley Parsonage* is not] either so brilliant or so well worth reading as *Barchester Towers,* of which it is too often merely a *réchauffé.* It stands to its predecessor very much as [Thackeray's] *Newcomes* stands to *Vanity Fair.* With fewer faults of taste, with more polish and geniality of tone, it is infinitely less forcible and striking. It is a curious thing to notice how soon, in the words of the poet, a successful author "rubs his social angles down." As Mr. Trollope becomes more successful, he becomes more tame. He improves in the refinement and delicacy of his touch, at the expense of his brilliancy and his fun. Belonging as he does to the "conversational" school, who address their readers from first to last in a tone of raillery and badinage, there is a slight danger that, with all his ability, he may at last degenerate into a mere *raconteur,* whose monthly mission is to gossip about things in general.

With some of the best characters in *Framley Parsonage* we are already acquainted. Mrs. Proudie, Miss Dunstable, the Greshams, and the Grantleys, are creations which belong to older and fresher works. It is astonishing how much a novelist loses in freshness and vigour by adopting the plan now so much in vogue, of borrowing from himself. . . . Mr. Trollope, it is true—whose art lies not in developing or creating character, but in depicting the behaviour of drawing-room company—suffers less than others might by his adoption of the practice. We are almost always glad to see Mrs. Proudie and Miss Dunstable in his book, just as we should be generally glad, for the sake of the fun, to go to an evening party if we knew they were to be there. But we simply are interested in them so far as they say something good to amuse us. About their inner life we have long known all that Mr. Trollope is able to tell us, and we do not care to watch them long unless they are going to be funny. . . .

It is because we are only slightly interested in the character of the people in the story, that Mr. Trollope is driven continually to amuse us by caricature. To paint the ordinary doings of ordinary men and women would be a stupid and uninteresting performance, unless either a shade of mystery and romance, or of psychological interest, was added to the picture, or unless everything is cleverly turned into fun. A dash of exaggeration and emphasis is needed to convert a commonplace scene into an amusing comedy. Perhaps the two wittiest scenes in *Framley Parsonage* are Mr. Harold Smith's lecture, and Miss Dunstable's conversazione. There are very few living writers who could exaggerage and caricature with so delicate and ingenious a touch as Mr. Anthony Trollope in these two chapters. . . . Mr. Trollope simply sees the amusing side of the scene, and relates the history of the proceedings as a good storyteller might. In fact, he is far less of a novelist than a good diner-out. Any of Mr. Trollope's admirers who has a strong sense of fun may do for himself in imagination what it is Mr. Trollope's charm that he has done so well on paper. Given Mrs. Proudie and Mrs. Grantley in a room, who does not know what they would say to one another? The difference between Mr. Trollope and his readers is that he not only knows what Mrs. Proudie and Mrs. Grantley would say, and how they would look, but can seize upon the most amusing points and write them down. As of course it is only worth his while to write down the amusing part of their conversation, which after all must be a fractional portion of the whole, his narrative is a caricature.

The plot of *Framley Parsonage* is really extremely poor, and the abruptness with which the third volume concludes leads us

to conjecture that the author was wearied of the society of the good people of Barsetshire, of whom, in the course of all his novels, he has seen so much. Mr. Trollope is not naturally a good constructor of plots, and writing month by month in a magazine is not the best way to make him so. . . . [It] is no doubt difficult to keep the spine of a novel strong and healthy, if the novel is twelve times a year divided into minute portions, and joined together at the end like a piece of patchwork. All unity of conception in the book too often gives way—the chapters become fragmentary and disjointed—and the novelist does little more than stroll on from month to month—preaching and teaching his own particular philosophy—catering for the amusement of the public, and piously hoping that something interesting may ultimately happen to his own hero. It is not in this way that great works are written. . . . Mr. Trollope, if he is a prudent man, will consider his ways. When next the author of *Framley Parsonage* comes before the public—an event to which all of us look forward with pleasure—we trust that it may be with new heroes and new heroines, and a new plot; and that *Tom Towers,* and *the Jupiter,* the gods and the giants, Barchester and its Bishop, may all be sleeping in a common grave. (p. 452)

> *A review of "Framley Parsonage," in* The Saturday Review, *London, Vol. II, No. 288, May 4, 1861, pp. 451-52.*

ELIZABETH BARRETT BROWNING   (letter date 1861)

[*A leading poet in Victorian England, Browning is best known for her cycle of love poetry,* Sonnets from the Portuguese.]

How admirably this last [*Orley Farm*] opens! We are both delighted with it. What a pity it is that so powerful and idiomatic a writer should be so incorrect grammatically and scholastically speaking! Robert insists on my putting down such phrases as these: 'The Cleeve was distant from Orley two miles, though it *could not be driven* under five.' '*One rises up the hill.*' 'As good as *him.*' 'Possessing more *acquirements* than he would have *learned* at Harrow.' *Learning acquirements!* Yes, they are faults, and should be put away by a first-rate writer like Anthony Trollope. It's always worth while to be correct. But do understand through the pedantry of these remarks that we are full of admiration for the book. The movement is so excellent and straightforward—walking like a man, and 'rising up-hill', and not going round and round, as Thackeray has taken to do lately.

> *Elizabeth Barrett Browning, in a letter to Miss Blagden in 1861, in* The Letters of Elizabeth Barrett Browning, *edited by Frederic G. Kenyon, The Macmillan Company, 1897 (and reprinted in* Trollope: The Critical Heritage, *edited by Donald Smalley, Routledge & Kegan Paul, 1969, p. 140).*

THE SPECTATOR   (essay date 1862)

[*The following was the first* Spectator *review of a work by Trollope after Richard Holt Hutton became an editor on the journal. Earlier* Spectator *reviews of Trollope's works are considered undistinguished, while critics agree that those published under Hutton's editorship are particularly insightful. Although no records exist to verify it, several Trollope scholars point to the style of the following review to support their claim that Hutton was its author. Donald Smalley, editor of* Trollope: The Critical Heritage, *termed this "one of the most penetrating critiques of a single novel of Trollope's to appear within a century since its publication."*]

Orley Farm is, in some respects, Mr. Trollope's greatest work; and in some respects, perhaps, his most defective. It is the nearest approach that he has made to the depth and force of tragedy, and for that very reason the light ripple of his habitually tranquil manner, the wide shadows, the arbitrary channels, and the ill-defined delta of this, as of nearly all his stories, come out into stronger relief. Mr. Trollope's imagination is not one that ever seems, to the critic's observation, at least, to brood long over visions that task its full power. As, one after another, his men and women pass out on to his literary stage, and become to us as the acquaintances we meet every day, neither less distinct nor better known, we gather the impression that his mind creates new varieties out of the faces and characters that flash by him in society almost as easily as a shaken kaleidoscope creates new patterns out of the same bits of coloured glass, and yet always within the same general limits of form, colour, and depth. There is nothing, apparently, of the agony of meditative travail about his mind. . . . Mr. Trollope does not give us so much the impression of conceiving and creating his own conceptions, as of very acutely observing them as they pass along the screen of some interior faculty. In this respect he differs from almost all his greater brother artists.

His mode of writing is uniformly, and even in the critical scenes, that of a spectator. He never loses himself so much in any situation as to lose even the dialectic tricks of a narrator. Open any page anywhere in *Orley Farm* and you are almost certain to find several sentences in it beginning, ''And then,'' in the true manner of a man who has minutely watched the succession of events, but not enough identified himself with any one character in the scene to make that so living a centre of interest that the little words which distinguish accurately the sequences of things almost become inappropriate. . . . [In] all the critical scenes of this book, Mr. Trollope never for a moment loses the nice discriminate style of ''articulately-speaking men,''—separating event from event, gesture from gesture, thought from thought, with the manner of a distinct witness who wishes to give the most perspicuous evidence, not of an artist the glow of whose conception has for the moment struck fire from his own mind. (pp. 1136-37)

[Much] of Mr. Trollope's secret charm generally consists in the spontaneous moderation with which he *limits* himself in regard to the leading characteristics of his *dramatis personae*, without in the least diminishing the emphasis or obscuring the meaning of his pictures, in the truthfulness with which he assigns a fixed verge within which the natural restraints of society and habit confine the swing of the individual passion or impulse he delineates. Thus, when he paints the cunning of a low attorney like Dockwrath, he confines it, and makes you feel his art in confining it, within the ordinary range of safe professional cunning. . . . In no place does he paint a passion or eccentricity without making you see the outer margin and natural orbit of it; he never indulges himself with a vague, wasteful infinitude of any quality, like novelists in general, but scarcely hints a characteristic at all before he allows you to see its scope and boundary. Now the great aim of his art in *Orley Farm* is to paint a naturally strong, and even noble character, stained by a great crime, with the same studious moderation. Lady Mason has committed, from maternal passion, a great forgery and robbery, and Mr. Trollope is exceedingly anxious to paint the exact limits within which the effect that crime is kept,—the effect it has, and the effect it does *not* have, in corrupting the other parts of her character. For the most part we think the picture, though the difficulty is for a long time evaded by a very cold external view of her demeanour

to others,—very powerful. There is certainly much art in the added vividness which her own sense of guilt takes the moment the pressure of constant concealment is removed, and she sees it reflected back from the minds of friends whom she reveres. But there are grave faults, we think, in the earlier picture of the guilty woman's manner while the self-restraint is still exerted and the crime kept down. She is by no means meant, even then, to be an evil woman; the coldness of her manner expresses the sense of her solitary position—of her wish to retain that solitary position; otherwise the seed of evil is meant to be almost latent. But the conception of Lady Mason is fluctuating and (what is very rare with Mr. Trollope) indistinct before the confession of her guilt. (p. 1137)

''Mr. Trollope's 'Orley Farm','' in The Spectator, *Vol. 33, No. 1789, October 11, 1862, pp. 1136-38.*

ANTHONY TROLLOPE   (letter date 1863)

[The following is excerpted from Trollope's letter to George Eliot in which he asks her to accept a copy of Rachel Ray; *Eliot's reply follows (1863). An often-quoted conversation between the two authors highlights the nature of the differences in their writing styles. After learning of the ease with which Trollope wrote (see excerpt from Trollope's* An Autobiography, 1883*), Eliot described her frequent struggles with failed inspiration and painstaking composition, concluding that ''there are days together when I cannot write a line.'' Trollope responded: ''With imaginative work like yours that is quite natural; but with my mechanical stuff it's a sheer matter of industry.'']*

In *Rachel Ray* I have attempted to confine myself absolutely to the commonest details of commonplace life among the most ordinary people, allowing myself no incident that would be even remarkable in every day life. I have shorn my fiction of all romance.

I do not know what you who have dared to handle great names & historic times will think of this. But you must not suppose that I think the little people are equal as subjects to the great names. Do you, who can do it, go on. I know you will not be deterred by the criticisms of people who cannot understand. Neither should you be deterred by internal criticism. That which you have in your flask you are bound to pour forth. (pp. 138-39)

Anthony Trollope, in a letter to George Eliot on October 18, 1863, in his The Letters of Anthony Trollope, *edited by Bradford Allen Booth (©Oxford University Press 1951; reprinted by permission of Oxford University Press), Oxford University Press, London, 1951, pp. 138-39.*

M. E. LEWES [GEORGE ELIOT]   (letter date 1863)

[The following is Eliot's response to Trollope's letter (1863). Eliot is considered to be one of the foremost English novelists of the nineteenth century. Her novels, like Trollope's, provide intimate pictures of everyday life informed by a profound insight into human character. Yet her novels also explore psychological and moral issues, elements which many critics have found lacking in Trollope's works.]

I am much struck in [''**Rachel Ray**''] with the skill with which you have organized thoroughly natural everyday incidents into a strictly related, well-proportioned whole, natty and complete as a nut on its stem. Such construction is among those subtleties of art which can hardly be appreciated except by those who have striven after the same result with conscious failure. Rachel herself is a sweet maidenly figure, and her poor mother's spiritual confusions are excellently observed.

But there is something else I care yet more about, which has impressed me very happily in all those writings of yours that I know—it is that people are breathing good bracing air in reading them—it is that they (the books) are filled with belief in goodness without the slightest tinge of maudlin. They are like pleasant public gardens, where people go for amusement and, whether they think of it or not, get health as well. (p. 110)

> *M. E. Lewes [George Eliot], in a letter to Anthony Trollope on October 23, 1863 (reprinted by permission of Princeton University Library, Parrish Collection), in* The George Eliot Letters: 1862-1868, *Vol. IV, edited by Gordon S. Haight, Yale University Press, 1955, pp. 110-11.*

THE SPECTATOR   (essay date 1864)

Mr. Trollope has written nothing more true or entertaining than [*The Small House at Allington,* an] admirable representation of our modern social world, with its special temptations, special vices, and special kinds of retribution. It is not so much a story, though it has a certain current of story quite sufficient to lead the reader on, as a fragment of complicated social strategy that he describes in these pages,—and describes with a delicacy of observation and a moral thoughtfulness which matters apparently so trifling probably never before received. (p. 197)

Mr. Trollope's intellectual grasp of his characters, so far as he goes (which is only now and then much below the surface), is nearly perfect; but then he chooses to display that grasp almost exclusively in the hold they get or fail to get over other characters, and in the hold they yield to other characters over them. It is in his command of what we may call the moral 'hooks and eyes' of life that Mr. Trollope's greatest power lies. And his characters are more or less interesting almost exactly in proportion to the degree in which their mode of influencing or failing to influence other people is unique and characteristic. (p. 198)

> *A review of "The Small House at Allington," in* The Spectator, *Vol. 37, No. 1867, April 9, 1864 (and reprinted in* Trollope: The Critical Heritage, *edited by Donald Smalley, Routledge & Kegan Paul, 1969, pp. 197-201).*

[HENRY JAMES]   (essay date 1865)

> *[James was an American-born English novelist, short story writer, critic, essayist, and playwright of the late nineteenth and early twentieth centuries who is considered to be one of the greatest novelists in the English language. Although best known for his novels, James is also admired as a lucid and insightful critic. His later essay (see excerpt below, 1883), considered to be one of the finest critical appraisals of Trollope, is a much more appreciative assessment than the following review.]*

This new novel of Mr. Trollope's ["**Can You Forgive Her?**"] has nothing new to teach us either about Mr. Trollope himself as a novelist, about English society as a theme for the novelist, or, failing information on these points, about the complex human heart. Take any one of his former tales, change the name of half the characters, leave the others standing, and transpose the incidents, and you will have "**Can You Forgive Her?**" It is neither better nor worse than the tale which you will select.

It became long ago apparent that Mr. Trollope had only one manner. In this manner he very soon showed us his *maximum*. He has recently, in "**Miss Mackenzie,**" showed us his *minimum*. In the work before us he has remained pretty constantly at his best. . . .

For so thick a book, there is certainly very little story. There are no less than three different plots, however, if the word can be applied to Mr. Trollope's simple machinations. That is, there is a leading story, which, being foreseen at the outset to be insufficient to protract the book during the requisite number of months, is padded with a couple of underplots, one of which comes almost near being pathetic, as the other falls very far short of being humorous. (p. 409)

Mr. Trollope's book presents no feature more remarkable than the inveteracy with which he just eludes being really serious; unless it be the almost equal success with which he frequently escapes being really humorous. Both of these results are the penalty of writing so rapidly; but as in much rapid writing we are often made to regret the absence of that sober second thought which may curtail an extravagance—that critical movement which, if you will only give it time, is sure to follow the creative one—so in Mr. Trollope we perpetually miss that sustained action of the imagination, that creative movement which in those in whom this faculty is not supreme *may,* if you will give it time, bear out the natural or critical one, which would intensify and animate his first conception. We are for ever wishing that he would go a little further, a little deeper. . . .

To Mr. Trollope all the possible incidents of society seem to be of equal importance and of equal interest. He has the same treatment, the same tone, for them all. After narrating the minutest particulars of a certain phase of his heroine's experience, he will dwell with equal length and great patience upon the proceedings of a vulgar widow (the heroine's aunt), who is engaged in playing fast and loose with a couple of vulgar suitors. With what authority can we invest the pen which treats of the lovely niece, when we see it devoted with the same good-will to the utterly prosaic and unlovely aunt? It is of course evident that Mr. Trollope has not intended to make the aunt either poetic or attractive. He has intended, in the first place, to swell his book into the prescribed dimensions, and, incidentally, to make the inserted matter amusing. A single chapter of it might be amusing; a dozen chapters are inexpressibly wearisome. (p. 410)

> *[Henry James], in a review of "Can You Forgive Her?" in* The Nation, *Vol. L, No. 13, September 28, 1865, pp. 409-10.*

THE SPECTATOR   (essay date 1867)

The art of *The Claverings* strikes us as of a very high class. There are far fewer unconnected side-pictures than is usual in Mr. Trollope's novels. Indeed, almost every side-picture is calculated to heighten the effect of the principal subject of the story. Harry Clavering's rather weak openness to the influence of any attractive woman with whom he is much thrown, is brought out in strong relief against the ungainly curate's (Mr. Saul's) manly dignity and intensity of purpose. Mr. Trollope has contrasted his rather soft, though in relation to all but feminine affairs perfectly manly, hero, with one who in many respects seems but half a man, and yet is, in relation to the dignity, depth, and constancy of his affection, immeasurably Harry Clavering's superior; and the effect of the contrast is a new force both in the mere vividness of the picture and in the clearness and truthfulness of Mr. Trollope's moral. . . . (p. 275)

The Claverings has, as we believe, a higher moral, and a more perfect artistic unity of the kind we have indicated, than any of Mr. Trollope's previous tales. There is scarcely a touch in it which does not contribute to the main effect, both artistic and moral, of the story, and not a character introduced, however slightly sketched, which does not produce its own unique and specific effect on the reader's imagination. (p. 276)

> *A review of "The Claverings," in* The Spectator, *Vol. 40, No. 2027, May 4, 1867 (and reprinted in* Trollope: The Critical Heritage, *edited by Donald Smalley, Routledge & Kegan Paul, 1969, pp. 275-76).*

J. HERBERT STACK (essay date 1869)

[In his] **"Last Chronicle of Barset"** [Mr. Trollope] has given us glimpses of a certain tragic and poetic power that place him far above any chronicler of young lady's thoughts. The story has all the good qualities of his other works—the exceeding naturalness of the dialogue, the homely fidelity to English character of the men and women, the absence of all coarse appeals to sympathy, the entire freedom from all straining after effect. But its superiority to his other stories arises from his selection of a situation as deep in its pain as any that could be brought within the range of ordinary English experience. . . . The depth of the [curate's] anguish as he tries to realise that he—with his high conscientiousness, his ever-rigid preaching of duty, and his stern views of the holiness of a moral life—is held to be a thief; the awful dread of the wife that this last crowning calamity, her husband's public disgrace as a felon, is coming on, and that he is perhaps insane, present a combination of as keen an agony as is possible in ordinary English life. . . . We do not remember any situation in any modern novel in which the pure tragedy of the circumstances is so deep. . . . (pp. 190-91)

But granting to Mr. Trollope very high praise for the genius, the conscientious art, the happy power, with which he has designed and elaborated this story of the Crawleys, we do think that hardly any words can be too strong to express our annoyance at finding what might have been a perfect work of literature disfigured by chapters of utterly irrelevant matter. Because Miss Lily Dale was a jilted young lady in the **"Small House of Allington,"** she must be trotted out again in this story as declining gracefully into the position of an old maid. Because Johnny Eames was a rather lubberly and lucky hobbledehoy in the one story, he must be Mr. John Eames in the second, still more lucky in the world, with *bonnes fortunes* in Bayswater, yet still besieging the impregnable Lily of his heart. We do not deny that, on the whole, Lily in her mature maidenhood is very natural, that she talks happily, that she is very like ten thousand other young English ladies of good style, and that faithful copies of John Eames are to be found by the score from ten to four in Somerset House; that half-silly women, like Mrs. Dobbs Broughton, with a substratum of the common-sense born of cowardice, are common enough; and that more than one Miss Demolines may inhabit handsome houses in the dissipated suburb of Bayswater. But why intrude those sketches of comedy and farce—very fair, as far as they go—into what might have been a very finished story—an enduring piece of English literary art? Ten thousand years hence, if our literature lives so long, the tragedy at Mr. Crawley's hearth will be easily understood; his character will stand clearly out; but we might

as well predict an immortality of art for the pictures in an illustrated paper as hope that Mr. John Eames or Miss Lily Dale will remain in literature as types of anything at all. If we had Mr. Trollope's leave, it seems that, with nothing but a knife, we could make his **"Last Chronicle"** one-half shorter and fifty-fold better worth preservation. We should simply cut out every chapter devoted to Miss Lily Dale, Mr. John Eames, Mr. Adolphus Crosbie, &c., &c., and make the story as it ought to have been, simply the tale of Mr. Crawley's trouble; how it affected himself, his wife, his daughter, his daughter's lover, his daughter's lover's father, his bishop, and his bishop's wife. With the one finely pathetic figure as the centre, a perfect story could be thus built up. (pp. 191-92)

In one respect Mr. Trollope deserves praise that even Dickens and Thackeray do not deserve. Many of his stories are more true throughout to that unity of design, that harmony of tone and colour, which are essential to works of art. In one of his Irish stories, **"The Kellys and the O'Kellys,"** the whole is steeped in Irish atmosphere; the key-note is admirably kept throughout; there is nothing irrelevant, nothing that takes the reader out of the charmed circle of the involved and slowly unwound bead-roll of incidents. We say nothing as to the other merits of the story—its truth to life, the excellence of the dialogue, the naturalness of the characters—for Mr. Trollope has these merits nearly always at his command. He has a true artist's idea of tone, of colour, of harmony; his pictures are one; are seldom out of drawing; he never strains after effect; is fidelity itself in expressing English life; is never guilty of caricature. Why then are many of his stories, with all their merits, not enduring works of art? Simply, in our opinion, because his choice of subjects is utterly wrong. The genteel public of the day may demand portraits of themselves as they demand photographs of surly-looking men and simpering women, which they call likenesses of themselves and their wives; but no amount of skill can make common-place men and common-place incidents and common-place feelings fit subjects of high or true literary art. (p. 196)

[Mr. Trollope] knows more, we think, of English parson life than any man in England. He has somehow got behind the clerical waistcoat, and can count its throbs: can he not, then, tell us something deeper and something more than he has yet done? We accept his revelation of Crawley struggling with poverty and shame, of Mark Robarts fighting off debt; but has he never heard of any conflict deeper, higher, fiercer, worse? (p. 197)

Then, again, we admit Mr. Trollope's power in describing young ladies in love and in doubt. He knows English girls by heart. We cannot well fancy him a Sylph like one of Pope's in the "Rape of the Lock," else we should suppose that he had often listened to a thousand talkee-talkee conversations, when young ladies in the seclusion of their bed-rooms or dressing-rooms unloose their thoughts to one another, and let down their back hair. But surely English ladies suffer occasionally other agony than doubts as to whether this or that lover is to be the man thrown over, accepted, subdued, encouraged, or drawn on. . . . [There] are deep chords in woman's nature that this kind of love does not touch; and as the prose laureate of English girls of the better class, why should not Mr. Trollope record something else beside flirtations that end well? Lady Glencora Palliser is pretty and true gliding over thin ice with her handsome lover; pretty and true in her candour to her cold spouse; pretty and true with her baby heir to the great dukedom. But suppose she had run away? Is there nothing deep, dark, and deadly in human nature and human sin to be painted vividly so that our souls may be purged by terror, and pity, and stronger thoughts than amusement at unmarried jilts, married flirts, and young mothers? (p. 198)

> J. Herbert Stack, "Mr. Anthony Trollope's Novels," in The Fortnightly Review *(reprinted by permission of Contemporary Review Company Limited), n.s. Vol. V, No. XXVI, February 1, 1869, pp. 188-98.*

[F. N. BROOME] (essay date 1869)

In *He Knew He Was Right* there is not a man or woman whom in real life we would greatly care to know, and there are certainly a great many we would rather not have anything to do with, and his readers would take it as a favour if Mr. Trollope would put a little vertebrate strength into his next literary creations. . . . Nor do we see why he should so frequently fly in the face of the proverb which associates gray hairs with wisdom; however often it may be the case in real life, there is in fiction a sort of impiety which should be seldom ventured on in making middle-age the synonym of silliness. Mr. Trollope's purpose, as we take it, is not satire; then why does he not show us a little more of the creditable side of human nature, instead of halting halfway between beauty and ugliness, and painting the commonplace? He gives us with ease and accuracy the pervading type, yet we cannot help wishing he would make a higher attempt at something, perhaps, less matter of fact, but certainly more alluring. (p. 330)

Mr. Trollope has never given a better illustration of all he is and all he is not than *He Knew He Was Right.* The Barsetshire series shows us his high merit; and they are so equal, so perfect in themselves, and so necessary to each other, that we wish for nothing else than they give us. But now that Barset, and the Bishop, and the Archdeacon, and all our old friends are done with, and we find Mr. Trollope still in the same vein, but with a little less vigour, and manifestly writing against time books that are pleasant reading for leisure hours, but are not such imperative claimants on the busiest lives as *Barchester Towers* and *Dr. Thorne* certainly were, we are apt to grow critical, and we think that most readers of *He Knew He Was Right* will agree with us when we say that, as coming from Mr. Trollope, there is something insufficient and unsatisfactory both in its conception and execution. . . . (pp. 330-31)

Mr. Trollope is one of the few novel writers the very excellence of whose work tends to produce hypercriticism. We cannot help wishing that a man who can do so much would do a little more; that he would give us something beyond a mere piece of realism; that, not content with the close and clear reflection of a square foot of the ground we all walk on, he would hold his mirror a little higher and include a larger area, some salient features of the country, and some sea and sky. (p. 332)

> [F. N. Broome], in a review of "He Knew He Was Right," in The Times, *London (© Times Newspapers Limited, 1869), August 26, 1869 (and reprinted in* Trollope: The Critical Heritage, *edited by Donald Smalley, Routledge & Kegan Paul, 1969, pp. 329-32).*

ANTHONY TROLLOPE (lecture date 1870)

> [*In the following excerpt, Trollope outlines his philosophy of the novel, focusing on the importance of the love story, which he*

describes as the "mainstay and the staff of (the novel's) existence."]

The book which we call a novel contains, we may say always, a love story. Indeed, taking the general character of novels as our guide, we may say that the love stories are their mainstay and the staff of their existence. They not only contain love stories, but they are written for the sake of the love stories. They have other attractions, and deal with every phase of life; but the other attractions hang round and depend on the love story as the planets depend upon the sun. There are novel worlds, no doubt, in which the planets are brighter than the sun; in which the love-making is less interesting than the life by which it is surrounded; but these are erratic worlds, novels out of the course of nature, and to be spoken of as exceptional. The love story is the thing. In what way did this special John make himself pleasant to that particular Jane;—how did Jane receive John's attentions, and what became of it at last? This is the nucleus of all this mass of ephemeral literature which is so voluminous;—and in which the wanderings of the planets round the centre sun are so various that it is hardly too much to say that in every action of our life we are more or less guided by what is so imparted to us. (pp. 108-09)

I think you must have chosen your novels unfortunately if you have found in them the bad and not the good lessons. That the novelist deals with the false and forward, as well as with the good and gracious, with lust as well as love, with the basest of characters as with the best, is of course true. How else shall he do his work as professor? Does not all our sacred teaching do the same? Are we not specially warned against murder, theft, adultery, and covetousness in the Scriptures? In treating of vice does the British novelist whom you know make vice alluring, or does he make it hideous? Which course does he recommend to you,—honour or dishonour? That happy ending with the normal marriage and the two children,—is it the lot of the good girl, who has restrained all her longings by the operations of her conscience, or of the bold, bad, scheming woman who has been unwomanly and rapacious? Which attracts you [in *Vanity Fair*], Amelia,—Thackeray's Amelia, who is not clever but good; or Becky Sharpe, who is all intellect and all vileness?

But there are many planets surrounding the suns in these novel-worlds. Much is intended to be inculcated quite independent of the love lessons. All the habits and ways of our domestic and public lives are portrayed to us in novels. We have political novels, social-science novels, law-life novels, civil-service novels, commercial novels, fashionable-life novels,—and I am told that novels even of clerical life have been written. In all of them there is probably some backbone of a love story; but, over and beyond that, lessons of life are being taught from the first page to the last. Looking back upon the novels which you know, can you say that the teaching is other than good, straightforward, and in the right direction? The novels may be bad novels, and yet the lessons taught may be in the right direction. (p. 110)

[One objection] has frequently been raised against me by those who disapprove of novel-reading. They say that novels are false;—meaning that they are untrue in the broadest sense, because they are fictions. The hero and the heroine, who are said by the novelist so to act or so to speak, never acted or spoke at all; and the whole thing is,—untrue. Of course it is all fiction; but fiction may be as true as fact. These objectors seem to me to misunderstand Truth and Untruth;—which consist in the desire of the speaker or actor to reveal or to deceive.

If I write for you a story, giving you a picture of life as true as I can make it, my story, though a fiction, is not false. It may be as true a book as ever was written. A novel indeed may be false,—hideously false. I could name to you novels that are very false. A novelist is false who, in dealing with this or that phase of life, bolsters up a theory of his own with pictures which are in themselves untrue. There is at this moment a great question forward as to the tenure of Land in Ireland. I may have my ideas upon it, and may desire to promulgate them in a novel. But if for the sake of promoting my theory, I draw a picture of Irish landlords which is not a true picture,—which I have no ground for believing to be true,—in which I make them out to be cruel, idle, God-abandoned reprobates, because I have a theory of my own to support in my novel, then my book is a false book, and I am a liar. In this way a novel may be false, and much of this falseness, sometimes in large and often in very small proportions, is to be found in novels; but to say that a novel is false because it deals with an imagined and not with a real world of people, seems to me to be an absurdity. (pp. 112-13)

Anthony Trollope, *"On English Prose Fiction As a Rational Amusement—Text" (originally a lecture delivered in Edinburgh on January 28, 1870), in his* Four Lectures: The Civil Service As a Profession (1861); the Present Condition of the Northern States of the American Union (1862 or 1863); Higher Education of Women (1868); On English Prose Fiction As a Rational Amusement (1870), *edited by Morris L. Parrish, Constable & Co., Ltd., 1938 (and reprinted by Norwood Editions, 1977), pp. 94-124.*

THE SPECTATOR   (essay date 1870)

Sir Harry Hotspur of Humblethwaite is one of Mr. Trollope's very best short tales. Mr. Trollope's genius demands space. He reels off his characters with almost unerring truthfulness, but then his touch is so light and his mode of portraiture so little intense, that you want the multiplication of details, the variety of situations, the change of lights, to make up for that *depth* of knowledge of them which Thackeray, or George Eliot, or sometimes Scott will contrive to give in a single scene and in a few sentences. Mr. Trollope's best figures are usually impressive in proportion to the scope he has had for painting them in a variety of different circumstances. (p. 341)

Trollope's picture of the irresolution of the haughty and usually absolute old baronet, and of the see-saw of policy into which this irresolution plunges him . . . is as good of its kind as any moral picture he has ever yet drawn for us. No subject ever suited Mr. Trollope better. He is, before all things, a man of the world, and as a man of the world he understands to the core every passion involved in this conflict,—the pride of blood, the sense of something like duty to the property and the title, the pride of honour, the sense of chivalry which compels Sir Harry to spurn a connection with a man of deficient honour, and then, again, the subtle twist which his wish to continue the old line through his daughter gives to his deep paternal love,—and he delineates these external effects with the most accurate and sure artistic touch. (p. 342)

Perhaps the least successful picture in the book is the drawing of Emily Hotspur. . . . In that picture Mr. Trollope impresses us as attempting what is in some sense, not in the least beyond his *conception*, but beyond the resources of his artistic style, to execute adequately. Mr. Trollope can tell you what a girl of Emily Hotspur's passion of nature would *do,* and how she

would do it, but he cannot tell you really what she feels. He needs an intensiveness of style to tell us this, on which he never ventures, and yet the picture is to our minds conspicuously incomplete without it. It is like the attempt of a geometrician to solve by plane geometry a problem which requires geometry of three dimensions. The figure of Emily Hotspur is really a very fine conception, but it is a conception which it needed something of Thackeray's power of condensing passion into words to delineate. (pp. 343-44)

A review of "Sir Harry Hotspur of Humblethwaite," in The Spectator, *Vol. 43, No. 2213, November 26, 1870 (and reprinted in* Trollope: The Critical Heritage, *edited by Donald Smalley, Routledge & Kegan Paul, 1969, pp. 341-44).*

[MEREDITH WHITE TOWNSEND]   (essay date 1875)

Mr. Trollope's novels are to us among the enjoyments of life, but it is with the greatest difficulty that we have read through **The Way We Live Now.** The author has made a mistake, which he made once before in the disagreeable story called **Brown, Jones, and Robinson,** and has surrounded his characters with an atmosphere of sordid baseness which prevents enjoyment like an effluvium. The novel, which is unusually long, is choked with characters, all of whom, with perhaps two exceptions, are seeking in dirty ways mean ends, working, playing, intriguing, making love, with the single object of obtaining, by dishonest means, either cash or a social position of the most vulgar and flaunting kind. (p. 397)

[We can not] say that the oppressive vulgarity of the characters is redeemed by many touches of Mr. Trollope's usual skill. Of course there is skill, for Mr. Trollope intended us to hate the greedy race he portrays, and we do hate them; and of course he cannot write a hundred chapters without some touches of his peculiar art, but they are very few, not enough to enliven the general atmosphere of the book. . . . Mr. Trollope is so rarely inaccurate, that we suppose there is somewhere a world like that he describes; and so somewhere among the marshes there is a sewage-farm, and we would as soon go there for a breath of fresh air as to **The Way We Live Now** for entertainment. (pp. 399-400)

[Meredith White Townsend], *in a review of "The Way We Live Now," in* The Spectator, *Vol. 48, No. 2452, June 26, 1875 (and reprinted in* Trollope: The Critical Heritage, *edited by Donald Smalley, Routledge & Kegan Paul, 1969, pp. 397-400).*

HARPER'S NEW MONTHLY MAGAZINE   (essay date 1875)

Mr. Anthony Trollope's novels are not only 'among the enjoyments of life' [see excerpt above by Meredith White Townsend, 1875], they are also among its instructors; for no modern novelist, and perhaps no novelist of any time, has depicted with such scrupulous fidelity to the truth the actual facts of society, the phases of our national and social life which almost inevitably escape the historian, and which are rarely caught even by the tourist or the essayist. There is nothing false about **The Way We Live Now** . . . but the title. There is a flavor of cynicism about that which is quite unlike Mr. Trollope. That Mr. Melmotte represents the ordinary type of enterprising capital or moneyed aristocracy, or Lady Carbury the average literary woman, or her worthless son the young man of the present age, or Miss Melmotte or the Longestaffe girls the best or even the average product of modern society, no one, we think, will be inclined to allow; and that Mr. Booker, Mr. Alf, or Mr. Broune fairly answers to the modern literary critic no reviewer could for an instant concede. It is true that the atmosphere of such a society as that which Mr. Trollope depicts is any thing but healthy. It is true that, with perhaps two exceptions, there is not a noble character in the book. But it is also true that the vices which Mr. Trollope so effectually uncovers are not only common, but, in their thin disguise, get ready admission and not infrequent respect in the society of both England and America.

> *A review of "The Way We Live Now," in* Harper's New Monthly Magazine, *Vol. LI, No. CCCV, October, 1875 (and reprinted in* Trollope: The Critical Heritage, *edited by Donald Smalley, Routledge & Kegan Paul, 1969, p. 414).*

[ALEXANDER INNES SHAND]   (essay date 1876)

The feeling we entertain towards Mr. Trollope's best-known personages shows at once the truthfulness and the geniality of the clever art to which they owe their existence. They are real enough to us; we repeatedly have their features recalled to us by the people we are habitually meeting in the world; and yet there is scarcely one of them, with all their faults and their failings, for whom we have not something of a kindly feeling. We even give a sigh to the memory of Mrs. Proudie for her own sake when she at length comes to her end in **'The Last Chronicles of Barset,'** although ever since our first introduction to her in **'Barchester Towers,'** she has been figuring as a noxious specimen of the most objectionable type of female. But, perhaps, Mr. Trollope has never given more convincing proof of his easy command of materials that are apparently anything but plastic than in developing the Duke of Omnium into the Prime Minister [in **'The Prime Minister'**]. Plantagenet Palliser, when we first met him, was as little interesting and almost as disagreeable as a man could be, who had the manners and feelings of a gentleman. We felt towards him as Arthur Pendennis felt towards Mr. Pynsent, when he remarked that he disliked that gentleman as he disliked cold boiled veal; and we feared that there was much of the tragic in the arrangement that had mated him with the impulsive, light-headed, and warm-hearted Lady Glencora. In **'Can You Forgive Her?'** we began to suspect Mr. Palliser has a heart, although we doubted whether he could ever win his wife, with his chilling rigidity of manner and prim correctness of feeling. In **'Phineas Finn'** and its sequel we slowly learnt to respect him, as an intelligent and indefatigable man of business, and a politician of punctilious honour and considerable patriotic ambition. If he could not mould men easily and pleasantly to his purpose, at least he had some art of commanding them and making them follow his lead at a respectful distance. So that, considering the social position of the Duke, his immense landed stake in the country, and the cool temperament that kept him clear of perilous extremes, there was nothing unnatural in his being chosen as the head of a Ministry of compromise. But we were scarcely prepared to find that Mr. Trollope should actually make us know him and like him better in that exalted post than we had ever done before. (pp. 424-25)

'The Prime Minister' is a novel that will be greatly enjoyed by people who can take an interest in its public personages, and who appreciate clever studies of political character; but we doubt whether it will ever be numbered among the favourites of those who delight in Mr. Trollope for his love stories. (p. 425)

> *[Alexander Innes Shand], in a review of "The Prime Minister," in* The Times, *London (© Times Newspapers Limited, 1876), August 18, 1876 (and reprinted in* Trollope: The Critical Heritage, *edited by Donald Smalley, Routledge & Kegan Paul, 1969, pp. 424-25).*

THE EXAMINER   (essay date 1877)

Mr. Trollope has not yet recovered from the attack of misanthropy from which he was suffering when he wrote **'The Way We Live Now.'** He seems still to keep a special inkstand supplied with gall, for use when describing fashionable society, against which his rancour appears to be unbounded. When he penned the character of the heroine of his present story [the **'American Senator'**], for instance, the very paper must have blanched under the withering impress of his quill. Arabella Trefoil is the name of this young lady, the conventional ballroom beauty of fiction. Mr. Trollope is not content with painting her heartless, mercenary, and unfilial, but, to make her moral deficiencies the more hideously glaring, contrasts with her the equally familiar character of the stereotyped country maiden, innocent and simple-minded to an almost imbecile pitch, the uncomplaining victim of maternal harshness. The chequered courses of the love affairs of each of these damsels, in alternate chapters, make the story. . . .

We can only hope that a tropical sun will reopen the petals of Mr. Trollope's imagination and elicit something more worthy than the **'American Senator.'**

> *A review of "The American Senator," in* The Examiner, *No. 3625, July 21, 1877 (and reprinted in* Trollope: The Critical Heritage, *edited by Donald Smalley, Routledge & Kegan Paul, 1969, p. 430).*

THE NATION   (essay date 1880)

As a whole [the **'Duke's Children'**] is one of Mr. Trollope's most successful novels. It is pitched in the usual quiet key which all readers of his books know so well, and which is maintained with the hand of a master to the end. . . . [We] do not think Mr. Trollope should be found fault with because his plots are faulty when compared with those which made the success of an entirely different school of fiction. If he has not the art of contriving plots he has that of telling stories, and this, after all, is the fundamental and essential thing. . . . There is nothing about [Mr. Trollope's novels] which, superficially, it seems difficult to imagine a dozen writers doing equally well. They all seem, as Hawthorne said, like slices cut off the huge English cheese, and presented for our microscopic inspection under a glass case [see excerpt above, 1860]. But the exhibition must be managed by Trollope himself or it is a failure. For bringing a quiet domestic scene before the eye, for ordinary conversation of any kind, for representing the everyday events of life without exaggeration or distortion, we cannot imagine a novelist superior to the author of the **'Duke's Children.'** If any one will examine such a chapter as the one which describes the breakfast-table of the duke and his two sons, and ask himself when he has read it how any detail could be altered so as to increase the reality of the scene, he will find that it is almost impossible to change a word without impairing the effect. (p. 138)

[Mr. Trollope is] the last of the realists, and, like a true Englishman, not even that on any theory. He paints the world as he sees it, but he sees it with just that amount of artistic vision which saves his picture from having the dull flatness of every-day life, and yet never makes the light and shade any lighter or any darker than everybody feels to be within the bounds of naturalness. No one ever, we fancy, read a novel of his without wishing that he might soon write another, and it is only born story-tellers who leave us in this frame of mind. (p. 139)

"Mr. Trollope's Last Novel," in The Nation, *Vol. XXXI, No. 790, August 19, 1880, pp. 138-39.*

[RICHARD HOLT HUTTON]   (essay date 1882)

[*Hutton, coeditor of the* Spectator *from 1861 to 1897, is noted for his insightful treatment of Trollope. In the obituary notice excerpted below, he praises Trollope as a novelist who faithfully depicted the English society of his time. Trollope's realism, according to Hutton, precluded an interest in the emotional depth of his characters, and dealt with "the surface of society."*]

Mr. Trollope's works will rank with those of other great novelists rather as works helping us to revive the past, than as works of which it is the great merit to interpret the relations in which we actually live.

That Mr. Trollope's name will live in English literature follows at once from the fact that his books are at once very agreeable to read, and contain a larger mass of evidence as to the character and aspects of English Society during Mr. Trollope's maturity than any other writer of his day has left behind him. (p. 505)

[It] is clear that there was little or no disposition in Mr. Trollope to pierce much deeper than the social surface of life. It is not often that he takes us into the world of solitary feeling at all, and of the power of the positive influence of their religion over men, you would hardly gain more knowledge from Mr. Trollope's stories than from those of the old-fashioned *régime*, when religion was thought too sacred to be touched-on at all as a real part of human life. The nearest thing which we can recall to any touch of a deeper kind in Mr. Trollope, is his pathetic picture of Bishop Proudie, after his wife's death, saying the little prayer which he thus describes:—'It may be doubted whether he quite knew for what he was praying. The idea of praying for her soul now that she was dead would have scandalized him. He certainly was not praying for his own soul. I think he was praying that God might save him from being glad that his wife was dead.' But touches as deep as that are very rare in Mr. Trollope.

That Mr. Trollope's humour has played a great part in the popularity of his novels, is evident enough, and yet his humour may be called rather a proper appreciation of the paradoxes of social life, than any very original faculty of his own. Mr. Trollope did not heighten, as Miss Austen does, the ludicrous elements in human life by those quaint turns of expression and those delicate contrasts which only a great genius of satiric touch could invent. Mr. Trollope's humour lay in his keen perception of the oddity of human motives, pursuits, and purposes, and his absolute truthfulness in painting them to the life. . . . [This] is a kind of humour which comes wholly from the keen insight into the little unconscious hypocrisies of worldly men's feelings. Mr. Trollope saw through all these little make-beliefs with the clearest vision, and his humour depended on the clearness of that vision. But he did not add to the humour of the facts, when seen, by any very unusual art in their presentation. What was absurd in the tactics of society, he seized and defined, but hardly ever heightened. Only there is so much that is absurd in the tactics of society, that to see and define

all that is absurd therein makes a man a humorist of no common power. Perhaps Mr. Trollope never showed this humour more effectually than when he delineated the romantic vein in very vulgar and very selfish people,—like Mrs. Greenow, in **'Can You Forgive Her?'** when she treats herself to a husband of a romantic kind. . . . Mr. Trollope's humour is thoroughly realistic. He sees the coarseness of human life in its close contrast with its ambitiousness, and simply shows us what he sees.

For a writer who dealt, and always professed to deal, chiefly with the surface of society, Mr. Trollope has been singularly sincere, never seeking to hide from us that there are deeper places of human nature into which he does not venture; nor his impression that the world and the motives of the world also penetrate into those places, and have perhaps as much to say to the practical result in conduct, as the higher motives themselves. Still, he cannot be called a satirist. He paints only a part of human life, but he paints that part precisely as he sees it, extenuating nothing and exaggerating nothing, but letting us know that he does not profess to see all, and does not try to divine by imaginative power what he cannot see. Probably no English writer of his day has amused Englishmen so much as Mr. Trollope, or has given them that amusement from sources so completely free from either morbid weaknesses or mischievous and dangerous taints. His name will live in our literature, and though it will certainly not represent the higher regions of imaginative life, it will picture the society of our day with a fidelity with which society has never been pictured before in the history of the world. (pp. 506-08)

[*Richard Holt Hutton*], *in a review of "Can You Forgive Her?" in* The Spectator, *Vol. 55, No. 2841, December 9, 1882 (and reprinted in* Trollope: The Critical Heritage, *edited by Donald Smalley, Routledge & Kegan Paul, 1969, pp. 504-08).*

ANTHONY TROLLOPE   (essay date 1883)

[*Trollope's* An Autobiography, *which appeared after his death, had a significant influence on his literary reputation. Published at a time when novelists and readers had come to value a harmonious prose style over plot,* An Autobiography *revealed Trollope's self-effacing estimate of his writing and lent credence to the growing opinion that Trollope's work lacked artistry. In his* Autobiography *Trollope outlines his method of composition and literary theories and judges his own successes and failures. The* Autobiography *is a chronicle of Trollope's creative life, and many critics agree that it is at all times informed by what Bradford A. Booth described as his "uncompromising honesty."*]

When I have commenced a new book, I have always prepared a diary, divided into weeks, and carried it on for the period which I have allowed myself for the completion of the work. In this I have entered, day by day, the number of pages I have written, so that if at any time I have slipped into idleness for a day or two, the record of that idleness has been there, staring me in the face, and demanding of me increased labour, so that the deficiency might be supplied. . . . I have allotted myself so many pages a week. The average number has been about 40. It has been placed as low as 20, and has risen to 112. And as a page is an ambiguous term, my page has been made to contain 250 words; and as words, if not watched, will have a tendency to straggle, I have had every word counted as I went. . . . I have prided myself on completing my work exactly within the proposed dimensions. But I have prided myself especially in completing it within the proposed time,—and I have always done so. There has ever been the record before me, and a week passed with an insufficient number of pages has been a blister to my eye, and a month so disgraced would have been a sorrow to my heart.

I have been told that such appliances are beneath the notice of a man of genius. I have never fancied myself to be a man of genius, but had I been so I think I might well have subjected myself to these trammels. Nothing surely is so potent as a law that may not be disobeyed. It has the force of the water-drop that hollows the stone. A small daily task, if it be really daily, will beat the labours of a spasmodic Hercules. (pp. 101-02)

Doctor Thorne has, I believe, been the most popular book that I have written,—if I may take the sale as a proof of comparative popularity. *The Bertrams* has had quite an opposite fortune. I do not know that I have ever heard it well spoken of even by my friends, and I cannot remember that there is any character in it that has dwelt in the minds of novel-readers. I myself think that they are of about equal merit, but that neither of them is good. They fall away very much from *The Three Clerks*, both in pathos and humour. There is no personage in either of them comparable to Chaffanbrass the lawyer. The plot of *Doctor Thorne* is good, and I am led therefore to suppose that a good plot,—which, to my own feeling, is the most insignificant part of a tale,—is that which will most raise it or most condemn it in the public judgment. . . . A novel should give a picture of common life enlivened by humour and sweetened by pathos. To make that picture worthy of attention, the canvas should be crowded with real portraits, not of individuals known to the world or to the author, but of created personages impregnated with traits of character which are known. To my thinking, the plot is but the vehicle for all this; and when you have a vehicle without the passengers, a story of mystery in which the agents never spring to life, you have but a wooden show. There must, however, be a story. You must provide a vehicle of some sort. That of *The Bertrams* was more than ordinarily bad; and as the book was relieved by no special character, it failed. Its failure never surprised me; but I have been surprised by the success of *Doctor Thorne*. (pp. 106-07)

Most of those among my friends who talk to me now about my novels, and are competent to form an opinion on the subject, say that [*Orley Farm*] is the best I have written. In this opinion I do not coincide. I think that the highest merit which a novel can have consists in perfect delineation of character, rather than in plot, or humour, or pathos. . . . The plot of *Orley Farm* is probably the best I have ever made; but it has the fault of declaring itself, and thus coming to an end too early in the book. When Lady Mason tells her ancient lover that she did forge the will, the plot of *Orley Farm* has unravelled itself;—and this she does in the middle of the tale. Independently, however, of this the novel is good. (p. 140)

Critics, if they ever trouble themselves with these pages, will, of course, say that . . . I have ignored altogether the one great evil of rapid production,—namely, that of inferior work. And of course if [my] work was inferior because of the too great rapidity of production, the critics would be right. Giving to the subject the best of my critical abilities, and judging of my own work as nearly as possible as I would that of another, I believe that the work which has been done quickest has been done the best. I have composed better stories—that is, have created better plots—than those of *The Small House at Allington* and *Can You Forgive Her?* and I have portrayed two or three better characters than are to be found in the pages of either of them; but taking these books all through, I do not think that I have ever done better work. Nor would these have been im-

proved by any effort in the art of story telling, had each of these been the isolated labour of a couple of years. How short is the time devoted to the manipulation of a plot can be known only to those who have written plays and novels;—I may say also, how very little time the brain is able to devote to such wearing work. There are usually some hours of agonising doubt, almost of despair,—so at least it has been with me,—or perhaps some days. And then, with nothing settled in my brain as to the final development of events, with no capability of settling anything but with a most distinct conception of some character or characters, I have rushed at the work as a rider rushes at a fence which he does not see. . . . [My] failures have not arisen from over-hurried work. When my work has been quicker done,—and it has sometimes been done very quickly—the rapidity has been achieved by hot pressure, not in the conception, but in the telling of the story. Instead of writing eight pages a day, I have written sixteen; instead of working five days a week, I have worked seven. I have trebled my usual average, and have done so in circumstances which have enabled me to give up all my thoughts for the time to the book I have been writing. . . . And I am sure that the work so done has had in it the best truth and the highest spirit that I have been able to produce. At such times I have been able to imbue myself thoroughly with the characters I have had in hand. I have wandered alone among the rocks and woods, crying at their grief, laughing at their absurdities, and thoroughly enjoying their joy. I have been impregnated with my own creations till it has been my only excitement to sit with the pen in my hand, and then drive my team before me at as quick a pace as I could make them travel. (pp. 146-48)

[That] which endears [*Can You Forgive Her?*] to me is the first presentation which I made in it of Plantagenet Palliser, with his wife, Lady Glencora.

By no amount of description or asseveration could I succeed in making any reader understand how much these characters with their belongings have been to me in my latter life; or how frequently I have used them for the expression of my political or social convictions. . . . In these personages and their friends, political and social, I have endeavoured to depict the faults and frailties and vices,—as also the virtues, the graces, and the strength of our highest classes; and if I have not made the strength and virtues predominant over the faults and vices, I have not painted the picture as I intended. (pp. 151-52)

In conducting these characters from one story to another I realised the necessity, not only of consistency,—which, had it been maintained by a hard exactitude, would have been untrue to nature,—but also of those changes which time always produces. . . . To do all this thoroughly was in my heart from first to last; but I do not know that the game has been worth the candle. To carry out my scheme I have had to spread my picture over so wide a canvas that I cannot expect that any lover of such art should trouble himself to look at it as a whole. Who will read *Can You Forgive Her? Phineas Finn, Phineas Redux,* and *The Prime Minister* consecutively, in order that they may understand the characters of the Duke of Omnium, of Plantagenet Palliser, and of Lady Glencora? Who will ever know that they should be so read? But in the performance of the work I had much gratification, and was enabled from time to time to have in this way that fling at the political doings of the day which every man likes to take, if not in one fashion then in another. I look upon this string of characters,—carried sometimes into other novels than those just named,—as the best work of my life. Taking him altogether, I think that Plantagenet Palliser stands more firmly on the ground than any other personage I have created. (pp. 154-55)

I think that Plantagenet Palliser, Duke of Omnium, is a perfect gentleman. If he be not, then am I unable to describe a gentleman. [Lady Glencora] is by no means a perfect lady; but if she be not all over a woman, then am I not able to describe a woman. I do not think it probable that my name will remain among those who in the next century will be known as the writers of English prose fiction;—but if it does, that permanence of success will probably rest on the character of Plantagenet Palliser, Lady Glencora, and the Rev. Mr. Crawley. (p. 300)

Anthony Trollope, in his An Autobiography, *Harper & Brothers, 1883 (and reprinted by University of California Press, 1947, 312 p.).*

HENRY JAMES (essay date 1883)

[In the opinion of many critics, the modern interpretation of Trollope begins with this essay. While James criticizes Trollope for sacrificing quality for quantity and for the intrusive nature of his authorial stance, he also praises Trollope's perceptive characterization. James's condemnation of Trollope's narrative technique is challenged by Chauncey Brewster Tinker (1947) and Edd Winfield Parks (1953); his comments on Trollope's style are disputed by Geoffrey Tillotson (1961-62) and Ruth apRoberts (1971).]

When, a few months ago, Anthony Trollope laid down his pen for the last time, it was a sign of the complete extinction of that group of admirable writers who, in England, during the preceding half century, had done so much to elevate the art of the novelist. The author of *The Warden,* of *Barchester Towers,* of *Framley Parsonage,* does not, to our mind, stand on the very same level as Dickens, Thackeray and George Eliot; for his talent was of a quality less fine than theirs. But he belonged to the same family—he had as much to tell us about English life; he was strong, genial and abundant. He published too much; the writing of novels had ended by becoming, with him, a perceptibly mechanical process. Dickens was prolific, Thackeray produced with a freedom for which we are constantly grateful; but we feel that these writers had their periods of gestation. They took more time to look at their subject; . . . they were able to wait for inspiration. Trollope's fecundity was prodigious; there was no limit to the work he was ready to do. It is not unjust to say that he sacrificed quality to quantity. Abundance, certainly, is in itself a great merit; almost all the greatest writers have been abundant. But Trollope's fertility was gross, importunate; he himself contended, we believe, that he had given to the world a greater number of printed pages of fiction than any of his literary contemporaries. (pp. 97-8)

The imagination that Trollope possessed he had at least thoroughly at his command. I speak of . . . this in order to explain (in part) why it was that, with his extraordinary gift, there was always in him a certain infusion of the common. He abused his gift, overworked it, rode his horse too hard. As an artist he never took himself seriously; many people will say this was why he was so delightful. The people who take themselves seriously are prigs and bores; and Trollope, with his perpetual "story," which was the only thing he cared about, his strong good sense, hearty good nature, generous appreciation of life in all its varieties, responds in perfection to a certain English ideal. According to that ideal it is rather dangerous to be explicitly or consciously an artist—to have a system, a doctrine, a form. Trollope, from the first, went in, as they say, for having

as little form as possible; it is probably safe to affirm that he had no "views" whatever on the subject of novel-writing. . . . With Trollope we were always safe; there were sure to be no new experiments.

His great, his inestimable merit was a complete appreciation of the usual. . . . [Trollope], with his eyes comfortably fixed on the familiar, the actual, was far from having invented a new category; his great distinction is that in resting there his vision took in so much of the field. And then he *felt* all daily and immediate things as well as saw them; felt them in a simple, direct, salubrious way, with their sadness, their gladness, their charm, their comicality, all their obvious and measurable meanings. He never wearied of the pre-established round of English customs—never needed a respite or a change—was content to go on indefinitely watching the life that surrounded him, and holding up his mirror to it. . . . This exact and on the whole becoming image, projected upon a surface without a strong intrinsic tone, constitutes mainly the entertainment that Trollope offered his readers. The striking thing to the critic was that his robust and patient mind had no particular bias, his imagination no light of its own. He saw things neither pictorially and grotesquely like Dickens; nor with that combined disposition to satire and to literary form which gives such "body," as they say, of wine, to the manner of Thackeray; nor with anything of the philosophic, the transcendental cast—the desire to follow them to their remote relations—which we associate with the name of George Eliot. Trollope had his elements of fancy, of satire, of irony; but these qualities were not very highly developed, and he walked mainly by the light of his good sense, his clear, direct vision of the things that lay nearest, and his great natural kindness. There is something remarkably tender and friendly in his feeling about all human perplexities; he takes the good-natured, temperate, conciliatory view—the humorous view, perhaps, for the most part, yet without a touch of pessimistic prejudice. As he grew older, and had sometimes to go farther afield for his subjects, he acquired a savour of bitterness and reconciled himself sturdily to treating of the disagreeable. A more copious record of disagreeable matters could scarcely be imagined, for instance, than *The Way We Live Now.* But, in general, he has a wholesome mistrust of morbid analysis, an aversion to inflicting pain. He has an infinite love of detail, but his details are, for the most part, the innumerable items of the expected. . . . [Trollope] represents in an eminent degree [the] natural decorum of the English spirit, and represents it all the better that there is not in him a grain of the mawkish or the prudish. He writes, he feels, he judges like a man, talking plainly and frankly about many things, and is by no means destitute of a certain saving grace of coarseness. But he has kept the purity of his imagination and held fast to old-fashioned reverences and preferences. He thinks it a sufficient objection to several topics to say simply that they are unclean. There was nothing in his theory of the story-teller's art that tended to convert the reader's or the writer's mind into a vessel for polluting things. He recognised the right of the vessel to protest, and would have regarded such a protest as conclusive. With a considerable turn for satire, though this perhaps is more evident in his early novels than in his later ones, he had as little as possible of the quality of irony. He never played with a subject, never juggled with the sympathies or the credulity of his reader, was never in the least paradoxical or mystifying. He sat down to his theme in a serious, business-like way, with his elbows on the table and his eye occasionally wandering to the clock. (pp. 99-103)

The source of [Trollope's] success in describing the life that lay nearest to him, and describing it without any of those artistic perversions that come . . . from a powerful imagination, from a cynical humour or from a desire to look, as George Eliot expresses it, for the suppressed transitions that unite all contrasts, the essence of this love of reality was his extreme interest in character. This is the fine and admirable quality in Trollope, this is what will preserve his best works in spite of those flatnesses which keep him from standing on quite the same level as the masters. Indeed this quality is so much one of the finest (to my mind at least), that it makes me wonder the more that the writer who had it so abundantly and so naturally should not have just that distinction which Trollope lacks, and which we find in his three brilliant contemporaries. If he was in any degree a man of genius (and I hold that he was), it was in virtue of this happy, instinctive perception of human varieties. His knowledge of the stuff we are made of, his observation of the common behaviour of men and women, was not reasoned nor acquired, not even particularly studied. All human doings deeply interested him, human life, to his mind, was a perpetual story; but he never attempted to take the so-called scientific view, the view which has lately found ingenious advocates among the countrymen and successors of Balzac. He had no airs of being able to tell you *why* people in a given situation would conduct themselves in a particular way; it was enough for him that he felt their feelings and struck the right note, because he had, as it were, a good ear. If he was a knowing psychologist he was so by grace; he was just and true without apparatus and without effort. He must have had a great taste for the moral question; he evidently believed that this is the basis of the interest of fiction. . . . We care what happens to people only in proportion as we know what people are. Trollope's great apprehension of the real, which was what made him so interesting, came to him through his desire to satisfy us on this point—to tell us what certain people were and what they did in consequence of being so. That is the purpose of each of his tales; and if these things produce an illusion it comes from the gradual abundance of his testimony as to the temper, the tone, the passions, the habits, the moral nature, of a certain number of contemporary Britons.

His stories, in spite of their great length, deal very little in the surprising, the exceptional, the complicated; as a general thing he has no great story to tell. The thing is not so much a story as a picture; if we hesitate to call it a picture it is because the idea of composition is not the controlling one and we feel that the author would regard the artistic, in general, as a kind of affectation. There is not even much description, in the sense which the present votaries of realism in France attach to that word. The painter lays his scene in a few deliberate, not especially pictorial strokes, and never dreams of finishing the piece for the sake of enabling the reader to hang it up. The finish, such as it is, comes later, from the slow and somewhat clumsy accumulation of small illustrations. These illustrations are sometimes of the commonest; Trollope turns them out inexhaustibly, repeats them freely, unfolds them without haste and without rest. But they are all of the most obvious sort, and they are none the worse for that. The point to be made is that they have no great spectacular interest (we beg pardon of the innumerable love-affairs that Trollope has described), like many of the incidents, say, of Walter Scott and of Alexandre Dumas: if we care to know about them (as repetitions of a usual case), it is because the writer has managed, in his candid, literal, somewhat lumbering way, to tell us that about the men and women concerned which has already excited on their behalf the impression of life. It is a marvel by what homely arts, by

what imperturbable button-holing persistence, he contrives to excite this impression. (pp. 104-07)

Trollope has described again and again the ravages of love, and it is wonderful to see how well, in these delicate matters, his plain good sense and good taste serve him. His story is always primarily a love-story, and a love-story constructed on an inveterate system. There is a young lady who has two lovers, or a young man who has two sweethearts; we are treated to the innumerable forms in which this predicament may present itself and the consequences, sometimes pathetic, sometimes grotesque, which spring from such false situations. Trollope is not what is called a colourist; still less is he a poet: he is seated on the back of heavy-footed prose. But his account of those sentiments which the poets are supposed to have made their own is apt to be as touching as demonstrations more lyrical. There is something wonderfully vivid in the state of mind of the unfortunate Harry Gilmore [in *The Vicar of Bullhampton*] . . . ; and his history, which has no more pretensions to style than if it were cut out of yesterday's newspaper, lodges itself in the imagination in all sorts of classic company. He is not handsome, nor clever, nor rich, nor romantic, nor distinguished in any way; he is simply rather a dense, narrow-minded, stiff, obstinate, common-place, conscientious modern Englishman, exceedingly in love and, from his own point of view, exceedingly ill-used. He is interesting because he suffers and because we are curious to see the form that suffering will take in that particular nature. Our good fortune, with Trollope, is that the person put before us will have, in spite of opportunities not to have it, a certain particular nature. The author has cared enough about the character of such a person to find out exactly what it is. (pp. 109-10)

He knew about bishops, archdeacons, prebendaries, precentors, and about their wives and daughters; he knew what these dignitaries say to each other when they are collected together, aloof from secular ears. . . . Trollope enlarged his field very speedily—there is, I remember that work, as little as possible of the ecclesiastical in the tale of *The Three Clerks,* which came after *Barchester Towers.* But he always retained traces of his early divination of the clergy; he introduced them frequently, and he always did them easily and well. There is no ecclesiastical figure, however, so good as the first—no creation of this sort so happy as the admirable Mr. Harding. *The Warden* is a delightful tale, and a signal instance of Trollope's habit of offering us the spectacle of a character. A motive more delicate, more slender, as well as more charming, could scarcely be conceived. It is simply the history of an old man's conscience. (pp. 112-13)

The question of Mr. Harding's resignation becomes a drama, and we anxiously wait for the catastrophe. Trollope never did anything happier than the picture of this sweet and serious little old gentleman, who on most of the occasions of life has shown a lamblike softness and compliance, but in this particular matter opposes a silent, impenetrable obstinacy to the arguments of the friends who insist on his keeping his sinecure—fixing his mild, detached gaze on the distance, and making imaginary passes with his fiddle-bow while they demonstrate his pusillanimity. The subject of *The Warden,* exactly viewed, is the opposition of the two natures of Archdeacon Grantley and Mr. Harding, and there is nothing finer in all Trollope than the vividness with which this opposition is presented. The archdeacon is as happy a portrait as the precentor—an image of the full-fed, worldly churchman, taking his stand squarely upon his rich temporalities, and regarding the church frankly as a fat social pasturage. It required the greatest tact and temperance to make the picture of Archdeacon Grantley stop just where it does. The type, impartially considered, is detestable, but the individual may be full of amenity. Trollope allows his archdeacon all the virtues he was likely to possess, but he makes his spiritual grossness wonderfully natural. No charge of exaggeration is possible, for we are made to feel that he is conscientious as well as arrogant, and expansive as well as hard. He is one of those figures that spring into being all at once, solidifying in the author's grasp. These two capital portraits are what we carry away from *The Warden*, which some persons profess to regard as our writer's masterpiece. (pp. 113-15)

[There] are certain precautions in the way of producing that illusion dear to the intending novelist which Trollope not only habitually scorned to take, but really, as we may say, asking pardon for the heat of the thing, delighted wantonly to violate. He took a suicidal satisfaction in reminding the reader that the story he was telling was only, after all, a make-believe. He habitually referred to the work in hand (in the course of that work) as a novel, and to himself as a novelist, and was fond of letting the reader know that this novelist could direct the course of events according to his pleasure. . . . [These little slaps at credulity] are very discouraging, but they are even more inexplicable; for they are deliberately inartistic, even judged from the point of view of that rather vague consideration of form which is the only canon we have a right to impose upon Trollope. It is impossible to imagine what a novelist takes himself to be unless he regard himself as an historian and his narrative as a history. It is only as an historian that he has the smallest *locus standi*. As a narrator of fictitious events he is nowhere; to insert into his attempt a back-bone of logic, he must relate events that are assumed to be real. This assumption permeates, animates all the work of the most solid story-tellers. . . . Trollope suddenly winks at us and reminds us that he is telling us an arbitrary thing, we are startled and shocked in quite the same way as if Macaulay or Motley were to drop the historic mask and intimate that William of Orange was a myth or the Duke of Alva an invention.

It is a part of this same ambiguity of mind as to what constitutes evidence that Trollope should sometimes endow his people with such fantastic names. Dr. Pessimist Anticant and Mr. Sentiment make, as we have seen, an awkward appearance in a modern novel; and Mr. Neversay Die, Mr. Stickatit, Mr. Rerechild and Mr. Fillgrave (the two last the family physicians), are scarcely more felicitous. . . . It is probably not unfair to say that if Trollope derived half his inspiration from life, he derived the other half from Thackeray; his earlier novels, in especial, suggest an honourable emulation of the author of *The Newcomes*. Thackeray's names were perfect; they always had a meaning, and (except in his absolutely jocose productions, where they were still admirable) we can imagine, even when they are most figurative, that they should have been borne by real people. But in this, as in other respects, Trollope's hand was heavier than his master's; though when he is content not to be too comical his appellations are sometimes fortunate enough. Mrs. Proudie is excellent, for Mrs. Proudie, and even the Duke of Omnium and Gatherum Castle rather minister to illusion than destroy it. Indeed, the names of houses and places, throughout Trollope, are full of colour. (pp. 115-18)

[For the most part, Trollope] should be judged by the productions of the first half of his career; later the strong wine was rather too copiously watered. His practice, his acquired facility, were such that his hand went of itself, as it were, and the thing

looked superficially like a fresh inspiration. But it was not fresh, it was rather stale; and though there was no appearance of effort, there was a fatal dryness of texture. It was too little of a new story and too much of an old one. Some of these ultimate compositions—*Phineas Redux* (*Phineas Finn* is much better), *The Prime Minister, John Caldigate, The American Senator, The Duke's Children*—betray the dull, impersonal rumble of the mill-wheel. . . . His fund of acquaintance with his own country—and indeed with the world at large—was apparently inexhaustible, and it gives his novels a spacious, geographical quality which we should not know where to look for elsewhere in the same degree, and which is the sign of an extraordinary difference between such an horizon as his and the limited world-outlook, as the Germans would say, of the brilliant writers who practise the art of realistic fiction on the other side of the Channel. Trollope was familiar with all sorts and conditions of men, with the business of life, with affairs, with the great world of sport, with every component part of the ancient fabric of English society. He had travelled more than once all over the globe, and for him, therefore, the background of the human drama was a very extensive scene. He had none of the pedantry of the cosmopolite; he remained a sturdy and sensible middle-class Englishman. But his work is full of implied reference to the whole arena of modern vagrancy. (pp. 119-22)

The contrast [between Trollope and the French naturalists] is complete, and it would be interesting . . . to see how far it goes. On one side a wide, good-humoured, superficial glance at a good many things; on the other a gimlet-like consideration of a few. Trollope's plan, as well as Zola's, was to describe the life that lay near him; but the two writers differ immensely as to what constitutes life and what constitutes nearness. For Trollope the emotions of a nursery-governess in Australia would take precedence of the adventures of a depraved *femme du monde* [woman of the world] in Paris or London. They both undertake to do the same thing—to depict French and English manners; but the English writer (with his unsurpassed industry) is so occasional, so accidental, so full of the echoes of voices that are not the voice of the muse. Gustave Flaubert, Emile Zola, Alphonse Daudet, on the other hand, are nothing if not concentrated and sedentary. Trollope's realism is as instinctive, as inveterate as theirs; but nothing could mark more the difference between the French and English mind than the difference in the application, on one side and the other, of this system. We say system, though on Trollope's part it is none. He has no visible, certainly no explicit care for the literary part of the business; he writes easily, comfortably, and profusely, but his style has nothing in common either with the minute stippling of Daudet or the studied rhythms of Flaubert. He accepted all the common restrictions, and found that even within the barriers there was plenty of material. . . . In spite of his want of doctrinal richness I think he tells us, on the whole, more about life than our sister republic. I say this with a full consciousness of the opportunities an artist loses in leaving so many corners unvisited, so many topics untouched, simply because I think his perception of character was naturally more just and liberal than that of the naturalists. (pp. 122-24)

But it would be hard to say (within the circle in which he revolved) what material he neglected. . . . I have spoken of *The Warden* not only because it made his reputation, but because, taken in conjunction with *Barchester Towers,* it is thought by many people to be his highest flight. *Barchester Towers* is admirable; it has an almost Thackerayan richness. Archdeacon

Grantley grows more and more into life, and Mr. Harding is as charming as ever. Mrs. Proudie is ushered into a world in which she was to make so great an impression. Mrs. Proudie has become classical; of all Trollope's characters she is the most often referred to. She is exceedingly true; but I do not think she is quite so good as her fame, and as several figures from the same hand that have not won so much honour. She is rather too violent, too vixenish, too sour. (pp. 125-26)

Trollope did not write for posterity; he wrote for the day, the moment; but these are just the writers whom posterity is apt to put into its pocket. So much of the life of his time is reflected in his novels that we must believe a part of the record will be saved; and the best parts of them are so sound and true and genial, that readers with an eye to that sort of entertainment will always be sure, in a certain proportion, to turn to them. Trollope will remain one of the most trustworthy, though not one of the most eloquent, of the writers who have helped the heart of man to know itself. . . . There are two kinds of taste in the appreciation of imaginative literature: the taste for emotions of surprise and the taste for emotions of recognition. It is the latter that Trollope gratifies, and he gratifies it the more that the medium of his own mind, through which we see what he shows us, gives a confident direction to our sympathy. His natural rightness and purity are so real that the good things he projects must be real. A race is fortunate when it has a good deal of the sort of imagination—of imaginative feeling—that had fallen to the share of Anthony Trollope; and in this possession our English race is not poor. (pp. 132-33)

> *Henry James, "Anthony Trollope" (originally published in* The Century, *Vol. 26, No. 3, July, 1883, in his* Partial Portraits, *Macmillan and Co., Limited, London, 1888 (and reprinted by Macmillan, 1899), pp. 97-133.*

[RICHARD HOLT HUTTON]   (essay date 1883)

[The absolute frankness of *An Autobiography*] is most characteristic of Mr. Trollope; and so is its unequalled,—manliness we were going to say,—but we mean something both more and less than manliness, covering more than the daring of manliness and something less than the quietness or equanimity which we are accustomed to include in that term, so we may call it, its unequalled masculineness. Mr. Trollope is not only candid in this autobiography; but of any deficiency of his own which he wishes to confess, he confesses himself almost defiantly. . . . There is a hurly-burly frankness about it, as of a man who is defying the public to prevent him from saying of himself precisely what he wants to say. And, no doubt, he does say precisely what he wants to say; and what he wants to say is most creditable to him; but it is thrust upon us somewhat too headlongly, too much after the fashion of the ardent hunting man he was, one who would ride straight across country, and was determined never to avail himself of any gap or gate which would furnish a more natural transition from one position to another. (p. 1377)

This book is characteristic also in the complete sincerity of its somewhat mundane ideal of life. Mr. Trollope seems to be one of the few men who have really reached their ideal, and enjoyed reaching it to the full. . . . Strangely enough, Mr. Trollope could create characters, and did create characters who, if they had written down their own ideals, would have painted something which seems to us infinitely higher than such an ideal as this. His own favourite, Plantagenet Palliser—not the Plantagenet Palliser of *Framley Parsonage,* but the Plantagenet Pal-

liser of *Can You Forgive Her?* and the subsequent novels, especially when he becomes Duke of Omnium, and has to manage unruly children after the death of his wife, had a far higher ideal than this. Mr. Harding had a far higher ideal than this. So had Mr. Crawley, and so even had Dean Arabin. But it is difficult, after reading this autobiography, not to feel that Mr. Trollope had a higher ideal when thinking the thoughts of some of the children of his own imagination, than he had when thinking his own. . . . Mr. Trollope was thoroughly in earnest in wishing to teach a high morality by his tales,—and no tales could be purer than his from anything like mischief; at the same time, we should say that what he understood as a high morality was a morality of a very limited kind, and involved little more for men and women in general than insisting that girls should be modest and loving, and that men should be honest and diligent, and should know their own minds. He hardly even teaches so much as that men should be pure as well as women, or that women should be courageous as well as men. . . . It is perfectly obvious that Mr. Trollope succeeded in embodying [his] ideal of the moral teaching of a novel in almost all his tales. But in how very few of them did he portray a character which puts before us a very high or delicate standard of motive and principle, such as that of the Duke in *The Duke's Children,* or that of Mr. Harding in all the Barchester stories, or that of Mr. Crawley in *The Last Chronicle of Barset,* or that of Dean Arabin in the same story. For the most part, Mr. Trollope is content with showing up the meanness of cowardice and dishonesty, and the misery of marrying without love, and he owes it rather to the force of his imagination than to his own personal ideal of what life should be, if he takes us into a finer and rarer atmosphere of spiritual feeling. (pp. 1378-79)

> *[Richard Holt Hutton], "Anthony Trollope's 'Autobiography'," in* The Spectator, *Vol. 56, No. 2887, October 27, 1883, pp. 1377-79.*

THE TIMES, LONDON   (essay date 1884)

A melancholy interest attaches to the last story we shall ever have from Anthony Trollope, and its excellence reawakens our regrets for his loss. '**An Old Man's Love**' is rather a novelette than a novel, and perhaps Trollope has seldom done himself justice in his more sketchy productions. He needed elbow-room for the effective display of his powers, and the most elaborately painted of his characters became our greatest favourite. But '**An Old Man's Love**' is unusually compact and complete; and we fancy that, with his practical turn of mind, he may have felt when he had finished it that he had been recklessly wasteful of good material. In the little group of personages who play their parts, there are two at least of rare capabilities; nor do we remember that in any of his equally unpretentious books he has shown so striking a command both of humour and pathos. As he might have written himself in his autobiography, and in the old housekeeper, Mrs. Baggett, 'I think there is a great deal of good comedy,' while Mr. Whittlestaff, the elderly gentleman who falls in love, is very nearly a masterpiece in his marvellous truth to nature. (p. 523)

As for Mrs. Baggett, the comic old housekeeper . . . , Trollope has shown all the familiar versatility in the completeness with which he has identified himself with the crusty but warm-hearted old woman who speaks her mind in season and out of season, both to her master and to the young intruder whom he admires. Yet, vulgar and coarsely indifferent to feelings as she is, Mrs. Baggett shows herself almost as self-sacrificing as her nobleminded master. . . . [Not withstanding] our regrets, we are glad to think that the last of Trollope's works should leave us with agreeable memories of its lamented writer almost at his very best. (p. 524)

> *A review of "An Old Man's Love," in* The Times, *London (© Times Newspapers Limited 1884), April 14, 1884 (and reprinted in* Trollope: The Critical Heritage, *edited by Donald Smalley, Routledge & Kegan Paul, 1969, pp. 523-24).*

GEORGE SAINTSBURY   (essay date 1895)

[*Saintsbury was an English literary historian and critic of the late nineteenth and early twentieth centuries. A prolific writer, he composed a number of histories of English and European literature as well as several critical works on individual authors, styles, and periods. In his essay on Trollope, excerpted below, Saintsbury maintains that Trollope's work lacks genius and is "doomed to pass." Saintsbury returns to Trollope and expresses a different opinion in his 1920 essay (see excerpt below).*]

I do not know that I myself ever took Mr. Trollope for one of the immortals; but really between 1860 and 1870 it might have been excusable so to take him. In **"Barchester Towers,"** especially, there are characters and scenes which go uncommonly near the characters and scenes that do not die. Years later the figure of Mr. Crawley and the scene of the final vanquishing of Mrs. Proudie simulate, if they do not possess, immortal quality. And in the enormous range of the other books earlier and later it would not be difficult to single out a number—a very considerable number—of passages not greatly inferior to these. From almost the beginning until quite the end, Mr. Trollope—whether by diligent contemplation of models, by dexterous study from the life, or by the mere persistent craftsman's practice which turns out pots till it turns them out flawlessly—showed the faculty of constructing a thoroughly readable story. You might not be extraordinarily enamoured of it; you might not care to read it again; you could certainly feel no enthusiastic reverence for or gratitude to its author. But it was eminently satisfactory; it was exactly what it held itself out to be. . . . (pp. 175-76)

And yet even such work is doomed to pass,—with everything that is of the day and the craftsman, not of eternity and art. It was not because Mr. Trollope had, as I believe he had in private life, a good deal of the genial Philistine about him, that his work lacks the certain vital signs. . . . The fault of the Trollopian novel is in the quality of the Trollopian art. It is shrewd, competent, not insufficiently supported by observation, not deficient in more than respectable expressive power, careful, industrious, active enough. But it never has the last exalting touch of genius, it is every-day, commonplace, and even not infrequently vulgar. These are the three things that great art never is; though it may busy itself with far humbler persons and objects than Mr. Trollope does, may confine itself even more strictly than he does to purely ordinary occurrences, may shun the exceptional, the bizarre, the *outré*, as rigidly as Miss Austen herself. Indeed, there is a very short road to vulgarity by affecting these last three things; and I think since Mr. Trollope's time it has been pretty frequently trodden by those who are hastening to the same goal of comparative oblivion which, I fear, he has already reached. (pp. 176-77)

> *George Saintsbury, "Three Mid-Century Novelists (Concluded)," in his* Corrected Impressions: Essays on Victorian Writers, *Dodd, Mead and Company, 1895, pp. 168-77.**

FREDERIC HARRISON   (essay date 1895)

One of Trollope's strong points and one source of his popularity was a command over plain English almost perfect for his own limited purpose. It is limpid, flexible, and melodious. It never rises into eloquence, poetry, or power; but it is always easy, clear, simple, and vigorous. Trollope was not capable of the sustained mastery over style that we find in [Thackeray's] *Esmond,* nor had he the wit, passion, and pathos at Thackeray's command. But of all contemporaries he comes nearest to Thackeray in easy conversations and in quiet narration of incidents and motives. Sometimes, but very rarely, Trollope is vulgar—for good old Anthony had a coarse vein: it was in the family:—but as a rule his language is conspicuous for its ease, simplicity, and unity of tone. This was one good result of his enormous rapidity of execution. His books read from cover to cover, as if they were spoken in one sitting by an *improvisatore* in one and the same mood, who never hesitated an instant for a word, and who never failed to seize the word he wanted. This ease and mastery over speech was the fruit of prodigious practice and industry both in office work and in literary work. It is a mastery which conceals itself, and appears to the reader the easiest thing in the world. (pp. 206-07)

His work has one special quality that has not been sufficiently noticed. It has the most wonderful unity of texture and a perfect harmony of tone. From the first line to the last, there is never a sentence or a passage which strikes a discordant note; we are never worried by a spasmodic phrase, nor bored by fine writing that fails to "come off." Nor is there ever a paragraph which we need to read over again, or a phrase that looks obscure, artificial, or enigmatic. This can hardly be said of any other novelist of this century, except of Jane Austen, for even Thackeray himself is now and then artificial in *Esmond,* and the vulgarity of *Yellowplush* at last becomes fatiguing. Now Trollope reproduces for us that simplicity, unity, and ease of Jane Austen, whose facile grace flows on like the sprightly talk of a charming woman, mistress of herself and sure of her hearers. This uniform ease, of course, goes with the absence of all the greatest qualities of style; absence of any passion, poetry, mystery, or subtlety. He never rises, it is true, to the level of the great masters of language. But, for the ordinary incidents of life amongst well-bred and well-to-do men and women of the world, the form of Trollope's tales is almost as well adapted as the form of Jane Austen.

In absolute realism of spoken words Trollope has hardly any equal. His characters utter quite literally the same words, and no more, than such persons utter in actual life. The characters, it is true, are the average men and women we meet in the educated world, and the situations, motives, and feelings described are seldom above or below the ordinary incidents of modern life. But within this very limited range of incident, and for this very common average of person and character, the conversations are photographic or stenographic reproductions of actual speech. His letters, especially his young ladies' letters, are singularly real, life-like, and characteristic. (pp. 207-08)

Trollope makes his people utter such phrases as the characters he presents to us actually use in real life—or rather such phrases as they did use thirty years ago. And yet, although he hardly ever rises into eloquence, wit, brilliancy, or sinks into any form of talk either unnaturally tall, or unnaturally low,—still, the conversations are just sufficiently pointed, humorous, or characteristic, to amuse the reader and develop the speaker's character. Trollope in this exactly hits the happy mean. . . .

Trollope's characters speaks with literal nature; and yet with enough of point, humour, vigour, to make it pleasant reading.

We may at once confess to his faults and limitations. They are plain enough, constant, and quite incapable of defence. Out of his sixty works, I should be sorry to pick more than ten as being worth a second reading, or twenty which are worth a first reading. Nor amongst the good books could I count any of the last ten years. The range of characters is limited. . . . The plots are neither new nor ingenious; the incidents are rarely more than commonplace; the characters are seldom very powerful, or original, or complex. There are very few "psychologic problems," very few dramatic situations, very few revelations of a new world and unfamiliar natures. (pp. 209-11)

But within this limited range of life, this uniformity of "genteel comedy," Trollope has not seldom given us pieces of inimitable truthfulness and curious delicacy of observation. The dignitaries of the cathedral close, the sporting squires, the county magnates, the country doctors, and the rectory home, are drawn with a precision, a refinement, an absolute fidelity that only Jane Austen could compass. There is no caricature, no burlesque, nothing improbable or over-wrought. The bishop, the dean, the warden, the curate, the apothecary, the duke, the master of fox-hounds, the bishop's wife, the archdeacon's lady, the vicar's daughter, the governess, the undergraduate—all are perfectly true to nature. So, too, are the men in the clubs in London, the chiefs, subordinates, and clerks in the public offices, the ministers and members of Parliament, the leaders, and rank and file of London "society." They never utter a sentence which is not exactly what such men and women do utter; they do and they think nothing but what such men and women think and do in real life. Their habits, conversation, dress, and interests are photographically accurate, to the point of illusion. It is not high art—but it is art. The field is a narrow one; the actors are ordinary. But the skill, grace, and humour with which the scenes are caught, and the absolute illusion of truthfulness, redeem it from the commonplace. (pp. 211-12)

> *Frederic Harrison, "Anthony Trollope" (originally published in a different form as "Anthony Trollope's Place in Literature," in* The Forum, *Vol. XIX, May, 1895), in his* Studies in Early Victorian Literature, *Edward Arnold, 1895, pp. 200-25.*

LESLIE STEPHEN (essay date 1901)

[Stephen is considered to be one of the most important commentators on Victorian fiction. In his criticism, Stephen argues that all literature is nothing more than an imaginative rendering, in concrete terms, of a writer's philosophy or beliefs. It is the role of criticism, he contends, to translate into intellectual terms what the writer has told the reader through character, symbol, and plot. Stephen's analyses often include biographical judgments of the writer as well as the work. As Stephen once observed: "The whole art of criticism consists in learning to know the human being who is partially revealed to us in his spoken or his written words." In the following essay he attempts to introduce Trollope to an unappreciative generation of readers. He begins with an examination of Trollope's life, working habits, and views on writing as they are presented in An Autobiography, *a work which Stephen considers essential to an understanding of Trollope's novels.]*

We can see plainly enough what we must renounce in order to enjoy Trollope. We must cease to bother ourselves about art. We must not ask for exquisite polish of style. We must be content with good homespun phrases which give up all their

meaning on the first reading. We must not desire brilliant epigrams suggesting familiarity with aesthetic doctrines or theories of the universe. A brilliant modern novelist is not only clever, but writes for clever readers. He expects us to understand oblique references to esoteric theories, and to grasp a situation from a delicate hint. We are not to be bothered with matter-of-fact details, but to have facts sufficiently adumbrated to enable us to accept the aesthetic impression. Trollope writes like a thorough man of business or a lawyer stating a case. We must know exactly the birth, parentage, and circumstances of all the people concerned, and have a precise statement of what afterwards happens to everybody mentioned in the course of the story. We must not care for artistic unity. Trollope admits that he could never construct an intricate plot to be gradually unravelled. That, in fact, takes time and thought. He got hold of some leading incident, set his characters to work, and followed out any series of events which happened to be involved. . . . He simply looks on, and only takes care to make his report consistent and intelligible. To accept such writing in the corresponding spirit implies, no doubt, the confession that you are a bit of a Philistine, able to put up with the plainest of bread and butter and dispense with all the finer literary essences. I think, however, that at times one's state is the more gracious for accepting the position. There is something so friendly and simple and shrewd about one's temporary guide that one is the better for taking a stroll with him and listening to gossiping family stories, even though they be rather rambling and never scandalous. . . . Hawthorne said at an early period that Trollope's novels precisely suited his taste [see excerpt above, 1860]. . . . Trollope was delighted, as he well might be, with such praise from so different a writer, and declares that this passage defined the aim of his novels "with wonderful accuracy." They represent, that is, the average English society of the time more faithfully even than memoirs of real persons, because there is no motive for colouring the motives of an imaginary person. (pp. 178-80)

Trollope's best achievement, I take it, was the series of Barsetshire novels. They certainly passed at the time for a marvel of fidelity. Trollope tells us that he was often asked when he had lived in a cathedral close and become intimate with archdeacons; and had been able to answer that he had never lived in a close and had never spoken to an archdeacon. He had evolved the character, he declares, "out of his moral consciousness," and is pleasantly complacent over his creation. (p. 181)

The prosaic person, it must remember, has a faculty for ignoring all the elements of life and character which are not prosaic, and if Trollope's picture is accurate it is not exhaustive. The weakness comes from misapplying a good principle. Trollope made it a first principle to keep rigorously to the realities of life. He inferred that nothing strange or improbable should ever be admitted. . . . Trollope inclines to make everybody an average specimen, and in his desire to avoid exaggeration inevitably exaggerates the commonplaceness of life. He is afraid of admitting any one into his world who will startle us by exhibiting any strength of character. His lovers, for example, have to win the heroine by showing superiority to the worldly scruples of their relations. . . . [The] heroes have all the vigour taken out of them that they may not shock us by diverging from the most commonplace standard. When a hero does something energetic, gives a thrashing, for example, to the man who has jilted a girl, we are carefully informed that he does it in a blundering and unsatisfactory way.

By the excision of all that is energetic, or eccentric, or impulsive, or romantic, you do not really become more lifelike; you only limit yourself to the common and uninteresting. That misconception injures Trollope's work, and accounts, I suspect, for the decline of our interest. An artist who systematically excludes all lurid colours or strong lights shows a dingy, whity-brown universe, and is not therefore more true to nature. Barsetshire surely has its heroes and its villains, its tragedy and its force, as well as its archdeacons and young ladies bound hand and foot by the narrowest rules of contemporary propriety. Yet, after all, Trollope's desire to be faithful had its good result in spite of this misconception. There are, in the first place, a good many commonplace people in the world; and, moreover, there were certain types into which he could throw himself with real vigour. He can appreciate energy when it does not take a strain of too obvious romance. His best novel, he thinks, and his readers must agree with him, was the *Last Chronicle of Barset.* The poor parson, Mr. Crawley, is at once the most lifelike and (in his sense) the most improbable of his characters. He is the embodiment of Trollope's own "doggedness." . . . [Mr. Crawley,] with his strange wrong-headed conscientiousness, his honourable independence, blended with bitter resentment against the more successful, and the strong domestic affections, which yet make him a despot in his family, is a real triumph of which more ambitious novelists might be proud. . . . [Mrs. Proudie] is one genuine type, albeit a very rare one, of the Englishwoman of the period, and Trollope draws her vigorously, because her qualities are only an excessive development of very commonplace failings. In such cases Trollope can deal with his characters vigorously and freely, and we do not feel that their vitality has been lowered from a mistaken desire to avoid a strain upon our powers of belief. He can really understand people on a certain plane of intelligence. His pompous officials at public offices, and dull members of Parliament, and here and there such disreputable persons as he ventures to sketch, as, for example, the shrewd contractor in *Dr. Thorne,* who is ruined by his love of gin, are solid and undeniable realities. We see the world as it was, only in a dark mirror which is incapable of reflecting the fairer shades of thought and custom.

Hawthorne's appreciation of Trollope's strain was perhaps due in part to his conviction that John Bull was a huge mass of solid flesh incapable of entering the more ethereal regions of subtle fancy of which he was himself a native. Trollope was to him a John Bull convicting himself out of his own mouth, and yet a good fellow in his place. When our posterity sits in judgment, it will discover, I hope, that the conventional John Bull is only an embodiment of one set of the national qualities, and by no means an exhaustive portrait of the original. But taking Trollope to represent the point of view from which there is a certain truthfulness in the picture—and no novelist can really do more than give one set of impressions—posterity may after all consider his novels as a very instructive document. . . . [Readers of the twenty-first century] will look back to the early days of Queen Victoria as a delightful time, when it was possible to take things quietly, and a good, sound, sensible optimism was the prevalent state of mind. How far the estimate would be true is another question; but Trollope, as representing such an epoch, will supply a soothing if rather mild stimulant for the imagination, and it will be admitted that if he was not among the highest intellects of his benighted time, he was as sturdy, wholesome, and kindly a human being as could be desired. (pp. 185-90)

Leslie Stephen, "Anthony Trollope" (originally published in The National Review, London, Vol. XXXVIII,

No. 223, September, 1901), in his Studies of a Biographer, Vol. IV, *G. P. Putnam's Sons, 1907, pp. 156-90.*

GEORGE SAINTSBURY (essay date 1920)

[*Although in his previous essay Saintsbury had declared Trollope's work "doomed to pass" (1895), here he reconsiders Trollope's achievement and praises the novelist for his accurate portrayal of a previous era and asserts that Trollope occupies a permanent place among Victorian writers.*]

The point at which decadence, real or alleged, begins [in Trollope's works], is perhaps itself a matter of some controversy. I have known some very good judges—though perhaps judges a little biassed by the fact of having begun with it—who see nothing decadent in *Phineas Finn.* I own that I see a sort of gap and drop between it and *The Last Chronicle*—which preceded it by not very many months—a gap and drop almost equal to a landslip—and that I do not think the higher level was ever recovered. It is true that Trollope did not now lose—that in fact he never lost—his remarkable faculty of telling a story. . . . [One of his latest], *Marion Fay,* is perhaps the weakest of all in this respect, though its predecessors by a year or two, *An Eye for an Eye, Cousin Henry,* and *Dr. Wortle's School,* are very far from strong. But a practised and judicial novel-critic will perceive in even the weakest of these something quite different from the case of the common circulating-library tale-teller who can't tell a tale. If you go back to *Is He Popenjoy?* [*sic*] or *John Caldigate* they will give you, though in changed degree, fresh evidence, and you may carry investigation further still through others including the 'Phineas-Eustace-Palliser' group itself, and, what is more, right back to weaklings of the greater period, always strengthening your provisional conclusion as you go. This conclusion will have been—at least if it agrees with the present critic's—that Trollope's novel-writing faculty, at its best of little below first-class quality, went through much the same vicissitudes as the mere physical faculties of other men, but that his economy or administration of it was peculiar and not always judicious. Before *The Warden,* and in that story and *The Three Clerks* to some extent, he did not know how to manage it at all, or how to direct it into his books. In *Dr. Thorne* he made a great advance. From *Barchester Towers* to *The Last Chronicle* he had it in fullest command and play in his greater books—*Barchester Towers* itself, *Framley Parsonage, Orley Farm* (not quite throughout), *The Small House, Can You Forgive Her?* and the [*Barsetshire Chronicle*]—less according to me in *The Bertrams, Castle Richmond,* and *The Claverings* (some good judges differ from me here but Trollope himself rather agreed), and least in the *Rachel Ray* group. (pp. 42-3)

Although Trollope has left a fair number of short stories he was not a good short-story-teller; and the slightly commercial view which he took of his art probably found support in a secret consciousness of this disability. The result was that he regularly made a short novel out of matter the substance of which was only enough for a short story; while the quality of it was not always suitable even for that. . . . Perhaps a born short-story-teller might have made short stories of *Rachel Ray, Miss Mackenzie,* and *The Belton Estate.* . . . But nobody could have made a good long or even short novel out of their material, nor out of that of *Sir Harry Hotspur* [or] *Lady Anna.* . . . The 'unequality' (as the elder Mr. Weller had it) of the spirit and the water in these compositions was too great. But the spirit itself remained. It gave itself in almost satisfactory quality in *Ayala's*

Angel only a year or two before the close; and in the actual concluding pair—the finished *Mr. Scarborough's Family* and the unfinished, remarkable, and just at this time really valuable *Landleaguers*—it ought not to be missed by any intelligent reader. Indeed, in these two it is 'left to itself' in an almost uncanny fashion, more particularly in *Mr. Scarborough's Family*. You don't care in the least for the clever heartless 'schemer' who gives it his name, or for the foolish *jeune premier,* or for the two sons (one a schemer like himself and the other a typical 'prodigal son') whom Mr. Scarborough plays off against each other, or for the heroine, or for anybody else. You don't very much want to know what is going to happen. And yet, if you have any sense of the particular art, you can't help feeling the skill with which the artist wheels you along till he feels inclined to turn you out of his barrow and then deposits you at his if not your destination. (pp. 44-5)

In respect, therefore, of the mere story, it may be possible to reply with some effect to the Devil's Advocate; in regard to all the weaker and not merely the later novels—let us for the moment pass from story to character. Here Trollope had always shown a curious inequality and uncertainty; an inequality and uncertainty which, let it be said at once, disqualifies him for the absolute front rank of novelists. Nothing distinguishes the members of this front rank so much as their unerring, or scarcely ever erring, grasp in creating and projecting personality. . . . But even in his early days Trollope had in this respect been unequal and uncertain. In almost all the books from the time when he made his mark with *The Warden* till *The Last Chronicle,* he maintains a high standard, though in *The Three Clerks* and *The Warden* itself he is by no means sure of hand. But in *Castle Richmond,* in *Miss Mackenzie,* in *Rachel Ray,* in *The Belton Estate,* all of them written before the Barsetshire series ceased, there is again a curious absence or at least relaxation of this grasp. Had Trollope's work ceased with *The Last Chronicle* there would have been a pretty opening for critics who like such things. In the cases where the command of character did not appear, was it real uncertainty of command or was it merely that the artist had not taken sufficient pains? (p. 45)

[There] were no doubt some minor reasons besides positive failure or exhaustion of power for the falling off. It may have been wise for Trollope to kill Mrs. Proudie (the death certainly produced some of his finest work) and even to turn off, almost entirely, the [*Barsetshire Chronicle*] tap of that fortunate county. But to some extent at the same time he drove himself out of Eden. The 'new faces, other ways' did not inspire him as the old ones did. It is very curious to see how, when he does allow himself and us renewal of old acquaintance, there is a momentary brightening up of the character-interest. (p. 46)

[There] is a cheerful theory that our faults always grow upon us, and Trollope had certain weaknesses which were likely to do so. One was, not coextensive with but a part result of, his fancy for dealing largely with love. In this fancy itself there was nothing reprehensible. Only very pretty or very ugly young ladies, very stupid or portentously clever young gentlemen disdain, or far more probably in two of the classes would pretend to disdain, love as motive. In fact a novel without love is, to adopt King Henry the Fifth's simile in less shocking fashion, 'like beef without mustard'. And Trollope had always recognized this truth: though even in his earlier days, as we may have to notice, his treatment of the subject was not impeccable. It grew much worse later. John Bold, Lucius Mason, and even Felix Graham, had been prigs; Mr. Slope was the modified villain for whose flogging at the gangway we cheer-

fully cheered; . . . Johnny Eames, though much the best of the lot as a lover, [was] not perfect. But they all (except the prigs) played their parts sympathetically enough (for it shows real sympathy in the villain to get himself flogged); and even the prigs were not quite despicable. Phineas Finn himself at the beginning of the decadence, and Lord Silverbridge in *The Duke's Children* near its end, are very despicable creatures indeed. Nothing short of kicking could fitly reward the Irishman for making Lady Laura Standish a confidante of his love (if you call it so) for Violet Effingham; kicking would perhaps be too much for Silverbridge's desertion of his first love—one of the most remarkable of Trollope's later characters—in favour of an American girl of whom we are told that she was pretty and rich, but who is not made actually attractive in any way whatever. Still, he deserves at least infinite contempt. On the other side of the account, it is undeniably true that women do manifest an inexplicable leaning towards 'bounders'. But, once more, the way in which *such* a bounder as Mr. Lopez in *The Prime Minister* made himself attractive to such a girl as Emily Wharton, and took in so acute a personage as that Lady Glencora whom one hardly cares to call 'the Duchess', is never even suggested. Now these failures all show a lost command of character-touches. There is almost nothing so bad or so disagreeable that a novelist may not make his personages do it if he can fix our attention on the naturalness and necessity of their doing it. It is when this naturalness and necessity do not make themselves felt that criticisms of the kind just made are justified. (pp. 46-8)

The Way We Live Now, with some good things, is hardly one of the rare instances in which an author's attempt to 'bring himself up to date' has been successful: and if there were nothing else to say (something has been said) against *The Duke's Children,* it would weigh against it that Lady Glencora had to be killed to make it possible. Trollope was rather fond of this kind of murder. One cannot blame him for killing off John Bold between *The Warden* and *Barchester Towers,* for John had already been much luckier than he deserved, and his sole reason for existence had been to start the theme of *The Warden* itself. . . . But the butchery of Lady Glencora—even of the somewhat faded 'Duchess' of *The Prime Minister*—for no other reason than the same, is really sad; for she had been perhaps the most *delightful* of all his heroines.

If it has seemed to anybody that our revisiting of Trollope has hitherto been not very prolific of blessings on him, let the very last sentence of the last paragraph serve as a hinge for turning the table of judgement. If one deplores, almost resents, the death of Lady Glencora it is because one has recognized and rejoiced in the fact that she lived. And this is, for her creator, the highest possible praise in kind, though the question of degrees may remain. . . . For the present writer the ultimate questions have been [simple]. . . . Is the romance such that you see the perilous seas and ride the *barrière* as in your own person? Are the folk of the novel such that you have met or feel that you might have met them in your life or in theirs? If so the work passes; with what degree of merit is again a second question.

If there be any soundness in this view Trollope has 'passed' already. . . . The way of romance he does not take with any success, nor as a rule does he attempt it; still less that highest way of all where the adventurer tries and wins the combined event, romance *and* novel. . . . But the novel prize, if not in the highest possible degree, he takes. (pp. 50-2)

I do not think that he will, by the best judges, ever be thought worthy of the very highest place among novelists or among

English novelists. He has something no doubt of the '*for* all time', but he is not exactly '*of* all time'. Or, to put the calculus the other way, he is by no means only '*for* an age'; but he is to a certain lowering though not disqualifying degree '*of* an age'. If you compare him with the really great novelists of his own century, all of whom were in actual drawing of breath his contemporaries, he cannot vie with Miss Austen in that quietly intense humanity which contends with and transcends a rather narrow scheme of manners and social habits; or with Scott in largeness of distinctly romantic conception. In absolute universality of '*this*-worldliness' Thackeray towers above him; as in a certain fantastic command of not impossible *other*-worldliness does Dickens. But short of these four I do not know any nineteenth-century English novelist whose superiority to him in some ways—Kingsley's in romance; Charles Reade's in a certain strange infusion of positive genius; George Eliot's in appeal to the *intelligentsia*—is not compensated by their inferiority in turning out personages and fitting them with incidents of the kind indicated in the foregoing survey—the personages and incidents, that is to say, of actual contemporary life, touched, if not to supreme, at any rate to more than competent freedom from commonplaceness of the disqualifying kind in one way and from mere eccentricity in another. (pp. 64-5)

George Saintsbury, "Trollope Revisited," in Essays and Studies by Members of the English Association, *Vol. VI, edited by A. C. Bradley, Oxford at the Clarendon Press, Oxford, 1920, pp. 41-66.*

MORRIS EDMUND SPEARE   (essay date 1924)

[*Speare discusses the six novels that form the Palliser series, in addition to* Ralph the Heir, *which recounts Trollope's experiences while running for Parliament. Speare asserts that Trollope's political novels were intended as a means for presenting everyday life rather than as a vehicle for his political philosophy.*]

[When] one surveys all that is to be found in Trollope's political novels, and seeks, so to speak, the common denominator of them, one is forced to the conclusion that Trollope's main interest, first and last, is to tell 'a rattling good story.' It was to weave a plot that would hold the reader's interest from first page to last, to infuse, wherever possible, a strong 'heart interest,' and to make all other things subordinate to that primary end. Long before he came to write his political novels Trollope had found his *métier* (which was to tell a straightforward English tale as Thackeray had told it), and he had found his audience, which was the world of average, normal human beings, less interested in psychological discernments and in the tracing of cause and effect than in the chronicles which dealt with broad surface values in human character and the portrayal of every-day domestic affections. Having therefore gained his reading public—a public which had learned to look for these definite things in him—Trollope, upon approaching the political *genre* of the novel, came to it with certain limitations already imposed upon him. The audience which had grown used to his 'style' necessarily sought only for those things which had interested them in his earlier novels and which they expected to find in these of the political *genre* as well. Had they missed here what they had learned to love in his other works . . . that reading public, always fickle, might easily have deserted him. Trollope, therefore, took no chances, but reproduced in this *genre* part of the world and much of the method which he had made popular in his earlier works. So, in [the] seven political novels we have again mainly the nar-

rative writer, the clever draftsman filling his canvasses with English squires, country gentlemen, lords of the chase and the hunt, grand ladies of the drawing-rooms, fine gentlemen of the clubs. In all of these the social emotions are more significant than the play of intellectual wit and fancy, and in depicting the social emotions Trollope was a master. In the political *milieu* Trollope found another, a new, background as a source for story-telling, and he took seven distinct novels in which to exhaust the material of it. Upon characters which he knew well, and had drawn elsewhere with great success, he imposed a political emphasis, without forgetting to deal here, too, with the domestic and social emotions, and the 'heart interest' which had earned him in his own day a very wide reading public. That he was successful, in spite of the limitations under which he worked here, in making some definite contributions to the *genre* of the political novel . . . is evidence of his great resourcefulness as a writer, and of his fertility as a storyteller, as well as of his acquaintance with widely-varying types of human beings.

Since the method of one is the method of all, let us take for our fuller analysis the two ***Phineas*** novels, and here discover in what consisted Trollope's art as a political novelist. (pp. 192-93)

As a study of the character of a rising young politician battling his way to high office and to power Phineas is of course a complete failure. But then Trollope was not interested in delineating ambition in public office. If Phineas lacks any of that wit, culture, refinement, all those graces and the supreme idealism and the poetic quality which characterizes Disraeli's youth, and by force of which they often attain high place enough 'to move the world,' we must remember that Trollope's imagination is not Disraeli's. That this prosaic, homespun, altogether worldly youth finally succeeds in making Commoners sit in wrapt attention while he rises to make his commonplace remarks, that lords of the Treasury confide their political philosophies to him, and a titled lady of a great family (having made an unfortunate marriage) acquires the bad habit of throwing her arms around his neck and burying her face upon his bosom for sympathy, are significant evidence that Trollope was less interested in drawing the character of a zealot touched by a great public cause, or a highly trained and highly spirited youth hungering to right great social or political injustices, than he was in setting forth a man made of common clay who was to be a focal point for as much as possible of domestic tragedy and romance, and one who would furnish 'copy' out of his political adventures for an absorbing tale. (p. 196)

If Trollope's knowledge of the intricacies of the political game is so imaginary, and his attachment to political convictions is so slight, as to make his primary political heroes altogether unconvincing (by which facts he stands at the very antipodes from Disraeli), we must, in his political novels, move away from the centre and seek for his contributions to the political *genre* in their 'outskirts' so to speak, upon the rim of the wheel which keeps the hub of it in motion. First in importance in the ***Phineas*** novels are the women. . . . [Lady Laura] is left by the author a pitifully broken wreck of her former high-minded self, without children or husband, a victim of her own ambition, suspicious, envious of others' good fortune,—a picture all the more pitiful to the reader who recalls her as the most high-minded, intelligent, perhaps the noblest woman character in all the political novels of Trollope, now completely fallen from her high estate. All this because she wished, in her own way, to be "politically powerful" and believed, after her father's straightened circumstances, that she could best remain so through a marriage. (pp. 197-99)

[In] drawing rising statesmen Trollope is altogether unsuccessful. This is shown clearly enough in the portrait of Phineas, who, when all is said and done, appears to be a young politician running amuck in public affairs, and leaves the reader with the final impression that he was a better model for a Lothario than he was for a promising politician with the ambitions of a Younger Pitt. Certainly, it would be a sad day for England if men of his weak moral fibre and mental flabbiness became samples of 'an ambitious younger generation' struggling with public affairs. Trollope's portrait of Lady Glencora's husband who gives his name to *The Prime Minister* is not more successful. A slow, plodding, unimaginative and therefore peculiarly conscientious aristocrat, who was never as happy as when in *Phineas Redux* he spent his days and nights, while Chancellor of the Exchequer, in studying decimal coinage, shy, fretful, a man of stiff reserve so that he was too cold for friendship, uncommunicative, sensitive to the point of morbidity at the attack of a single public organ upon the acts of his Ministry, we can never understand how such a fearful specimen of a statesman could ever have been made the Head of a Coalition Ministry. . . . All of Trollope's principal politicians have this same unconvincingness and unreality. Let us name Gresham, Daubeny . . . , Bonteen the politician who is useful, dull, unscrupulous, well-acquainted with all the back-doors and by-paths of official life and therefore 'invaluable' to his party. There is the poor, blundering Lord Fawn who represents the lay-figure in English public life; Sir Orlando Drought, type of sublime mediocrity of talent and energy. . . . Measure all these various types by those created by Disraeli and you see the *pastiche* in them, the counterfeits of their make-up, and with what little insight into political psychology their author was endowed when he created them or imitated them from some living characters about whom he read in his contemporary press or whom he knew.

With his women Trollope stands on firmer ground: here he deals not with silhouettes and shadows but with the substance. The Duchess of Omnium acting the proud wife of a Prime Minister, stirred into great political ambitions of her own, a wealthy woman whose feelings and convictions only help to keep her straight rather than her scruples, is blazing her way in the London social season in order to advance her husband's greatness and popularity. . . . [She reminds the reader] of another lady who came down the river Cydnus on a barge whose poop was "beaten gold, purple the sails," and by her ambition for her husband and herself, of Lady Macbeth.

> I was made to marry, . . . before I was old enough to assert myself. . . . He's Prime Minister, which is a great thing, and I begin to find myself filled to the full with political ambition. I feel myself to be a Lady Macbeth, prepared for the murder of any Duncan or any Daubeny who may stand in my Lord's way.
>
> (pp. 200-02)

It is easy enough to see that Trollope, who knew more about the domestic life of the English aristocracy than he did about the ways and means of the ruling classes at Downing Street and in the political clubs and committee rooms, had some definite convictions about the place of women in English public life. This he shows by both affirmative and negative methods. He shows it affirmatively in the fact that his two greatest 'political ladies,' Lady Laura and the Duchess of Omnium,

when they once over-reach that natural measure of influence which the laws of Victorian propriety permitted them, become not helpers but meddlers, and their meddling is fraught with danger and even ruin for him whom they would aid. Negatively he proves that he had definite convictions by the fact that Madame Goesler, who afterwards becomes the wife of Phineas Finn (a rising young statesman in the last novel in which he appears before us in the Parliamentary Series) seems to be his picture of a model wife for a politician. As Escott puts it in describing her, she "knows exactly when to help her husband by appearing in the foreground, and how to advance his interests by *unadvertised activity* behind the scenes." We see little of her maneuvering above board to give her husband place, but we remember, from her ingrained common sense and her practical measures taken in the *Phineas Redux* novel to save both the name and the life of her hero, . . . that in *her* Trollope paints the active woman with whom he had the greater sympathy. One of the most charming among the many women characters which Trollope knew so well how to draw, and which fill these novels, is Violet Effingham. (pp. 205-06)

It appears to me that as one looks later into the thoroughly happy home of this charming, keen-minded, altogether energetic matron, one finds in her the spokesman of Trollope's views upon woman's place in England. "I do not," she says in one place, "I do not think I shall marry Oswald. I shall knock under to Mr. Mill and go in for woman's rights, and look forward to stand for some female borough." But as a fact Mill's liberal views about Women's Rights was the very last thing that Violet ever thought of accepting. She wished rather to live a fuller life, a completer life, under the sure guidance of one whom she could trust, and whom therefore she could in turn help with her quick sympathies. When Lord Chiltern, as afterwards happens, turns out to be the man she hopes he might become, she appears to have found her complete happiness and the fulfillment of her desires. In the days of these novels, when Mill's theories of Feminism were beginning to startle some women, Trollope showed in these persons, for example, that a woman might live a broad and a full life under her husband's care, and so live it as to help him sanely and well. But her Liberty was to be guided according to him, we may be safe in saying, by an old-fashioned Puritan Principle: it was Liberty under the Law. If Trollope had some guiding conviction underlying his delineation of women who touched public life it seems to me that the conviction was embodied in some such Puritan ideal. To him Woman could be the greatest power in the affairs of England when she served a purpose, first, for which the Creator apparently chose her; to preside over the hearth and the home, and to make them the source of all that was true and of good report. . . . As soon as the woman began to have great public ambitions of her own, however, and began to over-reach herself by interfering with those things the intricacies of which she knew little or nothing, she became not a constructive force but a destructive influence. (p. 207)

[In] presenting his political figures one and all, Trollope never shows, in the political world at least, the interaction of character upon character; what help or injury there comes from one person upon another is always in material things. It is a misfortune that Trollope did not penetrate deep enough to paint these dramatic contrasts. . . . Trollope's political heroes are unconvincing *as* political characters: his prime minister, his Cabinet members, are men whose minds he shrewdly infers from their manners, and not because he knew them intimately; the slight reality they have for us is due to the fact that Trollope refrains from bringing them too close to the reader. Yet despite the fact that his political characters are unconvincing, there are still, in these novels, glimpses of profound knowledge of the parliamentary system of England. (p. 217)

Desirous first and always of picturing human nature as it shows itself in every-day, domestic surroundings, wishing to tell a good love-story in an easy, good-natured manner, he approaches his best characters (which are always the middle-class characters) with an observant, tolerant, and somewhat humorous outlook. Never offensive in his portraiture, with a comfortable interest in England and her sacred institutions, and the men who go up to make her laws in Parliament, he has no philosophy about public life, no ideas about what changes historical necessities call for, only opinions. . . . [Trollope was content] to *depict* his characters and his situations, to gratify his world of readers with the easily jogging narrative of sentiment to which they had already become accustomed in his earlier works. Dead earnestness and daring dreams of power in the mind of an aristocrat Trollope preferred to paint, or could paint merely, as the somewhat domestic and social manoeuvrings of the pale shades of the upper classes. The political life of England was never the integral part of Trollope's literary personality that it was of Disraeli's, to say the least. His political cabinets feed therefore always upon small talk and small ideas. His principal actors are somewhat mechanically-minded public leaders, when it is of them that he treats. Only when he steps down among the people that he knew most intimately, and whose daily fortunes, in their middle-class environment, he could easily follow, does he give us convincing situations and real flesh and blood. With the exception of the great ladies (whom he paints admirably, because he assumes them to be middle-class persons 'risen' to the level of 'high society,' but still with middle-class habits) his flesh-and-blood people are not the leaders in the fight, only the secondary characters. Trollope never took his politics more seriously than as a means of creating another background for the portrayal of human beings, for the telling of a good story, for the chance of reflecting more 'heart interest.' (pp. 218-19)

> *Morris Edmund Speare, "Anthony Trollope: The Victorian Realist in the Political Novel," in his* The Political Novel: Its Development in England and in America *(reprinted by permission of Oxford University Press, Inc.), Oxford University Press, New York, 1924 (and reprinted by Russell & Russell, 1966), pp. 185-220.*

MICHAEL SADLEIR   (essay date 1927)

[*Considered the best biography of Trollope, Sadleir's* Trollope: A Commentary *has been praised for its accuracy, thoroughness, and tact. Originally published in 1927, this study appeared when Trollope had fallen into a period of critical neglect. While modern critics agree that Sadleir's biography helped to revive interest in Trollope's work, many dispute his labeling of Trollope as "the supreme novelist of acquiescence." Sadleir's conclusion, excerpted below, defines Trollope's achievement and asserts that Trollope's greatness lies in his "profound understanding of ordinary life."*]

The initial obstacle to a sober-minded definition of Trollope's novels is that they provide a sensual rather than an intellectual experience. A smell, a pain or a sound is not more difficult to describe than the effect—at once soothing and exciting—produced on the reader's mind by the leisurely, nonchalant commentaries on English social life which carry his name on their title-pages.

The phenomenon is partly explicable by the fact that a Trollope novel is of the very essence of fiction. At its best it represents a distillation of that element in story-telling on which all other elements depend, without which no blend—however skilful—of fact, incident, idea and description can be recognised for fiction at all—the element of characterisation.

There are novels more spiritual than his, more heroic and more beautiful; but there are none more faultless in this most delicate of all novel-writing problems. (p. 366)

[Power of characterisation] is the superlative quality of Trollope as a novelist. And as revealed by him, it is not a power of observation nor of imagination; not a power of knowledge nor of intuition; but a compound of all four, with a something added of the author's personality, giving to the whole a peculiar but elusive flavour.

For even granted characterisation, Trollope's quality remains intangible, baffles resolution. In theme familiar, in treatment undistinguished, his work is nevertheless potent in appeal, unrivalled in its power to hold the attention of readers of any kind and of any generation. And its elusiveness is the more extreme for being unexpected. It seems hardly fitting that a being, who in himself was so definite and so solid, who—like a solitary tower upon a hill—was visible for miles around in the wide landscape of Victorian England, should as a literary phenomenon be so difficult to seize and to describe; it is almost irritating that books in themselves so lustily prosaic should be so hard of definition.

There are, of course, certain qualities that Trollope as a novelist emphatically does not possess. He is no great philanthropist like Dickens; he has not Thackeray's pointed brilliance nor George Eliot's grave enthusiasm; he does not, like Meredith, paint a familiar scene in colours so vivid as to be of themselves a challenge. . . . Even in comparison with Jane Austen—the writer nearest to him as a novelist of manners—his curiosity seems suave rather than searching, his observation to have more of scope than of discrimination.

But not by elimination only can the quality of Trollope be appraised. He may be neither teacher nor word-painter, neither pantheist nor social reformer, but he is definitely something. What is he? Wherein lies that strange potency, which renders work so featureless, so sober and so undemonstrative an entertainment than which few are more enthralling?

It lies surely in his acceptance and his profound understanding of ordinary daily life. In the tale of English literature he is—to put the matter in a phrase—the supreme novelist of acquiescence. (pp. 366-67)

[Trollope] seeks for no doorway of escape. He is content with life, engrossed in it, never weary of its kaleidoscope of good and evil, of tears and laughter. Not only does he agree to the terms proposed by life, but he glories in them. And yet his work is born of a desire for beauty. He finds all of romance and courage and achievement within the unpretentious limits of the social existence of his day. He believes in individual capacity for perfection, but in terms of things as they are; his ideal of beauty and of proportion, whether in character or in happening, lies in the suave adjustment of personality to circumstance.

Trollope, then, is never a writer of revolt. But so complete is his acquiescence that he is not even a critical despot over the society of his imagination. Like a man in a crowded street who views his fellow-men, he is at once genially disposed but fundamentally detached. Also, to the point inevitable in detachment, he is cynical. He is without superiority; without presumption of omniscience. (pp. 367-68)

The long series of his books—so drab yet so mysteriously alive, so obvious yet so impossible of imitation—evade every criterion of what has become an academic judgment. They will stand no schooltests save those of the school of real life. They cannot but violate the modish canons of good fiction, as continually and as shamelessly as does life itself. Like life, they are diffuse, often tedious, seldom arrestingly unusual. Their monotony is the monotony of ordinary existence, which, although while actually passing it provides one small sensation after another, emerges in retrospect as a dull sequence of familiar things.

For in this queer sense of the absorbing interest of normal occupations lies the true realism of Trollope. He can reproduce the fascination of the successive happenings of the daily round, in the absence of which the human spirit would perish or go mad. Existence is made up of an infinite number of tiny fragments of excitement, interest and provocation, which carry men on from day to day, ever expectant, ever occupied. It is the second part of Trollope's claim to be a novelist that, by building up from just such multifarious trivialities the big absorptions which are his books, he gives the illusion that is of all illusions the most difficult to create—the illusion of ordinary life.

The art of Trollope, therefore, has two predominant qualities: power of characterisation and power of dramatisation of the undramatic. Within the limits of these rare capacities he designed and peopled a second England, virtually a replica of the London and counties of his day. But although in his imaginary England life seems (as indeed it is) utterly, almost exasperatingly, a series of unsensational sensations, a slow progression of meals and small ambitions, of love-making and disappointments, of sport and business, it would be an error to regard the Trollopian world as—other than superficially—without violent happenings. . . . It is one aspect of his amazing truth to life that he could contrive at the same time to be a novelist for the *jeune fille* and a most knowledgeable realist. For his books are lifelike in this also—that though compounded both of innocent and guilty, the guilt (as in life) is shrouded from the innocent, so that only such as know the signs of it may realise its presence or its nature.

This fact indicates those two of his personal qualities which most influence his handling of an imaginary social scene—his worldly proficiency and his good manners. There is nothing that he does not know; there is very little that, in his quiet skilful diction, he is not prepared to say. Socially speaking he is the wisest of English novelists; but because a large part of social wisdom is restraint, alike of gesture and of word, his books are restrained—not in incident or necessarily in emotion—but in expression. He writes adult books for adult people. But because he writes in terms of polite society, because he is in the truest sense a "man of the world," he is too civilised and too experienced to forget the social decencies for the sake of the social sins.

And not only had he a well-bred man's distaste for ugly realism; he was himself more interested in the deceptive calm of society's surface than in details of the hidden whirlpools beneath. . . . [The] clash between conventional poise and secret catastrophe, the delicate adjustment of repute and disrepute which kept the life of upper-class England outwardly serene for all its inward hazard, appealed to Trollope's sophisticated and rather cynical mind.

For in all things he was sophisticated and in social things more than a little cynical. . . . Contrast his books with those of the sensation-writers of his day or with those of novelists from a later generation who have been praised for their courageous realism. Trollope in geniality, in satire or in bitterness is calm; but to the others, in one way or another, existence is perpetually and disproportionately exciting. . . . To him everything is material for observation, nothing for declamation or for vanity. He approves virtue and deprecates vice, but he refuses to become excited either over ugliness or beauty. Like a connoisseur of wine he sips at this vintage and at that, selects to his taste and lays a cellar down. We, who inherit it, have but to drink at will, and in the novels that he left behind to savour the essence of life as once it was, as it still is, as in all likelihood it will remain. (pp. 369-73)

> *Michael Sadleir, in his* Trollope: A Commentary *(reprinted by permission of Farrar, Straus and Giroux, Inc.; copyright 1927 by Michael Sadleir; copyright renewed © 1974 by Richard Sadleir), revised edition, Constable & Co., 1945 (and reprinted by Farrar, Straus and Giroux, 1947), 435 p.*

HUGH WALPOLE   (essay date 1928)

In all the honest downright pages of the *Autobiography* there is not a word to show that Anthony Trollope ever considered the novel as an Art. He considered it first as an impulse for his own entertainment and happiness; secondly as a means of livelihood; thirdly as his principal proof of self-justification.

Let us make no mistake about the first of these, his delight in his impulse of creation. That same impulse is now for us half his power. (pp. 177-78)

With Trollope it was not so much that he had a story to tell—indeed any kind of story would do, the same old story many times repeated—as that he had people to discover, and the first great quality of his charm and power lies just in this, that he is as deeply pleased as we are at the acquaintances and friendships that he is for ever making. We are there with him at the very moment of the first meeting. He does not, as Flaubert does, embalm his friends first, or, as Dickens does, turn them into a ghost, an Aunt Sally, or a Christmas pudding, or, as Balzac does, introduce them to us only after he has, by diligent detective work, discovered all the worst about them—no, we are there at the very moment of the first shake of the hand. We do not know, any more than he does, what is going to come of this. (p. 178)

[Whether] we allow ourselves to share Trollope's creative experiences or no—we may be temperamentally unfitted for it—we cannot deny the evidences of his own excitement. He is really, in these initial stages, not thinking of us at all, and so he rouses additionally our curiosity. We know him to be an honest man, not easily deceived, unlikely to be taken in by something of no sort of value, and so, as we watch him thus deeply absorbed, we want to share in his discoveries. . . .

Not even the most pedestrian of the Trollope novels—not *Lady Anna* nor *Marion Fay*—is altogether without this breath of creative stir. (p. 179)

[His] second impulse was mercenary. He wrote because he liked it and because he couldn't help himself, but he wrote also because he wanted money and because he wanted a good deal. And he got what he wanted.

His third impulse was one of self-justification. (p. 180)

Because he wrote creatively, commercially, and self-morally, his novels are amateur, commercial, and honest. (p. 182)

Trollope's creative zest was his finest quality, but because the amateur ignored too completely the powers of the technical professional he was prevented from being a novelist of the first class, of the class of Tolstoi, Fielding, Flaubert, and Balzac. (pp. 182-83)

[Even] in his most intense scenes, [Trollope] has the loose hold of the amateur on his material. His vision is not sufficiently fixed to be sufficiently intense. He sees things with the greatest vividness, but for a moment only. He passes as the scene passes, gaily, lightly, without any apprehension that he has not, perhaps, been artistic enough. . . .

[His] novels are commercial because he often sacrifices their artistic needs for money. (p. 183)

[It is] no artistic crime to permit your novel to be published serially—or at least it is not so until the serial necessities become of more importance than your novel. . . . But if Trollope in his desire to retain his serial market pads and lengthens his stories, corrects their incidents so that they do not shock possible readers, moulds his characters by his idea of serial moralities, then his commercial aim is interfering with his artistic aim. (pp. 183-84)

[However,] the honesty of his work very often saves him. Of all novelists the world has ever known, he is more free than any other from one of the curses of the novelist's psychology, humbug. (p. 184)

[It is] obvious that honesty alone is not enough to keep a book alive. . . . These novels of Trollope's must have some very great preservative qualities, qualities that have upheld and supported them when many far more pretentious volumes have passed utterly away.

The first of Trollope's great qualities is his sense of space. (pp. 184-85)

When Trollope adventured through the opening pages of *The Warden* he did not know where he would find himself next. We can see him fumbling at every page, stumbling into satire as he clothes the Grantley boys in the garments of three famous bishops of the moment or, rather feebly, throws paper darts at Carlyle. So he began, but when we, his readers, look back on the whole panorama of the Barsetshire and political novels we get something far wider, more generous, more enduring than a mere clever evocation of place. We get not only Barchester and its country roads and lanes, but all Mid-Victorian England, and then, beyond that again, a realisation of a whole world of human experience and intention. If it is "the sum total of bridges and frozen rivers, forests, roads, gardens, fields" which gives [Tolstoi's] *War and Peace* its sonority and amplitude, so it is the sum total of vicarage gardens, High Streets in sunlight, London rooms and corners, cathedral precincts, passages in the House of Commons, drawing-room tea-tables, the bars of public-houses and the sandy floors of country inns, the hedges, ditches, sloping fields of the Hunt driving the fox to his last lair, that gives these Barchester novels their great size and quality. (pp. 185-86)

Trollope had the gift because everything was of significance to him. It is true that this significance was material and nothing carried him farther than he could see it—nevertheless his vision of material things was infinite and swings us far beyond his immediate characters and narrative.

The value of his sense of space is greatly heightened by his constant preoccupation with average humanity. He is *the* supreme English novelist in this. (p. 186)

Acute though his observation of detail is, he does not psychologically notice very much more in his characters than the average man would notice. Having, from the first, discovered the almost fanatical personal pride of Mr. Crawley, combining this with his extreme poverty he has at once his motive for an immensely long novel. Almost anyone, meeting Mr. Crawley, must at once have discovered these same two things. Trollope makes no more discoveries about him. Crawley is not revealed to us in ever-deepening succession of motives, contrasts, elemental passions as [Dostoievsky's] old Karamazov is developed, or the heroine of *Smoke*, or the beautiful Kate Croy of *The Wings of the Dove*. These two elemental conditions of Crawley are emphasised for us again and again. . . . (pp. 187-88)

But just because there are so few psychological discoveries are we given a constant sense of rest and contentment. In a Trollope novel we discover as much about the characters as we discover about our fellow human beings. We are not startled or horrified, not plunged, as we so often are in a novel by Balzac or Dostoievsky, or even in a short story by Tchehov, into a kind of outer darkness of loneliness. . . .

Trollope reassures us, telling us that all is well; we know quite as much of the mystery as he himself does.

It is this reassurance about our common humanity that is responsible for so much of his extraordinarily effective reality. (p. 188)

Open a Trollope novel where you will and you will find dialogue of an astonishing realism, realism of word and accent and casual repetition. Realism, too, it must be confessed, of length and looseness. (p. 189)

[The naturalness of his dialogue] contains more than a revelation of character and an adroit furtherance of narrative. Trollope caught a certain natural rhythm of human speech and has never been excelled in this, save possibly by Henry James in his earlier novels. (p. 190)

[The] characters in Trollope talk as though their conversation has been reported for us in shorthand and *yet* at the same time the dialogue does forward the story and does reveal the characters.

It is also true that, in the later novels at least, this trick of natural dialogue was so easy to Trollope that he seriously betrayed his gift and tumbled into garrulity.

His further reality of surroundings is secured in the same way. He does not *appear* to be arranging the scenery for us. His country houses, for instance (and no one has ever given us, stone for stone and brick for brick, more real country houses), are introduced to us exactly as they are. They do not glow with the poetic light that novelists from Richardson to Henry James and Virginia Woolf have shone upon them, nor have they that bare sort of auctioneer's reality that the buildings in George Gissing and Arnold Bennett display. Trollope says about them the things that we (again allowing for his heightened genius of observation) might say were we on a country walk or paying an afternoon call. (p. 191)

His reality indeed is saved from being journalistic because of his excitement as creator, but it is often only just saved. When he is not excited (and there are such occasions), but is padding for the benefit of his serial, we might be seeing his fields and streets through the eyes of a contemporary newspaper, but our reward for some dreary passages is our ultimate conviction of his truth. He never betrays us, however pedestrian his novel may be, by deliberately falsifying his vision.

It is true, of course (as indeed of every artist it is true), that he has, very seriously, the defects of his qualities. . . .

Trollope's looseness is one of his gravest sins. It comes not only from the necessity of serial publications, but also from his own casual attitude as artist, which is again part of his early Victorian tradition. (p. 192)

[Much] of his monotony and repetition came from his serial necessities and his publication in monthly parts. Thackeray and Dickens, who were more exuberant artists than Trollope, found the publication of their novels in monthly parts a terrible trial, but the real trouble about Trollope was that he never found it a trial at all.

He went gaily and steadily forward, padding his very exiguous plot with still more exiguous comedy. How fine and tragic a work, for instance, might *He Knew He Was Right* have been had it not been lengthened to such spider-web thinness! How depressing and wearying is the comic element in *Can You Forgive Her?* how infinitely too long *Is He Popenjoy?* or *The American Senator.*

The easy rhythm of his dialogue tempts him to cover page after page with conversation so casual that it has finally no meaning at all. In many of the later novels his narrative tensity slackens to such a feebleness that when the big scenes do arrive he has lost the power of heightening his tone. In *The Way We Live Now* and some of the shorter stories that closed his career he remarkably recovered his early dramatic power, and it is noticeable that the majority of these later books were published neither serially nor in monthly numbers. (pp. 195-96)

None of Trollope's fine qualities—not his minute observation, nor his ''Englishness'', nor his humour, nor his gentle satire, nor the breadth and variety of his canvas would have kept him so magnificently alive had it not been for one virtue which runs like a silver thread through all the texture of his work, which makes him our companion and friend with an intimacy that is an intimacy of personality rather than of talent. (p. 197)

He has that greatest of all human gifts—love of his fellow human beings without consciousness that he loves them. He loves them as he breathes; he loves them and laughs at them and swears at them and preaches at them just as he loves and laughs and swears and preaches at himself. There are moods and thoughts and mean impulses, lusts and cruelties which he detests in himself just as he detests the Crosbies and the Kennedys in his novel world. There are weaknesses and follies in himself of which he is ashamed, but towards which he feels a certain friendliness just as he despises in a friendly manner his Sowerbys and Slopes.

There is the hobbledehoy in him, a legacy from his youth, so that he is himself John Eames; and there is something of the shy, affectionate, almost sentimental woman in him so that he understands with a beautiful sympathy the loneliness and pride of Lucy Robarts and Grace Crawley. But best of all does he have his being and live his life in sympathy with such men as Will Belton and Dr. Wortle, and they are men, too, who love their fellow human beings without knowing it, without pose, without self-satisfaction, almost without self-analysis.

Without poetry too, you may say. Yes, Trollope is the Commentator rather than the Poet, the Rationalist rather than the Enthusiast. He has exactly that temper of his own Mid-Victorian England, evenly balanced, commercially ambitious, believing in what he sees and in that alone, or at least resolving that this is all that he will believe.

And because he lived so exactly in the temper of his own time he has become for us the ideal day-by-day Novelist. . . . (pp. 197-98)

> *Hugh Walpole, in his* Anthony Trollope *(reprinted with permission of the Literary Estate of Hugh Walpole; copyright, 1928, by The Macmillan Company), Macmillan, 1928, 205 p.*

PAUL ELMER MORE (essay date 1928)

For many years I have felt a kind of obligation to write on Trollope. Through the most part of a lifetime his novels have been the chosen companions of my leisure, and, with the possible exception of Boswell's *Johnson,* have been oftener in my hands than the works of any other English author. I have not gone to them, naturally, for that which the great poets and philosophers and divines can give. But they have been like an unfailing voice of encouragement in times of joy and prosperity; they have afforded solace in hours of sickness and despondency and adversity; they have lightened the tedium of idleness and supplied refreshment after the fatigues of labour. (p. 89)

[Trollope] could not do, at any rate did not try to do, what Balzac and Dostoievsky and Turgeniev and Manzoni have done. He has his limitations. But who has not? Could Balzac or Dostoievsky or Turgeniev or Manzoni have written the chronicles of Barsetshire? Imagine the ''clumsiness'' and ''awkwardness'' and ''garrulity,''—epithets which Mr. Sadleir bestows on Trollope [see excerpt above, 1927],—if one of these geniuses had undertaken to fashion such a society as that in which Mrs. Proudie and Dr. Grantly and Mr. Crawley and Lily Dale and Mary Thorne play their parts. And these, I speak for myself, are the people amongst whom I am at home. Then, narrowing the field of comparison to England, I ask myself whether one ought to subscribe to the opinion of Mr. Newton: ''I do not say that Trollope is our greatest novelist; I know that he is not, but I can read him when I can't read anyone else.'' Now ''great'' is an ambiguous term, and it might be said that, among writers of fiction at least, he has a fair claim to be called greatest who can hold our interest when all others fail. But then I think of Thackeray, and suspend my judgement. I remember the heavy passages through which Trollope plods with leaden feet; but does Thackeray's lightness always save him from being tedious? . . . Trollope's language lacks the sustained urbanity and the fascinating charm of Thackeray's, his constant use (to descend to trifles that are not trivial) of ''proposition'' for ''proposal'' and ''predicate'' for ''predict,'' his abuse of ''commencement'' for ''beginning,'' grate like sand between the teeth; but in the long run I wonder whether his clear, manly, straightforward style is not the most satisfactory medium after all, and whether the softness of Thackeray's overworked ''kind'' and ''artless'' and ''honest'' does not end by exasperating us almost as much as Trollope's solecisms. (pp. 90-1)

[Trollope] may have boasted of his ability to put down so many words in so many minutes like a well constructed machine; in fact this was merely the mechanical act of recording what had been conceived and shaped and passionately felt through long hours of preliminary meditation. He was, besides his business of authorship, a much occupied man; yet somehow he contrived through the distractions of work and pleasure and during his incessant journeyings to and fro, to live with the people of his fictitious world as few other novelists have done. (p. 115)

[Any] reader of the *Autobiography* knows how masterfully this double life was carried on. . . . There is the passage which tells how Barsetshire, created by the author's imagination from several actual counties and cathedral towns, was all mapped out in his mind, with its roads and railways laid down and the relative position of its houses carefully plotted. And there is the warning given to the would-be writer that he can never make the creatures of his brain stand out like breathing persons to his reader unless he himself knows them, and can never know them unless he lives with them in the full reality of established intimacy, present to him when he lies down to sleep and when he wakes from his dreams, as people whom he has learned to love and hate, with whom he argues and quarrels and pleads and makes terms of pardon and submission. . . . (p. 116)

It is admittedly because Trollope held so vividly in his mind this fictitious society and possessed the art to make it real to his readers that he is loved and admired by those who profess to find him—though I think they do not quite believe what they say—so insensible to the higher claims of art and so devoid of ideas. And what a gallery! From the first and the second Duke of Omnium to Mr. Moulder and his commercial friends in *Orley Farm,* from Bishop Proudie and Dr. Grantly to the harassed Mr. Quiverful of Puddingdale, from Lady Glencora to the homeless Carry Brattle, what variety and precision and veracity of portrayal! From the agonized humiliation of Mr. Crawley, the tender piety of Mr. Harding, the devouring egotism of Lopez and George Vavasor, the tortured love of Lady Laura Standish, to the cringing criminality of Emilius, what range of passions and emotions and motives, how deftly the reactions of character and circumstance are adjusted, how cunningly the upward and downward paths of conscience are traced! There is nothing like it in any other English novelist except Scott and Dickens; and Trollope to me at least has this advantage that he is never paralysed, as the mighty Sir Walter sometimes was, by the grandeur of his noblemen or the sweetness of his heroines, and that his people are never, like some of Dickens', caricatures or mere gramophones limited to a single phrase.

Nor was this marvel of creation achieved by the mere mimicry of observation without reflection. If any novelist ever wove his plots with a definite idea before him about the meaning of life in general, it was this same "unideaed" Trollope; he is as clear in his conception of human destinies as George Eliot, and if anything truer to the facts. (p. 117)

I suspect that what is beginning to attract more and more attention to Trollope at the present time, what is winning the affection of an ever growing circle of readers and restoring him to his rightful place in the estimation of critics, is not so much his art in the telling of stories and his discernment into the vagaries of human character, as the incontestable fact that he is, of all the novelists of the Victorian era, the one most contrary to the desolating mood of the "futilitarians." To Trollope preeminently life presented itself as a game worth the candles. The goal which his heroes set before their eyes may not always have been of the most exalted type. His Dr. Grantly, scheming to marry his daughter to a marquis, and rejoicing in

his success, may be condemned as a worldly snob, and indeed his creator did not deal with him too gently; but even such an ambition, frankly and actively cherished, is something; it is nobler than the flabby indifference of our heroes who drift on the tides of temperament with no rudder at all. Success in politics or affairs may not seem the most exalted end of life. Nor did they so seem in themselves to Trollope. No one was more bitter against those who succeeded outwardly through grasping or dishonourable or hasty means. His Melmottes and Undy Scotts and Alaric Tudors are pilloried mercilessly in novel after novel; his excoriation of the devotees of "excelsior" at any cost extends at times to something like fanatical antipathy to the modern methods of business. What he held to be desirable, what he presented always as really worthy of respect, was the slow and unostentatious distinction that comes normally to strength of character and steadiness of purpose, checked by the humility of religious conviction. (pp. 118-19)

> *Paul Elmer More, "My Debt to Trollope," in his* The Demon of the Absolute *(copyright 1928, © renewed 1956 and assigned to Princeton University Press; excerpts reprinted by permission of Princeton University Press), Princeton University Press, 1928, pp. 89-125.*

VIRGINIA WOOLF   (essay date 1929)

[*A British novelist, essayist, and short story writer, Woolf is one of the most prominent literary figures of the twentieth century. The excerpt below is taken from Woolf's discussion of "the truth-tellers": Daniel Defoe, Jonathan Swift, George Borrow, W. E. Norris, Guy de Maupassant, and Trollope. Woolf comments that these writers' works directly mirror our own experience of life: "We get from their novels the same sort of refreshment and delight that we get from seeing something actually happen in the street below."*]

Certainly, the Barchester novels tell the truth. . . . Mr. Slope is a hypocrite, with a 'pawing, greasy way with him'. Mrs. Proudie is a domineering bully. The Archdeacon is well-meaning but coarse-grained and thick-cut. Thanks to the vigour of the author, the world of which these are the most prominent inhabitants goes through its daily rigmarole of feeding and begetting children and worshipping with a thoroughness, a gusto, which leaves us no loophole of escape. We believe in Barchester as we believe in the reality of our own weekly bills. Nor, indeed, do we wish to escape from the consequences of our belief, for the truth of the Slopes and the Proudies, the truth of the evening party where Mrs. Proudie has her dress torn off her back under the light of eleven gas jets, is entirely acceptable.

At the top of his bent Trollope is a big, if not first-rate, novelist, and the top of his bent came when he drove his pen hard and fast after the humours of provincial life and scored, without cruelty but with hale and hearty common sense, the portraits of those well-fed, black-coated, unimaginative men and women of the fifties. In his manner with them, and his manner is marked, there is an admirable shrewdness, like that of a family doctor or solicitor, too well acquainted with human foibles to judge them other then tolerantly and not above the human weakness of liking one person a great deal better than another for no good reason. Indeed, though he does his best to be severe and is at his best when most so, he could not hold himself aloof, but let us know that he loved the pretty girl and hated the oily humbug so vehemently that it is only by a great pull on his reins that he keeps himself straight. It is a family party over which he presides and the reader who becomes, as time goes on, one of Trollope's most intimate cronies has a seat at his right hand. Their relation becomes confidential.

All this, of course, complicates what was simple enough in Defoe and Maupassant. There, we were plainly and straight-forwardly asked to believe. Here, we are asked to believe, but to believe through the medium of Trollope's temperament and, thus, a second relationship is set up with Trollope himself which, if it diverts us, distracts us also. The truth is no longer quite so true. The clear cold truth, which seems to lie before us unveiled in *Gulliver's Travels* and *Moll Flanders* and *La Maison Tellier*, is here garnished with a charming embroidery. But it is not from this attractive embellishment of Trollope's personality that the disease comes which in the end proves fatal to the huge, substantial, well buttressed, and authenticated truth of the Barchester novels. Truth itself, however unpleasant, is interesting always. But, unfortunately, the conditions of story-telling are harsh; they demand that scene shall follow scene; that party shall be supported by another party, one parsonage by another parsonage; that all shall be of the same calibre; that the same values shall prevail. . . . But what will happen if, in process of solidifying the entire body of his story, the novelist finds himself out of facts or flagging in his invention? Must he then go on? Yes, for the story has to be finished: the intrigue discovered, the guilty punished, the lovers married in the end. The record, therefore, becomes at times merely a chronicle. Truth peters out into a thin-blooded catalogue. Better would it be, we feel, to leave a blank or even to outrage our sense of probability than to stuff the crevices with this makeshift substance: the wrong side of truth is a worn, dull fabric, un-steeped in the waters of imagination and scorched. But the novel has issued her orders; I consist, she says, of two and thirty chapters: and who am I, we seem to hear the sagacious and humble Trollope ask, with his usual good sense, that I should go disobeying the novel? And he manfully provides us with makeshifts. (pp. 62-4)

> *Virginia Woolf, "Phases of Fiction" (originally pub-lished in* The Bookman, *New York, Vol. LXIX, Nos. 2, 3, and 4, April, May, and June, 1929), in her* Granite and Rainbow: Essays *(© 1958 by Leonard Woolf; reprinted by permission of the Author's Lit-erary Estate and The Hogarth Press Ltd), Hogarth Press, 1958 (and reprinted in her* Collected Essays, *Vol. II, Hogarth Press, 1966, pp. 56-102.)**

DAVID CECIL (essay date 1934)

[*Cecil, an important modern British literary critic who has written extensively on eighteenth and nineteenth century authors, is highly acclaimed for his work on the Victorian era. Cecil does not follow any school of criticism; rather, his literary method has been de-scribed as appreciative and impressionistic. His essays are char-acterized by their lucid style, profound understanding, and con-scientious scholarship. Cecil describes Trollope as a typically Victorian novelist whose works often suffered from his adherence to the conventions of his chosen form. Thus, his novels are often diffuse, repetitious, incoherent, and of divided interest. Cecil as-serts that "it is in his style that Trollope's relative weakness of imagination shows itself most clearly" and declares that Trollope has no style at all; this view is disputed by Geoffrey Tillotson (1961-62), Ruth apRoberts (1971), and David Aitken (see Addi-tional Bibliography). However, as he compares Trollope with other Victorian novelists, Cecil finds much to admire, and praises Trollope's realism, his emotional range, and his humor.*]

Trollope is not only an admirable novelist, he is also conspic-uously free from some of the most characteristic Victorian faults. Not that he is un-Victorian. On the contrary, he was in himself a more typical Victorian than any of his famous con-temporaries. Dickens, Thackeray, and Charlotte Brontë were all in some degree opposed to their age—disapproved of some of its institutions, questioned some of its ideals. Trollope did nothing of the kind. He was brought up, an English gentleman with an English gentleman's standards, and his experience of the world only served to confirm him in the view that they were the right ones. (pp. 253-54)

His view of the novel was as orthodox as his other views. His books are constructed within the regular Victorian convention; panoramas of character and incident, drawn more from the outside than the inside, avoiding any mention of the spiritual and animal aspects of human nature. And even more frankly than any of his contemporaries, Trollope writes to entertain—altering his plot to please his readers, rounding every story unashamedly up with a happy marriage. This, coupled with a typical Victorian carelessness, meant that his books suffered from the customary Victorian faults of form: diffuseness, rep-etition, incoherence, divided interest. *The Last Chronicle of Barset* is as lacking in organic unity, as full of loose ends, and irrelevant sub-plots, as [Charles Dickens's] *Nicholas Nickleby* itself.

All the same, in an essential aspect his novels are not typically Victorian. For, consciously or not, he approaches his material from a different angle from that of the other Victorian authors. He was a realist. (pp. 254-55)

[Trollope] wrote to entertain. Only he thought that a novel was a picture of life, and therefore that it was entertaining in so far as it was an accurate picture of life. So that, unlike his contemporaries, he seeks to make his effects, not by embroi-dering fantasies on a ground of experience like Dickens, nor by imposing a moral order on experience like Thackeray, nor by distorting experience in the mirror of his own individuality like Charlotte Brontë; but simply by reproducing experience as exactly as possible. He draws always with his eye fixed on his object, never modifying its character, either to illustrate a theory or to improve his artistic effect.

And he had every qualification for doing this successfully. For one thing he had an extraordinary power of observation. It had its limitations; it was neither subtle nor microscopic. Trollope does not discern the convoluted intricacies of human conscious-ness like Proust, or of human impulse like Tolstoy, nor had he that command of circumstantial detail that enabled Defoe to give his incidents their eye-deceiving verisimilitude. His observing power was a broad straightforward affair. He stood at a little distance from character and incident, and noted only their outstanding features. But these he notices all the time; and always right. He stands in a central commanding position; his view is consistently correct, clear and sensible; he never fails to see the wood for the trees. (pp. 255-56)

[His] picture avoids many of the faults of Dickens' and Char-lotte Brontë's. It is never so unequal; the reader is never jarred by a sudden jolt from the true to the false. . . . Trollope's imagination is always supported and checked by reference to actual facts. He never allows it to run away with him, and if it fails him he has the facts to fall back upon. Again, his conception of what a novel should be makes it impossible for him to write outside his range. This, like that of most authors, is confined to the world he had himself seen. But since he is concerned only to write of what he saw, he always keeps to it. His limitations surround his books, they do not cut across them. Finally, the fact that he was a man of wide experience made his range wider than those of the other Victorians. He is most at home when writing about the small gentry from which he sprang, but he gives an adequate picture of the political world of Phineas Finn, the shabby lodging-house world of Mrs. Lupex, the flashy, dubious plutocracy that produced Mr. Dobbs Broughton, the shoddy, dissipated "bright young people" of *The Way We Live Now*. . . . Trollope's eye for facts, too, gave him a more varied emotional range than that of Dickens or Thackeray. There is no parallel in their works to the complex misery of Mr. Crawley, unjustly accused of theft, part wounded pride, part outraged rectitude, part self-pity; the agitation of Henry Clavering, torn between the old love and the new duty; the eating professional ambition of Phineas Finn. Trollope can describe love, too; Frank Gresham's first proposal to Mary on that sunny morning with the breeze stirring the creepers outside her window, Rachel Ray's walk in the sunset—these breathe an authentic, if gentle, note of lyrical emotion. Trollope can even—and here he is unique among Victorian novelists—describe a guilty love with understanding. His picture of Lady Glencora's passion for Burgo Fitzgerald is as convincing as his picture of Mrs. Proudie's temper. For though he disapproves of illicit passion as much as Thackeray himself, he does not allow his disapproval to distort the dispassionate accuracy with which he draws it. (pp. 256-58)

Even when he is writing of emotions within Dickens' and Thackeray's range, he does so with a more certain touch. Pathetic emotion, for instance; Trollope never spreads his pathos too thick, never tries to extract it from situations in which it is not inherent, in order the better to stir the reader's feelings. He is not concerned to stir the reader, but to tell the truth. With his eye fixed on his subject, he draws its plain facts for us; and leaves any pathos there may be in them to speak for itself. With the result that it always rings true. (p. 258)

Trollope's hold on dramatic emotion is equally sure. The drama in Dickens and Charlotte Brontë is exciting, but it tends to melodrama. . . . Trollope's characters are solid, daylight figures, the reverse of melodramatic; and for the most part they live very placid lives. But if they do by chance become involved in a dramatic situation, they do not lose their solidity. Mrs. Dobbs Broughton's reception of her husband's death is drawn with extraordinary reality. Its mixture of horror and suspense and squalor disturbs us with the discomfort that such a scene awakens in actual life. And Mrs. Broughton herself is not changed by disaster into a conventional figure of grief or heartlessness. For all her agony, we recognize her in manner and behavior as the same trivial vulgarian who roused our amusement at that dinner-party where she made her first appearance.

Indeed, Trollope's vigilant sense of reality prevents him from dividing his characters into comic and serious as his contemporaries did. Mr. Crawley has the grotesque mannerisms of a comic character part, but he is predominantly a dignified figure. . . . People are not exclusively comic or tragic in real life, nor are they in Trollope.

They are not exclusively good or bad either. Even Trollope's worst characters have their good points. Mrs. Proudie is genuinely compassionate of Mrs. Quiverful, Lady Carberry is disinterestedly devoted to a worthless son. And if Trollope shows us no irredeemable sinner, he also shows us no impeccable saint. . . . Most men novelists cannot resist idealizing their heroines, using them as illustrations of their own standards of feminine perfection. Not so Trollope. Mary Thorne has a hasty

temper, Rachel Ray is indiscreet. And these blemishes do not make them less sympathetic. On the contrary, the fact that they are not inhumanly faultless makes us believe in their merits. Indeed Trollope is the first novelist of his age in describing good people. (pp. 259-60)

Trollope's characters are, at their worst, probable. They never undergo incredible conversions like Mr. Micawber, or act in a manner inconsistent with their natures like Becky Sharp; none of them are dummies. Trollope—and here again he is exceptional among his contemporaries—can contrive to make the most commonplace character a live person. . . .

And his plots are as probable as his characters. They may be ill-constructed, he may twist them to provide a happy ending, stretch them to fit a required length, but his unfailing grip on reality enables him to do so without ever making them seem unlikely. Even if their development does not seem inevitable, it never seems unnatural. (p. 261)

Indeed, it is at once the final effect of Trollope's realism and the principal cause of his continued popularity that the literary conventions of his time are to him only machinery; they do not modify his conception. . . . Trollope, for all that the general scheme of his novels is the orthodox Victorian scheme, conceives his story not after a conventional ideal, but after his own observation of actual fact. So that the fabric of his book is as uniformly fresh as on the day it was made. The modern reader never has to adjust his mind to a Victorian angle in order to enjoy it. He can sit back and take the book just as it comes to him.

No wonder some people find him easier to read than his contemporaries. No wonder even that they think him better. All the same, he is not; and it is no service to his reputation to pretend that he is. His superiority to his contemporaries is mainly negative; he did not make their mistakes. His positive superiority resolves itself into one quality—he observed the surface of life more accurately than they did. But a great novelist is not just an accurate observer. Indeed, his greatness does not depend on his accuracy. It depends on his power to use his observation to make a new world in his creative imagination. It is the characteristic merit of the other Victorians that they possessed the creative imagination in an intense degree. With its help Dickens is able to create a living world in spite of a limited power of observation, Charlotte Brontë in spite of having hardly any power of observation at all. Now Trollope— it is perhaps the briefest way of defining his talent—was, in weakness as in strength, the opposite of Charlotte Brontë. He had creative imagination—he was not a mere photographer— but it was not always active; and even at its most active it was, compared to that of the greatest writers, a relatively low power of imagination. To paraphrase Johnson on Addison, Trollope imagined truly but he imagined faintly. (pp. 261-63)

[A] large number of his characters, for all their truth to fact, are not living creations in the fullest sense of the phrase. Such a character as Sir Roger Scatcherd in *Doctor Thorne,* for instance, is perfectly consistent and possible; he speaks and thinks and acts just as the rough, able, drunken, self-made man he is supposed to be would think and speak and act. But somehow he is without that indefinable spark of individuality which makes Mr. Pecksniff and Madame Beck as unmistakable as someone we have met in the flesh. We believe in his existence as we believe in the existence of a character in a history book; because the evidence seems to point to it. We believe in the existence of Mr. Pecksniff and Madame Beck as we believe in that of our friends, because we have seen them and heard them speak. Even when Trollope does succeed in "creating" a character, Archdeacon Grantly or Mrs. Proudie, they are without the preternatural vitality which boils in the veins of Mr. Pecksniff. They do not betray their identity so unfailingly by every word and gesture. (pp. 265-66)

Trollope's creative power shows itself even less in general plan than in detail. He does not impose an order on life; his books are formless. And this is not just because they are written by someone with little talent for form, but because they are not united by a central idea. Trollope, like Dickens, was an improviser; he started a story blithely ignorant of how it was going to work out; with the consequence that his stories are just unorganized groups of incident and character—sometimes divided into two or three plots, and as often as not wandering about indeterminately, till he shall see fit to bring them to a close. If, as in **Doctor Thorne,** his story is more concentrated, it is an artificial concentration. The action does not develop; Mary Thorne and Frank Gresham might have remained engaged but unmarried forever, if Mary had not, by a piece of good luck, come into a fortune. Indeed, Trollope did not have the ideas with which to knit a story together. He had a view of life—and a very sensible one—but it formed no part of his inspiration. Experience did not stimulate him to generalization. And, as a result, his imagination cannot show itself in the design of his book. He shows us the various scenes and characters that go to make up his world, one after another, separately and full-face. He does not, as Thackeray did, stand back and survey them as a whole and from a characteristic angle. So that they do not range themselves, as they do in *Vanity Fair,* in a characteristic proportion. (pp. 266-67)

Again, he recorded the surface of a character with conscientious accuracy; but his imagination was never fired to discover its guiding principle. This did not matter when he was writing of a simple character like Mr. Harding; beneath so transparent a surface we can see the guiding principle without help. But when Trollope comes to deal with a more complex and contradictory personality, it is a disadvantage. For unless we are made to penetrate beneath its surface, we are unable to reconcile its apparent inconsistencies. (p. 268)

Lady Arabella Gresham, during two-thirds of **Doctor Thorne,** is presented to us as a selfish snob, unsympathetic alike to her husband and to her children. Then, two chapters from the end, she is revealed to us as largely directed by a disinterested devotion to her son. That she should have possessed this better side is probable enough. But we have heard nothing about her that would have led us to expect it; so that it seems as if she had turned suddenly and surprisingly into someone else. The truth is that though Trollope observed the different sides of . . . Lady Arabella correctly enough, his mind was never stimulated to try to understand his observations, so that he never integrated them into a unified conception, and the result is that his picture leaves his reader baffled and unconvinced.

But it is in his style that Trollope's relative weakness of imagination shows itself most clearly. Style is the writer's power to incarnate his creative conceptions in a sensible form. And all the great writers have a very marked style. (pp. 269-70)

Now of style, in this sense, Trollope has none at all. He writes easily and unaffectedly—and his tone of voice has its own masculine friendliness. But that is all. He has no characteristic cadence, no typical unique use of image and epithet; even at his best we feel we could paraphrase him without losing any-

thing essential to his flavor. And at his worst he is as flat as a secretary writing the minutes of a meeting. (p. 270)

In consequence Trollope never achieved the highest expressiveness; never, even at his best, do we get the pleasure that comes from an inspiration perfectly incarnated in its medium. Besides, he has to depend entirely for his matter on his power to entertain. Jane Austen is never dull; for by the sheer quality of her writing she manages to make the most prosaic piece of narrative delightful. Trollope is entertaining if he is describing something entertaining, dull when he is describing something dull. And since his aim is to describe ordinary people just as they are, he is at times very dull indeed. (p. 272)

His dialogue is better than his narrative; indeed, it is extremely good. Realistic accuracy is a far greater asset in dialogue than in narrative, and Trollope's is the most realistic dialogue of any English novelist's. No one has solved so successfully the problem of evolving a form of speech which at once furthers the action and gives the illusion of actual conversation. But his dialogue is not free from his prevailing defects. If it is true to life, it is also sometimes as dull as life. Only now and again does he manage to transmute the dross of reality into the gold of art.

Here it is that Trollope falls short of his contemporaries—as an artist. The fact that his imagination was a relatively weak one meant that his books are, compared with the greatest novels, deficient in artistic quality. And since it is this artistic quality that most distinguishes the great from the lesser novelists, Trollope is, compared with the very greatest, a lesser novelist. (p. 273)

[Though] he was not creative in the highest sense of the phrase, he *was* creative. He makes a world of his own, he has imagination—and imagination of the typical Victorian kind. Like Dickens he improvised, and like Dickens in his own milder degree he had the spontaneous improviser's imagination. And since this is the type of imagination to whose development his period was most sympathetic, Trollope developed his to its fullest capacity. Like everything else about him it was substantial, well-found and consistent. It might be low-powered, it was never thin. It concerned itself not with the petty or the eccentric, but with the solid and the important. It is a pleasant imagination, too. Trollope is careful always to be true to the facts of his observation. But when his imagination is working he cannot help showing them to us through the light of his temperament. And this, though it is not bright, hardly brighter than the light of day, is a very agreeable one; it irradiates his whole picture with a ruddy, friendly, quiet glow. (pp. 274-75)

In the Barchester novels, as from some airplane of the spirit, we see a whole English county society laid out in ground plan before us. Our eye glides over each of the groups that go to its composition: its aristocratic magnates, de Courcys and Omniums; its squirearchy, Greshams, Thornes, Dales; its professional classes, doctors and clergy; . . . its *nouveaux riches,* Sir Roger Scatcherd, Miss Dunstable; the small urban society of the cathedral city which is its capital; the farmers and laborers who provide the base on which its feudal structure rests. The light of Trollope's imagination illuminates some of these groups more brightly than others; of the squires and parsons we are shown every characteristic idiosyncrasy; the aristocrats and peasants are shrouded in a mist which only permits us to discern their broad outlines.

But the light shines persistently and brilliantly clear on the relative position of each group to the other; on their comparative statures and influences, the peculiar characteristics which separate them, the common characteristics which unite them; the complex network of convention and custom and tradition which knits them all into a single whole. He shows us this organism in action, too. His plots usually turn on some clash between private desire and the pressure of the social order. Henry Grantly, son of the magnificent Archdeacon of the diocese, falls in love with Grace Crawley, daughter of a poverty-stricken clergyman who is suspected of theft. We are shown how their social positions react on the feelings of the two lovers, and of their respective family circles. Griselda Grantly becomes engaged to Lord Dumbello, the most eligible eldest son in England; we see how such a readjustment of the social balance alters Griselda's relations to her mother, to her grandfather, her old friends; her mother's relations to her neighbors, her father's relations to the other diocesan clergy. (pp. 275-76)

Trollope has an extraordinarily clear eye for the emotions of class-consciousness; pride of birth, social inferiority, the uneasy arrogance of upstarts. His snobs are among the best in our literature. They are not the most profoundly studied. Trollope cannot, as Thackeray can, penetrate the soul of the snob to expose his secret yearnings and vanities and mortifications. But, on the other hand, his power of accurate observation makes him paint their surface more truthfully. (p. 277)

This power of imagining the social scene never fails Trollope. Even if it does not show itself in individuals, it shows itself in his picture of their relation to the society of which they form part. The Duke of Omnium's dinner to his country neighbors, once read, remains in our memory forever. This is not because the individual figures in it are memorable. The duke and his guests are not among Trollope's most vivid figures. But their attitude to one another is portrayed with supreme vividness. The duke's bored contempt for his guests, the cynicism with which these guests—all but the sturdy, independent squire Frank Gresham—swallow the contempt and the excellent dinner that goes along with it, the assiduous courtesies of the duke's agent, all these go to make up one of the great comic scenes in our literature. Trollope's characters are sometimes uninteresting; their social relations to each other are always absorbing.

Indeed, that the characters are sometimes commonplace arises from the fact that he is primarily interested in people in their relation to the social structure, so that he prefers to write of those average characters that show those relations in their most universal form. He is concerned with the commonplace rule, not with the brilliant exception. (pp. 277-78)

Trollope's novels—and this is perhaps their outstanding distinction—combine to form a picture of a national social scene. Whatever their differences, the worlds they describe share those common traditions and characteristics which proclaim them part of a larger whole. Actually he brings many of the same characters into different books, but even when they are different, they are clearly part of one civilization. Barset is a rural district in the country of which the London of Phineas Finn is the capital. Littlebath is a spa to which Barsetshire people might go for their health; Rachel Ray's home is clearly in a neighboring county to Barset; while in *The Way We Live Now* Trollope shows us the same society in the throes of corruption produced by self-indulgence and foreign penetration. He has used his experience of England to create a complete new country of his own.

It is an extraordinary achievement, and it is unique in English literature. (p. 278)

Trollope's imagination appears most originally in his power to conceive the social structure, but it shows itself in other ways, too. Like all good novelists he can create living characters. He did not always do so, as we have seen; he was successful only with certain types. Neither the literary influences under which he had learned his art, nor the nature of his own talent, robust, masculine, oblivious of subtlety, disposed him to apprehend the deep or the delicate. He was no Rembrandt to penetrate the mysteries of the soul, no Gainsborough to capture the evanescent shimmer of feminine charm. He was rather a Raeburn, a shrewd, vigorous delineator of strongly featured, normal men and women. His great characters, Archdeacon Grantly, Mr. Crawley, Miss Dunstable, Mrs. Proudie, are all simple and positive, absorbed in the avocations of average human beings, devoid alike of psychological complexities and abstruse spiritual yearnings, made up of a few strongly marked qualities and idiosyncrasies. They are mostly elderly active men and women. And Trollope paints them in a manner as straightforward as themselves. He describes them as he describes everything, not by analysis, but by exhibiting them in action before us. (pp. 279-80)

Indeed, though Trollope's imagination does not show itself so consistently in his characters as in his picture of society, it rises to greater heights. (p. 280)

Moreover, now and again when his imagination is working at its hottest on these, his masterpieces, Trollope soars above his usual limitations. For a moment the characters seem, as only those of the greatest authors do, to get free from their creator; to act and speak, not at his command, but of their own volition. (p. 281)

No more than his picture of society and character is Trollope's humor of the very highest quality. At its finest it is not so exquisite as Jane Austen's, not so brilliant as that of Dickens. But it is infinitely vital and vigorous and easy, and it has a sort of genial, leisurely masculinity about it that makes it one of the pleasantest things in English literature. It is more like Jane Austen's humor than that of Dickens; a satirical humor concerned to comment on reality, not a fantastic excursion into the realms of pure laughter. And it is good satire. Trollope's power of observation makes him always hit his victim's weak spot. . . . But it is also good-tempered, and this makes it not only pleasanter, but more effective. (p. 282)

Trollope's liking for humanity makes him eminently cheerful and high-spirited. As a consequence, his humor carries us away with it, willing captives, in a way that the acid sparkles of more ill-humored writers rarely do. It is not that he is kind to the objects of his satire. He never weakens their absurdity by diluting it in sentimental rosewater. But, on the other hand, he is not primarily concerned to make them quiver under his lash. That would imply a wish to change them; and Trollope enjoys them too much to wish them different. He just wants to show how funny they are. And how funny that is set! (p. 283)

[Trollope's] satirical approach to character, his persistent good spirits, combine to make it impossible for him to remain for long unsmiling. And though he only achieves his highest flights now and again, he is, when he tries to be, unfailingly amusing. When all is said and done, his humor is his greatest glory. For this reason his humorous books are his best books. The political novels may cover a wider range, *The Way We Live Now* reveals a keener penetration of character, but his Barsetshire novels make us laugh the most; it is in them we find his most precious contribution to letters. Indeed, as they rise before our memory in all their substantial delightfulness, any criticisms we may make on Trollope seem beside the point. Admitted that he is not in the highest degree imaginative, admitted that his point of view is commonplace, his stories ill-constructed, his style pedestrian—his achievement is yet of a kind to justify him in facing the judgment of posterity with smiling confidence. He has bequeathed to mankind a legacy of enjoyment as solid and unfading and unalloyed as any in English literature. What is mankind that it should ask for more? (pp. 286-87)

> David Cecil, "Anthony Trollope," in his Early Victorian Novelists: Essays in Revaluation (copyright 1935 by The Bobbs-Merrill Company, Inc.; copyright renewed © 1962 by David Cecil; used by permission of the publisher, The Bobbs-Merrill Company, Inc.; in Canada by Constable & Company Limited), Constable, 1934 (and reprinted by Bobbs-Merrill, 1935, pp. 253-87).

BRADFORD ALLEN BOOTH   (essay date 1947)

[Booth is acknowledged as the premier Trollope scholar of his generation and was editor of both Trollope's letters and the journal The Trollopian. His Anthony Trollope: Artist and Moralist (see excerpt below, 1958) is considered the finest book-length study of Trollope.]

In world literature there are only a few masterpieces of autobiography. It is generally conceded that Anthony Trollope's is among them. Recognition of the merit of this book has come very slowly, however, for it has none of the sensationalism that makes for immediate and widespread interest. Trollope was not a hero of romance. His pages do not flame with the amorous adventures of Cellini, or Casanova, or Rousseau. Neither was he a mystic. There is nothing of the desperate soul-searching of St. Augustine, or Cardinal Newman, or even Henry Adams. Nor was he a scientist or philosopher. He cannot tell us, as do his contemporaries Huxley, Spencer, and Mill, of ideas which shook his age. He lacks the massive solidity of Gibbon, the chatty egoism of Leigh Hunt, the limpid ease of Ruskin.

What qualities of Trollope's **Autobiography,** then, have assured its permanence? Perhaps it is in part those same qualities which give lasting vitality to The Autobiography of Benjamin Franklin: a warm sense of the irreproachable integrity of the author and a lively appreciation of his simple, utterly lucid style. Trollope has always been admired for his uncompromising honesty. There is no posturing, no affectation, no attempt to exaggerate triumphs or to minimize defeats for the sake of dramatic emphasis. His pride in his accomplishment is boldly stated, undiminished by mealymouthed subterfuge. Yet with engaging modesty he never equates himself with his peers, so far underestimating his ability as to prophesy, "I do not think it probable that my name will remain among those who in the next century will be known as the writers of English prose fiction."

Were it not for one circumstance there would perhaps be more than an element of drabness in the chronicle history of Anthony Trollope. But in the story of the male Cinderella there is always the saving grace of romance, as well as the sympathy which Trollope felt to be one of the indispensable ingredients of a successful narrative. Only a callous nature could remain untouched by Trollope's pitiless account of himself as a dull, awkward, slovenly schoolboy. . . . Without mawkish sentiment Trollope enlists our interest in the career of the ugly

duckling whose maturation was more complete for its deliberateness, in the idle boy who became a dynamo of tireless energy, in the sluggish dullard who became one of the great English novelists. It is a pure, unvarnished tale that Trollope delivers, in a singularly pellucid style, without ornament, sparse to the point of bleakness, but economical and precise. (pp. v-vi)

An inferior man might conceivably write a superior poem, but I do not know that an inferior man ever wrote a superior autobiography. A self-revelatory book, even though, like Trollope's, it be not of the confessional type, demands from the writer an interesting career, a coherent philosophy, and a sympathetic as well as an illuminating understanding of life. It demands also a nice adjustment of the personal and the universal, as well as most of the virtues of a distinguished prose style. No need to ask why the masterpieces are so few. One man rarely possesses all the qualities to assure success. It suffices that Trollope had most of them. We do not find Santayana's subtlety of mind, or H. G. Wells's ingratiating candor, or John Buchan's heartwarming friendliness; but we do find stubborn idealism, patent sincerity, and clean, forthright exposition. That is perhaps enough for one masterpiece. (pp. xvii-xviii)

> Bradford Allen Booth, in an introduction to An Autobiography by Anthony Trollope, University of California Press, 1947, pp. v-xviii.

CHAUNCEY BREWSTER TINKER   (essay date 1947)

[Tinker defends Trollope's use of the omnipresent narrator, maintaining that these comments provide an ongoing, objective account of the action. His essay challenges the view presented by Henry James (1883) and others who find the narrator intrusive and anticipates the comments of Edd Winfield Parks (1953).]

Trollope's perfect clarity and unpretentiousness may . . . prove to be a saving grace, in that this very lack of manner keeps him from becoming antiquated. His style does not "date," like that of many of his contemporaries. It has no spot of decay, but has kept sweet as the decades have passed. . . .

Novel writing all seems—or is made to seem—incredibly easy. Mere plot never troubled him, and he has therefore been accused of formlessness. Although none of his works is remarkable for a classic roundness, for finish and economy of means, I cannot feel that this charge is apposite. He is guided only by what he conceives to be the reader's desire. He will not continue a story after the reader's interest has lapsed. He never leaves the reader guessing or stops the story midway. . . . (p. 108)

[Trollope] declared that the first duty of a novelist was to have a story to tell, and of this principle he was a scrupulous observer. Although he was indifferent to that smoothness and sequence of events which are found in the great masterpieces of plot, he was careful enough of the main problem, careful, that is, to lend a continuous interest to it. The presence of this feature may generally be detected by the question that is uppermost in the reader's mind. . . . [In *Is He Popinjoy?*] the recurrent question, "Is the Italian baby who was born abroad, in circumstances that cannot be investigated, the real heir to the name or is he illegitimate?" holds the entire story together and dominates the reader's attention throughout. And thus it is in other books. Can John Eames win the hand of Lily Dale? Did Lady Mason forge the codicil to her dying husband's will? Where did Mr. Crawley get the check which caused all the trouble in *The Last Chronicle of Barset*? . . . It is such questions as these that lead the reader on from chapter to thrilling chapter; and such problems may surely be said to constitute plot, if such a thing as plot there be.

Trollope never belittled the importance in fiction of exciting incidents. He defends sensationalism in his *Autobiography,* and contends that a good novel should be both realistic and sensational, and "in the highest degree." "If a novel fail in either," he adds, "there is a failure in art." People who think of Trollope as drab and rather unexciting do not sufficiently reckon with this feature of his work. . . . But Trollope was not so foolish as to suppose that incidents . . . were all-sufficient. Who cares about wills or diamonds or questions of legitimacy unless he is concerned for the persons whose lives are to be made or ruined by the disclosure of the truth? And, therefore, the author was primarily concerned with "realism," in that he was careful first to waken the reader's sympathy for the man or woman involved. (pp. 109-11)

[Why] is one justified in saying that *The Bertrams,* and even *Marion Fay* and *Sir Harry Hotspur,* may be read with a certain pleasure? What is the explanation of that vivid warming of the heart that one feels from time to time as one reads on? Is it not due to the association with the author himself, a man worldly-wise, yet kindly and, above all, fair-minded? Not even Henry Fielding associates with his readers on more agreeable terms. We do not care to lose ourselves wholly in the story, for we remember that Trollope is with us as a kind of chorus. This pleasant art he learned, it may be, from Thackeray, the god of his idolatry. But in Trollope there is none of Thackeray's pretension, no condescending to his characters, many of whom he frankly adores. He is forever saying what can be brought forward in extenuation of their actions; and at last the reader comes to feel that he would want for himself no more sympathetic and indulgent advocate.

Sometimes, to be sure, the author says too much. There are moments when he *will* be talking, though the reader wishes he would get on with the story. He insists on telling us about his travels. *Can You Forgive Her?* reflects two visits to Switzerland. *The Bertrams* is full of his travels to the Near East and the Holy Land. (pp. 114-15)

But when Trollope speaks to us out of the depths of his practical and kindly wisdom, no devoted reader will fail to give him a hearing. There is nothing very original or subversive in his opinions, but they are a kind of gracious common sense issuing from a warm heart and a large sympathy. (p. 115)

His views are set forth not as admonitions or newly discovered truths but as the natural sunshine of life. He reflects ordinary existence with such fidelity that his remarks never seem inopportune or dragged in to mend our morals or our daily conduct. Perhaps no subtler praise can be given than to call him companionable. He never sets himself up as arbiter or pretends to be wiser than we; but he is charitable and broad-minded, and it is a privilege to be with him.

Trollope never used his art to promote a particular reform or to bring a current scandal to public attention. He neither interrupted nor deflected the course of fiction in his own day, for he had no revolutionary theories or mannerisms, so that of all the great Victorian novelists he is the most engaging because of his very simplicity. He was content to be a storyteller and an entertainer, and saw no reason to blush for his profession, which he sometimes mischievously referred to as a trade. His aim was to depict life as he saw it all about him, "enlivened

by humour and sweetened by pathos," crowding his canvas with figures, and ranging with ease from the vulgar to the noble, from the commonplace to the sensational, from the streetwalker to the duchess, from a tout at the race course to the chancellor on the woolsack. He had a natural love of human beings, and his novels are a radiant reflection of it. These are the qualities that made him popular in his own generation; these are the qualities, construed as weaknesses, which clouded his reputation for a quarter of a century after his death, when he was reckoned among those who, even in their lifetime, had written themselves out, and were doomed to oblivion. And these are the very qualities which have enabled him in our own day to renew his strength, and demonstrate once again his happy skill in entertaining a host of readers. (pp. 116-17)

Chauncey Brewster Tinker, "Trollope," in The Yale Review *(copyright 1947, copyright renewed © 1975, by Yale University; reprinted by permission of the editors), Vol. XXXVI, No. 3, March, 1947 (and reprinted in his* Essays in Retrospect: Collected Articles and Addresses, *Yale University Press, 1948, pp. 105-17).*

BRADFORD ALLEN BOOTH (essay date 1950)

Trollope had an instinctive perception, in our day ratified by all critics, that a simple style is a good style. In everything he wrote he repudiated artificiality and complexity, emphasizing the virtues of sincerity and simplicity. But, above all, he worked for intelligibility, the *sine qua non* of good writing. In his *Autobiography* he put the matter succinctly:

> Any writer who has read even a little will know what is meant by the word intelligible. It is not sufficient that there be a meaning that may be hammered out of the sentence, but that the language should be so pellucid that the meaning should be rendered without an effort of the reader;—and not only some proportion of meaning, but the very sense, no more and no less, which the writer has intended to put into his words.
>
> (pp. xix-xx)

As a corollary to intelligibility Trollope named harmoniousness. The writer

> must so train his ear that he shall be able to weigh the rhythm of every word as it falls from his pen. This, when it has been done for a time, even for a short time, will become so habitual to him that he will have appreciated the metrical duration of every syllable before it shall have dared show itself upon paper.

Both of these qualities are characteristic of his letters. He knew what he wanted to say, and he had learned to say it in an uncomplicated and not unpleasing manner. Perhaps, realizing his limitations, he did not try to do more than this.

The letters which Trollope was so fond of inserting in his novels as to make them in some instances an integral part of the structure are often considered the best of their kind in English fiction. As the occasion demands, they are witty, or ponderous, or satiric, or frivolous, or gay. Clearly, Trollope put his very best into them. That he did not *always* put his literary best into his personal letters is perhaps unfortunate, but it assures the naturalness which we value in the type. He never tried to impress his correspondents with false dignity or false wit, with the far-sought allusion or the long-meditated quip. The letters are business-like: firm, precise, pointed. If in their intense purposefulness they are different from those of his literary contemporaries, they are by no means without positive qualities of rare merit.

It is not to be expected, however, that Trollope's letters will push their way into anthologies and 'treasuries'. They are not in the first place sufficiently dramatic. Further, they lack Walpole's infinite variety and undeniable charm, though they are free of course from his petty spitefulness. They do not have the stylistic grace of Lamb's or Meredith's, the ready facility of Stevenson's, the fecund imagination of Thackeray's, the amiable idiosyncrasy of FitzGerald's. But . . . they will interest students of Victorian literature in general and admirers of Trollope in particular. . . . [Most] of them have a biographical and critical relevance that makes them primary documents of the utmost importance for the full appreciation of Trollope's literary life and career. His relations with his publishers, with his literary contemporaries, with casual and with intimate friends are vividly re-created in a personal way. Trollope's correspondence is virtually a log-book of the busiest man of Victorian letters. There are materials for the analysis of character that the biographer will find instructive. There are commentaries on Trollope's own work and on that of his contemporaries that the critic will find penetrating. (pp. xx-xxi)

What Trollope inadvertently reveals of himself in his letters is not for the most part startlingly new, but while reinforcing well-grounded impressions it does serve to correct certain recent misconceptions of his character. If there is any novelty in the self-portrait it is in the softer lines, in the kindlier eyes, and in a less irritable expression than some of the biographical artists have given us. In the fine series of letters to Mary Holmes, for example, there is a sympathy and understanding that did not fail when the response was ungracious. The correspondence with John Blackwood illustrates the firm friendship that had its origin in mutual trust and respect. The letters to George Eliot show that in his open admiration for genius Trollope was without a shred of jealousy. (p. xxii)

[Among Trollope's letters] there are scores which make articulate the mind and heart of one of the finest of English novelists. We watch Trollope in moments of frustration, of exultation, of irritability, of serenity, of turmoil, and of peace. Through the most merciless lenses, the examination of letters written with no thought of publication, Trollope appears man-size, without distortion. Like his characters he is neither seraphic nor devilish, neither much wiser nor more foolish than the generality of educated Victorians. But with the great kindliness of spirit and the understanding compassion toward all men that grew out of his own early suffering, he peoples an imaginary county with men and women so sharply drawn with strokes of quiet humour and Horatian satire that his name has achieved a currency that would have amazed him. These letters will give us a fuller appreciation of his boundless activity, of his unaffected simplicity, and, perhaps, of his keen-eyed genius. (p. xxv)

Bradford Allen Booth, in an introduction to The Letters of Anthony Trollope *by Anthony Trollope, edited by Bradford Allen Booth, Oxford University Press, London, 1950, pp. xvii-xxv.*

EDD WINFIELD PARKS　(essay date 1953)

[*Parks's essay contributes to the discussion, begun by Henry James (1883) and continued by Chauncey Brewster Tinker (1947), on Trollope's narrative technique.*]

When he looked back upon his own writing with a cool dispassionate quality that is strangely disarming, Anthony Trollope assigned himself a rather low place in the rank of the English novelists. He knew his good qualities, and he recognized many of his poor ones. But it is surpassingly odd that in *An Autobiography* he never once mentions or even seems to hint at the quality for which he has been most frequently attacked or deprecated: his inability to keep himself out of his own novels. Apparently he was never troubled by that which has troubled so many admirers. . . . (p. 265)

[Even] a casual reader of his novels would hardly question the accusation that he was guilty, and that frequently, of authorial exegesis. (pp. 265-66)

He practiced exegesis on the grand scale, making himself as commentator an active participant in his novels. He was the creator of Barsetshire, but he was also a citizen of that imaginary county: its observer, its chronicler, its historian. He liked most of the characters that he had created, and he wanted his readers to like them also. (p. 266)

He lived much in company with many of his characters, and he never tired of pointing out the complex of good and bad qualities he had given to them. His role was that of a confidential personal guide as well as narrator. . . . (p. 267)

Trollope's manner is that of a skilled monologist speaking to an intimate, trusted, and trusting individual or group. Here is the story, he seems to be saying, told entirely for your pleasure and benefit. We have an entente together about these people, and you can trust me to work out the situations to your satisfaction. His clear, unadorned style reinforces this quality of seeming to tell all that he knows at the moment, holding back nothing that may be important. This air of improvisation has lulled and charmed many readers; it is effective partly because it is real. . . . Always he preferred to let a novel grow as he worked upon it. Never much interested in plot or tightly knit construction, and never in his own estimation good at this part of the work, he was somewhat naturally inclined to believe that "a good plot . . . is the most insignificant part of a tale"— a necessary vehicle, but of far less importance than the passengers it carried.

This indifference might lead at times to some peculiar creakings and groanings in the carelessly built vehicle, and to some strange and all-too-visible patchwork in and on the wheels and the body. But even to this he manages to give an air of openhanded and openhearted guilelessness, confessing his difficulties almost before they could be noticed. He did not hesitate to take the reader into his confidence on certain points. . . . The reader is made equal to the writer, and is flattered when he is let into the secrets of the author. . . . What Trollope does is to shift the interest from his characters and story over to himself. This is not an aside to the reader, but a direct confidence that his trustworthiness can be relied on. It gives to the novel something of the character of a human document: if it destroys the contained immediacy of the work of art, it substitutes a behind-the-stage relationship which disarms the critical faculties. (pp. 267-69)

Trollope uses exegesis to give readers [a] sense of participation in the novel—in its unfolding, and to a certain extent in its creation. Although he advised a younger writer to "sink the personal pronoun," he was never stingy about employing it himself. But the *I* in his pages is rarely if ever used to set the reader bluntly right; it is rather an invitation for the reader to join him in some secret of plot or character, some difficulty in the development of the story, or some entente as to more general views on life.

His subject matter lent itself easily to this treatment. He was interested in chronicling the doings of ordinary folk in everyday situations; his own work, at least, exemplifies his definition: "A novel should give a picture of common life enlivened by humour and sweetened by pathos." Rarely were his characters or situations so far outside the normal experiences of men that he could not safely invite his readers sympathetically if vicariously to share in the actions or to comprehend the dilemmas, failures, and triumphs of the persons he had created. As novelist he stayed mainly within the realm of normal experience, and his frequent invitations to his audience did not demand more than they were capable of giving. That both author and reader lost something in this process, however, seems inevitably true.

For the novelist exegesis is an easy method of solving problems of characterization and action. Inevitably it weakens a novel by shifting the emphasis from the primary to a secondary consideration, thus diluting the impact; and it constantly tempts the novelist to take the lazier way of explanation, avoiding the infinitely more complex task of resolving the work of art through characters in action. Trollope used it to the fullest extent, and his novels are blemished and to some degree vitiated by it. But in that use he made the reader feel himself so much a participant in the work that at times Trollope made a virtue out of a defect. (pp. 270-71)

> *Edd Winfield Parks, "Trollope and the Defense of Exegesis," in* Nineteenth-Century Fiction *(© 1953, copyright renewed © 1981, by The Regents of the University of California; reprinted by permission of The Regents), Vol. VII, No. 4, March, 1953, pp. 265-71.*

JOSEPH E. BAKER (essay date 1954)

[*Unlike the majority of critics, Baker praises Trollope as a great artist and delineates an "extra dimension" in Trollope's fiction, which he defines as the ability to make "us vividly aware of the* emotional *background against which the action and dialogue are carried on."*]

Trollope is as English as roast beef. He enables us to understand the unexpressed, to understand more about a social situation than he has yet put into words. I know of no other novelist whose art is quite so successful in achieving this particular effect. He makes us aware of the feelings of his characters, feelings more than thoughts. Often he brings this out explicitly; out in his best scenes we are aware of more than he is stating.

His appreciation of silence is beautifully illustrated [in *The Small House at Allington*] by the splendid scene at Courcy Castle when the beautiful, silent, Lady Dumbello (née Griselda Grantly) makes her appearance. By just the right amount of detail and action the novelist makes us dramatically aware of the excitement of a whole social group:

> There was immediately a commotion among them all. Even the gouty old lord shuffled up out of his chair, and tried, with a grin, to look sweet and pleasant. The countess [De Courcy]

came forward, looking very sweet and pleasant, making little complimentary speeches, to which the viscountess [Lady Dumbello] answered simply by a gracious smile. Lady Clandidlem, though she was very fat and heavy, left the viscount, and got up to join the group. Baron Potsneuf, a diplomatic German of great celebrity, crossed his hands upon his breast and made a low bow. The Honourable George, who had stood silent for the last quarter of an hour, suggested to her ladyship that she must have found the air rather cold; and the Ladies Margaretta and Alexandrina fluttered up with little complimentary speeches to their dear Lady Dumbello, hoping this and beseeching that, as though the "Woman in White" before them had been the dearest friend of their infancy.

> She was a woman in white, being dressed in white silk, with white lace over it, and with no other jewels upon her person than diamonds. Very beautifully she was dressed; doing infinite credit, no doubt, to those three artists who had, between them, succeeded in turning her out of hand. And her face, also, was beautiful, with a certain cold, inexpressive beauty. She walked up the room very slowly, smiling here and smiling there; but still with very faint smiles, and took the place which her hostess indicated to her. One word she said to the countess and two to the earl. Beyond that she did not open her lips. All the homage paid to her she received as though it were clearly her due. She was not in the least embarrassed, nor did she show herself to be in the slightest degree ashamed of her own silence. She did not look like a fool, nor was she even taken for a fool; but she contributed nothing to society but her cold, hard beauty, her gait, and her dress. We may say that she contributed enough, for society acknowledged itself to be deeply indebted to her.

This is very fine, very English, very Trollopian. And it rises to its climax in evoking the undemonstrative reaction of her husband, who, though the eldest son of a marquis, prides himself above all things in shining in the reflection of her greatness. (pp. 222-23)

It is not my claim that Trollope employs unusual technical devices, but that he achieves unusual success in a particular direction. This is not just a matter of words or even of style. You could translate every word into a foreign tongue; you could alter the style, even to the elimination of his delicious and appropriate figures of speech; and you would still have left the kind of thing I am now calling attention to. . . . We know we are not going to find a few quotable phrases or even paragraphs, but literary art of a more extensive nature, when he says,

> Before the evening of the party another memorable occurrence had taken place at Allington, which must be described, in order that the feelings of the different people on that evening may be understood.

And even when he is not promising us something like this explicitly, he is preparing the scene for us, or preparing us for the scene. (pp. 223-24)

Trollope's ability to make us feel, simultaneously, what various characters are experiencing, as they hear or see something, enables him to make good his implied contracts with the reader. But in scenes which are not *à faire*, this merit shows equally well. No build-up has led us to expect the rich delights that are heaped upon us in some of the passages of ***Barchester Towers***. In chapter eleven we had not been led to expect the delicious comedy of "that abominable young Stanhope," Bertie, when—ignoring the sensibilities of his audience—he dares to compare German professors with those of Oxford. It is our perception of the sensibilities of his audience that makes the scene so funny. This may also serve to exemplify Trollope's unequalled success in making us feel the embarrassment of a social situation. Often the reactions of several people are alive in our minds all at once. (p. 225)

[In countless examples] Trollope has made us vividly aware of the emotional *background* against which the action and dialogue are carried on. We are most likely to notice this quality, at first, in passages where the foreground does not absorb our attention. Silence, inarticulateness, movements that do not advance the plot, allow us to focus our awareness upon the unexpressed, the "undramatic"—which Trollope is making so dramatic.

But once we notice his skill in keeping us aware of emotional background, we realize that he is often creating the same effect for us when the foreground is articulate and dynamic. Or perhaps at such moments we find he *has already* created this background, which we are holding in the backs of our minds, feeling it almost unconsciously with our sensitive feelers of social emotional response, while our conscious minds think only of the dialogue or deeds. That is, we *think* we are thinking only of what happens on the page before us; but if we *stop to think*, we could say what else is there, in the penumbra.

Trollope's great art in giving us this extra dimension is most superb when he has availed himself of all his artistic resources. He has made us know his characters, he has arranged the situation, laid all the charges of dynamite, placed everything in context, stated feelings explicitly in previous scenes, articulated the dialogue, etc. . . . [The] evidence I have been offering, selected for its immediate intelligibility (and for its lack of foreground) cannot begin to demonstrate the richness and complexity of this delicious quality. Only a reading of a novel, as it develops, could do that. And then another novel. (p. 232)

> Joseph E. Baker, "Trollope's Third Dimension," in
> College English, *Vol. 16, No. 3, December, 1954,*
> pp. 222-25, 232.

A.O.J. COCKSHUT   (essay date 1955)

[*In his examination of Trollope's later novels, Cockshut challenges the widely held conception that Trollope's work reflects only the just and moral. Like Lucy Poate Stebbins and Richard Poate Stebbins (see Additional Bibliography), Cockshut emphasizes Trollope's negative world view. He asserts that "Trollope is a gloomier, more introspective, more satirical, and more profound writer than he is usually credited with being," a view disputed by Bradford A. Booth (1958). The Barsetshire chronicles, according to this critic, are not the best of Trollope's writings, nor are they the most characteristic. Cockshut devotes a chapter to each of the novels written after 1867, which he considers Trollope's "greatest achievement," and finds that each "reveals a further stage in the steepening curve of the author's pessimism." Cockshut's study initiated the emphasis on the darker* aspects of Trollope's work, an approach that is prevalent in recent commentary.]

Trollope's life can conveniently be divided into three periods. The first, which ended about 1847, was a period of suffering, self-reproach, and daydreaming. Though the dreams always seemed impossible of fulfilment, there was nothing napoleonic about them. To be liked, to make a good living, to have a family, to feel justified in one's own eyes, would seem to many people modest ambitions. It was in these long years of boyhood and adolescence . . . that the foundations were laid for the successes of the middle period which extends roughly from 1847 to 1868. Trollope had many literary gifts; but perhaps one, a direct result of his early experiences and dreams, has been the main cause of his popularity in his lifetime and in the twentieth century. Because the most ordinary pleasures had once seemed to him like whispers of an impossible paradise, he was able in his middle years to depict them with a strange mixture of detailed precision and visionary splendour. (p. 131)

The last period, from about 1868 to his death in 1882, is one of retreat, questioning, and satire. The leading books of this period deserve a detailed analysis, because they constitute his greatest achievement, and reveal, as the earlier ones do not, his deepest preoccupations. The change from the optimistic middle period, to the steadily-growing pessimism of the last corresponds with a decline in popularity.

The wheel would come full circle. The pleasures and successes which before 1847 had seemed unreal because unattainable, gradually drifted into another unreality. What, in the last analysis, was their moral nature? Were they so desirable after all? More and more his mind came to dwell on the ambiguity of things. Simple ideas like love and honesty turned out to be complex, and perhaps deceptive. The anger of a man who in his brightest times had well known how to be angry, was now turned against the agreed ideas of society. Unexpected objects for his pity came into view. These feelings brought him to his finest achievements. (pp. 131-32)

It is one of the drawbacks of Trollope's casual artistic methods that some of his characters and incidents seem only to occur when they do because he happened to think of them when he did. But [*The Way We Live Now*] has a unifying theme—the collapse of standards and of social order before new methods of finance—which unites almost all of it in a satisfying whole.

In many of his books, though his subject was ostensibly the present, Trollope had been influenced by memories of the past. In the Barsetshire novels, England is still an agricultural country in spite of the railways. . . . Now for the first time Trollope chose to be contemporary, even perhaps prophetic, and though he was all the time producing one or more books a year *The Way We Live Now* has the appearance of a great leap forward in time.

He never had spared the vices of the rich. But in the Barsetshire novels, money and rank still bore some relation to each other. The occasional *nouveau riche*, like Miss Dunstable, was easily absorbed by society, and partly adopted an aristocratic point of view. And so there was an element of responsibility even in the misuse of power. But now, almost everyone is tending to become irresponsible. Huge sums are won and lost in a moment and fortunes can be made out of non-existent enterprises. The origin of Melmotte, the central figure, is known to nobody, the source of his wealth is unknown, and his greatness so blinds with excess of light that people imagine that neither normal moral nor practical laws apply to him.

In outline, Melmotte's story is the great traditional story of fortune's wheel, the rise, the grandeur, and the fall of a great man. But the treatment has unique features which illustrate this disturbing suspension of ordinary laws. For neither his unprecedented commercial greatness, nor his collapse, represent much objective change in his prosperity. Credit makes him and loss of credit breaks him. The new financial system is a concourse of intangibles.

Credit is paradoxically separated from its own origins in personal confidence in a man's worth and solvency. Everybody is following everybody else's lead in accepting Melmotte. Excessive deference is paid to public opinion, and the result is that public opinion ceases to exist. Who is to say who the leader is when everyone is walking in a circle following the man in front? Most disturbing of all is the indirect power of money to influence people unawares. (pp. 204-05)

As credit becomes at the same time omnipotent and devoid of meaning, people trust Melmotte's bare word for large sums of money. It is ridiculous to trouble him to sign a cheque; and so money almost disappears from the dealings of a man whose only business is financial manipulation. (p. 205)

Though for a long time credit works only in his favour, Melmotte cannot control it. "He had contemplated great things; but the things which he was achieving were beyond his contemplation." These involuntary achievements bring about his fall; he is all the time a servant, not a master.

If, amid all these fluctuations, his real wealth does not alter much, his conduct and the generally accepted judgment on his character hardly alter at all. Here is no case of concealed villainy unmasked. It is true that at the height of his success he becomes a little more overbearing; when his fortunes begin to totter he is a little more reckless, though not more unscrupulous in his crimes. The time when the dinner for the Emperor of China is being planned is the apex of his career. But, endlessly discussed, endlessly admired though he is, no one suggests that he is, in the ordinary sense, honest. Some excuse dishonesty, some ignore it, same are faintly ill at ease, but very few, and they not people of fashion or importance, are surprised at the high honours he receives.

But in the few days before the banquet a great change occurs. There are rumours that Melmotte is not financially sound; it is hinted that he has committed forgery and may be arrested. . . . In describing the dilemma of all the invited guests, the author makes this comment, "No one wishes to dine with a swindler." An obvious remark, but its implications are wide. In his fall, as in his prosperity, Melmotte is always judged by unreal standards. As the case of Oscar Wilde would later illustrate in the realm of fact, wickedness, elegant or monstrous or magnificent, is one thing in the public mind, but the police court is quite another. The revulsion against Melmotte which leads to his disgrace and suicide is caused by the mere suspicion that he will turn out to be what he had always been supposed to be. A false signature is concrete; it recalls aristocratic minds, bemused by the contemplation of apparently unlimited wealth and power, to ordinary moral categories and definite legal penalties. (pp. 206-07)

As Melmotte's success and failure alike depend not on facts, but on reputations, newspapers play an important part in the story. Indeed, the book opens with an account of the three editors; the corruption of the word comes first. The semi-smart world of literary reviews is ruled by the same code as the commercial, which it imagines to be so different. . . . The

newspaper leaders about Melmotte hedge like the speculators on the stock exchange. In the same way the Beargarden set unconsciously imitates Melmotte's business methods with their gambling and cheating.

A series of inappropriate ideas about money poisons family life. Lady Carbury is driven to desperate and shady schemes by her son's gambling and extravagance until finally the two separate altogether. Melmotte's wish to buy a title for his daughter leads to cruelty which even prevents her from mourning his death. . . . The Grendalls form a sinister alliance in their parasitic attendance upon Melmotte, until they become accomplices, and the relationship of father and son is extinguished and forgotten by both.

What is the connection between this new commerce and the latter-day representatives of Barsetshire? They do not obtain the unqualified approval which we might expect; they can be corrupted too. There is Roger Carbury certainly, the honest Suffolk squire with his air of conscious virtue in decadent times. Trollope seems to have intended him to be the standard by which the other characters should be judged. But he made the mistake of allowing his own creation to be aware of the part assigned to him, and so he seems to be almost a prig, which was certainly not intended. (pp. 207-08)

It would be natural to suppose from this [novel] that Trollope was merely lamenting the half-imaginary glories of the past. But this would be a great mistake. Anyone, of course, would prefer the abuses of the Barsetshire system to those of the Melmotte system. But the latter are not entirely revolutionary or even wholly new. In some ways they only accentuate what the unsuspecting might consider the grand old anomalies of the past. The inequality of the sexes, instead of being lessened, has actually increased; whereas, under the old system women were expected to be quiet and almost idle, they are now bullied and insulted just because they are weak. The growth of ruthless competition is not confined to commerce.

Almost everyone in the book however degraded can strike an attitude and appeal to the good old days. Sir Felix Carbury, Hetta's dissolute brother, without a moral scruple to bless himself with, can still speak in the language of ancient chivalry in defence of his sister and believe in it himself. An appeal to the good old days is made by the members of the Beargarden Club when it has to close down. It strikes none of them as incongruous, though the club has been short-lived, and its traditions were only drinking and gambling all night, cheating and unpaid debts. Rootlessness can only be detected from outside. (p. 209)

It is the same with the lawyers. It seems at first sight that in his revulsion from Squercum, the sharp and disreputable lawyer of the new civilisation, a gentile masquerading as a Jew so that he may gain an advantage by working on Sundays, Trollope will grow almost sentimental about the stately delays of Slow and Bideawhile. These two had been satirised in the Barsetshire series, but with an easy, pleasant satire reserved for the incidental absurdities of a system, supposed at that time to be permanent and reasonably good. But we discover later with relief that we are not meant to be taken in by their venerable air. Their obstinate conviction that no one, least of all Squercum, can teach them anything about transacting legal business leads to serious loss for their clients. . . . These ardent traditionalists have, without realising it, underwritten Melmotte's business methods. They are more closely linked to the despised Squercum than they know. (p. 210)

But all this is subsidiary to the case of the elder Mr. Longestaffe and his daughter. The Longestaffes are an old family with a fine estate and a large income, who are embarrassed financially through their own foolishness. The head of the family fancies himself as a traditionalist, and is accustomed to blame everything on one single terrible departure from ancient standards of British virtue—the admission of the Jews into Parliament. . . . Having issued this charter of irresponsibility, he takes to dealing with Melmotte to raise the ready money he needs, and even welcomes social intercourse between the two families. He is far more modern than he realises, and in consequence he is confronted with what seems to him a story of horror.

Georgiana, his daughter, has been looking for a husband for ten years, always aiming a little too high in the social scale. . . . Melmotte introduces her to a rich Jewish merchant called Brehgert, a widower with grown-up children. Physically he is the very Platonic idea of what a Jew is popularly supposed to be, "a fat greasy man of fifty, conspicuous for hair-dye." Bertrand Russell has called Trollope anti-semitic. If, as seems probable, he was judging on this character, he might have read more carefully. For apart from Roger Carbury, Brehgert is the only genuinely honest man in the book, and behaves throughout with intelligence and forbearance. Instead of being a symbol of anti-semitism, Brehgert's disagreeable appearance helps to rehabilitate not only a Jew, but—a much more difficult matter—the popular idea of one. (pp. 210-11)

The contrast in delicacy and reasonableness between Longestaffe and Brehgert is underlined by their last meeting after the proposed marriage has been abandoned. Longestaffe, who has spoken with such thoughtless violence and even insulted Brehgert personally, is shocked and distressed that the other should refer to the past affair at all. In his unreal reticence as in his previous unwarranted outspokenness, he is out of touch with facts. Brehgert maintains throughout a calm and dignified attitude. Longestaffe, annoyed first by the man's calmness, then by his outspokenness, is like a weather-cock reproaching a compass needle for pointing first too far to the east, then too far to the west. (pp. 211-12)

The Longestaffes may be driven into [an] ecstasy of shame and anger [by Brehgert], but they are not ashamed of dealing with Melmotte. They can abandon moral considerations almost completely and then manufacture the fiercest indignation out of a mere prejudice. (p. 212)

To understand Trollope's intention [in *The Way We Live Now*], it is useful to consider the two permanent and opposite errors into which the satirist may fall. The more obvious is triteness. The more important vices are limited in number and in interest. To find an original method of attacking them is [difficult]. . . . Some writers, like Oscar Wilde, take refuge in what may prove an equally damaging error. They turn all the normal satirical judgments on their heads, and sometimes achieve no more than an irrelevant firework display. For satire devoid of its moral content is inevitably trivial. The story of Brehgert and the Longestaffes provides an example of Trollope's method of avoiding the dilemma. He takes what is in outline an ordinary story—similar to the plot of Thackeray's *Philip* and of several other well-known novels of the time. There are the same issues; the marriage market, wealth placed before love, disparity of age in marriage, and the sinister flirtation of a needy aristocracy with rich commercial upstarts. Then slowly and calmly, without self-conscious paradox, without any suggestion that moral categories can be neatly interchanged for literary purposes, the

author proceeds to falsify a number of time-honoured assumptions. The attempt to sell the girl for money is made by herself, instead of by her parents. The insolvent parents, though they are mercenary and care little for their daughter, are horrified, not for her sake, but for their own. The elderly man, with nothing but his money to recommend him, is in reality far superior to the proposed young bride in understanding and generosity. Finally, and this is the crucial point, all these surprises follow naturally from the original situation. Society and contemporary satirists are satirised at the same time; Trollope's indictment is formidable without being familiar, and avoids altogether the derivativeness of pure parody.

The Way We Live Now is among other things a sociological novel. It shows how part of the aristocracy and the gentry is drawn into the orbit of the financiers. Mr. Longestaffe sits for hours in Melmotte's antechamber while the nephew of a duke gives him soothing explanations. Trollope does not analyse this situation as Scott would probably have done. He is, so as to speak, a pictorial sociologist, not a scientific one. His mind was not given to weighing complicated sets of causes. His aristocratic characters do not ask themselves how they come to be in this strange position. But one reason emerges clearly. The insistence on useless luxuries, like powdered footmen, to copy men even richer than themselves, leads men of ample inherited wealth into financial difficulties as soon as circumstances cease to be ideal for the landed interest. (pp. 212-14)

[Of course, Longestaffe] is bored. The characters do not enjoy, or even expect to enjoy their own extravagances. A pervading boredom is indicated, without being stressed, by passages like this, as Melmotte, now a member of Parliament, approaches bankruptcy and death. "There were a great many members present, and a general feeling prevailed that the world was more than ordinarily alive because of Melmotte and his failures." There is domestic boredom as well, grey winter afternoons, dull tea-drinking and meaningless flirtation. Perhaps there was a change in the author as well as in his subject. The middle-aged Trollope had never been bored, and the Barsetshire characters were like him in this. Now, though he was only sixty, he felt old age coming on before its time.

Formally, Trollope came near to writing a masterpiece. That he did not is probably due to the fact, noticed by Mr. Michael Sadleir, that he had not fully prepared for Melmotte's central position when the book was begun. Still, the main characters are closely grouped round Melmotte. Their various connections with him do not strike us as contrived, complicated though they are. For they all depend in some way on the book's main subject—money, and every twist of plot is intended to illustrate the permeation of society by Melmotte's standards of conduct. In one case only does the connection seem forced—in Paul Montague's affair with Mrs. Hurtle. . . . [This] part of the book contributes nothing to its varied and subtle study of money. All the elements of a masterpiece are here except the editor's scissors. (pp. 214-15)

The Beargarden Club illustrates how ideas of money are modified by idleness and good nature. The principle of its existence is the combination of profligacy and parsimony. It has no morning papers, no library, no expensive front for other people to look at. But all this economy is devoted to the cause of reckless gambling. The members hate trouble and fuss so much that they give plenary power in all money matters to an agent so that they shall be cheated only by one man. The same dread dominates their relations to each other. No one expects Miles

Grendall to honour the IOUs he regularly issues for large gambling debts. (pp. 215-16)

[The Beargarden Club scenes] illustrate a main theme of the book—that money, when it becomes the centre of a man's universe, continually evades realisation. Mr. Longestaffe's embarrassments are due to money spent on powdered footmen, and the like, whom nobody enjoys. Melmotte's gigantic dealings are concluded without money transactions and make nonsense of work. So here these young men, whose life is devoted to making money at games of chance, are driven by habit to play with a man from whom they cannot win. For all of them money proves to be a phantom.

But the Beargarden scenes have another purpose also. Trollope understood very well the principle of literary relativity. When Othello strikes Desdemona, the act is as shocking as the blinding of Gloucester, because [William Shakespeare's] *Othello* presupposes a much higher level of civilisation than [his] *King Lear*. Trollope made use of this psychological fact in *Miss Mackenzie* where he succeeds in making the harmless dissipations of maiden ladies seem extremely daring. So here, but more effectively still, by comparison with Melmotte the somnolent good nature of the Beargarden seems almost sublime.

From this point of view the behaviour of Nidderdale is important. He is a modest man who moves among the Beargarden group without identifying himself with them. He gambles but without the real gambling fever. As the eldest son of a peer who wants money, he had had his fling and has now settled down with good-humoured pertinacity to his appointed task—marrying an heiress, Melmotte's daughter, Marie. But for all this, he becomes, relatively, a symbol of virtue.

Without probing into the moral nature of the proposed marriage, he sees it as a sound bargain, which he tries to perform in an honest spirit. When Melmotte is near to disgrace, and as it proves to death also, Nidderdale finds himself sitting next to him in the House of Commons. Disliking Melmotte personally and already abandoning the marriage in his own mind (because of the disturbing financial rumours about Melmotte), he still will not snub his neighbour. . . . In the end, though the marriage project has been abandoned, Marie comes to trust him as her only reliable friend. Nidderdale stands for fair dealing on an unquestioned basis of cynicism. On his lips and on others the word "love" echoes emptily, showing that it is much easier to alter ways of conduct than habits of thought.

Dolly Longestaffe is the central Beargarden figure, and he is the most apathetic of them all. Informed by Felix Carbury that Grendall has been cheating when they three and Nidderdale have been playing for high stakes, he is unimpressed. (pp. 216-17)

Trollope shows us the consequences of Melmotte as they are mirrored in [Longestaffe's] placid spirit. Vague disquiet in him is as startling as the destruction of empires. Melmotte is the first person he has ever taken the trouble to despise. He is driven to write letters, almost to fancy himself as a man of business, even to make a moral reflection. "'I've a sort of feeling,'" he says, "'that I don't like a family property going to pieces. A fellow oughtn't to let his family property go to pieces.'"

It is fitting that this moron should be the first to see through Melmotte. While all the clever people still believe in him, Dolly argues "'When I buy a thing and don't pay for it, it is because I haven't got the tin.'" He has not the brain to be

hypnotised like all the others by the bogus mysteries of credit. He alone is stupid enough to see the obvious truth. (p. 218)

A.O.J. Cockshut, in his Anthony Trollope: A Critical Study *(copyright A.O.J. Cockshut, 1955; reprinted by permission of William Collins Sons & Co. Ltd.), Collins, 1955 (and reprinted by New York University Press, 1968), 256 p.*

FRANK O'CONNOR (essay date 1956)

Trollope's style is weak compared with Hardy's or Dickens's. He had little or no feeling for poetry, and, what is considerably worse from my point of view, he also had little feeling for prose; his writing at its best never rises to the level of Stendhal's or Tolstoy's, which is Continental prose without benefit of poetry. Yet I think Trollope was as great a novelist as either, and a far greater novelist than Hardy. (pp. 166-67)

If one compares the realism of [Trollope and Jane Austen], one finds, I think, the quality that has kept Trollope so popular. She writes from a preconceived idea of conduct, where he does not. She is a moralist; Trollope is whatever the opposite of a moralist may be. Though [Lord David] Cecil declares that his standards were those of "the typical mid-Victorian gentleman" [see excerpt above, 1934], and though the statement could be liberally documented from the pages of the *Autobiography*, I do not for an instant think it is true.

If there is one phrase more than another which identifies a novel by Trollope it is a phrase like "With such censures I cannot profess that I completely agree." His favorite device is to lead his reader very gently up the garden path of his own conventions and prejudices and then to point out that the reader is wrong. This is not very like the behavior of a typical mid-Victorian gentleman. On the contrary, it is an original and personal approach to conduct, and I think that it is Trollope's approach, rather than his treatment, which pleases intelligent people in our time.

I do not mean that Trollope was a revolutionary figure. In fact, he was a persnickety and crusty conservative who distrusted all new views and methods. But, unlike most English novelists, he did not start out with a cut-and-dried system of morals and try to make his characters fit it. Instead, he made the system fit the characters.

For instance, to take a slight example, one of the conventions of the English novel is that of "one man, one girl," and such is the power of artistic convention that, whatever our own experience may have taught us, we never question this as we read. We could not conceive of [Jane Austen's] Mr. Knightley in love with Harriet Smith as well as with Emma. We certainly could not believe that, having been rejected by Emma, Mr. Knightley would ever immediately propose to Harriet. But Trollope's characters usually behave in that way. . . . And if the reader, forgetting his own errors, denounces Finn as a heartless rogue, Trollope, in that maddening way of his, chimes in with his pet phrase: "With such censures I cannot profess that I completely agree." Literature is one thing, life another. (pp. 167-69)

[He] expresses again and again his dislike for men of strong character. "The man who holds out," he says in *The Duke's Children*, "is not the man of the firmest opinions but the man of the hardest heart." . . . And here is the same thing in an even more striking passage:

In social life we hardly stop to consider how much of that daring spirit which gives mastery comes from hardness of heart rather than from high purpose or true courage. The man who succumbs to his wife, the mother who succumbs to her daughter, the master who succumbs to his servant, is as often brought to servility by the continual aversion to the giving of pain, by a softness which causes the fretfulness of others to be an agony to himself as by any actual fear which the firmness of the imperious one may have produced. There is an inner softness, a thinness of the mind's skin, an incapability of seeing or even of thinking of the troubles of others with equanimity which produces a feeling akin to fear; but which is compatible not only with courage but with absolute firmness of purpose when the demand for firmness arises so strongly as to assert itself.

There, in a paragraph, is the essential Trollope, the message of Trollope, if such a writer can be said to have a message. . . . (pp. 170-71)

This, then, rather than realism, represents Trollope's true quality as a novelist. Not merely loyalty to the facts, but loyalty to a certain attitude to the facts, to a humility and passivity in the face of life. I do not wish to suggest that artistically this is an unmixed blessing. When Trollope is not inspired by his subject, it gives his work a flabbiness and lack of energy that leave the reader feeling very flat indeed. Even on the trivial plane of "one man, one girl," it results in a lack of incisiveness. . . . (p. 172)

But it is important to remember that this very humility gives Trollope a quality not possessed to a similar degree by any other English novelist. That quality is range, and by range I do not mean merely the ability he shares with Tolstoy of handling great masses of material while keeping its elements distinct. I mean primarily the power of exploring his characters fully, of so understanding their interior perspective that by a simple change of lighting he can suddenly reveal them to us in a different way; as, for instance, in the scene in *Can You Forgive Her?* where Burgo Fitzgerald, the penniless and desperate adventurer whose only hope is to seduce Lady Glencora for her money, buys a meal for a prostitute. It is a most remarkable scene. In any other novelist of the period it would prove that Fitzgerald had a heart of gold, or, alternatively, that the prostitute had a heart of gold, or that both had hearts of gold. In Trollope it is merely one of those minor shocks by which he reminds us that life is not simple; it indicates to us that Lady Glencora is not altogether a fool, and that Fitzgerald, for all his faults, retains a capacity for spontaneous behavior which endears him to women. (p. 173)

But there is another sort of range which Trollope also had, and that is the power of describing extreme psychological types, types that are pathological or bordering on it. The principal character in *He Knew He Was Right*—a bad novel by Trollope's own standard—is a masterly presentation of pathological jealousy. Now, Proust can describe pathological jealousy with similar mastery, but Proust was the victim of what he described, and the fact that he described it so well meant that there were scores of other psychological states that he could not describe at all. Balzac could describe a variety of extreme psychological states, but his romantic imagination made it impossible for him to treat them from the point of view of simple normality, so

that ultimately they fail to impress us. Trollope, because his capacity came from the passiveness and humility with which he contemplated people, could describe scores of such types, but each one rises simple and sheer from a flat plain of normality. . . . Mr. Crawley of *The Last Chronicle* is the supreme example. He rises out of the commonplace and placid plane of the story, a giant figure who, even when we are looking elsewhere, still magnetizes us like some mountain peak. And of all these characters it is almost impossible to say when they pass the limits of sanity, so closely have they been observed, so carefully has each step been recorded.

The Last Chronicle is the final volume in the Barchester series, and I do not think anyone has ever analyzed the strange development in the works. (pp. 175-76)

In the manuscript of the *Autobiography,* Trollope deliberately deleted *The Small House at Allington.* This leaves us with five novels, of which four deal almost entirely with clerical life. The fifth, *Dr. Thorne,* is a book I find extremely dull. . . . Leave it in, and you have a panorama of English provincial life, centered on a cathedral city; take it out, and you have a saga of clerical life, all sections of it dealing in different ways with the same problem, the problem that in Mr. Crawley is presented to us in its most complex and tragic form. (pp. 176-77)

It is Lord David Cecil who lumps Mr. Crawley with the Archdeacon, Miss Dunstable, and Mrs. Proudie as "simple and positive, absorbed in the avocations of average human beings, devoid alike of psychological complexities and abstruse spiritual yearnings, made up of a few strongly marked qualities and idiosyncrasies." I do not think this describes Trollope's characters very well, and I certainly do not think it describes Mr. Crawley at all. He is one of the subtlest figures in all literature, and even between *Framley Parsonage* and *The Last Chronicle* Trollope continued to make discoveries about his character, and they still continue to astonish us. All the manifestations of his stern and ill-regulated piety we are familiar with, but who would suspect the sly and brutal humor or the childish pleasures of the true scholar? (pp. 181-82)

The thing that hindered [Trollope] from being a great writer and that makes the *Autobiography* so unrevealing was the same thing that made him the great novelist he certainly was: lack of self-consciousness. The only character this patient and humble observer could never observe was his own, and one element in that character was certainly the Reverend Josiah Crawley. (p. 183)

Frank O'Connor, "Trollope the Realist," in his The Mirror in the Roadway: A Study of the Modern Novel *(reprinted by permission of Joan Daves; copyright © 1956 by Frank O'Connor), Alfred A. Knopf, 1956, pp. 165-83.*

BRADFORD A. BOOTH (essay date 1958)

Trollope had little sympathy with Dickens's exaggerations, but like Dickens he considered humor one of the novel's necessary adjuncts. He apparently assumed, however, that there was about his work little, if any, Dickensian flavor. On this point he was self-deceived. . . . Trollope, in spite of his devotion to Jane Austen and Thackeray, produces unmistakable Dickensian overtones. Mrs. Proudie is out of Dickens. So probably are Ontario Moggs, Augustus Melmotte, Elias Gotobed, and a great many others. Furthermore, it is not likely that a number of Trollope's most successful scenes would have been cast in the form in which we find them without the example of Dickens. One thinks of the electors' dinner in *Rachel Ray,* the American Senator's speech in St. James's Hall, and Mrs. Proudie's soirée.

The last-named scene may be useful in pointing up the differences between Dickens and Trollope and between Jane Austen and Trollope. Dickens would no doubt have emphasized the farcical elements in the clash of personalities and in the absurdities of misunderstanding which Mrs. Proudie's entertainment produced. Jane Austen, establishing her humorous and satiric effects more subtly, would never have descended to the slapstick of Mrs. Proudie's torn dress. In spite of the fact that Trollope brings off this famous scene successfully his subsequent failures in depicting social high jinks indicate a basic uneasiness with farce material. In his treatment of this and similar plot situations Trollope stands midway between the tradition of the early nineteenth-century popular stage farce, which Dickens adopted and adapted, and the old-new tradition of the comedy of manners, intellectualized and enriched by the genius of Jane Austen. (pp. 208-09)

Trollope's admiration for Thackeray was perhaps based on a recognition of superb stylistic gifts which he himself did not have. His admiration for Jane Austen was probably based on a recognition of social insights which they shared. The indebtedness to Jane Austen, readily acknowledged, may have been greater than Trollope supposed; we see today, at any rate, the closest possible kinship. This is to be found, among other things, in their common appreciation of the humor of understatement—low pulsed, emotionally slack, apparently artless and naive, but ineffably sly. Trollope's humor, like Jane Austen's, grows out of the totality of character concepts. The source of our amusement at Archdeacon Grantly is not in what he says, but in what he *is.* (p. 209)

The archdeacon, a serious man, is a humorous creation, amply conceived and fully realized. Trollope presents him with masterly objectivity, implying, not stating, the amusing contradictions of his character. The hauteur of his pride is redeemed by the sincerity of his faith; his arrogance of office and his worldliness are softened by his spiritual and temporal loyalties. He is a complete human being, with Josiah Crawley Trollope's best character. But where the perpetual curate of Hogglestock is a somber study in implacable pride and embittered frustration, the Archdeacon of Barchester is a humorous study in self-complacency. Grantly is the quintessence of Trollopian characterization, and his discussion with his wife on one memorable occasion after they had retired for the night is the quintessence of Trollopian humor. Jane Austen might have written this scene, had she permitted herself such liberties, but it is out of Dickens's reach. This is not to say that Trollope is a keener humorist; but his purposes and his methods are different, and in this instance, I think, more artistic.

By instinct and to some extent by training Dickens wrote as a dramatist. His novels break structurally into acts and scenes. One will remember individual scenes long after their sequence and plot significance have been forgotten. . . . [Trollope's novels] have no particular form. Plot is improvised around the characters. This spontaneous composition, with its emphasis on character rather than on plot, promotes the relaxed ease of the informal essayist, and provides Trollope with a fine opportunity to indulge himself in humorous asides.

The genius of Dickens, like that of Shakespeare, was equally at home in high comedy and low comedy. . . . [His] incom-

parable versatility brought him success in many techniques. Trollope, a novelist of narrower talent, was not happy with broad comedy. Dickens's humor is in the main a swiftly moving surface current; Trollope's humor is a slow drifting undercurrent. Dickens can move the soberest reader to hilarity; Trollope rarely attempts to provoke more than a smile. (pp. 210-11)

[The] Trollopian formula for fiction calls for a story of common life to be enlivened by humor and sweetened by pathos. In point of fact, however, there is not a great deal of pathos in the novels. But it may be worth while to examine such scenes and characters as Trollope has given us, if only to note the distance that separates his practice from that of Dickens and Thackeray. (p. 212)

Since Trollope was fundamentally a creator of drawing-room comedy, he was not so frequently tempted toward the abyss of the false pathetic. But it is a fact of some importance in estimating his literary taste and discrimination that when his material called for pathetic treatment he never became maudlin. In the familiar matter of death scenes it is instructive to compare the passing of Septimus Harding with any similar scene in Victorian fiction. The quiet dignity of the Warden's death, deeply moving without a trace of mawkishness, is perfectly articulated with the simplicity and sincerity of his life. It would be difficult to find anything in Victorian fiction better than this chapter in *The Last Chronicle of Barset.* It might be noted, in passing, that Thackeray feels compelled to reiterate, principally by authorial intrusion, that Colonel Newcome's virtue is of a very special sort. Trollope, on the other hand, does not editorialize about Mr. Harding, content to develop his character dramatically.

In the *Autobiography* Trollope is characteristically reserved about his triumphs, but he does speak with affectionate approval of one of his pathetic scenes. . . . Trollope had every reason to be proud of his description of the parting of Charley and Katie [in *The Three Clerks*]. The scene skirts perilously near the area of unwholesome sentimentality, but Trollope's strong sense of decorum asserts the controls of realism with highly effective results. (p. 213)

By and large, however, Trollope's use of the pathetic, unlike Dickens's and Thackeray's, is to be found not in set scenes but in characters. Josiah Crawley, apostle of a stern faith, with his brilliant mind and prickly personality, unyielding martyr to a rigorous concept of truth and duty, homely and ineffective angel—where in literature is there a character so rich in his potential for good, so thin and meagre in his accomplishment? He is Trollope's most pathetic creation. (p. 214)

Orley Farm is, of course, not strictly a tragedy, but the pathos in the trial of Lady Mason is as genuine and as moving as Trollope ever created. In a desperate attempt to protect the interests of her son, Lady Mason . . . long ago forged a codicil to her elderly husband's will. The story of aroused suspicions, a trial, and an acquittal under shadowy circumstances has a dramatic intensity which Trollope never surpassed. It is out of the errors into which people are led by a selfless desire to aid others that the deepest tragedy is born. In Lady Mason Trollope has a good woman, a compassionate woman, essentially honest and law-abiding, who takes it upon herself illegally to right an obvious wrong. On this occasion, at least, Trollope enables us to see into not merely the heart but also the mind of one of his characters. Sympathy is created here, as one suffers with Lady Mason the tortures of a smirched conscience and the tensions developed from attacks on a false position. The pathos of her dilemma is spotlighted with subtlety and restraint, emphasizing, by force of contrast with the shoddy and conventional tragedies to come, the unevenness of Trollope's talent.

As we know, Trollope was no writer of tragedy. On a few occasions, however, he did vary the comic pattern—with indifferent results, except in the instance of the psychological novel *He Knew He Was Right*. Louis Trevelyan, protagonist of this novel, is one of Trollope's most vivid characters. Insanely jealous of his wife, brooding on fancied wrongs, his life hopelessly embittered and frustrated, Trevelyan evokes both pity and terror in the monomania to which he succumbs. . . . Disturbed perhaps by the darkness of his main plot, Trollope balanced the Trevelyan narrative with three colorful but conventional sub-plots. . . . [The] articulation of these plots is very weak, and it may be that Trollope's curious discontent with his work arises from his sense of the novel's diffuseness. Certainly the Trevelyan story is told with power and with an effective pathos, inherent but unexpressed. (pp. 214-15)

Trollope's lukewarm tragedies result from a timid and unimaginative reproduction of the patterns of romantic plotting. Apparently he did not see the incongruity of a master of the comedy of manners wrestling with a plot bad enough to be rejected by a librettist of Italian opera. (p. 216)

It is true that Trollope was not a stylist in the Meredithian sense. He lacked the lyric gifts of the poet, the flaming imagination, the lambent phrase. He almost never attempts a description of nature. . . . (p. 217)

It is clear that Trollope, knowing that he did not have the fancy for descriptive writing, chose to project his sense and character by other means. In an era when most successful novelists were working for startling effects through high-pitched tones and violent colors, Trollope was content with the blandest and most prosaic writing ever to come from a major novelist.

One may grant at once that Trollope is prosaic. To do so is not to deny his greatness. A poet, obviously, dares not be prosaic, and the informal essayist is so at his peril. But the values of fiction are such that other qualities may successfully counterbalance a stylistic deficiency. A knowledge of human behavior patterns, an understanding of the dynamics of plot, an ear for the rhythms of ordinary speech—all these may compensate for a style that is not highly imaginative. There is also a kind of story for which a poetic style would be quite unsuitable: the disreputable adventures of a picaro, a heated contest between political aspirants, a faithful narrative of the barracks and trenches. There should, of course, be congruity between subject matter and style. . . . Now, the social life of a few rural clergymen, though it might be handled poetically, can surely be approached on the level of an imaginative transcription of reality. Style need not be absent from even a factual transcription of reality; when the imagination plays a part, some kind of style other than the purely pedestrian must inevitably result. When such characters and materials as Trollope discovered are viewed with a humorous and lightly satiric eye, we have a highly individualized novel. (pp. 218-19)

The virtue of a restrained style, and it is a very great one, is that the author will not be caught in extremes of manner that make him ridiculous. So Trollope, who does not have eloquence and thus does not rise to the heights of expressed power often reached by Meredith and James, will not descend to bathos which greater writers occasionally touch. (p. 221)

Such a style as Trollope's, without any showy or flashy qualities, is . . . not intensely personal. In general, Trollope submits himself to the scale of values which he finds current in his world, and his style is accommodatingly cool and deliberate. An iconoclast like Thackeray views society subjectively through the filter of his own ironic personality, with the result that his style is warm and deeply personal. His purpose is to project *himself* by means of an interpretation of human action. . . . Trollope's purpose is chiefly to transcribe his sense of the world. This he does objectively and concretely. The authorial intrusions, of course, provide a personal statement, but they break in upon a method largely objective and do not seriously alter the impression of a realistic rendering of observation and experience. At his best, by means of a style muted and unobtrusive, Trollope gives a lucid, impersonal account of his age.

Unfortunately, however, Trollope does not always give us his best. At moments of mechanical writing the lean, functional style can lapse into pedestrian "officialese." . . . [He] does not often take himself or his task too seriously. If this is a defect, it is also a virtue; if he sacrifices a tension that is never absent from the greatest of novels, he gains a looseness which keeps his style easy rather than formal. Nevertheless, there are times when inspiration flags but the moving hand writes on. Such occasions are known to every prolific novelist. When this occurred Trollope dropped into the heavy jargon which among businessmen and politicians passes for an impressive prose style. . . . With his lighter tone and less formidable purposes Trollope is [usually] protected from the extremes of artificiality, bogus profundity, and self-conscious pedantry of diction. But examples of these errors can be found. . . . [Whatever] may have been Trollope's shortcomings as a stylist in the Meredithian sense, his good ear and innate sense of verbal appropriateness were such that one must hunt for such passages. (pp. 225-26)

It would be folly to argue that Trollope is a great stylist. He did not have the poetic imagination of Emily Brontë, the slashing wit of Thackeray, the incandescent humor of Dickens, or the deliberate intellectualism of George Eliot—all of which are expressed in terms of style. What is left to Trollope? A great deal: a fluency that . . . rarely becomes tedious; a level of practical competence which if it never rises to high passion infrequently sinks to irredeemable bathos; an easy grace that carries one along on a full tide of flowing narrative. One cannot read Meredith, or Melville, or Stevenson, or James without being conscious of style. On every page there are sentences which demand that we note how they are constructed and phrases which stimulate our laggard imagination. But in reading Trollope one rarely thinks of style. This is *not*, however, because, as Meredith suggested, Trollope has no style. It is rather because without verbal pyrotechnics he has talent enough to keep his story moving easily and his reader comfortably engrossed. It is a minor accomplishment of style, no doubt, the achievement of a journeyman novelist, but unlike some examples of more spectacular writing it has worn well through many generations of careful readers. (pp. 227-28)

> *Bradford A. Booth, in his* Anthony Trollope: Aspects of His Life and Art *(copyright © 1958 by Indiana University Press), Indiana University Press, 1958, 258 p.*

BRADFORD A. BOOTH (essay date 1958)

I do not know that anyone at all sympathetic to the Victorian novel has ever failed to like Trollope's *Orley Farm*. At all events, no unfavorable reaction has been recorded. Trollope thought the plot his best, and when he began to list the well-drawn characters, he could not stop much short of a total roll call. There is not, he says, "a dull page in the book." Such prideful language, so uncommon for Trollope that it is found nowhere else, is almost, if not quite, justified. On this occasion he had, as Henry James saw, an "admirable subject." It is one that not only suited perfectly his own mature temper but gave him a welcome opportunity to skirt certain mid-Victorian clichés and conventions in the design and development of a novel. The result is that *Orley Farm* is one of Trollope's richest and most satisfying books. If, like *The Last Chronicle of Barset*, it fails to attain true greatness, the failure is in large part the measure of his incomplete break with the familiar stereotypes of plotting. (p. 146)

Early in *Barchester Towers* Trollope invites the reader to turn to the last chapter, confident that such interest as his novel possesses does not rest on twists of plot. He might have made the same statement on behalf of *Orley Farm*, for again he breaks the Victorian stereotype by deliberately foregoing the interest that attaches to surprise. Lady Mason is guilty; indeed she soon avows her guilt to Sir Peregrine Orme. The power of the novel arises not from the shock of the unexpected, but from the skill with which Trollope explores the tenacity of a woman who will dare all for her son and who will break upon the rack of neither conscience nor the public tribunal. Trollope's main plot, secured and sustained by tensions of its own, needed no help from adventitious maneuverings and manipulations. (p. 147)

In such a novel as *Orley Farm*, which is the story of Lady Mason, nothing should have been permitted to deflect attention from her bitter problem. But Trollope fractioned his plot in deference to the Victorian stereotype of the huge, baggy monster. The inexorable demand for three volumes could not be refused, and the temper and experience of the reading public, still largely feminine and clerical, did not permit the close situational studies through which James imposed order on chaos. (p. 149)

Trollope's concern in *Orley Farm*, and in others of his most thoughtful novels, is not with what happens but with its effect upon the individuals most directly involved. Thus, in *The Warden-Barchester Towers* (it is useful to think of them as a single novel) Trollope interests himself in the analysis of a situation: the effect upon Septimus Harding, a man of impeccable honor, of the suggestion that his tenure of a sinecure is ethically indefensible. In *The Last Chronicle* it is the effect upon the Reverend Josiah Crawley, a man of stern, almost forbidding, rectitude, of the charge that he has stolen a sizable cheque. In *Orley Farm* it is the effect upon Lady Mason, an essentially good, if misguided, woman, of the growing certainty that she has ruined not only her own life but, more importantly, that of her son.

The three characters just named are, in my opinion, the best that Trollope created. By "best" I mean, of course, not the most colorful or most amusing or most ingratiating, but those through whom he got beneath the topsoil of superficial manners to the bedrock of fundamental human emotions. It should be noted that one is an old man and the other two are middle-aged. When Trollope broke through the stereotype love story, he did his most significant writing. . . . Trollope's young people take us into no new areas of self-knowledge, nor is it through them that he tries to enlarge the boundaries of man's sympathies.

Such sharpened perceptions as Trollope can give us of the dignity and the power of life, of its abnegations and renunciations, its terrors and humiliations, come through characters of mature years. The drama of young love did not move him greatly. . . . A realist who neither depreciated nor deified women, he wasted no emotion in Shelleyan longing for the unattainable. He preferred a plain girl of common sense to one of supernal beauty who was, to use his favorite adjective, "strong-minded." However wise such views may be, they do not suggest that the possessor will satisfy the taste for romance which largely determined the nature of the mid-Victorian novel. Trollope's observations of what is significant in life simply did not frame themselves in terms of young love.

It should also be remarked that Trollope came to the novel relatively late, with settled, middle-aged views of the decorum of life and of its ultimate values. *Orley Farm* is an early Trollope novel, but it was written in the author's forty-sixth year. (pp. 149-50)

Lady Mason, in whom is reflected the intensity with which the older characters are perceived, is one of the triumphs of Trollope's art, and one of the most moving characters of Victorian fiction. She is a forger, and has carried the gnawing secret of her guilt for twenty years, yet she is a good woman. The nature of the circumstances under which the crime was committed are such that only the sternest moralist would turn his face from Lady Mason, and only the most bitterly vindictive would pursue her with retributive justice. (p. 151)

Trollope had no consistent view of his character. Lady Mason was never intended to be evil, but there is an evident change after her guilt is established that cannot be accounted for solely in terms of the deepening of her nature. The change is in Trollope's attitude toward her. Hester Prynne [in Nathaniel Hawthorne's *The Scarlet Letter*] is shown to have become through her sin more thoughtful, more tolerant, more spiritual. Lady Mason's character, however, is relatively constant. Trollope has led us to a kindlier view because he has himself become more sympathetic. (p. 153)

Orley Farm is a characteristic Victorian novel. Its many-faceted plot is kept more rigorously under control than is traditional, and the tensions of the principal action are maintained with what is, for Trollope, unaccustomed tautness. The problem considered is worthy of a serious artist, and its resolution develops expectancy and invokes pity. If, as I believe, *The Last Chronicle* is a more satisfactory performance, the measure of its superiority must be sought in its leading character. *Orley Farm* fails, in part, because there is no greatness in Lady Mason. Her strength, and it is considerable, is exerted in support of a morally indefensible position. Her moment of renunciation is bitter indeed, but the pity she arouses is tempered by a recognition of her palpable weakness. Josiah Crawley, by contrast, though foundering in his social relationships because of grievous personality faults, has a nobility of soul that makes him a genuinely and impressively tragic figure. But the plot of *The Last Chronicle* is flawed beyond redemption. Each of these two novels, then, has what the other lacks; and Trollope, unable to bring all his powers to a focus in a single novel, left no perfect work of art. (p. 158)

Bradford A. Booth, "Trollope's 'Orley Farm': Artistry 'Manqué'" (© copyright 1958 by the University of Minnesota; reprinted by permission of the Literary Estate of Bradford A. Booth), in From Jane Austen to Joseph Conrad: Essays Collected in Memory of James T. Hillhouse, *edited by Robert C. Rathburn and Martin Steinmann, Jr., University of Minnesota Press, 1958, pp. 146-59.*

ARTHUR MIZENER (essay date 1958)

[Trollope did not] so much write novels as live with characters, and as a consequence, his powers are best seen in groups of books which deal with the same set of characters. . . . Of the leading characters in [the Palliser] novels Trollope said in the *Autobiography* that "by no amount of description or asseveration could I succeed in making any reader understand how much these characters with their belongings have been to me in my latter life." Characteristically, however, he is not at all sure that this intensity of imagination is not merely a private foible unlikely to be shared by his readers. "Who will read *Can You Forgive Her?, Phineas Finn, Phineas Redux,* and *The Prime Minister* [*The Duke's Children* is omitted from this list because it was written after the *Autobiography*] consecutively in order that they may understand the characters of the Duke of Omnium, of Plantagenet Palliser, and Lady Glencora? . . . But in the performance of the work I had much gratification. . . ." Perhaps not many people will read these books consecutively; they constitute a large order, something over four thousand pages. But they offer the reader much gratification and are the richest source of evidence for a study of the kind of greatness Trollope had.

It is a kind of greatness that is not so easy to see as it used to be; all Trollope's most evident weaknesses are in those very aspects of the novel that we are now accustomed to scan most attentively and demand the most of. He confessed with almost ostentatious innocence that he scarcely ever knew how a novel was going to end when he started it . . . ; he had so little interest in the delicate cabinet-making which fascinates artificers of the well-made novel that he hardly ever revised— seldom even read proofs with any care. . . . What he was prone to boast of was that he never but once (twice including *The Landleaguers,* which was left unfinished at his death) allowed a word of a novel to be printed until it was finished, that he always fulfilled his contracts on the dot, that if his career had any interest it was as an example "of the opening which a literary career offers to men and women for the earning of their bread."

Trollope was able to talk this way seriously because in those respects in which he was a great novelist he was so easily and naturally one and did so much of the work of imagination when he was not at his writing desk that when he sat down he could clock his two hundred and fifty words every quarter of an hour without diminishing his power, just as Jane Austen could write her novels amid the buzz of conversation in that incredibly tiny drawing room. Moreover, Trollope was, so far as these gifts took him, a novelist of a remarkably pure kind. For better and—in a minor sense—for worse, his gifts were never blurred by elaborate ideas, either about The Form of the Novel or about The Nature of Life. Trollope had a certain number of opinions, or perhaps only prejudices, which were organic outgrowths of his direct observation of experience; but he had no ideas in the proper sense; he never reasoned abstractly with any great success. (pp. 160-61)

About his limitations in these respects he always displayed that almost belligerent honesty of his on which critics of his novels have depended very heavily in defining their objections to his work. He thought of a plot as a piece of machinery, something that held together mechanically the incidents and characters,

"the most insignificant part of a tale," as he called it frankly. As such it was something he was conscientious about, because he was proud to be a good craftsman, and he was always the first to point out the defects in his plot. . . . He confesses that when he became a practiced novelist he "abandoned the effort to think, trusting myself, with the narrowest thread of a plot, to work the matter out when the pen is in my hands," and he is frank to say that "I am not sure that the construction of a perfected plot has been at any period within my power."

But if the structures of his novels are seldom perfected, they are nonetheless a good deal finer than is usually allowed. The dangers of proceeding as he did are, of course, disproportion, lack of economy, and the risk that the story may shift direction as it goes along and find itself encumbered by awkward commitments. . . . But the very fact that Trollope usually started with a group of characters and a situation and without a predetermined plot means that he seldom imagined an event until he had fully imagined the movements of thought and feeling in the characters which produced the event; situations are seldom forced on characters by the exigencies of plot in Trollope, and this is a very considerable merit.

But Trollope not only failed to plan his story in detail; he was much addicted to the Victorian custom of starting several stories and running them alternately throughout a book. In this way, as it seems to many theoreticians, he maximized the opportunities for trouble. How are the narrative links between the plots to be established without awkwardness unless they are planned ahead? More important, how are the large meanings of the various plots to be related when Trollope's hit-and-miss method of composition is followed? But it is a fact that Trollope does link his plots and, in his quiet and unsymbolic way, play their meanings off against one another. *The Prime Minister,* for example, has, if not three plots, at least three centers of action. There are the Duke and Duchess of Omnium, with their great houses in Carleton Gardens and at Matching and Gatherum, where the political and social life of the great world is lived. There are the Whartons, in Manchester Square and at Wharton, intermarried with the Fletchers at Longbarns, living their lives of country gentility and legal dignity. There is Ferdinand Lopez, floating commercially and socially from his very temporary flat in Westminster to Sexty Parker's office in Little Tankard Yard and thence to the Progress. They are all interlocked in a hundred ways, by Lopez's marriage to Emily, by the Duchess's taking up Lopez and persuading him to contest Silverbridge, where Arthur Fletcher runs, and so on. Each of these is an independent world with its own integrity, and we know each thoroughly, from inside. But they are nonetheless not only related in hundreds of ways but often parallel in character. Trollope had an extremely sharp eye for social differences; perhaps no English novelist has had a sharper one. But he knew very well that vanity, fear, and lust, unselfishness, courage, and love, are much the same everywhere. . . . It would not be easy to exhaust the parallels of this kind in any good Trollope novel; they are an important part of what the multiple plot structure exists for.

But Trollope was convinced that plot construction was a secondary matter. The main task of the novelist, he thought, was to make "the creations of his brain . . . speaking, moving" and therefore "living, human creatures" for the reader. Though he put his famous remark about Mrs. Proudie in his usual way, almost as if he were making ironic fun of himself for a silly habit, Trollope was telling the main secret of his art when he said in the *Autobiography* that "I have never dissevered myself from Mrs. Proudie, and still live much in company with her ghost.'' This was ten years after he had written the last word about Mrs. Proudie. (pp. 162-64)

It is easy, much too easy if one wishes to convey the full impressiveness of the achieved thing, to generalize the sources of the kind of understanding Trollope possessed. He was, in the first place, an indefatigable and inexhaustibly fascinated observer. . . . Trollope's kind of observation is an act of the imagination, charged with the excitement and the delight of the thing apprehended. In a way very characteristic of him, he used what he saw of the commonest objects of daily life modestly and quietly in his novels, with an almost perfect sense of when they were relevant to the wholeness of the reader's vision of the action. That is, he used objects, not for themselves, but as integral parts of the action. He seldom indulged in the vanity of being tricky about how he introduced such objects, but their force can be very subtle. Thus, when Phineas Finn meets Lady Laura above the falls at Loughlinter, Trollope gives us a straightforward description of how he was dressed: ''At the present moment he had on his head a Scotch cap with a grouse's feather in it, and he was dressed in a velvet shooting-jacket and dark knickerbockers.'' But the point of introducing these particulars is not so simple. This is not Trollope telling us what Phineas looked like for the sake of the fact. He goes on, ''He was certainly, in this costume, as handsome a man as any woman would wish to see.'' For a woman is seeing him, a woman who is going to love him all her life, and whose tragedy is that at this moment she does not even suspect that she cannot conquer her love for him and marry prudentially. This image of Phineas, with his beauty and his air of breeding, will haunt Lady Laura's imagination always; if we are to feel exactly what she felt, we must see exactly what she saw. (pp. 164-65)

[Because Trollope was] fascinated by and involved in the life he saw around him, he had what [Mr. A.O.J.] Cockshut has called an almost ''universal pity'' [see excerpt above, 1955]. He always understood the workings of the minds of even his worst characters and saw how they justified themselves to themselves. He also always saw how comically self-regarding and therefore illogical even the best of his characters were. (p. 166)

But if there is almost universal sympathy in Trollope's imagination, there is also unremitting judgment, so that his sympathetic understanding of men's self-evaluation is always balanced by his clear awareness of how common sense will judge them. There is a delicacy in the ironic balance of these two kinds of perception in his work which it would be hard to exaggerate. It is what makes us understand that so likeable a young man as Silverbridge is limited and, indeed, weak. (p. 167)

The characters Trollope thought of most highly, like Plantagenet Palliser, have some awareness of the distortions of self-judgment. Similarly, a man like Mr. Crawley understands most of his own faults of character, often as he is defeated by them, as he typically is when he tries to tell himself that others have suffered more than he:

> Of what sort had been the life of the man who had stood for years on the top of a pillar? But then the man on the pillar had been honoured by all around him. And thus, though he had thought of the man on the pillar to encourage himself by remembering how lamentable had been that man's sufferings, he came to reflect

that after all his own sufferings were perhaps keener than those of the man on the pillar.

But it is fundamental with Trollope that even the best men are incapable of seeing themselves with perfect clarity, and one of the finest things he regularly does is to add just a shade of self-deception to otherwise admirable characters. Thus, for instance, Emily Wharton is an intelligent, considerate, honest girl. But there is in her just a touch of overassurance about the rightness of her own judgment. She has no such radical overconfidence as Alice Vavasor; nonetheless, her assurance is enough to lead her, against all advice, into her disastrous marriage with Lopez and—finest of all—to make her cling with just her shade of assurance to her later conviction—an essentially self-regarding conviction—that as Lopez's widow she is not good enough for Arthur Fletcher.

What Trollope took the greatest delight in observing was the way people's egos and self-interest would lead them quite sincerely to find arguments of principle for what passion or willful prejudice made them believe. Even his villains are only extreme cases of self-deception; so Lopez, ''to give him his due, . . . did not know that he was a villain [and] conceived that he was grievously wronged by [Emily] in that she adhered to her father rather than to him.'' (pp. 168-69)

Characteristically, Trollope shows us the attitude of a character directly and balances it with the judgment of common sense by ironic overtone. Technically, he has two important ways of doing so, and he usually uses them together, as he does in the case of Mr. Spooner's proposal to Adelaide Palliser. . . . The first of these ways is to let us see and hear the character; the second is to offer us a summary of the thoughts which accompany the action. It is vital to Trollope's method that, however close he keeps to the original thoughts of the character, these passages should be given in summary, in his own words, because it is his own words which supply the balancing and ironic judgment of common sense. This is, of course, one of the major devices of Jane Austen's fiction, as the very famous first sentence of *Pride and Prejudice* is enough to show, and it is the reason why it is so disastrously wrong for critics to object out of hand to the intrusion of the novelist in a fiction. Of this method, Trollope was a great master. (pp. 169-70)

Trollope was, to borrow from [Mr. Michael] Sadleir a figure which was also a fact, a clumsy rider who had ''hands.'' He knew his characters intimately and he guided them very delicately. As long as he was telling what one of his fully imagined characters was thinking, he displayed an astonishing insight. Old Trollope, as Froude said in some irritation (Trollope beat him to the punch with a book on Africa), went banging about the world, but he never missed anything and his imagination was always tirelessly at work, so that both the inner and the outer natures of his characters were ''clear to me as are the stars on a summer night.'' (p. 172)

Arthur Mizener, ''Anthony Trollope: The Palliser Novels'' (© copyright 1958 by the University of Minnesota; reprinted by permission of the author), in From Jane Austen to Joseph Conrad: Essays Collected in Memory of James T. Hillhouse, *edited by Robert C. Rathburn and Martin Steinmann, Jr., University of Minnesota Press, 1958, pp. 160-76.*

JEROME THALE (essay date 1960)

[*In the following examination of Trollope's longer novels, Thale asserts that Trollope's method of organization allows him to reveal a broad and comprehensive vision of the complexity of life. Thale contends that unlike the conventional novel with a strong central plot, Trollope's novels are thematically structured, with many equally important characters; he maintains that this technique derives from a pattern of "parallels, contrasts, repetitions with slight variations."*]

Trollope's novels have always had a reputation for being loose and rambling. *The Way We Live Now,* for example, has three or four major plot strands and three or four subplots—and even in this accounting there are a good many characters and situations left over. Trollope himself said that he was not very concerned with plot, and spoke of it [in *An Autobiography*] as "but the vehicle," "the most insignificant part of a tale." . . . In Trollope's time, when most readers accepted the novel as a picture of life, this was well enough. But we have come to expect more from the novel: discursiveness and inclusiveness no longer seem virtues in themselves, and the lack of structure has become a radical fault. There is surely no question that Trollope presents one of the fullest and most interesting pictures of nineteenth-century England, and if this is his only accomplishment it is a considerable one. But if we accept his novels primarily as documents, we may begin to wonder whether by our standards his works are really novels, whether we ought to hedge about his greatness. (p. 147)

In speaking of the Trollope novel I am referring not so much to the familiar shorter books like *The Warden* and *Barchester Towers,* but principally to the longer and (as most critics now seem to feel) major Trollope novels, such books as *The Way We Live Now, He Knew He was Right, The Last Chronicle of Barset,* and *The Duke's Children.* Let me take, as a representative example, *The Last Chronicle of Barset.* (p. 148)

[It is clear that *The Last Chronicle*] does not have a single unified plot line. Even the central action, that about Mr. Crawley and the check, is not a dynamic one that springs from character and is resolved on the basis of change in it. It is largely mechanical and external. It is, to use Trollope's metaphor, the vehicle which allows for passengers and scenery, but whose destination is unimportant. It does not provide a vital organizing principle, an overall design to which parts are subordinated.

If the Trollope novel looks so centerless, if there is no single dramatic focus, if there are frequently four or five weakly related plots going at once, it is because plot, though present and not negligible, is not important. Or, to put it another way, time is not important. For what matters is not the succession of events but the accumulation of them, and the grouping of events and characters. A painting may be united through the repetition, echoing, contradiction, balancing, of such structural features as color, line, mass. In something of the same way, the Trollope novel depends upon parallels, contrasts, repetitions with slight variations. These things, which are present to some extent in any novel, become in Trollope the method of organization. In a Trollope novel, a large number of characters respond differently to the same situation, or do the same thing for different reasons. Half a dozen or a dozen people may fall in love and say "yes" or "no" in the same way but for different reasons, or in different ways but for the same reason. Thus the Trollope novel is the very opposite of the long comic strip, purely episodic; it is like a vast mural, one of those comprehensive images that cover walls, crammed with figures and united spatially.

If we examine the situations in *The Last Chronicle of Barset,* we discover that they are—to shift from a pictorial to a musical

metaphor—variations on the basic motif of honesty. At the center of the novel is Mr. Crawley, a man of great pride and almost painful integrity. When his honesty is questioned because he cannot account for the stolen check, he himself does not know what to think. Pride in his obedience to authority makes him answer the Bishop's somewhat arbitrary summons to the palace. The same pride makes him refuse to be lectured at by the Bishop's wife. . . . At last pride and mistaken honesty compel him, against the advice of his friends, to submit his resignation. Only when the mystery is solved are his honesty, his sanity, and his reputation re-established.

After Mr. Crawley, the most important variation on the motif of honesty is the love affair of Grace Crawley and Major Grantly. The impediment of Mr. Crawley's troubles raises for them a different kind of question of honesty. Just as Mr. Crawley's difficulty begins with honesty about money and becomes one of honesty toward his position, theirs begins with honesty in their relations with each other and ends in questions of integrity to themselves. Though Grace loves the Major she does not feel that it is fair to let him commit himself while her family is in such difficulty; though she cannot accept his love, she will not deny that she loves him, for she must remain honest to herself. Major Grantly after some hesitation feels that fidelity to Grace and honesty to himself require that he should not let his love be deterred by Mr. Crawley's situation, and so he makes the declaration which is rebuffed. . . . Trollope presents the Major's honesty in a very complex and satisfying way—showing the Major as at once true to his love and disturbed at the thought of losing his money and position.

The problem of honesty to one's love and to one's self is paralleled and reversed with Lily Dale and John Eames. Their story, which is the main business of *The Small House at Allington,* is here re-used and continued in terms of the over-all motif of *The Last Chronicle.* Lily still loves the man who had jilted her. John Eames, who has loved Lily for many years, resolves to press his suit again. If Johnny is persistent in being faithful to his love (even though it is becoming something of a joke), Lily is equally persistent in being faithful to her heart. Friends on both sides urge the match, the specter of old maidhood is facing Lily, and Johnny acquits himself manfully in extricating Crawley from his troubles. But Lily, though she acknowledges his merits, knows also that she does not love him, and so she will not marry him. (pp. 149-51)

An account of the large repetitions and variations on the main theme does not begin to indicate how thoroughly this method of repetition and variation pervades and organizes the novel, even in the presentation of subsidiary characters and situations. The novel opens, for example, with scenes in which we see the Walkers, the Grantlys, and the Crawleys at home, each discussing the incident of the check (and in each case we see how the wife—apparently under the control of a much stronger husband—manages him). The public response to Mr. Crawley's troubles is presented several times. The judgments come from a wide variety of characters and occur at various stages in the book; often of course they give us a double measure—of Mr. Crawley and of those who judge. . . .

The discussion of Mr. Crawley takes a formal and legal character when the magistrates meet. They do not want to bind Mr. Crawley over for trial, but the evidence seems against him, he offers no defense, and so they are compelled to bind him over. Later the Bishop appoints a clerical commission to investigate the matter, and a different set of judges examines the same material. The description of the meeting and the personalities is a miniature of the method of the novel, subtle and careful examination of the various possibilities for honesty and dishonesty. (p. 152)

In such situations as these, we see different people doing the same thing, being honest or dishonest but in different ways. In another type of situation a character repeats the same action—but under a different set of circumstances that gives us a different perspective on the action. When Mr. Crawley goes to the Bishop's he refuses to bend in the least to Mrs. Proudie and even to discuss the case with her. Our sympathies are all with him; he is being persecuted, and Mrs. Proudie is a meddlesome woman getting her comeuppance. But a few chapters later Mark Robarts goes to Mr. Crawley urging him to get legal help. Crawley refuses, and we are dismayed that he should so rudely reject the generous help of Robarts. If we reflect upon it, we realize that in spite of our different responses, Crawley's motive is essentially the same in both cases—stiff-necked pride, independence, assertion of his rights.

In its more complex uses, this method of repetition of an action under varying circumstances produces not simply a new perspective but a new meaning for the action. Sometimes the identical situation is repeated. John Eames proposes to Lily Dale at her home in Allington at about the same time that her old lover Crosbie writes that he still loves her; she decides against both of them. Later, on a visit to London, she comes to feel the attraction of a wider life and of marriage. John, in a wider circle himself, looks better to her, and she actually sees Crosbie. The earlier possibilities are repeated—John proposes again; Crosbie, who is more in love with her than ever, presents himself. With a larger and more direct experience, she comes to the same conclusion again—that she will not marry. Though she knows better what she is doing the second time, and her decision is more meaningful, the action is essentially the same. (pp. 153-54)

In all of these cases the method of variation is used for giving complexity of meaning to the main themes, for seeing actions and motives in many lights. Elsewhere in the novel, and often rather incidentally, Trollope uses the method not so much for moral perspective but as a compositional device for arranging characters and situations. Thus there are the two lawyers: one at the beginning, the other later in the book; one thinks Crawley guilty but is willing to stretch the law for him; the other is convinced of his innocence and also willing to stretch the law; one is sober and conservative, the other bustling and energetic; one a local man, the other from London. Each of the lawyers is basically honest (though in different ways), and each is willing to be a little dishonest (though again in different ways). (p. 154)

This same kind of structural principle that I have been describing in *The Last Chronicle of Barset* operates, as I have said, in most of the other large Trollope novels. It is by no means the most obvious or familiar structural principle in the English novel; whether it is the best of structural principles is unimportant. In Trollope's hands and in the hands of certain other novelists it is a way of examining a situation or problem with great breadth and complexity, of bringing a great deal of material into a vital relationship. It is a principle which makes the Trollope novel much more than a picture of life. The term panoramic suggests in a general way some of the features of this kind of novel. (pp. 154-55)

In trying to discern the structural principle which Trollope uses, I have not been trying to make his novels respectable by dem-

onstrating that they have structure. . . . In *The Last Chronicle* structure is the means through which Trollope's wonderful disenchanted clarity of vision, his tolerance and accuracy, operate to produce a remarkably complex and balanced vision of human life. The end result of the massive examination in *The Last Chronicle* is to indicate how complex a thing honesty is, how much there is involved in being honest or dishonest, and indeed how complex a thing human life is, viewed under this aspect. The method is static in the way that a mural is, taken in all at once, by a kind of exfoliation in which vision and technique are one. (p. 156)

Jerome Thale, "The Problem of Structure in Trollope," in Nineteenth-Century Fiction *(© 1960 by The Regents of the University of California; reprinted by permission of The Regents), Vol. 15, No. 2, September, 1960, pp. 147-57.*

GEOFFREY TILLOTSON (essay date 1961-62)

Now that I have read almost everything that Anthony Trollope wrote—he wrote some forty novels, most of them long—I see with increased clearness that he is a giant among novelists, that he is big not merely in girth but in height. He stands firmly among the dozen or so giants of English fiction. . . .

[Trollope's] style has no pretensions. It reveals its honesty in its preference for monosyllables. It likes plain words. It abhors the high-sounding. It creeps, and with the practised neatness of the centipede. But it is not the style of a man who abhors grace. Rather it is the style of one who knows how best to sustain grace without its seeming too much a thing of art. It has the beauty associated with the grey and white dress of Quaker women—. . . it could even transform a plain face into elegance. Trollope is so well satisfied with his one style that he scarcely used anything else. The upshot is that where his personages speak among themselves, or write letters to each other—and they do these things as often as possible—they speak and write, by and large, with his voice. I make the qualification 'by and large' because he does break up their spoken sentences a little, and leave some of them incomplete, when emotion or cunning and the like call for minor stoppages. But when there is nothing to arrest or complicate the spoken or written sentences of his personages, they flow on like Trollope's own. (p. 56)

[Most] of the speeches are beautifully shaped. Open the novels where you like and see if this is not so. The speeches are of the sort we should all like to be able to count on making—speeches that do not waste a word, which know exactly where they are going, and stride ahead with the utmost confidence. . . . Coleridge spoke of the prospective power that an educated man is supposed to have over his expression—he foresees the end of a sentence the moment of embarking upon it. Few educated men have his power, as a matter of fact. But we feel that everybody in the novels of Trollope has it even though few of his personages are more than ordinarily educated or clever. (p. 59)

But if Trollope's personages are usually Trollope himself when it comes to expressing their individual ideas, we can accept their unrealistic perfection of speech just because of the characteristics of Trollope's own style as described in my opening paragraph. That style is so pure and plain that it is indeed the style we should all prefer to speak and write if we had his sort of genius—Newman spoke of the simplicity that is an attribute of genius in general, and it certainly is an attribute of Trollope's in particular. It is a style for all purposes, being capable of handling the trivial and commonplace, and also the noble and splendid—it can indeed also handle the complicated when used by one who, like Trollope, always masters complexity so that it is reduced to its elements. (pp. 59-60)

Geoffrey Tillotson, ''Trollope's Style,'' in Ball State Teachers College Forum *(copyright 1961 by Ball State Teachers College; reprinted by permission), Vol. II, No. 2, Winter, 1961-62 (and reprinted in* Mid-Victorian Studies *by Geoffrey Tillotson and Kathleen Tillotson, The Athlone Press, 1965, pp. 56-61).*

JOHN E. DUSTIN (essay date 1962)

[*Dustin argues that the majority of Trollope's novels are limited in scope and can be classified by dividing them into two thematic groups: an ''A'' group which focuses on family hostilities that derive from a disputed inheritance, and a ''B'' group which features the rise and fall of a bright young man of the city. According to the critic, Trollope's use of theme is formulaic and mechanical in the early novels, while his later novels are much improved by the absence of this mechanical device. Dustin's analysis of theme in the later novels provides support for A.O.J. Cockshut's thesis (1955) that ''Trollope is a gloomier, more introspective, more satirical, and more profound writer than he is usually credited with being. . . .'' Dustin's thesis is challenged by William Cadbury (1963).*]

While chatting with Anthony Trollope one day, George Eliot lamented the occasional failure of her inspiration: ''There are days together when I cannot write a line.'' Trollope, in a rare moment of humility, replied: ''Oh, well, with imaginative work like yours that is quite natural; but with my mechanical stuff it's a sheer matter of industry.'' Perhaps it is unfair to accept Trollope's testimony against himself, but we do his workmanlike talents no disservice if we recognize that the same charge has often been brought against him by his critics, who allege a variety of ''mechanical'' practices. . . . However, one ''mechanical'' technique which he repeatedly employed has never been noticed. If we trace the appearance of the two principal sources of conflict in his fiction, we discover not only that two themes are very common but also that they appear with almost predictable regularity. The symmetry of this pattern is, I feel, significant and illuminating in understanding Trollope's literary fecundity, in classifying his novels, and in appreciating the exact nature of his artistic maturity, a matter of special concern in recent Trollope criticism. Paradoxically, this same pattern also suggests that those novels which are most popular at the moment were ''mechanically'' produced.

In eight of the early novels the main conflict originates in a single recurring problem. In chronological order these novels are **The Warden, Barchester Towers, Doctor Thorne, Castle Richmond, Orley Farm, Rachel Ray, Miss Mackenzie,** and **The Belton Estate.** Within what is generally a rural setting two, sometimes three, families are discovered in a state of extreme mutual hostility. Conflicting interpretations of an inheritance, the complications of entail—especially concealed illegitimacy as it affects entail—and successive wills are the specific bases for this hostility. Often the conflict is concretely introduced early in the novel through a collision of the opponents. When the dispute cannot be settled, the heads of the families then draw on the advice of a multitude of solicitous friends, counsellors, and lawyers. . . .

Because of its complex treatment of a disputed inheritance, **Orley Farm** is a good example of a novel of this type. Lady

Mason, the persecuted, somberly beautiful heroine, and her vindictive son-in-law, Sir Joseph Mason, quarrel over the legality of her late husband's will, through which she inherited his estate. Greatly disturbed, Lady Mason seeks advice first from several friends and then entrusts herself to the barrister Furnival. In this, the most litigious of Trollope's early novels, the solution is sought in court where, after a set-piece courtroom duel between the barristers, she is pronounced innocent. The eventual revelation of her guilt as a forger—for morally defensible reasons—affects several love affairs: she breaks her engagement, and her son, with self-conscious nobility, does the same.

The reader generally familiar with Trollope's fiction will recognize a repetition of this theme in the other novels of the group. **Castle Richmond, Doctor Thorne, Rachel Ray, Miss Mackenzie,** and **The Belton Estate** have a similar crux, the bitter disagreement over inherited titles (or names) or property. This hostility provides the unifying principle for the main narratives, and the action is shaped by the purely legal exigencies of the dispute. (p. 280)

Within this series, however, Trollope moved towards a more realistic, at least a less ingenuous employment of several of these principles. For example, the courtship of the lovers is conducted with increasing difficulty as their involvement in the main legal strategy becomes more intricate. In **The Warden** a simple antithesis exists: Eleanor Harding, daughter of an Anglican clergyman, loves John Bold, one of a group protesting the Church's use of endowments, from which her father directly benefits. Later, in **Rachel Ray** and **Castle Richmond,** this neat opposition was succeeded by a complicated interplay of hostile forces in which one of the lovers is forced to remain, at least part of the time, a non-combatant. . . .

There is a similar change in the general tone within this group. In the first novels, **The Warden, Barchester Towers,** and **Doctor Thorne,** the battle is waged with mock-heroic vigor. . . . However, this violence had considerably subsided by the time Trollope wrote **Orley Farm.** In **Rachel Ray** the wrath of Mr. Tappitt, the hero's enemy, is confused, sporadic, and unappreciated by members of his family; and in **Miss Mackenzie** and **The Belton Estate** acrimony is, much of the time, well concealed. . . .

Let us turn to those novels in which the second and alternate problem recurs: **The Three Clerks, The Bertrams, Framley Parsonage, The Small House at Allington, Can You Forgive Her?** and **The Claverings.** Trollope now considers the career of the bright young man of the city who early in the novel commits an error in moral judgment. Generally he succumbs to some form of temptation while he is on a trip. He may recover, properly penitent, before the end of the novel; but if he is basically evil, professional and occasionally physical annihilation will overtake him. The curve of his career following the mistake usually encompasses momentary regret, a temporary success, then financial troubles, involvement with money lenders, and a fall. (p. 281)

The Three Clerks is the prototype for these early novels. A young, intelligent civil servant, Alaric Tudor, no sooner wins promotion than he is seduced into misconduct by a friend, the speculator Undecimus Scott. The two form a partnership, enjoy a brief success, and Scott enters Parliament; but their schemes are finally detected, they quarrel, and Tudor is sent to prison. After serving a short sentence, he begins a remorseful existence in Australia. Throughout the novel the rectitude of his disapproving friend and unsuccessful rival in love, Henry Norman, contrasts with Alaric's easy morality.

The worldly opportunist dominates the action in the remaining five novels. In *The Bertrams, Framley Parsonage,* and *The Small House at Allington,* George Bertram, The Reverend Mark Robarts, and Adolphus Crosbie, all young men with an eye to the main chance, manage to go astray while on trips. . . . All these ambitious young men flourish for a time but then fall, although Bertram's and Robarts' punishment apparently offers no serious check to their careers. Crosbie, however, seems permanently doomed.

However, Trollope experimented within this series, just as he did in the other group; and again he progressed from the limiting, mechanical principles of the first novels towards a freer, less contrived realism. Tudor, Robarts, and Bertram succumb to the tempters Scott, Sowerby, and Sir Henry Harcourt; and in the first four novels a young man of slow intelligence but irreproachable virtue presents a monitory contrast to the hero. In the last novels of this series, *Can You Forgive Her?* and *The Claverings,* Trollope dropped both these figures to focus instead on the character of the hero himself.

The Claverings presents an apprentice engineer and honors graduate of Oxford, Harry Clavering, who is unable to decide between the daughter of his employer and a wealthy and highly desirable widow. The novel thus centers on his entanglement with women. The clever young man of the early four novels who commits a kind of moral misdemeanor and then founders is succeeded by an equally quick-witted individual who finds himself awkwardly promised to two women. To be sure, this side of the hero's personality was hinted at in *The Three Clerks* and then considerably developed in *The Small House at Allington.* Indeed, gallantry carried to various extremes repeatedly jeopardizes the heroes' fortunes in all the later novels of this type. George Vavasor, the young man of truly desperate aspiration in *Can You Forgive Her?* is of an entirely different breed. The first of Trollope's brooding, sometimes homicidal, egocentrics, Vavasor is a brutal, self-seeking rogue, who borrows money on his fiancée's signature and attempts murder. Nevertheless, his career describes the usual trajectory, and because it is a parliamentary career, this novel is important in tracing the final evolution of the novels of this series. With the completion of *The Claverings* Trollope brought to a halt this second series. (pp. 281-82)

[Within] the period 1863-67 Trollope began to feel a certain fatigue with the pattern which had served him so well. (p. 282)

[We] may observe Trollope undertaking at this time a whole range of completely new activities, literary and otherwise, which inevitably suggest that the period 1863-67 was one of reappraisal. . . .

Perhaps the most convincing evidence that Trollope was in an experimental mood in this middle period is the novels themselves: in terms of the "A" and "B" classifications they are plainly tentative and, for the classifier, intransigent. (p. 283)

In the late "A" novels disputed inheritances were less important than Trollope's concern for certain varieties of social amelioration. Similarly, a rigid classification of the last "B" novels in terms of their earlier principles cannot be insisted on without doing violence to the main themes. Although the careerist is present, as indicated, in *The Way We Live Now, The Prime Minister,* and *The Duke's Children,* he is now of only secondary interest. In *The Way We Live Now* Trollope denounces the whole "commercial profligacy of the age." *The Prime Minister* and *The Duke's Children* are dominated by Glencora and Plantagenet Palliser, two of Trollope's favorite

characters; and in these novels their portraits are blocked out in a full and final development. . . .

In his last years Trollope quite plainly turned to new themes, and like those which occupied Dickens and George Eliot in their maturity they were themes about the rules of human conduct. In the final novels he considered a variety of moral principles; and, like Dickens in another respect, Trollope often tested these principles in very bizarre settings. Occasionally the defender of a conventional moral precept will be one of Trollope's fanatics who, obsessed with his belief, argues with maniac logic. As a result a conditional note is introduced into a discussion of values which Trollope had never questioned earlier. (p. 285)

In Trollope's last novels, . . . he departed with an uncompromising finality from the "A" and "B" patterns to pursue his ethical studies, which had by now become paramount among his interests. In the last novels we find his final comment on the problem of the old man, both as parent (*The Fixed Period* and *The Landleaguers*), and as the aged lover (*Old Man's Love* and *Kept in the Dark*). But yet we look in vain for any center to his thinking. We find no ultimate solutions, only different, sometimes extreme points of view, tinged occasionally with bitterness. . . .

Trollope may also have proposed a purely subjective bitterness. Sometimes in his novels we seem to hear echoes, often dissonant, mocking echoes, of earlier themes. A figure or an idea, treated with a seeming seriousness at first, is presented later with an almost cavalier cynicism. In *The Landleaguers* Trollope returned to Ireland and her people, the subject of his first two novels, *The Macdermots of Ballycloran* and *The Kellys and O'Kellys.* The subtitle of the second is *Landlords and Tenants;* and, led by several parallels, one cannot but wonder if the stark tone of *The Landleaguers* does not present Trollope's deliberately brutal comment on the optimism of his second novel. (p. 286)

It seems to me that this perspective of Trollope's literary habits suggests certain conclusions. Undeniably, critical opinion now favors the novels of the early period, *Barchester Towers, Framley Parsonage,* and *Doctor Thorne.* This is the period of the scoundrel who tempts the hero and of the noble young man who admonishes him, of fierce animosities which separate households and of romances which reunite them. In this same period, of course, Trollope methodically alternated his "A" and "B" types with scarcely a break in the cycle. These early and very popular novels were produced by a formula which was then still reasonably fresh. At the same time I believe that my evidence gives substantial encouragement to a thesis recently advanced by A.O.J. Cockshut, whose book is devoted to an analysis of Trollope's late novels. Seeking to remedy what he feels is a critical unbalance which now favors the early novels, he states: "It is part of my thesis that Trollope is a gloomier, more introspective, more satirical, and more profound writer than he is usually credited with being; and further, the Barsetshire series, fine as it is, is not fully characteristic of his genius." . . . (pp. 286-87)

Like the novels of the mature Dickens, Trollope's last novels, then, are "dark," they have unsuspected profundities; and, Cockshut insists, they have a merit superior to that of the early novels. In terms of Trollope's gradual abandonment of his "mechanical" devices, a reevaluation of the late novels seems called for. Within the progression of both the "A" and "B" series there is a demonstrated improvement in technique; and, of course, after the 1863-67 interval the interchange of "A" and "B" themes is somewhat less automatic. We observe, moreover, that Trollope actually passed through two experimental periods, that of 1863-67, and then a final one, which began with the publication of *Kept in the Dark*. In both periods he departed from the patterns which had brought him popularity but which later seemed sterile to him or "mechanical." The experiments of 1863-67 were unsuccessful, and he returned to his earlier models, but after 1867 he subtly introduced philosophical and social comment in a manner which he had never ventured earlier. In these later "A" and "B" novels, the themes of disputed inheritances and compulsive ambition are often subordinated or adapted to his moral speculations; and it is of these novels and those of the second experimental period that Cockshut says: "[they] are among the most complex that I know." . . .

Cockshut's analysis is purely critical and evaluative, while this paper is not; but I feel that my evidence offers a *prima facie* confirmation of his theory. Trollope's self-liberation from his earlier "mechanical" practices is one consequence of the same artistic maturity that Cockshut sees in the late novels. Essentially we are dealing with Trollope's break with auto-plagiarism after 1867; and as he progressively rejects an automatic alternation of themes, as he breaks the symbiosis between his short stories and novels, and finally as he abandons altogether the "A" and "B" models, he develops new themes and subjects. His second experimental period was not a financial success. The period of his greatest popularity had long since passed. But Trollope persisted in his new interests, and now these products of his renewed inventiveness are beginning to receive, long overdue, the kind of close scrutiny they have always deserved. (p. 287)

> *John E. Dustin, "Thematic Alternation in Trollope," in PMLA, 77 (copyright © 1962 by the Modern Language Association of America; reprinted by permission of the Modern Language Association of America), Vol. LXXVII, No. 3, June, 1962, pp. 280-88.*

WILLIAM CADBURY (essay date 1963)

[*Cadbury disputes John E. Dustin's thematic division of Trollope's novels. He challenges Dustin's conception of theme, stating that "neither the plot nor the shape of the plot is the theme, which is the product of plot, character, setting, and the various other ingredients of the novelistic world." In addition, Cadbury declares that Dustin's system ignores "the importance of origins of conflict to the development of the whole action; the number, complexity, and relatedness of the various plots; and the nature, significance, and extent of the world presented."*]

John E. Dustin has set forth [Trollope's] novels in three groups based on adherence to or divergence from two "principal sources of conflict," and this system, in its postulate of "mechanical" alternation of "themes," tells us much . . . about Trollope's methods of creation. But sources of conflict manifest themselves primarily in outlines of plot, and the bare landmarks of plot are still a function of subject matter, raw material from which the finished novel is created. A system based on one such element not only excludes the consideration of other, equally important elements, but, more significantly, ignores the effective totality of each novel. The principal component of this effective totality, something we can call "shape," is a function of the *importance* of origins of conflict to the development of the whole action; the number, complexity, and re-

latedness of the various plots; and the nature, significance, and extent of the world presented. (p. 326)

Barchester Towers and *The Belton Estate* share an origin of conflict, the dispute over inheritances of position and property, but the uses to which the dispute is put differ widely in the two books. The plot of *Barchester Towers* revolves about the ramifications of succession to episcopal power, while in *The Belton Estate* the legal entanglement is merely an introduction to the real conflict of the novel. In *Barchester Towers* the conflict is social, a matter of conflicting motivations which are resolved in the course of the book as characters with different representative stances adjust their stances to the demands of society. But in *The Belton Estate* the conflict is personal; it goes on in Clara Amedroz' head, as she tries to decide between the rival values of character presented by her two suitors, Will Belton and Captain Aylmer. . . . Nothing could be more different from the careful explication of comic political action which is both plot and theme of *Barchester Towers* than the portrayal of a character making a moral choice between moral values which lies at the heart of *The Belton Estate*. Eleanor Bold's struggle to decide between suitors links itself in every case with the suitors' struggle for political power. . . . Clara's decision, on the other hand, denies specifically the validity of political considerations, and after the first she ignores them.

The differences between the novels are as great in the other two attributes of shape I have mentioned as in importance of origin of conflict to development of plot. In complexity and relatedness of plot, *The Belton Estate* differs from *Barchester Towers* in having two carefully distinguished actions unified only by the central character's importance to both—these are Clara's choice between suitors, and the search for social acceptance by her friends the Askertons. The plot of *Barchester Towers,* on the other hand, is full of actions which overlap at every conceivable point. Although there is a rough parallel between Clara's predicament and Eleanor Bold's, Eleanor is merely a focus for the main conflicts of the novel, while the conflict in Clara is the novel itself.

Finally, the natures of the worlds presented in the two books show superficial similarity but fundamental difference. Both novels have a provincial setting, but Barchester, while different in every way from London, is a thriving, bustling city with its own character. It is perhaps more clerical than the real world, but for that very reason works admirably as a microcosm of it, drawn with the slight distortion of realism which the comic vantage allows and demands. Belton, on the other hand, is an isolated pocket of rural life in which social contact, much limited by circumstance, is of infinitely less importance than the development of the self. These characteristics *The Belton Estate* shares with *An Eye for an Eye* or *Rachel Ray,* but certainly not with *Barchester Towers, Mr. Scarborough's Family,* or even *Doctor Thorne* [as John E. Dustin claims].

The narrative materials of *Framley Parsonage* and *The Small House at Allington* are, like those of *Barchester Towers* and *The Belton Estate,* in some ways alike, since they involve divergences from virtue of two ambitious young men, Mark Robarts and Aldophus Crosbie, but the situations are again developed in quite different ways. The main source of interest, and the reader's chief concern in *The Small House,* is the relationship between Lily Dale and Johnny Eames, not Adolphus Crosbie at all, whereas *Framley Parsonage* centers on Mark Robarts. Lily Dale is basically concerned with a question of value in love, based on the opposition of heart to head; while she chooses a virgin fidelity to her first love rather than honorable marriage to her second, her situation and the intricacies of its development are closely akin to those of Clara Amedroz, and we can legitimately label *The Small House* and *The Belton Estate* as of the same type.

But here a question arises which can best be settled by an analysis of themes: Is the similarity between *The Small House* and *The Belton Estate* proof that, as has been suggested, Trollope merely plugs in new names and places to old faces? Is the common shape proof of conventional, mechanical technique? Although we might allow that the shapes of the two were produced "mechanically," this is not to allow that the pattern of values established in both books is the same, or that the values in either are simple or naive, which would be the case with the conventionally mechanical. Within the framework of a love story which is conventional enough, two similar but not identical moral problems are worked out, and the working out of the two distinguishes their themes. In *The Belton Estate* the moral problem is the difficulty of choosing between two opposed sets of values, those of conventional sensibility and accomplishment, as seen in Captain Aylmer, and those of simplicity and directness governed by a sensitive ignorance, as seen in Will Belton. In *The Small House,* on the other hand, the moral issue is fidelity in love, worked out in terms of marriages of advantage, as in the cases of Crosbie and Bernard Dale, and in terms of continuity of commitment to affection, either when that affection is rejected, as is Johnny Eames's, or when it is shown to be falsely committed, as is Lily Dale's. The two novels explicate their themes with a sensitivity that points the differences and assures us of the independent worth of each. But they are also alike, in that they present variations on the more general theme of differences between social and moral worth. They espouse entirely conventional values. . . . (pp. 326-28)

As *The Belton Estate* and *The Small House* are similar in their general theme, so both are different from *Framley Parsonage,* in which the theme derives from a different structural principle. The center of *Framley Parsonage* is the rise and fall of the career of Mark Robarts. The book is essentially picaresque, since it traces the progress of a morally misguided hero through a world not his own but one to which he would like to belong. Its plot is linear; it moves from a stable to an unstable world, and only at the end returns, with hero purged, to further untroubled country sleep. *The Small House,* on the other hand, is radial in plot; it centers on Allington and the Dales, the residents of an original country world like Framley. Lily Dale is a kind of central intelligence, in function if not in Jamesian technique, to whom are brought for judgment representatives of various values. . . . As always in picaresque, the focus of *Framley Parsonage* is determined by the physical whereabouts of Mark Robarts, and Framley is felt only dimly in the background, as a paradise lost, like Scotland in *Roderick Random.* Themes, as we have seen, are determined by the shapes of the books which create them, despite apparent similarities of character situation—Lucy Robarts, in *Framley Parsonage,* might seem in a summary of plot landmarks to have the same place as Lily Dale in *The Small House,* but the shape of *Framley Parsonage* proves her function subsidiary to that of her brother Mark. Throughout *The Small House,* on the other hand, all events have principal reference to Allington, which remains in the front of our consciousness, if not of the summary, of the action.

The theme of *Framley Parsonage,* unlike that of *The Small House,* is political action. Although moral questions are implicit (our judgment of character is inevitably on moral grounds), the central interest is in Mark Robarts' attempt to adapt his character and his morals to his circumstances through politics. In so attempting, he falsifies himself—the larger world in which he tries to move is beyond the ideals of conduct which should govern his behavior; the political action necessary to his inclusion in that world unfits him for his pastoral duties. In the end, as befits a comedy, he comes to realize his error and the home society welcomes him again. Our interest, however, has been not so much in the moral regeneration, as in the ways in which politics contrasts with duty. In this sense the book is much like *Barchester Towers,* where the conflict between our ideas of appropriate clerical action and the political maneuvering in which the characters revel is also the cause of our delight. Nothing could be more different from the reflective, internalized conflicts of *The Belton Estate* and *The Small House at Allington* than this busy, bustling, scheming world of crosscurrents of motivation, a world whose evolution is governor of both shape and theme.

If we can classify at all the four novels discussed so far, it is clear that we must, on grounds of shape and theme, include *The Belton Estate* and *The Small House* in one part of our pattern, and *Barchester Towers* and *Framley Parsonage* in the other. From this argument it can be seen that John E. Dustin . . . avoids the error of treating Trollope as all of a piece, but in the process falls into cognate errors which prevent adequate assessment of the novels. Mr. Dustin argues an impressive case for a classification of the novels based on the alternation throughout Trollope's career of what he calls "themes." The place of a novel in his system is determined by the establishment of correspondences between distillations of only the main plots of the novels, or what Mr. Dustin arbitrarily takes as the main plots. . . . [In his "A" category] he places both *Barchester Towers* and *The Belton Estate,* on the grounds that their fundamental conflicts provide "the unifying principle for the main narratives, and the action is shaped by the purely legal exigencies of the dispute." . . . We have seen that this description of crux serves admirably for *Barchester Towers,* but only distorts *The Belton Estate.* Likewise, Mr. Dustin calls *The Small House* and *Framley Parsonage* "B" novels, since in both "young men with an eye to the main chance, manage to go astray while on trips." . . . Here again we have seen that *Framley Parsonage* is accurately described, but *The Small House* is distorted. Mr. Dustin is, then, confusing origin of conflict with the shape of a finished novel; he is, moreover, confusing origin of conflict with theme. Plot developments are not themes. . . . Neither the plot nor the shape of the plot is the theme, which is a product of plot, character, setting, and the various other ingredients of the novelistic world. Theme is more accurately described as the necessary interpretation of an action than as the action itself—it is manifested by plot, but is not the plot. (pp. 328-29)

The earlier novels which we have considered have a recognizable pattern of shape and theme which allows too many significant variations to be merely mechanical. But there is in them a common characteristic which must be taken into account in forming an overall classification of all the novels. They have an unashamedly moral bent; they are exempla, establishing patterns of behavior for emulation and avoidance. They thus tend to be comic, because the wish-fulfillment ending is the rule, showing good and virtuous lives to be rewarded. In this they have, paradoxically, far more concern with plot than with character. To those whose world is being presented in moral terms (here the Victorians), somewhat simplified characterizations of the people who make up that world—like Mark Robarts or Archdeacon Grantly—will seem to be the most real, because closest to a general idea of the possibilities of character. In his later novels . . . Trollope is out of tune with his audience and less concerned with holding a mirror up to it. Again paradoxically, this situation tends to lead to an appearance of greater contrivance in plot, since the characters are less predictable and what happens to them will seem more arbitrary.

The affinities of the earlier novels are with the epic, which treats of conventional morals in plots having the inevitability of moral truth; the affinities of the later novels are with romance, which deals with events which always seem a little arbitrary, though familiar and conventional enough in their outlines. The epic novel appeals to readers as members of a group and must universalize experience in a simple way for its general audience; the romantic novel appeals to readers as individual centers of consciousness, and so is more concerned with the singularities of experience than with the generalities. Both forms present moral truth manifested in plot, but they go about it in different ways—therefore the second, no less conventional, seems more daring than the first. But the manifestation of a clearly and generally accepted value system is as neat a trick as the presentation of peculiarities of moral vision like those in **Mr. Scarborough's Family,** and it is Trollope's particular gift that he manages in the early novels to speak to a general audience with a minimum of condescension and a maximum of conviction. The moral lessons taught are no less profound for all that they mirror the Victorian compromise, which we have learned to see as not very simple after all. Our aim should be to praise Trollope's mastery of the problems of presenting his teeming world in all its complexity, as well as to praise the peculiarities of the later renegade system of values.

The praise of the late, "dark" novels is then overpraise—they represent a difference, but not necessarily an improvement, in the creation of a rich and meaningful novelistic world. The plot materials of the earlier novels may alternate mechanically, as Mr. Dustin claims, but the plot materials themselves are subordinate to other ends, and their subordination makes them the vehicles for presentation of essentially serious matter, although in a predominantly comic form. Trollope is one of the greatest users of conventional plot materials for a serious purpose before James, and it is the use to which he puts the materials, not the materials themselves, which matters. (pp. 329-30)

Trollope's novels, finally, may be seen as . . . forming a pattern of alternative constructions which vary the uses of elements of shape and theme. Recent criticism has erred like the earlier in praising only one element of Trollope's diversity, though it has admitted that the diversity exists. All elements should be praised for their proper excellences, and although we can see a general pattern of change from light to dark according with Trollope's increasing dissatisfaction with the world around him, the change was not in the forms of his fiction, all of which he had established early in his career. Like most novelists, Trollope had a repertoire of shapes and themes to meet his fictional aims. These he combined to produce forms each pleasing in its own right, each useful in illuminating a particular set of experiences and problems which Trollope saw as central to his world. (p. 332)

William Cadbury, "Shape and Theme: Determinants of Trollope's Forms," in PMLA, 78 (copyright © 1963 by the Modern Language Association of America; reprinted by permission of the Modern Language Association of America), Vol. LXXVIII, No. 4, September, 1963, pp. 326-32.

V. S. PRITCHETT   (essay date 1964)

[*Pritchett, a modern British writer, is respected for his mastery of the short story and for what critics describe as his judicious, reliable, and insightful literary criticism. He writes in the conversational tone of the familiar essay, and he approaches literature from the viewpoint of an informed but not overly scholarly reader.*]

The comfort we get from Trollope's novels is the sedative of gossip. It is not cynical gossip for Trollope himself is the honest check on the self-deceptions of his characters, on their malicious lies or interested halftruths about each other. It is he, a workaday surrogate of God, sincere, sturdy, shrewd and unhopeful, who has the key. Trollope does not go with us into the dangerous region that lies just outside our affairs and from which we draw our will to live; rather, he settles lazily into that part of our lives which is a substitute, the part which avoids loneliness by living vicariously in other people. . . . There is something fervent, even extreme, in his admiration of endurance. He was a man whose temper could flare up. His preoccupation with what is normal is the intense one of a man who has had to gain acquaintance with normality from an abnormal situation outside it. His special eccentricities are his mania for work and his passion for spending energy. From his point of view, novel writing was obsessional. It convinced him that he, the outsider in a society of powerful groups of people, was justified in being alive. Even his most contented novels leave an aftertaste of flatness and sadness. He has succeeded in his assertions, to the point of conveying a personal satiety.

The plots of Trollope and Henry James have much in common. But if we compare a novel like **The Eustace Diamonds,** one of the most ingenious of Trollope's conundrums, with, say, Henry James's *The Spoils of Poynton,* we see the difference between a pragmatic gossip and an artist of richer sensibility. Sense, not sensibility, governs Trollope; it is fine good sense and, though he lumbers along, most notable for the subtlety of its timing. He is an excellent administrator and politician of private life. But whereas James saw how the magnificent spoils of the Poynton family could corrupt by their very beauty, Trollope did not envisage anything morally ambiguous in the imbroglio of the Eustace diamonds. The *Spoils* were treasure; the **Diamonds** are property. The former are made for the moral law; the latter for the courts. (pp. 128-29)

With all his mastery, Trollope is only interested in what people are like, not in what they are for. The limitation comes out most clearly in his political novels when we see how politics work and never for what purpose, beyond those of personal career. Some critics have put down this fundamental virtue of Trollope to his good-natured and sensible acceptance of mid-Victorian society, and would say that he accepted his world just as Jane Austen accepted hers. Others—and I think Mr. Cockshut would be among them—point to his constitutional melancholy. It has the effect of devitalizing his characters. . . . If we compare the portrait of Lady Eustace with Thackeray's Becky Sharp it is interesting to see how much passivity there is in Lady Eustace and how much greater is the adventuress than the stubborn fool. Lady Eustace drifts. Her wickednesses are many, but they are small. She is little more than a tedious *intrigante* who relies on chance. She, of course, succeeds with us because of her obstinacy, her wit, her courage, her seductiveness and her beauty and because her wickedness is that of a child. (pp. 129-30)

He Knew He Was Right and *The Eustace Diamonds* are not genial books. There is something savage in them. The values of society are rotten, the people are fools, brutes or lunatics. Lady Eustace may be bad; but what are we to say of the virtuous Mrs. Hittaway, the social climber, who does not scruple in the name of virtue to employ Lady Eustace's servants to spy upon her and who is so morally exalted by her own slanders that she does not even want to consider the evidence for them? They are a nasty, money-grubbing lot, no better than they should be. Their story is redeemed and "placed" by Trollope's smiling remark that the scandal managed to keep the old Duke of Omnium alive for three months and gave everybody in London something to talk about at dinner. Trollope may be pessimistic but he was too alert a comedian to be misled into rancor. His good nature was truthful if it grew less and less hopeful. Himself morbidly subject to loneliness and boredom and capable of portraying characters who were destroyed by these evils, he never fell into exaggeration—nor indeed rose to it. (p. 132)

[The critic] must admire Trollope's knowledge of the groups in the social hierarchy. He must notice how fertilizing was Trollope's own dilemma: that he was a man of liberal mind crossed by strong conservative feeling. There remain the serious limitations that his manner is slovenly, repetitive and pedestrian, that his scene has no vividness, that—as Mr. Cockshut says—the upper steps of his moral stairway are missing, that he lacks fantasy. There will be sin but no sanctity. It is after all Lady Eustace's crime that she was not the average woman and it is supposed to be Mrs. Hittaway's justification that she is. And so, when we emerge from Trollope's world, we, at first, define him as one of the masters who enables us to recognize average life for what it is. On second thoughts, we change the phrase: we recognize that he has drawn life as people say it is when they are not speaking about themselves. (pp. 133-34)

[*The Prime Minister*] is one of the chronicler's "failures." . . . It was the penultimate volume of what Trollope considered his best work: the series which begins with *Can You Forgive Her?* and runs on to the Phineas novels. As Mr. Amery says in his introduction [to *The Prime Minister*], it raises the question of politics in the novel. The failure of *The Prime Minister* is, of course, relative; no novel containing Lady Glencora could be called dull. But this one has no personable young hero like the frank and susceptible Phineas Finn and Emily Wharton is a bit of a stick as the meek but obstinate young bride in love. On the other hand, Lopez, the speculator and fortune hunter, is a genuine figure of the age; drama is created by his shifty fingers, he is bold and credible. The only bother with Lopez is that he is made the vehicle of Trollope's peculiar dislike of "outsiders" and foreigners . . . and a hostile lecturing tone comes into Trollope's voice when he writes of him, which is absent from the portrait of that other rapscallion—Burgo Fitzgerald. Yet Trollope tries very hard to be fair to Lopez, who is presented with objective care and is never all of a piece. . . . Trollope is very accurate as a psychologist of the uncomprehending rogue; a little cynical as he shows how mad it is to think of succeeding in England if you use your imagination and disobey the rules. It is a tremendous moment when Lopez attempts to blackmail the Duke of Omnium and the best kind of surprise: the brilliant Lopez has lost his head. We had forgotten how stupid cleverness can be. Finally, in the major

conflict between the lofty-minded Prime Minister and his wife, Lady Glencora, whose whole idea is to exploit her husband's political eminence socially, there is wit, and drama too.

Where is the specific failure, then? I do not mean the general criticism of Trollope that he is commonplace, that reading him is like walking down endless corridors of carpet, restful to walk on, but in the end enervating. What is the failure within Trollope's own honest terms? . . . [Controversy] is the living breath of politics, and Trollope leaves it out altogether. He purposely makes the Duke of Omnium Prime Minister of a Coalition, in which controversy is momentarily quiet. . . . [Though] we hear in detail of the machinery of Parliament, the intrigues for safe seats, the machinations of the drawing rooms and have an excellent picture of political comedy and humbug, we have no notion of politics as anything more than a career disputed between the "ins" and the "outs." (pp. 134-36)

Trollope is a detailed, rather cynical observer of a satisfied world. Honest, assertive, sensible, shrewd, good-humored, he is content. As Henry James said, he gives us the pleasure of recognition. But content is, so to speak, a summit that he has attained, not a torpor into which he has fallen. He grew worldliness like a second skin over the raw wounds of his youth, and the reason why he describes what is normally observable about people so well, is that he longed merely for the normal. . . . We feel about his people what we feel about our relatives: the curiosity that distracts us from a fundamental apathy. The sense of danger and extremity which alert us in the warlike compositions of Jane Austen, is dulled. His novels are social history, without the movements of history; life as we see it without having to think about it. It has no significance beyond itself; it is as pleasant, dull and restful as an afternoon in an armchair. The footpads in the London parks, the frightened family of the crooked bankrupt, the suicide on the suburban line, are there, not to frighten us unduly, but to give further assurance to normal people that normality is stronger than ever. Can we wonder, in these times, at the Trollope revival? (pp. 139-40)

V. S. Pritchett, "Trollope Was Right," in his The Living Novel & Later Appreciations (*copyright © 1964, 1975 by V. S. Pritchett; reprinted by permission of Literistic, Ltd.*), *revised edition, Random House, 1964, pp. 128-40.*

BRIGID BROPHY, MICHAEL LEVEY, AND CHARLES OSBORNE (essay date 1968)

In a sense, there is nothing wrong with Trollope—but he carries it to the point where that is what is wrong with him. He is always in perfect good taste.

That cannot be blamed on his period. Both Thackeray and Dickens were—sometimes distressingly, sometimes superbly—vulgar. Trollope avoided their excesses and also (with, one feels, even more of a shudder) their excess of genius. He treads the *via media* with what might pass for an eighteenth-century dislike of enthusiasm, except that in Trollope the dislike is not backed up by a classical and penetrating intellect, with the result that the *via media* turns out to be a suburban garden path. Indeed, Trollope *is* that nice, maundering spinster lady with a poke bonnet and a taste for cottagey gardens whom superficial readers *thought* they had got hold of when they had in fact got hold of the morally sabre-toothed Jane Austen.

Trollope's plots are as shamelessly wrenched as Dickens's but Trollope unfairly escapes the accusation of melodrama by confining them to domestic and miniaturistic settings. He dodges the accusation of sentimentality by squeezing instead of jerking his tears. By writing a plainish, porridge-like prose, he *seems* to avoid the crockets of Victorian gothic: but they're there all the same. . . . Likewise he *seems* not to caricature his characters; but the broadness of his character-drawing is obscured by the small proportion he gives of dialogue to narrative. What dialogue there is belongs to the un-telling, repetitively naturalistic type, and his narrative manner is condescending. . . . (pp. 63-4)

> *Brigid Brophy, Michael Levey, and Charles Osborne, '' 'The Warden','' in their* Fifty Works of English and American Literature We Could Do Without *(copyright © 1967 Brigid Brophy, Michael Levey, Charles Osborne; reprinted with permission of Stein and Day Publishers), Stein and Day, 1968, pp. 63-4.*

LOUIS KRONENBERGER (essay date 1969)

Barchester Towers is a novel wholly concerned with clerical politics and ambitions and pulling of strings, and with the life of the clergy in the community and in society. The clergy dominate the story, to begin with, from its being laid in a cathedral town; but as a cathedral town, Barchester is as distinctly a provincial capital as another town might be a provincial political capital or a banking or manufacturing center. That is to say, the gradations of rank, the customs of society, the sources of gossip, the center of thought pivot as much on the Church as elsewhere they might on the Parliament House or the stock exchange. An ecclesiastical crisis is Barchester's biggest news. A clerical feud is Barchester's biggest social predicament. A clerical faux pas is Barchester's choicest gossip. An invitation to dine at the Bishop's can be Barchester's social event of the month; being left out of his garden party can be the social disaster of the year. Moreover, there are all the internal politics among the Barchester clergy themselves, who are as distinctly hierarchy men as there are organization men today.

Being a cathedral town, Barchester breathes a certain air of decorum that may seem to set it apart, though it is not easy for us, after a hundred years and more, and in America rather than England, to know in what degree this is clerical rather than provincial decorum, or, more than either, mid-Victorian. But it would not seem that the decorum has undue clerical roots. . . . [Though] a Barchester might be immensely concerned with church going, nothing in *Barchester Towers* suggests overwhelming feelings of piety; and though the Barchester clergy might be greatly occupied with religious observance and matters of doctrine and ritual, there is no sense of great religious dedication. If most of the clergy have a sincere sort of belief, on the ecclesiastical side they have also a sharp eye to business, and an eye turned outward, to living in the world. As members of the cloth, they wear the Church's uniform, and to a degree it conditions their behavior, not least toward their superiors; but we cannot say, as we might of an army uniform, that it fully dominates their lives.

Barchester Towers, whatever shortcomings we may tax it with elsewhere, is a first-rate chronicle of clerical worldliness. It has the interest and, indeed, leaves the impression of a *social* novel. It reflects, to be sure, ecclesiastical issues that very much agitated the England of its time, or of just before that. We are not far distant from the Oxford Movement; and we breathe, right in Barchester, the air of High and Low Church factionalism. . . . And the general High-Low issue—some-

times High enough to arouse cries of Romanism, sometimes Low enough to provoke mutterings of Chapel—was a very real and persistent one which over a long period bored into the lives of parishoners and communities. In the light of that, however, we can the better judge its relatively minor role in Trollope's novel. Principles exist, and for all the more reputable members of Trollope's clergy, principles enter in; but the preeminent struggles are for personal victories—for place, for domination, for power.

Barchester Towers is, to begin with, chiefly a social novel because of the ticklishly varying social positions of its clerical participants. Bishop Proudie, Mrs. Proudie, and Dr. Stanhope have connections with the peerage; Archdeacon Grantly is rich and locally wellborn; his father-in-law, Mr. Harding, is well enough born but not rich; Bishop Proudie's chaplain, Mr. Slope, is a fiercely ambitious parvenu; Dr. Arabin has sound roots and the prestige of Oxford behind him. The lesser clergy of the novel are, except for the Quiverfuls, significantly lesser *characters,* but the Quiverfuls are significantly so much at the bottom as to belong to another race—their hideous struggle to exist centers on feeding their half-starved bodies, not on holding up their heads in the world. . . . [We] cannot fail to note how the ill-fed Quiverfuls, as part of the plotting and politics of *Barchester Towers,* come hair's-breadth close to being tragically ill-used as well: they are more than pawns in a game of bishops and rooks; they are at moments outright catspaws.

Church politics here, if of final importance for personal ambitions and ecclesiastical policy, merge with drawing-room contretemps. *Barchester Towers* is in the great English tradition of the social novel by being often a comedy of manners, very particularly of bad manners. This means that, however prominent the clerical collar, the Victorian bustle will very likely be more so. Mary Bold is the heroine of the book, with all the hub-like position of a heroine. She is the daughter of Mr. Harding, round whom rages the matter of the wardenship he has resigned; she is the sister-in-law of Dr. Grantly, the wealthy, doughty, opinionated archdeacon in command of the established High Church forces; she is, as an attractive widow of means, the object of Mr. Slope's matrimonial attempts and of Bertie Stanhope's matrimonial scheming; and she is the object, finally, of Dr. Arabin's love and desire. But though she is the heroine of the book, she is no vital part of its social comedy or political drama; it is Madeline Neroni and Mrs. Proudie who are memorable on these accounts, the first as a kind of disabled *femme fatale,* the other as a kind of overbearing *grande dame.* Mrs. Proudie is by all odds the book's most vivid character, and for long periods is its dramatic center, for she is not only the Bishop's wife, with all that signifies of social prestige, the Bishop is distinctly Mrs. Proudie's husband, with all that implies, for her, of political power. . . . [It is she] whom we have to thank for some of the best comedy of bad manners, and even the drama. Mrs. Proudie is an excellent kind of stage figure, whom Trollope has tailored to a particular role: she has real convictions about the Church and an interest in its concerns; she is not at all frivolous and has no wish to be fashionable, nor to have tea-table or dinner-party triumphs. Trollope tailors her, however, for a particular role without depriving her of a general one: of the dictatorial, interfering *grande dame,* cousin if not sister to Jane Austen's Lady Catherine and Wilde's Lady Bracknell.

Barchester Towers is a social novel, again, for portraying clerical life in terms of community life, the two things in a sense running parallel. A different kind of novelist . . . might make use of the community life to portray the clerical problems, or the clerical conscience, or the fight *against* worldliness and its temptations. And *it* would be very little a social novel. If *Barchester Towers* is very much one, the reason, very simply, is that Anthony Trollope is a social novelist. But that in no way denies the relevancy or truthfulness of his picture, or the fact that one whole side of the Church of England was a social organism and that in varying degrees a clergyman of that Church was a social animal. . . . That there is much more talk of parties in *Barchester Towers* than of prayer is one evidence of how true to life the book is. That Miss Thorne's fête champêtre occupies eighty pages of the book is, I grant, partly to be accounted for because it lets Trollope do a number of things, by way of story and background, that he wants to do. All the same, it truthfully illustrates the importance to the community of a party given by the most exalted member of it.

The hierarchical nature of clerical life in a cathedral town, with its own forms of rank and prestige, also brings into play the class structure of English life generally; it is not accidental that those in the upper strata of the hierarchy are in the upper strata of society as well, with most of the lesser clergy given just such walk-on roles as they would have occupied in Trollope's day. The great exception is Mr. Slope, and in Mr. Slope we get a good many of our thematic traits. We get first, in the best traditions of the social novel, the man on the make. But Mr. Slope is not simply a social climber who wants to make a good marriage and to sit at the right dinner tables; he is a clerical careerist who would sit very high in the Church and have not just position, but power. Mr. Slope is nothing more than Bishop Proudie's chaplain, and is that as Mrs. Proudie's protégé. Accordingly he needs to be a courtier as well as a politician; to insinuate himself to the point where he can manipulate others, then manipulate others to the point where he can install himself.

Climber and politician, he is also a hypocrite. I don't know that there is anything insincere in his Low Church views themselves. . . . But, however sincere, his clerical views must always ride pillion to his personal ambitions, and his views become blurred from looking in so many careerist directions at once. In any case, his doctrinal views are never reinforced by religious or ethical feelings, are not even tinged with honest bigotry. In the moral sense he seems, for being a churchman, all the more offensively ambitious and scheming. To be sure, his sliminess and utter lack of principle make him out at times almost too bad to be true, and almost too bad to be successful. Yet, overdrawn though he is, and tending though he may be to overreach himself, a good deal of him might be true, and the man as a whole is not untypical. But the psychological side of Mr. Slope, whatever its importance to Trollope's story, is not of great importance to our theme: what Mr. Slope tends to illustrate is a persisting ambitiousness in the Church of England's clergy. . . . Mr. Slope is no Trollopian Tartuffe; he is a representative figure. Moreover, his own crudities and unprincipledness, recalling to us his difficulties as a flagrant outsider, remind us of the smoother worldliness, the more sanctified plotting of the Dr. Grantlys. The Church of England very particularly offers careers to gentlemen because it is the Church of gentlemen, the lower-born qualifying for more dissentient and nonconformist theologies. But, as the Church of gentlemen, it attracts those who, like Mr. Slope, want secular rewards as well as ecclesiastical power. For, as the Church of gentlemen, it is also the Church of wealth. (pp. 222-29)

Trollope's own attitude is the realist's, not the reformer's. He is conversant with the world he treats of, which he portrays in

the form of comedy. He is in a fair degree critical of the world he treats of, which he impugns in the form of satire. He is not a master psychologist; he has no revolutionizing insights into man's inner nature. But he has much knowledge of general human nature and of how it is modified by particular environments and social climates. He knows our strongest desires and ambitions, our recurrent feelings and reactions, our likeliest masks and pretenses. He knows, above all, the Englishness of his people, which can mean all that is smug, ambitious, mealy-mouthed in Barchester, and in how many questionable ways these people can regard one another, judge one another, play-act for one another's benefit, conspire for one another's good or ill. His portrayal often constitutes an exposure but is almost never a protest. The impression he leaves is of social realism, social comedy, and satire—the way of the world in cathedrals as well as in clubs or country houses. And at times it offers, too, the way of the world among writers of fiction. "The end of a novel," Trollope begins the last chapter of *Barchester Towers,* "must be made up of sweetmeats and sugar-plums." This is but to echo the deliberately shameless happy ending of [John Gay's] *The Beggar's Opera* and to make us feel, just a little, that the author has joined hands with his own main-chance characters. But the fault with Trollope is perhaps less moral than artistic; there is something of the mere storyteller about him as well as a much larger element of the novelist. Certainly *Barchester Towers* is a true novel. Some of its cathedral-town atmosphere and detail has been questioned; but to an outsider, and after the lapse of a century, it has, I think, documentary as well as dramatic truth about it—which is to say that while particular characters and scenes palpably smack of fiction, the general scene seems rooted in fact, as the comedy of it seems ringed with criticism. (pp. 231-32)

> *Louis Kronenberger, "'Barchester Towers'," in his* The Polished Surface: Essays in the Literature of Worldliness *(copyright © 1969 by Louis Kronenberger; reprinted by permission of Alfred A. Knopf, Inc.), Knopf, 1969, pp. 217-32.*

JAMES GINDIN (essay date 1971)

Trollope's vision did not simply center on the creation of an island where all is ultimately ordered and happy. He began his literary career with three novels dominated by melodramatic intrigue. And even the Barchester series, from which the stereotype of Trollope's order is usually drawn, develops an interest in the psychology of people, in the complexities of their actions and reactions to others, and in the difficulties involved in judging them. Josiah Crawley, for example, the parson whose thorny integrity defies the society trying to help him, carries implications about human experience that go well beyond easy generalizations about the balms of gentle Barsetshire. Trollope's later work, however, the work of his last fifteen or twenty years, most clearly illustrates his far wider concerns and sympathies. This width is particularly visible in the social, political and psychological issues that help to shape the series called **"The Palliser Novels,"** . . . although almost all of Trollope's work from the mid-1860's until his death in 1882 demonstrates this deeper version of individual and social concern. (pp. 28-9)

[*An Autobiography*] reveals far less of the author's insight and sympathy than do many of his novels. His best work often modified the generalization or questioned the virtue it was trying to establish, but Trollope also sought in fiction the end he spoke of in *An Autobiography:* the arrangement of his characters and events around an ethical principle that could serve as a lesson. Always trying to describe the "good" man or the characteristics that made him "good," always concerned with matching his young lovers appropriately to people who deserved each other, Trollope attempted to demonstrate the importance of principles as simple and ancient as honesty, independence, concern for others. That his novels, at their best, seem to go beyond these principles, demonstrate a vitality, a sense of compassion, and an understanding far more searching than anything the principles demand, is not a statement designed to demonstrate that Trollope was a hasty or indifferent craftsman, nor a claim that he was unconscious of his sympathy and skill. Rather, the novels, more than instructive schemes, develop a comprehensiveness beyond their apparent boundaries.

Trollope's lessons were often involved with preserving order both in individual lives and in society, although he understood and charted both disruptive personal passion and disruptive public change. He was likely to satirize tenacious and inflexible allegiance to a past order, both personal and public, as in the character of Sir Roger Carbury in *The Way We Live Now* . . . , but a sense of order and control remain virtues even within a changing world or a personality exploring itself. As they introduce Trollope's world, the novels postulate a stratified and ordered society. (pp. 31-2)

More important than the world Trollope initially assumes is the demonstration in the endings of his novels of a sense of society's order. Trollope's novels are not instances of the open form. Questions are always resolved; balances restored; society summarized as, if not always just, always yielding a kind of rational sense. And seldom, in the later novels, is the resolution superficial—merely a luckily inherited fortune or a just dispensation by a higher power. Phineas Finn gets the career and the wealthy woman he has worked so hard for; in *The Prime Minister,* Lopez commits suicide and liberates his wife, Emily, to judge men and issues more soundly, and to marry the man she should have married in the first place. . . . The sense of acceptance at the conclusion of Trollope's novels does not always involve perfect happiness or complete moral justice; acceptance is a recognition of the way things are in a world where individual and social considerations must be carefully balanced.

Another indication of Trollope's emphasis on the need for order in human affairs is his enormous fear of (and, not surprisingly, fascination with) emotional violence and excess. Just under the surface a number of Trollope's characters and scenes give a sense of possible excess that might, if unchecked, tear the society apart. The Othello theme, the dangers of thwarted and excessive feelings, obviously fascinated Trollope, a fact apparent both in *An Autobiography* and in frequent references in the novels. Particularly in *The Prime Minister,* Trollope often compares his characters at their weakest moments, their moments of least rationality or control, to characters in [William Shakespeare's] *Othello.* (pp. 32-4)

Excessive intensity is not, in Trollope's terms, always to be equated with violence, for, although many of the object lessons about what is to be avoided are both intense and violent, other violent characters, such as John Crumb, the stalwart farmer in *The Way We Live Now,* and Lord Chiltern, the honest huntsman in the Palliser series, are highly praiseworthy. Violence is acceptable if it is sporadic, hot-blooded, an honest reaction to understandable circumstances, as it is for both John Crumb and Lord Chiltern. The violence that damns, for Trollope, is

the cold, the narcissistic, the calculated, the kind of intensity that rages inside, like that of Felix Carbury or Mr. Kennedy, and acknowledges no compromise or forgiveness. This unyielding intensity, this sense of excess, this kind of cold and intransigent self-assurance, destroys both the personal and social order so important in Trollope's fictional world.

Trollope's sense of order attempts to accommodate the complexity of human experience, but the sense of order and the awareness of complexity often work against each other. For example, Trollope's plots frequently pose the ancient question: should a young woman marry for love or for money? In one sense, marrying for money, along with all the social and parental approval that money implies, seems to support the idea of order, the idea of a stable basis for society's relationships. Yet, in another sense, for Trollope, marrying for love suggests a deeper order, a deeper sense of the importance of human relationships that should be established and conveyed to the next generation. . . . Trollope's ethical scheme grants approval only to those who marry for love. (pp. 36-7)

Treatment of women and their choices in the marriage market is not the only way in which the complexities of Trollope's world qualify his announced intention of providing guides for ethical conduct. Trollope's kind of satire often begins as the label, tag, or stereotype, the quick designation appropriate to pointing the lesson. Yet, frequently, even in the early Barchester series and more often in the later work, Trollope's quick labelling satire is funny only when one first encounters it, for he soon switches to explore a deeper humanity behind the stereotype. (p. 41)

[In] all Trollope's novels, money is tremendously important. Characters love and hate, assume airs and puncture them, but they are always aware of living in a world in which financial security matters. Many of the men who go down into the City or to the Law Courts to make money are worthy gentlemen. Trollope always admires hard and purposeful work. Cautious old Abel Wharton in *The Prime Minister* may seem rather penurious at first, but, after we see him working hard to accumulate his money, painfully parting with it, piece by piece, to try to bribe happiness for his daughter in a disastrous marriage he opposed in the first place, we are made to feel a good deal of sympathy for him. (p. 44)

The principal problem in almost all Trollope's later work, from *The Last Chronicle of Barset* . . . to *Ayala's Angel* is that of judgment, of learning to understand and evaluate the worth of all the varying issues and individuals one sees around him. Sometimes, as in *The Way We Live Now,* the questions of judgment are posed for the reader, leaving him skeptical and wondering if any clear guides for conduct can be extrapolated from the experience of the novel. At other times, Trollope (fairly early in the novels) gives the reader the standards on which the characters are to be judged, establishes a kind of ideal, but then depicts a world in which no one understands the issues as the author does, in which everyone, at least for a time, misjudges a central character or situation. This latter kind of novel, less completely skeptical than the other, still underlines the tremendous difficulty involved in establishing any applicable guide for ethical conduct. In *The Prime Minister,* for example, Trollope plants sufficient clues concerning Lopez' unprincipled exploitation of others early in the novel, but we gradually discover how and when the rest of society will see through him. The interest is in the process of coming to know, rather than in the suspense of what is to be known. . . . The whole texture of *The Way We Live Now* is one of misjudgment, and emphasizes our inability to use any known gauge to measure the worth of the characters in the novel. Financial and social reputations are governed by rumor and half-apprehended hint; the origins and principles of Melmotte are unknown; trusted people in responsible positions suddenly vanish with other people's money; Mrs. Hurtle has been violent and scheming, but we wonder if she really did kill a man and, more significantly, could kill another if provoked sufficiently. Even the kind of character supposedly easy to peg, the spoiled and indolent young aristocrat, is hard to judge, for the two principal examples in the novel, Adolphus Longestaff and young Lord Nidderdale, turn out to be very different from each other and Lord Nidderdale is far from the original cliché. In a novel in which almost everyone changes character, shifts opinions and convictions, only gradually discovers what he is and what his motives are, the dominant impression is that of the great difficulty and loneliness the sensible person undergoes in trying to find his way through contemporary experience. (pp. 47-9)

Trollope, in the later novels, places far more emphasis on man's accepting what he has to accept than on his establishing ethical principles that apply universally. And because man, half-ignorant and prone to mistakes, has to accept his world out of necessity, Trollope maintains a sense of compassion toward most human creatures. Especially toward the end of his career, the compassion dominates the novels, dominates them in direct proportion to the recognition that a meaningful code of virtue cannot be followed and applied within the unjust world. Compassion is a matter of emphasis, an attitude that fills the void left by all the codes, guides, and formulae that are inadequate for human experience. In the perspective of Trollope's later novels, only the very wise and the very fortunate could make their way successfully through a world that offered unequal possibilities. Man had no power to change his world, and, even if he had, he had no assurance that the changes would not involve inequities at least as great, or conditions that would destroy just as many individuals. He could only accept, follow whatever forms of order he could see and apply, remain resilient, and sympathize.

This kind of compassion was not entirely new with Trollope. . . . [In] the early novel, generally molded more by the instructive lesson than was the drama, writers like Jane Austen had substituted compassion for what they could not justify as truth. Yet, in Trollope's world, the emphasis on compassion increased, accelerated, as the attempt to provide lessons or guides for conduct became increasingly difficult to sustain. (p. 50)

Trollope writes most skillfully and profoundly when describing his characters interacting with one another, each helping to define and illuminate the other. The relationship between the Duke of Omnium and his Duchess, Lady Glencora, for example, is rich, complex, and humane. Lady Glencora had originally stayed with the Duke, in defiance of her love for Burgo Fitzgerald, because of the pressure of society and propriety. The pressure, in part, made the marriage work, and the constant memory of this makes the Duke, after Lady Glencora has died, apply so much pressure on his daughter to try to force his will to follow his will. Yet Trollope deliberately avoids the generalization. The kind of pressure that is desirable and that works in one instance is both undesirable and ineffective in another; people and circumstances differ. This realization of complexity allows Trollope to trace the constant shuttling, the constant turns of position and attitude that go on within a marriage. He carefully develops the marriage of the Duke and the Duchess

from its arranged beginnings in *Can You Forgive Her?*, through storms and the establishment of mutual although distant respect, to the genuine love and concern in *The Prime Minister*. (p. 51)

Trollope's kind of compassion, particularly in the work of his last fifteen years, seldom degenerates into sentimentality, is seldom shallow or superficially comforting. Rather, the later work gives an extensive and profound description of man as he relates to and operates in his social setting. The acute problems of man himself and man in society are depicted, despite all the gentle comedy and some of the apparently smooth resolutions. If, at times, the acceptance of society seems shallow or the conviction that it is impossible to change man and society seems shoddily developed or sentimentally conservative, still Trollope's acceptances and resolutions never obscure the relevance of the questions as he poses, as well as the fact that the questions have no complete or fully satisfactory answer. As in a great deal of fiction, from Jane Austen's to that of numerous twentieth century contemporaries, the questions are far more memorable than the resolutions. And, in Trollope's fiction, the range of the questions, the skepticism, prevents sentimentality. The resolutions become the graceful and compassionate means of emphasizing that, for most people, for all save the accidentally fortunate, the difficult questions—the social and personal displacements, the injustices—really have no answer. (p. 56)

James Gindin, "Trollope," in his Harvest of a Quiet Eye: The Novel of Compassion *(copyright © 1971 by Indiana University Press), Indiana University Press, 1971, pp. 28-56.*

RUTH ᴀᴘROBERTS   (essay date 1971)

[*apRoberts's study calls for a new approach to Trollope's work that integrates an analysis of his art with his moral concerns. In the portion excerpted below, she expresses dissatisfaction with older theories of fiction which she finds inadequate for an appreciation of Trollope. "Of all English novelists," she states, "Trollope seems to be the perfect example of the kind least served by our old theories." She turns to Phillip Rahv's essay, "Fiction and the Criticism of Fiction," published in* Kenyon Review, *1956, which argues against applying the aesthetic criteria of poetry to fiction. Although symbolism, style, and technical excellence are essential to poetry, according to Rahv, these are not valid standards for fiction. apRoberts's examination of Trollope's novels employs Rahv's theory: she praises Trollope's artistry while concluding that his work exhibits few of the qualities considered essential to poetry. apRoberts's study supports the arguments presented by Joseph E. Baker (1954), Geoffrey Tillotson (1961-62), and David Aitkins (see Additional Bibliography), and challenges David Cecil (1934).*]

There is something of a mystery in the case of Anthony Trollope. His novels constitute a phenomenon of acknowledged success and importance, but still go largely unexplained. Accepted, admired, and—above all—*read*, read widely and in depth . . . , by the sort of people who like to be able to explain things to themselves, people whom you can hardly call naïve, the novels have nevertheless not yet earned the dignity of a rationale. Trollope himself defended '**English Prose Fiction as a Rational Amusement**' [see excerpt above, 1870], and we might try to do the same by him. Not that we can pluck out the heart of his mystery, but we might be able to circumscribe, define, and perhaps reduce the mystery to a certain extent. I think the chances of some success are better now than they were; the inadequacies of our older theories of fiction have become embarrassing, and there have been many new openings made, and castings about for more serviceable aesthetics of fiction. . . . Of all English novelists Trollope seems to be the perfect example of the kind least served by our old theories; and for this very reason, to come to grips with his work may help us towards a new and more workable theory. In what way do his novels succeed for reasons that James, or Lubbock, or Leavis, do not recognise? By trying to answer this, we may do Trollope a service, and at the same time discover some things hitherto neglected in the study of the novel as genre. (pp. 11-12)

Philip Rahv, in 'Fiction and the Criticism of Fiction,' a good instance of a new kind of thinking about the novel, explains that the trouble lies in what has been an effort 'to deduce a prosaics from a poetics.' The effort to apply the criteria of poetry to fiction has saddled us with—he says—three critical biases, which have made us swerve off in various wrong directions. (pp. 14-15)

Trollope makes a good test case for Rahv's anti-poetics position. He is the least symbolic of novelists; he is least of a 'stylist'; and he exhibits little of those technical excellences the formalists admire beyond all else. I should like to suggest that on each of these counts he is all the more the artist of the novel proper, and we can characterise his particular art on each count.

Let us take him first as a non-symbolist. There are certainly symbols in Trollope's work, as there are in any phase of human life. But I think it can be said he is as little symbolic as an artist in words can be. The symbols we find in Trollope are symbols for his characters rather than for us. Certainly, his people make use of non-verbal communication. When Will Belton the farmer sends a courting present to Clara Amedroz, he makes his point eloquently. The present is, of all things, a cow. A real cow, particularly real. And the warm, pretty, milky thing is a good token of the earthiness of Will's real passion, clearly contrasted to the frigidity of Clara's other suitor, Captain Aylmer. The Captain's tepid and vacillating courtship, his avoidance of physical contact, and his subservience to his mother, all perfectly indicate his sexual inadequacy. Will is a little short on verbal eloquence and finds the cow an effective solution to the communication problem. The cow speaks to Clara; but he, Trollope, speaks to us in words. He glories in his own verbalism. His forte is the de-symbolising of things for us, clear, terse verbal exposition, often so witty that we hardly realise we have apprehended a subtle psychological fact. Joseph E. Baker quotes a good example of this in a stout-hearted and useful attempt to pin down Trollope's quality. He calls it 'Trollope's Third Dimension' and the passage he quotes [from *The Small House of Allington*] tells us something of the Countess de Courcy. . . .

> 'I dare say it will come to nothing,' said the countess, who liked to hear of girls being engaged and then losing their proposed husbands. She did not know she liked it, but she did; and already had pleasure in anticipating poor Lily's discomfiture. . . .

Surely there is something here that we can all recognise as the way a human being sometimes functions; and we may well recognise we have never had it anatomised before. Nothing is suggested, or connoted, or invoked, or adumbrated. It is precise descriptive analysis, verbal, plain and unequivocally clear. It may be that Trollope's 'third dimension,' his mysterious power,

is in fact plain non-metaphoric exposition. This is a possible excellence in fiction that we are not much used to respecting or analysing. Examples are everywhere in Trollope's work. Take, for instance, the occasion of an argument between Archdeacon Grantly and his wife [in *The Last Chronicle of Barset*]. The Archdeacon thought, at such times, 'that his wife took an unfair advantage of him by keeping her temper.' . . . We are inclined to enjoy these things, and ticket them as merely funny. But they are not *mere* at all. They are very important, and they are Trollope's quality, because they are really brilliant discoveries in psychology, recorded in baldest terms. We experience the joy of discovery in these analytical statements, that are witty just because they are both terse and true.

His method of descriptive analysis of the workings of men and women leaves no room for the novelistic set piece of 'description.' The early *Macdermots of Ballycloran* comes closest to it, perhaps: in it, Trollope does set a scene of the decay and ruin of real estate, for the playing out of a tragic story of the decay and ruin of a family. But in the main body of his work, this is not his way. There are virtually no atmospheric descriptions and no pathetic fallacies. He gives you a bald circumstantial description of a country house or a village because you have to know the geography to understand the action. Or he describes the furnishings of Madame Max Goesler's apartment because it helps to explain her character and her attractiveness. (pp. 15-18)

[What] description there is in Trollope is directly functional as exposition. No scene is written to put us in a mood, as music can; no coiling ubiquitous fog alerts us to a theme; no dust-heap suggests the corrupting power of riches. No sacred number suggests to us the Trinity or the Stations of the Cross. Trollope is, of all writers, the least legitimate ground for the search for symbols. (p. 18)

So much for Rahv's first count, the count of symbolism. On his second count, stylism, there is more to say, and some of it has recently been said, and said well. Already there is a new view of Trollope's style that stands in declared opposition to the old stylism Rahv deplores, and the new view indicates the trend both in Trollope studies and in critical theory. The main traditional pronouncement used to be that Trollope's style is plain, dull, and flat. Lord David Cecil goes so far as to say it is *nothing*. Trollope has *no style*. And of course this is taken to be a lack, a fault, a failing. (p. 19)

The old objections to his *nothing* style have recently been rejected. The most thoroughgoing rejection is David Aitkin's 'A Kind of Felicity'. . . . Aitkin demonstrates the apparent effortless simplicity of the writing, and the informality of the vocabulary, and the occasional spells of formal or ponderous words which were partly the doubtful humour of the time, partly Trollope's own little game. . . . [On] the whole, Aitkin insists, imagery is 'rather unimportant in the general scheme of his art.' Many of his images are repeated so often, and are so commonplace anyway—I would add to Aitkin's comment—that they simply do not function as images; the world is one's oyster, the beautiful woman is the candle to the moth, people row in the same boat, and so on. I might further add that this is a way Chaucer also had, in his stories—to draw on the common stock of conventional figures of speech. Such images are hardly what we are used to calling poetic, as all they do is maintain an air of comfortable ordinariness between teller and reader. And certainly the sum of all these things Aitkin remarks indicates a style that pointedly refuses to call attention to itself. Trollope scorns the novelist 'who thinks much of his words as he writes.' As though to support Philip Rahv, Trollope himself makes clear that he is speaking of fiction when he says this; he himself is quite clear that the case of poetry is altogether different. (pp. 20-1)

Can it be we have been so attuned to poetic style that we have been unable to appreciate an achievement in discursive statement, in prose? So often Trollope's rather tongue-in-cheek comments on his methods have been taken at face value; we have believed his work is like that of the shoemaker he is forever comparing himself to, when all he intends is to deflate the waiting-for-inspiration theory of composition, and to recommend a valiant discipline. Because his prose is easy to read, and because it was produced on time, we think it must have been easy to write. It is so simple and so clear that we incline to slight it. Of course that is just what he aimed at. He *masters complexity;* he makes us forget the words while we apprehend effortlessly the most tenuous delicacies of nuance in psychology, or social situations of the most extreme complexity. We grasp these and then cheat him of his praise, for he distracts us from the manner with his matter. It is a technique he practised tirelessly; every day he whittled and sharpened it. One can still see the journeyman in *The Warden* and *Barchester Towers;* here is manner and archness and uncertainty, at times. But the later writing hardly ever falters in its efficiency. Trollope himself says, in the terms of the latest technology of his day, 'The language used should be as ready and as *efficient* a conductor of the mind of the writer to the mind of the reader as is the electric spark which passes from one battery to another.' And again, *lucid,* or the intensive *pellucid,* is the word he uses most often to describe the best way for the novelist to write. *Lucid.* Let the medium be as glass, through which everything shows clear. Let the medium be as *nothing.* Trollope, says Lord David Cecil, has *no style.*

Tillotson says Trollope's style is like Dr. Johnson's. And he thinks that Dr. Johnson, much as he deprecated novels, would have approved of Trollope's. I think so too. Trollope does not offend in the way Johnson considered his contemporaries in the novel to offend. Johnson and Trollope have a similar sense of the decorous; they are both devoted conventional Anglicans, both great moralists; they both combine a grand and wide humour with a sympathetic sense of the tragic in life, and a sense of the doubleness of things. . . . Actually, Trollope himself tells us . . . who his master is.

> I hold that gentleman to be the best dressed whose dress no one observes. I am not sure but that the same may be said of an author's written language. Only, where shall we find an example of such perfection? Always easy, always lucid, always correct, we may find them; but who is the writer, easy, lucid and correct, who has not impregnated his writing with something of the personal flavour we call mannerism? To speak of authors well-known to all readers— Does not *The Rambler* taste of Johnson; *The Decline and Fall,* of Gibbon; . . . *The History of England,* of Macaulay . . .? I have sometimes thought that Swift has been nearest to the mark of any—writing English and not writing Swift.

That is what Trollope aimed at—the style so *lucid* that it does not show at all, writing which refuses attention to the words. By reason of this, 'the reality portrayed,' the *stuff* of the novel, is so much more insistently itself. (pp. 22-4)

I think it very significant that [Trollope's critics] have concertedly but independently overthrown the old stylism that Philip Rahv deplores. The plain, dull, flat style, the no-style style, has been declared to be a positive artistic advantage; in refusing to draw attention to itself it can the better display the reality of the content. We must once more deny the old idea of Trollope as a naïve writer. He knows what he is doing, in style as in other matters. The agreed-on excellence of his characterisation depends in fact on an extraordinarily subtle sense of styles. The vulgar Major Pountney addresses Plantagenet Palliser on the subject of his country seat at Matching:

> 'A noble pile, my Lord,' said the Major, stretching his hand gracefully towards the building.
>
> 'It is a big house,'

answers Palliser [in **The Prime Minister**]. . . . One feels it is only Trollope who could have so sharply ticked off these two characters in confrontation. (p. 26)

Albert Cook, another good instance of the new kind of thinking about fiction, is [a] rebel against technicism. James, Flaubert, and Lubbock, he says [in his *The Meaning of Fiction*], all 'begged the whole question of content.' Cook insists on an 'inductive approach to see the meaning of fiction through the whatness of individual novels.' His studies lead him to a very anti-formalist position: he suggests, at last, that the novel is the one genre which does not need 'good' structure. Indeed, 'the greater reality which the novelist discovers, the larger and more open his plots are likely to be.' Anyone acquainted with Trollope will be reminded that his plots are as 'large and open' as plots can be; that he never lays any claim to 'good' structure, and critics have not claimed it for him; that, at the same time, he seems to 'discover the greatest reality.' Dickens' plots can be said to be *large,* but perhaps not *open:* he aims for some sort of drum-roll conclusion and a falling curtain at the end. And although his plots may be bad, they are nevertheless an important element in his novels. George Eliot likes to end a novel with a bang—the flood ending of *The Mill on the Floss,* for example, is troublesome because it cheats the reader somewhat, as too easy a solution to the problem set up. Even *Middlemarch,* the most Trollopian of her novels, the largest and most open in plot, ends somewhat too pat, with a glimpse of the Comtean millennium. But Trollope will not sacrifice his realism to a tight plot or a pat ending. His comments on Wilkie Collins [in **An Autobiography**] reveal his own views on this. 'The novelist has other aims than the elucidation of his plot.' He admires the beautiful dovetailing of Collins' plots, but, he says, 'I can never lose the taste of the construction.' He cannot do such plots himself, he says, but it is perfectly clear that he does not want to, either. In him we see the high correlation of realism with the loose plot, the correlation Cook claims as a mark of kind of excellence in fiction. In fact, there seems to be no novelist that flouts more than Trollope those formal beauties we used to admire, and for this very reason, again, Trollope is the more liable to be useful to us as we try to discover new theory. (pp. 28-9)

[Just] as novelists have been admitted into our Pantheon for the effectiveness of their propaganda, so also have they been admitted for what we call Serious Thought. If a Victorian novel deals with Faith and Doubt urgently enough we put it on our literature list, even if it is a deadly novel. . . . [But propaganda] and doctrine and religious problems do not dignify Trollope's work. Perhaps in him, then, the art of the novel proper may be less dilute, and may better repay our study. Because we have not been able to talk about him in those non-aesthetic categories, and because our poetics-aesthetic has kept him out of ART, we have hardly known what to do with him. So we just read him. (pp. 29-30)

The investigation of [Trollope's] art is overdue. In sum, it is just because past criticism has failed so conspicuously with him that he may be highly useful to us in our attempts to evolve a new criticism. Just because he least lends himself to discussion of allegory and symbol, just because his style is the least of styles, and he appears deficient in the qualities called formal: just because he is no propagandist, and does not display 'Philosophy'—just because of all these things—Trollope is now our man. Maybe he can epitomise for us anew the Art of the Novel. (p. 31)

> *Ruth apRoberts, in her* The Moral Trollope (© *Ruth apRoberts 1971; reprinted by permission of Ohio University Press, Athens), Ohio University Press, 1971, 203 p.*

C. P. SNOW (essay date 1971)

[Trollope] was essentially and above all a psychological novelist: that is, he was preoccupied not with the Victorian scene which he observed so sensibly and took for granted, but with individual human beings and how they thought and felt. The difference in stress is patent, once and for all, in the first chapter of *Barchester Towers*. Trollope is well informed about the structure of a cathedral close. He is prepared to tell us how bishops operate and what a change of bishop may mean: but that isn't anywhere near the point. What he is really driving at, and this is true of all his most original work, is the need to understand Archdeacon Grantley. There he is, at what may be his father's death bed: he is deeply attached to his father: if his father dies, there is a chance that he may get his job: what is really, at all kinds of what we nowadays call levels, passing through his mind?

Which leads to a technical problem to which he, like all psychological novelists, had to find his own kind of solution. How do you express what is passing through anyone's mind? Not only in critical circumstances, such as Archdeacon Grantley's, but in any field of mental existence, when something is happening in each person's mind. What is it like? Flow or plasma or discontinuous jumps? How much does its nature vary from person to person? . . . How much is it to be communicated in words? How much is that worth doing? (pp. 10-11)

Trollope didn't find an elaborate way round [these problems] in the manner of Dostoyevskiy or Proust. His own mind was too direct for that. Things went on in people's thoughts, and had to be communicated—so one must have a shot at it. But it would not have occurred to him, even if he had written at a later period in the novel's history, to attempt a record of moment-by-moment mental events. Not that he was naïve: few men less naïve have ever lived. He was interested, however, in other mental activities: if he had thought about it at all, he would have assumed that a study of the immediate present . . . would cut out all in which he was most interested. Which was, in fact, the elements in mental processes which result in any moral choice and moral action.

It was for this purpose that he developed a form of psychological streaming. . . . (p. 13)

But that is irrelevant here. Trollope was not concerned about the present moment. He was trying to suggest the present experience *as it might be considered later* and as it impinged upon future action.

He loses something in the process: but any attempt to render mental experience loses something in the process. What he did not lose was what he most—or, at times, exclusively—wanted to do: that is, tell a continuous psychological history leading to a set of moral choices. For that, in its more sophisticated forms, his device of the psychological stream is beautifully adapted. The sedateness, the gentility, the steadiness, are all deceptive. No writer was more interested in psychological drama. It is that, and not the flavour of nostalgia, which makes him one of the most obsessively readable of novelists.

The lesson of **The Three Clerks** is that he found his way to a method which ultimately fitted, hand in glove, into the requirements of psychological drama. It looks so easy. No one has yet found a method which would have suited his purpose better. (pp. 15-16)

> *C. P. Snow, "Trollope: The Psychological Stream" (© C. P. Snow, "Trollope: The Psychological Stream," 1971; reprinted by permission of Curtis Brown Ltd., London, on behalf of the Literary Estate of C. P. Snow), in* On the Novel: A Present for Walter Allen on His 60th Birthday from His Friends and Colleagues, *edited by B. S. Benedikz, J. M. Dent & Sons Ltd, 1971, pp. 3-16.*

P. D. EDWARDS (essay date 1977)

> [*Edwards asserts that there are "two streams running through Trollope's work": the stream of everyday life and the more sensational stream of, in Trollope's words, "great and glowing incidents." Unlike such critics as J. Herbert Stack (1869), Henry James (1883), and Bradford A. Booth (1958), who maintain that Trollope's focus was the ordinary, Edwards stresses the importance of the sensational in Trollope's work. He concludes that Trollope's "unexcitable levelness of tone, his lumbering, strictly sequential unfolding of plot, his sameness of style in novel after novel have blinded most readers to the variety of his subject-matter and especially to his fondness for the sensational, the morally macabre, the exotic."*]

Though it has become fashionable to do so, . . . it is a mistake to regard Carlylean gloom, bitterness, and satirical rage, or a preoccupation with psychological abnormalities, as setting the dominant tone of Trollope's later work. Even in novels as satirical as **The Eustace Diamonds** and **The Way We Live Now,** a substratum of conservative decency persists; and it tends to come out on top in the end. But the tone of the novels is set above all by their comic energy and ingenuity, the excitement Trollope finds in the tortuosities of the human mind, the muted admiration that even the most antisocial deeds of his creatures appear to exact from him. Lizzie Eustace and Auguste Melmotte are great comic creations as well as social portents; and however degenerate the society that spawns and nourishes them, a good deal of its weakness for them, its subversive imaginative sympathy with them, clearly infects both Trollope himself and the reader. So that while, objectively, the world of the novels may often be ugly, vicious, even monstrous, their total effect is neither hysterical nor dispiriting.

Trollope, like James, takes the "great black things of life" for granted, neither wondering nor shuddering at them. He finds nothing unaccountable in monstrous evil any more than in simple goodness. Often it is only a slightly distorted version

land Press, 1977 (and reprinted by St. Martin's Press, 1978), 234 p.

JAMES R. KINCAID (essay date 1977)

The Barsetshire chronicle consists of a series of variations on the comic myth of renewal and preservation. Viewed as a sequence, the novels exhibit quite a wide variety, testing the comic proposition by probing it in different directions and with different means in each novel. Viewed against the background of the novels surrounding it, those whose publication was interspersed with the series, the chronicle's unity and basic stability become clear. Whereas the Barsetshire series moves carefully in different areas of comedy, the other early novels career wildly about and sometimes knock down the fences. The early novels outside the chronicle explore the limits of comedy with more abandon and often with the singleness of direction we associate with experiments. Though they are clearly more than just sketches preliminary to the chronicle novels, they define a wide range of themes and techniques which could be tested and refined for use within that chronicle. These early comic novels are less assured and less accomplished than the Barsetshire novels, but not for that reason always less interesting. (p. 69)

Trollope's first three novels—*The Macdermots, The Kellys,* and *La Vendée*—have had their defenders, at least the first two novels have, but they do seem to be the sorts of novels which are better in contemplation than in actual reading. . . . [That] each of these three novels seeks to exploit such radically different modes—first tragedy, then comedy, then historical romance—suggests that Trollope was searching very hard for his genre. He found it only with the publication of *The Warden,* five years after *La Vendée* failed so badly. (pp. 69-70)

The Three Clerks, published after the first two novels in the Barsetshire series, is as anomalous as *La Vendée,* but it is not a failure. It is as if Trollope had tried his hand at becoming a disciple of Dickens and then withdrew, not because the results were uninspiring but because he was attracted to other, far less inhabited territory. Trollope himself viewed *The Three Clerks* as 'certainly the best novel I had as yet written' (*Autobiography* . . .); and though we may find it difficult to see how the novel could be rated higher than *The Warden* or *Barchester Towers,* it has its own virtues. Unlike any other Trollope novel, it is 'a really brilliant tale' [according to E. S. Dallas]. This comment catches exactly the right note here and explains to us also how the novel differs from others in the Trollope canon. No other Trollope novel, with the possible exception of *Brown, Jones, and Robinson,* gives the impression of having the slightest desire to be thought 'brilliant'. But *The Three Clerks* does and is, and it is thus an anomaly.

It is very witty indeed, remarkably autobiographical, ethically and morally puristic; it is centred in London, reaches toward very drastic action and extreme solutions; it employs parody as a basic principle; it is didactic. In all these ways it is uncharacteristic. Perhaps it represents an experiment whose success was too easy, too 'brilliant' to be of further use. Or perhaps it is a novel written principally to test the methods and values of *Barchester Towers,* the major novel written just before this one. *The Three Clerks* extends some of the methods of *Barchester Towers* almost to the point of burlesque and seems thereby to establish the limits of the utility of broad satiric comedy, a method in which Trollope fast loses interest after this novel. *The Three Clerks* also inverts the values and many of the basic

assumptions of *Barchester Towers,* thus testing their validity and power. (pp. 71-2)

With *The Bertrams,* Trollope's novels begin more serious and doubtless more useful tests of the implications of the Barsetshire series. The variations on comedy developed in the chronicle are kept within a range defined by the broader excursions of these other novels. The chronicle, for all its variety, stays pretty much to the centre of the comic spectrum. The edges are explored, first in one direction and then in the other, by the six surrounding novels. *The Bertrams, Castle Richmond,* and *Orley Farm* all deal with dark, ironic comedy. All seem interested in testing the seriousness of opposition that can be erected and still overcome in comedy; they search for the deepest wounds that may still be healed, the grimmest effects that can be counterbalanced or smoothed over. Only the last of these, *Orley Farm,* really succeeds.

The Bertrams is perhaps the least controlled of Trollope's dark comedies. What appears at the beginning to be the main plot is submerged so deeply and for so long that it has to be hauled to the surface with much unpleasant straining at the end; the startling religious theme seems to be connected only loosely to the love stories; the sort of padding critics complain about, usually mysteriously, is for once really there, in the long descriptions of exotic cities of the east, whirling dervishes, and suchlike strangeness. Most serious, the comic form is never made sufficiently flexible to contain the great suffering and the pervasive sense of the arbitrary that abounds in the novel. The comedy thus seems superficial or even superadded. People are rescued from extremity but for no apparent reason. The rewards come to those who suffer, but why? Comedy is not usually logical, of course, but here Trollope moves us so far out of the comic environment that we certainly are not expecting comic miracles. We had thought we were in a different world.

It is a world marked by the decay of private sensitivity and public coherence. A representative citizen remarks, 'Poetry is all very well; but you can't create a taste for it if it doesn't exist. Nobody that I know cares a d— for Iphigenia'. . . . And if no one cares a damn for such fully dramatized sufferings as Iphigenia's, what sort of response can we hope for to the small, muffled sufferings of ordinary people? . . . [The] novel has to struggle desperately at the end to try and tuck in the loose corners which are wildly astray. It tries finally to look like a standard novel of vocation, but we have more likely responded to it as a novel of missed opportunities, whose standard is not comic fulfilment but the agonizing shortness of life and its pointlessness. (pp. 74-5)

Castle Richmond, the next novel in the group, is [one] of Trollope's recurrent geographical mistakes. The movement away from southern England again introduces materials that cannot be contained within the frame. Here it is the background of the Irish famine that works very oddly with the conventional love stories. . . . The details of the relief plans, the road work that accomplishes nothing, and the starvation are so starkly impressive that Trollope is forced to heighten the major plot to the point of ludicrous sensationalism in order to avoid making it appear trivial. But it still does. At one point in the action a character wanders out of the rain and out of the love story into a hovel which has been hit by the famine. When he sees the cringing mother there and the corpse of her small daughter, his own troubles strike him as remarkably small. When some Countess or other, then, worried about the financial and social prospects of her child, wails, 'O my daughter', he thinks only of the woman in the cottage. Marriage, class, money become almost as nothing to him; he never forgets this measurement, nor do we. Trollope has tried to incorporate a *memento mori* symbol far too dramatic and insistent for the context. As in *The Bertrams,* the comedy here is uncomfortably subverted.

Orley Farm goes beyond the ironic edge of comedy altogether, entering unmistakably the territory of 'the mythos of winter'. All appearances are wrong, and the best instincts are mistaken; the scoundrels have all the truth on their side. *Orley Farm* is concerned with mistakes and deceptions, heroic plans that go nowhere, the exercise of chivalric virtues that are now pointless. (pp. 77-8)

One of the subplots, the one involving the Staveley family, does follow a comic course, but this plot is so minor that Trollope almost forgot to complete it, and it is so overwhelmed by the ironic force of the other three plots that the good luck experienced there is made to seem just that: mere good luck. There is no essential comic rhythm, and the slight comic counterplot actually highlights this fact by forcing us to recognize the central patterns of denial. In this way the novel marks a great advance in Trollope's use of the commenting and defining subplot. Four plots are here interwoven with full success. Trollope's novels from this point on use this technique repeatedly and with great assurance. The next two chronicle novels after *Orley Farm, The Small House at Allington* and *Can You Forgive Her?,* owe a great deal to this experimental novel. (pp. 78-9)

With the next three non-chronicle novels, *Rachel Ray,* [*Miss Mackenzie,* and *The Belton Estate*] . . . , Trollope explores the possibilities of the art of full and simple satisfaction. These novels represent the alternate pole of comedy; just as the three novels already discussed are much darker than any of the Barsetshire novels, so are these three much lighter, less disturbed. They are all comedies of nature, positing a serene confidence in natural impulses and the natural working of things. The problems that arise, therefore, are principally confined to removing the obstacles that stand in the way of natural forces, love most especially or, to say the same thing, sex. These are all comedies of generation and renewal, only slightly disguised celebrations of the instincts for survival or procreation. The blocking figures, such as they are, are [like Shakespeare's Malvolio], enemies of youth, mirth, and pleasure; generally they are cast either as religious fanatics or class snobs. People are treated very gently; there are few outcasts and there is very little need for punishment. The world is harmonious and, for the most part, benign, and Trollope's traditional instruments of disruption—the narrator and the subplots—are here used not to upset, but to support, a basic unity of design and effect. Though the three comedies become progressively more complex and admit difficulties more ominous, the change is slight, not enough to disguise the fact that these novels represent the base from which Trollope worked, a world realized in art which offers opportunities for fulfilment and unified being which the other novels deny, seeing them as remote and dreamlike.

Rachel Ray takes a strong stand in favour of youth, sex, and good beer. It is an extremely simple story of how the young man, Luke Rowan, got the girl, Rachel Ray, and the brewery. Virtually everything is on his side, even the hostile brewer's own family and the rector—certainly the girl. . . . It is a novel about how to find 'the good times', an American phrase Trollope picked up and loved. In the process, society itself is cured of its slight neurosis, an uneasiness about sex, and is thus revitalized. Like the other two romantic comedies in this series, *Rachel Ray* is specifically a nationalistic novel, a pastoral that exalts not only nature but English nature, a celebration of that

particular 'air of homeliness which made the sweetness of her womanhood almost more attractive than the loveliness of her personal charms'. . . . (pp. 82-3)

England's natural beauty and natural sources of joy are clouded only slightly in this novel, and that cloud blows away by the end. It appears in the first place only because some people have grown distrustful of this world, have begun worrying about controls and future punishments, and have set up a false distinction between the wicked and the righteous. This morality is so stupidly self-destructive that it creates a division between marriage, which it wholly approves, and courtship, which it would ban entirely. The worthy vicar, appropriately named Mr. Comfort, asks the key question: 'And how are young people to get married if they are not allowed to see each other?' . . . (p. 83)

In this serene world the usual dilemmas in Trollope's novels are diminished, drained of their potential to cause suffering. The recurrent figure of a woman trapped in horrible masochism is here reduced to the comic Mrs. Prime, who has found sackcloth 'grateful to the skin'. . . . But she escapes from Mr. Prong and is clearly on her way to a rejuvenation in worldliness at the novel's close. More remarkable is Trollope's treatment of the hero, who is a gentle version of the usual wild absolutist. Luke's cause, the making of better beer, is comic. . . . His 'genuine radicalism' is only a version of Trollope's own belief in 'gradual progress'; he disdains 'equality'. . . . Even those who disrupt the sleepy world in order to bring new life to it are the mildest and least threatening of invaders.

This quiet and sheltered world is protected by a very skilful narrator, who begins, much as Dickens does in *Martin Chuzzlewit,* by encouraging our cynicism and giving it full rein. The novel opens by making fun of the very things it will finally hold dear—love, marriage, and Mrs. Ray. Love is seen as some sort of biological joke, marriage as a form of mutual support for neurotics, Mrs. Ray as a weak fool. The rhetoric deliberately defuses the sentimentality only to encourage it, tires our sarcasm by exercising it so vigorously. The sentimentality in this novel is not only effective but is so disguised that it does not seem like sentimentality at all. The narrator also helps protect us in the opposite direction, carefully distinguishing the absolute freedom he countenances from licentiousness or lust. (pp. 84-5)

It is a comedy so undisturbed that Luke, after he has won everything, cannot help thinking that the obstacles have been rather petty: 'he could not but wish that there had been some castles for him to storm in his career. Tapitt had made but poor pretence of fighting before he surrendered; and as to Rachel, it had not been in Rachel's nature to make any pretence'. . . . The world has been waiting for them all along. It is this easy confidence in the world and the corresponding full control of his art that made so many of Trollope's contemporaries become sunny over the warmth that was in the novel. (p. 85)

Miss Mackenzie is also a celebration of natural forces, and it admits also the opposition of social snobbery and low-church Puritanism. But there are new and darker problems here, too, namely, loneliness, age, and death. *Miss Mackenzie* enacts a fable of rejuvenation and rebirth, not of natural growth. Its models are works like *The Pickwick Papers* or *Persuasion,* and it narrates a similar magical story of the regaining of youth. Miss Mackenzie is nearly forty, 'neither beautiful nor clever', without particular softness or grace. She has spent all of her life around death and now struggles to find life before it is too late. This is a comedy which moves to a level of complexity and disturbance one step beyond *Rachel Ray,* where finally appearances were in full accord with reality and surfaces were depths. Miss Mackenzie's youth, however, is like her secret poetry, essential but hidden, and the novel is really a test of society and of this life to see if they can find that hidden self. (p. 86)

[*Miss Mackenzie*] is perhaps Trollope's most focused novel; it never takes its eyes off the central figure for a moment. The narrator, therefore, spends most of his time nudging us into identification with Miss Mackenzie, by mock apologies—'Where she has been weak, who among us is not, in that, weak also?' . . .—and by consistent generalization of her actions and motives: 'She was doing what we all do'. . . . He also artfully prepares the way for a comic resolution by parodying various idealized models of loneliness and patience, particularly Griselda and Mariana. . . . (p. 87)

The Belton Estate raises problems that are no more metaphysical [than those in *Miss Mackenzie*], but they are more serious. Despite its complexity, the novel has always seemed to be among Trollope's most forgettable. . . . The comedy is very warm and very controlled, certainly, but it seems on the whole to exclude far less and to work with more difficult issues than either *Rachel Ray* or *Miss Mackenzie.* (p. 88)

[Within its] simple lines there are very strong obstacles to . . . easy comic fulfilment, presented not so much by the narrative complication of the Aylmer engagement as by Clara's urgent need to preserve her own freedom. The very energy and power with which Will can rejuvenate the land are a threat to Clara and her desire to preserve that 'strong will of her own'. . . . The novel deals within its comic framework with the same feminism that was so disruptive in *Can You Forgive Her?* The treatment here is no less subtle. Will's energy and also his kindness are to Clara an assumption of power that must be resisted. She tries to hold herself distant from his authoritarian assumptions by insisting on his cousinly or brotherly relationship to herself. She resists also the dominance of romance, which seems to her an admission of emptiness. . . . She finds herself for a time in the usual masochism common to Trollope's strong women—'It was necessary [she thought] to her self-respect that she should be punished because of that mistake'. . . . But she is freed by the jokes of her friends, Will's gentleness, and the example of Will's sister, who calls him a 'despot', but who shows how very complete her own selfhood and her own powers are. Clara yields, then, with lots of comments about submission and victimization. Partly these are jokes, but the resolution is not at all easy; it is won with delicacy and tact. (pp. 88-9)

[But *The Belton Estate*] is not, despite this art, very memorable, primarily because the method it employs is so un-Trollopian. Trollope experiments here with a stylized and scenic novel, seeking to define issues and to create moods largely through symbolic images and through fixed pictorial attitudes. For once Trollope wants us to see, and the picture is simply not very sharp. It is an interesting experiment, but it is not a technique Trollope had refined, and the result is diffuse and unemphatic. (p. 89)

The diverse and often only partly successful experiments carried on during this period allow for the great control and assurance manifested in the Barsetshire chronicle. At least after the opening novel, the chronicle explores the possibilities of comedy within a range that is clearly defined. Ironic moments

and ironic themes are present, but they never range out of control; nor is the comedy ever so easy and undisturbed as to approach the sleepiness of *The Belton Estate.* The Barsetshire series works without any ponderous epic machinery, but it deals with an epic theme: the establishment and preservation of a civilization. The civilization is first erected and defended from outsiders, flourishes, decays, and is then revived. (p. 92)

It would, perhaps, be a mistake to claim for Trollope's chronicle a much tighter narrative organization than this. There are a few motifs that are repeated throughout, but they are not developed consistently or emphatically. The chronicle derives its unity not from a single narrative pattern or repeated themes but from the most obvious connections through geography and character. For the most part these novels hang together because they are set in the same general area and concern many of the same people. There is a sense that the novels are really just different perspectives on the same action, different lighting effects tried on the same subject. Correspondingly, the basic pattern and basic coherence are more clearly formal than thematic. More exactly, the novels conduct an exploration of the range of comedy.

But the explorations are, as I have said, conducted within safe grounds. The basic assumptions of that world and its values are established by tradition, the tradition of the pastoral. It is a very delicate and fragile world, certainly, subject to threats from within and without, but it is pastoral all the same, with Mr. Harding as chief shepherd. . . . The extraordinary thing about Trollope's pastoral is that it moves away from this reactionary tone after the first two novels, giving us a feeling in *Doctor Thorne* and *Framley Parsonage* that the values have been won and are in little need of protection. This solidity can be misleading, as the last two novels show, but running through the series is an unchanged belief that, at bottom, people's characters are firmly rooted in well-tried values and solid virtues. (pp. 92-3)

'Clergymen are only men', runs a dominant motif throughout. But what is in the first novels a comforting doctrine of unification becomes by the final novel a frightening one. 'All clergymen are men' in *Barchester Towers* means to the reader 'all men are clergymen', possessing in their common humility the source of all spirituality; in *The Last Chronicle,* 'all men are clergymen' seems to translate into 'all men are thieves'.

We notice a corresponding change in the position of women. Initially subject to a good deal of banter for not really understanding the full delicacies of moral behaviour, they are protected by the more refined sensitivies of men. By the end, the deep, if fairly murky, instincts of women hold together the society and give it a foundation from which to rebuild. As the genial surface falls apart, men tend to lose a sense of connection with the code, but women, though never grasping the intricacies of the code at its best moments of practice, are less likely to be led astray. The whole series moves inward, then, learning to distrust things as they are and formulating its comic base more and more on instincts that lie far below the surface.

The danger of this inward movement, as far as comedy is concerned, is that instincts tend to be incommunicable. A comedy established psychologically is less surely communal than one which collects its energies around the expulsion of an external threat, like Mr. Slope. In the early novels the tendency is to defend the sanctity of the private life against public invasion. There is such a confident sense of community that no need is felt to stress communal ties. . . . But in the last two novels the emphasis shifts in the opposite direction, and it is necessary to attempt to bring back the private self into public life. *The Warden* ends with Mr. Harding withdrawing from society, *The Last Chronicle* with Mr. Crawley entering it. These actions paradoxically suggest the shift from a great confidence in social virtue to a distrust of it. (pp. 93-4)

[The Barsetshire chronicle contains] a three-part pattern, consisting of the definition of pastoral values, their fulfilment, and their collapse and reconstruction. *The Warden* and *Barchester Towers* clear the way for the series by defining its central values. They ward off the threats from London and thus lay claim to the pastoral world. Both novels are concerned with telling us who Mr. Harding is and establishing his moral position as central, but they do this principally by indirection, by declaring with great clamour that all other moral systems are either invalid or incomplete. This loud, indelicate quality sets *The Warden* and *Barchester Towers* apart from all of Trollope's other novels. . . . These beginning novels in the chronicle are among Trollope's funniest novels, but it is an uncharacteristically simple (and for that reason highly successful) humour of expulsion that is employed. The villains are very clearly marked out, and Trollope only pretends to make them complex. (p. 95)

[*Doctor Thorne*] is likely to seem to us in many ways the first genuine Trollope novel. With this novel and *Framley Parsonage* there is a contented atmosphere provided by settled values. These values are not unchallenged, of course, and not everyone in the novels can live by them, but the reader now *is* assumed to understand and can therefore be urged quietly to participate in the action. The action in both novels involves recruitment, bolstering the ranks of the good. In both there is a sense of an expanding moral centre, and the confidence is very great. *Framley Parsonage* particularly carries an aura of luxuriance, fully deserving its characteristic tag, 'beautiful'. Its action is desultory, so much so that it is difficult to locate a central plot. But this very quality adds to its serenity, a serenity that is never dull because it is made so convincingly happy.

But in *The Small House at Allington* and *The Last Chronicle of Barset* a new invasion is mounted against the pastoral world, an invasion that so far succeeds that the full and easy confidence can never again be regained. Crosbie is different from Slope in that he fools everyone, not just women but even the Dales, staunch old conservative country gentry. As a result, virtue is twisted and turned inward. It is made perverse. In *The Small House,* the darkest novel in the series, confident and open love and the constancy of great honour are turned into a dangerous and rigid masochism. Natural values have little chance in an unnatural world, and Lily's rigidity ironically is made to appear the chief enemy of comedy. Everything yearns for her rebirth, but her virtue forbids her. Similarly, Mr. Crawley's great courage and heroism not only appear to be but are unnatural. Like Lily, he is forced into terrible psychological compensations, isolating himself and doing great damage. But Mr. Crawley is finally rescued—from poverty and from himself. As he comes back to life, so does society, and so does the code of the gentleman, of which he is the most extreme exemplification. The comic world is rebuilt with all its old values. . . . By reforming the pastoral values in this new world, a new pastoral is, in effect, created, one less protected and permanent but more mature and more capable of dealing with the fallen world.

The cycles of a civilization based on the generous and complex code of gentlemanly instincts is thus established. The series moves from an ironic comedy of withdrawal to full-hearted romantic comedy, and then, in the final stages, to a dark comedy of experience whose principal model is [Milton's] *Paradise Regained* or, in the nineteenth century, Tennyson's *In Memoriam.* Clergymen are central to Trollope's chronicle because it is, like his model, a spiritual guide and a definition of the Church's proper religious mission. The essential doctrine is stated in *Barchester Towers:* 'Till we can become divine, we must be content to be human, lest in our hurry for a change we sink to something lower'. . . . The dangers of slipping are there, but if we can put off the hurry for divinity, we can discover the grand contentment in being human. And that, Trollope's comedy insists, if not more wonderful than divinity, is great indeed—and a lot more certain. (pp. 95-7)

James R. Kincaid, in his The Novels of Anthony Trollope *(© Oxford University Press 1977; reprinted by permission of Oxford University Press), Oxford at the Clarendon Press, Oxford, 1977, 302 p.*

ROBERT TRACY (essay date 1978)

[*Like A.O.J. Cockshut (1955), Tracy considers Trollope's best work to be that written "during the 1870s, after he had attained his artistic maturity." Tracy disputes the popular view of Trollope's works as "pleasant enough to read but undistinguished in style, clumsy and rambling in structure, and uncertain in their moral and social attitudes." Instead, Tracy praises Trollope's technical skill and suggests "that Trollope has a consistent moral theory about society and its values; and that both the style and the structure of his novels effectively imply that theory."*]

Trollope's fear of exclusion and isolation is a constant element in his novels. Isolation tempts or threatens his characters. The isolated man receives his scorn or pity, while his heroes resist isolation. His typical protagonist has a generally recognized place in the social order, and accepts that place; or else the social order concedes a newcomer such a recognized place. Social integration depends on money, birth, an instinctive recognition of social laws, and an awareness of social tradition; it is synonymous with moral integration. Trollope's heroes do not criticize the social order, either explicitly or implicitly. They accept it and are accepted by it. They do not aspire to be anything but ordinary gentlemen; if they have other aspirations, they eventually abandon them. Ordinary decency is the heart of this moral and social doctrine, and in fact Trollope's moral and social doctrine are one. Morality consists in knowing one's proper place in the social order, and in conforming to society's demands. Acts that invoke exclusion or isolation are evil. . . .

In Trollope's pages, this status of being a gentleman—or a lady—is simultaneously a moral, a traditional, and an economic position. Moral excellence cannot confer a position in society, while a high social position does not automatically guarantee virtue. Gentle birth is useful, but it is not socially viable without a fortune to support it. (p. 73)

Although money is necessary to a gentleman, Trollope feels that too direct an involvement in getting it can be a social and moral disqualification. The man whose primary interest is in gaining a fortune risks corruption; the man whose primary interest lies in some occupation or profession that may bring him a fortune is comparatively safe. (p. 74)

It is this doctrine of the gentleman and his role as preserver and embodiment of order that Trollope means when he speaks of the novelist's task of inculcating morality. No attempt to understand his novels and their methods can succeed without striving to understand his doctrine, which is intimately related to his use of theme, plot, and structure. To the modern reader, Trollope's ideal social order may seem reactionary, but we cannot condemn him because he does not share the democratic ideas of another time and place.

Trollope's social ideas really do function within the novels, and the novels, in fact, depend upon those ideas. They may never have been realistic in terms of the real world, but in the imaginary world of the novels they are consistent. Since Trollope's created social world is governed by his social theories, his ideal gentleman is artistically valid.

Trollope is well aware that the word *gentleman*—like the words *lady* and *nobleman*—is both an abstract and specific noun. The difference between the two offers him continual opportunity for irony. Generally speaking, he does not separate the moral meaning of the word from its social meaning, and the term is not fully operative unless both are present. It is possible to condemn a man whose social rank is high when he lacks the gentle or noble virtues, but such a man is not easily condemned. (pp. 81-2)

The gentleman must have fine feelings, a good education, and social position. None of these qualities should be overdeveloped, for a man whose feelings are too fine becomes thin-skinned and useless. Palliser's sensitivity prevents that easy intercourse with his fellows which Cardinal Newman considered to be necessary if a group of men were to work together effectively. (p. 83)

Trollope defined the gentleman, then, not only as a virtuous individual, but also as participating actively in social and political life. Like Carlyle in *Sartor Resartus,* Trollope urges a move away from excessive self-consciousness—which leads to isolation—and toward integrating and working with society. The gentleman must accept social responsibilities. (p. 84)

For Trollope, *political* and *social* are almost interchangeable terms. Cousin Henry's brief and wretched reign as Squire of Llanfeare is a political as well as a social outrage because he lacks the social talents to rule as well as the right to rule. In the Palliser cycle, political power is closely involved with social relationships. . . . The anatomy of a small town like Dillsborough in *The American Senator,* and the analysis of the Scarborough family tree, reveal the intense politics of these miniature societies, the complicated stress and balance systems through which they exist.

The gentleman must serve society in order to justify his social privileges, for only by doing so can he prove his possession of the moral traits that should accompany his rank. His service will be political in character, whether he enters the Church, Parliament, or one of the other larger political complexes, or whether he remains in the country to govern his own little estate or parish. In either case, he must take care of his inferiors and live in harmony with his peers. (pp. 85-6)

For Trollope, the gentleman made society stable, and so it is essential that a gentleman share society's values, and conform to society's ways. He must think and act as do his peers. Like Tennyson's Sir Balin, he must feel "his being move / In music with his order" [from Tennyson's *Idylls of the King*]. This endorsement of conformity finds its antithesis in Trollope's unfavorable treatment of the individualist. When Trollope approves of a character who is independent or rebellious, it is almost invariably in a context of marriage. Some of his men and women refuse to marry as their guardians recommend, and

sometimes he endorses these refusals. But this endorsement does not indicate an approval of the social rebel. It often turns out that the guardian has projected a marriage that would in some way be socially wrong. The young man or woman in question is so placed that there is some discrepancy between their apparent and their true social status, usually because their habits and associates are not those to which they are formally entitled. In such cases, they "rebel" by conforming to their sense of their true social identity, and the general society eventually accepts them at their own valuation. For example, Lady Anna has been brought up in the household of a tailor, and chooses to marry the tailor's son rather than the earl her family prefers; despite her title, she does not feel at home among aristocrats. (pp. 92-3)

In all his works, he is hostile toward characters who possess traits associated with the Byronic hero, the individualist who refuses to conform. Such a character is, admittedly, more interesting than the ordinary worthy hero or heroine. We are more interested in Melmotte and Sir Felix Carbury than in Roger Carbury, more interested in bad Lizzie Eustace than in good Lucy Morris. But the very fact that these characters do stand out shows that they are refusing to conform. To attract interest is to be unusual. To be unusual is to be something other than an ordinary gentleman. "A man ought to be common," the hero of *An Old Man's Love* tells himself, in a remark that sums up Trollope's own belief. "A man who is uncommon is either a dandy or a buffoon."

The modern reader must remind himself that the man of ordinary goodness and ordinary talents who is endorsed in Trollope's novels represents a social ideal, just as Achilles and Odysseus do. The impulsive warrior, or the prudent explorer, were ideal types in Homeric Greece; the Victorian ideal was the decent, unobtrusive English gentleman, who sustained the nation morally and economically. . . . (pp. 93-4)

Trollope's acceptance of the world as he found it, and his dislike of romantic heroics, can easily become an impediment to taking him seriously as an artist. The modern reader is accustomed to regarding the artist as an outsider, a rebel. We have almost lost the ability to deal with writers who accept social and artistic conventions and create their art out of that acceptance. If we discuss them, we tend to emphasize their value as indices to social and cultural attitudes rather than as artists. Trollope does have undoubted value as a guide to the attitudes of his age, but he is not a passive recorder. In a sense, he is a propagandist, positively committed to the Victorian ideal of order, and his art is continually and systematically pervaded by this ideal. He saw Victorian civilization as a positive achievement, though it could be manipulated by outsiders and adventurers. . . . Trollope believed in his society and in its ability to enforce its standards and solve its problems. He believed that a man lived most freely when he conformed to the generally accepted idea of decent behavior. (pp. 95-6)

Trollope's rebels and outsiders fail to disturb society very much. They are either absorbed by society, or in some way they become incapable of causing further trouble. Trollope rarely treats them melodramatically; he domesticates them, so that they can fit into the real world of his novels. Wilkie Collins makes his weak wicked baronet, Sir Percival Glyde, die in a burning church; Trollope's Sir Felix Carbury, equally weak but capable of very little wickedness, goes tamely off to Germany to live on a small remittance. (p. 100)

In his novels, Trollope says little about the great political and intellectual issues of his day. He believed that both sides in any controversy were likely to be right; [Edith Simeox,] a contemporary reviewer of **Phineas Redux,** said that the novel illustrated "another form of the immortal thesis that there are two sides to every question, and that there is so much to be said for each of them that it is really rather hard to tell them apart." Though he stood for Parliament as a Liberal, he does not show the two political parties as essentially very different: Liberals are committed to moderate progress, Conservatives keep that progress from too rapid an acceleration. [In **The Duke's Children**] Lord Silverbridge cannot see much difference between Palliser, who is a conservative Liberal, and Frank Tregear, a liberal Conservative, and the reader is inclined to agree. (p. 101)

In the Palliser series, though Palliser is a Liberal politician we have only a vague notion of his politics. The important thing is his personal worth, and his desire to serve the nation. He proves that society can produce decent leaders, who can run the government competently. Society in fact governs itself. What happens in the House of Commons is simply a ratification of society's collective decisions. . . . (p. 102)

Trollope does not offer much commentary on the more complex political and intellectual issues of his day. His view of a coherent and placid social order, threatened by a few insignificant upstarts, would not find much agreement among modern students of the period. The class that he saw as essential to England's well-being, the landed gentry, was already in decline when he began to write, though this decline was not really apparent until the seventies; capital had already replaced land as the determinant of wealth and power. Trollope was improvising a social creed and ideal. Like the other great Victorian writers, he wrote with an awareness that the eighteenth century's optimism about the prevalence of order in the world was no longer possible. Revolution and the Romantic movement had shown him that order was neither universal nor permanent. There is a nostalgic element in his celebration of the gentleman, and in his attempt to define the gentleman by uniting the older insistence on gentle birth and "blood" to the Victorian insistence on virtuous behavior. His political and social theories were not very profound, and his ideal of the gentleman was not comprehensive enough or definite enough to perform the task of guaranteeing the social system. It remains a literary improvisation. . . . Trollope is not a deep or original thinker. But he is an accurate guide—in his very lack of political and intellectual analysis—to the opinions and attitudes of the average member of the middle and upper classes. "He reminds us," Max Beerbohm once said, "that sanity need not be Philistine."

There is an artistic corollary to Trollope's celebration of the ordinary unobtrusive gentleman. His style has been called undistinguished by some critics, who have not realized how deliberately he avoided individuality and distinction in his writing. He is capable of very idiosyncratic writing, as we see whenever he has occasion to write a letter that will reveal the personality of one of his characters, but his narrative style is not distinctive. It is difficult to analyze or parody, for it calls no attention to itself.

The discussion of style in the **Autobiography** is confined to a demand for ease and clarity, and in **Thackeray** Trollope simply asks that "A novel in style should be easy, lucid, and of course grammatical." . . . To Trollope a distinctive style was a disagreeable assertion of self, a romantic eccentricity. In his work such a style would have been out of harmony with the subject matter. A novel that celebrates the ordinary and unobtrusive

gentleman who conforms to society must be simply and clearly narrated in a style that is ordinary and unobtrusive. The denial of the right to be different must be accompanied by the author's abdication of the same right. (pp. 103-05)

> *Robert Tracy, in his* Trollope's Later Novels *(copyright © 1978 by The Regents of the University of California; reprinted by permission of the University of California Press), University of California Press, 1978, 350 p.*

ADDITIONAL BIBLIOGRAPHY

Aitken, David. "'A Kind of Felicity': Some Notes about Trollope's Style." *Nineteenth-Century Fiction* 20, No. 4 (March 1966): 337-53.
  A discussion of Trollope's style. After questioning whether Trollope's stylistic effects are evidence of artistry or instinctive skill developed after years of practice, Aitken concludes that Trollope's narratives "show little evidence of self-conscious artfulness."

Allen, Walter. "The Early Victorians." In his *The English Novel: A Short Critical History,* pp. 153-252. New York: E. P. Dutton & Co., 1954.*
  A survey of Trollope's novels that enumerates their strengths and weaknesses.

Auchincloss, Louis. "Americans in Trollope." In his *Reflections of a Jacobite,* pp. 113-25. Boston: Houghton Mifflin Co., 1961.
  Comments on Trollope's portraits of Americans. Auchincloss finds that these comprise three categories: "unscrupulous adventurers, . . . or grotesque, unsexed women who advocate radical causes, . . . or pompous political windbags, waving the stars and stripes in the disgusted eyes of their English cousins." Of all Trollope's Americans, only his young women, according to the critic, escape negative treatment.

Auden, W. H. "A Poet of the Actual." In his *Forewords and Afterwords,* edited by Edward Mendelson, pp. 262-67. New York: Random House, 1973.
  A brief, sympathetic discussion of Trollope's attitude toward money and writing. Auden states that, of all novelists, "Trollope best understands the role of money."

Banks, J. A. "The Way They Lived Then: Anthony Trollope and the 1870's." *Victorian Studies* XII, No. 2 (December 1968): 177-200.
  Assesses the value of Trollope's novels as historical evidence of the way people lived in the 1870s. Banks attempts to differentiate between Trollope's own opinions and those of his age and finds that "if in some sense his novels provide a mirror of his time it is because in this same sense he himself was representative of it."

Bareham, Tony, ed. *Anthony Trollope.* Barnes & Noble Critical Studies, edited by Anne Smith. New York: Barnes & Noble, 1980, 207 p.
  A collection of modern critical essays.

Beerbohm, Max. "Beerbohm on Trollope." *The Times Literary Supplement,* No. 3424 (12 October 1967): 968.
  A brief letter, written in 1928, praising *The Eustace Diamonds* as Trollope's best novel.

Belloc, H. "Anthony Trollope." *London Mercury* XXVII, No. 158 (December 1932): 150-57.
  Considers Trollope "the picture of that England which once was" and describes English society and manners during Trollope's era.

Booth, Bradford A. "Trollope." In *The English Novel: Selected Bibliographical Guides,* edited by A. E. Dyson, pp. 200-17. London: Oxford University Press, 1974.
  An excellent research guide that provides a comprehensive review of Trollope criticism from Henry James's 1883 essay through

1968. Booth, a noted Trollope scholar, also includes a concise summary of the author's reputation.

Bowen, Elizabeth. *Anthony Trollope: A New Judgement*. New York, London: Oxford University Press, 1946, 35 p.

A biographical, psychological, and critical evaluation of Trollope in dramatic form that analyzes his appeal to English readers during and after World War II. There are three characters in this short drama: William, an English soldier who takes one of Trollope's works into battle with him; his Uncle Jasper, who lends William the book and explains the literary climate at the time of Trollope's death and his subsequent unpopularity; and Trollope's ghost, who reminisces about his own youth, writings, and reputation. At the end of the piece, the narrator proposes that Trollope's troubled youth contributed to his longing for ordinary life and his ability to depict it: "*Were* there two Trollopes? . . . The anxious outcast, the successful man of the world—was the first, perhaps, never quite absorbed and lost in the second? Is it the wistful outsider, somewhere in Trollope's writings, who gives that mirage-illusion to the ordinary scene?"

Briggs, Asa. "Trollope, Bagehot, and the English Constitution." In *Victorian Literature: Selected Essays,* edited by Robert O. Preyer, pp. 37-52. The Contemporary Essays Series, edited by Leonard W. Levy. New York: Harper & Row, 1967.*

A social and historical assessment of mid-nineteenth-century England as presented in Trollope's novels. According to the editor of the collection, Robert O. Preyer, Briggs "attempts to define the special ethos of mid-Victorian England" through an analysis of the works of Trollope and Walter Bagehot, the writers whom Briggs considers most able to describe this period. The critic discusses Trollope and Bagehot's presentations of the issues of their day while providing an overview of the contemporary political situation.

Davies, Hugh Sykes. *Trollope*. Writers and Their Work, edited by Bonamy Dobrée, no. 118. London: Longmans, Green & Co., 1960, 40 p.

A brief introductory survey of Trollope's works. Davies contends that "all the essential qualities of Trollope are to be found in the two central series [the Barsetshire and Palliser series], and that there they are balanced in their right proportions. Outside them, only two novels appear to me to have a really strong claim on the general reader": *The Way We Live Now* and *The Claverings.*

Escott, T.H.S. *Anthony Trollope: His Public Services, Private Friends, and Literary Originals*. London: John Lane, The Bodley Head; New York: John Lane Co.; Toronto: Bell & Cockburn, 1913, 351 p.

The first Trollope biography, written by a friend of the author. Since Trollope's *An Autobiography* had provided the essential biographical information, Escott confined this study to the subjects indicated in the title.

Gerould, Winifred Gregory, and Gerould, James Thayer. *A Guide to Trollope*. Princeton: Princeton University Press, 1948, 256 p.

An alphabetical list of characters and significant locales in Trollope's novels.

Hall, N. John. *Trollope and His Illustrators*. New York: St. Martin's Press, 1980, 175 p.

A complete guide to the artists who illustrated Trollope's novels. Hall's study includes a critical introduction on the role of illustration in Victorian fiction, brief biographical-critical essays on each of Trollope's major illustrators, selected reproductions from their works, and commentary on the quality of various illustrations.

Hall, N. John, ed. *The Trollope Critics*. Totowa, N.J.: Barnes & Noble Books, 1981, 248 p.

A collection of essays by many of the most important Trollope critics, from Henry James in 1883 through the commentators of the 1970s.

Hall, N. John, and Stone, Donald D., eds. *Nineteenth-Century Fiction, Special Number: Anthony Trollope, 1882-1982* 37, No. 3 (December 1982): 255-496.

A special issue devoted to Trollope, published on the centenary of his death.

Halperin, John. *Trollope and Politics: A Study of the Pallisers and Others*. New York: Barnes & Noble, 1977, 318 p.*

A close study of Trollope's political novels. According to Halperin, these works provide information about Trollope's political beliefs and "tell us much about the politics of the time, the role of individuals in politics, and of politics in the lives of individuals, and the ways in which political and social systems interact and interdepend."

"Unsigned Notice." *Harper's Magazine* LV (October 1877): 790.

A review of *The American Senator* that illustrates the censorious American reaction to Trollope's negative portrayal of an American politician.

Harvey, Geoffrey. *The Art of Anthony Trollope*. New York: St. Martin's Press, 1980, 177 p.

An appraisal of Trollope as a literary artist. Harvey attempts to demonstrate how Trollope's "art draws its strength from its roots in the Victorian ethos and particularly from the critical debates on the form of the novel which were current during the peak of his writing career."

Hawk, Affable [pseudonym of Desmond MacCarthy]. "Review of *He Knew He Was Right*." *The New Statesman* XIX, No. 471 (22 April 1922): 67.

A brief review of *He Knew He Was Right* that praises Trollope's method of alternating several story lines in the novel.

Hawkins, Sherman. "Mr. Harding's Church Music." *ELH* 29, No. 2 (June 1962): 202-23.

Examines the music of the character Mr. Harding as a focus for an analysis of literary technique in *The Warden*. Hawkins asserts that "Trollope states his theme through a variety of techniques ranging from the personal allusions, parodies, and mock-heroic of Augustan satire to the symbols, allegories, and myths so dear to contemporary novelists. Thus he finds a precise symbolic notation for his pattern of conflict and reconciliation in the pervasive imagery of music."

Hawthorne, Julian. "The Maker of Many Books." In his *Confessions and Criticisms*, pp. 140-62. Boston: Ticknor and Co., 1887.

A personal reminiscence and biographical sketch by a friend of Trollope.

Helling, Rafael. *A Century of Trollope Criticism*. Port Washington, N.Y.: Kennikat Press, Inc., 1956, 203 p.

Traces Trollope's reputation and examines Trollope criticism from the publication of *The Warden* to the 1950s.

Hennedy, Hugh L. "Trollope on Reform and Change: *Barchester Towers*." In his *Unity in Barsetshire*, pp. 37-55. The Hague, Paris: Mouton, 1971.

Contradicts the common critical assumption that the Barsetshire novels are poorly constructed. Hennedy maintains that the individual novels and the series as a whole are thematically unified. Hennedy's argument supports those of Jerome Thale and Arthur Mizener (see excerpts above, 1958 and 1960).

Johnson, P. Hansford. "Trollope's Young Women." In *On the Novel*, edited by B. S. Benedikz, pp. 17-33. London: J. M. Dent & Sons, 1971.

A survey of Trollope's young female characters. Johnson states that "Trollope had the sharpest appreciation of women in their thoughts, actions, speech-rhythms and in their domestic routines."

Kendrick, Walter M. *The Novel-Machine: The Theory and Fiction of Anthony Trollope*. Baltimore, London: The Johns Hopkins University Press, 1980, 143 p.

Describes *An Autobiography* "as an undisguised theory of realistic fiction." The critic surveys Trollope's novels, particularly *He Knew He Was Right,* in light of this theory.

Koets, Christiaan Coenraad. *Female Characters in the Works of Anthony Trollope*. Gouda, Netherlands: T. Van Tilburg, 1933, 106 p.
Examines Trollope's conception of the ideal woman and identifies different types of female characters in his novels.

Laski, Audrey L. "Myths of Character: An Aspect of the Novel." *Nineteenth-Century Fiction* 14, No. 4 (March 1960): 333-43.*
Argues that novelists rely on four stock character types, or myths, that are based on the individual's relationship to society. Laski identifies these groups as the Myth of the Aristocrat, Hero, Burgess, and Clown and traces the history of the two dukes of Omnium from *Can You Forgive Her?* through the Palliser novels as representatives of the Myth of the Aristocrat.

McMaster, Juliet. *Trollope's Palliser Novels: Theme and Pattern*. New York: Oxford University Press, 1978, 242 p.
Debates the assertions of earlier critics, notably David Cecil (see excerpt above, 1934), that Trollope's work has no underlying meaning or coherent structure. McMaster contends that Trollope "does incorporate a vision of humanity in his novels, and it is often through the relation of his main plot to his subplots that this vision is best comprehended."

Murry, J. Middleton. "Trollope in *Autobiography*." *The Nation and the Athenaeum* XXXIII, No. 4 (28 April 1923): 120-21.
A laudatory review of *An Autobiography*.

"Trollope As the Voice of the English Middle Class." *National Review* XVI (January 1863): 27-40.
Responds to an article published in the French periodical *Revue des deux mondes* in 1862 in which E. D. Forgues claims that English novels are proof of society's corruption. Pointing to Trollope's *Orley Farm* as "the precise standard of English taste, sentiment, and conviction," the *National Review* critic refutes these charges, yet finds in Trollope's work another kind of degeneracy. According to the author, his portraits of society "are very low art; and while they do not corrupt the morals, they may degrade the tastes . . .". These charges of moral and artistic baseness are typical of those leveled at Trollope throughout the nineteenth century.

Pollard, Arthur. *Anthony Trollope*. London: Routledge & Kegan Paul, 1978, 208 p.
A laudatory survey of Trollope's work. Pollard concludes that "the secret of Trollope's success" is his intimacy with his characters and with the reader: "We feel, after reading him, that we are with a man we know and can trust, talking about people he knows and who through him we come to know."

Pope Hennessy, James. *Anthony Trollope*. London: Jonathan Cape, 1971, 400 p.
A detailed biography that provides commentary on Trollope's work and information about his critical reception.

Praz, Mario. "Anthony Trollope." In his *The Hero in Eclipse in Victorian Fiction*, translated by Angus Davidson, pp. 261-318. London: Oxford University Press, 1969.
Contends that Trollope detracted from the drama of his stories by refusing to exaggerate the characteristics of his heroes and villains so that they could become larger than life.

Pritchett, V. S. "Review of *An Autobiography*." *The New Statesman and Nation* XXXI, No. 798 (8 June 1946): 415.
A review of *An Autobiography* that claims that this is "the work of Trollope that is likely to last."

Raleigh, Sir Walter. "To Mrs. C. A. Ker, 15th April, 1905." In *The Letters of Sir Walter Raleigh (1879-1922), Vol. I*, edited by Lady Raleigh, pp. 271-72. London: Methuen & Co., 1926.
A brief but appreciative comment comparing Trollope with William Makepeace Thackeray.

Ray, Gordon N. "Trollope at Full Length." *The Huntington Library Quarterly* XXXI, No. 4 (August 1968): 313-37.
A quantitative study that asserts that "Trollope's major energies throughout his career were directed to his big books, and it is among them that we should seek his major accomplishments."

Rather than concentrating on a small group of characters, Trollope's larger novels, according to Ray, contain several sets of characters and intersecting narrative lines which lead to "amplification in breadth."

Sadleir, Michael. *Trollope: A Bibliography*. London: Constable & Co., 1928, 322 p.
The definitive bibliography of Trollope's works. Sadleir traces Trollope's publishing history by describing the early editions of his works and listing their publication in periodicals, where applicable. This bibliography is considered a landmark in the field of Victorian literature; its thorough descriptions of early publishing practices prompted Donald Smalley to describe it as "a history of Victorian book-making in miniature" [see annotation below, 1980].

Skilton, David. *Anthony Trollope and His Contemporaries: A Study in the Theory and Conventions of Mid-Victorian Fiction*. London: Longman, 1972, 170 p.*
An important study of contemporary reaction to Trollope's fiction. Skilton provides a chronological analysis of Trollope's reputation and extensive discussions of the most important concerns in Victorian criticism: "the hatred of realism" and the demand for tragedy, morality, and depth of characterization.

Skilton, David. "*The Fixed Period*: Anthony Trollope's Novel of 1980." *Studies in the Literary Imagination* VI, No. 2 (Fall 1973): 39-50.
Examines Trollope's ironic and futuristic novel *The Fixed Period*.

Smalley, Donald. "Anthony Trollope." In *Victorian Fiction: A Guide to Research*, edited by Lionel Stevenson, pp. 188-213. New York: The Modern Language Association, 1980.
A survey of Trollope criticism and an overview of his reputation.

Smalley, Donald, ed. *Trollope: The Critical Heritage*. The Critical Heritage Series, edited by B. C. Southam. London: Routledge & Kegan Paul; New York: Barnes & Noble, 1969, 572 p.
A compilation of early reviews of Trollope's works. This collection provides a reflection of his reception by his contemporaries.

Smalley, Donald, and Booth, Bradford Allen. "Introduction: Anthony Trollope in America." In *North America*, by Anthony Trollope, edited by Donald Smalley and Bradford Allen Booth, pp. v-xxxii. New York: Alfred A. Knopf, 1951.
An introduction to Trollope's *North America*, which recounts Trollope's experiences in the United States and his impressions of its people during the Civil War.

Snow, C. P. *Trollope: His Life and Art*. New York: Charles Scribner's Sons, 1975, 191 p.
A beautifully illustrated biography that includes detailed information on Trollope's life and early reputation. Snow's assessment of Trollope as a psychological novelist amplifies his 1971 essay (see excerpt above).

Stebbins, Lucy Poate, and Stebbins, Richard Poate. *The Trollopes: The Chronicle of a Writing Family*. New York: Columbia University Press, 1945, 394 p.
A biographical account of the Trollope family that focuses primarily on Anthony. The Stebbinses employ Freudian theory in depicting family relationships and individual personalities. Their view that Trollope became increasingly bitter with age is supported by A.O.J. Cockshut (see excerpt above, 1958).

Taylor, Robert H. Introduction to *Did He Steal It?*, by Anthony Trollope, pp. v-xiii. Princeton: Princeton University Library, 1952.
An introduction to Trollope's unsuccessful drama based on *The Last Chronicle of Barset*.

West, Rebecca. "A Nineteenth-Century Bureaucrat." In her *The Court and the Castle: Some Treatments of a Recurrent Theme*, pp. 133-64. New Haven: Yale University Press, 1957.
Praises Trollope's understanding and depiction of society. West asserts that Trollope "conceived his art as a celebration of society, rather than of the individual."

José Zorrilla y Moral

1817-1893

Spanish dramatist, poet, and novelist.

One of Spain's most beloved dramatists and poets, Zorrilla is best known for his drama *Don Juan Tenorio*. Written at the height of Spanish Romanticism, *Don Juan Tenorio* successfully recreates the famous character Don Juan. While other Spanish writers have achieved greater renown, Zorrilla remains important for his masterful descriptions and dramatic power. In the twentieth century, many critical sources still rank *Don Juan Tenorio* as one of the most popular plays in Spanish literature.

Zorrilla was born in Valladolid, Spain, where he attended the Real Seminario de Nobles, a Jesuit school that was also attended by the French novelist Victor Hugo. In 1833, he entered the University of Toledo and, at his father's encouragement, studied law. A year later, he returned to Valladolid and entered the local university, but he proved to be a poor student. Instead of studying, Zorrilla frequented graveyards where he read aloud from the works of such writers as Sir Walter Scott, James Fenimore Cooper, and Alexandre Dumas, *père*. He also wrote his own poems and stories, which he published in a Madrid newspaper.

Zorrilla became famous in 1837 for his dramatic behavior at the burial of the poet Mariano José de Larra. Witnesses reported that Zorrilla actually jumped into the grave and stood on the coffin as he read his own verses delineating the sacred mission of all poets. By 1840, his popularity had soared. Zorrilla composed eight volumes of unpublished verse and achieved respect as a literary figure. His marriage, however, was not as successful as his career; Zorrilla blamed his wife for his financial misfortunes and she, in turn, accused him of infidelity and desertion. He left her in 1850 and wandered through France, Mexico, and Spain.

Between 1839 and 1849, Zorrilla composed forty plays. His first drama, *Juan Dandolo*, was coauthored by Antonio García Gutiérrez and met with popular, though limited, success. His most enduring drama, *Don Juan Tenorio* brought Zorrilla little financial security, since he sold all the residual rights to the play after its first performance. In 1855, he became the director of the Mexican National Theatre in Mexico City, where he remained for eleven years. During this time, *Don Juan Tenorio* became a success in Spain. Distressed that he wasn't sharing in his play's profits, he wrote a *zarzuela,* or musical comedy satirizing his own work. The *zarzuela,* however, was virtually ignored by the public. In 1880, following the publication of his autobiography, *Recuerdos del tiempo viego*, Zorrilla received a government pension that enabled him to return to Spain.

By 1889 Zorrilla had regained his popularity in his native country. That year he was crowned Prince of National Poets in Granada, the city that inspired his popular poem, "Granada." 16,000 citizens attended the ceremony while the entire country celebrated his coronation, and for the first time, Zorrilla enjoyed prosperity. After his death in 1893, the Spanish Academy sponsored a magnificent funeral as a final tribute.

Though he wrote prolifically, Zorrilla's reputation depends primarily upon *Don Juan Tenorio*. Admired for its poetic beauty, *Don Juan Tenorio* is a *drama religioso-fantastico:* a work which depicts a condemned man miraculously saved from damnation by the love of a pure woman. In the play, Zorrilla both created characters who personify earthly and spiritual elements and elaborated on the Don Juan legend. Performed in Spanish theaters each year on All Saints' Day, the play still draws audiences today. Nineteenth-century critics considered the play Zorrilla's claim to immortality and applauded his recreation of an infamous folk hero. Recent commentators are generally more concerned with the technical aspects of the drama and find *Don Juan*'s theatricality to be its most appealing trait. Though some twentieth-century commentators find that *Don Juan Tenorio* is poorly constructed, hastily written, and too sentimental to deserve its widespread popularity, they do agree that it is, despite its faults, an engrossing work.

Zorrilla's legends in verse, collected in *Cantos del trovador*, are, with "Granada," his most enduring and popular poetry. Often called *leyendas,* or legends, the *Cantos* are the Spanish equivalent of the Arthurian tales in English literature.

While Zorrilla is considered an eminent writer in Spanish literary history, he is infrequently discussed by critics writing in English. In his own time, Zorrilla was regarded as an awesome literary force; his celebration as poet laureate was a tribute to both his literary distinction and his popularity. He is remembered for *Don Juan Tenorio* and for his contribution to the brief flourishing of Spanish Romanticism.

PRINCIPAL WORKS

Juan Dandolo [with Antonio García Gutiérrez]   (drama) 1839

Cantos del trovador. 3 vols.   (verse)   1840-41

El zapatero y el rey, Part I   (drama)   1840

El zapatero y el rey, Part II   (drama)   1842

El puñal del godo   (drama)   1843
   [*The Dagger of the Goth* published in journal *Poet Lore*, 1929]

Don Juan Tenorio   (drama)   1844
   [*Don Juan Tenorio*, 1944]

Translations from the Spanish Poet José Zorrilla y Moral (drama)   1846

Obras de d. José Zorrilla   (poetry)   1847

Traidor, inconfeso, y mártir   (drama)   1849

"*Granada*"   (unfinished poem)   1852

Obras de d. José Zorrilla   (poetry and drama)   1852

Obras completas   (poetry and drama)   1864

Recuerdos del tiempo viego   (autobiography)   1880

Obras dramaticas y liricas de Don José Zorrilla   (poetry and drama)   1895

THE ATHENAEUM   (essay date 1893)

In José Zorrilla one of the most eminent writers of modern Spain has passed away. . . . His commemorative ode, read at the grave of Mariano José de Larra [who wrote under the pseudonym "Figaro"], brought him into notice before he had completed his twentieth year. It contains passages of eloquence and beauty, but its vogue was chiefly due to the interest aroused by the tragic circumstances of Larra's suicide. Its opportuneness constitutes its highest merit. Zorrilla's '**Cantos del Trovador**' . . . show a great advance, and his versions of many of the national legends obtained a wide popularity, and their remarkable energy and fire distinguish them from the mass of contemporary Spanish poetry. His powers are, perhaps, seen at their highest point in his '**Granada,**' which, for private reasons, has been given to the public in only an incomplete form. His earliest drama, '**Juan Dandolo**'—written conjointly with Antonio García Gutiérrez—obtained a success as striking and immediate as his elegy, and was followed by a long series of plays, of which '**El zapatero y el rey,**' '**El puñal del godo,**' and '**Don Juan Tenorio**' are the best, though '**Traidor, inconfeso y mártir**' was the writer's favourite child. By '**Don Juan Tenorio**' . . . Zorrilla will be best remembered on the Spanish stage. The fascination which this subject had for him is shown in his '**Testigo de bronce**' and '**El desafío del diablo.**' (p. 121)

> "*Don José Zorrilla*," in The Athenaeum, *No. 3405, January 28, 1893, pp. 121-22.*

FANNY HALE GARDINER   (essay date 1898)

[*Gardiner calls Zorrilla's* Don Juan Tenorio "*the most important of his poetic productions*" *and maintains that it* "*encloses all his poetic personality.*" *Asserting that* Don Juan Tenorio *supersedes all earlier versions of the Don Juan legend, Gardiner explores the possible historical background for the play.*]

It does not appear that Zorilla ever passed through any "storm and stress" period, that the rights and wrongs of mankind ever drew painfully upon his sympathies, that the word *liberty* ever startled his inner consciousness, or that he was ever stung to resentment by the "reviewers." He might have written "My soul is an enchanted boat," but he certainly never attempted anything like [Percy Bysshe Shelley's] 'Queen Mab.' He was not an idle dreamer, however, but a diligent and earnest worker, who during his life-time produced seventeen volumes of lyric verse and twenty-four plays.

His most interesting lyric work, at least to a foreigner, is his Romancero. What Tennyson did for the Arthurian tales that did Zorilla for the favorite legends of Spanish history. (p. 508)

[Zorilla] produced his twenty-four plays in quick succession and to hearty applause. Many of them are frequently put on the stage to-day, but, in the words of a Spanish writer, "if we attend to the judgment of posterity rather than to that of authors and critics, Zorilla is the author of but one drama, namely, '**Don Juan Tenorio.**'"

Fifty years of unabated applause for what was the work of twenty days to a young man of twenty-seven years, seems an incontrovertible verdict for genius and renown. It is probably safe to predict for it another fifty years of the same popularity. Progress is in no haste in Spain, although her chariot is surely moving across the land. The public in any land may not be the best judge of a work of art, but perhaps the public grasps the larger aspects and, like Nature, is "careful of the type" while indifferent to detail. (pp. 509-10)

Although Zorilla has simply resurrected and rehabilitated a mass of old legend, his work has thrown all other versions into the shade. It is interesting to know that below the legend there is probably a basis of fact in connection with the history of a certain noble family of Seville named Tenorio, the site of whose palaces and gardens, now occupied by a convent, is still pointed out to visitors. But in a larger sense it was true of the typical hidalgo of southern Spain after the final conquest of the Moors had left him no further career for his energies, and the Inquisition had suppressed any attempt at intellectual expansion; thenceforth he must kill time by recounting ancient deeds of valor, and work off his energies by acts of audacity, recklessness, and vice. The simplest form of the story . . . seems to be that Don Juan Tenorio killed the Comendador Ulloa, whose daughter he had stolen away. The Comendador was buried in the chapel of the Franciscan convent, into which, it was rumored, Don Juan forced his way for the purpose of insulting the tomb of his victim, whereupon the effigy, descending from its niche, seized upon the offender and bore him body and soul to the infernal regions; the most probable explanation being, however, that the monks, in order to check the atrocious career of Don Juan, enticed him within their walls,—whence he never again came forth. (pp. 510-11)

[The] original "belle legende" received new life under the touch of Zorilla. He delighted in the opportunities it afforded to his romantic imagination, and he presented it to his sympathetic countrymen with the result already shown. Yet even in this modern dress both story and setting are so foreign to Anglo-Saxon taste that it would be far from commanding a "hundred-nights' run" at any theatre in England or the United States, and it were vain even to publish a translation of it. We are not accustomed to public mention of an amount and kind of lawlessness that is boasted between Don Juan and his friend Don Luis. . . . (p. 512)

The nun-like, dove-like lady of the play, the daughter of the Comendador de Ulloa, whom Don Juan steals from her cloister (in the good old-fashioned romantic way, with a rope-ladder) is a picture dear to the hearts of Spaniards of both sexes. Bred to a life of blissful ignorance of the world, and perhaps dedicated to the "more excellent way" of the cloister, she yet longs to be loved by the daring and passionate lover who clasps her shrinking form and fascinates her fainting senses. Even when the body of her father (who comes to rescue her) lies at her feet, slain by this lover, who then escapes and abandons her, she begs her avengers to spare Don Juan and prays for him with her latest breath.

Don Juan's colloquy with the sculptor in the cemetery suggests Hamlet and the grave-digger, although in dignity and breadth of thought and expression the former bears no comparison. It is when Don Juan, alone with the marble company that counterfeit the dead, addresses the statue of Doña Inés, that Zorilla does his best lyric work. Both here and in Don Juan's passionate pleading with the living Inés, Zorilla makes use of the *refrain* which the Spanish ear so dearly loves. Given the full, sonorous cadences of the Spanish language, and the chanting style of declamation in vogue on the Spanish stage, it would be difficult for any ear to resist the sensuous thrall, though in soberer moments one may rebel against the fascination and the artificiality. The whole play is written in stanzas of four or five lines, four stresses to the line, rhyming irregularly; this becomes very monotonous, and seems, moreover, quite inadequate to the varying moods and scenes of the play.

And the moral! When at last the statue of the old Comendador points Don Juan to the last sands running through the hourglass, and gives him only so much time for repentance and a *credo,* the precious hero tardily admits that "the light of faith at last penetrates his heart." (pp. 512-13)

We are told that "no critic has been or could be so cruel toward this drama as Zorilla himself. He has written all that vehemence could formulate against it, but his protest will not be heard. **'Don Juan Tenorio'** is the most important of his poetic productions, the greatest of his legends, and it encloses all his poetic personality. Its characters are even now national; any Spaniard believes himself capable of being a Don Juan, any Spanish lady may be a Doña Inés." (p. 513)

Zorrilla had outlived his times, and his coronation [as national poet of Spain in 1889] was the tribute of reverence rather than of popularity, of old friends rather than of new. But that the nation honored him to the last is manifest in the official announcement of his death in the public press, which stated that "The Government of His Majesty, the Royal Spanish Academy, Doña Juana Pacheco, his widow, and other relations, Pray his friends and the lovers of letters that they commend him to God, and be present at the removal of the body from the Academy to the Cemetery of San Justo, on the 25th day of January, 1893 at two in the afternoon." (p. 514)

Fanny Hale Gardiner, "A Spanish Poet-Laureate: José Zorrilla," in Poet Lore *(copyright, 1898, by Poet Lore, Inc.; reprinted by permission of Heldref Publications, a publication of the Helen Dwight Reid Educational Foundation), Vol. X, No. 4, 1898, pp. 506-14.*

ELLA CROSBY-HEATH   (essay date 1926)

[*Although Heath feels that Zorrilla's work is "often lacking in unity, and weak in construction," she still considers him a great poet who offers a "fresh and spontaneous interpretation" of age-old legends and themes. In the following essay, Heath outlines several of Zorrilla's major works and briefly describes their importance.*]

Zorrilla was undoubtedly a great poet, no less great because others were greater. He was a lyric poet, a religious poet, a national poet, and, above all, a Spanish poet. He has been called "the incarnation of the vast national legend." He had a marvellous memory and a phenomenal imagination; he possessed a rich vocabulary in one of the richest languages of the world. He was tender, sympathetic and devout, with the simplicity of a child, and the passionate emotions of a man. . . . [He] was not a thinker, but he was a man of deep and sincere feeling, and it was this quality that endeared him to his people, to the masses, who are never thinkers, but whose emotions are strong and easily roused.

He is never profound, and always diffuse, never satisfied with one word where ten can be used. He wrote almost as much as Lope de Vega, but he said less. Amidst his careless profusion it is difficult to distinguish the grain from the chaff. But the grain is there, and it is precious.

His work is often lacking in unity, and weak in construction, but when the foundations were laid, and the structure indicated, as in the national legends, his facility of execution and his felicity of phrase gave the theme new life and fresh beauty. (pp. 188-89)

The supreme explanation of his power over his countrymen, of his popularity and of his enduring fame, lies in the fact that at the outset of his career he struck the superlatively Spanish note. His *Songs of a Troubadour* were a clarion call to Spain, the call of chivalry and of romance. He lived in the beginning of a new epoch in Spanish poetry. The spread of education was bringing its philosophies, its sciences, its doubts, its denials, into the national life. Foreign influence was altering the current of thought, and while he once attained to the stature of the early poets, much admirable work was being done by a brilliant group of writers who left Spanish tradition behind. Zorrilla was the last mouthpiece of the Church and of the nation. He stood for God and for Spain, and he will always be remembered in the literature of his country as its Cid and its Champion. (p. 189)

The *Cantos del trovador* [*Songs of a Troubadour*] are the earliest revelation of Zorrilla's true genius. In them he shows himself to be a great narrative poet. He could put a long and detailed story into verse as flowing and natural as prose. In his hands the buried and forgotten legends spring to life, and to read his fresh and spontaneous interpretation is like listening to tales of those one knows and loves.

Don Juan Tenorio, Zorrilla's supreme claim to immortality, is one of the most surprising plays ever penned. Only a Spaniard could have written it, and only in Spain can it be entirely understood and appreciated. It begins on a spirited note of brilliant comedy which develops into a farcical but equally brilliant flippancy; it passes from comedy to romantic and tragic drama. . . . (pp. 342-43)

The *Drama del alma* is a notable poem, careless and inconsequent as it often is, and it well repays reading in the original Spanish, which alone can reveal its intrinsic charm.

In [the long, unfinished poem,] *Granada,* we find a more per-fect technique, a deeper feeling for construction and a more controlled sense of beauty. The subject was Zorrilla's own—the glorious history of Spain; and, as an integral part of that glory, he discerned the power and the guidance of an omni-potent God, and the triumph of the Catholic church. (p. 399)

> Ella Crosby-Heath, "Zorrilla I," "Zorrilla II," and "Zorrilla III," in Poetry Review (copyright © The Poetry Society 1926), Vol. XVII, Nos. 3, 5, 6, May-June, September-October, and November-December, 1926, pp. 173-89; 339-58; 393-416.

E. ALLISON PEERS   (essay date 1935)

[*Peers provides a critical survey of Zorrilla's dramas and analyzes his verse* leyendas, *or legends, which Peers considers to be among Zorrilla's greatest contributions. The critic briefly evaluates Zorrilla's characterization, narrative technique, imagery, and metre, and stresses his role in popularizing the chronicles of the Middle Ages, asserting that Zorrilla should be considered the "greatest poet of the Mediaeval Revival in Spain."*]

The three-act comedy *Ganar perdiendo* . . . , though its action is set in Toledo at the end of the seventeenth century, is not strictly an historical play, nor is it comparable in merit with the best of Zorrilla's dramas. To the student of those dramas it has a double interest: first, it reveals the growing influence upon the young author of Golden Age technique, and secondly, it is evidently a preliminary sketch for a much maturer work, *Don Juan Tenorio.* Zorrilla may not, in 1839, have planned, or even thought of, his later play, but it is clear that his mind is inclining in the direction of the Don Juan legend and the incident on which turns the action of *Ganar perdiendo* is com-pletely in harmony with it. (p. 177)

The composition of verse *leyendas* [legends] was an unsuitable and even a demoralizing apprenticeship for an incipient dra-matist, and its deleterious effect upon Zorrilla is evident from the diffuseness of *El Zapatero y el Rey.* To this defect, which he never entirely remedied, must be added those of inverisi-militude in characterization and failure to maintain an interest in his plot which the early scenes certainly stimulate. From the end of the second act (some might say even earlier) the nature of the *dénouement* becomes obvious and as a result plot-interest diminishes almost to vanishing point. The arrangement of the characters for the grand final scene is from the third act onward as obviously preoccupying the dramatist as though he were discussing it openly. In all respects which are applicable equally to drama and to narrative, on the other hand, this first part of *El Zapatero y el Rey* is quite effective. The domination of the play by a single character, which Zorrilla was shortly to achieve with great *éclat,* is attempted with some degree of success, Peter the Cruel, represented as the Rey Justiciero, being quite a suitable figure for experiment. Emotional suggestions are well conveyed—especially the suggestions of fear in the ex-position of the play and of mystery here and there throughout the first two acts. Contrasts abound—notably objective char-acter-contrasts between noble and *villano* [wicked], *zapatero* and *rey* [shoemaker and king], and psychological contrasts of attraction and repulsion in the spectator. This last characteristic is even more marked in the second part of the play . . . , which is more properly a second play, taking over from its predecessor two of the principal *dramatis personae*: Don Pedro himself and Blas Pérez, the shoemaker's son who has been given a cap-taincy in the army. Here the action, though still unsatisfactory, is more closely knit than before; the nature of the conclusion

is something of a surprise to the spectator; and the historical incidents leading to the death of Don Pedro lose nothing in interest from the free and highly dramatic treatment which the author gives them.

Besides the second part of *El Zapatero y el Rey* Zorrilla pro-duced three plays in the year 1842, of which only one, *El Puñal del Godo,* the shortest of the four, is of any great significance in the history of the Romantic movement. More substantial, and in some respects more praiseworthy as a whole, is the three-act "tragic composition", *Sancho García,* which has fre-quently been reprinted, both in Zorrilla's day and in our own. Here, . . . Zorrilla was seeking to make terms with that eclec-ticism of taste which was becoming more marked in the public, and the sub-title, if not the nature of his play, testifies to the skill of his tactics. In colour, however, as in the abandon of its tone, in much of its characterization and often in its lan-guage, it preserves a close connection with Romantic drama, and its success, which, though not remarkable, was quite sat-isfactory to its author, was probably due largely to this con-nection and to his growing fame.

The merit and the interest of *El Eco del Torrente,* another of the plays of 1842, are both completely eclipsed by those of *El Puñal del Godo,* a one-act drama written (according to its au-thor's own testimony) in twenty-four hours. This is a more important specimen of Zorrilla's art than its length might sug-gest, as indicating the direction which he took and the type of work he produced when he was obliged to write rapidly. Sr Menéndez Pidal [the Spanish medievalist] has shown that the play, though not the result of deep and careful study, is by no means, as had previously been supposed, a purely imaginative treatment of a few lines of Mariana, but is indebted to a number of earlier versions of the Roderick-legend. . . . There is much exaggerated language; much thunder and lightning; much talk of phantoms, stars, and the *fuerza del sino* [power of fate]. Rodrigo, in the limelight, becomes at times extraordinarily like an eighth-century Don Álvaro, while the dagger that gives the play its title is almost a symbol of the unseen power which he feels to be dogging his footsteps. . . . A word should be added on the ease and melody of the versification, an art of which Zorrilla was now a master. Not only is it admirable in its variety, and skilfully adapted to the lyrico-dramatic style which Zorrilla loved, but it lends itself well to the sprightly and vehement dialogue in the penultimate scene, between Rodrigo and the Count, where the tension rises quickly till it reaches breaking-point. (pp. 178-80)

Higher praise is merited by *El Caballo del Rey Don Sancho.* This is a lively treatment of a story from Mariana—of how the sons of Sancho the Great of Navarre accused their own mother of adultery on account of a dispute concerning a horse be-longing to the King. . . . With great dramatic skill, Zorrilla contrives to impart an impressive significance to his horse by making it a symbol of the royal power. But the play has other qualities which recommend it to lovers of the Romantic. The chief of these is the antagonism, which forms the principal theme, between the attractive royal villain, Don García, and the mysterious royal hero, Don Ramiro. The latter is our old friend the Romantic hero in a slightly altered guise. As an omniscient and anonymous apparition he makes Don García's flesh creep in the approved manner. . . . Half-way through the play, [Don Ramiro] appears in the conventional Romantic dis-guise of a pilgrim, and from this point to the end of the play we have a combination of the *décor* of a Scott novel and the plot of a Romantic drama. Replete with incident, atmosphere and the interest of the unknown, its dramatic qualities more than compensate for its somewhat obvious deficiencies and from the playgoer's point of view it was a pity that it fell into oblivion. (pp. 180-82)

[*Don Juan Tenorio*] marks for Zorrilla the limit of ultra-Romantic drama: its immediate and striking success at a time when the Romantic movement was declining proves, as the popularity of Zorrilla's *leyendas* proved, that it need never have declined had it but had leaders of courage, conviction and ability; the persistence of the vogue of the play down to the present is one more illustration of the inherently Romantic temperament of the Spaniard. What can be said in a short space of Zorrilla's new choice of a hero has been said more frequently than anything else about Romantic drama. Don Juan is the Romantic hero carried to the highest degree of dramatic effectiveness. . . . No play in the whole history of Spanish literature is more completely dominated by its hero than *Don Juan Tenorio:* the nature of his character subserves the interest of the action and the dramatic skill which the author puts into the action enhances the appeal of the character. Zorrilla's Don Juan is neither Tirso's nor Molière's nor Dumas', but his own. His audacity, verve and abandon, and his exaggerated cynicism contrasted with his tardy remorse and repentance, mark him out from all his other incarnations. He may not be—is not, indeed—great art, but he is certainly effective drama.

All the other traits of the play illumine its central figure: the religious *motif*, which, even if we demur to it as Christians we must applaud as playgoers; the bold and dramatic use of the supernatural; the contrast between the mundane, realistic and brilliant scenes of Part I and the shadowy, eerie scenes of Part II; the considerable mastery of theatrical effect . . . and, not least, the irresistible melody of his easy, tripping verse. Once more, it will be observed, he has taken truly Romantic liberties with the constructional conventions of drama: his two "parts" are in no sense, as they are in *El Zapatero y el Rey,* two plays on closely related themes, but one enormous play, with a gap of five years in the middle. Somehow, though the critics frown on it, this seems perfectly in keeping with the other characteristics of the drama. About *Don Juan Tenorio* there is a greatness which an Englishman can best describe as Marlovian. True, Zorrilla cannot (and would not if he could) wield Marlowe's mighty line, and he has none of that elemental ruggedness and crudeness of Marlowe, which, after all, belong not only to the man but to his epoch. (pp. 182-83)

The chief title to fame of the author of *Don Juan Tenorio* is his creation of verse "legends" and his popularization of the Middle Ages. Where his lyrics approach greatness, this is generally due rather to narrative or descriptive passages interpolated in them than to their distinctively lyrical qualities. (p. 244)

The peculiarly incoherent form which we associate with the *leyenda* is of the type which we should expect to have been evolved by one who wrote "sin rumbo ni puerto"[without direction or port], though Zorrilla was not in fact the first to use it. Undefined, like the ballad, as to length, it admits of unlimited digressions and may be rhymed or assonanced at the author's will. Over the ballad the *leyenda* has the further advantage that it can use the most widely divergent measures, and thus, besides completely avoiding monotony, it is able with some subtlety to register frequent changes of emotional tone. Zorrilla took full advantage of this new freedom. His *leyendas* correspond approximately in structure with the *Estudiante de Salamanca* but exaggerate some of its formal characteristics. In particular, Zorrilla's "cuadros dramáticos" [dramatic sketches] are not confined to any particular divisions of the poem: at any moment, as we turn a page, we may expect to find a few lines of the narrative cast in dramatic form, or to be switched back into narrative as abruptly as we were carried away from it.

A number of other semi-formal devices will be found to occur frequently in the *leyendas:* such are the repetition of words and phrases in a somewhat artificial and oratorical manner, the use of colloquial digressions and asides to the reader and the alternation of reflective and narrative passages, often a shade too systematic for the truest art. But far more characteristic than any of these is Zorrilla's favourite device of calling in Nature to provide an emotional background for the principal scenes of his narrative. If he did it less regularly he might be said to do it well. . . . But the procedure too easily becomes familiar. Zorrilla's method is not that of associating particular types of scene with particular aspects of scenery but that of prefacing most of his principal incidents with descriptions of Nature which may either be in harmony with them or stand out in striking contrast. . . . This is not to say that Zorrilla cannot . . . evoke thunder and lightning where effectiveness seems to demand it. The fine description of the storm at the climax in the Hoffmanesque story **"La Pasionaria"** is a case in point. But Zorrilla is at his best in this respect when his evocations of Nature are carefully worked up and elaborated, as happens increasingly in his later *leyendas,* notably in **"La Azucena Silvestre".**

Since space forbids fuller treatment of these interesting but minor features of Zorrilla's narrative poems, we must be content with evaluating them as a whole. Granted their superficiality, which, except that they emphasize their author's favourite principles and ideas, is complete, there is little to be given them but praise. Their worst fault is a somewhat frequent diffuseness; for, though Zorrilla could find the *mot propre* [correct word] when he chose, he often preferred what to him was the easier alternative of running riot with Romantic *clichés,* and, as a result, whole pages of description may be little better than a mass of verbiage. This, after all, is the defect of one of his great qualities: the consummate ease with which he wrote, and can be read. He uses some measure for rapid narrative and it at once strikes the reader as pre-eminently the measure for that narrative. Then he turns the same measure to the purpose of leisurely description and immediately it seems the only measure appropriate to that purpose. No doubt the consciousness of his own powers helped to put him on good terms with his readers. His confidential asides to them are perfectly natural; he constantly talks to them for their good but never preaches to them; he is often obviously artifical but seldom pompous. (pp. 245-47)

It would be mere self-indulgence to expatiate on Zorrilla's magnificently loaded descriptions, on the soaring images conceived by his fancy and on the striking scenes and figures by which all remember him. More relevant here is the observation that, though he succeeded to the Romantic heritage, he fell comparatively seldom into Romantic exaggerations of phraseology or portraiture. True, his plots are often "fantastic", and confessedly so, and he loves to puzzle his presumably impressionable audiences with mysterious castles, masked figures, unknown pilgrims, and the like, as though they were entirely composed of children. Compare the language of his narrative poetry, however, with that of the drama of the same period: the frequent "infernal pasión" [blazing passion] of the plots is seldom reflected in the phraseology. . . . (p. 247)

Zorrilla was at least as much the poet of the Middle Ages as the poet of Spain. The suggestion conveys less than the truth. Nearly all his stories are taken from the history or legend of that fertile period or woven into its texture by his no less fertile imagination. He knew less of it than a superficial reading might lead one to suppose, and certainly less than many a contemporary poet of not half his skill. He was never a student, either of the Middle Ages or of anything else. . . . [He] never, like some of his contemporaries, loads his narratives with learned footnotes or bulky historical appendices of doubtful reliability. But he lives in the Middle Ages for so long as he is writing of them and he writes *con amore*. Such mediaeval types as the troubadour, the knight, and the pilgrim are his familiar friends, clothed, not always recognizably, in attractive garments of his own fancy. In every way he is entitled to be considered the greatest poet of the Mediaeval Revival in Spain. . . . (p. 249)

All the outstanding characteristics of Zorrilla's poetry are to be found in [*Granada*]: the patriotic and religious *motifs*, a great wealth and profusion of imagery, an unusual metrical variety, a passion for the picturesque and the skilful presentation of it, and so on. . . . In *Granada* as a whole the poet for once took some care with his sources, and went for his local colour not only to his imagination but to mediaeval and modern historians. Occasionally he overdoes his effects. . . . But the general impression made by the whole poem is certainly not one of erudition. . . . It should be added that this poem contains some of Zorrilla's best and most familiar lyric passages. Always happiest as a lyrist when engaged mainly upon narrative, he had ample scope in a theme so near his heart and developed upon a scale which encouraged lengthy digression. (pp. 254-55)

> *E. Allison Peers, "The Continuance of Romanticism, 1837-1860," in his* A History of the Romantic Movement in Spain, Vol. II, *Cambridge University Press, 1935 (and reprinted by Hafner Publishing Company, 1964, pp. 160-258.**

CARLOS FEAL (essay date 1981)

[*In his analysis of* Don Juan Tenorio, *Feal examines Zorrilla's Romantic attitudes, his character development, and his treatment of the Don Juan myth.*]

The most striking feature of [Zorrilla's] Don Juan is his exaggerated theatricality. (p. 375)

The theatrical quality of [*Don Juan Tenorio*] shows itself through the emphatic tone of the dialogue and through the seemingly unreal, illusory nature of the events. The phantasmagoric elements, particularly striking in the second part, permeate the play. Phantasmagoria, coupled with theatricality, furthers the similarity between the suppers, which frame the representation. . . .

Zorrilla skillfully establishes close parallels between the fathers of Don Juan and of Don Juan's beloved. . . . The paternal figure, split into two characters, sets itself up as Don Juan's true rival. In this light, Don Luis proves merely the apparent rival, over whom Don Juan triumphs easily, aided by an intimate familiarity with that individual's world. Don Juan, instead, succumbs to the character from the other world, a supernatural world and a world of human values diametrically opposed to those of Donjuanism. In other words, the emissary from beyond into whom the Commander becomes transformed is inextricably linked to the paternal figure, whose realm is sup-

posedly based on a divine order. By defying the father, Don Juan also defies God. Don Diego Tenorio's words underscore the same idea: . . .

> Don Juan, I'll listen to you no longer! I'm sure that Heaven is saving a bolt of lightning especially for you. . . .
>
> (p. 376)

Zorrilla's mentality does not differ from that of . . . other Romantics. Woman's innocence is considered more valuable than the revelation of dormant desires. The sleeping beauty, therefore, should not be awakened. In Zorrilla's legend, we also see that Don Juan, once he has conquered Margarita, tires of her. He abandons her for a woman who is apparently at the other extreme: the lascivious woman. The Romantic soul oscillates between these two poles, purity and lasciviousness. Once Margarita loses her purity, at the hands of Don Juan, she ceases to attract Don Juan. Since it is he who conquers Margarita, he contributes to the ruin of his own ideal. Margarita's disenchantment is obvious. Having escaped from the convent, she faces only a new jail. . . . Would not Doña Inés have experienced a similar deception?

The character of Inés has been interpreted in excessively idealistic terms. . . . It seems that the ability to guide and pacify (*encauzar*), which Zorrilla attributes to Inés, is one that he (and Don Juan) would like to see in her. Yet there is no doubt that she is also given to outbursts of passion: . . .

> I come to you as certainly as that river is sucked into the sea. Your presence robs me of reason; your words cast a spell on me, and your eyes entrance me, and your breath poisons me. . . .

Don Juan and Zorrilla seem to shut their eyes to this conduct, insofar as such a vision, no matter how much it satisfies man's vanity, destroys the image of the pure woman. By insisting on her chastity and finally having her die before her love is consummated, Zorrilla desexualizes Inés; in a way, he acts like the Commander. Nonetheless, he cannot prevent Inés from showing passions contrary to that angelic image. The character slips away from its author. In other words, Inés rebels not only against her father but also against Zorrilla. One can only wonder whether she would also have revolted against Don Juan. (pp. 381-82)

[In] ***Don Juan Tenorio,*** Inés is grateful, despite her misfortunes. She plays a decisive role in the salvation of Don Juan. The duel for Don Juan's soul must be settled between Inés and the Commander, and it is she who triumphs. In this way, she repays Don Juan for liberating the instincts her father had repressed. After Don Juan partially liberates Inés, she liberates him; both times, the oppressor or enemy is the Commander. Nevertheless, love may challenge, but it does not overthrow, patriarchal order. Don Gonzalo's opposition at the end of the play is not justifiable, since his law has been obeyed by the prodigal son. . . .

[A close model for Don Juan's salvation is found in Prosper] Mérimée's *Les Ames du purgatoire,* in which Don Juan witnesses his own funeral. He then repents, as does the legendary Mañara, whose surname he bears. The souls that pray before Don Juan's coffin are those brought forth from purgatory by the prayers of Mañara's mother. . . . Don Juan is finally saved thanks to the intervention of woman, his mother, whose emissaries, so to speak, have opened his eyes to the other life; in Zorrilla, the redeeming woman is the loved one, even though

Inés is also a mother figure. Don Juan's maternal superego (to use Erich Fromm's term) shows less severity than the paternal superego. If Don Juan's mother instilled in him a moral conscience, by means of the image of the souls that filled the child with terror, these same souls are responsible for his salvation. His sense of guilt and his forgiveness have a common origin. . . .

The originality of Zorrilla's work further stands out if the comparison with Mérimée's is extended. For Zorrilla, salvation is not at odds with love. Don Juan is neither converted to religion, like Mañara, who renounces women, nor condemned. But for love to triumph, Inés must die. The love between Don Juan and Inés is consummated in the world beyond. The spirit ultimately conquers the flesh, whose misery should be seen in both moral and metaphysical terms. (p. 382)

In the light of Zorrilla's creation, some salient features of the Don Juan myth can be pointed out. Marriage as the play's end, insinuated by Zorrilla, triumphs years later in George Bernard Shaw's *Man and Superman* . . . and in Max Frisch's *Don Juan oder Die Liebe zur Geometrie.* . . . This ending supposes a true surrender on the parts of Don Juan and his English equivalent, John Tanner, who by marrying show (without need of the Commander) their inability to escape the law of the father, whose representatives they become.

Nonetheless, that Zorrilla's Don Juan is saved against the Commander's will proves that God does not side with the paternal figure, despite the Commander's assertions. To some extent, the tension between the heavenly and the terrestrial fathers already exists in [Tirso de Molina's play, *El burlador de Sevilla*], in which the Commander rejects Don Juan's tardy repentance and leads Don Juan to his death with a false gesture of friendship: "Dame esa mano; / no temas" 'Give me your hand; do not fear'. . . . True, Tirso does not challenge the Commander's behavior, even though it is questionable. Not many years later, however, in Molière's *Dom Juan* . . . , the mechanical nature of the Commander's apparition turns Don Juan's punishment into a comedy. There is no dissociation of God and his surrogate, but authorial disrespect for both. From Molière on, desire gains ground in its fight against authority. That Don Juan finally defers to authority is an irony, an inescapable evil. Therefore, the condemnation of the modern Don Juan, when it occurs, runs parallel to the denunciation of the norms that Don Juan violates. In Shaw's and Frisch's plays the Commander meets with open sarcasm.

Zorrilla's Don Juan, like Tirso's, repents too late in the eyes of the Commander . . . , who as a messenger from the other world continues to ignore the hero's pleas. At the same time, however, Inés intervenes to break the alliance between God and his agent. Her intervention suggests that the law of the father yields to the rule of woman, or the "law of the heart." Paradoxically, it is in the name of Don Juan that Inés opposes men's law, thus advocating her own cause. Perhaps here lies another reason for the perplexing fact that Inés and Don Juan were destined to meet with the same final judgment.

Don Juan, then embodies a desire for love in defiance of the established order. But this type of love cannot be fulfilled. Law (marriage or death) finally entraps those who endeavor to be exempt from it. Thus, Don Juan either perishes completely or, if he survives as an individual, dies as Don Juan. His continuous artistic reincarnations express the need both to create and to destroy him. On the one hand, Don Juan is a perpetual threat, but on the other he is an indispensable component that

a man has to assimilate if he wishes to win a woman's heart. He must incorporate Don Juan to destroy him—his myth—effectively. (p. 383)

> *Carlos Feal, "Conflicting Names, Conflicting Laws: Zorrilla's 'Don Juan Tenorio'," in PMLA, 96 (copyright © 1981 by the Modern Language Association of America; reprinted by permission of the Modern Language Association of America), Vol. 96, No. 3, May, 1981, pp. 375-87.*

ADDITIONAL BIBLIOGRAPHY

Abrams, Fred. "The Death of Zorrilla's *Don Juan* and the Problem of Catholic Orthodoxy." *Romance Notes* VI, No. I (Autumn 1964): 42-6.

Discusses the religious implications in *Don Juan Tenorio*. In particular, Abrams addresses the issues of Don Juan's repentance after death and subsequent salvation. He disagrees with critics who conclude that Don Juan's repentance violates Catholic doctrine.

Brett, Lewis E. "Zorrilla." In *Nineteenth Century Spanish Plays,* edited by Lewis E. Brett, pp. 283-86. New York, London: D. Appleton-Century Co., 1935.

A concise overview of Zorrilla's career. Brett briefly appraises Zorrilla's dramas and poetic legends, as well as his ill-received *zarzuela,* or parody, of *Don Juan Tenorio.*

Firmat, Gustavo Pérez. "Carnival in *Don Juan Tenorio.*" *Hispanic Review* 51, No. 3 (Summer 1983): 269-81.

Discounts the "vaunted defects" of *Don Juan Tenorio*. Firmat contends that the alleged flaws in the play's structure are actually "harmonious elements in a coherent, if unusual, design." Firmat concentrates specifically on two aspects of the drama: the letter Don Juan writes to Inés and the carnival which goes on throughout the action.

Leslie, John Kenneth. "Towards the Vindication of Zorrilla: The Dumas-Zorrilla Question." *Hispanic Review* XIII, No. IV (October 1945): 288-93.*

A defense of Zorrilla. Leslie maintains that Zorrilla's *Don Juan Tenorio* does not duplicate *Don Juan de Marana* by Alexandre Dumas, père, but instead reflects several ideas which recur throughout Spanish Romantic drama.

Mansour, George P. "Parallelism in *Don Juan Tenorio.*" *Hispania* 61, No. 2 (May 1978): 245-53.

A structural and thematic analysis of *Don Juan Tenorio*. Mansour examines, in particular, the parallels between Zorrilla's use of the themes of life, death, love, and human justice in the first and second parts of the play.

Nozick, Martin. "Some Parodies of *Don Juan Tenorio.*" *Hispania* XXXIII, No. 2 (May 1950): 105-12.*

An informative essay outlining the major works that satirize Zorrilla's *Don Juan Tenorio*. The play itself, a popular subject for caricatures, is discussed briefly in light of its many parodies.

[Ogden, R.] "Zorrilla's Apotheosis." *The Nation* XLIX, No. 1255 (18 July 1889): 46-8.

Highlights Zorrilla's literary career.

Sánchez, Roberto G. "Between Macías and Don Juan: Spanish Romantic Drama and the Mythology of Love." *Hispanic Review* 44, No. 1 (Winter 1976): 27-44.*

A comparison of Mariano José de Larra's drama *Macías* and Zorrilla's *Don Juan Tenorio*. Sánchez explores the similarities between the two Spanish romance dramas and concludes that the works portray "the hidden fears and desires of the society of the time."

Ter Horst, Robert. ''Ritual Time Regained in Zorrilla's *Don Juan Tenorio*.'' *The Romantic Review* LXX, No. 1 (January 1979): 80-95.
   An examination of time in *Don Juan Tenorio*. Ter Horst submits that ''the logic of Don Juan Tenorio's fate principally derives from the nature of his engagement with time'' and suggests that the character's salvation results from this ''fundamental posture.''

Weiner, Hadassah Ruth. ''A Note on Zorrilla's *Traidor, inconfeso, y mártir*.'' *Romance Notes* XVIII, No. 3 (Spring 1978): 343-48.
   A detailed analysis of the characterization in *Traidor, inconfeso, y mártir*. Weiner discusses the protagonist of Zorrilla's play and compares him with Duque de Riva's Don Alvaro and García Gutiérrez's Manrique.

Appendix

THE EXCERPTS IN NCLC, VOLUME 6, WERE REPRINTED FROM THE FOLLOWING PERIODICALS:

The Academy
The Academy and Literature
The American Monthly Review
The American Review
The American Review of Reviews
The Antigonish Review
Ariel
The Athenaeum
The Atlantic Monthly
Ball State Teachers College Forum
Belgravia
Blackwood's Edinburgh Magazine
The Book Buyer
The Bookman, *New York*
Burton's Gentleman's Magazine
The Century
College English
Commonweal
The Cornhill Magazine
The Critic, *New York*
The Critical Review
The Denver Quarterly
The Dial
The Eclectic Magazine
The Eclectic Review
The Edinburgh Review
English
English Literature in Transition
Essays by Divers Hands
Every Saturday
The Examiner
The Foreign Quarterly Review
The Fortnightly Review

The Forum
Forum for Modern Language Studies
The French Review
Harper's New Monthly Magazine
Harper's Weekly
Hartford Studies in Literature
The Harvard Monthly
Horizon
The Irish Quarterly Review
John Bull
The Journal of Narrative Technique
Journal of Popular Culture
The Leader
Lippincott's Magazine of Popular Literature
 & Science
The London and Westminster Review
The London Magazine
Macmillan's Magazine
The Magazine of Art
The Monthly Anthology and Boston Review
The Monthly Review, *London*
The Nation
The National Review, *London*
The New England Quarterly
New England Weekly Review
The New Englander
The New Monthly Magazine
The New Republic
The New Statesman & Nation
The New York Herald Tribune
The New York Times
The New York Times Book Review
The North American Review

Overland Monthly
Partisan Review
Philological Quarterly
PMLA
Poet Lore
Poetry Review
The Prospective Review
The Quarterly Review
The Review of English Studies
The Round Table
The Saturday Review, *London*
Scribner's Monthly
Scrutiny
The Sewanee Review
Sharpe's London Magazine
South Atlantic Quarterly
The Southern Literary Messenger
The Southern Review
The Spectator
Studies in English Literature, 1500-1900
The Sunday Times, *London*
Symposium
The Times, *London*
The Times Literary Supplement
Tomorrow, *London*
TriQuarterly
The United States Literary Gazette
The University of Kansas City Review
The Westminster and Foreign Quarterly
 Review
The Westminster Review
The Yale Review

THE EXCERPTS IN NCLC, VOLUME 6, WERE REPRINTED FROM THE FOLLOWING BOOKS:

Alcott, Bronson. The Journals of Bronson Alcott. *Edited by Odell Shepard. Little, Brown, 1938.*

Alcott, Louisa May. An Old-Fashioned Girl. *Roberts Brothers, 1870.*

Alcott, Louisa May. Hospital Sketches and Camp and Fireside Stories. *Roberts Brothers, 1872.*

Allen, Gay Wilson. American Prosody. *American Book Company, 1935.*

Anderson, Warren D. Matthew Arnold and Classical Tradition. *The University of Michigan Press, 1965.*

apRoberts, Ruth. The Moral Trollope. *Ohio University Press, 1971.*

Arnold, Matthew. The Poems of Matthew Arnold: 1840 to 1866. *E. P. Dutton & Co., 1908.*

Auerbach, Erich. Scenes from the Drama of European Literature: Six Essays. *Meridian Books, 1959.*

Axton, William F. Introduction to Melmoth the Wanderer, *by Charles Robert Maturin. University of Nebraska Press, 1961.*

Baker, Ernest A. The History of the English Novel: The Novel of Sentiment and the Gothic Romance, Vol. 5. *H. F. & G. Witherby, 1934, Barnes & Noble, 1957.*

Barthes, Roland. Critical Essays. *Translated by Richard Howard. Northwestern University Press, 1972.*

Beach, Joseph Warren. The Concept of Nature in Nineteenth-Century English Poetry. *The Macmillan Publishing Company, 1936, Pageant Book Company, 1956.*

Benedikz, B. S., ed. On the Novel: A Present for Walter Allen on His 60th Birthday from His Friends and Colleagues. *J. M. Dent & Sons Ltd, 1971.*

Bennett, Joseph D. Baudelaire: A Criticism. *2d ed. Princeton University Press, 1944.*

Birkhead, Edith. The Tale of Terror: A Study of the Gothic Romance. *Constable & Company Ltd., 1921, Russell & Russell, Inc., 1963.*

Birley, Robert. Sunk without Trace: Some Forgotten Masterpieces Reconsidered. *Rupert Hart-Davis, 1962.*

Booth, Bradford A. Anthony Trollope: Aspects of His Life and Art. *Indiana University Press, 1958.*

Boynton, Percy H.; Jones, Howard M.; Sherburn, George W.; and Webster, Frank M., eds. American Poetry. *Charles Scribner's Sons, 1918, Granger Books, 1978.*

Bradley, A. C., ed. Essays and Studies by Members of the English Association, Vol. VI. *Oxford at the Clarendon Press, Oxford, 1920.*

Bradley, William Aspenwall. William Cullen Bryant. *Macmillan, 1905.*

Brandes, George. Main Currents in Nineteenth Century Literature: Naturalism in England, Vol. IV. *Translated by Mary Morison. William Heinemann, 1905.*

Brandes, George. Main Currents in Nineteenth Century Literature: The Emigrant Literature, Vol. I. *Translated by Diana White and Mary Morison. William Heinemann, 1923.*

Brandes, George. Main Currents in Nineteenth Century Literature: The Romantic School in France, Vol. V. *Translated by Diana White and Mary Morison. William Heinemann, 1924.*

Brandes, George. Naturalism in Nineteenth Century English Literature. *Russell & Russell, 1957.*

Brophy, Brigid. Don't Never Forget: Collected Views and Reviews. *Holt, Rinehart and Winston, 1967.*

Brophy, Brigid. Black and White: A Portrait of Aubrey Beardsley. *Cape, 1968, Stein and Day, 1969.*

Brophy, Brigid; Levey, Michael; and Osborne, Charles. Fifty Works of English and American Literature We Could Do Without. *Stein and Day, 1968.*

Brownell, W. C. Victorian Prose Masters: Thackeray—Carlyle—George Eliot—Matthew Arnold—Ruskin—George Meredith. *Charles Scribner's Sons, 1901.*

Browning, Elizabeth Barrett. The Letters of Elizabeth Barrett Browning. *Edited by Frederic G. Kenyon. The Macmillan Company, 1897.*

Burdett, Osbert. The Beardsley Period: An Essay in Perspective. *Boni and Liveright, 1925.*

Campbell, Ian, ed. Nineteenth-Century Scottish Fiction: Critical Essays. *Carcanet New Press, 1979.*

Carlyle, Thomas. Critical and Miscellaneous Essays: Collected and Republished, Vol. IV. *Brown and Taggard, 1860.*

Carrère, Jean. Degeneration in the Great French Masters: Rousseau—Chateaubriand—Balzac—Stendhal—Sand—Musset—Baudelaire—Flaubert—Verlaine—Zola. *Translated by Joseph McCabe. T. Fisher Unwin, Limited, 1922.*

Cecil, David. Early Victorian Novelists: Essays in Revaluation. *Constable, 1934, Bobbs-Merrill, 1935.*

Cecil, David. Poets and Story-Tellers: A Book of Critical Essays. *Constable, 1949.*

Cheney, John Vance. That Dome in Air: Thoughts on Poetry and the Poets. *A. C. McClurg and Company, 1895.*

Chesterton, G. K. The Victorian Age in Literature. *Holt, Rinehart and Winston, 1913.*

Chesterton, G. K. A Handful of Authors: Essays on Books and Writers. *Edited by Dorothy Collins. Sheed and Ward, Inc., 1953.*

Child, Lydia Maria. An Appeal in Favor of That Class of Americans Called Africans. *Allen and Ticknor, 1833.*

Child, Lydia Maria. Philothea: A Romance. *Otis, Broaders & Co., 1836.*

Child, Lydia Maria. Letters of Lydia Maria Child. *Edited by Harriet Winslow Sewall. Houghton Mifflin and Company, 1883.*

Cockshut, A.O.J. Anthony Trollope: A Critical Study. *Collins, 1955, New York University Press, 1968.*

Coleridge, Samuel Taylor. Coleridge's Miscellaneous Criticism. *Edited by Thomas Middleton Raysor. Harvard University Press, 1936.*

Cowie, Alexander. The Rise of the American Novel. *American Book Company, 1951.*

Craig, David. Introduction to Some Passages in the Life of Mr. Adam Blair, Minister of the Gospel at Cross-Meikle, *by J. G. Lockhart. Edinburgh University Press, 1963.*

Croce, Benedetto. European Literature in the Nineteenth Century. *Translated by Douglas Ainslie. Alfred A. Knopf, 1924.*

Culler, A. Dwight. Imaginative Reason: The Poetry of Matthew Arnold. *Yale University Press, 1966.*

De Bellis, Jack. Sidney Lanier. *Twayne, 1972.*

Dickey, James. Master Poems of the English Language: Over One Hundred Poems Together with Introductions by Leading Poets and Critics of the English-Speaking World. *Edited by Oscar Williams. Trident Press, 1966.*

Dickey, James. Babel to Byzantium: Poets and Poetry Now. *Grosset & Dunlap, 1971.*

Edwards, P. D. Anthony Trollope: His Art and Scope. *University of Queensland Press, 1977, St. Martin's Press, 1978.*

Eells, John Shepard, Jr. The Touchstones of Matthew Arnold. *Bookman Associates, 1955, College and University Press, 1963.*

Eliot, George. The George Eliot Letters: 1862-1868, Vol. IV. *Edited by Gordon S. Haight. Yale University Press, 1955.*

Eliot, T. S. Selected Essays: 1917-1932. *Harcourt, Brace Jovanovich, 1932.*

Eliot, T. S. The Use of Poetry and the Use of Criticism to Poetry in England. *Harvard University Press, 1933, Faber and Faber, 1933, Barnes & Noble, Inc., 1959.*

Eliot, T. S. Selected Essays. *Harcourt Brace Jovanovich, 1950.*

Elliott, G. R. The Cycle of Modern Poetry: A Series of Essays toward Clearing Our Present Poetic Dilemma. *Princeton University Press, 1929.*

Emerson, Ralph Waldo. Journals of Ralph Waldo Emerson: 1864-1876. *Edited by Edward Waldo Emerson and Waldo Emerson Forbes. Houghton Mifflin, 1914.*

Essays on the Eighteenth Century: Presented to David Nichol Smith in Honour of His Seventieth Birthday. *Oxford at the Clarendon Press, Oxford, 1945.*

Evans, Bertrand. Gothic Drama from Walpole to Shelley. *University of California Press, 1947.*

Fairlie, Alison. Imagination and Language: Collected Essays on Constant, Baudelaire, Nerval, and Flaubert. *Edited by Malcolm Bowie. Cambridge University Press, 1981.*

Fletcher, Ian, ed. Romantic Mythologies. *Barnes & Noble, 1967.*

Foerster, Norman. Nature in American Literature: Studies in the Modern View of Nature. *Russell & Russell, 1958.*

Fowlie, Wallace. Clowns and Angels: Studies in Modern French Literature. *Sheed and Ward, Inc., 1943.*

France, Anatole. The Latin Genius. *Translated by Wilfrid S. Jackson. Dodd, Mead, 1924.*

Freeman, R. Austin. Introduction to The Mysteries of Udolpho, Vol. I, *by Ann Radcliffe. J. M. Dent & Sons Ltd, 1959.*

Fry, Roger Eliot. Vision and Design. *Wm. Clowes & Son, 1920.*

Garber, Frederick. Introduction to The Italian; or, The Confessional of the Black Penitents, *by Ann Radcliffe. Edited by Frederick Garber. Oxford University Press, London, 1968.*

Gautier, Théophile. The Complete Works of Théophile Gautier, Vol. XII. *Edited and translated by F. C. DeSumichrast. Bigelow, Smith & Co., 1903.*

Gerould, Katharine Fullerton. Modes and Morals. *Charles Scribner's Sons, 1920.*

Gindin, James. Harvest of a Quiet Eye: The Novel of Compassion. *Indiana University Press, 1971.*

Goethe, Johann Wolfgang von. Conversations of Goethe with Eckermann and Soret. *Rev. ed. Edited by John Peter Eckermann. Translated by John Oxenford. George Bell & Sons, 1883.*

Gohdes, Clarence. Introduction to The Centennial Edition of the Works of Sidney Lanier: ''The English Novel'' and Essays on Literature, Vol. IV, *by Sidney Lanier. Edited by Clarence Gohdes and Kemp Malone. The Johns Hopkins University Press, 1945.*

Gosse, Edmund. Questions at Issue. *William Heinemann, 1893.*

Grant, Douglas. Introduction to Melmoth the Wanderer: A Tale, *by Charles Robert Maturin. Edited by Douglas Grant. Oxford University Press, London, 1968.*

Greever, Garland. *Introduction to* The Centennial Edition of the Works of Sidney Lanier: ''Tiger-Lillies'' and Southern Prose, Vol. V, *by Sidney Lanier. Edited by Garland Greever and Cecil Abernethy. The Johns Hopkins University Press, 1945.*

Grierson, Herbert. Essays and Addresses. *Chatto & Windus, 1940.*

Griswold, Rufus Wilmot. The Prose Writers of America: With a Survey of the History, Condition, and Prospects of American Literature. *Carey and Hart, 1847.*

Guérard, Albert Leon. French Prophets of Yesterday: A Study of Religious Thought Under the Second Empire. *D. Appleton and Company, 1913.*

Gwynn, Stephen. Thomas Moore. *Macmillan, 1905.*

Harrison, Frederic. Studies in Early Victorian Literature. *Edward Arnold, 1895.*

Hart, Francis R. Lockhart As Romantic Biographer. *Edinburgh University Press, 1971.*

Hart, Francis Russell. The Scottish Novel: From Smollett to Spark. *Harvard University Press, 1978.*

Hazlitt, William. Political Essays, with Sketches of Public Characters. *W. Hone, 1819.*

Hazlitt, William. The Spirit of the Age; or, Contemporary Portraits. *H. Colburn, 1825, Oxford University Press, 1947.*

Hazlitt, William. The Complete Works of William Hazlitt: Political Essays, with Sketches of Public Characters, Vol. 7. *Edited by P. P. Howe. J. M. Dent and Sons, Ltd., 1932.*

Hearn, Lafcadio. Interpretations of Literature, Vol. 1. *Edited by John Erskine. Dodd, Mead, 1915, Kennikat Press, 1965.*

Higginson, Thomas Wentworth. Contemporaries. *Houghton Mifflin and Company, 1899.*

Hildyard, M. Clive. *Introduction to* Lockhart's Literary Criticism, *by John Gibson Lockhart. Edited by M. Clive Hildyard. Basil Blackwell, 1931.*

Hilles, F. W., ed. The Age of Johnson: Essays Presented to Chauncey Brewster Tinker. *Yale University Press, 1949.*

Holdheim, William W. Benjamin Constant. *Hillary House Publishers, Ltd, 1961.*

Holloway, John. The Victorian Sage: Studies in Argument. *Macmillan, 1953, Archon Books, 1962.*

Howells, Coral Ann. Love, Mystery, and Misery: Feeling in Gothic Fiction. *The Athlone Press, 1978.*

Hubbell, Jay B. The South in American Literature: 1607-1900. *Duke University Press, 1954.*

Hunt, Leigh. Leigh Hunt's Dramatic Criticism: 1808-1831. *Edited by Lawrence Huston Houtchens and Carolyn Washburn Houtchens. Columbia University Press, 1948.*

Hutton, Richard Holt. Literary Essays. *Rev. ed. Macmillan and Co., Limited, 1896, Gregg International Publishers Limited, 1969.*

Huysmans, J. K. Against Nature. *Translated by Robert Baldick. Penguin Books, Inc., 1959.*

Idman, Niilo. Charles Robert Maturin: His Life and Works. *Constable & Co Ltd, 1923.*

Jackson, Holbrook. The Eighteen Nineties: A Review of Art and Ideas at the Close of the Nineteenth Century. *Grant Richards, 1913, Humanities Press, 1976.*

James, Henry, Jr. Hawthorne. *Macmillan and Co., London, 1879, Harper & Brothers, Publishers, 1880.*

James, Henry. Partial Portraits. *Macmillan and Co., Limited, London, 1899.*

James, Henry. Literary Reviews and Essays: On American, English, and French Literature. *Edited by Albert Mordell. Twayne Publishers, 1957.*

Johnson, W. Stacy. The Voices of Matthew Arnold: An Essay in Criticism. *Yale University Press, 1961.*

Jones, Howard Mumford. The Harp that Once—A Chronicle of the Life of Thomas Moore. *Holt, 1937.*

Jones, P. Mansell. Baudelaire. *Bowes & Bowes, 1952.*

Ker, William Paton. The Art of Poetry: Seven Lectures, 1920-1922. *Oxford at the Clarendon Press, Oxford, 1923.*

Kiely, Robert. The Romantic Novel in England. *Harvard University Press, 1972.*

Kilmer, Joyce. The Circus and Other Essays. *Gomme, 1916.*

Kilmer, Joyce. The Circus and Other Essays and Fugitive Pieces. *Edited by Robert Cortes Holliday. Doran, 1921.*

Kincaid, James R. The Novels of Anthony Trollope. *Oxford at the Clarendon Press, Oxford, 1977.*

Kronenberger, Louis. The Polished Surface: Essays in the Literature of Worldliness. *Knopf, 1969.*

Lanier, Sidney. The Centennial Edition of the Works of Sidney Lanier: "The Science of English Verse" and Essays on Music, Vol. II. *Edited by Paull Franklin Baum. The Johns Hopkins University Press, 1945.*

Le Gallienne, Richard. Attitudes and Avowals: With Some Retrospective Reviews. *John Lane Company, 1910.*

Lockhart, J. G. Memoirs of the Life of Sir Walter Scott, Bart. *R. Cadell, 1837-38.*

Lockhart, J. G. The Life of Sir Walter Scott, Bart.: 1779-1832. *Rev. ed. Adam & Charles Black, 1893.*

Lockhart, John. Lockhart's Literary Criticism. *Edited by M. Clive Hildyard. Basil Blackwell, 1931.*

Lougy, Robert E. Charles Robert Maturin. *Bucknell University Press, 1975.*

Lowell, James Russell. A Fable for Critics: A Glance at a Few of Our Literary Progenies. *2d ed. G. P. Putnam, 1849.*

MacBeth, Gilbert. John Gibson Lockhart. *University of Illinois Press, 1935.*

Macy, John. The Spirit of American Literature. *Doubleday, Page & Company, 1913.*

Madden, David, ed. Rediscoveries: Informal Essays in Which Well-Known Novelists Rediscover Neglected Works of Fiction by One of Their Favorite Authors. *Crown, 1971.*

Maturin, Charles Robert. Women; or, Pour et Contre, Vol. I. *A. Constable, 1818, Garland Publishing, Inc., 1979.*

McDowell, Tremaine. Introduction to William Cullen Bryant: Representative Selections, *by William Cullen Bryant. Edited by Tremaine McDowell. American Book Company, 1935.*

McLean, Albert F., Jr. William Cullen Bryant. *Twayne, 1964.*

Meigs, Cornelia. Introduction to Little Women; or, Meg, Jo, Beth and Amy, *by Louisa May Alcott. Little, Brown, 1968.*

Mencken, H. L. Prejudices, third series. *Knopf, 1924.*

Mérimée, Prosper. The Writings of Prosper Mérimée: Letters to an Unknown, Vol. 7. *Translated by Olive Edwards Palmer. Croscup & Holby Company, 1905.*

Michelson, Peter. The Aesthetics of Pornography. *Herder and Herder, 1971.*

Mims, Edwin. Sidney Lanier. *Houghton Mifflin, 1905.*

Moers, Ellen. Literary Women. *Doubleday, 1976.*

Montgomery, H. R. Thomas Moore: His Life, Writings, and Contemporaries. *Thomas Cautley Newby, Publisher, 1860.*

More, Paul Elmer. The Demon of the Absolute. *Princeton University Press, 1928.*

Morse, David. Romanticism: A Structural Analysis. *Barnes & Noble, 1982.*

Mossop, D. J. Baudelaire's Tragic Hero: A Study of the Architecture of ''Les fleurs du mal.'' *Oxford University Press, London, 1961.*

Murry, John Middleton. Countries of the Mind: Essays in Literary Criticism, first series. *Rev. ed. Oxford University Press, London, 1931, Books for Libraries Press, 1968.*

O'Connor, Frank. The Mirror in the Roadway: A Study of the Modern Novel. *Alfred A. Knopf, 1956.*

Oliphant, Mrs. The Victorian Age of English Literature, Vol. II. *Lovell, Coryell & Company, 1892.*

Omond, T. S. English Metrists: Being a Sketch of English Prosodical Criticism from Elizabethan Times to the Present Day. *Oxford at the Clarendon Press, Oxford, 1921, Phaeton Press, 1968.*

Osborne, William S. Lydia Maria Child. *Twayne, 1980.*

Nalbantian, Suzanne. The Symbol of the Soul from Hölderlin to Yeats: A Study in Metonymy. *Columbia University Press, 1977.*

Parker, Gail. Introduction to The Oven Birds: American Women on Womanhood, 1820-1920. *Edited by Gail Parker. Anchor Press, 1972.*

Parks, Edd Winfield. Introduction to Southern Poets. *Edited by Edd Winfield Parks. American Book Company, 1936.*

Parrington, Vernon Louis. Main Currents in American Thought, an Interpretation of American Literature from the Beginnings to 1920: The Romantic Revolution in America, 1800-1860, Vol. 2. *Harcourt Brace Jovanovich, 1958.*

Pater, Walter. Miscellaneous Studies: A Series of Essays. *Macmillan and Co., Limited, 1895, Johnson Reprint Corporation, 1967.*

Pattee, Fred Lewis. The Development of the American Short Story: An Historical Survey. *Harper & Brothers, 1923.*

Payne, William Morton. The Greater English Poets of the Nineteenth Century. *Henry Holt and Company, 1907, Books for Libraries Press, 1967.*

Payne, William Morton, ed. American Literary Criticism. *Longmans, Green, and Co., 1904, Books for Libraries Press, 1968.*

Pearce, Roy Harvey, ed. Experience in the Novel: Selected Papers from the English Institute. *Columbia University Press, 1968.*

Peers, E. Allison. A History of the Romantic Movement in Spain, Vol. II. *Cambridge University Press, 1935, Hafner Publishing Company, 1964.*

Peyre, Henri. Connaissance de Baudelaire. *Corti, 1951.*

Peyre, Henri, ed. Baudelaire: A Collection of Critical Essays. *Prentice-Hall, Inc., 1962.*

Phelps, William Lyon. Howells, James, Bryant and Other Essays. *The Macmillan Company, 1924.*

Phillips, Wendell. Appendix to Letters of Lydia Maria Child, *by Lydia Maria Child. Edited by Harriet Winslow Sewall. Houghton Mifflin and Company, 1883.*

Poe, Edgar Allan. Literary Criticism of Edgar Allan Poe. *Edited by Robert L. Hough. University of Nebraska Press, 1965.*

Poulet, Georges. The Metamorphoses of the Circle. Translated by Carley Dawson, Elliott Coleman, and Georges Poulet. The Johns Hopkins University Press, 1966.

Powell, Thomas. The Living Authors of America, first series. Stringer and Townsend, 1850.

Pritchett, V. S. The Living Novel & Later Appreciations. Rev. ed. Random House, 1964.

Proust, Marcel. Marcel Proust on Art and Literature 1896-1919. Translated by Sylvia Townsend Warner. Meridian Books, 1958.

Radcliffe, Ann. Gaston de Blondeville; or, The Court of Henry III, Vol. I. Henry Colburn, 1826, Arno Press, Inc., 1972.

Raitt, A. W. Introduction to The Venus of Ille and Other Stories, by Prosper Mérimée. Translated by Jean Kimber. Oxford University Press, London, 1966.

Raleigh, Walter. The English Novel: Being a Short Sketch of Its History from the Earliest Times to the Appearance of "Waverley." 5th ed. Charles Scribner's Sons, 1911.

Raleigh, Walter. Introduction to Essays in Criticism, by Matthew Arnold. Gowans and Gray, 1912.

Raleigh, Walter. Some Authors: A Collection of Literary Essays, 1896-1916. Oxford at the Clarendon Press, Oxford, 1923.

Rathburn, Robert C., and Steinmann, Martin, Jr., eds. From Jane Austen to Joseph Conrad: Essays Collected in Memory of James T. Hillhouse. University of Minnesota Press, 1958.

Raymond, E. T. Portraits of the Nineties. Charles Scribner's Sons, 1921.

Rhodes, S. A. The Cult of Beauty in Charles Baudelaire, Vols. I & II. Columbia University Press, 1929.

Ringe, Donald A. The Pictorial Mode: Space & Time in the Art of Bryant, Irving & Cooper. University Press of Kentucky, 1971.

Rothenstein, John K. M. The Artists of the 1890's. Routledge, 1928.

Rubin, Louis D., Jr. William Elliott Shoots a Bear: Essays on the Southern Literary Imagination. Louisiana State University Press, 1975.

Sadleir, Michael. Trollope: A Commentary. Rev. ed. Constable & Co., 1945, Farrar, Straus and Giroux, 1947.

Saintsbury, George. Corrected Impressions: Essays on Victorian Writers. Dodd, Mead and Company, 1895.

Saintsbury, George. A History of Criticism and Literary Taste in Europe from the Earliest Texts to the Present Day: Modern Criticism, Vol. III. William Blackwood & Sons Ltd., 1904.

Saintsbury, George. Introduction to The Writings of Prosper Mérimée: Carmen, Arsène Guillot, Abbé Aubain, Vol. 1, by Prosper Mérimée. Translated by Emily Mary Weller, The Lady Mary Loyd, and Edmund Burke Thompson. Croscup & Holby Company, 1905.

Saintsbury, George. The English Novel. J. M. Dent & Sons Ltd., 1913.

Saintsbury, George. The Collected Essays and Papers of George Saintsbury: 1875-1920, Vol. II. J. M. Dent & Sons Ltd., 1923, Johnson Reprint Corporation, 1969.

Saintsbury, George. A History of English Prosody from the Twelfth Century to the Present Day: From Blake to Mr. Swinburne, Vol. III. 2d ed. Macmillan and Co., Limited, London, 1923, Russell & Russell, 1961.

Sartre, Jean-Paul. Baudelaire. Translated by Martin Turnell. Gallimard, 1947, New Directions, 1950.

Scott, Sir Walter. Introduction to The Novels of Ann Radcliffe, by Ann Radcliffe. Ballantyne Publishers, 1824.

Scott, Sir Walter, and Maturin, Charles Robert. The Correspondence of Sir Walter Scott and Charles Robert Maturin. University of Texas Press, 1937.

Scott, Sir Walter. On Novels and Novelists. *Edited by Ioan Williams. Routledge & Kegan Paul, 1968.*

Smalley, Donald, ed. Trollope: The Critical Heritage. *Routledge & Kegan Paul, 1969.*

Smiles, Samuel, ed. Memoir and Correspondence of the Late John Murray, Vol. II. *John Murray, 1891.*

Spacks, Patricia Meyer. The Female Imagination. *Knopf, 1975.*

Speare, Morris Edmund. The Political Novel: Its Development in England and in America. *Oxford University Press, New York, 1924, Russell & Russell, 1966.*

Starke, Aubrey Harrison. Sidney Lanier: A Biographical and Critical Study. *University of North Carolina Press, 1933.*

Stedman, Edmund Clarence. Genius and Other Essays. *Moffat, Yard and Company, 1911.*

Stedman, Edmund Clarence. Poets of America. *Houghton Mifflin Company, 1913.*

Steiner, George. Language and Silence: Essays on Language, Literature and the Inhuman. *Atheneum, 1967.*

Stendhal [pseudonym of Henri Beyle]. Selected Journalism from the English Reviews. *Edited by Geoffrey Strickland. John Calder Ltd, 1959.*

Stephen, Leslie. Studies of a Biographer, Vol. IV. *G. P. Putnam's Sons, 1907.*

Strong, L.A.G. The Minstrel Boy: A Portrait of Tom Moore. *Knopf, 1937.*

Symons, Arthur. Studies in Prose and Verse. *J M Dent & Sons Ltd, 1904.*

Symons, Arthur. Charles Baudelaire: A Study. *Elkin Mathews, 1920.*

Talfourd, Sir Thomas Noon. Critical and Miscellaneous Writings of T. Noon Talfourd. *2d ed. A. Hart, 1850.*

Tate, Allen. Reason in Madness: Critical Essays. **G. P. Putnam's Sons, 1941.**

Tate, Allen. Limits of Poetry: Selected Essays, 1928-1948. *Swallow Press, 1949.*

Thayer, William Roscoe. Throne-Makers. *Houghton Mifflin Company, 1899.*

Tillotson, Geoffrey. Criticism and the Nineteenth Century. *The Athlone Press, 1951.*

Tillotson, Geoffrey, and Tillotson, Kathleen. Mid-Victorian Studies. *The Athlone Press, 1965.*

Tinker, Chauncey Brewster. Essays in Retrospect: Collected Articles and Addresses. *Yale University Press, 1948.*

Tompkins, J.M.S. The Popular Novel in England: 1770-1800. *Constable & Company, Ltd, 1932, University of Nebraska Press, 1961.*

Tracy, Robert. Trollope's Later Novels. *University of California Press, 1978.*

Trent, William Peterfield, & others, eds. The Cambridge History of American Literature, Early National Literature, Part I, Vol. I. *Macmillan, 1933.*

Trollope, Anthony. An Autobiography. *Harper & Brothers, 1883, University of California Press, 1947.*

Trollope, Anthony. The Letters of Anthony Trollope. *Edited by Bradford Allen Booth. Oxford University Press, London, 1951.*

Turnell, Martin. The Novel in France: Mme. de la Fayette, Laclos, Constant, Stendhal, Balzac, Flaubert, Proust. *Hamish Hamilton, 1950.*

Turnell, Martin. Baudelaire: A Study of His Poetry. *Hamilton, 1953, New Directions, 1954.*

Valéry, Paul. Variety, second series. *Translated by William Aspenwall Bradley. Harcourt Brace Jovanovich, 1938.*

Varma, Devendra P. The Gothic Flame. *Arthur Barker Ltd, 1957.*

Wagenknecht, Edward. Cavalcade of the English Novel: From Elizabeth to George VI. *Holt, Rinehart and Winston, 1943.*

Wagenknecht, Edward. Cavalcade of the English Novel. *Rev. ed. Henry Holt and Company, 1954.*

Waggoner, Hyatt H. American Poets: From the Puritans to the Present. *Houghton Mifflin Company, 1968.*

Wain, John, ed. Interpretations: Essays on Twelve English Poems. *Routledge & Kegan Paul, 1955.*

Walpole, Hugh. Anthony Trollope. *Macmillan, 1928.*

Webb, Richard, and Coulson, Edwin R. Sidney Lanier: Poet and Prosodist. *University of Georgia Press, 1941.*

Weintraub, Stanley. Beardsley: A Biography. *George Braziller, 1967.*

Welch, Robert. Irish Poetry from Moore to Yeats. *Smythe, 1980.*

Wellek, René. A History of Modern Criticism, 1750-1950: The Later Nineteenth Century. *Yale University Press, 1965.*

Whipple, Edwin P. Literature and Life. *7th ed. Houghton Mifflin and Company, 1885.*

Whitman, Walt. Specimen Days & Collect. *Rees Welsh & Co., 1882-1883.*

Whitman, Walt. Rivulets of Prose: Critical Essays. *Edited by Carolyn Welts and Alfred F. Goldsmith. Greenberg Publishers. 1928.*

Whittier, John Greenleaf. Introduction to Letters of Lydia Maria Child, *by Lydia Maria Child. Edited by Harriet Winslow Sewall. Houghton Mifflin and Company, 1883.*

Whittier, John Greenleaf. Whittier on Writers and Writing: The Uncollected Critical Writings of John Greenleaf Whittier. *Edited by Edwin Harrison Cady and Harry Hayden Clark. Syracuse University Press, 1950.*

Wilson, Edmund. Patriotic Gore: Studies in the Literature of the American Civil War. *Oxford University Press, New York, 1962.*

Wolff, Robert Lee. Introduction to The Milesian Chief, Vol. I, *by Charles Robert Maturin. Garland Publishing, Inc., 1979.*

Woolf, Virginia. The Moment and Other Essays. *Harcourt Brace Jovanovich, 1948.*

Woolf, Virginia. Granite and Rainbow: Essays. *Hogarth Press, 1958.*

Woolf, Virginia. Collected Essays, Vol. II. *Hogarth Press, 1966.*

Yeats, W. B. Memoirs. *Edited by Denis Donoghue. Macmillan, 1972.*